Big Java

Big Java

Cay Horstmann

San Jose State University

John Wiley & Sons, Inc.

ACQUISITIONS EDITOR: Paul Crockett

EDITORIAL ASSISTANT: Susannah Barr

MARKETING MANAGER: Katherine Hepburn

SENIOR PRODUCTION EDITOR: Valerie Vargas

PRODUCTION SERVICES MANAGER: Jeanine Furino

SENIOR DESIGNER: Harry Nolan

PHOTO EDITOR: Lisa Gee

PRODUCTION MANAGEMENT SERVICES: Publication Services

This book was set in 10.5/12 Adobe Caslon Regular by Publication Services and printed and bound by RR Donnelley & Sons Company. The cover was printed by The Lehigh Press, Inc.

This book is printed on acid-free paper ∞

Horstmann, Cay S., 1959-
    Big Java : programming and practice / Cay Horstmann.
      p. cm.
    ISBN 0-471-40248-6 (cloth : alk. paper)
    1. Java (Computer program language) I. Title.

  QA76.73.J38 H674 2002
  005.13'3--dc21   2001045305

Printed in the United States of America

10 9 8 7 6 5 4

Preface

This book is an introductory text in computer science, focusing on programming principles and practices. Why should you choose this book for your first course in computer science? Here are the key reasons:

- I take a point of view that goes beyond language syntax and focuses on computer science concepts.

- I stress the object-oriented paradigm, starting with the first example—an object-oriented version of the traditional "Hello, World" program.

- I motivate students to master the practical aspects of programming, with lots of useful tips and a chapter on testing and debugging.

- I present a carefully selected subset of the Java library that is accessible to beginners and rich enough to create interesting programs.

- I use the standard Java language, library, and tools—not a specialized "training wheels" environment.

- In the final chapters of the book, I cover important techniques for server-side program development such as database programming, XML and Java Server Pages.

The Use of Java

This book is based on the Java programming language. I chose Java for four reasons:

- Object orientation

- Safety

- Simplicity

- Breadth of the standard library

At this point, the object-oriented point of view is the predominant paradigm for software design. I strongly believe that object orientation enables students to spend more time on the design of their programs and less time coding and debugging. In this book, I start out with objects and classes early. Students learn how to manipulate objects and build simple classes in Chapter 2.

I rarely use static methods other than `main`. As a result, students think in terms of objects from the outset—they don't have to spend the second half of the course unlearning bad habits developed in the first half.

When designing classes, I strictly separate the classes from the test driver programs. (In fact, if you use an environment such as BlueJ, then you don't need the test driver programs at all. This book doesn't require that you use BlueJ or any other particular environment, but it works very well with BlueJ. Give it a try and you too may become a convert—my students were delighted when they were able to interact with their objects in an intuitive fashion.)

Another notable aspect of this book is that I cover interfaces before subclasses. This has a great advantage: Students see the power of polymorphism before having to worry about technicalities of extending classes.

Of course, there are many object-oriented programming languages besides Java. In principle, one can teach object-oriented programming using the C++ language. However, Java has a fundamental advantage over C++, namely its safety. Students can—and do—make an amazing number of errors when using C++, many of which lead to mysterious and irreproducible program behavior. When using C++, an instructor must spend a great deal of class time on safe programming habits, or students will end up with a well-deserved lack of confidence in their creations—hardly an ideal situation for a beginning course.

Another major advantage of Java is its simplicity. Although it is not a reasonable goal to cover all constructs of Java in the first course, instructors can master all of the syntax and semantics of the Java language and can answer student questions with complete confidence. In contrast, the C++ language is so complex that very few people can truthfully state that they understand all features of the language. Even though I have used C++ extensively for over a dozen years, I regularly get stumped by freshmen who show me a particularly baffling compiler error message. Simplicity is important, especially for a foundational course. It is not a good practice to choose as a foundational tool a programming language that students and instructors cannot master with confidence.

Finally, the standard Java library has sufficient breadth that it can be used for most courses in a computer science curriculum. Graphics, user interface construction, database access, multithreading, and network programming are all part of the standard library. Thus, the skills that students learn in the beginning course will serve them well throughout the curriculum. Again, C++ falls notably short in this regard. There are no standard toolkits for any of the above-mentioned programming domains in C++. The Java library subset that this book covers enables students to handle a wide variety of common programming tasks.

A Tour of the Book

The book can be naturally grouped into four parts. Figure 1 shows the dependencies among the chapters.

Part A

Chapters 1 through 8 cover the fundamentals of object-based programming: objects, methods, classes, variables, number types, strings, and control structures. Students learn how to build very simple classes in Chapter 2. Chapter 7 takes up the subject of class design in a more systematic fashion.

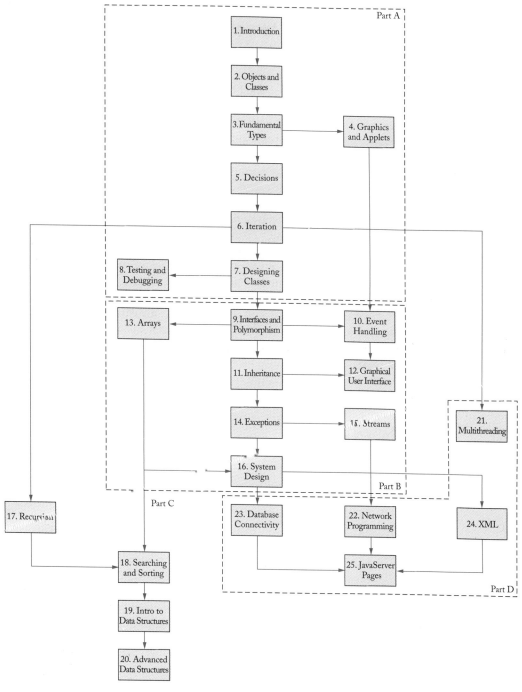

Figure 1

Chapter Dependencies

Starting with Chapter 7, I use a very small subset of the UML notation—just class diagrams and four arrow types for dependency, realization of interfaces, inheritance, and directed association. That small subset is useful for visualizing the relationships between classes, but it minimizes issues that beginners find complex, such as when to choose association, aggregation, or attributes.

I cover graphics very early, in Chapter 4, because many students enjoy writing programs that create drawings, and because rectangles, ellipses, and lines are good examples of objects. I use the "2D graphics" classes in the `java.awt.geom` package throughout, not the outdated procedural methods in the `Graphics` class. Calling `g.drawRect(x,y,w,h)` is *not* object-oriented. Manipulating geometric objects is both object-oriented and fun for the students. I use applets because students can program them with very little technical knowledge.

However, coverage of graphics is entirely optional. All material has been carefully presented so that you can skip all chapters that cover graphics and graphical user interfaces.

Chapter 8 covers testing and debugging, a subject that is unfortunately given short shrift in many textbooks.

As explained in Chapter 3, you can either use the `JOptionPane` class to read input from a dialog box (even in a console program), or you can use a `BufferedReader`. The latter forces you to tag the `main` method with `throws IOException`, which I used to find unacceptable until I reorganized all programs so that the `main` method is just a "throwaway" test driver class. I don't find it problematic if methods in a test driver class throw exceptions. (By the end of the first semester, students will know how to catch exceptions.)

Part B

Chapters 9 through 16 cover inheritance, arrays, exceptions, streams and, optionally, graphical user interface (GUI) programming.

The discussion of inheritance is split into two chapters. Chapter 9 covers interfaces and polymorphism, whereas Chapter 11 covers inheritance. Introducing interfaces before inheritance pays off in several ways. Students immediately see polymorphism before getting bogged down with superclass construction. It becomes possible to discuss event-driven programming at an early stage. Students are naturally led to local inner classes for event handlers, a more robust technique than the "opportunistic" realization of event interfaces that one still finds in older textbooks.

GUI programming is split into two chapters. Chapter 10 covers event-driven programming, relying just on the notion of an interface introduced in Chapter 9. Chapter 12 covers GUI components and their layout. This chapter requires some knowledge of inheritance (extending frames and panels and invoking `super.paintComponent`). It is possible to cover both of these chapters together, either before or after Chapter 11.

Again, let me stress that coverage of graphics and graphical user interfaces is entirely optional. One alternative is to cover graphics and applets (which are quite simple to program) and skip GUIs and event handling.

I cover arrays and streams after inheritance. From an object-oriented point of view, inheritance is a crucial concept, and I find that it helps to introduce it as early as possible. However, if you prefer to cover arrays and streams earlier, you can simply switch the chapters without incurring any problems.

I prefer to cover array lists first before covering arrays. In my experience, students find the `get`/`set` syntax perfectly natural and have surprisingly little attachment to the [] operator. They aren't even overly bothered by the cast required when using the `get` method. By using array lists, you avoid the unpleasantness of partially filled arrays altogether—it is no wonder that most professional programmers use array lists (or vectors) all the time and rarely resort to arrays. Of course, you need arrays for numbers, but lists of numbers aren't all that common in object-oriented programs.

I highly recommend covering object streams and serialization, especially if the course involves significant programming projects. In my experience, students are delighted when they discover that they can store the entire state of their application with a single `writeObject` call and retrieve it again just as easily.

Part C

Chapters 17 through 20 contain an introduction to algorithms and data structures, covering recursion, sorting and searching, linked lists, binary trees, and hash tables. These topics are probably outside the scope of a one-semester course.

When discussing recursion, I find that the object-oriented point of view is very helpful. In my introductory examples, an object that solves a problem recursively constructs another object of the same class that solves a simpler problem. Having the other object do the simpler job is much more plausible to students than having a function call itself.

I place the data structures into the context of the standard Java collections library. Students will learn the essential abstractions of the standard library (such as iterators, sets, and maps) as well as the performance characteristics of the various collections. However, a detailed discussion of the implementation of data structures is beyond the scope of this book.

Part D

Chapters 21 through 25 cover advanced Java programming techniques that definitely go beyond a first course in Java. Although, as already mentioned, a comprehensive coverage of the Java library would span many volumes, many instructors suggested that a textbook should give students additional reference material of lasting value beyond their first course. Some institutions also teach a second-semester course that covers more practical programming aspects such as database and network programming, rather than the more traditional in-depth material on data structures and algorithms. Personally, I think this is a very viable approach. Thus, this book can be used in a two-semester course to give students an introduction into programming fundamentals *and* a broad coverage of applications. Alternatively, the material in the final chapters can be useful for student projects.

When selecting topics for the latter part of the book, I purposefully included those technologies that are of particular interest to *server-side programming*, such as networking, databases, XML, JavaServer Pages, and servlets, rather than including more advanced material on user interface construction. The Internet has made it possible to deploy many useful applications on servers, often accessed by nothing more than a browser. This new server-centric approach to application development was in part made possible by the Java language and libraries, and today, most of the industrial use of Java is in server-side programming.

Appendices

Appendix A1 contains a style guide for use with this book. I have found it highly beneficial to require a consistent style for all assignments. If this style guide conflicts with instructor sentiment or local customs, it can be modified. The style guide is available in electronic form for this purpose. Other appendices contain an overview over the parts of the standard library that this book covers, as well as quick references on HTML, UML, Java syntax, Unicode, the applet viewer, and javadoc.

The Pedagogical Structure

The beginning of each chapter has the customary overview of chapter objectives and motivational introduction. Throughout each chapter, margin notes show the places at which new concepts are introduced. The notes are summarized at the end of the chapter.

> To help students locate key concepts easily, margin notes show the place at which new concepts are introduced.

Throughout the chapters, there are five sets of notes to help your students, namely those entitled "Common Errors", "Productivity Hints", "Quality Tips", "Advanced Topics", and "Random Facts". These notes are specially marked so that they don't interrupt the flow of the main material. I expect that most instructors cover only a few of these notes in class and assign others for home reading. Some notes are quite short; others extend over a page. I decided to give each note the space that is needed for a full and convincing explanation, rather than attempting to fit them into one-paragraph "tips".

- **Common Errors** describe the kinds of errors that students often make, with an explanation of why the errors occur, and what to do about them. Most students quickly discover the Common Errors sections and read them on their own.

- **Quality Tips** explain good programming practices. Since most of them require an initial investment of effort, these notes carefully motivate the reason behind the advice, and explain why the effort will be repaid later.

- **Productivity Hints** teach students how to use their tools more effectively. Many beginning students put little thought into their use of computers and software. They are often unfamiliar with tricks of the trade such as keyboard shortcuts, global search and replace, or automation of common tasks with scripts.

- **Advanced Topics** cover nonessential or more difficult material. Some of these topics introduce alternative syntactical constructions that are not necessarily technically advanced. In many cases, the book uses one particular language construct but explains alternatives as Advanced Topics. Instructors and students should feel free to use those constructs in their own programs if they prefer them. It has, however, been my experience that many students are grateful for the "keep it simple" approach, because it greatly reduces the number of gratuitous decisions they have to make.

- **Random Facts** provide historical and social information on computing, as required to fulfill the "historical and social context" requirements of the ACM curriculum guidelines, as well as capsule reviews of advanced computer science topics. Many students will read the Random Facts on their own while pretending to follow the lecture.

- New to this edition is a set of **HOWTO** sections, inspired by the Linux HOWTO guides. These sections are intended to answer the common student question: "Now what do I do?", by giving step-by-step instructions for common tasks.

Web Resources

Additional resources are found on the book's web site at http://www.wiley.com/college/horstmann. These resources include:

- Solutions to selected exercises (accessible to students)
- Solutions to all exercises (for instructors only)
- A test bank
- A laboratory manual
- A list of frequently asked questions
- Help with common compilers
- Presentation slides for lectures
- Discussion boards for instructors and students
- Source code for all examples in the book
- The programming style guide in electronic form, so you can modify it to suit local preferences
- A "crash course in C++" that takes students rapidly from the material covered in this book to C++ programming

Acknowledgments

Many thanks to Paul Crockett, Bill Zobrist, Katherine Hepburn and Lisa Gee at John Wiley & Sons and Jerome Colburn, Lori Martinsek, and the team at Publication Services for their hard work and support for this book project.

I am very grateful to the many individuals who reviewed the manuscript, made valuable suggestions and brought an embarrassingly large number of errors and omissions to my attention. They include:

Sven Anderson, University of North Dakota, Robert Burton, Brigham Young University, Bruce Ellinbogen, University of Michigan-Dearborn, John Franco, University of Cincinnati, Rick Giles, Acadia University, John Gray, University of Hartford, Joann Houlihan, John Hopkins University, Richard Kick, Hinsdale Central High School, Michael Kölling, University of Southern Denmark, Miroslaw Majewski, Zayed University, Blaine Mayfield, Oklahoma State University, Hugh McGuire, University of California-Santa Barbara, Jim Miller, Bradley University, Jim Miller, University of Kansas, Don Needham, US Naval Academy, Ben Nystin, University of Colorado at Colorado Springs, Hugh O'Brien, University of California-Santa Barbara, Kathleen O'Brien, West Valley College, Michael Overton, New York University, Richard Pattis, Carnegie

Mellon University, Pete Peterson, Texas A&M University, Sarah Pham, SGI, Stuart Reges, University of Arizona, Jim Roberts, Carnegie Mellon University, John Rose, University of South Carolina-Columbia, Kenneth Slonneger, University of Iowa, and Monica Sweck, University of Florida.

Finally, as always, my gratitude goes to my family—Hui-Chen, Thomas and Nina—for their never-ending encouragement and patience.

Contents

Introduction

CHAPTER GOALS

CHAPTER GOALS

To understand the activity of programming

▶ To learn about the architecture of computers

▶ To learn about machine code and high-level programming languages

▶ To become familiar with your computing environment and your compiler

▶ To compile and run your first Java program

▶ To recognize syntax and logic errors

CHAPTER CONTENTS

1.1 What Is a Computer?

You have probably used a computer for work or fun. Many people use computers for everyday tasks such as balancing a checkbook or writing a term paper. Computers are good for such tasks. They can handle repetitive chores, such as totaling up numbers or placing words on a page, without getting bored or exhausted. More importantly, the computer presents you with the checkbook or the term paper on the screen and lets you fix up mistakes easily. Computers also make good game machines because they can play sequences of sounds and pictures, involving the human user in the process.

> A computer must be programmed to perform tasks. Different tasks require different programs.

What makes all this possible is not just the computer. The computer must be *programmed* to perform these tasks. A computer itself is a machine that stores data (numbers, words, pictures), interacts with devices (the monitor screen, the sound system, the printer), and executes programs. Programs are sequences of instructions and decisions that the computer carries out to achieve a task. One program balances checkbooks; a different program, perhaps designed and constructed by a different company, processes words; and a third program, probably from yet another company, plays a game.

> A computer program executes a sequence of very basic operations in rapid succession.

Today's computer programs are so sophisticated that it is hard to believe that they are all composed of extremely primitive operations. A typical operation may be one of the following:

- Put a red dot onto this screen position.

- Send the letter A to the printer.

- Get a number from this location in memory.

- Add up these two numbers.

- If this value is negative, continue the program at that instruction.

Only because a program contains a huge number of such operations, and because the computer can execute them at great speed, does the computer user have the illusion of smooth interaction.

The flexibility of a computer is quite an amazing phenomenon. The same machine can balance your checkbook, print your term paper, and play a game. In contrast, other machines carry out a much narrower range of tasks; a car drives, and a toaster toasts. Computers can carry out a wide range of tasks because they execute different programs, each of which directs the computer to work on a specific task.

1.2 What Is Programming?

> Programmers develop computer programs to make computers perform new tasks.

A computer program tells a computer, in minute detail, the sequence of steps that are needed to fulfill a task. The act of designing and implementing these programs is called computer programming. As you work through this book, you will learn how to program a computer—that is, how to direct the computer to execute tasks.

To use a computer you do not need to do any programming. When you write a term paper with a word processor, that software package has been programmed by the manufacturer and is ready for you to use. That is only to be expected—you can drive a car without being a mechanic and toast bread without being an electrician. Many people who use computers every day in their careers never need to do any programming.

Of course, a professional computer scientist or software engineer does a great deal of programming. You are reading this introductory computer science book, so your career goal may well be to become such a professional. Programming is not the only skill required of a computer scientist or software engineer; indeed, programming is not the only skill required to create successful computer programs. Nevertheless, the activity of programming is an important part of computer science. It is also a fascinating and pleasurable activity that continues to attract and motivate students. The discipline of computer science is particularly fortunate that it can make such an interesting activity the foundation of the learning path.

Writing a computer game with motion and sound effects or a word processor that supports fancy fonts and pictures is a complex task that requires a team of many highly skilled programmers. Your first programming efforts will be more mundane. The concepts and skills you learn in this book form an important foundation, and you should not be disappointed if your first programs do not rival the sophisticated software that is familiar to you. Actually, you will find that there is an immense thrill even in simple programming tasks. It is an amazing experience to see the computer precisely and quickly carry out a task that would take you hours of drudgery, to make small changes in a program that lead to immediate improvements, and to see the computer become an extension of your mental powers.

1.3 The Anatomy of a Computer

To understand the programming process, you need to have a rudimentary understanding of the building blocks that make up a computer. We will look at a personal computer. Larger computers have faster, larger, or more powerful components, but they have fundamentally the same design.

> At the heart of the computer lies the central processing unit (CPU).

At the heart of the computer lies the *central processing unit* (CPU) (see Figure 1). It consists of a single *chip* (integrated circuit) or a small number of chips. A computer chip is a component with a plastic or metal housing, metal connectors, and inside wiring made principally from silicon. For a CPU chip, the inside wiring is enormously complicated. For example, the Pentium III chip (a popular CPU for personal computers at the time of this writing) contains over 28 million structural elements called *transistors*—the elements that enable electrical signals to control other electrical signals, making automatic computing possible. The CPU performs program control, arithmetic, and data movement. That is, the CPU locates and executes the program instructions; it carries out arithmetic operations such as addition, subtraction, multiplication, and division; it fetches data from external memory or devices or stores data back. All data must travel through the CPU whenever it is moved from one location to another. (There are a few technical exceptions to this rule; some devices can interact directly with memory.)

Figure 1

Central Processing Unit

> Data and programs are stored in primary storage (memory) and secondary storage (such as a hard disk).

The computer keeps data and programs in *storage*. There are two kinds of storage. *Primary storage,* also called *random-access memory* (*RAM*) or simply *memory,* is fast but expensive; it is made from memory chips (see Figure 2). Primary storage has two disadvantages. It is comparatively expensive, and it loses all its data when the power is turned off. *Secondary storage,* usually a *hard disk* (see Figure 3), provides less expensive storage that persists without electricity. A hard disk consists of rotating platters, which are coated with a magnetic material, and read/write heads, which can detect and change

Figure 2

A Memory Module with Memory Chips

Figure 3

A Hard Disk

the patterns of varying magnetic flux on the platters. This is essentially the same recording and playback process that is used in audio or video tapes.

Some computers are self-contained units, whereas others are interconnected through *networks*. Home computers are usually intermittently connected to the Internet via a modem. The computers in your computer lab are probably permanently connected to a local area network. Through the network cabling, the computer can read programs from central storage locations or send data to other computers. For the user of a networked computer, it may not even be obvious which data reside on the computer itself and which are transmitted through the network.

Most computers have *removable storage* devices that can access data or programs on media such as floppy disks, tapes, or compact discs (CDs).

The most common use for a floppy disk is to move data from one computer to another; you can copy data from your home computer and bring the disk to school to continue working with it. Now that network connections have become commonplace, some computer manufacturers have discontinued the use of floppy disk drives, because email or a network-based file-sharing service can transport data between networked computers much more quickly and easily.

Compact discs originally served as read-only memories (CD-ROMs), which, like a commercial audio CD, could only be "played back" to bring the data on them into memory, but more and more new computers support CDs that a personal computer user can record (CD-Rs) or even overwrite with new data (CD-RWs).

Figure 4

A Motherboard

To interact with a human user, a computer requires other peripheral devices. The computer transmits information to the user through a display screen, loudspeakers, and printers. The user can enter information and directions to the computer by using a keyboard or a pointing device such as a mouse.

The CPU, the RAM, and the electronics controlling the hard disk and other devices are interconnected through a set of electrical lines called a *bus*. Data travel along the bus from the system memory and peripheral devices to the CPU and back. Figure 4 shows a *motherboard*, which contains the CPU, the RAM, and *card slots*, through which cards that control peripheral devices connect to the bus.

▼ **Random Fact**

The ENIAC and the Dawn of Computing

The ENIAC (*e*lectronic *n*umerical *i*ntegrator *a*nd *c*omputer) was the first usable electronic computer. It was designed by J. Presper Eckert and John Mauchly at the University of Pennsylvania and was completed in 1946. Instead of transistors, which were not invented until two years after it was built, the ENIAC contained about 18,000 *vacuum tubes* in many cabinets housed in a large room (see Figure 5). Vacuum tubes burned out at the rate of several tubes per day. An attendant with a shopping cart full of tubes con-

Figure 5

The ENIAC

stantly made the rounds and replaced defective ones. The computer was programmed by connecting wires on panels. Each wiring configuration would set up the computer for a particular problem. To have the computer work on a different problem, the wires had to be replugged.

Work on the ENIAC was supported by the U.S. Navy, which was interested in computations of ballistic tables that would give the trajectory of a projectile, depending on the wind resistance, initial velocity, and atmospheric conditions. To compute the trajectories, one must find the numerical solutions of certain differential equations; hence the name "numerical integrator". Before machines like ENIAC were developed, humans did this kind of work, and until the 1950s the word "computer" referred to these people. The ENIAC was later used for peaceful purposes such as the tabulation of U.S. census data.

Figure 6 gives a schematic overview of the architecture of a computer. Program instructions and data (such as text, numbers, audio, or video) are stored on the hard disk, on a CD, or elsewhere on the network. When a program is started, it is brought into memory, from which the CPU can read it. The CPU reads the program an instruction at a time. As directed by these instructions, the CPU reads data, modifies them, and writes them back to

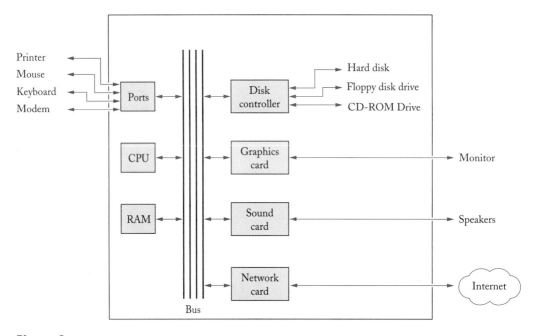

Figure 6

Schematic Diagram of a Computer

> The CPU reads machine instructions from memory. The instructions direct it to communicate with memory, secondary storage, and peripheral devices.

RAM or to secondary storage. Some program instructions will cause the CPU to place dots on the display screen or to vibrate the speaker. As these actions happen many times over and at great speed, the human user will perceive images and sound. Similarly, the CPU can send instructions to a printer to mark the paper with patterns of closely spaced dots, which a human recognizes as text characters and pictures. Some program instructions read user input from the keyboard or mouse. The program analyzes the nature of these inputs and then executes the next appropriate instructions.

1.4 Translating Human-Readable Programs to Machine Code

> Generally, machine code depends on the CPU type. However, the instruction set of the Java virtual machine (JVM) can be executed on many CPUs.

On the most basic level, computer instructions are extremely primitive. The processor executes *machine instructions*. CPUs from different vendors, such as the Intel Pentium or the Sun SPARC, have different sets of machine instructions. To enable Java applications to run on multiple CPUs without modification, most Java programs contain machine instructions for a so-called "Java virtual machine" (JVM), an idealized CPU that is then simulated by a program run on the actual CPU. The difference between actual and virtual machine instructions is not important to us—all you need to know is that machine instructions are very simple and can be executed very quickly.

A typical sequence of machine instructions is

1. Load the contents of memory location 40.

2. Load the value 100.

3. If the first value is greater than the second value, continue with the instruction that is stored in memory location 240.

Actually, machine instructions are encoded as numbers so that they can be stored in memory. On the Java virtual machine, this sequence of instruction is encoded as the sequence of numbers

```
21 40 16 100 163 240
```

> Because machine instructions are encoded as numbers, it is difficult to write programs in machine code.

On a processor such as a Pentium or SPARC, the encoding would be quite different.

When the virtual machine fetches this sequence of numbers, it decodes them and executes the associated sequence of commands.

How can you communicate the command sequence to the computer? The simplest method is to place the actual numbers into the computer memory. This is, in fact, how the very earliest computers worked. However, a long program is composed of thousands of individual commands, and it is tedious and error-prone to look up the numeric codes for all commands and place the codes manually into memory. As we said before, computers are really good at automating tedious and error-prone activities, and it did not take long for computer programmers to realize that the computers themselves could be harnessed to help in the programming process.

The first step was to assign short names to the commands. For example, `iload` denotes "integer load", `bipush` means "push integer constant", and `if_icmpgt` means "if integers compare greater". Using these commands, the instruction sequence becomes

```
iload 40
bipush 100
if_icmpgt 240
```

> Assembly language makes it easier to generate machine instructions by translating mnemonics and symbolic names.

That is a lot easier to read for humans. To get the instruction sequences accepted by the computer, though, the names must be translated into the machine codes. Early computers used a computer program called an *assembler* to carry out these translations. An assembler takes the sequence of characters such as `iload`, translates it into the command code 21, and carries out similar operations on the other commands. Assemblers have another feature: They can give names to *memory locations* as well as to instructions. Our program sequence might have checked that some interest rate was greater than 100 percent, and the interest rate was stored in memory location 40. It is usually not important where a value is stored; any available memory location will do. When symbolic names are used instead of memory addresses, the program gets even easier to read:

```
iload      intRate
bipush     100
if_icmpgt  intError
```

It is the job of the assembler program to find suitable numeric addresses for the symbolic names and to put those addresses into the generated code sequence.

Assembler instructions were a major advance over programming with raw machine instructions, but they suffer from two problems: It still takes a great many instructions to achieve even the simplest goals, and the exact instruction sequence differs from one processor to another.

> High-level languages let you describe tasks at a higher conceptual level than machine code.

In the mid-1950s, *high-level* programming languages began to appear. In these languages, the programmer expresses the idea behind the task that needs to be performed, and a special computer program, called a *compiler,* translates the high-level description into machine instructions for a particular processor.

For example, in Java, the high-level programming language that you will use in this book, you might give the following instruction:

```
if (intRate > 100)
    System.out.print("Interest rate error");
```

This means, "If the interest rate is over 100, display an error message." It is then the job of the compiler program to look at the sequence of characters if (intRate > 100) and translate that into

```
21 40 16 100 163 240
```

> A compiler translates programs written in a high-level language into machine code.

Compilers are quite sophisticated programs. They have to translate logical statements, such as the if, into sequences of computations, tests, and jumps, and they must find memory locations for *variables*—items of information identified by symbolic names—like intRate. In this course, we will generally take the existence of a compiler for granted. If you decide to become a professional computer scientist, you may well learn more about compiler-writing techniques later in your studies.

1.5   Programming Languages

> Each programming language has its own set of rules for forming instructions. Compilers enforce these rules strictly.

High-level programming languages are independent of specific computer architecture, but they are human creations. As such, they follow certain conventions. To ease the translation process, those conventions are much stricter than they are for human languages. When you talk to another person, and you scramble or omit a word or two, your conversation partner will usually still understand what you have to say. Compilers are less forgiving. For example, if you omit the quotation mark close to the end of the instruction,

```
if (intRate > 100)
    System.out.print("Interest rate error);
```

the Java compiler will get quite confused and complain that it cannot translate an instruction containing this error. That is actually a good thing. If the compiler were to try to guess what you did wrong and tried to fix it, it might not guess your intentions correctly. In that case, the resulting program would do the wrong thing—quite possibly with disastrous effects, if that program controlled a device on whose functions someone's well-being depends. When a compiler reads programming instructions in a programming language, it will translate them into machine code only if the input follows the language conventions exactly.

Just as there are many human languages, there are many programming languages. Consider the instruction

```
if (intRate > 100)
   System.out.print("Interest rate error");
```

This is how you must express a decision in Java. Java is a very popular programming language, and it is the one we use in this book. But in Pascal (another programming language that was in common use in the 1970s and 1980s) the same instruction would be written as

```
if intRate > 100 then write('Interest rate error');
```

In this case, the differences between the Java and Pascal versions are slight. For other constructions, there will be far more substantial differences. Compilers are language-specific. The Java compiler will translate only Java code, whereas a Pascal compiler will reject anything but legal Pascal code. For example, if a Java compiler reads the instruction `if intRate > 100 then ...`, it will complain, because the condition of the `if` statement isn't surrounded by parentheses () and the compiler doesn't expect the word `then`. The choice of the layout for a language construct like the `if` statement is somewhat arbitrary, and the designers of different languages choose different tradeoffs among readability, easy translation, and consistency with other languages.

1.6   The Java Programming Language

In 1991, a group led by James Gosling and Patrick Naughton at Sun Microsystems designed a language that they code-named "Green" for use in consumer devices such as intelligent television "set-top" boxes. The language was designed to be simple and architecture-neutral, so that it could be executed on a variety of hardware. No customer was ever found for this technology.

> Java was originally designed for programming consumer devices, but it was first successfully used to write Internet applets.

Gosling recounts that in 1994 the team realized, "We could write a really cool browser. It was one of the few things in the client/server mainstream that needed some of the weird things we'd done: architecture neutral, real-time, reliable, secure." The HotJava browser, which was shown to an enthusiastic crowd at the SunWorld exhibition in 1995, had one unique property: It could download programs, called *applets,* from the web and run them. Applets, written in the language now called Java, let web developers provide a variety of animation and interaction that can greatly extend the capabilities of a web page (see Figure 7). Since 1996, both Netscape and Microsoft have supported Java in their browsers.

Java has grown at a phenomenal rate. Programmers have embraced the language because it is simpler than its closest rival, C++. In addition to the programming language itself, Java has a rich *library* that makes it possible to write portable programs that can

Figure 7

An Applet for Visualizing Molecules (`http://www.openscience.org/jmol`)

bypass proprietary operating systems—a feature that was eagerly sought by those who wanted to be independent of those proprietary systems and was bitterly fought by their vendors.

Some of the early expectations that were placed on the Java language were overly optimistic, and the slogan "write once, run anywhere" turned into "write once, debug everywhere" for the early adopters of Java, who had to deal with less-than-perfect implementations. Since then, Java has come a long way. The Java 2 language and library, released in 1998, has brought a much greater level of stability to Java development. A "micro edition" and an "enterprise edition" of the Java library make Java programmers at home on hardware ranging from the smallest embedded devices to the largest Internet servers.

> Java was designed to be safe and portable, benefitting both Internet users and students.

Because Java was designed for the Internet, it has two attributes that make it very suitable for beginners: safety and portability. If you visit a web page that contains applets, those applets automatically start running. It is important that you can trust that applets are inherently safe. If an applet could do something evil, such as damaging data or reading personal information on your computer, then you would be in real danger every time you browsed the Web—an unscrupulous designer might put up a web page containing dangerous code that would execute on your machine as soon as you visited the page. The Java language has an assortment of security features that guarantee that no evil applets can run on your computer. As an added benefit, these features also help you to learn the language faster. The Java virtual machine can catch many kinds of beginners' mistakes and report them accurately. (In contrast, many beginners' mistakes in the C language merely produce programs that act in random and confusing ways.) The other benefit of Java is portability. The same Java program will run, without change, on Windows, UNIX, Linux, or the Macintosh. This too is a requirement for applets. When you visit a web page, the web server that serves up the page contents has no idea what computer you are using to browse the Web. It simply returns you the portable code that was generated by the Java compiler. The virtual machine on your computer executes that portable code. Again, there is a benefit for the student. You do not have to learn how to write programs for different computers' operating systems.

At this time, Java has already established itself as one of the most important languages for general-purpose programming as well as for computer science instruction. However, although Java is a good language for beginners, it is not perfect, for two reasons.

Because Java was not specifically designed for students, no thought was given to make it really simple to write basic programs. A certain amount of technical machinery is necessary in Java to write even the simplest programs. To understand what this technical machinery does, you need to know something about programming. This is not a problem for a professional programmer with prior experience in another programming language, but not having a linear learning path is a drawback for the student. As you learn how to program in Java, there will be times when you will be asked to be satisfied with a preliminary explanation and wait for complete details in a later chapter.

> Java has a very large library. Focus on learning those parts of the library that you need for your programming projects.

Furthermore, you cannot hope to learn all of Java in one semester. The Java language itself is relatively simple, but Java contains a vast set of *library packages* that are necessary to write useful programs. There are packages for graphics, user interface design, cryptography, networking, sound, database storage, and many other purposes. Even expert Java programmers do not know the contents of all of the packages—they just use those that they need for particular projects. Using this book, you should expect to learn a good deal about the Java language and about the most important packages. Keep in mind that the central goal of this book is not to make you memorize Java minutiae, but to teach you how to think about programming.

1.7   Becoming Familiar with Your Computer

> Set aside some time to become familiar with the computer system and the Java compiler that you will use for your class work.

You may be taking your first programming course as you read this book, and you may well be doing your work on an unfamiliar computer system. You should spend some time making yourself familiar with the computer. Because computer systems vary widely, this book can only give an outline of the steps you need to follow. Using a new and unfamiliar computer system can be frustrating, especially if you are on your own. Look for training courses that your campus offers, or just ask a friend to give you a brief tour.

Step 1. Log In

If you use your own home computer, you probably don't need to worry about this step. Computers in a lab, however, are usually not open to everyone. Access is usually restricted

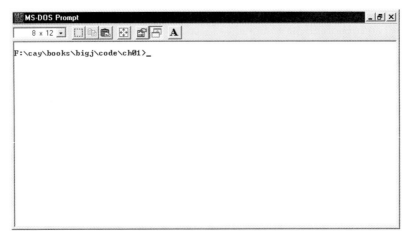

Figure 8

A Shell Window

to those who have paid the necessary fees, and often each student account has permissions and restrictions that enable the student to do class work but not mess up the system for others. You will need an account name or number and a password to gain access to such a system.

Step 2. Locate the Java Compiler

Computer systems differ greatly in this regard. On some systems you must open a *shell window* (see Figure 8) and type commands to launch the compiler. Other systems have an *integrated development environment* in which you can write and test your programs (see Figure 9). Many university labs have information sheets and tutorials that walk you through the tools that are installed in the lab. The companion web site for this book (reference [1] at the end of this chapter) contains instructions for several popular compilers.

Step 3. Understand Files and Folders

As a programmer, you will write Java programs, try them out, and improve them. You will be provided a place in secondary storage to store them, and you need to find out where that place is. Information in secondary storage is kept in *files*. A file is a collection of items of information that are kept together, such as the text of a word processing document or the instructions of a Java program. Files have names, and the rules for legal names differ from one system to another. Some systems allow spaces in file names; others don't. Some distinguish between upper- and lowercase letters; others don't. Most Java compilers require that Java files end in an *extension* `.java`; for example, `Test.java`. Java file names cannot contain spaces, and the distinction between upper- and lowercase letters is important.

Files are stored in *folders* or *directories*. These file containers can be *nested*. That is, a folder can contain not only files but also other folders, which themselves can contain

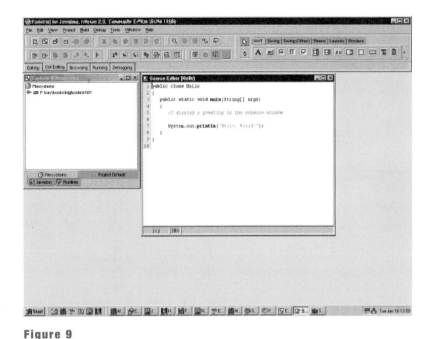

Figure 9

An Integrated Development Environment

more files and folders (see Figure 10). This hierarchy can be quite large, especially on networked computers, where some of the files may be on your local disk, others elsewhere on the network. While you need not be concerned with every branch of the hierarchy, you should familiarize yourself with your local environment. Different systems have different ways of showing files and directories. Some use a graphical display and let you move around by clicking the mouse on folder icons. In other systems, you must enter commands to visit or inspect different locations.

Step 4. Write a Simple Program

In the next section, we will introduce a very simple program. You will need to learn how to type it in, how to run it, and how to fix mistakes.

Step 5. Save Your Work

You will spend many hours typing Java program code and improving it. The resulting program files have some value, and you should treat them as you would other important property. A conscientious safety strategy is particularly important for computer files. They are more fragile than paper documents or other more tangible objects. It is easy to delete a file by accident, and occasionally files are lost because of a computer malfunction. Unless you kept another copy, you must then retype the contents. Because you probably won't remember the entire file, you will likely find yourself spending almost as much time again as you did to enter and improve it in the first place. This costs time, and it may cause you to miss deadlines. It is therefore crucially important that you learn how

Figure 10

Nested Folders

to safeguard files and that you get in the habit of doing so *before* disaster strikes. You can make safety or *backup* copies of files by saving copies on a floppy, into another folder, or to a different computer on your local area network or the Internet.

Productivity Hint   1.1

Backup Copies

Backing up on floppy disks is the easiest and most convenient method for most people. Another increasingly popular form of backup is Internet file storage. Here are a few pointers to keep in mind.

> Develop a strategy for keeping backup copies of your work before disaster strikes.

- *Back up often.* Backing up a file takes only a few seconds, and you will hate yourself if you have to spend many hours recreating work that you could have saved easily. Back up your work once every thirty minutes, and every time before you test one of your programs.

- *Rotate backups.* Use more than one floppy disk for backups, and rotate them. That is, first back up onto the first floppy disk and put it aside. Then back up onto the second floppy disk. Then use the third, and then go back to the first. That way you always have three recent backups. Even if one of the floppy disks has a defect, you can use one of the others.

▼

▼

- *Back up source files only.* The compiler translates the files that you write into files consisting of machine code. There is no need to back up the machine code files, since you can recreate them easily by running the compiler again. Focus your backup activity on those files that represent your effort. That way your backup disks won't fill up with files that you don't need.

▼

- *Pay attention to the backup direction.* Backing up involves copying files from one place to another. It is important that you do this right—that is, copy from your work location to the backup location. If you do it the wrong way, you will over-write a newer file with an older version.

▼

- *Check your backups once in a while.* Double-check that your backups are where you think they are. There is nothing more frustrating than to find out that the backups are not there when you need them. This is particularly true if you use a backup program that stores files on an unfamiliar device (such as data tape) or in a compressed format.

▼

- *Relax, then restore.* When you lose a file and need to restore it from backup, you are likely to be in an unhappy, nervous state. Take a deep breath and think through the recovery process before you start. It is not uncommon for an agitated computer user to wipe out the last backup when trying to restore a damaged file.

▼

1.8   ## Compiling a Simple Program

You are now ready to write and run your first Java program. The traditional choice for the very first program in a new programming language is a program that displays a simple greeting: "Hello, World!". Let us follow that tradition. Here is the "Hello, World!" program in Java.

File Hello.java

```
1  public class Hello
2  {
3     public static void main(String[] args)
4     {
5        // display a greeting in the console window
6
7        System.out.println("Hello, World!");
8     }
9  }
```

We will examine this program in a minute. For now, you should make a new program file and call it `Hello.java`. Enter the program instructions and compile and run the program, following the procedure that is appropriate for your compiler.

> Java is case-sensitive. You must be careful about distinguishing between upper- and lowercase letters.

Java is *case-sensitive*. You must enter upper- and lowercase letters exactly as they appear in the program listing. You cannot type `MAIN` or `PrintLn`. If you are not careful, you will run into problems—see Common Error 1.1.

On the other hand, Java has *free-form layout*. You can use any number of spaces and line breaks to separate words. You can cram as many words as possible into each line,

```
public class Hello{public static void main(String[]
args){// display a greeting in the console window
System.out.println("Hello, World!");}}
```

You can even write every word and symbol on a separate line,

```
public
class
Hello
{
public
static
void
main
(
   . . .
```

> Lay out your programs so that they are easy to read.

However, good taste dictates that you lay out your programs in a readable fashion. Chapters 2 and 3 contain recommendations for good layout.

When you run the program, the message

```
Hello, World!
```

> Classes are the fundamental building blocks of Java programs.

will appear somewhere on the screen (see Figures 11 and 12). The exact location depends on your programming environment.

Now that you have seen the program working, it is time to understand its makeup. The first line,

```
public class Hello
```

> Each class contains definitions of methods. Each method contains a sequence of instructions.

starts a new *class*. Classes are a fundamental concept in Java, and you will begin to study them in Chapter 2. In Java, every program consists of one or more classes.

The keyword `public` denotes that the class is usable by the "public". You will later encounter `private` features, which are not.

At this point, you should simply regard the

```
public class ClassName
{
   . . .
}
```

as a necessary part of the "plumbing" that is required to write any Java program. In Java, every source file can contain at most one public class, and the name of the public class must match the name of the file containing the class. For example, the class `Hello` *must be* contained in a file Hello.java. It is very important that the names *and the capitalization* match exactly. You can get strange error messages if you call the class `HELLO` or the file `hello.java`.

Figure 11

Running the Hello Program in a Console Window

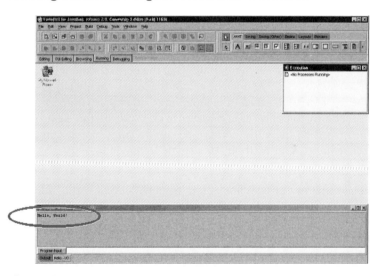

Figure 12

Running the Hello Program in an Integrated Development
Environment

The construction

```
public static void main(String[] args)
{
}
```

defines a *method* called main. A method contains a collection of programming instructions that describe how to carry out a particular task. Every Java application must have a main method. Most Java programs contain other methods besides main, and you will see in Chapter 2 how to write other methods.

> Every Java application contains a class with a main method. When the application starts, the instructions in the main method are executed.

The *parameter* `String[]  args` is a required part of the `main` method. (It contains *command line arguments*, which we will not discuss until Chapter 16.) The keyword `static` indicates that the `main` method does not operate on an *object*. (As you will see in Chapter 2, most methods in Java do operate on objects, and `static` methods are not common in large Java programs. Nevertheless, `main` must always be `static`, because it starts running before the program can create objects.)

At this time, simply consider

```
public class ClassName
{
    public static void main(String[] args)
    {
        . . .
    }
}
```

as yet another part of the "plumbing". Our first program has all instructions inside the `main` method of a class.

> Use comments to help human readers understand your program.

The first line inside the `main` method is a *comment*

// display a greeting in the console window

This comment is purely for the benefit of the human reader, to explain in more detail what the next statement does. Any text enclosed between `//` and the end of the line is completely ignored by the compiler. Comments are used to explain the program to other programmers or to yourself.

The instructions or *statements* in the *body* of the `main` method—that is, the statements inside the curly braces {}—are executed one by one. Each statement ends in a semicolon ;. Our method has a single statement:

```
System.out.println("Hello, World!");
```

This statement prints a line of text, namely "Hello, World!". However, there are many places where a program can send that string: to a window, to a file, or to a networked computer on the other side of the world. You need to specify that the destination for the string is the *standard output*—that is, a console window. The console window is represented in Java by an object called `out`. Just as you needed to place the `main` method in a `Hello` class, the designers of the Java library needed to place the `out` object into a class. They placed it in the `System` class, which contains useful objects and methods to access system resources. To use the `out` object in the `System` class, you must refer to it as `System.out`.

> You call a method by specifying an object, the method name, and the method parameters.

To use an object such as `System.out`, you specify what you want to do to it. In this case, you want to print a line of text. The `println` method carries out this task. You do not have to implement this method—the programmers who wrote the Java library already did that for us—but you do need to *call* the method.

Whenever you call a method in Java, you need to specify three items:

1. The object that you want to use (in this case, `System.out`)

2. The name of the method you want to use (in this case, `println`)

3. A pair of parentheses, containing any other information the method needs (in this case, `("Hello, World!")`)

Note that the two periods in `System.out.println` have different meanings. The first period means "locate the `out` object in the `System` class". The second period means "apply the `println` method to that object".

Syntax 1.1: Method Call

object.methodName (*parameters*)

Example:

```
System.out.println("Hello, Dave!");
```

Purpose:

To invoke a method on an object and supply any additional parameters

---

A sequence of characters enclosed in quotation marks

```
"Hello, World!"
```

is called a *string*. You must enclose the contents of the string inside quotation marks so that the compiler knows you literally mean `"Hello, World!"`. There is a reason for this requirement. Suppose you need to print the word *main*. By enclosing it in quotation marks, `"main"`, the compiler knows you mean the sequence of characters m a i n, not the method named `main`. The rule is simply that you must enclose all text strings in quotation marks, so that the compiler considers them plain text and does not try to interpret them as program instructions.

> A string is a sequence of characters enclosed in quotation marks.

You can also print numerical values. For example, the statement

```
System.out.println(3 + 4);
```

displays the number 7.

The `println` method prints a string or a number and then starts a new line. For example, the sequence of statements

```
System.out.println("Hello");
System.out.println("World!");
```

prints two lines of text:

```
Hello
World!
```

There is a second method, called `print`, that you can use to print an item without starting a new line afterward. For example, the output of the two statements

```
System.out.print("00");
System.out.println(3 + 4);
```

is the single line

```
007
```

⊗ Common Error   1.1

Omitting Semicolons

In Java every statement must end in a semicolon. Forgetting to type a semicolon is a common error. It confuses the compiler, because the compiler uses the semicolon to find where one statement ends and the next one starts. The compiler does not use line breaks or closing braces to recognize the end of statements. For example, the compiler considers

```
System.out.println("Hello")
System.out.println("World!");
```

a single statement, as if you had written

```
System.out.println("Hello") System.out.println("World!");
```

Then it doesn't understand that statement, because it does not expect the word `System` following the closing parenthesis after `"Hello"`. The remedy is simple. Scan every statement for a terminating semicolon, just as you would check that every English sentence ends in a period.

Advanced Topic   1.1

Alternative Comment Syntax

In Java there are two methods for writing comments. You already learned that the compiler ignores anything that you type between `//` and the end of the current line. The compiler also ignores any text between a `/*` and `*/`.

```
/* A simple Java program */
```

The `//` comment is easier to type if the comment is only a single line long. If you have a comment that is longer than a line, then the `/* . . . */` comment is simpler:

```
/*
This is a simple Java program that you can use to try out
your compiler and interpreter.
*/
```

It would be somewhat tedious to add the `//` at the beginning of each line and to move them around whenever the text of the comment changes.

In this book, we use `//` for comments that will never grow beyond a line, and `/* . . . */` for longer comments. If you prefer, you can always use the `//` style. The readers of your code will be grateful for *any* comments, no matter which style you use.

▼ Advanced Topic   1.2

Escape Sequences

Suppose you want to display a string containing quotation marks, such as

```
Hello, "World"!
```

You can't use

```
System.out.println("Hello, "World"!");
```

As soon as the compiler reads `"Hello, "`, it thinks the string is finished, and then it gets all confused about `World` followed by two quotation marks. A human would probably realize that the second and third quotation marks were supposed to be part of the string, but compilers have a one-track mind. If a simple analysis of the input doesn't make sense to them, they just refuse to go on, and they report an error. Well, how do you then display quotation marks on the screen? You precede the quotation marks inside the string with a *backslash* character. Inside a string, the sequence `\"` denotes a literal quote, not the end of a string. The correct display statement is therefore

```
System.out.println("Hello, \"World\"!");
```

The backslash character is used as an *escape* character, and the character sequence `\"` is called an escape sequence. The backslash does not denote itself; instead, it is used to encode other characters that would otherwise be difficult to include in a string.

Now, what do you do if you actually want to print a backslash (for example, to specify a Windows file name)? You must enter two `\\` in a row, like this:

```
System.out.println(
    "The secret message is in C:\\Temp\\Secret.txt");
```

This statement prints

```
The secret message is in C:\Temp\Secret.txt
```

Another escape sequence occasionally used is `\n`, which denotes a *newline* or line feed character. Printing a newline character causes the start of a new line on the display. For example, the statement

```
System.out.print("*\n**\n***\n");
```

prints the characters

```
*
**
***
```

on three separate lines. Of course, you could have achieved the same effect with three separate calls to `println`.

Finally, escape sequences are useful for including international characters in a string. For example, suppose you want to print "All the way to San José!", with an accented letter é. If you use a U.S. keyboard, you may not have a key to generate that letter. Java uses

▼   the *Unicode* encoding scheme to denote international characters. For example, the é character has Unicode encoding 00E9. You can include that character inside a string by writing \u, followed by its Unicode encoding:

▼

```
System.out.println("All the way to San Jos\u00E9!");
```

▼   You can look up the codes for the U.S. English and Western European characters in Appendix A6, and codes for thousands of characters in reference [2].

1.9   Errors

Experiment a little with the Hello program. What happens if you make a typing error such as

```
System.ouch.println("Hello, World!");
System.out.println("Hello, World!);
System.out.println("Hell, World!");
```

> A syntax error is a violation of the rules of the programming language. The compiler detects syntax errors.

In the first case, the compiler will complain. It will say that it has no clue what you mean by ouch. The exact wording of the error message is dependent on the compiler, but it might be something like "Undefined symbol ouch". This is a *compile-time error* or *syntax error*. Something is wrong according to the language rules, and the compiler finds it. When the compiler finds one or more errors, it refuses to translate the program to Java virtual machine instructions, and as a consequence you have no program that you can run. You must fix the error and compile again. In fact, the compiler is quite picky, and it is common to go through several rounds of fixing compile-time errors before compilation succeeds for the first time.

If the compiler finds an error, it will not simply stop and give up. It will try to report as many errors as it can find, so you can fix them all at once. Sometimes, however, one error throws it off track. This is likely to happen with the error in the second line. Because the closing quotation mark is missing, the compiler will think that the) ; characters are still part of the string. In such cases, it is common for the compiler to emit bogus error reports for neighboring lines. You should fix only those error messages that make sense to you and then recompile.

The error in the third line is of a different kind. The program will compile and run, but its output will be wrong. It will print

```
Hell, World!
```

> A logic error causes a program to take an action that the programmer did not intend. You must test your programs to find logic errors.

This is a *run-time error* or *logic error*. The program is syntactically correct and does something, but it doesn't do what it is supposed to do. The compiler cannot find the error. You, the programmer, must flush out this type of error. Run the program, and carefully look at its output.

During program development, errors are unavoidable. Once a program is longer than a few lines, it requires superhuman concentration to enter it correctly without slipping up once. You will find yourself omitting semicolons or quotes more often than you would like, but the compiler will track down these problems for you.

Logic errors are more troublesome. The compiler will not find them—in fact, the compiler will cheerfully translate any program as long as its syntax is correct—but the resulting program will do something wrong. It is the responsibility of the program author to test the program and find any logic errors. Testing programs is an important topic that you will encounter many times in this book. Another important aspect of good craftsmanship is *defensive programming:* structuring programs and development processes in such a way that an error in one place of a program does not trigger a disastrous response.

The error examples that you saw so far were not difficult to diagnose or fix, but as you learn more sophisticated programming techniques, there will also be much more room for error. It is an uncomfortable fact that locating all errors in a program is very difficult. Even if you can observe that a program exhibits faulty behavior, it may not at all be obvious what part of the program caused it and how you can fix it. Special software tools (so-called *debuggers*) let you trace through a program to find *bugs*—that is, logic errors. In this course you will learn how to use a debugger effectively.

Note that all these errors are different from the kind of errors that you are likely to make in calculations. If you total up a column of numbers, you may miss a minus sign or accidentally drop a carry, perhaps because you are bored or tired. Computers do not make these kinds of errors. When a computer adds up numbers, it will get the correct answer. Admittedly, computers can make overflow or roundoff errors, just as pocket calculators do when you ask them to perform computations whose result falls outside their numeric range. An overflow error occurs if the result of a computation is very large or very small. For example, most computers and pocket calculators overflow when you try to compute 10^{1000}. A roundoff error occurs when a value cannot be represented precisely. For example, 1/3 may be stored in the computer as 0.3333333, a value that is close to, but not exactly equal to, 1/3. If you compute $1 - (3 \times 1/3)$, you may obtain 0.0000001, not 0, as a result of the roundoff error. We will consider such errors logic errors, because the programmer should have chosen a more appropriate calculation scheme that handles overflow or roundoff correctly.

You will learn a three-part error management strategy in this book. First, you will learn about common errors and how to avoid them. Then you will learn defensive programming strategies to minimize the likelihood and impact of errors. Finally, you will learn debugging strategies to flush out those errors that remain.

▼ ⊗ **Common Error**   **1.2**

Misspelling Words

▼

If you accidentally misspell a word, then strange things may happen, and it may not always be completely obvious from the error messages what went wrong. Here is a good example of how simple spelling errors can cause trouble:

▼

```
public class Hello
{
```

```
public static void Main(String[] args)
{
    System.out.println("Hello, World!");
}
}
```

This class defines a method called `Main`. The compiler will not consider this to be the same as the `main` method, because `Main` starts with an uppercase letter and the Java language is *case-sensitive*. Upper- and lowercase letters are considered to be completely different from each other, and to the compiler `Main` is no better match for `main` than `rain`. The compiler will cheerfully compile your `Main` method, but when the Java interpreter reads the compiled file, it will complain about the missing `main` method and refuse to run the program. Of course, the message "missing main method" should give you a clue where to look for the error.

If you get an error message that seems to indicate that the compiler is on the wrong track, it is a good idea to check for spelling and capitalization. All Java keywords use only lowercase letters. Names of classes usually start with an uppercase letter, names of methods and variables with a lowercase letter. If you misspell the name of a symbol (for example, `ouch` instead of `out`), the compiler will complain about an "undefined symbol". That error message is usually a good clue that you made a spelling error.

1.10   The Compilation Process

Some Java development environments are very convenient to use. You just enter the code in one window, click on a button to compile, and click on another button to execute your program. Error messages show up in a second window, and the program runs in a third window. With such an environment you are completely shielded from the details of the compilation process. On other systems you must carry out every step manually, by typing commands such as

```
edit Hello.java
javac Hello.java
java Hello
```

into a shell window.

> An editor is a program for entering and modifying text, such as a Java program.

No matter which compilation environment you use, you begin your activity by typing in the program statements. The program that you use for entering and modifying the program text is called an *editor*. Remember to *save* your work to disk frequently, because otherwise the text editor stores the text only in the computer's memory. If something goes wrong with the computer and you need to restart it, the contents of the primary memory (including your program text) are lost, but anything stored on a hard disk or floppy disk is permanent even if you need to restart the computer.

> The Java compiler translates source code into instructions for the Java virtual machine, called bytecode.

When you compile your program, the compiler translates the Java *source code* (that is, the statements that you wrote) into *bytecode*, which consists of virtual machine instructions and some other pieces of information on how to load the program into memory prior to execution. The bytecode for a program is stored in a separate file, with extension `.class`. For example, the bytecode for the Hello program will be stored in a file `Hello.class`. However, the compiler produces a class file only after you have corrected all syntax errors.

The class file contains the translation of only the instructions that you wrote. That is not enough actually to run the program. To display a string on a window, quite a bit of low-level activity is necessary. The authors of the `System` and `PrintStream` classes (which define the `out` object and the `println` method) have implemented all necessary actions and placed the required bytecode into a *library*. A library is a collection of code that has been programmed and translated by someone else, ready for you to use in your program. (More complicated programs are built from more than one class file and more than one library.)

The *Java interpreter* loads the bytecode of the program that you wrote, starts your program, and loads the necessary library files as they are required.

> The Java interpreter runs a program, loading the necessary bytecode from class files and library files.

The steps of compiling and running your program are outlined in Figure 13.

Your programming activity centers around these steps. You start in the editor, writing the source file. You compile the program and look at the error messages. You go back to the editor and fix the syntax errors. When the compiler succeeds, you run your program. If you find an error, you can run the debugger to execute it a line at a time. Once you find the cause of the error, you go back to the editor and fix it. You compile and run again to see whether the error has gone away. If not, you go back to the editor. This is called the *edit–compile–test loop* (see Figure 14). You will spend a substantial amount of time in this loop whenever you work on programming assignments.

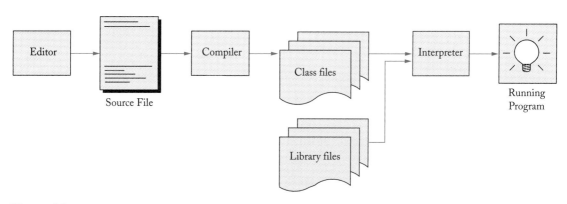

Figure 13

From Source Code to Running Program

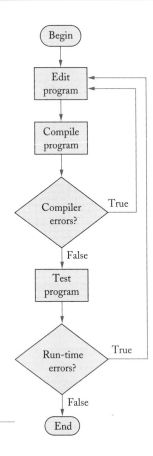

Figure 14

The Edit-Compile-Test Loop

CHAPTER SUMMARY

1. A computer must be programmed to perform tasks. Different tasks require different programs.

2. A computer program executes a sequence of very basic operations in rapid succession.

3. Programmers develop computer programs to make computers perform new tasks.

4. At the heart of the computer lies the central processing unit (CPU).

5. Data and programs are stored in primary storage (memory) and secondary storage (such as a hard disk).

6. The CPU reads machine instructions from memory. The instructions direct it to communicate with memory, secondary storage, and peripheral devices.

7. Generally, machine code depends on the CPU type. However, the instruction set of the Java virtual machine (JVM) can be executed on many CPUs.

8. Because machine instructions are encoded as numbers, it is difficult to write programs in machine code.

9. Assembly language makes it easier to generate machine instructions by translating mnemonics and symbolic names.

10. High-level languages let you describe tasks at a higher conceptual level than machine code.

11. A compiler translates programs written in a high-level language into machine code.

12. Each programming language has its own set of rules for forming instructions. Compilers enforce these rules strictly.

13. Java was originally designed for programming consumer devices, but it was first successfully used to write Internet applets.

14. Java was designed to be safe and portable, benefitting both Internet users and students.

15. Java has a very large library. Focus on learning those parts of the library that you need for your programming projects.

16. Set aside some time to become familiar with the computer system and the Java compiler that you will use for your class work.

17. Develop a strategy for keeping backup copies of your work before disaster strikes.

18. Java is case-sensitive. You must be careful about distinguishing between upper- and lowercase letters.

19. Lay out your programs so that they are easy to read.

20. Classes are the fundamental building blocks of Java programs.

21. Each class contains definitions of methods. Each method contains a sequence of instructions.

22. Every Java application contains a class with a `main` method. When the application starts, the instructions in the `main` method are executed.

23. Use comments to help human readers understand your program.

24. You call a method by specifying an object, the method name, and the method parameters.

25. A string is a sequence of characters enclosed in quotation marks.

26. A syntax error is a violation of the rules of the programming language. The compiler detects syntax errors.

27. A logic error causes a program to take an action that the programmer did not intend. You must test your programs to find logic errors.

28. An editor is a program for entering and modifying text, such as a Java program.

29. The Java compiler translates source code into instructions for the Java virtual machine, called bytecode.

30. The Java interpreter runs a program, loading the necessary bytecode from class files and library files.

Further Reading

[1] http://www.horstmann.com/bigjava/help/compilers.html Instructions for using several popular Java compilers.
[2] http://www.unicode.org/ The web site of the Unicode Consortium. It contains character tables that show the Unicode values of characters from many scripts.

CLASSES, OBJECTS, AND METHODS INTRODUCED IN THIS CHAPTER

Here is a list of all classes, methods, static variables, and constants introduced in this chapter. Turn to the documentation in Appendix A6 for more information.

```
java.io.PrintStream
    print
    println
java.lang.String
    length
java.lang.System
    out
```

REVIEW EXERCISES

Exercise R1.1. Explain the difference between using a computer program and programming a computer.

Exercise R1.2. What distinguishes a computer from a typical household appliance?

Exercise R1.3. Rank the storage devices that can be part of a computer system by (*a*) speed, (*b*) cost, and (*c*) storage capacity.

Exercise R1.4. What is the Java virtual machine?

Exercise R1.5. What is an applet?

Exercise R1.6. Explain two benefits of higher-level programming languages over assembler code.

Exercise R1.7. List the programming languages mentioned in this chapter.

Exercise R1.8. What is an integrated programming environment?

Exercise R1.9. What is a console window?

Exercise R1.10. Describe *exactly* what steps you would take to back up your work after you have typed in the Hello.java program.

Exercise R1.11. On your own computer or on your lab computer, find the exact location (folder or directory name) of

- The sample file Hello.java, which you wrote with the editor
- The Java interpreter java.exe
- The library file rt.jar that contains the runtime library

Exercise R1.12. Explain the special role of the \ escape character in Java character strings.

Exercise R1.13. Write three versions of the Hello.java program that have different syntax errors. Write a version that has a logic error.

Exercise R1.14. How do you discover syntax errors? How do you discover logic errors?

PROGRAMMING EXERCISES

Exercise P1.1. Write a program that displays your name inside a box on the console screen, like this:

```
+----+
|Dave|
+----+
```

Do your best to approximate lines with characters like | - +.

Exercise P1.2. Write a program that prints a face, using text characters, hopefully better looking than this one:

Use *comments* to indicate when you print the hair, ears, mouth, and so on.

Exercise P1.3. Write a program that prints a Christmas tree:

Remember to use escape sequences to print the \ and " characters.

Exercise P1.4. Write a program that prints a staircase:

```
                +---+
                |   |
            +---+---+
            |   |   |
        +---+---+---+
        |   |   |   |
    +---+---+---+---+
    |   |   |   |   |
+---+---+---+---+---+
|   |   |   |   |   |
+---+---+---+---+---+
```

Exercise P1.5. Write a program that computes the sum of the first ten positive integers, $1 + 2 + \cdots + 10$. *Hint:* Write a program of the form

```
public class Sum10
{
   public static void main(String[] args)
   {
      System.out.println(              );
   }
}
```

Exercise P1.6. Write a program that computes the sum of the reciprocals $1/1 + 1/2 + \cdots + 1/10$. This is harder than it sounds. Try writing the program, and check the result. The program's result isn't likely to be correct. Then write the numbers as *floating-point* numbers, 1.0, 2.0, ..., 10.0, and run the program again. Can you explain the difference in the results? We will explore this phenomenon in Chapter 3.

An Introduction to Objects and Classes

To understand the concepts of classes and objects

▶ To realize the difference between objects and object references

▶ To become familiar with the process of implementing classes

▶ To be able to implement simple methods

▶ To understand the purpose and use of constructors

▶ To understand how to access instance fields and local variables

▶ To appreciate the importance of documentation comments

Most useful programs don't just manipulate numbers and strings. Instead, they deal with data items that are more complex and that more closely represent entities in the real world. Examples of these data items include bank accounts, employee records, and graphical shapes.

The Java language is ideally suited for designing and manipulating such data items, or *objects*. In Java, you define *classes* that describe the behavior of these objects. In this chapter, you will learn how to define classes that describe objects with very simple behavior. As you learn more about Java programming in subsequent chapters, you will be able to implement classes whose objects carry out more sophisticated actions.

2.1   Using and Constructing Objects

Objects and classes are central concepts for Java programming. It will take you some time to master these concepts fully, but since every Java program uses at least a couple of objects and classes, it is a good idea to have a basic understanding of these concepts right away.

An *object* is an entity that you can manipulate in your program, generally by calling *methods*. For example, you saw in Chapter 1 that System.out refers to an object, and you saw how to manipulate it by calling the println method. (Actually, several different methods are available, all called println: one for printing strings, one for printing integers, one for printing floating-point numbers, and so on; the reason is discussed in Section 2.8.) When you call the println method, some activities occur inside the object, and the ultimate effect is that the object causes text to appear in the console window.

> Objects are entities in your program that you manipulate by invoking methods.

You should think of the object as a "black box" with a public *interface* (the methods you can call) and a hidden *implementation* (the code and data that are necessary to make these methods work).

> The public interface of a class specifies what you can do with its objects. The hidden implementation describes how these actions are carried out.

Different objects support different sets of methods. For example, you can apply the println method to the System.out object, but not to the string object "Hello, World!". That is, it would be an error to call

```
"Hello, World!".println(); // This method call is an error
```

The reason is simple. The System.out and "Hello, World!" objects belong to different *classes*. The System.out object is an object of the class PrintStream, but the "Hello, World!" object is an object of class String. You can apply the println method to *any* object of the PrintStream class, but the String class does not support the println method. The String class supports a good number of other methods; you will see many of them in Chapter 3. For example, the length method counts the number of characters in a string. You can apply that method to any object of type String. Thus,

        "Hello, World!".length() // This method call is OK

is a correct method call—it computes the number of characters in the string object "Hello, World!" and returns the result, 13. (The quotation marks are not counted.) You can verify that the length method does return the length of a String object by writing a short test program

```
public class LengthTest
{
    public static void main(String[] args)
    {
        System.out.println("Hello, World!".length());
    }
}
```

Every object belongs to a class. The class defines the methods for the objects. Thus, the PrintStream class defines the print and println methods. The String class defines the length method and many other methods.

> Classes are factories for objects. You construct a new object of a class with the new operator.

The System.out object is created automatically when a Java program loads the System class. String objects are created when you specify a string enclosed in quotation marks. However, in most Java programs, you want to create more objects.

To see how to create new objects, let us turn to another class: the Rectangle class in the Java class library. Objects of type Rectangle describe rectangular shapes—see Figure 1.

Note that a Rectangle object isn't a rectangular shape—it is a set of numbers that describe the rectangle (see Figure 2). Each rectangle is described by the *x*- and *y*-coordinates of its top left corner, its width, and its height. To make a new rectangle, you

Figure 1

Rectangular Shapes

Figure 2

A Rectangle Object

Rectangle
x = 5
y = 10
width = 20
height = 30

need to specify these four values. For example, you can make a new rectangle with top left corner at (5, 10), width 20, and height 30 as follows:

```
new Rectangle(5, 10, 20, 30)
```

The **new** operator causes the creation of an object of type `Rectangle`. The process of creating a new object is called *construction*. The four values 5, 10, 20, and 30 are called the *construction parameters*. Different classes will require different construction parameters. For example, to construct a `Rectangle` object, you supply four numbers that describe the position and size of the rectangle. To construct a `Car` object, you might supply the model name and year.

Actually, some classes let you construct objects in multiple ways. For example, you can also obtain a `Rectangle` object by supplying no construction parameters at all (but you must still supply the parentheses):

```
new Rectangle()
```

This constructs a (rather useless) rectangle with top left corner at the origin (0, 0), width 0, and height 0.

To construct any object, you do the following:

1. Use the **new** operator.
2. Give the name of the class.
3. Supply construction parameters (if any) inside parentheses.

What can you do with a `Rectangle` object? Not much, for now. In Chapter 4, you will learn how to display rectangles and other shapes in a window. You can pass a rectangle object to the `System.out.println` or `print` method, which just prints a description of the rectangle object onto the console window:

```
public class RectangleTest
{
   public static void main(String[] args)
   {
      System.out.println(new Rectangle(5, 10, 20, 30));
   }
}
```

This program prints the line

```
java.awt.Rectangle[x=5,y=10,width=20,height=30]
```

More specifically, this program creates an object of type `Rectangle`, then passes that object to the `println` method. Afterward, that object is no longer used.

Syntax 2.1: Object Construction

new *ClassName* (*parameters*)

Example:

```
new Rectangle(5, 10, 20, 30)
new Car("BMW 540ti", 2004)
```

Purpose:

To construct a new object, initialize it with the construction parameters, and return a reference to the constructed object

---

2.2   Object Variables

> You store object locations in object variables.

Of course, usually you want to do something more to an object than just create it, print it, and forget it. To remember an object, you need to hold it in an *object variable*. As was mentioned in Chapter 1, a variable is an item of information in memory whose location is identified by a symbolic name. An object variable is a container that stores the location of an object.

In Java, every variable has a particular *type* that identifies what kind of information it can contain. You create a variable by giving its type followed by a name for the variable. For example,

```
Rectangle cerealBox;
```
(handwritten annotations: Type · object variable · Now you give it a type · This statement is 'defined')

This statement defines an object variable, cerealBox. The type of this variable is Rectangle. That is, after the cerealBox variable has been defined by the preceding statement, thereafter in the program it must always contain the location of a Rectangle object, never a Car or String object.

Figure 3   cerealBox = [   ]

An Uninitialized Object Variable

Figure 4

An Object Variable Containing an Object Reference

You can choose any variable names you like, provided you follow a few simple rules.

- Names can be made up of letters, digits, and the underscore (_) character. They cannot start with a digit, though.

- You cannot use other symbols such as ? or % in variable names.

- Spaces are not permitted inside names, either.

- Furthermore, you cannot use *reserved words* such as `public` as names; these words are reserved exclusively for their special Java meanings. Appendix A4 lists all reserved words.

- Variable names are also *case-sensitive;* that is, `cerealBox` and `Cerealbox` are *different* names.

> All object variables must be initialized before you access them.

Look again at the declaration of the `cerealBox` variable. So far, the variable is not *initialized*—it doesn't yet contain any object location at all (see Figure 3). You need to set `cerealBox` to an object location. How do you get an object location? The `new` operator creates a new object and returns its location. Use that value to initialize the variable.

```
Rectangle cerealBox = new Rectangle(5, 10, 20, 30);
```

> An object reference describes the location of an object.

You may wonder what happens if you leave the `cerealBox` variable uninitialized. See Common Error 2.1 for an answer. Figure 4 shows the result.

An object location is also often called an object *reference*. When a variable contains the location of an object, we say that it *refers* to an object. For example, `cerealBox` refers to the `Rectangle` object that the `new` operator constructed.

> Multiple object variables can contain references to the same object.

It is very important that you remember that the `cerealBox` variable *does not contain* the object. It *refers to* the object. You can have two object variables refer to the same object:

```
Rectangle r = cerealBox;
```

Now you can access the same `Rectangle` object both as `cerealBox` and as r, as shown in Figure 5.

Usually, your programs use objects in the following ways:

1. Construct an object with the `new` operator.
2. Store the object reference in an object variable.
3. Call methods on the object variable.

The `Rectangle` class has over 50 methods, some useful, some less so. To give you a flavor of manipulating `Rectangle` objects, let us look at a method of the `Rectangle` class. The `translate` method *moves* a rectangle by a certain distance in the *x*- and *y*-directions. For example,

```
cerealBox.translate(15, 25);
```

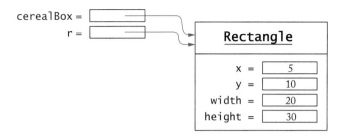

Figure 5

Two Object Variables Referring to the Same Object

moves the rectangle by 15 units in the *x*-direction and 25 units in the *y*-direction. Moving a rectangle doesn't change its width or height, but it changes the top left corner. The code fragment

```
Rectangle cerealBox = new Rectangle(5, 10, 20, 30);
cerealBox.translate(15, 25);
System.out.println(cerealBox);
```

prints

```
java.awt.Rectangle[x=20,y=35,width=20,height=30]
```

Let's turn this code fragment into a complete program. As with the Hello program, you need to carry out three steps:

1. Invent a new class, say MoveTest.
2. Supply a main method.
3. Place instructions inside the main method.

> Java classes are grouped into packages. If you use a class from another package (other than the java.lang package), you must import the class.

For this program, you need to carry out another step in addition to those: You need to *import* the Rectangle class from a *package*. A package is a collection of classes with a related purpose. All classes in the standard library are contained in packages. The Rectangle class belongs to the package java.awt (where awt is an abbreviation for "Abstract Windowing Toolkit"), which contains many classes for drawing windows and graphical shapes.

To use the Rectangle class from the java.awt package, simply place the following line at the top of your program:

```
import java.awt.Rectangle;
```

Why didn't you have to import the System and String classes that were used in the Hello program? The reason is that the System and String classes are in the java.lang package, and all classes from this package are automatically imported, so you never need to import them yourself.

Thus, the complete program is:

File MoveTest.java

```
1  import java.awt.Rectangle;
2
3  public class MoveTest
4  {
5     public static void main(String[] args)
6     {
7        Rectangle cerealBox = new Rectangle(5, 10, 20, 30);
8
9        // move the rectangle
10       cerealBox.translate(15, 25);
11
12       // print the moved rectangle
13       System.out.println(cerealBox);
14    }
15 }
```

Syntax 2.2: Variable Definition

TypeName variableName;
TypeName variableName = *expression*;

Example:

```
Rectangle cerealBox;
String name = "Dave";
```

Purpose:

To define a new variable of a particular type and optionally supply an initial value

---

Syntax 2.3: Importing a Class from a Package

import *packageName*.*ClassName*;

Example:

```
import java.awt.Rectangle;
```

Purpose:

To import a class from a package for use in a program

Common Error   2.1

Forgetting to Initialize Variables

You just learned how to store an object reference in a variable so that you can manipulate the object in your program. This is a very common step, and it can lead to one of the most common programming errors—using a variable that you forgot to initialize.

Suppose your program contains the lines

```
Rectangle cerealBox;
cerealBox.translate(15, 25);
```

Now you have a variable `cerealBox`. An object variable is a container for an object reference. But you haven't put anything into the variable—it is not initialized. Thus, there is no rectangle to translate.

The compiler spots these problems. If you make this mistake, the compiler will complain that you are trying to use an uninitialized variable.

The remedy is to initialize the variable. You can initialize a variable with any object reference, either a reference to a new object or an existing object.

```
// initialize with new object reference
Rectangle cerealBox = new Rectangle(5, 10, 20, 30);
// initialize with existing object reference
Rectangle cerealBox = anotherRectangle;
```

Advanced Topic   2.1

Importing Classes

You have seen the simplest and clearest method for importing classes from packages. Simply use an `import` statement that names the package and class for each class that you want to import. For example,

```
import java.awt.Rectangle;
import java.awt.Point;
```

There is a shortcut that many programmers find convenient. You can import *all* classes from a package name with the construct

```
import packagename.*;
```

For example, the statement

```
import java.awt.*;
```

imports all classes from the `java.awt` package. This is less trouble to type, but we won't use this style in this book, for a simple reason. If a program imports multiple packages

▼

and you encounter an unfamiliar class name, then you have to look up all of those packages to find the class. For example, suppose you see a program that imports

▼

```
import java.awt.*;
import java.io.*;
```

Furthermore, suppose you see a class name Image. You would not know whether the Image class is in the java.awt package or the java.io package. Why do you care in which package it is? You need to know if you want to use the class in your own programs.

▼

Note that you cannot import multiple packages with a single import statement. For example,

▼

```
import java.*.*; // Error
```

is a syntax error.

You can avoid all import statements by using the *full* name (both package name and class name) whenever you use a class. For example,

▼

```
java.awt.Rectangle cerealBox =
    new java.awt.Rectangle(5, 10, 20, 30);
```

▼

That is pretty tedious, and you won't find many programmers doing it.

2.3   Defining a Class

In this section, you will learn how to define your own classes. Recall that a class defines the methods that you can apply to its objects. We will start with a very simple class that contains a single method.

```
public class Greeter
{
    public String sayHello()
    {
        String message = "Hello, World!";
        return message;
    }
}
```

A method definition contains the following parts:

- An *access specifier* (such as public)

- The *return type* of the method (such as String)

- The name of the method (such as sayHello)

- A list of the *parameters* of the method, enclosed in parentheses (the sayHello method has no parameters)

- The *body* of the method: a sequence of statements enclosed in braces

The access specifier controls which other methods can call this method. Most methods should be declared as public. That way, all other methods in your program can call them.

> A method definition specifies the method name, parameters, and the statements for carrying out the method's actions.

(Occasionally, it can be useful to have methods that are not so widely callable—turn to Chapter 11 for more information on this issue.)

The return type is the type of the value that the method returns to its caller. The `sayHello` method returns an object of type `String` (namely, the string `"Hello, World!"`).

Some methods just execute some statements without returning a value. Those methods are tagged with a return type of `void`.

Many methods depend on other information. For example, the `translate` method of the `Rectangle` class needs to know how far you want to move the rectangle horizontally and vertically. These items are called the *parameters* of the method. Each parameter is a variable, with a type and a name. Parameter variables are separated by commas. For example, the implementors of the Java library defined the `translate` method like this:

```
public class Rectangle
{  . . .
    public void translate(int x, int y)
    {
        method body
    }
    . . .
}
```

Syntax 2.4: Method Implementation

```
public class ClassName
{

    . . .

    accessSpecifier returnType methodName(parameterType parameterName,  ... )
    {
        method body
    }
    . . .
}
```

Example:

```
public class Greeter
{
    public String sayHello()
    {
        String message = "Hello, World!";
        return message;
    }
}
```

Purpose:

To define the behavior of a method

The method body contains the statements that the method executes. The `sayHello` method body, for example, contains two statements. The first statement initializes a `String` variable with a `String` object:

```
String message = "Hello, World!";
```

> Use the `return` statement to specify the value that a method returns to its caller.

The second statement is a special statement that terminates the method. When the `return` statement is executed, the method exits. If the method has a return type other than `void`, then the `return` statement must contain a *return value*, namely the value that the method sends back to its caller. The `sayHello` method returns the object reference stored in `message`—that is, a reference to the `"Hello, World!"` string object.

Now you have seen how to define a class that contains a method. In the next section, you will see what you can do with the class.

Syntax 2.5: The `return` Statement

`return` *expression*;

or

`return`;

Example:

`return message;`

Purpose:

To specify the value that a method returns, and exit the method immediately. The return value becomes the value of the method call expression.

2.4   Testing a Class

In the preceding section, you saw the definition of a simple `Greeter` class. What can you do with it? Of course, you can compile the file `Greeter.java`. However, you can't *execute* the resulting `Greeter.class` file. It doesn't contain a `main` method. That is normal—most classes don't contain a `main` method.

> To test a class, use an environment for interactive testing, or write a second class to execute test instructions.

To do something with your class, you have two choices. Some development environments, such as the excellent BlueJ program, let you create objects of a class and call methods on those objects. Figure 6 shows the result of creating an object of the `Greeter` class and invoking the `sayHello` method. The dialog box contains the return value of the method.

Alternatively, if you don't have a development environment that lets you test a class interactively, you can write a *test class*. A test class is a class with a `main` method that contains statements to test another class. A test class typically carries out the following steps:

1. Construct one or more objects of the class that is being tested.
2. Invoke one or more methods.
3. Print out one or more results.

Figure 6

Testing a Class in the BlueJ Environment

The RectangleTest class in Section 2.1 is a good example of a test class. That class tests the Rectangle class—a class in the Java library.

Here is a class to test the Greeter class. The main method constructs an object of type Greeter, invokes the sayHello method, and displays the result on the console.

```java
public class GreeterTest
{
    public static void main(String[] args)
    {
        Greeter worldGreeter = new Greeter();
        System.out.println(worldGreeter.sayHello());
    }
}
```

To produce a program, you need to combine these two classes. The details for building the program depend on your compiler and development environment. In most environments, you need to carry out these steps:

1. Make a new subfolder for your program.
2. Make two files, one for each class.
3. Compile both files.
4. Run the test program.

For example, if you use the Java SDK command line tools, the steps are like this:

```
mkdir greeter
cd greeter
edit Greeter.java
edit GreeterTest.java
javac Greeter.java
javac GreeterTest.java
java GreeterTest
```

Many students are surprised that such a simple program contains two classes. However, this is normal. The two classes have entirely different purposes. The `Greeter` class (which we will make more interesting in the next section) describes objects that can utter greetings. The `GreeterTest` class runs a test that puts a `Greeter` object through its paces. The `GreeterTest` program is necessary only if your development environment does not have a facility for interactive testing.

Productivity Hint   2.1

Using the Command Line Effectively

If your programming environment lets you accomplish all routine tasks with menus and dialog boxes, you can skip this note. However, if you need to invoke the editor, the compiler, the linker, and the program to test manually, then it is well worth learning about *command line editing*.

Most operating systems (UNIX, DOS, OS/2) have a *command line interface* to interact with the computer. (In Windows, you can use the DOS command line interface by double-clicking the "MS-DOS Prompt" icon, or, if that icon doesn't appear on your "Programs" menu, clicking "Run..." and typing `command.com`.) You launch commands at a *prompt*. The command is executed, and on completion you get another prompt.

When you develop a program, you find yourself executing the same commands over and over. Wouldn't it be nice if you didn't have to type beastly commands like

```
javac MyProg.java
```

more than once? Or if you could fix a mistake rather than having to retype the command in its entirety? Many command line interfaces have an option to do just that, but they don't always make it obvious. If you use Windows, you need to install a program called `doskey`. If you use UNIX, some shells let you cycle through your old commands. If your default configuration does not have that feature, ask how you can change to a better shell, such as `bash` or `tcsh`.

Once you have your shell configured properly, you can use the up and down arrow keys to recall old commands and the left and right arrow keys to edit lines. You can also perform *command completion*. For example, to reissue the same `javac` command, type `javac` and press F8 (Windows) or type `!javac` (UNIX).

2.5   Instance Fields

Right now, our `Greeter` class isn't very interesting, because all objects act in the same way. Suppose you construct two objects:

```
Greeter greeter1 = new Greeter();
Greeter greeter2 = new Greeter();
```

> An object uses instance fields to store its state—the data that it needs to execute its methods.

Then both `greeter1` and `greeter2` return exactly the same result when you invoke the `sayHello` method. Let's modify the `Greeter` class so that one object can return the message `"Hello, World!"` and another can return `"Hello, Dave!"`.

To achieve this purpose, each `Greeter` object must store *state*. The state of an object is the set of values that determine how an object reacts to method calls. In the case of our improved `Greeter` object, the state is the name that we want to use in the greeting, such as `"World"` or `"Dave"`.

An object stores its state in one or more variables called *instance fields*. You declare the instance fields for an object in the class.

```
public class Greeter
{
    . . .
    private String name;
}
```

Instance field

An instance field declaration consists of the following parts:

- An *access specifier* (usually private)
- The *type* of the variable (such as `String`)
- The name of the variable (such as `name`)

> Each object of a class has its own set of instance fields.

Each object of a class has its own set of instance fields. For example, if `worldGreeter` and `daveGreeter` are two objects of the `Greeter` class, then each object has its own `name` field, called `worldGreeter.name` and `daveGreeter.name` (see Figure 7).

> Encapsulation is the process of hiding object data and providing methods for data access.

Instance fields are generally declared with the access specifier `private`. That specifier means that they can be accessed only by the methods of the *same class*, not by any other method. In particular, the `name` variable can be accessed only by the `sayHello` method.

> You should declare all instance fields as private.

In other words, if the instance fields are declared private, then all data access must occur through the public methods. Thus, the instance fields of an object are effectively hidden from the programmer who uses a class. They are of concern only to the programmer who implements the class. The process of hiding the data and providing methods for data access is called *encapsulation*. Although it is theoretically possible in Java to leave instance fields public, that is very uncommon in practice. We will always make all instance fields private in this book.

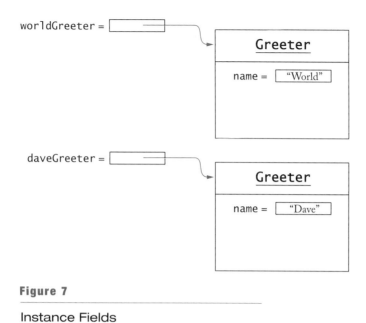

Figure 7

Instance Fields

For example, because the `name` instance field is private, you cannot access the instance field in methods of another class:

```
public class GreeterTest
{
   public static void main(String[] args)
   {
      . . .
      System.out.println(daveGreeter.name); // ERROR
   }
}
```

Only the `sayHello` method can access the private `name` variable. If we later add other methods to the `Greeter` class, such as a `sayGoodbye` method, then those methods can access the private instance field as well.

Here is the implementation of the `sayHello` method of the improved `Greeter` class.

```
public String sayHello()
{
   String message = "Hello, " + name + "!";
   return message;
}
```

The + symbol denotes *string concatenation*, an operation that forms a new string by putting shorter strings together one after another.

This method computes a string `message` by combining three strings: `"Hello, "`, the string stored in the `name` instance field, and the string consisting of an exclamation point "!". If the name variable refers to the string "Dave", then the resulting string is "Hello, Dave!".

Note that this method uses two separate object variables: the *local variable* message and the instance field name. A local variable belongs to an individual method, and you can use it only in the method in which you declare it. An instance field belongs to an object, and you can use it in all methods of its class.

Syntax 2.6: Instance Field Declaration

accessSpecifier class *ClassName*
{

   . . .

   accessSpecifier fieldType fieldName;
   . . .

}

Example:

```
public class Greeter
{
    . . .
    private String name;
    . . .
}
```

Purpose:

To define a field that is present in every object of a class

2.6   Constructors

To complete the improved Greeter class, we need to be able to construct objects with different values for the name instance field. We want to specify the name when constructing the object:

> Constructors contain instructions to initialize objects. The constructor name is always the same as the class name.

```
Greeter worldGreeter = new Greeter("World");
Greeter daveGreeter = new Greeter("Dave");
```

To accomplish this, we need to supply a *constructor* in the class definition. A constructor specifies how an object should be initialized. In our example, we have one construction parameter—a string describing the name. Here is the code for the constructor.

```
public Greeter(String aName)
{
    name = aName;
}
```

A constructor always has the same name as the class of the objects it constructs. Similar to methods, constructors are generally declared as `public` to enable any code in a program to construct new objects of the class. Unlike methods, though, constructors do not have return types.

> The new operator invokes the constructor.

The `new` operator invokes the constructor:

```
new Greeter("Dave")
```

This expression constructs a new object whose `name` instance field is set to the string `"Dave"`.

Constructors are not methods. You cannot invoke a constructor on an existing object. For example, the call

```
worldGreeter.Greeter("Harry"); // Error
```

is illegal. You can use a constructor only in combination with the `new` operator.

Here is the complete code for the enhanced `Greeter` class.

File Greeter.java

```
1  public class Greeter
2  {
3     public Greeter(String aName)
4     {
5        name = aName;
6     }
7
8     public String sayHello()
9     {
10        String message = "Hello, " + name + "!";
11        return message;
12     }
13
14     private String name;
15 }
```

Here is a test class that you can use to confirm that the `Greeter` class works correctly.

File GreeterTest.java

```
1  public class GreeterTest
2  {
3     public static void main(String[] args)
4     {
5        Greeter worldGreeter = new Greeter("World");
6        System.out.println(worldGreeter.sayHello());
7
8        Greeter daveGreeter = new Greeter("Dave");
9        System.out.println(daveGreeter.sayHello());
10     }
11 }
```

> **Syntax 2.7: Constructor Implementation**
>
> *accessSpecifier* `class` *ClassName*
> ```
> {
>    . . .
>    accessSpecifier ClassName(parameterType parameterName, . . .)
>    {
>        constructor implementation
>    }
>    . . .
> }
> ```
>
> **Example:**
>
> ```
> public class Greeter
> {
>    . . .
>    public Greeter(String aName)
>    {
>       name = aName;
>    }
>    . . .
> }
> ```
>
> **Purpose:**
>
> To define the behavior of a constructor, which is used to initialize the instance fields of newly created objects

2.7 Designing the Public Interface of a Class

The purpose of the `Greeter` class was to show you the mechanics of defining classes, methods, instance fields, and constructors. Frankly, that class was not very useful. In this section we will create a more interesting class that describes the behavior of a *bank account*. More importantly, we will go through the thought process that is required when you design a new class.

Before you start programming, you need to understand how the objects of your class behave. Consider what kind of operations you can carry out with a bank account. You can

- Deposit money
- Withdraw money
- Get the current balance

In Java, these operations are expressed as method calls. Let's suppose the variable `harrysChecking` contains a reference to an object of type `BankAccount`. You'll want to be able to call methods such as the following:

```
harrysChecking.deposit(2000);
harrysChecking.withdraw(500);
System.out.println(harrysChecking.getBalance());
```

That is, the `BankAccount` class should define three methods:

- `deposit`
- `withdraw`
- `getBalance`

Next, you need to determine the parameters and return types of these methods. As you can see from the code samples, the `deposit` and `withdraw` methods receive a number (the dollar amount) and return no values. The `getBalance` method has no parameter and returns a number.

Java has several number types—you will learn about them in the next chapter. The most flexible number type is called `double`, which stands for "double precision floating-point number". Think of a number in `double` format as any number that can appear in the display panel of a calculator, such as `250`, `6.75`, or `-0.333333333`.

Now that you know that you can use the `double` type for numbers, you can write down the methods of the `BankAccount` class:

```
public void deposit(double amount)
public void withdraw(double amount)
public double getBalance()
```

Now let's do the same for the constructors of the class. How do we want to construct a bank account? It seems reasonable that a call

```
BankAccount harrysChecking = new BankAccount();
```

should construct a new bank account with a zero balance. What if we want to start out with another balance? A second constructor would be useful that sets the balance to an initial value:

```
BankAccount harrysChecking = new BankAccount(5000);
```

That gives us two constructors:

```
public BankAccount()
public BankAccount(double initialBalance)
```

The compiler figures out which constructor to call by looking at the parameters. For example, if you call

```
new BankAccount()
```

then the compiler picks the first constructor. If you call

```
new BankAccount(5000)
```

then the compiler picks the second constructor. But if you call

```
new BankAccount("lotsa moolah")
```

then the compiler generates an error message—for this class there is no constructor that takes a parameter of type `String`.

> Overloaded methods are methods with the same name but different parameter types.

You may think that it is strange to have two constructors that have the same name and that differ only in the parameter type. (The first constructor has no parameters; the second one has one parameter, a number.) If a name is used to denote more than one constructor or method, that name is *overloaded*. See Advanced Topic 2.2 for more information on name overloading. Name overloading is common in Java, especially for constructors. After all, we have no choice what to call the constructor. The name of a constructor must be identical to the name of the class.

The constructors and methods of a class form the *public interface* of the class. These are the operations that any code in your program can access to create and manipulate BankAccount objects. Here is a complete listing of the public interface of the BankAccount class:

```
public BankAccount()
public BankAccount(double initialBalance)
public void deposit(double amount)
public void withdraw(double amount)
public double getBalance()
```

The behavior of our BankAccount class is simple, but it lets you carry out all of the important operations that commonly occur with bank accounts. For example, here is how you can transfer an amount from one bank account to another:

```
// transfer from one account to another
double transferAmount = 500;
momsSavings.withdraw(transferAmount);
harrysChecking.deposit(transferAmount);
```

And here is how you can add interest to a savings account:

```
double interestRate = 5; // 5% interest
double interestAmount =
    momsSavings.getBalance() * interestRate / 100;
momsSavings.deposit(interestAmount);
```

> Abstraction is the process of finding the essential feature set for a class.

As you can see, you can use objects of the BankAccount class to carry out meaningful tasks, without knowing how the BankAccount objects store their data or how the BankAccount methods do their work. This is an important aspect of object-oriented programming. The process of determining the feature set for a class is called *abstraction*. Think about how an abstract painting strips away extraneous details and tries to represent only the essential features of an object. When you design the public interface of a class, you also need to find what operations are essential to manipulate objects in your program.

 Advanced Topic **2.2**

Overloading

When the same name is used for more than one method or constructor, the name is *overloaded*. This is particularly common for constructors, because all constructors must have the same name—the name of the class. In Java you can overload methods and constructors, provided the parameter types are different. For example, the PrintStream class defines many methods, all called println, to print various number types and to print objects:

```
class PrintStream
{
```

```
      public void println(String s) { . . . }
      public void println(double a) { . . . }
      . . .

}
```

When the `println` method is called,

```
   system.out.println(x);
```

the compiler looks at the type of x. If x is a `String` value, the first method is called. If x is a `double` value, the second method is called. If x does not match the parameter type of any of the methods, the compiler generates an error.

For overloading purposes, the type of the *return value* does not matter. You cannot have two methods with identical names and parameter types but different return values.

2.8   Commenting the Public Interface

> Use documentation comments to describe the classes and public methods of your programs.

When you define classes and methods, you should get into the habit of thoroughly *commenting* their behavior. In Java there is a very useful standard form for *documentation comments*. If you use this form in your classes, a program called `javadoc` can automatically generate a neat set of HTML pages that describe them. (See Productivity Hint 2.2 for a description of this utility.)

A documentation comment starts with a /**, a special comment delimiter used by the `javadoc` utility. Then you describe the method's *purpose*. Then, for each method parameter, you supply a line that starts with @param, followed by the parameter name and a short explanation. Finally, you supply a line that starts with @return, describing the return value. You omit the @param tag for methods that have no parameters, and you omit the @return tag for methods whose return type is `void`.

The `javadoc` utility copies the *first* sentence of each comment to a summary table. Therefore, it is best to write that first sentence with some care. It should start with an uppercase letter and end with a period. It does not have to be a grammatically complete sentence, but it should be meaningful when it is pulled out of the comment and displayed in a summary.

Here are two typical examples.

```
/**
      Withdraws money from the bank account.
      @param amount  the amount to withdraw
*/
public void withdraw(double amount)
{
      implementation—filled in later
}
/**
      Gets the current balance of the bank account.
      @return  the current balance
*/
public double getBalance()
{
      implementation—filled in later
}
```

The comments you have just seen explain individual *methods*. You should also supply a brief comment for each *class,* explaining its purpose. The comment syntax for class comments is very simple: Just place the documentation comment above the class.

```
/**
    A bank account has a balance that can be changed by
    deposits and withdrawals.
*/
public class BankAccount
{
    . . .
}
```

Your first reaction may well be "Whoa! Am I supposed to write all this stuff?" These comments do seem pretty repetitive. But you should still take the time to write them, even if it feels silly at times. There are three reasons.

First, the `javadoc` utility will format your comments into a neat set of documents that you can view in a web browser. It makes good use of the seemingly repetitive phrases. The first sentence of the comment is used for a *summary table* of all methods of your class (see Figure 8). The `@param` and `@return` comments are neatly formatted in the detail description of each method (see Figure 9). If you omit any of the comments, then `javadoc` generates documents that look strangely empty.

Next, it is actually easy to spend more time pondering whether a comment is too trivial to write than it takes just to write it. In practical programming, very simple methods are rare. It is harmless to have a trivial method overcommented, whereas a complicated method without

Figure 8

A Method Summary Generated by `javadoc`

Figure 9

Method Details Generated by `javadoc`

> Provide documentation comments for every class, every method, every parameter, and every return value.

any comment can cause real grief to future maintenance programmers. According to the standard Java documentation style, *every* class, *every* method, *every* parameter, and *every* return value should have a comment.

Finally, it is always a good idea to write the method comment *first*, before writing the method code. This is an excellent test to see that you firmly understand what you need to program. If you can't explain what a class or method does, you aren't ready to implement it.

Productivity Hint 2.2

The `javadoc` Utility

You should always insert documentation comments in your code, whether or not you use `javadoc` to produce HTML documentation. But most people find the HTML documentation convenient, so it is worth learning how to run `javadoc`.

From a command shell, you invoke the `javadoc` utility with the command

```
javadoc MyClass.java
```

or

```
javadoc *.java
```

The `javadoc` utility then produces files `MyClass.html` in HTML format, which you can inspect in a browser. If you know HTML (see Chapter 4), you can embed HTML tags into the comments to specify fonts or add images. Perhaps most importantly, `javadoc` automatically provides *hyperlinks* to other classes and methods.

You can actually run `javadoc` before implementing any methods. Just leave all the method bodies empty. Don't run the compiler—it would complain about missing return values. Simply run `javadoc` on your file to generate the documentation for the public interface that you are about to implement.

The `javadoc` tool is wonderful because it does one thing right: It lets you put the documentation *together with your code*. That way, when you update your programs, you can see right away which documentation needs to be updated. Hopefully, you will update it right then and there. Afterward, run `javadoc` again and get updated information that is both timely and nicely formatted.

Productivity Hint 2.3

Keyboard Shortcuts for Mouse Operations

Programmers spend a lot of time with the keyboard and the mouse. Programs and documentation are many pages long and require a lot of typing. The constant switching among the editor, compiler, and debugger takes up quite a few mouse clicks. The designers of programs such as a Java integrated development environment have added some features to make your work easier, but it is up to you to discover them.

Just about every program has a user interface with menus and dialog boxes. Click on a menu and click on a submenu to select a task. Click on each field in a dialog box, fill in the requested answer, and click on the OK button. These are great user interfaces for the beginner, because they are easy to master, but they are terrible user interfaces for the regular user. The constant switching between the keyboard and the mouse slows you down. You need to move a hand off the keyboard, locate the mouse, move the mouse, click the mouse, and move the hand back onto the keyboard. For that reason, most user interfaces have *keyboard shortcuts:* combinations of keystrokes that allow you to achieve the same tasks without having to switch to the mouse at all.

All Microsoft Windows applications use the following conventions:

- The Alt key plus the underlined letter in a menu name (such as the F in "File") pulls down that menu. Inside a menu, just type the underlined character in the name of a submenu to activate it. For example, Alt+F followed by O selects "File" "Open". Once your fingers know about this combination, you can open files faster than the fastest mouse artist.

- Inside dialog boxes, the Tab key is important; it moves from one option to the next. The arrow keys move within an option. The Enter key accepts the entire dialog, and Esc cancels it.

- In a program with multiple windows, Ctrl+Tab usually toggles through the windows managed by that program, for example between the source and error window.

▼ • Alt+Tab toggles between applications, letting you toggle quickly between, for example, the text editor and a command shell window.

▼ • Hold down the Shift key and press the arrow keys to highlight text. Then use Ctrl+X to cut the text, Ctrl+C to copy it, and Ctrl+V to paste it. These keys are easy to remember. The V looks like an insertion mark that an editor would use to insert text. The X should remind you of crossing out text. The C is just the first letter in "Copy". (OK, so it is also the first letter in "Cut"—no mnemonic rule is perfect.) You find these reminders in the Edit menu of most text editors.

▼ Of course, the mouse has its use in text processing: to locate or select text that is on the same screen but far away from the cursor.

▼ Take a little bit of time to learn about the keyboard shortcuts that the designers of your programs provided for you, and the time investment will be repaid many times during your programming career. When you blaze through your work in the computer lab

▼ with keyboard shortcuts, you may find yourself surrounded by amazed onlookers who whisper, "I didn't know you could do *that.*"

2.9   Specifying the Implementation of a Class

Now that you understand the public interface of the `BankAccount` class, let's provide the implementation. As you already know, you need to supply a class with these ingredients:

```
public class BankAccount
{
    constructors
    methods
    fields
}
```

We have seen which constructors and methods we need. Let us turn to the instance fields. The instance fields are used to store the object state. In the case of our simple bank account objects, the state is the current balance of the bank account. (A more complex bank account might have a richer state—perhaps the current balance together with the interest rate paid, the date for mailing out the next statement, and so on.) For now, a single instance field suffices:

```
public class BankAccount
{
    . . .
    private double balance;
}
```

Note that the instance field is declared with the access specifier `private`. That means, the bank balance can be accessed only by the constructors and methods of the *same class*—namely, `deposit`, `withdraw`, and `getBalance`—and not by any constructor or method of another class. How the state of a bank account is maintained is a private implementation detail of the class. Recall that the practice of hiding the implementation details and providing methods for data access is called encapsulation.

The BankAccount class is so simple that it is not obvious what benefit you gain from the encapsulation. After all, you can always find out the current balance by calling the getBalance method. You can set the balance to any value by calling deposit with an appropriate amount.

The primary benefit of the encapsulation mechanism is the guarantee that an object cannot accidentally be put into an incorrect state. For example, suppose you want to make sure that a bank account is never overdrawn. You can simply implement the withdraw method so that it refuses to carry out a withdrawal that would result in a negative balance. (You will need to wait until Chapter 5 to see how to implement that protection.) On the other hand, if any code could freely modify the balance instance field of a BankAccount object, then it would be an easy matter to store a negative number in the variable.

Now that you know what methods you need, and how the object state is represented, it is an easy matter to implement each of the methods. For example, here is the deposit method:

```
public void deposit(double amount)
{
    double newBalance = balance + amount;
    balance = newBalance;
}
```

Here is the constructor with no parameters.

```
public BankAccount()
{
    balance = 0;
}
```

You will find the complete BankAccount class, with the implementations of all methods, at the end of this section.

If your development environment lets you construct objects interactively, then you can test this class immediately. Figures 10 and 11 show how to test the class in BlueJ. Otherwise, you need to supply a test class. The BankAccountTest class at the end of this section constructs a bank account, deposits and withdraws some money, and prints the remaining balance.

File BankAccount.java

```
 1  /**
 2      A bank account has a balance that can be changed by
 3      deposits and withdrawals.
 4  */
 5  public class BankAccount
 6  {
 7      /**
 8          Constructs a bank account with a zero balance.
 9      */
10      public BankAccount()
11      {
12          balance = 0;
```

Figure 10

Calling the `withdraw` Method in BlueJ

```
13    }
14
15    /**
16        Constructs a bank account with a given balance.
17        @param initialBalance the initial balance
18    */
19    public BankAccount(double initialBalance)
20    {
21        balance = initialBalance;
22    }
23
24    /**
25        Deposits money into the bank account.
26        @param amount the amount to deposit
27    */
28    public void deposit(double amount)
29    {
30        double newBalance = balance + amount;
31        balance = newBalance;
32    }
33
34    /**
```

Figure 11

The Return Value of the getBalance Method in BlueJ

```
35          Withdraws money from the bank account.
36          @param amount the amount to withdraw
37       */
38       public void withdraw(double amount)
39       {
40          double newBalance = balance - amount;
41          balance = newBalance;
42       }
43
44       /**
45          Gets the current balance of the bank account.
46          @return the current balance
47       */
48       public double getBalance()
49       {
50          return balance;
51       }
52
53       private double balance;
54 }
```

File BankAccountTest.java

```
1  /**
2      A class to test the BankAccount class.
3  */
4  public class BankAccountTest
5  {
6     /**
7         Tests the methods of the BankAccount class.
8         @param args not used
9     */
10    public static void main(String[] args)
11    {
12       BankAccount harrysChecking = new BankAccount();
13       harrysChecking.deposit(2000);
14       harrysChecking.withdraw(500);
15       System.out.println(harrysChecking.getBalance());
16    }
17 }
```

▼

 Common Error   2.2

Trying to Reset an Object by Calling a Constructor

▼

The constructor is invoked only when an object is first created. You cannot call the constructor to reset an object:

▼
```
BankAccount harrysChecking = new BankAccount();
harrysChecking.withdraw(500);
harrysChecking.BankAccount(); // Error—can't reconstruct object
```

▼

The constructor sets a *new* account object to a zero balance, but you cannot invoke a constructor on an *existing* object. The remedy is simple: Make a new object and overwrite the current one.

▼
```
harrysChecking = new BankAccount(); // OK
```

? **HOWTO**   2.1

▼

Designing and Implementing a Class

▼

This is the first of several "HOWTO" sections in this book. Users of the Linux operating system have HOWTO guides that give answers to the common questions "How do I get started?" and "What do I do next?" in solving a variety of problems. Similarly, the HOWTO

▼

sections in this book give you step-by-step procedures for carrying out specific tasks.

You will often be asked to design and implement a class. For example, a homework assignment might ask you to design a Car class.

▼ **Step 1** Find out what you are asked to do with an object of the class

▼ For example, suppose you are asked to implement a `Car` class. You won't have to model every feature of a real car—there are too many. The assignment should tell you *which aspects* of a car your class should simulate. Make a list, in plain English, of the operations that an object of your class should carry out, such as this one:

▼ - Add gas to gas tank.
   - Drive a certain distance.
   - Check the amount of gas left in the tank.

▼ **Step 2** Find names for the methods

▼ Come up with method names and apply them to a sample object, like this:

```
Car myBeemer = new Car(. . .);
myBeemer.addGas(20);
myBeemer.drive(100);
myBeemer.getGas();
```

Step 3 Document the public interface

▼ Here is the documentation, with comments that describe the class and its methods:

```
/**
    A car can drive and consume fuel.
*/
public class Car
{
    /**
        Adds gas to the tank.
        @param amount  the amount of fuel to add
    */
    public void addGas(double amount)
    {
    }

    /**
        Drives a certain amount, consuming gas.
        @param distance  the distance driven
    */
    public void drive(double distance)
    {
    }

    /**
        Gets the amount of gas left in the tank.
        @return  the amount of gas
    */
    public double getGas()
    {
    }
}
```

▼ Step 4 Determine instance variables

▼ Ask yourself what information an object needs to store to do its job. Remember, the methods can be called in any order! The object needs to have enough internal memory to be able to process every method, using just its instance fields and the method parameters. Go through each method, perhaps starting with a simple one or an interesting one, and ask yourself what you need to carry out the method's task. Make instance fields to store the information that the method needs.

In the car example, we need to know (or compute) the amount of gas in the tank—the `getGas` method asks for it. It makes sense for a `Car` object to store it:

```
public class Car
{
    . . .
    private double gas;
}
```

▼ Then the `addGas` method simply adds to that value. The `drive` method must reduce the gas in the tank. By how much? That depends on the fuel efficiency of the car. If you drive 100 miles, and the car can drive 20 miles per gallon, then 5 gallons are consumed. We don't get the efficiency as part of the `drive` method, so the car must store it:

```
public class Car
{
    . . .
    private double gas;
    private double efficiency;
}
```

▼ Step 5 Determine constructors

▼ Ask yourself what you need to construct an object. Often, you can just set all fields to 0 or a constant value. Sometimes, you need some essential information. Then you need to set that information in a constructor. Sometimes you will want two constructors: one that sets all fields to a default and one that sets them to user-supplied values. Design constructors as needed.

▼ In the case of the car example, we can start out with an empty gas tank, but we need the efficiency of the car. There is no good default for it, so it should be a construction parameter. It is common to prefix construction parameter names with "a" or "an" so that you don't conflict with instance variable names.

```
/**
    Constructs a car with a given fuel efficiency.
    @param anEfficiency the fuel efficiency of the car
*/
public Car(double anEfficiency)
{
}
```

▼ Step 6 Implement methods

▼ Implement the methods and constructors in your class, one at a time, starting with the easiest ones. If you find that you have trouble with the implementation, you may need to go back to a previous step. Maybe your set of methods from steps 1 through 3 wasn't good? Maybe you didn't have the right instance fields? It is common for a beginner to run into a couple of problems that require backtracking.

Compile your class and fix any compiler errors.

Step 7   Test your class

Write a short test program and run it. The test program can just carry out the method calls that you found in step 2.

```
public class CarTest
{
   public static void main(String[] args)
   {
      Car myBeemer = new Car(20); // 20 miles per gallon
      myBeemer.addGas(20);
      myBeemer.drive(100);
      double gasLeft = myBeemer.getGas();
      System.out.println(gasLeft);
   }
}
```

Alternatively, if you use a program that lets you test objects interactively, such as BlueJ, construct an object and apply the method calls (see Figure 12).

Figure 12

Testing a Class with BlueJ

2.10 Variable Types

You have seen three different types of variables in this chapter:

1. Instance fields, such as the `balance` variable of the `BankAccount` class
2. Local variables, such as the `newBalance` variable of the `deposit` method
3. Parameter variables, such as the `amount` variable of the `deposit` method

> Instance fields belong to an object. Parameter variables and local variables belong to a method—they die when the method exits.

These variables are similar—they all hold a value of a particular type. But they have a couple of important differences. The first difference is their *lifetime*.

An instance field belongs to an object. Each object has its own copy of each instance field. For example, if you have two `BankAccount` objects (say, `harrysChecking` and `momsSavings`), then each of them has its own `balance` field. When an object is constructed, its instance fields are created. They stay alive until no method uses the object any longer.

Local and parameter variables belong to a method. When the method starts, these variables come to life. When the method exits, they die. For example, if you call

```
harrysChecking.deposit(500);
```

then a parameter variable called `amount` is created and initialized with the parameter value, 500. When the method returns, that variable dies. When you make another method call,

```
momsSavings.deposit(1000);
```

a different parameter variable, also called `amount`, is created. It too dies at the end of the method. The same holds for the local variable `newBalance`. When the `deposit` method reaches the line

```
double newBalance = balance + amount;
```

the variable comes to life and is initialized with the sum of the object's balance and the deposit amount. The lifetime of that variable extends to the end of the method. However, the `deposit` method has a lasting effect. Its next line,

```
balance = newBalance;
```

> Instance fields are initialized to a default value, but you must initialize local variables.

sets the `balance` instance field, and that variable lives beyond the end of the `deposit` method, as long as the `BankAccount` object is in use.

The second major difference between instance and local variables is *initialization*.

You must initialize all local variables. If you don't initialize a local variable, the compiler complains when you try to use it.

Parameter variables are initialized with the values that are supplied in the method call.

Instance fields are initialized with a default value if you don't explicitly set them in a constructor. Instance fields that are numbers are initialized to 0. Object references are set to a special value called `null`. If an object reference is `null`, then it refers to no object at all. We will discuss the `null` value in greater detail in Section 5.2. Inadvertent initialization with 0 or `null` is a common cause of errors. Therefore, it is a matter of good style to initialize *every* instance field explicitly in every constructor.

⊗ **Common Error**   **2.3**

Forgetting to Initialize Object References in a Constructor

Just as it is a common error to forget to initialize a local variable, it is easy to forget about instance fields. Every constructor needs to ensure that all instance fields are set to appropriate values.

If you do not initialize an instance field, the Java compiler will initialize it for you. Numbers are initialized with 0, but object references—such as string variables—are set to the `null` reference.

Of course, 0 is often a convenient default for numbers. However, `null` is hardly ever a convenient default for objects. Consider this "lazy" constructor for the `Greeter` class:

```
public class Greeter
{
    public Greeter() {} // do nothing
    . . .
    private String name;
}
```

The `name` field is set to a `null` reference. When you call `sayHello`, it will return `"Hello, null!"`.

If you forget to initialize a *local* variable in a *method*, the compiler flags this as an error, and you must fix it before the program runs. If you make the same mistake with an instance field, the compiler provides a default initialization, and the error becomes apparent only when the program runs.

To avoid this problem, make it a habit to initialize every instance field in every constructor.

2.11   Explicit and Implicit Method Parameters

Have a look at a particular invocation of the `deposit` method:
```
momsSavings.deposit(500);
```
implicit

Now look again at the code of the `deposit` method:
```
public void deposit(double amount)
{
    double newBalance = balance + amount;
    balance = newBalance;
}
```
implicit

The parameter variable `amount` is set to 500 when the `deposit` method starts. But what does `balance` mean exactly? After all, our program may have multiple `BankAccount` objects, and *each of them* has its own balance.

> The implicit parameter of a method is the object on which the method is invoked. The `this` reference denotes the implicit parameter.

Of course, since we deposit the money into `momsSavings`, `balance` must mean `momsSavings.balance`. In general, when you refer to an instance field inside a method, it means the instance field of the object on which the method was called.

Thus, the call to the `deposit` method depends on two values: the object to which `momsSavings` refers, and the value `500`. The `amount` parameter inside the parentheses is called an *explicit* parameter, because it is explicitly named in the method definition. However, the reference to the bank account object is not explicit in the method definition—it is called the *implicit parameter* of the method.

If you need to, you can access the implicit parameter—the object on which the method is called—with the keyword `this`. For example, in the preceding method invocation, `this` was set to `momsSavings` and `amount` to 500.

Every method has one implicit parameter. You don't give the implicit parameter a name. It is always called `this`. (There is one exception to the rule that every method has an implicit parameter: `static` methods do not. We will discuss them in Chapter 7.) In contrast, methods can have any number of explicit parameters, which you can name any way you like, or no explicit parameter at all.

Next, look again closely at the implementation of the `deposit` method. The statement

```
double newBalance = balance + amount;
```

actually means

```
double newBalance = this.balance + amount;
```

> Use of an instance field name in a method denotes the instance field of the implicit parameter.

When you refer to an instance field in a method, the compiler automatically applies it to the `this` parameter. Some programmers actually prefer to manually insert the `this` parameter before every instance field because they find it makes the code clearer. Here is an example:

```
public void deposit(double amount)
{
    double newBalance = this.balance + amount;
    this.balance = newBalance;
}
```

You may want to try it out and see if you like that style.

Common Error 2.4

Trying to Call a Method Without an Implicit Parameter

Suppose your `main` method contains the instruction

```
withdraw(30); // Error
```

The compiler will not know which account to access to withdraw the money. You need to supply an object reference of type `BankAccount`:

```
BankAccount harrysChecking = new BankAccount();
harrysChecking.withdraw(30);
```

However, there is one situation in which it is legitimate to invoke a method without, seemingly, an implicit parameter. Consider the following modification to the BankAccount class. Add a method to apply the monthly account fee:

```
class BankAccount
{  . . .
    public void monthlyFee()
    {                    10 is the implicit parameter of monthly fee
        withdraw(10); // withdraw $10 from this account
    }
}
```

That means to withdraw from the *same* account object that is carrying out the monthlyFee operation. In other words, the implicit parameter of the withdraw method is the (invisible) implicit parameter of the monthlyFee method.

If you find it confusing to have an invisible parameter, you can always use the this parameter to make the method easier to read:

```
class BankAccount
{  . . .
    public void monthlyFee()
    {
        this.withdraw(10); // withdraw $10 from this account
    }
}
```

AT Advanced Topic   2.3

Calling One Constructor from Another

Consider the BankAccount class. It has two constructors: a constructor without parameters to initialize the balance with zero, and another constructor to supply an initial balance. Rather than explicitly setting the balance to zero, one constructor can call another constructor of the same class instead. There is a shorthand notation to achieve this result:

```
class BankAccount
{
    public BankAccount (double initialBalance)
    {
        balance = initialBalance;
    }

    public BankAccount()
    {
        this(0);
    }
    . . .
}
```

The command `this(0);` means "Call another constructor of this class and supply the value 0." Such a constructor call can occur only *as the first line in another constructor.*

This syntax is a minor convenience. We will not use it in this book. Actually, the use of the keyword `this` is a little confusing. Normally, `this` denotes a reference to the implicit parameter, but if `this` is followed by parentheses, it denotes a call to another constructor of this class.

Random Fact   2.1

Mainframes—When Dinosaurs Ruled the Earth

When the International Business Machines Corporation, a successful manufacturer of punched-card equipment for tabulating data, first turned its attention to designing computers in the early 1950s, its planners assumed that there was a market for perhaps 50 such devices, for installation by the government, the military, and a few of the country's largest corporations. Instead, they sold about 1,500 machines of their System 650 model and went on to build and sell more powerful computers.

The so-called *mainframe* computers of the 1950s, 1960s, and 1970s were huge. They filled up whole rooms, which had to be climate-controlled to protect the delicate equipment (see Figure 13). Today, because of miniaturization technology, even mainframes are getting smaller, but they are still very expensive. (At the time of this writing, the cost for a midrange IBM 3090 is approximately 4 million dollars.)

Figure 13

A Mainframe Computer

▼   These huge and expensive systems were an immediate success when they first
appeared, because they replaced many roomfuls of even more expensive employees, who
had previously performed the tasks by hand. Few of these computers do any exciting
▼   computations. They keep mundane information, such as billing records or airline reservations; they just keep lots of them.

        IBM was not the first company to build mainframe computers; that honor belongs to
▼   the Univac Corporation. However, IBM soon became the major player, partially because
of technical excellence and attention to customer needs and partially because it exploited
its strengths and structured its products and services in a way that made it difficult for
▼   customers to mix them with those of other vendors. In the 1960s, IBM's competitors,
the so-called "Seven Dwarfs"—GE, RCA, Univac, Honeywell, Burroughs, Control
Data, and NCR—fell on hard times. Some went out of the computer business alto-
▼   gether, while others tried unsuccessfully to combine their strengths by merging their
computer operations. It was generally predicted that they would eventually all fail. It was
in this atmosphere that the U.S. government brought an antitrust suit against IBM in
▼   1969. The suit went to trial in 1975 and dragged on until 1982, when the Reagan
Administration abandoned it, declaring it "without merit".

        Of course, by then the computing landscape had changed completely. Just as the
▼   dinosaurs gave way to smaller, nimbler creatures, three new waves of computers had
appeared: the minicomputers, workstations, and microcomputers, all engineered by new
companies, not the Seven Dwarfs. Today, the importance of mainframes in the market-
▼   place has diminished, and IBM, while still a large and resourceful company, no longer
dominates the computer market.

        Mainframes are still in use today for two reasons. They still excel at handling large
▼   data volumes. More importantly, the programs that control the business data have
been refined over the last 20 or more years, fixing one problem at a time. Moving these
programs to less expensive computers, with different languages and operating systems,
▼   is difficult and error-prone. Sun Microsystems, a leading manufacturer of workstations, was eager to prove that its mainframe system could be "downsized" and replaced
by its own equipment. Sun eventually succeeded, but it took over five years—far longer
▼   than it expected.

CHAPTER SUMMARY

1. Objects are entities in your program that you manipulate by invoking methods.

2. The public interface of a class specifies what you can do with its objects. The hidden
   implementation describes how these actions are carried out.

3. Classes are factories for objects. You construct a new object of a class with the **new**
   operator.

4. You store object locations in object variables.

5. All object variables must be initialized before you access them.

6. An object reference describes the location of an object.

7. Multiple object variables can contain references to the same object.

8. Java classes are grouped into packages. If you use a class from another package (other than the `java.lang` package), you must import the class.

9. A method definition specifies the method name, parameters, and the statements for carrying out the method's actions.

10. Use the `return` statement to specify the value that a method returns to its caller.

11. To test a class, use an environment for interactive testing, or write a second class to execute test instructions.

12. An object uses instance fields to store its state—the data that it needs to execute its methods.

13. Each object of a class has its own set of instance fields.

14. Encapsulation is the process of hiding object data and providing methods for data access.

15. You should declare all instance fields as private.

16. Constructors contain instructions to initialize objects. The constructor name is always the same as the class name.

17. The `new` operator invokes the constructor.

18. Overloaded methods are methods with the same name but different parameter types.

19. Abstraction is the process of finding the essential feature set for a class.

20. Use documentation comments to describe the classes and public methods of your programs.

21. Provide documentation comments for every class, every method, every parameter, and every return value.

22. Instance fields belong to an object. Parameter variables and local variables belong to a method—they die when the method exits.

23. Instance fields are initialized to a default value, but you must initialize local variables.

24. The implicit parameter of a method is the object on which the method is invoked. The `this` reference denotes the implicit parameter.

25. Use of an instance field name in a method denotes the instance field of the implicit parameter.

Review Exercises

Exercise R2.1. Explain the difference between an object and an object reference.

Exercise R2.2. Explain the difference between an object and an object variable.

Exercise R2.3. Explain the difference between an object and a class.

Exercise R2.4. Explain the difference between a constructor and a method.

Exercise R2.5. Give the Java code for an *object* of class `BankAccount` and for an *object variable* of class `BankAccount`.

Exercise R2.6. Explain the difference between an instance field and a local variable.

Exercise R2.7. Explain the difference between a local variable and a parameter variable.

Exercise R2.8. Explain the difference between

```
new BankAccount(5000);
```

and

```
BankAccount b = new BankAccount(5000);
```

Exercise R2.9. Explain the difference between

```
BankAccount b;
```

and

```
BankAccount b = new BankAccount(5000);
```

Exercise R2.10. What are the construction parameters for a `BankAccount` object?

Exercise R2.11. Give Java code to construct the following objects:

- A rectangle with center (100, 100) and all side lengths equal to 50
- A greeter who will say `"Hello, Mars!"`
- A bank account with a balance of $5000

Create just objects, not object variables.

Exercise R2.12. Repeat the preceding exercise, but now define object variables that are initialized with the required objects.

Exercise R2.13. Find the errors in the following statements:

```
Rectangle r = (5, 10, 15, 20);

double x = BankAccount(10000).getBalance();

BankAccount b;
b.deposit(10000);

b = new BankAccount(10000);
b.add("one million bucks");
```

Exercise R2.14. Describe all constructors of the `BankAccount` class. List all methods that can be used to change a `BankAccount` object. List all methods that don't change the `BankAccount` object.

Exercise R2.15. What is the value of `b` after the following operations?

```
BankAccount b = new BankAccount(10);
b.deposit(5000);
b.withdraw(b.getBalance() / 2);
```

Exercise R2.16. If b1 and b2 store objects of class BankAccount, consider the following instructions.

```
b1.deposit(b2.getBalance());
b2.deposit(b1.getBalance());
```

Are the balances of b1 and b2 now identical? Explain.

Exercise R2.17. What is the this reference?

Exercise R2.18. What does the following method do? Give an example of how you can call the method.

```
public class BankAccount
{
   public void mystery(BankAccount that, double amount)
   {
      this.balance = this.balance - amount;
      that.balance = that.balance + amount;
   }
      . . . // other bank account methods
}
```

PROGRAMMING EXERCISES

Exercise P2.1. Write a program that constructs a Rectangle object, prints it, and then translates and prints it three more times, so that, if the rectangles were drawn, they would form one large rectangle:

Exercise P2.2. The intersection method computes the *intersection* of two rectangles—that is, the rectangle that is formed by two overlapping rectangles:

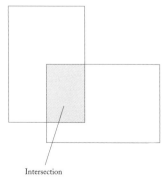

Intersection

You call this method as follows:

```
Rectangle r3 = r1.intersection(r2);
```

Write a program that constructs two rectangle objects, prints them, and then prints the rectangle object that describes the intersection. What happens when the rectangles do not overlap?

Exercise P2.3. Add a method sayGoodbye to the Greeter class.

Exercise P2.4. Add a method refuseHelp to the Greeter class. It should return a string such as "I am sorry, Dave. I am afraid I can't do that."

Exercise P2.5. Write a program that constructs a bank account, deposits $1000, withdraws $500, withdraws another $400, and then prints the remaining balance.

Exercise P2.6. Add a method

```
void addInterest(double rate)
```

to the BankAccount class that adds interest at the given rate. For example, after the statements

```
BankAccount momsSavings = new BankAccount(1000);
momsSavings.addInterest(10); // 10% interest
```

the balance in momsSavings is $1,100.

Exercise P2.7. Write a class SavingsAccount that is similar to the BankAccount class, except that it has an added instance variable interest. Supply a constructor that sets both the initial balance and the interest rate. Supply a method addInterest (with no explicit parameter) that adds interest to the account. Write a program that constructs a savings account with an initial balance of $1,000 and interest rate 10%. Then apply the addInterest method five times and print the resulting balance.

Exercise P2.8. Implement a class Employee. An employee has a name (a string) and a salary (a double). Write a default constructor, a constructor with two parameters (name and salary), and methods to return the name and salary. Write a small program that tests your class.

Exercise P2.9. Enhance the class in the preceding exercise by adding a method raiseSalary (double byPercent) that raises the employee's salary by a certain percentage. Sample usage:

```
Employee harry = new Employee("Hacker, Harry", 55000);
harry.raiseSalary(10); // Harry gets a 10% raise
```

Exercise P2.10. Implement a class Car with the following properties. A car has a certain fuel efficiency (measured in miles/gallon or liters/km—pick one) and a certain amount of fuel in the gas tank. The efficiency is specified in the constructor, and the initial fuel level is 0. Supply a method drive that simulates driving the car for a certain distance, reducing the fuel level in the gas tank, and methods getGas, returning the current fuel level, and addGas, to tank up. Sample usage:

```
Car myBeemer = new Car(29); // 29 miles per gallon
myBeemer.addGas(20); // tank 20 gallons
myBeemer.drive(100); // drive 100 miles
System.out.println(myBeemer.getGas());
// print fuel remaining
```

Exercise P2.11. Implement a class `Student`. For the purpose of this exercise, a student has a name and a total quiz score. Supply an appropriate constructor and methods `getName()`, `addQuiz(int score)`, `getTotalScore()`, and `getAverageScore()`. To compute the latter, you also need to store the *number of quizzes* that the student took.

Exercise P2.12. Implement a class `Product`. A product has a name and a price, for example `new Product("Toaster", 29.95)`. Supply methods `getName()`, `getPrice()`, and `setPrice()`. Write in a program that makes two products, prints the name and price, reduces their prices by $5.00, and then prints them again.

Exercise P2.13. Implement a class `Circle` that has methods `getArea()` and `getPerimeter()`. In the constructor, supply the radius of the circle.

Exercise P2.14. Implement a class `Square` that has methods `getArea()` and `getPerimeter()`. In the constructor, supply the width of the square.

Exercise P2.15. Implement a class `SodaCan` with methods `getSurfaceArea()` and `getVolume()`. In the constructor, supply the height and radius of the can.

Exercise P2.16. Implement a class `RoachPopulation` that simulates the growth of a roach population. The constructor takes the size of the initial roach population. The `waitForDoubling` method simulates a period in which the population doubles. The `spray` method simulates spraying with insecticide, which reduces the population by 10%. The `getRoaches` method returns the current number of roaches. Implement the class and a test program that simulates a kitchen that starts out with 10 roaches. Wait, spray, print the roach count. Repeat three times.

Exercise P2.17. Implement a class `RabbitPopulation` that simulates the growth of a rabbit population. The rules are as follows: Start with one pair of rabbits. Rabbits are able to mate at the age of one month. A month later, each female produces another pair of rabbits. Assume that rabbits never die and that the female always produces one new pair (one male, one female) every month from the second month on. Implement a method `waitAMonth` that waits for one month, and a method `getPairs` that prints the current number of rabbit pairs. Write a test program that shows the growth of the rabbit population for ten months. *Hint:* Keep one instance field for the newborn rabbit pairs and another one for the rabbit pairs that are at least one month old.

Fundamental Data Types

CHAPTER GOALS

To understand integer and floating-point numbers

▶ To recognize the limitations of the `int` and `double` types and the overflow and roundoff errors that can result

▶ To write arithmetic expressions in Java

▶ To use the `String` type to define and manipulate character strings

▶ To learn about the `char` data type

▶ To learn how to read program input

▶ To understand the copy behavior of primitive types and object references

This chapter teaches how to manipulate numbers and character strings in Java. The goal of this chapter is to gain a firm understanding of the fundamental Java data types.

3.1   Number Types

In this chapter, we will use a `Purse` class to demonstrate several important concepts. We won't yet reveal the implementation of the purse, but here is the public interface:

```
public class Purse
{
   /**
      Constructs an empty purse.
   */
   public Purse()
   {
      // implementation
   }

   /**
      Add nickels to the purse.
      @param count the number of nickels to add
   */
   public void addNickels(int count)
   {
      // implementation
   }

   /**
      Add dimes to the purse.
      @param count the number of dimes to add
```

```
*/
public void addDimes(int count)
{
    // implementation
}


/**
    Add quarters to the purse.
    @param  count the number of quarters to add
*/
public void addQuarters(int count)
{
    // implementation
}


/**
    Get the total value of the coins in the purse.
    @return  the sum of all coin values
*/
public double getTotal()
{
    // implementation
}

    // private instance variables
}
```

Read through the public interface and ask yourself whether you can figure out how to use `Purse` objects. You should find this straightforward. There is a constructor to make a new, empty purse:

```
Purse myPurse = new Purse();
```

You can add nickels, dimes, and quarters. (For simplicity, we don't bother with pennies, half dollars, or dollar coins.)

```
myPurse.addNickels(3);
myPurse.addDimes(1);
myPurse.addQuarters(2);
```

Now you can ask the purse object about the total value of the coins in the purse:

```
double totalValue = myPurse.getTotal(); // returns 0.75
```

> The `int` type denotes integers: numbers without fractional parts.

If you look closely at the methods to add coins, you will see an unfamiliar data type. The `count` parameter has type `int`, which denotes an *integer* type. An integer is a number without a fractional part. For example, 3 is an integer, but 0.05 is not. The number zero and negative numbers are integers. Thus, the `int` type is more restrictive than the `double` type that you saw in Chapter 2.

Why have both integer and floating-point number types? Your calculator doesn't have a separate integer type. It uses floating-point numbers for all calculations. Why don't we just use the `double` type for the coin counts?

There are two reasons for having a separate integer type: one philosophical and one pragmatic. In terms of philosophy, when we think about real purses and modern American coins, we recognize that there can be only a whole number of nickels, say, in a purse. If we were to saw a nickel in half, the halves would be worthless, and dropping one of them into a purse would not increase the amount of money in the purse. By specifying that the number of nickels is an integer, we make that observation into an explicit assumption in our model. The program would have worked just as well with floating-point numbers to count the coins, but it is generally a good idea to choose programming solutions that document one's intentions. Pragmatically speaking, integers are more efficient than floating-point numbers. They take less storage space, are processed faster on some platforms, and don't cause rounding errors.

Now let's start implementing the `Purse` class. Any `Purse` object can be described by the number of nickels, dimes, and quarters that the purse currently contains. Thus, we use three instance variables to represent the state of a `Purse` object:

```
public class Purse
{
   . . .
   private int nickels;
   private int dimes;
   private int quarters;
}
```

Now we can implement the `getTotal` method simply:

```
public double getTotal()
{
   return nickels * 0.05 + dimes * 0.1 + quarters * 0.25;
}
```

In Java, multiplication is denoted by an asterisk *, not a raised dot · or a cross ×, because there are no keys for these symbols on most keyboards. For example, $d \cdot 10$ is written as `d  *  10`. Do not write commas or spaces in numbers in Java. For example, 10,150.75 must be entered as `10150.75`. To write numbers in exponential notation in Java, use E n instead of "$\times 10^n$". For example, 5.0×10^{-3} is written as `5.0E-3`.

The `getTotal` method computes the value of the expression

```
nickels * 0.05 + dimes * 0.1 + quarters * 0.25
```

That value is a floating-point number, because multiplying an integer (such as `nickels`) by a floating-point number (such as `0.05`) yields a floating-point number. The `return` statement returns the computed value as the method result, and the method exits.

▼   3.1
Quality Tip

Choose Descriptive Variable Names

In algebra, variable names are usually just one letter long, such as p or A, maybe with a subscript such as p_1. You might be tempted to save yourself a lot of typing by using shorter variable names in your Java programs as well:

```
public class Purse
{
   . . .
   private int n;
   private int d;
   private int q;
}
```

Compare this with the previous one, though. Which one is easier to read? There is no comparison. Just reading `nickels` is a lot less trouble than reading n and then *figuring out* that it must mean "nickels".

In practical programming, descriptive variable names are particularly important when programs are written by more than one person. It may be obvious to *you* that n must stand for nickels, but is it obvious to the person who needs to update your code years later, long after you were promoted (or laid off)? For that matter, will you remember yourself what n means when you look at the code six months from now?

Of course, you could use comments:

```
public class Purse
{
   . . .
   private int n; // nickels
   private int d; // dimes
   private int q; // quarters
}
```

That makes the definitions pretty clear. But in the `getTotal` method, you'd still have a rather cryptic computation n * 0.05 + d * 0.1 + q * 0.25. Descriptive variable names are a better choice, because they make your code easy to read without requiring comments.

 Advanced Topic **3.1**

Numeric Ranges and Precisions

Unfortunately, `int` and `double` values do suffer from one problem: They cannot represent arbitrarily large integer or floating-point numbers. Integers have a range of $-2{,}147{,}483{,}648$ (about -2 billion) to $+2{,}147{,}483{,}647$ (about 2 billion). See Advanced Topic 3.4 for an explanation of these values. If you need to refer to these boundaries in your program, use the constants `Integer.MIN_VALUE` and `Integer.MAX_VALUE`, which are defined in a class called `Integer`. If you want to represent the world population, you can't use an `int`. Double-precision floating-point numbers are somewhat less limited; they can go up to more than 10^{300}. However, `double` floating-point numbers suffer from a different problem: *precision*. They store only about 15 significant digits. Suppose your customers might find the price of three hundred trillion dollars ($\$300{,}000{,}000{,}000{,}000$) for your product a bit excessive, so you want to reduce it by five cents to a more reasonable-looking $\$299{,}999{,}999{,}999{,}999.95$. Try running the following program:

```
class AdvancedTopic3_1
{
```

```
public static void main(String[] args)
{
    double originalPrice = 3E14;
    double discountedPrice = originalPrice - 0.05;
    double discount = originalPrice - discountedPrice;
        // should be 0.05;
    System.out.println(discount);
        // prints 0.0625;
}
}
```

The program prints out `0.0625`, not `0.05`. It is off by more than a penny!

For most of the programming projects in this book, the limited range and precision of `int` and `double` are acceptable. Just bear in mind that overflows or loss of precision can occur.

Advanced Topic   3.2

Other Number Types

If `int` and `double` are not sufficient for your computational needs, there are other data types to which you can turn. When the range of integers is not sufficient, the simplest remedy is to use the `long` type. *Long integers* have a range from −9,223,372,036,854,775,808 to +9,223,372,036,854,775,807.

To specify a long integer constant, you need to append the letter `L` after the number value. For example,

```
long price = 300000000000000L;
```

There is also an integer type `short` with shorter-than-normal integers, having a range of −32,768 to 32,767. Finally, there is a type `byte` with a range of −128 to 127.

The `double` type can represent about 15 decimal digits. There is a second floating-point type, called `float`, whose values take half the storage space. Computations involving `float` execute a bit faster than those involving `double`, but the precision of `float` values—about 7 decimal digits—is insufficient for many programs. However, some graphics routines require you to use `float` values.

By the way, the name "floating-point" comes from the fact that the numbers are represented in the computer as a sequence of the significant digits and an indication of the position of the decimal point. For example, the numbers 250, 2.5, 0.25, and 0.025 all have the same decimal digits: 25. When a floating-point number is multiplied or divided by 10, only the position of the decimal point changes; it "floats". This representation corresponds to numbers written in "exponential" or "scientific" notation, such as 2.5×10^2. (Actually, internally the numbers are represented in base 2, as binary numbers, but the principle is the same. See Advanced Topic 3.4 for more information on binary numbers.) Sometimes `float` values are called "single-precision", and of course `double` values are "double-precision" floating-point numbers.

If you want to compute with really large numbers, you can use *big number objects*. Big number objects are objects of the `BigInteger` and `BigDecimal` classes in the `java.math` package. Unlike the number types such as `int` or `double`, big number objects have essentially no limits on their size and precision. However, computations with big number objects are much slower than those that involve number types. Perhaps more importantly, you can't use the familiar arithmetic operators (+ - * /) with them. Instead, you have to use methods called `add`, `subtract`, `multiply`, and `divide`. Here is an example of how to create two big numbers and how to multiply them.

```
BigInteger a = new BigInteger("123456789");
BigInteger b = new BigInteger("987654321");
BigInteger c = a.multiply(b);
System.out.println(c); // prints 121932631112635269
```

Random Fact 3.1

The Pentium Floating-Point Bug

In 1994, Intel Corporation released what was then its most powerful processor, the first of the Pentium series. Unlike previous generations of Intel's processors, the Pentium had a very fast floating-point unit. Intel's goal was to compete aggressively with the makers of higher-end processors for engineering workstations. The Pentium was an immediate huge success.

In the summer of 1994, Dr. Thomas Nicely of Lynchburg College in Virginia ran an extensive set of computations to analyze the sums of reciprocals of certain sequences of prime numbers. The results were not always what his theory predicted, even after he took into account the inevitable roundoff errors. Then Dr. Nicely noted that the same program did produce the correct results when run on the slower 486 processor, which preceded the Pentium in Intel's lineup. This should not have happened. The optimal roundoff behavior of floating-point calculations has been standardized by the Institute of Electrical and Electronics Engineers (IEEE), and Intel claimed to adhere to the IEEE standard in both the 486 and the Pentium processors. Upon further checking, Dr. Nicely discovered that indeed there was a very small set of numbers for which the product of two numbers was computed differently on the two processors. For example,

$$4{,}195{,}835 - ((4{,}195{,}835 \,/\, 3{,}145{,}727) \times 3{,}145{,}727)$$

is mathematically equal to 0, and it did compute as 0 on a 486 processor. On a Pentium processor, however, the result was 256.

As it turned out, Intel had independently discovered the bug in its testing and had started to produce chips that fixed it. (Subsequent versions of the Pentium, such as the Pentium III and IV, are free of the problem.) The bug was caused by an error in a table that was used to speed up the floating-point multiplication algorithm of the processor. Intel determined that the problem was exceedingly rare. They claimed that under normal use a typical consumer would only notice the problem once every 27,000 years. Unfortunately for Intel, Dr. Nicely had not been a normal user.

▼   Now Intel had a real problem on its hands. It figured that replacing all the Pentium processors that it had already sold would cost it a great deal of money. Intel
▼   already had more orders for the chip than it could produce, and it would be particularly galling to have to give out the scarce chips as free replacements instead of selling them. Intel's management decided to punt on the issue and initially offered
▼   to replace the processors only for those customers who could prove that their work required absolute precision in mathematical calculations. Naturally, that did not go over well with the hundreds of thousands of customers who had paid retail prices
▼   of $700 and more for a Pentium chip and did not want to live with the nagging feeling that perhaps, one day, their income tax program would produce a faulty return.
▼   Ultimately, Intel had to cave in to public demand and replaced all defective chips, at a cost of about 475 million dollars.
    What do you think? Intel claims that the probability of the bug occurring in any calculation is extremely small—smaller than many chances you take every day, such as driv-
▼   ing to work in an automobile. Indeed, many users had used their Pentium computers for many months without reporting any ill effects, and the computations that Professor Nicely was doing are hardly examples of typical user needs. As a result of its public rela-
▼   tions blunder, Intel ended up paying a large amount of money. Undoubtedly, some of that money was added to chip prices and thus actually paid by Intel's customers. Also, a large number of processors, whose manufacture consumed energy and caused some envi-
▼   ronmental impact, were destroyed without benefiting anyone. Could Intel have been justified in wanting to replace only the processors of those users who could reasonably be expected to suffer an impact from the problem?
▼   Suppose that, instead of stonewalling, Intel had offered you the choice of a free replacement processor or a $200 rebate. What would you have done? Would you have replaced your faulty chip, or would you have taken your chance and pocketed the
▼   money?

3.2   ## Assignment

Here is the constructor of the Purse class:

```
public Purse()
{
    nickels = 0;   Expression
    dimes = 0;     Expression
    quarters = 0;  Expression
}
```

The = operator is called the *assignment* operator. On the left, you need a variable name. The right-hand side can be a single value or an expression. The assignment operator sets the variable to the given value. So far, that's straightforward. But now let's look at a more interesting use of the assignment operator, in the addNickels method.

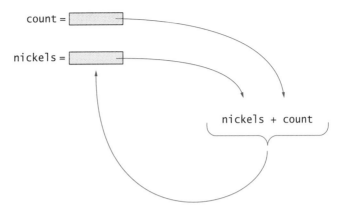

Figure 1

Assignment

```
public void addNickels(int count)
{
    nickels = nickels + count;
}
```

It means, "Compute the value of the expression nickels + count, *and place the result again into the variable* nickels." (See Figure 1.)

The = sign doesn't mean that the left-hand side is *equal* to the right-hand side but that the right-hand-side value is copied into the left-hand-side variable. You should not confuse this *assignment operation* with the = used in algebra to denote *equality*. The assignment operator is an instruction to do something, namely place a value into a variable. The mathematical equality states the fact that two values are equal. For example, in Java it is perfectly legal to write

```
nickels = nickels + 1;
```

It means to look up the value stored in the variable nickels, to add 1 to it, and to stuff the sum back into nickels. (See Figure 2.) The net effect of executing this

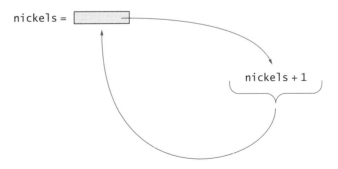

Figure 2

Incrementing a Variable

> Assignment to a variable
> is not the same as
> mathematical equality.

> The ++ and -- operators
> increment and decrement
> a variable.

statement is to increment `nickels` by 1. Of course, in mathematics it would make no sense to write that $n = n + 1$; no integer can equal itself plus 1.

The concepts of assignment and equality have no relationship with each other, and it is a bit unfortunate that the Java language (following C and C++) uses = to denote assignment. Other programming languages use a symbol such as <- or :=, which avoids the confusion.

Consider once more the statement `nickels = nickels + 1`. This statement increments the `nickels` variable. For example, if `nickels` was 3 before execution of the statement, it is set to 4 afterwards. This increment operation is so common when writing programs that there is a special shorthand for it, namely

```
nickels++;
```

This statement has exactly the same effect—namely, to add 1 to `nickels`—but it is easier to type. As you might have guessed, there is also a decrement operator --. The statement

```
nickels--;
```

subtracts 1 from `nickels`.

Advanced Topic   3.3

Combining Assignment and Arithmetic

In Java you can combine arithmetic and assignment. For example, the instruction

```
nickels += count;
```

is a shortcut for

```
nickels = nickels + count;
```

Similarly,

```
nickels *= 2;
```

is another way of writing

```
nickels = nickels * 2;
```

Many programmers find this a convenient shortcut. If you like it, go ahead and use it in your own code. For simplicity, we won't use it in this book, though.

▼ **Productivity Hint** 3.1

Avoid Unstable Layout

▼

You should arrange program code and comments so that the program is easy to read. For example, you should not cram all statements on a single line, and you should make sure
▼
that braces { } line up.

However, you should be careful when you embark on beautification efforts. Some programmers like to line up the = signs in a series of assignments, like this:

▼
```
nickels  = 0;
dimes    = 0;
quarters = 0;
```

▼
This looks very neat, but the layout is not *stable*. Suppose you add a line like the one at the bottom of this:

▼
```
nickels  = 0;
dimes    = 0;
quarters = 0;
halfDollars = 0;
```

▼
Oops, now the = signs no longer line up, and you have the extra work of lining them up *again*.

▼
Here is another example. Suppose you have a comment that goes over multiple lines:

```
// In this test class, we compute the value of a set of coins.
// We add a number of nickels, dimes, and quarters
▼
// to a purse. We then get and display the total value.
```

When the program is extended to work for half-dollar coins as well, you must modify
▼
the comment to reflect that change.

```
// In this test class, we compute the value of a set of coins.
// We add a number of nickels, dimes, quarters, and
▼
half-dollars // to a purse. We then get and display the total
value.
```

Now you need to rearrange the // to fix up the comment. This scheme is a *disincentive* to
▼
keep comments up to date. Don't do it. Instead, for comments that are longer than one line,
use the /* . . . */ style for comments, and block off the entire comment like this:

▼
```
/*
   In this test class, we compute the value of a set of coins.
   We add a number of nickels, dimes, and quarters
▼
   to a purse. We then get and display the total value.
*/
```

▼
You may not care about these issues. Perhaps you plan to beautify your program just before it is finished, when you are about to turn in your homework. That is not a

▼

▼

particularly useful approach. In practice, programs are never finished. They are continuously improved and updated. It is better to develop the habit of laying out your programs well from the start and keeping them legible at all times. As a consequence, you should avoid layout schemes that are hard to maintain.

3.3 Constants

Consider once again the getTotal method, paying attention to whether it is easy to understand the code.

```java
public double getTotal()
{
    return nickels * 0.05 + dimes * 0.1 + quarters * 0.25;
}
```

Most of the code is self-documenting. However, the three numeric quantities, 0.05, 0.1, and 0.25, are included in the arithmetic expression without any explanation. Of course, in this case, you know that the value of a nickel is five cents, which explains the 0.05, and so on. However, the next person who needs to maintain this code may live in another country and may not know that a nickel is worth five cents.

Thus, it is a good idea to use symbolic names for *all* values, even those that appear obvious. Here is a clearer version of the computation of the total:

```java
double nickelValue = 0.05;
double dimeValue = 0.1;
double quarterValue = 0.25;
return nickels * nickelValue
    + dimes * dimeValue
    + quarters * quarterValue;
```

> A final variable is a constant. Once its value has been set, it cannot be changed.

> Use named constants to make your programs easier to read and maintain.

There is another improvement we can make. There is a difference between the nickels and nickelValue variables. The nickels variable can truly vary over the life of the program, as more coins are added to the purse. But nickelValue is *always* 0.05. It is a *constant*. In Java, constants are identified with the keyword final. A variable tagged as final can never change after it has been set. If you try to change the value of a final variable, the compiler will report an error and your program will not compile.

Many programmers use all-uppercase names for constants (final variables), such as NICKEL_VALUE. That way, it is easy to distinguish between variables (with mostly lowercase letters) and constants. We will follow this convention in this book. However, this rule is a matter of good style, not a requirement of the Java language. The compiler will not complain if you give a final variable a name with lowercase letters.

Here is the improved version of the `getTotal` method:

```
public double getTotal()
{
    final double NICKEL_VALUE = 0.05;
    final double DIME_VALUE = 0.1;
    final double QUARTER_VALUE = 0.25;
    return nickels * NICKEL_VALUE
        + dimes * DIME_VALUE
        + quarters * QUARTER_VALUE;
}
```

In this example, the constants are needed only inside one method of the class. Frequently, a constant value is needed in several methods. Then you need to declare it together with the instance variables of the class and tag it as `static final`. The meaning of the keyword `static` will be explained in Chapter 6.

```
public class Purse
{
    // methods
    . . .

    // constants
    private static final double NICKEL_VALUE = 0.05;
    private static final double DIME_VALUE = 0.1;
    private static final double QUARTER_VALUE = 0.25;

    // instance variables
    private int nickels;
    private int dimes;
    private int quarters;
}
```

Here we defined the constants to be `private` because we didn't think they were of interest to users of the `Purse` class. However, it is also possible to declare constants as `public`:

```
public static final double NICKEL_VALUE = 0.05;
```

Then methods of other classes can access the constant as `Purse.NICKEL_VALUE`.
The `Math` class from the standard library defines a couple of useful constants:

```
public class Math
{
    . . .
    public static final double E = 2.7182818284590452354;
    public static final double PI = 3.14159265358979323846;
}
```

You can refer to these constants as `Math.PI` and `Math.E` in any of your methods. For example,

```
double circumference = Math.PI * diameter;
```

Syntax 3.1: Constant Definition

In a method:

final *typeName* *variableName* = *expression*;

In a class:

accessSpecifier static final *typeName* *variableName* = *expression*;

Example:

```
final double NICKEL_VALUE = 0.05;
public static final double LITERS_PER_GALLON = 3.785;
```

Purpose:

To define a constant of a particular type

File Purse.java

```
 1  /**
 2      A purse computes the total value of a collection of coins.
 3  */
 4  public class Purse
 5  {
 6      /**
 7          Constructs an empty purse.
 8      */
 9      public Purse()
10      {
11          nickels = 0;
12          dimes = 0;
13          quarters = 0;
14      }
15
16      /**
17          Add nickels to the purse.
18          @param count the number of nickels to add
19      */
20      public void addNickels(int count)
21      {
22          nickels = nickels + count;
23      }
24      /**
25          Add dimes to the purse.
26          @param count the number of dimes to add
```

```
27      */
28      public void addDimes(int count)
29      {
30          dimes = dimes + count;
31      }
32
33      /**
34          Add quarters to the purse.
35          @param count  the number of quarters to add
36      */
37      public void addQuarters(int count)
38      {
39          quarters = quarters + count;
40      }
41
42      /**
43          Get the total value of the coins in the purse.
44          @return the sum of all coin values
45      */
46      public double getTotal()
47      {
48          return nickels * NICKEL_VALUE
49              + dimes * DIME_VALUE + quarters * QUARTER_VALUE;
50      }
51
52      private static final double NICKEL_VALUE = 0.05;
53      private static final double DIME_VALUE = 0.1;
54      private static final double QUARTER_VALUE = 0.25;
55
56      private int nickels;
57      private int dimes;
58      private int quarters;
59  }
```

File PurseTest.java

```
1   /**
2       This program tests the Purse class.
3   */
4   public class PurseTest
5   {
6       public static void main(String[] args)
7       {
8           Purse myPurse = new Purse();
9
10          myPurse.addNickels(3);
11          myPurse.addDimes(1);
12          myPurse.addQuarters(2);
13          double totalValue = myPurse.getTotal();
```

```
14        System.out.print("The total is ");
15        System.out.println(totalValue);
16    }
17 }
```

▼ ▲ Quality Tip   3.2 ▶

Do Not Use Magic Numbers

▼ A *magic number* is a numeric constant that appears in your code without explanation. For example, consider the following scary example that actually occurs in the Java library source:

▼
```
h = 31 * h + ch;
```

Why 31? The number of days in January? One less than the number of bits in an integer?

▼ Actually, this code computes a "hash code" from a string—a number that is derived from the characters in such a way that different strings are likely to yield different hash codes. The value 31 turns out to scramble the character values nicely.

▼ You should use a named constant instead:

```
final int HASH_MULTIPLIER = 31;
h = HASH_MULTIPLIER * h + ch;
```

▼ You should *never* use magic numbers in your code. Any number that is not completely self-explanatory should be declared as a named constant. Even the most reasonable cosmic con-

▼ stant is going to change one day. You think there are 365 days in a year? Your customers on Mars are going to be pretty unhappy about your silly prejudice. Make a constant

```
final int DAYS_PER_YEAR = 365;
```

▼ By the way, the device

```
final int THREE_HUNDRED_AND_SIXTY_FIVE = 365;
```

is counterproductive and frowned upon.

▼

3.4   Arithmetic and Mathematical Functions

You already saw how to add, subtract, and multiply values. Division is indicated with a /, not a fraction bar. For example,

$$\frac{a + b}{2}$$

becomes

```
(a + b) / 2
```

Parentheses are used just as in algebra: to indicate in which order the subexpressions should be computed. For example, in the expression (a + b) / 2, the sum a + b is computed first, and then the sum is divided by 2. In contrast, in the expression

```
a + b / 2
```

only b is divided by 2, and then the sum of a and b / 2 is formed. Just as in regular algebraic notation, multiplication and division *bind more strongly* than addition and subtraction. For example, in the expression a + b / 2, the / is carried out first, even though the + operation occurs further to the left.

> If both arguments of the / operator are integers, the result is an integer and the remainder is discarded.

Division works as you would expect, as long as at least one of the numbers involved is a floating-point number. That is,

```
7.0 / 4.0
7 / 4.0
7.0 / 4
```

all yield 1.75. However, if *both* numbers are integers, then the result of the division is always an integer, with the remainder discarded. That is,

```
7 / 4
```

evaluates to 1, because 7 divided by 4 is 1 with a remainder of 3 (which is discarded). This can be a source of subtle programming errors—see Common Error 3.1.

If you are interested only in the remainder of an integer division, use the % operator:

```
7 % 4
```

> The % operator computes the remainder of a division.

is 3, the remainder of the integer division of 7 by 4. The % symbol has no analog in algebra. It was chosen because it looks similar to /, and the remainder operation is related to division.

Here is a typical use for the integer / and % operations. Suppose you want to know the value of the coins in a purse in dollars and cents. You can compute the value as an integer, denominated in cents, and then compute the whole dollar amount and the remaining change:

```
final int PENNIES_PER_NICKEL = 5;
final int PENNIES_PER_DIME = 10;
final int PENNIES_PER_QUARTER = 25;
final int PENNIES_PER_DOLLAR = 100;

// compute total value in pennies

int total = nickels * PENNIES_PER_NICKEL
   + dimes * PENNIES_PER_DIME
   + quarters * PENNIES_PER_QUARTER;

// use integer division to convert to dollars, cents

int dollars = total / PENNIES_PER_DOLLAR;
int cents = total % PENNIES_PER_DOLLAR;
```

For example, if total is 243, then dollars is set to 2 and cents to 43.

To take the square root of a number, you use the Math.sqrt method. For example, $\sqrt{x}$ is written as Math.sqrt(x). To compute x^n, you write Math.pow(x, n). However, to compute x^2 it is significantly more efficient simply to compute x * x.

⊗ Common Error   3.1

Integer Division

It is unfortunate that Java uses the same symbol, namely /, for both integer and floating-point division. These are really quite different operations. It is a common error to use integer division by accident. Consider this program segment that computes the average of three integers.

```
int s1 = 5; // score of test 1
int s2 = 6; // score of test 2
int s3 = 3; // score of test 3
double average = (s1 + s2 + s3) / 3;   // Error
System.out.print("Your average score is ");
System.out.println(average);
```

What could be wrong with that? Of course, the average of s1, s2, and s3 is

$$\frac{s_1 + s_2 + s_3}{3}$$

Here, however, the / does not mean division in the mathematical sense. It denotes integer division, because the values s1 + s2 + s3 and 3 are both integers. For example, if the scores add up to 14, the average is computed to be 4, the result of the integer division of 14 by 3. That integer 4 is then moved into the floating-point variable average. The remedy is to make the numerator or denominator into a floating-point number:

```
double total = s1 + s2 + s3;
double average = total / 3;
```

or

```
double average = (s1 + s2 + s3) / 3.0;
```

> The Math class contains methods sqrt and pow to compute square roots and powers.

As you can see, the visual effect of the /, Math.sqrt, and Math.pow notations is to flatten out mathematical terms. In algebra, you use fractions, superscripts for exponents, and radical signs for roots to arrange expressions in a compact two-dimensional form. In Java, you have to write all expressions in a linear arrangement. For example, the subexpression

$$\frac{-b + \sqrt{b^2 - 4ac}}{2a}$$

of the quadratic formula becomes

```
(-b + Math.sqrt(b * b - 4 * a * c)) / (2 * a)
```

Figure 3 shows how to analyze such an expression. With complicated expressions like these, it is not always easy to keep the parentheses (...) matched—see Common Error 3.2.

Table 1 shows additional methods of the Math class. Inputs and outputs are floating-point numbers.

Figure 3

Analyzing an Expression

$$(-b + \texttt{Math.sqrt(b * b - 4 * a * c))} / (2 * a)$$

with braces indicating:
b^2 $4ac$ $2a$

$$b^2 - 4ac$$

$$\sqrt{b^2 - 4ac}$$

$$-b + \sqrt{b^2 - 4ac}$$

$$\frac{-b + \sqrt{b^2 - 4ac}}{2a}$$

Function	Returns
`Math.sqrt(x)`	Square root of x (≥ 0)
`Math.pow(x,y)`	x^y ($x > 0$, or $x=0$ and $y>0$, or $x<0$ and y is an integer)
`Math.sin(x)`	Sine of x (x in radians)
`Math.cos(x)`	Cosine of x
`Math.tan(x)`	Tangent of x
`Math.asin(x)`	Arc sine ($\sin^{-1}x \in [-\pi/2, \pi/2]$, $x \in [-1,1]$)
`Math.acos(x)`	Arc cosine ($\cos^{-1}x \in [0,\pi]$, $x \in [-1,1]$)
`Math.atan(x)`	Arc tangent ($\tan^{-1}x \in (-\pi/2, \pi/2)$)
`Math.atan2(y,x)`	Arc tangent ($\tan^{-1}(y/x) \in [-\pi,\pi]$, ($x$ may be 0)
`Math.toRadians(x)`	Convert x degrees to radians (i.e., returns $x \cdot \pi/180$)
`Math.toDegrees(x)`	Convert x radians to degrees (i.e., returns $x \cdot 180/\pi$)
`Math.exp(x)`	e^x
`Math.log(x)`	Natural log ($\ln(x)$, $x > 0$)
`Math.round(x)`	Closest integer to x (as a `long`)
`Math.ceil(x)`	Smallest integer $\geq x$ (as a `double`)
`Math.floor(x)`	Largest integer $\leq x$ (as a `double`)
`Math.abs(x)`	Absolute value $|x|$
`Math.max(x, y)`	The larger of x and y
`Math.min(x, y)`	The smaller of x and y

Table 1

Mathematical Methods

▼ ⊗ **Common Error** ▶ **3.2**

Unbalanced Parentheses

▼

Consider the expression

```
1.5 * ((-(b - Math.sqrt(b * b - 4 * a * c)) / (2 * a))
```

▼

What is wrong with it? Count the parentheses. There are five opening parentheses (and four closing parentheses). The parentheses are *unbalanced*. This kind of typing error is very common with complicated expressions. Now consider this expression.

▼

```
1.5 * (Math.sqrt(b * b - 4 * a * c))) - ((b / (2 * a))
```

This expression has five opening parentheses (and five closing parentheses), but it is still not correct. In the middle of the expression,

▼

```
1.5 * (Math.sqrt(b * b - 4 * a * c))) - ((b / (2 * a))
```

▼

there are only two opening parentheses (but three closing parentheses), which is an error. In the middle of an expression, the count of opening parentheses (must be greater than or equal to the count of closing parentheses), and at the end of the expression the two counts must be the same.

▼

Here is a simple trick to make the counting easier without using pencil and paper. It is difficult for the brain to keep two counts simultaneously, so keep only one count when scanning the expression. Start with 1 at the first opening parenthesis; add 1 whenever you see an opening parenthesis; and subtract 1 whenever you see a closing parenthesis. Say the numbers aloud as you scan the expression. If the count ever drops below zero, or if it is not zero at the end, the parentheses are unbalanced. For example, when scanning the previous expression, you would mutter

▼

```
1.5 * (Math.sqrt(b * b - 4 * a * c) )  ) - ((b / (2 * a))
         1          2              1 0 −1
```

▼

and you would find the error.

▼ ⊘ **Productivity Hint** ▶ **3.2**

On-Line Help

▼

The Java library has hundreds of classes and thousands of methods. It is neither necessary nor useful trying to memorize them. Instead, you should become familiar with using the on-line documentation. You can download the documentation from http://java.sun.com/ j2se/1.3/docs.html. Install the documentation set and point your browser to your Java installation directory /docs/api/index.html. Alternatively, you can browse http:// java.sun.com/j2se/1.3/docs/api/index.html. For example, if you are not sure how the pow method works, or cannot remember whether it was called pow or power, the on-line help

Figure 4

On-Line Help

can give you the answer quickly. Click on the Math class in the class window on the left, and look at the method summary in the main window (see Figure 4).

If you use javadoc to document your own classes, then this documentation format will look extremely familiar to you. The programmers who implement the Java library use javadoc themselves. They too document every class, every method, every parameter, and every return value, and then use javadoc to extract the documentation in HTML format.

Quality Tip   3.3

White Space

The compiler does not care whether you write your entire program onto a single line or place every symbol onto a separate line. The human reader, though, cares very much. You should use blank lines to group your code visually into sections. For example, you can signal to the reader that an output prompt and the corresponding input statement belong together by inserting a blank line before and after the group. You will find many examples in the source code listings in this book.

White space inside expressions is also important. It is easier to read

```
x1 = (-b + Math.sqrt(b * b - 4 * a * c)) / (2 * a);
```

than

```
X1=(-b+Math.sqrt(b*b-4*a*c))/(2*a);
```

Simply put spaces around all operators + - * / % =. However, don't put a space after a *unary* minus: a - used to negate a single quantity, as in -b. That way, it can be easily distinguished from a *binary* minus, as in a - b. Don't put spaces between a method name and the parentheses, but do put a space after every Java keyword. That makes it easy to see that the sqrt in Math.sqrt(x) is a method name, whereas the if in if (x > 0)... is a keyword.

Quality Tip   3.4

Factor Out Common Code

Suppose you want to find both solutions of the quadratic equation $ax^2 + bx + c = 0$. The quadratic formula tells us that the solutions are

$$x_{1,2} = \frac{-b \pm \sqrt{b^2 - 4ac}}{2a}$$

In Java, there is no analog to the $\pm$ operation, which indicates how to obtain two solutions simultaneously. Both solutions must be computed separately:

```
x1 = (-b + Math.sqrt(b * b - 4 * a * c)) / (2 * a);
x2 = (-b - Math.sqrt(b * b - 4 * a * c)) / (2 * a);
```

This approach has two problems. First, the computation of Math.sqrt(b * b - 4 * a * c) is carried out twice, which wastes time. Second, whenever the same code is replicated, the possibility of a typing error increases. The remedy is to *factor out* the common code:

```
double root = Math.sqrt(b * b - 4 * a * c);
x1 = (-b + root) / (2 * a);
x2 = (-b - root) / (2 * a);
```

You could go even further and factor out the computation of 2 * a, but the gain from factoring out very simple computations is too small to warrant the effort.

3.5   Calling Static Methods

In the preceding section, you encountered the Math class, which contains a collection of helpful methods for carrying out mathematical computations.

There is one important difference between the methods of the Math class, such as the sqrt method, and the methods that you have seen so far (such as getTotal or *method sqrt example only operates on Maths*

println). The getTotal and println methods, as you have seen, operate on an object such as myPurse or System.out. In contrast, the sqrt method does not operate on any object. That is, you don't call

```
double x = 4;
double root = x.sqrt(); // Error
```

> A static method does
> not operate on an object.

Math.sqrt(x);

The reason is that, in Java, numbers are not objects, so you can never invoke a method on a number. Instead, you pass a number as an explicit parameter to a method, enclosing the number in parentheses after the method name. For example, the number value x can be a parameter of the Math.sqrt method: Math.sqrt(x).

This call makes it appear as if the sqrt method is applied to an object called Math, because Math precedes sqrt just as myPurse precedes getTotal in a method call myPurse.getTotal(). However, Math is a class, not an object. A method such as Math.round that does not operate on any object is called a *static* method. (The term "static" is a historical holdover from C and C++ that has nothing to do with the usual meaning of the word.) Static methods do not operate on objects, but they are still defined inside classes. You must specify the class to which the sqrt method belongs—hence the call is Math.sqrt(x).

How can you tell whether Math is a class or an object? All classes in the Java library start with an uppercase letter (such as System). Objects and methods start with a lowercase letter (such as out and println). You can tell objects and methods apart because method calls are followed by parentheses. Therefore, System.out.println() denotes a call of the println method on the out object inside the System class. On the other hand, Math.sqrt(x) denotes a call to the sqrt method inside the Math class. This use of upper- and lowercase letters is merely a *convention*, not a rule of the Java language. It is, however, a convention that the authors of the Java class libraries follow consistently. You should do the same in your programs. If you give names to objects or methods that start with an uppercase letter, you will likely confuse your fellow programmers. Therefore, we strongly recommend that you follow the standard naming convention.

Syntax 3.2: Static Method Call

ClassName.methodName(parameters)

Example:

Math.sqrt(4) *= static method*

Purpose:

To invoke a static method (a method that does not operate on an object) and supply its parameters

3.6   Type Conversion

When you make an assignment of an expression into a variable, the *types* of the variable and the expression must be compatible. For example, it is an error to assign

```
double total = "a lot"; // Error
```

because `total` is a floating-point variable and `"a lot"` is a string. It is, however, legal to store an integer expression in a `double` variable:

```
int dollars = 2;
double total = dollars; // OK
```

In Java, you cannot assign a floating-point expression to an integer variable.

```
double total = . . . .;
int dollars = total; // Error
```

You must convert the floating-point value to integer with a *cast*:

```
int dollars = (int)total;
```

> You use a cast (*typeName*) to convert a value to a different type.

The cast `(int)` converts the floating-point value `total` to an integer. The effect of the cast is to discard the fractional part. For example, if `total` is 13.75, then `dollars` is set to 13. If you want to convert the value of a floating-point expression to an integer, you need to enclose the expression in parentheses to ensure that it is computed first:

```
int pennies = (int)(total * 100);
```

This is different from the expression

```
int pennies = (int)total * 100;
```

In the second expression, `total` is *first* converted to an integer, and then the resulting integer is multiplied by 100. For example, if `total` is 13.75, then the first expression computes `total * 100`, or 1375, and then converts that value to the integer 1375. In the second expression, `total` is first cast to the integer 13, and then the integer is multiplied by 100, yielding 1300. Normally, you will want to apply the integer conversion *after* all other computations, so that your computations use the full precision of their input values. That means you should enclose your computation in parentheses and apply the cast to the expression in parentheses.

There is a good reason why you must use a cast in Java when you convert a floating-point number to an integer: The conversion *loses information*. You must confirm that you agree to that information loss. Java is quite strict about this. You must use a cast whenever there is the possibility of information loss. A cast always has the form (*typeName*), for example `(int)` or `(float)`.

Actually, simply using an `(int)` cast to convert a floating-point number to an integer is not always a good idea. Consider the following example:

```
double price = 44.95;
int dollars = (int)price; // sets dollars to 44
```

What did you want to achieve? Did you want to get the number of dollars in the price? Then dropping the fractional part is the right thing to do. Or did you want to get the approximate dollar amount? Then you really want to *round up* when the fractional part is 0.5 or larger.

One way to round to the nearest integer is to add 0.5, then cast to an integer:

```
double price = 44.95;
int dollars = (int)(price + 0.5); // OK for positive values
System.out.print("The price is approximately $")
System.out.println(dollars); // prints 45
```

> Use the Math.round method to round a floating-point number to the nearest integer.

Adding 0.5 and casting to the int type works, because it turns all values that are between 44.50 and 45.4999... into 45.

Actually, there is a better way. Simply adding 0.5 works fine for positive numbers, but it doesn't work correctly for negative numbers. Instead, use the Math.round method in the standard Java library. It works for both positive and negative numbers. However, that method returns a long integer, because large floating-point numbers cannot be stored in an int. You need to cast the return value to an int:

```
int dollars = (int)Math.round(price); // better
```

Syntax 3.3: Cast

(*typeName*) *expression*

Examples

```
(int)(x + 0.5)
(int)Math.round(100 * f)
```

Purpose:

To convert an expression to a different type

? HOWTO   3.1

Carrying Out Computations

Many programming problems require that you use mathematical formulas to compute values. It is not always obvious how to turn a problem statement into a sequence of mathematical formulas and, ultimately, statements in the Java programming language.

Step 1 Understand the problem: What are the inputs? What are the desired outputs?

For example, suppose you are asked to simulate a postage stamp vending machine. A customer inserts money into the vending machine. Then the customer pushes a "First class stamps" button. The vending machine gives out as many first-class stamps as the customer paid for. (A first-class stamp cost 34 cents at the time this book was written.) Finally, the customer pushes a "Penny stamps" button. The machine gives the change in penny (1-cent) stamps.

In this problem, there is one input:

- The amount of money the customer inserts

There are two desired outputs:

- The number of first-class stamps that the machine returns
- The number of penny stamps that the machine returns

Step 2   Work out examples by hand

This is a very important step. If you can't compute a couple of solutions by hand, it's unlikely that you'll be able to write a program that automates the computation.

Let's assume that a first-class stamp costs 34 cents and the customer inserts $1.00. That's enough for two stamps (68 cents) but not enough for three stamps ($1.02). Therefore, the machine returns 2 first-class stamps and 32 penny stamps.

Step 3   Find mathematical equations that compute the answers

Given an amount of money and the price of a first-class stamp, how can you compute how many first-class stamps can be purchased with the money? Clearly, the answer is related to the quotient

$$\frac{\text{amount of money}}{\text{price of first-class stamp}}$$

For example, suppose the customer paid $1.00. Use a pocket calculator to compute the quotient: $1.00/$0.34 ≈ 2.9412.

How do you get "2 stamps" out of 2.9412? It's the integer part. By discarding the fractional part, you get the number of whole stamps that the customer has purchased.

In mathematical notation,

$$\text{number of first-class stamps} = \left\lfloor \frac{\text{money}}{\text{price of first-class stamp}} \right\rfloor$$

where $\lfloor x \rfloor$ denotes the largest integer $\leq x$. That function is sometimes called the "floor function".

You now know how to compute the number of stamps that are given out when the customer pushes the "First-class stamps" button. When the customer gets the stamps, the amount of money is reduced by the value of the stamps purchased. For example, if the customer gets two stamps, the remaining money is $0.32. It is the difference between $1.00 and 2 · $0.34. Here is the general formula:

remaining money = money − number of first-class stamps · price of first-class stamp

How many penny stamps does the remaining money buy? That's easy. If $0.32 is left, the customer gets 32 stamps. In general, the number of penny stamps is

number of penny stamps = 100 · remaining money

Step 4 Turn the mathematical equations into Java statements

In Java, you can compute the integer part of a nonnegative floating-point value by applying an (int) cast. Therefore, you can compute the number of first-class stamps with the following statement:

```
firstClassStamps =
    (int)(money / FIRST_CLASS_STAMP_PRICE);
money = money -
    firstClassStamps * FIRST_CLASS_STAMP_PRICE;
```

Finally, the number of penny stamps is

```
pennyStamps = 100 * money;
```

That's not quite right, though. The value of pennyStamps should be an integer, but the right hand side is a floating-point number. Therefore, the correct statement is

```
pennyStamps = (int)Math.round(100 * money);
```

Step 5 Build a class that carries out your computations

HOWTO 2.1 explains how to develop a class by finding methods and instance variables. In our case, we can find three methods:

- void insert(double amount)
- int giveFirstClassStamps()
- int givePennyStamps()

The state of a vending machine can be described by the amount of money that the customer has available for purchases. Therefore, we supply one instance variable, money.
Here is the implementation:

```
public class StampMachine
{
    public StampMachine()
    {
        money = 0;
    }

    public void insert(double amount)
    {
        money = money + amount;
    }

    public int giveFirstClassStamps()
    {
        int firstClassStamps =
            (int)(money / FIRST_CLASS_STAMP_PRICE);
        money = money -
            firstClassStamps * FIRST_CLASS_STAMP_PRICE;
```

```
      return firstClassStamps;
   }

   public int givePennyStamps()
   {
      int pennyStamps = (int)Math.round(100 * money);
      money = 0;
      return pennyStamps;
   }

   private double money;
   private static final double FIRST_CLASS_STAMP_PRICE =
      0.34;
}
```

Step 6 Test your class

Run a test program (or use BlueJ) to verify that the values that your class computes are the same values that you computed by hand. In our example, try the statements

```
StampMachine machine = new StampMachine();
machine.insert(1);
System.out.println("First class stamps: " +
   machine.giveFirstClassStamps());
System.out.println("Penny stamps: " +
   machine.givePennyStamps());
```

Check that the result is

```
First class stamps: 2
Penny stamps: 32
```

⊗ Common Error   3.3 ▶

Roundoff Errors

Roundoff errors are a fact of life when calculating with floating-point numbers. You probably have encountered that phenomenon yourself with manual calculations. If you calculate 1/3 to two decimal places, you get 0.33. Multiplying again by 3, you obtain 0.99, not 1.00.

In the processor hardware, numbers are represented in the binary number system, not in decimal. You still get roundoff errors when binary digits are lost. They just may crop up at different places than you might expect. Here is an example:

```
double f = 4.35;
int n = (int)(100 * f);
System.out.println(n); // prints 434!
```

Of course, one hundred times 4.35 is 435, but the program prints 434.

▼

Computers represent numbers in the binary system (see Advanced Topic 3.4). In the binary system, there is no exact representation for 4.35, just as there is no exact representation for 1/3 in the decimal system. The representation used by the computer is just a

▼

little less than 4.35, so 100 times that value is just a little less than 435. When a floating-point value is converted to an integer, the entire fractional part is discarded, even if it is almost 1. As a result, the integer 434 is stored in n. Remedy: Use Math.round to convert

▼

floating-point numbers to integers:

```
int n = (int)Math.round(100 * f);
```

▼

Note that the wrong result of the first computation is *not* caused by lack of precision. The problem lies with the wrong choice of rounding method. Dropping the fractional part, no matter how close it may be to 1, is not a good rounding method.

▼   **AT** **Advanced Topic**   **3.4**

Binary Numbers

▼

You are familiar with *decimal* numbers, which use the digits 0, 1, 2, . . . , 9. Each digit has a place value of 1, 10, 100 = 10^2, 1000 = 10^3, and so on. For example,

▼

$$435 = 4 \cdot 10^2 + 3 \cdot 10^1 + 5 \cdot 10^0$$

Fractional digits have place values with negative powers of ten: $0.1 = 10^{-1}$,

▼

$0.01 = 10^{-2}$, and so on. For example,

$$4.35 = 4 \cdot 10^0 + 3 \cdot 10^{-1} + 5 \cdot 10^{-2}$$

▼

Computers use *binary* numbers instead, which have just two digits (0 and 1) and place values that are powers of 2. Binary numbers are easier for computers to manipulate, because it is easier to build logic circuits that differentiate between "off" and "on" than it

▼

would be to build circuits that can accurately tell ten different voltage levels apart.

It is easy to transform a binary number into a decimal number. Just compute the powers of two that correspond to ones in the binary number. For example,

▼

$$1101 \text{ binary} = 1 \cdot 2^3 + 1 \cdot 2^2 + 0 \cdot 2^1 + 1 \cdot 2^0 = 8 + 4 + 1 = 13$$

Fractional binary numbers use negative powers of two. For example,

▼

$$1.101 \text{ binary} = 1 \cdot 2^0 + 1 \cdot 2^{-1} + 0 \cdot 2^{-2} + 1 \cdot 2^{-3} = 1 + 0.5 + 0.125 = 1.625$$

Converting decimal numbers to binary numbers is a little trickier. Here is an algo-

▼

rithm that converts a decimal integer into its binary equivalent: Keep dividing the integer by 2, keeping track of the remainders. Stop when the number is 0. Then write the remainders as a binary number, starting with the *last* one. For example,

▼

$100 \div 2 = 50$ remainder 0
$50 \div 2 = 25$ remainder 0
$25 \div 2 = 12$ remainder 1
$12 \div 2 = 6$ remainder 0

$6 \div 2 = 3$ remainder 0
$3 \div 2 = 1$ remainder 1
$1 \div 2 = 0$ remainder 1

Therefore, 100 in decimal is 1100100 in binary.

To convert a fractional number <1 to its binary format, keep multiplying by 2. If the result is >1, subtract 1. Stop when the number is 0. Then use the digits before the decimal points as the binary digits of the fractional part, starting with the *first* one. For example,

$0.35 \cdot 2 = 0.7$
$0.7 \cdot 2 = 1.4$
$0.4 \cdot 2 = 0.8$
$0.8 \cdot 2 = 1.6$
$0.6 \cdot 2 = 1.2$
$0.2 \cdot 2 = 0.4$

Here the pattern repeats. That is, the binary representation of 0.35 is 0.01 0110 0110 0110 . . .

To convert any floating-point number into binary, convert the whole part and the fractional part separately. For example, 4.35 is 100.01 0110 0110 0110 . . . in binary.

You don't actually need to know about binary numbers to program in Java, but at times it can be helpful to understand a little about them. For example, knowing that an `int` is represented as a 32-bit binary number explains why the largest integer that you can represent in Java is 0111 1111 1111 1111 1111 1111 1111 1111 binary = 2,147,483,647 decimal. (The first bit is the sign bit. It is off for positive values.)

To convert an integer into its binary representation, you can use the static `toString` method of the `Integer` class. The call `Integer.toString(n, 2)` returns a string with the binary digits of the integer n. Conversely, you can convert a string containing binary digits into an integer with the call `Integer.parseInt(digitString, 2)`. In both of these method calls, the second parameter denotes the base of the number system. It can be any number between 0 and 36. You can use these two methods to convert between decimal and binary *integers*. However, the Java library has no convenient method to do the same for floating-point numbers.

Now you can see why we had to fight with a roundoff error when computing 100 times 4.35 in Common Error 3.3. If you actually carry out the long multiplication, you get:

```
1 1 0 0 1 0 0 * 1 0 0.0 1|0 1 1 0|0 1 1 0|0 1 1 0 . . .

1 0 0.0 1|0 1 1 0|0 1 1 0|0 1 1 0 . . .
 1 0 0.0 1|0 1 1 0|0 1 1 0|0 1 1 . . .
 0
   0
     1 0 0.0 1|0 1 1 0|0 1 1 0 . . .
       0
         0

1 1 0 1 1 0 0 1 0.1 1 1 1 1 1 1 1 . . .
```

▼   That is, the result is 434, followed by an infinite number of 1s. The fractional part of the
           product is the binary equivalent of an infinite decimal fraction 0.999999 . . . , which is
           equal to 1. But the CPU can store only a finite number of 1s, and it discards them all
▼   when converting the result to an integer.

3.7   Strings

Next to numbers, *strings* are the most important data type that most programs use. A
string is a sequence of characters, such as "Hello, World!". In Java, strings are
enclosed in quotation marks, which are not themselves part of the string. Note that,
unlike numbers, strings are objects. (You can tell that `String` is a
class name because it starts with an uppercase letter. The basic types
`int` and `double` start with a lowercase letter.)

> A string is a sequence of characters. Strings are objects of the `String` class.

The number of characters in a string is called the *length* of the
string. For example, the length of "Hello, World!" is 13. You can
compute the length of a string with the `length` method.

```
int n = message.length();
```

A string of length zero, containing no characters, is called the *empty string* and is written
as "".

You already saw in Chapter 2 how to put strings together to form a longer string.

```
String name = "Dave";
String message = "Hello, " + name;
```

> Strings can be concatenated, that is, put end to end to yield a new longer string. String concatenation is denoted by the + operator.

The + operator concatenates two strings. The concatenation operator in Java is very powerful. If *one of the expressions*, either to the left or
the right of a + operator, is a string, then the other one is automatically
forced to become a string as well, and both strings are concatenated.

For example, consider this code:

```
String a = "Agent";
int n = 7;
String bond = a + n;
```

> Whenever one of the arguments of the + operator is a string, the other argument is converted to a string.

Since a is a string, n is converted from the integer 7 to the string "7".
Then the two strings "Agent" and "7" are concatenated to form the
string "Agent7".

This concatenation is very useful to reduce the number of
`System.out.print` instructions. For example, you can combine

```
System.out.print("The total is ");
System.out.println(total);
```

to the single call

```
System.out.println("The total is " + total);
```

If a string contains the digits of a number, you use the `Integer.parseInt` or `Double.parseDouble` method to obtain the number value.

The concatenation `"The total is " + total` computes a single string that consists of the string `"The total is "`, followed by the string equivalent of the number `total`.

Sometimes you have a string that contains a number, usually from user input. For example, suppose that the string variable `input` has the value `"19"`. To get the integer value 19, you use the static `parseInt` method of the `Integer` class.

```
int count = Integer.parseInt(input);
   // count is the integer 19
```

To convert a string containing floating-point digits to its floating-point value, use the static `parseDouble` method of the `Double` class. For example, suppose `input` is the string `"3.95"`.

```
double price = Double.parseDouble(input);
   // price is the floating-point number 3.95
```

The `toUpperCase` and `toLowerCase` methods make strings with only upper- or lower-case characters. For example,

```
String greeting = "Hello";
System.out.println(greeting.toUpperCase());
System.out.println(greeting.toLowerCase());
```

This code segment prints HELLO and hello. Note that the `toUpperCase` and `toLowerCase` methods do not change the original `String` object `greeting`. They return new `String` objects that contain the uppercased and lowercased versions of the original string. In fact, *no* `String` methods modify the string object on which they operate. For that reason, strings are called *immutable* objects.

The `substring` computes substrings of a string. The call

```
s.substring(start, pastEnd)
```

Use the `substring` method to extract a part of a string.

returns a string that is made up from the characters in the string `s`, starting at character `start`, and containing all characters up to, but not including, the character `pastEnd`. Here is an example:

```
String greeting = "Hello, World!";
String sub = greeting.substring(0, 4);
   // sub is "Hell"
```

String positions are counted starting with 0.

The `substring` operation makes a string that consists of four characters taken from the string `greeting`. A curious aspect of the `substring` operation is the numbering of the starting and ending positions. Starting position 0 means "start at the beginning of the string". For technical reasons that used to be important but are no longer relevant, Java string position numbers start at 0. The first string position is labeled 0, the second one 1, and so on. For example, Figure 5 shows the position numbers in the `greeting` string.

The position number of the last character (12 for the string `"Hello, World!"`) is always 1 less than the length of the string.

Figure 5

String Positions

H	e	l	l	o	,		W	o	r	l	d	!
0	1	2	3	4	5	6	7	8	9	10	11	12

Figure 6

Extracting a Substring

H	e	l	l	o	,		W	o	r	l	d	!
0	1	2	3	4	5	6	7	8	9	10	11	12

Let us figure out how to extract the substring "World". Count characters starting at 0, not 1. You find that W, the 8th character, has position number 7. The first character that you *don't* want, !, is the character at position 12 (see Figure 6). Therefore, the appropriate substring command is

```
String w = greeting.substring(7, 12);
```

It is curious that you must specify the position of the first character that you do want and then the first character that you don't want. There is one advantage to this setup. You can easily compute the *length* of the substring: it is `pastEnd - start`. For example, the string "World" has length 12 − 7 = 5.

If you omit the second parameter of the `substring` method, then all characters from the starting position to the end of the string are copied. For example,

```
String tail = greeting.substring(7);
   // copies all characters from position 7 on
```

sets `tail` to the string "World!".

Advanced Topic **3.5**

Formatting Numbers

The default format for printing numbers is not always what you would like. For example, consider the following code segment:

```
int quarters = 2;
int dollars = 3;
double total = dollars + quarters * 0.25; // price is 3.5
final double TAX_RATE = 8.5; // tax rate in percent
double tax = total * TAX_RATE / 100; // tax is 0.2975
System.out.println("Total: $" + total);
System.out.println("Tax:    $" + tax);
```

The output is

```
Total: $3.5
Tax:    $0.2975
```

You may prefer the numbers to be printed with two digits after the decimal point, like this:

```
Total: $3.50
Tax:   $0.30
```

You can achieve this with the `NumberFormat` class in the `java.text` package. First, you must use the static method `getNumberInstance` to obtain a `NumberFormat` object. Then you set the maximum number of fraction digits to 2:

```
NumberFormat formatter =
    NumberFormat.getNumberInstance();
formatter.setMaximumFractionDigits(2);
```

Then the numbers are rounded to two digits. For example, 0.2875 will be converted to the string `"0.29"`. On the other hand, 0.2975 will be converted to `"0.3"`, not `"0.30"`. If you want trailing zeroes, you *also* have to set the minimum number of fraction digits to 2:

```
formatter.setMinimumFractionDigits(2);
```

Then you use the `format` method of that object. The result is a string that you can print.

```
formatter.format(tax)
```

returns the string `"0.30"`. The statement

```
System.out.println("Tax:    $" + formatter.format(tax));
```

rounds the value of `tax` to two digits after the decimal point and prints: `Tax: $0.30`.

The "number instance" formatter is useful because it lets you print numbers with as many fraction digits as desired. If you just want to print a currency value, the `getCurrencyInstance` method of the `NumberFormat` class produces a more convenient formatter. The "currency instance" formatter generates currency value strings, with the local currency symbol (such as $ in the United States) and the appropriate number of digits after the decimal point (for example, two digits in the United States).

```
NumberFormat formatter = NumberFormat.getCurrencyInstance();
System.out.print(formatter.format(tax));
    // prints "$0.30"
```

3.8   Reading Input

The Java programs that you have constructed so far have constructed objects, called methods, printed results, and exited. They were not interactive and took no user input. In this section, you will learn one method for reading user input.

> The JOptionPane .showInputDialog method prompts the user for an input string.

The `JOptionPane` class has a static method `showInputDialog` that displays an input dialog (see Figure 7). The user can type any string into the input field and click the "OK" button. Then the `showInputDialog` method returns the string that the user entered. You should capture the user input in a string variable. For example,

```
String input =
    JOptionPane.showInputDialog("How many nickels do you have?");
```

Figure 7

An Input Dialog

Often you want the input as a number, not a string. Use the `Integer.parseInt` and `Double.parseDouble` methods to convert the string to a number:

```
int count = Integer.parseInt(input);
```

If the user doesn't type in a number, then the `parseInt` method *throws an exception*. An exception is a way for a method to indicate an error condition. You will see in Chapter 15 how to handle exceptions. Until then, we will simply rely on the default mechanism for exception handling. That mechanism terminates the program with an error message.

```
Exception in thread "main"
java.lang.NumberFormatException: x
        at java.lang.Integer.parseInt(Unknown Source)
        at java.lang.Integer.parseInt(Unknown Source)
        at InputTest.main(InputTest.java:10)
```

That doesn't make your programs very user-friendly. You will simply have to wait until Chapter 15 to make your programs bulletproof. In the meantime, you should assume that the user is cooperative and types in an actual number when you prompt for one. Since the users of your first programs are likely to be just yourself, your instructor, and your grader, that should not be a problem.

> You must call `System.exit(0)` to exit a program that has a graphical user interface.

Finally, whenever you call `JOptionPane.showInputDialog` in your programs, you need to add a line

```
System.exit(0)
```

to the end of your `main` method. The `showInputDialog` method starts a user interface *thread* to handle user input. When the `main` method reaches the end, that thread is still running, and your program won't exit automatically. (See Chapter 20 for more information on threads.) To force the program to exit, you need to call the `exit` method of the `System` class. The parameter of the `exit` method is the status code of the program. A code of 0 denotes successful completion; you can use nonzero status codes to denote various error conditions.

Here is an example of a test class that takes user input. This class tests the `Purse` class and lets the user supply the numbers of nickels, dimes, and quarters.

File InputTest.java

```
1 import javax.swing.JOptionPane;
2
3 /**
4     This program tests input from an input dialog.
```

```
 5  */
 6  public class InputTest
 7  {
 8     public static void main(String[] args)
 9     {
10        Purse myPurse = new Purse();
11
12        String input = JOptionPane.showInputDialog(
13           "How many nickels do you have?");
14        int count = Integer.parseInt(input);
15        myPurse.addNickels(count);
16
17        input = JOptionPane.showInputDialog(
18           "How many dimes do you have?");
19        count = Integer.parseInt(input);
20        myPurse.addDimes(count);
21
22        input = JOptionPane.showInputDialog(
23           "How many quarters do you have?");
24        count = Integer.parseInt(input);
25        myPurse.addQuarters(count);
26
27        double totalValue = myPurse.getTotal();
28        System.out.println("The total is " + totalValue);
29
30        System.exit(0);
31     }
32  }
```

Admittedly, the program is not very elegant. It pops up three dialog boxes to collect input and then displays the output in the console window. You will learn in Chapter 12 how to write programs with more sophisticated graphical user interfaces.

Productivity Hint 3.3

Reading Exception Reports

▼

You will often have programs that terminate and display an error message such as

```
Exception in thread "main" java.lang.NumberFormatException: x
        at java.lang.Integer.parseInt(Unknown Source)
        at java.lang.Integer.parseInt(Unknown Source)
        at InputTest.main(InputTest.java:10)
```

▼

An amazing number of students simply give up at that point, saying "it didn't work", or "my program died", without ever reading the error message. Admittedly, the format of the exception report is not very friendly. But it is actually easy to decipher it.

▼ When you have a close look at the error message, you will notice two pieces of useful information:

▼ 1. The name of the exception, such as `NumberFormatException`

2. The line number of the code that contained the statement that caused the exception, such as `InputTest.java:10`

▼ The name of the exception is always in the first line of the report, and it ends in `Exception`. If you get a `NumberFormatException`, then there was a problem with the format of some number. That is useful information.

▼ The line number of the offending code is a little harder to determine. The exception report contains the entire *stack trace*—that is, the names of all methods that were pending when the exception hit. The first line of the stack trace is the method that actually generated the exception. The last line of the stack trace is a line in `main`. Often, the exception was thrown by a method that is in the standard library. Look for the first line in *your code* that appears in the exception report. For example, skip the lines that refer to

▼ `java.lang.Integer.parseInt(Unknown Source)`.

Once you have the line number in your code, open up the file, go to that line, and look at it! In the great majority of cases, knowing the name of the exception and the line that caused it makes it completely obvious what went wrong, and you can easily fix your error.

▼ **Advanced Topic** **3.6**

Reading Console Input

▼ You just saw how to read input from an input dialog. Admittedly, it is a bit strange to have dialogs pop up for every input. Some programmers prefer to read the input from the console window. Console input has one great advantage. As you will see in Chapter 6, you can put all your input strings into a file and redirect the console input to read from a file. That's a great help for program testing. However, console input is somewhat cumbersome to program. This note explains the details.

▼ Console input reads from the `System.in` object. However, unlike `System.out`, which was ready-made for printing numbers and strings, `System.in` can only read *bytes*. Keyboard input consists of characters. To get a reader for characters, you have to turn `System.in` into an `InputStreamReader` object, like this:

```
InputStreamReader reader =
    newInputStreamReader(System.in);
```

▼ Wrap `System.in` inside a `BufferedReader` to read input from the console window.

An input stream reader can read characters, but it can't read a whole string at a time. That makes it pretty inconvenient—you wouldn't want to piece together every input line from its individual characters. To overcome this limitation, you can turn an input stream reader into a `BufferedReader` object:

```
BufferedReader console =
    new BufferedReader(reader);
```

▼   If you like, you can combine the two constructors:

```
BufferedReader console = new BufferedReader(
    new InputStreamReader(System.in));
```

▼

Now you use the readLine method to read an input line, like this:

▼
```
System.out.println(
    "How many nickels do you have?");
String input = console.readLine();
int count = Integer.parseInt(input);
```

▼

> When calling the readLine method of the BufferedReader class, you must tag the calling methods with throws IOException.

There is one remaining problem. When there is a problem with reading input, the readLine method generates an exception, just as the parseInt method does when you give it a string that isn't an integer. However, the readLine method generates an IOException, which is a *checked exception*, a more severe kind of exception than the NumberFormatException that the parseInt method generates. The Java compiler insists that you take one of two steps when you call a method that can throw a checked exception.

▼   1. Handle the exception. You will see how to do that in Chapter 15

2. Acknowledge that you are not handling the exception. Then you have to indicate that your method can cause a checked exception because it calls another method
▼   that can cause that exception. You do that by tagging your method with a **throws** specifier, like this:

▼   ```
public static void main(String[] args) throws IOException
```

or

▼    ```
public void readInput(BufferedReader reader) throws IOException
```

There is no shame associated with acknowledging that your method might throw a checked exception—it is just "truth in advertising". Of course, in a professional program,
▼   you do need to handle all exceptions somewhere, and the main method won't throw any exceptions. You'll have to wait for Chapter 15 for the details.

Following this note is another version of the test program for the Purse class, this
▼   time reading input from the console. Figure 8 shows a typical program run.

File ConsoleInputTest.java

```
1  import java.io.BufferedReader;
2  import java.io.InputStreamReader;
3  import java.io.IOException;
4
5  /**
6     This program tests input from a console window.
7  */
```

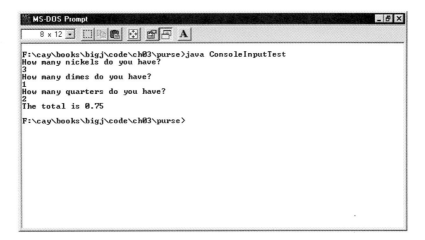

Figure 8

Reading Input from the Console

```
 8 public class ConsoleInputTest
 9 {
10    public static void main(String[] args) throws IOException
11    {
12       Purse myPurse = new Purse();
13
14
15       BufferedReader console = new BufferedReader(
16          new InputStreamReader(System.in));
17       System.out.println(
18          "How many nickels do you have?");
19       String input = console.readLine();
20       int count = Integer.parseInt(input);
21       myPurse.addNickels(count);
22
23       System.out.println("How many dimes do you have?");
24       input = console.readLine();
25       count = Integer.parseInt(input);
26       myPurse.addDimes(count);
27
28       System.out.println(
29          "How many quarters do you have?");
30       input = console.readLine();
31       count = Integer.parseInt(input);
32       myPurse.addQuarters(count);
33
34       double totalValue = myPurse.getTotal();
35       System.out.println("The total is " + totalValue);
```

```
36    }
37 }
```

3.9   Characters

> A char value denotes a single character. Character constants are enclosed in single quotes.

Strings are composed of individual characters. Characters are values of the char type. A variable of type char can hold a single character.

Character constants look like string constants, except that character constants are delimited by single quotes: 'H' is a character, "H" is a string containing a single character. You can use escape sequences (see Advanced Topic 1.1) inside character constants. For example, '\n' is the newline character, and '\u00E9' is the character é. You can find the values of the character constants that are used in Western European languages in Appendix A6.

Characters have numeric values. For example, if you look at Appendix A6, you can see that the character 'H' is actually encoded as the number 72.

The charAt method of the String class returns a character from a string. As with the substring method, the positions in the string are counted starting at 0. For example, the statement

```
String greeting = "Hello";
char ch = greeting.charAt(0);
```

sets ch to the character 'H'.

Random Fact   3.2

International Alphabets

The English alphabet is pretty simple: upper- and lowercase a to z. Other European languages have accent marks and special characters. For example, German has three *umlaut* characters (ä, ö, ü) and a double-s character (ß). These are not optional frills; you couldn't write a page of German text without using these characters a few times. German computer keyboards have keys for these characters (see Figure 9).

This poses a problem for computer users and designers. The American standard character encoding (called ASCII, for American Standard Code for Information Interchange) specifies 128 codes: 52 upper- and lowercase characters, 10 digits, 32 typographical symbols, and 34 control characters (such as space, newline, and 32 others for controlling printers and other devices). The umlaut and double-s are not among them. Some German data processing systems replace seldom-used ASCII characters with German letters: [\ ] { | } ~ are replaced with Ä Ö Ü ä ö ü ß.

Figure 9

German Keyboard

Most people can live without those ASCII characters, but programmers using Java definitely cannot. Other encoding schemes take advantage of the fact that one byte can encode 256 different characters, but only 128 are standardized by ASCII. Unfortunately, there are multiple incompatible standards for using the remaining 128 characters, such as those used by the Windows and Macintosh operating systems, resulting in a certain amount of aggravation among European computer users and their American email correspondents.

Many countries don't use the Roman script at all. Russian, Greek, Hebrew, Arabic, and Thai letters, to name just a few, have completely different shapes (see Figure 10). To complicate matters, scripts like Hebrew and Arabic are written from right to left instead of from left to right, and many of these scripts have characters that stack above or below other characters, as those marked with a dotted circle in Figure 10 do in Thai. Each of these alphabets has between 30 and 100 letters, and the countries using them have established encoding standards for them.

The situation is much more dramatic in languages that use the Chinese script: the Chinese dialects, Japanese, and Korean. The Chinese script is not alphabetic but *ideographic*—a character represents an idea or thing rather than a single sound. (See Figure 11; can you identify the characters for soup, chicken, and wonton?) Most words are made up of one, two, or three of these ideographic characters. Over 50,000 ideographs are known, of which about 20,000 are in active use. Therefore, two bytes are needed to encode them. China, Taiwan, Japan, and Korea have incompatible encoding standards for them. (Japanese and Korean writing use a mixture of native syllabic and Chinese ideographic characters.)

The inconsistencies among character encodings have been a major nuisance for international electronic communication and for software manufacturers vying for a global market. Between 1988 and 1991 a consortium of hardware and software manufacturers developed a uniform 16-bit encoding scheme called *Unicode* that is capable of encoding text in essentially all written languages of the world (see reference [1]). About 39,000 characters have been given codes, including 21,000 Chinese ideographs. A 16-bit code

	ฐ	ภ	ะ	เ	๐		เ◌
ก	ฑ	ม	◌ั	แ	๑		แ◌
ข	ฒ	ย	า	โ	๒		โ◌
ฃ	ณ	ร	◌ํา	ใ	๓		ใ◌
ค	ด	ฤ	◌ิ	ไ	๔		ไ◌
ฅ	ต	ล	◌ี	ๅ	๕		
ฆ	ถ	ฦ	◌ึ	ๆ	๖		
ง	ท	ว	◌ื	◌ุ	๗		
จ	ธ	ศ	◌ิ	◌ุ	๘		
ฉ	น	ษ	◌ุ	◌ู	๙		
ช	บ	ส	◌ฺ	◌ฺ	๚		
ซ	ป	ห		◌็	๛		
ฌ	ผ	ฬ		◌่			
ญ	ฝ	อ		◌้			
ฎ	พ	ฮ		◌๊			
ฏ	ฟ	ๆ					

Figure 10

The Thai Alphabet

▼

			CLASSIC SOUPS	Sm.	Lg.
清燉雞湯		57.	House Chicken Soup (Chicken, Celery, Potato, Onion, Carrot)	1.50	2.75
雞飯湯		58.	Chicken Rice Soup	1.85	3.25
雞麵湯		59.	Chicken Noodle Soup	1.85	3.25
廣東雲吞		60.	Cantonese Wonton Soup	1.50	2.75
蕃茄蛋湯		61.	Tomato Clear Egg Drop Soup	1.65	2.95
雲吞湯		62.	Regular Wonton Soup	1.10	2.10
酸辣湯		63. ✿	Hot & Sour Soup	1.10	2.10
蛋花湯		64.	Egg Drop Soup	1.10	2.10
雲蛋湯		65.	Egg Drop Wonton Mix	1.10	2.10
豆腐菜湯		66.	Tofu Vegetable Soup	NA	3.50
雞玉米湯		67.	Chicken Corn Cream Soup	NA	3.50
蟹肉玉米湯		68.	Crab Meat Corn Cream Soup	NA	3.50
海鮮湯		69.	Seafood Soup	NA	3.50

Figure 11

A Menu with Chinese Characters

can incorporate 65,000 codes, so there is ample space for expansion. Future versions of the standard will be able to encode such scripts as Egyptian hieroglyphs and the ancient script used on the island of Java.

All Unicode characters can be stored in Java strings, but which ones can actually be displayed depends on your computer system.

3.10 Comparing Primitive Types and Objects

> Number variables hold values. Object variables hold references.

In Java, every value is either a primitive type or an object reference. Primitive types are numbers (such as `int`, `double`, `char`, and the other number types listed in Advanced Topic 3.2) and the `boolean` type that you will encounter in Chapter 5. There is an important difference between primitive types and objects in Java. Primitive type variables hold values, but object variables don't hold objects—they hold references to objects. You can see the difference when you make a copy of a variable. When you copy a primitive type value, the original and the copy of the number are independent values. But when you copy an object reference, both the original and the copy are references to the same object.

> A copy of an object reference is another reference to the same object.

Consider the following code, which copies a number and then adds an amount to the copy (see Figure 12):

```
double balance1 = 1000;
double balance2 = balance1; // see Figure 12
balance2 = balance2 + 500;
```

Now the variable `balance1` contains the value 1000, and `balance2` contains 1500.

Figure 12

Copying Numbers

Figure 13

Copying Object References

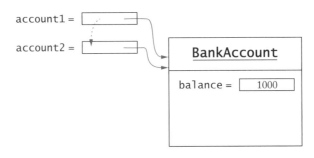

Now consider the seemingly analogous code with `BankAccount` objects.

```
BankAccount account1 = new BankAccount(1000);
BankAccount account2 = account1; // see Figure 13
account2.deposit(500);
```

Unlike the preceding code, now *both* `account1` and `account2` have a balance of $1500.

What can you do if you actually need to make a true copy of an object—that is, a new object whose state is identical to an existing object? As you will see in Chapter 13, you can define a `clone` method for your classes to make such a copy. But in the meantime, you will simply have to construct a new object:

```
BankAccount account2 = new
    BankAccount(account1.getBalance());
```

Strings are objects; therefore, if you copy a `String` variable, you get two references to the same string object. However, unlike bank accounts, strings are *immutable*. None of the methods of the `String` class change the state of a `String` object. Thus, there is no problem in sharing string references.

CHAPTER SUMMARY

1. The `int` type denotes integers: numbers without fractional part.

2. Assignment to a variable is not the same as mathematical equality.

3. The `++` and `--` operators increment and decrement a variable.

4. A `final` variable is a constant. Once its value has been set, it cannot be changed.

5. Use named constants to make your programs easier to read and maintain.

6. If both arguments of the / operator are integers, the result is an integer and the remainder is discarded.

7. The % operator computes the remainder of a division.

8. The Math class contains methods sqrt and pow to compute square roots and powers.

9. A static method does not operate on an object.

10. You use a cast (*typeName*) to convert a value to a different type.

11. Use the Math.round method to round a floating-point number to the nearest integer.

12. A string is a sequence of characters. Strings are objects of the String class.

13. Strings can be concatenated, that is, put end to end to yield a new longer string. String concatenation is denoted by the + operator.

14. Whenever one of the arguments of the + operator is a string, the other argument is converted to a string.

15. If a string contains the digits of a number, you use the Integer.parseInt or Double.parseDouble method to obtain the number value.

16. Use the substring method to extract a part of a string.

17. String positions are counted starting with 0.

18. The JOptionPane.showInputDialog method prompts the user for an input string.

19. You must call System.exit(0) to exit a program that has a graphical user interface.

20. Wrap System.in inside a BufferedReader to read input from the console window.

21. When calling the readLine method of the BufferedReader class, you must tag the calling methods with throws IOException.

22. A char value denotes a single character. Character constants are enclosed in single quotes.

23. Number variables hold values. Object variables hold references.

24. A copy of an object reference is another reference to the same object.

Further Reading

[1] http://www.unicode.org/ The web site of the Unicode consortium. It contains character tables that show the Unicode values of characters from many scripts.

Classes, Objects, and Methods Introduced in This Chapter

```
java.io.BufferedReader
    readLine
java.io.InputStreamReader
java.lang.Double
    parseDouble
    toString
java.lang.Integer
    parseInt
    toString
    MAX_VALUE
    MIN_VALUE
java.lang.Math
    E
    PI
    abs
    acos
    asin
    atan
    atan2
    ceil
    cos
    exp
    floor
    log
    max
    min
    pow
    round
    sin
    sqrt
    tan
    toDegrees
    toRadians
java.lang.String
    length
    substring
    toLowerCase
    toUpperCase
java.lang.System
    exit
    in
java.math.BigDecimal
    add
    divide
    multiply
    subtract
```

```
java.math.BigInteger
   add
   divide
   multiply
   subtract
java.text.NumberFormat
   format
   getCurrencyInstance
   getNumberInstance
   setMaximumFractionDigits
   setMinimumFractionDigits
javax.swing.JOptionPane
   showInputDialog
```

REVIEW EXERCISES

Exercise R3.1. Write the following mathematical expressions in Java.

$$s = s_0 + v_0 t + \frac{1}{2} g t^2$$

$$G = 4\pi^2 \frac{a^3}{P^2(m_1 + m_2)}$$

$$FV = PV \cdot \left(1 + \frac{INT}{100}\right)^{YRS}$$

$$c = \sqrt{a^2 + b^2 - 2ab\cos\gamma}$$

Exercise R3.2. Write the following Java expressions in mathematical notation.

```
dm = m * ((Math.sqrt(1 + v / c) / Math.sqrt(1 - v / c)) - 1);
volume = Math.PI * r * r * h;
volume = 4 * Math.PI * Math.pow(r, 3) / 3;
p = Math.atan2(z, Math.sqrt(x * x + y * y));
```

Exercise R3.3. What is wrong with this version of the quadratic formula?

```
x1 = (-b - Math.sqrt(b * b - 4 * a * c)) / 2 * a;
x2 = (-b + Math.sqrt(b * b - 4 * a * c)) / 2 * a;
```

Exercise R3.4. Give an example of integer overflow. Would the same example work correctly if you used floating-point? Give an example of a floating-point roundoff error. Would the same example work correctly if you used integers? For this exercise, you should assume that the values are represented in a sufficiently small unit, such as cents instead of dollars, so that the values don't have a fractional part.

Exercise R3.5. Write a test program that executes the following code:

```
Purse myPurse = new Purse();
myPurse.addNickels(3);
```

```
myPurse.addDimes(2);
myPurse.addQuarters(1);
System.out.println(myPurse.getTotal());
```

The program prints the total as 0.6000000000000001. Explain why. Give a recommendation to improve the program so that users will not be confused.

Exercise R3.6. Let n be an integer and x a floating-point number. Explain the difference between

```
n = (int)x;
```

and

```
n = (int)Math.round(x);
```

Exercise R3.7. Let n be an integer and x a floating-point number. Explain the difference between

```
n = (int)(x + 0.5);
```

and

```
n = (int)Math.round(x);
```

For what values of x do they give the same result? For what values of x do they give different results?

Exercise R3.8. Explain the differences between 2, 2.0, '2', "2", and "2.0".

Exercise R3.9. Explain what each of the following two program segments computes:

```
x = 2;
y = x + x;
```

and

```
s = "2";
t = s + s;
```

Exercise R3.10. Uninitialized variables can be a serious problem. Should you *always* initialize every variable with zero? Explain the advantages and disadvantages of such a strategy.

Exercise R3.11. True or false? (x is an int and s is a String)

- Integer.parseInt("" + x) is the same as x
- "" + Integer.parseInt(s) is the same as s
- s.substring(0, s.length()) is the same as s

Exercise R3.12. How do you get the first character of a string? The last character? How do you *remove* the first character? The last character?

Exercise R3.13. How do you get the last digit of an integer? The first digit? That is, if n is 23456, how do you find out that the first digit is 2 and the last digit is 6? Do not convert the number to a string. *Hint:* %, Math.log.

Exercise R3.14. This chapter contains several recommendations regarding variables and constants that make programs easier to read and maintain. Summarize these recommendations.

Exercise R3.15. What is a `final` variable? Can you define a `final` variable without supplying its value? (Try it out.)

Exercise R3.16. What are the values of the following expressions? In each line, assume that

```
double x = 2.5;
double y = -1.5;
int m = 18;
int n = 4;
String s = "Hello";
String t = "World";
```

- `x + n * y - (x + n) * y`

- `m / n + m % n`

- `5 * x - n / 5`

- `Math.sqrt(Math.sqrt(n))`

- `(int)Math.round(x)`

- `(int)Math.round(x) + (int)Math.round(y)`

- `s + t`

- `s + n`

- `1 - (1 - (1 - (1 - (1 - n))))`

- `s.substring(1, 3)`

- `s.length() + t.length()`

Exercise R3.17. Explain the similarities and differences between copying numbers and copying object references.

Exercise R3.18. What are the values of a, b, c, and d after these statements?

```
double a = 1;
double b = a;
a++;
Purse p = new Purse();
Purse q = p;
p.addNickels(5);
double c = p.getTotal();
double d = q.getTotal();
```

Exercise R3.19. When you copy a `BankAccount` reference, the original and the copy share the same object. That can be significant because you can modify the state of the object through either of the references. Explain why this is not a problem for `String` references.

Programming Exercises

Exercise P3.1. Enhance the `Purse` class by adding methods `addPennies` and `addDollars`.

Exercise P3.2. Add methods `getDollars` and `getCents` to the `Purse` class. The `get-Dollars` method should return the number of whole dollars in the purse, as an integer. The `getCents` method should return the number of cents, as an integer. For example, if the total value of the coins in the purse is $2.14, `getDollars` returns 2 and `getCents` returns 14.

Exercise P3.3. Write a program that prints the values

```
1
10
100
1000
10000
100000
1000000
10000000
100000000
1000000000
10000000000
100000000000
```

Implement a class

```java
public class PowerGenerator
{
    /**
       Constructs a power generator.
       @param aFactor the number that will be multiplied by itself
    */
    public PowerGenerator(int aFactor) { . . . }
    /**
       Computes the next power.
    */
    public double nextPower() { . . . }
    . . .
}
```

Then supply a test class `PowerGeneratorTest` that calls `System.out.println(myGenerator.nextPower())` twelve times.

Exercise P3.4. Write a program that prompts the user for two integers and then prints

- The sum
- The difference
- The product
- The average

- The distance (absolute value of the difference)
- The maximum (the larger of the two)
- The minimum (the smaller of the two)

Implement a class

```
public class Pair
{
    /**
        Constructs a pair.
        @param aFirst the first value of the pair
        @param aSecond the second value of the pair
    */
    public Pair(double aFirst, double aSecond) { . . . }
    /**
        Computes the sum of the values of this pair.
        @return the sum of the first and second values
    */
    public double getSum() { . . . }
    . . .
}
```

Then implement a class `PairTest` that reads in two numbers (using either a `JOption-Pane` or a `BufferedReader`), constructs a `Pair` object, invokes its methods, and prints the results.

Exercise P3.5. Write a program that reads in four integers and prints their sum and average. Define a class `DataSet` with methods

```
void addValue(int x)
int getSum()
double getAverage()
```

Hint: Keep track of the sum and the count of the values. Then write a test program `DataSetTest` that reads four numbers and calls `addValue` four times.

Exercise P3.6. Write a program that reads in four integers and prints the largest and smallest value that the user entered. Use a class `DataSet` with methods

- `void addValue(int x)`
- `int getLargest()`
- `int getSmallest()`

Keep track of the smallest and largest value that you've seen so far. Then use the `Math.min` and `Math.max` methods to update it in the `addValue` method. What should you use as initial values? *Hint:* `Integer.MIN_VALUE`, `Integer.MAX_VALUE`.

Write a test program `DataSetTest` that reads four numbers and calls `addValue` four times.

Exercise P3.7. Write a program that prompts the user for a measurement in meters and then converts it into miles, feet, and inches. Use a class

```
public class Converter
{
```

```
    /**
        Constructs a converter that can convert between two units.
        @param aConversionFactor the factor with which to multiply
        to convert to the target unit
    */
    public Converter(double aConversionFactor) { . . . }
    /**
        Converts from a source measurement to a target measurement.
        @param fromMeasurement the measurement
        @return the input value converted to the target unit
    */
    public double convertTo(double fromMeasurement) { . . . }
}
```

Then construct three instances, such as

```
final double MILE_TO_KM = 1.609; // from Appendix A7
Converter metersToMiles = new Converter(1000 * MILE_TO_KM);
```

Exercise P3.8. Write a program that prompts the user for a radius and then prints

- The area and circumference of the circle with that radius
- The volume and surface area of the sphere with that radius

Define classes `Circle` and `Sphere`.

Exercise P3.9. Implement a class `SodaCan` whose constructor receives the height and diameter of the soda can. Supply methods `getVolume` and `getSurfaceArea`. Supply a `SodaCanTest` class that tests your class.

Exercise P3.10. Write a program that asks the user for the length of the sides of a square. Then print

- The area and perimeter of the square
- The length of the diagonal (use the Pythagorean theorem)

Define a class `Square`.

Exercise P3.11. *Giving change.* Implement a program that directs a cashier how to give change. The program has two inputs: the amount due and the amount received from the customer. Compute the difference, and compute the dollars, quarters, dimes, nickels, and pennies that the customer should receive in return.

First transform the difference into an integer balance, denominated in pennies. Then compute the whole dollar amount. Subtract it from the balance. Compute the number of quarters needed. Repeat for dimes and nickels. Display the remaining pennies.

Define a class `Cashier` with methods

- `setAmountDue`
- `receive`
- `returnDollars`
- `returnQuarters`

- `returnDimes`
- `returnNickels`
- `returnPennies`

For example,

```
Cashier harry = new Cashier();
harry.setAmountDue(9.37);
harry.receive(10);
double quarters = harry.returnQuarters(); // returns 2
double dimes = harry.returnDimes(); // returns 1
double nickels = harry.returnNickels(); // returns 0
double pennies = harry.returnPennies(); // returns 3
```

Exercise P3.12. Write a program that reads in an integer and breaks it into a sequence of individual digits in reverse order. For example, the input 16384 is displayed as

```
4
8
3
6
1
```

You may assume that the input has no more than five digits and is not negative.

Define a class `DigitExtractor`:

```
public class DigitExtractor
{
    /**
        Constructs a digit extractor that gets the digits
        of an integer in reverse order.
        @param anInteger the integer to break up into digits
    */
    public DigitExtractor(int anInteger) { . . . }
    /**
        Returns the next digit to be extracted.
        @return the next digit
    */
    public int nextDigit() { . . . }
}
```

Then call `System.out.println(myExtractor.nextDigit())` five times.

Exercise P3.13. Implement a class `QuadraticEquation` whose constructor receives the coefficients a, b, c of the quadratic equation $ax^2 + bx + c = 0$. Supply methods `getSolution1` and `getSolution2` that get the solutions, using the quadratic formula. Write a test class `QuadraticEquationTest` that prompts the user for the values of a, b, and c, constructs a `QuadraticEquation` object, and prints the two solutions.

Exercise P3.14. Write a program that reads two times in military format (0900, 1730) and prints the number of hours and minutes between the two times. Here is a sample run. User input is in color.

```
Please enter the first time: 0900
Please enter the second time: 1730
8 hours 30 minutes
```

Extra credit if you can deal with the case where the first time is later than the second time:

```
Please enter the first time: 1730
Please enter the second time: 0900
15 hours 30 minutes
```

Implement a class `TimeInterval` whose constructor takes two military times. The class should have two methods `getHours` and `getMinutes`.

Exercise P3.15. *Writing large letters.* A large letter H can be produced like this:

```
*   *
*   *
*****
*   *
*   *
```

Define a class `LetterH` with a method

```
String getLetter()
{
    return "*   *\n*   *\n*****\n*   *\n*   *\n";
}
```

Do the same for the letters E, L, and O. Then write the message

```
H
E
L
L
O
```

in large letters.

Exercise P3.16. Write a program that transforms numbers 1, 2, 3, ... , 12 into the corresponding month names `January`, `February`, `March`, ... , `December`. *Hint:* Make a very long string `"January February March. . ."`, in which you add spaces such that each month name has *the same length*. Then use `substring` to extract the month you want. Implement a class `Month` whose constructor parameter is the month number and whose `getName` method returns the month name.

Exercise P3.17. Write a program to compute the date of Easter Sunday. Easter Sunday is the first Sunday after the first full moon of Spring. Use this algorithm, invented by the mathematician Carl Friedrich Gauss in 1800:

1. Let y be the year (such as 1800 or 2001)
2. Divide y by 19 and call the remainder a. Ignore the quotient.
3. Divide y by 100 to get a quotient b and a remainder c
4. Divide b by 4 to get a quotient d and a remainder e
5. Divide 8 * b + 13 by 25 to get a quotient g. Ignore the remainder.

6. Divide 19 * a + b - d - g + 15 by 30 to get a remainder h. Ignore the quotient.
7. Divide c by 4 to get a quotient j and a remainder k
8. Divide a + 11 * h by 319 to get a quotient m. Ignore the remainder.
9. Divide 2 * e + 2 * j - k - h + m + 32 by 7 to get a remainder r. Ignore the quotient.
10. Divide h - m + r + 90 by 25 to get a quotient n. Ignore the remainder.
11. Divide h - m + r + n + 19 by 32 to get a remainder p. Ignore the quotient.

Then Easter falls on day p of month n. For example, if y is 2001:

```
a = 6
b = 20
c = 1
d = 5, e = 0
g = 6
h = 18
j = 0, k = 1
m = 0
r = 6
n = 4
p = 15
```

Therefore, in 2001, Easter Sunday fell on April 15. Write a class `Year` with methods `getEasterSundayMonth` and `getEasterSundayDay`.

4

Applets and Graphics

▶ To display graphical shapes such as lines and ellipses

▶ To use colors

▶ To display text in multiple fonts

▶ To select appropriate units for drawing

▶ To develop test cases that validate the correctness of your programs

There are three kinds of Java programs that you will learn to write: *console applications*, *graphical applications*, and *applets*. Console applications run in a single, usually rather plain-looking terminal window (see Figure 1). Applications with a graphical user interface use one or more windows filled with *user interface components* such as buttons, text input fields, and menus (see Figure 2). *Applets* are similar to applications with a graphical user interface, but they run *inside a web browser*.

Console programs are simpler to write than programs with a graphical user interface, and we will continue to use console programs frequently in this book to learn about fundamental concepts. Graphical user interface programs can show more interesting output, however, and are often more fun to develop. In this chapter you will learn how to write simple applets that display graphical shapes.

CHAPTER CONTENTS

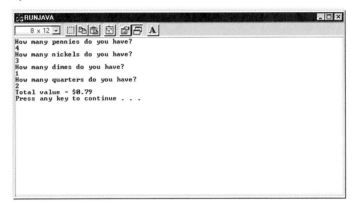

Figure 1

A Console Application

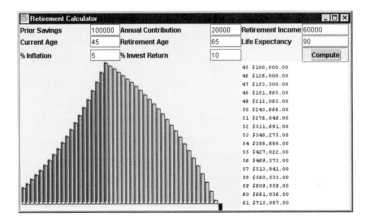

Figure 2

A Graphical Application

4.1   Why Applets?

> There are three types of Java programs: *console applications, applets,* and *graphics applications.*

The World Wide Web makes a huge amount of information available to anyone with a web browser. When you use a web browser, you connect to a *web server*, which sends web pages and images to your browser (see Figure 3). Because the web pages and images have standard formats, your web browser can display them. To retrieve the daily news or your bank balance, you don't have to be at home, in front of your own computer. You can use a browser at school or in an airport terminal or Web café anywhere in the world. This ubiquitous access to information is one reason why the World Wide Web is so hugely popular.

> Applets are programs that run inside a web browser.

Applets are programs that run inside a web browser. The code for an applet is stored on a web server and downloaded into the browser whenever you access a web page that contains the applet. That has one big advantage: You don't have to be at your own computer to run a program that is implemented as an applet. There is also an obvious disadvantage: You have to wait for the applet code to download into the browser, which can take a long time if you have a slow Internet connection. For that reason, complex applets are rare in web pages with a wide audience. Applets work very nicely, however, over a fast connection. For example, employees in a company often have a fast local area network connection. Then the company can deploy applets for schedule planning, health benefit access, product catalog lookup, and so on, and gain a big cost savings over the traditional process of developing corporate applications to be rolled out on the desktop of every user. When the program application changed, a system administrator had to make sure that every desktop was updated—a real hassle. When an applet changes, on the other hand, the code needs to be updated in one location: on the web server.

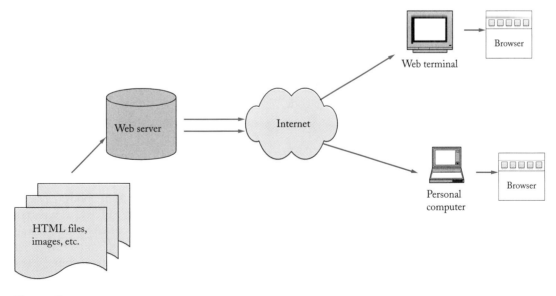

Figure 3

Web Browsers Accessing a Web Server

Web browser programs run on PCs, Macintoshes, UNIX workstations, and special web devices. For this reason, it is important that the applet code be able to execute on multiple platforms. Most traditional programs (such as word processors, computer games, and browsers) are written for a single platform, or perhaps written twice, for the two most popular platforms. Applets, on the other hand, are delivered as Java bytecode. Any computer or device that can execute Java bytecode can execute the applet.

> The applet security mechanisms let you safely execute applets on your computer.

Whenever you run a program on your computer, you run a risk that the program might do some kind of damage either because it is poorly written or because it is outright malicious. A poorly written program might accidentally corrupt or erase some of your files. A virus program might do the same intentionally. In the old days, before computers were networked, you had to install every program yourself, and it was a relatively easy matter to check for viruses on the floppy disks that you used to add new programs or data to your computer. Nowadays, programs can come from anywhere—from another machine on a local area network, as email attachments, or as code that is included in a web page. Code that is part of a web page is particularly troublesome, because it starts running immediately when the browser loads the page. It would be an easy matter for a malicious person to set up a web page with enticing content, have many people visit the page, and attempt to infect each visitor with a virus. The designers of Java anticipated this problem and came up with two safeguards: Java applets can run at specified *security privileges*, and they can be *signed*. If you allow a machine language program to run, there is no control over what it can do, and it can create many kinds of problems. In contrast, the Java virtual machine can limit the actions of an applet. By default, an applet runs in a *sandbox*, where it can display information and get user input, but it can't read or touch anything else on the user's computer. You can give an applet more privileges, such as the ability to read and write local files, if you notify your browser that the applet is *trusted*. An applet can carry a *certificate* with a *signature* from an authentication firm such as VeriSign, which tells you where the applet originated. If the applet comes from a source you trust, such as a vendor who has delivered quality code to you in the past, you can tell the browser that you trust it. Signatures are not limited to applets; some browsers support certificates for machine language code.

4.2 A Brief Introduction to HTML

Applets are embedded inside web pages, so you need to know a few facts about the structure of web pages. A web page is written in a language called HTML (Hypertext Markup Language). Like Java code, HTML code is made up of text that follows certain strict rules. When a browser reads a web page, the browser *interprets* the code and *renders* the page, displaying characters, fonts, paragraphs, tables, and images.

> Web pages are written in HTML, using tags to format text and include images.

HTML files are made up of text and *tags* that tell the browser how to render the text. Nowadays, there are dozens of HTML tags. Fortunately, you need only a few to get started. Most HTML tags come in pairs consisting of an opening tag and a closing tag, and each pair applies to the text between the two tags. Here is a typical example of a tag pair:

```
Java is an <i>object-oriented</i> programming language.
```

The tag pair `<i> </i>` directs the browser to display the text inside the tags as *italics:* Java is an *object-oriented* programming language.

The closing tag is just like the opening tag, but it is prefixed by a slash (/). For example, bold-faced text is delimited by `<b> </b>`, and a paragraph is delimited by the tag pair `<p> </p>`.

```
<p><b>Java</b> is an <i>object-oriented</i>
programming language.</p>
```

The result is the paragraph

Java is an *object-oriented* programming language.

Another common construct is a bulleted list.
Java is

- object-oriented

- safe

- platform-independent

Here is the HTML code to display it:

```
<p>Java is</p>
<ul><li>object-oriented</li>
<li>safe</li>
<li>platform-independent</li></ul>
```

Each item in the list is delimited by `<li> </li>` (for "list item"), and the whole list is surrounded by `<ul> </ul>` (for "unnumbered list").

As in Java code, you can freely use white space (spaces and line breaks) in HTML code to make it easier to read. For example, you can lay out the code for a list as follows:

```
<p>Java is</p>
<ul>
    <li>object-oriented</li>
    <li>safe</li>
    <li>platform-independent</li>
</ul>
```

The browser ignores the white space.

If you omit a tag (such as a `</li>`), most browsers will try to guess the missing tags—sometimes with differing results. It is always best to include all tags.

You can include images in your web pages with the `img` tag. In its simplest form, an image tag has the form

```
<img src="hamster.jpeg" />
```

This code tells the browser to load and display the image that is stored in the file hamster.jpeg. This is a slightly different type of tag. Rather than text inside a tag pair `<img> </img>`, the `img` tag uses an *attribute* to specify a file name. Attributes have names and values. For example, the `src` attribute has the value `"hamster.jpeg"`. It is considered polite to use several additional attributes with the `img` tag, namely the *image size* and an *alternate description:*

```
<img src="hamster.jpeg" width="640" height="480"
alt="A photo of Harry, the Horrible Hamster" />
```

These additional attributes help the browser lay out the page and display a temporary description while gathering the data for the image (or if the browser cannot display images, such as a voice browser for blind users). Users with slow network connections really appreciate this extra effort.

Because there is no closing `</img>` tag, we put a slash / before the closing >. This is not a requirement of HTML, but it is a requirement of the emerging XHTML standard, the XML-based successor to HTML. See [1] for more information on XHTML.

The most important tag in web pages is the `<a>` `</a>` tag pair, which makes the enclosed text into a *link* to another file. The links between web pages are what makes the Web into, well, a web. The browser displays a link in a special way (for example, underlined text in blue color). Here is the code for a typical link:

```
<a href="http://java.sun.com">Java</a> is an object-oriented
programming language.
```

When the viewer of the web page clicks on the word <u>Java</u>, the browser loads the web page located at `java.sun.com`. (The value of the `href` attribute is a *Universal Resource Locator (URL)*, which tells the browser where to go. The prefix `http:`, for *Hypertext Transfer Protocol*, tells the browser to fetch the file as a web page. Other protocols allow different actions, such as `ftp:` to download a file, `mailto:` to send email to a user, and `file:` to view a local HTML file.)

> To run an applet, you need an HTML page with the `applet` tag.

Finally, the `applet` tag includes an applet in a web page. To display an applet, you need first to write and compile a Java file to generate the applet code—you will see how in the next section. Then you tell the browser how to find the code for the applet and how much screen space to reserve for the applet. Here is an example:

```
<applet code="HamsterApplet.class" width="400" height="300">An
animation of Harry, the Horrible Hamster</applet>
```

The text between the `<applet>` and `</applet>` tags is only displayed in lieu of the actual applet by browsers that can't run Java applets.

You have noticed that tags are enclosed in angle brackets (less-than and greater-than signs). What if you want to show an angle bracket on a web page? HTML provides the notations `&lt;` and `&gt;` produce the < and > symbols, respectively. Other codes of this kind produce symbols such as accented letters. The & (ampersand) symbol introduces these codes; to get that symbol itself, use `&amp;`.

You may already have created web pages with a web editor that works like a word processor, giving you a WYSIWYG (what you see is what you get) view of your web page. But the tags are still there, and you can see them when you load the HTML file into a text editor. If you are comfortable using a WYSIWYG web editor, and if your editor can insert applet tags, you don't need to memorize HTML tags at all. But many programmers and professional web designers prefer to work directly with the tags at least some of the time, because it gives them more control over their pages.

Random Fact   4.1

The Evolution of the Internet

Home computers and laptops are usually self-contained units with no permanent connection to other computers. Office and lab computers, however, are usually connected with each other and with larger computers: so-called *servers*. A server can store application programs and make them available on all computers on the network. Servers can also store data, such as schedules and mail messages, that everyone can retrieve. Networks that connect the computers in one building are called local area networks, or LANs.

Other networks connect computers in geographically dispersed locations. Such networks are called *wide area networks* or WANs. The most prominent wide area network is the *Internet*. At the time of this writing, the Internet is in a phase of explosive growth. Nobody knows for certain how many users have access to the Internet, but the user population is estimated in the hundreds of millions. The Internet grew out of the ARPAnet, a network of computers at universities that was funded by the Advanced Research Planning Agency of the U.S. Department of Defense. The original motivation behind the creation of the network was the desire to run programs on remote computers. Using remote execution, a researcher at one institution would be able to access an underutilized computer at a different site. It quickly became apparent, though, that remote execution was not what the network was actually used for. Instead, the "killer application" was *electronic mail:* the transfer of messages between computer users at different locations. To this day, electronic mail is one of the most compelling applications of the Internet.

Over time, more and more *information* became available on the Internet. The information was created by researchers and hobbyists and made freely available to anyone, either out of the goodness of their hearts or for self-promotion. For example, the *GNU* (GNU's Not UNIX) project is producing a set of high-quality operating system utilities and program development tools that can be used freely by anyone (ftp://prep.ai.mit.edu/pub/gnu), and Project Gutenberg makes available the text of important classical books, whose copyright has expired, in computer-readable form (http://www.gutenberg.org).

The first interfaces to retrieve this information were clumsy and hard to use. All that changed with the appearance of the *World Wide Web* (WWW). The World Wide Web brought two major advances to Internet information. The information could contain *graphics* and *fonts*—a great improvement over the older text-only format—and it became possible to embed *links* to other information pages. Using a *browser* such as Netscape or Internet Explorer, surfing the Web becomes easy and fun (Figure 4).

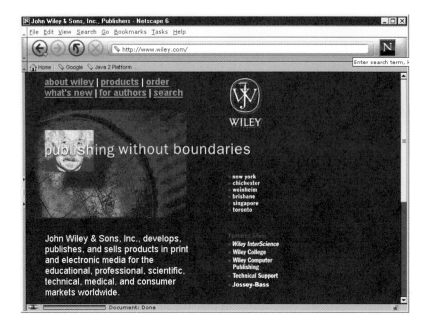

Figure 4

A Web Browser

A Simple Applet

In our first applet we will simply draw a couple of rectangles (see Figure 5). You'll soon see how to produce more interesting drawings. The purpose of this applet is to show you the basic outline of an applet that creates a drawing.

This applet will be implemented in a single class `RectangleApplet`. To run this applet, you need an HTML file with an `applet` tag. Here is the simplest possible file to display the applet:

File RectangleApplet.html

```
1 <applet code="RectangleApplet.class" width="300" height="300">
2 </applet>
```

Or you can proudly explain your creation, by adding text and more HTML tags:

File RectangleAppletExplained.html

```
1 <p>Here is my <i>first applet</i>:</p>
2 <applet code="RectangleApplet.class" width="300" height="300">
3 </applet>
```

Figure 5

The Rectangle Applet in the Applet Viewer

An HTML file can have multiple applets. For example, you can place all your homework solutions into a single HTML file.

You can give the HTML file any name you like. It is easiest to give the HTML file the same name as the applet. But some development environments already generate an HTML file with the same name as your project to hold your project notes; then you must give the HTML file containing your applet a different name.

> You view applets with the applet viewer or a Java-enabled browser.

To run the applet, you have two choices. You can use the *applet viewer*, a program that is included with the Java Software Development Kit from Sun Microsystems. You simply start the applet viewer, giving it the name of the HTML file that contains your applets:

```
appletviewer RectangleApplet.html
```

The applet viewer brings up one window for each applet in the HTML file. It ignores all other HTML tags. Figure 5 shows the applet inside the applet viewer.

> Your applet class needs to extend the Applet class.

You can also show the applet inside any Java 2–enabled web browser such as Netscape 6 (or later) or Opera. Figure 6 shows the applet running in a browser. As you can see, both the text and the applet are displayed.

An applet is programmed as a class, like any other program in Java. However, the class is declared public, and it *extends* Applet. That means that our rectangle applet *inherits* the behavior of the Applet class. We will discuss inheritance in Chapter 11.

```
public class RectangleApplet extends Applet
{
   public void paint(Graphics g)
   {
      . . .
   }
}
```

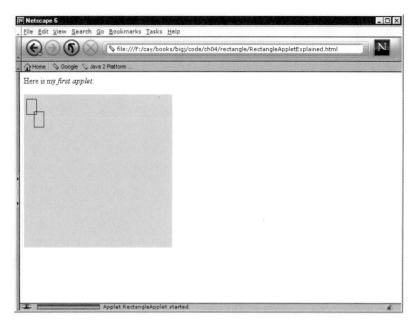

Figure 6

The Rectangle Applet in a Browser

> You draw graphical shapes in an applet by placing the drawing code inside the paint method. The paint method is called whenever the applet needs to be refreshed.

Unlike applications, applets don't have a main method. The web browser (or applet viewer) is responsible for starting up the Java virtual machine, for loading the applet code, and for starting the applet. This applet implements only one method: paint. There are other methods that you *may* implement; see Advanced Topic 4.3.

The window manager calls the paint method whenever the surface of the applet needs to be filled in. Of course, when the applet is shown for the first time, its contents need to be painted. If the user visits another web page and then goes back to the web page containing the applet, the surface must be painted again, and the window manager calls the paint method once more. Thus, you must put all drawing instructions inside the paint method, and you must be aware that the window manager can call the paint method many times.

> The Graphics2D class stores the graphics state (such as the current color) and has methods to draw shapes. You need to cast the Graphics parameter of the paint method to Graphics2D to use these methods.

The paint method receives an object of type Graphics. The Graphics object stores the *graphics state:* the current color, font, and so on, that are used for the drawing operations. For the drawing programs that we explore in this book, we always convert the Graphics object to an object of the Graphics2D class:

```
public class RectangleApplet extends Applet
{
    public void paint(Graphics g)
```

```
    {
        // recover Graphics2D
        Graphics2D g2 = (Graphics2D)g;
        . . .
    }
}
```

To understand why, you need to know a little about the history of these classes. The `Graphics` class was included with the first version of Java. It is suitable for very basic drawings, but it does not use an object-oriented approach. After some time, programmers clamored for a more powerful graphics package, and the designers of Java created the `Graphics2D` class. They did not want to inconvenience those programmers who had produced programs that used simple graphics, so they did not change the `paint` method. Instead, they made the `Graphics2D` class extend the `Graphics` class, a process that will be discussed in Chapter 9. Whenever the window manager calls the `paint` method, it actually passes a parameter of type `Graphics2D`. Programs with simple graphics needs do not need to know about this, but if you want to use the more sophisticated 2D graphics methods, you recover the `Graphics2D` reference by using a cast as discussed in Chapter 3.

You use the `draw` method of the `Graphics2D` class to draw shapes such as rectangles, ellipses, line segments, polygons, and arcs. Here we draw a rectangle:

```
public class RectangleApplet extends Applet
{
    public void paint(Graphics g)
    {
        . . .
        Rectangle cerealBox = new Rectangle(5, 10, 20, 30);
        g2.draw(cerealBox);
        . . .
    }
}
```

The `Graphics`, `Graphics2D`, and `Rectangle` classes are part of the `java.awt` package. As was mentioned in Chapter 1, the acronym AWT stands for Abstract Windowing Toolkit. This is the original user interface toolkit that Sun supplied for Java. It defines many classes for graphics programming, a mechanism for event handling, and a set of user interface components. In this chapter, we focus on the graphics classes of the AWT.

Here is the complete applet for displaying the rectangle shapes.

File RectangleApplet.java

```
1  import java.applet.Applet;
2  import java.awt.Graphics;
3  import java.awt.Graphics2D;
4  import java.awt.Rectangle;
5
6  /**
7     An applet that draws two rectangles.
```

```
 8  */
 9  public class RectangleApplet extends Applet
10  {
11     public void paint(Graphics g)
12     {
13        // recover Graphics2D
14
15        Graphics2D g2 = (Graphics2D)g;
16
17        // construct a rectangle and draw it
18
19        Rectangle cerealBox = new Rectangle(5, 10, 20, 30);
20        g2.draw(cerealBox);
21
22        // move rectangle 15 units sideways and 25 units down
23
24        cerealBox.translate(15, 25);
25
26        // draw moved rectangle
27
28        g2.draw(cerealBox);
29     }
30  }
```

▼ ▎**Advanced Topic** ▎ 4.1
▶

The Java Runtime Environment and Java Plug-ins

▼
You can run applets inside the applet viewer program, but applets are meant to be executed inside a browser. The first versions of browser programs that supported Java contained a built-in Java virtual machine to execute the downloaded Java applets. That

▼
turned out not to be a good idea. New versions of Java appeared rapidly, and the browser manufacturers were unable to keep up. Also, browser manufacturers made minor changes to the Java implementations, causing compatibility problems.

▼
In 1998, Sun Microsystems, the company that invented the Java language, realized that it is best to separate the browser and the virtual machine. Sun now packages the virtual machine as the "Java Runtime Environment", which is to be installed in a standard

▼
place on each computer that supports Java. Browser manufacturers are encouraged to use the Java Runtime Environment, not their own Java implementation, to execute applets. That way, users can update their Java implementations and browsers separately. If your

▼
browser uses this approach, then it will be able to execute your Java applets without problems. As of this writing, Netscape 6 and Opera work in this way.

▼
However, Microsoft's Internet Explorer browser does not currently support a modern version of the Java virtual machine. To solve this problem, Sun Microsystems provided a second tool, the "Java Plug-in". The Java Plug-in uses the Microsoft ActiveX component

▼   architecture to add Java support to Internet Explorer. If you want to display your applets inside Internet Explorer, you need to download the Java Plug-in from http://java.sun.com/products/plugin/index.html.

▼   Unfortunately, the HTML required to activate the browser extension is quite a bit more arcane than the simple `applet` tag. Sun has developed a program, the "Java Plug-in HTML Converter", that can translate HTML pages containing `applet` tags to HTML

▼   pages with the appropriate tags to launch the Java Plug-in. You can download the converter from http://java.sun.com/products/plugin/1.3/converter.html.

4.4   Graphical Shapes

In Section 4.3 you learned how to write an applet that draws rectangles. In this section you will learn how to draw other shapes: ellipses and lines. With these graphical elements you can draw quite a few interesting pictures.

> The `Rectangle2D.Double`, `Ellipse2D.Double`, and `Line2D.Double` classes describe graphical shapes.

To draw an ellipse, you specify its *bounding box* (see Figure 7) in the same way that you would specify a rectangle, namely by the *x*- and *y*-coordinates of the top-left corner and the width and height of the box.

However, there is no simple `Ellipse` class that you can use. Instead, you must use one of the two classes `Ellipse2D.Float` and `Ellipse2D.Double`, depending on whether you want to store the ellipse coordinates as `float` or as `double` values. Since `double` values are more convenient to use than `float` values in Java, we will always use the `Ellipse2D.Double` class. Here is how you construct an ellipse:

```
Ellipse2D.Double easterEgg = new Ellipse2D.Double(5, 10, 15, 20);
```

The class name `Ellipse2D.Double` looks different from the class names that you have encountered up to now. It consists of two class names `Ellipse2D` and `Double` separated by a period (`.`). This indicates that `Ellipse2D.Double` is a so-called *inner* class inside `Ellipse2D`. When constructing and using ellipses, you don't actually need to worry about the fact that `Ellipse2D.Double` is an inner class—just think of it as a class with a long name. However, in the `import` statement at the top of your program, you must be careful that you import only the *outer* class:

```
import java.awt.geom.Ellipse2D;
```

You may wonder why an ellipse would want to store its size as `double` values when the screen coordinates are measured in pixels. As you'll see later in this chapter, working with pixel coordinates can be cumbersome. It is often a good idea to switch to different units, and then it can be handy to use floating-point coordinates. (Note that the `Rectangle` class uses integer coordinates, so you will need to use a separate class called `Rectangle2D.Double` whenever you use rectangles with floating-point coordinates.)

Drawing an ellipse is easy: You use exactly the same `draw` method of the `Graphics2D` class that you used for drawing rectangles.

```
g2.draw(easterEgg);
```

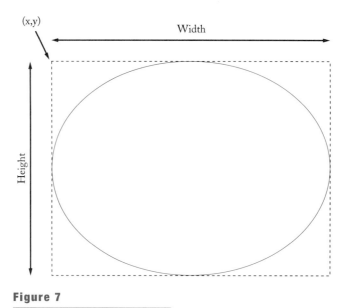

Figure 7

An Ellipse and Its Bounding Box

To draw a circle, simply set the width and height to the same value:

```
Ellipse2D.Double circle =
    new Ellipse2D.Double(x, y, diameter, diameter);
g2.draw(circle);
```

Notice that (x, y) is the top-left corner of the bounding box, *not* the center of the circle.

To draw a line, you use an object of the `Line2D.Double` class. You construct a line by specifying its two end points. You can do this in two ways. You can simply give the *x*- and *y*-coordinates of both end points:

```
Line2D.Double segment = new Line2D.Double(x1, y1, x2, y2);
```

Or you can specify each endpoint as an object of the `Point2D.Double` class:

```
Point2D.Double from = new Point2D.Double(x1, y1);
Point2D.Double to = new Point2D.Double(x2, y2);

Line2D.Double segment = new Line2D.Double(from, to);
```

The latter is more object-oriented, and it is also often more useful, in particular if the point objects can be reused elsewhere in the same drawing.

To draw thicker lines, supply a different *stroke* object to the `Graphics2D` parameter. For example, to get lines that are 4 pixels thick, you call

```
g2.setStroke(new BasicStroke(4.0F));
```

All shapes that you draw after making that call will be drawn with thicker lines.

4.5   Colors

When you first start drawing, all shapes are drawn with a black pen. To change the color, you need to supply an object of type `Color`. Java uses the *RGB color model*. That is, you specify a color by the amounts of the *primary colors*—red, green, and blue—that make up the color. The amounts are given as `float` values, which you must identify by a suffix F. They vary from `0.0F` (primary color not present) to `1.0F` (maximum amount present). For example,

```
Color magenta = new Color(1.0F, 0.0F, 1.0F);
```

> When you set a new color in the graphics context, it is used for subsequent drawing operations.

constructs a `Color` object with maximum red, no green, and maximum blue, yielding a bright purple color called magenta.

For your convenience, a variety of colors have been predefined in the `Color` class. Table 1 shows those predefined colors and their RGB values. For example, `Color.pink` has been predefined to be the same color as new `Color(1.0F, 0.7F, 0.7F)`.

Color	RGB Value
`Color.black`	0.0F, 0.0F, 0.0F
`Color.blue`	0.0F, 0.0F, 1.0F
`Color.cyan`	0.0F, 1.0F, 1.0F
`Color.gray`	0.5F, 0.5F, 0.5F
`Color.darkGray`	0.25F, 0.25F, 0.25F
`Color.lightGray`	0.75F, 0.75F, 0.75F
`Color.green`	0.0F, 1.0F, 0.0F
`Color.magenta`	1.0F, 0.0F, 1.0F
`Color.orange`	1.0F, 0.8F, 0.0F
`Color.pink`	1.0F, 0.7F, 0.7F
`Color.red`	1.0F, 0.0F, 0.0F
`Color.white`	1.0F, 1.0F, 1.0F
`Color.yellow`	1.0F, 1.0F, 0.0F

Table 1

Predefined Colors and Their RGB Values

Once you have an object of type Color, you can change the *current color* of the Graphics2D object with the setColor method. For example, the following code draws a rectangle in black, then switches the color to red, and draws the next rectangle in red:

```
public void paint(Graphics g)
{
    Graphics2D g2 = (Graphics2D)g;

    Rectangle cerealBox = new Rectangle(5, 10, 20, 30);
    g2.draw(cerealBox); // draws in black

    cerealBox.translate(15, 25); // move rectangle

    g2.setColor(Color.red); // set current color to red
    g2.draw(cerealBox); // draws in red
}
```

If you want to color the inside of the shape, you use the fill method instead of the draw method. For example,

```
g2.fill(cerealBox);
```

fills the inside of the rectangle with the current color.

4.6 Fonts

> The drawString method of the Graphics2D class draws a string, starting at its basepoint.

You often want to put text inside a drawing, for example to label some of the parts. You use the drawString method of the Graphics2D class to draw a string anywhere in a window. You must specify the string and the *x*- and *y*-coordinates of the *basepoint* of the first character in the string (see Figure 8). For example,

```
g2.drawString("Applet", 50, 100);
```

Baseline

Basepoint

Figure 8

Basepoint and Baseline

> A font is described by its face name, style, and point size.

You can select different fonts. The procedure is similar to setting the drawing color. You create a `Font` object and call the `setFont` method of the `Graphics2D` class. To construct a `Font` object, you specify

- The font face name
- The *style* (one of `Font.PLAIN`, `Font.BOLD`, `Font.ITALIC`, or `Font.BOLD + Font.ITALIC`)
- The point size

The font face name is either one of the five *logical face names* in Table 2 or a *typeface name*, the name of a typeface that is available on your computer, such as "Times Roman" or "Helvetica". "Times Roman" and "Helvetica" are the names of popular typefaces that were designed many years ago and are in very widespread use today. These fonts differ in the shapes of their letters. The most visible difference is that the characters of the Times Roman font are composed of strokes with small cross segments at the ends, called *serifs*. The characters of the Helvetica font do not have serifs (see Figure 9). A typeface such as Helvetica is called a *sans-serif* font. It is generally believed that the serifs help make text easier to read. In

Name	Sample	Description
`Serif`	The quick brown fox	A serif-style font such as Times Roman
`SansSerif`	The quick brown fox	A sans-serif font such as Helvetica
`Monospaced`	The quick brown fox	A font in which all characters have the same width, such as Courier
`Dialog`	**The quick brown fox**	A screen font suitable for labels in dialogs
`DialogInput`	The quick brown fox	A screen font suitable for user input in text field

Table 2

Logical Font Names

Helvetica

Times Roman

Figure 9

Common Fonts

Courier

fact, the Times Roman font was designed specifically for the London *Times* newspaper, to be easy to read on newsprint paper. Most books (including this one) use a serif typeface for the body text. Sans-serif typefaces are appropriate for headlines, figure labels, and so on. Many other typefaces have been designed over the centuries, with and without serifs. For example, Garamond is another popular serif-style typeface. A third kind of typeface that you will commonly see is Courier, a font that was originally designed for typewriters.

The design of a good typeface requires artistic judgment and substantial experience. However, in the United States, the shapes of letters are considered industrial design that cannot be protected by copyright. For that reason, typeface designers protect their rights by trademarking the *names* of the fonts. For example, the names "Times Roman" and "Helvetica" are trademarks of the Linotype Corporation. Although other companies can create lookalike fonts (just as certain companies create imitations of famous perfumes), they have to give them different names. That's why you find fonts with names such as "Times New Roman" or "Arial". That makes it bit of a bother to select fonts by their names, especially if you don't know what fonts are available on a particular computer. For that reason, we will specify fonts by their *logical* face names. Java recognizes five logical font names (see Table 2) that are mapped to fonts that exist on every computer system. For example, if you request the "SansSerif" font, then the Java font mapper will go and search for the best general-purpose sans-serif font available. On a computer running the Windows operating system, you will get the "Arial" font. On a Macintosh, you will get "Helvetica".

To create a font, you must specify the *point size:* the height of the font in the typesetter's unit called *points*. The height of a font is measured from the top of the *ascender* (the top part of letters such as *b* and *l*) to the bottom of the *descender* (the bottom part of letters such as *g* and *p*). There are 72 points per inch. For example, a 12-point font has a height of $\frac{1}{6}$ inch. Actually, the point size of a font is only an approximate measure, and you can't necessarily be sure that two fonts with the same point size have matching character sizes. The actual sizes will in any case depend on the size and resolution of your monitor screen. Without getting into fine points of typography, it is best if you simply remember a few typical point sizes: 8 point ("small"), 12 point ("medium"), 18 point ("large"), and 36 point ("huge").

Here is how you can write "Applet" in huge pink letters:

```
final int HUGE_SIZE = 36;
String message = "Applet";
Font hugeFont = new Font("Serif", Font.BOLD, HUGE_SIZE);
g2.setFont(hugeFont);
g2.setColor(Color.pink);
g2.drawString(message, 50, 100);
```

The *x*- and *y*-positions in the `drawString` method can be specified either as `int` or as `float`.

▼ **Advanced Topic** 4.2

Accurate Positioning of Text

▼

When drawing strings on the screen, you usually need to position them accurately. For example, if you want to draw two lines of text, one below the other, then you need to

Ascent

Descent

Figure 10

Text Layout Measurements

know the distance between the two basepoints. Of course, the size of a string depends on the shapes of the letters, which in turn depends on the font face and point size. You will need to know a few typographical measurements (see Figure 10):

- The *ascent* of a font is the height of the largest letter above the baseline.

- The *descent* of a font is the depth below the baseline of the letter with the lowest descender.

These values describe the *vertical* extent of strings. The *horizontal* extent depends on the individual letters in a string. In a monospaced font, all letters have the same width. Monospaced fonts are still used for computer programs, but for plain text they are as outdated as the typewriter. In a *proportionally spaced font,* different letters have different widths. For example, the letter *l* is much narrower than the letter *m*.

To measure the size of a string, you need to construct a FontRenderContext object, which you obtain from the Graphics2D object by calling getFontRenderContext. A font render context is an object that knows how to transform letter shapes (which are described as curves) into pixels. In general, a "context" object is usually an object that has some specialized knowledge how to carry out complex tasks. You don't have to worry how the context object works; you just create it and pass it along as required. The Graphics2D object is another example of a context object—many people call it a "graphics context".

To get the size of a string, you call the getStringBounds method of the Font class. For example,

```
String message = "Applet";
FontRenderContext context = g2.getFontRenderContext();
Rectangle2D bounds = hugeFont.getStringBounds(message, context);
```

The returned rectangle is positioned so that the origin (0, 0) falls on the basepoint (see Figure 8). Therefore, you can get the ascent, descent, height, and width as

```
double yMessageAscent = -bounds.getY();
double yMessageDescent = bounds.getHeight() + bounds.getY();
double yMessageHeight = bounds.getHeight();
double xMessageWidth = bounds.getWidth();
```

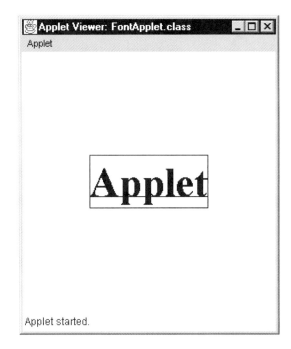

Figure 11

The Font Applet Displays a Centered String

The following program uses these measurements to center a string precisely in the middle of the applet window (see Figure 11). To center the string, you need to know the size of the applet. (The user might have resized it, so you can't simply use the values of `width` and `height` in the HTML file.) The `getWidth` and `getHeight` methods return the applet size in pixels. To center the string horizontally, think of the amount of blank space that you have available. The width of the applet window is `getWidth()`. The width of the string is `xMessageWidth`. Therefore, the blank space is the difference,

```
getWidth() - xMessageWidth
```

Half of that blank space should be distributed on either side. Therefore, the string should start at

```
double xLeft = (getWidth() - xMessageWidth) / 2;
```

For the same reason, the top of the string is at

```
double yTop = (getHeight() - yMessageHeight) / 2;
```

But the `drawString` method needs the basepoint of the string. You get to the baseposition by adding the ascent:

```
double yBase = yTop + yMessageAscent;
```

Following this note is the complete program. When you run it in the applet viewer, try resizing the applet window and observe that the string always stays centered.

File FontApplet.java

```
1  import java.applet.Applet;
2  import java.awt.Font;
3  import java.awt.Graphics;
4  import java.awt.Graphics2D;
5  import java.awt.font.FontRenderContext;
6  import java.awt.geom.Line2D;
7  import java.awt.geom.Rectangle2D;
8
9  /**
10     This applet draws a string that is centered in the
11     applet window.
12  */
13 public class FontApplet extends Applet
14 {
15    public void paint(Graphics g)
16    {
17       Graphics2D g2 = (Graphics2D)g;
18
19       // select the font into the graphics context
20
21       final int HUGE_SIZE = 48;
22       Font hugeFont =
23          new Font("Serif", Font.BOLD, HUGE_SIZE);
24       g2.setFont(hugeFont);
25
26       String message = "Applet";
27
28       // measure the string
29
30       FontRenderContext context =
31          g2.getFontRenderContext();
32       Rectangle2D bounds =
33          hugeFont.getStringBounds(message, context);
34
35       double yMessageAscent = -bounds.getY();
36       double yMessageDescent =
37          bounds.getHeight() + bounds.getY();
38       double yMessageHeight = bounds.getHeight();
39       double xMessageWidth = bounds.getWidth();
40
41       // center the message in the window
42
43       double xLeft = (getWidth() - xMessageWidth) / 2;
44       double yTop = (getHeight() - yMessageHeight) / 2;
45       double yBase = yTop + yMessageAscent;
46
47       g2.drawString(message, (float)xLeft, (float)yBase);
48       // draw bounding rectangle
49
```

```
50        g2.draw(new Rectangle2D.Double(xLeft, yTop,
51           xMessageWidth, yMessageHeight));
52
53        // draw base line
54        g2.draw(new Line2D.Double(xLeft, yBase,
55           xLeft + xMessageWidth, yBase));
56     }
57 }
```

4.7   Drawing Complex Shapes

> It is a good idea to make a class for each complex graphical shape.

The next program shows how you can put shapes together to draw a simple figure of a car—see Figure 12. It is a good idea to make a separate class for each complex shape that you want to draw. For example, the program at the end of this section defines a Car class.

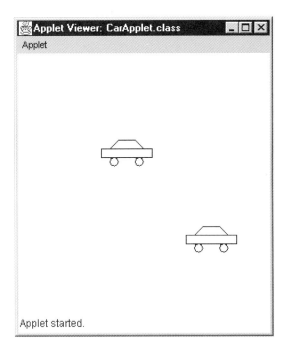

Figure 12

The Car Applet Draws Two Car Shapes

Figure 13

Using Graph Paper to Find Shape Coordinates

```
class Car
{
    . . .
    public void draw(Graphics2D g2)
    {
        // drawing instructions
        . . .
    }
}
```

The coordinates of the car parts seem a bit arbitrary. To come up with suitable values, you want to draw the image on graph paper and read off the coordinates—see Figure 13.

Here is the program. Unfortunately, in programs such as these it is difficult to avoid the "magic numbers" for the coordinates of the various shapes.

> To figure out how to draw a complex shape, make a sketch on graph paper.

File CarApplet.java

```
1  import java.applet.Applet;
2  import java.awt.Graphics;
3  import java.awt.Graphics2D;
```

```
 4  /**
 5      This applet draws two car shapes.
 6  */
 7  public class CarApplet extends Applet
 8  {
 9      public void paint(Graphics g)
10      {
11          Graphics2D g2 = (Graphics2D)g;
12
13          Car car1 = new Car(100, 100);
14          Car car2 = new Car(200, 200);
15
16          car1.draw(g2);
17          car2.draw(g2);
18      }
19  }
```

File Car.java

```
 1  import java.awt.Graphics2D;
 2  import java.awt.geom.Ellipse2D;
 3  import java.awt.geom.Line2D;
 4  import java.awt.geom.Point2D;
 5  import java.awt.geom.Rectangle2D;
 6
 7  /**
 8      A car shape that can be positioned anywhere on the screen.
 9  */
10  public class Car
11  {
12      /**
13          Constructs a car with a given top left corner.
14          @param x the x-coordinate of the top left corner
15          @param y the y-coordinate of the top left corner
16      */
17      public Car(double x, double y)
18      {
19          xLeft = x;
20          yTop = y;
21      }
22
23      /**
24          Draws the car.
25          @param g2 the graphics context
26      */
27      public void draw(Graphics2D g2)
28      {
29          Rectangle2D.Double body  = new
```

```
30              Rectangle2D.Double(xLeft, yTop + 10, 60, 10);
31          Ellipse2D.Double frontTire  = new
32              Ellipse2D.Double(xLeft + 10, yTop + 20, 10, 10);
33          Ellipse2D.Double rearTire = new
34              Ellipse2D.Double(xLeft + 40, yTop + 20, 10, 10);
35
36          // the bottom of the windshield
37          Point2D.Double r1
38              = new Point2D.Double(xLeft + 10, yTop + 10);
39          // the front of the roof
40          Point2D.Double r2
41              = new Point2D.Double(xLeft + 20, yTop);
42          // the rear of the roof
43          Point2D.Double r3
44              = new Point2D.Double(xLeft + 40, yTop);
45          // the bottom of the rear window
46          Point2D.Double r4
47              = new Point2D.Double(xLeft + 50, yTop + 10);
48
49          Line2D.Double frontWindshield
50              = new Line2D.Double(r1, r2);
51          Line2D.Double roofTop
52              = new Line2D.Double(r2, r3);
53          Line2D.Double rearWindow
54              = new Line2D.Double(r3, r4);
55
56          g2.draw(body);
57          g2.draw(frontTire);
58          g2.draw(rearTire);
59          g2.draw(frontWindshield);
60          g2.draw(roofTop);
61          g2.draw(rearWindow);
62      }
63
64      private double xLeft;
65      private double yTop;
66 }
```

▼ **?** HOWTO 4.1 ▶

Drawing Graphical Shapes

You can program applets that display a wide variety of graphical shapes. These instructions give you a step-by-step procedure how to decompose a drawing into parts and implement a program that produces the drawing.

▼ **Step 1** Determine the shapes that you need for the drawing

You can use the following shapes:

▼

- Squares and rectangles
- Circles and ellipses

▼

- Lines

You can draw the outlines of these shapes in any color, or you can fill the insides of these shapes with any color.

▼

You can also use text to label parts of your drawing.

For example, many national flag designs consist of three equally wide sections of different colors, side by side:

▼

▼

You could draw such a flag using three rectangles. But if the middle rectangle is white, as it is, for example, in the flag of Italy (green, white, red), it is easier and looks better just to draw two lines on the top and bottom of the middle portion:

▼

Two lines

▼

Two rectangles

Step 2 Find the coordinates for the shapes

▼

You now need to find the exact positions for the geometric shapes.

- For rectangles, you need the *x*- and *y*-position of the top left corner, the width, and height.

▼

- For ellipses, you need the top left corner, width, and height of the bounding rectangle.

▼   • For lines, you need the *x*- and *y*-positions of the starting point and the end point.

▼   • For text, you need the *x*- and *y*-positions of the basepoint.

▼ A typical size for an applet is 300 by 300 pixels. You may not want the flag crammed all the way to the top, so perhaps the upper left corner of the flag should be at the point (100, 100).

Many flags, such as the flag of Italy, have a width : height ratio of 3 : 2. (You can often find exact proportions for a particular flag by doing a bit of Internet research on

▼ one of several Flags of the World sites.) For example, if you make the flag 90 pixels wide, then it should be 60 pixels tall. (Why not make it 100 pixels wide? Then the height would be 100 · 2 / 3 ≈ 67, which seems more awkward.)

▼ Now you can compute the coordinates of all the important points of the shape:

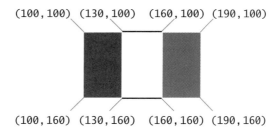

```
(100,100)  (130,100)   (160,100) (190,100)
```

```
(100,160)  (130,160)   (160,160) (190,160)
```

▼ **Step 3**   Write Java statements to draw the shapes

▼ In our example, there are two rectangles and two lines:

```
Rectangle2D.Double leftRectangle
    = new Rectangle2D.Double(100, 100, 30, 60);
Rectangle2D.Double rightRectangle
    = new Rectangle2D.Double(160, 100, 30, 60);
Line2D.Double topLine
    = new Line2D.Double(130, 100, 160, 100);
Line2D.Double bottomLine
    = new Line2D.Double(130, 160, 160, 160);
```

▼ If you are more ambitious, then you can express the coordinates in terms of a few variables. In the case of the flag, we have arbitrarily chosen the top left corner and the width. All other coordinates follow from those choices. If you decide to follow the ambitious

▼ approach, then the rectangles and lines are determined as follows:

```
Rectangle2D.Double leftRectangle
    = new Rectangle2D.Double(xLeft, yTop,
        width / 3, width * 2 / 3);
Rectangle2D.Double rightRectangle
    = new Rectangle2D.Double(xLeft + 2 * width / 3, yTop,
        width / 3, width * 2 / 3);
Line2D.Double topLine
    = new Line2D.Double(xLeft + width / 3, yTop,
        xLeft + width * 2 / 3, yTop);
```

```
Line2D.Double bottomLine
   = new Line2D.Double(
       xLeft + width / 3, yTop + width * 2 / 3,
       xLeft + width * 2 / 3, yTop + width * 2 / 3);
```

Now you need to fill the rectangles and draw the lines. For the flag of Italy, the left rectangle is green and the right rectangle is red. Remember to switch colors before the filling and drawing operations:

```
g2.setColor(Color.green);
g2.fill(leftRectangle);
g2.setColor(Color.red);
g2.fill(rightRectangle);
g2.setColor(Color.black);
g2.draw(topLine);
g2.draw(bottomLine);
```

Step 4   Combine the drawing statements with the applet "plumbing"

The simplest form of the "plumbing" looks like this:

```
public class MyApplet extends Applet
{
   public void paint(Graphics g)
   {
      Graphics2D g2 = (Graphics2D)g;
      // your drawing code goes here
      . . .
   }
}
```

In our example, you can simply add all shapes and drawing instructions inside the paint method:

```
public class ItalianFlagApplet extends Applet
{
   public void paint(Graphics g)
   {
      Graphics2D g2 = (Graphics2D)g;
      Rectangle2D.Double leftRectangle
         = new Rectangle2D.Double(100, 100, 30, 60);
      . . .
      g2.setColor(Color.green);
      g2.fill(leftRectangle);
      . . .
   }
}
```

That approach is acceptable for simple drawings, but it is not very object-oriented. After all, a flag is an object. It is better to make a separate class for the flag. Then you can draw different flags at different positions and sizes. Specify the sizes in a constructor and supply a **draw** method:

```
public class ItalianFlag
{
   public ItalianFlag(double x, double y, double aWidth)
   {
      xLeft = x;
      yTop = y;
      width = aWidth;
   }

   public void draw(Graphics2D g2)
   {
      Rectangle2D.Double leftRectangle
         = new Rectangle2D.Double(xLeft, yTop,
            width / 3, width * 2 / 3);
      . . .
      g2.setColor(Color.green);
      g2.fill(leftRectangle);
      . . .
   }

   private double xLeft;
   private double yTop;
   private double width;
}
```

You still need a separate class for the applet, but it is very simple:

```
public class ItalianFlagApplet extends Applet
{
   public void paint(Graphics g)
   {
      Graphics2D g2 = (Graphics2D)g;
      ItalianFlag flag = new ItalianFlag(100, 100, 90);
      flag.draw(g2);
   }
}
```

You may wish to modify this code to make the flag fit comfortably in the applet area even if the applet is not 300 by 300. Use the applet getWidth() and getHeight() methods to find the actual size of the applet window, and use these dimensions to compute the constructor parameters, similar to what was done for text in Advanced Topic 4.2.

Step 5   Write the HTML file for the applet

To show an applet in the applet viewer or a Java 2-enabled browser, you need an HTML file that specifies the name of the applet class and the desired width and height of the applet. Here is a minimal HTML file for the Italian flag applet:

```
<applet code="ItalianFlagApplet.class"
   width="300" height="300"></applet>
```

▼ If you like, you can add more HTML code around the `applet` tag to describe your applet. The description shows up when you view the HTML file in a browser, but the applet viewer displays only the applet.

▼ **Random Fact** 4.2 ▶

Computer Graphics

▼ Generating and manipulating visual images are among the most exciting applications of the computer. We distinguish different kinds of graphics.

▼ *Diagrams, such as numeric charts or maps, are artifacts that convey information to the viewer* (see Figure 14). They do not directly depict anything that occurs in the natural world but are a tool for visualizing information.

▼ *Scenes* are computer-generated images that attempt to depict images of the real or an imagined world (see Figure 15). It turns out to be quite challenging to render light and shadows accurately. Special effort must be taken so that the images do not look overly

Figure 14

Diagrams

Figure 15

Scene

neat and simple; clouds, rocks, leaves, and dust in the real world have a complex and somewhat random appearance. The degree of realism in these images is constantly improving.

Manipulated images are photographs or film footage of actual events that have been converted to digital form and edited by the computer (see Figure 16). For example, film

Figure 16

Manipulated Image

▼   sequences of the movie *Apollo 13* were produced by starting from actual images and changing the perspective, showing the launch of the rocket from a more dramatic viewpoint.

▼   Computer graphics is one of the most challenging fields in computer science. It requires processing of massive amounts of information at very high speed. New algorithms are constantly invented for this purpose. Displaying an overlapping set of three-dimensional objects with curved boundaries requires advanced mathematical tools. Realistic modeling of textures

▼   and biological entities requires extensive knowledge of mathematics, physics, and biology.

4.8   Reading Text Input

The applets that you have seen so far are quite nice for drawing, but they aren't interactive—you can't change the positions of the shapes that are drawn on the screen. Interactive input in a graphical program turns out to be more complex than in a console program. In a console program, the programmer dictates the control flow and forces the user to enter input in a predetermined order. A graphical program, however, generally makes available to the program user a large number of controls (buttons, input fields, scroll bars, and so on), which users can manipulate in any order they please. Therefore, the program must be prepared to process input from multiple sources in random order. You will learn how to do that in Chapter 10.

In the meantime, we will simply read input with the `JOptionPane.showInputDialog` method that you saw in Chapter 3.

You should place any calls to the `showInputDialog` method into the applet constructor, not the `paint` method. That way, the user is prompted for input once, when the applet is first displayed. (If you place the calls to `showInputDialog` inside the `paint` method, then you are prompted for new input every time the applet is repainted.) To get another chance to supply input, select "Reload" or "Refresh" from the browser or applet viewer menu.

If you put the call to `showInputDialog` inside the applet constructor, then your applet needs to remember the user input in one or more instance fields and refer to these variables in the `paint` method. The following program is an example. It prompts the user for red, green, and blue values, and then fills a rectangle with the color that the user specified. For example, if you enter 1.0, 0.7, 0.7, then the rectangle is filled with pink color.

File ColorApplet.java

```
1  import java.applet.Applet;
2  import java.awt.Color;
3  import java.awt.Graphics;
4  import java.awt.Graphics2D;
5  import java.awt.Rectangle;
6  import javax.swing.JOptionPane;
7
8  /**
9      An applet that lets a user choose a color by specifying
10     the fractions of red, green, and blue.
11  */
12  public class ColorApplet extends Applet
13  {
```

```
14      public ColorApplet()
15      {
16         String input;
17         // ask the user for red, green, blue values
18
19         input = JOptionPane.showInputDialog("red:");
20         float red = Float.parseFloat(input);
21
22         input = JOptionPane.showInputDialog("green:");
23         float green = Float.parseFloat(input);
24
25         input = JOptionPane.showInputDialog("blue:");
26         float blue = Float.parseFloat(input);
27
28         fillColor = new Color(red, green, blue);
29      }
30
31      public void paint(Graphics g)
32      {
33         Graphics2D g2 = (Graphics2D)g;
34
35         // select color into graphics context
36
37         g2.setColor(fillColor);
38
39         // construct and fill a square whose center is
40         // the center of the window
41
42         Rectangle square = new Rectangle(
43            (getWidth() - SQUARE_LENGTH) / 2,
44            (getHeight() - SQUARE_LENGTH) / 2,
45            SQUARE_LENGTH,
46            SQUARE_LENGTH);
47
48         g2.fill(square);
49      }
50
51      private static final int SQUARE_LENGTH = 100;
52
53      private Color fillColor;
54 }
```

When you run this program, you will note that the input dialog has a label identifying it as an "applet window" (see Figure 17). That is an applet security feature. It would be an easy matter for a cracker to write an applet that pops up a dialog "Your password has expired. Please reenter your password." and then sends the input back to the web server. If you should happen to visit the web page containing that applet, you might be confused and reenter the password to your computer account, giving it to the cracker. The window label tips you off that it is an applet, and not your operating system, that displays the dialog. All windows that pop up from an applet have this warning label.

Figure 17

Applet Dialog with Warning Label

While the input dialog window is on the screen, the user is not allowed to do anything in the browser except type input and click on the OK or Cancel button. This kind of dialog is called a *modal dialog*. A sequence of modal input dialogs can be frustrating to the user, so it is not really a good user interface design. However, it is easy to program, and it makes sense for you to use it until you learn how to gather input in a more professional way—the topic of Chapter 12.

AT Advanced Topic   4.3

Applet Parameters

You have seen how to use the `showInputDialog` method of the `JOptionPane` class to supply user input to an applet. Another way of supplying input is sometimes useful: Use the `param` tag in the HTML page that loads the applet. The `param` tag has the form

```
<param name="..." value="..." />
```

You place one or more `param` tags between the `<applet>` and `</applet>` tags, like this:

```
<applet code="ColorApplet.class" width="300" height="300">
<param name="Red" value="1.0" />
<param name="Green" value="0.7" />
<param name="Blue" value="0.7" />
</applet>
```

The applet can read these values with the `getParameter` method. For example, when the `ColorApplet` is loaded with the HTML tags given above, then `getParameter("Blue")` returns the string `"0.7"`. Of course, you then need to convert the string into a number.

You cannot call the `getParameter` method in the applet constructor. When the applet is first constructed, the parameters are not yet ready. Instead, you can read them either in the `paint` method or in a special `init` method. The applet viewer or browser calls the `init` method after the constructor but before the first call to `paint`.

```
public class ColorApplet extends Applet
{
    public void init()
```

▼

▼

```
    {
        float r = Float.parseFloat(getParameter("Red"));
        float g = Float.parseFloat(getParameter("Green"));
        float b = Float.parseFloat(getParameter("Blue"));
        fillColor = new Color(r, g, b);
    }
```

▼

```
    public void paint(Graphics g)
    {
        . . .
    }
```

▼

```
    private Color fillColor;
}
```

▼

Now you can change the color values simply by editing the HTML page.

4.9   Comparing Visual and Numerical Information

The next example shows how one can look at the same problem both visually and numerically. You want to figure out the intersection between a circle and a line. The circle has radius 100 and center (100, 100). Ask the user to specify the position of a vertical line. Then draw the circle, the line, and the intersection points (see Figure 18). Label them to display the exact locations.

Exactly where do the two shapes intersect? We need a bit of mathematics. The equation of a circle with radius r and center point (a, b) is

$$(x - a)^2 + (y - b)^2 = r^2$$

If you know x, then you can solve for y:

$$(y - b)^2 = r^2 - (x - a)^2$$

or

$$y - b = \pm\sqrt{r^2 - (x - a)^2}$$

hence

$$y = b \pm \sqrt{r^2 - (x - a)^2}$$

That is easy to compute in Java:

```
double root = Math.sqrt(r * r - (x - a) * (x - a));
double y1 = b + root;
double y2 = b - root;
```

But how do you know that you did both the math and the programming right?

Figure 18

Intersection of a Line and a Circle

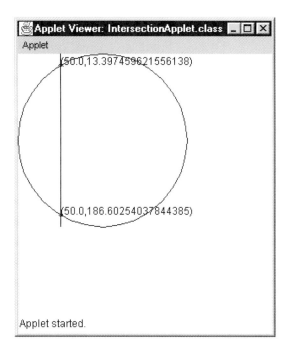

If your program is correct, these two points will show up right on top of the actual intersections in the picture. If not, the two points will be at the wrong place.

If you look at Figure 18, you will see that the results match perfectly, which gives us confidence that everything is correct. See Quality Tip 4.1 for more information on verifying that this program works correctly.

Here is the complete program.

File IntersectionApplet.java

```
 1  import java.applet.Applet;
 2  import java.awt.Graphics;
 3  import java.awt.Graphics2D;
 4  import java.awt.geom.Ellipse2D;
 5  import java.awt.geom.Line2D;
 6  import javax.swing.JOptionPane;
 7
 8  /**
 9      An applet that computes and draws the intersection points
10      of a circle and a line.
11  */
12  public class IntersectionApplet extends Applet
13  {
14      public IntersectionApplet()
15      {
```

```
16        String input
17            = JOptionPane.showInputDialog("x:");
18        x = Integer.parseInt(input);
19    }
20
21    public void paint(Graphics g)
22    {
23        Graphics2D g2 = (Graphics2D)g;
24
25        double r = 100;  // the radius of the circle
26
27        // draw the circle
28
29        Ellipse2D.Double circle  = new
30            Ellipse2D.Double(0, 0, 2 * RADIUS, 2 * RADIUS);
31        g2.draw(circle);
32
33        // draw the vertical line
34
35        Line2D.Double line
36            = new Line2D.Double(x, 0, x, 2 * RADIUS);
37        g2.draw(line);
38
39        // compute the intersection points
40
41        double a = RADIUS;
42        double b = RADIUS;
43
44        double root =
45            Math.sqrt(RADIUS * RADIUS - (x - a) * (x - a));
46        double y1 = b + root;
47        double y2 = b - root;
48
49        // draw the intersection points
50
51        LabeledPoint p1 = new LabeledPoint(x, y1);
52        LabeledPoint p2 = new LabeledPoint(x, y2);
53
54        p1.draw(g2);
55        p2.draw(g2);
56    }
57
58    private static final double RADIUS = 100;
59    private double x;
60 }
```

File LabeledPoint.java

```
1 import java.awt.Graphics2D;
2 import java.awt.geom.Ellipse2D;
```

```
 3  /**
 4      A point with a label showing the point's coordinates.
 5  */
 6  public class LabeledPoint
 7  {
 8      /**
 9          Construct a labeled point.
10          @param anX the x-coordinate
11          @param aY the y-coordinate
12      */
13      public LabeledPoint(double anX, double aY)
14      {
15          x = anX;
16          y = aY;
17      }
18
19      /**
20          Draws the point as a small circle with a coordinate label.
21          @param g2 the graphics context
22      */
23      public void draw(Graphics2D g2)
24      {
25          // draw a small circle centered around (x, y)
26
27          Ellipse2D.Double circle = new Ellipse2D.Double(
28                  x - SMALL_CIRCLE_RADIUS,
29                  y - SMALL_CIRCLE_RADIUS,
30                  2 * SMALL_CIRCLE_RADIUS,
31                  2 * SMALL_CIRCLE_RADIUS);
32
33          g2.draw(circle);
34
35          // draw the label
36
37          String label = "(" + x + "," + y + ")";
38
39          g2.drawString(label, (float)x, (float)y);
40      }
41
42      private static final double SMALL_CIRCLE_RADIUS = 2;
43
44      private double x;
45      private double y;
46  }
```

At this point you should be careful to specify only lines that intersect the circle. If the line doesn't meet the circle, then the program will attempt to compute a square root of a negative number, and a math error will occur. We have not yet discussed how to implement a test to protect against this situation. That will be the topic of the next chapter.

Quality Tip   4.1

Calculate Sample Data Manually

> You should calculate test cases by hand to double-check that your program computes the correct answers.

It is usually difficult or impossible to prove that a given program functions correctly in all cases. For gaining confidence in the correctness of a program, or for understanding why it does not function as it should, manually calculated sample data are invaluable. If the program arrives at the same results as the manual calculation, our confidence in it is strengthened. If the manual results differ from the program results, we have a starting point for the debugging process.

Surprisingly, many programmers are reluctant to perform any manual calculations as soon as a program carries out the slightest bit of algebra. Their math phobia kicks in, and they irrationally hope that they can avoid the algebra and beat the program into submission by random tinkering, such as rearranging the + and - signs. Random tinkering is always a great time sink, but it rarely leads to useful results.

It is much smarter to look for test cases that are representative and easy to compute. In our example, let us look for three easy cases that we can compute by hand and then compare against program runs.

First, let the vertical line pass through the center of the circle. That is, x is 100. Then we expect the distance between the center and the intersection point to be the same as the radius of the circle. Now root = Math.sqrt(100 * 100 - 0 * 0), which is 100. Therefore, y1 is 0 and y2 is 200. Those are indeed the top and bottom points on the circle. Now, that wasn't so hard.

Next, let the line touch the circle on the right. Then x is 200 and root = Math .sqrt(100 * 100 - 100 * 100), which is 0. Therefore, y1 and y2 are both equal to 100, and indeed (200, 100) is the rightmost point of the circle. That also was pretty easy.

The first two cases were *boundary cases* of the problem. A program may work correctly for several special cases but still fail for more typical input values. Therefore we must come up with an intermediate test case, even if it means a bit more computation. Let us pick a simple value for x, say x = 50. Then root = Math.sqrt(100 * 100 - 50 * 50) = Math.sqrt(7500). Using a calculator, you get approximately 86.6025. That yields y1 = 100 − 86.6025 = 13.3975 and y2 = 100 + 86.6025 = 186.6025. So what? Run the program and enter 50. First, you will find that the program also computes the same x- and y-values that you computed by hand. That is good—it confirms that you probably typed in the formulas correctly, and the intersection points really do fall on the right place.

4.10   Coordinate Transformations

By default, the draw method of the Graphics2D class uses *pixels* to measure screen locations. A pixel (short for "picture element") is a dot on the screen. For example, the point (50, 100) is 50 pixels to the right and 100 pixels down from the top left corner of the panel. This default coordinate system is fine for simple test programs, but it is

Figure 19

Plotting Temperature Data

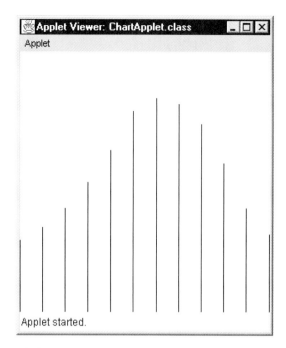

tedious when dealing with real-world data. For example, suppose you want to show a chart plotting the average temperature (degrees Celsius) in Phoenix, Arizona, for every month of the year (see Figure 19). The temperature ranges from 11 degrees Celsius in January to 33 degrees Celsius in July (see Table 3).

Here, the x-values range from 1 to 12 and the y-values range from 11 to 33. The applet pixel coordinates range from 0 to getWidth() - 1 and 0 to getHeight() - 1. If the width and height of the applet are 300 pixels each, then we can't just use pixel coordinates for the data, or the graph would only occupy a tiny area of the window.

> Pixel coordinates are not useful for real-world data sets. Pick convenient user coordinates and convert to pixels.

In such a situation, you need to define *user coordinates* that makes sense for your particular application and then transform them to pixel coordinates. Suppose the application coordinates range from $x_{\min}$ to $x_{\max}$ and $y_{\min}$ to $y_{\max}$. Then you can transform user coordinates to pixel coordinates, by using the following equations:

$$x_{\text{pixel}} = (x_{\text{user}} - x_{\min}) \cdot (\text{width} - 1) / (x_{\max} - x_{\min})$$

$$y_{\text{pixel}} = (y_{\text{user}} - y_{\max}) \cdot (\text{height} - 1) / (y_{\min} - y_{\max})$$

To see that these equations make sense, plug in $x_{\text{user}} = x_{\min}$ and $x_{\text{user}} = x_{\max}$ and check that you get $x_{\text{pixel}} = 0$ and $x_{\text{pixel}} = \text{width} - 1$. Do the same for the y values.

Note that for the y-coordinates, the roles for $y_{\min}$ and $y_{\max}$ are reversed. In Java, y-coordinates increase when moving down, whereas in mathematics, they increase when moving up. That is, $y_{\max}$ corresponds to pixel 0 and $y_{\min}$ to pixel height −1.

Let's apply this to our temperature chart. The month range is

$$x_{\min} = 1, x_{\max} = 12$$

Table 3

Average Temperatures in Phoenix, Arizona

Month	Temperature
January	11
February	13
March	16
April	20
May	25
June	31
July	33
August	32
September	29
October	23
November	16
December	12

We'll choose a temperature range

$$y_{min} = 0, y_{max} = 40$$

We draw each data point as a line from (month, 0) to (month, temperature) in user coordinates. Here is how you compute the pixel coordinates.

```
final double XMIN = 1;
final double XMAX = 12;
final double YMIN = 0;
final double YMAX = 40;

double xpixel = (month - XMIN) * (getWidth() - 1) /
    (XMAX - XMIN);
double y1pixel = getHeight() - 1; // 0 in user coordinates
double y2pixel = (temperature - YMAX)
    * (getHeight() - 1) / (YMIN - YMAX);

Line2D.Double bar =
    new Line2D.Double(xpixel, y1pixel, xpixel, y2pixel);
```

This approach works, but it is tedious and can make your code hard to read. It is better to write a couple of simple helper methods for the coordinate transformation.

```
public class Phoenix extends Applet
{
   . . .
   public double xpixel(double xuser)
   {
      return
         (xuser - XMIN) * (getWidth() - 1) / (XMAX - XMIN);
   }

   public double ypixel(double yuser)
   {
      return
         (yuser - YMAX) * (getHeight() - 1) / (YMIN - YMAX);
   }

   private static final double XMIN = 1;
   private static final double XMAX = 12;
   private static final double YMIN = 0;
   private static final double YMAX = 40;
}
```

Now you can compute pixel coordinates conveniently:

```
Line2D.Double stick = new Line2D.Double(
   xpixel(month), ypixel(0),
   xpixel(month), ypixel(temperature));
```

Advanced Topic 4.4 shows another solution that is even more elegant.

Here is the complete program for drawing the temperature bar chart. Figure 18 shows the output.

File ChartApplet.java

```
 1  import java.applet.Applet;
 2  import java.awt.Graphics;
 3  import java.awt.Graphics2D;
 4  import java.awt.geom.Line2D;
 5
 6  /**
 7      This applet draws a chart of the average monthly
 8      temperatures in Phoenix, AZ.
 9  */
10  public class ChartApplet extends Applet
11  {
12     public void paint(Graphics g)
13     {
14        Graphics2D g2 = (Graphics2D)g;
15
16        month = 1;
```

```
17        drawBar(g2, JAN_TEMP);
18        drawBar(g2, FEB_TEMP);
19        drawBar(g2, MAR_TEMP);
20        drawBar(g2, APR_TEMP);
21        drawBar(g2, MAY_TEMP);
22        drawBar(g2, JUN_TEMP);
23        drawBar(g2, JUL_TEMP);
24        drawBar(g2, AUG_TEMP);
25        drawBar(g2, SEP_TEMP);
26        drawBar(g2, OCT_TEMP);
27        drawBar(g2, NOV_TEMP);
28        drawBar(g2, DEC_TEMP);
29     }
30
31     /**
32         Draws a bar for the current month and increments
33         the month.
34         @param g2  the graphics context
35         @param temperature  the temperature for the month
36     */
37     public void drawBar(Graphics2D g2, int temperature)
38     {
39        Line2D.Double bar
40           = new Line2D.Double(xpixel(month), ypixel(0),
41               xpixel(month), ypixel(temperature));
42
43        g2.draw(bar);
44
45        month++;
46     }
47
48     /**
49         Converts from user coordinates to pixel coordinates.
50         @param xuser  an x value in user coordinates
51         @return  the corresponding value in pixel coordinates
52     */
53     public double xpixel(double xuser)
54     {
55        return
56           (xuser - XMIN) * (getWidth() - 1) /
57           (XMAX - XMIN);
58     }
59
60     /**
61         Converts from user coordinates to pixel coordinates.
62         @param yuser  a y-value in user coordinates
63         @return  the corresponding value in pixel coordinates
64     */
65     public double ypixel(double yuser)
66     {
```

```
67        return
68            (yuser - YMAX) * (getHeight() - 1) /
69            (YMIN - YMAX);
70    }
71
72    private static final int JAN_TEMP = 11;
73    private static final int FEB_TEMP = 13;
74    private static final int MAR_TEMP = 16;
75    private static final int APR_TEMP = 20;
76    private static final int MAY_TEMP = 25;
77    private static final int JUN_TEMP = 31;
78    private static final int JUL_TEMP = 33;
79    private static final int AUG_TEMP = 32;
80    private static final int SEP_TEMP = 29;
81    private static final int OCT_TEMP = 23;
82    private static final int NOV_TEMP = 16;
83    private static final int DEC_TEMP = 12;
84
85    private static final double XMIN = 1;
86    private static final double XMAX = 12;
87    private static final double YMIN = 0;
88    private static final double YMAX = 40;
89
90    private int month;
91 }
```

▲▼ Advanced Topic 4.4

Let the Graphics Context Transform the Coordinates

You can change the coordinate system of the graphics context. At the beginning of the paint method, insert the following two calls:

```
double xscale = (getWidth() - 1.0) / (XMAX - XMIN);
double yscale = (getHeight() - 1.0) / (YMIN - YMAX);
g2.scale(xscale, yscale);
g2.translate(-XMIN, -YMAX);
g2.setStroke(new BasicStroke(0));
```

Now the graphics context translates user coordinates to pixels, leaving the programmer to focus on more important issues. You simply draw objects in user coordinates, such as

```
Line2D.Double rect =
    new Line2D.Double(month, 0, month, temperature);
```

The call to setStroke is necessary to set the line thickness. The default drawing operation draws lines of width 1 in user coordinates, which would result in lines that are much

▼   too fat. A stroke with thickness zero is always drawn one pixel wide. Font size is also
     specified in user coordinates. If your drawing contains fonts, you need to divide the point
     size by `Math.max(xscale, -yscale)`.
▼   The program after this note shows how the chart applet is implemented with graphics
     context transformations. Note that the `xpixel` and `ypixel` methods are no longer required.

File ChartApplet.java

```java
 1 import java.applet.Applet;
 2 import java.awt.BasicStroke;
 3 import java.awt.Graphics;
 4 import java.awt.Graphics2D;
 5 import java.awt.geom.Line2D;
 6
 7 /**
 8    This applet draws a chart of the average monthly
 9    temperatures in Phoenix, AZ.
10 */
11 public class ChartApplet extends Applet
12 {
13    public void paint(Graphics g)
14    {
15       Graphics2D g2 = (Graphics2D)g;
16
17       double xscale =
18          (getWidth() - 1.0) / (XMAX - XMIN);
19       double yscale =
20          (getHeight() - 1.0) / (YMIN - YMAX);
21       g2.scale(xscale, yscale);
22       g2.translate(-XMIN, -YMAX);
23       g2.setStroke(new BasicStroke(0));
24
25       month = 1;
26
27       drawBar(g2, JAN_TEMP);
28       drawBar(g2, FEB_TEMP);
29       drawBar(g2, MAR_TEMP);
30       drawBar(g2, APR_TEMP);
31       drawBar(g2, MAY_TEMP);
32       drawBar(g2, JUN_TEMP);
33       drawBar(g2, JUL_TEMP);
34       drawBar(g2, AUG_TEMP);
35       drawBar(g2, SEP_TEMP);
36       drawBar(g2, OCT_TEMP);
37       drawBar(g2, NOV_TEMP);
38       drawBar(g2, DEC_TEMP);
39    }
```

```
40    /**
41        Draws a bar for the current month and increments
42        the month.
43        @param g2  the graphics context
44        @param temperature  the temperature for the month
45    */
46    public void drawBar(Graphics2D g2, int temperature)
47    {
48        Line2D.Double bar = new
49            Line2D.Double(month, 0, month, temperature);
50
51        g2.draw(bar);
52
53        month++;
54    }
55
56    private static final int JAN_TEMP = 11;
57    private static final int FEB_TEMP = 13;
58    private static final int MAR_TEMP = 16;
59    private static final int APR_TEMP = 20;
60    private static final int MAY_TEMP = 25;
61    private static final int JUN_TEMP = 31;
62    private static final int JUL_TEMP = 33;
63    private static final int AUG_TEMP = 32;
64    private static final int SEP_TEMP = 29;
65    private static final int OCT_TEMP = 23;
66    private static final int NOV_TEMP = 16;
67    private static final int DEC_TEMP = 12;
68
69    private static final double XMIN = 1;
70    private static final double XMAX = 12;
71    private static final double YMIN = 0;
72    private static final double YMAX = 40;
73
74    private int month;
75 }
```

▼ **Productivity Hint**   4.1 ▶

Choose Convenient Units for Drawing

▼

Whenever you deal with real-world data, you should use units that are matched to the data. Figure out which range of x- and y-coordinates is most appropriate for the program data. For example, suppose you want to display a tic-tac-toe board (see Figure 20) that is

▼

supposed to fill the entire applet.

▼ **Figure 20**

A Tic-Tac-Toe Board

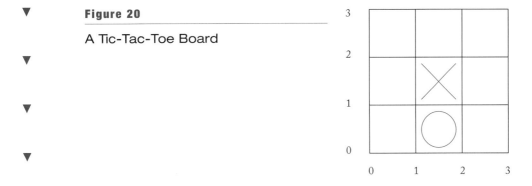

▼

▼

▼

▼

▼

Of course, you could labor mightily and figure out where the lines are in relation to the default pixel coordinate system. Or you can simply set your own units with both x and y going from 0 to 3.

```
g2.draw(new Line2D.Double(
    xpixel(0), ypixel(1), xpixel(3), ypixel(1)));
g2.draw(new Line2D.Double(
    xpixel(0), ypixel(2), xpixel(3), ypixel(2)));
g2.draw(new Line2D.Double(
    xpixel(2), ypixel(0), xpixel(1), ypixel(3)));
g2.draw(new Line2D.Double(
    xpixel(2), ypixel(0), xpixel(2), ypixel(3)));
```

Some people have horrible memories about coordinate transformations from their high-school geometry class and have taken a vow never to think about coordinates again for the remainder of their lives. If you are among them, you should reconsider. If pixel coordinates are a poor match for your drawing, you may end up spending a lot of time fussing with coordinates to get the drawing right. Pick the right coordinate system and use the standard conversion functions (or, even better, let the graphics context do them, as described in Advanced Topic 4.4). Then all the horrible algebra is done automatically for you, so you don't have to program it by hand.

CHAPTER SUMMARY

1. There are three types of Java programs: *console applications*, *applets*, and *graphics applications*.

2. Applets are programs that run inside a web browser.

3. The applet security mechanisms let you execute applets safely on your computer.

4. Web pages are written in HTML, using tags to format text and include images.

5. To run an applet, you need an HTML page with the `applet` tag.

6. You view applets with the applet viewer or a Java-enabled browser.

7. Your applet class needs to extend the `Applet` class.

8. You draw graphical shapes in an applet by placing the drawing code inside the `paint` method. The `paint` method is called whenever the applet needs to be refreshed.

9. The `Graphics2D` class stores the graphics state (such as the current color) and has methods to draw shapes. You need to cast the `Graphics` parameter of the `paint` method to `Graphics2D` to use these methods.

10. The `Rectangle2D.Double`, `Ellipse2D.Double`, and `Line2D.Double` classes describe graphical shapes.

11. When you set a new color in the graphics context, it is used for subsequent drawing operations.

12. The `drawString` method of the `Graphics2D` class draws a string, starting at its basepoint.

13. A font is described by its face name, style, and point size.

14. It is a good idea to make a class for each complex graphical shape.

15. To figure out how to draw a complex shape, make a sketch on graph paper.

16. An applet can obtain input by displaying a `JOptionPane` in its constructor.

17. You should calculate test cases by hand to double-check that your application computes the correct answer.

18. Pixel coordinates are not useful for real-world data sets. Pick convenient user coordinates and convert to pixels.

References

[1] For details about the XHTML standard, see http://www.w3.org/MarkUp/.

CLASSES, OBJECTS, AND METHODS INTRODUCED IN THIS CHAPTER

```
java.applet.Applet
   getHeight
   getWidth
   init
   paint
java.awt.BasicStroke
java.awt.Color
java.awt.Font
```

```
        getStringBounds
java.awt.Graphics
java.awt.Graphics2D
    draw
    drawString
    fill
    getFontRenderContext
    getParameter
    scale
    setColor
    setFont
    setStroke
    translate
java.awt.font.FontRenderContext
java.awt.geom.Ellipse2D.Double
java.awt.geom.Line2D.Double
    getX1
    getX2
    getY1
    getY2
    setLine
java.awt.geom.Point2D.Double
    getX
    getY
    setLocation
java.awt.geom.Rectangle2D.Double
java.awt.geom.RectangularShape
    getCenterX
    getCenterY
    getMaxX
    getMaxY
    getMinX
    getMinY
    getWidth
    getHeight
    setFrameFromDiagonal
java.lang.Float
    parseFloat
javax.swing.JOptionPane
    showInputDialog
```

REVIEW EXERCISES

Exercise R4.1. What is the difference between an applet and an application?

Exercise R4.2. What is the difference between a browser and the applet viewer?

Exercise R4.3. Why do you need an HTML page to run an applet?

Exercise R4.4. Who calls the `paint` method of an applet? When does the call to the `paint` method occur?

Exercise R4.5. Why does the parameter of the `paint` method have type `Graphics` and not `Graphics2D`?

Exercise R4.6. What is the purpose of a graphics context?

Exercise R4.7. How do you specify a text color?

Exercise R4.8. What is the difference between a font and a font face?

Exercise R4.9. What is the difference between a monospaced font and a proportionally spaced font?

Exercise R4.10. What are serifs?

Exercise R4.11. What is a logical font?

Exercise R4.12. How do you determine the pixel dimensions of a string in a particular font?

Exercise R4.13. Which classes are used in this chapter for drawing graphical shapes?

Exercise R4.14. What are the four different classes for specifying rectangles in the Java library?

Exercise R4.15. You want to plot a bar chart showing the grade distribution of all students in your class (where A = 4.0, F = 0). What coordinate system would you choose to make the plotting as simple as possible?

Exercise R4.16. Let **e** be any ellipse. Write Java code to plot the ellipse **e** and another ellipse of the same size that touches **e**. *Hint:* You need to look up the accessors that tell you the dimensions of an ellipse.

Exercise R4.17. Write Java instructions to display the letters X and T in a graphics window, by plotting line segments.

Exercise R4.18. Introduce an error in the program `Intersect.java`, by computing `double root = Math.sqrt(r * r + (x - a) * (x - a));`. Run the program. What happens to the intersection points?

Exercise R4.19. Suppose you run the `Intersect` program and give a value of 30 for the *x*-position of the vertical line. Without actually running the program, determine what values you will obtain for the intersection points.

PROGRAMMING EXERCISES

Exercise P4.1. Write a graphics program that draws your name in red, centered inside a blue rectangle.

Exercise P4.2. Write a graphics program that draws your name four times, in a large serif font, in plain, bold, italic, and bold italic. The names should be stacked on top of each other, with equal distance between them. Each of them should be centered horizontally, and the entire stack should be centered vertically.

Exercise P4.3. Write a graphics program that draws twelve strings, one each for the 12 standard colors besides `Color.white`, each in its own color.

Exercise P4.4. Write a graphics program that prompts the user to enter a radius. Draw a circle with that radius.

Exercise P4.5. Write a program that draws two solid circles: one in pink and one in purple. Use a standard color for one of them and a custom color for the other.

Exercise P4.6. Draw a "bull's eye"—a set of concentric rings in alternating black and white colors. *Hint:* Fill a black circle, then fill a smaller white circle on top, and so on.

Exercise P4.7. Write a program that fills the applet window with a large ellipse, filled with your favorite color, that touches the window boundaries. The ellipse should resize itself when you resize the window.

Exercise P4.8. Write a program that draws the picture of a house. It could be as simple as the accompanying figure, or if you like, make it more elaborate (3-D, skyscraper, marble columns in the entryway, whatever).

Implement a class `House` and supply a method `draw(Graphics2D g2)` that draws the house.

Exercise P4.9. Extend Exercise 4.8 by allowing the user to specify houses of different sizes in the `House` constructor. Then populate your screen with a few houses of different sizes.

Exercise P4.10. Write a program to plot the following face.

Exercise P4.11. Write a program to plot the string "HELLO", using just lines and circles. Do not call `drawString`, and do not use `System.out`. Make classes `LetterH`, `LetterE`, `LetterL` and `LetterO`.

Exercise P4.12. *Plotting a data set.* Make a bar chart to plot the following data set:

Bridge Name	Longest Span (ft)
Golden Gate	4,200
Brooklyn	1,595
Delaware Memorial	2,150
Mackinac	3,800

Make the bars horizontal for easier labeling. *Hint:* Set the window coordinates to 5,000 in the *x*-direction and 4 in the *y*-direction.

Exercise P4.13. Write a graphics program that displays the values of Exercise 4.12 as a *pie chart*. Just draw a circle and the edges of the pie slices. You don't have to color the slices. (If you want to color them, look at the online API documentation for the `Arc2D` class.)

Exercise P4.14. Write a program that displays the Olympic rings.

Color the rings in the Olympic colors.

Exercise P4.15. Write a graphics program that draws a clock face with a time that the user enters in a text field. (The user must enter the time in the format hh:mm, for example 09:45.)

Hint: You need to find out the angles of the hour hand and the minute hand. The angle of the minute hand is easy: The minute hand travels 360 degrees in 60 minutes. The angle of the hour hand is harder; it travels 360 degrees in 12 × 60 minutes.

Design a class `Clock` and supply a method `draw(Graphics2D g2)` that draws the clock.

Exercise P4.16. Change the `CarApplet` program to make the cars appear twice the size of the original example.

Exercise P4.17. Change the `CarApplet` program to make the cars appear in different colors. Each `Car` object should store its own color.

Exercise P4.18. Design a class `Truck` whose constructor takes the top left corner point of the truck. Supply a method `draw(Graphics2D g2)` that draws the truck. Then populate your screen with a few cars and trucks.

Decisions

CHAPTER GOALS

To be able to implement decisions using if statements

▶ To understand how to group statements into blocks

▶ To learn how to compare integers, floating-point numbers, strings, and objects

▶ To recognize the correct ordering of decisions in multiple branches

▶ To program conditions using Boolean operators and variables

The programs we have seen so far were able to do fast computations and render graphs, but they were very inflexible. Except for variations in the input, they worked the same way with every program run. One of the essential features of nontrivial computer programs is the ability to make decisions and to carry out different actions, depending on the nature of the inputs. The goal of this chapter is to learn how to program simple and complex decisions.

5.1 The if Statement

Consider the bank account class of Chapter 3. The withdraw method allows you to withdraw as much money from the account as you like. The balance just moves ever further into the negatives. That is not a realistic model for a bank account. Let's implement the withdraw method so that you cannot withdraw more money than you have in the account. That is, the withdraw method must make a *decision:* whether to allow the withdrawal or not.

> The if statement lets a program carry out different actions depending on the outcome of a condition.

The if statement is used to implement a decision. The if statement has two parts: a *test* and a *body.* If the test succeeds, the body of the statement is executed. The body of the if statement consists of a statement:

```
if (amount <= balance)
    balance = balance - amount;
```

The assignment statement is carried out only when the amount to be withdrawn is less than or equal to the balance. (See Figure 1.)

Let us make the withdraw method of the BankAccount even more realistic. Most banks not only disallow withdrawals that exceed your account balance; they also—adding insult to injury—charge you a penalty for every attempt to do so.

You can't simply program that by providing two complementary if statements:

```
if (amount <= balance)
    balance = balance - amount;
if (amount > balance) // NO
    balance = balance - OVERDRAFT_PENALTY;
```

There are two problems with this approach. First, if you need to modify the condition amount <= balance for some reason, you must remember to update the condition

Figure 1

Flowchart for an if Statement

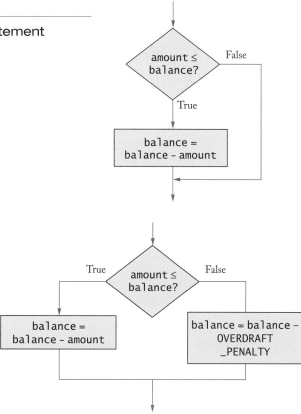

Figure 2

Flowchart for an if/else Statement

amount > balance as well. If you do not, the logic of the program will no longer be correct. More importantly, if you modify the value of balance in the body of the first if statement (as in this example), then the second condition uses the new value.

To implement a choice between alternatives, use the if/else statement:

```
if (amount <= balance)
    balance = balance - amount;
else
    balance = balance - OVERDRAFT_PENALTY;
```

Now there is only one condition. If it is satisfied, the first statement is executed. Otherwise, the second is executed. The flowchart in Figure 2 gives a graphical representation of the branching behavior.

> A block statement groups together several statements.

Quite often, however, the body of the if statement consists of multiple statements that must be executed in sequence whenever the test is successful. These statements must be grouped together to form a *block statement* by enclosing them in braces { }. Here is an example.

```
if (amount <= balance)
{
    double newBalance = balance - amount;
    balance = newBalance;
}
```

Syntax 5.1: The if Statement

```
if (condition)
    statement
```

```
if (condition)
    statement
else
    statement
```

Example:

```
if (amount <= balance)
    balance = balance - amount;
```

```
if (amount <= balance)
    balance = balance - amount;
else
    balance = balance - OVERDRAFT_PENALTY;
```

Purpose:

To execute a statement when a condition is true or false

Syntax 5.2: Block Statement

```
{
    statement
    statement
    . . .
}
```

Example:

```
{
    double newBalance = balance - amount;
    balance = newBalance;
}
```

Purpose:

To group several statements together to form a single statement

A statement such as

```
balance = balance - amount;
```

is called a *simple statement*. A conditional statement such as

```
if (x >= 0) y = x;
```

is called a *compound statement*. In Chapter 6, you will encounter loop statements; they too are compound statements.

The body of an if statement or the else alternative must be a statement—that is, a simple statement, a compound statement (such as another if statement), or a block statement.

▼ Advanced Topic 5.1

The Selection Operator

Java has a selection operator of the form

test ? *value1* : *value2*

The value of that expression is either *value1* if the test passes or *value2* if it fails. For example, we can compute the absolute value as

```
y = x >= 0 ? x : -x;
```

which is a convenient shorthand for

```
if (x >= 0)
    y = x;         [handwritten: Expression with value]
else
    y = -x;        [handwritten annotations: statement, statement]
```

The selection operator is similar to the if/else statement, but it works on a different syntactical level. The selection operator combines *expressions* and yields another expression. The if/else statement combines statements and yields another statement.

Expressions have values. For example, balance + amount is an expression, as is x >= 0 ? x : -x. Any expression can be made into a statement by adding a semicolon. For example, y = x is an expression (with value x), but y = x; is a statement. Statements do not have values. Since if/else forms a statement and does not have a value, you cannot write

```
y = if (x > 0) x; else -x; // Error
```

We don't use the selection operator in this book, but it is a convenient and legitimate construct that you will find in many Java programs.

▼ Quality Tip 5.1

Brace Layout

The compiler doesn't care where you place braces, but we strongly recommend that you follow a simple rule: *Line up* { and }.

```
if (amount <= balance)
{
   double newBalance = balance - amount;
   balance = newBalance;
}
```

This scheme makes it easy to spot matching braces.

Some programmers put the opening brace on the same line as the `if`:

```
if (amount <= balance) {
   double newBalance = balance - amount;
   balance = newBalance;
}
```

That saves a line of code, but it makes it harder to match the braces.

It is important that you pick a layout scheme and stick with it consistently. Which scheme you choose may depend on your personal preference or a coding style guide that you need to follow.

Productivity Hint   5.1

Indentation and Tabs

When writing Java programs, you use *indentation to indicate nesting levels:*

```
public class BankAccount
{
|  . . .
|  public void withdraw(double amount)
|  {
|  |  if (amount <= balance)
|  |  {
|  |  |  double newBalance = balance - amount;
|  |  |  balance = newBalance;
|  |  }
|  }
|  . . .
}
0  1  2  3
```
Indentation level

How many spaces should you use per indentation level? Some programmers use eight spaces per level, but that isn't a good choice:

```
public class BankAccount
{
        . . .
        public void withdraw(double amount)
        {
                if (amount <= balance)
                {
```

```
                                    double newBalance =
                                            balance - amount;
                                    balance = newBalance;
                          }
                }
                    . . .
            }
```

It crowds the code too much to the right side of the screen. As a consequence, long expressions frequently must be broken into separate lines. More common values are two, three, or four spaces per indentation level.

How do you move the cursor from the leftmost column to the appropriate indentation level? A perfectly reasonable strategy is to hit the space bar a sufficient number of times. However, many programmers use the Tab key instead. A tab moves the cursor to the next tab stop. By default, there are tab stops every eight columns, but most editors let you change that value; you should find out how to set your editor's tab stops to, say, every three columns.

Some editors actually help you out with an *autoindent* feature. They automatically insert as many tabs or spaces as the preceding line had, because the new line is quite likely to belong to the same logical indentation level. If it isn't, you must add or remove a tab, but that is still faster than tabbing all the way from the left margin.

As nice as tabs are for data entry, they have one disadvantage: They can mess up printouts. If you send a file with tabs to a printer, the printer may either ignore the tabs altogether or set tab stops every eight columns. It is therefore best to save and print your files with spaces instead of tabs. Most editors have settings that convert tabs to spaces before you save or print a file.

5.2   Comparing Values

5.2.1   Relational Operators

Every `if` statement performs a test. In many cases, the test compares two values. For example, in the previous example we tested `amount <= balance`. Comparison operators such as `<=` are called *relational operators*. Java has six relational operators:

Java	Math Notation	Description
>	$>$	Greater than
>=	$\geq$	Greater than or equal
<	$<$	Less than
<=	$\leq$	Less than or equal
==	$=$	Equal
!=	$\neq$	Not equal

> Relational operators compare values. The == operator tests for equality.

As you can see, only two Java relational operators (> and <) look as you would expect from the mathematical notation. Computer keyboards do not have keys for $\geq$, $\leq$, or $\neq$, but the >=, <=, and != operators are easy to remember because they look similar.

The == operator is initially confusing to most newcomers to Java. In Java, the = symbol already has a meaning, namely assignment. The == operator denotes equality testing:

```
a = 5; // assign 5 to a
if (a == 5) ... //  test whether a equals 5
```

You will have to remember to use == for equality testing and to use = for assignment.

5.2.2 — Comparing Floating-Point Numbers

Floating-point numbers have only a limited precision, and calculations can introduce roundoff errors. For example, the following code multiplies the square root of 2 by itself and then subtracts 2.

```
double r = Math.sqrt(2);
double d = r * r - 2;
if (d == 0)
   System.out.println("sqrt(2) squared minus 2 is 0");
else
   System.out.println(
      "sqrt(2) squared minus 2 is not 0 but " +  d);
```

Even though the laws of mathematics tell us that equals 0, this program fragment prints

```
sqrt(2) squared minus 2 is not 0 but 4.440892098500626E-16
```

> When comparing floating-point numbers, don't test for equality. Instead, check whether they are *close enough*.

Unfortunately, such roundoff errors are unavoidable. It plainly does not make sense in most circumstances to compare floating-point numbers exactly. Instead, we should test whether they are *close enough*.

To test whether a number x is close to zero, you can test whether the absolute value $|x|$ (that is, the number with its sign removed) is less than a very small threshold number. That threshold value is often called ε (the Greek letter epsilon). It is common to set ε to 10^{-14} when testing double numbers.

In Java, we program the test as follows: x is close to 0 if

```
Math.abs(x) <= EPSILON
```

where we define

```
final double EPSILON = 1E-14;
```

Similarly, you can test whether two numbers are close to each other by checking whether their difference is close to 0.

$$|x - y| \leq \varepsilon$$

However, this is not always good enough. Suppose x and y are rather large, say a few billion each. Then they could be the same, except for a roundoff error, even if their difference was quite a bit larger than 10^{-14}. To overcome this problem, you need to divide by the magnitude of the numbers before comparing how close they are. Here is the formula: x and y are close enough if

$$\frac{|x - y|}{\max(|x|, |y|)} \le \varepsilon$$

In Java, the code for this test is

```
Math.abs(x-y) / Math.max(Math.abs(x), Math.abs(y))
    <= EPSILON;
```

For this test to work, both x and y must be nonzero. If one of the values is zero, you lose the magnitude information. Then all you can do is test whether the absolute value of the other number is at most ε.

5.2.3 — Comparing Strings

Do not use the == operator to compare strings. Use the equals method instead.

To test whether two strings are equal to each other, you must use the method called equals:

```
if (string1.equals(string2)) ...
```

Do not use the == operator to compare strings! The expression

```
if (string1 == string2) // not useful
```

has an unrelated meaning. It tests whether the two string variables refer to the *identical* string object. You can have strings with identical contents stored in different objects, so this test never makes sense in actual programming; see Common Error 5.1.

In Java, letter case matters. For example, "Harry" and "HARRY" are not the same string. To ignore the letter case, use the equalsIgnoreCase method:

```
if (string1.equalsIgnoreCase(string2)) ...
```

The compareTo method compares strings in dictionary order.

If two strings are not identical to each other, you still may want to know the relationship between them. The compareTo method compares strings in dictionary order. If

```
string1.compareTo(string2) < 0
```

then the string string1 comes before the string string2 in the dictionary. For example, this is the case if string1 is "Harry", and string2 is "Hell". If

```
string1.compareTo(string2) > 0
```

then string1 comes after string2 in dictionary order. Finally, if

```
string1.compareTo(string2) == 0
```

then string1 and string2 are equal.

Actually, the "dictionary" ordering used by Java is slightly different from that of a normal dictionary. Java is case-sensitive and sorts characters by putting numbers first, then uppercase characters, then lowercase characters. For example, 1 comes before B, which comes before a. The space character comes before all other characters.

Figure 3

Lexicographic Comparison

Letters   r comes
match   before t

Let us investigate the comparison process closely. When Java compares two strings, corresponding letters are compared until one of the strings ends or the first difference is encountered. If one of the strings ends, the longer string is considered the later one. If a character mismatch is found, the characters are compared to determine which string comes later in the dictionary sequence. This process is called *lexicographic* comparison. For example, let's compare `"car"` with `"cargo"`. The first three letters match, and we reach the end of the first string. Therefore `"car"` comes before `"cargo"` in the lexicographic ordering. Now compare `"cathode"` with `"cargo"`. The first two letters match. In the third character position, t comes after r, so the string `"cathode"` comes after `"cargo"` in lexicographic ordering. (See Figure 3.)

⊗ Common Error

Using `==` to Compare Strings

It is an extremely common error in Java to write `==` when `equals` is intended. This is particularly true for strings. If you write

```
if (nickname == "Rob")
```

then the test succeeds only if the variable `nickname` refers to the exact same string object as the string constant `"Rob"`. For efficiency, Java makes only one string object for every string constant. Therefore, the following test will pass:

```
String nickname = "Rob";
...
if (nickname == "Rob") // test is true
```

However, if the string with the letters R o b has been assembled in some other way, then the test will fail:

```
String name = "Robert";
String nickname = name.substring(0, 3);
...
if (nickname == "Rob") // test is false
```

This is a particularly distressing situation: The wrong code will sometimes do the right thing, sometimes the wrong thing. Since string objects are always constructed by the compiler, you never have an interest in whether two string objects are shared. You must remember never to use `==` to compare strings. Always use `equals` or `compareTo` to compare strings.

5.2.4 — Comparing Objects

If you compare two object references with the == operator, you test whether the references refer to the same *object*. Here is an example:

```
Rectangle cerealBox = new Rectangle(5, 10, 20, 30);
Rectangle r = cerealBox;
Rectangle oatmealBox = new Rectangle(5, 10, 20, 30);
```

The comparison

```
cerealBox == r
```

is true. Both object variables refer to the same object. But the comparison

```
cerealBox == oatmealBox
```

is false. The two object variables refer to *different* objects (see Figure 4). It does not matter that the objects have identical contents.

> The == operator tests whether two object references are identical. To compare the contents of objects, you need to use the equals method.

You can use the equals method to test whether two rectangles have the same *contents*, that is, whether they have the same upper left corner and the same width and height. For example, the test

```
cerealBox.equals(oatmealBox)
```

is true.

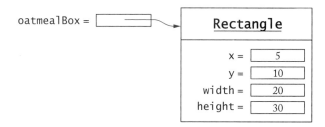

Figure 4

Comparing Object References

However, you must be careful when using the `equals` method. It works correctly only if the implementors of the class have defined it. The `Rectangle` class has an `equals` method that is suitable for comparing rectangles.

For your own classes, you need to supply an appropriate `equals` method. You will learn how to do that in Chapter 9. Until that point, you should not use the `equals` method to compare objects of your own classes.

5.2.5 — Testing for `null`

An object reference can have the special value `null` if it refers to no object at all. You use the `==` operator (and not `equals`) to test whether an object reference is a `null` reference:

```
if (account == null) . . .
    // account is a null reference
```

> The `null` reference refers to no object.

Frequently, methods return `null` if they are not able to return a valid object. For example, the `showInputDialog` method of the `JOptionPane` class returns `null` if the user hits the "Cancel" button of the input dialog.

```
String input = JOptionPane.showInputDialog(
    "How many nickels do you have?");
if (input == null) . . .
    // user canceled dialog
```

Note that the `null` reference is *not the same* as the empty string `""`. The empty string is a valid string of length 0, whereas a `null` indicates that a string variable refers to no string at all. For example, the `showInputDialog` method returns an empty string if the user leaves the input field of an input dialog blank and hits the "Ok" button.

▼ 🎗 Quality Tip   5.2

Avoid Conditions with Side Effects

In Java, it is legal to nest assignment statements inside test conditions:

```
if ((d = b * b - 4 * a * c) >= 0) r = Math.sqrt(d);
```

It is legal to use the decrement operator inside other expressions:

```
if (n-- > 0)  . . .
```

These are bad programming practices, because they mix a test with another activity. The other activity (setting the variable d, decrementing n) is called a *side effect* of the test.

As you will see in Advanced Topic 6.2, conditions with side effects can occasionally be helpful to simplify *loops*. For `if` statements they should always be avoided.

5.3   Multiple Alternatives

5.3.1 — Sequences of Comparisons

Multiple conditions can be combined to evaluate complex decisions. The correct arrangement depends on the logic of the problem to be solved.

The following program asks for a value describing the magnitude of an earthquake on the Richter scale and prints a description of the likely impact of the quake. The Richter scale is a measurement for the strength of an earthquake. Every step in the scale, for example from 6.0 to 7.0, signifies a tenfold increase in the strength of the quake. The 1989 Loma Prieta earthquake that damaged the Bay Bridge in San Francisco and destroyed many buildings in several Bay Area cities registered 7.1 on the Richter scale.

File Earthquake.java

```
1   /**
2       A class that describes the effects of an earthquake.
3   */
4   public class Earthquake
5   {
6       /**
7           Constructs an Earthquake object.
8           @param magnitude the magnitude on the Richter scale
9       */
10      public Earthquake(double magnitude)
11      {
12          richter = magnitude;
13      }
14
15      /**
16          Gets a description of the effect of the earthquake.
17          @return the description of the effect
18      */
19      public String getDescription()
20      {
21          String r;
22          if (richter >= 8.0)
23              r = "Most structures fall";
24          else if (richter >= 7.0)
25              r = "Many buildings destroyed";
26          else if (richter >= 6.0)
27              r = "Many buildings considerably damaged;"
28                  + "some collapse";
29          else if (richter >= 4.5)
30              r = "Damage to poorly constructed buildings";
31          else if (richter >= 3.5)
32              r = "Felt by many people, no destruction";
```

```
33          else if (richter >= 0)
34              r = "Generally not felt by people";
35          else
36              r = "Negative numbers are not valid";
37          return r;
38      }
39
40      private double richter;
41  }
```

File EarthquakeTest.java

```
1  import javax.swing.JOptionPane;
2
3  /**
4      A class to test the Earthquake class.
5  */
6  public class EarthquakeTest
7  {
8      public static void main(String[] args)
9      {
10         String input = JOptionPane.showInputDialog(
11             "Enter a magnitude on the Richter scale:");
12         double magnitude = Double.parseDouble(input);
13         Earthquake quake = new Earthquake(magnitude);
14         System.out.println(quake.getDescription());
15         System.exit(0);
16     }
17 }
```

Here we must sort the conditions and test against the largest cutoff first. Suppose we reverse the order of tests:

```
if (richter >= 0) // Tests in wrong order
    r = "Generally not felt by people";
else if (richter >= 3.5)
    r = "Felt by many people, no destruction";
else if (richter >= 4.5)
    r = "Damage to poorly constructed buildings";
else if (richter >= 6.0)
    r = "Many buildings considerably damaged;"
        + "some collapse";
else if (richter >= 7.0)
    r = "Many buildings destroyed";
else if (richter >= 8.0)
    r = "Most structures fall";
```

This does not work. All positive values of richter fall into the first case, and the other tests will never be attempted.

In this example, it is also important that we use an if/else/else test, not just multiple independent if statements. Consider this sequence of independent tests:

```
if (richter >= 8.0) // Didn't use else
    r = "Most structures fall";
if (richter >= 7.0)
    r = "Many buildings destroyed";
if (richter >= 6.0)
    r = "Many buildings considerably damaged;"
        + "some collapse";
if (richter >= 4.5)
    r = "Damage to poorly constructed buildings";
if (richter >= 3.5)
    r = "Felt by many people, no destruction";
if (richter >= 0)
    r = "Generally not felt by people";
```

Now the alternatives are no longer exclusive. If richter is 6.0, then the last *four* tests all match, and r is set four times.

▼ AT Advanced Topic   5.2 ▶

▼ The switch Statement

A sequence of if/else/else that compares a *single integer value* against several *constant* alternatives can be implemented as a switch statement. For example,

```
int digit;
. . .
switch (digit)
{
    case 1: System.out.print("one"); break;
    case 2: System.out.print("two"); break;
    case 3: System.out.print("three"); break;
    case 4: System.out.print("four"); break;
    case 5: System.out.print("five"); break;
    case 6: System.out.print("six"); break;
    case 7: System.out.print("seven"); break;
    case 8: System.out.print("eight"); break;
    case 9: System.out.print("nine"); break;
    default: System.out.print("error"); break;
}
```

This is a shortcut for

```
int digit;
. . .
if (digit == 1) System.out.print("one");
else if (digit == 2) System.out.print("two");
else if (digit == 3) System.out.print("three");
else if (digit == 4) System.out.print("four");
else if (digit == 5) System.out.print("five");
```

```
else if (digit == 6) System.out.print("six");
else if (digit == 7) System.out.print("seven");
else if (digit == 8) System.out.print("eight");
else if (digit == 9) System.out.print("nine");
else System.out.print("error");
```

Using the `switch` statement has one advantage. It is obvious that all branches test the *same* value, namely `digit`.

The `switch` statement can be applied only in narrow circumstances. The test cases must be constants, and they must be integers or characters. You cannot use a `switch` to branch on floating-point or string values. For example, the following is an error:

```
switch (name)
{
    case "one": ... break; // Error
    ...
}
```

Note how every branch of the switch was terminated by a `break` instruction. If the `break` is missing, execution *falls through* to the next branch, and so on, until finally a `break` or the end of the `switch` is reached. For example, consider the following `switch` statement:

```
switch (digit)
{
    case 1: System.out.print("one"); // oops—no break
    case 2: System.out.print("two"); break;
    . . .
}
```

If `digit` has the value 1, then the statement after the `case 1:` label is executed. Since there is no `break`, the statement after the `case 2:` label is executed as well. The program prints `"onetwo"`.

There are a few cases in which this fall-through behavior is actually useful, but they are very rare. Peter van der Linden [1, p. 38] describes an analysis of the `switch` statements in the Sun C compiler front end. Of the 244 `switch` statements, each of which had an average of 7 cases, only 3 percent used the fall-through behavior. That is, the default—falling through to the next case unless stopped by a `break`—was *wrong 97 percent of the time*. Forgetting to type the `break` is an exceedingly common error, yielding wrong code.

We leave it to you to use the `switch` statement for your own programs or not. At any rate, you need to have a reading knowledge of `switch` in case you find it in the code of other programmers.

Productivity Hint 5.2

Copy and Paste in the Editor

When you see code like

```
if (richter >= 8.0)
    r = "Most structures fall";
else if (richter >= 7.0)
```

```
            r = "Many buildings destroyed";
        else if (richter >= 6.0)
            r = "Many buildings considerably damaged;"
                + "some collapse";
        else if (richter >= 4.5)
            r = "Damage to poorly constructed buildings";
        else if (richter >= 3.5)
            r = "Felt by many people, no destruction";
```

you should think "copy and paste".

Make a template

```
        else if (richter >= )
            r = "";
```

and copy it. That is usually done by highlighting with the mouse and then selecting Edit and then Copy from the menu bar. (If you follow Productivity Hint 3.1, you are smart and use the keyboard. Hit Shift+End to highlight the entire line, then Ctrl+C to copy it. Then paste it (Ctrl+V) multiple times and fill the text into the copy. Of course, your editor may use different commands, but the concept is the same.)

The ability to copy and paste is always useful when you have code from an example or another project that is similar to your current needs. To copy, paste, and modify is faster than to type everything from scratch. You are also less likely to make typing errors.

Random Fact 5.1

Minicomputers and Workstations

Within 20 years after the first computers became operational, they had become indispensable for organizing the customer and financial data of every major corporation in America. Corporate data processing required a centralized computer installation and high staffing levels to ensure the round-the-clock availability of the data. These installations were enormously expensive, but they were vital to running a modern business. Major universities and large research institutions could also afford the installation of these expensive computers, but many scientific and engineering organizations and corporate divisions could not.

In the mid-1960s, when integrated circuits first became available, the cost of computers could be brought down for users who did not require as high a level of support and services (or data storage volume) as corporate data processing installations. Such users included scientists and engineers who had the expertise to operate computers. (At that time, to "operate" a computer did not just mean to turn it on. Computers came with little off-the-shelf software, and most tasks had to be programmed by the computer users.) In 1965 Digital Equipment Corporation introduced the PDP-8 *minicomputer*, housed in a single cabinet (see Figure 5) and thus small enough for departmental use. In 1978, the first 32-bit minicomputer, the VAX, was released, also by DEC. Other companies, such as Data General, brought out competing designs; the book [2] contains a fascinating description of the engineering work at Data General to bring out a machine that could compete with the VAX. Minicomputers were not just used for engineering applications, however. System integration companies would buy these machines, supply software, and resell them to smaller

Figure 5

An Early Minicomputer

companies for business data processing. Minicomputers such as IBM's successful AS/400 line are still in use today, but they face stiff competition from workstations and personal computers, which are much less expensive and have increasingly powerful software.

In the early 1980s, engineering users became increasingly disenchanted with having to share computers with other users. Computers did divide up their attention among multiple users who were currently logged on, a process known as *time sharing*. However, graphical terminals were becoming available, and the fast processing of graphics was more than could be done in the allotted time slices. The technology had again advanced to the point where an entire computer could be put into a box that would fit on a desk. A new breed of manufacturers, such as Sun Microsystems, started producing *workstations* (Figure 6). These computers are used by individuals with high computing demands—for example, electronic-circuit designers, aerospace engineers, and, more recently, cartoon artists. Workstations typically run an operating system called *UNIX*. Although each workstation manufacturer had its own brand of UNIX, with slight differences in each version, it became economical for software manufacturers to produce programs that could run on several hardware platforms. This was aided by the fact that most workstation manufacturers standardized on the *X Window system* for displaying graphics.

Not all workstation manufacturers were successful. The book [3] tells the story of NeXT, a company that tried to build a workstation and failed, losing over $250 million of its investors' money in the process.

Nowadays workstations are used mainly for two distinct purposes: as fast graphics processors and as *servers* to store data such as electronic mail, sales information, or web pages.

Figure 6

A Workstation

5.3.2 — Nested Branches

In the United States, taxpayers pay federal income tax at different rates depending on their incomes and marital status. There are two main tax schedules: one for single taxpayers and one for married taxpayers "filing jointly", meaning that the married taxpayers add their incomes together and pay taxes on the total. (In fact, there are two other schedules, "head of household" and "married filing separately", which we will ignore for simplicity.) Table 1 gives the tax rate computations for each of the filing categories, using the values for the 1992 federal tax return. (We're using the 1992 tax rate schedule in this illustration because of its simplicity. Legislation in 1993 increased the number of rates in each status and added more complicated rules. By the time that you read this, the tax laws may well have become even more complex.)

Now let us compute the taxes due, given a filing status and an income figure. The key point is that there are two *levels* of decision making. First, we must branch on the filing status. Then, for each filing status, we must have another branch on income level.

File TaxReturn.java

```
1  /**
2      A tax return of a taxpayer in 1992.
3  */
4  class TaxReturn
5  {
6      /**
```

If your filing status is Single

If the taxable income is over	But not over	The tax is	Of the amount over
$0	$21,450	15%	$0
$21,450	$51,900	$3,217.50 + 28%	$21,450
$51,900		$11,743.50 + 31%	$51,900

If your filing status is Married filing jointly

If the taxable income is over	But not over	The tax is	Of the amount over
$0	$35,800	15%	$0
$35,800	$86,500	$5,370.00 + 28%	$35,800
$86,500		$19,566.00 + 31%	$86,500

Table 1

Federal Tax Rate Schedule (1992)

```
7           Constructs a TaxReturn  object for a given income and
8           marital status.
9           @param anIncome  the taxpayer income
10          @param aStatus either SINGLE or MARRIED
11       */
12       public TaxReturn(double anIncome, int aStatus)
13       {
14          income = anIncome;
15          status = aStatus;
16       }
17
18       public double getTax()
19       {
20          double tax = 0;
21
22          if (status == SINGLE)
23          {
24             if (income <= SINGLE_CUTOFF1)
25                tax = RATE1 * income;
26             else if (income <= SINGLE_CUTOFF2)
27                tax = SINGLE_BASE2
28                   + RATE2 * (income - SINGLE_CUTOFF1);
29             else
30                tax = SINGLE_BASE3
31                   + RATE3 * (income - SINGLE_CUTOFF2);
32          }
```

```
33          else
34          {
35             if (income <= MARRIED_CUTOFF1)
36                tax = RATE1 * income;
37             else if (income <= MARRIED_CUTOFF2)
38                tax = MARRIED_BASE2
39                   + RATE2 * (income - MARRIED_CUTOFF1);
40             else
41                tax = MARRIED_BASE3
42                   + RATE3 * (income - MARRIED_CUTOFF2);
43          }
44
45          return tax;
46       }
47
48       public static final int SINGLE = 1;
49       public static final int MARRIED = 2;
50
51       private static final double RATE1 = 0.15;
52       private static final double RATE2 = 0.28;
53       private static final double RATE3 = 0.31;
54
55       private static final double SINGLE_CUTOFF1 = 21450;
56       private static final double SINGLE_CUTOFF2 = 51900;
57
58       private static final double SINGLE_BASE2 = 3217.50;
59       private static final double SINGLE_BASE3 = 11743.50;
60       private static final double MARRIED_CUTOFF1 = 35800;
61       private static final double MARRIED_CUTOFF2 = 86500;
62
63       private static final double MARRIED_BASE2 = 5370;
64       private static final double MARRIED_BASE3 = 19566;
65
66       private double income;
67       private int status;
68    }
```

File TaxReturnTest.java

```
1  import javax.swing.JOptionPane;
2
3  /**
4     A class to test the TaxReturn class.
5  */
6  public class TaxReturnTest
7  {
8     public static void main(String[] args)
9     {
10        String input = JOptionPane.showInputDialog(
11           "Please enter your income:");
12        double income = Double.parseDouble(input);
13
```

```
14          input = JOptionPane.showInputDialog(
15             "Please enter S (single) or M (married)");
16          int status = 0;
17
18          if (input.equalsIgnoreCase("S"))
19             status = TaxReturn.SINGLE;
20          else if (input.equalsIgnoreCase("M"))
21             status = TaxReturn.MARRIED;
22          else
23          {
24             System.out.println("Bad input.");
25             System.exit(0);
26          }
27
28          TaxReturn aTaxReturn =
29             new TaxReturn(income, status);
30
31          System.out.println("The tax is "
32             + aTaxReturn.getTax());
33
34          System.exit(0);
35       }
36 }
```

The two-level decision process is reflected in two levels of if statements. We say that the income test is *nested* inside the test for filing status. (See Figure 7 for a flowchart.)

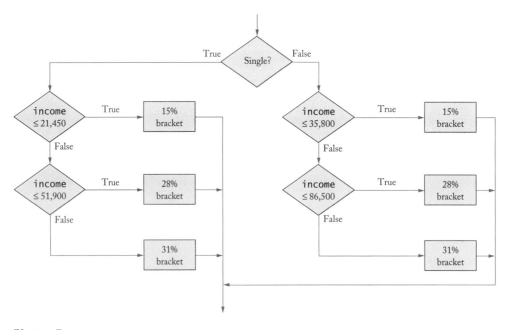

Figure 7

Income Tax Computation Using 1992 Schedule

Quality Tip 5.3

Prepare Test Cases Ahead of Time

Let us consider how we can test the tax computation program. Of course, we cannot try out all possible inputs of filing status and income level. Even if we could, there would be no point in trying them all. If the program correctly computes one or two tax amounts in a given bracket, then we have a good reason to believe that all amounts within that bracket will be correct. We want to aim for complete *coverage* of all cases.

There are two possibilities for the filing status and three tax brackets for each status. That makes six test cases. Then we want to test a handful of *error conditions,* such as a negative income. That makes seven test cases. For the first six, we need to compute manually what answer we expect. For the remaining one, we need to know what error reports we expect. We write down the test cases and then start coding.

Should you really test seven inputs for this simple program? You certainly should. Furthermore, if you find an error in the program that wasn't covered by one of the test cases, make another test case and add it to your collection. After you fix the known mistakes, *run all test cases again.* Experience has shown that the cases that you just tried to fix are probably working now, but that errors that you fixed two or three iterations ago have a good chance of coming back! If you find that an error keeps coming back, that is usually a reliable sign that you did not fully understand some subtle interaction between features of your program.

It is always a good idea to design test cases *before* starting to code. There are two reasons for this. Working through the test cases gives you a better understanding of the algorithm that you are about to program. Furthermore, it has been noted that programmers instinctively shy away from testing fragile parts of their code. That seems hard to believe, but you will often make that observation about your own work. Watch someone else test your program. There will be times when that person enters input that makes you very nervous because you are not sure that your program can handle it, and you never dared to test it yourself. This is a well-known phenomenon, and making the test plan before writing the code offers some protection.

Productivity Hint 5.3

Make a Schedule and Make Time for Unexpected Problems

Commercial software is notorious for being delivered later than promised. For example, Microsoft originally promised that the successor to its Windows 3 operating system would be available early in 1994, then late in 1994, then in March 1995; it finally was released in August 1995. Some of the early promises might not have been realistic. It was in Microsoft's interest to let prospective customers expect the imminent availability of the product. Had customers known the actual delivery date, they might have switched to a different product in the meantime. Undeniably, though, Microsoft had not anticipated the full complexity of the tasks it had set itself to solve.

Microsoft can delay the delivery of its product, but it is likely that you cannot. As a student or a programmer, you are expected to manage your time wisely and to finish your assignments on time. You can probably do simple programming exercises the night before the due date, but an assignment that looks twice as hard may well take four times as long, because more things can go wrong. You should therefore make a schedule whenever you start a programming project.

First, estimate realistically how much time it will take you to

- Design the program logic

- Develop test cases

- Type the program in and fix syntax errors

- Test and debug the program

For example, for the income tax program I might estimate 30 minutes for the design, because it is mostly done; 30 minutes for developing test cases; one hour for data entry and fixing syntax errors; and 2 hours for testing and debugging. That is a total of 4 hours. If I work 2 hours a day on this project, it will take me two days.

Then think of things that can go wrong. Your computer might break down. The lab might be crowded. You might be stumped by a problem with the computer system. (That is a particularly important concern for beginners. It is *very* common to lose a day over a trivial problem just because it takes time to track down a person who knows the "magic" command to overcome it.) As a rule of thumb, *double* the time of your estimate. That is, you should start four days, not two days, before the due date. If nothing goes wrong, great; you have the program done two days early. When the inevitable problem occurs, you have a cushion of time that protects you from embarrassment and failure.

⊗ Common Error   5.2

The Dangling else Problem

When an if statement is nested inside another if statement, the following error may occur.

```
if (richter >= 0)
    if (richter <= 4)
        System.out.println("The earthquake is harmless");
else // Pitfall!
    System.out.println("Negative value not allowed");
```

The indentation level seems to suggest that the `else` is grouped with the test `richter >= 0`. Unfortunately, that is not the case. The compiler ignores all indentation and follows the rule that an `else` always belongs to the closest `if`. That is, the code is actually

```
if (richter >= 0)
    if (richter <= 4)
        System.out.println("The earthquake is harmless");
    else // Pitfall!
        System.out.println("Negative value not allowed");
```

That isn't what we want. We want to group the `else` with the first `if`. For that, we must use braces.

```
if (richter >= 0)
{
    if (richter <= 4)
        System.out.println("The earthquake is harmless");
}
else
    System.out.println("Negative value not allowed");
```

To avoid having to think about the pairing of the `else`, we recommend that you *always* use a set of braces when the body of an `if` contains another `if`. In the following example, the braces are not strictly necessary, but they help clarify the code:

```
if (richter >= 0)
{
    if (richter <= 4)
        System.out.println("The earthquake is harmless");
    else
        System.out.println("Damage may occur");
}
```

The ambiguous `else` is called a *dangling* `else`, and it is enough of a syntactical blemish that some programming language designers developed an improved syntax that avoids it altogether. For example, Algol 68 uses the construction

if *condition* then *statement* else *statement* fi;

The `else` part is optional, but since the end of the `if` statement is clearly marked, the grouping is unambiguous if there are two `if`s and only one `else`. Here are the two possible cases:

if *c1* then if *c2* then *s1* else *s2* fi fi;

if *c1* then if *c2* then *s1* fi else *s2* fi;

By the way, `fi` is just `if` backwards. Other languages use `endif`, which has the same purpose but is less fun.

5.4 Using Boolean Expressions

5.4.1 — The boolean Type

> The boolean type has two values: true and false.

In Java, an expression such as amount < 1000 has a value, just as the expression amount + 1000 has a value. The value of a relational expression is either true or false. For example, if amount is 500, then the value of amount < 1000 is true. Try it out: The program fragment

```
double amount = 0;
System.out.println(amount < 1000);
```

prints true. The values true and false are not numbers, nor are they objects of a class. They belong to a separate type, called boolean. The Boolean type is named after the mathematician George Boole (1815–1864), a pioneer in the study of logic.

5.4.2 — Predicate Methods

> A predicate method returns a Boolean value.

A *predicate method* is a method that returns a boolean value. Here is an example of a predicate method:

```
public class BankAccount
{
```

```
public boolean isOverdrawn()
{
   return balance < 0;
}
}
```

You can use the return value of the method as the condition of an `if` statement:

```
if (harrysChecking.isOverdrawn()) . . .
```

There are several useful static predicate methods in the `Character` class:

```
isDigit
isLetter
isUpperCase
isLowerCase
```

that let you test whether a character is a digit, a letter, an uppercase letter, or a lowercase letter:

```
if (Character.isUpperCase(ch)) . . .
```

It is a common convention to give a prefix "`is`" to the name of a predicate method.

5.4.3 — The Boolean Operators

> You can form complex tests with the Boolean operators && (and), || (or) and ! (not).

Suppose you want to find whether `amount` is between 0 and 1000. Then two conditions have to be true: `amount` must be greater than 0, *and* it must be less than 1000. In Java you use the `&&` operator to represent the *and* to combine test conditions. That is, you can write the test as follows:

```
if (0 < amount && amount < 1000) . . .
```

The `&&` operator combines several tests into a new test that passes only when all conditions are true. An operator that combines test conditions is called a *logical* operator.

The `||` (*or*) logical operator also combines two or more conditions. The resulting test succeeds if at least one of the conditions is true. For example, here is a test to check whether the string `input` is a "S" or "M":

```
if (input.equals("S") || input.equals("M")) . . .
```

Figure 8 shows flowcharts for these examples.

Sometimes you need to *invert* a condition with the `!` (*not*) logical operator. For example, we may want to carry out a certain action only if two strings are *not* equal:

```
if (!input.equals("S")) . . .
```

The `!` operator takes a single condition and evaluates to `true` if that condition is false and to `false` if the condition is true.

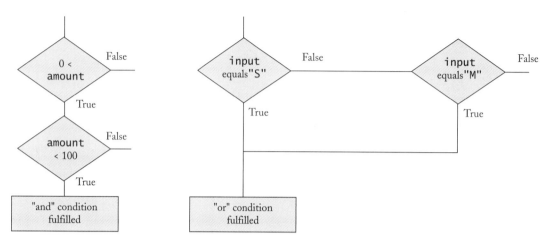

Figure 8

Flowcharts for && and || Combinations

Here is a summary of the three logical operations:

A	B	A && B
true	true	true
true	false	false
false	*Any*	false

A	B	A || B
true	*Any*	true
false	true	true
false	false	false

A	!A
true	false
false	true

⊗ Common Error 5.3

Multiple Relational Operators

Consider the expression

```
if (0 < amount < 1000) ... // Error
```

This looks just like the mathematical notation for "amount is between 0 and 1000". But in Java, it is a syntax error.

Let us dissect the condition. The first half, 0 < amount, is a test with outcome true or false. The outcome of that test (true or false) is then compared against 1000. This seems to make no sense. Can one compare truth values and numbers? Is true larger than 1000 or not? In Java, you cannot. The Java compiler rejects this statement.

Instead, use **&&** to combine two separate tests:

```
if (0 < amount && amount < 1000) ...
```

Another common error, along the same lines, is to write

```
if (ch == 'S' || 'M') ... // Error
```

to test whether ch is 'S' or 'M'. Again, the Java compiler flags this construct as an error. You cannot apply the || operator to characters. You need to write two Boolean expressions and join them with the || operator:

```
if (ch == 'S' || ch == 'M') ...
```

⊗ Common Error 5.4

Confusing && and || Conditions

It is a surprisingly common error to confuse *and* and *or* conditions. A value lies between 0 and 100 if it is at least 0 *and* at most 100. It lies outside that range if it is less than 0 *or* greater than 100. There is no golden rule; you just have to think carefully.

Often the *and* or *or* is clearly stated, and then it isn't too hard to implement it. Sometimes, though, the wording isn't as explicit. It is quite common that the individual conditions are nicely set apart in a bulleted list, but with little indication how they should be combined. The instructions for the 1992 tax return say that you can claim single filing status if any one of the following is true:

- You were never married.

- You were legally separated or divorced on December 31, 1992.

- You were widowed before January 1, 1992, and did not remarry in 1992.

Since the test passes if *any one* of the conditions is true, you must combine the conditions with *or*. Elsewhere, the same instructions state that you may use the more advantageous status of married filing jointly if all five of the following conditions are true:

▼
- Your spouse died in 1990 or 1991 and you did not remarry in 1992.

- You have a child whom you can claim as dependent.

▼
- That child lived in your home for all of 1992.

- You paid over half the cost of keeping up your home for this child.

▼
- You filed (or could have filed) a joint return with your spouse the year he or she died.

Because *all* of the conditions must be true for the test to pass, you must combine them

▼
with an *and*.

▼ **AT** **Advanced Topic** **5.3**

Lazy Evaluation of Boolean Operators

▼
The **&&** and **||** operators in Java are computed using *lazy* (or *short circuit*) evaluation. In other words, logical expressions are evaluated from left to right, and evaluation stops as soon as the truth value is determined. When an *and* is evaluated and the first condition is

▼
false, then the second condition is skipped—no matter what it is, the combined condition must be false. When an *or* is evaluated and the first condition is true, the second condition

▼
is not evaluated, because it does not matter what the outcome of the second test is. Here is an example:

```
if (input != null && Integer.parseInt(input) > 0) . . .
```

▼
If `input` is `null`, then the first condition is false, and thus the combined statement is false, no matter what the outcome of the second test is. The second test is never evaluated if `input` is `null`, and there is no danger of parsing a `null` string (which would

▼
cause an exception).

If you do need to evaluate both conditions, then use the **&** and **|** operators. When evaluated with Boolean arguments, these operators always evaluate both arguments.

▼

5.4.4 — De Morgan's Law

> De Morgan's law shows how to simplify expressions in which a ! operator is applied to terms joined by the && or || operator.

In the preceding section, we programmed a test to see whether `amount` was between 0 and 1000. Let's find out whether the opposite is true:

```
if (!(0 < amount && amount < 1000)) . . .
```

This test is a little bit complicated, and you have to think carefully through the logic. "When it is *not* true that 0 < `amount` and `amount` < 1000 . . ." Huh? It is not true that some people won't be confused by this code.

The computer doesn't care, but humans generally have a hard time comprehending logical conditions with *not* operators applied to *and/or* expressions. De Morgan's law, named after the logician Augustus de Morgan (1806–1871), can be used to simplify these Boolean expressions. De Morgan's law has two forms: one for the negation of an *and* expression and one for the negation of an *or* expression:

`!(A && B)` is the same as `!A || !B`

`!(A || B)` is the same as `!A && !B`

Pay particular attention to the fact that the *and* and *or* operators are *reversed* by moving the *not* inwards. For example, the negation of "the input is S or the input is M",

```
!(input.equals("S") || input.equals("M"))
```

is "the input is not S *and* the input is not M":

```
!input.equals("S") && !input.equals("M")
```

Let us apply the law to the negation of "the amount is between 0 and 1000":

```
!(0 < amount && amount < 1000)
```

is equivalent to

```
!(0 < amount) || !(amount < 1000)
```

which can be further simplified to

```
0 >= amount || amount >= 1000
```

Note that the opposite of `<` is `>=`, not `>`!

5.4.5 — Using Boolean Variables

> You can store the outcome of a condition in a Boolean variable.

You can use a Boolean variable if you know that there are only two possible values. Have another look at the tax program in Section 5.3.2. The marital status is either single or married. Instead of using an integer, you can use a variable of type `boolean`:

```
private boolean married;
```

The advantage is that you can't accidentally store a third value in the variable.

Then you can use the Boolean variable in a test:

```
if (married)
    . . .
else
    . . .
```

Sometimes Boolean variables are called *flags* because they can have just two states: "up" and "down".

It pays to think carefully about the naming of Boolean variables. In our example, it would not be a good idea to give the name `maritalStatus` to the Boolean variable.

What does it mean that the marital status is `true`? With a name like `married` there is no ambiguity; if `married` is `true`, the taxpayer is married.

By the way, it is considered gauche to write a test such as

```
if (married == true) ... // Don't
```

Just use the simpler test

```
if (married) ...
```

In Chapter 6 we will use Boolean variables to control complex loops.

Random Fact   **5.2**

Artificial Intelligence

When one uses a sophisticated computer program such as a tax preparation package, one is bound to attribute some intelligence to the computer. The computer asks sensible questions and makes computations that we find a mental challenge. After all, if doing our taxes were easy, we wouldn't need a computer to do it for us.

As programmers, however, we know that all this apparent intelligence is an illusion. Human programmers have carefully "coached" the software in all possible scenarios, and it simply replays the actions and decisions that were programmed into it.

Would it be possible to write computer programs that are genuinely intelligent in some sense? From the earliest days of computing, there was a sense that the human brain might be nothing but an immense computer, and that it might well be feasible to program computers to imitate some processes of human thought. Serious research into *artificial intelligence* (*AI*) began in the mid-1950s, and the first twenty years brought some impressive successes. Programs that play chess—surely an activity that appears to require remarkable intellectual powers—have become so good that they now routinely beat all but the best human players. In 1975 an *expert-system* program called Mycin gained fame for being better in diagnosing meningitis in patients than the average physician. *Theorem-proving* programs produced logically correct mathematical proofs. *Optical character recognition* software can read pages from a scanner, recognize the character shapes (including those that are blurred or smudged), and reconstruct the original document text, even restoring fonts and layout.

However, there were serious setbacks as well. From the very outset, one of the stated goals of the AI community was to produce software that could translate text from one language to another, for example from English to Russian. That undertaking proved to be enormously complicated. Human language appears to be much more subtle and interwoven with the human experience than had originally been thought. Even the grammar-checking programs that come with many word processors today are more a gimmick than a useful tool, and analyzing grammar is just the first step in translating sentences.

From 1982 to 1992, the Japanese government embarked on a massive research project, funded at over 50 billion Japanese yen. It was known as the *Fifth-Generation Project*. Its goal was to develop new hard- and software to greatly improve the performance of expert systems. At its outset, the project created great fear in other countries that the Japanese computer industry was about to become the undisputed leader in the field. However, the end results were disappointing and did little to bring artificial intelligence applications to market.

One reason that artificial intelligence programs have not performed as well as it was hoped seems to be that they simply don't know as much as humans do. In the early 1990s, Douglas Lenat and his colleagues decided to do something about it and initiated the CYC project (from en*cyc*lopedia), an effort to codify the implicit assumptions that underly human speech and writing. The team members started out analyzing news articles and asked themselves what unmentioned facts are necessary to actually understand the sentences. For example, consider the sentence "Last fall she enrolled in Michigan State." The reader automatically realizes that "fall" is not related to falling down in this context, but refers to the season. While there is a State of Michigan, here Michigan State denotes the university. A priori, a computer program has none of this knowledge. The goal of the CYC project was to extract and store the requisite facts—that is, (1) people enroll in universities; (2) Michigan is a state; (3) a state X is likely to have a university named X State University, often abbreviated as X State; (4) most people enroll in a university in the fall. In 1995, the project had codified about 100,000 common-sense concepts and about a million facts of knowledge relating them. Even this massive amount of data has not proven sufficient for useful applications.

Successful artificial intelligence programs, such as chess-playing programs, do not actually imitate human thinking. They are just very fast in exploring many scenarios and have been tuned to recognize those cases that do not warrant further investigation. *Neural networks* are interesting exceptions: coarse simulations of the neuron cells in animal and human brains. Suitably interconnected cells appear to be able to "learn". For example, if a network of cells is presented with letter shapes, it can be trained to identify them. After a lengthy training period, the network can recognize letters, even if they are slanted, distorted, or smudged.

When artificial intelligence programs are successful, they can raise serious ethical issues. There are now programs that can scan résumés, select those that look promising, and show only those to a human for further analysis. How would you feel if you knew that your résumé had been rejected by a computer, perhaps on a technicality, and that you never had a chance to be interviewed? When computers are used for credit analysis, and the analysis software has been designed to deny credit systematically to certain groups of people (say, all applicants with certain ZIP codes), is that illegal discrimination? What if the software has not been designed in this fashion, but a neural network has "discovered" a pattern from historical data? These are troubling questions, especially because those that are harmed by such processes have little recourse.

CHAPTER SUMMARY

1. The `if` statement lets a program carry out different actions depending on the outcome of a condition.

2. A block statement groups together several statements.

3. Relational operators compare values. The == operator tests for equality.

4. When comparing floating-point numbers, don't test for equality. Instead, check whether they are *close enough*.

5. Do not use the == operator to compare strings. Use the `equals` method instead.

6. The `compareTo` method compares strings in dictionary order.

7. The == operator tests whether two object references are identical. To compare the contents of objects, you need to use the `equals` method.

8. The `null` reference refers to no object.

9. Multiple conditions can be combined to evaluate complex decisions. The correct arrangement depends on the logic of the problem to be solved.

10. The `boolean` type has two values: `true` and `false`.

11. A predicate method returns a Boolean value.

12. You can form complex tests with the Boolean operators **&&** (and), **| |** (or), and **!** (not).

13. De Morgan's law shows how to simplify expressions in which a **!** operator is applied to terms joined by the **&&** or **| |** operator.

14. You can store the outcome of a condition in a Boolean variable.

Further Reading

[1] Peter van der Linden, *Expert C Programming*, Prentice-Hall, 1994.
[2] Tracy Kidder, *The Soul of a New Machine*, Little, Brown and Co., 1981.
[3] Randall E. Stross, *Steven Jobs and the NeXT Big Thing*, Atheneum, 1993.
[4] William H. Press et al., *Numerical Recipes in C*, Cambridge, 1988.

CLASSES, OBJECTS, AND METHODS INTRODUCED IN THIS CHAPTER

```
java.lang.Character
    isDigit
    isLetter
    isUpperCase
    isLowerCase
java.lang.Object
    equals
java.lang.String
    equalsIgnoreCase
    compareTo
```

REVIEW EXERCISES

Exercise R5.1. Find the errors in the following `if` statements.

- `if quarters > 0 then System.out.println(quarters + " quarters");`
- `if (1 + x > Math.pow(x, Math.sqrt(2)) y = y + x;`
- `if (x = 1) y++; else if (x = 2) y = y + 2;`
- `if (x && y == 0) { x = 1; y = 1; }`
- ```
  if (1 <= x <= 10)
     System.out.println(x);
  ```
- ```
  if (s != "nickels" || s != "pennies"
     || s != "dimes" || s != "quarters")
     System.out.print("Input error!");
  ```
- ```
  if (input.equalsIgnoreCase("N") || "NO")
     return;
  ```
- ```
  int x = Integer.parseInt(input);
  if (x != null) y = y + x;
  ```
- ```
  language = "English";
  if (country.equals("US"))
     if (state.equals("PR")) language = "Spanish";
  else if (country.equals("China"))
     language = "Chinese";
  ```

Exercise R5.2. Explain the following terms, and give an example for each construct:

- Expression
- Condition
- Statement
- Simple statement
- Compound statement
- Block

Exercise R5.3. Explain the difference between an `if/else /else` statement and nested `if` statements. Give an example for each.

Exercise R5.4. Give an example for an `if/else /else` statement where the order of the tests does not matter. Give an example where the order of the tests matters.

Exercise R5.5. Of the following pairs of strings, which comes first in lexicographic order?

- `"Tom"`, `"Dick"`
- `"Tom"`, `"Tomato"`
- `"church"`, `"Churchill"`
- `"car manufacturer"`, `"carburetor"`
- `"Harry"`, `"hairy"`
- `"C++"`, `" Car"`
  ```

- "Tom", "Tom"
- "Car", "Carl"
- "car", "bar"

Exercise R5.6. Complete the following truth table by finding the truth values of the Boolean expressions for all combinations of the Boolean inputs p, q, and r.

p	q	r	(p && q) || !r	!(p && (q || !r))
false	false	false		
false	false	true		
false	true	false		
...				
5 more combinations				
...				

Exercise R5.7. Before you implement any complex algorithm, it is a good idea to understand and analyze it. The purpose of this exercise is to gain a better understanding of the tax computation algorithm of Section 5.3.2.

Some people object to the fact that the tax rates increase with higher incomes, claiming that certain taxpayers are then better off *not* to work hard and get a raise, since they would then have to pay a higher tax rate and actually end up with less money after taxes. Can you find such an income level, and if not, why not?

Another feature of the tax code is the *marriage penalty*. Under certain circumstances, a married couple pays higher taxes than the sum of what the two partners would pay if they both were single. Find examples for such income levels.

Exercise R5.8. True or false? *A* && *B* is the same as *B* && *A* for any Boolean conditions *A* and *B*.

Exercise R5.9. Explain the difference between

```
s = 0;
if (x > 0) s++;
if (y > 0) s++;
```

and

```
s = 0;
if (x > 0) s++;
else if (y > 0) s++;
```

Exercise R5.10. Use De Morgan's law to simplify the following Boolean expressions.

- !(x > 0 && y > 0)
- !(x != 0 || y != 0)

- `!(country.equals("US") && !state.equals("HI")`
  `&& !state.equals("AK"))`

- `!(x % 4 != 0 || !(x % 100 == 0 && x % 400 == 0))`

Exercise R5.11. Make up another Java code example that shows the dangling-`else` problem, using the following statement. A student with a GPA of at least 1.5, but less than 2, is on probation. With less than 1.5, the student is failing.

Exercise R5.12. Explain the difference between the `==` operator and the `equals` method when comparing strings.

Exercise R5.13. Explain the difference between the tests

```
r == s
```
and
```
r.equals(s)
```
where both `r` and `s` are of type `Rectangle`.

Exercise R5.14. What is wrong with this test to see whether `r` is `null`? What happens when this code runs?

```
Rectangle r;
. . .
if (r.equals(null))
   r = new Rectangle(5, 10, 20, 30);
```

Exercise R5.15. Explain how the lexicographic ordering of strings differs from the ordering of words in a dictionary or telephone book. *Hint:* Consider strings like IBM, `wiley.com`, Century 21, While-U-Wait, 7-11.

Exercise R5.16. Write Java code to test whether two objects of type `Line2D.Double` represent the same line when displayed on the graphics screen. *Do not* use `a.equals(b)`.

```
Line2D.Double a;
Line2D.Double b;

if (your condition goes here)
   g2.drawString("They look the same!", x, y);
```
Hint: If p and q are points, then `Line2D.Double(p, q)` and `Line2D.Double(q, p)` look the same.

Exercise R5.17. Explain why it is more difficult to compare floating-point numbers than integers. Write Java code to test whether an integer `n` equals 10 and whether a floating-point number `x` equals 10.

Exercise R5.18. Give an example for two floating-point numbers `x` and `y` such that `Math.abs(x - y)` is larger than 1000, but `x` and `y` are still identical except for a round-off error.

Exercise R5.19. Give a set of test cases for the tax program in Section 5.3.2. Compute the expected results manually.

Exercise R5.20. Consider the following test to see whether a point falls inside a rectangle.

```
Point2D.Double p = . . .
Rectangle2D.Double r = . . .
boolean xInside = false;
if (r.getX() <= p.getX() &&
      p.getX() <= r.getX() + r.getWidth())
   xInside = true;
boolean yInside = false;
if (r.getY() <= p.getY() && p.getY() <= r.getY())
   yInside = true;
if (xInside && yInside)
   g2.drawString("p is inside the rectangle.",
      p.getX(), p.getY());
```

Rewrite this code to eliminate the explicit `true` and `false` values, by setting `xInside` and `yInside` to the values of Boolean expressions.

PROGRAMMING EXERCISES

Exercise P5.1. Write a program that prints all real solutions to the quadratic equation $ax^2 + bx + c = 0$. Read in a, b, c and use the quadratic formula. If the *discriminant* $b^2 - 4ac$ is negative, display a message stating that there are no real solutions.

Implement a class `QuadraticEquation` whose constructor receives the coefficients a, b, c of the quadratic equation. Supply methods `getSolution1` and `getSolution2` that get the solutions, using the quadratic formula. Supply a method

```
boolean hasSolutions()
```

that returns `false` if the discriminant is negative.

Exercise P5.2. Write a program that takes user input describing a playing card in the following shorthand notation:

Notation	Meaning
A	Ace
2...10	Card values
J	Jack
Q	Queen
K	King
D	Diamonds
H	Hearts
S	Spades
C	Clubs

Your program should print the full description of the card. For example,

```
Enter the card notation:
QS
Queen of spades
```

Implement a class `Card` whose constructor takes the card letters and whose `get-Description` method returns a description of the card.

Exercise P5.3. As in the `IntersectionApplet` program of Chapter 4, compute and plot the intersection of a line and a circle. However, if the line and the circle do not intersect, do not plot the intersection points but display a message instead.

Exercise P5.4. Write a program that reads in three floating-point numbers and prints the three inputs in sorted order. For example:

```
Please enter three numbers:
4
9
2.5
The inputs in sorted order are
2.5
4
9
```

Exercise P5.5. Write a program that draws a circle with radius 100 and center (110, 120). Ask the user to specify the x- and y-coordinates of a point. If the point lies inside the circle, then show a message "Congratulations." Otherwise, show a message "You missed." In your excercise, define a class `Circle` and a method `boolean isInside( Point2D.Double p)`.

Exercise P5.6. Write a graphics program that asks the user to specify the radii of two circles. The first circle has center (100, 200), and the second circle has center (200, 100). Draw the circles. If they intersect, then display a message "Circles intersect." Otherwise, display "Circles don't intersect." *Hint:* Compute the distance between the centers and compare it to the radii. Your program should draw nothing if the user enters a negative radius. In your excercise, define a class `Circle` and a method `boolean intersects( Circle other)`.

Exercise P5.7. Write a program that prints the question "Do you want to continue?" and reads a user input. If the user input is "Y", "Yes", "OK", "Sure", or "Why not?", print out "OK". If the user input is "N" or "No", then print out "Terminating." Otherwise, print "Bad input." The case of the user input should not matter. For example, "y" or "yes" are also valid inputs. Write a class `InputChecker` for this purpose.

Exercise P5.8. Write a program that translates a letter grade into a number grade. Letter grades are A B C D F, possibly followed by + or -. Their numeric values are 4, 3, 2, 1, and 0. There is no F+ or F-. A + increases the numeric value by 0.3, a - decreases it by 0.3. However, an A+ has value 4.0.

```
Enter a letter grade:
B-
The numeric value is 2.7.
```

Use a class Grade with a method getNumericGrade.

Exercise P5.9. Write a program that translates a number between 0 and 4 into the closest letter grade. For example, the number 2.8 (which might have been the average of several grades) would be converted to B-. Break ties in favor of the better grade; for example, 2.85 should be a B.

Use a class Grade with a method getLetterGrade.

Exercise P5.10. Write a program that reads in four strings and prints the lexicographically smallest and largest one:

```
Enter four strings:
Charlie
Able
Delta
Baker
The lexicographic minimum is Able
The lexicographic maximum is Delta
```

Hint: Use a class that keeps track of the current maximum and minimum.

Exercise P5.11. If you look at the tax tables in Section 5.3.2, you will note that the percentages 15%, 28%, and 31% are identical for both single and married taxpayers, but the cutoffs for the tax brackets are different. Married people get to pay 15% on their first $35,800, then pay 28% on the next $50,700, and 31% on the remainder. Single people pay 15% on their first $21,450, then pay 28% on the next $30,450, and 31% of the remainder. Write a TaxReturn class with the following logic. Set variables cutoff1 and cutoff2 that depend on the marital status. Then have a single formula that computes the tax, depending on the incomes and the cutoffs. Verify that your results are identical to that of the TaxReturn class in this chapter.

Exercise P5.12. A year with 366 days is called a leap year. A year is a leap year if it is divisible by 4 (for example, 1980). However, since the introduction of the Gregorian calendar on October 15, 1582, a year is not a leap year if it is divisible by 100 (for example, 1900); however, it is a leap year if it is divisible by 400 (for example, 2000). Write a program that asks the user for a year and computes whether that year is a leap year. Implement a class Year with a predicate method boolean isLeapYear().

Exercise P5.13. Write a program that asks the user to enter a month (1 = January, 2 = February, and so on) and then prints the number of days of the month. For February, print "28 days".

```
Enter a month:
5
31 days
```

Implement a class Month with a method int getDays().

Exercise P5.14. Write a program that reads in two floating-point numbers and tests whether they are the same when rounded to two decimal places. Here are two sample runs.

```
Enter two floating-point numbers:
2.0
1.99998
They are the same when rounded to two decimal places.
```

```
Enter two floating-point numbers:
2.0
1.98999
They are different.
```

Exercise P5.15. Enhance the `BankAccount` class of Chapter 2 by

- Rejecting negative amounts in the `deposit` and `withdraw` methods
- Rejecting withdrawals that would result in a negative balance

Exercise P5.16. Write a program that reads in the name and hourly wage of an employee. Then ask how many hours the employee worked in the past week. Be sure to accept fractional hours. Compute the pay. Any overtime work (over 40 hours per week) is paid at 150 percent of the regular wage. Solve this problem by implementing a class `Paycheck`.

Exercise P5.17. Write a unit conversion program using the conversion factors of Appendix A7. Ask the users the unit from which they want to convert and the unit to which they want to convert. Legal units are in, ft, mi, mm, cm, m, km. *Hint:* Define objects of a class `UnitConverter` that convert from and to meters.

```
Convert from?
in
Convert to?
mm
Value?
10
10 in = 254 mm
```

Exercise P5.18. Implement a *combination lock* class. A combination lock has a dial with 26 positions labeled A . . . Z. The dial needs to be set three times. If it is set to the correct combination, the lock can be opened. When the lock is closed again, the combination can be entered again. If a user sets the dial more than three times, the last three settings determine whether the lock can be opened. Support the following interface:

```java
public class CombinationLock
{
    /**
        Constructs a lock with a given combination.
        @param aCombination the combination; a string
        with three uppercase letters A . . . Z
```

```
    */
    public CombinationLock(String aCombination) { . . . }

    /**
        Set the dial to a position.
        @param aPosition a string consisting of a single uppercase
        letter A . . . Z
    */
    void setPosition(String aPosition) { . . . }

    /**
        Try unlocking the lock.
    */
    void unlock() { . . . }

    /**
        Check whether the lock is unlocked.
        @return true if the lock is currently open.
    */
    boolean isOpen() { . . . }

    /**
        Close the lock.
    */
    void lock() { . . . }
}
```

Chapter 6

Iteration

CHAPTER GOALS

To be able to program loops with the while, for, and do statements

▶ To avoid infinite loops and off-by-one errors

▶ To understand nested loops

▶ To learn how to process input

▶ To implement simulations

CHAPTER CONTENTS

6.1   while Loops

In this chapter you will learn how to write programs that repeatedly execute one or more statements. We will illustrate these concepts by looking at typical investment situations. Consider a bank account with an initial balance of $10,000 that earns 5% interest. The interest is computed at the end of every year on the current balance and then deposited into the bank account. For example, after the first year, you earned $500 (5% of $10,000). The interest gets added to your bank account. Next year, the interest is $525 (5% of $10,500), and your balance is $11,025. Table 1 shows how the balance grows in the first five years:

Year	Balance
0	$10,000.00
1	$10,500.00
2	$11,025.00
3	$11,576.25
4	$12,155.06
5	$12,762.82

Table 1

Growth of an Investment

> A while statement executes a block of code repeatedly. A termination condition controls how often the loop is executed.

How many years does it take for the balance to reach $20,000? Of course, it won't take longer than 20 years, because at least $500 is added to the bank account each year. But it may take less than 20 years, because interest is computed on increasingly larger balances.

In Java, the while statement implements such a repetition. The code

```
while (condition)
      statement
```

keeps executing the statement while the condition is true. Most commonly, the statement is a block statement, that is, a set of statements delimited by { ... }.

In our case, we want to know when the bank account has reached a particular balance. While the balance is less, we keep adding interest and incrementing the year counter:

```
while (balance < targetBalance)
{
   years++;
   double interest = balance * rate / 100;
   balance = balance + interest;
}
```

Here is the program that solves our investment problem:

File Investment.java

```
 1  /**
 2      A class to monitor the growth of an investment that
 3      accumulates interest at a fixed annual rate.
 4  */
 5  public class Investment
 6  {
 7      /**
 8          Constructs an Investment object from a starting balance and
 9          interest rate.
10          @param aBalance the starting balance
11          @param aRate the interest rate in percent
12      */
13      public Investment(double aBalance, double aRate)
14      {
15          balance = aBalance;
16          rate = aRate;
17          years = 0;
18      }
19
20      /**
21          Keeps accumulating interest until a target balance has
22          been reached.
23          @param targetBalance the desired balance
24      */
25      public void waitForBalance(double targetBalance)
26      {
27          while (balance < targetBalance)
28          {
29              years++;
30              double interest = balance * rate / 100;
31              balance = balance + interest;
32          }
33      }
34
35      /**
36          Gets the current investment balance.
37          @return the current balance
38      */
39      public double getBalance()
40      {
41          return balance;
42      }
43
44      /**
45          Gets the number of years this investment has accumulated
46          interest.
47          @return the number of years since the start of the investment
```

```
48      */
49      public int getYears()
50      {
51          return years;
52      }
53
54      private double balance;
55      private double rate;
56      private int years;
57  }
```

File InvestmentTest.java

```
1   /**
2       This program computes how long it takes for an investment
3       to double.
4   */
5   public class InvestmentTest
6   {
7       public static void main(String[] args)
8       {
9           final double INITIAL_BALANCE = 10000;
10          final double RATE = 5;
11          Investment invest =
12              new Investment(INITIAL_BALANCE, RATE);
13          invest.waitForBalance(2 * INITIAL_BALANCE);
14          int years = invest.getYears();
15          System.out.println("The investment doubled after "
16              + years + " years");
17      }
18  }
```

A `while` statement is often called a *loop*. If you draw a flowchart, you will see that the control loops backward to the test after every iteration (see Figure 1).

The following loop,

```
while (true)
{
    body
}
```

executes the *body* over and over, without ever terminating. Whoa! Why would you want that? The program would never stop. There are two reasons. Some programs indeed never stop; the software controlling an automated teller machine, a telephone switch, or a microwave oven doesn't ever stop (at least not until the device is turned off). Our programs aren't usually of that kind, but even if you can't terminate the loop, you can exit from the method that contains it. This can be helpful when the termination test naturally falls into the middle of the loop (see Advanced Topic 6.5).

Figure 1

Flowchart of a while Loop

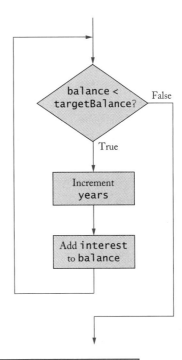

Syntax 6.1: The while **Statement**

while (*condition*)
   statement

Example:

```
while (balance < targetBalance)
{
    years++;
    double interest = balance * rate / 100;
    balance = balance + interest;
}
```

Purpose:

To execute a statement while a condition is true

▼ ⊗ **Common Error**   **6.1** ▶

Infinite Loops

▼

The most annoying loop error is an infinite loop: a loop that runs forever and can be stopped only by killing the program or restarting the computer. If there are output state-ments in the loop, then reams and reams of output flash by on the screen. Otherwise, the

▼

program just sits there and *hangs*, seeming to do nothing. On some systems you can kill a

▼ hanging program by hitting Ctrl+Break or Ctrl+C. On others, you can close the window in which the program runs.

▼ A common reason for infinite loops is forgetting to advance the variable that controls the loop:

```
int years = 0;
while (years < 20)
{
   double interest = balance * rate / 100;
   balance = balance + interest;
}
```

Here the programmer forgot to add a years++ command in the loop. As a result, the value of years always stays 0, and the loop never comes to an end.

▼ Another common reason for an infinite loop is accidentally incrementing a counter that should be decremented (or vice versa). Consider this example:

```
int years = 20;
while (years > 0)
{
   years++; // Oops, should have been years--
   double interest = balance * rate / 100;
   balance = balance + interest;
}
```

▼ The years variable really should have been decremented, not incremented. This is a common error, because incrementing counters is so much more common than decrementing that your fingers may type the ++ on autopilot. As a consequence, years is always larger ▼ than 0, and the loop never terminates. (Actually, eventually years will exceed the largest representable positive integer and *wrap around* to a negative number. Then the loop exits— of course, that takes a long time, and the result is completely wrong.)

▼ ⊗ **Common Error**   **6.2** ▶

Off-by-1 Errors

▼ Consider our computation of the number of years that are required to double an investment:

```
int years = 0;
while (balance < 2 * initialBalance)
{
   years++;
   double interest = balance * rate / 100;
   balance = balance + interest;
}
System.out.println(
   "The investment reached the target after "
   + years + " years.");
```

Should years start at 0 or at 1? Should you test for balance < 2 * initialBalance or for balance <= 2 * initialBalance? It is easy to be *off by 1* in these expressions.

> An off-by-one error is a common error when programming loops. Think through simple test cases to avoid this type of error.

Some people try to solve off-by-1 errors by randomly inserting + 1 or – 1 until the program seems to work. That is, of course, a terrible strategy. It can take a long time to compile and test all the various possibilities. Expending a small amount of mental effort is a real time saver.

Fortunately, off-by-1 errors are easy to avoid, simply by thinking through a couple of test cases and using the information from the test cases to come up with a rationale for your decisions.

Should `years` start at 0 or at 1? Look at a scenario with simple values: an initial balance of $100 and an interest rate of 50%. After year 1, the balance is $150, and after year 2 it is $225, or over $200. So the investment doubled after 2 years. The loop executed two times, incrementing `years` each time. Hence `years` must start at 0, not at 1.

In other words, the `balance` variable denotes the balance *after* the end of the year. At the outset, the `balance` variable contains the balance after year 0 and not after year 1.

Next, should you use a < or <= comparison in the test? That is harder to figure out, because it is rare for the balance to be exactly twice the initial balance. Of course, there is one case when this happens, namely when the interest is 100%. The loop executes once. Now `years` is 1, and `balance` is exactly equal to `2 * initialBalance`. Has the investment doubled after one year? It has. Therefore, the loop should *not* execute again. If the test condition is `balance < 2 * initialBalance`, the loop stops, as it should. If the test condition had been `balance <= 2 * initialBalance`, the loop would have executed once more.

In other words, you keep adding interest while the balance *has not yet doubled*.

AT Advanced Topic 6.1

do **Loops**

Sometimes you want to execute the body of a loop at least once and perform the loop test after the body was executed. The do loop serves that purpose:

```
do
    statement
while (condition);
```

The *statement* is executed while the *condition* is true. The condition is tested after the statement is executed, so the statement is executed at least once.

For example, suppose you want to make sure that a user enters a positive number. As long as the user enters a negative number or zero, just keep prompting for a correct input. In this situation, a do loop makes sense, because you need to get a user input before you can test it.

```
double value;
do
{
    String input = JOptionPane.showInputDialog(
        "Please enter a positive number");
    value = Double.parseDouble(input);
}
while (value <= 0);
```

See Figure 2 for a flowchart.

Figure 2

Flowchart of a do Loop

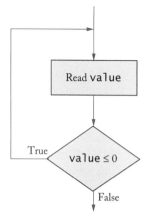

In practice, this situation is not very common. You can always replace a do loop with a `while` loop, by introducing a `boolean` control variable.

```
boolean done = false;
while (!done)
{
    String input = JOptionPane.showInputDialog(
        "Please enter a positive number");
    value = Double.parseDouble(input);
    if (value > 0) done = true;
}
```

Random Fact   6.1

Spaghetti Code

In this chapter we are using flowcharts to illustrate the behavior of the loop statements. It used to be common to draw flowcharts for every method, on the theory that flow-charts were easier to read and write than the actual code (especially in the days of machine-language and assembler programming). Nowadays, flowcharts are no longer routinely used for program development and documentation.

Flowcharts have one fatal flaw. Although it is possible to express the `while` and do loops with flowcharts, it is also possible to draw flowcharts that cannot be programmed with loops. Consider the chart in Figure 3. The top of the flowchart is simply a statement

```
years = 1;
```

The lower part is a do loop:

```
do
{
    years++;
    double interest = balance * rate / 100;
    balance = balance + interest;
}
while (balance < targetBalance);
```

Figure 3

Spaghetti Code

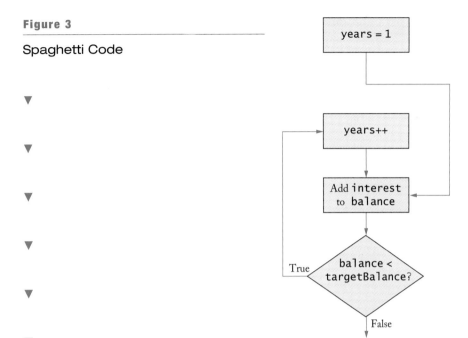

But how can you join these two parts? According to the flowchart, you are supposed to jump from the first statement into the middle of the loop, skipping the first statement.

```
years = 1;
goto a; // not an actual Java statement
do
{
    years++;
    a:

    double interest = balance * rate / 100;
    balance = balance + interest;
}
while (balance < targetBalance);
```

In fact, why even bother with the do loop? Here is a faithful interpretation of the flowchart:

```
years = 1;
goto a; // not an actual Java statement
b:
years++;
a:
double interest = balance * rate / 100;
balance = balance + interest;
if (balance < targetBalance) goto b;
```

This *nonlinear* control flow turns out to be extremely hard to read and understand if you have more than one or two goto statements. Because the lines denoting the goto

▼

▼

▼

▼

statements weave back and forth in complex flowcharts, the resulting code is named *spaghetti code.*

In 1968 the influential computer scientist Edsger Dijkstra wrote a famous note, entitled "Goto Statements Considered Harmful" [1], in which he argued for the use of loops instead of unstructured jumps. Initially, many programmers who had been using goto for years were mortally insulted and promptly dug out examples in which the use of goto does lead to clearer or faster code. Some languages offer weaker forms of goto that are less harmful, such as the break statement in Java, discussed in Advanced Topic 6.5. Nowadays, most computer scientists accept Dijkstra's argument and fight bigger battles than optimal loop design.

6.2 for Loops

Far and away the most common loop has the form

```
i = start;
while (i <= end)
{
    . . .
    i++;
}
```

Because this loop is so common, there is a special form for it that emphasizes the pattern:

```
for (i = start; i <= end; i++)
{
    . . .
}
```

You can also *declare* the loop counter variable inside the for loop header. That convenient shorthand restricts the use of the variable to the body of the loop (as will be discussed further in Advanced Topic 6.2).

```
for (int i = start; i <= end; i++)
{
    . . .
}
```

> You use a for loop when a variable runs from a starting to an ending value with a constant increment or decrement.

Let us use this loop to find out the size of our $10,000 investment if 5% interest is compounded for 20 years. Of course, the balance will be larger than $20,000, because at least $500 is added every year. You may be surprised to find out just how much larger the balance is.

In our loop, we let i go from 1 to n, the number of years for which we want to compound interest.

```
for (int i = 1; i <= n; i++)
{
    double interest = balance * rate / 100;
    balance = balance + interest;
}
```

Figure 4 shows the corresponding flowchart.

Figure 4

Flowchart of a for Loop

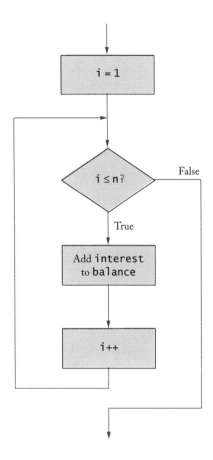

File Investment.java

```
1  /**
2      A class to monitor the growth of an investment that
3      accumulates interest at a fixed annual rate.
4  */
5  public class Investment
6  {
7      /**
8          Constructs an Investment object from a starting balance and
9          interest rate.
10         @param aBalance  the starting balance
11         @param aRate  the interest rate in percent
12     */
13     public Investment(double aBalance, double aRate)
14     {
15         balance = aBalance;
16         rate = aRate;
```

```
17          years = 0;
18       }
19
20       /**
21          Keeps accumulating interest until a target balance has
22          been reached.
23          @param targetBalance the desired balance
24       */
25       public void waitForBalance(double targetBalance)
26       {
27          while (balance < targetBalance)
28          {
29             years++;
30             double interest = balance * rate / 100;
31             balance = balance + interest;
32          }
33       }
34
35       /**
36          Keeps accumulating interest for a given number of years.
37          @param n the number of years
38       */
39       public void waitYears(int n)
40       {
41          for (int i = 1; i <= n; i++)
42          {
43             double interest = balance * rate / 100;
44             balance = balance + interest;
45          }
46          years = years + n;
47       }
48
49       /**
50          Gets the current investment balance.
51          @return the current balance
52       */
53       public double getBalance()
54       {
55          return balance;
56       }
57
58       /**
59          Gets the number of years this investment has accumulated
60          interest.
61          @return the number of years since the start of the investment
62       */
63       public int getYears()
64       {
65          return years;
66       }
```

```
67
68    private double balance;
69    private double rate;
70    private int years;
71 }
```

File InvestmentTest.java

```
1 /**
2     This program computes how much an investment grows in
3     a given number of years.
4 */
5 public class InvestmentTest
6 {
7     public static void main(String[] args)
8     {
9        final double INITIAL_BALANCE = 10000;
10       final double RATE = 5;
11       final int YEARS = 20;
12       Investment invest =
13          new Investment(INITIAL_BALANCE, RATE);
14       invest.waitYears(YEARS);
15       double balance = invest.getBalance();
16       System.out.println("The balance after " + YEARS +
17          " years is " + balance);
18    }
19 }
```

Syntax 6.2: The for Statement

for (*initialization*; *condition*; *update*)
   statement

Example:
```
for (i = 1; i <= n; i++)
{
    double interest = balance * rate / 100;
    balance = balance + interest;
}
```

Purpose:

To execute an initialization, then keep executing a statement and updating an expression while a condition is true

---

The three slots in the for header can contain any three expressions. You can count down instead of up:

```
for (years = n; years > 0; years--)
```

The increment or decrement need not be in steps of 1:

```
for (x = -10; x <= 10; x = x + 0.5) . . .
```

It is possible—but a sign of unbelievably bad taste—to put unrelated conditions into the loop:

```
for (rate = 5; years-- > 0; System.out.println(balance))
    . . . // Bad taste
```

We won't even begin to decipher what that might mean. You should stick with `for` loops that initialize, test, and update a single variable.

Quality Tip · 6.1

Use `for` Loops for Their Intended Purpose Only

A `for` loop is an *idiom* for a `while` loop of a particular form. A counter runs from the start to the end, with a constant increment:

```
for (set counter to start; test whether counter at end;
        update counter by increment)
{   . . .
    // counter, start, end, increment  not changed here
}
```

If your loop doesn't match this pattern, don't use the `for` construction. The compiler won't prevent you from writing idiotic `for` loops:

```
// bad style—unrelated header expressions
for (System.out.println("Inputs:");
        (x = Double.parseDouble(console.readLine())) > 0;
        sum = sum + x)
    count++;

for (int i = 1; i <= years; i++)
{
    // bad style—modifies counter
    if (balance >= targetBalance)
        i = years + 1;
    else
    {
        double interest = balance * rate / 100;
        balance = balance + interest;
    }
}
```

These loops will work, but they are plainly bad style. Use a `while` loop for iterations that do not fit into the `for` pattern.

▼ ▒▒▒ **Advanced Topic**   **6.2**

Scope of Variables Defined in a for **Loop Header**

As mentioned, it is legal in Java to declare a variable in the header of a for loop. Here is the most common form of this syntax:

```
for (int i = 1; i <= n; i++)
{
    . . .
}
```

```
// i  no longer defined here
```

The scope of the variables extends to the end of the for loop. Therefore, i is no longer defined after the loop ends. If you need to use the value of the variable beyond the end of the loop, then you need to define it outside the loop. In this loop, you don't need the value of i—you know it is years + 1 when the loop is finished. (Actually, that is not quite true—it is possible to break out of a loop before its end; see Advanced Topic 6.5). When you have two or more exit conditions, though, you may still need the variable. For example, consider the loop

```
for (i = 1; balance < targetBalance && i <= n; i++)
{
    . . .
}
```

You want the balance to reach the target, but you are willing to wait only a certain number of years. If the balance doubles sooner, you may want to know the value of i. Therefore, in this case, it is not appropriate to define the variable in the loop header.

Note that the variables named i in the following pair of for loops are independent:

```
for (int i = 1; i <= 10; i++)
    System.out.println(i * i);
for (int i = 1; i <= 10; i++) // declares a new variable i
    System.out.println(i * i * i);
```

In the loop header, you can declare multiple variables, as long as they are of the same type, and you can include multiple update expressions, separated by commas:

```
for (int i = 0, j = 10; i <= 10; i++, j--)
{
    . . .
}
```

However, many people find it confusing if a for loop controls more than one variable. I recommend that you not use this form of the for statement (see Quality Tip 6.1). Instead, make the for loop control a single counter, and update the other variable explicitly:

```
int j = 10;
```

```
for (int i = 0; i <= 10; i++)
{
    . . .
    j--;
}
```

Common Error   6.3

Forgetting a Semicolon

It occasionally happens that all the work of a loop is already done in the loop header. Suppose you ignored Quality Tip 6.1. Then you could write the investment doubling loop as follows:

```
for (years = 1;
        (balance = balance + balance * rate / 100)
            < targetBalance;
        years++)
    ;
return years;
```

The body of the `for` loop is completely empty, containing just one empty statement terminated by a semicolon.

If you do run into a loop without a body, it is important that you really make sure the semicolon is not forgotten. If the semicolon is accidentally omitted, then the next line becomes part of the loop statement!

```
for (years = 1;
        (balance = balance + balance * rate / 100)
            < targetBalance;
        years++)
    return years;
```

To make the semicolon really stand out, place it on a line all by itself, as shown in the first example.

Common Error   6.4

A Semicolon Too Many

What does the following loop print?

```
sum = 0;
for (i = 1; i <= 10; i++);
    sum = sum + i;
System.out.println(sum);
```

Of course, this loop is supposed to compute $1 + 2 + \cdots + 10 = 55$. But actually, the print statement prints 11!

Why 11? Have another look. Did you spot the semicolon at the end of the `for` loop? This loop really is a loop with an empty body.

```
for (i = 1; i <= 10; i++)
    ;
```

The loop does nothing ten times, and when it is finished, sum is still 0 and i is 11. Then the statement

```
sum = sum + i;
```

is executed, and sum is 11. The statement was indented, which fools the human reader. But the compiler pays no attention to indentation.

Of course, the semicolon at the end of the statement was a typing error. Someone's fingers were so used to typing a semicolon at the end of every line that a semicolon was added to the for loop by accident. The result was a loop with an empty body.

Quality Tip   6.2

Don't Use != to Test the End of a Range

Here is a loop with a hidden danger:

```
for (i = 1; i != n; i++)
{
    . . .
}
```

The test i != n is a poor idea. What would happen if n happened to be negative? Then the test i != n is never false, because i starts at 1 and increases with every step.

The remedy is simple. Test

```
for (i = 1; i <= n; i++) . . .
```

For floating-point values, there is another reason not to use !=: Because of roundoff errors, the exact termination point may never be reached.

Of course, you would never write

```
for (rate = 5; rate != 10; rate = rate + 0.3333333) . . .
```

because it is highly unlikely that rate would match 10 exactly after 15 steps. But the same problem may happen for the harmless-looking

```
for (rate = 5; rate != 10; rate = rate + 0.1) . . .
```

The number 0.1 is exactly representable in the decimal system, but the computer represents floating-point numbers in binary. There is a slight error in any finite binary representation of 1/10, just as there is a slight error in a decimal representation 0.3333333 of 1/3. Maybe rate is exactly 10 after 50 steps; maybe it is off by a tiny amount. There is no point in taking chances. Just use < instead of !=:

```
for (rate = 5; rate < 10; rate = rate + 0.1) . . .
```

6.3   Nested Loops

Suppose you need to print the following triangle shape:

```
[]
[][]
[][][]
[][][][]
[][][][][]
[][][][][][]
[][][][][][][]
```

The basic idea is simple. You have to generate a number of rows:

```
for (int i = 1; i <= width; i++)
{
    // make triangle row
    . . .
}
```

> Loops can be nested. A typical example for nested loops is printing a table with rows and columns.

How do you make a triangle row? Use another loop to concatenate the squares [] for that row. Then add a newline at the end of the row. The ith row has i symbols, so the loop counter goes from 1 to i.

```
for (int j = 1; j <= i; j++)
    r = r + "[]";
r = r + "\n";
```

Putting both loops together yields two *nested loops:*

```
String r = "";
for (int i = 1; i <= width; i++)
{
    // make triangle row
    for (int j = 1; j <= i; j++)
        r = r + "[]";
    r = r + "\n";
}
return r;
```

Here is the complete program:

File Triangle.java

```
1  /**
2      This class describes triangle objects that can be displayed
3      as shapes like this:
4      []
5      [][]
6      [][][]
```

```
 7 */
 8 public class Triangle
 9 {
10    /**
11       Constructs a triangle.
12       @param aWidth the number of [] in the last row of the triangle
13    */
14    public Triangle(int aWidth)
15    {
16       width = aWidth;
17    }
18
19    /**
20       Computes a string representing the triangle.
21       @return a string consisting of [] and newline characters
22    */
23    public String toString()
24    {
25       String r = "";
26       for (int i = 1; i <= width; i++)
27       {
28          // make triangle row
29          for (int j = 1; j <= i; j++)
30             r = r + "[]";
31          r = r + "\n";
32       }
33       return r;
34    }
35    private int width;
36 }
```

File TriangleTest.java

```
 1 /**
 2    This program tests the Triangle class.
 3 */
 4 public class TriangleTest
 5 {
 6    public static void main(String[] args)
 7    {
 8       Triangle small = new Triangle(3);
 9       System.out.println(small.toString());
10
11       Triangle large = new Triangle(15);
12       System.out.println(large.toString());
13    }
14 }
```

▼ ▲Ⅱ Advanced Topic 6.3 ▶

▼ String Buffers

▼ It is somewhat inefficient to form a string by concatenating many small strings. Each intermediate string is a new object that is only used once. The `StringBuffer` class offers
▼ a more efficient way. Start with an empty string buffer, then keep calling the `append` method to add characters to the end of the string buffer. When you are done, call the `toString` method to obtain the string whose characters are stored in the string buffer.

▼
```
StringBuffer r = new StringBuffer();
for (int i = 1; i <= width; i++)
{
    // make triangle row
    for (int j = 1; j <= i; j++)
        r.append("[]");
    r.append("\n");
}
return r.toString();
```

▼ To keep our programs as simple as possible, we will not use string buffers in this book.
▼ However, for "real-world" programs it is a good idea to use a string buffer whenever you build up a long string from many individual pieces.
▼

6.4 Processing Input

6.4.1 — Reading a Set of Values

Suppose you want to process a set of values, for example a set of measurements, to compute some property, such as the average of the values or the largest value. For reading input, you can use the `showInputDialog` method of the `JOptionPane` class or the `readLine` method of the `BufferedReader` class (see Advanced Topic 3.6).

This loop reads through input data:

```
boolean done = false;
while (!done)
{
    String input = read input;
    if (end of input indicated)
        done = true;
    else
    {
        process input
    }
}
```

Processing input is complicated by the fact that checking for the end of input occurs in the middle of the loop.

This loop is a little different from the ones you saw before, because the test condition is a variable done. That variable stays false until you reach the end of the input data; then it is set to true. The next time the loop starts at the top, done is true, and the loop exits.

There is a reason for using a variable. The test for loop termination occurs in the *middle* of the loop, not at the top or the bottom.

You must first try to read input before you can test whether you have reached the end of input. In Java, there isn't a ready-made control structure for the pattern "do work, then test, then do more work". Therefore, we use a combination of a while loop and a boolean variable. This pattern is sometimes called "loop and a half". Some programmers find it clumsy to introduce a control variable for such a loop. Advanced Topic 6.5 shows a few alternatives.

Let's write a program that analyzes a set of values. To decouple the input handling from the computation of the average and the maximum, we'll introduce a class DataSet. You add values to a DataSet object with the add method. The getAverage method returns the average of all added data and the getMaximum method returns the largest.

File DataSet.java

```
1  /**
2      Computes the average of a set of data values.
3  */
4  public class DataSet
5  {
6      /**
7          Constructs an empty data set.
8      */
9      public DataSet()
10     {
11         sum = 0;
12         count = 0;
13         maximum = 0;
14     }
15
16     /**
17         Adds a data value to the data set.
18         @param x a data value
19     */
20     public void add(double x)
21     {
22         sum = sum + x;
23         if (count == 0 || maximum < x) maximum = x;
24         count++;
25     }
26
27     /**
28         Gets the average of the added data.
29         @return the average or 0 if no data have been added
```

```
30      */
31      public double getAverage()
32      {
33         if (count == 0) return 0;
34         else return sum / count;
35      }
36
37      /**
38         Gets the largest of the added data.
39         @return the maximum or 0 if no data have been added
40      */
41      public double getMaximum()
42      {
43         return maximum;
44      }
45
46      private double sum;
47      private double maximum;
48      private int count;
49   }
```

We use JOptionPane input dialogs to collect the inputs. The showInputDialog method returns null if the user clicks the "Cancel" button of the dialog. Thus, we can ask the user to keep entering numbers, or to click on "Cancel" to end the input.

You read the input as a string, but you want to interpret it as a number. Therefore, you must use the Integer.parseInt or Double.parseDouble method to convert the input data from a string to a number. Here is the program to compute the average of a set of input data.

File InputTest.java

```
1   import javax.swing.JOptionPane;
2
3   /**
4      This program computes the average and maximum of a set
5      of input values.
6   */
7   public class InputTest
8   {
9      public static void main(String[] args)
10     {
11        DataSet data = new DataSet();
12
13        boolean done = false;
14        while (!done)
15        {
16           String input = JOptionPane.showInputDialog(
17              "Enter value, Cancel to quit");
18           if (input == null)
19              done = true;
20           else
```

```
21              {
22                  double x = Double.parseDouble(input);
23                  data.add(x);
24              }
25          }
26
27          System.out.println("Average = " +
28              data.getAverage());
29          System.out.println("Maximum = " +
30              data.getMaximum());
31          System.exit(0);
32      }
33  }
```

This program pops up a set of input dialogs, which makes for rather tedious data entry. Advanced Topic 6.6 shows you how to read the data from the console window instead. For even more efficient input, use Productivity Hint 6.1 to read data from a file.

Advanced Topic 6.4

The "Loop and a Half" Problem

When reading data from input, we always used to use a loop like the following, which is somewhat unsightly:

```
boolean done = false;
while (!done)
{
    String input = JOptionPane.showInputDialog(
        "Enter value, Cancel to quit");
    if (input == null)
        done = true;
    else
    {
        process data
    }
}
```

The true test for loop termination is in the middle of the loop, not at the top. This is called a "loop and a half", because one must go halfway into the loop before knowing whether one needs to terminate.

Some programmers dislike the introduction of an additional Boolean variable for loop control. Two Java language features can be used to alleviate the "loop and a half" problem. I don't think either is a superior solution, but both approaches are fairly common, so it is worth knowing about them when reading other people's code.

You can combine an assignment and a test in the loop condition:

```
while ((input = JOptionPane.showInputDialog(
        "Enter value, Cancel to quit")) != null)
```

```
{
    process data
}
```

The expression (input = JOptionPane.showInputDialog("Enter value, Cancel to quit")) != null means, "First read a line; then test whether the end of the input has been reached." This is an expression with a side effect. The primary purpose of the expression is to serve as a test for the while loop, but it also actually does some work—namely, reading the input and storing it in the variable input. In general, it is always a bad idea to use side effects, because they make a program hard to read and maintain. In this case, however, that practice is somewhat seductive, because it eliminates the control variable done, which also makes the code hard to read and maintain.

The other solution is to exit the loop from the middle, either by a return statement or by a break statement (see Advanced Topic 6.5). Here is an example. This loop reads input data, and the method containing the loop returns value when the end of input is encountered.

```
while (true)
{
    String input = JOptionPane.showInputDialog(
        "Enter value, Cancel to quit");
    if (input == null) // leave loop in the middle
        return data;
    double x = Double.parseDouble(input);
    data.add(x);
}
```

Advanced Topic 6.5

The break and continue Statements

You already encountered the break statement in Advanced Topic 5.2, where it was used to exit a switch statement. In addition to breaking out of a switch statement, a break statement can also be used to exit a while, for, or do loop. For example, the break statement in the following loop terminates the loop when the end of input is reached.

```
while (true)
{
    String input = JOptionPane.showInputDialog(
        "Enter value, Cancel to quit");
    if (input == null) // leave loop in the middle
        break;
    double x = Double.parseDouble(input);
    data.add(x);
}
```

▼ In general, a `break` is a very poor way of exiting a loop. In 1990, a misused `break` caused
an AT&T 4ESS telephone switch to fail, and the failure propagated through the entire
U.S. network, rendering it nearly unusable for about nine hours. A programmer had used
▼ a `break` to terminate an `if` statement. Unfortunately, `break` cannot be used with `if`, so
the program execution broke out of the enclosing `switch` statement, skipping some variable initializations and running into chaos [2, p. 38]. Using `break` statements also makes
▼ it difficult to use *correctness proof* techniques (see Advanced Topic 6.8).

However, when faced with the bother of introducing a separate loop control variable,
some programmers find that `break` statements are beneficial in the "loop and a half"
▼ case. This issue is often the topic of heated (and quite unproductive) debate. In this
book, we won't use the `break` statement, and we leave it to you to decide whether you
like to use it in your own programs.

▼ In Java, there is a second form of the `break` statement that is used to break out of a
nested statement. The statement `break` *label*; immediately jumps to the *end* of the statement that is tagged with a label. Any statement (including `if` and block statements) can
▼ be tagged with a label—the syntax is

    label: *statement*

The labeled `break` statement was invented to break out of a set of nested loops.

```
outerloop:
while (outer loop condition)
{  . . .
    while (inner loop condition)
    {  . . .
        if (something really bad happened)
            break outerloop;
    }
}
jumps here if something really bad happened
```

Naturally, this situation is quite rare. We recommend that you try to introduce additional
methods instead of using complicated nested loops.

▼ Finally, there is another `goto`-like statement, the `continue` statement, which jumps
to the end of the *current iteration* of the loop. Here is a possible use for this statement:

```
do
{
    input = JOptionPane.showInputDialog(
        "Enter value, Cancel to quit");
    if (input == null) continue; // jump to the end of the loop body
    double x = Double.parseDouble(input);
    data.add(x);
    // continue statement jumps here
}
while (input != null);
```

▼ By using the `continue` statement, you don't need to place the remainder of the loop
code inside an `else` clause. This is a minor benefit. Few programmers use this statement.

Reading Data from the Console

In Advanced Topic 3.6, you saw how to use a `BufferedReader` to read input from the console window. It is easier to enter a large quantity of data in the console window than it is to type the data into a sequence of input dialogs. More importantly, Productivity Hint 6.1 shows how console input can be *redirected* to read from a file. That is a true time saver that is impossible to achieve with input dialogs.

Recall from Advanced Topic 3.6 that you need to turn `System.in` into a `BufferedReader` as follows:

```
BufferedReader console = new BufferedReader(
    new InputStreamReader(System.in));
```

You use the `readLine` method to read a line of input. The `readLine` method returns `null` at the end of input.

Since `readLine` throws an `IOException`, you need to tag the method in which you call `readLine` with a `throws IOException` specifier.

Here is the `InputTest` program, rewritten to read from the console. The changes are in color.

```
public class InputTest
{
    public static void main(String[] args)
        throws IOException
    {
        BufferedReader console = new BufferedReader(
            new InputStreamReader(System.in));
        DataSet data = new DataSet();

        System.out.println(
            "Enter value, close input to quit");
        boolean done = false;
        while (!done)
        {
            String input = console.readLine();
            if (input == null)
                done = true;
            else
            {
                double x = Double.parseDouble(input);
                data.add(x);
            }
        }

        System.out.println(
            "Average = " + data.getAverage());
```

```
                    System.out.println(
                        "Maximum = " + data.getMaximum());
                }
            }
```

To supply data to the program, you type the input data, a line at a time. When you are done typing, you must indicate to the operating system that all console input for this program has been supplied. The mechanism for this differs from one operating system to another. For example, in DOS you type Ctrl+Z, whereas on UNIX you type Ctrl+D, to indicate the end of console input. This special keystroke combination is a signal to the *operating system* (and not to Java) to close console input. The `System.in` stream never sees this special character. Instead, it just senses that console input has been closed. The `readLine` method returns a `null` string (and not a string containing a control character) at the end of input.

Of course, typing a long set of numbers at the console is tedious and error-prone. Productivity Hint 6.1 shows you how you can prepare the input data in a file and use input redirection to have the `System.in` stream read the characters from that file. In that case you do not terminate the file with a control character, because the operating system knows the size of the file and therefore knows where it ends. But the operating system, not being clairvoyant, cannot know the end of keyboard input—hence the need for the special control character. (Some ancient versions of DOS did terminate text files on disk with a Ctrl+Z, and you will still find some "experts" who tell you that all files have a special end-of-file character at the end. This is plainly not the case—the operating system uses the size of a disk file to determine its end.)

Productivity Hint   6.1

Redirection of Input and Output

> Use input redirection to avoid repetitive typing during testing. Use output redirection to save your program output in a file.

It is tedious to test programs by typing data in for every test run. Testing is far easier if the program reads its input from a *file*. You can then prepare the file once and reuse it for many tests. The command line interfaces of most operating systems provide a way to link a file to the input of a program, as if all the characters in the file had actually been typed by a user. If you type

```
java Average < data.txt
```

the `Average` program is executed. Its input instructions no longer expect input from the keyboard. The `readLine` method gets the input from the file `data.txt`.

This mechanism works for any program that reads its input from the standard input stream `System.in`. By default, the standard input is tied to the keyboard, but it can be tied to any file by specifying *input redirection* on the command line.

If you have always launched your program from the integrated environment, you need to find out whether your environment supports input redirection. If it does not, you need to learn how to open a command window (often called a *shell*) and launch the program in the command window by typing its name and redirection instructions.

▼   You can also redirect output. In this program, that is not terribly useful. If you run

```
java Average < data.txt > output.txt
```

▼   the file output.txt contains two lines ("Enter value, close input to quit" and something like "Average = . . ."). However, redirecting output is obviously useful for programs that produce lots of it. You can print the file containing the output or edit it before you turn it in for grading.

6.4.2 — ## String Tokenization

In the last examples, input data were provided a line at a time. However, sometimes it is convenient to have an input line that contains *several* items of input data. Suppose an input line contains two numbers:

```
5.5 10000
```

You can't convert the string "5.5 10000" to a number, because the parsing method would complain that this string is not a legal number and throw an exception. Instead, you need to break the input line into a sequence of strings, each of which represents a separate input item. There is a special class, the StringTokenizer, that can break up a string into items or, as they are sometimes called, *tokens*. By default, the string tokenizer uses white space (spaces,

> You can break a line into words by using a StringTokenizer.

tabs, and newlines) as delimiters. For example, the string "5.5 10000" will be decomposed into two tokens: "5.5" and "10000". The delimiting white space is discarded.

Here is how you break up a string. Construct a StringTokenizer object and supply the string to be broken up in the constructor:

```
StringTokenizer tokenizer = new StringTokenizer(input);
```

Then keep calling the nextToken method to get the next token.

However, if the entire string has been consumed and there are no more tokens, the nextToken method is a bit hostile and throws an exception rather than returning a null string. Therefore, you need to call the hasMoreTokens method to ensure that there still are tokens to be processed. The following loop traverses all tokens in a string:

```
while (tokenizer.hasMoreTokens())
{
    String token = tokenizer.nextToken();
    do something with token
}
```

If you want to use another separator, such as a comma, to separate the individual values, then you can specify the separator as a second argument when you construct the StringTokenizer object:

```
StringTokenizer tokenizer =
    new StringTokenizer(input, ",");
```

If you use this option, you should make sure that there are no extra white spaces in the input file between the commas and your tokens; otherwise the white spaces will be included in the tokens.

Here is a program that computes the average and the maximum of input values that are all specified on a single line. Naturally, that is a reasonable option only for a small data set.

File InputTest.java

```
1  import java.util.StringTokenizer;
2  import javax.swing.JOptionPane;
3
4  /**
5     This program computes the average and maximum of a set
6     of input values that are entered on a single line.
7  */
8  public class InputTest
9  {
10    public static void main(String[] args)
11    {
12       DataSet data = new DataSet();
13
14       String input =
15          JOptionPane.showInputDialog("Enter values:");
16       StringTokenizer tokenizer =
17          new StringTokenizer(input);
18       while (tokenizer.hasMoreTokens())
19       {
20          String token = tokenizer.nextToken();
21
22          double x = Double.parseDouble(token);
23          data.add(x);
24       }
25
26       System.out.println("Average = " +
27          data.getAverage());
28       System.out.println("Maximum = " +
29          data.getMaximum());
30       System.exit(0);
31    }
32 }
```

6.4.3 — Traversing the Characters in a String

You can access the individual characters of a string with the charAt method.

In the last section, you learned how to decompose a string into tokens. Sometimes, you need to go further and analyze the individual characters of a string. The charAt method of the String class returns an individual character as a value of the char type. Recall from Chapter 3 that string positions are counted starting from 0. That is, the parameter i in the call s.charAt(i) must be a value between 0 and s.length() - 1.

Therefore, the general pattern to traverse all characters in a string is

```
for (int i = 0; i < s.length(); i++)
{
   char ch = s.charAt(i);
   do something with ch
}
```

Suppose you want to count the number of vowels in a string. The following loop carries out that task.

```
int vowelCount = 0;
String vowels = "aeiouy";
for (int i = 0; i < s.length(); i++)
{
    char ch = Character.toLowerCase(s.charAt(i));
    if (vowels.indexOf(ch) >= 0)
        vowelCount++;
}
```

Here we use the `indexOf` method of the string class. The call

```
s.indexOf(ch)
```

returns the position of the first occurrence of the character `ch` in the string `s`, or −1 if `ch` doesn't occur in `s`. For example, `"Mississippi".indexOf('s')` is 2.

Quality Tip 6.3

Symmetric and Asymmetric Bounds

It is easy to write a loop with i going from 1 to n:

```
for (i = 1; i <= n; i++) . . .
```

The values for i are bounded by the relation $1 \le i \le n$. Because there are $\le$ comparisons on both bounds, the bounds are called *symmetric*.

When traversing the characters in a string, the bounds are *asymmetric*.

```
for (i = 0; i < s.length(); i++) . . .
```

The values for i are bounded by $0 \le i < s.length()$, with a $\le$ comparison to the left and a $<$ comparison to the right. That is appropriate, because `s.length()` is not a valid position.

It is not a good idea to force symmetry artificially:

```
for (i = 0; i <= s.length() - 1; i++) . . .
```

> Make a choice between symmetric and asymmetric bounds for each `for` loop.

That is more difficult to read and understand.

For every loop, consider which form is most natural according to the needs of the problem, and use that.

Quality Tip 6.4

Count Iterations

Finding the correct lower and upper bounds for an iteration can be confusing. Should I start at 0? Should I use `<= b` or `< b` as a termination condition?

Counting the number of iterations is a very useful device for better understanding a loop. Counting is easier for loops with asymmetric bounds. The loop

```
for (i = a; i < b; i++) . . .
```

▼   is executed b - a times. For example, the loop traversing the characters in a string,

```
for (i = 0; i < s.length(); i++) . . .
```

▼   runs `s.length()` times. That makes perfect sense, because there are `s.length()` characters in a string.

The loop with symmetric bounds,

```
for (i = a; i <= b; i++)
```

▼   is executed b - a + 1 times. That "+ 1" is the source of many programming errors. For example,

```
for (x = 0; x <= 10; x++)
```

▼   runs 11 times. Maybe that is what you want; if not, start at 1 or use < 10.

One way to visualize this "+1" error is to think of the posts and sections of a fence. Suppose the fence has ten sections (=). How many posts (|) does it have?

▼ |=|=|=|=|=|=|=|=|=|=|

> Count the number of iterations of a `for` loop to check that your loop is correct.

A fence with ten sections has *eleven* posts. Each section has one post to the left, *and* there is one more post after the last section. Forgetting to count the last iteration of a "<=" loop is often called a "fence post error".

If the increment is a value c other than 1, then the counts are

$$(b - a) / c \qquad \text{for the asymmetric loop}$$

$$(b - a) / c + 1 \qquad \text{for the symmetric loop}$$

▼   For example, the loop `for (i = 10; i <= 40; i += 5)` executes $(40 - 10)/5 + 1 = 7$ times.

▼ ？ **HOWTO**   6.1

Implementing Loops

▼   You write a loop because your program needs to repeat an action multiple times. As you have seen in this chapter, there are several loop types, and it isn't always obvious how to structure loop statements. This HOWTO walks you through the thought process that is involved when programming a loop.

Step 1   List the work that needs to be done in every step of the loop body

▼   For example, suppose you need to read in input values in gallons and convert them to liters, until the end of input is reached. Then the operations are:

▼   • Read input.

   • Convert the input to liters.

▼   • Print out the response.

Suppose you need to scan through the characters of a string and count the vowels. Then the operations are:

- Get the next character.

- If it's a vowel, increase a counter.

Step 2 Find out how often the loop is repeated

Typical answers might be:

- Ten times

- Once for each character in the string

- Until the end of input is reached

- While the balance is less than the target balance

If a loop is executed for a definite number of times, a `for` loop is usually appropriate. The first two loops lead to `for` loops, such as

```
for (int i = 1; i <= 10; i++) . . .
for (int i = 0; i < str.length(); i++) . . .
```

The other two loops need to be implemented as `while` loops—you don't know how many times the loop body is going to be repeated.

Step 3 With a `while` loop, find out where you can determine that the loop is finished

There are three possibilities:

- Before entering the loop

- In the middle of the loop

- At the end of the loop

For example, if you execute a loop while the balance is less than the target balance, you can check for that condition at the beginning of the loop. If the balance is less than the target balance, you enter the loop. If not, you are done. In such a case, your loop has the form

```
while (condition)
{
    do work
}
```

However, checking for input requires that you first *read* the input. That means, you'll need to enter the loop, read the input, and then decide whether you want to go any further. Then your loop has the form

```
boolean done = false;
while (!done)
```

```
{
    do the work needed to check the condition
    if (condition)
        done = true;
    else
    {
        do more work
    }
}
```

This loop structure is sometimes called a "loop and a half".

Finally, if you know whether you need to go on after you have gone through the loop once, then you use a do/while loop:

```
do
{
    do work
}
while (condition)
```

However, these loops are very rare in practice.

Step 4   Implement the loop by putting the operations from Step 1 into the loop body

When you write a for loop, you usually use the loop index inside the loop body. For example, "get the next character" is implemented as the statement

```
char ch = str.charAt(i);
```

Step 5   Double-check your variable initializations

If you use a Boolean variable done, make sure it is initialized to false. If you accumulate a result in a sum or count variable, make sure that you set it to 0 before entering the loop for the first time.

Step 6   Check for off-by-one errors

Consider the simplest possible scenarios:

- If you read input, what happens if there is no input at all? Exactly one input?

- If you look through the characters of a string, what happens if the string is empty? If it has one character in it?

- If you accumulate values until some target has been reached, what happens if the target is 0? A negative value?

Manually walk through every instruction in the loop, including all initializations. Carefully check all conditions, paying attention to the difference between comparisons such as < and <=. Check that the loop is not traversed at all, or only once, and that the final result is what you expect.

If you write a for loop, check to see whether your bounds should be symmetric or asymmetric (see Quality Tip 6.3) and count the number of iterations (see Quality Tip 6.4).

▼ 🄰🄣 Advanced Topic 6.7 ▶

Pipes

In many operating systems, output of one program can become the input of another program. Here is a simple program that writes each word of the input file onto a separate line:

File Split.java

```
 1  import java.io.BufferedReader;
 2  import java.io.InputStreamReader;
 3  import java.io.IOException;
 4  import java.util.StringTokenizer;
 5
 6  /**
 7     This program splits the lines read from System.in into
 8     individual words.
 9  */
10  public class Split
11  {
12     public static void main(String[] args)
13        throws IOException
14     {
15        BufferedReader console = new BufferedReader(
16           new InputStreamReader(System.in));
17        boolean done = false;
18        while (!done)
19        {
20           String inputLine = console.readLine();
21           if (inputLine == null)
22              done = true;
23           else
24           {
25              // break input line into words
26
27              StringTokenizer tokenizer =
28                 new StringTokenizer(inputLine);
29              while (tokenizer.hasMoreTokens())
30              {
31                 // print each word
32                 String word = tokenizer.nextToken();
33                 System.out.println(word);
34              }
35           }
36        }
37     }
38  }
```

▼   Then

```
java Split < article.txt
```

▼   lists the words in the file article.txt, one on each line. That isn't too exciting, but it
becomes useful when combined with another program: *sort*. You don't yet know how to
write a program that sorts strings, but most operating systems have a sort program. A
▼   sorted list of the words in a file would be quite useful—for example, for making an index.
You can save the unsorted words in a temporary file:

```
java Split < article.txt > temp.txt
```
▼
```
sort < temp.txt > sorted.txt
```

Now the sorted words are in the file sorted.txt.

Because this operation is so common, there is a command line shorthand for it.

▼
```
java Split < article.txt | sort > sorted.txt
```

The split program runs first, reading input from article.txt. Its output becomes the input
of the sort program. The output of `sort` is saved in the file sorted.txt. The | operator
▼   instructs the operating system to construct a *pipe* that links the output of the first program to the input of the second.

The file sorted.txt has one blemish. It is likely to contain runs of repeated words, like

▼
```
a
a
a
▼   an
an
anteater
▼   asia
```

This is easy to fix with another program that removes *adjacent* duplicates. Removing
duplicates in arbitrary positions is quite hard, but adjacent duplicates are easy to handle:

▼
File Unique.java

```
 1  import java.io.BufferedReader;
 2  import java.io.InputStreamReader;
 3  import java.io.IOException;
 4
 5  /**
 6     This program removes adjacent duplicate lines from
 7     the input read from System.in.
 8  */
 9  public class Unique
10  {
11     public static void main(String[] args)
12        throws IOException
13     {
14        BufferedReader console = new BufferedReader(
15           new InputStreamReader(System.in));
16
17        String lastLine = "";
18
```

Figure 5

A Series of Pipes

```
19        boolean done = false;
20
21        while(!done)
22        {
23            String inputLine = console.readLine();
24            if (inputLine == null)
25                done = true;
26            else if (!inputLine.equals(lastLine))
27            {
28                // it's a different line from its predecessor
29                System.out.println(inputLine);
30                lastLine = inputLine;
31            }
32        }
33    }
34 }
```

The sorted word list, with duplicates removed, is obtained as the series of pipes (see Figure 5).

```
java Split < article.txt | sort | java Unique >
sorted.txt
```

Redirection and pipes make it possible to combine simple programs to do useful work. This approach was pioneered in the UNIX operating system, which comes with dozens of commands that perform common tasks and are designed to be combined with each other.

6.5   Random Numbers and Simulations

> In a simulation, you repeatedly generate random numbers and use them to simulate an activity.

In a simulation you generate random events and evaluate their outcomes. Here is a typical problem that can be decided by running a simulation: the *Buffon needle experiment*, devised by Comte Georges-Louis Leclerc de Buffon (1707–1788), a French naturalist. On each *try*, a needle of length 1 inch is dropped onto paper that is ruled with lines 2 inches apart. If the needle drops onto a line, count it as a hit. Buffon conjectured that the quotient *tries/hits* approximates π. (See Figure 6.)

Now, how can you run this experiment in the computer? You don't actually want to build a robot that drops needles on paper. The Random class of the Java library implements

Figure 6

The Buffon Needle Experiment

a *random number generator*, which produces numbers that appear to be completely random. To generate random numbers, you construct an object of the Random class, and then apply one of the following methods:

Method	Returns
nextInt(n)	A random integer between the integers 0 (inclusive) and n (exclusive)
nextDouble()	A random floating-point number between 0 (inclusive) and 1 (exclusive)

For example, you can simulate the cast of a die as follows:

```
Random generator = new Random();
int d = 1 + generator.nextInt(6);
```

The call generator.nextInt(6) gives you a random number between 0 and 5 (inclusive). Add 1 to obtain a number between 1 and 6.

To give you a feeling for the random numbers, run the following program a few times:

File Die.java

```
1  import java.util.Random;
2
3  /**
4     This class models a die that, when cast, lands on a random
5     face.
6  */
7  public class Die
8  {
9     /**
10        Constructs a die with a given number of sides.
11        @param s the number of sides, e.g. 6 for a normal die
12     */
13     public Die(int s)
14     {
15        sides = s;
16        generator = new Random();
17     }
18
```

```
19    /**
20        Simulates a throw of the die.
21        @return the face of the die
22    */
23    public int cast()
24    {
25        return 1 + generator.nextInt(sides);
26    }
27
28
29    private Random generator;
30    private int sides;
31 }
```

File DieTest.java

```
1  /**
2      This program simulates casting a die ten times.
3  */
4  public class DieTest
5  {
6     public static void main(String[] args)
7     {
8        Die d = new Die(6);
9        final int TRIES = 10;
10       for (int i = 1; i <= TRIES; i++)
11       {
12          int n = d.cast();
13          System.out.print(n + " ");
14       }
15       System.out.println();
16    }
17 }
```

Here are a few typical program runs.

```
6 5 6 3 2 6 3 4 4 1
3 2 2 1 6 5 3 4 1 2
4 1 3 2 6 2 4 3 3 5
```

As you can see, this program produces a different stream of simulated die casts every time it is run. Actually, the numbers are not completely random. They are drawn from very long sequences of numbers that don't repeat for a long time. These sequences are actually computed from fairly simple formulas; they just behave like random numbers. For that reason, they are often called *pseudorandom* numbers. How to generate good sequences of numbers that behave like truly random sequences is an important and well-studied problem in computer science. We won't investigate this issue further, though; we'll just use the random numbers produced by the Random class.

To run the Buffon needle experiment, we have to work a little harder. When you throw a die, it has to come up with one of six faces. When throwing a needle, however, there are many possible outcomes. You must generate *two* random numbers: one to

Figure 7

When Does the Needle Fall on a Line?

describe the starting position and one to describe the angle of the needle with the *x*-axis. Then you need to test whether the needle touches a grid line. Stop after 10,000 tries.

Let us agree to generate the *lower* point of the needle. Its *x*-coordinate is irrelevant, and you may assume its *y*-coordinate y_{low} to be any random number between 0 and 2. However, because it can be a random *floating-point* number, we use the `nextDouble` method of the `Random` class. It returns a random floating-point number between 0 and 1. Multiply by 2 to get a random number between 0 and 2.

The angle α between the needle and the *x*-axis can be any value between 0 degrees and 180 degrees. The upper end of the needle has *y*-coordinate

$$y_{high} = y_{low} + \sin(\alpha)$$

The needle is a hit if y_{high} is at least 2. See Figure 7.

Here is the program to carry out the simulation of the needle experiment.

File Needle.java

```
 1  import java.util.Random;
 2
 3  /**
 4      This class simulates a needle in the Buffon needle experiment.
 5  */
 6  public class Needle
 7  {
 8      /**
 9          Constructs a needle.
10      */
11      public Needle()
12      {
13          hits = 0;
14          tries = 0;
15          generator = new Random();
16      }
17
18      /**
19          Drops the needle on the grid of lines and
```

```
20          remembers whether the needle hit a line.
21      */
22      public void drop()
23      {
24          double ylow = 2 * generator.nextDouble();
25          double angle = 180 * generator.nextDouble();
26
27          // compute high point of needle
28
29          double yhigh = ylow
30              + Math.sin(Math.toRadians(angle));
31          if (yhigh >= 2) hits++;
32          tries++;
33      }
34
35      /**
36          Gets the number of times the needle hit a line.
37          @return the hit count
38      */
39      public int getHits()
40      {
41          return hits;
42      }
43
44      /**
45          Gets the total number of times the needle was dropped.
46          @return the try count
47      */
48      public int getTries()
49      {
50          return tries;
51      }
52
53      private Random generator;
54      private int hits;
55      private int tries;
56  }
```

File NeedleTest.java

```
1  public class NeedleTest
2  {
3      public static void main(String[] args)
4      {
5          Needle n = new Needle();
6          final int TRIES1 = 10000;
7          final int TRIES2 = 100000;
8
9          for (int i = 1; i <= TRIES1; i++)
10             n.drop();
11         System.out.println("Tries / Hits = "
```

```
12              + (double)n.getTries() / n.getHits());
13
14          for (int i = TRIES1 + 1; i <= TRIES2; i++)
15              n.drop();
16          System.out.println("Tries / Hits = "
17              + (double)n.getTries() / n.getHits());
18      }
19  }
```

On one computer I obtained the result 3.10 when running 10,000 iterations and 3.1429 when running 100,000 iterations.

The point of this program is *not* to compute π—there are far more efficient ways for that purpose. Rather, the point is to show how a physical experiment can be simulated on the computer. Buffon had to drop the needle physically thousands of times and record the results, which must have been a rather dull activity. You can have the computer execute the experiment quickly and accurately.

Simulations are very common computer applications. Many simulations use essentially the same pattern as the code of this example: In a loop, a large number of sample values are generated, and the values of certain observations are recorded for each sample. When the simulation is completed, the averages, or other statistics of interest from the observed values are printed out.

A typical example of a simulation is the modeling of customer queues at a bank or a supermarket. Rather than observing real customers, one simulates their arrival and their transactions at the teller window or checkout stand in the computer. One can try out different staffing or building layout patterns in the computer simply by making changes in the program. In the real world, making many such changes and measuring their effect would be impossible, or at least very expensive.

▼ 𝔸𝕋 Advanced Topic   6.8 ▶

Loop Invariants

Consider the task of computing a^n, where a is a floating-point number and n is a positive integer. Of course, you can multiply $a \cdot a \cdot \cdots \cdot a$, n times, but if n is large, you'll end up doing a lot of multiplications. The following loop computes a^n in far fewer steps:

```
double a = . . .;
int n = . . .;
double r = 1;
double b = a;
int i = n;
while (i > 0)
{
    if (i % 2 == 0) // n is even
    {
        b = b * b;
        i = i / 2;
    }
```

```
            else
            {
                r = r * b;
                i--
            }
        }
        // now r equals a to the nth power
```

Consider the case n = 100. The method performs the following steps.

b	i	r
a	100	1
a^2	50	
a^4	25	
	24	a^4
a^8	12	
a^{16}	6	
a^{32}	3	
	2	a^{36}
a^{64}	1	
	0	a^{100}

Amazingly enough, the algorithm yields exactly a^{100}. Do you understand why? Are you convinced it will work for all values of n? Here is a clever argument to show that the method always computes the correct result. We will demonstrate that whenever the program reaches the top of the while loop, it is true that

$$r \cdot b^i = a^n \qquad (I)$$

Certainly, it is true the first time around, because b == a and i == n. Suppose that (I) holds at the beginning of the loop. We label the values of r, b, and i as "old" when entering the loop, as "new" when exiting the loop. We assume that upon entry

$$r_{old} \cdot b_{old}^{i_{old}} = a^n$$

In the loop we have to distinguish two cases: i_{old} even and i_{old} odd. If i_{old} is even, the loop performs the following transformations:

$$r_{new} = r_{old}$$
$$b_{new} = b_{old}^2$$
$$i_{new} = i_{old} / 2$$

Therefore,

$$r_{new} \cdot b_{new}^{i_{new}} = r_{old} \cdot b_{old}^{2 \cdot i_{old}/2}$$

$$= r_{old} \cdot b_{old}^{i_{old}}$$

$$= a^n$$

On the other hand, if i_{old} is odd, then

$$r_{new} = r_{old} \cdot a_{old}$$

$$b_{new} = b_{old}$$

$$i_{new} = i_{old} - 1$$

Therefore,

$$r_{new} \cdot b_{new}^{i_{new}} = r_{old} \cdot b_{old} \cdot b_{old}^{i_{old} - 1}$$

$$= r_{old} \cdot b_{old}^{i_{old}}$$

$$= a^n$$

In either case, the new values for r, b, and i fulfill the *loop invariant* (I). So what? When the loop finally exits, (I) holds again:

$$r \cdot b^i = a^n$$

Furthermore, we know that i = 0, because the loop is terminating. But because i = 0, $r \cdot b^i = r \cdot b^0 = r$. Hence $r = a^n$, and the method really does compute the nth power of a.

This technique is quite useful, because it can explain an algorithm that is not at all obvious. The condition (I) is called a loop invariant because it is true when the loop is entered, at the top of each pass, and when the loop is exited. If a loop invariant is chosen skillfully, you may be able to deduce correctness of a computation. See [3] for another nice example.

Random Fact   6.2

Correctness Proofs

In Advanced Topic 6.8 we introduced the technique of loop invariants. If you skipped that note, have a glance at it now. That technique can be used to prove rigorously that a loop computes exactly the value that it is supposed to compute. Such a proof is far more valuable than any testing. No matter how many test cases you try, you always worry whether another case that you haven't tried yet might show a bug. A proof settles the correctness for *all possible inputs.*

For some time, programmers were very hopeful that proof techniques such as loop invariants would greatly reduce the need of testing. You would prove that each simple method is correct, and then put the proven components together and prove that they work together as they should. Once it is proved that `main` works correctly, no testing is required at all! Some researchers were so excited about these techniques that they tried to

▼ omit the programming step altogether. The designer would write down the program requirements, using the notation of formal logic. An automatic prover would prove that such a program could be written and generate the program as part of its proof.

▼ Unfortunately, in practice these methods never worked very well. The logical notation to describe program behavior is complex. Even simple scenarios require many formulas. It is easy enough to express the idea that a method is supposed to compute a^n, but

▼ the logical formulas describing all methods in a program that controls an airplane, for instance, would fill many pages. These formulas are created by humans, and humans make errors when they deal with difficult and tedious tasks. Experiments showed that

▼ instead of buggy programs, programmers wrote buggy logic specifications and buggy program proofs.

Van der Linden [2, p. 287], gives some examples of complicated proofs that are much

▼ harder to verify than the programs they are trying to prove.

Program proof techniques are valuable for proving the correctness of individual methods that make computations in nonobvious ways. At this time, though, there is no

▼ hope to prove any but the most trivial programs correct in such a way that the specification and the proof can be trusted more than the program. There is hope that correctness proofs will become more applicable to real-life programming situations in the future. At

▼ this point, however, engineering and management are at least as important as mathematics and logic for the successful completion of large software projects.

CHAPTER SUMMARY

1. A `while` statement executes a block of code repeatedly. A termination condition controls how often the loop is executed.

2. An off-by-one error is a common error when programming loops. Think through simple test cases to avoid this type of error.

3. You use a `for` loop when a variable runs from a starting to an ending value with a constant increment or decrement.

4. Loops can be nested. A typical example for nested loops is printing a table with rows and columns.

5. Processing input is complicated by the fact that checking for the end of input occurs in the middle of the loop.

6. Use input redirection to avoid repetitive typing during testing. Use output redirection to save your program output in a file.

7. You can break a line into words by using a `StringTokenizer`.

8. You can access the individual characters of a string with the `charAt` method.

9. Make a choice between symmetric and asymmetric bounds for each `for` loop.

10. Count the number of iterations of a `for` loop to check that your loop is correct.

11. In a simulation, you repeatedly generate random numbers and use them to simulate an activity.

Further Reading

[1] E. W. Dijkstra, "Goto Statements Considered Harmful", *Communications of the ACM*, vol. 11, no. 3 (March 1968), pp. 147–148.
[2] Peter van der Linden, *Expert C Programming*, Prentice-Hall, 1994.
[3] Jon Bentley, *Programming Pearls*, Addison-Wesley, 1986, Chapter 4, "Writing Correct Programs".
[4] Kai Lai Chung, *Elementary Probability Theory with Stochastic Processes*, Undergraduate Texts in Mathematics, Springer-Verlag, 1974.
[5] Rudolf Flesch, *How to Write Plain English*, Barnes & Noble Books, 1979.

CLASSES, OBJECTS, AND METHODS INTRODUCED IN THIS CHAPTER

```
java.lang.String
    indexOf
java.util.Random
    nextDouble
    nextInt
java.util.StringTokenizer
    countTokens
    hasMoreTokens
    nextToken
```

REVIEW EXERCISES

Exercise R6.1. Which loop statements does Java support? Give simple rules when to use each loop type.

Exercise R6.2. What does the following code print?

```
for (int i = 0; i < 10; i++)
{
    for (int j = 0; j < 10; j++)
        System.out.print(i * j % 10);
    System.out.println();
}
```

Exercise R6.3. How often do the following loops execute? Assume that i is an integer variable that is not changed in the loop body.

- `for (i = 1; i <= 10; i++) ...`
- `for (i = 0; i < 10; i++) ...`

- `for (i = 10; i > 0; i--) ...`
- `for (i = -10; i <= 10; i++) ...`
- `for (i = 10; i >= 0; i++) ...`
- `for (i = -10; i <= 10; i = i + 2) ...`
- `for (i = -10; i <= 10; i = i + 3) ...`

Exercise R6.4. Rewrite the following `for` loop into a `while` loop.

```
int s = 0;
for (int i = 1; i <= 10; i++) s = s + i;
```

Exercise R6.5. Rewrite the following `do` loop into a `while` loop.

```
int n = 1;
double x = 0;
double s;
do
{
   s = 1.0 / (n * n);
   x = x + s;
   n++;
}
while (s > 0.01);
```

Exercise R6.6. What is an infinite loop? On your computer, how can you terminate a program that executes an infinite loop?

Exercise R6.7. There are two ways to supply input to `System.in`. Describe both methods. Explain how the "end of input" is signaled in both cases.

Exercise R6.8. In UNIX and Windows, there is no special "end of file" character stored in a file. Verify that statement by producing a file with known character count—for example, a file consisting of the following three lines

```
Hello
cruel
world
```

Then look at the directory listing. How many characters does the file contain? Remember to count the newline characters. (In DOS, you may be surprised that the count is not what you expect. DOS text files store each newline as a two-character sequence. The input readers and output streams automatically translate between this carriage return/line feed sequence used by files and the '\n' character used by Java programs, so you don't need to worry about it.) Why does this prove that there is no "end of file" character? Why do you nevertheless need to type Ctrl+D/Ctrl+Z to end console input?

Exercise R6.9. Show how to use a string tokenizer to break up the string `"Hello, cruel world!"` into tokens. What are the resulting tokens?

Exercise R6.10. How do you break up the string `"Hello, cruel world!"` into characters? What are the resulting characters?

Exercise R6.11. What is a "loop and a half"? Give three strategies to implement the following "loop and a half":

```
loop
{
    read name of bridge
    if not OK, exit loop
    read length of bridge in feet
    if not OK, exit loop
    convert length to meters
    print bridge data
}
```

Use a Boolean variable, a `break` statement, and a method with multiple `return` statements. Which of these three approaches do you find clearest?

Exercise R6.12. Give a strategy for reading input of the form

name of bridge   length of bridge

Here the name of the bridge can be a single word ("Brooklyn") or consist of several words ("Golden Gate"). The length is a floating-point number. Unlike the preceding exercise, the entire input is provided on a single line.

Exercise R6.13. Sometimes students write programs with instructions such as "Enter data, 0 to quit" and exit the data entry loop when the user enters the number 0. (Such a value is called a sentinel value.) Explain why that is usually a poor idea.

Exercise R6.14. How would you use a random number generator to simulate the drawing of a playing card?

Exercise R6.15. What is an "off by one" error? Give an example from your own programming experience.

Exercise R6.16. Give an example of a `for` loop in which symmetric bounds are more natural. Give an example of a `for` loop in which asymmetric bounds are more natural.

Exercise R6.17. What are nested loops? Give an example where a nested loop is typically used.

PROGRAMMING EXERCISES

Exercise P6.1. *Currency conversion.* Write a program that asks the user to enter today's exchange rate between U.S. dollars and the Euro. Then the program reads U.S. dollar values and converts each to Euro values. Stop when the user hits the "Cancel" button of the input dialog (or when the user closes input if you read from `System.in`).

Exercise P6.2. *Random walk.* Simulate the wandering of an intoxicated person in a square street grid. Draw a grid of 10 streets horizontally and 10 streets vertically. Represent the simulated drunkard by a dot, placed in the middle of the grid to start. For 100 times, have the simulated drunkard randomly pick a direction (east, west, north, south), move one block in the chosen direction, and redraw the dot. After the iterations, display the distance that the drunkard has covered. (One might expect that on average the person might not get anywhere because the moves to different directions cancel another out in the long run, but in fact it can be shown that with probability 1 the person eventually moves outside any finite region. See, for example, [4], Chapter 8, for more details.) Use classes for the grid and the drunkard.

Exercise P6.3. *Projectile flight.* Suppose a cannonball is propelled vertically into the air with a starting velocity v_0. Any calculus book will tell us that the position of the ball after t seconds is $s(t) = -0.5 \cdot g \cdot t^2 + v_0 \cdot t$, where $g = 9.81$ m/sec^2 is the gravitational force of the earth. No calculus book ever mentions why someone would want to carry out such an obviously dangerous experiment, so we will do it in the safety of the computer.

In fact, we will confirm the theorem from calculus by a simulation. In our simulation, we will consider how the ball moves in very short time intervals Δt. In a short time interval the velocity v is nearly constant, and we can compute the distance the ball moves as $\Delta s = v \cdot \Delta t$. In our program, we will simply set

```
double deltaT = 0.01;
```

and update the position by

```
s = s + v * deltaT;
```

The velocity changes constantly—in fact, it is reduced by the gravitational force of the earth. In a short time interval, v decreases by $g \cdot \Delta t$, and we must keep the velocity updated as

```
v = v - g * deltaT;
```

In the next iteration the new velocity is used to update the distance.

Now run the simulation until the cannonball falls back onto the earth. Get the initial velocity as an input (100 m/sec is a good value). Update the position and velocity 100 times per second, but print out the position only every full second. Also print out the values from the exact formula $s(t) = -0.5 \cdot g \cdot t^2 + v_0 \cdot t$ for comparison. Use a class `Cannonball`.

What is the benefit of this kind of simulation when an exact formula is available? Well, the formula from the calculus book is *not* exact. Actually, the gravitational force diminishes the further the cannonball is away from the surface of the earth. This complicates the algebra sufficiently that it is not possible to give an exact formula for the actual motion, but the computer simulation can simply be extended to apply a variable gravitational force. For cannonballs, the calculus-book formula is actually good enough, but computers are necessary to compute accurate trajectories for higher-flying objects such as ballistic missiles.

Exercise P6.4. Most cannonballs are not shot upright but at an angle. If the starting velocity has magnitude v and the starting angle is α, then the velocity is actually a vector with components $v_x = v \cdot \cos(\alpha)$, $v_y = v \cdot \sin(\alpha)$. In the x-direction the velocity does not change. In the y-direction the gravitational force takes its toll. Repeat the simulation from the previous exercise, but update the x and y components of the location and the velocity separately. Every full second, plot the location of the cannonball on the graphics display. Repeat until the cannonball has reached the earth again. Again, use a class `Cannonball`.

This kind of problem is of historical interest. The first computers were designed to carry out just such ballistic calculations, taking into account the diminishing gravity for high-flying projectiles and wind speeds.

Exercise P6.5. The *Fibonacci sequence* is defined by the following rule. The first two values in the sequence are 1 and 1. Every subsequent value is the sum of the two values preceding it. For example, the third value is $1 + 1 = 2$, the fourth value is $1 + 2 = 3$, and the fifth is $2 + 3 = 5$. If f_n denotes the nth value in the Fibonacci sequence, then

$$f_1 = 1$$
$$f_2 = 1$$
$$f_n = f_{n-1} + f_{n-2} \text{ if } n > 2$$

Write a program that prompts the user for n and prints the nth value in the Fibonacci sequence. Use a class `FibonacciGenerator` with a method `nextNumber`.

Hint: There is no need to store all values for f_n. You only need the last two values to compute the next one in the series:

```
fold1 = 1;
fold2 = 1;
fnew = fold1 + fold2;
```

After that, discard `fold2`, which is no longer needed, and set `fold2` to `fold1` and `fold1` to `fnew`.

Exercise P6.6. Write a program that draws a *bar chart* from a data set. The program should be a graphics applet that prompts the user for the values, all to be entered into a single option dialog, separated by spaces (for example, 40 60 50). Assume all values are between 0 and 100. Then draw a bar chart like this:

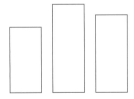

Exercise P6.7. *Mean and standard deviation.* Write a program that reads a set of floating-point data values from the input. When the end of file is reached, print out the count of the values, the average, and the standard deviation. The average of a data set $x_1, \ldots, x_n$ is

$$\bar{x} = \frac{\sum x_i}{n}$$

where $\sum x_i = x_1 + \cdots + x_n$ is the sum of the input values. The standard deviation is

$$S = \sqrt{\frac{\sum (x_i - \bar{x})^2}{n - 1}}$$

However, that formula is not suitable for our task. By the time you have computed the mean, the individual x_i are long gone. Until you know how to save these values, use the numerically less stable formula

$$S = \sqrt{\frac{\sum x_i^2 - (\sum x_i)^2 / n}{n - 1}}$$

You can compute this quantity by keeping track of the count, the sum, and the sum of squares in the `DataSet` class as you process the input values.

Exercise P6.8. Write a graphical applet that prompts a user to enter a number n and that draws n circles with random center and random radius.

Exercise P6.9. *Flesch Readability Index.* The following index [5] was invented by Flesch as a simple tool to gauge the legibility of a document without linguistic analysis.

- Count all words in the file. A *word* is any sequence of characters delimited by white space, whether or not it is an actual English word.

- Count all syllables in each word. To make this simple, use the following rules: Each *group* of adjacent vowels (a,e,i,o,u,y) counts as one syllable (for example, the "ea" in "real" contributes one syllable, but the "e..a" in "regal" count as two syllables). However, an "e" at the end of a word doesn't count as a syllable. Also, each word has at least one syllable, even if the previous rules give a count of 0.

- Count all sentences. A sentence is ended by a period, colon, semicolon, question mark, or exclamation mark.

- The index is computed by

  Index = 206.835

       $-84.6 \times$ (Number of syllables / Number of words)

       $-1.015 \times$ (Number of words / Number of sentences)

  rounded to the nearest integer.

This index is a number, usually between 0 and 100, indicating how difficult the text is to read. Some examples for random material for various publications are

Comics	95
Consumer ads	82
Sports Illustrated	65
Time	57
New York Times	39
Auto insurance policy	10
Internal Revenue Code	−6

Translated into educational levels, the indices are

91–100	5th grader
81–90	6th grader
71–80	7th grader
66–70	8th grader
61–66	9th grader
51–60	High school student
31–50	College student
0–30	College graduate
Less than 0	Law school graduate

The purpose of the index is to force authors to rewrite their text until the index is high enough. This is achieved by reducing the length of sentences and by removing long words. For example, the sentence

> The following index was invented by Flesch as a simple tool to estimate the legibility of a document without linguistic analysis.

can be rewritten as

> Flesch invented an index to check whether a text is easy to read. To compute the index, you need not look at the meaning of the words.

His book [5] contains delightful examples of translating government regulations into "plain English".

Your program should read a text file in, compute the legibility index, and print out the equivalent educational level. Use classes `Word` and `Document`.

Exercise P6.10. *Factoring of integers.* Write a program that asks the user for an integer and then prints out all its factors. For example, when the user enters 150, the program should print

```
2
3
5
5
```

Use a class `FactorGenerator` with methods `nextFactor` and `hasMoreFactors`.

Exercise P6.11. *Prime numbers.* Write a program that prompts the user for an integer and then prints out all prime numbers up to that integer. For example, when the user enters 20, the program should print

```
2
3
5
7
11
13
17
19
```

Recall that a number is a prime number if it is not divisible by any number except 1 and itself.

Use a class `PrimeGenerator` with a method `nextPrime`.

Exercise P6.12. The *Heron method* is a method for computing square roots that was known to the ancient Greeks. If x is a guess for the value $\sqrt{a}$, then the average of x and a/x is a better guess.

Implement a class `RootApproximator` that starts with an initial guess of 1 and whose `nextGuess` method produces a sequence of increasingly better guesses. Supply a method `hasMoreGuesses` that returns `false` if two successive guesses are sufficiently close to each other. Then test your class like this:

```
RootApproximator r = new RootApproximator(n);
while (r.hasMoreGuesses())
    System.out.println(r.nextGuess());
```

Exercise P6.13. The best known iterative method for computing the *roots* of a function f (that is, the x-values for which $f(x)$ is 0) is *Newton–Raphson approximation*. To find the zero of a function whose derivative is also known, compute

$$x_{new} = x_{old} - f(x_{old}) / f'(x_{old}).$$

For this exercise, write a program to compute nth roots of floating-point numbers. Prompt the user for a and n, then obtain $\sqrt[n]{a}$ by computing a zero of the function $f(x) = x^n - a$. Follow the approach of the preceding exercise.

Exercise P6.14. The value of e^x can be computed as the power series

$$e^x = \sum_{n=0}^{\infty} \frac{x^n}{n!}$$

where $n! = 1 \cdot 2 \cdot 3 \cdot \cdots \cdot n$.

Write a program that computes e^x using this formula. Of course, you can't compute an infinite sum. Just keep adding values until an individual summand (term) is less than a certain threshold. At each step, you need to compute the new term and add it to the total. Update these terms as follows:

```
term = term * x / n;
```

Follow the approach of the preceding two exercises, by implementing a class `ExpApproximator`.

Exercise P6.15. Write a graphical applet that displays a checkerboard with 64 squares, alternating white and black.

Exercise P6.16. *The game of Nim.* This is a well-known game with a number of variants. We will consider the following variant, which has an interesting winning strategy. Two players alternately take marbles from a pile. In each move, a player chooses how many marbles to take. The player must take at least one but at most half of the marbles. Then the other player takes a turn. The player who takes the last marble loses.

Write a program in which the computer plays against a human opponent. Generate a random integer between 10 and 100 to denote the initial size of the pile. Generate a random integer between 0 and 1 to decide whether the computer or the human takes the first turn. Generate a random integer between 0 and 1 to decide whether the computer plays *smart* or *stupid*. In stupid mode, the computer simply takes a random legal value (between 1 and $n/2$) from the pile whenever it has a turn. In smart mode the computer takes off enough marbles to make the size of the pile a power of two minus 1—that is, 3, 7, 15, 31, or 63. That is always a legal move, except if the size of the pile is currently one less than a power of 2. In that case, the computer makes a random legal move.

Note that the computer cannot be beaten in smart mode when it has the first move, unless the pile size happens to be 15, 31, or 63. Of course, a human player who has the first turn and knows the winning strategy can win against the computer.

Exercise P6.17. Program the following simulation: Darts are thrown at random points onto the square with corners (1,1) and (−1,−1). If the dart lands inside the unit circle (that is, the circle with center (0,0) and radius 1), it is a hit. Otherwise it is a miss. Run this simulation and use it to determine an approximate value for π. Explain why this is a better method for estimating π than the Buffon needle program.

Exercise P6.18. It is easy and fun to draw graphs of curves with the Java graphics library. Simply draw a hundred line segments joining the points $(x, f(x))$ and $(x + d, f(x + d))$, where x ranges from x_{min} to x_{max} and $d = (x_{max} - x_{min})/100$. Draw the curve $f(x) = x^3/100 - x + 10$, where x ranges from -10 to 10 in this fashion.

Exercise P6.19. Draw a picture of the "four-leaved rose" whose equation in polar coordinates is $r = \cos(2\theta)$. Let θ go from 0 to 2π in 100 steps. Each time, compute r and then compute the (x,y) coordinates from the polar coordinates by using the formula

$$x = r\cos\theta, \quad y = r\sin\theta$$

You can get extra credit if you can vary the number of petals.

Exercise P6.20. The series of pipes in Advanced Topic 6.7 has one final problem: The output file contains upper- and lowercase versions of the same word, such as "The" and "the". Modify the procedure, either by changing one of the programs or, in the true spirit of piping, by writing another short program and adding it to the series.

Designing Classes

CHAPTER GOALS

To learn how to choose appropriate classes to implement

▶ To understand the concepts of cohesion and coupling

▶ To minimize the use of side effects

▶ To document the responsibilities of methods and their callers with preconditions and postconditions

▶ To understand the difference between instance methods and static methods

▶ To introduce the concept of static fields

▶ To understand the scope rules for local variables and instance fields

▶ To learn about packages

In this chapter you will learn more about designing classes. First, we will discuss the process of discovering classes and defining methods. Next, we will discuss how the concepts of pre- and postconditions enable you to specify, implement, and invoke methods correctly. You will also learn about several more technical issues, such as static methods and variables. Finally, you will see how to use packages to organize your classes.

7.1   Choosing Classes

You have used a good number of classes in the preceding chapters and probably designed a few classes yourself as part of your programming assignments. Designing a class can be a challenge—it is not always easy to tell how to start or whether the result is of good quality.

Students who have prior experience with programming in another programming language are used to programming *functions*. A function carries out an action. In object-oriented programming, the actions appear as methods. Each method, however, belongs to a class. Classes are collections of objects, and objects are not actions—they are entities. So you have to start the programming activity by identifying objects and the classes to which they belong.

> A class should represent a single concept from the problem domain, such as business, science, or mathematics.

Remember the rule of thumb from Chapter 2: Class names should be nouns, and method names should be verbs.

What makes a good class? Most importantly, a class should *represent a single concept*. Some of the classes that you have seen represent concepts from mathematics:

- `Point`
- `Rectangle`
- `Ellipse`

Other classes are abstractions of real-life entities.

- `BankAccount`
- `Purse`

For these classes, the properties of a typical object are easy to understand. A `Rectangle` object has a width and height. Given a `BankAccount` object, you can deposit and withdraw money. Generally, concepts from the part of the universe that our program concerns, such as science, business, or a game, make good classes. The name for such a class should be a noun that describes the concept. Some of the standard Java class names are a bit strange, such as `Ellipse2D.Double`, but you can choose better names for your own classes.

Another useful category of classes can be described as *actors*. Objects of an actor class does some kind of work for you. Examples of actors are the `StringTokenizer` class of Chapter 6 and the `Random` class in Chapter 4. A `StringTokenizer` object breaks up strings. A `Random` object generates random numbers. It is a good idea to choose class names for actors that end in "-er" or "-or". (A better name for the `Random` class might be `RandomNumberGenerator`.)

Very occasionally, a class has no objects, but it contains a collection of related static methods and constants. The `Math` class is a typical example. Such a class is called a *utility class*.

Finally, you have seen classes with just a `main` method. Their sole purpose is to start a program. From a design perspective, these are somewhat degenerate examples of classes.

What might not be a good class? If you can't tell from the class name what an object of the class is supposed to do, then you are probably not on the right track. For example, your homework assignment might ask you to write a program that prints paychecks. Suppose you start by trying to design a class `PaycheckProgram`. What would an object of this class do? An object of this class would have to do everything that the homework needs to do. That doesn't simplify anything. A better class would be `Paycheck`. Then your program can manipulate one or more `Paycheck` objects.

Another common mistake, particularly by students who are used to writing programs that consist of functions, is to turn an action into a class. For example, if your homework assignment is to compute a paycheck, you may consider writing a `ComputePaycheck` class. But can you visualize a "ComputePaycheck" object? The fact that "ComputePaycheck" isn't a noun tips you off that you are on the wrong track. On the other hand, a `Paycheck` class makes intuitive sense. The word "paycheck" is a noun. You can visualize a paycheck object. You can then think about useful methods of the `Paycheck` class, such as `compute`, that help you solve the assignment.

7.2   Cohesion and Coupling

> The public interface of a class is cohesive if all of its features are related to the concept that the class represents.

In this section you will learn a couple of useful criteria for analyzing the quality of the public interface of a class.

A class should represent a single concept. The public methods and constants that the public interface exposes should be *cohesive*. That is, all interface features should be closely related to the single concept that the class represents.

If you find that the public interface of a class refers to multiple concepts, then that is a good sign that it may be time to use separate classes instead. Consider, for example, the public interface of the `Purse` class in Chapter 3:

```
public class Purse
{
```

```
        public Purse() { . . . }
        public void addNickels(int count)  { . . . }
        public void addDimes(int count)  { . . . }
        public void addQuarters(int count)  { . . . }
        public double getTotal()  { . . . }
        public static final double NICKEL_VALUE = 0.05;
        public static final double DIME_VALUE = 0.1;
        public static final double QUARTER_VALUE = 0.25;
        . . .
    }
```

There are really two concepts here: a purse that holds coins and computes their total, and the values of individual coins. It would make more sense to have a separate `Coin` class and have coins responsible for knowing their values.

```
    public class Coin
    {
        public Coin(double aValue, String aName) { . . . }
        public double getValue() { . . . }
        . . .
    }
```

Then the `Purse` class can be simplified:

```
    public class Purse
    {
        public Purse() { . . . }
        public void add(Coin aCoin) { . . . }
        public double getTotal()  { . . . }
        . . .
    }
```

This is clearly a better solution, because it separates the responsibilities of the purse and the coins. The only reason we didn't follow this approach in Chapter 3 was to keep the `Purse` example simple.

> A class depends on another class if it uses objects of that other class.

Many classes need other classes to do their job. For example, the restructured `Purse` class now depends on the `Coin` class to determine the total value of the coins in the purse.

To visualize relationships such as dependence between classes, programmers draw class diagrams. In this book, we use the UML ("Unified Modeling Language") notation for objects and classes. UML is a notation for object-oriented analysis and design invented by Grady Booch, Ivar Jacobson, and James Rumbaugh, three leading researchers in object-oriented software development. The UML notation distinguishes between *object diagrams* and class diagrams. In an object diagram the class names are <u>underlined</u>; in a class diagram the class names are not underlined. In a class diagram, you denote dependency by a dashed line with a >-shaped open arrow tip that points to the dependent class. Figure 1 shows a class diagram that indicates that the `Purse` class depends on the `Coin` class.

Note that the `Coin` class does *not* depend on the `Purse` class. Coins have no idea that they are being collected in purses, and they can carry out their work without ever calling any method in the `Purse` class.

Figure 1

Dependency Relationship between the
Purse and Coin Classes

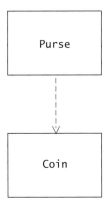

It is a good practice to
minimize the coupling (i.e.,
dependency) between classes.

If many classes of a program depend on each other, then we say
that the *coupling* between classes is high. Conversely, if there are few
dependencies between classes, then we say that the coupling is low
(see Figure 2).

Low coupling

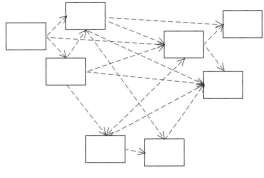

High coupling

Figure 2

High and Low Coupling between Classes

Why does coupling matter? If the `Coin` class changes in the next release of the program, all the classes that depend on it may be affected. If the change is drastic, the coupled classes must all be updated. Furthermore, if we would like to use a class in another program, we have to take with it all the classes on which it depends. Thus, we want to remove unnecessary coupling between classes.

✖ Quality Tip   7.1

Consistency

In this section you learned of two criteria to analyze the quality of the public interface of a class. You should maximize cohesion and remove unnecessary coupling. There is another criterion that we would like you to pay attention to—consistency. When you have a set of methods, follow a consistent scheme for their names and parameters. This is simply a sign of good craftsmanship.

Sadly, you can find any number of inconsistencies in the standard library. Here is an example. To show an input dialog, you call

```
JOptionPane.showInputDialog(promptString)
```

To show a message dialog, you call

```
JOptionPane.showMessageDialog(null, messageString)
```

What's the `null` parameter? It turns out that the `showMessageDialog` method needs a parameter to specify the parent window, or `null` if no parent window is required. But the `showInputDialog` method requires no parent window. Why the inconsistency? There is no reason. It would have been an easy matter to supply a `showMessageDialog` method that exactly mirrors the `showInputDialog` method.

Inconsistencies such as these are not a fatal flaw, but they are an annoyance, particularly because they can be so easily avoided.

7.3   Accessor and Mutator Methods

> An accessor method does not change the state of its implicit parameter. A mutator method can change the state.

In this section we introduce a useful terminology for the methods of a class. A method that accesses an object and returns some information about it, without changing the object, is called an *accessor* method. In contrast, a method whose purpose is to modify the state of an object is called a *mutator* method. For example, in the `BankAccount` class, `getBalance` is an accessor method, because getting the account balance does not change the account. In contrast, the `deposit` and `withdraw` methods are mutator methods.

As a rule of thumb, it is a good idea for mutators to have return type `void`. This is not a rule of the Java language, but just a recommendation to make it easy to differentiate between mutators and accessors. The `BankAccount` methods follow this recommendation. The `getBalance` method returns the current balance without changing it. The `deposit` and `withdraw` methods change the object state, and they have return type `void`.

> An immutable class has no mutator methods.

You can call an accessor method as many times as you like—you always get the same answer, and it does not change the state of your object. That is clearly a desirable property, because it makes the behavior of such a method very predictable. Some classes have been designed to have only accessor methods and no mutator methods at all. Such classes are called *immutable*. An example is the `String` class. Once a string has been constructed, its contents never change. No method in the `String` class can modify the contents of a string. For example, the `substring` method does not remove characters from the original string. Instead, it constructs a *new* string that contains the substring characters.

An immutable class has a major advantage: It is safe to give out references to its objects freely. If no method can change the object's value, then no code can modify the object at an unexpected time. In contrast, if you give out a `BankAccount` reference to any other method, you have to be aware that the state of your object may change—the other method can call the `deposit` and `withdraw` methods on the reference that you gave it.

7.4   Side Effects

> A side effect of a method is any externally observable behavior outside the implicit parameter. You should minimize side effects.

We have classified methods as accessors or mutators depending on what effect they have on their implicit parameters. If a method modifies some outside value other than its implicit parameter, we call that modification a *side effect*. A side effect of a method is *any kind of observable behavior* outside the object.

Here is an example of a method whose side effect is the updating of an explicit parameter:

```java
public class BankAccount
{
    /**
        Transfers money from this account to another account.
        @param amount  the amount of money to transfer
        @param other  the account into which to transfer the money
    */
    public void transfer(double amount, BankAccount other)
    {
        balance = balance - amount;
        other.balance = other.balance + amount;
    }
    . . .
}
```

As a rule of thumb, updating an explicit parameter can be surprising to programmers, and it is best to avoid it whenever possible.

Note that a method can update only *object* parameters. Primitive type parameters are safe—a method can never change them. See Common Error 7.1 for more information.

Another example of a side effect is output. Consider how we have always printed a bank balance:

```
System.out.println("The balance is now $" +
    momsSavings.getBalance());
```

Why don't we simply have a printBalance method?

```
public void printBalance() // not recommended
{
    System.out.println("The balance is now $" + balance);
}
```

That would be more convenient when you actually want to print the value. But, of course, there are cases when you want the value for some other purpose. Thus, you can't simply drop the getBalance method in favor of printBalance.

More importantly, the printBalance method forces strong assumptions on the BankAccount class.

- The message is in English—you assume that the user of your software reads English. The majority of people on the planet don't.

- You rely on System.out. A method that relies on System.out won't work in an embedded system, such as the computer inside an automatic teller machine.

A method with a side effect introduces additional dependencies, thus violating the rule of minimizing the coupling of the classes. For example, the printBalance method couples the BankAccount class with the System and PrintStream classes. It is best to decouple input/output from the actual work of your classes.

One particularly reprehensible practice is printing error messages inside methods. You should never do that:

```
public void deposit(double amount)
{
    if (amount < 0)
        System.out.println("Bad value of amount");
        // bad style
    else
        balance = balance + amount;
}
```

You will learn in Section 7.5 and in Chapter 14 how a method can use *exceptions* to indicate problems.

Quality Tip   7.2

Minimize Side Effects

In an ideal world, all methods would be accessors that simply return an answer without changing any value at all. (In fact, programs that are written in so-called *functional* programming languages, such as Scheme and ML, come close to this ideal.) Of course, in an object-oriented programming language, we use objects to remember state changes. Therefore, a method that just changes the state of its implicit parameter is certainly acceptable. A method that does anything else is said to have a side effect, as described in Section 7.4. Although side effects cannot be completely eliminated, they can be the cause of surprises and problems and should be minimized. Here is a classification of method behavior.

- *Best:* Accessor methods with no changes to any explicit parameters—no side effects. Example: `getBalance`.

- *Good:* Mutator methods with no changes to any explicit parameters—no side effects: Example: `withdraw`.

- *Fair:* Methods that change an explicit parameter. Example: `transfer`.

- *Poor:* Methods that change a static field of another class such as `System.out`. (See Section 7.6 for more information on static fields.)

Common Error   7.1

Trying to Modify Primitive Type Parameters

In Java, a method can never change parameters of primitive type.

Methods can't update parameters of primitive type (numbers and `boolean`). To illustrate this point, let us try to write a method that updates a number parameter:

```
public class BankAccount
{
    /**
        Transfers money from this account and tries to add it to a balance.
        @param amount the amount of money to transfer
        @param otherBalance balance to add the amount to
    */
    void transfer(double amount, double otherBalance)
    {
```

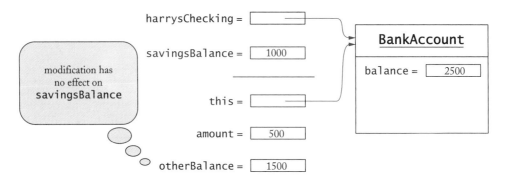

Figure 3

Modifying a Numeric Parameter Has No Effect on Caller

```
        balance = balance - amount;
        otherBalance = otherBalance + amount; // won't work
    }
      . . .
    }
```

This doesn't work. Let's consider a method call.

```
    double savingsBalance = 1000;
    harrysChecking.transfer(500, savingsBalance);
```

As the method starts, the parameter variable `otherBalance` is set to the same value as `savingsBalance`. Then the value of the `otherBalance` value is modified, but that modification had no effect on `savingsBalance`, because `otherBalance` is a separate variable (see Figure 3). When the method terminates, the `otherBalance` variable dies, and `savingsBalance` isn't increased.

Why did the example at the beginning of Section 7.4 work, where the second explicit parameter was a `BankAccount` reference? Then the parameter variable contained a copy of the object reference. Through that reference, the method is able to modify the object.

You already saw this difference between objects and primitive types in Chapter 3. As a consequence, a Java method can *never* modify numbers that are passed to it.

Advanced Topic 7.1

Call by Value and Call by Reference

In Java, method parameters are *copied* into the parameter variables when a method starts. Computer scientists call this call mechanism "call by value". There are some limitations to the "call by value" mechanism. As you saw in Common Error 7.1, it is not possible to implement methods that modify the contents of number variables. Other programming

▼ languages such as C++ support an alternate mechanism, called "call by reference". For
▼ example, in C++ it would be an easy matter to write a method that modifies a number, by
using a so-called *reference parameter*. Here is the C++ code, for those of you who know
▼ C++:

```
// this is C++
class BankAccount
{
public:
    void transfer(double amount, double& otherBalance)
        // otherBalance is a double&, a reference to a double
    {
        balance = balance - amount;
        otherBalance = otherBalance + amount; // works in C++
    }
    . . .
};
```

You will sometimes read in Java books that "numbers are passed by value, objects are
▼ passed by reference". That is technically not quite correct. In Java, objects themselves are
never passed as parameters; instead, both numbers and *object references* are copied by
value. To see this clearly, let us consider another scenario. This method tries to set the
▼ otherAccount parameter to a new object:

```
public class BankAccount
{
    public void transfer(double amount,
        BankAccount otherAccount)
    {
        balance = balance - amount;
        double newBalance = other.balance + amount;
        otherAccount = new BankAccount(newBalance); // won't work
    }
}
```

In this situation, we are not trying to change the state of the object to which the
parameter variable otherAccount refers; instead, we are trying to replace the
object with a different one (see Figure 4). Now the parameter variable other-
Account is replaced with a reference to a new account. But if you call the method
▼ with

```
harrysChecking.transfer(500, savingsAccount);
```

> In Java, a method can
> change the state of an
> object reference parameter,
> but it cannot replace the
> object reference with another.

then that change does not affect the savingsAccount variable that
is supplied in the call.

As you can see, a Java method can update an object's state, but it
cannot *replace* the contents of an object reference. This shows that
object references are passed by value in Java.

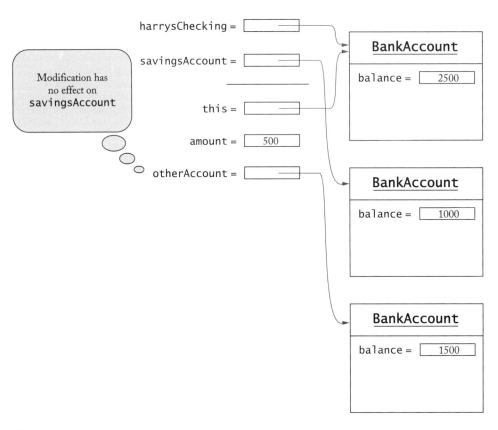

Figure 4

Modifying an Object Reference Parameter Has No Effect on the Caller

Quality Tip 7.3

Don't Change the Contents of Parameter Variables

As you saw in Common Error 7.1 and Advanced Topic 7.1, a method can treat its parameter variables like any other local variables and change their contents. However, that change affects only the parameter variable within the method itself—not any values supplied in the method call. Some programmers take "advantage" of the temporary nature of the parameter variables and use them as "convenient" holders for intermediate results, as in this example:

```
public void deposit(double amount) // poor style
{
    // using the parameter variable to hold an intermediate value
    amount = balance + amount;
    balance = amount;
}
```

▼

▼

That code would produce errors if another statement in the method referred to `amount` expecting it to be the value of the parameter, and it will confuse later programmers maintaining this method. You should always treat the parameter variables as if they were constants. Don't assign new values to them. Instead, introduce a new local variable.

▼

```
public void deposit(double amount)
{
    double newBalance = balance + amount;
    balance = newBalance;
}
```

▼

7.5   Preconditions and Postconditions

> A precondition is a requirement that the caller of a method must meet. If a method is called in violation of a precondition, the method is not responsible for computing the correct result.

A *precondition* is a requirement that the caller of a method must obey. For example, the `deposit` method of the `BankAccount` class has a precondition that the amount to be deposited should not be negative. It is the responsibility of the caller never to call a method if one of its preconditions is violated. If the method is called anyway, it is not responsible for producing a correct result.

Therefore, a precondition is an important part of the method, and you must document it. Here we document the precondition that the `amount` parameter must not be negative.

```
/**
    Deposits money into this account.
    @param amount  the amount of money to deposit
    (Precondition: amount >= 0)
*/
```

Some `javadoc` extensions support a `@precondition` or `@requires` tag, but it is not a part of the standard `javadoc` program. Because the standard `javadoc` tool skips all unknown tags, we simply add the precondition to the method explanation or the appropriate `@param` tag.

Preconditions are typically stated for one of two reasons:

1. To restrict the parameters of a method
2. To require that a method is only called when it is in the appropriate *state*

For example, once a `StringTokenizer` has run out of tokens, it is no longer legal to call the `nextToken` method. Thus, a precondition for the `nextToken` methods is that the `hasMoreTokens` method returns `true`.

A method is responsible only for operating correctly when its caller has fulfilled all preconditions. The method is free to do *anything* if a precondition is not fulfilled. It would be perfectly legal if the method reformatted the hard disk every time it was called with a wrong input. Naturally, that isn't reasonable. What should a method actually do when it is called with inappropriate inputs? For example, what should `account.deposit(-1000)` do? There are two good choices.

1. A method can check for the violation and *throw an exception.* Then the method does not return to its caller; instead, control is transferred to an exception handler. If no handler is present, then the program terminates.

2. If it is too cumbersome to carry out the check, the method can simply work under the assumption that the preconditions are fulfilled. If they aren't, then any data corruption (such as a negative balance) or other failures are the caller's fault.

You'll see in Chapter 14 how to program exception handlers. Right now, we'll show you how to throw an exception to indicate that a method has been called with inappropriate parameters.

```
public double deposit(double amount)
{
    if (amount < 0)
        throw new IllegalArgumentException();
    balance = balance + amount;
}
```

When the method is called with an illegal argument, the program aborts with an error message

```
java.lang.IllegalArgumentException
        at BankAccount.deposit(BankAccount.java:14)
```

If a method is called when the object is in an inappropriate state, you can throw an `IllegalStateException` instead.

Many beginning programmers think that it isn't "nice" to abort the program. Why not simply return to the caller instead?

```
public void deposit(double amount)
{
    if (amount < 0)
        return;  // not as good as throwing an exception
    balance = balance + amount;
}
```

That is legal—after all, a method can do anything if its preconditions are violated. But it is not as good as throwing an exception. If the program calling the deposit method has a few bugs that cause it to pass a negative amount as an input value, then the version that throws the exception will make the bugs very obvious during testing—it is hard to ignore when the program aborts. The quiet version, on the other hand, will not alert you, and you may not notice that it performs some wrong calculations as a consequence. Think of exceptions as the "tough love" approach to precondition checking.

If you test for the precondition, then you might as well throw an exception. However, sometimes the cost of testing is too high. It might slow down the method too much, or it might make it too confusing. Then you may simply go ahead and assume that the precondition is fulfilled:

```
public void deposit(double amount)
{
```

```
// no test, for maximum efficiency
// if this makes the balance negative, it's the caller's fault
balance = balance + amount;
}
```

When a method is called in accordance with its preconditions, then the method promises to do its job correctly. A different kind of promise that the method makes is called a *postcondition*. There are two kinds of postconditions:

1. That the return value is computed correctly

2. That the object is in a certain state after the method call is completed

Here is a postcondition that makes a statement about the object state after the `deposit` method is called.

```
/**
    Deposits money into this account.
    (Postcondition: getBalance() >= 0)
    @param amount  the amount of money to deposit
    (Precondition: amount >= 0)
*/
```

As long as the precondition is fulfilled, this method guarantees that the balance after the deposit is not negative.

Some `javadoc` extensions support a `@postcondition` or `@ensures` tag. However, just as with preconditions, we simply add postconditions to the method explanation or the `@return` tag, because the standard `javadoc` program skips all tags that it doesn't know.

Some programmers feel that they must specify a postcondition for every method. When you use `javadoc`, however, you already specify a part of the postcondition in the `@return` tag, and you shouldn't repeat it in a postcondition.

```
// this postcondition statement is overly repetitive
/**
    Returns the current balance of this account.
    @return  the account balance
    (Postcondition: the return value equals the account balance)
*/
```

Note that we formulate pre- and postconditions only in terms of the *interface* of the class. Thus, we state the precondition of the `withdraw` method as `amount <= getBalance()`, not `amount <= balance`. After all, the caller, which needs to check the precondition, has access only to the public interface, not the private implementation.

Bertrand Meyer [1] compares preconditions and postconditions to contracts. In real life, contracts spell out the obligations of the contracting parties. For example, your mechanic may promise to fix the brakes of your car, and you promise in turn to pay a certain amount of money. If either party breaks the promise, then the other is not bound by the terms of the contract. In the same fashion, pre- and postconditions are contractual terms between a method and its caller. The method promises to fulfill the postcondition for all inputs that fulfill the precondition. The caller promises never to call the method with illegal inputs. If the caller fulfills its promise and gets a wrong answer, it can take the method to "programmer's court". If the caller doesn't fulfill its promise and something terrible happens as a consequence, it has no recourse.

▼ **AT** **Advanced Topic** **7.2** ▶

Class Invariants

Advanced Topic 6.8 introduced the concept of loop invariants. A loop invariant is established when the loop is first entered, and it is preserved by all loop iterations. We then know that the loop invariant must be true when the loop exits, and we can use that information to reason about the correctness of a loop.

Class invariants fulfill a similar purpose. A class invariant is a statement about an object that is true after every constructor and that is preserved by every mutator (provided that the caller respects all preconditions). We then know that the class invariant must always be true, and we can use that information to reason about the correctness of our program.

Here is a simple example. Consider a `BankAccount` class with the following preconditions for the constructor and the mutators:

```
public class BankAccount
{
    /**
        Constructs a bank account with a given balance.
        @param initialBalance the initial balance
        (Precondition: initialBalance >= 0)
    */
    public BankAccount(double initialBalance) { . . . }
    {
        balance = initialBalance;
    }

    /**
        Deposits money into the bank account.
        @param amount the amount to deposit
        (Precondition: amount >= 0)
    */
    public void deposit(double amount) { . . . }

    /**
        Withdraws money from the bank account.
        @param amount the amount to withdraw
        (Precondition: amount <= getBalance())
    */
    public void withdraw(double amount) { . . . }

    . . .
}
```

Now we can formulate the following invariant:

```
getBalance() >= 0
```

▼ To see why this invariant is true, we first check the constructor. Since the precondition of the constructor is

▼
```
initialBalance >= 0
```

we can prove that the invariant is true after the constructor has set `balance` to `initialBalance`.

▼ Next, check the mutators. The precondition of the `deposit` method is

```
amount >= 0
```

We can assume that the invariant condition holds before calling the method. Thus, we
▼ know that `balance >= 0` before the method executes. The laws of mathematics tell us that the sum of two nonnegative numbers is again nonnegative, so we can conclude that `balance >= 0` after the completion of the `deposit`. Thus, the `deposit` method pre-
▼ serves the invariant.

A similar argument shows that the `withdraw` method preserves the invariant.

Since the invariant is a property of the class, you document it with the class description:

▼
```
/**
    A bank account has a balance that can be changed by
    deposits and withdrawals.
    (Invariant: getBalance() >= 0)
▼ */
public class BankAccount
▼ {
        . . .
    }
```
▼

7.6   Static Methods

A static method has
no implicit parameter.

Sometimes you write methods that don't need an implicit parameter. Such a method is called a *static method* or a *class method*. In contrast, the methods that you wrote up to now are often called *instance methods* because they operate on a particular instance of an object. You encountered static method calls in Chapter 3. For example, the `sqrt` method in the `Math` class is a static method. When you call `Math.sqrt(x)`, you don't supply any implicit parameter. (Recall that `Math` is the name of a class, not an object.) And, of course, every application has a static `main` method (however, applets do not).

Why would you want to write a method without an implicit parameter? The most common reason is that you want to encapsulate some computations that involve only numbers. Since numbers aren't objects, you can't pass them as implicit parameters.

Here is a typical example of a static method that carries out some simple algebra. Recall from Chapter 5 that two floating-point numbers x and y are approximately equal if

$$\frac{|x - y|}{\max(|x|, |y|)} \le \varepsilon$$

where ε is a small number, typically chosen to be 10^{-14}.

However, if *x* or *y* is zero, then you need to test whether the absolute value of the other quantity is at most ε.

Of course, this computation is just complex enough that it makes a lot of sense to encapsulate it in a method. Since the parameters are numbers, the method doesn't operate on any objects at all, so we make it into a `static` method:

```
/**
    Tests whether two floating-point numbers are
    equal, except for a roundoff error.
    @param x  a floating-point number
    @param y  a floating-point number
    @return true if x and y are approximately equal
*/
public static boolean approxEqual(double x, double y)
{
    final double EPSILON = 1E-14;
    if (x == 0) return Math.abs(y) <= EPSILON;
    if (y == 0) return Math.abs(x) <= EPSILON;
    return Math.abs(x - y) /
        Math.max(Math.abs(x), Math.abs(y))
        <= EPSILON;
}
```

You need to find a home for this method. You have two choices. You can simply add this method to a class whose methods need to call it. Or you can come up with a new class (similar to the `Math` class of the standard Java library) to contain this method. In this book, we will generally use the latter approach. Since this method has to do with numbers, we'll design a class `Numeric` to hold the `approxEqual` method. Here is the class:

```
class Numeric
{
    public static boolean approxEqual(double x, double y)
    {
        . . .
    }
    // more numeric methods can be added here
}
```

When calling a static method, you supply the name of the class containing the method so that the compiler can find it. For example,

```
double r = Math.sqrt(2);
if (Numeric.approxEqual(r * r, 2))
    System.out.println("Math.sqrt(2) squared is approximately 2");
```

Note that you do not supply an object of type `Numeric` when you call the method. Static methods have no implicit parameter—in other words, they don't have a `this` parameter.

Now we can tell you why the `main` method is static. When the program starts, there aren't any objects yet. Therefore, the *first* method in the program must be a static method.

In general, you want to minimize the use of static methods. If you find yourself using lots of static methods, then that's an indication that you may not have found the right classes to solve your problem in an object-oriented way.

You may well wonder why these methods are called `static`. The normal meaning of the word *static* ("staying fixed at one place") does not seem to have anything to do with what static methods do. Indeed, it's used by accident. Java uses the `static` keyword because C++ uses it in the same context. C++ uses `static` to denote class methods because the inventors of C++ did not want to invent another keyword. Someone noted that there was a relatively rarely used keyword, `static`, that denotes certain variables that stay in a fixed location for multiple method calls. (Java does not have this feature, nor does it need it.) It turned out that the keyword could be reused to denote class methods without confusing the compiler. The fact that it can confuse humans was apparently not a big concern. You'll just have to live with the fact that "`static` method" means "class method": a method that does not operate on an object and that has only explicit parameters.

7.7   Static Fields

Consider a slight variation of our `BankAccount` class: a bank account that has both a balance and an *account number*:

```
public class BankAccount
{
    . . .
    private double balance;
    private int accountNumber;
}
```

We want to assign account numbers sequentially. That is, we want the bank account constructor to construct the first account with number 1, the next with number 2, and so on. Therefore, we must store the last assigned account number somewhere.

It makes no sense, though, to make this value into an instance field:

```
public class BankAccount
{
    . . .
    private double balance;
    private int accountNumber;
    private int lastAssignedNumber; // NO—won't work
}
```

> A static field belongs to the class, not to any object of the class.

In that case each *instance* of the `BankAccount` class would have its own value of `lastAssignedNumber`.

Instead, we need to have a single value of `lastAssigned Number` that is the same for the entire *class*. Such a field is called a *class field* or a `static` field, because you declare it using the `static` keyword.

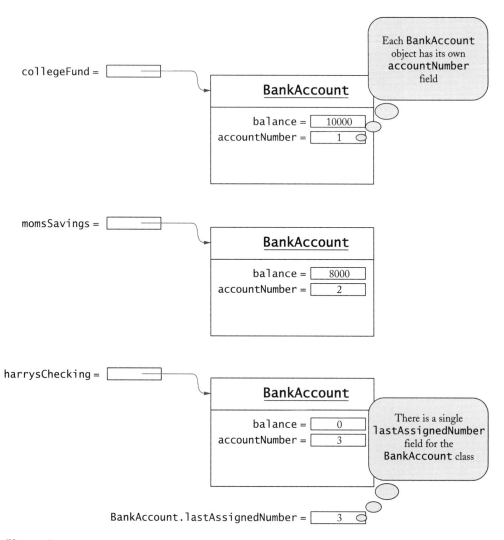

Figure 5

A Static Field and Instance Fields

```
public class BankAccount
{
    . . .
    private double balance;
    private int accountNumber;
    private static int lastAssignedNumber;
}
```

Every BankAccount object has its own balance and accountNumber instance fields, but there is only a single copy of the lastAssignedNumber variable (see Figure 5).

Every method of a class can access its static fields. Here is the constructor of the BankAccount class, which increments the last assigned number and then uses it to initialize the account number of the object to be constructed:

```
class BankAccount
{
   public BankAccount()
   {
      // generate next account number to be assigned

      lastAssignedNumber++; // updates the static field

      // assign to account number of this bank account

      accountNumber = lastAssignedNumber;
         // sets the instance field
   }
   . . .
}
```

How do you initialize static fields? You can't initialize them in the class constructor:

```
public BankAccount()
{
   lastAssignedNumber = 0; // NO—would reset to 0 for each new object
   . . .
}
```

Then the initialization would occur each time a new instance is constructed. Instead, use an explicit initializer:

```
public class BankAccount
{
   . . .
   private static lastAssignedNumber = 0;
}
```

The initialization is executed once when the class is loaded.

There are three ways to initialize a static field:

1. Do nothing. The static field is then initialized with 0 (for numbers), false (for boolean values) or null (for objects).
2. Use an explicit initializer.
3. Use a static initialization block (see Advanced Topic 7.3).

In general, static fields are considered undesirable. Methods that modify static fields have side effects, and the behavior of methods that read static fields does not simply depend on their inputs. If you call such a method twice, with the exact same inputs, it may still act differently, because the settings of the static fields are different.

In the preceding example, getting two different results from calling the BankAccount constructor twice in a row was the whole point of introducing the static lastAssignedNumber variable. However, in practical programs, static fields are rarely useful. If your program relies on a static field, you should think carefully whether you merely used that static field as a momentary convenience to "park" a value so that it can be picked up by another method. That is a bad strategy, because many other methods can also access and change that static field.

Like instance fields, static fields, when used at all, should always be declared as `private` to ensure that methods of other classes do not change their values. However, static *constants* are often declared public. For example, the `BankAccount` class may want to define a public constant value, such as

```
public class BankAccount
{
    . . .
    public static final double OVERDRAFT_FEE = 5;
}
```

Methods from any class refer to such a constant as `BankAccount.OVERDRAFT_FEE`.

It makes sense to declare constants as `static`—you wouldn't want every object of the `BankAccount` class to have its own set of variables with these constant values. It is sufficient to have one set of them for the class.

Why are class variables called `static`? As with static methods, the `static` keyword itself is just a meaningless holdover from C++. But static fields and static methods have much in common: they apply to the entire *class*, not to specific instances of the class.

Quality Tip 7.4

Do Not Abuse Static Fields

We have purposefully not covered static fields earlier in this book. They make it possible to write programs that are hard to understand and maintain. Consider the following bad example. The `Sorter` class sorts three numbers in increasing order. The `setMinMax` "helper" method sorts two numbers by setting the static fields `min` and `max` to hold the smaller and the larger values.

```
class Sorter // bad code inside
{
    public Sorter(double a, double b, double c)
    {
        setMinMax(a, b);
        if (c < min)
            smallest = c; // c is the smallest of the three
        else
        {
            smallest = min; // min is the smallest of the three
            setMinMax(c, max); // sort c and max
        }
        middle = min;
        largest = max;
    }

    public double getSmallest()
    {
```

```
        return smallest;
    }

    public double getMiddle()
    {
        return middle;
    }

    public double getLargest()
    {
        return largest;
    }

    public static void setMinMax(double a, double b)
    {
        if (a < b) { min = a; max = b; }
        else { min = b; max = a; }
    }

    private double smallest;
    private double middle;
    private double largest;

    private static double min;
    private static double max;
}
```

The writer of this class had a problem. The `setMinMax` method computes both the smaller and the larger of its input values, but it can't return both. Therefore, the programmer chose to return neither value and instead stored them in static fields. In this example, the code will work correctly, but there is a danger. If you don't *immediately* retrieve the answers from the static fields, some other part of the program may overwrite them. When static fields are used in larger programs, they get accidentally overwritten with distressing regularity, and therefore they are best avoided.

Advanced Topic 7.3

Alternative Forms of Field Initializations

As you have seen, instance fields are initialized with a default value (0, `false`, or `null`, depending on their type). You can then set them to any desired value in a constructor, and that is the style that we prefer in this book.

However, there are two other mechanisms to specify an initial value for a field. Just as with local variables, you can specify initialization values for fields. For example,

```
public class Coin
{
    . . .
    private double value = 1;
```

```
        private String name = "Dollar";
    }
```

These default values are used for *every* object that is being constructed.

There is also another, much less common, syntax. You can place one or more *initialization blocks* inside the class definition. All statements in that block are executed whenever an object is being constructed. Here is an example:

```
    public class Coin
    {
        . . .
        {
            value = 1;
            name = "Dollar";
        }
        private double value;
        private String name;
    }
```

For static fields, you use a static initialization block:

```
    public class BankAccount
    {
        . . .
        private static lastAssignedNumber;

        static
        {
            lastAssignedNumber = 0;
        }
    }
```

All statements in the static initialization block are executed once when the class is loaded. Initialization blocks are rarely used in practice.

When an object is constructed, the initializers and initialization blocks are executed in the order in which they appear. Then the code in the constructor is executed. Since the rules for the alternative initialization mechanisms are somewhat complex, we recommend that you simply use constructors to do the job of construction.

7.8 Scope

7.8.1 — Scope of Local Variables

It sometimes happens that the same variable name is used in two methods. Consider the variables r in the following example:

```
    public static double area(Rectangle rect)
    {
        double r = rect.getWidth() * rect.getHeight();
```

```
            return r;
        }

        public static void main(String[] args)
        {
            Rectangle r = new Rectangle(5, 10, 20, 30);
            double a = area(r);
            . . .
        }
```

> The scope of a variable is the region of a program in which you can refer to the variable by its name.

These variables are independent from each other. You can have local variables with the same name r in different methods, just as you can have different motels with the same name "Bates Motel" in different cities.

The *scope* of a variable is the region of a program in which you can refer to the variable by its name. The scope of a local variable extends from the point of its declaration to the end of the block that encloses it. Variables declared in a `for` loop are a special case. Their scope extends to the `for` loop but not beyond.

```
        for (int i = 1; i <= years; i++)
        {
            . . .
        } // scope of i ends here
```

> In Java, you cannot have two local variables with overlapping scope.

You can never have two local variables with overlapping scope. If you try to define a second local variable within the scope of the first, then the compiler reports an error. For example, the following is an error:

```
        Rectangle r = new Rectangle(5, 10, 20, 30);
        if (x >= 0)
        {
            double r = Math.sqrt(x);
            // Error—can't declare another variable called r here
            . . .
        }
```

However, you can have local variables with identical names if their scopes do not overlap, such as

```
        if (x >= 0)
        {
            double r = Math.sqrt(-x);
            . . .
        } // scope of r ends here
        else
        {
            Rectangle r = new Rectangle(5, 10, 20, 30);
            // OK—this is a different r
            . . .
        }
```

7.8.2 — Scope of Class Members

A qualified name is prefixed by its class name or by an object reference, such as `Math.sqrt` or `other.balance`.

An unqualified instance field or method name refers to the implicit parameter `this`.

Within a method of a class, you can access all fields and methods of the class by their simple name. However, if you want to use a field or method outside its class, you must *qualify* the name. You qualify a static field or method by specifying the class name, such as `Math.sqrt` or `Math.PI`. You qualify an instance field or method by specifying the object to which the field or method should be applied, such as `harrysChecking.getBalance()`.

Inside a method, you don't need to qualify fields or methods of their own class. Instance fields automatically refer to the implicit parameter of the method. For example, inside the `transfer` method

```
public void transfer(double amount, BankAccount other)
{
    balance = balance - amount; // i.e., this.balance
    other.balance = other.balance + amount;
}
```

the unqualified name `balance` means `this.balance`.

The same rule applies to methods. Thus, another implementation of the `transfer` method is

```
public void transfer(double amount, BankAccount other)
{
    withdraw(amount); // i.e., this.withdraw(amount);
    other.deposit(amount);
}
```

Whenever you see an instance method call without an implicit parameter, then the method is called on the `this` parameter. Such a method call is called a "self-call".

Similarly, you can use a static field or method of the same class without a qualifier. For example, if `OVERDRAFT_FEE` is a static field of the `BankAccount` class, then the statement

```
if (balance < 0) balance = OVERDRAFT_FEE;
```

in a `BankAccount` method refers to `BankAccount.OVERDRAFT_FEE`.

7.8.3 — Overlapping Scope

Problems arise if you have two variable names with overlapping scope. This can never occur with local variables, but the scopes of a local variable and an instance field can overlap. Here is a purposefully bad example.

```
public class Coin
{
    . . .
```

```
public void draw(Graphics2D g2)
{
    String name = "SansSerif"; // local variable
    int size = 18;
    . . .
}

private String name; // field with the same name
private double value;
}
```

> A local variable can shadow a field with the same name. You can access the shadowed field name by qualifying it with the `this` reference.

Inside the `draw` method, the variable name `name` could potentially have two meanings: the local variable or the instance field. The Java language specifies that in this situation the *local* variable wins out. It *shadows* the instance field. This sounds pretty arbitrary, but there is actually a good reason: You can still refer to the instance field as `this.name`.

```
g2.setFont(new Font(name, Font.BOLD, size));
    // accesses local variable
g2.drawString(this.name, x, y);
    // accesses field
```

Some people use this trick on purpose so that they don't have to come up with new variable names:

```
public Coin(double value, String name)
{
    this.value = value;
    this.name = name;
}
```

It isn't necessary to write code like this. You can easily change the name of the local variable to something else, such as `fontName` or `aName`. Then you, and the other readers of your code, don't have to remember that local variables shadow instance fields.

⊗ Common Error   7.2

Shadowing

Using the same name accidentally for a local variable and an instance field is a surprisingly common error. As you saw in the preceding section, the local variable then *shadows* the instance field. Even though you may have meant to access the instance field, the local variable is quietly accessed. For some reason, this problem is most common in constructors. Look at this example of a wrong constructor:

```
public class Coin
{
```

```
public Coin(double aValue, String aName)
{
   value = aValue;
   String name = aName; // oops...
}

   . . .

private double value;
private String name;
}
```

The programmer declared a local variable `name` in the constructor. In all likelihood, that was just a typo—the programmer's fingers were on autopilot and typed the keyword `String`, even though the programmer all the time intended to access the instance field. Unfortunately, the compiler gives no warning in this situation and quietly sets the local variable to the value of `aName`. The instance field of the object that is being constructed is never touched, and remains `null`. Some programmers give all instance field names a special prefix to distinguish them from other variables. A common convention is to prefix all instance field names with the prefix `my`, such as `myValue` or `myName`.

Productivity Hint   7.1

Global Search and Replace

Suppose you chose an unfortunate name for a method—say `ae` instead of `approx-Equal`—and you regret your choice. Of course, you can locate all occurrences of `ae` in your code and replace them manually. However, most programming editors have a command to search for the `ae`'s automatically and replace them with `approxEqual`.

You need to specify some details about the search:

- Do you want it to ignore case? That is, should `Ae` be a match? In Java you usually don't want that.

- Do you want it to match whole words only? If not, the `ae` in `maelstrom` is also a match. In Java you usually want to match whole words.

- Is this a regular-expression search? No, but regular expressions can make searches even more powerful—see Productivity Hint 7.2.

- Do you want to confirm each replace, or simply go ahead and replace all matches? I usually confirm the first three or four, and when I see that it works as expected, I give the go-ahead to replace the rest. (By the way, a *global* replace means to replace all occurrences in the document.) Good text editors can undo a global replace that has gone awry. Find out whether yours will.

- Do you want the search to go from the cursor to the rest of the program file, or should it search the currently selected text? Restricting replacement to a portion of the file can be very useful, but in this example you would want to move the cursor to the top of the file and then replace until the end of the file.

Not every editor has all these options. You should investigate what your editor offers.

Productivity Hint 7.2

Regular Expressions

Regular expressions describe character patterns. For example, numbers have a simple form. They contain one or more digits. The regular expression describing numbers is [0-9]+. The set [0-9] denotes any digit between 0 and 9, and the + means "one or more".

What good is it? Several utility programs use regular expressions to locate matching text. Also, the search commands of some programming editors understand regular expressions. The most popular program that uses regular expressions is *grep* (which stands for "generalized regular expression pattern"). You can run grep from a command prompt or from inside some compilation environments. Grep is part of the UNIX operating system, but versions are available for Windows and MacOS. It needs a regular expression and one or more files to search. When grep runs, it displays a set of lines that match the regular expression.

Suppose you want to look for all magic numbers (see Quality Tip 2.2) in a file. The command

```
grep [0-9]+ Homework.java
```

lists all lines in the file Homework.java that contain sequences of digits. That isn't terribly useful; lines with variable names x1 will be listed. OK, you want sequences of digits that do *not* immediately follow letters:

```
grep [^A-Za-z][0-9]+ Homework.java
```

The set [^A-Za-z] denotes any characters that are *not* in the ranges A ro Z and a to z. This works much better, and it shows only lines that contain actual numbers.

There are a bewildering number of symbols (sometimes called *wildcards*) with special meanings in the regular expression syntax, and unfortunately, different programs use different styles of regular expressions. It is best to consult the program documentation for details.

Advanced Topic 7.4

Calling One Constructor from Another

Consider the following Coin class. It has two constructors: a constructor with no parameters to make a dollar coin, and another constructor to supply the coin name and value.

▼
▼
▼
▼
▼
▼

```
public class Coin
{
   public Coin(double aValue, String aName)
   {
      value = aValue;
      name = aName;
   }

   public Coin()
   {
      this(1, "dollar");
   }
   . . .
}
```

The command `this(1, "dollar");` means: Call another constructor of this class and supply the values 1 and `"dollar"`. Such a constructor call can occur only *as the first line in another constructor*.

This syntax is a minor convenience, and we will not use it in this book. Actually, the use of the keyword `this` is a little confusing, because normally `this` denotes a reference to the implicit parameter. However, if `this` is followed by parentheses, it denotes a call to another constructor of *this class*.

7.9 Packages

7.9.1 — Organizing Related Classes into Packages

A Java program consists of a collection of classes. So far, most of your programs have consisted of a small number of classes.

> A package is a set of related classes.

As programs get larger, however, simply distributing the classes over multiple files isn't enough. An additional structuring mechanism is needed. In Java, packages provide this structuring mechanism. A Java package is a set of related classes. For example, the Java library consists of dozens of packages, some of which are listed in Table 1.

To put classes in a package, you must place a line

`package` *packagename*;

as the first instruction in the source file containing the classes. As you can see from the examples in the Java library, a package name consists of one or more identifiers separated by periods.

For example, consider the `Numeric` class that we introduced in this chapter. For maximum simplicity, you can include the class together with your own programs whenever you need it. However, it would be much more professional to place the class into a separate

Package	Purpose	Sample Classes
java.lang	Language support	Math
java.util	Utilities	Random
java.io	Input and output	PrintStream
java.awt	Abstract Windowing Toolkit	Color
java.applet	Applets	Applet
java.net	Networking	Socket
java.sql	Database access through Structured Query Language	ResultSet
javax.swing	Swing user interface	JButton
omg.org.CORBA	Common Object Request Broker Architecture for distributed objects	ORB

Table 1

Important Packages in the Java Library

package. That way, the classes that are specific to a particular program are clearly separated from the utility classes that you share between different programs.

Let us place the Numeric class into a package named com.horstmann.bigjava. (See Section 7.9.3 for an explanation of how to construct package names.) Each source file in that package must start with the instruction

```
package com.horstmann.bigjava;
```

For example, the Numeric.java file starts out as follows:

```
package com.horstmann.bigjava;

public class Numeric
{
   . . .
}
```

Not only must the package name be placed into the source file; the class file itself must be placed in a special location. We'll show you later where to place the class file.

In addition to the named packages (such as java.util), there is a special package, called the *default package*, which has no name. If you did not include any package statement at the top of your source file, its classes are placed in the default package.

Syntax 7.1: Package Specification

package *packageName*;

Example:

package com.horstmann.bigjava;

Purpose:

To declare that all classes in this file belong to a particular package

---

7.9.2 — Importing Packages

> The import directive lets you refer to a class of a package by its class name, without the package prefix.

If you want to use a class from a package, you can refer to it by its full name (package name plus class name). For example, java.awt.Color refers to the Color class in the java.awt package, and com.horstmann.bigjava.Numeric refers to the Numeric class in the com.horstmann.bigjava package:

```
java.awt.Color backgroundColor =
    new java.awt.Color(1.0, 0.7, 0.7);
```

Naturally, that is somewhat inconvenient. You can instead *import* a name with an import statement:

```
import java.awt.Color;
import com.horstmann.bigjava.Numeric;
```

Then you can refer to the classes as Color and Numeric without the package prefixes.

You can import *all classes* of a package with an import statement that ends in .*. For example, you can use the statement

```
import java.awt.*;
```

to import all classes from the java.awt package. That statement lets you refer to classes like Graphics2D or Color without a java.awt prefix. This is the most convenient method for importing classes. If a program starts with multiple imports of this form, however, it can be harder to guess to which package a class belongs. Suppose for example a program imports

```
import java.awt.*;
import java.io.*;
```

Then suppose you see a class name Image. You would not know whether the Image class is in the java.awt package or the java.io package. For that reason, we prefer to use an explicit import statement for each class, though many programmers like the convenience of importing all classes in a package.

However, you never need to import the classes in the java.lang package explicitly. That is the package containing the most basic Java classes, such as Math and Object. These classes are always available to you. In effect, an automatic import java.lang.*; statement has been placed into every source file.

Finally, you don't import the other classes in the same package. For example, when you implement the class `homework1.Test`, you don't need to import the class `homework1.Bank`. The compiler will find the class without an import statement because it is located in the same package.

▼ ⊗ **Common Error**   **7.3**

Confusing Dots

In Java, the dot symbol (.) is used as a separator in the following situations:

- Between package names (`java.util`)
- Between package and class names (`homework1.Bank`)
- Between class and inner class names (`Ellipse2D.Double`)
- Between class and instance variable names (`Math.PI`)
- Between objects and methods (`account.getBalance()`)

When you see a long chain of dot-separated names, it can be a challenge to find out which part is the package name, which part is the class name, which part is an instance variable name, and which part is a method name. Consider

```
java.lang.System.out.println(x);
```

Since the `println` is followed by an opening parenthesis, it must be a method name. Therefore, `out` must be either an object or a class with a `static println` method. (Of course, we know that `out` is an object reference of type `PrintStream`.) Again, it is not at all clear, without context, whether `System` is another object, with a public variable `out`, or a class with a `static` variable. Judging from the number of pages that the Java reference manual [1] devotes to this issue, even the compiler has trouble interpreting these dot-separated sequences of strings.

To avoid problems, it is helpful to adopt a strict coding style. If class names always start with an uppercase letter, while variable, method, and package names always start with a lowercase letter, then confusion can be avoided.

7.9.3 — Package Names

Placing related classes into a package is clearly a convenient mechanism to organize classes. However, there is a more important reason for packages: to avoid *name clashes*. In a large project, it is inevitable that two people will come up with the same name for the same concept. This even happens in the standard Java class library (which has now grown to thousands of classes). There is a class `Object` in the `java.lang` package and an interface, also called `Object`, in the `org.omg.CORBA` package. Fortunately, you never need to import both packages. If you did, then the name `Object` would be *ambiguous*.

However, thanks to the package concept, not all is lost. You can still tell the Java compiler exactly which `Object` class you need, simply by referring to them as `java.lang.Object` and `org.omg.CORBA.Object`.

> Use a domain name in reverse to construct unambiguous package names.

Of course, for the package-naming convention to work, there must be some way to ensure that package names are unique. It wouldn't be good if the car maker BMW placed all its Java code into the package `bmw`, and some other programmer (perhaps Bertha M. Walters) had the same bright idea. To avoid this problem, the inventors of Java recommend that you use a package-naming scheme that takes advantage of the uniqueness of Internet domain names.

If your company or organization has an Internet domain name, then you have an identifier that is guaranteed to be unique—the organizations who assign domain names take care of that. For example, I have a domain name `horstmann.com`, and there is nobody else on the planet with the same domain name. (I was lucky that the domain name `horstmann.com` had not been taken by anyone else when I applied. If your name is Walters, you will sadly find that someone else beat you to `walters.com`.) To get a package name, turn the domain name around, to produce a package name prefix:

```
org.omg
com.horstmann
```

Then it is up to the owner of the domain name to subdivide package names further. For example, the Object Management Group, the holder of the `omg.org` domain name, decided to use the package name `org.omg.CORBA` for the Java classes that implement their Common Object Request Broker Architecture (a mechanism for communication between objects that are distributed on different computers).

If you don't have your own domain name, you can still create a package name that has a high probability of being unique, by writing your email address backwards. For example, if Bertha Walters has an email address `walters@cs.sjsu.edu`, then she can use a package name `edu.sjsu.cs.walters` for her own classes.

Some instructors will want you to place each of your assignments into a separate package, such as `homework1`, `homework2`, and so on. The reason is again to avoid name collision. You can have two classes, `homework1.Bank` and `homework2.Bank`, with slightly different properties.

7.9.4 — How Classes Are Located

> The path of a class file must match its package name.

If the Java compiler has been properly set up on your system, and you use only the standard classes, you ordinarily need not worry about the location of class files and can safely skip this section. If you want to add your own packages, however, or if the compiler cannot locate a particular class or package, you need to understand the mechanism.

A package is located in a subdirectory that matches the package name. The parts of the name between periods represent successively nested directories. For example, the package `com.horstmann.bigjava` would be placed in a subdirectory `com/horstmann/bigjava`. If the package is to be used only in conjunction with a single program, then you can place the subdirectory inside the directory holding that program's files. For example, if you do your homework assignments in a *base directory* `/home/walters`, then you can place

the class files for the `com.horstmann.bigjava` package into the directory /home/
walters/com/horstmann/bigjava, as shown in Figure 6. (Here, we are using UNIX-style
file names. Under Windows, you might use `c:\home\walters\com\horstmann\bigjava`.)

However, if you want to place your programs into many different directories, such as
/home/walters/hw1, /home/walters/hw2, . . . , then you probably don't want to have
lots of identical subdirectories /home/walters/hw1/com/horstmann/bigjava, /home/
walters/hw2/com/horstmann/bigjava, and so on. In that case, you want to make a
single directory with a name such as /home/walters/lib/com/horstmann/bigjava,
place all class files for the package in that directory, and tell the Java compiler once and
for all how to locate the class files.

You need to add the directories that might contain packages to the *class path*. In the preceding example, you add the /home/walters/lib directory to that class path. The details
for doing this depend on your compilation environment; consult the documentation for your
compiler, or your instructor. If you use the Sun Java SDK, you need to set the class path.
The exact command depends on the operating system. In UNIX, the command might be

        export CLASSPATH=/home/walters/lib:.

This setting places both the /home/walters/lib directory and the current directory .
onto the class path.

A typical example for Windows would be

        set CLASSPATH=c:\home\walters\lib;.

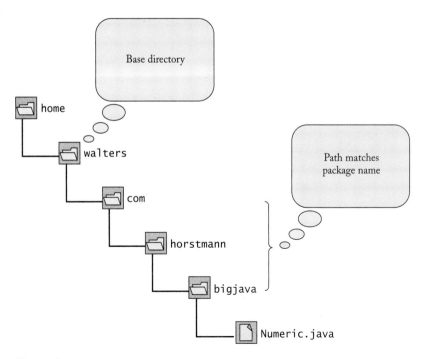

Figure 6

Base Directories and Subdirectories for Packages

Note that the class path contains the *base directories* that may contain package directories. It is a common error to place the complete package address in the class path. If the class path mistakenly contains /home/walters/lib/com/horstmann/bigjava, then the compiler will attempt to locate the com.horstmann.bigjava package in /home/walters/lib/com/horstmann/bigjava/com/horstmann/bigjava and won't find the files.

? HOWTO 7.1

Programming with Packages

This HOWTO explains in detail how to place your programs into packages. For example, your instructor may ask you to place each homework assignment into a separate package. That way, you can have classes with the same name but different implementations in separate packages (such as homework1.Bank and homework2.Bank).

Step 1   Come up with a package name

Your instructor may give you a package name to use, such as homework1. Or, perhaps you want to use a package name that is unique to you only. Start with your email address, written backwards. For example, walters@cs.sjsu.edu becomes edu.sjsu.cs.walters. Then add a subpackage that describes your project or homework, such as edu.sjsu.cs.walters.homework1.

Step 2   Pick a *base directory*

The base directory is the directory that contains the directories for your various packages, for example /home/walters or c:\cs1.

Step 3   Make a subdirectory from the base directory that matches your package name

The subdirectory must be contained in your base directory. Each segment must match a segment of the package name. For example,

```
mkdir /home/walters/homework1
```

If you have multiple segments, build them up one by one:

```
mkdir c:\cs1\edu
mkdir c:\cs1\edu\sjsu
mkdir c:\cs1\edu\sjsu\cs
mkdir c:\cs1\edu\sjsu\cs\walters
mkdir c:\cs1\edu\sjsu\cs\walters\homework1
```

Step 4   Place your source files into the package subdirectory

For example, if your homework consists of the files Test.java and Bank.java, then you place them into

```
/home/walters/homework1/Test.java
/home/walters/homework1/Bank.java
```

or
```
c:\cs1\edu\sjsu\cs\walters\homework1\Test.java
c:\cs1\edu\sjsu\cs\walters\homework1\Bank.java
```

Step 5 Use the `package` statement in each source file

The first noncomment line of each file must be a `package` statement that lists the name of the package, such as
```
package homework1;
```
or
```
package edu.sjsu.cs.walters.homework1;
```

Step 6 Compile your source files *from the base directory*

Change to the base directory (from Step 2) to compile your files. For example,
```
cd /home/walters
javac homework1/Test.java
```
or
```
cd \cs1
javac edu\sjsu\cs\walters\homework1\Test.java
```
Note that the Java compiler needs the source *filename and not the class name. That is, you need to supply file separators (/* on UNIX, \ on Windows) and a file extension (`.java`).

Step 7 Run your program *from the base directory*

Unlike the Java compiler, the Java interpreter needs the *class name (and not a file name) of the class containing the* `main` *method. That is, use periods as package separators, and don't use a file extension. For example,
```
cd /home/walters
java homework1.Test
```
or
```
cd \cs1
java edu.sjsu.cs.walters.homework1.Test
```

Random Fact 7.1

The Explosive Growth of Personal Computers

In 1971, Marcian E. "Ted" Hoff, an engineer at Intel Corporation, was working on a chip for a manufacturer of electronic calculators. He realized that it would be a better idea to develop a *general-purpose* chip that could be *programmed* to interface with the keys and display of a calculator, rather than to do yet another custom design. Thus, the *microprocessor* was born. At the time, its primary application was as a controller for calculators, washing machines, and the like. It took years for the computer industry to notice that a genuine central processing unit was now available as a single chip.

Hobbyists were the first to catch on. In 1974 the first computer *kit*, the Altair 8800, was available from MITS Electronics for about $350. The kit consisted of the micropro- cessor, a circuit board, a very small amount of memory, toggle switches, and a row of dis- play lights. Purchasers had to solder and assemble it, then program it in machine language through the toggle switches. It was not a big hit.

The first big hit was the Apple II. It was a real computer with a keyboard, a monitor, and a floppy disk drive. When it was first released, users had a $3000 machine that could play Space Invaders, run a primitive bookkeeping program, or let users program it in BASIC. The original Apple II did not even support lowercase letters, making it worthless for word processing. The breakthrough came in 1979 with a new *spreadsheet* program, VisiCalc. In a spreadsheet, you enter financial data and their relationships into a grid of rows and columns (see Figure 7). Then you modify some of the data and watch in real time how the others change. For example, you can see how changing the mix of widgets in a manufacturing plant might affect estimated costs and profits. Mid- dle managers in companies, who understood computers and were fed up with having to wait for hours or days to get their data runs back from the computing center, snapped up VisiCalc and the computer that was needed to run it. For them, the computer was a spreadsheet machine.

The next big hit was the IBM Personal Computer, ever after known as the PC. It was the first widely available personal computer that used Intel's 16-bit processor, the 8086, whose successors are still being used in personal computers today. The success of the PC was based not on any engineering breakthroughs but on the fact that it was easy to *clone*. IBM published specifications for plug-in cards, and it went one step fur- ther. It published the exact source code of the so-called BIOS (Basic Input/Output System), which controls the keyboard, monitor, ports, and disk drives and must be installed in ROM form in every PC. This allowed third-party vendors of plug-in cards to ensure that the BIOS code, and third-party extensions of it, interacted correctly with the equipment. Of course, the code itself was the property of IBM and could not be copied legally. Perhaps IBM did not foresee that functionally equivalent versions of the BIOS nevertheless could be recreated by others. Compaq, one of the first clone vendors, had fifteen engineers, who certified that they had never seen the original IBM code, write a new version that conformed precisely to the IBM specifications. Other companies did the same, and soon a variety of vendors were selling computers that ran the same software as IBM's PC but distinguished themselves by a lower price, increased portability, or better performance. In time, IBM lost its dominant position in the PC market. It is now one of many companies producing IBM PC–compatible computers.

IBM never produced an *operating system* for its PCs—that is, the software that organizes the interaction between the user and the computer, starts application pro- grams, and manages disk storage and other resources. Instead, IBM offered customers the option of three separate operating systems. Most customers couldn't care less about the operating system. They chose the system that was able to launch most of the few applications that existed at the time. It happened to be DOS (Disk Operating System) by Microsoft. Microsoft cheerfully licensed the same operating system to

Figure 7

A Spreadsheet

other hardware vendors and encouraged software companies to write DOS applications. A huge number of useful application programs for PC-compatible machines was the result.

PC applications were certainly useful, but they were not easy to learn. Every vendor developed a different *user interface:* the collection of keystrokes, menu options, and settings that a user needed to master to use a software package effectively. Data exchange between applications was difficult, because each program used a different data format. The Apple Macintosh changed all that in 1984. The designers of the Macintosh had the vision to supply an intuitive user interface with the computer and to force software developers to adhere to it. It took Microsoft and PC-compatible manufacturers years to catch up.

The book [2] is highly recommended for an amusing and irreverent account of the emergence of personal computers.

At the time of this writing, it is estimated that two in three U.S. households own a personal computer and that one in two uses the Internet at least occasionally. Most personal computers are used for word processing, home finance (banking, budgeting, taxes), accessing information from CD-ROM and online sources, and entertainment. Some analysts predict that the personal computer will merge with the television set and cable network into an entertainment and *information appliance.*

CHAPTER SUMMARY

1. A class should represent a single concept from the problem domain, such as business, science, or mathematics.

2. The public interface of a class is cohesive if all of its features are related to the concept that the class represents.

3. A class depends on another class if it uses objects of that other class.

4. It is a good practice to minimize the coupling (i.e., dependency) between classes.

5. An accessor method does not change the state of its implicit parameter. A mutator method can change the state.

6. An immutable class has no mutator methods.

7. A side effect of a method is any externally observable behavior outside the implicit parameter. You should minimize side effects.

8. In Java, a method can never change parameters of primitive type.

9. In Java, a method can change the state of an object reference parameter, but it cannot replace the object reference with another.

10. A precondition is a requirement that the caller of a method must meet. If a method is called in violation of a precondition, the method is not responsible for computing the correct result.

11. If a method has been called in accordance with its preconditions, then it must ensure that its postconditions are valid.

12. A static method has no implicit parameter.

13. A static field belongs to the class, not to any object of the class.

14. The scope of a variable is the region of a program in which you can refer to the variable by its name.

15. In Java, you cannot have two local variables with overlapping scope.

16. A qualified name is prefixed by its class name or by an object reference, such as `Math.sqrt` or `other.balance`.

17. An unqualified instance field or method name refers to the implicit parameter `this`.

18. A local variable can shadow a field with the same name. You can access the shadowed field name by qualifying it with the `this` reference.

19. A package is a set of related classes.

20. The `import` directive lets you refer to a class of a package by its class name, without the package prefix.

21. Use a domain name in reverse to construct unambiguous package names.

22. The path of a class file must match its package name.

Further Reading

[1] Bertrand Meyer, *Object-Oriented Software Construction*, Prentice-Hall, 1989, chapter 7.
[2] Robert X. Cringely, *Accidental Empires*, Addison-Wesley, 1992.

CLASSES, OBJECTS, AND METHODS INTRODUCED IN THIS CHAPTER

```
java.lang.IllegalArgumentException
```

REVIEW EXERCISES

Exercise R7.1. Consider the following problem description:

> Users place coins in a vending machine and select a product by pushing a button. If the inserted coins are sufficient to cover the purchase price of the product, the product is dispensed and change is given. Otherwise, the inserted coins are returned to the user.

What classes should you use to implement it?

Exercise R7.2. Consider the following problem description:

> Employees receive their biweekly paycheck. They are paid their hourly for each hour worked; however, if they worked more than 40 hours per week, they are paid overtime at 150% of their regular wage.

What classes should you use to implement it?

Exercise R7.3. Consider the following problem description:

> Customers order products from a store. Invoices are generated to list the items and quantities ordered, payments received and amounts still due. Products are shipped to the shipping address of the customer, and invoices are sent to the billing address.

What classes should you use to implement it?

Exercise R7.4. Look at the public interface of the System class and discuss whether or not it is cohesive.

Exercise R7.5. Suppose an Invoice object contains descriptions of the products ordered, and the billing and the shipping address of the customer. Draw a UML diagram showing the dependencies between the classes Invoice, Address, Customer, and Product.

Exercise R7.6. Suppose a vending machine contains products, and users insert coins into the vending machine to purchase products. Draw a UML diagram showing the dependencies between the classes VendingMachine, Coin, and Product.

Exercise R7.7. On which classes does the class Integer in the standard library depend?

Exercise R7.8. On which classes does the class Rectangle in the standard library depend?

Exercise R7.9. Classify the methods of the class `StringTokenizer` as accessors and mutators.

Exercise R7.10. Classify the methods of the class `Rectangle` as accessors and mutators.

Exercise R7.11. Which of the following classes are immutable?
- `Rectangle`
- `String`
- `Random`

Exercise R7.12. Which of the following classes are immutable?
- `PrintStream`
- `Date`
- `Integer`

Exercise R7.13. What side effect, if any, do the following three methods have:

```
public class Coin
{
   public void print()
   {
      System.out.println(name + " " + value);
   }

   public void print(PrintStream stream)
   {
      stream.println(name + " " + value);
   }

   public String toString()
   {
      return name + " " + value;
   }
   . . .
}
```

Exercise R7.14. Ideally, a method should have no side effect. Can you write a program in which no method has a side effect? Would such a program be useful?

Exercise R7.15. Write preconditions for the following methods. Do not implement the methods.
- `public static double sqrt(double x)`
- `public static String romanNumeral(int n)`
- `public static double slope(Line2D.Double a)`
- `public static String weekday(int day)`

Exercise R7.16. What preconditions do the following methods from the standard Java library have?
- `Math.sqrt`
- `Math.tan`
- `Math.log`
- `Math.exp`

- `Math.pow`
- `Math.abs`

Exercise R7.17. What preconditions do the following methods from the standard Java library have?

- `Integer.parseInt(String s)`
- `StringTokenizer.nextToken()`
- `Random.nextInt(int n)`
- `String.substring(int m, int n)`

Exercise R7.18. When a method is called with parameters that violate its precondition, it can throw an exception, or it can return to its caller. Give two examples of library methods (standard or the library methods used in this book) that return some result to their callers when called with invalid parameters, and give two examples of library methods that throw an exception.

Exercise R7.19. Consider a `Purse` class with methods

- `public void addCoin(Coin aCoin)`
- `public double getTotal()`

Give a reasonable postcondition of the `addCoin` method. What preconditions would you need so that the `Purse` class can ensure that postcondition?

Exercise R7.20. Consider the following method that is intended to swap the values of two floating-point numbers:

```
public static void falseSwap(double a, double b)
{
   double temp = a;
   a = b;
   b = temp;
}

public static void main(String[] args)
{
   double x = 3;
   double y = 4;
   falseSwap(x, y);
   System.out.println(x + " " + y);
}
```

Why doesn't the method swap the contents of x and y?

Exercise R7.21. How *can* you write a method that swaps two floating-point numbers? *Hint:* `Point2D.Double`.

Exercise R7.22. Try compiling the following program. Explain the error message that you get.

```
public class Exercise7_22
{
   public void print(int x)
   {
      System.out.println(x);
```

```
        }
    public static void main(String[] args)
    {
        int n = 13;
        print(13);
    }
}
```

Exercise R7.23. Look at the methods in the Integer class. Which are static? Why?

Exercise R7.24. Look at the methods in the String class (but ignore the ones that take a parameter of type char[]). Which are static? Why?

Exercise R7.25. The in and out fields of the System class are public static fields of the System class. Is that good design? If not, how could you improve on it?

Exercise R7.26. In the following class, the variable n occurs in multiple scopes. Which declarations of n are legal and which are illegal?

```
public class X
{
    public int f()
    {
        int n = 1;
        return n;
    }

    public int g(int k)
    {
        int a;
        for (int n = 1; n <= k; n++)
            a = a + n;
        return a;
    }

    public int h(int n)
    {
        int b;
        for (int n = 1; n <= 10; n++)
            b = b + n;
        return b + n;
    }

    public int k(int n)
    {
        if (n < 0)
        {
            int k = -n;
            int n = (int)(Math.sqrt(n));
            return n;
        }
        else return n;
```

```
   }

   public int m(int k)
   {
      int a;
      for (int n = 1; n <= k; n++)
         a = a + n;
      for (int n = k; n >= 1; n++)
         a = a + n;
      return a;
   }

   private int n;
}
```

Exercise R7.27. What is a qualified name? What is an unqualified name?

Exercise R7.28. When you access an unqualified name in a method, what does that access mean? Discuss both instance and static features.

Exercise R7.29. Every Java program can be rewritten to avoid `import` statements. Explain how, and rewrite IntersectionApplet.java from Chapter 4 to avoid `import` statements.

Exercise R7.30. What is the default package? Have you used it before this chapter in your programming?

Programming Exercises

Exercise P7.1. Implement the `Purse` and `Coin` classes described in Section 7.2.

Exercise P7.2. Enhance the `BankAccount` class by adding preconditions for the constructor and the `deposit` method that require the `amount` parameter to be at least zero, and a precondition for the `withdraw` method that requires `amount` to be at most the current balance. Throw exceptions if the precondition is not fulfilled.

Exercise P7.3. Write static methods

- `public static double sphereVolume(double r)`
- `public static double sphereSurface(double r)`
- `public static double cylinderVolume(double r, double h)`
- `public static double cylinderSurface(double r, double h)`
- `public static double coneVolume(double r, double h)`
- `public static double coneSurface(double r, double h)`

that compute the volume and surface area of a sphere with radius r, a cylinder with circular base with radius r and height h, and a cone with circular base with radius r and height h. Place them into an appropriate class. Then write a program that prompts the user for the values of r and h, calls the six methods, and prints the results.

Exercise P7.4. Solve the preceding exercise by implementing classes `Sphere`, `Cylinder`, and `Cone`. Which approach is more object-oriented?

Exercise P7.5. Write methods

```
public static double perimeter(Ellipse2D.Double e);
public static double area(Ellipse2D.Double e);
```

that compute the area and the perimeter of the ellipse **e**. Use these methods in an applet that prompts the user to specify an ellipse. Then display messages with the perimeter and area of the ellipse. Why does it make sense to use a static method in this case?

Exercise P7.6. Write a method

```
public static double distance(Point2D.Double p,
    Point2D.Double q)
```

that computes the distance between two points. Add the method to a suitable class. Write a test program that asks the user to enter two points. Then display the distance. Why does it make sense to use a static method in this case?

Exercise P7.7. Write a method

```
public static boolean isInside(Point2D.Double p,
    Ellipse2D.Double e)
```

that tests whether a point is inside an ellipse. Add the method to a suitable class. Write a test program that asks the user to enter a point and an ellipse. Then print whether the point is contained inside the ellipse.

Exercise P7.8. Write a method

```
public static int readInt(String prompt,
    int min, int max)
```

that displays the prompt string, reads an integer and tests whether it is between the minimum and maximum. If not, print an error message and repeat reading the input. Also, if the user cancels the input dialog, print an error message and keep reading. Add the method to an appropriate class and provide a test program.

Exercise P7.9. Write methods

- ```
  public static void drawH(Graphics2D g2,
      Point2D.Double p);
  ```
- ```
  public static void drawE(Graphics2D g2,
      Point2D.Double p);
  ```
- ```
  public static void drawL(Graphics2D g2,
      Point2D.Double p);
  ```
- ```
  public static void drawO(Graphics2D g2,
      Point2D.Double p);
  ```

that show the letters H, E, L, O on the graphics window, where the point **p** is the top left corner of the letter. Then call the methods to draw the words "HELLO" and "HOLE" on the graphics display. Draw lines and ellipses. Do not use the **drawString** method. Do not use **System.out**.

Exercise P7.10. Repeat the preceding exercise by designing classes **LetterH**, **LetterE**, **LetterL** and **LetterO**, each with a constructor that takes a **Point2D.Double** (the top left corner) and a method **draw(Graphics2D g2)**. Which solution is more object-oriented?

Figure 8

A Postal Bar Code

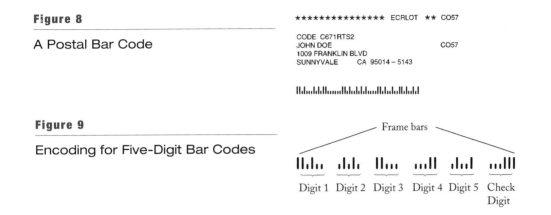

```
*************** ECRLOT ** CO57

CODE C671RTS2
JOHN DOE                              CO57
1009 FRANKLIN BLVD
SUNNYVALE      CA 95014 – 5143
```

Figure 9

Encoding for Five-Digit Bar Codes

Digit 1 Digit 2 Digit 3 Digit 4 Digit 5 Check Digit

Exercise P7.11. *Postal bar codes.* For faster sorting of letters, the United States Postal Service encourages companies that send large volumes of mail to use a bar code denoting the ZIP code (see Figure 8).

The encoding scheme for a five-digit ZIP code is shown in Figure 9. There are full-height frame bars on each side. The five encoded digits are followed by a correction digit, which is computed as follows: Add up all digits, and choose the correction digit to make the sum a multiple of 10. For example, the ZIP code 95014 has sum of digits 19, so the correction digit is 1 to make the sum equal to 20.

Each digit of the ZIP code, and the correction digit, is encoded according to the following table:

	7	4	2	1	0
1	0	0	0	1	1
2	0	0	1	0	1
3	0	0	1	1	0
4	0	1	0	0	1
5	0	1	0	1	0
6	0	1	1	0	0
7	1	0	0	0	1
8	1	0	0	1	0
9	1	0	1	0	0
0	1	1	0	0	0

where 0 denotes a half bar and 1 a full bar. Note that they represent all combinations of two full and three half bars. The digit can be easily computed from the bar code using the column weights 7, 4, 2, 1, 0. For example, 01100 is $0 \cdot 7 + 1 \cdot 4 + 1 \cdot 2 + 0 \cdot 1 + 0 \cdot 0 = 6$. The only exception is 0, which would yield 11 according to the weight formula.

Write a program that asks the user for a ZIP code and prints the bar code. Use : for half bars, | for full bars. For example, 95014 becomes

```
||:|:::|:|:||:::::::||:|::|:::|||
```

Use classes `BarCode` and `Digit` in your solution.

Exercise P7.12. Write a program that displays the bar code, using actual bars, on your graphic screen. In addition to the classes of the preceding exercise, use a class `Bar` with a method `void draw(Graphics2D g2)`.

Exercise P7.13. Write a program that reads in a bar code (with : denoting half bars and | denoting full bars) and prints out the ZIP code it represents. Print an error message if the bar code is not correct.

Exercise P7.14. Consider the following algorithm for computing x^n for an integer n. If $n < 0$, x^n is $1 / x^{-n}$. If n is positive and even, then $x^n = (x^{n/2})^2$. If n is positive and odd, then $x^n = x^{n-1} \cdot x$. Implement a static method `intPower(double x, int n)` that uses this algorithm. Add it to the `Numeric` class.

Exercise P7.15. Consider the `Die` class of Chapter 6. Turn the `generator` field into a static field so that all dice share a single random number generator.

Exercise P7.16. This exercise assumes that you have an email address. Write `Greeter` and `GreeterTest` classes in a package whose name is derived from your email address, as described in Section 7.9.

Exercise P7.17. Implement the `Purse` and `Coin` classes described in Section 7.2. Place them into a package called `money`. Write a test class `MoneyTest` in the default package.

8

Testing and Debugging

▶ To understand the principles of test case selection and evaluation

▶ To learn how to use logging and assertions

▶ To become familiar with the debugger

▶ To learn strategies for effective debugging

A complex program never works right the first time; it will contain errors, commonly called *bugs*, and will need to be tested. It is easier to test a program if it has been designed with testing in mind. This is a common engineering practice: On television circuit boards or in the wiring of an automobile, you will find lights and wire connectors that serve no direct purpose for the TV or car but are put in place for the repair person in case something goes wrong. In the first part of this chapter you will learn how to instrument your programs in a similar way. It is a little more work up-front, but that work is amply repaid by shortened debugging times.

In the second part of this chapter you will learn how to run the debugger to cope with programs that don't do the right thing.

8.1   Unit Tests

> Use unit tests to test classes in isolation.

> Write a test harness to run a test.

The single most important testing tool is the *unit test* of a method or a set of cooperating methods.

For a unit test, the classes to be tested are compiled outside the program in which they will be used, together with a simple method called a *test harness* that feeds parameters to the methods.

The test arguments can come from one of several sources: from user input, by running through a range of values in a loop, as random values, and as values that are stored in a file or database.

In the following sections we will use a simple example for a method to test, namely an approximation algorithm to compute square roots that was known to the ancient Greeks. The algorithm, which was mentioned in Exercise P6.12, starts by guessing a value x that might be somewhat close to the desired square root $\sqrt{a}$. The initial value doesn't have to be very close; $x = a$ is a perfectly good choice. Now consider the quantities x and a / x. If $x < \sqrt{a}$, then $a / x > a/\sqrt{a} = \sqrt{a}$. Similarly, if $x > \sqrt{a}$, then $a / x < a/\sqrt{a} = \sqrt{a}$. That is, $\sqrt{a}$ lies between x and a / x. Make the *midpoint* of that interval our improved guess of the square root (see Figure 1). Therefore set $x_{new} = (x + a / x) / 2$ and repeat the procedure—that is, compute the midpoint between x_{new} and a / x_{new}. Stop when two successive approximations differ from each other by a very small amount.

This method converges very rapidly. To compute $\sqrt{100}$, only 8 steps are required:

```
Guess #1: 50.5
Guess #2: 26.24009900990099
Guess #3: 15.025530119986813
Guess #4: 10.840434673026925
Guess #5: 10.032578510960604
Guess #6: 10.000052895642693
Guess #7: 10.000000000139897
```

Figure 1

Approximating a Square Root

```
        Guess #8: 10.0
        Guess #9: 10.0
        Guess #10: 10.0
```

Here is a class that implements the root approximation algorithm. Construct a Root-Approximator to extract a square root of a given number. The nextGuess method computes the next guess, and the getRoot method keeps calling nextGuess until two guesses are sufficiently close.

File RootApproximator.java

```
1   /**
2       Computes approximations to the square root of
3       a number, using Heron's algorithm.
4   */
5   public class RootApproximator
6   {
7       /**
8           Constructs a root approximator for a given number.
9           @param aNumber  the number from which to extract the square root
10          (Precondition: aNumber >= 0)
11      */
12      public RootApproximator(double aNumber)
13      {
14          a = aNumber;
15          xold = 1;
16          xnew = a;
17      }
18
19      /**
20          Compute a better guess from the current guess.
21          @return  the next guess
22      */
23      public double nextGuess()
24      {
25          xold = xnew;
26          if (xold != 0)
27              xnew = (xold + a / xold) / 2;
28          return xnew;
29      }
30
31      /**
32          Compute the root by repeatedly improving the current
33          guess until two successive guesses are approximately equal.
34          @return  the computed value for the square root
35      */
36      public double getRoot()
37      {
38          while (!Numeric.approxEqual(xnew, xold))
39              nextGuess();
40          return xnew;
```

```
41     }
42
43     private double a; // the number whose square root is computed
44     private double xnew; // the current guess
45     private double xold; // the old guess
46 }
```

The guesses for $\sqrt{100}$ were computed by this test program.

File RootApproximatorTest.java

```
1  import javax.swing.JOptionPane;
2
3  /**
4     This program prints ten approximations for a square root.
5  */
6  public class RootApproximatorTest
7  {
8     public static void main(String[] args)
9     {
10        String input
11           = JOptionPane.showInputDialog("Enter a number");
12        double x = Double.parseDouble(input);
13        RootApproximator r = new RootApproximator(x);
14        final int MAX_TRIES = 10;
15        for (int tries = 1; tries <= MAX_TRIES; tries++)
16        {
17           double y = r.nextGuess();
18           System.out.println("Guess #"
19              + tries + ": " + y);
20        }
21        System.exit(0);
22     }
23 }
```

Does the `RootApproximator` class work correctly? Let us approach this question systematically.

If you use an environment such as BlueJ that allows you to create objects and call methods, you can easily run a few quick tests by constructing a few objects and calling methods—see Figure 2.

Alternatively, if you don't have such a development environment, it is an easy matter to write a test harness that supplies individual values for testing. Here is an example.

File RootApproximatorTest2.java

```
1  import javax.swing.JOptionPane;
2
3  /**
4     This program computes square roots of user-supplied inputs.
5  */
6  public class RootApproximatorTest2
```

Figure 2

Testing a Class with BlueJ

```
 7  {
 8      public static void main(String[] args)
 9      {
10          boolean done = false;
11          while (!done)
12          {
13              String input = JOptionPane.showInputDialog(
14                  "Enter a number, Cancel to quit");
15
16              if (input == null)
17                  done = true;
18              else
19              {
20                  double x = Double.parseDouble(input);
21                  RootApproximator r = new RootApproximator(x);
22                  double y = r.getRoot();
23
24                  System.out.println("square root of " + x
25                      + " = " + y);
26              }
27          }
```

```
28          System.exit(0);
29      }
30 }
```

> If you read test inputs from a file, you can easily repeat the test.

Now you can type values in and check that the `getRoot` method computes the correct values for the square root.

There is just one problem with this test approach. Suppose you detect and fix an error in your code. Of course, you will want to test the class again. The test harness program is still usable, which is good. But you have to retype all the inputs.

Therefore, it is a better idea to read the inputs from a file. That way, you can simply place the inputs into a file once and then run the test harness program whenever you want to test a new version of your code. The simplest way of reading input from a file is redirection of `System.in` (see Productivity Hint 6.1). First, you need to make a minor change to the test harness and read from a `BufferedReader` (see Advanced Topic 3.6). The following program listing shows the change.

File RootApproximatorTest3.java

```
1  import java.io.BufferedReader;
2  import java.io.InputStreamReader;
3  import java.io.IOException;
4
5  /**
6      This program computes square roots of inputs supplied
7      through System.in.
8  */
9  public class RootApproximatorTest3
10 {
11     public static void main(String[] args)
12         throws IOException
13     {
14         BufferedReader console  = new BufferedReader(
15             new InputStreamReader(System.in));
16         boolean done = false;
17         while (!done)
18         {
19             String input = console.readLine();
20             if (input == null) done = true;
21             else
22             {
23                 double x = Double.parseDouble(input);
24                 RootApproximator r = new RootApproximator(x);
25                 double y = r.getRoot();
26
27                 System.out.println("square root of " + x
28                     + " = " + y);
29             }
30         }
```

```
31    }
32 }
```

Then prepare a file with test inputs, such as this one:

```
100
20
4
1
0.25
0.01
```

Run the program like this. (Recall from Productivity Hint 6.1 that the < symbol denotes redirection of the file test.in to System.in.)

```
java RootApproximatorTest3 < test.in
```

The output is

```
square root of 100.0 = 10.0
square root of 20.0 = 4.47213595499958
square root of 4.0 = 2.0
square root of 1.0 = 1.0
square root of 0.25 = 0.5
square root of 0.01 = 0.1
```

It is also possible to generate test cases automatically. If there are few possible inputs, it is feasible to run through a representative number of them with a loop.

File RootApproximatorTest4.java

```
1  /**
2      This program computes square roots of input values
3      supplied by a loop.
4  */
5  public class RootApproximatorTest4
6  {
7      public static void main(String[] args)
8      {
9          final double MIN = 1;
10         final double MAX = 10;
11         final double INCREMENT = 0.5;
12         for (double x = MIN; x <= MAX; x = x + INCREMENT)
13         {
14             RootApproximator r = new RootApproximator(x);
15             double y = r.getRoot();
16             System.out.println("square root of " + x
17                 + " = " + y);
18         }
19     }
20 }
```

The output is:

```
square root of 1.0 = 1.0
square root of 1.5 = 1.224744871391589
square root of 2.0 = 1.414213562373095
. . .
square root of 9.0 = 3.0
square root of 9.5 = 3.0822070014844885
square root of 10.0 = 3.162277660168379
```

Unfortunately, this test is restricted to only a small subset of values. To overcome that limitation, random generation of test cases can be useful:

File RootApproximatorTest5.java

```
 1  import java.util.Random;
 2
 3  /**
 4     This program computes square roots of random inputs.
 5  */
 6  public class RootApproximatorTest5
 7  {
 8     public static void main(String[] args)
 9     {
10        final double SAMPLES = 100;
11        Random generator = new Random();
12        for (int i = 1; i <= SAMPLES; i++)
13        {  // generate random test value
14
15           double x = 1.0E6 * generator.nextDouble();
16           RootApproximator r = new RootApproximator(x);
17           double y = r.getRoot();
18           System.out.println("square root of " + x
19              + " = " + y);
20        }
21     }
22  }
```

A sample run looks like this:

```
square root of 298042.3906807571 = 545.932588036982
square root of 552836.0182932373 = 743.5294333738493
square root of 751687.182520626 = 866.9989518567056
square root of 872344.1056077272 = 933.9936325306116
. . .
```

Selecting good test cases is an important skill for debugging programs. Of course, you want to test your program with inputs that a typical user might supply.

You should test all program features. In the square root computation program, you should check typical test cases such as 100, 1/4, 0.01, 2, 10E12, and so on. These tests are *positive* tests. They consist of legitimate inputs, and you expect the program to handle them correctly.

> Boundary test cases are test
> cases that are at the boundary
> of acceptable inputs.

Next, you should include *boundary cases:* values that lie at the boundary of the set of acceptable inputs. For the root approximator, test what happens if the input is 0. Boundary cases are still legitimate inputs, and you expect that the program will handle them correctly—often in some trivial way or through special cases. Testing boundary cases is important, because programmers often make mistakes dealing with boundary conditions. Division by zero, extracting characters from empty strings, and accessing null pointers are common sources of errors.

Finally, gather *negative* test cases. These are inputs that you expect the program to reject. Examples are the square root of −2. However, in this case you need to be a little careful. If the precondition of a method doesn't allow an input, the method need not produce an output. In fact, if you try to compute the square root of −2 with the root approximator, the loop in the `getRoot` method never terminates. You can see why, by calling `getNext` a few times:

```
Guess #1: -0.5
Guess #2: 1.75
Guess #3: 0.3035714285714286
Guess #4: -3.142331932773109
Guess #5: -1.2529309672222557
Guess #6: 0.1716630854488237
Guess #7: -5.739532701343778
Guess #8: -2.6955361385562107
Guess #9: -0.976784358209916
Guess #10: 0.5353752385394334
```

No matter how you generate the test cases, the important point is that you test individual classes thoroughly before you put them into your program. If you have ever put together a computer or fixed a car, you probably followed a similar process. Rather than simply throwing all the parts together and hoping for the best, you probably first tested each part in isolation. It takes a little longer at the beginning, but it greatly reduces the possibility of complete and mysterious failure once the parts are put together.

8.2   Test Case Evaluation

In the last section we worried about how to get test *inputs*. Now let us consider what to do with the *outputs*. How do you know whether the output is correct?

Sometimes you can verify the output by calculating the correct values by hand. For example, for a payroll program you can compute taxes manually.

Sometimes a computation does a lot of work, and it is not practical to do the computation manually. That is the case with many approximation algorithms, which may run through dozens or hundreds of iterations before they arrive at the final answer. The square root method of Section 8.1 is an example of such an approximation.

How can you test that the square root method works correctly? You can supply test inputs for which you know the answer, such as 4 and 100, and also 1/4 and 0.01, so that you don't just restrict the inputs to integers.

Alternatively, you can write a test harness that verifies that the output values fulfill certain properties. For the square root program you can compute the square root, compute the square of the result, and verify that you obtain the original input:

File RootApproximatorTest6.java

```java
1  import java.util.Random;
2
3  /**
4     This program verifies the computation of square root values
5     by checking a mathematical property of square roots.
6  */
7  public class RootApproximatorTest6
8  {
9     public static void main(String[] args)
10    {
11       final double SAMPLES = 100;
12       int passcount = 0;
13       int failcount = 0;
14       Random generator = new Random();
15       for (int i = 1; i <= SAMPLES; i++)
16       {
17          // generate random test value
18
19          double x = 1.0E6 * generator.nextDouble();
20          RootApproximator r = new RootApproximator(x);
21          double y = r.getRoot();
22          System.out.println("square root of " + x
23             + " = " + y);
24
25          // check that test value fulfills square property
26
27          if (Numeric.approxEqual(y * y, x))
28          {
29             System.out.println("Test passed.");
30             passcount++;
31          }
32          else
33          {
34             System.out.println("Test failed.");
35             failcount++;
36          }
37       }
38       System.out.println("Pass: " + passcount);
39       System.out.println("Fail: " + failcount);
40    }
41 }
```

Finally, there may be a less efficient way of computing the same value that a method produces. You can then run a test harness that computes the method to be tested, together with the slower process, and compares the answers. For example, $\sqrt{x} = x^{1/2}$, so you can use the slower Math.pow method to generate the same value. Such a slower but reliable method is called an *oracle*. The following example program shows how to compare the result of the method to be tested with the outcome of an oracle. Alternatively, you

> An oracle is a slow but reliable method to compute a result for testing purposes.

can write a separate program that writes the oracle values to a file, and then compare the results of your method against the precomputed oracle values.

File RootApproximatorTest7.java

```java
1  import java.util.Random;
2
3  /**
4     This program verifies the computation of square root values
5     by using an oracle.
6  */
7  public class RootApproximatorTest7
8  {
9     public static void main(String[] args)
10    {
11       final double SAMPLES = 100;
12       int passcount = 0;
13       int failcount = 0;
14       Random generator = new Random();
15       for (int i = 1; i <= SAMPLES; i++)
16       {
17          // generate random test value
18
19          double x = 1.0E6 * generator.nextDouble();
20          RootApproximator r = new RootApproximator(x);
21          double y = r.getRoot();
22          System.out.println("square root of " + x
23             + " = " + y);
24
25          double oracleValue = Math.pow(x, 0.5);
26
27          // check that test value approximately equals oracle value
28
29          if (Numeric.approxEqual(y, oracleValue))
30          {
31             System.out.println("Test passed.");
32             passcount++;
33          }
34          else
35          {
36             System.out.println("Test failed.");
37             failcount++;
38          }
39       }
40       System.out.println("Pass: " + passcount);
41       System.out.println("Fail: " + failcount);
42    }
43 }
```

8.3   Regression Testing and Test Coverage

How should you collect test cases? This is easy for programs that get all their input from standard input. Just make each test case into a file—say, test1.in, test2.in, test3.in. These files contain the keystrokes that you would normally type at the keyboard when the program runs. Feed the files into the program to be tested, using redirection:

```
java Program < test1.in > test1.out
java Program < test2.in > test2.out
java Program < test3.in > test3.out
```

> A test suite is a set of tests for repeated testing.

Then study the outputs and see whether they are correct.

Keeping a test case in a file is smart, because you can then use it to test every version of the program. In fact, it is a common and useful practice to make a test file whenever you find a program bug. You can use that file to verify that your bug fix really works. Don't throw it away; feed it to the next version after that and all subsequent versions. Such a collection of test cases is called a *test suite*.

> Regression testing involves repeating previously run tests to ensure that known failures of prior versions do not appear in new versions of the software.

You will be surprised how often a bug that you fixed will reappear in a future version. This is a phenomenon known as *cycling*. Sometimes you don't quite understand the reason for a bug and apply a quick fix that appears to work. Later, you apply a different quick fix that solves a second problem but makes the first problem appear again. Of course, it is always best to think through what really causes a bug and fix the root cause instead of doing a sequence of "Band-Aid" solutions. If you don't succeed in doing that, however, at least you want to have an honest appraisal of how well the program works. By keeping all old test cases around and testing them all against every new version, you get that feedback. The process of testing against a set of past failures is called *regression testing*.

> Black-box testing describes a testing method that does not take the structure of the implementation into account.

Testing the functionality of the program without consideration of its internal structure is called *black-box testing*. That is an important part of testing, because, after all, the users of a program do not know its internal structure. If a program works perfectly on all positive inputs and fails gracefully on all negative ones, then it does its job.

> White-box testing uses information about the structure of a program.

However, it is impossible to ensure absolutely that a program will work correctly on all inputs just by supplying a finite number of test cases. As the famous computer scientist Edsger Dijkstra pointed out, testing can show only the presence of bugs—not their absence. To gain more confidence in the correctness of a program, it is useful to consider its internal structure. Testing strategies that look inside a program are called *white-box testing*. Performing unit tests of each method is a part of white-box testing.

> Test coverage is a measure of how many parts of a program have been tested.

You want to make sure that each part of your program is exercised at least once by one of your test cases. This is called *test coverage*. If some code is never executed by any of your test cases, you have no way of knowing whether that code would perform correctly if it ever were executed by user input. That means that you need to look at every `if/else` branch to see that each of them is reached by some test case. Many conditional branches are in the code only to take care of strange and abnormal inputs, but they still do something. It is a common phenomenon that they end up doing something incorrect, but that those faults are never discovered during testing, because nobody supplied the strange and abnormal inputs. Of course, these flaws become immediately apparent when the program is released and the first user types in a bad input and is incensed when the program crashes. A test suite should ensure that each part of the code is covered by some input.

For example, in testing the `getTax` method of the tax program in Chapter 5, you want to make sure that every `if` statement is entered for at least one test case. You should test both single and married taxpayers, with incomes in each of the three tax brackets.

It is a good idea to write the first test cases *before* the program is written completely. Designing a few test cases can give you insight into what the program should do, which is valuable for implementing it. You will also have something to throw at the program when it compiles for the first time. Of course, the initial set of test cases will be augmented as the debugging process progresses.

Modern programs can be quite challenging to test. In a program with a graphical user interface, the user can click random buttons with a mouse and supply input in random order. Programs that receive their data through a network connection need to be tested by simulating occasional network delays and failures. All this is much harder, because you cannot simply place keystrokes in a file. You need not worry about these complexities as you study this book, and there are tools to automate testing in these scenarios. The basic principles of regression testing (never throwing a test case away) and complete coverage (executing all code at least once) still hold.

Productivity Hint   8.1

Batch Files and Shell Scripts

If you need to perform the same tasks repeatedly on the command line, then it is worth learning about the automation features offered by your operating system.

Under DOS, you use *batch files* to execute a number of commands automatically. For example, suppose you need to test a program with three inputs:

```
java Program < test1.in
java Program < test2.in
java Program < test3.in
```

Then you find a bug, fix it, and run the tests again. Now you need to type the three commands once more. There has to be a better way. Under DOS, put the commands in a text file and call it test.bat:

File test.bat

```
1 java Program < test1.in
2 java Program < test2.in
3 java Program < test3.in
```

▼   Then you just type

```
test
```

▼   and the three commands in the batch file execute automatically.

It is easy to make the batch file more useful. If you are done with Program and start working on Program2, you can of course write a batch file test2.bat, but you can do bet-
▼   ter than that. Give the test batch file a *parameter*. That is, call it with

```
test Program
```

or
▼

```
test Program2
```

You need to change the batch file to make this work. In a batch file, %1 denotes the first
▼   string that you type after the name of the batch file, %2 the second string, and so on:

File test.bat
▼

```
1 java %1 < test1.in
2 java %1 < test2.in
3 java %1 < test3.in
```

▼   What if you have more than three test files? DOS batch files have a very primitive for loop:

File test.bat
▼

```
1 for %%f in (test*.in) do java %1 < %%f
```

If you work in a computer lab, you will want a batch file that copies all your files onto a
▼   floppy disk when you are ready to go home. Put the following lines in a file gohome.bat:

File gohome.bat
▼

```
1 copy *.java a:
2 copy *.txt a:
3 copy *.in a:
```

▼   There are lots of uses for batch files, and it is well worth it to learn more about them.

Batch files are a feature of the DOS operating system, not of Java. On a UNIX sys-
▼   tem, *shell scripts* are used for the same purpose.

8.4   Program Traces, Logging, and Assertions

> A program trace consists of trace messages that show the path of execution.

Sometimes you run a program and you are not sure where it spends its time. To get a printout of the program flow, you can insert trace messages into the program, such as this one:

```
public double getTax()
{
    . . .
```

```
if (status == SINGLE)
{
   System.out.println("status is SINGLE");
   . . .
}
. . .
```

You may also want to print out a *stack trace* that tells you how you got to this point. Use these instructions:

```
Throwable t = new Throwable();
t.printStackTrace(System.out);
```

A stack trace looks like this:

```
java.lang.Throwable
        at TaxReturn.getTax(TaxReturn.java:26)
        at TaxReturnTest.main(TaxReturnTest.java:30)
```

> A stack trace consists of a list of all pending method calls at a particular point in time.

This is very useful information—the trace message was generated inside the getTax method of the TaxReturn class (specifically, in line 26 of the TaxReturn.java file). That method was called from line 30 in TaxReturnTest.java.

However, there is a problem with trace messages. When you are done testing the program, you need to remove all print statements that produce trace messages. If you find another error, however, you need to stick the print statements back in.

To overcome this problem, you can use the Logger class, which allows you to turn off the trace messages. Support for logging is included in the standard Java library version 1.4 and above.

Instead of printing directly to System.out, use the global logger object

```
Logger logger = Logger.getLogger("global");
```

and call

```
logger.info("status is SINGLE");
```

By default, the message is printed. But if you call

```
logger.setLevel(Level.OFF);
```

all log message printing is suppressed. Thus, you can turn off the log messages when your program works fine, and you can turn them back on if you find another error.

When you are tracing execution flow, the most important events are entering and exiting a method. At the beginning of a method, print out the parameters:

```
public TaxReturn(double anIncome, int aStatus)
{
   Logger logger = Logger.getLogger("global");
   logger.info("Parameters: anIncome = " + anIncome
      + " aStatus = " + aStatus);
   . . .
}
```

At the end of a method, print out the return value:

```
public double getTax()
{
    . . .
    logger.info("Return value = " + tax);
    return tax;
}
```

To get a proper trace, you must locate *each* method exit point. Be sure to locate any `return` statements in the middle of the method.

Of course, you aren't restricted to "enter/exit" messages. You can report on progress inside a method. The `Logger` class has many other options for industrial-strength logging. You may want to check out the API documentation if you want to have more control over logging.

Program traces can be useful to analyze the behavior of a program, but they have some definite disadvantages. It can be quite time-consuming to find out which trace messages to insert. If you insert too many messages, you produce a flurry of output that is hard to analyze; if you insert too few, you may not have enough information to spot the cause of the error. If you find that a hassle, you are not alone. Most professional programmers use a *debugger*, not trace messages, to locate errors in their code. The debugger is covered in the next section.

Programs often contain implicit assumptions. For example, an interest rate should not be negative. Surely nobody would ever deposit money in an account that earns negative interest, but such a value might creep into a program due to an input or processing error. Sometimes, it is useful to check that no such error has occurred before continuing with the program. For example, before extracting the square root of a number that you know can't possibly be negative, you may want to check your assumption.

> An assertion is a logical condition in a program that you believe to be true.

An assumption that you believe to be true is called an *assertion*. An assertion test checks whether an assertion is true and terminates the program with an error report if it is not. Here is a typical assertion check:

```
public void computeIntersection()
{   . . .
    double y = r * r - (x - a) * (x - a);
    assert y >= 0;
    root = Math.sqrt(y);
    . . .
}
```

In this program excerpt, the programmer expects that the quantity y can never be negative. When the assertion is correct, no harm is done, and the program works in the normal way. If, for some reason, the assertion fails, then the programmer would rather have the program terminate than go on, compute the square root of a negative number, and cause greater harm later.

A common use for assertions is to monitor pre- and postconditions (see Section 7.5). For example, here is how you can monitor the precondition of the `deposit` method of the `Bank` class:

```
public double deposit (double amount)
{
    assert amount >= 0;
    balance = balance + amount;
}
```

Assertions are part of the Java language version 1.4 and above. To compile a program with assertions, run the Java compiler as

```
javac -source 1.4 MyProg.java
```

To execute the program with assertion checking turned on, use this command:

```
java -enableassertions MyProg
```

8.5   The Debugger

As you have undoubtedly realized by now, computer programs rarely run perfectly the first time. At times, it can be quite frustrating to find the bugs. Of course, you can insert trace messages to show the program flow as well as the values of key variables, run the program, and try to analyze the printout. If the printout does not clearly point to the problem, you may need to add and remove print commands and run the program again. That can be a time-consuming process.

> A debugger is a program that you can use to execute another program and analyze its runtime behavior.

Modern development environments contain special programs, called *debuggers,* that help you locate bugs by letting you follow the execution of a program. You can stop and restart your program and see the contents of variables whenever your program is temporarily stopped. At each stop, you have the choice of what variables to inspect and how many program steps to run until the next stop.

Some people feel that debuggers are just a tool to make programmers lazy. Admittedly some people write sloppy programs and then fix them up with the debugger, but the majority of programmers make an honest effort to write the best program they can before trying to run it through the debugger. These programmers realize that the debugger, while more convenient than print statements, is not cost-free. It does take time to set up and carry out an effective debugging session.

In actual practice, you cannot avoid using the debugger. The larger your programs get, the harder it is to debug them simply by inserting print statements. You will find that the time investment to learn about the debugger is amply repaid in your programming career.

Like compilers, debuggers vary widely from one system to another. On some systems they are quite primitive and require you to memorize a small set of arcane commands; on others they have an intuitive window interface. The screen shots in this chapter show the debugger in the Forte Community Edition development environment, presently downloadable for free from Sun Microsystems.

You will have to find out how to prepare a program for debugging and how to start the debugger on your system. If you use an integrated development environment, which contains an editor, compiler, and debugger, this step is usually very easy. You just build the program in the usual way and pick a menu command to start debugging. On some systems, you must manually build a debug version of your program and invoke the debugger.

> You can make effective use of the debugger by mastering just three concepts: breakpoints, single-stepping, and inspecting variables.

Once you have started the debugger, you can go a long way with just three debugging commands: "set breakpoint", "single step", and "inspect variable". The names and keystrokes or mouse clicks for these commands differ widely between debuggers, but all debuggers

Figure 3

The Debugger Stopping at a Breakpoint

> When the debugger executes a program, the execution is suspended whenever a breakpoint is reached.

support these basic commands. You can find out how, either from the documentation or a lab manual, or by asking someone who has used the debugger before.

When you start the debugger, it runs at full speed until it reaches a *breakpoint*. Then execution stops, and the breakpoint that causes the stop is displayed (see Figure 3). You can now inspect variables and step through the program a line at a time, or continue running the program at full speed until it reaches the next breakpoint. When the program terminates, the debugger stops as well.

Breakpoints stay active until you remove them, so you should periodically clear the breakpoints that you no longer need.

Once the program has stopped, you can look at the current values of variables. Again, the method for selecting the variables differs among debuggers. Some debuggers always show you a window with the current local variables (see Figure 4). On other debuggers you issue a command such as "inspect variable" and type in or click on the variable. The debugger then displays the contents of the variable. If all variables contain what you expected, you can run the program until the next point where you want to stop.

When inspecting objects, you often need to give a command to "open up" the object, for example by clicking on a tree node. Once the object is opened up, you see its instance variables (see Figure 4).

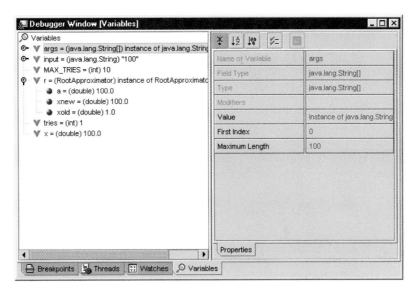

Figure 4

Inspecting Variables

> The single-step command executes the program one line at a time.

Running to a breakpoint gets you there speedily, but you don't know how the program got there. You can also step through the program a line at a time. Then you know how the program flows, but it can take a long time to step through it. The "single step" command executes the current line and stops at the next program line. Most debuggers have two "single step" commands, one called "step inside", which steps inside method calls, and one called "step over", which skips over method calls.

For example, suppose the current line is

```
String token = tokenizer.nextToken();
Word w = new Word(token);
int syllables = w.countSyllables();
System.out.println("Syllables in "
   + w.getText() + ": "
   + syllables);
```

When you "step over" method calls, you get to the next line:

```
String token = tokenizer.nextToken();
Word w = new Word(token);
int syllables = w.countSyllables();
System.out.println("Syllables in "
   + w.getText() + ": "
   + syllables);
```

However, if you "step into" method calls, you enter the first line of the `countSyllables` method.

```
public int countSyllables()
{
   int count = 0;
   int end = text.length() - 1;
}
```

You should step into a method to check whether it carries out its job correctly. You should step over a method if you know it works correctly.

Finally, when the program has completed running, the debug session is also finished. You can no longer inspect variables. To run the program again, you may be able to reset the debugger, or you may need to exit the debugging program and start over. Details depend on the particular debugger.

8.6   A Sample Debugging Session

To have a realistic example for running the debugger, we will study a Word class whose primary purpose is to count the number of syllables in a word. The class uses this rule for counting syllables:

Each *group* of adjacent vowels (a,e,i,o,u,y) counts as one syllable (for example, the "ea" in "real" contributes one syllable, but the "e..a" in "regal" count as two syllables). However, an "e" at the end of a word doesn't count as a syllable. Also, each word has at least one syllable, even if the previous rules give a count of 0.

Also, when you construct a word from a string, any characters at the beginning or the end of the string that aren't letters are stripped off. That is useful when you use a string tokenizer to break up a sentence into tokens. Tokens can still contain quotation marks and punctuation marks, and we don't want them as part of the word.

Here is the source code. There are a couple of bugs in this class.

File Word.java

```
 1 public class Word
 2 {
 3    /**
 4       Constructs a word by removing leading and trailing nonletter
 5       characters, such as punctuation marks.
 6       @param s the input string
 7    */
 8    public Word(String s)
 9    {
10       int i = 0;
11       while (i < s.length()
12             && !Character.isLetter(s.charAt(i)))
13          i++;
14       int j = s.length() - 1;
15       while (j > i
16             && !Character.isLetter(s.charAt(j)))
17          j--;
18       text = s.substring(i, j);
19    }
```

```
20
21      /**
22          Returns the text of the word, after removal of the
23          leading and trailing nonletter characters.
24          @return the text of the word
25      */
26      public String getText()
27      {
28          return text;
29      }
30
31      /**
32          Counts the syllables in the word.
33          @return the syllable count
34      */
35      public int countSyllables()
36      {
37          int count = 0;
38          int end = text.length() - 1;
39          if (end < 0) return 0; // the empty string has no syllables
40
41          // an e at the end of the word doesn't count as a vowel
42          char ch = Character.toLowerCase(text.charAt(end));
43          if (ch == 'e') end--;
44
45          boolean insideVowelGroup = false;
46          for (int i = 0; i <= end; i++)
47          {
48              ch = Character.toLowerCase(text.charAt(i));
49              if ("aeiouy".indexOf(ch) >= 0)
50              {
51                  // ch is a vowel
52                  if (!insideVowelGroup)
53                  {
54                      // start of new vowel group
55                      count++;
56                      insideVowelGroup = true;
57                  }
58              }
59          }
60
61          // every word has at least one syllable
62          if (count == 0)
63              count = 1;
64
65          return count;
66      }
67
68      private String text;
69  }
```

Here is a simple test class. Type in one or more words into the input dialog, and the syllable counts of all words are displayed.

File WordTest.java

```
1  import java.util.StringTokenizer;
2  import javax.swing.JOptionPane;
3
4  public class WordTest
5  {
6     public static void main(String[] args)
7     {
8        String input = JOptionPane.showInputDialog(
9           "Enter a sentence");
10       StringTokenizer tokenizer =
11          new StringTokenizer(input);
12       while (tokenizer.hasMoreTokens())
13       {
14          String token = tokenizer.nextToken();
15          Word w = new Word(token);
16          int syllables = w.countSyllables();
17          System.out.println("Syllables in "
18             + token + ": "
19             + syllables);
20       }
21       System.exit(0);
22    }
23 }
```

When you run this program with an input of `hello regal real`, then the output is

```
Syllables in hello: 1
Syllables in regal: 1
Syllables in real: 1
```

That is not very promising.

First, set a breakpoint in the first line of the `countSyllables` method of the `Word` class, in line 35 of `Word.java`. Then start the program. The program will prompt you for the input. For now, just supply the input value `hello`. The program will stop at the breakpoint you just set.

First, the `countSyllables` method checks the last character of the word to see if it is a letter `'e'`. Let's just verify that this works correctly. Run the program to line 41 (see Figure 5).

Now inspect the variable `ch`. This particular debugger has a handy display of all current local and instance variables—see Figure 6. If yours doesn't, you may need to inspect `ch` manually. You can see that `ch` contains the value `'l'`. That is strange. Look at the source code. The `end` variable was set to `text.length()` - 1, the last position in the `text` string, and `ch` is the character at that position.

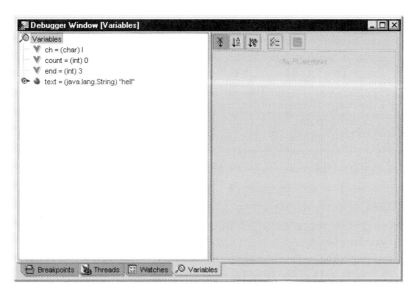

Figure 5

Debugging the countSyllables Method

Figure 6

The Current Values of the Local and Instance Variables

Looking further, you will find that end is set to 3, not 4, as you would expect. And text contains the string "hell", not "hello". Thus, it is no wonder that countSyllables returns the answer 1. We'll need to look elsewhere for the culprit. Apparently, the Word constructor contains an error.

Figure 7

Debugging the `Word` Constructor

Unfortunately, a debugger cannot go back in time. Thus, you must stop the debugger, set a breakpoint in the `Word` constructor, and restart the debugger. Supply the `"hello"` input once again. The debugger will stop at the beginning of the `Word` constructor. The constructor sets two variables `i` and `j`, skipping past any nonletters at the beginning and the end of the input string. Set a breakpoint past the end of the second loop (see Figure 7) so that you can inspect the values of `i` and `j`.

At this point, inspecting `i` and `j` shows that `i` is 0 and `j` is 4. That makes sense—there were no punctuation marks to skip. So why is `text` being set to `"hell"`? Recall that the `substring` method counts positions up to *but not including* the second parameter. Thus, the correct call should be

```
text = s.substring(i, j + 1);
```

This is a very typical "off by one" error.

Fix this error, recompile the program, and try the three test cases again. You will now get the output

```
Syllables in hello: 1
Syllables in regal: 1
Syllables in real: 1
```

Unfortunately, there still is a problem. Erase all breakpoints and set a breakpoint in the `countSyllables` method. Start the debugger and supply the input `"regal"`. When the debugger stops at the breakpoint, start single-stepping through the lines of the method. Here is the code of the loop that counts the syllables:

```
boolean insideVowelGroup = false;
for (int i = 0; i <= end; i++)
{
```

```
ch = Character.toLowerCase(text.charAt(i));
if ("aeiouy".indexOf(ch) >= 0)
{
    // ch is a vowel
    if (!insideVowelGroup)
    {
        // start of new vowel group
        count++;
        insideVowelGroup = true;
    }
}
}
```

In the first iteration through the loop, the debugger skips the `if` statement. That makes sense, because the first letter, `'r'`, isn't a vowel. In the second iteration, the debugger enters the `if` statement, as it should, because the second letter, `'e'`, is a vowel. The `inside-VowelGroup` variable is set to `true`, and the vowel counter is incremented. In the third iteration, the `if` statement is again skipped, because the letter `'g'` is not a vowel. But in the fourth iteration, something weird happens. The letter `'a'` is a vowel, and the `if` statement is entered. But the second `if` statement is skipped, and `count` is not incremented again.

Why? The `insideVowelGroup` variable is still true, even though the first vowel group was finished when the consonant `'g'` was encountered. Reading a consonant should set `insideVowelGroup` back to `false`. This is a more subtle logic error, but not an uncommon one when designing a loop that keeps track of the processing state. To fix it, stop the debugger and add the following clause:

```
if ("aeiouy".indexOf(ch) >= 0)
{
    . . .
}
else insideVowelGroup = false;
```

Now recompile and run the test once again. The output is:

```
Syllables in hello: 2
Syllables in regal: 2
Syllables in real: 1
```

> The debugger can be used only to analyze the presence of bugs, not to show that a program is bug-free.

Is the program now free from bugs? That is not a question the debugger can answer. Remember: Testing can show only the presence of bugs, not their absence.

▼ Random Fact 8.1 ▶

The First Bug

▼

According to legend, the first bug was one found in 1947 in the Mark II, a huge electromechanical computer at Harvard University. It really was caused by a bug—a moth was trapped

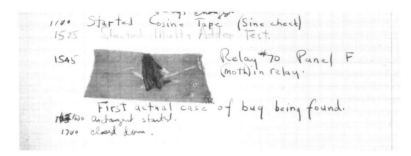

Figure 8

The "First Bug"

in a relay switch. Actually, from the note that the operator left in the log book next to the moth (see Figure 8), it appears as if the term "bug" had already been in active use at the time.

The pioneering computer scientist Maurice Wilkes wrote: "Somehow, at the Moore School and afterwards, one had always assumed there would be no particular difficulty in getting programs right. I can remember the exact instant in time at which it dawned on me that a great part of my future life would be spent finding mistakes in my own programs."

HOWTO   8.1

Debugging

Now you know about the mechanics of debugging, but all that knowledge may still leave you helpless when you fire up the debugger to look at a sick program. There are a number of strategies that you can use to recognize bugs and their causes.

Step 1   Reproduce the error

As you test your program, you notice that your program sometimes does something wrong. It gives the wrong output, it seems to print something completely random, it goes in an infinite loop, or it crashes. Find out exactly how to *reproduce* that behavior. What numbers did you enter? Where did you click with the mouse?

Run the program again; type in exactly the same answers, and click with the mouse on the same spots (or as close as you can get). Does the program exhibit the same behavior? If so, then it makes sense to fire up the debugger to study this particular problem. Debuggers are good for analyzing particular failures. They aren't terribly useful for studying a program in general.

Step 2   Simplify the error

Before you fire up the debugger, it makes sense to spend a few minutes trying to come up with a simpler input that also produces an error. Can you use shorter words or simpler numbers and still have the program misbehave? If so, use those values during your debugging session.

▼   Step 3   Divide and conquer

▼   Now that you have a particular failure, you want to get as close to the failure as possible.
           The key point of debugging is to locate the code that produces the failure. Just as with
           real insect pests, finding the bug can be hard, but once you find it, squashing it is usually
           the easy part. Suppose your program dies with a division by 0. Since there are many divi-
▼   sion operations in a typical program, it is often not feasible to set
           breakpoints to all of them. Instead, use a technique of *divide and con-*
           quer. Step over the methods in `main`, but don't step inside them.

> Use the "divide-and-
> conquer" technique to
> locate the point of failure
> of a program.

           Eventually, the failure will happen again. Now you know which
           method contains the bug: It is the last method that was called from
           `main` before the program died. Restart the debugger and go back to
           that line in `main`, then step inside that method. Repeat the process.
▼   Eventually, you will have pinpointed the line that contains the bad division. Maybe it
           is completely obvious from the code why the denominator is not correct. If not, you need
▼   to find the location where it is computed. Unfortunately, you can't go *back* in the debug-
           ger. You need to restart the program and move to the point where the denominator com-
           putation happens.

▼   Step 4   Know what your program should do

> During debugging,
> compare the actual
> contents of variables
> against the values
> that you know they
> should have.

           The debugger shows you what the program *does* do. You must know
           what the program *should* do, or you will not be able to find bugs.
           Before you trace through a loop, ask yourself how many iterations you
           expect the program to make. Before you inspect a variable, ask yourself
           what you expect to see. If you have no clue, set aside some time and
           think first. Have a calculator handy to make independent computa-
           tions. When you know what the value should be, inspect the variable.
           This is the moment of truth. If the program is still on the right track,
▼   then that value is what you expected, and you must look further for the bug. If the value is
           different, you may be on to something. Double-check your computation. If you are sure
           your value is correct, find out why your program comes up with a different value.
▼   In many cases, program bugs are the result of simple errors such as loop termination
           conditions that are off by 1. Quite often, however, programs make computational errors.
           Maybe they are supposed to add two numbers, but by accident the code was written to
▼   subtract them. Unlike your calculus instructor, programs don't make a special effort to
           ensure that everything is a simple integer (and neither do real-world problems). You will
           need to make some calculations with large integers or nasty floating-point numbers.
▼   Sometimes these calculations can be avoided if you just ask yourself, "Should this quan-
           tity be positive? Should it be larger than that value?" Then inspect variables to verify
           those theories.

▼   Step 5   Look at all details

▼   When you debug a program, you often have a theory about what the problem is. Neverthe-
           less, keep an open mind and look around at all details. What strange messages are displayed?

Why does the program take another unexpected action? These details count. When you run a debugging session, you really are a detective who needs to look at every clue available.

If you notice another failure on the way to the problem that you are about to pin down, don't just say, "I'll come back to it later". That very failure may be the original cause for your current problem. It is better to make a note of the current problem, fix what you just found, and then return to the original mission.

Step 6 Make sure you understand each bug before you fix it

Once you find that a loop makes too many iterations, it is very tempting to apply a "Band-Aid" solution and subtract 1 from a variable so that the particular problem doesn't appear again. Such a quick fix has an overwhelming probability of creating trouble elsewhere. You really need to have a thorough understanding of how the program should be written before you apply a fix.

It does occasionally happen that you find bug after bug and apply fix after fix, and the problem just moves around. That usually is a symptom of a larger problem with the program logic. There is little you can do with the debugger. You must rethink the program design and reorganize it.

Random Fact   8.2

The Therac-25 Incidents

The Therac-25 is a computerized device to deliver radiation treatment to cancer patients (see Figure 9). Between June 1985 and January 1987, several of these machines delivered serious overdoses to at least six patients, killing some of them and seriously maiming the others.

The machines were controlled by a computer program. Bugs in the program were directly responsible for the overdoses. According to [1], the program was written by a single programmer, who had since left the manufacturing company producing the device and could not be located. None of the company employees interviewed could say anything about the educational level or qualifications of the programmer.

The investigation by the federal Food and Drug Administration (FDA) found that the program was poorly documented and that there was neither a specification document nor a formal test plan. (This should make you think. Do you have a formal test plan for your programs?)

The overdoses were caused by an amateurish design of the software that had to control different devices concurrently, namely the keyboard, the display, the printer, and of course the radiation device itself. Synchronization and data sharing between the tasks were done in an ad hoc way, even though safe multitasking techniques were known at the time. Had the programmer enjoyed a formal education that involved these techniques, or taken the effort to study the literature, a safer machine could have been built. Such a machine would have probably involved a commercial multitasking system, which might have required a more expensive computer.

The same flaws were present in the software controlling the predecessor model, the Therac-20, but that machine had hardware interlocks that mechanically prevented overdoses.

Figure 9

Typical Therac-25 Facility

The hardware safety devices were removed in the Therac-25 and replaced by checks in the software, presumably to save cost.

Frank Houston of the FDA wrote in 1985 [1]: "A significant amount of software for life-critical systems comes from small firms, especially in the medical device industry; firms that fit the profile of those resistant to or uninformed of the principles of either system safety or software engineering."

Who is to blame? The programmer? The manager who not only failed to ensure that the programmer was up to the task but also didn't insist on comprehensive testing? The hospitals that installed the device, or the FDA, for not reviewing the design process? Unfortunately, even today there are no firm standards of what constitutes a safe software design process.

CHAPTER SUMMARY

1. Use unit tests to test classes in isolation.

2. Write a test harness to run a test.

3. If you read test inputs from a file, you can easily repeat the test.

4. Boundary test cases are test cases that are at the boundary of acceptable inputs.

5. An oracle is a slow but reliable method to compute a result for testing purposes.

6. A test suite is a set of tests for repeated testing.

7. Regression testing involves repeating previously run tests to ensure that known failures of prior versions do not appear in new versions of the software.

8. Black-box testing describes a testing method that does not take the structure of the implementation into account.

9. White-box testing uses information about the structure of a program.

10. Test coverage is a measure of how many parts of a program have been tested.

11. A program trace consists of trace messages that show the path of execution.

12. A stack trace consists of a list of all pending method calls at a particular point in time.

13. An assertion is a logical condition in a program that you believe to be true.

14. A debugger is a program that you can use to execute another program and analyze its runtime behavior.

15. You can make effective use of the debugger by mastering just three concepts: breakpoints, single-stepping, and inspecting variables.

16. When the debugger executes a program, the execution is suspended whenever a breakpoint is reached.

17. The single-step command executes the program one line at a time.

18. The debugger can be used only to analyze the presence of bugs, not to show that a program is bug-free.

19. Use the "divide-and-conquer" technique to locate the point of failure of a program.

20. During debugging, compare the actual contents of variables against the values that you know they should have.

Further Reading

[1] Nancy G. Leveson and Clark S. Turner, "An Investigation of the Therac-25 Accidents," *IEEE Computer,* July 1993, pp. 18–41.

CLASSES, OBJECTS, AND METHODS INTRODUCED IN THIS CHAPTER

```
java.lang.Throwable
    printStackTrace
java.util.logging.Logger
    getLogger
    info
    setLevel
```

REVIEW EXERCISES

Exercise R8.1. Define the terms *unit test* and *test harness*.

Exercise R8.2. What is an oracle?

Exercise R8.3. Define the terms *regression testing* and *test suite*.

Exercise R8.4. What is the debugging phenomenon known as "cycling"? What can you do to avoid it?

Exercise R8.5. The arc sine function is the inverse of the sine function. That is, $y = \arcsin(x)$ if $x = \sin(y)$. It is defined only if $-1 \le x \le 1$. Suppose you need to write a Java method to compute the arc sine. List three positive test cases and one boundary test case with their expected return values, and two negative test cases.

Exercise R8.6. What is a program trace? When does it make sense to use a program trace, and when does it make more sense to use a debugger?

Exercise R8.7. Explain the differences between these debugger operations:
- Stepping into a method
- Stepping over a method

Exercise R8.8. Explain in detail how to inspect the information stored in a `Point2D.Double` object in your debugger.

Exercise R8.9. Explain in detail how to inspect the string stored in a `String` object in your debugger.

Exercise R8.10. Explain in detail how to use your debugger to inspect the balance stored in a `BankAccount` object.

Exercise R8.11. Explain the "divide-and-conquer" strategy to get close to a bug in the debugger.

Exercise R8.12. True or false:
- If a program has passed all tests in the test suite, it has no more bugs.
- If a program has a bug, that bug always shows up when running the program through the debugger.
- If all methods in a program were proven correct, then the program has no bugs.

PROGRAMMING EXERCISES

Exercise P8.1. The arc sine function is the inverse of the sine function. That is,

$$y = \arcsin(x) \text{ if } x = \sin(y)$$

where y is in radians. For example,

$$\arcsin(0) = 0$$
$$\arcsin(0.5) = \pi/6$$

$$\arcsin(\sqrt{2}/2) = \pi/4$$
$$\arcsin(\sqrt{3}/2) = \pi/3$$
$$\arcsin(1) = \pi/2$$
$$\arcsin(-1) = \pi/2$$

The arc sine is defined only for values between −1 and 1. There is a Java standard library method to compute the arc sine, but you should not use it for this exercise. Write a Java class `ArcSinApproximator` that computes the arc sine from its Taylor series expansion

$$\arcsin(x) = x + \frac{x^3}{3!} + \frac{3^2 \cdot x^5}{5!} + \frac{3^2 \cdot 5^2 \cdot x^7}{7!} + \frac{3^2 \cdot 5^2 \cdot 7^2 \cdot x^9}{9!} + \cdots$$

Hint: Don't compute the powers and factorials explicitly. Instead, compute each term from the value of the preceding term.

You should compute the sum until a new term is $< 10^{-6}$. This method will be used in subsequent exercises.

Exercise P8.2. Write a simple test harness for the `ArcSinApproximator` class that reads floating-point numbers from standard input and computes their arc sines, until the end of the input is reached. Then run that program and verify its outputs against the arc sine function of a scientific calculator.

Exercise P8.3. Write a test harness that automatically generates test cases for the `ArcSinApproximator` class, namely numbers between −1 and 1 in a step size of 0.1.

Exercise P8.4. Write a test harness that generates 10 random floating-point numbers between −1 and 1 and feeds them to `ArcSinApproximator`.

Exercise P8.5. Write a test harness that automatically tests the validity of the `ArcSinApproximator` class by verifying that

```
Math.sin(new ArcSinApproximator(x).getArcSin())
```

is approximately equal to x. Test with 100 random inputs.

Exercise P8.6. The arc sine function can be computed from the arc tangent function, according to the formula

$$\arcsin(x) = \arctan\left(x / \sqrt{1 - x^2}\right)$$

Use that expression as an *oracle* to test that your arc sine method works correctly. Test your method with 100 random inputs and verify against the oracle.

Exercise P8.7. The domain of the arc sine function is $-1 \le x \le 1$. Test your class by computing arcsin(1.1). What happens?

Exercise P8.8. Place logging messages into the loop of the arc sine method that computes the power series. Print the value of the exponent of the current term, the value of the current term, and the current approximation to the result. What trace output do you get when you compute arcsin(0.5)?

Exercise P8.9. Add logging messages to the buggy Word class. Log relevant values such as instance variable values, return values, and loop counters. Run your program with the same sample inputs used for the debugging session. Are the messages informative enough to spot the bug?

Exercise P8.10. Run a test harness of the ArcSinApproximator class through the debugger. Step inside the computation of arcsin(0.5). Step through the computation until the x^7 term has been computed and added to the sum. What is the value of the current term and of the sum at this point?

Exercise P8.11. Run a test harness of the arcsin method through the debugger. Step inside the computation of arcsin(0.5). Step through the computation until the x^n term has become smaller than 10^{-6}. Then inspect n. How large is it?

Exercise P8.12. The following class has two bugs:

```
public class RootApproximator
{
   public RootApproximator(double aNumber)
   {
      a = aNumber;
      x1 = aNumber;
   }

   public double nextGuess()
   {
      x1 = x0;
      x0 = (x1 + a / x1) / 2;
      return x1;
   }

   public double getRoot()
   {
      while (!Numeric.approxEqual(x0, x1))
         nextGuess();
      return x1;
   }

   private double a; //  the number whose square root is computed
   private double x0;
   private double x1;
}
```

Create a series of test cases to flush out the bugs. Then run a debugging session to find them. What changes did you make to the class to fix the bugs?

Interfaces and Polymorphism

CHAPTER GOALS

To learn about interfaces

▶ To be able to convert between supertype and subtype references

▶ To understand the concept of polymorphism

▶ To appreciate how interfaces can be used to decouple classes

▶ To learn how to implement helper classes as inner classes

▶ To understand how inner classes access variables from the surrounding scope

▶ To implement event listeners for timer events

CHAPTER CONTENTS

9.1 Developing Reusable Solutions

Consider the DataSet class of Chapter 6. We used that class to compute the average and maximum of a set of input values. However, the class was suitable only for computing the average of a set of *numbers*. If we wanted to process bank accounts to find the bank account with the highest balance, we would have to modify the class, like this:

```
public class DataSet // modified for BankAccount objects
{
    . . .
    public void add(BankAccount x)
    {
        sum = sum + x.getBalance();
        if (count == 0
                || maximum.getBalance() < x.getBalance())
            maximum = x;
        count++;
    }

    public BankAccount getMaximum()
    {
        return maximum;
    }

    private double sum;
    private BankAccount maximum;
    private int count;
}
```

Or suppose we wanted to find the coin with the highest value among a set of coins. We would need to modify the DataSet class again.

```
public class DataSet // modified for Coin objects
{
    . . .
    public void add(Coin x)
    {
        sum = sum + x.getValue();
        if (count == 0
                || maximum.getValue() < x.getValue())
            maximum = x;
        count++;
    }

    public Coin getMaximum()
    {
        return maximum;
    }

    private double sum;
```

```
        private Coin maximum;
        private int count;
    }
```

Clearly, the fundamental mechanics of analyzing the data is the same in all cases, but the details of measurement differ.

Suppose that the various classes could agree on a single method `getMeasure` that obtains the measure to be used in the data analysis, such as the balance for bank accounts, value for coins, and so on. Then we could implement a single reusable `DataSet` class. The `add` method would look like this:

```
    sum = sum + x.getMeasure();
    if (count == 0 || maximum.getMeasure() < x.getMeasure())
        maximum = x;
    count++;
```

What is the type of the variable x? Ideally, x should refer to any class that has a `getMeasure` method. In Java, an *interface type* expresses that concept. Here is the interface type declaration for a `Measurable` type.

```
    public interface Measurable
    {
        double getMeasure();
    }
```

> A Java interface declares a set of methods and their signatures. Unlike a class, it provides no implementation.

The interface declaration lists all methods that the interface requires. This interface requires a single method, but in general, an interface can require multiple methods.

An interface is similar to a class, but there are several important differences:

- All methods in an interface are *abstract;* that is, they have a name, parameters, and a return type, but they don't have an implementation.

- All methods in an interface are automatically public.

- An interface does not have instance variables.

Now we can use the type `Measurable` to declare the variables x and `maximum`.

```
    public class DataSet
    {
        . . .
        public void add(Measurable x)
        {
            sum = sum + x.getMeasure();
            if (count == 0
                    || maximum.getMeasure() < x.getMeasure())
                maximum = x;
            count++;
        }

        public Measurable getMaximum()
```

```
    {
        return maximum;
    }

    private double sum;
    private Measurable maximum;
    private int count;
}
```

> To realize an interface, a class must supply all methods that the interface requires.

This `DataSet` class is usable for analyzing objects of any class that *realizes* the `Measurable` interface. A class realizes an interface if it declares the interface in an `implements` clause, and if it implements the method or methods that the interface requires.

```
class ClassName implements Measurable
{
    public double getMeasure()
    {
        implementation
    }

    additional methods and fields
}
```

A class can realize more than one interface. Of course, the class must then define all the methods that are required by all the interfaces it realizes.

Let us modify the `BankAccount` class to realize the `Measurable` interface.

```
public class BankAccount implements Measurable
{
    public double getMeasure()
    {
        return balance;
    }
    . . .
}
```

Note that the class must declare the method as `public`, whereas the interface does not—all methods in an interface are public.

Similarly, it is an easy matter to modify the `Coin` class to realize the `Measurable` interface.

```
public class Coin implements Measurable
{
    public double getMeasure()
    {
        return value;
    }
    . . .
}
```

Now `DataSet` objects can be used to analyze collections of bank accounts or coins. Here is a test program that illustrates the fact.

File DataSetTest.java

```
1  /**
2      This program tests the DataSet class.
3  */
4  public class DataSetTest
5  {
6     public static void main(String[] args)
7     {
8
9        DataSet bankData = new DataSet();
10
11       bankData.add(new BankAccount(0));
12       bankData.add(new BankAccount(10000));
13       bankData.add(new BankAccount(2000));
14
15       System.out.println("Average balance = "
16          + bankData.getAverage());
17       Measurable max = bankData.getMaximum();
18       System.out.println("Highest balance = "
19          + max.getMeasure());
20
21       DataSet coinData = new DataSet();
22
23       coinData.add(new Coin(0.25, "quarter"));
24       coinData.add(new Coin(0.1, "dime"));
25       coinData.add(new Coin(0.05, "nickel"));
26
27       System.out.println("Average coin value = "
28          + coinData.getAverage());
29       max = coinData.getMaximum();
30       System.out.println("Highest coin value = "
31          + max.getMeasure());
32    }
33 }
```

> Interfaces can reduce the coupling between classes.

Figure 1 shows the relationships between the classes and interfaces. In the UML notation, interfaces are tagged with a "stereotype" indicator «interface». A dotted arrow with a triangular tip denotes the realization relationship between a class and an interface. You have to look carefully at the arrow tips—a dotted line with an open v-shaped arrow tip denotes dependency.

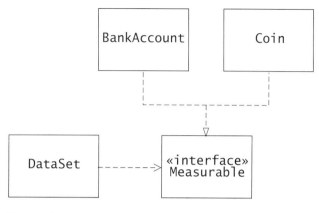

Figure 1

UML Diagram of the `DataSet` Class and the
Classes That Realize the `Measurable` Interface

This diagram shows that the `DataSet` class depends only on the `Measurable` interface. It is decoupled from the `BankAccount` and `Coin` classes. This decoupling makes the `DataSet` class reusable. Any class that is willing to implement the `Measurable` interface can be used with the `DataSet` class.

Syntax 9.1: Defining an Interface

```
public interface InterfaceName
{
    method signatures
}
```

Example:

```
public interface Measurable
{
    double getMeasure();
}
```

Purpose:

To define an interface and its method signatures. The methods are automatically public.

Syntax 9.2: Implementing an Interface

```
public class ClassName
    implements InterfaceName, InterfaceName, ...
{
    methods
    instance variables
}
```

Example:

```
public class BankAccount
    implements Measurable
{
    // other BankAccount methods
    public double getMeasure()
    {
        // method implementation
    }
}
```

Purpose:

To define a new class that implements the methods of an interface

---

▼ ⊗ Common Error   9.1 ▶

Forgetting to Define Implementing Methods as Public

▼   The methods in an interface are not declared as `public`, because they are public by default. However, the methods in a class are not public by default—their default access level is "package" access, which we discuss in Chapter 11. It is a common error to forget

▼   the `public` keyword when defining a method from an interface:

```
public class BankAccount implements Measurable
{
```
▼
```
    double getMeasure() // oops—should be public
    {
        return balance;
```
▼
```
    }
    . . .
}
```

▼   Then the compiler complains that the method has a weaker access level, namely package access instead of public access. The remedy is to declare the method as public.

9.2 Converting between Types

Have a close look at the call

```
bankData.add(new BankAccount(10000));
```

from the test program of the preceding section. Here we pass an object of type Bank-
Account to the add method of the DataSet class. However, that

> You can convert from a class type to an interface type, provided the class realizes the interface.

method has a parameter of type Measurable! Is it legal to convert
from the BankAccount type to the Measurable type?

In Java, such a type conversion is legal. You can convert from a
class type to the type of any interface that the class realizes. For
example,

```
BankAccount account = new BankAccount(10000);
Measurable x = account; // OK
```

Alternatively, x can refer to a Coin object, provided the Coin class has been modified to
realize the Measurable interface.

```
Coin dime = new Coin(0.1, "dime");
x = dime; // also OK
```

Thus, when you have an object variable of type Measurable, you don't actually know
the exact type of the object to which x refers. All you know is that the object has a get-
Measure method.

However, you cannot convert between unrelated types:

```
x = new Rectangle(5, 10, 20, 30); // ERROR
```

That assignment is an error, because the Rectangle class doesn't realize the Measurable
interface.

Occasionally, it happens that you convert an object to an interface reference and you
need to convert it back. This happens in the getMaximum method of the DataSet class.
The DataSet stores the object with the largest measure, *as a* Measurable *reference*.

```
DataSet coinData = new DataSet();
coinData.add(new Coin(0.25, "quarter"));
coinData.add(new Coin(0.1, "dime"));
coinData.add(new Coin(0.05, "nickel"));
Measurable max = coinData.getMaximum();
```

Now what can you do with the max reference? *You* know it refers to a Coin object, but
the compiler doesn't. Thus, you cannot call the getName method:

```
String name = max.getName(); // ERROR
```

> You need a cast to convert from an interface type to a class type.

That call is an error, because the Measurable type has no getName
method.

However, as long as you are absolutely sure that max really refers
to a Coin object, you can use the *cast* notation to convert it back:

```
Coin maxCoin = (Coin)max;
String name = maxCoin.getName();
```

If you are wrong, and the object doesn't actually refer to a coin, your program will throw an exception and terminate.

This cast notation is the same notation that you saw in Chapter 3 to convert between number types. For example, if x is a floating-point number, then (int)x is the integer part of the number. The intent is similar—to convert from one type to another. However, there is one big difference between casting of number types and casting of class types. When casting number types, you *lose information*, and you use the cast to tell the compiler that you agree to the information loss. When casting object types, on the other hand, you *take a risk* of causing an exception, and you tell the compiler that you agree to that risk.

> The instanceof operator tests whether an object belongs to a particular type.

You saw one example of using casts in graphics programs, when you had to cast the Graphics object to a Graphics2D object. That cast is really not a sign of good programming; the library designers used the cast as a quick fix for a compatibility problem. At any rate, situations for casts occasionally arise. When they do, it is best to play it safe and test whether a cast will succeed before carrying out the cast. For that purpose, you use the instanceof operator. It tests whether an object belongs to a particular type. For example,

```
max instanceof Coin
```

returns true if the type of max is Coin, false if it is not. Therefore, a safe cast can be programmed as follows:

```
if (max instanceof Coin)
{
    Coin maxCoin - (Coin)max;
    . . .
}
```

***

Syntax 9.3: The instanceof **Operator**

object instanceof *ClassName*

Example:

```
if (x instanceof Coin)
{
    Coin c = (Coin)x;
    . . .
}
```

Purpose:

To return true if the *object* is an instance of *ClassName* (or one of its subclasses), and false otherwise

▼

▼ ⚇ **Advanced Topic** ▶ **9.1**

Constants in Interfaces

▼

Interfaces cannot have variables, but you can specify *constants*, which will be inherited by all classes that implement the interface.

▼

For example, the `SwingConstants` interface defines various constants such as `Swing-Constants.NORTH`, `SwingConstants.EAST`, and so on. Several classes implement this interface. For example, since `JLabel` implements the `SwingConstants` interface, users can refer to them as `JLabel.NORTH`, `JLabel.EAST`, and so on, when using these con-

▼

stants in conjunction with `JLabel` objects.

When defining a constant in an interface, you can (and should) omit the keywords

▼

`public static final`, because all variables in an interface are automatically `public static final`. For example,

```
public interface SwingConstants
```

▼

```
{
    int NORTH = 1;
    int NORTHEAST = 2;
    int EAST = 3;
```

▼

```
    . . .
}
```

9.3   Polymorphism

It is worth emphasizing once again that it is perfectly legal—and in fact very common—to have variables whose type is an interface, such as

```
Measurable x;
```

Just remember that the object to which x refers doesn't have type `Measurable`. In fact, *no object* has type `Measurable`. Instead, the type of the object is some class that realizes the `Measurable` interface, such as `BankAccount` or `Coin`.

Note that x can refer to objects of *different* types during its lifetime. Here the variable x first contains a reference to a bank account, later to a coin.

```
x = new BankAccount(10000); // OK
x = new Coin(0.1, "dime"); // OK
```

However, you can *never* construct an interface:

```
x = new Measurable(); // ERROR
```

Interfaces aren't classes, so you can't construct interface *objects*.

What can you do with an interface variable, given that you don't know the class of the object that it references? You can invoke the methods of the interface:

```
double m = x.getMeasure();
```

The DataSet class took advantage of this capability by computing the measure of the added object, without worrying exactly what kind of object was added.

Now let's think through the call to the getMeasure method more carefully. *Which* getMeasure method? The BankAccount and Coin classes provide two *different* implementations of that method. How did the correct method get called if the caller didn't even know the exact class to which x belongs?

The Java virtual machine makes a special effort to locate the correct method that belongs to the class of the actual object. That is, if x refers to a BankAccount object, then the BankAccount.getMeasure method is called. If x refers to a Coin object, then the Coin.getMeasure method is called.

That means that one method call

```
double m = x.getMeasure();
```

can call different methods depending on the momentary contents of x.

> Polymorphism denotes the principle that behavior can vary depending on the actual type of an object.

The principle that the actual type of the object determines the method to be called is called *polymorphism*. The term "polymorphism" comes from the Greek words for "many shapes". The same computation works for objects of many shapes, and adapts itself to the nature of the objects. In Java, all instance methods are polymorphic.

When you see a polymorphic method call, such as x.getMeasure(), there are several possible getMeasure methods that can be called. You have already seen another case in which the same method name can refer to different methods, namely when a method name is *overloaded:* that is, when a single class has several methods with the same name but different parameter types. For example, you can have two constructors BankAccount() and BankAccount(double). Then the compiler selects the appropriate method when compiling the program, simply by looking at the types of the parameters:

```
account = new BankAccount();
    // compiler selects BankAccount()
account = new BankAccount(10000);
    // compiler selects BankAccount(double)
```

> Early binding of methods occurs if the compiler selects a method from several possible candidates. Late binding occurs if the method selection takes place when the program runs.

There is an important difference between polymorphism and overloading. The compiler picks an overloaded method when translating the program, before the program ever runs. This method selection is called *early binding*. However, when selecting the appropriate getMeasure method in a call x.getMeasure(), the compiler does not make any decision when translating the method. The program has to run before anyone can know what is stored in x. Therefore, the virtual machine, and not the compiler, selects the appropriate method. This method selection is called *late binding*.

9.4   Using a Strategy Interface for Improving Reusability

The interface concept that we explored up to now is a useful step towards writing reusable classes. However, as a practical matter, there are serious limitations to using the Measurable interface.

- You can add the `Measurable` interface only to classes under your control. If you want to process a set of `Rectangle` objects, you cannot make the `Rectangle` class realize another interface—it is a system class, which you cannot change.

- You can measure an object in only one way. If you want to analyze a set of savings accounts both by bank balance and by interest rate, you are stuck.

Therefore, let us rethink the `DataSet` class. The data set needs to be able to measure the objects that are added. When the objects are required to be of type `Measurable`, the responsibility of measuring lies with the added objects themselves, which is the cause of the limitations that we noted. It would be better if another object could carry out the measurement. Therefore, let's move the measurement method into a different interface:

```
public interface Measurer
{
    double measure(Object anObject);
}
```

The `measure` method measures an object and returns its measurement. Here we use the fact that all objects can be converted to the type `Object`, the "lowest common denominator" of all classes in Java. We will discuss the `Object` type in greater detail in Chapter 11.

The improved `DataSet` class is constructed with a `Measurer` object (that is, an object of some class that realizes the `Measurer` interface). That object is saved in a `measurer` instance variable and used to carry out the measurements, like this:

```
public void add(Object x)
{
    sum = sum + measurer.measure(x);
    if (count == 0
            || measurer.measure(maximum) < measurer.measure(x))
        maximum = x;
    count++;
}
```

You can find the complete source code for the `DataSet` class at the end of this section.

Now you can define measurers to take on any kind of measurement. For example, here is how you can measure rectangles by area. Define a class

```
class RectangleMeasurer implements Measurer
{
    public double measure(Object anObject)
    {
        Rectangle aRectangle = (Rectangle)anObject;
        double area = aRectangle.getWidth()
            * aRectangle.getHeight();
        return area;
    }
}
```

Note that the `measure` method must accept a parameter of type `Object`, even though this particular measurer just wants to measure rectangles. The method signature must match the signature of the `measure` method in the `Measurer` interface. Therefore, the `Object` parameter is cast to the `Rectangle` type:

```
Rectangle aRectangle = (Rectangle)anObject;
```

Now construct an object of the `RectangleMeasurer` class and pass it to the `DataSet` constructor.

```
Measurer m = new RectangleMeasurer();
DataSet data = new DataSet(m);
```

Next, add rectangles to the data set. The `RectangleMeasurer` object will measure them by area.

```
data.add(new Rectangle(5, 10, 20, 30));
data.add(new Rectangle(10, 20, 30, 40));
. . .
```

What would happen if you added an object of some other type, say a coin, to this data set? The `add` method does not complain—it will take any object. But when the measurer tries to convert the `Coin` reference to a `Rectangle` reference, then an exception is generated and the program terminates.

An object such as the `measurer` object of the `DataSet` class is called a *strategy* object, because it carries out a particular strategy for a computation. For a different strategy, simply use a different strategy object. For example, it is a simple matter to define a different strategy for measuring the perimeter of a rectangle.

Figure 2 shows the UML diagram of the classes and interfaces of this solution. As in Figure 1, the `DataSet` class is decoupled from the `Rectangle` class whose objects it processes. However, unlike in Figure 1, the `Rectangle` class is no longer coupled with another class. Instead, to process rectangles, you have to come up with a small "helper" class `RectangleMeasurer`.

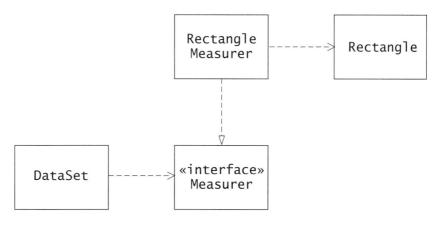

Figure 2

UML Diagram of the `DataSet` Class and the `Measurer` Interface

The `RectangleMeasurer` class is a very trivial class. Its objects don't carry any state at all. We needed this class only because the `DataSet` needs an object of some class that implements the `Measurer` interface. When you have a class that serves a very tactical purpose, such as this one, you can declare the class inside the method that needs it:

```
public static void main(String[] args)
{
   class RectangleMeasurer implements Measurer
   {
      . . .
   }

   Measurer m = new RectangleMeasurer();
   DataSet data = new DataSet(m);
   . . .
}
```

> An inner class is declared inside another class. Inner classes are commonly used for tactical classes that should not be visible elsewhere in a program.

Such a class is called an *inner class*. An inner class is any class that is defined inside another class. This arrangement signals to the reader of your program that the `RectangleMeasurer` class is not interesting beyond the scope of this method. Since an inner class inside a method is not a publicly accessible feature, you don't need to document it as thoroughly.

When you compile the source files for this program, have a look at the class files on your disk—you will find that the inner classes are stored in files with curious names, such as `DataSetTest$1$RectangleMeasurer.class`. The exact names aren't important. The point is that the compiler turns an inner class into a regular class file.

File DataSet.java

```
 1  /**
 2      Computes the average of a set of data values.
 3  */
 4  public class DataSet
 5  {
 6     /**
 7         Constructs an empty data set with a given measurer.
 8         @param aMeasurer  the measurer that is used to measure data values
 9     */
10     public DataSet(Measurer aMeasurer)
11     {
12        sum = 0;
13        count = 0;
14        maximum = null;
15        measurer = aMeasurer;
```

```
16      }
17
18      /**
19          Adds a data value to the data set.
20          @param x  a data value
21      */
22      public void add(Object x)
23      {
24          sum = sum + measurer.measure(x);
25          if (count == 0
26                  || measurer.measure(maximum) < measurer.measure(x))
27              maximum = x;
28          count++;
29      }
30
31      /**
32          Gets the average of the added data.
33          @return  the average, or 0 if no data have been added
34      */
35      public double getAverage()
36      {
37          if (count == 0) return 0;
38          else return sum / count;
39      }
40
41      /**
42          Gets the largest of the added data.
43          @return  the maximum, or 0 if no data have been added
44      */
45      public Object getMaximum()
46      {
47          return maximum;
48      }
49
50      private double sum;
51      private Object maximum;
52      private int count;
53      private Measurer measurer;
54 }
```

File DataSetTest.java

```
1 import java.awt.Rectangle;
2
3 /**
4     This program demonstrates the use of a Measurer.
```

```
 5  */
 6  public class DataSetTest
 7  {
 8     public static void main(String[] args)
 9     {
10        class RectangleMeasurer implements Measurer
11        {
12           public double measure(Object anObject)
13           {
14              Rectangle aRectangle = (Rectangle)anObject;
15              double area = aRectangle.getWidth()
16                 * aRectangle.getHeight();
17              return area;
18           }
19        }
20
21        Measurer m = new RectangleMeasurer();
22
23        DataSet data = new DataSet(m);
24
25        data.add(new Rectangle(5, 10, 20, 30));
26        data.add(new Rectangle(10, 20, 30, 40));
27        data.add(new Rectangle(20, 30, 5, 10));
28
29        System.out.println("Average area = "
30           + data.getAverage());
31        Rectangle max = (Rectangle)data.getMaximum();
32        System.out.println("Maximum area = " + max);
33     }
34  }
```

File Measurer.java

```
 1  /**
 2      Describes any class whose objects can measure other objects.
 3  */
 4  public interface Measurer
 5  {
 6     /**
 7         Computes the measure of an object.
 8         @param anObject  the object to be measured
 9         @return  the measure
10     */
11     double measure(Object anObject);
12  }
```

Syntax 9.4: Inner Classes

Declared inside a method

```
class OuterClassName
{
    method signature
    {
        . . .
        class InnerClassName
        {
            methods
            fields
        }
        . . .
    }
    . . .
}
```

Declared inside the class:

```
class OuterClassName
{
    methods
    fields
    accessSpecifier class InnerClassName
    {
        methods
        fields
    }
    . . .
}
```

Example:

```
public class Test
{
    public static void main(String[] args)
    {
        class RectangleMeasurer implements Measurer
        {
            . . .
        }
        . . .
    }
}
```

Purpose:

To define an inner class whose methods have access to the same variables and methods as the outer-class methods

▼ ## Advanced Topic 9.2

Anonymous Inner Classes

An entity is *anonymous* if it does not have a name. In a program, something that is only used once doesn't usually need a name. For example, you can replace

```
Coin aCoin = new Coin(0.1, "dime");
data.add(aCoin);
```

with

```
data.add(new Coin(0.1, "dime"));
```

if the coin is not used elsewhere in the same method. The object `new Coin("dime", 0.1)` is an *anonymous object*. Programmers like anonymous objects, because they don't have to go through the trouble of coming up with a name. If you have struggled with the decision whether to call a coin `c`, `dime`, or `aCoin`, you'll understand this sentiment.

Inner classes often give rise to a similar situation. After a single object of the `RectangleMeasurer` has been constructed, the class is never used again. In Java, it is possible to define *anonymous classes* if all you ever need is a single object of the class.

```
public static void main(String[] args)
{
    Measurer m = new Measurer()
        // construct an object of anonymous class
        // class definition starts here
        {
            public double measure(Object anObject)
            {
                Rectangle aRectangle = (Rectangle)anObject;
                double area =
                    aRectangle.getWidth()
                    * aRectangle.getHeight();
                return area;
            }
        };

    DataSet data = new DataSet(m);
    . . .
}
```

This means: Construct an object of a class that implements the `Measurer` interface by defining the `measure` method as specified.

Some programmers like this style, but many newcomers find it quite bewildering. We will not cover it further in this book—you can find more information in reference [1].

9.5   Processing Timer Events

In this section we will study timer events, because the event handling uses interfaces in the same way as buttons and menus in a graphical program. However, since timers are simpler than graphical programs, we can focus on the essential mechanism without being distracted by the code for placing buttons or building menus.

Timers are also useful for programming animations (see Exercise P9.13).

> A timer generates timer events at fixed intervals.

The Timer class in the javax.swing package generates a sequence of *events*, spaced apart at even time intervals. This is useful whenever you want to have an object updated in regular intervals. For example, in an animation, you may want to update a scene 10 times per second and redisplay the image, to give the illusion of movement.

> An event listener is notified when a particular event occurs.

When a timer event occurs, the timer needs to notify some object, called the *event listener*. The designers of the Timer class had no idea how you would want to use the Timer, yet they had to specify a type for the listener object and call a specific method. They chose the ActionListener interface for this purpose:

```
public interface ActionListener
{
    void actionPerformed(ActionEvent event);
}
```

When you use a timer, you need to define a class that realizes the ActionListener interface. Place whatever action you want to occur inside the actionPerformed method. Construct an object of that class. Pass it to the Timer constructor. Finally, start the timer.

```
class MyListener implements ActionListener
{
    public void actionPerformed(ActionEvent event)
    {
        // this action will be executed at each timer event
        place listener action here
    }
}

MyListener listener = new MyListener();
Timer t = new Timer(interval, listener);
t.start();
```

Then the timer calls the actionPerformed method of the listener object every interval milliseconds. The event parameter of the actionPerformed method contains more detailed information about the timer event. However, in practice, many listeners ignore this parameter.

Here is a somewhat silly example program—a timer that counts down to zero.

```
10
9
. . .
```

```
2
1
0
Liftoff!
```

However, unlike a for loop, which would print all lines immediately, there is a one second delay between decrements.

To keep the program alive after setting up the timer, the program displays a message dialog. Click the "Ok" button to quit the program.

File TimerTest.java

```
1  import java.awt.event.ActionEvent;
2  import java.awt.event.ActionListener;
3  import javax.swing.JOptionPane;
4  import javax.swing.Timer;
5
6  /**
7     This program tests the Timer class.
8  */
9  public class TimerTest
10 {
11    public static void main(String[] args)
12    {
13       class CountDown implements ActionListener
14       {
15          public CountDown(int initialCount)
16          {
17             count = initialCount;
18          }
19
20          public void actionPerformed(ActionEvent event)
21          {
22             if (count >= 0)
23                System.out.println(count);
24             if (count == 0)
25                System.out.println("Liftoff!");
26             count--;
27          }
28
29          private int count;
30       }
31
32       CountDown listener = new CountDown(10);
33
34       final int DELAY = 1000; // milliseconds between timer ticks
35       Timer t = new Timer(DELAY, listener);
36       t.start();
37
38       JOptionPane.showMessageDialog(null, "Quit?");
39       System.exit(0);
40    }
41 }
```

The preceding example is somewhat oversimplified. Usually, the event listener needs to modify other objects in the `actionPerformed` method. That can make the design of the listener classes more complex, because they need to store instance variables to access the various objects that need to be manipulated when an event occurs. Fortunately, the Java compiler can *automatically* generate some of these variables when you use inner classes for listeners. Here is an example.

To simulate the growth of an investment, we want to add interest to a bank account once per second. The program prints the balance once a second, like this:

```
Balance = 1050.0
Balance = 1102.5
Balance = 1157.625
Balance = 1215.50625
  . . .
```

Here is the `BankAccount` object:

```java
public class TimerTest
{
   public static void main(String[] args)
   {
      final BankAccount account = new BankAccount(1000);
         . . .
   }

   private static final double RATE = 5;
}
```

You will see soon why the account variable is declared as `final`. The `actionPerformed` method of the listener class adds interest to the account and prints the new balance.

```java
class InterestAdder implements ActionListener
{
   public void actionPerformed(ActionEvent event)
   {
      double interest = account.getBalance()
         * RATE / 100;
      account.deposit(interest);
      System.out.println("Balance = "
         + account.getBalance());
   }
}
```

> Methods of an inner class can access variables from the surrounding scope.

As you can see, the `actionPerformed` method needs access to the `BankAccount` object. Of course, you can add a `BankAccount` instance variable and set it in the `InterestAdder` constructor. However, for inner classes there is a convenient shortcut. An inner class can access variables that are defined at the place of the class definition. When the `InterestAdder` definition is placed inside the `main` method, below the definition of the `account` variable, then it can access that local variable of the `main` method!

```
public static void main(String[] args)
{
    final BankAccount account = new BankAccount(1000);

    class InterestAdder implements ActionListener
    {
        public void actionPerformed(ActionEvent event)
        {
            double interest = account.getBalance()
                * RATE / 100;
                // OK to access account
            . . .
        }
    }

    . . .
}
```

When the compiler builds the `InterestAdder` class, it notes that one of its methods accesses variables from the surrounding scope. It then automatically provides an instance variable inside the class and initializes it with the value from the outer variables. That's very convenient for the programmer. It significantly reduces the burden of supplying tactical helper classes. You don't actually have to think about the process that the compiler goes through when building an inner class. Simply access any variables of the surrounding scope and let the compiler worry about the details.

> Local variables that are accessed by an inner-class method must be declared as `final`.

There is a technical wrinkle. An inner class can access any *fields* of the surrounding scope without restrictions. But it can access *local variables* only if they are declared as `final`. Then there is no ambiguity about the values of local variables that the inner-class methods use. That sounds like a restriction, but it is usually not an issue in practice. Keep in mind that an object variable is `final` when the variable always refers to the same object. The state of the object can change, but the variable can't refer to a different object. For example, in our program, we never intended to have the `account` variable refer to multiple bank account objects, so there was no harm in declaring it as `final`.

Figure 3 shows the UML diagram of the classes and interfaces. Note how the `Timer` class and the `BankAccount` class are completely decoupled from another. Neither class knows about the other. The `InterestAdder` helper class forms the bridge between the two.

Here is the source code for the program.

File TimerTest.java

```
 1 import java.awt.event.ActionEvent;
 2 import java.awt.event.ActionListener;
 3 import javax.swing.JOptionPane;
 4 import javax.swing.Timer;
 5
 6 /**
 7     This program uses a timer to add interest to a bank
 8     account once per second.
```

```
 9  */
10  public class TimerTest
11  {
12     public static void main(String[] args)
13     {
14        final BankAccount account = new BankAccount(1000);
15
16        class InterestAdder implements ActionListener
17        {
18           public void actionPerformed(ActionEvent event)
19           {
20              double interest = account.getBalance()
21                 * RATE / 100;
22              account.deposit(interest);
23              System.out.println("Balance = "
24                 + account.getBalance());
25           }
26        }
27
28        InterestAdder listener = new InterestAdder();
29
30        final int DELAY = 1000; // milliseconds between timer ticks
31        Timer t = new Timer(DELAY, listener);
32        t.start();
33
34        JOptionPane.showMessageDialog(null, "Quit?");
35        System.exit(0);
36     }
37
38     private static final double RATE = 5;
39  }
```

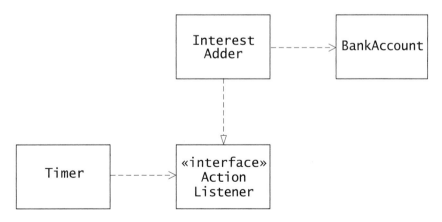

Figure 3

The Classes and Interfaces for Processing Timer Events

You have now seen how to build an event listener. This is a very common task when you program graphical user interfaces. Buttons, sliders, checkboxes, the mouse, timers, and other sources generate events. You need to attach an event listener to every event source that you want to track. For example, if your program should do something when a button is clicked, attach an event listener to the button. You will learn more about this process in the next chapter.

Common Error 9.2

Modifying the Signature in the Implementing Method

When you implement an interface, you must define each method *exactly* as it is specified in the interface. Making small changes accidentally to the parameter or return types is a common error. Here is the classical example,

```
class MyAction implements ActionListener
{
    public void actionPerformed()
    // oops . . . forgot ActionEvent parameter
    {
        . . .
    }
}
```

As far as the compiler is concerned, this class has two methods:

```
public void actionPerformed(ActionEvent event)
public void actionPerformed()
```

The first method is undefined. The compiler will complain that the method is missing. However, you have to read the error message carefully and pay attention to the parameter and return types.

Random Fact 9.1

Operating Systems

Without an operating system, a computer would not be useful. Minimally, you need an operating system to locate files and to start programs. The programs that you run need services from the operating system to access devices and to interact with other programs. Operating systems on large computers need to provide more services than those on personal computers do. Here are some typical services:

▼ • *Program loading.* Every operating system provides some way of launching application programs. The user indicates what program should be run, usually by typing
the name of the program in or by clicking on an icon. The operating system
▼ locates the program code, loads it in memory, and starts it.

▼ • *Managing files.* A storage device such as a hard disk is, electronically, simply a
device capable of storing a huge sequence of zeroes and ones. It is up to the oper-
▼ ating system to bring some structure to the storage layout and organize it into
files, folders, and so on. The operating system also needs to impose some amount
▼ of security and redundancy into the file system so that a power outage does not
jeopardize the contents of an entire hard disk. Some operating systems do a better
job in this regard than others.

▼ • *Virtual memory.* RAM is expensive, and few computers have enough RAM to
hold all programs and their data that a user would like to run simultaneously.
Most operating systems extend the available memory by storing some data on the
▼ hard disk. The application programs do not realize whether a particular data item
is in memory or in the virtual memory disk storage. When a program accesses a
data item that is currently not in RAM, the processor senses this and notifies the
▼ operating system. The operating system swaps the needed data from the hard disk
into RAM, simultaneously swapping out a memory block of equal size that had
▼ not been accessed for some time.

• *Handling multiple users.* The operating systems of large and powerful computers
allow simultaneous access by multiple users. Each user is connected to the com-
▼ puter through a separate terminal. The operating system authenticates users by
checking that each one has a valid account and password. It gives each user a
small slice of processor time, then serves the next user.
▼

• *Multitasking.* Even if you are the sole user of a computer, you may want to run multiple applications—for example, to read your email in one window and run the Java
▼ compiler in another. The operating system is responsible for dividing processor time
between the applications you are running, so that each can make progress.

▼ • *Printing.* The operating system queues up the print requests that are sent by multiple applications. This is necessary to make sure that the printed pages do not
contain a mixture of words sent simultaneously from separate programs.

▼ • *Windows.* Many operating systems present their users with a desktop made up of
multiple windows. The operating system manages the location and appearance of
the window frames; the applications are responsible for the interiors.
▼

• *Fonts.* To render text on the screen and the printer, the shapes of characters must
be defined. This is especially important for programs that can display multiple
▼ type styles and sizes. Modern operating systems contain a central font repository.

• *Communicating between programs.* The operating system can facilitate the transfer
of information between programs. That transfer can happen through *cut and paste*

Figure 4

A Graphical Software Environment for the Linux Operating System

or *interprocess communication*. Cut and paste is a user-initiated data transfer in which the user copies data from one application into a transfer buffer (often called a "clipboard") managed by the operating system and inserts the buffer's contents into another application. Interprocess communication is initiated by applications that transfer data without direct user involvement.

- *Networking.* The operating system provides protocols and services for enabling applications to reach information on other computers attached to the network.

Today, the most popular operating systems are UNIX (and its variants such as Linux; see Figure 4), Windows, and the MacOS.

CHAPTER SUMMARY

1. A Java interface declares a set of methods and their signatures. Unlike a class, it provides no implementation.

2. To realize an interface, a class must supply all methods that the interface requires.

3. Interfaces can reduce the coupling between classes.

4. You can convert from a class type to an interface type, provided the class realizes the interface.

5. You need a cast to convert from an interface type to a class type.

6. The `instanceof` operator tests whether an object belongs to a particular type.

7. Polymorphism denotes the principle that behavior can vary depending on the actual type of an object.

8. Early binding of methods occurs if the compiler selects a method from several possible candidates. Late binding occurs if the method selection takes place when the program runs.

9. An inner class is declared inside another class. Inner classes are commonly used for tactical classes that should not be visible elsewhere in a program.

10. A timer generates timer events at fixed intervals.

11. An event listener is notified when a particular event occurs.

12. Methods of an inner class can access variables from the surrounding scope.

13. Local variables that are accessed by an inner-class method must be declared as `final`.

Further Reading

[1] Cay S. Horstmann and Gary Cornell, *Core Java Fundamentals*, 5th Edition, Prentice-Hall, 2001.

CLASSES, OBJECTS, AND METHODS INTRODUCED IN THIS CHAPTER

```
java.awt.event.ActionEvent
java.awt.event.ActionListener
    actionPerformed
javax.swing.Timer
    start
```

REVIEW EXERCISES

Exercise R9.1. Suppose C is a class that realizes the interfaces I and J. Which of the following assignments require a cast?

```
C c = . . .;
I i = . . .;
J j = . . .;
c = i; // 1
j = c; // 2
i = j; // 3
```

Exercise R9.2. Suppose C is a class that realizes the interfaces I and J. Which of the following assignments will throw an exception?

```
C c = new C();
I i = c; // 1
J j = (J)i; // 2
C d = (C)i; // 3
```

Exercise R9.3. Suppose the class Sandwich implements the Edible interface. Which of the following assignments are legal?

```
Sandwich sub = new Sandwich();
Edible e = sub; // 1
Rectangle cerealBox = new Rectangle(5, 10, 20, 30);
Edible f = cerealBox; // 2
f = (Edible)cerealBox; // 3
sub = e; // 4
sub = (Sandwich)e; // 5
sub = (Sandwich)cerealBox; // 6
```

Exercise R9.4. How does a cast such as (BankAccount)x differ from a cast of number values such as (int)x?

Exercise R9.5. The classes Rectangle2D.Double, Ellipse2D.Double and Line2D.Double realize the Shape interface. The Graphics2D class depends on the Shape interface but not on the rectangle, ellipse, and line classes. Draw a UML diagram denoting these facts.

Exercise R9.6. Suppose r contains a reference to a new Rectangle(5, 10, 20, 30). Which of these conditions returns true? (*Hint:* Check the API documentation for the interfaces that the Rectangle class realizes.)

- r instanceof Rectangle
- r instanceof Shape
- r instanceof Point
- r instanceof Object
- r instanceof ActionListener
- r instanceof Serializable

Exercise R9.7. Classes such as Rectangle2D.Double, Ellipse2D.Double, and Line2D.Double realize the Shape interface. The Shape interface has a method

```
Rectangle getBounds()
```

that returns a rectangle completely enclosing the shape. Consider the method call:

```
Shape s = . . .;
Rectangle r = s.getBounds();
```

Explain why this is an example of polymorphism.

Exercise R9.8. In Java, a method call such as x.f() uses late binding—the exact method to be called depends on the type of the object to which x refers. Give two kinds of method calls that use early binding in Java.

Exercise R9.9. Suppose you need to process an array of employees to find the average and the highest salary. Discuss what you need to do to use the first implementation of the `DataSet` class (which processes `Measurable` objects). What do you need to do to use the second implementation? Which is easier?

Exercise R9.10. What happens if you add a `String` object to the first implementation of the `DataSet`? What happens if you add a `String` object to a `DataSet` object of the second implementation that uses a `RectangleMeasurer` class?

Exercise R9.11. How would you reorganize the test program that uses the `Rectangle-Measurer` class if you needed to make `RectangleMeasurer` into a top-level class (that is, not an inner class)?

Exercise R9.12. How would you reorganize the test program that uses the `Interest-Adder` class if you needed to make `InterestAdder` into a top-level class (that is, not an inner class)?

Exercise R9.13. What is a strategy object? Can you think of another useful strategy object for the `DataSet` class? (*Hint:* Exercise P9.8.)

Exercise R9.14. What is the difference between an event and an event listener?

Exercise P9.15. Can a `Timer` object notify multiple event listeners? If so, how? (Check the API documentation.)

Exercise R9.16. Consider this top-level and inner class. Which variables can the `f` method access?

```java
public class T
{
   public void m(final int x, int y)
   {
      int a;
      final int b;

      class C implements I
      {
         public void f()
         {
            . . .
         }
      }

      final int c;
      . . .
   }

   private int t;
}
```

Exercise R9.17. What happens when an inner class tries to access a non-`final` local variable? Try it out and explain.

Programming Exercises

Exercise P9.1. Have the `Die` class of Chapter 6 implement the `Measurable` interface. Generate dice, cast them, and add them to the first implementation of the `DataSet` class. Display the average.

Exercise P9.2. Define a class `Quiz` that implements the `Measurable` interface. A quiz has a score and a letter grade (such as B+). Use the first implementation of the `DataSet` class to process a collection of quizzes. Display the average score and the quiz with the highest score (both letter grade and score).

Exercise P9.3. Define a class `Person`. A person has a name and a height in centimeters. Use the second implementation of the `DataSet` class to process a collection of `Person` objects. Display the average height and the name of the tallest person.

Exercise P9.4. Modify the first implementation of the `DataSet` (the one processing `Measurable` objects) to also compute the minimum data element.

Exercise P9.5. Modify the second implementation of the `DataSet` (the one using a `Measurer` object) to also compute the minimum data element.

Exercise P9.6. Using a different `Measurer` object, process a set of `Rectangle` objects to find the rectangle with the largest perimeter.

Exercise P9.7. Enhance the `DataSet` class so that it can be used either with a `Measurer` object or for processing `Measurable` objects. *Hint:* Supply a default constructor that implements a `Measurer` that can process `Measurable` objects.

Exercise P9.8. Define an interface `Filter` as follows:

```
public interface Filter
{
    boolean accept(Object x)
}
```

Modify the second implementation of the `DataSet` class to use both a `Measurer` and a `Filter` object. Only objects that the filter accepts should be processed. Demonstrate your modification by having a data set process a collection of bank accounts, filtering out all accounts whose balance is less than $1,000.

Exercise P9.9. Use the interface

```
public interface Drawable
{
    void draw(Graphics2D g2)
}
```

Implement classes `Car` and `House` that realize this interface. The `Car` and `House` constructors should receive the position of the car or house, just as in Section 4.7.

Then write a method `randomDrawable` that randomly generates `Drawable` references. Randomly choose between a car and a house, then pick random positions. Call the method 10 times and draw all of the shapes.

Exercise P9.10. Write a method randomShape that randomly generates objects implementing the Shape interface: some mixture of rectangles, ellipses, and lines, with random positions. Call it 10 times and draw all of them.

Exercise P9.11. Write a program that uses a timer to print the current time once a second. *Hint:* The following code prints the current time:

```
Date now = new Date();
System.out.println(now);
```

The Date class is in the java.util package.

Exercise P9.12. Enhance the program that uses a timer to increment a bank account balance once per second by adding a second bank account with a balance of $2,000 and a second timer that increments it every two seconds.

Exercise P9.13. Write an applet that uses a timer to display an animation of a moving car. Ten times a second, have the actionPerformed method of a timer listener

• Move the car to the right by one pixel.
• Call the repaint method of the applet.

Exercise P9.14. Use the interface

```
public interface InputReader
{
    String readLine(String prompt) throws IOException
}
```

Define two classes, OptionPaneReader and ConsoleReader, that implement this interface. An OptionPaneReader reads input by displaying input dialogs. The ConsoleReader reads from a buffered reader attached to System.in.

Then define a static method

```
public Coin readCoin(InputReader reader)
```

that prompts the user for the name and value of a coin (which may be a foreign coin, not just a nickel, dime, or quarter). Demonstrate that this method can get user input both through dialog boxes and from the console window.

Exercise P9.15. Look up the definition of the standard Comparable interface in the API documentation. Modify the DataSet class to accept Comparable objects. With this interface, it is no longer meaningful to compute the average. The DataSet class should record the minimum and maximum data value. Test your modified DataSet class by adding a number of String objects. (The String class implements the Comparable interface.)

Exercise P9.16. Modify the Coin and Purse classes introduced in Chapter 3 to have them implement the Comparable interface.

10

Event Handling

► To install mouse and action event listeners

► To accept mouse and text input

► To display frame windows

► To show text output in a text area with a scroll bar

In the console applications and applets you have written so far, user input was under control of the *program*. The program asked the user for input in a specific order. For example, a program might ask the user to supply first a name, then some dollar amount. But the programs that you use every day on your computer don't work like that. In a program with a modern graphical user interface, the *user* is in control. The user can use both the mouse and the keyboard and can manipulate many parts of the user interface in any desired order. For example, the user can enter information into text fields, pull down menus, click buttons, and drag scroll bars, in any order. The program must react to the user commands, in whatever order they arrive. Having to deal with many possible inputs in random order is quite a bit harder than simply forcing the user to supply input in a fixed order.

In this chapter you will learn how to write Java programs that can react to user interface events such as keystrokes, mouse clicks, and button pushes. The Java window toolkit has a very sophisticated mechanism that allows a program to specify the events in which it is interested and which objects to notify when one of these events occurs.

10.1 Events, Event Listeners, and Event Sources

> User interface events include key presses, mouse moves, button presses, menu selections, and so on.

Whenever the user of a graphical program types characters or uses the mouse anywhere inside one of the windows of the program, the Java window manager sends a notification to the program that an *event* has occurred. The window manager can generate huge numbers of events. For example, whenever the mouse moves a tiny interval over a window, a "mouse move" event is generated. Most programs have no interest in many of these events.

> You supply *event listeners* for the events about which you care. You need to implement methods for handling the event. You construct listener objects and attach them to the event sources.

So as not to be flooded by boring events, every program must indicate which events it likes to receive. It does that by installing *event listener* objects. Furthermore, there are different *kinds* of events, such as keyboard events, mouse move events, and mouse click events. To make event listening more organized, you use different event listener classes to listen to different kinds of events.

> *Event source* classes report on events. When an event occurs, the event source notifies all event listeners.

To install a listener, you need to know the *event source*. The event source is the user interface component that generates a particular event. For example, a button is an event source for button click events; a menu item is an event source for a menu selection event; and a scrollbar is an event source for a scrollbar adjustment event.

> Event notifications happen in event listener classes. An event listener class implements an *event listener interface*. The interface lists all possible notifications for a particular event category.

Once you have determined the event source, you attach one or more listeners to it. Each listener is an object of a *listener class,* which you must supply. In the methods for that class, you determine what should happen whenever the particular event occurs.

Once an event occurs for which there is a listener, the event source will call the methods you supplied in the listener and supply detailed information about the event in an *event class* object.

> *Event classes* contain detailed information about various kinds of events.

This sounds somewhat complex, so let's run through an example. We will listen to mouse clicks in an applet. There are three classes involved:

1. *The event source.* This is the component that generates the mouse event and that manages the listeners. In our case, the event source is the applet. When the user clicks anywhere inside an applet, the applet tells the attached mouse listeners where the mouse was clicked.

2. *The listener class.* In the case of mouse clicks, this must be a class that implements the `MouseListener` interface. The mouse listener interface has several methods, which we will discuss below. These methods are called when the mouse button is depressed, when it is released, and so on.

3. *The event class.* In the case of mouse clicks, this is the class `MouseEvent`. Each listener method has a `MouseEvent` parameter that tells you details about the event. For example, the `getX` and `getY` methods return the *x*- and *y*-position of the mouse pointer.

> You use a *mouse listener* to capture mouse events.

The most complex part of Java event handling is to come up with the listener. A mouse listener must implement the `MouseListener` interface, which comprises the following five methods:

```
public interface MouseListener
{
    void mousePressed(MouseEvent event);
        // Called when a mouse button has been pressed on a component
    void mouseReleased(MouseEvent event);
        // Called when a mouse button has been released on a component
    void mouseClicked(MouseEvent event);
        // Called when the mouse has been clicked on a component
    void mouseEntered(MouseEvent event);
        // Called when the mouse enters a component
    void mouseExited(MouseEvent event);
        // Called when the mouse exits a component
}
```

Right now, we just want to "spy" on the mouse events and print them out as they occur. For that purpose, we'll implement a particular listener:

```
public class MouseSpy implements MouseListener
{
    public void mousePressed(MouseEvent event)
    {
        System.out.println("Mouse pressed. x = "
            + event.getX() + " y = " + event.getY());
    }

    public void mouseReleased(MouseEvent event)
    {
        System.out.println("Mouse released. x = "
            + event.getX() + " y = " + event.getY());
    }

    public void mouseClicked(MouseEvent event)
```

```
    {
        System.out.println("Mouse clicked. x = "
            + event.getX() + " y = " + event.getY());
    }

    public void mouseEntered(MouseEvent event)
    {
        System.out.println("Mouse entered. x = "
            + event.getX() + " y = " + event.getY());
    }

    public void mouseExited(MouseEvent event)
    {
        System.out.println("Mouse exited. x = "
            + event.getX() + " y = " + event.getY());
    }
}
```

The listener methods simply print out the cause of the event and the x- and y-positions of the mouse.

Now let's install the listener. You need to call the addMouseListener method of the event source. In our case, the event source is the applet that receives the mouse clicks. Construct a mouse spy object and pass it as the parameter to the addMouseListener method.

```
public class MouseSpyApplet extends Applet
{
    public MouseSpyApplet()
    {
        MouseSpy listener = new MouseSpy();
        addMouseListener(listener);
    }
}
```

As the applet senses mouse events, it calls the appropriate methods of the listener object. For example, when the user clicks with the mouse in the applet area, the applet calls listener.mousePressed(event1) and listener.mouseReleased(event2), where event1 and event2 are mouse event objects that describe the mouse position at the time of the mouse button press and release. If the press and release were in quick succession, the applet also calls listener.mouseClicked(event3). You can try this out by opening a console window, starting the applet viewer from that console window, clicking with the mouse in the applet, and watching the messages in the console window (see Figure 1).

10.2   Processing Mouse Input

In the preceding example, our mouse listener simply printed all mouse events to System.out. In practice, you want something more interesting to happen when the user presses the mouse. For example, suppose we want to write a program that moves a rectangle to the mouse press position.

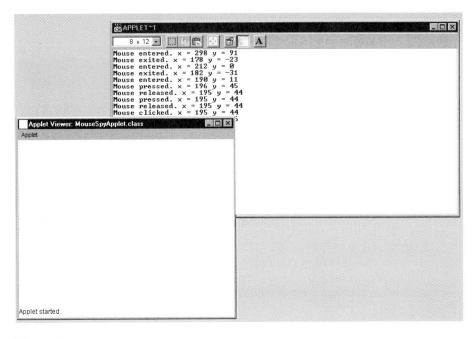

Figure 1

Spying on Mouse Events

Here is a program that draws a rectangle on the screen. The rectangle is stored as an instance variable so that we can later modify it:

```java
import java.applet.Applet;
import java.awt.Graphics;
import java.awt.Graphics2D;
import java.awt.Rectangle;

public class MouseApplet extends Applet
{
   public MouseApplet()
   {
      // the rectangle that the paint method draws
      box = new Rectangle(BOX_X, BOX_Y,
         BOX_WIDTH, BOX_HEIGHT);
   }

   public void paint(Graphics g)
   {
      Graphics2D g2 = (Graphics2D)g;
```

```
        g2.draw(box);
    }

    private Rectangle box;
    private static final int BOX_X = 100;
    private static final int BOX_Y = 100;
    private static final int BOX_WIDTH = 20;
    private static final int BOX_HEIGHT = 30;
}
```

Now, let us add a mouse listener that listens to a mouse press and moves the rectangle.

```
public class MouseApplet extends Applet
{
    public MouseApplet()
    {
        . . .
        // add mouse press listener

        class MousePressListener implements MouseListener
        {
            public void mousePressed(MouseEvent event)
            {
                int x = event.getX();
                int y = event.getY();
                box.setLocation(x, y);
                repaint();
            }

            // do-nothing methods
            public void mouseReleased(MouseEvent event) {}
            public void mouseClicked(MouseEvent event) {}
            public void mouseEntered(MouseEvent event) {}
            public void mouseExited(MouseEvent event) {}
        }

        MouseListener listener = new MousePressListener();
        addMouseListener(listener);
    }
```

You often install event listeners as *inner classes*. Recall that the inner-class methods can have access to the surrounding fields, methods, and final variables.

As you saw in Chapter 9, we define the listener class as an inner class inside the MouseApplet constructor. That gives the mousePressed the same access to fields and methods that the MouseApplet constructor enjoys.

As you can see, the mousePressed method of the inner class accesses the box field. Since the inner class has no field called box (in fact, it has no fields at all), the compiler interprets box to mean "the box field of the outer-class object that constructed this inner-class object".

When a mouse click occurs, we call `setLocation` on the rectangle object. However, that call has no effect on the screen display. The `setLocation` method merely updates the Java object that stores the rectangle's position. We need to redraw the applet. We could call the `paint` method, but then we would need a `Graphics` object, which we don't have. It is possible to get such an object, but that is actually not a good idea. You should never call `paint` directly—it can interfere with the window manager. Instead, you should *tell the applet to repaint itself* at the next convenient moment. You do that by calling the `repaint` method, which causes the `paint` method to be called, at an opportune moment, with an appropriate `Graphics` object.

> The `repaint` method causes a window to repaint itself as soon as possible.

Let us have another look at the call to `repaint` in the `mousePressed` method of the `MousePressListener` class. Of course, the inner class doesn't have a method called `repaint`. Therefore, the compiler looks in the outer applet class, where it does find a `repaint` method (which is inherited from its superclass `Component`). It invokes the method. On which object? Again, on the outer-class object that created the inner-class object—namely, the applet that constructed the listener.

Programming listener classes is somewhat involved. You may simply want to recognize and reuse the following template:

```
class MyClass
{
    public MyClass()
    {
        . . .
        class MyListener implements ListenerInterface
        {
            public void eventOccurred(EventClass event)
            {
                event action goes here
            }
        }

        MyListener listener = new MyListener();
        anEventSource.addAListener(listener);
    }
}
```

Finally, we are ready to put all the pieces together. Note how the use of inner classes makes the program easy to read—the rather specialized event listener class is placed out of the way and hidden inside the applet constructor. Furthermore, all the information about the event is kept together in one place.

Go ahead and run the program. Whenever you click the mouse on the applet, the top left corner of the rectangle moves to the mouse pointer (see Figure 2). While perhaps not the most exciting program that you have ever used, it does demonstrate how to provide mouse input to a graphical application.

Figure 2

The Mouse Applet

File MouseApplet.java

```
 1  import java.applet.Applet;
 2  import java.awt.Graphics;
 3  import java.awt.Graphics2D;
 4  import java.awt.Rectangle;
 5  import java.awt.event.MouseListener;
 6  import java.awt.event.MouseEvent;
 7
 8  /**
 9      This applet lets the user move a rectangle by clicking
        the mouse.
10  */
11  public class MouseApplet extends Applet
12  {
13      public MouseApplet()
14      {
15          // the rectangle that the paint method draws
16          box = new Rectangle(BOX_X, BOX_Y,
17              BOX_WIDTH, BOX_HEIGHT);
18
19          // add mouse press listener
20
21          class MousePressListener implements MouseListener
22          {
23              public void mousePressed(MouseEvent event)
24              {
25                  int x = event.getX();
26                  int y = event.getY();
```

```
27                    box.setLocation(x, y);
28                    repaint();
29                }
30
31                // do-nothing methods
32                public void mouseReleased(MouseEvent event) {}
33                public void mouseClicked(MouseEvent event) {}
34                public void mouseEntered(MouseEvent event) {}
35                public void mouseExited(MouseEvent event) {}
36            }
37
38            MouseListener listener = new MousePressListener();
39            addMouseListener(listener);
40        }
41
42        public void paint(Graphics g)
43        {
44            Graphics2D g2 = (Graphics2D)g;
45            g2.draw(box);
46        }
47
48        private Rectangle box;
49        private static final int BOX_X = 100;
50        private static final int BOX_Y = 100;
51        private static final int BOX_WIDTH = 20;
52        private static final int BOX_HEIGHT = 30;
53 }
```

Common Error 10.1

Forgetting to Repaint

A drawing program stores the data that are necessary to repaint the window. The `paint` method retrieves the data; generates geometric shapes such as lines, ellipses, and rectangles; and draws them. When you make a change to the data, your drawing is *not* automatically updated. You must tell the window manager that the data have changed, by calling the `repaint` method. Do not call the `paint` method directly. Only the window manager should call `paint`.

Advanced Topic 10.1

Event Adapters

In the preceding section you saw how to install a mouse listener into a mouse event source and how the listener methods are called when an event occurs. Usually, a program is not interested in all listener notifications. For example, a program may only be interested in mouse clicks and may not care that these mouse clicks are composed of "mouse pressed" and "mouse released" events. Of course, the program could supply a listener that defines all those methods in which it has no interest as "do-nothing" methods, for example:

```
class MouseClickListener implements MouseListener
{
    public void mouseClicked(MouseEvent event)
    {
        // mouse click action here
    }

    // four do-nothing methods
    public void mouseEntered(MouseEvent event) {}
    public void mouseExited(MouseEvent event) {}
    public void mousePressed(MouseEvent event) {}
    public void mouseReleased(MouseEvent event) {}
}
```

This is boring. For that reason, some friendly soul has created a `MouseAdapter` class that implements the `MouseListener` interface such that all methods do nothing. You can *extend* that class, inheriting the "do-nothing" methods and overriding just the methods that you care about, like this:

```
class MouseClickListener extends MouseAdapter
{
    public void mouseClicked(MouseEvent event)
    {
        // mouse click action here
    }
}
```

See Chapter 11 for more information on the process of extending classes.

10.3   Processing Text Input

In the preceding section you saw how to obtain input from the mouse. Let us next turn to text input. So far, your applets received text input by calling the `showInputDialog` method of the `JOptionPane` class, but that was not a very natural user interface. Most graphical programs collect text input through *text fields* (see Figure 3). In this section, you will learn how to add a control panel with text fields to an applet, and how to read what the user types into it.

In this book, we use the user interface components from the *Swing* toolkit, the most advanced user interface toolkit that Sun Microsystems has created for Java. Before the creation of Swing, Java used components in the AWT (Abstract Windowing Toolkit) for graphical applications. Both AWT and Swing components are *multiplatform*—that is, programs can run on Windows, the Macintosh, UNIX, and other platforms without modification. This behavior is often described as "write once, run anywhere". However, the toolkits achieved this goal in different ways. The AWT uses the *native* user interface

Figure 3

An Applet with a Control Panel for Text Input

elements (buttons, text fields, menus, and so on) of the host platform. This turned out not to work very well. There are slight differences in behavior on each platform, and programmers soon began complaining that the promised "write once, run anywhere" turned out in fact to be "write once, debug everywhere". Swing takes a different approach—it *paints* the shapes for buttons, text fields, menus, and so on. That is slower but more consistent.

The Swing classes are placed in the `javax.swing` package, where the `javax` package name denotes a *standard extension* of Java. Swing was first released as a standard extension to an earlier version of Java, and it became a standard part of Java 2. For compatibility reasons, the package name was not changed from `javax` to `java`. Swing uses some parts of the AWT, such as the parts for drawing graphical shapes and handling events, so you use some classes from the `java.awt` package in Swing programs.

> Use `JTextField` components to provide space for user input. Place a `JLabel` next to each text field.

The class names for most Swing user interface components start with the letter `J`. For example, `JTextField` is a Swing text field. There is also a `TextField` class—the (now obsolete) AWT text field.

When you construct a text field, you need to supply the width—the approximate number of characters that you expect the user to type.

```
JTextField xField = new JTextField(5);
```

Users can type additional characters, but then a part of the contents of the field becomes invisible.

You will want to *label* each text field so that the user knows what to type into it. You need to construct a `JLabel` object for each label:

```
JLabel xLabel = new JLabel("x = ");
```

Use JButton components for buttons. Attach an ActionListener to each button.

Finally, you want to give the user an opportunity to enter information into all text fields before processing it. Therefore, you also need to supply a button that the user can press to indicate that the input is ready for processing.

You construct a button by supplying a label string, an icon, or both. Here are the alternatives:

```
moveButton = new JButton("Move");
moveButton = new JButton(new ImageIcon("hand.gif"));
moveButton = new JButton("Move", new ImageIcon("hand.gif"));
```

When a button is clicked, it sends an action event. To capture it, you need to install an action listener. Here is the action listener for the Move button. The actionPerformed method reads the user input from the text fields, using the getText method of the JTextField class. It turns the resulting string into a number, moves the rectangle, and repaints the applet.

```
public class ButtonApplet extends Applet
{
    public ButtonApplet()
    {
        . . .
        class MoveButtonListener implements ActionListener
        {
            public void actionPerformed(ActionEvent event)
            {
                int x = Integer.parseInt(xField.getText());
                int y = Integer.parseInt(yField.getText());
                box.setLocation(x, y);
                repaint();
            }
        };
        ActionListener listener = new MoveButtonListener();
        moveButton.addActionListener(listener);
        . . .
    }
    . . .
}
```

The actionPerformed method accesses the xField and yField variables from the ButtonApplet constructor. As you saw in Chapter 9, those local variables must be declared as final:

```
final JTextField xField = new JTextField(5);
        final JTextField yField = new JTextField(5);
```

Use a JPanel container to group multiple user interface components together.

The method also accesses the box field of the ButtonApplet class. Inner classes can access all fields of the surrounding class.

To finish up this program, we need to place the labels, text fields, and button into the control panel. Construct a JPanel object—it is a container for user interface components.

```
JPanel panel = new JPanel();
```

Then add all components into the panel.

```
panel.add(xLabel);
panel.add(xField);
panel.add(yLabel);
panel.add(yField);
panel.add(moveButton);
```

> A JFrame corresponds to a window with a border and title bar.

Finally, show the panel in its own *frame*. A frame is a window with a title bar. You set the panel as the *content pane* of the frame. The content pane is a container that holds all of the user interface components. Then you call the **pack** method. That method sets the size of the frame just large enough to show all components. Finally, call show to display the frame.

```
JFrame frame = new JFrame();
frame.setContentPane(panel);
frame.pack();
frame.show();
```

It is also possible to show the control panel inside the applet. You will see how in Chapter 12.

Here is the complete program.

File ButtonApplet.java

```
 1  import java.applet.Applet;
 2  import java.awt.Graphics;
 3  import java.awt.Graphics2D;
 4  import java.awt.Rectangle;
 5  import java.awt.event.ActionEvent;
 6  import java.awt.event.ActionListener;
 7  import javax.swing.ImageIcon;
 8  import javax.swing.JButton;
 9  import javax.swing.JFrame;
10  import javax.swing.JLabel;
11  import javax.swing.JPanel;
12  import javax.swing.JTextField;
13
14  /**
15      This applet lets the user move a rectangle by specifying
16      the x- and y-position of the top left corner.
17  */
18  public class ButtonApplet extends Applet
19  {
20      public ButtonApplet()
21      {
22          // the rectangle that the paint method draws
23          box = new Rectangle(BOX_X, BOX_Y,
24              BOX_WIDTH, BOX_HEIGHT);
```

```
25
26          // the text fields for entering the x- and y-coordinates
27          final JTextField xField = new JTextField(5);
28          final JTextField yField = new JTextField(5);
29
30          // the button to move the rectangle
31          JButton moveButton = new JButton("Move",
32             new ImageIcon("hand.gif"));
33
34          class MoveButtonListener implements ActionListener
35          {
36             public void actionPerformed(ActionEvent event)
37             {
38                int x = Integer.parseInt(xField.getText());
39                int y = Integer.parseInt(yField.getText());
40                box.setLocation(x, y);
41                repaint();
42             }
43          }
44
45          ActionListener listener = new MoveButtonListener();
46          moveButton.addActionListener(listener);
47
48          // the labels for labeling the text fields
49          JLabel xLabel = new JLabel("x = ");
50          JLabel yLabel = new JLabel("y = ");
51
52          // the panel for holding the user interface components
53          JPanel panel = new JPanel();
54
55          panel.add(xLabel);
56          panel.add(xField);
57          panel.add(yLabel);
58          panel.add(yField);
59          panel.add(moveButton);
60
61          // the frame for holding the component panel
62          JFrame frame = new JFrame();
63          frame.setContentPane(panel);
64          frame.pack();
65          frame.show();
66       }
67
68       public void paint(Graphics g)
69       {
70          Graphics2D g2 = (Graphics2D)g;
71          g2.draw(box);
72       }
73
74       private Rectangle box;
```

```
75     private static final int BOX_X = 100;
76     private static final int BOX_Y = 100;
77     private static final int BOX_WIDTH = 20;
78     private static final int BOX_HEIGHT = 30;
79  }
```

10.4 Multiple Buttons with Similar Behavior

Often, your program needs to process inputs from multiple buttons. Look at Figure 4—the program has four buttons to control the movement of the rectangle.

The buttons carry out similar tasks, so the code to define the buttons is very repetitive. Here is the definition of the left button:

```
JButton leftButton = new JButton("Left");

class LeftButtonListener implements ActionListener
{
   public void actionPerformed(ActionEvent event)
   {
      box.translate(-BOX_WIDTH, 0);
      repaint();
   }
};

LeftButtonListener leftListener = new ButtonListener();
leftButton.addActionListener(leftListener);
```

Figure 4

An Applet with Multiple
Buttons

And here is the definition of the right button:

```
JButton rightButton = new JButton("Right");

class RightButtonListener implements ActionListener
{
   public void actionPerformed(ActionEvent event)
   {
      box.translate(BOX_WIDTH, 0);
      repaint();
   }
};

RightButtonListener rightListener = new ButtonListener();
rightButton.addActionListener(rightListener);

// two more to go...
```

> Factor out similar event handlers into a separate method.

This is, of course, intensely boring. Let's factor out the common code (see Quality Tip 3.4) into a method. When we do, we find that the code differs from button to button in only these parameters:

- The button label

- The amounts by which to move the rectangle in the *x*- and *y*-directions

The method can construct any of the buttons, given the parameter values:

```
public JButton makeButton(String label,
   final int dx, final int dy)
{
   JButton button = new JButton(label);

   class ButtonListener implements ActionListener
   {
      public void actionPerformed(ActionEvent event)
      {
         box.translate(dx, dy);
         repaint();
      }
   }

   ButtonListener listener = new ButtonListener();
   button.addActionListener(listener);
   return button;
}
```

Note that the dx and dy parameters are declared as final because they are accessed in the actionPerformed method of the inner class.

We call this method four times:

```
panel.add(makeButton("Left", -BOX_WIDTH, 0));
panel.add(makeButton("Right", BOX_WIDTH, 0));
panel.add(makeButton("Up", 0, -BOX_HEIGHT));
panel.add(makeButton("Down", 0, BOX_HEIGHT));
```

Each call to the method makes a listener object of type `ButtonListener`. In other words, each button has a separate listener, but all four listener objects are instances of the same listener class. Recall from Chapter 9 that the compiler automatically turns local variables that an inner class accesses into instance fields of the inner class. That is, the four listener objects have different states for dx and dy, namely the four combinations supplied in the method calls.

Sharing a listener class among buttons with the same behavior is an effective way to reduce complexity. When you find yourself implementing multiple listener classes with essentially the same functionality, place the listener class inside a separate method.

Here is the whole program:

File ButtonApplet.java

```
 1  import java.applet.Applet;
 2  import java.awt.Graphics;
 3  import java.awt.Graphics2D;
 4  import java.awt.Rectangle;
 5  import java.awt.event.ActionEvent;
 6  import java.awt.event.ActionListener;
 7  import javax.swing.JButton;
 8  import javax.swing.JFrame;
 9  import javax.swing.JPanel;
10
11  /**
12      This applet lets the user move a rectangle by clicking
13      on buttons labeled "Left", "Right", "Up", and "Down".
14  */
15  public class ButtonApplet extends Applet
16  {
17      public ButtonApplet()
18      {
19          // the rectangle that the paint method draws
20          box = new Rectangle(BOX_X, BOX_Y,
21              BOX_WIDTH, BOX_HEIGHT);
22
23          // the panel for holding the user interface components
24          JPanel panel = new JPanel();
25
26          panel.add(makeButton("Left", -BOX_WIDTH, 0));
27          panel.add(makeButton("Right", BOX_WIDTH, 0));
28          panel.add(makeButton("Up", 0, -BOX_HEIGHT));
29          panel.add(makeButton("Down", 0, BOX_HEIGHT));
30
31          // the frame for holding the component panel
32          JFrame frame = new JFrame();
33          frame.setContentPane(panel);
34          frame.pack();
35          frame.show();
36      }
37
38      public void paint(Graphics g)
39      {
```

```
40          Graphics2D g2 = (Graphics2D)g;
41          g2.draw(box);
42       }
43
44       /**
45          Makes a button that moves the box.
46          @param label the label to show on the button
47          @param dx the amount by which to move the box in the x-direction
48          when the button is clicked
49          @param dy the amount by which to move the box in the y-direction
50          when the button is clicked
51          @return the button
52       */
53       public JButton makeButton(String label, final int dx,
54          final int dy)
55       {
56          JButton button = new JButton(label);
57
58          class ButtonListener implements ActionListener
59          {
60             public void actionPerformed(ActionEvent event)
61             {
62                box.translate(dx, dy);
63                repaint();
64             }
65          }
66
67          ButtonListener listener = new ButtonListener();
68          button.addActionListener(listener);
69          return button;
70       }
71
72       private Rectangle box;
73       private static final int BOX_X = 100;
74       private static final int BOX_Y = 100;
75       private static final int BOX_WIDTH = 20;
76       private static final int BOX_HEIGHT = 30;
77    }
```

⊗ Common Error   10.2

Forgetting to Attach a Listener

If you run your program and find that your buttons seem to be dead, double-check that you attached the button listener. The same holds for other user interface components. It is a surprisingly common error to program the listener class and the event handler action without actually attaching it to the event source.

Productivity Hint 10.1

Share Listener Classes, Not Listener Objects

You saw in the preceding section how to make a listener *class* so that each button can have its own customized listener object. You will see some programmers use another approach in which a single listener *object* is shared among buttons. Then the `action-Performed` method must find out which button was clicked, by calling the `getSource` method of the `ActionEvent` parameter.

```
class DirectionListener implements ActionListener
{
   public void actionPerformed(ActionEvent event)
   {
      // find the button that was clicked
      // this approach is not recommended
      Object source = event.getSource();
      if (source == leftButton)
         box.translate(-BOX_WIDTH, 0);
      else if (source == rightButton)
         box.translate(BOX_WIDTH, 0);
      else if (source == upButton)
         box.translate(0, -BOX_HEIGHT);
      else if (source == downButton)
         box.translate(0, BOX_HEIGHT);
      repaint();
   }
}
```

This solution is still quite repetitive and therefore not as good as the one we used in the preceding section, where each button had its own listener. When you find yourself calling `getSource`, check whether you can instead use a separate object for each event source.

Productivity Hint 10.2

Don't Use a Container as a Listener

In this book, we use inner classes for interface listeners. That approach works for many different event types, and once you master the technique, you don't have to think about it anymore. Many development environments automatically generate code with inner classes, so it is a good idea to be familiar with them.

However, some programmers bypass the event listener classes and instead turn a container (such as an applet) into a listener. Here is a typical example. The `action-Performed` method is added to the applet class. That is, the applet implements the `ActionListener` interface.

```
public class ButtonApplet extends Applet
    implements ActionListener // this approach is not recommended
{
    public ButtonApplet()
    {
        . . .
        JButton moveButton = new JButton("Move",
            new ImageIcon("hand.gif"));
        moveButton.addActionListener(this);
        . . .
    }

    public void actionPerformed(ActionEvent event)
    {
        int x = Integer.parseInt(xField.getText());
        int y = Integer.parseInt(yField.getText());
        box.setLocation(x, y);
        repaint();
    }
    . . .
    private JTextField xField;
    private JTextField yField;
}
```

Now the `actionPerformed` method is a part of the `ButtonApplet` class rather than in a separate listener class. The listener is installed as `this`.

This technique has two major flaws. First, it separates the button definition from the button action. Also, it doesn't *scale* well. If the container contains two buttons that each generate action events, then the `actionPerformed` method must investigate the event source—which is not a good idea, according to Productivity Hint 10.1.

? HOWTO   **10.1** ▶

Handling Mouse and Action Events

Handling input from the mouse and from buttons is more challenging than processing keyboard input from the console. Follow these steps to implement the event handling code.

Step 1 Implement the *data that your program manipulates*

The data might be stored in a simple object, such as a `Rectangle` or a `Car`, or the data may be more complex, such as a collection of points.

Implement the data as instance variables of an applet, or, as you will see in Chapter 12, a panel. For example,

```
public class CarApplet
{
```

```
      . . .
   private Car myCar;
}
```

Step 2   Implement the *visual representation of the data*

A graphical program usually draws the data in a `paint` method. The `paint` method is called whenever the data need to be displayed, either because the window needs repainting or because the data have changed. For example,

```
public class CarApplet extends Applet
{
   . . .
   public void paint(Graphics g)
   {
      Graphics2D g2;
      myCar.draw(g2);
   }
   . . .
}
```

Step 3   Design a user interface for manipulating the data

So far, you have seen two user interface techniques:

- Clicking with the mouse in a window
- Clicking a button in a control panel

In Chapter 12 you will learn more about placement of buttons and other user interface components.

If you decide to use a control panel, sketch it. What text fields and buttons do you need?

Then ask yourself: How should the visual representation change when the user clicks with the mouse in the window, or when the user presses a button? What change in the data is necessary to cause that change in the visual representation?

For example, consider this simple interface for the car applet.

- When the user presses the mouse, the car is moved to the horizontal position of the mouse press. The vertical position of the car doesn't change. That means, the x-coordinate of the car is set to the x-coordinate of the mouse press.

- A control panel contains two buttons, marked "Left" and "Right". When the user clicks one of the buttons, the car moves 10 pixels to the left or right. That means, 10 is added to the x-coordinate of the car.

Step 4   Supply the user interface components

Use the following "plumbing" in the applet constructor:

```
// the panel for holding the user interface components
JPanel panel = new JPanel();

// add buttons and text fields
```

```
      panel.add(. . .);
      panel.add(. . .);
      . . .

      // the frame for holding the component panel
      JFrame frame = new JFrame();
      frame.setContentPane(panel);
      frame.pack();
      frame.show();
```

In Chapter 12 you will see how to add user interface components to a frame.

If your program takes only mouse inputs and doesn't require any text fields or buttons, skip this step.

Step 5 Supply event handler classes

For each event that you identified in step 3, you need to add an event handler.

You use classes that implement an `ActionListener` for buttons or a `MouseListener` for mouse events. (For convenience, you may want to extend the `MouseAdapter` interface instead—see Advanced Topic 10.1.)

In the event-handling method, update the data, then call `repaint` so that the visual representation is also updated.

The most basic coding style is to supply a class for every event. For example,

```
class MousePressListener extends MouseAdapter
{
   public void mousePressed(MouseEvent event)
   {
      car.setPosition(event.getX(), car.getY());
      repaint();
   }
}

class LeftButtonListener implements ActionListener
{
   public void actionPerformed(ActionEvent event)
   {
      car.setPosition(car.getX() - 10, car.getY());
      repaint();
   }
}
class RightButtonListener implements ActionListener
{
   public void actionPerformed(ActionEvent event)
   {
      car.setPosition(car.getX() + 10, car.getY());
      car.repaint();
   }
}
```

If several events have closely related actions, you can share the same listener class and supply the varying values either in a constructor or, most concisely, as parameters of a method, like this:

```
public JButton makeMoveButton(
   String title, final int amount)
{
   class MoveButtonListener implements ActionListener
   {
      public void actionPerformed(ActionEvent event)
      {
         car.setPosition(
            car.getX() + amount, car.getY());
         car.repaint();
      }
   }
   . . .
}
```

Step 6   Make listener objects and attach them to the event sources

For mouse events, the event source is the window on which you click—usually an applet or a panel. For action events, the event source is a button or other user interface component, or a timer. You need to add a listener object to each event source, like this:

```
public class CarApplet extends Applet
{
   public CarApplet()
   {
      MousePressListener listener =
         new MousePressListener();
      addMouseListener(listener);

      JButton leftButton =
         new makeMoveButton("Left", -10);
      JButton rightButton =
         new makeMoveButton("Right", 10);
      . . .
   }
   . . .
   public JButton makeMoveButton(
      String title, final int amount)
   {
      . . .
      JButton button = new JButton(title);
      ActionListener listener = new MoveButtonListener();
      button.addActionListener(listener);
   }
}
```

10.5   Frame Windows

Up to now, all the graphical programs that you wrote have been *applets*, programs that run inside a browser or the applet viewer. You can also write regular graphical programs in Java that do not run inside another program. In this section, you will learn how to write such *graphical applications*.

> A graphical application displays one or more frame windows.

Every graphical application puts up one or more frame windows, just like the window that we used as a control panel in the preceding examples. You can put up a frame window inside the `main` method of a program:

```
public class FrameTest
{
   public static void main(String[] args)
   {
      JFrame frame = new JFrame();
      . . .
      frame.show();
   }
}
```

After you construct a frame, you should set its *default close operation*.

```
JFrame frame = new JFrame();
frame.setDefaultCloseOperation(JFrame.EXIT_ON_CLOSE);
```

When the user closes the frame, the program automatically exits. This setting is useful for very simple programs. For more complex programs, you might want to perform some shutdown actions before allowing the program to exit.

To add some interest to the frame, let's add a couple of decorative labels, one a graphic icon, the other a string of text (see Figure 5).

```
JLabel iconLabel =
   new JLabel(new ImageIcon("world.gif"));
JLabel textLabel = new JLabel("Hello, World!");
```

As in the preceding examples, add the user interface components to a panel and set that panel as the content pane of the frame.

```
JPanel panel = new JPanel();
panel.add(iconLabel);
panel.add(textLabel);
frame.setContentPane(panel);
```

Figure 5

A Frame with Two Labels

Finally, pack and show the frame:

```
frame.pack();
frame.show();
```

Here is the complete program:

File FrameTest.java

```
1  import javax.swing.ImageIcon;
2  import javax.swing.JFrame;
3  import javax.swing.JLabel;
4  import javax.swing.JPanel;
5
6  /**
7     This program displays a frame with an image and a text label.
8  */
9  public class FrameTest
10 {
11    public static void main(String[] args)
12    {
13       JFrame frame = new JFrame();
14
15       frame.setDefaultCloseOperation(JFrame.EXIT_ON_CLOSE);
16
17       JLabel iconLabel =
18          new JLabel(new ImageIcon("world.gif"));
19       JLabel textLabel = new JLabel("Hello, World!");
20
21       JPanel panel = new JPanel();
22       panel.add(iconLabel);
23       panel.add(textLabel);
24       frame.setContentPane(panel);
25
26       frame.pack();
27       frame.show();
28    }
29 }
```

10.6   Text Components

> Use a JTextArea
> to show multiple
> lines of text.

You already saw in Section 10.3 how to construct text fields. A text field holds a single line of text. To display multiple lines of text, you use the JTextArea class.

When constructing a text area, you can specify the number of rows and columns:

```
JTextArea textArea = new JTextArea(10, 30);
```

You use the setText method to set the text of a text field or text area. The append method adds text to the end of a text area. Use newline characters to separate lines, like this:

```
textArea.append(account.getBalance() + "\n");
```

To find the current contents of a text field or text area, use the `getText` method.

If you want to use a text field or text area for display purposes only, then you can use the `setEditable` method:

```
textArea.setEditable(false);
```

> You can add scroll bars to any component with a `JScrollPane`.

Now the user can no longer edit the contents of the field, but your program can still call `setText` and `append` to change it.

You can set the font of a text component with the `setFont` method:

```
textArea.setFont(new Font(. . .));
```

To add scroll bars to a text area, use a `JScrollPane`, like this:

```
JTextArea textArea = new JTextArea(10, 30);
JScrollPane scrollPane = new JScrollPane(textArea);
frame.setContentPane(scrollPane);
```

Figure 6 shows the result.

The following sample program puts these concepts together. A user can enter numbers into the interest rate text field and then click on the "Add Interest" button (see Figure 7). The interest rate is applied, and the updated balance is appended to the text area. The text area has scroll bars and is not editable. (The scroll bars are displayed only when the text area fills up with text.)

This application is a useful prototype for a graphical user interface front end for arbitrary calculations. You can easily modify it for your own needs. Place other input components into the control panel. Change the contents of the `actionPerformed` method to carry out other calculations. Display the results in the text area.

Figure 6

A Text Area with Scroll Bars

Figure 7

The Control Panel for Adding Interest to the Bank Account

File TextAreaTest.java

```
1  import java.awt.event.ActionEvent;
2  import java.awt.event.ActionListener;
3  import javax.swing.JButton;
4  import javax.swing.JFrame;
5  import javax.swing.JLabel;
6  import javax.swing.JPanel;
7  import javax.swing.JScrollPane;
8  import javax.swing.JTextArea;
9  import javax.swing.JTextField;
10
11 /**
12     This program shows a frame with a text area that displays
13     the growth of an investment. A second frame holds a text
14     field to specify the interest rate.
15 */
16 public class TextAreaTest
17 {
18     public static void main(String[] args)
19     {
20        // the application adds interest to this bank account
21        final BankAccount account =
22           new BankAccount(INITIAL_BALANCE);
23        // the text area for displaying the results
24        final JTextArea textArea = new JTextArea(10, 30);
25        textArea.setEditable(false);
26        JScrollPane scrollPane = new JScrollPane(textArea);
27
28        // construct the frame for displaying the text area
29        JFrame frame = new JFrame();
30        frame.setDefaultCloseOperation(
31           JFrame.EXIT_ON_CLOSE);
32        frame.setContentPane(scrollPane);
33        frame.pack();
34        frame.show();
35
36        // the label and text field for entering the interest rate
37        JLabel rateLabel = new JLabel("Interest Rate: ");
38
```

```
39        final JTextField rateField = new JTextField(10);
40        rateField.setText("" + DEFAULT_RATE);
41
42        // the button to trigger the calculation
43        JButton calculateButton =
44           new JButton("Add Interest");
45
46        class CalculateListener implements ActionListener
47        {
48           public void actionPerformed(ActionEvent event)
49           {
50              double rate = Double.parseDouble(
51                 rateField.getText());
52              double interest = account.getBalance()
53                 * rate / 100;
54              account.deposit(interest);
55              textArea.append(account.getBalance() + "\n");
56           }
57        }
58
59        ActionListener listener = new CalculateListener();
60        calculateButton.addActionListener(listener);
61
62        // the control panel that holds the input components
63        JPanel controlPanel = new JPanel();
64        controlPanel.add(rateLabel);
65        controlPanel.add(rateField);
66        controlPanel.add(calculateButton);
67
68        // the frame to hold the control panel
69        JFrame controlFrame = new JFrame();
70        controlFrame.setContentPane(controlPanel);
71        controlFrame.pack();
72        controlFrame.show();
73     }
74
75     private static final double DEFAULT_RATE = 10;
76     private static final double INITIAL_BALANCE = 1000;
77  }
```

Productivity Hint 10.3

Code Reuse

Suppose you are given the task to write another graphical user interface program that reads input from a couple of text fields and displays the result of some calculations in a text area. You don't have to start from scratch. Instead, you can—and often should—*reuse* the outline of an existing program, such as the foregoing TextAreaTest program.

▼   To reuse program code, simply make a copy of a program file and give the copy a new name. For example, you may want to copy `TextAreaTest.java` to a file `MyProg.java`.

▼   Then remove the code that is clearly specific to the old problem, but leave the outline in place. That is, keep the panel, text field, event listener, and so on. Fill in the code for your new calculations. Finally, rename classes, buttons, frame titles, and so on.

▼   Once you understand the principles behind event listeners, frames and panels, there is no need to rethink them every time. Reusing the structure of a working program makes your work more efficient.

▼   However, reuse by "copy and rename" is still a mechanical and somewhat error-prone approach. It is even better to package reusable program structures into a set of common classes. The inheritance mechanism lets you design classes for reuse without copy and paste. We will cover inheritance in the next chapter.

▼ **Random Fact**   **10.1**

▼   **Programming Languages**

Many hundreds of programming languages exist today. That is actually quite surprising. The idea behind a high-level programming language is to provide a medium for program-

▼   ming that is independent from the instruction set of a particular processor, so that one can move programs from one computer to another without rewriting them. Moving a program from one programming language to another is a difficult process, however, and it is rarely

▼   done. Thus, it seems that there would be little use for so many programming languages.

Unlike human languages, programming languages are created with specific purposes. Some programming languages make it particularly easy to express tasks from a particular

▼   problem domain. Some languages specialize in database processing; others in "artificial intelligence" programs that try to infer new facts from a given base of knowledge; others in multimedia programming. The Pascal language was purposefully kept simple because

▼   it was designed as a teaching language. The C language was developed to be translated efficiently into fast machine code, with a minimum of housekeeping overhead. The C++ language builds on C by adding features for object-oriented programming. The Java lan-

▼   guage was designed for deploying programs across the Internet.

In the early 1970s the U.S. Department of Defense (DoD) was seriously concerned about the high cost of the software components of its weapons equipment. It was estimated that

▼   more than half of the total DoD budget was spent on the development of this *embedded-systems* software—that is, software that is embedded in some machinery, such as an airplane or missile, to control it. One of the perceived problems was the great diversity of programming

▼   languages that were used to produce that software. Many of these languages, such as TACPOL, CMS-2, SPL/1, and JOVIAL, were virtually unknown outside the defense sector.

In 1976 a committee of computer scientists and defense industry representatives was

▼   asked to evaluate existing programming languages. The committee was to determine whether any of them could be made the DoD standard for all future military programming. To nobody's surprise, the committee decided that a new language would need to be created.

▼   Contractors were then invited to submit designs for such a new language. Of 17 initial proposals, four were chosen to develop their languages. To ensure an unbiased evaluation, the languages received code names: Red (by Intermetrics), Green (by CII Honeywell Bull), Blue (by Softech), and Yellow (by SRI International). All four languages were based on Pascal. The Green language emerged as the winner in 1979. It was named Ada in honor of the world's first programmer, Ada Lovelace (see Random Fact 15.1).

The Ada language was roundly derided by academics as a typical bloated Defense Department product. Military contractors routinely sought, and obtained, exemptions from the requirement that they had to use Ada on their projects. Outside the defense industry, few companies used Ada. Perhaps that is unfair. Ada had been *designed* to be complex enough to be useful for many applications, whereas other, more popular languages, notably C++, have *grown* to be just as complex and ended up being unmanageable.

The initial version of the C language was designed about 1972. Unlike Ada, C is a simple language that lets you program "close to the machine". It is also quite unsafe. Because different compiler writers added different features, the language actually sprouted various dialects. Some programming instructions were understood by one compiler but rejected by another. Such divergence is an immense pain to a programmer who wants to move code from one computer to another, and an effort got underway to iron out the differences and come up with a standard version of C. The design process ended in 1989 with the completion of the ANSI (American National Standards Institute) Standard. In the meantime, Bjarne Stroustrup of AT&T added features of the language Simula (an object-oriented language designed for carrying out simulations) to C. The resulting language was called C++. From 1985 until today, C++ has grown by the addition of many features, and a standardization process was completed in 1998. C++ has been enormously popular because programmers can take their existing C code and move it to C++, with only minimal changes. In order to keep compatibility with existing code, every innovation in C++ had to work around the existing language constructs, yielding a language that is powerful but somewhat cumbersome to use.

In 1995, Java was designed to be conceptually simpler and more internally consistent than C++, while retaining the syntax that is familiar to millions of C and C++ programmers. The Java *language* was a great design success. It is indeed clean and simple. As for the Java *library*, you know from your own experience that it is neither.

Keep in mind that a programming language is only a part of the technology for writing programs. To be successful, a programming language needs feature-rich libraries, powerful tools, and a community of knowledgeable and enthusiastic users. Several very well-designed programming languages have withered on the vine, whereas other programming languages whose design was merely "good enough" have thrived in the marketplace.

CHAPTER SUMMARY

1. User interface events include key presses, mouse moves, button presses, menu selections, and so on.

2. You supply *event listeners* for the events about which you care. You need to implement methods for handling the event. You construct listener objects and attach them to the event sources.

3. *Event source* classes report on events. When an event occurs, the event source notifies all event listeners.

4. Event notifications happen in event listener classes. An event listener class implements an *event listener interface*. The interface lists all possible notifications for a particular event category.

5. *Event classes* contain detailed information about various kinds of events.

6. You use a *mouse listener* to capture mouse events.

7. You often install event listeners as *inner classes*. Recall that the inner-class methods can have access to the surrounding fields, methods, and final variables.

8. The `repaint` method causes a window to repaint itself as soon as possible.

9. Use `JTextField` components to provide space for user input. Place a `JLabel` next to each text field.

10. Use `JButton` components for buttons. Attach an `ActionListener` to each button.

11. Use a `JPanel` container to group multiple user interface components together.

12. A `JFrame` corresponds to a window with a border and title bar.

13. Factor out similar event handlers into a separate method.

14. A graphical application displays one or more frame windows.

15. Use a `JTextArea` to show multiple lines of text.

16. You can add scroll bars to any component with a JScrollPane

Further Reading

[1] Cay S. Horstmann and Gary Cornell, *Core Java 1.2 Volume 1: Fundamentals,* Prentice Hall, 1999.

CLASSES, OBJECTS, AND METHODS INTRODUCED IN THIS CHAPTER

```
java.awt.Component
    addActionListener
    addMouseListener
    repaint
java.awt.Container
    add
java.awt.Rectangle
    setLocation
java.awt.Window
    show
java.awt.event.ActionListener
    actionPerformed
java.awt.event.ActionEvent
```

```
java.awt.event.MouseEvent
    getX
    getY
java.awt.event.MouseListener
    mousePressed
javax.swing.ImageIcon
javax.swing.JButton
javax.swing.JFrame
    EXIT_ON_CLOSE
    setContentPane
    setDefaultCloseOperation
    pack
javax.swing.JLabel
javax.swing.JPanel
javax.swing.JScrollPane
javax.swing.JTextArea
    append
javax.swing.JTextField
javax.swing.text.JTextComponent
    getText
    isEditable
    setEditable
    setText
```

Review Exercises

Exercise R10.1. What is an event object? An event source? An event listener?

Exercise R10.2. From a programmer's perspective, what is the most important difference between the user interfaces of a console application and a graphical application?

Exercise R10.3. What is the difference between an `ActionEvent` and a `MouseEvent`?

Exercise R10.4. Why does the `ActionListener` interface have only one method, whereas the `MouseListener` has five methods?

Exercise R10.5. Can a class be an event source for multiple event types?

Exercise R10.6. What information does an action event object carry? What additional information does a mouse event object carry?

Exercise R10.7. Why are we using inner classes for event listeners? If Java did not have inner classes, could we still implement event listeners? How?

Exercise R10.8. What is the difference between the `paint` and `repaint` methods?

Exercise R10.9. What is the difference between an applet and a graphical user interface application?

Exercise R10.10. What is the difference between a frame and a panel?

Exercise R10.11. What is the difference between a text field and a text area?

PROGRAMMING EXERCISES

Exercise P10.1. Reimplement the `MouseSpy` program as an application. Display the frame's mouse events in the console window.

Exercise P10.2. Implement the `MousePressListener` in the `MouseApplet` as a regular class (that is, not an inner class). *Hint:* Store a reference to the applet object in the listener, add to the listener a constructor that sets that reference, and add a public method for moving the box position to the applet.

Exercise P10.3. Write an applet that prompts the user for an integer and then draws as many rectangles at random positions as the user requested. Place a text field and a "Draw" button into an external frame.

Exercise P10.4. Write an applet that prompts the user to enter the *x*- and *y*-positions of the center and a radius. When the user clicks a "Draw" button, draw a circle with that center and radius.

Exercise P10.5. Write an applet that lets a user specify a circle by typing the radius in a text field and then clicking on the center. Note that you don't need a "Draw" button.

Exercise P10.6. Write an applet that lets a user specify a circle with two mouse presses, the first one on the center and the second on a point on the periphery. *Hint:* In the mouse press handler, you must keep track of whether you already received the center point in a previous mouse press.

Exercise P10.7. Write an applet that lets a user specify a triangle with three mouse clicks. *Hint:* In the mouse click handler, you must keep track of how many corners you already received. When the user clicks for the first time, draw a small circle to mark the position. When the user clicks for the second time, draw a line joining the two points. Finally, after the third click, draw the entire triangle.

Exercise P10.8. Write an applet that prompts the user to click on three points. Then draw a circle passing through the three points.

Exercise P10.9. Write an applet that prompts the user to click on two points. Then draw a line joining the points and write a message displaying the *slope* of the line; that is, the "rise over run" ratio. The message should be displayed at the *midpoint* of the line.

Exercise P10.10. Write an applet that prompts the user to click on two points. Then draw a line joining the points and write a message displaying the *length* of the line. The message should be displayed at the *midpoint* of the line.

Exercise P10.11. Write an applet that plots a *regression line;* that is, the line with the best fit through a collection of points. The regression line is the line with equation

$$y = \bar{y} + m(x - \bar{x}),$$

where

$$m = \frac{\sum x_i y_i - n\bar{x}\bar{y}}{\sum x_i^2 - n\bar{x}^2}$$

$\bar{x}$ is the mean of the *x*-values, and $\bar{y}$ is the mean of the *y*-values.

The user keeps clicking on points. You don't need to store the individual points, but you need to keep track of

- The count of input values
- The sum of x, y, x^2, and xy values

To draw the regression line, compute its endpoints at the left and right edges of the screen and draw a segment. Each time the user clicks on another point, you update the screen again.

Exercise P10.12. Write an applet that draws a clock face with a time that the user enters in two text fields (one for the hours, one for the minutes).

Hint: You need to find out the angles of the hour hand and the minute hand. The angle of the minute hand is easy: The minute hand travels 360 degrees in 60 minutes. The angle of the hour hand is harder; it travels 360 degrees in 12 × 60 *minutes*.

Exercise P10.13. Write an applet that asks the user to enter an integer n, and then draw an n-by-n grid on the panel. Whenever the user clicks inside one of the grid squares on the panel, color that grid square in black.

Exercise P10.14. Write an applet that asks the user for a number of sticks, and then generate a random stick chart (similar to the temperature chart in Chapter 4) with the given number of sticks.

Exercise P10.15. Write an applet that asks the user to enter data values in a text area. Then draw a stick chart showing the data values. *Hint:* Use a string tokenizer to break the text into tokens.

Exercise P10.16. Write a graphical application front end for a bank account class. Supply text fields and buttons for depositing and withdrawing money, and for displaying the current balance in a text area.

Exercise P10.17. Write a graphical application front end for a `Purse` class. Supply buttons for adding various coins, and for displaying the total amount of money in the purse. Make sure to use a single method for the event listeners for the various coin buttons.

Exercise P10.18. Write a graphical application front end for a `VendingMachine` class. Supply a text field and button for adding money and buttons for selecting products. Display messages such as "Here is your chocolate bar" or "Insufficient money" in a text area.

Exercise P10.19. Write a graphical application front end for an `Earthquake` class. Supply a text field and button for entering the strength of the earthquake. Display the earthquake description in a text area.

Exercise P10.20. Write a graphical application front end for a `DataSet` class. Supply text fields and buttons for adding values, and display the current minimum, maximum, and average in a text area.

Inheritance

CHAPTER GOALS

To learn about inheritance

▶ To understand how to inherit and override superclass methods

▶ To be able to invoke superclass constructors

▶ To learn about protected and package access control

▶ To understand the common superclass Object and to override its toString, equals, and clone methods

CHAPTER CONTENTS

11.1 An Introduction to Inheritance

> Inheritance is a method for extending existing classes by adding methods and fields.

Inheritance is a mechanism for enhancing existing, working classes. If you need to implement a new class and a class representing a more general concept is already available, then the new class can inherit from the existing class. For example, suppose you need to define a class `SavingsAccount` to model an account that pays a fixed interest rate on deposits. You already have a class `BankAccount`, and a savings account is a special case of a bank account. In this case, it makes sense to use the language construct of inheritance. Here is the syntax for the class definition:

```
class SavingsAccount extends BankAccount
{
    new methods
    new instance fields
}
```

In the `SavingsAccount` class definition you specify only new methods and instance fields. All methods and instance fields of the `BankAccount` class are *automatically inherited* by the `SavingsAccount` class. For example, the `deposit` method automatically applies to savings accounts:

```
SavingsAccount collegeFund = new SavingsAccount(10);
    // savings account with 10% interest
collegeFund.deposit(500);
    // OK to use BankAccount method with SavingsAccount object
```

> The more general class is called a superclass. The more specialized class that inherits from the superclass is called the subclass.

You have already encountered inheritance in Chapter 4, where your applets all belonged to classes that inherited from the `Applet` class.

We must introduce some more terminology here. The more general class that forms the basis for inheritance is called the *superclass*. The more specialized class that inherits from the superclass is called the *subclass*. In our example, `BankAccount` is the superclass and `SavingsAccount` is the subclass.

> Every class extends the Object class either directly or indirectly.

In Java, every class that does not specifically extend another class is a subclass of the class `Object`. For example, the `BankAccount` class extends the class `Object`. The `Object` class has a small number of methods that make sense for all objects, such as the `toString` method, which you can use to obtain a string that describes the state of an object.

> Inheriting from a class differs from realizing an interface: The subclass inherits behavior and state from the superclass.

Figure 1 is a class diagram showing the relationship between the three classes `Object`, `BankAccount`, and `SavingsAccount`. In a class diagram, you denote inheritance by a solid arrow with a "hollow triangle" tip that points to the superclass.

You may wonder at this point in what way inheritance differs from realizing an interface. An interface is not a class. It has *no state and no behavior*. It merely tells you which methods you should implement. A superclass has state and behavior, and the subclasses inherit them.

Figure 1

An Inheritance Diagram

> One advantage of inheritance is code reuse.

One important reason for inheritance is *code reuse*. By inheriting from an existing class, you do not have to replicate the effort that went into designing and perfecting that class. For example, when implementing the SavingsAccount class, you can rely on the withdraw, deposit, and getBalance methods of the BankAccount class without touching them.

> When defining a subclass, you specify added instance fields, added methods, and changed or *overridden* methods.

Let us see how our savings account objects are different from BankAccount objects. We will set an interest rate in the constructor, and then we need a method to apply that interest periodically. That is, in addition to the three methods that can be applied to every account, there is an additional method addInterest. These new methods and instance fields must be defined in the subclass.

```
public class SavingsAccount extends BankAccount
{
    public SavingsAccount(double rate)
    {
        constructor implementation
    }

    public void addInterest()
    {
        method implementation
    }

    private double interestRate;
}
```

Figure 2

Layout of a Subclass Object

Figure 2 shows the layout of a SavingsAccount object. It inherits the balance instance field from the BankAccount superclass, and it gains one additional instance field: interestRate.

Next, you need to implement the new addInterest method. This method computes the interest due on the current balance and deposits that interest to the account.

```java
public class SavingsAccount extends BankAccount
{
    public SavingsAccount(double rate)
    {
        interestRate = rate;
    }

    public void addInterest()
    {
        double interest = getBalance()
            * interestRate / 100;
        deposit(interest);
    }

    private double interestRate;
}
```

Note how the addInterest method calls the getBalance and deposit methods of the superclass. Because no object is specified for the calls to getBalance and deposit, the calls apply to the implicit parameter of the addInterest method. In other words, the following statements are executed:

```java
double interest = this.getBalance()
    * this.interestRate / 100;
this.deposit(interest);
```

For example, if you call

```java
collegeFund.addInterest();
```

then the following instructions are executed:

```java
double interest = collegeFund.getBalance()
    * collegeFund.interestRate / 100;
collegeFund.deposit(interest);
```

Syntax 11.1: Inheritance

```
class SubclassName extends    SuperclassName
{
    methods
    instance fields
}
```

Example:

```java
public class SavingsAccount extends BankAccount
{
    public SavingsAccount(double rate)
    {
        interestRate = rate;
    }

    public void addInterest()
    {
        double interest =
            getBalance() * interestRate / 100;
        deposit(interest);
    }

    private double interestRate;
}
```

Purpose:

To define a new class that inherits from an existing class, and define the methods and instance fields that are added in the new class

---

▼ **Common Error** 11.1 ▶

Confusing Super- and Subclasses

If you compare an object of type SavingsAccount with an object of type BankAccount, then you find that

- The keyword extends suggests that the SavingsAccount object is an extended version of a BankAccount.

- The SavingsAccount object is larger; it has an added instance field interest-Rate.

- The SavingsAccount object is more capable; it has an addInterest method.

▼

▼

▼

It seems a superior object in every way. So why is SavingsAccount called the *subclass* and BankAccount the *superclass*?

The *super/sub* terminology comes from set theory. Look at the set of all bank accounts. Not all of them are SavingsAccount objects; some of them are other kinds of bank accounts. Therefore, the set of SavingsAccount objects is a *subset* of the set of all BankAccount objects, and the set of BankAccount objects is a *superset* of the set of SavingsAccount objects. The more specialized objects in the subset have richer state and more capabilities.

11.2 Inheritance Hierarchies

In the real world, you often categorize concepts into *hierarchies*. Hierarchies are frequently represented as trees, with the most general concepts at the root of the hierarchy and more specialized ones towards the branches. Figure 3 shows a typical example.

> Sets of classes can form complex inheritance hierarchies.

In Java it is equally common to group classes in complex *inheritance hierarchies*. The classes representing the most general concepts are near the root, more specialized classes towards the branches. For example, Figure 4 shows part of the hierarchy of Swing user interface components in Java.

When designing a hierarchy of classes, you ask yourself which features and behavior are common to all the classes that you are designing. Those common properties are col-

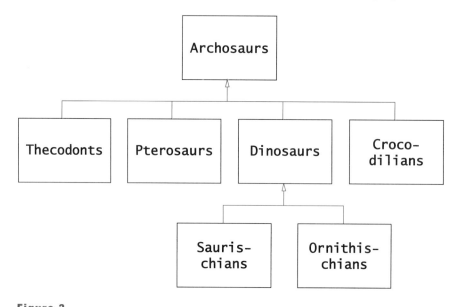

Figure 3

A Part of the Hierarchy of Ancient Reptiles

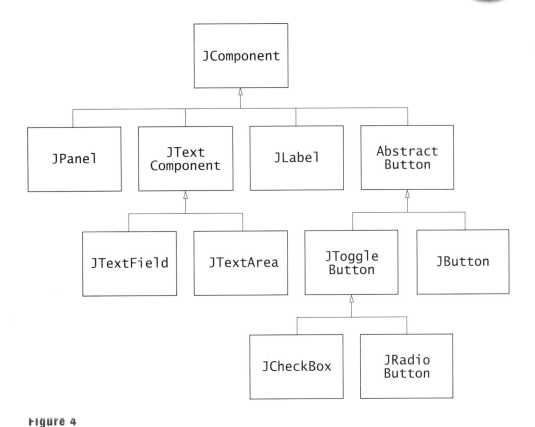

Figure 4

A Part of the Hierarchy of Swing User Interface Components

lected in a superclass. For example, all user interface components have a width and height, and the getWidth and getHeight methods of the JComponent class return the component's dimensions. More specialized properties can be found in subclasses. For example, buttons can have text and icon labels. The class AbstractButton, but not the superclass JComponent, has methods to set and get the button text and icon, and instance fields to store them. The individual button classes (such as JButton, JRadioButton, and JCheckBox) inherit these properties. In fact, the AbstractButton class was created to express the commonality between these buttons.

We will use a simpler example of a hierarchy in our study of inheritance concepts. Consider a bank that offers its customers the following account types:

1. The checking account has no interest, gives you a small number of free transactions per month, and charges a transaction fee for each additional transaction.

2. The savings account earns interest that compounds monthly. (In our implementation, the interest is compounded using the balance of the last day of the month, which is somewhat unrealistic. Typically, banks use either the average or the minimum daily balance. Exercise P11.1 asks you to implement this enhancement.)

Figure 5

Inheritance Hierarchy for Bank Account
Classes

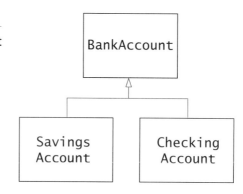

Figure 5 shows the inheritance hierarchy. Exercise P11.2 asks you to add another class to this hierarchy.

Next, let us determine the behavior of these classes. All bank accounts support the get-Balance method, which simply reports the current balance. They also support the deposit and withdraw methods, although the details of the implementation differ. For example, a checking account must keep track of the number of transactions to account for the transaction fees. A time deposit account must reject withdrawals for other than the full balance.

The checking account needs a method deductFees to deduct the monthly fees and to reset the transaction counter. The deposit and withdraw methods must be redefined to count the transactions.

The savings account needs a method addInterest to add interest.

11.3   Inheriting Instance Fields and Methods

When you form a subclass of a given class, you can specify additional instance fields and methods. In this section we will discuss this process in detail.

Let us look at methods first. When defining the methods for a subclass, there are three possibilities.

1. You can *override* methods from the superclass. If you specify a method with the same *signature* (that is, the same name and the same parameter types), it overrides the method of the same name in the superclass. Whenever the method is applied to an object of the subclass type, the overriding method, and not the original method, is executed. For example, CheckingAccount.deposit overrides BankAccount.deposit.

2. You can *inherit* methods from the superclass. If you do not explicitly override a superclass method, you automatically inherit it. The superclass method can be applied to the subclass objects. For example, the CheckingAccount class inherits the BankAccount.getBalance method.

3. You can define new methods. If you define a method that did not exist in the superclass, then the new method can be applied only to subclass objects. For example, CheckingAccount.deductFees is a new method that does not exist in the superclass BankAccount.

The situation for instance fields is quite different. You can never override instance fields. When defining instance fields for a subclass, there are only two cases:

1. You can inherit fields from the superclass. All instance fields from the superclass are automatically inherited. For example, all subclasses of the `BankAccount` class inherit the instance field `balance`.

2. You can define new fields. Any new instance fields that you define in the subclass are present only in subclass objects. For example, the subclass `SavingsAccount` defines a new instance field `interestRate`.

What happens if you define a new field with the same name as a superclass field? For example, what happens if you define another field named `balance` in the `Savings-Account` class? Then each `SavingsAccount` object has *two* instance fields of the same name. The newly defined subclass field *shadows* the superclass field. That is, the superclass field is still present, but it cannot be accessed from the `SavingsAccount` methods. Shadowing instance fields can be a source of confusion (see Common Error 11.2).

We already implemented the `BankAccount` and `SavingsAccount` classes. Now we will implement the subclass `CheckingAccount` so that you can see in detail how methods and instance fields are inherited. Recall that the `BankAccount` class has three methods and one instance field:

```
public class BankAccount
{
   public double getBalance() { . . . }
   public void deposit(double d) { . . . }
   public void withdraw(double d) { . . . }

   private double balance;
}
```

The `CheckingAccount` has an added method `deductFees` and an added instance field `transactionCount`, and it overrides the `deposit` and `withdraw` methods to increment the transaction count:

```
public class CheckingAccount extends BankAccount
{
   public void deposit(double d) { . . . }
   public void withdraw(double d) { . . . }
   public void deductFees() { . . . }

   private int transactionCount;
}
```

Each object of class `CheckingAccount` has two instance fields:

- `balance` (inherited from `BankAccount`)

- `transactionCount` (new to `CheckingAccount`)

You can apply four methods to `CheckingAccount` objects:

- `getBalance()` (inherited from `BankAccount`)
- `deposit(double)` (overrides `BankAccount` method)
- `withdraw(double)` (overrides `BankAccount` method)
- `deductFees()` (new to `CheckingAccount`)

Next, let us implement these methods. The `deposit` method increments the transaction count and deposits the money:

```
public class CheckingAccount extends BankAccount
{
   public void deposit(double amount)
   {
      transactionCount++;
      // now add amount to balance
      . . .
   }
   . . .
}
```

Now we have a problem. We can't simply add `amount` to `balance`:

```
public class CheckingAccount extends BankAccount
{
   public void deposit(double amount)
   {
      transactionCount++;
      // now add amount to balance
      balance = balance + amount; // ERROR
   }
   . . .
}
```

> A subclass has no access to private fields of its superclass.

Although every `CheckingAccount` object has a `balance` instance field, that instance field is *private* to the superclass `BankAccount`. Subclass methods have no more access rights to the private data of the superclass than any other methods. If you want to modify a private superclass field, you must use a public method of the superclass, just like everyone else.

How can we add the deposit amount to the balance, using the public interface of the `BankAccount` class? There is a perfectly good method for just that purpose—namely, the `deposit` method of the `BankAccount` class. So we have to invoke the `deposit` on some object. On which object? The checking account into which the money is deposited—that is, the implicit parameter of the `deposit` method of the `CheckingAccount` class. As you saw in Chapter 3, to invoke another method on the implicit parameter, you don't specify the parameter but just write the method name:

```
public class CheckingAccount extends BankAccount
{
   public void deposit(double amount)
   {
      transactionCount++;
      // now add amount to balance
      deposit(amount); // not complete
   }
   . . .
}
```

But this won't quite work. The compiler interprets

```
deposit(amount);
```

as

```
this.deposit(amount);
```

The `this` parameter is of type `CheckingAccount`. There is a method called `deposit` in the `CheckingAccount` class. Therefore, that method will be called—but that is just the method we are currently writing! The method will call itself over and over, and the program will die in an infinite recursion (discussed in Chapter 17).

> Use the super keyword to call a method of the superclass.

Instead, we must be more specific that we want to invoke only the *superclass's* `deposit` method. There is a special keyword `super` for this purpose:

```
public class CheckingAccount extends BankAccount
{
   public void deposit(double amount)
   {
      transactionCount++;
      // now add amount to balance
      super.deposit(amount);
   }
   . . .
}
```

This version of the `deposit` method is correct. To deposit money into a checking account, update the transaction count and then call the `deposit` method of the superclass.

The remaining methods are now straightforward.

```
public class CheckingAccount extends BankAccount
{
   . . .
   public void withdraw(double amount)
   {
      transactionCount++;
      // now subtract amount from balance
```

```
        super.withdraw(amount);
    }

    public void deductFees()
    {
        if (transactionCount > FREE_TRANSACTIONS)
        {
            double fees = TRANSACTION_FEE
                * (transactionCount - FREE_TRANSACTIONS);
            super.withdraw(fees);
        }
        transactionCount = 0;
    }
    . . .
    private static final int FREE_TRANSACTIONS = 3;
    private static final double TRANSACTION_FEE = 2.0;
}
```

Syntax 11.2: Calling a Superclass Method

super.*methodName*(*parameters*);

Example:

```
public void deposit(double amount)
{
    transactionCount++;
    super.deposit(amount);
}
```

Purpose:

To call a method of the superclass instead of the
method of the current class

▼ ⊗ Common Error 11.2

Shadowing Instance Fields

▼

A subclass has no access to the private instance fields of the superclass. For example, the
methods of the CheckingAccount class cannot access the balance field:

▼
```
public class CheckingAccount extends BankAccount
{
    public void deposit(double amount)
    {
        transactionCount++;
```

Figure 6

Shadowing Instance Fields

```
        balance = balance + amount; // ERROR
    }
    . . .
}
```

It is a common beginner's error to "solve" this problem by adding *another* instance field with the same name.

```
public class CheckingAccount extends BankAccount
{
    public void deposit(double amount)
    {
        transactionCount++;
        balance = balance + amount;
    }
    . . .
    private double balance; // DON'T
    private double interestRate;
}
```

Sure, now the deposit method compiles, but it doesn't update the correct balance! Such a CheckingAccount object has two instance fields, both named balance (see Figure 6). The getBalance method of the superclass retrieves one of them, and the deposit method of the subclass updates the other.

⊗ Common Error   11.3

Failing to Invoke the Superclass Method

A common error in extending the functionality of a superclass method is to forget the super. qualifier. For example, to withdraw money from a checking account, update the transaction count and then withdraw the amount:

```
public void withdraw(double amount)
{
    transactionCount++;
```

▼
```
            withdraw(amount);
            // Error—should be super.withdraw(amount)
        }
```

▼ Here withdraw(amount) refers to the withdraw method applied to the implicit parameter of the method. The implicit parameter is of type CheckingAccount, and the
▼ CheckingAccount class has a withdraw method, so that method is called. Of course, that just calls the current method all over again, which will call itself yet again, over and over, until the program runs out of memory. Instead, you must be precise which withdraw method you want to call.

▼   Another common error is to forget to call the superclass method altogether. Then the functionality of the superclass mysteriously vanishes.

11.4 ## Subclass Construction

Let us define a constructor to set the initial balance of a checking account.

```
public class CheckingAccount extends BankAccount
{
    public CheckingAccount(double initialBalance)
    {
        // construct superclass
        . . .
        // initialize transaction count
        transactionCount = 0;
    }
    . . .
}
```

We want to invoke the BankAccount constructor to set the balance to the initial balance. There is a special instruction to call the superclass constructor from a subclass constructor. You use the keyword super, followed by the construction parameters in parentheses:

```
public class CheckingAccount extends BankAccount
{
    public CheckingAccount(double initialBalance)
    {
        // construct superclass
        super(initialBalance);
        // initialize transaction count
        transactionCount = 0;
    }
    . . .
}
```

> To call the superclass constructor, you use the super keyword in the first statement of the subclass constructor.

When the keyword super is followed by a parenthesis, it indicates a call to the superclass constructor. When used in this way, the constructor call must be *the first statement of the subclass constructor*. If super is followed by a period and a method name, on the other hand, it indicates a call to a superclass method, as you saw in the preceding section. Such a call can be made anywhere in any subclass method. The dual use of the super keyword is analogous to the dual use of the this keyword (see Advanced Topic 7.4).

If a subclass constructor does not call the superclass constructor, the superclass is constructed with its default constructor. If the superclass does not have a default constructor, then the compiler reports an error.

For example, you can implement the CheckingAccount constructor without calling the superclass constructor. Then the BankAccount class is constructed with its default constructor, which sets the balance to zero. Of course, then the CheckingAccount constructor must explicitly deposit the initial balance.

Most commonly, however, subclass constructors have some parameters that they pass on to the superclass and others that they use to initialize subclass fields.

Syntax 11.3: Calling a Superclass Constructor

ClassName(*parameters*)
{
    super(*parameters*);
    . . .
}

Example:

```
public CheckingAccount(double initialBalance)
{
    super(initialBalance);
    transactionCount = 0;
}
```

Purpose:

To invoke the constructor of the superclass. Note that this statement must be the first statement of the subclass constructor.

11.5   Converting from Subclasses to Superclasses

> Subclass references can be converted to superclass references.

The class SavingsAccount extends the class BankAccount. In other words, a SavingsAccount object is a special case of a BankAccount object. Therefore, you can store a reference to a SavingsAccount object into an object field of type BankAccount. Furthermore, all object references can be stored in a variable of type Object.

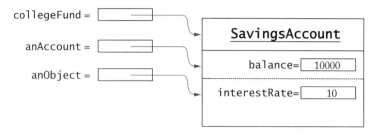

Figure 7

Variables of Different Types Refer to the Same Object

```
SavingsAccount collegeFund = new SavingsAccount(10);
BankAccount anAccount = collegeFund;
Object anObject = collegeFund;
```

Now the three object references stored in `collegeFund`, `anAccount`, and `anObject` all refer to the same object of type `SavingsAccount` (see Figure 7).

However, the object field `anAccount` knows less than the full story about the object to which it refers. Because `anAccount` is an object of type `BankAccount`, you can use the `deposit` and `withdraw` methods to change the balance of the savings account. You cannot use the `addInterest` method, though—it is not a method of the `BankAccount` superclass:

```
anAccount.deposit(1000); // OK
anAccount.addInterest();
    // No—not a method of the class to which anAccount belongs
```

And, of course, the field `anObject` knows even less. You can't even apply the `deposit` method to it—`deposit` is not a method of the `Object` class.

Conversion from a subclass type to a superclass type is very similar to the conversion from a class type to an interface type. As you saw in Chapter 9, you can convert from a class to an interface that the class realizes. For example, if `BankAccount` realizes the `Comparable` interface, then you can store a `BankAccount` object (as well as any object of a subclass of `BankAccount`) in a field of type `Comparable`.

Why would anyone *want* to know less about an object and store a reference in an object field of a superclass? This can happen if you want to reuse code that knows about the superclass but not the subclass. Here is a typical example. Consider a `transfer` method that transfers money from one account to another:

```
public void transfer(double amount, BankAccount other)
{
   withdraw(amount);
   other.deposit(amount);
}
```

You can use this method to transfer money from one bank account to another:

```
BankAccount momsAccount = . . . ;
BankAccount harrysAccount = . . . ;
momsChecking.transfer(1000, harrysAccount);
```

You can *also* use the method to transfer money into a CheckingAccount:

```
CheckingAccount harrysChecking = . . . ;
momsAccount.transfer(1000, harrysChecking);
    // OK to pass a CheckingAccount reference to a
    // method expecting a BankAccount
```

The transfer method expects a reference to a BankAccount, and it gets a reference to the subclass CheckingAccount. Fortunately, rather than complaining about a type mismatch, the compiler simply copies the subclass reference harrysChecking to the superclass reference other. The transfer method doesn't actually know that, in this case, other refers to a CheckingAccount reference. It knows only that other is a BankAccount, and it doesn't need to know anything else. All it cares about is that the other object can carry out the deposit method.

Now let us follow the method call more precisely. *Which* deposit method? The other parameter has type BankAccount, so it would appear as if BankAccount.deposit is called. On the other hand, the CheckingAccount class provides its own deposit method that updates the transaction count. The other field actually refers to an object of the subclass CheckingAccount, so it would be appropriate if the CheckingAccount.deposit method were called instead.

As you already saw in Chapter 9, method calls *are always determined by the type of the actual object*, not the type of the object reference. That is, if the actual object has the type CheckingAccount, then the CheckingAccount.deposit method is called. It does not matter that the object reference is stored in a field of type BankAccount. Recall that this mechanism is called late binding, and that the other field's ability to refer to objects of multiple types with varying behavior is called polymorphism.

Why don't we store all account references in variables of type Object? The compiler still needs the BankAccount type to confirm that there are methods such as deposit and withdraw. Those methods are defined only in the BankAccount class, not the Object class.

The following program calls the polymorphic withdraw and deposit methods. You should manually calculate what the program should print for each account balance, and confirm that the correct methods have in fact been called.

File AccountTest.java

```
 1  /**
 2      This program tests the BankAccount class and
 3      its subclasses.
 4  */
 5  public class AccountTest
 6  {
 7      public static void main(String[] args)
 8      {
 9          SavingsAccount momsSavings
10              = new SavingsAccount(0.5);
11
12          CheckingAccount harrysChecking
13              = new CheckingAccount(100);
14
15          momsSavings.deposit(10000);
```

```
16
17        momsSavings.transfer(harrysChecking, 2000);
18        harrysChecking.withdraw(1500);
19        harrysChecking.withdraw(80);
20
21        momsSavings.transfer(harrysChecking, 1000);
22        harrysChecking.withdraw(400);
23
24        // simulate end of month
25        momsSavings.addInterest();
26        harrysChecking.deductFees();
27
28        System.out.println("Mom's savings balance = $"
29           + momsSavings.getBalance());
30
31        System.out.println("Harry's checking balance = $"
32           + harrysChecking.getBalance());
33     }
34 }
```

File BankAccount.java

```
 1 /**
 2     A bank account has a balance that can be changed by
 3     deposits and withdrawals.
 4 */
 5 public class BankAccount
 6 {
 7     /**
 8         Constructs a bank account with a zero balance.
 9     */
10     public BankAccount()
11     {
12        balance = 0;
13     }
14
15     /**
16         Constructs a bank account with a given balance.
17         @param initialBalance the initial balance
18     */
19     public BankAccount(double initialBalance)
20     {
21        balance = initialBalance;
22     }
23
24     /**
25         Deposits money into the bank account.
26         @param amount the amount to deposit
27     */
28     public void deposit(double amount)
29     {
30        balance = balance + amount;
```

```java
31      }
32
33      /**
34          Withdraws money from the bank account.
35          @param amount the amount to withdraw
36      */
37      public void withdraw(double amount)
38      {
39          balance = balance - amount;
40      }
41
42      /**
43          Gets the current balance of the bank account.
44          @return the current balance
45      */
46      public double getBalance()
47      {
48          return balance;
49      }
50
51      /**
52          Transfers money from the bank account to another account.
53          @param other the other account
54          @param amount the amount to transfer
55      */
56      public void transfer(BankAccount other, double amount)
57      {
58          withdraw(amount);
59          other.deposit(amount);
60      }
61
62      private double balance;
63  }
```

File CheckingAccount.java

```java
1  /**
2      A checking account that charges transaction fees.
3  */
4  public class CheckingAccount extends BankAccount
5  {
6      /**
7          Constructs a checking account with a given balance.
8          @param initialBalance the initial balance
9      */
10      public CheckingAccount(int initialBalance)
11      {
12          // construct superclass
13          super(initialBalance);
14
15          // initialize transaction count
16          transactionCount = 0;
```

```
17      }
18
19      public void deposit(double amount)
20      {
21         transactionCount++;
22         // now add amount to balance
23         super.deposit(amount);
24      }
25
26      public void withdraw(double amount)
27      {
28         transactionCount++;
29         // now subtract amount from balance
30         super.withdraw(amount);
31      }
32
33      /**
34         Deducts the accumulated fees and resets the
35         transaction count.
36      */
37      public void deductFees()
38      {
39         if (transactionCount > FREE_TRANSACTIONS)
40         {
41            double fees = TRANSACTION_FEE *
42               (transactionCount - FREE_TRANSACTIONS);
43            super.withdraw(fees);
44         }
45         transactionCount = 0;
46      }
47
48      private int transactionCount;
49
50      private static final int FREE_TRANSACTIONS = 3;
51      private static final double TRANSACTION_FEE = 2.0;
52   }
```

File SavingsAccount.java

```
1    /**
2       An account that earns interest at a fixed rate.
3    */
4    public class SavingsAccount extends BankAccount
5    {
6       /**
7          Constructs a bank account with a given interest rate.
8          @param rate the interest rate
9       */
10      public SavingsAccount(double rate)
11      {
12         interestRate = rate;
13      }
```

```
14
15    /**
16        Adds the earned interest to the account balance.
17    */
18    public void addInterest()
19    {
20       double interest = getBalance()
21          * interestRate / 100;
22       deposit(interest);
23    }
24
25    private double interestRate;
26 }
```

▼ Advanced Topic 11.1

Abstract Classes

When you extend an existing class, you have the *choice* whether or not to redefine the methods of the superclass. Sometimes, it is desirable to *force* programmers to redefine a method. That happens when there is no good default for the superclass, and only the subclass programmer can know how to implement the method properly.

Here is an example. Suppose the First National Bank of Java decides that every account type must have some monthly fees. Therefore, a `deductFees` method should be added to the `BankAccount` class:

```
public class BankAccount
{
   public void deductFees() { . . . }
   . . .
}
```

But what should this method do? Of course, we could have the method do nothing. But then a programmer implementing a new subclass might simply forget to implement the `deduct-Fees` method, and the new account would inherit the do-nothing method of the superclass. There is a better way: namely, to declare the `deductFees` method as an *abstract method:*

```
public abstract void deductFees();
```

> An abstract method is a method whose implementation is not specified.

An abstract method has no implementation. This forces the implementors of subclasses to specify concrete implementations of this method. (Of course, some subclasses might decide to implement a do-nothing method, but then that is their choice—not a silently inherited default.)

You cannot construct objects of classes with abstract methods. For example, once the `BankAccount` class has an abstract method, the compiler will flag an attempt to create a `new BankAccount()` as an error. Of course, if the `CheckingAccount` subclass overrides the `deductFees` method and supplies an implementation, then you can create `CheckingAccount` objects.

> An abstract class is a class that cannot be instantiated.

A class for which you cannot create objects is called an *abstract class*. A class for which you can create objects is sometimes called a *concrete class*. In Java, you must declare all abstract classes with the keyword `abstract`:

```
public abstract class BankAccount
{
    public abstract void deductFees();
    . . .
}
```

A class that defines an abstract method, or that inherits an abstract method without overriding it, *must* be declared as abstract. You can also declare classes with no abstract methods as abstract. Doing so prevents programmers from creating instances of that class but allows them to create their own subclasses.

Note that you cannot construct an *object* of an abstract class, but you can still have an *object reference* whose type is an abstract class. Of course, the actual object to which it refers must be an instance of a concrete subclass:

```
BankAccount anAccount; // OK
anAccount = new BankAccount(); // Error—BankAccount is abstract
anAccount = new SavingsAccount(); // OK
anAccount = null; // OK
```

The reason for using abstract classes is to force programmers to create subclasses. By specifying certain methods as abstract, you avoid the trouble of coming up with useless default methods that others might inherit by accident.

Abstract classes differ from interfaces in an important way—they can have instance fields, and they can have some concrete methods.

Advanced Topic   11.2

Final Methods and Classes

In Advanced Topic 11.1 you saw how you can force other programmers to create subclasses of abstract classes and override abstract methods. Occasionally, you may want to do the opposite and *prevent* other programmers from creating subclasses or from overriding certain methods. In these situations, you use the `final` keyword. For example, the `String` class in the standard Java library has been declared as

```
public final class String { . . . }
```

That means that nobody can extend the `String` class. The reason is twofold. The compiler can generate more efficient method calls if it knows that it doesn't have to worry about late binding. Also, the `String` class is meant to be *immutable*—string objects can't be modified by any of their methods. Since the Java language does not enforce this, the class designers did. Nobody can create subclasses of `String`; therefore, you know that all `String` references can be copied without the risk of mutation.

▼ You can also declare individual methods as final:

▼
```
public class MyApplet extends Applet
{
   . . .
   public final boolean checkPassword(String password)
   {
      . . .
   }
}
```

▼

▼

This way, nobody can override the `checkPassword` method with another method that simply returns `true`.

11.6   Access Control

Java has four levels of controlling access to fields, methods, and classes:

- `public` access

- `private` access

- `protected` access (see Advanced Topic 11.3)

- Package access (the default, when no access modifier is given)

You have already used the `private` and `public` modifiers extensively. Private features can be accessed only by the methods of their own class. Public features can be accessed by methods of all classes. We will discuss protected access in Advanced Topic 11.3—we will not need it in this book.

> A field or method that is not declared as `public`, `private`, or `protected` can be accessed by all classes in the same package, which is usually not desirable.

If you do not supply an access control modifier, then the default is *package access*. That is, all methods of classes in the same package can access the feature. For example, if a class is declared as `public`, then all other classes in all packages can use it. But if a class is declared without an access modifier, then only the other classes in the same package can use it. Package access is a good default for classes, but it is extremely unfortunate for fields. Instance and static fields of classes should always be `private`. There are a few exceptions:

- Public constants (`public static final` fields) are useful and safe.

- Some objects, such as `System.out`, need to be accessible to all programs and therefore should be public.

- Very occasionally, several classes in a package must collaborate very closely. In that case, it may make sense to give some fields package access. But inner classes are usually a better solution—you will see examples in Chapter 19.

However, it is a common error to *forget* the keyword `private`, thereby opening up a potential security hole. For example, at the time of this writing, the `Window` class in the `java.awt` package contained the following declaration:

```
public class Window extends Container
{
    String warningString;
    . . .
}
```

The programmer was careless and didn't make the field private. There actually was no good reason to grant package access to the `warningString` field—*no other class accesses it.* It is a security risk. Packages are not closed entities—any programmer can make a new class, add it to the `java.awt` package, and gain access to the `warningString` fields of all `Window` objects! (Actually, this possibility bothered the Java implementors so much that recent versions of the class loader refuse to load classes whose package name starts with "`java.`". Your own packages, however, do not enjoy this protection.)

Package access for fields is very rarely useful, and most fields are given package access by accident because the programmer simply forgot the `private` keyword.

Methods should generally be `public` or `private`. Public methods are the norm. Private methods make sense for implementation-dependent tasks that should be carried out only by methods of the same class. Methods with package access can be called by any other method in the same package. That can occasionally make sense if a package consists of a small number of closely collaborating classes, but more often than not, it is simply an accident—the programmer forgot the `public` modifier. We recommend that you do not use package-visible methods.

Classes and interfaces can have public or package access. Classes that are generally useful should have public access. Classes that are used for implementation reasons should have package access. You can hide them even better by turning them into inner classes; you saw examples of inner classes in Chapter 9. There are a few examples of public inner classes, such as the familiar `Ellipse.Float` and `Ellipse.Double` classes. However, in general, inner classes should be private.

Common Error 11.4

Accidental Package Access

It is very easy to forget the `private` modifier for instance fields.

```
public class BankAccount
{
    . . .
    double balance; // Package access really intended?
}
```

Most likely, this was just an oversight. Probably the programmer never intended to grant access to this field to other classes in the same package. The compiler won't complain, of course. Much later, some other programmer may take advantage of the access privilege, either out of convenience or out of evil intent. This is a serious problem, and you must get into the habit of scanning your field declarations for missing `private` modifiers.

⊗ Common Error   11.5

Making Inherited Methods Less Accessible

If a superclass declares a method to be publicly accessible, you cannot override it to be more private. For example,

```
public class BankAccount
{
    public void withdraw(double amount) { . . . }
    . . .
}

public CheckingAccount
{
    private void withdraw(double amount) { . . . }
        // Error—subclass method cannot be more private
    . . .
}
```

The compiler does not allow this, because the increased privacy would be an *illusion*. Anyone can still call the method through a superclass reference:

```
BankAccount account = new CheckingAccount();
account.withdraw(100000); // calls CheckingAccount.withdraw
```

Because of late binding, the subclass method is called.

These errors are usually an oversight. If you forget the `public` modifier, your subclass method has package access, which is more restrictive. Simply restore the `public` modifier, and the error will go away.

Advanced Topic   11.3

Protected Access

> Protected features can be accessed by all subclasses and all classes in the same package.

We ran into some degree of grief when trying to implement the `deposit` method of the `CheckingAccount` class. That method needed access to the `balance` instance field of the superclass. Our remedy was to use the appropriate methods of the superclass to set the balance.

▼ Java offers another solution to this problem. The superclass can declare an instance field as *protected:*

▼
```
public class BankAccount
{
    . . .
    protected double balance;
}
```

▼ Protected data in an object can be accessed by the methods of the object's class and all its subclasses. For example, CheckingAccount inherits from BankAccount, so its methods can access the protected instance fields of the BankAccount class. Furthermore, protected data can be accessed by all methods of classes in the same package.

▼ Some programmers like the protected access feature because it seems to strike a balance between absolute protection (making all fields private) and no protection at all (making all fields public). However, experience has shown that protected fields are subject to the same kind of problems as public fields. The designer of the superclass has no control over the authors of subclasses. Any of the subclass methods can corrupt the superclass data. Furthermore, classes with protected fields are hard to modify. Even if the author of the superclass would like to change the data implementation, the protected fields cannot be changed, because someone somewhere out there might have written a subclass whose code depends on them.

▼ In Java, protected field have another drawback—they are accessible not just by subclasses but also by other classes in the same package.

It is best to leave all data private. If you want to grant access to the data only to subclass methods, consider making the *accessor* method protected.

11.7 Object: The Cosmic Superclass

In Java, every class that does not extend another class automatically extends the class Object. That is, the class Object is the direct or indirect superclass of *every* class in Java (see Figure 8).

Of course, the methods of the Object class are very general. Here are the most useful ones:

Method	Purpose
String toString()	Returns a string representation of the object
boolean equals(Object otherObject)	Tests whether the object equals another object
Object clone()	Makes a full copy of an object

It is a good idea for you to override these in your classes.

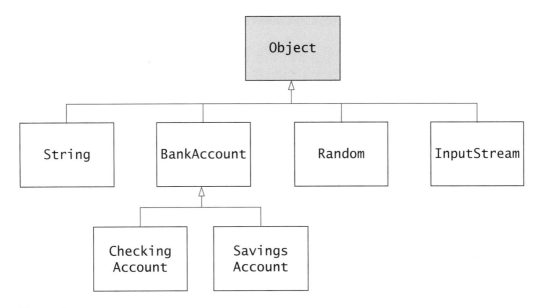

Figure 8

The Object Class Is the Superclass of Every Java Class

11.7.1 — Overriding the toString Method

> You should define the toString method to yield a string that describes the object state.

The toString method returns a string representation for each object. It is used for debugging. For example,

```
Rectangle cerealBox = new Rectangle(5, 10, 20, 30);
String s = cerealBox.toString();
/* sets s to
     "java.awt.Rectangle[x=5,y=10,width=20,height=30]"
*/
```

In fact, this toString method is called whenever you concatenate a string with an object. Consider the concatenation

```
"cerealBox=" + cerealBox;
```

On one side of the + concatenation operator is a string, but on the other side is an object reference. The Java compiler automatically invokes the toString method to turn the object into a string. Then both strings are concatenated. In this case, the result is the string

```
"cerealBox=java.awt.Rectangle[x=5,y=10,width=20,height=30]"
```

This works only if one of the objects is already a string. If you try to apply the + operator to two objects, neither of which is a string, then the compiler reports an error.

The compiler can invoke the toString method, because it knows that *every* object has a toString method: Every class extends the Object class, and that class defines toString.

As you know, numbers are also converted to strings when they are concatenated with other strings. For example,

```
int age = 18;
String s = "Harry's age is " + age;
    // sets s to "Harry's age is 18"
```

In this case, the `toString` method is not involved. Numbers are not objects, and there is no `toString` method for them. There is only a small set of primitive types, however, and the compiler knows how to convert them to strings.

Let's try the `toString` method for the `BankAccount` class:

```
BankAccount momsSavings = new BankAccount(5000);
String s = momsSavings.toString();
    // sets s to something like "BankAccount@d24606bf"
```

That's disappointing—all that's printed is the name of the class, followed by the address of the object in memory. We don't care *where* the object is in memory. We want to know what is inside the object, but, of course, the `toString` method of the `Object` class does not know what is inside our `BankAccount` class. Therefore, we have to override the method and supply our own version in the `BankAccount` class. We'll follow the same format that the `toString` method of the `Rectangle` class uses: First print the name of the class, and then the values of the instance fields inside brackets.

```
public class BankAccount
{
    . . .
    public String toString()
    {
        return "BankAccount[balance=" + balance + "]";
    }
}
```

This works better:

```
BankAccount momsSavings = new BankAccount(5000);
String s = momsSavings.toString();
    // sets s to "BankAccount[balance=5000]"
```

Productivity Hint 11.1

Supply `toString` in All Classes

If you have a class whose `toString()` method returns a string that describes the object state, then you can simply call `System.out.println(x)` whenever you need to inspect the current state of an object x. This works because the `println` method of the `Print-Stream` class invokes `x.toString()` when it needs to print an object. That is extremely helpful if there is an error in your program and your objects don't behave the way you

▼ think they should. You can simply insert a few print statements and peek inside the object state during the program run. Some debuggers can even invoke the `toString` method on objects that you inspect.

▼   Sure, it is a bit more trouble to write a `toString` method when you aren't sure your program ever needs one—after all, it might just work correctly on the first try. Then again, many programs don't work on the first try. As soon as you find out that yours doesn't, con-

▼ sider adding those `toString` methods so that you can easily print out objects.

▼   **AT**   **Advanced Topic**   **11.4**

Inheritance and the `toString` Method

▼ You just saw how to write a `toString` method: Form a string consisting of the class name and the names and values of the instance fields. However, if you want your

▼ `toString` method to be usable by subclasses of your class, you need to work a bit harder. Instead of hard-coding the class name, you should call the `getClass` method to obtain a *class* object, an object of the `Class` class that describes classes and their properties. Then

▼ invoke the `getName` method to get the name of the class:

```
public String toString()
{
   return getClass().getName() + "[balance="
      + balance + "]";
}
```

Then the `toString` method prints the correct class name when you apply it to a sub-class, say a `SavingsAccount`.

```
SavingsAccount momsSavings = . . .;
System.out.println(momsSavings);
// prints "SavingsAccount[balance=10000]"
```

▼ Of course, in the subclass, you should override `toString` and add the values of the sub-class instance fields. Note that you must call `super.toString` to get the superclass field values—the subclass can't access them directly.

```
public class SavingsAccount extends BankAccount
{
   public String toString()
   {
      return super.toString() +
         "[interestRate=" + interestRate + "]";
   }
}
```

▼ Now a savings account is converted to a string such as `SavingsAccount[balance=10000][interestRate=10]`. The brackets show which fields belong to the superclass.

11.7.2 — Overriding the equals Method

> You should define the equals method to test whether two objects have equal state.

The equals method is called whenever you want to compare whether two objects have the same contents:

```
if (coin1.equals(coin2)) . . .
    // contents are the same—see Figure 9
```

That is different from the test with the == operator. That operator tests whether the two references are to the *same* object:

```
if (coin1 == coin2) . . .
    // objects are the same—see Figure 10
```

Let us implement the equals method for the Coin class. You need to override the equals method of the Object class:

```
public class Coin
{
    . . .
    public boolean equals(Object otherObject)
    {
        . . .
    }
    . . .
}
```

Figure 9

Two References to Equal Objects

Figure 10

Two References to the Same Object

Now you have a slight problem. The Object class knows nothing about bank accounts, so it defines the otherObject parameter of the equals method to have the type Object. When redefining the method, you are not allowed to change the object signature. Cast the parameter to the class Coin:

```
Coin other = (Coin)otherObject;
```

Then you can compare the two coins.

```
public boolean equals(Object otherObject)
{
   Coin other = (Coin)otherObject;
   return name.equals(other.name)
      && value == other.value;
}
```

Note that you must use equals to compare object fields, but you use == to compare number fields.

▼ **Advanced Topic** **11.5**

Inheritance and the equals Method

You just saw how to write an equals method: Cast the otherObject parameter to the type of your class, and then compare the fields of the implicit parameter and the other parameter.

But what if someone called coin1.equals(x) where x wasn't a Coin object? Then the bad cast would generate an exception, and the program would die. Therefore, you first want to test whether otherObject really is an instance of the Coin class. The easiest test would be with the instanceof operator. However, that test is not specific enough. It would be possible for otherObject to belong to some subclass of Coin. To rule out that possibility, you should test whether the two objects belong to the *same class*. If not, return false.

```
if (getClass() != otherObject.getClass()) return false;
```

Moreover, the Java language specification [1] demands that the equals method return false when otherObject is null.

Here is an improved version of the equals method that takes these two points into account:

```
public boolean equals(Object otherObject)
{
   if (otherObject == null) return false;
   if (getClass() != otherObject.getClass())
      return false;

   Coin other = (Coin)otherObject;
   return name.equals(other.name)
      && value == other.value;
}
```

When you define equals in a subclass, you should first call equals in the superclass, like this:

```
public CollectibleCoin extends Coin
{
```

▼
```
    . . .
    public boolean equals(Object otherObject)
    {
        if (!super.equals(otherObject)) return false;
```
▼
```
        CollectibleCoin other =
            (CollectibleCoin)otherObject;
        return year == other.year;
    }
```
▼
```
    private int year;
}
```
▼

11.7.3 — Overriding the clone Method

> The clone method makes a new object with the same state as an existing object.

You know that copying an object reference simply gives you two references to the same object:

```
BankAccount account1 = new BankAccount(1000);
BankAccount account2 = account1;
account2.deposit(500);
    // now both account1 and account2 have a balance of 1500
```

What can you do if you actually want to make a copy of an object? That is the purpose of the clone method. The clone method must return a *new* object that has identical state to the existing object (see Figure 11). Here is a clone method for the Bank-Account class.

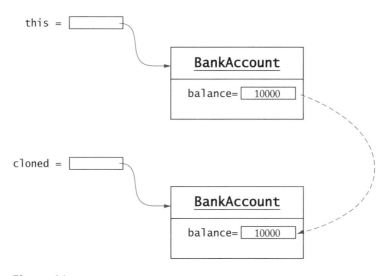

Figure 11

Cloning Objects

```
public class BankAccount
{  . . .
   public Object clone()
   {
      BankAccount cloned = new BankAccount();
      cloned.balance = balance;
      return cloned;
   }
}
```

It is more difficult to define the clone method for subclasses. See Advanced Topic 11.6 for details.

Since the clone method is defined in the Object class, it cannot know the *type* of the object to be returned. Therefore, its return type is Object. That is not a problem when implementing the clone method. But when you call the method, you must use a cast to convince the compiler that account1.clone() really has the same type as account1. Here is an example:

```
BankAccount account2 = (BankAccount)account1.clone();
```

▼ **Common Error** **11.6**

Forgetting to Clone

▼

In Java, object fields contain references to objects, not actual objects. This can be convenient for giving *two names to the same object:*

▼
```
BankAccount harrysChecking = new BankAccount();
BankAccount slushFund = harrysChecking;
    // Use Harry's checking account for the slush fund
▼
slushFund.deposit(80000)
    // a lot of money ends up in Harry's checking account
```

However, if you don't intend two references to refer to the same object, then this is a
▼
problem. In that case, you should use the clone method:

```
BankAccount slushFund = (BankAccount)harrysChecking.clone();
```

▼ **Quality Tip** **11.1**

Clone Mutable Instance Fields in Accessor Methods

▼

Consider the following class:

```
public class Customer
{
▼
   public Customer(String aName)
```

```
      {
         name = aName;
         account = new BankAccount();
      }

      public String getName()
      {
         return name;
      }

      public BankAccount getAccount();
      {
         return account;
      }

      private String name;
      private BankAccount account;
   }
```

This class looks very boring and normal, but the `getAccount` method has a curious property. It *breaks encapsulation*, because anyone can modify the object state without going through the public interface:

```
   Customer harry = new Customer("Harry Handsome");
   BankAccount account = harry.getAccount();
      // anyone can withdraw money!
   account.withdraw(100000);
```

Maybe that wasn't what the designers of the class had in mind? Maybe they wanted class users only to inspect the account? In such a situation, you should *clone* the object reference:

```
   public BankAccount getAccount();
   {
      return (BankAccount)account.clone();
   }
```

Do you also need to clone the `getName` method? No—that method returns a string, and strings are immutable. It is safe to give out a reference to an immutable object.

The rule of thumb is that a class should clone all references to mutable objects that it gives out.

Advanced Topic 11.6

Inheritance and the `clone` Method

You saw how to clone an object by constructing a new object with the same state:

```
   public Object clone()
   {
```

```
            BankAccount cloned = new BankAccount();
            cloned.balance = balance;
            return cloned;
        }
```

This method has an important limitation: It doesn't work for subclasses.

```
        SavingsAccount momsSavings = . . .;
        Object clonedAccount = momsSavings.clone();
```

The clone method constructs a new *bank account*, not a savings account!

It is better to use the Object.clone method to do the cloning. That method creates a new object of the same type as the original object. It also automatically copies the instance fields from the original object to the cloned object.

```
        public class BankAccount
        {  . . .
            public Object clone()
            {
                // not complete
                Object clonedAccount = super.clone();
                return clonedAccount;
            }
        }
```

However, this Object.clone method must be used with care. It only shifts the problem of cloning by one level; it does not completely solve it. Specifically, if an object contains a reference to another object, then the Object.clone method makes a copy of that object reference, not a clone of that object. Figure 12 shows how the Object.clone method works with a Customer object that has references to a String object and a BankAccount object.

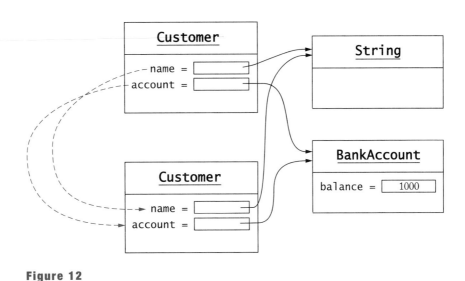

Figure 12

The Object.clone Method Makes a Shallow Copy

As you can see, the `Object.clone` method copies the references to the cloned `Customer` object and does not clone the objects to which they refer. Such a copy is called a *shallow copy*.

There is a reason why the `Object.clone` method does not systematically clone all subobjects. In some situations, it is unnecessary. For example, if an object contains a reference to a string, there is no harm in copying the string reference, because Java string objects can never change their contents. The `Object.clone` method does the right thing if an object contains only numbers, Boolean values, and strings. But it must be used with caution when an object contains references to other objects.

For that reason, there are two safeguards built into the `Object.clone` method to ensure that it is not used accidentally. First, the method is declared `protected` (see Advanced Topic 11.3). This prevents you from accidentally calling `x.clone()` if the class to which x belongs hasn't redefined `clone` to be public.

As a second precaution, `Object.clone` checks that the object being cloned implements the `Cloneable` interface. If not, it throws an exception. That is, the `Object.clone` method looks like this:

```java
public class Object
{
    protected Object clone()
        throws CloneNotSupportedException
    {
        if (this instanceof Cloneable)
        {
            // copy the instance fields
            . . .
        }
        else
            throw new CloneNotSupportedException();
    }
}
```

Unfortunately, all that safeguarding means that the legitimate callers of `Object.clone()` pay a price—they must catch that exception *even if their class implements* `Cloneable`.

```java
public class BankAccount implements Cloneable
{
    . . .
    public Object clone()
    {
        try
        {
            return super.clone();;
        }
        catch (CloneNotSupportedException e)
        {
            // can't happen because we implement Cloneable
            // but we still must catch it
            return null;
        }
```

```
      }
   }
```

If an object contains a reference to another mutable object, then you need to call `clone` for that reference. For example, suppose the `Customer` class has an instance field of class `BankAccount`. Then you can implement `Customer.clone` as follows:

```
public class Customer implements Cloneable
{
   . . .
   public Object clone()
   {
      try
      {
         Customer cloned = (Customer)super.clone();
         cloned.account = (BankAccount)account.clone();
         return cloned;
      }
      catch(CloneNotSupportedException e)
      {
         // can't ever happen because we implement Cloneable
         return null;
      }
   }

   private String name;
   private BankAccount account;
}
```

Random Fact   11.1

Scripting Languages

Suppose you work for an office where you have to help with the bookkeeping. Suppose that every sales person sends in a weekly spreadsheet with sales figures. One of your jobs is to copy and paste the individual figures into a master spreadsheet and then copy and paste the totals into a word processor document that gets emailed to several managers. This kind of repetitive work can be intensely boring. Can you automate it?

It would be a real challenge to write a Java program that can help you—you'd have to know how to read a spreadsheet file, how to format a word processor document, and how to send email.

Fortunately, many office software packages nowadays include *scripting languages*. These are programming languages that are integrated with the software for the purpose of automating repetitive tasks. The best-known of these scripting languages is Visual Basic Script, which is a part of the Microsoft Office suite. The Macintosh operating system has a language called AppleScript for the same purpose.

In addition, scripting languages are available for many other purposes. JavaScript is used for web pages. (There is no relationship between Java and JavaScript—the name JavaScript was chosen for marketing reasons.) Tcl (short for "tool control language" and pronounced "tickle") is an open source scripting language that has been ported to many platforms and is often used for scripting software test procedures. Productivity Hint 8.1 has more information about shell scripts.

Scripting languages have two features that makes them easier to use than full-fledged programming languages such as Java. First, they are *interpreted*. The interpreter program reads each line of program code and executes it immediately without compiling it first. That makes experimenting much more fun—you get immediate feedback. Also, scripting languages are usually *loosely typed*. That means, you don't have to declare the types of variables. Every variable can hold values of any type. For example, Figure 13 shows a scripting session with BeanShell, a scripting language for Java objects. The script stores frame and button objects in variables that are declared just by using them. It then sets a couple of properties and calls methods that are executed immediately—the frame pops up as soon as the line with the show command is typed. (You can download BeanShell from http://www.beanshell.org.)

In recent years, authors of computer viruses have discovered how scripting languages simplify their life. The famous "love bug" is a Visual Basic Script program that is sent as an attachment to an email. The email has an enticing subject line "I love you" and asks the recipient to click on an attachment masquerading as a love letter. In fact, the attachment is a script file that is executed when the user clicks on it. The script creates some damage on the recipient's computer and then, through the power of the scripting language, uses the Outlook email client to mail itself to all addresses found in the address book. Try programming that in Java! By the way, the person suspected of

Figure 13

Writing a BeanShell Script

▼ authoring that virus was a student who had submitted a proposal to write a thesis researching how to write such programs. Perhaps not surprisingly, the proposal was rejected by the faculty.

▼ Why do we still need Java if scripting is easy and fun? Scripts often have poor error checking and are difficult to adapt to new circumstances. Scripting languages lack many of the structuring and safety mechanisms (such as classes and type checking by the compiler) that are important for building robust and scalable programs.

CHAPTER SUMMARY

1. Inheritance is a method for extending existing classes by adding methods and fields.

2. The more general class is called a superclass. The more specialized class that inherits from the superclass is called the subclass.

3. Every class extends the `Object` class either directly or indirectly.

4. Inheriting from a class differs from realizing an interface: The subclass inherits behavior and state from the superclass.

5. One advantage of inheritance is code reuse.

6. When defining a subclass, you specify added instance fields, added methods, and changed or *overridden* methods.

7. Sets of classes can form complex inheritance hierarchies.

8. A subclass has no access to private fields of its superclass.

9. Use the `super` keyword to call a method of the superclass.

10. To call the superclass constructor, you use the `super` keyword in the first statement of the subclass constructor.

11. Subclass references can be converted to superclass references.

12. An abstract method is a method whose implementation is not specified.

13. An abstract class is a class that cannot be instantiated.

14. A field or method that is not declared as `public`, `private`, or `protected` can be accessed by all classes in the same package, which is usually not desirable.

15. Protected features can be accessed by all subclasses and all classes in the same package.

16. You should define the `toString` method to yield a string that describes the object state.

17. You should define the `equals` method to test whether two objects have equal state.

18. The `clone` method makes a new object with the same state as an existing object.

Further Reading

[1] James Gosling, Bill Joy, and Guy Steele, *The Java Language Specification*, Addison-Wesley, 1996.

CLASSES, OBJECTS, AND METHODS INTRODUCED IN THIS CHAPTER

```
java.lang.Cloneable
java.lang.Comparable
    compareTo
java.lang.Object
    clone
    toString
```

REVIEW EXERCISES

Exercise R11.1. What is the balance of b after the following operations?

```
SavingsAccount b = new SavingsAccount(10);
b.deposit(5000);
b.withdraw(b.getBalance() / 2);
b.addInterest();
```

Exercise R11.2. Describe all constructors of the SavingsAccount class. List all methods that are inherited from the BankAccount class. List all methods that are added to the SavingsAccount class.

Exercise R11.3. Can you convert a superclass reference into a subclass reference? A subclass reference into a superclass reference? If so, give an example. If not, explain why.

Exercise R11.4. In the following pairs of classes, identify the superclass and the subclass:

- Employee, Manager
- Polygon, Triangle
- GraduateStudent, Student
- Person, Student
- Employee, GraduateStudent
- BankAccount, CheckingAccount
- Vehicle, Car
- Vehicle, Minivan
- Car, Minivan
- Truck, Vehicle

Exercise R11.5. Suppose the class Sub extends the class Sandwich. Which of the following assignments are legal?

```
Sandwich x = new Sandwich();
Sub y = new Sub();
x = y;
y = x;
y = new Sandwich();
x = new Sub();
```

Exercise R11.6. Draw an inheritance diagram that shows the inheritance relationships between the classes

- `Person`
- `Employee`
- `Student`
- `Instructor`
- `Classroom`
- `Object`

Exercise R11.7. In an object-oriented traffic simulation system, we have the following classes:

- `Vehicle`
- `Car`
- `Truck`
- `Sedan`
- `Coupe`
- `PickupTruck`
- `SportUtilityVehicle`
- `Minivan`
- `Bicycle`
- `Motorcycle`

Draw an inheritance diagram that shows the relationships between these classes.

Exercise R11.8. What inheritance relationships would you establish among the following classes?

- `Student`
- `Professor`
- `TeachingAssistant`
- `Employee`
- `Secretary`
- `DepartmentChair`
- `Janitor`
- `SeminarSpeaker`
- `Person`
- `Course`
- `Seminar`
- `Lecture`
- `ComputerLab`

Exercise R11.9. Which of these conditions returns `true`? Check the Java documentation for the inheritance patterns.

```
Rectangle r = new Rectangle(5, 10, 20, 30);
if (r instanceof Rectangle) . . .
if (r instanceof Point) . . .
if (r instanceof Rectangle2D.Double) . . .
if (r instanceof RectangularShape) . . .
if (r instanceof Object) . . .
if (r instanceof Shape) . . .
```

Exercise R11.10. Explain the two meanings of the `super` keyword. Explain the two meanings of the `this` keyword. How are they related?

Exercise R11.11. (Tricky.) Consider the two calls

```
public class D extends B
{
   public void f()
   {
      this.g(); // 1
   }
   public void g()
   {
      super.g(); // 2
   }
   . . .
}
```

Which of them is an example of early binding? Which of them is an example of late binding?

Exercise R11.12. Consider this program:

```
public class AccountTest
{
   public static void main(String[] args)
   {
      SavingsAccount momsSavings
         = new SavingsAccount(0.5);

      CheckingAccount harrysChecking
         = new CheckingAccount(0);

      . . .
      endOfMonth(momsSavings);
      endOfMonth(harrysChecking);
      printBalance(momsSavings);
      printBalance(harrysChecking);
   }

   public static void endOfMonth(SavingsAccount savings)
   {
      savings.addInterest();
   }

   public static void endOfMonth(CheckingAccount checking)
   {
      checking.deductFees();
   }

   public static void printBalance(BankAccount account)
   {
      System.out.println("The balance is $"
         + account.getBalance());
   }
}
```

Are the calls to the endOfMonth methods resolved by early binding or late binding? Inside the printBalance method, is the call to getBalance resolved by early binding or late binding?

Exercise R11.13. Explain the terms *shallow copy* and *deep copy*.

Exercise R11.14. What access attribute should instance fields have? What access attribute should static fields have? How about static final fields?

Exercise R11.15. What access attribute should instance methods have? Does the same hold for static methods?

Exercise R11.16. The fields System.in and System.out are static public fields. Is it possible to overwrite them? If so, how?

Exercise R11.17. Why are public fields dangerous? Are public static fields more dangerous than public instance fields?

PROGRAMMING EXERCISES

Exercise P11.1. Enhance the addInterest method of the SavingsAccount class to compute the interest on the *minimum* balance since the last call to addInterest. *Hint:* You need to modify the withdraw method as well, and you need to add an instance field to remember the minimum balance.

Exercise P11.2. Add a TimeDepositAccount class to the bank account hierarchy. The time deposit account is just like a savings account, but you promise to leave the money in the account for a particular number of months, and there is a penalty for early withdrawal. Construct the account with the interest rate and the number of months to maturity. In the addInterest method, decrement the count of months. If the count is positive during a withdrawal, charge the withdrawal penalty.

Exercise P11.3. Implement a subclass Square that extends the Rectangle class. In the constructor, accept the *x*- and *y*-positions of the *center* and the side length of the square. Call the setLocation and setSize methods of the Rectangle class. Look up these methods in the documentation for the Rectangle class. Also supply a method getArea that computes and returns the area of the square. Write a sample program that asks for the center and side length, then prints out the square (using the toString method that you inherit from Rectangle) and the area of the square.

Exercise P11.4. Implement a superclass Person. Make two classes, Student and Instructor, inherit from Person. A person has a name and a year of birth. A student has a major, and an instructor has a salary. Write the class definitions, the constructors, and the methods toString for all classes. Supply a test program that tests these classes and methods.

Exercise P11.5. Make a class Employee with a name and salary. Make a class Manager inherit from Employee. Add an instance field, named department, of type String.

Supply a method `toString` that prints the manager's name, department, and salary. Make a class `Executive` inherit from `Manager`. Supply appropriate `toString` methods for all classes. Supply a test program that tests these classes and methods.

Exercise P11.6. Write a superclass `Worker` and subclasses `HourlyWorker` and `Salaried-Worker`. Every worker has a name and a salary rate. Write a method `computePay(int hours)` that computes the weekly pay for every worker. An hourly worker gets paid the hourly wage for the actual number of hours worked, if `hours` is at most 40. If the hourly worker worked more than 40 hours, the excess is paid at time and a half. The salaried worker gets paid the hourly wage for 40 hours, no matter what the actual number of hours is. Supply a test program that uses polymorphism to test these classes and methods.

Exercise P11.7. Implement a superclass `Vehicle` and subclasses `Car` and `Truck`. A vehicle has a position on the screen. Write methods `draw` that draw cars and trucks as follows:

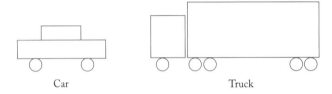

Car   Truck

Then write a method `randomVehicle` that randomly generates `Vehicle` references, with an equal probability for constructing cars and trucks, with random positions. Call it 10 times and draw all of them.

Exercise P11.8. Implement the `toString`, `equals`, and `clone` methods for all three bank account classes used in this chapter.

Exercise P11.9. Implement the `toString`, `equals`, and `clone` methods for the `Coin` and `Purse` classes of Chapter 7.

Exercise P11.10. Reorganize the bank account classes as follows. In the `BankAccount` class, introduce an abstract method `endOfMonth` with no implementation. Rename the `addInterest` and `deductFees` methods into `endOfMonth` in the subclasses. Which classes are now abstract and which are concrete? Write a static method `void test(BankAccount account)` that makes five random transactions, prints out the balance after each of them, and then calls `endOfMonth` and prints the balance once again. Test it with instances of all concrete account classes.

Graphical User Interfaces

To use inheritance to customize panels and frames

▶ To understand how user interface components are added to a container

▶ To understand the use of layout managers to arrange user interface components in a container

▶ To become familiar with common user interface components such as buttons, text components, combo boxes, and menus

▶ To build programs that handle events from user interface components

▶ To learn how to browse the Java documentation

U p to now, your graphical programs received user input from an option dialog or a mouse. The graphical applications with which you are familiar, on the other hand, have a large number of visual gadgets for information entry: buttons, scroll bars, menus, and so on. In this chapter, you will learn how to use the most common user interface components in the Java Swing user interface toolkit. However, Swing has many more components than you can master in a first course, and even the basic components have many advanced options that we cannot cover here. In fact, few programmers ever try to learn everything about a particular user interface component. It is much better to understand the concepts and to search the Java documentation for the details. This chapter walks you through one example to show you how the Java documentation is organized and how you can rely on it for your own programming.

CHAPTER CONTENTS

12.1   Using Inheritance to Customize Panels

In Chapter 10 you saw how to implement applications that show results in a text area. However, those applications were not able to produce any graphical output. In this section, you will learn how to add graphics to a Java application.

Recall how you produce graphics in an applet. You extend the Applet class and override the paint method:

```
public class MyApplet extends Applet
{
    public void paint(Graphics g)
    {
        // your drawing instructions go here
        . . .
    }
    . . .
}
```

This approach does not work for frames, however. You should not directly draw onto the surface of a frame. Frames have been designed to arrange *user interface components* such as buttons, menus, and scroll bars. Drawing directly on the frame interferes with the display of the user interface components. If you want to show graphics in a frame, you draw the graphics onto a JPanel and add it to the frame. A JPanel is completely blank, and you can draw onto it what you like.

> You can draw graphical shapes on a panel by overriding the paintComponent method of a JPanel subclass.

Drawing on a panel is a bit different from drawing on an applet. You override the paintComponent method. There is a second important difference. When implementing your own paintComponent method, you *must* call the paintComponent method of the superclass. This gives the superclass method a chance to erase the old contents of the panel.

Here is an outline of the paintComponent method:

```
public class MyPanel extends JPanel
{
    public void paintComponent(Graphics g)
    {
```

```
        super.paintComponent(g);
        Graphics2D g2 = (Graphics2D)g;

        // your drawing instructions go here
        . . .
    }
}
```

Once you have called `super.paintComponent` and obtained a `Graphics2D` object, you are ready to draw graphical shapes in the usual way.

By default, panels have a size of 0 by 0 pixels. Therefore, a panel should set its *preferred size* in its constructor, like this:

```
public class MyPanel
{
    public MyPanel()
    {
        setPreferredSize(
            new Dimension(PANEL_WIDTH, PANEL_HEIGHT));
        . . .
    }
    . . .
    private static final int PANEL_WIDTH = 300;
    private static final int PANEL_HEIGHT = 300;
}
```

Recall the `MouseApplet` program from Chapter 10. That applet draws a rectangle at the position of a mouse click. Let us turn the applet into an application.

We need a panel to do the drawing. In the constructor, we set the preferred size and add a mouse listener.

```
public class RectanglePanel extends JPanel
{
    public RectanglePanel()
    {
        setPreferredSize(
            new Dimension(PANEL_WIDTH, PANEL_HEIGHT));

        // add mouse press listener
        . . .
    }

    public void paintComponent(Graphics g)
    {
        super.paintComponent(g);
        Graphics2D g2 = (Graphics2D)g;
        . . .
    }

    . . .
}
```

> A panel class that paints a drawing on the panel should store all data that it needs to repaint itself.

When implementing a panel such as the `RectanglePanel`, you need to think about minimizing the interrelationship between the component and the rest of your program. If you store information in the wrong place, you keep handing it back and forth all the time. A good rule of thumb is: *A panel should store the data that it needs to repaint itself.* In our case, the information is simple—just a rectangle. For more complex drawings, the panel needs to store the collection of all elements that are needed for recreating the drawing.

```java
public class RectanglePanel extends JPanel
{
    public RectanglePanel()
    {
        // the rectangle that the paint method draws
        box = new Rectangle(. . .);
        . . .
    }

    public void paintComponent(Graphics g)
    {
        super.paintComponent(g);
        Graphics2D g2 = (Graphics2D)g;
        g2.draw(box);
    }

    private Rectangle box;
    . . .
}
```

You will find the code for the complete class at the end of this section.

Now you need a second class to launch an application that displays this panel in a frame:

File RectangleTest.java

```java
 1  import javax.swing.JButton;
 2  import javax.swing.JFrame;
 3  import javax.swing.JLabel;
 4  import javax.swing.JPanel;
 5  import javax.swing.JTextField;
 6
 7  /**
 8     This program displays a frame containing a RectanglePanel.
 9  */
10  public class RectangleTest
11  {
12     public static void main(String[] args)
13     {
14        RectanglePanel rectPanel =
15           new RectanglePanel();
```

```
16
17        JFrame appFrame = new JFrame();
18        appFrame.setDefaultCloseOperation(
19            JFrame.EXIT_ON_CLOSE);
20        appFrame.setContentPane(rectPanel);
21        appFrame.pack();
22        appFrame.show();
23    }
24 }
```

Figure 1 shows the layout of the application. Figure 2 shows the relationships between the classes.

The result is a program that acts exactly like the MouseApplet. Because this is an application, you don't need to use the applet viewer, and you don't need to produce an HTML file.

File RectanglePanel.java

```
1 import java.awt.event.MouseEvent;
2 import java.awt.event.MouseListener;
3 import java.awt.Dimension;
4 import java.awt.Graphics;
5 import java.awt.Graphics2D;
6 import java.awt.Rectangle;
7 import javax.swing.JPanel;
8
```

Figure 1

The Layout of the RectangleTest Application

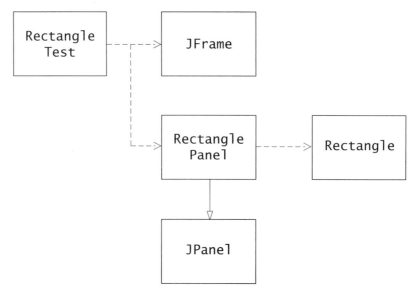

Figure 2

The Classes Used in the RectangleTest Application

```
 9  /**
10      A rectangle panel displays a rectangle that a user can
11      move by clicking the mouse.
12  */
13  public class RectanglePanel extends JPanel
14  {
15      /**
16          Constructs a rectangle panel with the rectangle at a
17          default location.
18      */
19      public RectanglePanel()
20      {
21          setPreferredSize(
22             new Dimension(PANEL_WIDTH, PANEL_HEIGHT));
23
24          // the rectangle that the paint method draws
25          box = new Rectangle(BOX_X, BOX_Y,
26             BOX_WIDTH, BOX_HEIGHT);
27
28          // add mouse press listener
29
30          class MousePressListener implements MouseListener
31          {
32              public void mousePressed(MouseEvent event)
```

```
33                {
34                    int x = event.getX();
35                    int y = event.getY();
36                    box.setLocation(x, y);
37                    repaint();
38                }
39
40                // do-nothing methods
41                public void mouseReleased(MouseEvent event) {}
42                public void mouseClicked(MouseEvent event) {}
43                public void mouseEntered(MouseEvent event) {}
44                public void mouseExited(MouseEvent event) {}
45            }
46
47            MouseListener listener = new MousePressListener();
48            addMouseListener(listener);
49        }
50
51        public void paintComponent(Graphics g)
52        {
53            super.paintComponent(g);
54            Graphics2D g2 = (Graphics2D)g;
55            g2.draw(box);
56        }
57
58        private Rectangle box;
59        private static final int BOX_X = 100;
60        private static final int BOX_Y = 100;
61        private static final int BOX_WIDTH = 20;
62        private static final int BOX_HEIGHT = 30;
63
64        private static final int PANEL_WIDTH = 300;
65        private static final int PANEL_HEIGHT = 300;
66    }
```

▼ ⊗ **Common Error**   **12.1** ▶

▼

Overriding the paint Method of a Panel

▼

When you implement an applet, you need to override the paint method. To draw on a panel, on the other hand, you override paintComponent. But panels also have a paint method for internal use by the Swing library. If you accidentally override that paint method, then painting of the panel will be erratic.

▼ ⊗ Common Error 12.2 ▶

Forgetting to Call the paintComponent Method of the Superclass

▼

The paintComponent method of every subclass of a Swing component must call super.paintComponent in order to give the superclass paintComponent method a

▼

chance to draw the background, draw borders and decorations, and set the attributes of the Graphics object. If you forget to call super.paintComponent, then the background may not be erased, or your drawing instructions may show up in the wrong position.

12.2 Layout Management

> You arrange user interface components by placing them inside containers. Containers can be placed inside larger containers.

> Each container has a *layout manager* that directs the arrangement of its components.

> Three useful layout managers are the border layout, flow layout, and grid layout.

> When adding a component to a container with the border layout, specify NORTH, EAST, SOUTH, WEST, or CENTER position.

Up to now, we have simply added user interface components such as buttons and text fields into a container, such as a panel. The panel arranges the components from the left to the right. However, in many applications, you need to stack some of the components top to bottom, or have some other arrangement.

In Java, you build up user interfaces by adding components into containers such as panels. Each container has its own *layout manager*, which determines how the components are laid out.

By default, a JPanel uses a *flow layout*. A flow layout simply arranges its components from left to right and starts a new row when there is no more room in the current row.

Another commonly used layout manager is the *border layout*. The border layout groups the container into five areas: center, north, west, south, and east (see Figure 3). You don't usually fill all five areas at the same time.

You can set the layout manager of a panel to a border layout:

```
panel.setLayout(new BorderLayout());
```

When you add a component to a container with a border layout, you must specify the position, like this:

```
panel.add(label, BorderLayout.CENTER);
```

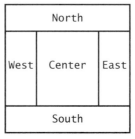

Figure 3

Border Layout Areas

> The content pane of a frame or applet has a border layout by default. A panel has a flow layout by default.

> With the flow layout, the individual components stay at their preferred size. The border layout and grid layout grow components to fill the area allotted for them.

Instead of using a panel and setting its layout manager to a border layout, you can also use the default content pane of a frame—it already uses a border layout. You retrieve it with the `getContent-Pane` method:

```
frame.getContentPane().add(label, BorderLayout.CENTER);
```

There is one important difference between the border layout and the flow layout. The border layout expands each component to fill all available space in its area. For example, Figure 4 shows how a button looks when it is placed in the South area of a border layout. In contrast, the flow layout leaves each component at its *preferred* size. That is why the buttons inside a panel stay at their natural size. Therefore, even if you have a single button, if you want to protect it from being resized, place it inside a new panel.

The *grid layout* is a third layout that is sometimes useful. The grid layout arranges components in a grid with a fixed number of rows and columns, resizing each of the components so that they all have the same size. Like the border layout, it also expands each component to fill the entire allotted area. (If that is not desirable, you need to place each component inside a panel, as described previously.) Figure 5 shows a number pad panel that uses a grid layout. To create a grid layout, you supply the number of rows and columns in the constructor. Then you add the components, row by row, left to right:

```
JPanel numberPanel = new JPanel();
numberPanel.setLayout(new GridLayout(4, 3));
numberPanel.add(button7);
numberPanel.add(button8);
numberPanel.add(button9);
numberPanel.add(button4);
. . .
```

Figure 4

Components Expanded to Fill Space in Border Layout

Figure 5

The Grid Layout

Sometimes you want to have a tabular arrangement of the components where columns have different sizes or one component spans multiple columns. A more complex layout manager called the grid bag layout can handle these situations. The grid bag layout is quite complex to use, however, and we do not cover it in this book; see, for example, [1] for more information. Using the border layout, flow layout, and grid layout, along with panels, you can create acceptable-looking layouts in nearly all situations (see, for example, Figure 6). The borders around the panels don't show up in the

Content Pane
with `BorderLayout`

`RectanglePanel`
in CENTER position

Panel
with `FlowLayout`
in SOUTH position

Figure 6

Combining Layout Managers

actual frame window—they are just added to the figure to show you the extent of the containers.

If you want more control over component layout, you can check out the grid bag layout, or you can use a development environment with a layout tool that lets you place the components visually and then generates the appropriate Java code.

12.3 Using Inheritance to Customize Frames

> Define a JFrame subclass for a complex frame.

As you add more user interface components to a frame, the frame can get quite complex. You should use inheritance for a frame that contains multiple components. Here is a typical example. Let's add a control panel to set the position of a rectangle in a frame, such as in Figure 6.

Design a subclass of JFrame and add the user interface components in the constructor. If a set of user interface components gets complex, then write a separate method for building up that set. In our example, we have a separate method to build the control panel at the bottom of the frame.

```
public class RectangleFrame extends JFrame
{
    public RectangleFrame()
    {
        // the panel that draws the rectangle
        rectPanel = new RectanglePanel();
        getContentPane().add(
            rectPanel, BorderLayout.CENTER);

        createControlPanel();

        pack();
    }

    private void createControlPanel()
    {
        // the text fields for entering the x- and y-coordinates
        final JTextField xField = new JTextField(5);
        final JTextField yField = new JTextField(5);;

        class MoveButtonListener implements ActionListener
        {
            public void actionPerformed(ActionEvent event)
            {
                int x = Integer.parseInt(xField.getText());
                int y = Integer.parseInt(yField.getText());
                rectPanel.setLocation(x, y);
            }
        }

        // create button and attach listener
```

```
        . . .

        // the panel for holding the user interface components
        JPanel controlPanel = new JPanel();

        // add components to control panel
        . . .
        getContentPane().add(
            controlPanel, BorderLayout.SOUTH);
    }

    private RectanglePanel rectPanel;
}
```

Turn any components that must be shared among these methods into instance variables of the class. For example, the rectPanel is needed both in the RectangleFrame constructor and the createControlPanel method.

Now you need a separate program class to display the frame:

```
public class RectangleTest
{
    public static void main(String[] args)
    {
        JFrame appFrame = new RectangleFrame();
        appFrame.setDefaultCloseOperation(
            JFrame.EXIT_ON_CLOSE);
        appFrame.show();
    }
}
```

There is an added complexity. The action listener of the "Move" button has no direct access to the rectangle inside the RectanglePanel. Therefore, you need to add a method to the RectanglePanel that allows others to set the rectangle location.

```
public class RectanglePanel extends JPanel
{
    public RectanglePanel()
    {
        . . .
        box = new Rectangle(. . .);
    }

    public void setLocation(int x, int y)
    {
        box.setLocation(x, y);
        repaint();
    }

    public void paintComponent(Graphics g)
    {
        super.paintComponent(g);
```

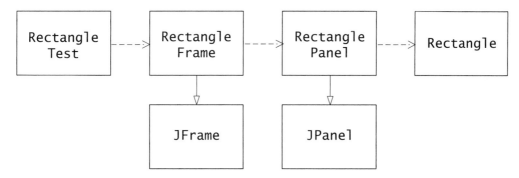

Figure 7

Classes in the Rectangle Frame Application

```
        Graphics2D g2 = (Graphics2D)g;
        g2.draw(box);
    }

    private Rectangle box;
}
```

This is very typical for a panel that displays graphics. Generally, the graphics changes through some external event. The panel class needs to supply methods to change the graphics state. These methods should apply the appropriate settings and then call repaint to trigger a redisplay of the drawing.

Figure 7 shows the classes of this application.

File RectangleTest.java

```
1  import javax.swing.JFrame;
2
3  /**
4      This program tests the RectangleFrame.
5  */
6  public class RectangleTest
7  {
8      public static void main(String[] args)
9      {
10         JFrame appFrame = new RectangleFrame();
11         appFrame.setDefaultCloseOperation(
12             JFrame.EXIT_ON_CLOSE);
13         appFrame.show();
14     }
15 }
```

File RectangleFrame.java

```
1  import java.awt.BorderLayout;
2  import java.awt.event.ActionEvent;
```

```
 3  import java.awt.event.ActionListener;
 4  import javax.swing.JButton;
 5  import javax.swing.JFrame;
 6  import javax.swing.JLabel;
 7  import javax.swing.JPanel;
 8  import javax.swing.JTextField;
 9
10  /**
11     This frame contains a panel that displays a rectangle
12     and a panel of text fields to specify the rectangle position.
13  */
14  public class RectangleFrame extends JFrame
15  {
16     /**
17        Constructs the frame.
18     */
19     public RectangleFrame()
20     {
21        // the panel that draws the rectangle
22        rectPanel = new RectanglePanel();
23
24        // add panel to content pane
25        getContentPane().add(
26           rectPanel, BorderLayout.CENTER);
27
28        createControlPanel();
29
30        pack();
31     }
32
33     /**
34        Creates the control panel with the text fields
35        at the bottom of the frame.
36     */
37     private void createControlPanel()
38     {
39        // the text fields for entering the x- and y-coordinates
40        final JTextField xField = new JTextField(5);
41        final JTextField yField = new JTextField(5);
42
43        // the button to move the rectangle
44        JButton moveButton = new JButton("Move");
45
46        class MoveButtonListener implements ActionListener
47        {
48           public void actionPerformed(ActionEvent event)
49           {
50              int x = Integer.parseInt(xField.getText());
51              int y = Integer.parseInt(yField.getText());
52              rectPanel.setLocation(x, y);
```

```
53              }
54          }
55
56          ActionListener listener = new MoveButtonListener();
57          moveButton.addActionListener(listener);
58
59          // the labels for labeling the text fields
60          JLabel xLabel = new JLabel("x = ");
61          JLabel yLabel = new JLabel("y = ");
62
63          // the panel for holding the user interface components
64          JPanel controlPanel = new JPanel();
65
66          controlPanel.add(xLabel);
67          controlPanel.add(xField);
68          controlPanel.add(yLabel);
69          controlPanel.add(yField);
70          controlPanel.add(moveButton);
71
72          getContentPane().add(
73              controlPanel, BorderLayout.SOUTH);
74      }
75
76      private RectanglePanel rectPanel;
77  }
```

File RectanglePanel.java

```
 1  import java.awt.Dimension;
 2  import java.awt.Graphics;
 3  import java.awt.Graphics2D;
 4  import java.awt.Rectangle;
 5  import javax.swing.JPanel;
 6
 7  /**
 8      This panel displays a rectangle.
 9  */
10  public class RectanglePanel extends JPanel
11  {
12      /**
13          Constructs a rectangle panel with the rectangle at a
14          default location.
15      */
16      public RectanglePanel()
17      {
18          setPreferredSize(
19              new Dimension(PANEL_WIDTH, PANEL_HEIGHT));
20          // the rectangle that the paint method draws
21          box = new Rectangle(BOX_X, BOX_Y,
22              BOX_WIDTH, BOX_HEIGHT);
```

```
23      }
24
25      /**
26          Sets the location of the rectangle and repaints the panel
27          @param x the x-coordinate of the top left corner of the rectangle
28          @param y the y-coordinate of the top left corner of the rectangle
29      */
30      public void setLocation(int x, int y)
31      {
32          box.setLocation(x, y);
33          repaint();
34      }
35
36      public void paintComponent(Graphics g)
37      {
38          super.paintComponent(g);
39          Graphics2D g2 = (Graphics2D)g;
40          g2.draw(box);
41      }
42
43      private Rectangle box;
44      private static final int BOX_X = 100;
45      private static final int BOX_Y = 100;
46      private static final int BOX_WIDTH = 20;
47      private static final int BOX_HEIGHT = 30;
48
49      private static final int PANEL_WIDTH = 300;
50      private static final int PANEL_HEIGHT = 300;
51  }
```

⚠ Advanced Topic   ▌12.1

Adding the main Method to the Frame Class

Have another look at the RectangleTest program. We have two classes: RectangleTest, a class with only a main method that constructs and shows the frame, and the class RectangleFrame, which contains the frame's constructor, helper methods, and instance variables. Some programmers prefer to combine these two classes, simply by adding the main method to the frame class:

```
public class RectangleFrame extends JFrame
{
    public static void main(String[] args)
    {
        JFrame appFrame = new RectangleFrame();
        appFrame.setDefaultCloseOperation(
            JFrame.EXIT_ON_CLOSE);
        appFrame.show();
```

▼   }

▼   public RectangleFrame()
            {
                . . .
            }
                . . .
▼   }

▼ This is a convenient shortcut that you will find in many programs, but it does muddle the responsibilities between the frame class and the program. Therefore, we do not use this approach in this book.

▼   **AT Advanced Topic**   **12.2**

Converting a Frame to an Applet

▼   If you enjoyed placing your applets onto a web page, then you will want to know how to convert a graphical application into an applet. The `javax.swing` package supplies a class `JApplet` that is very similar to a `JFrame`. Unlike a plain `Applet`, a `JApplet` also has a content pane whose default is the border layout. Therefore, laying out components in a `JApplet` works exactly the same as for a `JFrame`.

▼   Thus, there are only a few steps to convert from a frame to an applet:

1. Drop the class with the `main` method that shows the frame.
2. Inherit from `JApplet`, not `JFrame`.
▼ 3. Remove any calls to `setSize`. You need to set the size in the applet's HTML page.
4. Remove any calls to `setTitle`. If you want to show a title, supply it in HTML around the applet tag.

▼ Keep in mind that the visitors to your web site need a Java 2-enabled browser such as Netscape 6 or Opera. Older browsers cannot display Java 2 applets.

12.4   Choices

12.4.1 — Radio Buttons

> For a small set of mutually exclusive choices, use a group of radio buttons or a combo box.

In this section you will see how to present a finite set of choices to the user. If the choices are mutually exclusive, you use a set of *radio buttons*. In a radio button set, only one button can be selected at one time. When the user selects another button in the same set, the previously selected button is automatically turned off. (These buttons are called radio buttons because they work like the station selector buttons on a car radio: If you select a new station, the old station is automatically deselected.) For example, in Figure 8, the font sizes are mutually exclusive. You can select small, medium, or large, but not a combination of them.

Figure 8

A Combo Box, Check Boxes, and
Radio Buttons

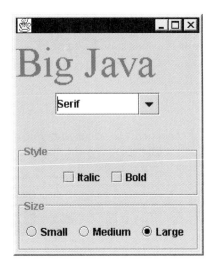

> Add radio buttons into a
> ButtonGroup so that only
> one button in the group is
> on at any time.

To create a set of radio buttons, you first create each button individually, and then you add all buttons of the set to a ButtonGroup
object:

```
JRadioButton smallButton = new JRadioButton("Small");
JRadioButton mediumButton = new JRadioButton("Medium");
JRadioButton largeButton = new JRadioButton("Large");

ButtonGroup group = new ButtonGroup();
group.add(smallButton);
group.add(mediumButton);
group.add(largeButton);
```

Note that the button group does *not* place the buttons close to each other on the container. The purpose of the button group is simply to find out which buttons to turn off
when one of them is turned on. It is still your job to arrange the buttons on the screen.

Your program can turn a button on or off, without the user clicking on it, by calling
the setSelected method. If you have a reference to a button, you can call the isSelected
method to find out whether the button is currently selected or not. For example,

```
if (largeButton.isSelected()) size = LARGE_SIZE;
```

> You can place a border
> around a panel to
> group its contents visually.

You should call setSelected(true) on one of the radio buttons in
each radio button group before showing the container.

If you have multiple button groups in a container, it is a good idea
to group them together visually. You probably use panels to build up
your user interface, but the panels themselves are invisible. You can
add a border to a panel to make it visible. In Figure 8, for example; the panels containing
the Size radio buttons and Style check boxes have borders.

There are a large number of border types. We will show only one variation and leave it to the border enthusiasts to look up the others in the Swing documentation. The `EtchedBorder` class yields a border with a 3-D "etched" effect. You can add a border to any component, but most commonly you apply it to a panel:

```
JPanel panel = new JPanel();
panel.setBorder(new EtchedBorder());
```

If you want to add a title to the border (as in Figure 8), you need to construct a `TitledBorder`. Swing borders can be layered, similar to stream objects (discussed in Chapter 15). You make a titled border by supplying a basic border and then the title you want. Here is a typical example:

```
panel.setBorder(new TitledBorder(
    new EtchedBorder(), "Size"));
```

12.4.2 — Check Boxes

> For a binary choice, use a check box.

The choices for "Bold" and "Italic" in Figure 8 are *not* exclusive. You can choose either, both, or neither. Therefore, they are implemented as a set of separate check boxes. Radio buttons and check boxes have different visual appearances. Radio buttons are round and have a black dot when selected. Check boxes are square and have a check mark when selected. (Strictly speaking, the appearance depends on the chosen look and feel. It is possible to create a different look and feel in which check boxes have a different shape or in which they give off a particular sound when selected.)

You construct a check box by giving the name in the constructor:

```
JCheckBox italicCheckBox = new JCheckBox("Italic");
```

Do not place check boxes inside a button group.

12.4.3 — Combo Boxes

> For a large set of mutually exclusive choices, use a combo box.

If you have a large number of choices, you don't want to make a set of radio buttons, because that would take up a lot of space. Instead, you can use a *combo box*. This component is called a combo box because it is a combination of a list and a text field. The text field displays the name of the current selection. When you click on the arrow to the right of the text field of a combo box, a list of selections drops down, and you can choose one of items on the list (see Figure 9).

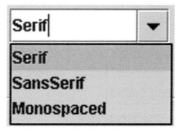

Figure 9

An Opened Combo Box

If the combo box is *editable*, you can also type in your own selection. To make a combo box editable, call the `setEditable` method.

You add strings to a combo box with the `addItem` method.

```
JComboBox facenameCombo = new JComboBox();
facenameCombo.addItem("Serif");
facenameCombo.addItem("SansSerif");
. . .
```

You get the item that the user has selected by calling the `getSelectedItem` method. However, since combo boxes can store other objects besides strings, the `getSelectedItem` method has return type `Object`. Hence you must cast the returned value back to `String`.

```
String selectedString =
    (String)facenameCombo.getSelectedItem();
```

> Radio buttons, check boxes, and combo boxes generate action events, just as buttons do.

You can select an item for the user with the `setSelectedItem` method.

Radio buttons, check boxes, and combo boxes generate an `ActionEvent` whenever the user selects an item. In the following program, we don't care which component was clicked—all components notify the same listener object. Whenever the user clicks on any one of them, we simply ask each component for its current content, using the `isSelected` and `getSelectedItem` methods. We then redraw the text sample with the new font.

Figure 10 shows how the components are arranged in the frame. Figure 11 shows the UML diagram.

Figure 10

The Components of the `ChoiceFrame`

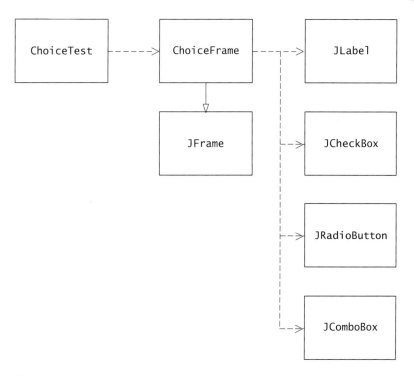

Figure 11

Classes of the ChoiceTest Program

File ChoiceTest.java

```
1  import javax.swing.JFrame;
2
3  /**
4     This program tests the ChoiceFrame.
5  */
6  public class ChoiceTest
7  {
8     public static void main(String[] args)
9     {
10       JFrame frame = new ChoiceFrame();
11       frame.setDefaultCloseOperation(
12          JFrame.EXIT_ON_CLOSE);
13       frame.show();
14    }
15 }
```

File ChoiceFrame.java

```
1  import java.awt.BorderLayout;
2  import java.awt.Container;
```

```java
 3  import java.awt.Font;
 4  import java.awt.GridLayout;
 5  import java.awt.event.ActionEvent;
 6  import java.awt.event.ActionListener;
 7  import java.awt.event.WindowAdapter;
 8  import java.awt.event.WindowEvent;
 9  import javax.swing.ButtonGroup;
10  import javax.swing.JButton;
11  import javax.swing.JCheckBox;
12  import javax.swing.JComboBox;
13  import javax.swing.JFrame;
14  import javax.swing.JLabel;
15  import javax.swing.JPanel;
16  import javax.swing.JRadioButton;
17  import javax.swing.border.EtchedBorder;
18  import javax.swing.border.TitledBorder;
19
20  /**
21      This frame contains a text field and a control panel
22      to change the font of the text.
23  */
24  public class ChoiceFrame extends JFrame
25  {
26      /**
27          Constructs the frame.
28      */
29      public ChoiceFrame()
30      {
31          // construct text sample
32          sampleField = new JLabel("Big Java");
33          getContentPane().add(
34              sampleField, BorderLayout.CENTER);
35
36          // this listener is shared among all components
37          class ChoiceListener implements ActionListener
38          {
39              public void actionPerformed(ActionEvent event)
40              {
41                  setSampleFont();
42              }
43          }
44
45          listener = new ChoiceListener();
46
47          createControlPanel();
48          setSampleFont();
49          pack();
50      }
```

```
51
52    /**
53       Creates the control panel to change the font.
54    */
55    public void createControlPanel()
56    {
57       JPanel facenamePanel = createComboBox();
58       JPanel sizeGroupPanel = createCheckBoxes();
59       JPanel styleGroupPanel = createRadioButtons();
60
61       // line up component panels
62
63       JPanel controlPanel = new JPanel();
64       controlPanel.setLayout(new GridLayout(3, 1));
65       controlPanel.add(facenamePanel);
66       controlPanel.add(sizeGroupPanel);
67       controlPanel.add(styleGroupPanel);
68
69       // add panels to content pane
70
71       getContentPane().add(
72          controlPanel, BorderLayout.SOUTH);
73    }
74
75    /**
76       Creates the combo box with the font style choices.
77       @return the panel containing the combo box
78    */
79    public JPanel createComboBox()
80    {
81       facenameCombo = new JComboBox();
82       facenameCombo.addItem("Serif");
83       facenameCombo.addItem("SansSerif");
84       facenameCombo.addItem("Monospaced");
85       facenameCombo.setEditable(true);
86       facenameCombo.addActionListener(listener);
87
88       JPanel panel = new JPanel();
89       panel.add(facenameCombo);
90       return panel;
91    }
92
93    /**
94       Creates the check boxes for selecting bold and italic style.
95       @return the panel containing the check boxes
96    */
97    public JPanel createCheckBoxes()
98    {
99       italicCheckBox = new JCheckBox("Italic");
```

```
100         italicCheckBox.addActionListener(listener);
101
102         boldCheckBox = new JCheckBox("Bold");
103         boldCheckBox.addActionListener(listener);
104
105         JPanel panel = new JPanel();
106         panel.add(italicCheckBox);
107         panel.add(boldCheckBox);
108         panel.setBorder
109            (new TitledBorder(new EtchedBorder(), "Style"));
110
111         return panel;
112      }
113
114      /**
115         Creates the radio buttons to select the font size.
116         @return the panel containing the radio buttons
117      */
118      public JPanel createRadioButtons()
119      {
120         smallButton = new JRadioButton("Small");
121         smallButton.addActionListener(listener);
122
123         mediumButton = new JRadioButton("Medium");
124         mediumButton.addActionListener(listener);
125
126         largeButton = new JRadioButton("Large");
127         largeButton.addActionListener(listener);
128         largeButton.setSelected(true);
129
130         // add radio buttons to button group
131
132         ButtonGroup group = new ButtonGroup();
133         group.add(smallButton);
134         group.add(mediumButton);
135         group.add(largeButton);
136
137         JPanel panel = new JPanel();
138         panel.add(smallButton);
139         panel.add(mediumButton);
140         panel.add(largeButton);
141         panel.setBorder
142            (new TitledBorder(new EtchedBorder(), "Size"));
143
144         return panel;
145      }
146
147      /**
```

```
148         Gets user choice for font name, style, and size.
149         and sets the font of the text sample.
150      */
151      public void setSampleFont()
152      {   // get font name
153
154          String facename
155              = (String)facenameCombo.getSelectedItem();
156
157          // get font style
158
159          int style = 0;
160          if (italicCheckBox.isSelected())
161              style = style + Font.ITALIC;
162          if (boldCheckBox.isSelected())
163              style = style + Font.BOLD;
164
165          // get font size
166
167          int size = 0;
168
169          final int SMALL_SIZE = 24;
170          final int MEDIUM_SIZE = 36;
171          final int LARGE_SIZE = 48;
172
173          if (smallButton.isSelected())
174              size = SMALL_SIZE;
175          else if (mediumButton.isSelected())
176              size = MEDIUM_SIZE;
177          else if (largeButton.isSelected())
178              size = LARGE_SIZE;
179
180          // set font of text field
181
182          sampleField.setFont(
183              new Font(facename, style, size));
184          sampleField.repaint();
185      }
186
187      private JLabel sampleField;
188      private JCheckBox italicCheckBox;
189      private JCheckBox boldCheckBox;
190      private JRadioButton smallButton;
191      private JRadioButton mediumButton;
192      private JRadioButton largeButton;
193      private JComboBox facenameCombo;
194      private ActionListener listener;
195  }
```

▼ **? HOWTO**

Layout Management

A graphical user interface is made up of components such as buttons and text fields. The Swing library uses containers and layout managers to arrange these components. This HOWTO explains how to group components into containers and how to pick the right layout managers.

Step 1 Make a sketch of your desired component layout.

Draw all the buttons, labels, text fields, and borders on a sheet of paper. Graph paper works best.

Here is an example—a user interface for ordering pizza. The user interface contains

- Three radio buttons
- Two check boxes
- A label: "Your Price:"
- A text field
- A border

```
┌─ Size ──────────────┐
│   ◉  Small      ☒ Pepperoni
│   ○  Medium
│   ○  Large      ☒ Anchovies
└─────────────────────┘

     Your Price:  [            ]
```

Step 2 Find groupings of adjacent components with the same layout

Usually, the component arrangement is complex enough that you need to use several panels, each with its own layout manager. Start by looking at adjacent components that

▼ are arranged top to bottom or left to right. If several components are surrounded by a border, they should probably all be grouped together.

▼ Here are the groupings from the pizza user interface:

▼

▼

▼

▼

▼

▼

▼ **Step 3** Identify layouts for each group

When components are arranged horizontally, choose a flow layout. When components
▼ are arranged vertically, use a grid layout. The grid has as many rows as you have components, and it has one column.

In the pizza user interface example, you would choose

▼ • A (3, 1) grid layout for the radio buttons

• A (2, 1) grid layout for the check boxes

▼ • A flow layout for the label and text field

Step 4 Group the groups together
▼
Look at each group as one blob, and group the blobs together into larger groups, just as
you grouped the components in the preceding step. If you note one large blob sur-
▼ rounded by smaller blobs, you can group them together in a border layout.

You may have to repeat the grouping again if you have a very complex user interface.
You are done if you have arranged all groups in a single container.

▼ For example, the three component groups of the pizza user interface can be arranged
as follows:

• A group containing the first two component groups, placed in the center of a con-
▼ tainer with a border layout

• The third component group, in the southern area of that container

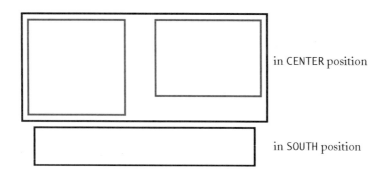

in CENTER position

in SOUTH position

In this step, you may run into a couple of complications. The group "blobs" tend to vary in size more than the individual components. If you place them inside a grid layout, the grid layout forces them all to be the same size. Also, you occasionally would like a component from one group to line up with a component from another group, but there is no way for you to communicate that intent to the layout managers.

These problems can be overcome by using more sophisticated layout managers or implementing a custom layout manager. However, those techniques are beyond the scope of this book. Sometimes, you may want to start over with step 1, using a component layout that is easier to manage. Or you can decide to live with minor imperfections of the layout. Don't worry about achieving the perfect layout—after all, you are learning programming, not user interface design.

Step 5 Write the code to generate the layout

This step is straightforward but potentially tedious, especially if you have a large number of components.

Start by constructing the components. Then construct a panel for each component group and set its layout manager if it is not a flow layout (the default for panels). Add a border to the panel if required. Finally, add the components to the panel.

Continue in this fashion until you reach the outermost container. Instead of constructing another panel, use the content pane of the surrounding JFrame or JApplet.

Of course, you also need to add event handlers to the components. That is the topic of HOWTO 10.1.

Here is an outline of the code required for the pizza user interface.

```
JPanel radioButtonPanel = new JPanel();
radioButtonPanel.setLayout(new GridLayout(3, 1));
radioButton.setBorder(new TitledBorder(
   new EtchedBorder(), "Size"));
radioButtonPanel.add(smallButton);
radioButtonPanel.add(mediumButton);
radioButtonPanel.add(largeButton);

JPanel checkBoxPanel = new JPanel();
checkBoxPanel.setLayout(new GridLayout(2, 1));
```

▼
```
        checkBoxPanel.add(pepperoniButton());
        checkBoxPanel.add(anchoviesButton());
```

▼
```
        JPanel pricePanel = new JPanel(); // uses FlowLayout
        pricePanel.add(new JLabel("Your Price:"));
        pricePanel.add(priceTextField);
```

▼
```
        JPanel centerPanel = new JPanel(); // uses FlowLayout
        centerPanel.add(radioButtonPanel);
        centerPanel.add(checkBoxPanel);
```
▼

▼
```
        // use content pane as top-level container
        // content pane uses BorderLayout by default
        getContentPane().add(centerPanel, BorderLayout.CENTER);
        getContentPane().add(pricePanel, BorderLayout.SOUTH);
```

12.5   Menus

> A frame contains a menu bar. The menu bar contains menus. A menu contains submenus and menu items.

Anyone who has ever used a graphical user interface is familiar with pull-down menus (see Figure 12). In Java it is easy to create these menus.

The container for the top-level menu items is called a *menu bar* in the Java world. First, you construct a menu bar and attach it to the frame:

```
public class MyFrame extends JFrame
{
    public MyFrame()
    {
        JMenuBar menuBar = new JMenuBar();
        setJMenuBar(menuBar);
        . . .
    }
}
```

Then you add menus to the menu bar:

```
JMenu fileMenu = new JMenu("File");
menuBar.add(fileMenu);
```

A menu is a collection of *menu items* and more menus (submenus). You add menu items and submenus with the add method:

```
JMenuItem fileNewMenuItem = new JMenuItem("New");
fileMenu.add(fileNewMenuItem);
```

> Menu items generate action events.

A menu item has no further submenus. When the user selects a menu item, the menu item sends an action event. Therefore, you want to add a listener to each menu item:

```
fileNewMenuItem.addActionListener(listener);
```

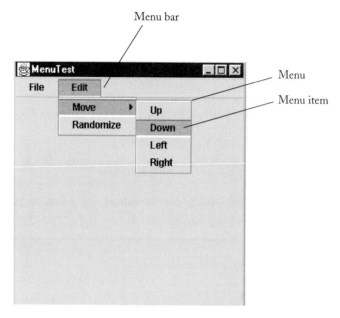

Figure 12

Pull-Down Menus

You add action listeners only to menu items, not to menus or the menu bar. When the user clicks on a menu name and a submenu opens, no action event is sent.

The following program builds up a small but typical menu and traps the action events from the menu items. To keep the program readable, it is a good idea to use a separate method for each menu or set of related menus. Have a look at the `createMoveItem` method, which creates a menu item to move up, down, left, or right. The same action listener class takes care of the four cases, with the `dx` and `dy` values varying for each menu item.

File MenuTest.java

```
1  import javax.swing.JFrame;
2
3  /**
4     This program tests the MenuFrame.
5  */
6  public class MenuTest
7  {
8     public static void main(String[] args)
9     {
10        JFrame frame = new MenuFrame();
11        frame.setDefaultCloseOperation(
12           JFrame.EXIT_ON_CLOSE);
13        frame.show();
14     }
15  }
```

File MenuFrame.java

```java
1  import java.awt.BorderLayout;
2  import java.awt.event.ActionEvent;
3  import java.awt.event.ActionListener;
4  import java.util.Random;
5  import javax.swing.JFrame;
6  import javax.swing.JMenu;
7  import javax.swing.JMenuBar;
8  import javax.swing.JMenuItem;
9
10 /**
11    This frame has a menu with commands to set the position of
12    a rectangle.
13 */
14 public class MenuFrame extends JFrame
15 {
16    /**
17       Constructs the frame.
18    */
19    public MenuFrame()
20    {
21       generator = new Random();
22
23       // add drawing panel to content pane
24
25       panel = new RectanglePanel();
26       getContentPane().add(panel, BorderLayout.CENTER);
27
28       // construct menu
29
30       JMenuBar menuBar = new JMenuBar();
31       setJMenuBar(menuBar);
32
33       menuBar.add(createFileMenu());
34       menuBar.add(createEditMenu());
35       pack();
36    }
37
38    /**
39       Creates the File menu.
40       @return the menu
41    */
42    public JMenu createFileMenu()
43    {
44       JMenu menu = new JMenu("File");
45       menu.add(createFileNewItem());
46       menu.add(createFileExitItem());
47       return menu;
48    }
49
```

```
50      /**
51          Creates the Edit menu.
52          @return the menu
53      */
54      public JMenu createEditMenu()
55      {
56          JMenu menu = new JMenu("Edit");
57          menu.add(createMoveMenu());
58          menu.add(createEditRandomizeItem());
59          return menu;
60      }
61
62      /**
63          Creates the Move submenu.
64          @return the menu
65      */
66      public JMenu createMoveMenu()
67      {
68          JMenu menu = new JMenu("Move");
69          menu.add(createMoveItem("Up", 0, -1));
70          menu.add(createMoveItem("Down", 0, 1));
71          menu.add(createMoveItem("Left", -1, 0));
72          menu.add(createMoveItem("Right", 1, 0));
73          return menu;
74      }
75
76      /**
77          Creates the File->New menu item and sets its action listener.
78          @return the menu item
79      */
80      public JMenuItem createFileNewItem()
81      {
82          JMenuItem item = new JMenuItem("New");
83          class MenuItemListener implements ActionListener
84          {
85              public void actionPerformed(ActionEvent event)
86              {
87                  panel.reset();
88              }
89          }
90          ActionListener listener = new MenuItemListener();
91          item.addActionListener(listener);
92          return item;
93      }
94
95      /**
96          Creates the File->Exit menu item and sets its action listener.
97          @return the menu item
98      */
99      public JMenuItem createFileExitItem()
```

```
100     {
101         JMenuItem item = new JMenuItem("Exit");
102         class MenuItemListener implements ActionListener
103         {
104             public void actionPerformed(ActionEvent event)
105             {
106                 System.exit(0);
107             }
108         }
109         ActionListener listener = new MenuItemListener();
110         item.addActionListener(listener);
111         return item;
112     }
113
114     /**
115         Creates a menu item to move the rectangle and sets its
116         action listener.
117         @param label the menu label
118         @param dx the amount by which to move the rectangle in the x-direction
119         @param dy the amount by which to move the rectangle in the y-direction
120         @return the menu item
121     */
122     public JMenuItem createMoveItem(String label,
123         final int dx, final int dy)
124     {
125         JMenuItem item = new JMenuItem(label);
126         class MenuItemListener implements ActionListener
127         {
128             public void actionPerformed(ActionEvent event)
129             {
130                 panel.moveRectangle(dx, dy);
131             }
132         }
133         ActionListener listener = new MenuItemListener();
134         item.addActionListener(listener);
135         return item;
136     }
137
138     /**
139         Creates the Edit->Randomize menu item and sets its action listener.
140         @return the menu item
141     */
142     public JMenuItem createEditRandomizeItem()
143     {
144         JMenuItem item = new JMenuItem("Randomize");
145         class MenuItemListener implements ActionListener
146         {
147             public void actionPerformed(ActionEvent event)
148             {
149                 int width = panel.getWidth();
```

```
150                     int height = panel.getHeight();
151                     int dx = -1 + generator.nextInt(2);
152                     int dy = -1 + generator.nextInt(2);
153                     panel.moveRectangle(dx, dy);
154                 }
155             }
156         ActionListener listener = new MenuItemListener();
157         item.addActionListener(listener);
158         return item;
159     }
160
161     private RectanglePanel panel;
162     private Random generator;
163 }
```

File RectanglePanel.java

```
 1  import java.awt.Dimension;
 2  import java.awt.Graphics;
 3  import java.awt.Graphics2D;
 4  import java.awt.Rectangle;
 5  import javax.swing.JPanel;
 6
 7  /**
 8      A panel that shows a rectangle.
 9  */
10  class RectanglePanel extends JPanel
11  {
12      /**
13          Constructs a panel with the rectangle in the top left corner.
14      */
15      public RectanglePanel()
16      {
17          setPreferredSize(
18              new Dimension(PANEL_WIDTH, PANEL_HEIGHT));
19          // the rectangle that the paint method draws
20          box = new Rectangle(0, 0, BOX_WIDTH, BOX_HEIGHT);
21      }
22
23      public void paintComponent(Graphics g)
24      {
25          super.paintComponent(g);
26          Graphics2D g2 = (Graphics2D)g;
27          g2.draw(box);
28      }
29
30      /**
31          Resets the rectangle to the top left corner.
32      */
33      public void reset()
34      {
```

```
35          box.setLocation(0, 0);
36          repaint();
37       }
38
39       /**
40          Moves the rectangle and repaints it. The rectangle
41          is moved by multiples of its full width or height.
42          @param dx the number of width units
43          @param dy the number of height units
44       */
45       public void moveRectangle(int dx, int dy)
46       {
47          box.translate(dx * BOX_WIDTH, dy * BOX_HEIGHT);
48          repaint();
49       }
50
51       private Rectangle box;
52       private static final int BOX_WIDTH = 20;
53       private static final int BOX_HEIGHT = 30;
54       private static final int PANEL_WIDTH = 300;
55       private static final int PANEL_HEIGHT = 300;
56    }
```

12.6   Exploring the Swing Documentation

> You should learn to navigate the API documentation to find out more about user interface components.

In the preceding sections, you saw the basic properties of the most common user interface components. We purposefully omitted many options and variations to simplify the discussion. You can go a long way by using only the simplest properties of these components. If you want to implement a more sophisticated effect, you can look inside the Swing documentation. You will probably find the documentation quite intimidating at first glance, though. The purpose of this section is to show you how you can use the documentation to your advantage without becoming overwhelmed.

Recall the Color class that was introduced in Chapter 4. Every combination of red, green, and blue values represents a different color. It should be fun to mix your own colors, with a slider for the red, green, and blue values (see Figure 13).

The Swing user interface toolkit has a large set of user interface components. How do you know whether there is a slider? You can buy a book that illustrates all Swing components, such as [2]. Or you can run the sample application included in the Java Development Kit that shows off all Swing components (see Figure 14). Or you can look at the names of all of the classes that start with J and decide that JSlider may be a good candidate.

Next, you need to ask yourself a few questions:

- How do I construct a JSlider?

- How can I get notified when the user has moved it?

- How can I tell to which value the user has set it?

Figure 13

A Color Mixer

Figure 14

The Swing Set Demo

Figure 15

A Mysterious Method Description from the API Documentation

If you can answer these questions, then you can put a slider to good use. Once you achieve that, you can fritter away more time and find out how to set tick marks or otherwise enhance the visual beauty of your creation.

When you look at the documentation of the `JSlider` class, you will probably not be happy. There are over 50 methods in the `JSlider` class and over 250 inherited methods, and some of the method descriptions look downright scary, such as the one in Figure 15. Apparently some folks out there are concerned about the `valueIsAdjusting` property, whatever that may be, and the designers of this class felt it necessary to supply a method to tweak that property. Until you too feel that need, your best bet is to ignore this method. As the author of an introductory book, it pains me to tell you to ignore certain facts. But the truth of the matter is that the Java library is so large and complex that nobody understands it in its entirety, not even the designers of Java themselves. You need to develop the ability to separate fundamental concepts from ephemeral minutiae. For example, it is important that you understand the concept of event handling. Once you understand the concept, you can ask the question, "What event does the slider send when the user moves it?" But it is not important that you memorize how to set tick marks or that you know how to implement a slider with a custom look and feel.

Let us go back to our fundamental questions. In Java 2, there are six constructors for the `JSlider` class. (There may well be more by the time you read this.) You want to learn about one or two of them. You need to strike a balance somewhere between the trivial and the bizarre. Consider

```
public JSlider()
```
       Creates a horizontal slider with the range 0 to 100 and an initial value of 50

Maybe that is good enough for now, but what if you want another range or initial value? It seems too limited.

On the other side of the spectrum, there is

```
public JSlider(BoundedRangeModel brm)
```
       Creates a horizontal slider using the specified `BoundedRangeModel`

Whoa! What is that? You can click on the BoundedRangeModel link to get a long explanation of this class. This appears to be some internal mechanism for the Swing implementors. Let's try to avoid this constructor if we can. Looking further, we find

> public **JSlider**(int min, int max, int value)
> Creates a horizontal slider using the specified min, max, and value

This sounds general enough to be useful and simple enough to be usable. You might want to stash away the fact that you can have vertical sliders as well.

Next, you want to know what events a slider generates. There is no addActionListener method. That makes sense. Adjusting a slider seems different from clicking a button, and Swing uses a different event type for these events. There is a method

> public void **addChangeListener**(ChangeListener l)

Click on the ChangeListener link to find out more about this interface. It has a single method

> void **stateChanged**(ChangeEvent e)

Apparently, that method is called whenever the user moves the slider. What is a ChangeEvent? Once again, click on the link, to find out that this event class has *no* methods of its own, but it inherits the getSource method from its superclass EventObject. Now we have a plan: Add a change event listener to each slider. When the slider is changed, the stateChanged method is called. Find out the new value of the slider. Recompute the color value and repaint the color panel. That way, the color panel is continually repainted as the user moves one of the sliders.

To compute the color value, you will still need to get the current value of the slider. Look at all the methods that start with get. Sure enough, you find

> public int **getValue**()
> Returns the slider's value

Now you know everything to write the program. The program uses one new constructor, two new methods, and one event listener of a new type. Of course, now that you have "tasted blood", you may want to add those tick marks—see Exercise P12.15.

Figure 16 shows how the components are arranged in the frame. Figure 17 shows the UML diagram.

File SliderTest.java

```
1  import javax.swing.JFrame;
2
3  public class SliderTest
4  {
5     public static void main(String[] args)
6     {
7        SliderFrame frame = new SliderFrame();
8        frame.setDefaultCloseOperation(
9           JFrame.EXIT_ON_CLOSE);
10       frame.show();
11    }
12 }
```

Figure 16

The Components of the SliderFrame

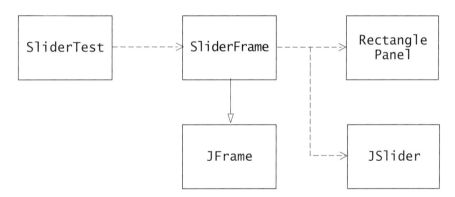

Figure 17

Classes of the SliderTest Program

File SliderFrame.java

```
1 import java.awt.BorderLayout;
2 import java.awt.Color;
3 import java.awt.Container;
4 import java.awt.Dimension;
5 import java.awt.GridLayout;
6 import java.awt.event.WindowAdapter;
7 import java.awt.event.WindowEvent;
8 import javax.swing.JFrame;
```

```
 9  import javax.swing.JLabel;
10  import javax.swing.JPanel;
11  import javax.swing.JSlider;
12  import javax.swing.SwingConstants;
13  import javax.swing.event.ChangeListener;
14  import javax.swing.event.ChangeEvent;
15
16  class SliderFrame extends JFrame
17  {
18     public SliderFrame()
19     {
20        colorPanel = new JPanel();
21        colorPanel.setPreferredSize(
22           new Dimension(PANEL_WIDTH, PANEL_HEIGHT));
23
24        getContentPane().add(colorPanel,
25           BorderLayout.CENTER);
26        createControlPanel();
27        setSampleColor();
28        pack();
29     }
30
31     public void createControlPanel()
32     {
33        class ColorListener implements ChangeListener
34        {
35           public void stateChanged(ChangeEvent event)
36           {
37              setSampleColor();
38           }
39        }
40
41        ChangeListener listener = new ColorListener();
42
43        redSlider = new JSlider(0, 100, 100);
44        redSlider.addChangeListener(listener);
45
46        greenSlider = new JSlider(0, 100, 70);
47        greenSlider.addChangeListener(listener);
48
49        blueSlider = new JSlider(0, 100, 70);
50        blueSlider.addChangeListener(listener);
51
52        JPanel controlPanel = new JPanel();
53        controlPanel.setLayout(new GridLayout(3, 2));
54
55        controlPanel.add(new JLabel("Red",
56           SwingConstants.RIGHT));
57        controlPanel.add(redSlider);
58
59        controlPanel.add(new JLabel("Green",
```

```
60              SwingConstants.RIGHT));
61          controlPanel.add(greenSlider);
62
63          controlPanel.add(new JLabel("Blue",
64              SwingConstants.RIGHT));
65          controlPanel.add(blueSlider);
66
67          getContentPane().add(controlPanel,
68              BorderLayout.SOUTH);
69      }
70
71
72      /**
73          Reads the slider values and sets the panel to
74          the selected color.
75      */
76      public void setSampleColor()
77      {   // read slider values
78
79          float red = 0.01F * redSlider.getValue();
80          float green = 0.01F * greenSlider.getValue();
81          float blue = 0.01F * blueSlider.getValue();
82
83          // set panel background to selected color
84
85          colorPanel.setBackground(
86              new Color(red, green, blue));
87          colorPanel.repaint();
88      }
89
90      private JPanel colorPanel;
91      private JSlider redSlider;
92      private JSlider greenSlider;
93      private JSlider blueSlider;
94
95      private static final int PANEL_WIDTH = 300;
96      private static final int PANEL_HEIGHT = 300;
97  }
```

▼ **Random Fact**

12.1

Visual Programming

Programming as you know it involves typing code into a text editor and then running it. A programmer must be familiar with the programming language to write even the simplest of programs. When programming in graphics, one must compute every screen position.

A new *visual* style of programming makes this much easier. When you use a visual programming environment, such as Visual Café or JBuilder, you use your mouse to specify

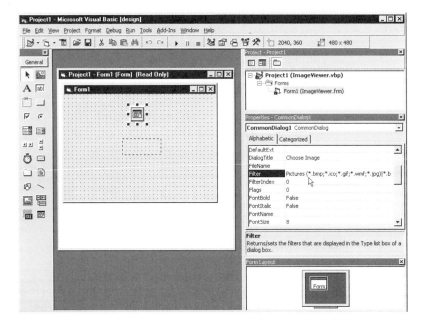

Figure 18

A Visual Programming Environment

where text, buttons, and other fields should appear on the screen (see Figure 18). You still need to do some programming. You need to write code for every event. For example, you can drag a button to its desired location, but you still need to specify what should happen when the user clicks on it.

Visual programming offers two benefits. It is much easier to lay out a screen by dragging buttons and images with the mouse than it is to compute the coordinates in a program. The visual programming environment also makes it easy to place objects with sophisticated behavior onto the screen. For example, a calendar object can show the current month's calendar, with buttons to move to the next or previous month; all of that has been preprogrammed by someone (usually the hard way, using a traditional programming language), but you can add a fully working calendar to your program simply by dragging it off a toolbar and dropping it into your program.

A prebuilt component, such as a calendar chooser, usually has a large number of *properties* that you can simply choose from a table. For example, you can simply check whether you want the calendar to be weekly or monthly. The provider of the calendar component had to work hard to include both cases in the code, but the programmer using the component does not have to care. When written in Java, these prepackaged components are called *JavaBeans*.

User interface design in a visual environment is *much* easier than writing the equivalent code in Java. In days a programmer can design an attractive user interface that would take weeks to complete by writing code. These systems are highly recommended for user interface programming.

CHAPTER SUMMARY

1. You can draw graphical shapes on a panel by overriding the `paintComponent` method of a `JPanel` subclass.

2. A panel class that paints a drawing on the panel should store all data that it needs to repaint itself.

3. You arrange user interface components by placing them inside containers. Containers can be placed inside larger containers.

4. Each container has a *layout manager* that directs the arrangement of its components.

5. Three useful layout managers are the border layout, flow layout, and grid layout.

6. When adding a component to a container with the border layout, specify the NORTH, EAST, SOUTH, WEST, or CENTER position.

7. The content pane of a frame or applet has a border layout by default. A panel has a flow layout by default.

8. With the flow layout, the individual components stay at their preferred size. The border layout and grid layout grow components to fill the area allotted for them.

9. Define a `JFrame` subclass for a complex frame.

10. For a small set of mutually exclusive choices, use a group of radio buttons or a combo box.

11. Add radio buttons into a `ButtonGroup` so that only one button in the group is on at any time.

12. You can place a border around a panel to group its contents visually.

13. For a binary choice, use a check box.

14. For a large set of mutually exclusive choices, use a combo box.

15. Radio buttons, check boxes, and combo boxes generate action events, just as buttons do.

16. A frame contains a menu bar. The menu bar contains menus. A menu contains submenus and menu items.

17. Menu items generate action events.

18. You should learn to navigate the API documentation to find out more about user interface components.

Further Reading

[1] Cay S. Horstmann and Gary Cornell, *Core Java 2 Volume 1: Fundamentals*, Prentice Hall, 2000.
[2] Kim Topley, *Core Java Foundation Classes*, Prentice Hall, 1998.

Classes, Objects, and Methods Introduced in This Chapter

```
java.awt.BorderLayout
    CENTER
    EAST
    NORTH
    SOUTH
    WEST
java.awt.Component
    setLayout
    setPreferredSize
    setSize
java.awt.FlowLayout
java.awt.GridLayout
javax.swing.AbstractButton
    addActionListener
    isSelected
    setSelected
javax.swing.ButtonGroup
    add
javax.swing.JComponent
    paintComponent
javax.swing.JFrame
    getContentPane
javax.swing.EtchedBorder
javax.swing.ImageIcon
javax.swing.JCheckBox
javax.swing.JComboBox
    addItem
    getSelectedItem
    isEditable
    setEditable
javax.swing.JComponent
    setBorder
    setFont
javax.swing.JLabel
javax.swing.JMenu
    add
javax.swing.JMenuBar
    add
javax.swing.JMenuItem
javax.swing.JRadioButton
javax.swing.JSlider
    addChangeListener
    getValue
javax.swing.border.TitledBorder
javax.swing.event.ChangeEvent
javax.swing.event.ChangeListener
    stateChanged
```

REVIEW EXERCISES

Exercise R12.1. What is the difference between the `paint` and `paintComponent` methods?

Exercise R12.2. What happens if you don't call `super.paintComponent` in a class that extends `JPanel`? Try it out with the `RectangleTest` program. Can you find out how the program misbehaves when you comment out that call?

Exercise R12.3. What happens when you paint directly on a frame? Try it out—rewrite the `RectanglePanel` application and move the `paintComponent` method directly into the `RectangleFrame` class.

Exercise R12.4. What is a layout manager? What is the advantage of a layout manager over telling the container "place this component at position (x,y)"?

Exercise R12.5. What happens when you place a single button into the CENTER area of a container that uses a border layout? Try it out, by writing a small sample program, if you aren't sure about the answer.

Exercise R12.6. What happens if you place multiple buttons into the SOUTH area? Try it out, by writing a small sample program, if you aren't sure about the answer.

Exercise R12.7. What happens when you add a button to a container that uses a border layout and omit the position? Try it out and explain.

Exercise R12.8. What happens when you try to add a component directly to a `JFrame` and not the content pane? Try it out and explain.

Exercise R12.9. The `SliderTest` program uses a grid layout manager. Explain a drawback of the grid that is apparent from Figure 16. What could you do to overcome this drawback?

Exercise R12.10. What is the difference between an `Applet` and a `JApplet`?

Exercise R12.11. Can you add icons to check boxes, radio buttons, and combo boxes? Browse the Java documentation to find out. Then write a small test program to verify your findings.

Exercise R12.12. What is the difference between radio buttons and check boxes?

Exercise R12.13. Why do you need a button group for radio buttons but not for check boxes?

Exercise R12.14. What is the difference between a menu bar, a menu, and a menu item?

Exercise R12.15. When browsing through the Java documentation for more information about sliders, we ignored the `JSlider` default constructor. Why? Would it have worked in our sample program?

Exercise R12.16. How do you construct a vertical slider? Consult the Swing documentation for an answer.

Exercise R12.17. Why doesn't a slider send out action events?

Exercise R12.18. What component would you use to show a set of choices, just as in a combo box, but so that several items are visible at the same time? Run the Swing demo app or look at a book with Swing example programs to find the answer.

Exercise R12.19. How many Swing user interface components are there? Look at the Java documentation to get an approximate answer.

Exercise R12.20. How many methods does the `JProgressBar` component have? Be sure to count inherited methods. Look at the Java documentation.

PROGRAMMING EXERCISES

Exercise P12.1. Write an application with three buttons labeled "Red", "Green", and "Blue" that changes the background color of a panel in the center of the content pane to red, green, or blue.

Exercise P12.2. Add icons to the buttons of the preceding Exercise.

Exercise P12.3. Write a calculator application. Use a grid layout to arrange buttons for the digits and for the + - × ÷ operations. Add a text field to display the result.

Exercise P12.4. Write an application with three radio buttons labeled "Red", "Green", and "Blue" that changes the background color of a panel in the center of the content pane to red, green, or blue.

Exercise P12.5. Write an application with three check boxes labeled "Red", "Green", and "Blue" that adds a red, green, or blue component to the the background color of a panel in the center of the content pane. This application can display a total of eight color combinations.

Exercise P12.6. Write an application with a combo box containing three items labeled "Red", "Green", and "Blue" that changes the background color of a panel in the center of the content pane to red, green, or blue.

Exercise P12.7. Change the `RectangleTest` program so that the rectangle position is moved by the values entered in two text fields for the offsets in the x- and y-directions.

Exercise P12.8. Write a program that displays a number of rectangles at random positions. Supply buttons "Fewer" and "More" that generate fewer or more random rectangles. Each time the user clicks on "Fewer", the count should be halved. Each time the user clicks on "More", the count should be doubled.

Exercise P12.9. Modify the program of the preceding exercise to replace the buttons with a slider to generate fewer or more random rectangles.

Exercise P12.10. Write an application with three labeled text fields, one each for the initial amount of a savings account, the annual interest rate, and the number of years. Add a button "Calculate" and a read-only text area to display the result, namely, the balance of the savings account after the given number of years.

Exercise P12.11. Add a bar graph to the preceding exercise that shows the balance after the end of each year.

Exercise P12.12. Write a program that contains a text area, a button "Draw Graph", and a panel that draws a bar chart of the numbers that a user typed into the text area. Use a string tokenizer to break up the text in the text area.

Exercise P12.13. Write a program that lets users design charts such as the following:

```
┌─────────────────────────────────────┐
│Golden Gate                          │
└─────────────────────────────────────┘
┌───────────────────┐
│Brooklyn           │
└───────────────────┘
┌──────────────────────┐
│Delaware Memorial     │
└──────────────────────┘
┌───────────────────────────────┐
│Mackinac                       │
└───────────────────────────────┘
```

Use appropriate components to ask for the length, label, and color, then apply them when the user clicks an "Add Bar" button.

Exercise P12.14. Write a program that lets users create pie charts. Design your own user interface.

Exercise P12.15. In the slider test program, add a set of tick marks to each slider that show the exact slider position.

Exercise P12.16. Write a graphical application front end for an `Earthquake` class. Supply a slider for entering the strength of the earthquake. Display the earthquake description in a text field that you continually update.

Array Lists and Arrays

CHAPTER CONTENTS

13.1 Array Lists

Consider again the `Purse` class from Chapter 7. You can add `Coin` objects to the purse. However, the purse doesn't actually remember the individual coins that you add, only the total value. It would be more realistic if we could actually store the individual coins.

If you knew that there were always ten coins in the purse, then you could store the objects in ten fields `coin1`, `coin2`, `coin3`, . . . , `coin10`. But such a sequence of variables is not very practical to use. You would have to write quite a bit of code ten times, once for each of the variables, and you'd still not be able to model a purse that holds twenty coins. Fortunately, there is a better way of storing a collection of objects: the `ArrayList` class.

> An array list is a sequence of objects.

An *array list* is a sequence of objects. Every element of the sequence can be accessed separately. Here is how you define an array list and fill it with coins:

```
ArrayList coins = new ArrayList();
coins.add(new Coin(0.1, "dime"));
coins.add(new Coin(0.25, "quarter"));
. . .
```

> Each object in an array list has an integer position number, called the index.

To get objects out of the array list, use the `get` method and specify which position in the array list you want to access. For example, `coins.get(4)` retrieves the coin in position number 4. The position number is called the *index* of the array list element.

> When retrieving an element from an array list, you need to cast the return value of the get method to the element class.

However, since an `ArrayList` stores `Object` references, the return type of the `get` method is `Object`. You need to cast the returned reference to the correct class.

```
Coin aCoin = (Coin)coins.get(4);
```

> Position numbers of an array range from 0 to size() − 1. Accessing a nonexistent position results in a bounds error.

For unfortunate historical reasons, the positions of array lists are numbered *starting at 0*. That is,

> `coins.get(0)` gets the first object
> `coins.get(1)` gets the second object
> `coins.get(2)` gets the third object

and so on.

In "ancient" times there was a technical reason why this setup was a good idea. So many programmers got used to it in C and C++ that Java follows it too. It is, however, a major source of grief for the newcomer.

If you try to access a position that does not exist, then an exception is thrown. For example, if `coins` holds ten objects, then the statement

```
Coin aCoin = (Coin)coins.get(20);
```

is a *bounds error*. To avoid bounds errors, you will want to know how many elements are in an array list. The `size` method returns the number of elements.

The most common bounds error is to use the following:

```
int i = coins.size();
aCoin = (Coin)coins.get(i);   // ERROR
```

Suppose `coins.size()` is 10. There is no element with index 10. Because the first element has index 0, the legal subscripts are 0 through 9. Thus, the call to `coins.get(10)` is a bounds error.

It is extremely common to step through *all* elements of an array list. For example, the following loop computes the total value of all coins:

```
double total = 0;
for (int i = 0; i < coins.size(); i++)
{
    Coin aCoin = (Coin)coins.get(i);
    total = total + aCoin.getValue();
}
```

Note that i is a legal index for the array list if $0 \leq$ i and i `< coins.size()`.
Don't write the test as

```
for (int i = 0; i <= coins.size() - 1; i++) // DON'T
```

The condition i `<= coins.size() - 1` means the same thing as i `< coins.size()`, but it is harder to read (see Quality Tip 6.3).

To set an array list element to a new value, use the `set` method.

```
Coin aNickel = new Coin(0.05, "nickel");
coins.set(4, aNickel);
```

This call sets position 4 of the coins array list to aNickel, overwriting whatever value was there before.

The `set` method can only overwrite existing values. To add a new object to the end of the array list, call the `add` method. You can also insert an object in the middle of an array list. The call `coins.add(i, c)` adds the object c at position i and moves all elements by one position, from the current element at position i to the last element in the array list. After each call to the `add` method, the size of the array list increases by 1 (see Figure 1).

Conversely, the call `coins.remove(i)` removes the element at position i, moves all elements after the removed element down by one position, and reduces the size of the array list by 1 (see Figure 2).

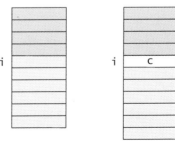

Figure 1

Adding an Element in the Middle of
an Array List

Before   After

Figure 2

Removing an Element from the Middle
of an Array List

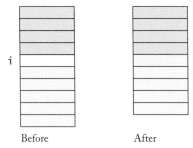

i

Before   After

Here is an implementation of the `Purse` class that uses an array list to store the coins. We will enhance the functionality of this class in the next section.

File Purse.java

```java
1  import java.util.ArrayList;
2
3  /**
4      A purse holds a collection of coins.
5  */
6  public class Purse
7  {
8      /**
9          Constructs an empty purse.
10     */
11     public Purse()
12     {
13         coins = new ArrayList();
14     }
15
16     /**
17         Adds a coin to the purse.
18         @param aCoin the coin to add
19     */
20     public void add(Coin aCoin)
21     {
22         coins.add(aCoin);
23     }
24
25     /**
26         Get the total value of the coins in the purse.
27         @return the sum of all coin values
28     */
29     public double getTotal()
30     {
31         double total = 0;
32         for (int i = 0; i < coins.size(); i++)
33         {
34             Coin aCoin = (Coin)coins.get(i);
```

```
35              total = total + aCoin.getValue();
36          }
37          return total;
38      }
39
40      private ArrayList coins;
41 }
```

Common Error   13.1

▼

Bounds Errors

▼

The most common array list error is attempting to access a nonexistent position.

```
ArrayList coins = new ArrayList();
coins.add(new Coin(0.1, "dime"));
coins.add(new Coin(0.25, "quarter"));
Coin c = (Coin)coins.get(2);
// ERROR—only have positions #0 and #1
```

▼

When the program runs, an out-of-bounds subscript generates an exception and terminates the program.

▼

This is a great improvement over languages such as C and C++. With those languages there is no error message; instead, the program will quietly (or not so quietly) corrupt some memory. Except for very short programs, in which the problem may go unnoticed, that corruption will make the program act flaky or cause a horrible death many instructions later. These are serious errors that make C and C++ programs difficult to debug.

▼

Common Error   13.2

▼

Inserting Objects of the Wrong Type into an Array List

▼

An array list is a "one size fits all" data structure. It manages a sequence of elements of type `Object`. As a result, you can use the `add` and `set` methods to add objects of any class into an array list. If you accidentally insert an element of the wrong type, then no error occurs until you retrieve the object.

```
coins.add(new Rectangle(5, 10, 20, 30)); // no error here
```

▼

The call to `add` is technically correct—a `Rectangle` value can be converted to `Object`, and therefore it can be inserted into the array list. For that reason, the compiler will not complain. This was still a programming error, though, because the programmer's intention is that `coins` contain coins.

▼

▼

The error is reported when the rectangle object is cast to the `Coin` class.

```
for (int i = 0; i < coins.size(); i++)
{
    Coin aCoin = (Coin)coins.get(i); // error reported here
    total = total + aCoin.getValue();
}
```

▼

▼

13.2 Simple Array List Algorithms

13.2.1 — Finding a Value

> To find a value in an array list, check all elements until you have found a match.

Suppose you want to know whether you have a particular coin in your purse. You simply inspect each element until you find a match or reach the end of the array list. Note that the loop might fail to find an answer, namely if none of the coins match. This search process is called a *linear search* through the array list.

```
public class Purse
{
    public boolean find(Coin aCoin)
    {
        for (int i = 0; i < coins.size(); i++)
        {
            Coin c = (Coin)coins.get(i);
            if (c.equals(aCoin)) return true; // found a match
        }
        return false; // no match in the entire array list
    }
    . . .
}
```

13.2.2 — Counting

> To count values in an array list, check all elements and count the matches, until you reach the end of the array list.

Suppose you want to find *how many* coins of a certain type you have. Then you must go through the entire array list and increment a counter each time you find a match.

```
public class Purse
{
    public int count(Coin aCoin)
    {
        int matches = 0;
        for (int i = 0; i < coins.size(); i++)
        {
```

```
                        Coin c = (Coin)coins.get(i);
                        if (c.equals(aCoin)) matches++; // found a match
                  }
                  return matches;
            }
            . . .
      }
```

13.2.3 — Finding the Maximum or Minimum

To compute the maximum or minimum value of an array list, initialize a candidate with the starting element. Then compare the candidate with the remaining elements and update it if you find a larger or smaller value.

Suppose you want to find the coin with the largest value currently in the purse. Keep a candidate for the maximum. Visit all elements of the array. If you find an element with a larger value, then replace the candidate with that value. When you have reached the end of the array, you have found the maximum.

There is just one problem. When you visit the beginning of the array, you don't yet have a candidate for the maximum. The easiest way to overcome that is to set the candidate to the starting element of the array and start the comparison with the next element.

```
      public class Purse
      {
         public Coin getMaximum()
         {
            Coin max = (Coin)coins.get(0);
            for (int i = 1; i < coins.size(); i++)
            {
               Coin c = (Coin)coins.get(i);
               if (c.getValue() > max.getValue())
                  max = c;
            }
            return max;
         }
         . . .
      }
```

Note that the for loop starts with 1, not with 0.

Of course, this method works only if there is at least one element in the array list. It doesn't make a lot of sense to ask for the largest element of an empty collection. We can return null in that case, or else we can declare a precondition that the purse must not be empty when calling the getMaximum method. Recall from Chapter 7 that it is better to establish a reasonable precondition than to return a bogus value.

However, then the Purse class needs a method that can tell whether there are any coins in the purse—it isn't fair to set a precondition that the class user can't test. For that reason, the class at the end of this section has a method count that returns the coin count of the purse.

To compute the minimum of a data set, keep a candidate for the minimum, initialize it with the beginning data value, and replace it whenever you encounter a smaller value. At the end of the data set, you have found the minimum.

File Purse.java

```
1  import java.util.ArrayList;
2
3  /**
4      A purse holds a collection of coins.
5  */
6  public class Purse
7  {
8      /**
9          Constructs an empty purse.
10     */
11     public Purse()
12     {
13         coins = new ArrayList();
14     }
15
16     /**
17         Adds a coin to the purse.
18         @param aCoin the coin to add
19     */
20     public void add(Coin aCoin)
21     {
22         coins.add(aCoin);
23     }
24
25     /**
26         Gets the total value of the coins in the purse.
27         @return the sum of all coin values
28     */
29     public double getTotal()
30     {
31         double total = 0;
32         for (int i = 0; i < coins.size(); i++)
33         {
34             Coin aCoin = (Coin)coins.get(i);
35             total = total + aCoin.getValue();
36         }
37         return total;
38     }
39
40     /**
41         Counts the number of coins in the purse.
42         @return the number of coins
43     */
44     public int count()
45     {
46         return coins.size();
47     }
48
49     /**
```

```
50          Tests whether the purse has a coin that matches a given coin.
51          @param aCoin  the coin to match
52          @return true  if there is a coin equal to aCoin
53      */
54      public boolean find(Coin aCoin)
55      {
56         for (int i = 0; i < coins.size(); i++)
57         {
58            Coin c = (Coin)coins.get(i);
59            if (c.equals(aCoin)) return true; // found a match
60         }
61         return false; // no match in the entire array list
62      }
63
64      /**
65          Counts the number of coins in the purse that match
66          a given coin.
67          @param aCoin  the coin to match
68          @return  the number of coins equal to aCoin
69      */
70      public int count(Coin aCoin)
71      {
72         int matches = 0;
73         for (int i = 0; i < coins.size(); i++)
74         {
75            Coin c = (Coin)coins.get(i);
76            if (c.equals(aCoin)) matches++; // found a match
77         }
78         return matches;
79      }
80
81      /**
82          Finds the coin with the largest value.
83          (Precondition: The purse is not empty)
84          @return  a coin with maximum value in this purse
85      */
86      Coin getMaximum()
87      {
88         Coin max = (Coin)coins.get(0);
89         for (int i = 1; i < coins.size(); i++)
90         {
91            Coin c = (Coin)coins.get(i);
92            if (c.getValue() > max.getValue())
93               max = c;
94         }
95         return max;
96      }
97
98      private ArrayList coins;
99   }
```

13.3 Storing Numbers in Array Lists

To store primitive type values in an array list, you must use wrapper classes.

Because numbers are not objects in Java, you cannot directly insert them into array lists. To store sequences of integers, floating-point numbers, or `boolean` values in an array list, you must use *wrapper classes*. The classes `Integer`, `Double`, and `Boolean` wrap numbers and truth values inside objects. These wrapper objects can be stored inside array lists.

The `Double` class is a typical number wrapper. There is a constructor that makes a `Double` object out of a `double` value:

```
Double d = new Double(29.95);
```

Conversely, the `doubleValue` method retrieves the `double` value that is stored inside the `Double` object.

```
double x = d.doubleValue();
```

Here is how you can add a floating-point number into an array list. First construct a wrapper object, then add the object:

```
ArrayList data = new ArrayList();
double x = 29.95;
Double wrapper = new Double(x);
data.add(wrapper);
```

To retrieve the number, you need to cast the return value of the `get` method to `Double`, then call the `doubleValue` method:

```
Double wrapper = (Double)data.get(0);
double x = wrapper.doubleValue();
```

As you can see, using wrapper classes to store numbers in an array list is also a considerable hassle. You will see in the next section how to use arrays to store sequences of numbers.

By the way, the `Integer` and `Double` classes should look familiar. You have used their `parseInt` and `parseDouble` method many times. These static methods really have nothing to do with wrapper objects for numbers; they were just put inside these classes because it seemed to be a convenient place.

13.4 Declaring and Accessing Arrays

An array is a fixed-length sequence of values of the same type.

An *array* is a fixed-length sequence of values of the same type, which can be an object type or a primitive type. For example, here is how you construct an array of ten `double` values:

```
new double[10]
```

In most cases you will want to store a reference to the array in a variable so that you can access it later. The type of an array variable is the element type, followed by `[]`. In this example, the type is `double[]`, because the element type is `double`. Here is the declaration of an array variable:

```
double[] data = new double[10];
```

Figure 3

An Array Reference and an Array

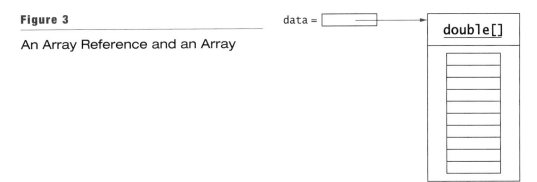

That is, `data` is a reference to an array of floating-point numbers. The call

```
new double[10]
```

creates the actual array of 10 numbers. (See Figure 3.)

Arrays differ from array lists in two aspects:

1. An array has a fixed length. In contrast, an array list starts out with length 0, grows when you add elements, and shrinks when you remove them.

2. An array has elements of a specified type, whereas an array list holds a collection of `Object` references.

When an array is first created, all values are initialized with 0 (for an array of numbers such as `int[]` or `double[]`), `false` (for a `boolean[]` array), or `null` (for an array of objects).

To change a value in the `data` array, you need to specify which position in the array you want to access. That is done with the `[]` operator, which follows the name of the array and encloses the index expression:

```
data[4] = 29.95;
```

> You access array elements with an integer index, using the notation `a[i]`.

Now the position with index 4 of `data` is filled with the value 29.95.

To read out the data value at index 4, you simply use the expression `data[4]` as you would any variable of type `double`:

```
System.out.println("The price of this item is "
    + data[4]);
```

This is an advantage of arrays over array lists. The `[]` notation is more compact than calls to the `set` and `get` methods.

As with array lists, the positions of arrays are numbered starting at 0. That is, the legal positions for the `data` array run from `data[0]`, the first position, up to `data[9]`, the tenth position.

As with array lists, it is an error to try to access nonexistent positions.

```
int i = 10;
double x = data[i]; // ERROR
```

There is no `data[10]`. Remember, the array has length 10, so the index values range from 0 to 9. The compiler does not catch this error. Generally, it is too difficult for the compiler to follow the current contents of `data` and `i`. However, when an invalid index is detected during the execution of a program, an exception is generated and the program terminates.

Another common error is to forget to initialize the array variable:

```
double[] data; // not initialized
data[0] = 29.95;
```

> Use the length field to find the number of elements in an array.

When an array variable is defined, it must be initialized with an array such as new double[10] before any array elements can be accessed.

A Java array has an instance variable length, which you can access to find out the size of the array. For example, here is how you can find out the lowest price in an array of prices:

```
double lowest = data[0];
for (int i = 1; i < data.length; i++)
   if (data[i] < lowest)
      lowest = data[i];
```

Note that there are *no parentheses* following length—it is an instance variable of the array object, not a method. However, you cannot assign a new value to this instance variable. In other words, length is a final public instance variable. This is quite an anomaly. Normally, Java programmers use a method to inquire about the properties of an object. You just have to remember to omit the parentheses in this case.

Using length is a much better idea than using a number such as 10, even if you know that the array has ten elements. If the program changes later, and there are now 20 values, then the loop automatically stays valid. This principle is another case of avoiding magic numbers, as discussed in Quality Tip 3.2.

Syntax 13.1 : Array Construction

new *typeName*[*length*]

Example:

new double[10]

Purpose:

To construct an array with a given number of elements

Syntax 13.2 : Array Element Access

arrayReference[*index*]

Example:

```
a[4] = 29.95;
double x = a[4];
```

Purpose:

To access an element in an array

Common Error 13.3

Uninitialized Arrays

A common error is to allocate an array reference, but not an actual array.

```
double[] data;
data[0] == 29.95; // Error—data not initialized
```

Array variables work exactly like object variables—they are only references to the actual array. To construct the actual array, you must use the new operator:

```
double[] data = new double[10];
```

Common Error 13.4

Length and Size

Unfortunately, the Java syntax for determining the number of elements in an array, an array list, and a string is not at all consistent.

Data type	Number of elements
Array	a.length
Array list	a.size()
String	a.length()

It is a common error to confuse these. You just have to remember the correct syntax for every data type.

Advanced Topic 13.1

Array Initialization

You can initialize an array by allocating it and then filling each entry:

```
int[] primes = new int[5];
primes[0] = 2;
primes[1] = 3;
primes[2] = 5;
primes[3] = 7;
primes[4] = 11;
```

▼ However, if you already know all the elements that you want to place in the array, there is an easier way. You can list all elements that you want to include in the array, enclosed in braces and separated by commas:

▼
```
int[] primes = { 2, 3, 5, 7, 11 };
```

The Java compiler counts how many elements you want to place in the array, allocates an array of the correct size, and fills it with the elements that you specify.

▼ If you want to construct an array and pass it on to a method that expects an array parameter, you can initialize an *anonymous array* as follows:

▼
```
new int[] { 2, 3, 5, 7, 11 }
```

13.5   Copying Arrays

> An array variable stores a reference to the array. Copying the variable yields a second reference to the same array.

Array variables work just like object variables—they hold a *reference* to the actual array. If you copy the reference, you get another reference to the same array (see Figure 4):

```
double[] data = new double[10];
. . . // fill array
double[] prices = data;
```

> Use the clone method to copy the elements of an array.

If you want to make a true copy of an array, call the clone method (see Figure 5).

```
double[] prices = (double[])data.clone();
```

Note that you need to cast the return value of the clone method from the type Object to the type double[].

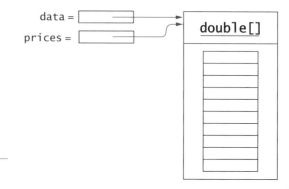

Figure 4

Two References to the Same Array

Figure 5

Cloning an Array

data =

double[]

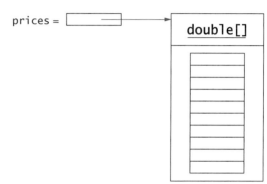

prices =

double[]

> Use the
> `System.arraycopy`
> method to copy elements
> from one array to another.

Occasionally, you need to copy elements from one array into another array. You can use the static `System.arraycopy` method for that purpose (see Figure 6):

```
System.arraycopy(from, fromStart, to, toStart, count);
```

One use for the `System.arraycopy` method is to add or remove elements in the middle of an array. To add a new element at position i into `data`, first move all elements from i onward one position up. Then insert the new value.

```
System.arraycopy(data, i, data, i + 1,
    data.length - i - 1);
data[i] = x;
```

Note that the last element in the array is lost (see Figure 7).

To remove the element at position i, copy the elements above the position downward (see Figure 8).

```
System.arraycopy(data, i + 1, data, i,
    data.length - i - 1);
```

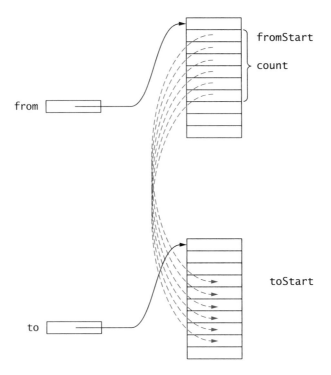

Figure 6

The System.arraycopy Method

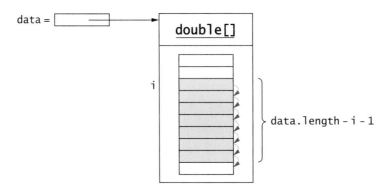

Figure 7

Inserting a New Element into an Array

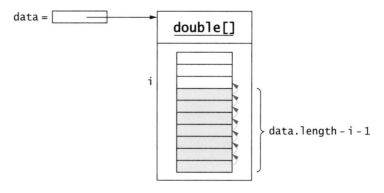

Figure 8

Removing an Element from an Array

13.6 Partially Filled Arrays

Suppose you write a program that reads a sequence of numbers into an array. How many numbers will the user enter? You can't very well ask the user to count the items for us before entering them—that is just the kind of work that the user expects the computer to do. Unfortunately, you now run into a problem. You need to set the size of the array before you know how many elements you need. Once the array size is set, it cannot be changed.

> Arrays are often *partially filled*. Then you need to remember the number of elements that you actually placed in the array.

To solve this problem, you can sometimes make an array that is guaranteed to be larger than the largest possible number of entries, and *partially fill it*. For example, you can decide that the user will never enter more than 100 data points. Then allocate an array of size 100:

```
final int DATA_LENGTH = 100;
double[] data = new double[DATA_LENGTH];
```

Then keep a *companion variable* that tells how many elements in the array are actually used. It is an excellent idea *always* to name this companion variable by adding the suffix Size to the name of the array.

```
int dataSize = 0;
```

Now data.length is the *capacity* of the array data, and dataSize is the *current size* of the array (see Figure 9). Keep adding elements into the array, incrementing the size variable each time.

```
data[dataSize] = x;
dataSize++;
```

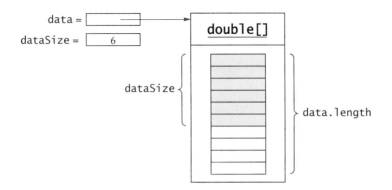

Figure 9

A Partially Filled Array

This way, dataSize always contains the correct element count. When inspecting the array elements, you must be careful to stop at dataSize, not at data.length:

```
for (int i = 0; i < dataSize; i++)
    sum = sum + data[i];
```

You must be careful not to overfill the array. Insert elements only if there is still room for them! If the array fills up, there are two approaches you can take. The simple way out is to refuse additional entries:

```
if (dataSize >= data.length)
    System.out.println("Sorry, the array is full.");
```

If you run out of space in an array, you need to allocate a larger array and copy the elements into it.

Of course, refusing to accept all input is often unreasonable. Users routinely use software on larger data sets than the original developers ever imagined. Therefore, you will need to work a little harder for a realistic program. When you run out of space in an array, you can create a new, larger array; copy all elements into the new array; and then attach the new array to the old array variable.

```
if (dataSize >= data.length)
{
    // make a new array of twice the size
    double[] newData = new double[2 * data.length];
    // copy over all elements from data to newData
    System.arraycopy(data, 0, newData, 0, data.length);
    // abandon the old array and store in data
    // a reference to the new array
    data = newData;
}
```

Figure 10 shows the process.

At the end of this section, you will find an implementation of the DataSet class that stores an arbitrary number of elements. We test it with a program that feeds in 10,000 random numbers.

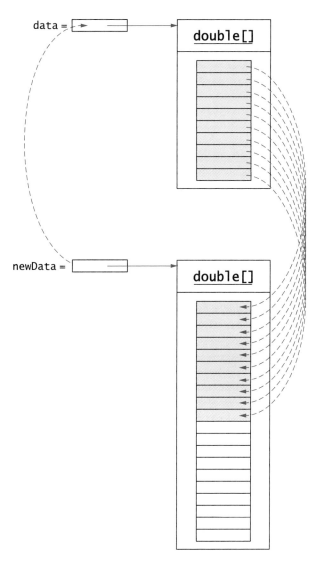

Figure 10

Growing an Array

The `ArrayList` class contains an `Object[]` array to hold a sequence of objects. When the array runs out of space, the `ArrayList` class allocates a larger array, using exactly the same technique that you just saw.

Frankly, it is a hassle to track array sizes and to grow arrays when they run out of space. If you collect *objects*, then you can avoid that hassle, simply by using an array list. You should generally use array lists to collect objects.

Fortunately, in most object-oriented programs, you collect objects, not numbers. However, when you collect numbers, you need to make a hard choice. Is it more of a hassle to track array sizes, or to use wrapper classes? An array of numbers is much more efficient than an array list of wrapper objects that contain numbers, so most programmers will choose arrays.

File DataSet.java

```
1  /**
2      This class computes the average of a set of data values.
3  */
4  public class DataSet
5  {
6     /**
7         Constructs an empty data set.
8     */
9     public DataSet()
10    {
11       final int DATA_LENGTH = 100;
12       data = new double[DATA_LENGTH];
13       dataSize = 0;
14    }
15
16    /**
17        Adds a data value to the data set.
18        @param x a data value
19    */
20    public void add(double x)
21    {
22       if (dataSize >= data.length)
23       {
24          // make a new array of twice the size
25          double[] newData = new double[2 * data.length];
26          // copy over all elements from data to newData
27          System.arraycopy(data, 0, newData, 0,
28             data.length);
29          // abandon the old array and store in data
30          // a reference to the new array
31          data = newData;
32       }
33       data[dataSize] = x;
34       dataSize++;
35    }
36
37    /**
38        Gets the average of the added data.
39        @return the average or 0 if no data have been added
40    */
41    public double getAverage()
42    {
43       if (dataSize == 0) return 0;
44       double sum = 0;
```

```
45        for (int i = 0; i < dataSize; i++)
46            sum = sum + data[i];
47        return sum / dataSize;
48    }
49
50    private double[] data;
51    private int dataSize;
52 }
```

File DataSetTest.java

```
1  import java.util.Random;
2
3  /**
4      This program tests the DataSet class by adding 10,000 numbers
5      to the data set and computing the average.
6  */
7  public class DataSetTest
8  {
9      public static void main(String[] args)
10     {
11         Random generator = new Random();
12         DataSet data = new DataSet();
13         final int COUNT = 10000;
14         System.out.println("Adding " +
15             COUNT + " random numbers.");
16         for (int i = 0; i < COUNT; i++)
17         {
18             double x = generator.nextDouble();
19             data.add(x);
20         }
21         double average = data.getAverage();
22         System.out.println("average=" + average);
23     }
24 }
```

▼ ⊗ **Common Error**   **13.5**
▶

▼

Underestimating the Size of a Data Set

▼

Programmers commonly underestimate the amount of input data that a user will pour
into an unsuspecting program. The most common problem caused by underestimating
the amount of input data results from the use of fixed-sized arrays. Suppose you write a

▼ program to search for text in a file. You store each line in a string, and keep an array of
strings. How big do you make the array? Surely nobody is going to challenge your program with an input that is more than 100 lines. Really? A smart grader can easily feed in

▼ the entire text of *Alice in Wonderland* or *War and Peace* (which are available on the Internet).

▼ All of a sudden, your program has to deal with tens or hundreds of thousands of lines. What will it do? Will it handle the input? Will it politely reject the excess input? Will it crash and burn?

▼ A famous article [1] analyzed how several UNIX programs reacted when they were fed large or random data sets. Sadly, about a quarter didn't do well at all, crashing or hanging without a reasonable error message. For example, in some versions of UNIX the

▼ tape backup program *tar* cannot handle file names that are longer than 100 characters, which is a pretty unreasonable limitation. Many of these shortcomings are caused by features of the C language that, unlike Java, makes it difficult to store strings of arbitrary

▼ size.

▼ ## Random Fact   13.1

An Early Internet Worm

▼ In November 1988, a graduate student at Cornell University launched a virus program that infected about 6,000 computers connected to the Internet across the United States. Tens of thousands of computer users were unable to read their email or otherwise use

▼ their computers. All major universities and many high-tech companies were affected. (The Internet was much smaller then than it is now.)

▼ The particular kind of virus used in this attack is called a *worm*. The virus program crawled from one computer on the Internet to the next. The entire program is quite complex; its major parts are explained in [2]. However, one of the methods used in the attack is of interest here. The worm would attempt to connect to *finger*, a program in the

▼ UNIX operating system for finding information on a user who has an account on a particular computer on the network. Like many programs in UNIX, *finger* was written in the C language. C does not have array lists, only arrays, and when you construct an array

▼ in C, as in Java, you have to make up your mind how many elements you need. To store the user name to be looked up (say, `walters@cs.sjsu.edu`), the *finger* program allocated an array of 512 characters, under the assumption that nobody would ever provide such a long input. Unfortunately, C, unlike Java, does not check that an array index is less than the length of the array. If you write into an array, using an index that is too large, you simply overwrite memory locations that belong to some other objects. In some

▼ versions of the *finger* program, the programmer had been lazy and had not checked whether the array holding the input characters was large enough to hold the input. So the worm program purposefully filled the 512-character array with 536 bytes. The excess

▼ 24 bytes would overwrite a return address, which the attacker knew was stored just after the line buffer. When that function was finished, it didn't return to its caller but to code supplied by the worm. That code ran under the same super-user privileges as *finger*,

▼ allowing the worm to gain entry into the remote system.

Had the programmer who wrote *finger* been more conscientious, this particular attack would not be possible. In C++ and C, all programmers must be especially careful

▼ not to overrun array boundaries.

▼   One may well wonder what would possess a skilled programmer to spend many
weeks or months to plan the antisocial act of breaking into thousands of computers and
disabling them. It appears that the break-in was fully intended by the author, but the dis-
▼   abling of the computers was a side effect of continuous reinfection and efforts by the
worm to avoid being killed. It is not clear whether the author was aware that these moves
would cripple the attacked machines.
▼   In recent years, the novelty of vandalizing other people's computers has worn off
somewhat, and there are fewer jerks with programming skills who write new viruses.
Other attacks by individuals with more criminal energy, whose intent has been to steal
▼   information or money, have surfaced. Reference [3] gives a very readable account of the
discovery and apprehension of one such person.

▼   **Quality Tip**   **13.1**

Make Parallel Arrays into Arrays of Objects

▼

> Avoid parallel arrays
> by changing them
> into arrays of objects.

Programmers who are familiar with arrays but unfamiliar with object-
oriented programming sometimes distribute information across separate arrays. Here is a typical example. A program needs to manage
employee data, consisting of employee names and salaries. Don't store
the names and salaries in separate arrays.

```
// don't do this
String[] names;
double[] salaries;
```

▼

▼   In such a program, related information is distributed in separate arrays. The ith *slice*
(names[i] and salaries[i]) contains data that needs to be processed together. These
arrays are called *parallel arrays* (Figure 11).

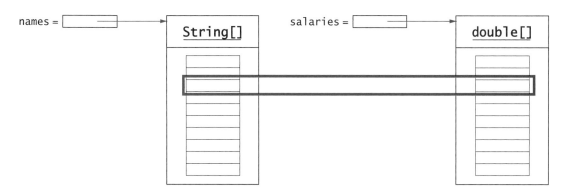

Figure 11

Avoid Parallel Arrays

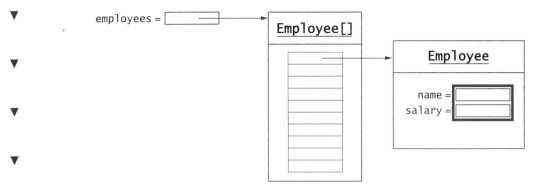

Figure 12

Reorganizing Parallel Arrays into an Array of Objects

If you find yourself using two arrays that have the same length, ask yourself whether you couldn't replace them with a single array of a class type. Look at a slice and find the *concept* that it represents. Then make the concept into a class. In our example each slice contains a name and a salary, describing an *employee*. Therefore, it is an easy matter to use a single array of objects

```
Employee[] staff;
```

(See Figure 12.) Or, even better, use an `ArrayList` of `Employee` objects.

Why is this beneficial? Think ahead. Maybe your program will change and you will need to store the job title of the employees as well. It is a simple matter to update the `Employee` class. It may well be quite complicated to add a new array and make sure that all methods that accessed the original two arrays now also correctly access the third one.

13.7   Two-Dimensional Arrays

> Two-dimensional arrays form a tabular, two-dimensional arrangement. You access elements with an index pair a[i][j].

Arrays and array lists can store linear sequences. Occasionally you want to store collections that have a two-dimensional layout. The traditional example is the tic-tac-toe board (see Figure 13).

Such an arrangement, consisting of rows and columns of values, is called a *two-dimensional array* or *matrix*. When constructing a two-dimensional array, you specify how many rows and columns you need. In this case, ask for 3 rows and 3 columns:

```
final int ROWS = 3;
final int COLUMNS = 3;
char[][] board = new char[ROWS][COLUMNS];
```

This yields a two-dimensional array with 9 elements

```
board[0][0]    board[0][1]    board[0][2]
board[1][0]    board[1][1]    board[1][2]
board[2][0]    board[2][1]    board[2][2]
```

Figure 13

A Tic-Tac-Toe Board

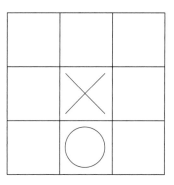

To access a particular element, specify two subscripts in separate brackets:

```
board[i][j] = 'x';
```

When filling or searching a two-dimensional array, it is common to use two nested loops. For example, this pair of loops sets all elements in the array to spaces.

```
for (int i = 0; i < ROWS; i++)
   for (int j = 0; j < COLUMNS; j++)
      board[i][j] = ' ';
```

Here is a class and a test program for playing tic-tac-toe. This class does not check whether a player has won the game. That is left as the proverbial exercise to the reader—see Exercise P13.15.

File TicTacToe.java

```
 1  /**
 2     A 3 × 3 tic-tac-toe board.
 3  */
 4  public class TicTacToe
 5  {
 6     /**
 7        Constructs an empty board.
 8     */
 9     public TicTacToe()
10     {
11        board = new char[ROWS][COLUMNS];
12
13        // fill with spaces
14        for (int i = 0; i < ROWS; i++)
15           for (int j = 0; j < COLUMNS; j++)
16              board[i][j] = ' ';
17     }
18
```

```
19      /**
20          Sets a field in the board. The field must be unoccupied.
21          @param i  the row index
22          @param j  the column index
23          @param player  the player ('x' or 'o')
24      */
25      public void set(int i, int j, char player)
26      {
27          if (board[i][j] != ' ')
28              throw new IllegalArgumentException(
29                  "Position occupied");
30          board[i][j] = player;
31      }
32
33      /**
34          Creates a string representation of the board such as
35          |x  o|
36          |  x |
37          |   o|.
38          @return  the string representation
39      */
40      public String toString()
41      {
42          String r = "";
43          for (int i = 0; i < ROWS; i++)
44          {
45              r = r + "|";
46              for (int j = 0; j < COLUMNS; j++)
47                  r = r + board[i][j];
48              r = r + "|\n";
49          }
50          return r;
51      }
52
53      private char[][] board;
54      private static final int ROWS = 3;
55      private static final int COLUMNS = 3;
56 }
```

File TicTacToeTest.java

```
1 import javax.swing.JOptionPane;
2
3 /**
4     This program tests the TicTacToe class by prompting the
5     user to set positions on the board and printing out the
6     result.
7 */
```

```
 8  public class TicTacToeTest
 9  {
10     public static void main(String[] args)
11     {
12        char player = 'x';
13        TicTacToe game = new TicTacToe();
14        while (true)
15        {
16           System.out.println(game); // calls game.toString()
17           String input = JOptionPane.showInputDialog(
18              "Row for " + player + " (Cancel to exit)");
19           if (input == null) System.exit(0);
20           int row = Integer.parseInt(input);
21           input = JOptionPane.showInputDialog(
22              "Column for " + player);
23           int column = Integer.parseInt(input);
24           game.set(row, column, player);
25           if (player == 'x') player = 'o';
26           else player = 'x';
27        }
28     }
29  }
```

▼ **ᴀᴛ Advanced Topic**   **13.2**

Two-Dimensional Arrays with Variable Row Lengths

▼
When you declare a two-dimensional array with the command

```
int[][] a = new int[5][5];
```

▼
then you get a 5-by-5 matrix that can store 25 elements:

```
a[0][0] a[0][1] a[0][2] a[0][3] a[0][4]
a[1][0] a[1][1] a[1][2] a[1][3] a[1][4]
a[2][0] a[2][1] a[2][2] a[2][3] a[2][4]
a[3][0] a[3][1] a[3][2] a[3][3] a[3][4]
a[4][0] a[4][1] a[4][2] a[4][3] a[4][4]
```

▼
In this matrix, all rows have the same length. In Java it is possible to declare arrays in which the row length varies. For example, you can store an array that has triangular shape, such as this one:

```
b[0][0]
b[1][0] b[1][1]
b[2][0] b[2][1] b[2][2]
b[3][0] b[3][1] b[3][2] b[3][3]
b[4][0] b[4][1] b[4][2] b[4][3] b[4][4]
```

▼

To allocate such an array, you must work harder. First, you allocate space to hold five rows. You indicate that you will manually set each row by leaving the second array index empty:

▼

```
int[][] b = new int[5][];
```

Then you need to allocate each row separately.

▼

```
for (int i = 0; i < b.length; i++)
    b[i] = new int[i + 1];
```

▼

You can access each array element as b[i][j], but you must now be careful that j is less than b[i].length.

Naturally, such "ragged" arrays are not very common.

▼

Chapter Summary

1. An array list is a sequence of objects.

2. Each object in an array list has an integer position number, called the index.

3. When retrieving an element from an array list, you need to cast the return value of the get method to the element class.

4. Position numbers of an array range from 0 to size() - 1. Accessing a nonexistent position results in a bounds error.

5. To find a value in an array list, check all elements until you have found a match.

6. To count values in an array list, check all elements and count the matches, until you reach the end of the array list.

7. To compute the maximum or minimum value of an array list, initialize a candidate with the starting element. Then compare the candidate with the remaining elements and update it if you find a larger or smaller value.

8. To store primitive type values in an array list, you must use wrapper classes.

9. An array is a fixed-length sequence of values of the same type.

10. You access array elements with an integer index, using the notation a[i].

11. Use the length field to find the number of elements in an array.

12. An array variable stores a reference to the array. Copying the variable yields a second reference to the same array.

13. Use the clone method to copy the elements of an array.

14. Use the System.arraycopy method to copy elements from one array to another.

15. Arrays are often *partially filled*. Then you need to remember the number of elements that you actually placed in the array.

16. If you run out of space in an array, you need to allocate a larger array and copy the elements into it.

17. Avoid parallel arrays by changing them into arrays of objects.

18. Two-dimensional arrays form a tabular, two-dimensional arrangement. You access elements with an index pair `a[i][j]`.

Further Reading

[1] Barton P. Miller, Louis Fericksen, and Bryan So, "An Empirical Study of the Reliability of Unix Utilities", *Communications of the ACM*, vol. 33, no. 12 (December 1990), pp. 32–44.
[2] Peter J. Denning, *Computers under Attack*, Addison-Wesley, 1990.
[3] Cliff Stoll, *The Cuckoo's Egg*, Doubleday, 1989.

CLASSES, OBJECTS, AND METHODS INTRODUCED IN THIS CHAPTER

```
java.lang.Boolean
    booleanValue
java.lang.Double
    doubleValue
java.lang.Integer
    intValue
java.lang.System
    arrayCopy
java.util.ArrayList
    add
    get
    remove
    set
    size
```

REVIEW EXERCISES

Exercise R13.1. What is an index? What are the bounds of an array list? What is a bounds error?

Exercise R13.2. Write a program that contains a bounds error. Run the program. What happens on your computer? How does the error message help you locate the error?

Exercise R13.3. Write Java code for a loop that simultaneously computes the maximum and minimum value of an array list. Use an array list of coins as an example.

Exercise R13.4. Write a loop that reads ten strings and inserts them into an array list. Write a second loop that prints out the strings in the opposite order from which they were entered.

Exercise R13.5. For each of the following sets of values, write code that fills an array a with the values.

- 1 2 3 4 5 6 7 8 9 10
- 0 2 4 6 8 10 12 14 16 18 20
- 1 4 9 16 25 36 49 64 81 100
- 0 0 0 0 0 0 0 0 0 0
- 1 4 9 16 9 7 4 9 11

Use a loop when appropriate.

Exercise R13.6. Write a loop that fills an array a with ten random numbers between 1 and 100. Write code (using one or more loops) to fill a with ten *different* random numbers between 1 and 100.

Exercise R13.7. What is wrong with the following loop?

```
double[] data = new double[10];
for (int i = 1; i <= 10; i++) data[i] = i * i;
```

Explain two ways of fixing the error.

Exercise R13.8. Write a program that fills an array of 20 integers with the numbers 1, 4, 9, . . . , 100. Compile it and launch the debugger. After the array has been filled with three numbers, *inspect it*. What are the contents of the elements in the array beyond those that you filled?

Exercise R13.9. Give an example of

- A useful method that has an array of integers as a parameter that is not modified
- A useful method that has an array of integers as a parameter that is modified
- A useful method that has an array of integers as a return value

Just describe each method. Don't implement the methods.

Exercise R13.10. A method that has an array list as a parameter can change the contents in two ways. It can change the contents of individual array elements, or it can rearrange the elements. Describe two useful methods with `ArrayList` parameters that change an array list of `Employee` objects in each of the two ways just described.

Exercise R13.11. What are parallel arrays? Why are parallel arrays indications of poor programming? How can they be avoided?

Exercise R13.12. How do you perform the following tasks with arrays in Java?

- Test that two arrays contain the same elements in the same order.
- Copy one array to another.
- Fill an array with zeroes, overwriting all elements in it.
- Remove all elements from an array list.

Exercise R13.13. True or false?

- All elements of an array are of the same type.
- Array subscripts must be integers.
- Arrays cannot contain strings as elements.
- Arrays cannot use strings as subscripts.
- Parallel arrays must have equal length.
- Two-dimensional arrays always have the same numbers of rows and columns.
- Two parallel arrays can be replaced by a two-dimensional array.
- Elements of different columns in a two-dimensional array can have different types.
- Elements in an array list can have different types.

Exercise R13.14. True or false?

- A method cannot return a two-dimensional array.
- A method can change the length of an array parameter.
- A method can change the length of an array list that is passed as a parameter.
- An array list can hold values of any type.

PROGRAMMING EXERCISES

Exercise P13.1. Implement a class `Bank` that contains an array list of `BankAccount` objects. Support methods

```
public void addAccount(double initialBalance)
public void deposit(int account, double amount)
public void withdraw(int account, double amount)
public double getBalance(int account)
```

An account number is simply an index into the array list.

Exercise P13.2. Add a method `toString` to the `Purse` class that prints the coins in the purse in the format

```
Purse[Quarter,Dime,Nickel,Dime]
```

Exercise P13.3. Write a method `reverse` that reverses the sequence of coins in a purse. Use the `toString` method of the preceding assignment to test your code. For example, if `reverse` is called with a purse

```
Purse[Quarter,Dime,Nickel,Dime]
```

then the purse is changed to

```
Purse[Dime,Nickel,Dime,Quarter]
```

Exercise P13.4. Add a method

```
public void transfer(Purse other)
```

that transfers the contents of one purse to another. For example, if `a` is

```
Purse[Quarter,Dime,Nickel,Dime]
```

and b is

```
Purse[Dime,Nickel]
```

then after the call `a.append(b)`, a is

```
Purse[Quarter,Dime,Nickel,Dime,Dime,Nickel]
```

and b is empty.

Exercise P13.5. Write an `equals` method for the `Purse` class

```
public boolean equals(Object other)
```

that checks whether the other purse has the same coins in the same order.

Exercise P13.6. Write an `equals` method for the `Purse` class

```
public boolean equals(Object other)
```

that checks whether the other purse has the same coins in *some* order. For example, the purses

```
Purse[Quarter,Dime,Nickel,Dime]
```

and

```
Purse[Nickel,Dime,Dime,Quarter]
```

should be considered equal.

You will probably need one or more helper methods.

Exercise P13.7. Implement a class `Cloud` that contains an array list of `Point2D.Double` objects. Support methods

```
public void add(Point2D.Double aPoint)
public void draw(Graphics2D g2)
```

Draw each point as a tiny circle.

Write an applet that draws a cloud of 20 random points.

Exercise P13.8. Implement a class `Polygon` that contains an array list of `Point2D.Double` objects. Support methods

```
public void add(Point2D.Double aPoint)
public void draw(Graphics2D g2)
```

Draw the polygon by joining adjacent points by a line, and then closing it up by joining the end and start points.

Write an applet that draws a square and a pentagon using two `Polygon` objects.

Exercise P13.9. Write methods of the `Polygon` class of the preceding exercise

```
public double perimeter()
```

and

```
public double area()
```

that compute the circumference and the area of a polygon. To compute the perimeter, compute the distance between adjacent points, and total up the distances. The area of a polygon with corners $(x_0, y_0), \ldots, (x_{n-1}, y_{n-1})$ is

$$\tfrac{1}{2}(x_0 y_1 + x_1 y_2 + \cdots + x_{n-1} y_0 - y_0 x_1 - y_1 x_2 - \cdots - y_{n-1} x_0)$$

As test cases, compute the perimeter and area of a rectangle and of a regular hexagon.

Exercise P13.10. Add a method that computes the *alternating sum* of all elements in the DataSet class of section 13. 6. For example, if alternatingSum is called with the data

$$1 \quad 4 \quad 9 \quad 16 \quad 9 \quad 7 \quad 4 \quad 9 \quad 11$$

then it computes

$$1 - 4 + 9 - 16 + 9 - 7 + 4 - 9 + 11 = -2$$

Exercise P13.11. Write a program that produces random permutations of the numbers 1 to 10. To generate a random permutation, you need to fill an array with the numbers 1 to 10 so that no two entries of the array have the same contents. You could do it by brute force, by calling Random.nextInt until it produces a value that is not yet in the array. Instead, you should implement a smart method. Make a second array and fill it with the numbers 1 to 10. Then pick one of those at random, *remove it*, and append it to the permutation array. Repeat ten times. Implement a class PermutationGenerator with a method

```
int[] nextPermutation
```

Exercise P13.12. Write a class Chart with methods

```
public void add(int value)
public void draw(Graphics2D g2)
```

that displays a stick chart of the added values, similar to the chart in Section 4.10. You may assume that the values are pixel positions.

Exercise P13.13. Write a class BarChart with methods

```
public void add(double value)
public void draw(Graphics2D g2)
```

that displays a chart of the added values. You may assume that all values in data are positive. *Hint:* You must figure out the maximum of the values. Set the coordinate system so that the x-range equals the number of bars and the y-range goes from 0 to the maximum.

Exercise P13.14. Improve the BarChart class of the preceding exercise to work correctly when data contains negative values.

Exercise P13.15. Write a class PieChart with methods

```
public void add(double value)
public void draw(Graphics2D g2)
```

that displays a pie chart of the values in data. You may assume that all values in data are positive.

Exercise P13.16. Add a method `getWinner` to the `TicTacToe` class of Section 13.7. It should return `'x'` or `'o'` to indicate a winner, or `' '` if there is no winner yet. Recall that a winning position has three matching marks in a row, column, or diagonal.

Exercise P13.17. Write an applet that plays tic-tac-toe. Your program should draw the game board, accept mouse clicks into empty squares, change players after every successful move, and pronounce the winner.

Exercise P13.18. *Magic squares.* An $n \times n$ matrix that is filled with the numbers 1, 2, 3, . . . , n^2 is a magic square if the sum of the elements in each row, in each column, and in the two diagonals is the same value. For example,

16	3	2	13
5	10	11	8
9	6	7	12
4	15	14	1

Write a program that reads in n^2 values from the keyboard and tests whether they form a magic square when arranged as a square matrix. You need to test three features:

- Did the user enter n^2 numbers for some n?
- Does each of the numbers 1, 2, . . . , n^2 occur exactly once in the user input?
- When the numbers are put into a square, are the sums of the rows, columns, and diagonals equal to each other?

If the size of the input is a square, test whether all numbers between 1 and n are present. Then compute the row, column, and diagonal sums. Implement a class `Square` with methods

```
public void add(int i)
public boolean isMagic()
```

Exercise P13.19. Implement the following algorithm to construct magic n-by-n squares; it works only if n is odd. Place a 1 in the middle of the bottom row. After k has been placed in the (i, j) square, place $k + 1$ into the square to the right and down, wrapping around the borders. However, if the square to the right and down has already been filled, or if you are in the lower right corner, then you must move to the square straight up instead. Here is the 5×5 square that you get if you follow this method:

11	18	25	2	9
10	12	19	21	3
4	6	13	20	22
23	5	7	14	16
17	24	1	8	15

Write a program whose input is the number *n* and whose output is the magic square of order *n* if *n* is odd. Implement a class `MagicSquare` with a constructor that constructs the square and a `toString` method that returns a representation of the square.

Exercise P13.20. The *Game of Life* is a well-known mathematical game that gives rise to amazingly complex behavior, although it can be specified by a few simple rules. (It is not actually a game in the traditional sense, with players competing for a win.) Here are the rules. The game is played on a rectangular board. Each square can be either empty or occupied. At the beginning, you can specify empty and occupied cells in some way; then the game runs automatically. In each *generation*, the next generation is computed. A new cell is born on an empty square if it is surrounded by exactly three occupied neighbor cells. A cell dies of overcrowding if it is surrounded by four or more neighbors, and it dies of loneliness if it is surrounded by zero or one neighbors. A neighbor is an occupant of an adjacent square to the left, right, top, or bottom or in a diagonal direction. Figure 14 shows a cell and its neighbor cells.

Many configurations show interesting behavior when subjected to these rules. Figure 15 shows a *glider*, observed over five generations. Note how it moves. After four generations, it is transformed into the identical shape, but located one square to the right and below.

One of the more amazing configurations is the *glider gun:* a complex collection of cells that, after 30 moves, turns back into itself and a glider. (See Figure 16.)

Program the game to eliminate the drudgery of computing successive generations by hand. Use a two-dimensional array to store the rectangular configuration. Write a program that shows successive generations of the game. You may get extra credit if you implement an applet that lets the user add or remove cells by clicking with the mouse.

Figure 14

Neighborhood of a Cell in the Game of Life

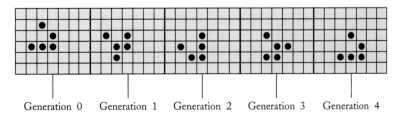

Generation 0   Generation 1   Generation 2   Generation 3   Generation 4

Figure 15

Glider

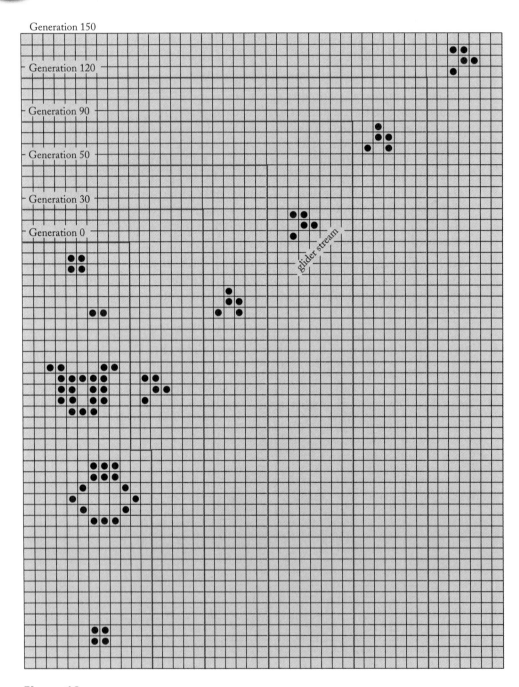

Figure 16

Glider Gun

Exception Handling

CHAPTER GOALS

To learn how to throw exceptions

▶ To be able to design your own exception classes

▶ To understand the difference between checked and unchecked exceptions

▶ To learn how to catch exceptions

▶ To know when and where to catch an exception

As you probably know from your own experience, programs can fail for a variety of reasons. Bad input and programmer error are just two of many possible causes. A program should deal with failure in a predictable manner. There are two aspects to handling failure: *detection* and *recovery*. A major challenge of error handling is that the point of detection is usually decoupled from the point of recovery. For example, the get method of the ArrayList class may detect that a nonexistent element is being accessed, and the parseInt method of the Integer class may detect that the string that it is processing can't be an integer, but neither of these methods has enough information to decide what to do about this failure. Should the user be asked to try a different operation? Should the program be aborted after saving the user's work? The logic for these actions is completely independent from the normal processing that these methods do. In Java, *exception handling* provides a flexible mechanism for passing control from the point of error detection to a competent recovery handler. This short chapter discusses the exception handling mechanism in detail and shows you how to use it appropriately in your programs.

14.1   Throwing Exceptions

When a method detects a problematic situation, what should it do? The traditional solution is that the method returns an indicator whether it succeeded or failed. For example, the showInputDialog method of the JOptionPane class returns either a string or null if the user canceled the dialog instead of supplying an input string. However, this approach has two problems.

1. The calling method may forget to check the return value.
2. The calling method may not be able to do anything about the failure.

If the calling method forgets to check the return value, a failure notification may go completely undetected. Then the program keeps going, processing faulty information and mysteriously failing later.

If the caller knows about the failure but it cannot do anything about it, it can fail too and let *its* caller worry about it. That would be a real hassle for the programmer, because many method calls would need to be checked for failure. Instead of programming for success,

```
x.doStuff();
```

you would always be programming for failure:

```
if (!x.doStuff()) return false;
```

That is fine when done occasionally, but if you have to check *every* method call, then your programs become very hard to read.

The exception handling mechanism has been designed to solve these two problems:

1. Exceptions can't be overlooked.
2. Exceptions can be handled by a *competent* handler—not just the caller of the failed method.

> To signal an exceptional condition, use the `throw` statement to throw an exception object.

Let us look into the details of this mechanism. When you detect an error condition, your job is really easy. You just `throw` an appropriate exception object, and you are done. For example, suppose someone tries to withdraw too much money from a bank account.

```
public class BankAccount
{
    public void withdraw(double amount)
    {
        if (amount > balance)
            // now what?
        . . .
    }
    . . .
}
```

First look for an appropriate exception class. The Java library provides many classes to signal all sorts of exceptional conditions. Figure 1 shows the most useful ones.

Look around for an exception type that might describe your situation. How about the `IllegalStateException`? Is the bank account in an illegal state for the `withdraw` operation? Not really—some `withdraw` operations could succeed. Is the argument illegal? Indeed it is. It is just too large. Therefore, let's throw an `IllegalArgumentException`.

```
public class BankAccount
{
    public void withdraw(double amount)
    {
        if (amount > balance)
        {
            IllegalArgumentException exception
                = new IllegalArgumentException(
                    "Amount exceeds balance");
            throw exception;
        }
        balance = balance - amount;
    }
    . . .
}
```

Actually, you don't have to store the exception object in a variable. You can just throw the object that the **new** operator returns:

```
throw new IllegalArgumentException(
    "Amount exceeds balance");
```

> When you throw an exception, the current method terminates immediately.

When you throw an exception, the method exits immediately, just as with a `return` statement. Execution does not continue with the method's caller but with an *exception handler*. For now, we won't worry about the handling of the exception. That is the topic of Section 14.4.

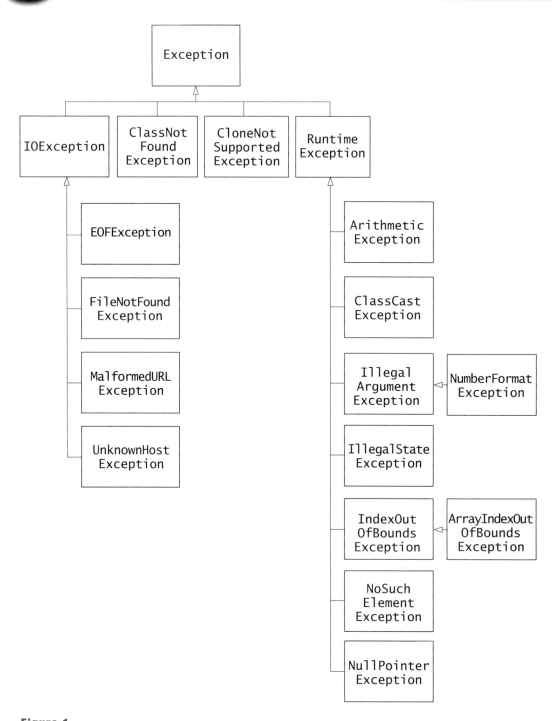

Figure 1

The Hierarchy of Exception Classes

> ### Syntax 14.1: Throwing an Exception
>
> `throw` *exceptionObject*;
>
> **Example:**
>
> `throw new IllegalArgumentException();`
>
> **Purpose:**
>
> To throw an exception and transfer control to a handler for this exception type

---

 Quality Tip `14.1`

Throw Exceptions Only in Exceptional Cases

Consider the `readLine` method of the `BufferedReader` class. It returns `null` at the end of the input. Why doesn't it throw an `EOFException`?

The designers of this method did the right thing. Every input must come to an end. In other words, the end of input is a normal condition, not an exceptional one. Whenever you read a line of input, you must be prepared to deal with the possibility that you reached the end. However, if the end of input occurs inside a data record that should be complete, then you can throw an `EOFException` to indicate that the input came to an *unexpected* end. This must have been caused by some exceptional event, perhaps a corrupted file.

In particular, you should *never* use exceptions as a "`break` statement on steroids". Don't throw an exception to exit a deeply nested loop or a set of recursive method calls. That is considered an abuse of the exception mechanism.

14.2 Checked Exceptions

> There are two kinds of exceptions:
> checked exceptions
> and unchecked exceptions.
> Unchecked exceptions
> extend the class
> `RuntimeException`
> or `Error`.

Java exceptions fall into two categories, called *checked* and *unchecked* exceptions. When you call a method that throws a checked exception, you *must* tell the compiler what you are going to do about the exception if it is ever thrown. For example, all subclasses of `IOException` are checked exceptions. On the other hand, the compiler does not require you to keep track of unchecked exceptions. Exceptions such as `NumberFormatException`, `IllegalArgumentException`, and `NullPointerException` are unchecked exceptions. More generally, all exceptions that belong to subclasses of `RuntimeException` are unchecked, and all other subclasses of the class `Exception` are checked (see Figure 2). There is a second category of internal errors that are reported by throwing objects of type `Error`. One example is the `OutOfMemoryError`, which is thrown when all available

> Checked exceptions are due to external circumstances that the programmer cannot prevent. The compiler checks that your program handles these exceptions.

memory has been used up. These are fatal errors that happen rarely and are beyond your control. They too are unchecked.

Why have two kinds of exceptions? A checked exception describes a problem that is likely to occur at times, no matter how careful you are. The unchecked exceptions, on the other hand, are *your fault*. For example, an unexpected end of file can be caused by forces beyond your control, such as a disk error or a broken network connection. But you are to blame for a `NullPointerException`, because your code was wrong when it tried to use a `null` reference.

The compiler doesn't check whether you handle a `NullPointer-Exception`, because you should test your references for `null` before using them instead of installing a handler for that exception. The compiler does insist that your program be able to handle error conditions that you cannot *prevent*.

Actually, those categories aren't perfect. For example, it isn't your fault if a user enters an incorrect number, but `Integer.parseInt` throws an unchecked `NumberFormatException`.

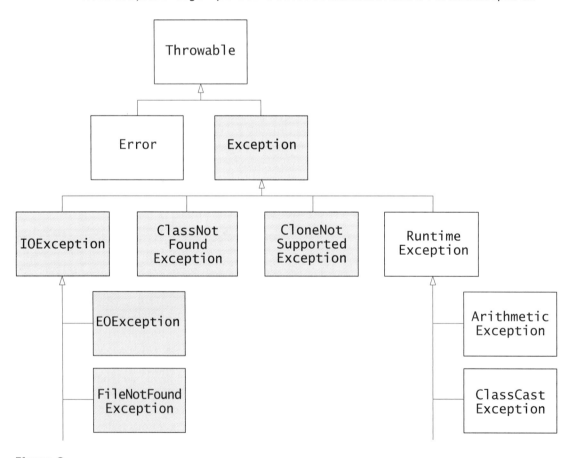

Figure 2

Checked and Unchecked Exceptions

As you can see from Figure 2, the majority of checked exceptions occur when you deal with input and output. That is a fertile ground for external failures beyond your control—a file might have been corrupted or removed, a network connection might be overloaded, a server might have crashed, and so on. Therefore, you will need to deal with checked exceptions principally when programming with files and streams.

Advanced Topic 3.6 showed you how to use a `BufferedReader` class to read console input from `System.in`. First, construct the reader object:

```
BufferedReader console = new BufferedReader(
    new InputStreamReader(System.in));
```

Then call the `readLine` method to read a line of input from the console window.

```
String input = console.readLine();
```

As you will see in greater detail in the next chapter, reading text from a file is very similar:

```
String filename = . . .;
BufferedReader reader = new BufferedReader(
    new FileReader(filename));
```

Suppose you write a method that calls the `readLine` method, which can throw an `IOException`. The `IOException` is a checked exception, so you need to tell the compiler what you are going to do about it. You have two choices. You can handle the exception in the same method that contains the call to `readLine`, using the techniques that you will see in Section 14.4. Or you can simply tell the compiler that you are aware of this exception and that you want your method to be terminated when it occurs. The method that reads input rarely knows what to do about an unexpected error, so that is usually the better option.

Here is an example of a method that reads a two-line coin description, like this:

```
0.5
half dollar
```

> Add a `throws` specifier to a method that can throw a checked exception.

The method calls `readLine` and therefore needs to declare that it might throw an `IOException`. If that happens, we want the `read` method to terminate. To declare that a method should be terminated when a checked exception occurs within it, tag the method with a `throws` specifier.

```
public class Coin
{
    public void read(BufferedReader in) throws IOException
    {
        value = Double.parseDouble(in.readLine());
        name = in.readLine();
    }
    . . .
}
```

The `throws` clause in turn signals the caller of your method that it may encounter an `IOException`. Then the caller needs to make the same decision—handle the exception, or tell its caller that the exception may be thrown. For example, consider the `read` method of a `Purse` class:

```
public class Purse
{
   public void read(BufferedReader in) throws IOException
   {
      while (. . .)
      {
         Coin c = new Coin();
         c.read(in);
         add(c);
      }
   }
   . . .
}
```

Even though the read method doesn't call readLine, it calls Coin.read, and that method declares that it might throw an IOException. Since the Purse.read method does not handle that exception, it too declares that it might throw it.

If your method can throw multiple checked exceptions, you separate them by commas:

```
public void read(BufferedReader in)
   throws IOException, ClassNotFoundException
```

It sounds somehow irresponsible not to handle an exception when you know that it happened. Actually, though, it is usually best not to catch an exception if you don't know how to *remedy* the situation. After all, what can you do in a low-level read method? Can you tell the user? How? By sending a message to System.out? You don't know whether this method is called in an applet or maybe an embedded system (such as a vending machine), where the user may never see System.out. And even if your users can see your error message, how do you know that they can understand English? Your class may be used to build an application for users in another country. Or can you perhaps fix up the object and keep going? How? If you set a variable to null or an empty string, that may just cause the program to break later, with much greater mystery.

Of course, *some* methods in the program know how to communicate with the user or take other remedial action. By allowing the exception to reach those methods, you make it possible for the exception to be processed by a *competent* handler.

Syntax 14.2: Exception Specifications

accessSpecifier returnType methodName
          (*parameterType parameterName*, . . .)
     throws *ExceptionClass*, *ExceptionClass*, . . .

Example:

```
public void read(BufferedReader in)
   throws IOException
```

Purpose:

To indicate the checked exceptions that this method can throw

---

Designing Your Own Exception Types

Sometimes none of the standard exception types describes your particular error condition well enough. In that case, you can design your own exception class. Consider a bank account. Let's report an `InsufficientFundsException` when an attempt is made to withdraw an amount from a bank account that exceeds the current balance.

```
if (amount > balance)
{
    throw new InsufficientFundsException(
        "withdrawal of " + amount +
        " exceeds balance of " + balance);
}
```

> You can design your own exception types–subclasses of `Exception` or `RuntimeException`.

Now you need to define the `InsufficientFundsException` class. Should it be a checked or an unchecked exception? Is it the fault of some external event, or is it the fault of the programmer? We take the position that the programmer could have prevented the exceptional condition—after all, it would have been an easy matter to check whether `amount <= account.getBalance()` before calling the `withdraw` method. Therefore, the exception should be an unchecked exception and extend the `RuntimeException` class or one of its subclasses.

It is customary to provide two constructors for an exception class: a default constructor and a constructor that accepts a message string describing the reason for the exception. Here is the definition of the exception class.

```
public class InsufficientFundsException
    extends RuntimeException
{
    public InsufficientFundsException()
    {
    }

    public InsufficientFundsException(String reason)
    {
        super(reason);
    }
}
```

Catching Exceptions

Every exception should be handled *somewhere* in your program. If an exception has no handler, an error message is printed, and your program terminates. That may be fine for a student program. But you would not want a professionally written program to die just because some method detected an unexpected error. Therefore, you must install exception handlers for all exceptions that your program might throw.

In a method that is ready to handle a particular exception type, place the statements that can cause the exception inside a `try` block, and the handler inside a `catch` clause.

You install an exception handler with the `try` statement. Each `try` block contains one or more method calls that may cause an exception, and `catch` clauses for all possible exception types that the `try` block is willing to handle. Here is an example:

```
try
{
    BufferedReader in = new BufferedReader(
        new InputStreamReader(System.in));
    System.out.println("How old are you?");
    String inputLine = in.readLine();
    int age = Integer.parseInt(inputLine);
    age++;
    System.out.println("Next year, you'll be " + age);
}
catch (IOException exception)
{
    System.out.println("Input/output error "
        + exception);
}
catch (NumberFormatException exception)
{
    System.out.println("Input was not a number");
}
```

In this example, the `try` block contains six statements. Two exceptions may be thrown in this code: The `readLine` method can throw an `IOException`, and `Integer.parseInt` can throw a `NumberFormatException`. If either of these exceptions is actually thrown, then the rest of the instructions in the `try` block are skipped, and the appropriate `catch` clause is executed immediately. In that case, we inform the user of the source of the problem. (A better way of dealing with the exception would be to give the user another chance to provide a correct input—see Section 14.6 for a solution.)

When the `catch (IOException exception)` block is executed, then some method in the `try` block has failed with an `IOException`, and that exception object is stored in the variable `exception`. The `catch` clause can analyze that object to find out more details about the failure. For example, you can get a printout of the chain of method calls that lead to the exception, by calling

```
exception.printStackTrace()
```

Note that the caught object may belong to a *subclass* of `IOException` (such as `EOFException`).

Because all exceptions are subclasses of the class `Throwable`, you can catch all exceptions with a `catch (Throwable t)` clause. However, that is actually not a good idea (see Quality Tip 14.2).

It is important to remember that you should place `catch` clauses *only* in methods in which you can competently handle the particular exception type.

Syntax 14.3: General Try Block

```
try
{
    statement
    statement
     . . .
}
catch (ExceptionClass exceptionObject)
{
    statement
    statement
     . . .
}
catch (ExceptionClass exceptionObject)
{
    statement
    statement
     . . .
}
 . . .
```

Example:

```
try
{
    System.out.println("What is your name?");
    String name = console.readLine();
    System.out.println("Hello, " + name + "!");
}
catch (IOException exception)
{
    exception.printStackTrace();
    System.exit(1);
}
```

Purpose:

To execute one or more statements that may generate exceptions. If an exception of a particular type occurs, then stop executing those statements and instead go to the matching `catch` clause. If no exception occurs, then skip the `catch` clauses. In all cases, execute the `finally` clause if one is present.

Quality Tip 14.2

Do Not Squelch Exceptions

> It is better to declare that a method throws a checked exception than handle the exception poorly.

When you call a method that throws a checked exception, the compiler complains. In your eagerness to continue your work, it is an understandable impulse to shut the compiler up by *squelching* the exception:

▼
```
try
{
    input = in.readLine();
    // compiler complained about IOException
}
catch (Exception e) {} // so there!
```

▼ The do-nothing exception handler fools the compiler into thinking that the exception has been handled. In the long run, this is clearly a bad idea. Exceptions were designed to transmit problem reports to a *competent* handler. Installing an incompetent handler simply hides an error condition that could be serious.

14.5 The finally Clause

Occasionally, you need to take some action whether or not an exception is thrown. The finally construct is used to handle this situation. Here is a typical situation. Suppose a method opens a file, calls one or more methods, and then closes the file:

```
BufferedReader in;
in = new BufferedReader(new FileReader(filename));
purse.read(in);
in.close();
```

Now suppose that one of the methods before the last line throws an exception. Then the call to close is never executed! You solve this problem by placing the call to close inside a finally clause:

```
BufferedReader in = null;
try
{
    in = new BufferedReader(new FileReader(filename));
    purse.read(in);
}
finally
{
    if (in != null) in.close();
}
```

> Once a try block is entered, the statements in a finally clause are guaranteed to be executed, whether or not an exception is thrown.

In the normal case, there will be no problem. When the try block is completed, the finally clause is executed, and the file is closed. However, if an exception occurs, the finally clause is also executed before the exception is passed to its handler.

Notice that the finally clause closes the file only when in is not null. Of course, if the read method throws an exception, then in is not null. If the FileReader constructor throws an exception, however (usually because there is no file with the given name), then in has not yet been set, and you cannot close it. Also note that the in variable must be declared outside the try block so that it can be accessed in the finally clause.

Use the finally clause whenever you need to do some cleanup, such as closing a file, to ensure that the cleanup happens no matter how the method exits.

It is also possible to have a finally clause following one or more catch clauses. Then the code in the finally clause is executed whenever the try block is exited through any of three ways:

1. After completing the last statement of the try block
2. When an exception was thrown in the try block that is being passed to this method's caller
3. When an exception was thrown in the try block that was handled by one of the catch clauses

However, we will not use finally in such a complex situation in this book.

Syntax 14.4: finally **Clause**

```
try
{
    statement
    statement
    . . .
}
finally
{
    statement
    statement
    . . .
}
```

Example:

```
BufferedReader in = null;
try
{
    in = new BufferedReader(new
        FileReader(filename));
    purse.read(in);
}
finally
{
    if (in != null) in.close();
}
```

Purpose:

To execute one or more statements that may generate exceptions. If an exception of a particular type occurs, then stop executing those statements and instead go to the matching catch clause. If no exception occurs, then skip the catch clauses. In all cases, execute the finally clause if one is present.

14.6   A Complete Example

Let us walk through a complete example of a program with exception handling. The program asks a user for the name of a file, reads a sequence of coin descriptions from the file, adds coins to a purse, and then prints out the total of the purse.

What can go wrong? There are two principal risks.

- The file might not exist.

- The file might have data in the wrong format.

Who can detect these faults? The `FileReader` constructor will throw an exception when the file does not exist. We need to make sure that the `read` method of the `Coin` class throws an exception when it finds an error in the data format.

Who can remedy these faults? The `main` method of the `PurseTest` program interacts with the user. It should catch any exceptions and give the user another chance to enter a correct file.

Here is the `read` method of the `Coin` class.

```
public boolean read(BufferedReader in)
   throws IOException
{
   String input = in.readLine();
   if (input == null) return false;
   value = Double.parseDouble(input);
   name = in.readLine();
   if (name == null)
      throw new EOFException("Coin name expected");
   return true;
}
```

The method passes along all exceptions of type `IOException` that `readLine` may throw. Furthermore, when the method encounters an unexpected end of file, it reports it as an `EOFException`.

Note that the method differentiates between an *expected* end of file and an *unexpected* end of file. All files must come to an end. The method is prepared for the case that the end of the file has been reached before the *start* of a record. In that case, the method simply returns `false`. However, if the file ends in the *middle* of a record, then the method throws an exception.

Now let us put this method to use. The following `read` method of the `Purse` class reads coin records and adds them into a purse. It is completely unconcerned with any exceptions. If there is a problem with the input file, it simply passes the exception to its caller.

```
public void read(BufferedReader in)
   throws IOException
{
   boolean done = false;
   while (!done)
```

```
      {
         Coin c = new Coin();
         if (c.read(in))
            add(c);
         else
            done = true;
      }
   }
```

Next, here is the `readFile` method of the `Purse` class that opens the file and invokes the method you just saw. Note how the `finally` clause ensures that the file is closed even when an exception occurs.

```
   public void readFile(String filename)
      throws IOException
   {
      BufferedReader in = null;
      try
      {
         in = new BufferedReader(
            new FileReader(filename));
         read(in);
      }
      finally
      {
         if (in != null) in.close();
      }
   }
```

To complete the program, let's implement the user interaction in the `main` method. We ask the user for a file name, read the file, and print the total value of the coins. If there is a problem, we report the nature of the problem. The program is not terminated, and the user has a chance to open a different file.

```
   boolean done = false;
   String filename
      = JOptionPane.showInputDialog("Enter file name");

   while (!done)
   {
      try
      {
         Purse myPurse = new Purse();
         myPurse.readFile(filename);
         System.out.println("total="
            + myPurse.getTotal());
         done = true;
      }
      catch (IOException exception)
      {
         System.out.println("Input/output error "
            + exception);
```

```
      }
      catch (NumberFormatException exception)
      {
         exception.printStackTrace();
      }

      if (!done)
      {
         filename = JOptionPane.showInputDialog(
            "Try another file:");
         if (filename == null) done = true;
      }
   }
```

Let us look at a specific scenario.

1. `PurseTest.main` calls `Purse.readFile`.

2. `Purse.readFile` calls `Purse.read`.

3. `Purse.read` calls `Coin.read`.

4. `Coin.read` throws an `EOFException`.

5. `Coin.read` has no handler for the exception and terminates immediately.

6. `Purse.read` has no handler for the exception and terminates immediately.

7. `Purse.readFile` has no handler for the exception and terminates immediately after executing the `finally` clause and closing the file.

8. `PurseTest.main` has a handler for an `IOException`, a superclass of `EOFException`. That handler prints a message to the user. Afterwards, the user is given another chance to enter a file name. Note that the statement printing the purse total has been skipped.

This example shows the separation between error detection (in the `Coin.read` method) and error handling (in the `main` method). In between the two are the `Purse.read` and `Purse.readFile` methods, which just pass exceptions along.

File PurseTest.java

```
 1 import javax.swing.JOptionPane;
 2 import java.io.IOException;
 3
 4 /**
 5    This program prompts the user to enter a file name
 6    with coin values. A Purse object is filled with
 7    the coins specified in the file. In case of an exception,
 8    the user can choose another file.
 9 */
10 public class PurseTest
11 {
12    public static void main(String[] args)
13    {
14       boolean done = false;
```

```
15        String filename
16            = JOptionPane.showInputDialog(
17                "Enter file name");
18
19        while (!done)
20        {
21            try
22            {
23                Purse myPurse = new Purse();
24                myPurse.readFile(filename);
25                System.out.println("total="
26                    + myPurse.getTotal());
27                done = true;
28            }
29            catch (IOException exception)
30            {
31                System.out.println("Input/output error "
32                    + exception);
33            }
34            catch (NumberFormatException exception)
35            {
36                exception.printStackTrace();
37            }
38
39            if (!done)
40            [
41                filename = JOptionPane.showInputDialog(
42                    "Try another file:");
43                if (filename == null) done = true;
44            }
45        }
46        System.exit(0);
47    }
48 }
```

File Purse.java

```
1 import java.io.BufferedReader;
2 import java.io.FileReader;
3 import java.io.IOException;
4
5 /**
6     A purse computes the total of a collection of coins.
7 */
8 public class Purse
9 {
10    /**
11        Constructs an empty purse.
12    */
13    public Purse()
14    {
```

```
15         total = 0;
16      }
17
18      /**
19         Reads a file with coin descriptions and adds the coins
20         to the purse.
21         @param filename the name of the file
22      */
23      public void readFile(String filename)
24         throws IOException
25      {
26         BufferedReader in = null;
27         try
28         {
29            in = new BufferedReader(
30               new FileReader(filename));
31            read(in);
32         }
33         finally
34         {
35            if (in != null) in.close();
36         }
37      }
38
39      /**
40         Reads a file with coin descriptions and adds the coins
41         to the purse.
42         @param in the buffered reader for reading the input
43      */
44      public void read(BufferedReader in)
45         throws IOException
46      {
47         boolean done = false;
48         while (!done)
49         {
50            Coin c = new Coin();
51            if (c.read(in))
52               add(c);
53            else
54               done = true;
55         }
56      }
57
58      /**
59         Adds a coin to the purse.
60         @param aCoin the coin to add
61      */
62      public void add(Coin aCoin)
63      {
64         total = total + aCoin.getValue();
```

```
65     }
66
67     /**
68         Gets the total value of the coins in the purse.
69         @return  the sum of all coin values
70     */
71     public double getTotal()
72     {
73         return total;
74     }
75
76     private double total;
77 }
```

File Coin.java

```
 1 import java.io.BufferedReader;
 2 import java.io.EOFException;
 3 import java.io.IOException;
 4
 5 /**
 6     A coin with a monetary value.
 7 */
 8 public class Coin
 9 {
10     /**
11         Constructs a default coin.
12         Use the read method to fill in the value and name
13     */
14     public Coin()
15     {
16         value = 0;
17         name = "";
18     }
19
20     /**
21         Constructs a coin.
22         @param aValue  the monetary value of the coin
23         @param aName  the name of the coin
24     */
25     public Coin(double aValue, String aName)
26     {
27         value = aValue;
28         name = aName;
29     }
30
31     /**
32         Reads a coin value and name.
33         @param in  the reader
34         @return true  if the data were read,
```

```
35          false if the end of the stream was reached
36       */
37       public boolean read(BufferedReader in)
38          throws IOException
39       {
40          String input = in.readLine();
41          if (input == null) return false;
42          value = Double.parseDouble(input);
43          name = in.readLine();
44          if (name == null)
45             throw new EOFException("Coin name expected");
46          return true;
47       }
48
49       /**
50          Gets the coin value.
51          @return the value
52       */
53       public double getValue()
54       {
55          return value;
56       }
57
58       /**
59          Gets the coin name.
60          @return the name
61       */
62       public String getName()
63       {
64          return name;
65       }
66
67       private double value;
68       private String name;
69  }
```

Random Fact 14.1

The Ariane Rocket Incident

The European Space Agency, Europe's counterpart to NASA, had developed a rocket model called Ariane that it had successfully used several times to launch satellites and scientific experiments into space. However, when a new version, the Ariane 5, was launched on June 4, 1996, from ESA's launch site in Kourou, French Guiana, the rocket veered off course about 40 seconds after liftoff. Flying at an angle of more than 20 degrees, rather than straight up, exerted such an aerodynamic force that the boosters separated, which triggered the automatic self-destruction mechanism. The rocket blew itself up.

Figure 3

The Explosion of the Ariane Rocket

The ultimate cause of this accident was an unhandled exception! The rocket contained two identical devices (called inertial reference systems) that processed flight data from measuring devices and turned the data into information about the rocket position. The onboard computer used the position information for controlling the boosters. The same inertial reference systems and computer software had worked fine on the Ariane 4 predecessor.

However, due to design changes of the rocket, one of the sensors measured a larger acceleration force than had been encountered in the Ariane 4. That value, expressed as a floating-point value, was stored in a 16-bit integer (like a short variable in Java). Unlike Java, the Ada language, used for the device software, generates an exception if a floating-point number is too large to be converted to an integer. Unfortunately, the programmers of the device had decided that this situation would never happen and didn't provide an exception handler.

When the overflow did happen, the exception was triggered and, since there was no handler, the device shut itself off. The onboard computer sensed the failure and switched over to the backup device. However, that device had shut itself off for exactly the same reason, something that the designers of the rocket had not expected. They figured that the devices might fail for mechanical reasons, and the chances of two devices having the same mechanical failure was considered remote. At that point, the rocket was without reliable position information and went off course.

Perhaps it would have been better if the software hadn't been so thorough? If it had ignored the overflow, the device wouldn't have been shut off. It would have just computed bad data. But then the device would have reported wrong position data, which could have been just as fatal. Instead, a correct implementation should have caught overflow exceptions and come up with some strategy to recompute the flight data. Clearly, giving up was not a reasonable option in this context.

The advantage of the exception-handling mechanism is that it makes these issues explicit to programmers—something to think about when you curse the Java compiler for complaining about uncaught exceptions.

CHAPTER SUMMARY

1. To signal an exceptional condition, use the throw statement to throw an exception object.

2. When you throw an exception, the current method terminates immediately.

3. There are two kinds of exceptions: checked exceptions and unchecked exceptions. Unchecked exceptions extend the class `RuntimeException` or `Error`.

4. Checked exceptions are due to external circumstances that the programmer cannot prevent. The compiler checks that your program handles these exceptions.

5. Add a `throws` specifier to a method that can throw a checked exception.

6. You can design your own exception types—subclasses of `Exception` or `Runtime-Exception`.

7. In a method that is ready to handle a particular exception type, place the statements that can cause the exception inside a `try` block, and the handler inside a `catch` clause.

8. It is better to declare that a method throws a checked exception than to handle the exception poorly.

9. Once a `try` block is entered, the statements in a `finally` clause are guaranteed to be executed, whether or not an exception is thrown.

CLASSES, OBJECTS, AND METHODS INTRODUCED IN THIS CHAPTER

```
java.io.EOFException
java.io.FileNotFoundException
java.lang.IllegalStateException
java.lang.NullPointerException
java.lang.NumberFormatException
java.lang.RuntimeException
```

REVIEW EXERCISES

Exercise R14.1. What is the difference between throwing and catching an exception?

Exercise R14.2. What is a checked exception? What is an unchecked exception? Is a `NullPointerException` checked or unchecked? Which exceptions do you need to declare with the `throws` keyword?

Exercise R14.3. Why don't you need to declare that your method might throw a `NullPointerException`?

Exercise R14.4. When your program executes a `throw` statement, which statement is executed next?

Exercise R14.5. What happens if an exception does not have a matching `catch` clause?

Exercise R14.6. What can your program do with the exception object that a `catch` clause receives?

Exercise R14.7. Is the type of the exception object always the same as the type declared in the `catch` clause that catches it?

Exercise R14.8. What kind of objects can you throw? Can you throw a string? An integer?

Exercise R14.9. What is the purpose of the `finally` clause? Give an example of how it can be used.

Exercise R14.10. What happens when an exception is thrown, the code of a `finally` clause executes, and that code throws an exception of a different kind than the original one? Which one is caught by a surrounding `catch` clause? Write a sample program to try it out.

PROGRAMMING EXERCISES

Exercise P14.1. Modify the `BankAccount` class to throw an `IllegalArgumentException` when the account is constructed with a negative balance, when a negative amount is deposited, or when an amount that is not between 0 and the current balance is withdrawn. Write a test program that causes all three exceptions to occur and that catches them all.

Exercise P14.2. Repeat the preceding exercise, but throw exceptions of three exception types that you define yourself.

Exercise P14.3. Write a program that asks the user to input a set of coin values and names. When the user enters a coin value that is not a number, give the user a second chance to enter the value. After two chances, quit the program. Add all correctly specified coins to a purse, and print its total value when the user is done entering data. Use a `JOptionPane` to prompt for the input.

Exercise P14.4. Repeat the preceding problem, but give the user as many chances as necessary to enter a correct coin value. Quit the program only when the user cancels an input dialog.

Exercise P14.5. Define a class `ConsoleReader` with a method

```
String readLine(String prompt) { . . . }
```
that throws no exception. The `ConsoleReader` reads from a buffered reader attached to `System.in`. You need to catch the `IOException` that the `readLine` method may throw. Return a `null` in that case. Write a test program that tests the class.

Exercise P14.6. Enhance the class from the preceding problem to include two additional methods.

```
int readInt(String prompt)
double readDouble(String prompt)
```
As long as the conversion from the string to a number throws a `NumberFormatException`, repeat the prompt and give the user another chance to enter a correct value. Write a test program that tests the class.

Exercise P14.7. Repeat the preceding exercise, except read the input from a `JOptionPane`.

Exercise P14.8. You can read the contents of a text file with this sequence of commands.

```
String filename = "myfile.txt";
BufferedReader reader =
  new BufferedReader(new FileReader(filename));
```

```
boolean done = false;
while (!done)
{
    String input = reader.readLine();
    if (input == null) done = true;
    else do something with input
}
```

Design a class `TextFileReader` whose constructor receives the name of a file and whose `readLine` method returns the next line of input from the text file or `null` if the end of the file has been reached. Don't have these methods catch any exceptions, but use `throws` specifiers to report the exceptions that may occur. You may need to consult the API documentation for the exceptions. Be sure to close the file when any exception occurs. Write a test program that tests your class.

Exercise P14.9. You can read the contents of a web page with this sequence of commands.

```
String address = "http://java.sun.com/index.html";
URL u = new URL(address);
URLConnection connection = u.openConnection(u);
InputStream in = connection.getInputStream();
BufferedReader reader =
    new BufferedReader(new InputStreamReader(in));
boolean done = false;
while (!done)
{
    String input = reader.readLine();
    if (input == null) done = true;
    else do something with input
}
```

Design a class `WebPageReader`, whose constructor receives an address string and whose `readLine` method returns the next line of input from the web page or `null` if the end of the page has been reached. Don't have these methods catch any exceptions, but use `throws` specifiers to report the exceptions that may occur. You may need to consult the API documentation for the exceptions. Write a test program that tests your class.

Exercise P14.10. Design a class `Bank` that contains a number of bank accounts. Each account has an account number and a current balance. Add an `accountNumber` field to the `BankAccount` class. Store the bank accounts in an array list. Write a `readFile` method of the `Bank` class for reading a file with the format

```
accountNumber1   balance1
accountNumber2   balance2
. . .
```

Follow the design of the sample program in Section 14.6 and implement `read` methods for the `Bank` and `BankAccount` classes. Write a sample program to read in a file with bank accounts. Afterwards, print the account with the highest balance. If the file is not properly formatted, give the user another chance to select another file.

Streams

CHAPTER GOALS

To be able to read and write files

▶ To become familiar with the concepts of text and binary formats

▶ To be able to read and write objects using serialization

▶ To be able to process the command line

▶ To learn about encryption

▶ To understand when to use sequential and random file access

All of the programs we have discussed until now read their input from the keyboard and mouse and displayed their output on the screen. For console programs, you can read from a file or write to a file by using redirection (see Productivity Hint 6.1). That method for accessing files is useful but still limited. In this chapter you will learn how to write Java programs that interact with disk files and other sources of bytes and characters.

15.1 Streams, Readers, and Writers

There are two fundamentally different ways to store data: in *text* or *binary* format. In text format, data items are represented in human-readable form, as a sequence of *characters*. For example, the integer 12,345 is stored as the sequence of five characters:

```
'1' '2' '3' '4' '5'
```

In binary form, data items are represented in *bytes*. A byte is composed of 8 bits and can denote one of 256 values. For example, in binary format, the integer 12,345 is stored as a sequence of four *bytes:*

```
0 0 48 57
```

> Streams access sequences of bytes. Readers and writers access sequences of characters.

(because $12{,}345 = 48 \cdot 256 + 57$).

If you store information in text form, as a sequence of characters, you need to use the `Reader` and `Writer` class and their subclasses to process input and output. If you store information in binary form, as a sequence of bytes, you use the `InputStream` and `OutputStream` classes and their subclasses.

Text input and output are more convenient for humans, because it is easier to produce input (just use a text editor) and it is easier to check that output is correct (just look at the output file in an editor). However, binary storage is more compact and more efficient.

> Use `FileReader`, `FileWriter`, `FileInputStream`, and `FileOutputStream` classes to read and write disk files.

To read text data from a disk file, you create a `FileReader` object:

```
FileReader reader =
    new FileReader("input.txt");
```

To read binary data from a disk file, you create a `FileInputStream` object instead:

```
FileInputStream inputStream =
    new FileInputStream("input.dat");
```

Similarly, you use `FileWriter` and `FileOutputStream` objects to write data to a disk file in text or binary form:

```
FileWriter writer = new FileWriter("output.txt");
FileOutputStream outputStream =
    new FileOutputStream("output.dat");
```

> The read method returns an integer, either −1, at the end of the file, or another value, which you need to cast to a char or byte.

All these classes are defined in the java.io package.

The Reader class has a method, read, to read a single character at a time. (The FileReader class overrides this method to obtain the characters from a disk file.) However, the read method actually returns an int so that it can signal either that a character has been read or that the end of input has been reached. At the end of input, read returns −1. Otherwise it returns the character (as an integer between 0 and 65,535). You should test the return value and, if it is not −1, cast it to a char:

```
Reader reader = . . .;
int next = reader.read();
char c;
if (next != -1)
    c = (char)next;
```

The InputStream class also has a method, read, to read a single byte. The method also returns an int, namely either the byte that was input (as an integer between 0 and 255) or the integer −1 if the end of the input stream has been reached. You should test the return value and, if it is not −1, cast it to a byte:

```
InputStream in = . . .;
int next = in.read();
byte b;
if (next != -1)
    b = (byte)next;
```

> You must close all files that you no longer need.

Similarly, the Writer and FileOutputStream classes have a write method to write a single character or byte.

When you are done reading or writing from a file or reader, you should call the close method. This is particularly important when writing to a file. Only when you close it can you be assured that all changes are committed to the disk file. For example,

```
writer.close();
```

> Basic streams, readers, and writers can process only individual bytes or characters. You need to combine them with other classes to process lines of text or entire objects.

These basic methods are the only input and output methods that the file input and output classes provide. The Java stream package is built on the principle that each class should have a very focused responsibility. The job of a FileInputStream is to interact with files. Its job is to *get* bytes, not to analyze them. If you want to read numbers, strings, or other objects, you have to combine the class with other classes whose responsibility is group individual bytes or characters together into numbers, strings, and objects. You will see those classes later in this chapter.

▼ **Common Error** 15.1

▼

Backslashes in File Names

▼ When you specify a file name as a constant string, and the name contains backslash characters (as in a Windows filename), you must supply each backslash *twice:*

▼
```
in = new FileReader("c:\\homework\\input.dat");
```

Recall that a single backslash inside quoted strings is an *escape character* that is combined
▼ with another character to form a special meaning, such as \n for a newline character. The
\\ combination denotes a single backslash.

When a user supplies a file name to a program, however, the user should not type the
▼ backslash twice.

▼ **Common Error** 15.2

Negative byte Values

▼ In Java, the byte type is a *signed* type. There are 256 values of the byte type, from −128
to 127. The starting bit of the byte is the *sign bit*. If it is on, the number is negative. In
converting an integer into a byte, only the least significant byte of the integer is taken,
▼ and the remaining bytes are ignored. The result can be negative even if the integer is positive. For example,

▼
```
int n = 233; // binary 00000000 00000000 00000000 11101001
byte b = (byte)n; // binary 11101001, sign bit is on
if (b == n) . . . // not true! b is negative, n is positive
```

When the byte is converted back to an integer, then the result is still negative. In partic-
▼ ular, it is *different* from the original.

Here is an even trickier case. Consider this test:

▼
```
int next = in.read();
byte b = (byte)next;
if (b == 'é') . . .
```

▼ This test is *never* true, *even if* next was equal to the Unicode value for the 'é' character.
That Unicode value happens to be 233, but a single byte is always a value between −128
and 127. American readers won't be too concerned, because all characters and symbols
▼ used in American English have Unicode values in the "safe" range between 1 and 127,
but international programmers who use characters with Unicode values between 128 and
▼ 255 find this a source of continual frustration.

15.2   Reading and Writing Text Files

> When writing text files, use the `PrintWriter` class and the `print/println` methods.

In the previous section, you saw how to write data to a text file. You construct a `FileWriter` object from the file name:

```
FileWriter writer = new FileWriter("output.txt");
```

Now you can send your output to the file, a character at a time, by calling the `write` method.

Of course, you don't have the output available a character at a time. You have the output in the form of numbers or strings. For that reason, you need another class whose task it is to break up numbers and strings into individual characters and send them to a writer. That class is called a `PrintWriter`. You construct a `PrintWriter` from any `Writer` object:

```
PrintWriter out = new PrintWriter(writer);
```

Now you can use the familiar `print` and `println` methods to print numbers, objects, and strings:

```
out.println(29.95);
out.println(new Rectangle(5, 10, 15, 25));
out.println("Hello, World!");
```

The `print` and `println` methods convert numbers to their decimal string representations and use the `toString` method to convert objects to strings; break up the strings into individual characters; and give each character to the `FileWriter` object through its `write` method. The `FileWriter` then sends them off to a file, a network connection, or some other destination.

> When reading text files, use the `BufferedReader` class and the `readLine` method.

Reading text files is unfortunately much less convenient. The Java library supplies no classes to read numbers directly. The best you can do is use the `BufferedReader` class, which has a `readLine` method that lets you read a line at a time. The `readLine` method keeps calling the `read` method of the reader object that you supplied in the constructor, until it has collected an entire input line. Then it returns that line. When all input has been consumed, the `readLine` method returns `null`.

After reading a line of input, you can use the `Integer.parseInt` and `Double.parseDouble` methods to convert the strings you find in the input to numbers.

```
FileReader reader = new FileReader("input.txt");
BufferedReader in = new BufferedReader(reader);
String inputLine = in.readLine();
double x = Double.parseDouble(inputLine);
```

If there are several items in a single input line, you can use the `StringTokenizer` class to break up the input line into multiple strings.

15.3 File Dialogs

> The JFileChooser dialog lets users select a file by navigating through directories.

In this section we show you how you can have a user supply a file name through a file dialog such as the one shown in Figure 1. The JFileChooser class implements a file dialog for the Swing user interface toolkit.

The JFileChooser class relies on another class, File, which describes disk files and directories. For example,

```
File inputFile = new File("input.txt");
```

> A File object describes a file or directory.

> You can pass a File object to the constructor of a file reader, writer, or stream.

describes the file input.txt in the current directory. The File class has methods to delete or rename the file. The file does not actually have to exist—you may want to pass the File object to an output stream or writer so that the file can be created. The exists method returns true if the file already exists.

You cannot directly use a File object for reading or writing. You still need to construct a file reader, writer, or stream from the File object. Simply pass the File object in the constructor.

```
FileReader in = new FileReader(inputFile);
```

The JFileChooser class has many options to fine-tune the display of the dialog, but in its most basic form it is quite simple: Construct a file chooser object; then call the showOpenDialog or showSaveDialog method. Both methods show the same dialog, but the button for selecting a file is labeled "Open" or "Save", depending on which method you call. For better placement of the dialog on the screen, you can specify the user interface component over which to pop up the dialog. If you don't care where the dialog pops up, you can simply pass null. These methods return either JFileChooser.APPROVE_OPTION, if the user has chosen a file, or JFileChooser.CANCEL_OPTION, if the user canceled the selection. If a file was chosen,

Figure 1

A JFileChooser Dialog

then you call the `getSelectedFile` method to obtain a `File` object that describes the file. Here is a complete example:

```
JFileChooser chooser = new JFileChooser();
FileReader in = null;
if (chooser.showOpenDialog(null)
    == JFileChooser.APPROVE_OPTION)
{
    File selectedFile = chooser.getSelectedFile();
    in = new FileReader(selectedFile);
}
```

15.4   An Encryption Program

Let us write a program that *encrypts* a file—that is, scrambles it so that it is unreadable except to those who know the decryption method and the secret keyword. Ignoring over 2000 years of progress in the field of encryption, we will use a method familiar to Julius Caesar. The person performing any encryption chooses an *encryption key;* here the key is a number between 1 and 25 that indicates the shift to be used in encrypting each letter. For example, if the key is 3, replace A with D, B with E, and so on (see Figure 2).

To decrypt, simply use the negative of the encryption key. For example, to decrypt the message of Figure 2, use a key of −3.

In this program we process binary data—we read each byte separately, encrypt it, and write the encrypted byte.

```
int next = in.read();
if (next == -1)
    done = true;
else
{
    byte b = (byte)next;
    byte c = encrypt(b);
    out.write(c);
}
```

In a more complex encryption program, you would read a block of bytes, encrypt the block, and write it out.

Because the program reads binary data, it uses streams, not readers and writers.

Here is the program. We put the `JFileChooserDialog` class to work to ask the user to specify the input and output files. Try out the program on a file of your choice. You will find that the encrypted file is unreadable. In fact, because the newline characters are

Figure 2

The Caesar Cipher

Plain text

M	e	e	t		m	e		a	t		t	h	e	

Encrypted text

P	h	h	w	#	p	h	#	d	w	#	w	k	h	#

transformed, you may not be able to read the encrypted file in a text editor. To decrypt, simply run the program again and supply the negative of the encryption key.

Program Encryptor.java

```
 1  import java.io.File;
 2  import java.io.FileInputStream;
 3  import java.io.FileOutputStream;
 4  import java.io.InputStream;
 5  import java.io.OutputStream;
 6  import java.io.IOException;
 7
 8  /**
 9      An encryptor encrypts files using the Caesar cipher.
10      For decryption, use an encryptor whose key is the
11      negative of the encryption key.
12  */
13  public class Encryptor
14  {
15      /**
16          Constructs an encryptor.
17          @param aKey  the encryption key
18      */
19      public Encryptor(int aKey)
20      {
21          key = aKey;
22      }
23
24      /**
25          Encrypts the contents of a file.
26          @param inFile  the input file
27          @param outFile  the output file
28      */
29      public void encryptFile(File inFile, File outFile)
30          throws IOException
31      {
32          InputStream in = null;
33          OutputStream out = null;
34
35          try
36          {
37              in = new FileInputStream(inFile);
38              out = new FileOutputStream(outFile);
39              encryptStream(in, out);
40          }
41          finally
42          {
43              if (in != null) in.close();
44              if (out != null) out.close();
45          }
```

```
46      }
47
48      /**
49          Encrypts the contents of a stream.
50          @param in  the input stream
51          @param out  the output stream
52      */
53      public void encryptStream(InputStream in,
54          OutputStream out)
55          throws IOException
56      {
57          boolean done = false;
58          while (!done)
59          {
60              int next = in.read();
61              if (next == -1) done = true;
62              else
63              {
64                  byte b = (byte)next;
65                  byte c = encrypt(b);
66                  out.write(c);
67              }
68          }
69      }
70
71      /**
72          Encrypts a byte.
73          @param b  the byte to encrypt
74          @return  the encrypted byte
75      */
76      public byte encrypt(byte b)
77      {
78          return (byte)(b + key);
79      }
80
81      private int key;
82  }
```

Program EncryptorTest.java

```
1  import java.io.File;
2  import java.io.IOException;
3  import javax.swing.JFileChooser;
4  import javax.swing.JOptionPane;
5
6  /**
7      A program to test the Caesar cipher encryptor.
8  */
9  public class EncryptorTest
10 {
```

```
11    public static void main(String[] args)
12    {
13       try
14       {
15          JFileChooser chooser = new JFileChooser();
16          if (chooser.showOpenDialog(null)
17              != JFileChooser.APPROVE_OPTION)
18              System.exit(0);
19
20          File inFile = chooser.getSelectedFile();
21          if (chooser.showSaveDialog(null)
22              != JFileChooser.APPROVE_OPTION)
23              System.exit(0);
24          File outFile = chooser.getSelectedFile();
25          String input =
26              JOptionPane.showInputDialog("Key");
27          int key = Integer.parseInt(input);
28          Encryptor crypt = new Encryptor(key);
29          crypt.encryptFile(inFile, outFile);
30       }
31       catch (NumberFormatException exception)
32       {
33          System.out.println("Key must be an integer: "
34              + exception);
35       }
36       catch (IOException exception)
37       {
38          System.out.println("Error processing file: "
39              + exception);
40       }
41       System.exit(0);
42    }
43 }
```

Random Fact   15.1

Encryption Algorithms

The exercises at the end of this chapter give a few algorithms to encrypt text. Don't actually use any of those methods to send secret messages to your lover. Any skilled cryptographer can *break* these schemes in a very short time—that is, reconstruct the original text without knowing the secret keyword.

In 1978 Ron Rivest, Adi Shamir, and Leonard Adleman introduced an encryption method that is much more powerful. The method is called RSA encryption, after the last names of its inventors. The exact scheme is too complicated to present here, but it is not actually difficult to follow. You can find the details in [2].

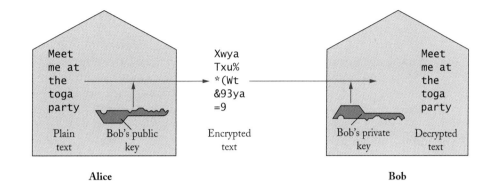

Alice   Bob

Figure 3

Public Key Encryption

RSA is a remarkable encryption method. There are two keys: a public key and a private key. (See Figure 3.) You can print the public key on your business card (or in your email signature block) and give it to anyone. Then anyone can send you messages that only you can decrypt. Even though everyone else knows the public key, and even if they intercept all the messages coming to you, they cannot break the scheme and actually read the messages. In 1994, hundreds of researchers, collaborating over the Internet, cracked an RSA message encrypted with a 129-digit key. Messages encrypted with a key of 230 digits or more are expected to be secure.

The inventors of the algorithm obtained a *patent* for it. That means that for a period of 20 years, anyone using it had to seek a license from the inventors. They have given permission for most noncommercial usage, but companies that implemented RSA in a product that they sold had to get the patent holder's permission and pay substantial royalties. The RSA patent expired on September 20, 2000, so you are now free to use the algorithm without restriction.

A patent is a deal that society makes with an inventor. For a period of 20 years after the filing date, the inventor has an exclusive right for its commercialization, may collect royalties from others wishing to manufacture the invention, and may even stop competitors from marketing it altogether. In return, the inventor must publish the invention, so that others may learn from it, and must relinquish all claim to it after the protection period ends. The presumption is that in the absence of patent law, inventors would be reluctant to go through the trouble of inventing, or they would try to cloak their techniques to prevent others from copying their devices.

What do you think? Are patents a fair deal? Unquestionably, some companies have chosen not to implement RSA, and instead chose a less capable method, because they could not or would not pay the royalties. Thus, it seems that the patent may have hindered, rather than advanced, commerce. Had there not been patent protection, would the inventors have published the method anyway, thereby giving the benefit for society without the cost of the 20-year monopoly? In this case, the answer is probably yes; the inventors were academic researchers, who live on salaries rather than sales receipts and are usually rewarded for their discoveries by a boost in their reputation and careers.

▼ Would their followers have been as active in discovering (and patenting) improvements? There is no way of knowing, of course.

▼ Further, is an algorithm even patentable in the first place? Or is it a mathematical fact that belongs to nobody? The patent office did take the latter attitude for a long time. The RSA inventors and many others described their inventions in terms of imaginary electronic devices, rather than algorithms, to circumvent that restriction. Nowadays, the patent office will award software patents.

▼ There is another fascinating aspect to the RSA story. A programmer named Phil Zimmermann developed a program called PGP (for *Pretty Good Privacy*) [3]. PGP implements RSA. That is, you can have it generate a pair of public and private keys, publish the public key, receive encrypted messages from others who use their copy of PGP and your public key, and decrypt them with your private key. Even though the encryption can be performed on any personal computer, decryption is not feasible even with the most powerful computers. You can get a copy of PGP from `http://web.mit.edu/network/pgp.html`. As long as it is for personal use, there is no charge, courtesy of Phil Zimmermann and the folks at MIT and RSA.

▼ The existence of PGP bothers the government to no end. They worry that criminals use the package to correspond by email and that the police cannot tap those "conversations". Foreign governments can send communications that the National Security Agency (the premier electronic spy organization of the United States) cannot decipher. In the 1990s, the U.S. government unsuccessfully attempted to standardize on a different encryption scheme, called *Skipjack*, to which government organizations hold a decryption key that—of course—they promise not to use without a court order. There have been serious proposals to make it illegal to use any other encryption method in the United States. At one time, the government considered charging Mr. Zimmermann with breaching another law that forbids the unauthorized export of munitions as a crime and defines cryptographic technology as "munitions". They made the argument that, even though Mr. Zimmermann never exported the program, he should have known that it would immediately spread through the Internet when he released it in the United States.

▼ What do you think? Will criminals and terrorists be harder to detect and convict once encryption of email and phone conversations is widely available? Should the government therefore have a backdoor key to any legal encryption method? Or is this a gross violation of our civil liberties? Is it even possible to put the genie back into the bottle at this time?

15.5 Command Line Arguments

Depending on the operating system and Java development system used, there are different methods of starting a program—for example, by selecting "Run" in the compilation environment, by clicking on an icon, or by typing the name of the program at a prompt in a terminal or shell window. The latter method is called "invoking the program from the command line". When you use this method, you must of course type the name of the program, but you can also type in additional information that the program can use.

These additional strings are called *command line arguments*. For example, if you start a program with the command line

```
java MyProgram -d file.txt
```

> When you launch a program from the command line, you can specify arguments after the program name. The program can access these strings by processing the args parameter of the main method.

then the program receives two command line arguments: the strings "-d" and "file.txt". It is entirely up to the program what to do with these strings. It is customary to interpret strings starting with a – as options and other strings as file names.

Only application programs receive command line arguments; you cannot pass a command line to an applet. (The corresponding mechanism for applets is the HTML param tag; see Advanced Topic 4.3.)

Command line arguments are placed in the args parameter of the main method:

```
class MyProgram
{
   public static void main(String[] args)
   {
      . . .
   }
}
```

Now you finally know the use of the args array that you have seen in so many programs. In our example, args contains the two strings

args[0]	"-d"
args[1]	"file.txt"

To put command line processing to work, let us write a driver for the Encryptor class that reads the file names and encryption key from the command line rather than prompting the user. The program takes the following command line arguments:

- An optional -d flag to indicate decryption instead of encryption

- An optional encryption key, specified with a -k flag

- The input file name

- The output file name

If no key is specified, then 3 is used. For example,

```
java Crypt input.txt encrypt.txt
```

encrypts the file input.txt with a key of 3 and places the result into encrypt.txt. On the other hand,

```
java Crypt -d -k11 encrypt.txt output.txt
```

decrypts the file encrypt.txt with a key of 11 and places the result into output.txt.

What is better for the user? A graphical user interface with file chooser dialogs, or a command-line interface where files need to be specified on the command line? For a casual and infrequent user, the graphical user interface is much better. The user interface guides the user along and makes it possible to navigate the application without much knowledge. But for a frequent user, graphical user interfaces have a major drawback—they are hard to automate. If you need to process hundreds of files every day, you could spend all your time typing file names into file chooser dialogs. But it is not difficult to call a program multiple times automatically with different command-line arguments. Productivity Hint 8.1 discusses how to use shell scripts (also called batch files) for this purpose.

Here is the front end for the encryption program. Combine it with the `Encryptor` class of the preceding section.

File Crypt.java

```
1  import java.io.File;
2  import java.io.IOException;
3
4  /**
5     A program to run the Caesar cipher encryptor with
6     command line arguments.
7  */
8  public class Crypt
9  {
10    public static void main(String[] args)
11    {
12       boolean decrypt = false;
13       int key = DEFAULT_KEY;
14       File inFile = null;
15       File outFile = null;
16
17       if (args.length < 2 || args.length > 4) usage();
18
19       try
20       {
21          for (int i = 0; i < args.length; i++)
22          {
23             if (args[i].charAt(0) == '-')
24             {
25                // it is a command line option
26                char option = args[i].charAt(1);
27                if (option == 'd')
28                   decrypt = true;
29                else if (option == 'k')
30                   key = Integer.parseInt(
31                      args[i].substring(2));
32             }
33             else
34             {
35                // it is a file name
36                if (inFile == null)
37                   inFile = new File(args[i]);
38                else if (outFile == null)
```

```
39                        outFile = new File(args[i]);
40                    else usage();
41                  }
42              }
43              if (decrypt) key = -key;
44              Encryptor crypt = new Encryptor(key);
45              crypt.encryptFile(inFile, outFile);
46          }
47          catch (NumberFormatException exception)
48          {
49              System.out.println("Key must be an integer: "
50                  + exception);
51          }
52          catch (IOException exception)
53          {
54              System.out.println("Error processing file: "
55                  + exception);
56          }
57      }
58
59      /**
60          Prints a message describing proper usage and exits.
61      */
62      public static void usage()
63      {
64          System.out.println(
65              "Usage: java Crypt [-d] [-kn] infile outfile");
66          System.exit(1);
67      }
68
69      public static final int DEFAULT_KEY = 3;
70  }
```

15.6   Object Streams

Use object streams to save and restore all instance fields of an object automatically.

In the sample program of Section 14.6, you read Coin objects by processing strings that describe the coin data. To save a set of coins in the same format, you would need to write code to break up coin objects into strings and numbers. Actually, in Java, there is an easier way. The ObjectOutputStream class can save entire objects out to disk, and the ObjectInputStream class can read them back in. Objects are saved in binary format; hence, you use streams and not writers.

For example, you can write a Coin object to a file as follows:

```
Coin c = . . .;
ObjectOutputStream out = new ObjectOutputStream
    (new FileOutputStream("coins.dat"));
out.writeObject(c);
```

The object output stream automatically saves all instance variables of the object to the stream. When reading the object back in, you use the `readObject` method of the `ObjectInputStream` class. That method returns an `Object` reference, so you need to remember the types of the objects that you saved and use a cast:

```
ObjectInputStream in = new ObjectInputStream
    (new FileInputStream("coins.dat"));
Coin c = (Coin)in.readObject();
```

The `readObject` method can throw a `ClassCastException`—it is a checked exception, so you need to catch or declare it.

You can do even better than that, though. You can store a whole bunch of objects in an array list or array, or inside another object, and then save that object:

```
ArrayList a = new ArrayList();
// now add many Coin objects into a
out.writeObject(a);
```

With one instruction, you can save the array list and *all the objects that it references*. You can read all of them back with one instruction:

```
ArrayList a = (ArrayList)in.readObject();
```

Of course, if the `Purse` class contains an `ArrayList` of coins, then you can simply save and restore the `Purse` object. Then its array list, and all the `Coin` objects that it contains, are automatically saved and restored as well. The sample program at the end of this section uses this approach.

> Objects saved to an object stream must belong to classes that implement the `Serializable` interface.

This is a truly amazing capability that is highly recommended (see Productivity Hint 15.1).

To place objects of a particular class into an object stream, the class must implement the `Serializable` interface. That interface has no methods, so there is no effort involved in implementing it:

```
class Coin implements Serializable
{
    . . .
}
```

The process of saving objects to a stream is called *serialization* because each object is assigned a serial number on the stream. If the same object is saved twice, only the serial number is written out the second time. When the objects are read back in, duplicate serial numbers are restored as references to the same object.

Why don't all classes implement `Serializable`? For security reasons, some programmers may not want to serialize classes with confidential contents. Once a class is serializable, anyone can write its objects to disk and analyze the disk file. There are also some classes that contain values that are meaningless once a program exits, such as operating-system-specific font descriptors. These values should not be serialized.

Here is a sample program that puts serialization to work. The `Coin` and `Purse` classes are identical to those of Chapter 13, except that they both implement the `Serializable` interface. Run the program several times. Whenever the program exits, it saves the `Purse` object (and all coin objects that the purse contains) into a file `purse.dat`. When the program starts again, the file is loaded, and your additional coins are added. However, if the file is missing (either because the program is running for the first time, or because the file was erased), then the program starts with a new purse.

File PurseTest.java

```java
1  import java.io.File;
2  import java.io.IOException;
3  import java.io.FileInputStream;
4  import java.io.FileOutputStream;
5  import java.io.ObjectInputStream;
6  import java.io.ObjectOutputStream;
7  import javax.swing.JOptionPane;
8
9  /**
10     This program tests serialization of a Purse object.
11     If a file with serialized purse data exists, then it is
12     loaded. Otherwise the program starts with a new purse.
13     More coins are added to the purse. Then the purse data
14     are saved.
15  */
16 public class PurseTest
17 {
18    public static void main(String[] args)
19       throws IOException, ClassNotFoundException
20    {
21       Purse myPurse;
22
23       File f = new File("purse.dat");
24       if (f.exists())
25       {
26          ObjectInputStream in = new ObjectInputStream
27             (new FileInputStream(f));
28          myPurse = (Purse)in.readObject();
29          in.close();
30       }
31       else myPurse = new Purse();
32
33       // add coins to the purse
34       myPurse.add(new Coin(NICKEL_VALUE, "nickel"));
35       myPurse.add(new Coin(DIME_VALUE, "dime"));
36       myPurse.add(new Coin(QUARTER_VALUE, "quarter"));
37
38       double totalValue = myPurse.getTotal();
39       System.out.println("The total is " + totalValue);
40
41       ObjectOutputStream out = new ObjectOutputStream
42          (new FileOutputStream(f));
43       out.writeObject(myPurse);
44       out.close();
```

```
45      }
46
47      private static double NICKEL_VALUE = 0.05;
48      private static double DIME_VALUE = 0.1;
49      private static double QUARTER_VALUE = 0.25;
50  }
```

Productivity Hint   15.1

Use Object Streams

Object streams have a huge advantage over other data file formats. You don't have to come up with a way of breaking objects up into numbers and strings when writing a file. You don't have to come up with a way of combining numbers and strings back into objects when reading a file. The serialization mechanism takes care of this automatically. You simply write and read objects. For this to work, you need to have each of your classes implement the `Serializable` interface, which is trivial to do.

To save your data to disk, it is best to put them all into one large object (such as an array list or an object that describes your entire program state) and save that object. When you need to read the data back, read that object back in. It is easier for you to retrieve data from an object than it is to search for them in a file.

Advanced Topic   15.1

Serializing Geometric Objects

Many classes in the standard library are serializable—after all, it is a simple matter for class designers to add `implements Serializable` to their classes. Unfortunately, the geometry classes `Point2D.Double`, `Rectangle2D.Double`, `Ellipse2D.Double`, and `Line2D.Double` are not. There is no good reason for this. It was just an oversight.

The `Point` and `Rectangle` classes are serializable. If you can get by with integer coordinates, then you may want to use them instead of `Point2D.Double` and `Rectangle2D.Double`.

If you have classes with instance fields that are not serializable, you have to work a bit harder to make serialization work. Follow these steps.

First, mark the nonserializable instance fields with the keyword `transient`:

```
public class Car implements Serializable
{
    . . .
    private Rectangle body; // ok, Rectangle is serializable
    private transient Ellipse2D.Double frontTire;
    private transient Ellipse2D.Double rearTire;
}
```

▼   Then add two methods to save and restore the transient fields explicitly, like this:

```
private void writeObject(ObjectOutputStream out)
   throws IOException
{
   out.defaultWriteObject();

   out.writeDouble(frontTire.getX());
   out.writeDouble(frontTire.getY());
   out.writeDouble(frontTire.getWidth());
   out.writeDouble(frontTire.getHeight());

   out.writeDouble(rearTire.getX());
   out.writeDouble(rearTire.getY());
   out.writeDouble(rearTire.getWidth());
   out.writeDouble(rearTire.getHeight());
}

private void readObject(ObjectInputStream in)
   throws IOException, ClassNotFoundException
{
   in.defaultReadObject();

   double x = in.readDouble();
   double y = in.readDouble();
   double width = in.readDouble();
   double height = in.readDouble();
   frontTire = new Ellipse2D.Double(x, y, width, height);

   x = in.readDouble();
   y = in.readDouble();
   width = in.readDouble();
   height = in.readDouble();
   rearTire = new Ellipse2D.Double(x, y, width, height);
}
```

These special methods *must* be private, and they must call `defaultWriteObject`/
`defaultReadObject` before saving and restoring the additional information.

15.7   Random Access

Consider a file that contains a set of bank accounts. We want to change the balances of
some of the accounts. Of course, we can read all account data into an array list, update
the information that has changed, and save the data out again. If the data set in the file is
very large, we may end up doing a lot of reading and writing just to update a handful of
records. It would be better if we could locate the changed information in the file and just
replace it.

In sequential file access, a file is processed a byte at a time. Random access allows access at arbitrary locations in the file, without first reading the bytes preceding the access location.

This is quite different from the file access you have programmed up to now. In the past, you read from a file, starting at the beginning and reading the entire contents until you reached the end. That access pattern is called *sequential access*. Now we would like to access specific locations in a file and change just those locations. This access pattern is called random access (see Figure 4). There is nothing "random" about random access—the term just means that you can read and modify any byte stored at any location in the file.

Only disk files support random access; the System.in and System.out streams, which are attached to the keyboard and the terminal window, do not. Each disk file has a special *file pointer* position. Normally, the file pointer is at the end of the file, and any output is appended to the end. However, if you move the file pointer to the middle of the file and write to the file, the output overwrites what is already there. The next read command starts reading input at the file pointer location. You can move the file pointer just beyond the last byte currently in the file but no further.

In Java, you use a RandomAccessFile object to access a file and move a file pointer. To open a random-access file, you supply a file name and a string to specify the *open mode*. You can open a file either for reading only ("r") or for reading and writing ("rw"). For example, the following command opens the file accounts.dat for both reading and writing:

```
RandomAccessFile f =
    new RandomAccessFile("bank.dat", "rw");
```

The method call

```
f.seek(n);
```

moves the file pointer to byte n counted from the beginning of the file. To find out the current position of the file pointer (counted from the beginning of the file), use

```
n = f.getFilePointer();
```

A file pointer is a position in a random-access file. Because files can be very large, the file pointer is of type long.

Because files can be very large, the file pointer values are long integers. To find out the number of bytes in a file, use the length method:

```
long fileLength = f.length();
```

Figure 4

Sequential and Random Access

In the example program at the end of this section, we use a random-access file to store a set of savings accounts, each of which has a current balance and an interest rate. The test program lets you pick a random account and add the interest.

If you want to manipulate a data set in a file, you have to pay special attention to the formatting of the data. Suppose you just store the data as text. Say the balance is $950, and the interest rate is 10%.

```
950 10
```

If the balance is increased by 10% or $95, the new price has more digits. Suppose you place the file pointer to the first character of the old value.

```
950 10
```

If you now simply write out the new value, the result is

```
104510
```

That is not working too well. The update is overwriting the space that separates the fields.

In order to be able to update a file, you must give each field a *fixed* size that is sufficiently large. As a result, every record in the file has the same size. That has another advantage: It is then easy to skip quickly to, say, the 50th record, without having to read the first 49 records in. Just set the file pointer to 50 × the record size.

When storing numbers in a file with fixed record sizes, it is easier to store them in binary format, rather than text format. For that reason, the RandomAccessFile class stores binary data. The readInt and writeInt methods read and write integers as four-byte quantities. The readDouble and writeDouble methods process double-precision floating-point numbers as eight-byte quantities

```
double x = f.readDouble();
f.writeDouble(x);
```

If we save the balance and interest rate as double values, then each savings account record consists of 16 bytes: 8 bytes for each double-precision value.

Now that we have determined the file layout, we can implement our random-access file methods. In the program at the end of this section, we use a BankData class to translate between the random-access file format and savings account objects. The size method determines the total number of accounts by dividing the file length by the size of a record.

```
public int size() throws IOException
{
    return (int)(file.length() / RECORD_SIZE);
}
```

To read the nth account in the file, the read method positions the file pointer to the offset n * RECORD_SIZE, then reads the data, and constructs a savings account object:

```
public SavingsAccount read(int n)
    throws IOException
```

```
    {
        file.seek(n * RECORD_SIZE);
        double balance = file.readDouble();
        double interestRate = file.readDouble();
        SavingsAccount account =
            new SavingsAccount(interestRate);
        account.deposit(balance);
        return account;
    }
```

Writing an account works the same way:

```
    public void write(int n, SavingsAccount account)
        throws IOException
    {
        file.seek(n * RECORD_SIZE);
        file.writeDouble(account.getBalance());
        file.writeDouble(account.getInterestRate());
    }
```

The test program asks the user to enter the position of the account that should be updated and the amount of the deposit or withdrawal. The user can also add new accounts to the database.

Program BankDataTest.java

```
 1  import java.io.IOException;
 2  import java.io.RandomAccessFile;
 3  import javax.swing.JOptionPane;
 4
 5  /**
 6      This program tests random access. You can access existing
 7      accounts and add interest, or create new accounts. The
 8      accounts are saved in a random-access file.
 9  */
10  public class BankDataTest
11  {
12      public static void main(String[] args)
13          throws IOException
14      {
15          BankData data = new BankData();
16          try
17          {
18              data.open("bank.dat");
19
20              boolean done = false;
21              while (!done)
22              {
23                  String input = JOptionPane.showInputDialog(
24                      "Account number or " + data.size()
25                      + " for new account");
26                  if (input == null) done = true;
```

```
27              else
28              {
29                  int pos = Integer.parseInt(input);
30
31                  if (0 <= pos && pos < data.size())
32                  // add interest
33                  {
34                      SavingsAccount account =
35                          data.read(pos);
36                      System.out.println("balance="
37                          + account.getBalance()
38                          + ",interest rate="
39                          + account.getInterestRate());
40                      account.addInterest();
41                      data.write(pos, account);
42                  }
43                  else // add account
44                  {
45                      input = JOptionPane.showInputDialog(
46                          "Balance");
47                      double balance =
48                          Double.parseDouble(input);
49                      input = JOptionPane.showInputDialog(
50                          "Interest Rate");
51                      double interestRate =
52                          Double.parseDouble(input);
53                      SavingsAccount account
54                          = new SavingsAccount(interestRate);
55                      account.deposit(balance);
56                      data.write(data.size(), account);
57                  }
58              }
59          }
60      }
61      finally
62      {
63          data.close();
64          System.exit(0);
65      }
66  }
67 }
```

Program BankData.java

```
1 import java.io.IOException;
2 import java.io.RandomAccessFile;
3
4 /**
5    This class is a conduit to a random-access file
6    containing savings account data.
7 */
```

```
 8  public class BankData
 9  {
10     /**
11         Constructs a BankData object that is not associated
12         with a file.
13     */
14     public BankData()
15     {
16         file = null;
17     }
18
19     /**
20         Opens the data file.
21         @param filename the name of the file containing savings
22         account information
23     */
24     public void open(String filename)
25         throws IOException
26     {
27         if (file != null) file.close();
28         file = new RandomAccessFile(filename, "rw");;
29     }
30
31     /**
32         Gets the number of accounts in the file.
33         @return the number of accounts
34     */
35     public int size()
36         throws IOException
37     {
38         return (int)(file.length() / RECORD_SIZE);
39     }
40
41     /**
42         Closes the data file.
43     */
44     public void close()
45         throws IOException
46     {
47         if (file != null) file.close();
48         file = null;
49     }
50
51     /**
52         Reads a savings account record.
53         @param n the index of the account in the data file
54         @return a savings account object initialized with the file data
55     */
56     public SavingsAccount read(int n)
57         throws IOException
58     {
59         file.seek(n * RECORD_SIZE);
```

```
60          double balance = file.readDouble();
61          double interestRate = file.readDouble();
62          SavingsAccount account =
63             new SavingsAccount(interestRate);
64          account.deposit(balance);
65          return account;
66       }
67
68       /**
69          Writes a savings account record to the data file.
70          @param n  the index of the account in the data file
71          @param account  the account to write
72       */
73       public void write(int n, SavingsAccount account)
74          throws IOException
75       {
76          file.seek(n * RECORD_SIZE);
77          file.writeDouble(account.getBalance());
78          file.writeDouble(account.getInterestRate());
79       }
80
81       private RandomAccessFile file;
82
83       public static final int DOUBLE_SIZE = 8;
84       public static final int RECORD_SIZE
85          = 2 * DOUBLE_SIZE;
86  }
```

? HOWTO   15.1

Using Files and Streams

Suppose your program needs to process data in files. This HOWTO walks you through
the steps that are involved.

Step 1 Select a data format

The most important question you need to ask yourself concerns the format to use for
saving your data.

- Does your program need to save and restore objects? Then use object streams.

- Does your program manipulate text, such as a plain text files? Then use readers
  and writers.

- Does your program manipulate binary data, such as image files or encrypted data?
  Then use binary streams.

We don't discuss random-access files here since they are not commonly needed for student projects. If you need to have fast access to data, use a database—see Chapter 23.

Step 2 If you use object streams, make your classes implement the `Serializable` interface

Simply go through your classes and tag them with `implements Serializable`. You don't need to add any additional methods.

Also go to the online API documentation to check that the library classes that you are using implement the `Serializable` interface. Fortunately, many of them do. In particular, `String` and `ArrayList` are serializable.

If your classes use geometric objects (such as `Point2D.Double`, `Rectangle2D.Double`, and so on), then you have to work harder, because those classes are unfortunately not serializable—see Advanced Topic 15.1.

Step 3a Use object streams if you are processing objects

Now simply put all the objects you want to save into a class (or an array or array list—but why not make another class containing that?).

Saving all program data is a trivial operation:

```
ProgramData data = . . .;
ObjectOutputStream out = new ObjectOutputStream
    (new FileOutputStream("program.dat"));
out.writeObject(data);
out.close();
```

Similarly, to restore the program data, you use an `ObjectInputStream` and call

```
ProgramData data = (ProgramData)in.readObject();
```

The `readObject` method can throw a `ClassNotFoundException`. You must catch or declare that exception.

Step 3b Use readers and writers if you are processing text

You need to turn the file input stream into a buffered reader:

```
BufferedReader in = new BufferedReader(
    new FileReader("input.txt"));
```

Now you can read the input a line at a time:

```
boolean done = false;
while (!done)
{
    String input = in.readLine();
    if (input == null)
        done = true;
    else
    {
        process input
    }
}
```

Of course, you need to use `Integer.parseInt` and `Double.parseDouble` to read any numbers in the text file. But wait—if you have numbers in the text file, are you converting numbers and strings into objects? If so, you should probably use object streams instead.

▼ To write output, turn the file output stream into a `PrintWriter`:

```
PrintWriter out = new PrintWriter(
    new FileWriter("output.txt"));
```

▼ Then use the familiar `print` and `println` methods:

```
out.println(text);
```

▼ **Step 3c** Use streams if you are processing bytes

▼ Use this loop to process input a byte at a time:

```
BufferedReader in = new BufferedReader(
    new FileReader("input.txt"));
```

▼ Now you can read the input a byte at a time:

```
InputStream in = new FileInputStream("input.bin");
boolean done = false;
while (!done)
{
    int next = in.read();
    if (next = -1)
        done = true;
    else
    {
        byte b = (byte)next;
        process input
    }
}
in.close();
```

▼ Similarly, write the output a byte at a time:

```
OutputStream out = new FileOutputStream("output.bin");
. . .
byte b = . . .;
out.write(b);
. . .
out.close();
```

▼ You want to use binary streams only if you are ready to process the input a byte at a time. This makes sense for encryption/decryption or processing the pixels in an image. In other situations, binary streams are not appropriate.

Chapter Summary

1. Streams access sequences of bytes. Readers and writers access sequences of characters.

2. Use `FileReader`, `FileWriter`, `FileInputStream`, and `FileOutputStream` classes to read and write disk files.

3. The `read` method returns an integer, either −1, at the end of the file, or another value, which you need to cast to a `char` or `byte`.

4. You must close all files that you no longer need.

5. Basic streams, readers, and writers can process only individual bytes or characters. You need to combine them with other classes to process lines of text or entire objects.

6. When writing text files, use the `PrintWriter` class and the `print/println` methods.

7. When reading text files, use the `BufferedReader` class and the `readLine` method.

8. The `JFileChooser` dialog lets users select a file by navigating through directories.

9. A `File` object describes a file or directory.

10. You can pass a `File` object to the constructor of a file reader, writer, or stream.

11. When you launch a program from the command line, you can specify arguments after the program name. The program can access these strings by processing the `args` parameter of the `main` method.

12. Use object streams to save and restore all instance fields of an object automatically.

13. Objects saved to an object stream must belong to classes that implement the `Serializable` interface.

14. In sequential file access, a file is processed a byte at a time. Random access allows access at arbitrary locations in the file, without first reading the bytes preceding the access location.

15. A file pointer is a position in a random-access file. Because files can be very large, the file pointer is of type `long`.

Further Reading

[1] Bruce Schneier, *Applied Cryptography,* John Wiley & Sons, 1994.
[2] Phillip R. Zimmermann, *The Official PGP User's Guide,* MIT Press, 1995.
[3] David F. Linowes, *Privacy in America,* University of Illinois Press, 1989.
[4] Abraham Sinkov, *Elementary Cryptanalysis,* Mathematical Association of America, 1966.

CLASSES, OBJECTS, AND METHODS INTRODUCED IN THIS CHAPTER

```
java.io.EOFException
java.io.File
   exists
java.io.FileInputStream
java.io.FileNotFoundException
```

```
java.io.FileOutputStream
java.io.FileReader
java.io.FileWriter
java.io.InputStream
    read
    close
java.io.ObjectInputStream
    readObject
java.io.ObjectOutputStream
    writeObject
java.io.OutputStream
    write
    close
java.io.PrintWriter
    print
    println
java.io.RandomAccessFile
    getFilePointer
    length
    readChar
    readDouble
    readInt
    seek
    writeChar
    writeChars
    writeDouble
    writeInt
java.io.Reader
    read
    close
java.io.Writer
    write
    close
java.lang.Serializable
javax.swing.JFileChooser
    getSelectedFile
    showOpenDialog
    showSaveDialog
```

REVIEW EXERCISES

Exercise R15.1. What is the difference between a stream and a reader?

Exercise R15.2. How can you open a file for both reading and writing in Java?

Exercise R15.3. What happens if you try to write to a file reader? What happens if you try to write to a random-access file that you opened only for reading? Try it out if you don't know.

Exercise R15.4. What happens if you try to open a file for reading that doesn't exist? What happens if you try to open a file for writing that doesn't exist?

Exercise R15.5. What happens if you try to open a file for writing, but the file or device is write-protected (sometimes called read-only)? Try it out with a short test program.

Exercise R15.6. How do you open a file whose name contains a backslash, like `c:\temp\output.dat`?

Exercise R15.7. How can you break the Caesar cipher? That is, how can you read a document that was encrypted with the Caesar cipher, even though you don't know the key?

Exercise R15.8. What is a command line? How can a program read its command line arguments?

Exercise R15.9. Give two examples of programs on your computer that read arguments from the command line.

Exercise R15.10. If a program Woozle is started with the command

```
java Woozle -DNAME=Piglet -I\eeyore -v heff.txt a.txt lump.txt
```

what are the values of `args[0]`, `args[1]`, and so on?

Exercise R15.11. What happens if you try to save in an object stream an object that is not serializable? Try it out and report your results.

Exercise R15.12. Of the classes that you encountered in this book, which implement the `Serializable` interface?

Exercise R15.13. Why is it better to save an entire `ArrayList` to an object stream instead of programming a loop that writes each element?

Exercise R15.14. What is the difference between sequential access and random access?

Exercise R15.15. What is the file pointer in a file? How do you move it? How do you tell the current position? Why is it a long integer?

Exercise R15.16. How do you move the file pointer to the first byte of a file? To the last byte? To the exact middle of the file?

Exercise R15.17. What happens if you try to move the file pointer past the end of a file? Can you move the file pointer of `System.in`? Try it out and report your results.

PROGRAMMING EXERCISES

Exercise P15.1. Write a program that asks the user for a file name and prints the number of characters, words, and lines in that file. Then the program asks for the name of the next file. When the user enters a file that doesn't exist (such as the empty string), the program exits.

Exercise P15.2. *Random monoalphabet cipher.* The Caesar cipher, which shifts all letters by a fixed amount, is ridiculously easy to crack—just try out all 25 possible keys. Here is a better idea. For the key, don't use numbers but words. Suppose the key word is FEATHER. Then first remove duplicate letters, yielding FEATHR, and append the other letters of the alphabet in reverse order: Now encrypt the letters as follows:

A	B	C	D	E	F	G	H	I	J	K	L	M	N	O	P	Q	R	S	T	U	V	W	X	Y	Z
↓	↓	↓	↓	↓	↓	↓	↓	↓	↓	↓	↓	↓	↓	↓	↓	↓	↓	↓	↓	↓	↓	↓	↓	↓	↓
F	E	A	T	H	R	Z	Y	X	W	V	U	S	Q	P	O	N	M	L	K	J	I	G	D	C	B

Write a program that encrypts or decrypts a file using this cipher. For example,

```
java Crypt -d -kFEATHER encrypt.txt output.txt
```

decrypts a file using the keyword FEATHER. It is an error not to supply a keyword.

Exercise P15.3. *Letter frequencies.* If you encrypt a file using the cipher of the preceding exercise, it will have all of its letters jumbled up, and it doesn't look as if there was any hope of decrypting it without knowing the keyword. Guessing the keyword seems hopeless too. There are just too many possible keywords. However, someone who is trained in decryption will be able to break this cipher in no time at all. The average letter frequencies of English letters are well known. The most common letter is E, which occurs about 13% of the time. Here are the average frequencies of the letters (see [5]).

A	8%	N	8%
B	<1%	O	7%
C	3%	P	3%
D	4%	Q	<1%
E	13%	R	8%
F	3%	S	6%
G	2%	T	9%
H	4%	U	3%
I	7%	V	1%
J	<1%	W	2%
K	<1%	X	<1%
L	4%	Y	2%
M	3%	Z	<1%

Write a program that reads an input file and prints the letter frequencies in that file. Such a tool will help a code breaker. If the most frequent letters in an encrypted file are H and K, then there is an excellent chance that they are the encryptions of E and T.

Exercise P15.4. *Vigenère cipher.* The trouble with a monoalphabetic cipher is that it can be easily broken by frequency analysis. The so-called Vigenère cipher overcomes this problem by encoding a letter into one of several cipher letters, depending on its position in the input document. Choose a keyword, for example TIGER. Then encode the first letter of the input text like this:

A	B	C	D	E	F	G	H	I	J	K	L	M	N	O	P	Q	R	S	T	U	V	W	X	Y	Z
↓	↓	↓	↓	↓	↓	↓	↓	↓	↓	↓	↓	↓	↓	↓	↓	↓	↓	↓	↓	↓	↓	↓	↓	↓	↓
T	U	V	W	X	Y	Z	A	B	C	D	E	F	G	H	I	J	K	L	M	N	O	P	Q	R	S

That is, the encoded alphabet is just the regular alphabet shifted to start at T, the first letter of the keyword TIGER. The second letter is encrypted according to the map

The third, fourth, and fifth letters in the input text are encrypted using the alphabet sequences beginning with characters G, E, and R, and so on. Because the key is only five letters long, the sixth letter of the input text is encrypted in the same way as the first.

Write a program that encrypts or decrypts an input text according to this cipher.

Exercise P15.5. *Playfair cipher.* Another way of thwarting a simple letter frequency analysis of an encrypted text is to encrypt *pairs* of letters together. A simple scheme to do this is the Playfair cipher. You pick a keyword and remove duplicate letters from it. Then you fill the keyword, and the remaining letters of the alphabet, into a 5 × 5 square. (Since there are only 25 squares, I and J are considered the same letter.) Here is such an arrangement with the keyword PLAYFAIR:

```
P L A Y F
I R B C D
E G H K M
N O Q S T
U V W X Z
```

To encrypt a letter pair, say AT, look at the rectangle with corners A and T:

```
P L A Y F
I R B C D
E G H K M
N O Q S T
U V W X Z
```

The encoding of this pair is formed by looking at the other two corners of the rectangle—in this case, FQ. If both letters happen to be in the same row or column, such as GO, simply swap the two letters. Decryption is done in the same way.

Write a program that encrypts or decrypts an input text according to this cipher.

Exercise P15.6. Write a program CopyFile that copies one file to another. The file names are specified on the command line. For example,

```
java CopyFile report.txt report.sav
```

Exercise P15.7. Write a program that *concatenates* the contents of several files into one file. For example,

```
java CatFiles chapter1.txt chapter2.txt chapter3.txt book.txt
```

makes a long file, book.txt, that contains the contents of the files chapter1.txt, chapter2.txt, and chapter3.txt. The output file is always the last file specified on the command line.

Exercise P15.8. Write a program `Find` that searches all files specified on the command line and prints out all lines containing a keyword. For example, if you call

```
java Find Buff report.txt address.txt Homework.java
```

then the program might print

```
report.txt: Buffet style lunch will be available at the
address.txt: Buffet, Warren|11801 Trenton Court|Dallas|TX
address.txt: Walters, Winnie|59 Timothy Circle|Buffalo|MI
Homework.java: BufferedReader in;
```

The keyword is always the first command line argument.

Exercise P15.9. Write a program that checks the spelling of all words in a file. It should read each word of a file and check whether it is contained in a word list. A word list is available on most UNIX systems in the file /usr/dict/words. (If you don't have access to a UNIX system, your instructor should be able to get you a copy.) The program should print out all words that it cannot find in the word list.

Exercise P15.10. Write a program that opens a file for reading and writing, and replaces each line with its reverse. For example, if you run

```
java Reverse Hello.java
```

then the contents of Hello.java are changed to

```
olleH ssalc cilbup
)sgra ][gnirtS(niam diov citats cilbup  {
;"n\\!dlroW ,olleH" = gniteerg gnirtS   {
;)gniteerg(tnirp.tuo.metsyS
}
}
```

Of course, if you run `Reverse` twice on the same file, you get back the original file.

Exercise P15.11. Write a program that reads a file from standard input and rewrites the file to standard output, replacing all tab characters `'\t'` with the *appropriate* number of spaces. Make the distance between tab columns a constant and set it to 3, the value we use in this book for Java programs. Then expand tabs to the number of spaces necessary to move to the next tab column. *That may be less than three spaces.* For example, consider the line containing `"\t|\t||\t|"`. The first tab is changed to three spaces, the second to two spaces, and the third to one space.

Exercise P15.12. Reimplement the `BankData` class of Section 15.7 by storing all savings accounts in an `ArrayList` and by using serialization. Change only the implementation of the class, not the public interface.

Exercise P15.13. Write a graphical application in which the user clicks on a panel to add car shapes at the mouse click location. The shapes are stored in an array list. When the user selects File→Save from the menu, save the selection of shapes in a file. When the user selects File→Open, load in a file. Use serialization.

Exercise P15.14. The program in Section 15.7 only locates one bank account and adds interest. Add an option to the program that adds interest to all bank accounts.

Exercise P15.15. Implement a graphical user interface for the program in Section 15.6.

System Design

▶ To learn how to discover new classes and methods

▶ To understand the use of CRC cards for class discovery

▶ To be able to identify inheritance, aggregation, and dependency relationships between classes

▶ To master the use of UML class diagrams to describe class relationships

▶ To learn how to use object-oriented design to build complex programs

To implement a software system successfully, be it as simple as your next homework project or as complex as the next air traffic monitoring system, some amount of planning, design, and testing is required. In fact, for larger projects, the amount of time spent on planning is much higher than the amount of time spent on programming and testing.

If you find that most of your homework time is spent in front of the computer, keying code in and fixing bugs, you are probably spending more time on your homework than you should. You could cut down your total time by spending more on the planning and design phase. This chapter tells you how to approach these tasks in a systematic manner.

16.1 The Software Life Cycle

> The life cycle of software encompasses all activities from initial analysis until obsolescence.

> A formal process for software development describes phases of the development process and gives guidelines for how to carry out the phases.

In this section we will discuss the *software life cycle:* the activities that take place between the time a software program is first conceived and the time it is finally retired.

A software project usually starts because some customer has some problem and is willing to pay money to have it solved. The Department of Defense, the customer of many programming projects, was an early proponent of a *formal process* for software development. A formal process identifies and describes different phases and gives guidelines how to carry out the phases and when to move from one phase to the next.

Many software engineers break the development process down into the following five phases:

- Analysis
- Design
- Implementation
- Testing
- Deployment

In the *analysis* phase, you decide *what* the project is supposed to accomplish; you do not think about *how* the program will accomplish its tasks. The output of the analysis phase is a *requirements document*, which describes in complete detail what the program will be able to do once it is completed. Part of this requirements document can be a user manual that tells how the user will operate the program to derive the promised benefits. Another part sets performance criteria—how many inputs the program must be able to handle in what time, or what its maximum memory and disk storage requirements are.

In the *design* phase, you develop a plan for how you will implement the system. You discover the structures that underlie the problem to be solved. When you use object-oriented design, you decide what classes you need and what their most important methods are. The output of this phase is a description of the classes and methods, with diagrams that show the relationships among the classes.

In the *implementation* phase, you write and compile program code to implement the classes and methods that were discovered in the design phase. The output of this phase is the completed program.

In the *testing* phase, you run tests to verify that the program works correctly. The output of this phase is a report describing the tests that you carried out and their results.

> The waterfall model of software development describes a sequential process of analysis, design, implementation, testing, and deployment.

In the *deployment* phase, the users of the program install it and use it for its intended purpose.

When formal development processes were first established in the early 1970s, software engineers had a very simple visual model of these phases. They postulated that one phase would run to completion, its output would spill over to the next phase, and the next phase would begin. This model is called the *waterfall model* of software development (see Figure 1).

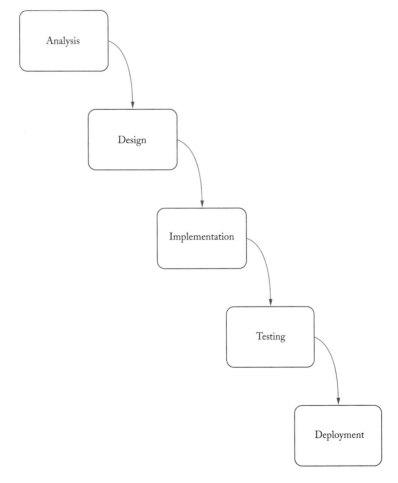

Figure 1

The Waterfall Model

In an ideal world the waterfall model has a lot of appeal: You figure out what to do; then you figure out how to do it; then you do it; then you verify that you did it right; then you hand the product to the customer. When rigidly applied, though, the waterfall model simply did not work. It was very difficult to come up with a perfect requirement specification. It was quite common to discover in the design phase that the requirements were not consistent or that a small change in the requirements would lead to a system that was both easier to design and more useful for the customer, but the analysis phase was over, so the designers had no choice—they had to take the existing requirements, errors and all. This problem would repeat itself during implementation. The designers may have thought they knew how to solve the problem as efficiently as possible, but when the design was actually implemented, it turned out that the resulting program was not as fast as the designers had thought. The next transition is one with which you are surely familiar. When the program was handed to the quality assurance department for testing, many bugs were found that would best be fixed by reimplementing, or maybe even redesigning, the program, but the waterfall model did not allow for this. Finally, when the customers received the finished product, they were often not at all happy with it. Even though the customers typically were very involved in the analysis phase, often they themselves were not sure exactly what they needed. After all, it can be very difficult to describe how you want to use a product that you have never seen before. But when the customers started using the program, they began to realize what they would have liked. Of course, then it was too late, and they had to live with what they got.

> The spiral model of software development describes an iterative process in which design and implementation are repeated.

Having some level of iteration is clearly necessary. There simply must be a mechanism to deal with errors from the preceding phase. The *spiral model*, proposed by Barry Boehm in 1988, breaks the development process down into multiple phases (see Figure 2). Early phases focus on

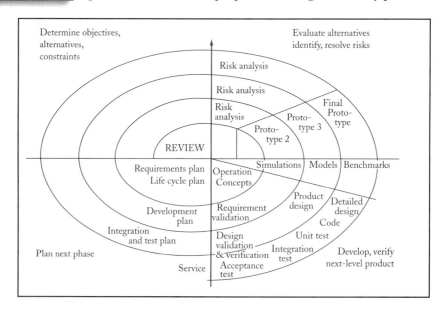

Figure 2

The Spiral Model

the construction of *prototypes*. A prototype is a small system that shows some aspects of the final system. Because prototypes model only a part of a system and do not need to withstand customer abuse, they can be implemented quickly. It is common to build a *user interface prototype* that shows the user interface in action. This gives customers an early chance to become more familiar with the system and to suggest improvements before the analysis is complete. Other prototypes can be built to validate interfaces with external systems, to test performance, and so on. Lessons learned from the development of one prototype can be applied to the next iteration of the spiral.

By building in repeated trials and feedback, a development process that follows the spiral model has a greater chance of delivering a satisfactory system. However, there is also a danger. If engineers believe that they don't have to do a good job because they can always do another iteration, then there will be many iterations, and the process will take a very long time to complete.

> Extreme Programming is a development methodology that strives for simplicity by removing formal structure and focusing on best practices.

Figure 3 (from [1]) shows activity levels in the "Rational Unified Process", a development process methodology by the inventors of UML. You can see that this is a complex process involving multiple iterations.

Even complex development processes with many iterations have not always met with success. In 1999, Kent Beck published an influential book [2] on *Extreme Programming*, a development methodology that strives for simplicity by cutting out most of the formal trappings of a traditional development methodology and instead focusing on a set of *practices:*

- *Realistic planning:* Customers are to make business decisions, programmers are to make technical decisions. Update the plan when it conflicts with reality.

- *Small releases:* Release a useful system quickly, then release updates on a very short cycle.

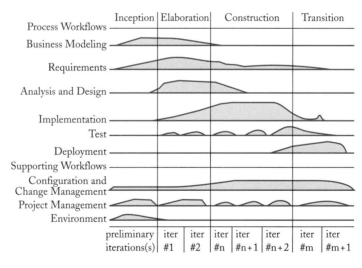

Figure 3

Activity Levels in the Rational Unified Process Methodology

- *Metaphor:* All programmers should have a simple shared story that explains the system under development.

- *Simplicity:* Design everything to be as simple as possible instead of preparing for future complexity.

- *Testing:* Both programmers and customers are to write test cases. The system is continuously tested.

- *Refactoring:* Programmers are to restructure the system continuously to improve the code and eliminate duplication.

- *Pair programming:* Put programmers together in pairs, and require each pair to write code on a single computer.

- *Collective ownership:* All programmers are to have permission to change all code as it becomes necessary.

- *Continuous integration:* Whenever a task is completed, build the entire system and test it.

- *40-hour week:* Don't cover up unrealistic schedules with bursts of heroic effort.

- *On-site customer:* An actual customer of the system is to be accessible to team members at all times.

- *Coding standards:* Programmers are to follow standards that emphasize self-documenting code.

Many of these practices are common-sense. Others, such as the pair programming requirement, are surprising. Beck claims that the value of the Extreme Programming approach lies in the synergy of these practices—the sum is bigger than the parts.

In your first programming course, you will not yet develop systems that are so complex that you need a full-fledged methodology to solve your homework problems. This introduction to the development process should, however, show you that successful software development involves more than just coding. In the remainder of this chapter we will have a closer look at the *design phase* of the software development process.

▼ Random Fact 16.1

Programmer Productivity

If you talk to your friends in this programming class, you will find that some of them consistently complete their assignments much more quickly than others. Perhaps they have more experience. However, even when programmers with the same education and experience are compared, wide variations in competence are routinely observed and measured. It is not uncommon to have the best programmer in a team be five to ten times as productive as the worst, using any of a number of reasonable measures of productivity [3].

That is a staggering range of performance among trained professionals. In a marathon race, the best runner will not run five to ten times faster than the slowest one. Software product managers are acutely aware of these disparities. The obvious solution is, of

▼   course, to hire only the best programmers, but even in recent periods of economic slow-
down the demand for good programmers has greatly outstripped the supply.

▼   Fortunately for all of us, joining the rank of the best is not necessarily a question of
raw intellectual power. Good judgment, experience, broad knowledge, attention to
detail, and superior planning are at least as important as mental brilliance. These skills
can be acquired by individuals who are genuinely interested in improving themselves.

▼   Even the most gifted programmer can deal with only a finite number of details in a
given time period. Suppose a programmer can implement and debug one method every
two hours, or one hundred methods per month. (This is a generous estimate. Few pro-

▼   grammers are this productive.) If a task requires 10,000 methods (which is typical for a
medium-sized program), then a single programmer would need 100 months to complete
the job. Such a project is sometimes expressed as a "100-man-month" project. But as

▼   Fred Brooks explains in his famous book [4], the concept of "man-month" is a myth. One
cannot trade months for programmers. One hundred programmers cannot finish the task
in one month. In fact, 10 programmers probably couldn't finish it in 10 months. First of

▼   all, the 10 programmers need to learn about the project before they can get productive.
Whenever there is a problem with a particular method, both the author and its users need
to meet and discuss it, taking time away from all of them. A bug in one method may have

▼   other programmers twiddling their thumbs until it is fixed.

It is difficult to estimate these inevitable delays. They are one reason why software is
often released later than originally promised. What is a manager to do when the delays

▼   mount? As Brooks points out, adding more personnel will make a late project even later,
because the productive people have to stop working and train the newcomers.

You will experience these problems when you work on your first team project with

▼   other students. Be prepared for a major drop in productivity, and be sure to set ample
time aside for team communications.

There is, however, no alternative to teamwork. Most important and worthwhile

▼   projects transcend the ability of one single individual. Learning to function well in a
team is as important for your education as it is to become a competent programmer.

16.2   Discovering Classes

> In object-oriented design, you discover classes, determine the responsibilities of classes, and describe the relationships between classes.

In the design phase of software development, your task is to discover structures that make it possible to implement a set of tasks on a computer. When you use the object-oriented design process, you carry out the following tasks:

1. Discover classes.
2. Determine the responsibilities of each class.
3. Describe the relationships between the classes.

A class represents some useful concept. You have seen classes for concrete entities such as bank accounts, ellipses, and products. Other classes represent abstract concepts such as streams and

INVOICE

Sam's Small Appliances
100 Main Street
Anytown, CA 98765

Item	Qty	Price	Total
Toaster	3	$29.95	$89.85
Hair Dryer	1	$24.95	$24.95
Car Vacuum	2	$19.99	$39.98

AMOUNT DUE: **$154.78**

Figure 4

An Invoice

windows. A simple rule for finding classes is to look for *nouns* in the task description. For example, suppose your job is to print an invoice such as the one in Figure 4. Obvious classes that come to mind are Invoice, Item, and Customer. It is a good idea to keep a list of *candidate classes* on a whiteboard or a sheet of paper. As you brainstorm, simply put all ideas for classes onto the list. You can always cross out the ones that weren't useful after all.

Once a set of classes has been identified, you need to define the behavior for each class. That is, you need to find out what methods each object needs to carry out to solve the programming problem. A simple rule for finding these methods is to look for *verbs* in the task description, and then match the verbs to the appropriate objects. For example, in the invoice program, some class needs to compute the amount due. Now you need to figure out *which class* is responsible for this method. Do customers compute what they owe? Do invoices total up the amount due? Do the items total themselves up? The best choice is to make "compute amount due" the responsibility of the Invoice class.

> A CRC card describes a class, its responsibilities, and its collaborating classes.

An excellent way to carry out this task is the so-called *CRC* card method. "CRC" stands for "classes", "responsibilities", "collaborators", and in its simplest form, the method works as follows. Use an index card for each *class* (see Figure 5). As you think about verbs in the task description that indicate methods, you pick the card of the class that

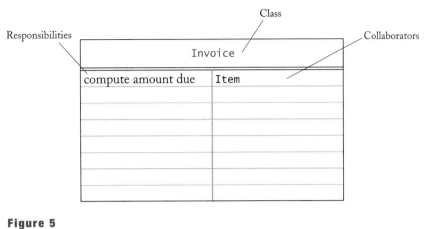

Figure 5

A CRC Card

you think should be responsible, and write that *responsibility* onto the card. For each responsibility, you record which other classes are needed to fulfill it. Those classes are the *collaborators*.

For example, suppose you decide that an invoice should compute the amount due. Then you write "compute amount due" on the left-hand side of an index card with the title `Invoice`.

If a class can carry out that responsibility all by itself, you do nothing further. But if the class needs the help of other classes, you write the names of these collaborators on the right-hand side of the card.

To compute the total, the invoice needs to ask each item about its total price. Therefore, the `Item` class is a collaborator.

This is a good time to look up the index card for the `Item` class. Does it have a "get total price" method? If not, add one:

How do you know that you are on the right track? For each responsibility, ask yourself how it can actually be done, using just the responsibilities written on the various cards. Many people find it helpful to group the cards on a table so that the collaborators are close to each other, and to simulate tasks by moving a token (such as a coin) from one card to the next to indicate which object is currently active.

Keep in mind that the responsibilities that you list on the CRC card are on a *high level*. Sometimes a single responsibility may need two or more Java methods for carrying it out. Some researchers say that a CRC card should have no more than three distinct responsibilities.

The CRC card method is informal on purpose, so that you can be creative and discover classes and their properties. Once you find that you have settled on a good set of classes, you will want to know how they are related to each other. Can you find classes with common properties, so that some responsibilities can be taken care of by a common superclass? Can you organize classes into clusters that are independent of each other? Finding class relationships and documenting them with diagrams is the topic of the next section.

16.3 Relationships between Classes

When designing a program, it is useful to document the relationships between classes. This helps you in a number of ways. For example, if you find classes with common behavior, you can save effort by placing the common behavior into a superclass. If you know that some classes are *not* related to each other, you can assign different programmers to implement each of them, without worrying that one of them has to wait for the other.

You have seen the inheritance relationship between classes many times in this book. Inheritance is a very important relationship between classes, but, as it turns out, it is not the only useful relationship, and it can be overused.

Inheritance is a relationship between a more general class (the superclass) and a more specialized class (the subclass). This relationship is often described as the *is-a* relationship. Every truck is a vehicle. Every savings account is a bank account. Every circle is an ellipse (with equal width and height).

> Inheritance (the "is-a" relationship) is sometimes inappropriately used when the "has-a" relationship would be more appropriate.

Inheritance is sometimes abused, however. For example, consider a `Tire` class that describes a car tire. Should the class `Tire` be a subclass of a class `Circle`? It sounds convenient. There are probably quite a few useful methods in the `Circle` class—for example, the `Tire` class may inherit methods that compute the radius, perimeter, and center point. All that should come in handy when drawing tire shapes. Yet though it may be convenient for the programmer, this arrangement makes no sense conceptually. It isn't true that every tire is a circle. Tires are car parts, whereas circles are geometric objects.

There is a relationship between tires and circles, though. A tire *has* a circle as its boundary. Java lets us model that relationship, too. Use an instance variable:

```
class Tire
{
   . . .
   private String rating;
   private Circle boundary;
}
```

The technical term for this relationship is *association*. Each `Tire` object is associated with a `Circle` object.

Here is another example. Every car *is a* vehicle. Every car *has a* tire (in fact, it has four or, if you count the spare, five). Thus, you would use inheritance from `Vehicle` and use association of `Tire` objects:

```
class Car extends Vehicle
{
   . . .
   private Tire[] tires;
}
```

In this book, we use the UML notation for class diagrams. You have already seen many examples of the UML notation for inheritance—an arrow with an open triangle

> A class is associated with another class if you can navigate from its objects to objects of the other class, usually by following object references.

> Dependency is another name for the "uses" relationship.

pointing to the superclass. In the UML notation, association is denoted by a solid line with an open arrow tip. Figure 6 shows a class diagram with an inheritance and an association relationship.

A class is associated with another if you can *navigate* from objects of one class to objects of the other class. For example, given a Car object, you can navigate to the Tire objects, simply by accessing the tires instance field. When a class has an instance field whose type is another class, then the two classes are associated.

The association relationship is related to the *dependency* relationship, which you saw in Chapter 7. Recall that a class depends on another if one of its methods *uses* an object of the other class in some way.

For example, all of our applet classes depend on the Graphics class, because they receive a Graphics object in the paint method and then use it to draw various shapes. The console applications depend on the System class, because they use the static variable System.out.

Association is a stronger form of dependency. If a class is associated with another, it also depends on the other class.

However, the converse is not true. If a class is associated with another, objects of the class can locate objects of the associated class, usually because they store references to those objects. If a class depends on another, it comes in contact with objects of the other class in some way, not necessarily through navigation. For example, an applet depends on the Graphics class, but it is not associated with the Graphics class. Given an applet object, you can't navigate to a Graphics object. You have to wait for the paint method to pass a Graphics object as a parameter.

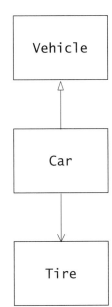

Figure 6

UML Notation for Inheritance and Association

> You need to be able to distinguish the UML notations for inheritance, realization, association, and dependency.

As you saw in Chapter 7, the UML notation for dependency is a dashed line with an open arrow that points to the dependent class.

The arrows in the UML notation can get confusing. Table 1 shows a summary of the four UML relationship symbols that we use in this book.

Relationship	Symbol	Line style	Arrow tip
Inheritance	——————▷	Solid	Closed
Realization	- - - - - - -▷	Dotted	Closed
Association	——————>	Solid	Open
Dependency	- - - - - - ->	Dotted	Open

▼ AT Advanced Topic 16.1

Attributes and Methods in UML Diagrams

Sometimes it is useful to indicate class *attributes* and *methods* in a class diagram. An *attribute* is an externally observable property that objects of a class have. For example, name and price would be attributes of the Product class. Usually, attributes correspond to instance variables. But they don't have to—a class may have a different way of organizing its data. Consider the ellipse class from the Java library. Conceptually, it has attributes center, width, and height, but it doesn't actually store the center of the ellipse. Instead, it stores the top left corner and computes the center from it.

You can indicate attributes and methods in a class diagram by dividing a class rectangle into three compartments, with the class name in the top, attributes in the middle, and methods in the bottom (see Figure 7). You need not list *all* attributes and methods in a particular diagram. Just list the ones that are helpful to understand whatever point you are making with a particular diagram.

Also, don't list as an attribute what you also draw as an association. If you denote by association the fact that a Car has Tire objects, don't add an attribute tires.

Figure 7

Attributes and Methods in a Class Diagram

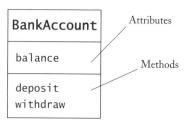

▼ 𝔸𝕋 Advanced Topic 16.2 ▶

Association, Aggregation, and Composition

The association relationship is the most complex relationship in the UML notation. It is also the least standardized. As you read other books and see class diagrams produced by fellow programmers, you may encounter quite a few different flavors of the association relationship.

The association relationship that we use in this book is called a *directed* association. It implies that you can navigate from one class to another, but not the other way around. For example, given a Car object, you can navigate to Tire objects. But if you have a Tire object, then there is no indication to which car it belongs.

Of course, a Tire object may contain a reference back to the Car object so that you can navigate from the tire back to the car to which it belongs. Then the association is *bidirectional.* For cars and tires, this is an unlikely implementation. But consider the example of Person and Company objects. The company may keep a list of people working for it, and each person object may keep a reference to the current employer.

According to the UML standard, a bidirectional association is drawn as a solid line with *no* arrow tips. (See Figure 8 for this and other variations of the association notation.) But some designers interpret an association without arrow tips as an "undecided" association, where it is not yet known in which direction the navigation can happen.

Some designers like to add *adornments* to the association relationships. An association can have a name, roles, or multiplicities. A name describes the nature of the relationship. Role adornments express specific roles that the associated classes have toward each other. Multiplicities state how many objects can be reached when navigating the association relationship. The example in Figure 8 expresses the fact that every tire is associated with 0 or 1 car, whereas every car must have 4 or more tires.

Aggregation is a stronger form of association. A class aggregates another if there is a "whole-part" relationship between the classes. For example, the Company class aggregates the Person class because a company (the "whole") is made up from people (the "parts"), namely its employees and contractors. But a BankAccount class does not aggregate a Person class, even though it may be possible to navigate from a bank customer object to a person object—the owner of the account. Conceptually, a person is not a part of the bank account.

Composition is an even stronger form of aggregation that denotes that a "part" can belong to only one "whole" at a given point in time. For example, a tire can be in only one car at a time, but a person can work for two companies at the same time.

Frankly, the differences between association, aggregation, and composition are confusing, even to experienced designers. If you find the distinctions helpful, by all means use them. But don't spend time pondering subtle differences between these concepts. From the practical point of view of a Java programmer, it is useful to know when one class stores a reference to another class. Directed associations accurately describe this phenomenon.

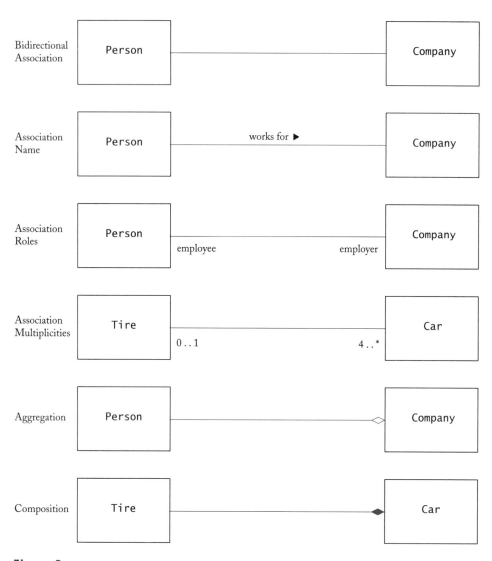

Bidirectional Association

Association Name

Association Roles

Association Multiplicities

Aggregation

Composition

Figure 8

Variations of the Association Notation

CRC Cards and UML Diagrams

Before writing code for a complex problem, you need to design a solution. The methodology introduced in this chapter suggests that you follow a design process that is composed of the following tasks:

▼   1. Discover classes.

      2. Determine the responsibilities of each class.

▼   3. Describe the relationships between the classes.

CRC cards and UML diagrams help you discover and record this information.

▼   **Step 1   Discover classes**

Highlight the nouns in the problem description. Make a list of the nouns. Cross out those that don't seem reasonable candidates for classes.

▼

Step 2   Discover responsibilities

▼   Make a list of the major tasks that your system needs to fulfill. From those tasks, pick one that is not trivial and that is intuitive to you. Find a class that is responsible for carrying out that task. Make an index card and write the name and the task on it. Now ask yourself

▼   how an object of the class can carry out the task. It probably needs help from other objects. Then make CRC cards for the classes to which those objects belong and write the responsibilities on them.

▼   Don't be afraid to cross out, move, split, or merge responsibilities. Rip up cards if they become too messy. This is an informal process.

      You are done when you have walked through all major tasks and satisfied yourself

▼   that they can all be solved with the classes and responsibilities that you discovered.

Step 3   Discover relationships

▼   Make a class diagram that shows the relationships between all the classes that you discovered.

      Start with inheritance—the "is-a" relationship between classes. Is any class a special-

▼   ization of another? If so, draw inheritance arrows. Keep in mind that many designs, especially for simple programs, don't use inheritance extensively.

      The "collaborators" column of the CRC cards tell you which classes use another.

▼   Draw usage arrows for the collaborators on the CRC cards.

      For each of the dependency relationships, ask yourself: How does the object locate its collaborator? Does it navigate to it directly because it stores a reference? Does it ask

▼   another object to locate the collaborator? Is the collaborator passed as a parameter to a method? Only in the first case is the collaborating class an associated class. In those cases, draw association arrows.

16.4   # Example: Printing an Invoice

In this chapter, we discuss a five-part development process that is recommended for you to follow:

   1. Gather requirements.

   2. Use CRC cards to find classes, responsibilities, and collaborators.

   3. Use UML diagrams to record class relationships.

4. Use `javadoc` to document method behavior.

5. Implement your program.

This process is particularly well suited for beginning programmers. There isn't a lot of notation to learn. The class diagrams are simple to draw. The deliverables of the design phase are obviously useful for the implementation phase—you simply take the source files and start adding the method code. Of course, as your projects get more complex, you will want to learn more about formal design methods. There are many techniques to describe object scenarios, call sequencing, the large-scale structure of programs, and so on, that are very beneficial even for relatively simple projects. The book [1] gives a good overview of these techniques.

In this section, we will walk through the object-oriented design technique with a very simple example. In this case, the methodology will certainly feel overblown, but it is a good introduction to the mechanics of each step. You will then be better prepared for the more complex example that follows.

16.4.1 — Requirements

The task of this program is to print out an *invoice*. An invoice describes the charges for a set of products in certain quantities. (We omit complexities such as dates, taxes, and invoice and customer numbers.) The program simply prints the billing address, all line items, and the amount due. Each line item contains the description and unit price of a product, the quantity ordered, and the total price.

```
                    I N V O I C E

    Sam's Small Appliances
    100 Main Street
    Anytown, CA 98765

    Description              Price  Qty  Total
    Toaster                  29.95   3   89.85
    Hair dryer               24.95   1   24.95
    Car vacuum               19.99   2   39.98

    AMOUNT DUE: $154.78
```

Also, in the interest of simplicity, we do not provide a user interface. We just supply a test program that adds items to the invoice and then prints it.

16.4.2 — CRC Cards

First, you need to discover classes. Classes correspond to nouns in the problem description. In this problem, it is pretty obvious what the nouns are:

```
Invoice
Address
Item
Product
Description
Price
Quantity
Total
Amount Due
```

(Of course, `Toaster` doesn't count—it is the description of an `Item` object and therefore a data value, not the name of a class.)

The product description and price are fields of the `Product` class. What about the quantity? The quantity is not an attribute of a `Product`. Just as in the printed invoice, let's have a class `Item` that records the product and the quantity (such as "3 toasters").

The total and amount due are computed—not stored anywhere. Thus, they don't lead to classes.

After this process of elimination, we are left with four candidates for classes:

```
Invoice
Address
Item
Product
```

Each of them represents a useful concept, so let's make them all into classes.

The purpose of the program is to print an invoice. However, the `Invoice` class won't necessarily know whether to display the output in `System.out`, in a text area, or in a file. Therefore, let's relax the task slightly and make the invoice responsible for *formatting* the invoice. The result is a string (containing multiple lines) that can be printed out or displayed. Record that responsibility in a CRC card:

Invoice
format the invoice

How does an invoice format itself? It must format the billing address, format all items, and then add the amount due. How can the invoice format an address? It can't—that really is the responsibility of the `Address` class. This leads to a second CRC card:

Address
format the address

Similarly, formatting of an item is the responsibility of the `Item` class.

The `format` method of the `Invoice` class calls the `format` methods of the `Address` and `Item` classes. Whenever a method uses another class, you list that other class as a collaborator. In other words, `Address` and `Item` are collaborators of `Invoice`:

Invoice	
format the invoice	`Address`
	`Item`

When formatting the invoice, the invoice also needs to compute the total amount due. To obtain that amount, it must ask each item about the total price of the item.

How does an item obtain that total? It must ask the product for the unit price, and then multiply it by the quantity. That is, the `Product` class must reveal the unit price, and it is a collaborator of the `Item` class.

Product	
get description	
get unit price	

Item	
format the item	`Product`
get total price	

Finally, the invoice must be populated with products and quantities, so that it makes sense to format the result. That too is a responsibility of the `Invoice` class.

Invoice	
format the invoice	`Address`
add a product and quantity	`Item`
	`Product`

We now have a set of CRC cards that completes the CRC card process.

16.4.3 — UML Diagrams

You get the dependency relationships from the collaboration column in the CRC cards. Each class depends on the classes with which it collaborates. In our example, the `Invoice` class collaborates with the `Address`, `Item`, and `Product` classes. The `Item` class collaborates with the `Product` class.

Now ask yourself which of these dependencies are actually associations. How does an invoice know about the address, item, and product objects with which it collaborates? An invoice object must hold references to the address and the items when it formats the invoice. But an invoice object need not hold a reference to a product object when adding a product. The product is turned into an item, and then it is the item's responsibility to hold a reference to it.

Therefore, the `Invoice` class is associated with the `Address` class and the `Item` class. The `Item` class is associated with the `Product` class. However, you cannot directly navigate from an invoice to a product. An invoice doesn't store products directly—they are stored in the `Item` objects.

There is no inheritance in this example.

Figure 9 shows the class relationships that we discovered.

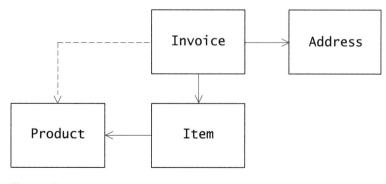

Figure 9

The Relationships between the Invoice Classes

16.4.4— Method Documentation

> You can use javadoc documentation comments (with the bodies of the methods left blank) to record formally the behavior of the classes that you discovered.

The final step of the design phase is to write the documentation of the discovered classes and methods. Simply write a Java source file for each class, write the method comments for those methods that you have discovered, and leave the bodies of the methods blank.

```java
/**
    Describes an invoice for a set of purchased products.
*/
public class Invoice
{
    /**
        Adds a charge for a product to this invoice.
        @param aProduct  the product that the customer ordered
        @param quantity  the quantity of the product
    */
    public void add(Product aProduct, int quantity)
    {
    }

    /**
        Formats the invoice.
        @return  the formatted invoice
    */
    public String format()
    {
    }
}


/**
    Describes a quantity of an article to purchase and its price.
*/
public class Item
{
    /**
        Computes the total cost of this item.
        @return  the total price
    */
    public double getTotalPrice()
    {
    }

    /**
        Formats this item.
        @return  a formatted string of this item
```

```
    */
    public String format()
    {
    }
}


/**
    Describes a product with a description and a price.
*/
public class Product
{
    /**
        Gets the product description.
        @return the description
    */
    public String getDescription()
    {
    }

    /**
        Gets the product price.
        @return the unit price
    */
    public double getPrice()
    {
    }
}


/**
    Describes a mailing address.
*/
public class Address
{
    /**
        Formats the address.
        @return the address as a string with 3 lines
    */
    public String format()
    {
    }
}
```

Then run the `javadoc` program to obtain a prettily formatted version of your documentation in HTML format (see Figure 10).

This approach for documenting your classes has a number of advantages. You can share the HTML documentation with others if you work in a team. You use a format that is immediately useful—Java source files that you can carry into the implementation phase. And, most importantly, you supply the comments of the key methods—a task that less prepared programmers leave for later, and then often neglect for lack of time.

Figure 10

The Class Documentation in the HTML Format

16.4.5— Implementation

Finally, you are ready to implement the classes.

You already have the method signatures and comments from the previous step. Now look at the UML diagram to add instance variables. Associated classes yield instance variables. Start with the `Invoice` class. An invoice is associated with `Address` and `Item`. Every invoice has one billing address, but it can have many items. To store multiple `Item` objects, you can use an array list. Now you have the instance variables of the `Invoice` class:

```
public class Invoice
{
    . . .
    private Address billingAddress;
    private ArrayList items;
}
```

As you can see from the UML diagram, the `Item` class is associated with a product. Also, you need to store the product quantity. That leads to the following instance variables:

```
public class Item
{
    . . .
    private Product theProduct;
    private int quantity;
}
```

The methods themselves are now very easy. Here is a typical example. You already know what the `getTotalPrice` method of the `Item` class needs to do—get the unit price of the product and multiply it with the quantity.

```
/**
    Computes the total cost of this item.
    @return the total price
*/
public double getTotalPrice()
{
    return theProduct.getPrice() * quantity;
}
```

We will not discuss the other methods in detail—they are equally straightforward.
Finally, you need to supply constructors, another routine task.

Here is the entire program. It is a good practice to go through it in detail and match
up the classes and methods against the CRC cards and UML diagram.

File InvoiceTest.java

```java
1  import java.util.Vector;
2
3  /**
4      This program tests the invoice classes by printing
5      a sample invoice.
6  */
7  public class InvoiceTest
8  {
9      public static void main(String[] args)
10     {
11         Address samsAddress = new Address(
12             "Sam's Small Appliances", "100 Main Street",
13             "Anytown", "CA", "98765");
14
15         Invoice samsInvoice = new Invoice(samsAddress);
16         samsInvoice.add(new Product("Toaster", 29.95), 3);
17         samsInvoice.add(
18             new Product("Hair dryer", 24.95), 1);
19         samsInvoice.add(
20             new Product("Car vacuum", 19.99), 2);
21
22         System.out.println(samsInvoice.format());
23     }
24 }
```

File Invoice.java

```java
1  import java.util.ArrayList;
2
3  /**
4      Describes an invoice for a set of purchased products.
5  */
6  class Invoice
7  {
8      /**
9          Constructs an invoice.
```

```
10           @param anAddress  the billing address
11       */
12       public Invoice(Address anAddress)
13       {
14           items = new ArrayList();
15           billingAddress = anAddress;
16       }
17
18       /**
19           Adds a charge for a product to this invoice.
20           @param aProduct  the product that the customer ordered
21           @param quantity  the quantity of the product
22       */
23       public void add(Product aProduct, int quantity)
24       {
25           Item anItem = new Item(aProduct, quantity);
26           items.add(anItem);
27       }
28
29       /**
30           Formats the invoice.
31           @return  the formatted invoice
32       */
33       public String format()
34       {
35           String r =
36               "                          I N V O I C E\n\n"
37               + billingAddress.format()
38               + "\n\nDescription                    Price    "
39               + "Qty  Total\n";
40           for (int i = 0; i < items.size(); i++)
41           {
42               Item nextItem = (Item)items.get(i);
43               r = r + nextItem.format() + "\n";
44           }
45
46           r = r + "\nAMOUNT DUE: $" + getAmountDue();
47
48           return r;
49       }
50
51       /**
52           Computes the total amount due.
53           @return  the amount due
54       */
55       public double getAmountDue()
56       {
57           double amountDue = 0;
58           for (int i = 0; i < items.size(); i++)
59           {
60               Item nextItem = (Item)items.get(i);
61               amountDue = amountDue
```

```
62                    + nextItem.getTotalPrice();
63          }
64          return amountDue;
65       }
66
67       private Address billingAddress;
68       private ArrayList items;
69 }
```

File Item.java

```
1  /**
2      Describes a quantity of an article to purchase and its price.
3  */
4  class Item
5  {
6      /**
7          Constructs an item from the product and quantity.
8          @param aProduct  the product
9          @param aQuantity  the item quantity
10     */
11     public Item(Product aProduct, int aQuantity)
12     {
13         theProduct = aProduct;
14         quantity = aQuantity;
15     }
16
17     /**
18         Computes the total cost of this item.
19         @return  the total price
20     */
21     public double getTotalPrice()
22     {
23         return theProduct.getPrice() * quantity;
24     }
25
26     /**
27         Formats this item.
28         @return  a formatted string of this item
29     */
30     public String format()
31     {
32         final int COLUMN_WIDTH = 30;
33         String description = theProduct.getDescription();
34
35         String r = description;
36
37         // pad with spaces to fill column
38
39         int pad = COLUMN_WIDTH - description.length();
40         for (int i = 1; i <= pad; i++)
```

```
41              r = r + " ";
42
43        r = r + theProduct.getPrice()
44           + "    " + quantity
45           + "    " + getTotalPrice();
46
47        return r;
48     }
49
50     private int quantity;
51     private Product theProduct;
52 }
```

File Product.java

```
 1 /**
 2     Describes a product with a description and a price.
 3 */
 4 class Product
 5 {
 6    /**
 7        Constructs a product from a description and a price.
 8        @param aDescription the product description
 9        @param aPrice the product price
10    */
11    public Product(String aDescription, double aPrice)
12    {
13       description = aDescription;
14       price = aPrice;
15    }
16
17    /**
18        Gets the product description.
19        @return the description
20    */
21    public String getDescription()
22    {
23       return description;
24    }
25
26    /**
27        Gets the product price.
28        @return the unit price
29    */
30    public double getPrice()
31    {
32       return price;
33    }
34
35    private String description;
36    private double price;
37 }
```

File Address.java

```
 1  /**
 2      Describes a mailing address.
 3  */
 4  class Address
 5  {
 6      /**
 7          Constructs a mailing address.
 8          @param aName  the recipient name
 9          @param aStreet  the street
10          @param aCity  the city
11          @param aState  the 2-letter state code
12          @param aZip  the ZIP postal code
13      */
14      public Address(String aName, String aStreet,
15          String aCity, String aState, String aZip)
16      {
17          name = aName;
18          street = aStreet;
19          city = aCity;
20          state = aState;
21          zip = aZip;
22      }
23
24      /**
25          Formats the address.
26          @return  the address as a string with 3 lines
27      */
28      public String format()
29      {
30          return name + "\n" + street + "\n"
31              + city + ", " + state + " " + zip;
32      }
33
34      private String name;
35      private String street;
36      private String city;
37      private String state;
38      private String zip;
39  }
```

16.5   Example: An Automatic Teller Machine

16.5.1 — Requirements

The purpose of this project is to design a simulation of an automatic teller machine
(ATM). The ATM has a keypad to enter numbers, a display to show messages, and a set
of buttons, labeled A, B, and C, whose function depends on the state of the machine (see
Figure 11).

The ATM is used by the customers of a bank. Each customer has two accounts: a checking account and a savings account. Each customer also has a customer number and a personal identification number (PIN). Both are required to gain access to the accounts. (In a real ATM, the customer number would be recorded on the magnetic strip of the ATM card. In this simulation, the customer will need to type it in.) With the ATM, customers can select an account (checking or savings). The balance of the selected account is displayed. Then the customer can deposit and withdraw money. This process is repeated until the customer chooses to exit.

Specifically, the user interaction is as follows. When the ATM starts up, it expects a user to enter a customer number. The display shows the following message:

```
Enter customer number
A = OK
```

The user enters the customer number on the keypad and presses the A button. The display message changes to

```
Enter PIN
A = OK
```

Next, the user enters the PIN and presses the A button again. If the customer number and ID match those of one of the customers in the bank, then the customer can proceed. If not, the user is again prompted to enter the customer number.

If the customer has been authorized to use the system, then the display message changes to

```
Select Account
A = Checking
B = Savings
C = Exit
```

If the user presses the C button, the ATM reverts to its original state and asks the next user to enter a customer number.

If the user presses the A or B button, the ATM remembers the selected account, and the display message changes to

```
Balance = balance of selected account
Enter amount and select transaction
A = Withdraw
B = Deposit
C = Cancel
```

If the user presses the A or B button, the value entered in the keypad is withdrawn from or deposited into the selected account. (This is just a simulation, so no money is dis-

Figure 11

User Interface of the Automatic Teller Machine

pensed and no deposit is accepted.) Afterwards, the ATM reverts to the preceding state, allowing the user to select another account or to exit.

If the user presses the C button, the ATM reverts to the preceding state without executing any transaction.

Since this is a simulation, the ATM does not actually communicate with a bank. It simply loads a set of customer numbers and PINs from a file. All accounts are initialized with a zero balance.

16.5.2 — CRC Cards

We will again follow the recipe of Section 16.2 and show how to discover classes, responsibilities, and relationships and how to obtain a detailed design for the ATM program.

Recall that the first rule for finding classes is "Look for nouns in the problem description". Here is a list of the nouns:

```
ATM
User
Keypad
Display
Display message
Button
State
Bank account
Checking account
Savings account
Customer
Customer number
PIN
Bank
```

Of course, not all of these nouns will become names of classes, and we may yet discover the need for classes that aren't in this list, but it is a good start.

Let's start simply with a noncontroversial choice. A Keypad sounds like an excellent idea for a class. A keypad is a component with buttons and a text field that lets the user type in a value. What can we do with a keypad? There is one essential method: get the value the user entered. (Of course, the keypad will end up using one or more internal methods to track the button clicks, but we are not concerned with such an implementation detail now.) Here is the CRC card for the Keypad class:

Keypad
get value

On the other hand, there is already a good class for the display, namely JTextArea. Thus we won't need to create a separate Display class. Similarly, there is no need for a class to encapsulate display messages—we will just use strings. Also, we will use the existing JButton class for buttons.

Users and customers represent the same concept in this program. Let's use a class Customer. A customer has two bank accounts, and a customer object must be able to tell us the accounts. A customer also has a customer number and a PIN. We can, of course, require that a customer object give us the customer number and the PIN. But perhaps that isn't so secure. Instead, let us simply require that a customer object, when given a customer number and a PIN, will tell us whether it matches its own information or not.

Customer
get accounts
match number and PIN

A bank contains a collection of customers. When a user walks up to the ATM and enters a customer number and PIN, it is the job of the bank to find the matching customer. How can the bank do this? It needs to check for each customer whether its customer number and PIN match. Thus, it needs to call the match number and PIN method of the Customer class that we just discovered. Because the find customer method calls a Customer method, it collaborates with the Customer class. We record that fact in the right-hand column of the CRC card.

Bank	
find customer	Customer
read customers	

When the simulation starts up, the bank must also be able to read a collection of customers and PINs.

The BankAccount class is our familiar class, with methods to get the balance and to deposit and withdraw money:

In this program there is nothing that distinguishes checking accounts from savings accounts. The ATM does not add interest or deduct fees. Therefore, we decide not to implement separate subclasses for checking and savings accounts.

Finally, we are left with the ATM class itself. An important notion of the ATM is the state. Whenever the state changes, the display needs to be updated, and the meaning of the buttons changes. There are four states:

1. START: Enter customer ID
2. PIN: Enter PIN
3. ACCOUNT: Select account
4. TRANSACT: Select transaction

To understand how to move from one state to the next, it is useful to draw a *state diagram* (Figure 12). The UML notation has standardized shapes for state diagrams. Draw states

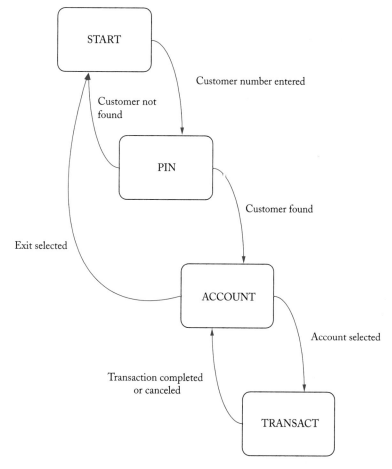

Figure 12

State Diagram for the ATM Class

as rectangles with rounded corners. Draw state changes as arrows, with labels that indicate the reason for the change.

We will implement a setState method that sets the system to a new state and updates the display.

The user must type a valid customer number and PIN. Then the ATM can ask the bank to find the customer. This calls for a select customer method. It collaborates with the bank, asking the bank for the customer that matches the customer number and PIN. Next, there must be a select account method that asks the current customer for the checking or savings account. Finally, the deposit and withdraw methods carry out the selected transaction on the current account.

ATM	
set state	Customer
select customer	Bank
select account	BankAccount
execute transaction	Keypad

Of course, discovering these classes and methods was not as neat and orderly as it appears from this discussion. When I designed these classes for this book, it took me several trials and tearing up of cards to come up with a satisfactory design. It is also important to remember that there is seldom one best design.

This design has several advantages. The classes describe clear concepts. The methods are sufficient to implement all necessary tasks. (I mentally walked through every ATM usage scenario to verify that.) There are not too many collaboration dependencies between the classes. Thus, I was satisfied with this design and proceeded to the next step.

16.5.3 — UML Diagram

Figure 13 shows the relationship between these classes. There are two examples of inheritance. The keypad is a panel. The ATM is a frame.

To draw the dependencies, use the "collaborator" columns from the CRC cards. Looking at those columns, you find that the dependencies are as follows:

- ATM uses KeyPad, Bank, Customer, and BankAccount.

- Bank uses Customer.

It is easy to see the association relationships. Given a bank, we can navigate to its customers. Given a customer, we can navigate to its bank accounts. The ATM can navigate to the keypad, the bank, the current customer, and the current bank account.

In this case, it turns out that all of the collaboration relationships are associations, so there are no additional dependency relationships to draw.

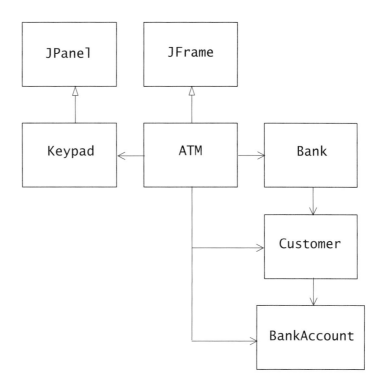

Figure 13

Relationships between the ATM Classes

The class diagram is a good tool to visualize dependencies. Look at the Keypad class. It is completely independent from the rest of the ATM system—you could take out the Keypad class and use it in another application. Also, the Bank, BankAccount, and Customer classes, although dependent on each other, don't know anything about the ATM class. That makes sense—you can have banks without ATMs. As you can see, when you analyze relationships, you look for the absence of relationships just as much as for their presence.

16.5.4 Method Documentation

Now you are ready for the final step of the design phase: to document the classes and methods that you discovered. Here is the documentation for the ATM class:

```
public class ATM
{
   /**
      Gets PIN from keypad, finds customer in bank.
      If found sets state to ACCOUNT, else to START
   */
   public void selectCustomer()
   {
   }
```

```
/**
    Sets current account to checking or savings.
    Sets state to TRANSACT.
    @param account one of CHECKING_ACCOUNT
        or SAVINGS_ACCOUNT
*/
public void selectAccount(int account)
{
}


/**
    Withdraws amount typed in keypad from current account.
    Sets state to ACCOUNT
*/
public void withdraw()
{
}

/**
    Deposits amount typed in keypad to current account.
    Sets state to ACCOUNT
*/
public void deposit()
{
}

/**
    Sets state and updates display message.
    @param state the next state
*/
public void setState(int newState)
{
}
}
```

Then run the `javadoc` utility to turn this documentation into HTML format.

For conciseness, we omit the documentation of the other classes.

16.5.5 — Implementation

Finally, the time has come to implement the ATM simulator. You will find that the implementation phase is very straightforward and should take *much less time than the design phase.*

A good strategy for implementing the classes is to go "bottom-up". Start with the classes that don't depend on others, such as `Keypad` and `BankAccount`. Then implement a class such as `Customer` that depends only on the `BankAccount` class. This "bottom-up" approach allows you to test your classes individually. You will find the implementations of these classes at the end of this section.

The most complex class is the `ATM` class. In order to implement the methods, you need to define the necessary instance variables. From the class diagram, you can tell that the ATM has a keypad and a bank object. They become instance variables of the class:

```
class ATM
{   . . .
    private Bank theBank;
    private Keypad pad;
    . . .
}
```

From the description of the ATM states, it is clear that we require additional instance variables to store the current state, customer, and bank account.

```
class ATM
{   . . .
    private int state;
    private Customer currentCustomer;
    private BankAccount currentAccount;
    . . .
}
```

Most methods are very straightforward to implement. Consider the `withdraw` method. From the design documentation, we have the description

```
/**
    Withdraws amount typed in keypad from current account.
    Sets state to ACCOUNT
*/
```

This description can be almost literally translated to Java instructions:

```
public void withdraw()
{
    currentAccount.withdraw(pad.getValue());
    setState(ACCOUNT_STATE);
}
```

Much of the remaining complexity in the ATM program results from the user interface. The ATM constructor has many statements to lay out components, and there are three button handlers that laboriously call the various ATM methods, depending on the state. This code is lengthy but straightforward.

We won't go through a method-by-method description of the ATM program. You should take some time and compare the actual implementation against the CRC cards and the UML diagram.

File ATMSimulation.java

```
1  import javax.swing.JFrame;
2
3  /**
4      A simulation of an automatic teller machine.
5  */
6  public class ATMSimulation
7  {
8      public static void main(String[] args)
9      {
10         JFrame frame = new ATM();
```

```
11        frame.setTitle("First National Bank of Java");
12        frame.setDefaultCloseOperation(
13           JFrame.EXIT_ON_CLOSE);
14        frame.pack();
15        frame.show();
16     }
17 }
```

File ATM.java

```
 1 import java.awt.Container;
 2 import java.awt.FlowLayout;
 3 import java.awt.GridLayout;
 4 import java.awt.event.ActionEvent;
 5 import java.awt.event.ActionListener;
 6 import java.awt.event.WindowEvent;
 7 import java.awt.event.WindowAdapter;
 8 import java.io.IOException;
 9 import javax.swing.JButton;
10 import javax.swing.JFrame;
11 import javax.swing.JOptionPane;
12 import javax.swing.JPanel;
13 import javax.swing.JTextArea;
14
15 /**
16    A frame displaying the components of an ATM.
17 */
18 class ATM extends JFrame
19 {
20    /**
21       Constructs the user interface of the ATM application.
22    */
23    public ATM()
24    {
25       // initialize bank and customers
26
27       theBank = new Bank();
28       try
29       {
30          theBank.readCustomers("customers.txt");
31       }
32       catch(IOException e)
33       {
34          JOptionPane.showMessageDialog(null,
35             "Error opening accounts file.");
36       }
37
38       // construct components
39
40       pad = new KeyPad();
```

```
41
42        display = new JTextArea(4, 20);
43
44        aButton = new JButton("  A  ");
45        aButton.addActionListener(new AButtonListener());
46
47        bButton = new JButton("  B  ");
48        bButton.addActionListener(new BButtonListener());
49
50        cButton = new JButton("  C  ");
51        cButton.addActionListener(new CButtonListener());
52
53        // add components to content pane
54
55        JPanel buttonPanel = new JPanel();
56        buttonPanel.setLayout(new GridLayout(3, 1));
57        buttonPanel.add(aButton);
58        buttonPanel.add(bButton);
59        buttonPanel.add(cButton);
60
61        Container contentPane = getContentPane();
62        contentPane.setLayout(new FlowLayout());
63        contentPane.add(pad);
64        contentPane.add(display);
65        contentPane.add(buttonPanel);
66
67        setState(START_STATE);
68     }
69
70     /**
71        Sets the current customer number to the keypad value
72        and sets state to PIN.
73     */
74     public void setCustomerNumber()
75     {
76        customerNumber = (int)pad.getValue();
77        setState(PIN_STATE);
78     }
79
80     /**
81        Gets PIN from keypad, finds customer in bank.
82        If found, sets state to ACCOUNT, else to START.
83     */
84     public void selectCustomer()
85     {
86        int pin = (int)pad.getValue();
87        currentCustomer = theBank.findCustomer(
88           customerNumber, pin);
89        if (currentCustomer == null)
90           setState(START_STATE);
```

```
91          else
92              setState(ACCOUNT_STATE);
93      }
94
95      /**
96          Sets current account to checking or savings. Sets
97          state to TRANSACT.
98          @param account one of CHECKING_ACCOUNT
99              or SAVINGS_ACCOUNT
100     */
101     public void selectAccount(int account)
102     {
103         if (account == CHECKING_ACCOUNT)
104             currentAccount =
105                 currentCustomer.getCheckingAccount();
106         else
107             currentAccount =
108                 currentCustomer.getSavingsAccount();
109         setState(TRANSACT_STATE);
110     }
111
112     /**
113         Withdraws amount typed in keypad from current account.
114         Sets state to ACCOUNT.
115     */
116     public void withdraw()
117     {
118         currentAccount.withdraw(pad.getValue());
119         setState(ACCOUNT_STATE);
120     }
121
122     /**
123         Deposits amount typed in keypad to current account.
124         Sets state to ACCOUNT.
125     */
126     public void deposit()
127     {
128         currentAccount.deposit(pad.getValue());
129         setState(ACCOUNT_STATE);
130     }
131
132     /**
133         Sets state and updates display message.
134         @param state the next state
135     */
136     public void setState(int newState)
137     {
138         state = newState;
139         pad.clear();
140         if (state == START_STATE)
```

```
141            display.setText(
142                "Enter customer number\nA = OK");
143         else if (state == PIN_STATE)
144            display.setText("Enter PIN\nA = OK");
145         else if (state == ACCOUNT_STATE)
146            display.setText("Select Account\n"
147               + "A = Checking\nB = Savings\nC = Exit");
148         else if (state == TRANSACT_STATE)
149            display.setText("Balance = "
150               + currentAccount.getBalance()
151               + "\nEnter amount and select transaction\n"
152               + "A = Withdraw\nB = Deposit\nC = Cancel");
153      }
154
155      private class AButtonListener
156         implements ActionListener
157      {
158         public void actionPerformed(ActionEvent event)
159         {
160            if (state == START_STATE)
161               setCustomerNumber();
162            else if (state == PIN_STATE)
163               selectCustomer();
164            else if (state == ACCOUNT_STATE)
165               selectAccount(CHECKING_ACCOUNT);
166            else if (state == TRANSACT_STATE)
167               withdraw();
168         }
169      }
170
171      private class BButtonListener
172         implements ActionListener
173      {
174         public void actionPerformed(ActionEvent event)
175         {
176            if (state == ACCOUNT_STATE)
177               selectAccount(SAVINGS_ACCOUNT);
178            else if (state == TRANSACT_STATE)
179               deposit();
180         }
181      }
182
183      private class CButtonListener
184         implements ActionListener
185      {
186         public void actionPerformed(ActionEvent event)
187         {
188            if (state == ACCOUNT_STATE)
189               setState(START_STATE);
190            else if (state == TRANSACT_STATE)
```

```
191                    setState(ACCOUNT_STATE);
192         }
193      }
194
195      private int state;
196      private int customerNumber;
197      private Customer currentCustomer;
198      private BankAccount currentAccount;
199      private Bank theBank;
200
201      private JButton aButton;
202      private JButton bButton;
203      private JButton cButton;
204
205      private KeyPad pad;
206      private JTextArea display;
207
208      private static final int START_STATE = 1;
209      private static final int PIN_STATE = 2;
210      private static final int ACCOUNT_STATE = 3;
211      private static final int TRANSACT_STATE = 4;
212
213      private static final int CHECKING_ACCOUNT = 1;
214      private static final int SAVINGS_ACCOUNT = 2;
215 }
```

File KeyPad.java

```
 1 import java.awt.BorderLayout;
 2 import java.awt.GridLayout;
 3 import java.awt.event.ActionEvent;
 4 import java.awt.event.ActionListener;
 5 import javax.swing.JButton;
 6 import javax.swing.JPanel;
 7 import javax.swing.JTextField;
 8
 9 /**
10    A component that lets the user enter a number, using
11    a button pad labeled with digits.
12 */
13 public class KeyPad extends JPanel
14 {
15    /**
16       Constructs the keypad panel.
17    */
18    public KeyPad()
19    {
20       setLayout(new BorderLayout());
21
22       // add display field
23
```

```
24          display = new JTextField();
25          add(display, "North");
26
27          // make button panel
28
29          buttonPanel = new JPanel();
30          buttonPanel.setLayout(new GridLayout(4, 3));
31
32          // add digit buttons
33
34          addButton("7");
35          addButton("8");
36          addButton("9");
37          addButton("4");
38          addButton("5");
39          addButton("6");
40          addButton("1");
41          addButton("2");
42          addButton("3");
43          addButton("0");
44          addButton(".");
45
46          // add clear entry button
47
48          clearButton = new JButton("CE");
49          buttonPanel.add(clearButton);
50
51          class ClearButtonListener implements ActionListener
52          {
53             public void actionPerformed(ActionEvent event)
54             {
55                display.setText("");
56             }
57          }
58          ActionListener listener =
59             new ClearButtonListener();
60
61          clearButton.addActionListener(new
62             ClearButtonListener());
63
64          add(buttonPanel, "Center");
65       }
66
67       /**
68          Adds a button to the button panel.
69          @param label  the button label
70       */
71       private void addButton(final String label)
72       {
73          class DigitButtonListener implements ActionListener
```

```
74          {
75              public void actionPerformed(ActionEvent event)
76              {
77
78                  // don't add two decimal points
79                  if (label.equals(".")
80                      && display.getText().indexOf(".") != -1)
81                      return;
82
83                  // append label text to button
84                  display.setText(display.getText() + label);
85              }
86          }
87
88          JButton button = new JButton(label);
89          buttonPanel.add(button);
90          ActionListener listener =
91              new DigitButtonListener();
92          button.addActionListener(listener);
93      }
94
95      /**
96          Gets the value that the user entered.
97          @return the value in the text field of the keypad
98      */
99      public double getValue()
100     {
101         return Double.parseDouble(display.getText());
102     }
103
104     /**
105         Clears the display.
106     */
107     public void clear()
108     {
109         display.setText("");
110     }
111
112     private JPanel buttonPanel;
113     private JButton clearButton;
114     private JTextField display;
115 }
```

File Bank.java

```
1  import java.io.BufferedReader;
2  import java.io.FileReader;
3  import java.io.IOException;
4  import java.util.ArrayList;
5  import java.util.StringTokenizer;
6
```

```
 7  /**
 8      A bank contains customers with bank accounts.
 9  */
10  public class Bank
11  {
12      /**
13          Constructs a bank with no customers.
14      */
15      public Bank()
16      {
17          customers = new ArrayList();
18      }
19
20      /**
21          Reads the customer numbers and PINs
22          and initializes the bank accounts.
23          @param filename the name of the customer file
24      */
25      public void readCustomers(String filename)
26          throws IOException
27      {
28          BufferedReader in = new BufferedReader
29              (new FileReader(filename));
30          boolean done = false;
31          while (!done)
32          {
33              String inputLine = in.readLine();
34              if (inputLine == null) done = true;
35              else
36              {
37                  StringTokenizer tokenizer
38                      = new StringTokenizer(inputLine);
39                  int number
40                      = Integer.parseInt(tokenizer.nextToken());
41                  int pin
42                      = Integer.parseInt(tokenizer.nextToken());
43
44                  Customer c = new Customer(number, pin);
45                  addCustomer(c);
46              }
47          }
48          in.close();
49      }
50
51      /**
52          Adds a customer to the bank.
53          @param c the customer to add
54      */
55      public void addCustomer(Customer c)
56      {
```

```
57            customers.add(c);
58        }
59
60        /**
61            Finds a customer in the bank.
62            @param aNumber a customer number
63            @param aPin a personal identification number
64            @return the matching customer, or null if no customer
65            matches
66        */
67        public Customer findCustomer(int aNumber, int aPin)
68        {
69            for (int i = 0; i < customers.size(); i++)
70            {
71                Customer c = (Customer)customers.get(i);
72                if (c.match(aNumber, aPin))
73                    return c;
74            }
75            return null;
76        }
77
78        private ArrayList customers;
79 }
```

File Customer.java

```
1 /**
2      A bank customer with a checking and savings account.
3 */
4 public class Customer
5 {
6     /**
7         Constructs a customer with a given number and PIN.
8         @param aNumber the customer number
9         @param aPin the personal identification number
10    */
11    public Customer(int aNumber, int aPin)
12    {
13        customerNumber = aNumber;
14        pin = aPin;
15        checkingAccount = new BankAccount();
16        savingsAccount = new BankAccount();
17    }
18
19    /**
20        Tests whether this customer matches a customer number
21        and PIN.
22        @param aNumber a customer number
23        @param aPin a personal identification number
24        @return true if the customer number and PIN match
```

```
25     */
26     public boolean match(int aNumber, int aPin)
27     {
28        return customerNumber == aNumber && pin == aPin;
29     }
30
31     /**
32        Gets the checking account of this customer.
33        @return the checking account
34     */
35     public BankAccount getCheckingAccount()
36     {
37        return checkingAccount;
38     }
39
40     /**
41        Gets the savings account of this customer.
42        @return the checking account
43     */
44     public BankAccount getSavingsAccount()
45     {
46        return savingsAccount;
47     }
48
49     private int customerNumber;
50     private int pin;
51     private BankAccount checkingAccount;
52     private BankAccount savingsAccount;
53 }
```

In this chapter, you learned a *systematic* approach for building a relatively complex program. However, object-oriented design is definitely not a spectator sport. To really learn how to design and implement programs, you have to gain experience by repeating this process with your own projects. It is quite possible that you don't immediately home in on a good solution and that you need to go back and reorganize your classes and responsibilities. That is normal and only to be expected. The purpose of the object-oriented design process is to spot these problems in the design phase, when they are still easy to rectify, instead of in the implementation phase, when massive reorganization is more difficult and time-consuming.

Random Fact   16.2

Computing—Art or Science?

There has been a long discussion whether the discipline of computing is a science or not. We call the field "computer science", but that doesn't mean much. Except possibly for librarians and sociologists, few people believe that library science and social science are scientific endeavors.

A scientific discipline aims to discover certain fundamental principles dictated by the laws of nature. It operates on the *scientific method:* by posing hypotheses and testing them with experiments that are repeatable by other workers in the field. For example, a physicist may have a theory on the makeup of nuclear particles and attempt to confirm or refute that theory by running experiments in a particle collider. If an experiment cannot be confirmed, such as the "cold fusion" research in the early 1990s, then the theory dies a quick death.

Some programmers indeed run experiments. They try out various methods of computing certain results or of configuring computer systems, and measure the differences in performance. However, their aim is not to discover laws of nature.

Some computer scientists discover fundamental principles. One class of fundamental results, for instance, states that it is impossible to write certain kinds of computer programs, no matter how powerful the computing equipment is. For example, it is impossible to write a program that takes as its input any two Java program files and as its output prints whether or not these two programs always compute the same results. Such a program would be very handy for grading student homework, but nobody, no matter how clever, will ever be able to write one that works for all input files. However, the majority of computer scientists are not researching the limits of computation.

Some people view programming as an *art* or *craft*. A programmer who writes elegant code that is easy to understand and runs with optimum efficiency can indeed be considered a good craftsman. Calling it an art is perhaps far-fetched, because an art object requires an audience to appreciate it, whereas the program code is generally hidden from the program user.

Others call computing an *engineering discipline*. Just as mechanical engineering is based on the fundamental mathematical principles of statics, computing has certain mathematical foundations. There is more to mechanical engineering than mathematics, though, such as knowledge of materials and of project planning. The same is true for computing.

In one somewhat worrisome aspect, computing does not have the same standing as other engineering disciplines. There is little agreement as to what constitutes professional conduct in the computer field. Unlike the scientist, whose main responsibility is the search for truth, the engineer must strive to satisfy the conflicting demands of quality, safety, and economy. Engineering disciplines have professional organizations that hold their members to standards of conduct. The computer field is so new that in many cases we simply don't know the correct method for achieving certain tasks. That makes it difficult to set professional standards.

What do you think? From your limited experience, do you consider the discipline of computing an art, a craft, a science, or an engineering activity?

CHAPTER SUMMARY

1. The life cycle of software encompasses all activities from initial analysis until obsolescence.

2. A formal process for software development describes phases of the development process and gives guidelines for how to carry out the phases.

3. The waterfall model of software development describes a sequential process of analysis, design, implementation, testing, and deployment.

4. The spiral model of software development describes an iterative process in which design and implementation are repeated.

5. Extreme Programming is a development methodology that strives for simplicity by removing formal structure and focusing on best practices.

6. In object-oriented design, you discover classes, determine the responsibilities of classes, and describe the relationships between classes.

7. A CRC card describes a class, its responsibilities, and its collaborating classes.

8. Inheritance (the "is-a" relationship) is sometimes inappropriately used when the "has-a" relationship would be more appropriate.

9. A class is associated with another class if you can navigate from its objects to objects of the other class, usually by following object references.

10. Dependency is another name for the "uses" relationship.

11. You need to be able to distinguish the UML notations for inheritance, realization, association, and dependency.

12. You can use `javadoc` documentation comments (with the bodies of the methods left blank) to record formally the behavior of the classes that you discovered.

Further Reading

[1] Grady Booch, James Rumbaugh, and Ivar Jacobson, *The Unified Modeling Language User Guide,* Addison-Wesley, 1999.
[2] Kent Beck, *Extreme Programming Explained,* Addison-Wesley, 1999.
[3] F. Brooks, *The Mythical Man-Month,* Addison-Wesley, 1975.
[4] W. H. Sackmann, W. J. Erikson, and E. E. Grant, "Exploratory Experimental Studies Comparing Online and Offline Programming Performance", *Communications of the ACM, vol. 11, no. 1* (January 1968), pp. 3–11.

REVIEW EXERCISES

Exercise R16.1. What is the software life cycle?

Exercise R16.2. Explain the process of object-oriented design that this chapter recommends for student use.

Exercise R16.3. Give a rule of thumb for how to find classes when designing a program.

Exercise R16.4. Give a rule of thumb for how to find methods when designing a program.

Exercise R16.5. After discovering a method, why is it important to identify the object that is *responsible* for carrying out the action?

Exercise R16.6. What relationship is appropriate between the following classes: association, inheritance, or neither?

- University–Student
- Student–TeachingAssistant
- Student–Freshman
- Student–Professor
- Car–Door
- Truck–Vehicle
- Traffic–TrafficSign
- TrafficSign–Color

Exercise R16.7. Every BMW is a car. Should a class BMW inherit from the class Car? BMW is a car manufacturer. Does that mean that the class BMW should inherit from the class CarManufacturer?

Exercise R16.8. Some books on object-oriented programming recommend deriving the class Circle from the class Point. Then the Circle class inherits the setLocation method from the Point superclass. Explain why the setLocation method need not be redefined in the subclass. Why is it nevertheless not a good idea to have Circle inherit from Point? Conversely, would deriving Point from Circle fulfill the "is-a" rule? Would it be a good idea?

Exercise R16.9. Write CRC cards for the Coin and Purse classes of Chapter 3.

Exercise R16.10. Write CRC cards for the bank account classes in Chapter 11.

Exercise R16.11. Draw a UML diagram for the Coin and Purse classes of Chapters 3 and 13.

Exercise R16.12. Draw a UML diagram for the classes in the ChoiceTest program in Chapter 12. Use associations when appropriate.

Exercise R16.13. A file contains a set of records describing countries. Each record consists of the name of the country, its population, and its area. Suppose your task is to write a program that reads in such a file and prints

- The country with the largest area
- The country with the largest population
- The country with the largest population density (people per square kilometer)

Think through the problems that you need to solve. What classes and methods will you need? Produce a set of CRC cards, a UML diagram, and a set of javadoc comments.

Exercise R16.14. Discover classes and methods for generating a student report card that lists all classes, grades, and the grade point average for a semester. Produce a set of CRC cards, a UML diagram, and a set of javadoc comments.

PROGRAMMING EXERCISES

Exercise P16.1. Enhance the invoice-printing program by providing for two kinds of line items: One kind describes products that are purchased in certain numerical quantities (such as "3 toasters"), another describes a fixed charge (such as "shipping: $5.00"). *Hint:* Use inheritance. Produce a UML diagram of your modified implementation.

Exercise P16.2. The invoice-printing program is somewhat unrealistic because the formatting of the Item objects won't lead to good visual results when the prices and quantities have varying numbers of digits. Enhance the format method in two ways: Accept an int[] array of column widths as a parameter. Use the NumberFormat class to format the currency values.

Exercise P16.3. The invoice-printing program has an unfortunate flaw—it mixes "business logic", the computation of total charges, and "presentation", the visual appearance of the invoice. To appreciate this flaw, imagine the changes that would be necessary to draw the invoice in HTML for presentation on the web. Reimplement the program, using a separate InvoiceFormatter class to format the invoice. That is, the Invoice and Item methods are no longer responsible for formatting. However, they will acquire other responsibilities, because the InvoiceFormatter class needs to query them for the values that it requires.

Exercise P16.4. Implement a program to teach your baby sister to *read the clock*. In the game, present an analog clock such as the one in Figure 14. Generate random times and display the clock. Accept guesses from the player. Reward the player for correct guesses. After two incorrect guesses, display the correct answer and make a new random time. Implement several levels of play. In level 1, only show full hours. In level 2, show quarter hours. In level 3, show five-minute multiples, and in level 4, show any number of minutes. After a player has achieved five correct guesses at one level, advance to the next level.

Exercise P16.5. Write a program that implements a different game, to teach arithmetic to your younger brother. The program tests addition and subtraction. In level 1 it tests only addition of numbers less than 10 whose sum is less than 10. In level 2 it tests addition of arbitrary one-digit numbers. In level 3 it tests subtraction of one-digit numbers with a nonnegative difference. Generate random problems and get the player input. The player gets up to two tries per problem. Advance from one level to the next when the player has achieved a score of five points. Your user interface can be text-based or graphical.

Figure 14

An Analog Clock

Exercise P16.6. Write a bumper car game with the following rules. A bumper car starts moving in a random direction, either left, right, up, or down. If it reaches a boundary, then it reverses direction. If it is about to bump into another bumper car, it reverses direction. Supply a user interface to add bumper cars, and to run the simulation. Use at least four classes in your program.

Exercise P16.7. Write a program that can be used to design a suburban scene, with houses, streets, and cars. Users can add houses and cars of various colors to a street. Design a user interface that firms up the requirements, discover classes and methods, provide UML diagrams, and implement your program.

Exercise P16.8. Design a simple email messaging system. A message has a recipient, a sender, and a message text. A mailbox can store messages. Supply a number of mailboxes for different users and a user interface for users to log in, send messages to other users, read their own messages, and log out. Your user interface can be text-based or graphical. Follow the design process that was described in this chapter.

Exercise P16.9. Write a program that simulates a vending machine. Products can be purchased by inserting the correct number of coins into the machine. A user selects a product from a list of available products, adds coins, and either gets the product or gets the coins returned if insufficient money was supplied or if the product is sold out. Products can be restocked and money removed by an operator. Follow the design process that was described in this chapter.

Exercise P16.10. Write a program to design an appointment calendar. An appointment includes the starting time, ending time, and a description; for example,

```
Dentist 2001/10/1 17:30 18:30
CS1 class 2001/10/2 08:30 10:00
```

Supply a user interface to add appointments, remove canceled appointments, and print out a list of appointments for a particular day. Your user interface can be text-based or graphical. Follow the design process that was described in this chapter.

Exercise P16.11. *Airline seating.* Write a program that assigns seats on an airplane. Assume the airplane has 20 seats in first class (5 rows of 4 seats each, separated by an aisle) and 180 seats in economy class (30 rows of 6 seats each, separated by an aisle). Your program should take three commands: add passengers, show seating, and quit. When passengers are added, ask for the class (first or economy), the number of passengers traveling together (1 or 2 in first class; 1 to 3 in economy), and the seating preference (aisle or window in first class; aisle, center, or window in economy). Then try to find a match and assign the seats. If no match exists, print a message. Your user interface can be text-based or graphical. Follow the design process that was described in this chapter.

Exercise P16.12. Write a simple graphics editor that allows users to add a mixture of shapes (ellipses, rectangles, lines, and text in different colors) to a panel. Supply commands to load and save the picture. For simplicity, you may use a single text size, and you don't have to fill any shapes. Design a user interface, discover classes, supply a UML diagram, and implement your program.

Exercise P16.13. Write a tic-tac-toe game that lets a human player play against the computer. Your program will play many turns against a human opponent, and it will learn. When it is the computer's turn, the computer randomly selects an empty field, except that it won't ever choose a losing combination. For that purpose, your program must keep an array of losing combinations. Whenever the human wins, the immediately preceding combination is stored as losing. For example, suppose that x = computer and o = human. Suppose the current combination is

```
 O | X | X
---+---+---
   | O |
---+---+---
   |   |
```

Now it is the human's turn, who will of course choose

```
 O | X | X
---+---+---
   | O |
---+---+---
   |   | O
```

The computer should then remember the preceding combination

```
 O | X | X
---+---+---
   | O |
---+---+---
   |   |
```

as a losing combination. As a result, the computer will never again choose that combination from

```
 O | X |
---+---+---
   | O |
---+---+---
   |   |
```

or

```
 O |   | X
---+---+---
   | O |
---+---+---
   |   |
```

Discover classes and supply a UML diagram before you begin to program. *Hint:* Make a class Combination that contains an int[][] array. Each element in that two-dimensional array is EMPTY, FILLED_X, or FILLED_O. Write an equals method that tests whether two combinations are identical.

Recursion

To learn about the method of recursion

▶ To understand the relationship between recursion and iteration

▶ To analyze problems that are much easier to solve by recursion than by iteration

▶ To learn to "think recursively"

▶ To be able to use recursive helper methods

▶ To understand when the use of recursion affects the efficiency of an algorithm

The method of recursion is a powerful technique to break up complex computational problems into simpler ones. The term "recursion" refers to the fact that the same computation recurs, or occurs repeatedly, as the problem is solved. Recursion is often the most natural way of thinking about a problem, and there are some computations that are very difficult to perform without recursion. This chapter shows you both simple and complex examples of recursion and teaches you how to "think recursively".

17.1   Triangle Numbers

In this example, we will look at triangle shapes such as the ones from Section 6.3. We'd like to compute the area of a triangle of width n, assuming that each [] square has area 1. This value is sometimes called the nth *triangle number*. For example, as you can tell from looking at

```
[]
[][]
[][][]
```

the third triangle number is 6.

You may know that there is a very simple formula to compute these numbers, but you should pretend for now that you don't know about it. The ultimate purpose of this section is not to compute triangle numbers, but to learn about the concept of recursion in a simple situation.

Here is the outline of the class that we will develop:

```java
public class Triangle
{
    public Triangle(int aWidth)
    {
        width = aWidth;
    }

    public int getArea()
    {
        . . .
    }

    private int width;
}
```

If the width of the triangle is 1, then the triangle consists of a single square, and its area is 1. Let's take care of this case first.

```java
public int getArea()
{
    if (width == 1) return 1;
    . . .
}
```

To deal with the general case, consider this picture.

```
[]
[][]
[][][]
[][][][]
```

Suppose we knew the area of the smaller, colored triangle. Then we could easily compute the area of the larger triangle as

```
smallerArea + width
```

How can we get the smaller area? Let's just make a smaller triangle and ask it!

```
Triangle smallerTriangle = new Triangle(width - 1);
int smallerArea = smallerTriangle.getArea();
```

Now we can complete the `getArea` method:

```
public int getArea()
{
   if (width == 1) return 1;
   Triangle smallerTriangle = new Triangle(width - 1);
   int smallerArea = smallerTriangle.getArea();
   return smallerArea + width;
}
```

> A recursive computation solves a problem by using the solution of the same problem with simpler inputs.

Here is an illustration of what happens when we compute the area of a triangle of width 4.

- The `getArea` method makes a smaller triangle of width 3.
  - It calls `getArea` on that triangle.
    - That method makes a smaller triangle of width 2.
      - It calls `getArea` on that triangle.
        - That method makes a smaller triangle of width 1.
        - It calls `getArea` on that triangle.
        - That method returns 1.
      - The method returns `smallerArea` + `width` = 1 + 2 = 3.
    - The method returns `smallerArea` + `width` = 3 + 3 = 6.
  - The method returns `smallerArea` + `width` = 6 + 4 = 10.

This solution has one remarkable aspect. To solve the area problem for a triangle of a given width, we use the fact that we can solve the same problem for a lesser width. This is called a *recursive* solution.

The call pattern of a recursive method looks complicated, and the key to the successful design of a recursive method is *not to think about it*. Instead, look at the `area` method one more time and notice how utterly reasonable it is. If the width is 1, then of course the area is 1. The next part is just as reasonable. Compute the area of the smaller triangle *and don't think about why that works*. Then the area of the larger triangle is clearly the sum of the smaller area and the width.

There are two key requirements to make sure that the recursion is successful:

- Every recursive call must simplify the computation in some way.

- There must be special cases to handle the simplest computations directly.

The `getArea` method calls itself again with smaller and smaller width values. Eventually the width must reach 1, and there is a special case for computing the area of a triangle with width 1. Thus, the `getArea` method always succeeds.

> For a recursion to terminate, there must be special cases for the simplest inputs.

Actually, you have to be careful. What happens when you call the area of a triangle with width −1? It computes the area of a triangle with width −2, which computes the area of a triangle with width −3, and so on. To avoid this, the `getArea` method should return 0 if the width is <= 0.

Recursion is not really necessary to compute the triangle numbers. The area of a triangle equals the sum

```
1 + 2 + 3 + . . . + width
```

Of course, we can program a simple loop:

```
double area = 0;
for (int i = 1; i <= width; i++)
   area = area + i;
```

Many simple recursions can be computed as loops. However, loop equivalents for more complex recursions—such as the one in our next example—can be complex.

Actually, in this case, you don't even need a loop to compute the answer. The sum of the first n integers can be computed as

$$1 + 2 + \cdots + n = n \times (n + 1) / 2$$

Thus, the area equals

```
width * (width + 1) / 2
```

Therefore, neither recursion nor a loop are required to solve this problem. The recursive solution is intended as a "warm-up" for the next section.

File Triangle.java

```
1  /**
2     A triangular shape composed of stacked unit squares like this:
3     []
4     [][]
5     [][][]
6     . . .
7  */
8  public class Triangle
9  {
```

```
10     /**
11         Constructs a triangular shape.
12         @param aWidth the width (and height) of the triangle
13     */
14     public Triangle(int aWidth)
15     {
16         width = aWidth;
17     }
18
19     /**
20         Computes the area of the triangle.
21         @return the area
22     */
23     public int getArea()
24     {
25         if (width <= 0) return 0;
26         if (width == 1) return 1;
27         Triangle smallerTriangle = new Triangle(width - 1);
28         int smallerArea = smallerTriangle.getArea();
29         return smallerArea + width;
30     }
31
32     private int width;
33 }
```

File TriangleTest.java

```
1  import javax.swing.JOptionPane;
2
3  public class TriangleTest
4  {
5      public static void main(String[] args)
6      {
7          String input =
8              JOptionPane.showInputDialog("Enter width");
9          int width = Integer.parseInt(input);
10         Triangle t = new Triangle(width);
11         int area = t.getArea();
12         System.out.println("Area = " + area);
13     }
14 }
```

Common Error 17.1

Infinite Recursion

A common programming error is an infinite recursion: a method calling itself over and over with no end in sight. The computer needs some amount of memory for bookkeeping for each call. After some number of calls, all memory that is available for this purpose is exhausted. Your program shuts down and reports a "stack fault".

▼

▼

Infinite recursion happens either because the parameter values don't get simpler or because a special terminating case is missing. For example, suppose the `getArea` method computes the area of a triangle with width 0. If it wasn't for the special test, the method would have constructed triangles with −1, −2, −3, and so on.

17.2   Permutations

We will now turn to a more complex example of recursion that would be difficult to program with a simple loop. We will design a class that lists all *permutations* of a string. A permutation is simply a rearrangement of the letters. For example, the string `"eat"` has six permutations (including the original string itself):

```
"eat"
"eta"
"aet"
"ate"
"tea"
"tae"
```

Our `PermutationGenerator` class will have a public interface that is similar to the `StringTokenizer` class.

```
class PermutationGenerator
{
    public PermutationGenerator(String s) { . . . }
    public String nextPermutation() { . . . }
    public boolean hasMorePermutations() { . . . }
}
```

Here is the test program that prints out all permutations of the string `"eat"`:

File PermutationGeneratorTest.java

```
1  /**
2      This program tests the permutation generator.
3  */
4  public class PermutationGeneratorTest
5  {
6      public static void main(String[] args)
7      {
8          PermutationGenerator generator
9              = new PermutationGenerator("eat");
10         while (generator.hasMorePermutations())
11             System.out.println(generator.nextPermutation());
12     }
13 }
```

Now we need an idea how to generate the permutations recursively. Consider the string `"eat"` and let's simplify the problem. First, we'll generate all permutations that start with the letter 'e', then those that start with 'a', and finally those that start with 't'. How do we generate the permutations that start with 'e'? We need to know the permutations of the substring "at". But that's the same problem—to generate all permutations—with a simpler input, namely the shorter string "at". Thus, we can use recursion. Make another PermutationGenerator object that generates the permutations of the substring "at". That generator will produce

```
"at"
"ta"
```

For each permutation of that substring, prepend the letter 'e' to get the permutations of "eat" that start with 'e', namely

```
"eat"
"eta"
```

Now let's turn our attention to the permutations of "eat" that start with 'a'. We need to create a permutation generator that produces the permutations of the remaining letters, "et". That generator will produce:

```
"et"
"te"
```

We add the letter 'a' to the front of the strings and obtain

```
"aet"
"ate"
```

We generate the permutations that start with t in the same way

That's the idea. To carry it out, we have to implement the nextPermutation method, which gets just one permutation, not all permutations at once. To do that, the PermutationGenerator needs to remember the *state* of the permutation computation. Each call to nextPermutation produces a new permutation and advances the state so that the next call to nextPermutation can pick up where the current call left off.

Clearly, an important part of the state is the character that we currently put in front. We'll call the position of that character current. As we generate more permutations, current moves from 0 to word.length() - 1, where word is the word whose letters we permute.

We also need to store the permutation generator of the substring. Let's call it tail-Generator. Now we are ready to compute the next permutation. Simply ask tailGenerator what *its* next permutation is, and then return

```
word.charAt(current) + tailGenerator.nextPermutation()
```

For the most part, that will work just fine. However, there is one special case. When the tail generator runs out of permutations, we have exhausted all permutations that start with the current letter. Then we need to

- Increment the current position.

- Compute the tail string that contains all letters except for the current one.

- Make a new permutation generator for the tail string.

When are we done? When `current` has reached `word.length()`. Here is the next-Permutation method:

```
public String nextPermutation()
{
   . . .

   String r = word.charAt(current)
      + tailGenerator.nextPermutation();

   if (!tailGenerator.hasMorePermutations())
   {
      current++;
      if (current < word.length())
      {
         String tailString =
            word.substring(0, current)
                  + word.substring(current + 1);
         tailGenerator =
            new PermutationGenerator(tailString);
      }
   }

   return r;
}
```

The `hasMorePermutations` method simply checks whether `current` has moved past the end of the word:

```
public boolean hasMorePermutations()
{  return current < word.length();  }
```

The permutation generation algorithm is recursive—it uses the fact that we can generate the permutations of shorter words. When does the recursion stop? We need to build in a stopping point, as a special case to handle words of length 1. A word of length 1 has a single permutation, namely itself. The `nextPermutation` method needs to recognize that as a special case, and not generate permutations of the (empty) tail. Here is the added code to handle a word of length 1.

```
public String nextPermutation()
{
   if (word.length() == 1)
   {
      current++;
      return word;
   }
   . . .
}
```

By advancing `current`, we make sure that `hasMorePermutations` returns `false` after `nextPermutations` has been called once.

Here is the complete PermutationGenerator class.

File PermutationGenerator.java

```
1  /**
2      This class generates permutations of a word.
3  */
4  class PermutationGenerator
5  {
6      /**
7          Constructs a permutation generator.
8          @param aWord  the word to permute
9      */
10     public PermutationGenerator(String aWord)
11     {
12        word = aWord;
13        current = 0;
14        if (word.length() > 1)
15           tailGenerator =
16              new PermutationGenerator(word.substring(1));
17     }
18
19     /**
20         Computes the next permutation of the word.
21         @return  the next permutation
22     */
23     public String nextPermutation()
24     {
25        if (word.length() == 1)
26        {
27           current++;
28           return word;
29        }
30
31        String r = word.charAt(current)
32           + tailGenerator.nextPermutation();
33
34        if (!tailGenerator.hasMorePermutations())
35        {
36           current++;
37           if (current < word.length())
38           {
39              String tailString =
40                 word.substring(0, current)
41                    + word.substring(current + 1);
42              tailGenerator =
43                 new PermutationGenerator(tailString);
44           }
45        }
46
47        return r;
48     }
```

```
49
50      /**
51          Tests whether there are more permutations.
52          @return true if more permutations are available
53      */
54      public boolean hasMorePermutations()
55      {
56          return current < word.length();
57      }
58
59      private String word;
60      private int current;
61      private PermutationGenerator tailGenerator;
62  }
```

Compare the PermutationGenerator and Triangle classes. Both of them work on the same principle. When they work on a more complex input, they generate another object of the same class that works on a simpler input. Then they combine the work of that object with their own work to deliver the results for the more complex input. There really is no particular complexity behind that process as long as you think about the solution on that level only. However, behind the scenes, the object with the simpler input creates yet another object that works on even simpler input, which creates yet another, and so on, until one object's input is so simple that it can compute the results without further help. It is interesting to think about that process, but it can also be confusing. What's important is that you can focus on the one level that matters—putting a solution together from the slightly simpler problem, ignoring the fact that it also uses recursion to get its results.

▼ ⊗ **Common Error**   **17.2**

Tracing through Recursive Methods

Debugging a recursive method can be somewhat challenging. When you set a breakpoint in a recursive method, the program stops as soon as that program line is encountered in *any call to the recursive method.* Suppose you want to debug the recursive getArea method of the Triangle class. Debug the TriangleTest program with an input of 4. Run until the beginning of the getArea method (Figure 1). Inspect the width instance variable. It is 4.

Remove the breakpoint and now run until the statement return smallerArea + width;. When you inspect width again, its value is 2! That makes no sense. There was no instruction that changed the value of width! Is that a bug with the debugger?

No. The program stopped in the first *recursive* call to getArea that reached the return statement. If you are confused, look at the *call stack* (Figure 2). You will see that three calls to getArea are pending.

You can debug recursive methods with the debugger. You just need to be particularly careful, and watch the call stack to understand in which nested call you currently are.

```
Source Editor [Triangle]                                              _ □ ✕
  6    */
  7    public Triangle(int aWidth)
  8    {
  9       width = aWidth;
 10    }
 11
 12    /**
 13       Computes the area of the triangle.
 14       @return the area
 15    */
 16    public int getArea()
 17    {
 18       if (width == 1) return 1;
 19       Triangle smallerTriangle = new Triangle(width - 1);
 20       int smallerArea = smallerTriangle.getArea();
 21       return smallerArea + width;
 22    }
 23
 24    private int width;
 25 }
 19:7    INS
 Triangle  TriangleTest
```

Figure 1

Debugging a Recursive Method

```
Debugger Window [Threads]                                            _ □ ✕
 Threads                                    ┃  ↓  ↓   ≠   ▦
 system
   main                                     Name          main
     main (Running)                         State         Running
       CallStack                            Class         Triangle
         Triangle.getArea : 21              Method        getArea
         Triangle.getArea : 20              Line Number   21
         Triangle.getArea : 20              Stack Depth   4
         TriangleTest.main : 10             Suspended     True
       Locals
     AWT-EventQueue-0 (Wait)
     SunToolkit.PostEventQueue-0 (Wait)
     AWT-Windows (Running)
     TimerQueue (Wait)
     Screen Updater (Running)
   Signal dispatcher (Running)
   Reference Handler (Wait)
   Finalizer (Wait)
                                            Properties
 Breakpoints   Threads   Watches   Variables
```

Figure 2

Call Stack Display

? HOWTO   17.1

Thinking Recursively

To solve a problem recursively requires a different mindset than to solve it by programming loops. In fact, it helps if you are, or pretend to be, a bit lazy and like others to do most of the work for you. If you need to solve a complex problem, pretend that "someone else" will do most of the heavy lifting and solve the problem for all simpler inputs. Then you only need to figure out how you can turn the solutions with simpler inputs into a solution for the whole problem.

To illustrate the method of recursion, let us consider the following problem. We want to test whether a sentence is a *palindrome*—a string that is equal to itself when you reverse all characters. Typical examples of palindromes are

- A man, a plan, a canal—Panama!

- Go hang a salami, I'm a lasagna hog

and, of course, the oldest palindrome of all:

- Madam, I'm Adam

When testing for a palindrome, match upper-and lowercase letters, and ignore all spaces and punctuation marks.

We want to implement the `isPalindrome` method in the following class:

```
public class Sentence
{
    /**
        Constructs a sentence.
        @param aText a string containing all characters of the sentence.
    */
    public Sentence(String aText)
    {
        text = aText;
    }

    /**
        Tests whether this sentence is a palindrome.
        @return true if this sentence is a palindrome, false otherwise
    */
    public isPalindrome()
    {
        . . .
    }

    private String text;
}
```

▼   **Step 1** Consider various ways for simplify inputs

▼   In your mind, fix a particular input or set of inputs for the problem that you want to
         solve.
                 Think how you can simplify the inputs in such a way that the same problem can be
         applied to the simpler input.
▼   When you consider simpler inputs, you may want to remove just a little bit from the
         original input—maybe remove one or two characters from a string, or remove a small
         portion of a geometric shape. But sometimes it is more useful to cut the input in half and
▼   then see what it means to solve the problem for both halves.
                 In the palindrome test problem, the input is the string that we need to test. How can
         you simplify the input? Here are several possibilities:

▼
              • Remove the first character.

              • Remove the last character.
▼
              • Remove both the first and the last character.

              • Remove a character from the middle.
▼
              • Cut the string into two halves.

         These simpler inputs are all potential inputs for the palindrome test.
▼
         Step 2 Combine solutions with simpler inputs to a solution of the original problem

▼   In your mind, consider the solutions of your problem for the simpler inputs that you have
         discovered in Step 1. Don't worry *how* those solutions are obtained. Simply have faith
         that the solutions are readily available. Just say to yourself: These are simpler inputs, so
▼   someone else will solve the problem for me.
                 Now think how you can turn the solution for the simpler inputs into a solution for
         the input that you are currently thinking about. Maybe you need to add a small quantity,
▼   related to the quantity that you lopped off to arrive at the simpler input. Maybe you cut
         the original input in two halves and have solutions for both halves. Then you may need
         to add both solutions to arrive at a solution for the whole.
▼   Consider the methods for simplifying the inputs for the palindrome test. Cutting the
         string in half doesn't seem a good idea. If you cut

             `"Madam, I'm Adam"`
▼
         in half, you get two strings:

             `"Madam, I"`
▼
         and

             `"'m Adam"`
▼
         Neither of them is a palindrome. Cutting the input in half and testing whether the
         halves are palindromes seems a dead end.
▼   The most promising simplification is to remove the first *and* last characters.

▼ Removing the M at the front and the m at the back yields

```
"adam, I'm Ada"
```

▼ Suppose you can verify that the shorter string is a palindrome. Then *of course* the original string is a palindrome—we put the same letter in the front and the back. That's extremely promising. A word is a palindrome if

▼ • The first and last letters match (ignoring letter case)

and

▼ • The word obtained by removing the first and last letters is a palindrome.

Again, don't worry how the test works for the shorter string. It just works.

▼ There is one other case to consider. What if the first or last letter of the word is not a letter? For example, the string

```
"A man, a plan, a canal, Panama!"
```

▼ ends in a '!' character, which does not match the 'A' in the front. But we should ignore nonletters when testing for palindromes. Thus, when the last character is not a letter but the first character is a letter, it doesn't make sense to remove both the first and the last

▼ characters. That's not a problem. Remove just the last character. If the shorter string is a palindrome, then it stays a palindrome when you attach a nonletter.

▼ The same argument applies if the first character is not a letter. Now we have a complete set of cases.

• If the first and last character are both letters, then check whether they match. If so, remove both and test the shorter string.

▼ • Otherwise, if the last character isn't a letter, remove it and test the shorter string.

▼ • Otherwise, the first character isn't a letter. Remove it and test the shorter string.

In all three cases, you can use the solution to the simpler problem to arrive at a solution to your problem.

▼ **Step 3** Find solutions to the simplest inputs

▼ A recursive computation keeps simplifying its inputs. Eventually it arrives at very simple inputs. To make sure that the recursion comes to a stop, you must deal with the simplest inputs separately. Come up with special solutions for them. That is usually very easy.

▼ However, sometimes you get into philosphical questions dealing with *degenerate* inputs: empty strings, shapes with no area, and so on. Then you may want to investigate a slightly larger input that gets reduced to such a trivial input and see what value you should attach to the degenerate inputs so that the simpler value, when used according to the rules you discovered in Step 2, yields the correct answer.

▼ Let's look at the simplest strings for the palindrome test:

• Strings with two characters

• Strings with a single character

• The empty string

▼ We don't have to come up with a special solution for strings with two characters. Step 2 still applies to those strings—either or both of the characters are removed. But we do need to worry about strings of length 0 and 1. In those cases, Step 2 can't apply. There aren't two characters to remove.

▼ A string with a single character, such as `"I"`, is a palindrome. It doesn't matter whether or not the character is a letter. The string `"!"` is also a palindrome.

▼ The empty string is a palindrome—it's the same string when you read it backwards. If you find that too artificial, consider a string `"mm"`. According to the rule discovered in Step 2, this string is a palindrome if the first and last character of that string match and the remainder—that is, the empty string—is also a palindrome. Therefore, it makes sense to consider the empty string a palindrome.

Thus, all strings of length 0 or 1 are palindromes.

▼

Step 4 Implement the solution by combining the simple cases and the reduction step

▼ Now you are ready to implement the solution. Make separate cases for the simple inputs that you considered in Step 3. If the input isn't one of the simplest cases, then implement the logic you discovered in Step 2.

▼ Here is the `isPalindrome` method.

```
public boolean isPalindrome()
{
   // separate case for shortest strings
   if (text.length() <= 1) return true;

   // get first and last character, converted to lowercase
   char first = Character.toLowerCase(text.charAt(0));
   char last = Character.toLowerCase(
      text.charAt(text.length() - 1));

   if (Character.isLetter(first)
      && Character.isLetter(last))
   {
      // both are letters
      if (first == last)
      {
         // remove both first and last character
         Sentence shorter = new Sentence(
            text.substring(1, text.length() - 2));
         return shorter.isPalindrome();
      }
      else
         return false;
   }
   else if (!Character.isLetter(last))
   {
      // remove last character
      Sentence shorter = new Sentence(
         text.substring(0, text.length() - 2));
```

▼

```
      return shorter.isPalindrome();
   }
   else
   {
      // remove first character
      Sentence shorter = new Sentence(
         text.substring(1, text.length() - 1));
      return shorter.isPalindrome();
   }
}
```

▼

▼

▼

17.3 Recursive Helper Methods

> Sometimes it is easier to find a recursive solution if you make a slight change to the original problem.

Sometimes it is easier to find a recursive solution if you change the original problem slightly. Then the original problem can be solved by calling a recursive helper method.

Here is a typical example. Consider the palindrome test of HOWTO 17.1. It is a bit inefficient to construct new Sentence objects in every step. Now consider the following change in the problem. Rather than testing whether the entire sentence is a palindrome, let's check whether a substring is a palindrome:

```
/** Tests whether a substring of the sentence is a palindrome.
   @param start the index of the first character of the substring
   @param end the index of the last character of the substring
   @return true if the substring is a palindrome
*/
boolean isPalindrome(int start, int end)
```

This method turns out to be even easier to implement than the original test. In the recursive calls, simply adjust the start and end parameters to skip over matching letter pairs and characters that are not letters. There is no need to construct new Sentence objects to represent the shorter strings.

```
public boolean isPalindrome(int start, int end)
{
   // separate case for substrings of length 0 and 1
   if (start >= end) return true;

   // get first and last character, converted to lowercase
   char first = Character.toLowerCase(
      text.charAt(start));
   char last = Character.toLowerCase(text.charAt(end));

   if (Character.isLetter(first)
      && Character.isLetter(last))
```

```
      {
         if (first == last)
         {
            // test substring that doesn't contain the matching letters
            return isPalindrome(start + 1, end - 1);
         }
         else
            return false;
      }
      else if (!Character.isLetter(last))
      {
         // test substring that doesn't contain the last character
         return isPalindrome(start, end - 1);
      }
      else
      {
         // test substring that doesn't contain the first character
         return isPalindrome(start + 1, end);
      }
   }
```

You should still supply a method to solve the whole problem—the user of your method shouldn't have to know about the trick with the substring positions. Simply call the helper method with positions that test the entire string:

```
public boolean isPalindrome()
{
   return isPalindrome(0, text.length() - 1);
}
```

Note that this call is *not* a recursive method. The isPalindrome() method calls a different method, isPalindrome(int, int). The latter method is recursive.

Use the technique of recursive helper methods whenever it is easier to solve a recursive problem that is slightly different from the original problem.

17.4   Mutual Recursions

> In a mutual recursion, a set of cooperating methods calls each other repeatedly.

In the preceding examples, a method called itself to solve a simpler problem. Sometimes, a set of cooperating methods calls each other in a recursive fashion. In this section, we will explore a typical situation of such a mutual recursion.

We will develop a program that can compute the values of arithmetic expressions such as

```
3 + 4 * 5
(3 + 4) * 5
1 - (2 - (3 - (4 - 5)))
```

Computing such an expression is complicated by the fact that * and / bind more strongly than + and -, and that parentheses can be used to group subexpressions.

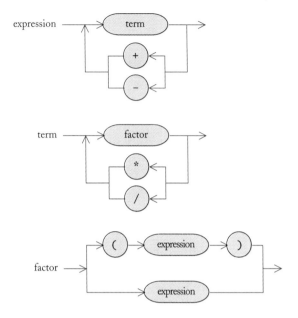

Figure 3

Syntax Diagrams for Evaluating an Expression

Figure 3 shows a set of *syntax diagrams* that describes the syntax of these expressions. An expression is either a term, or a sum or difference of terms. A term is either a factor, or a product or quotient of factors. Finally, a factor is either a number or an expression enclosed in parentheses.

Figure 4 shows how the expressions 3 + 4 * 5 and (3 + 4) * 5 are derived from the syntax diagram.

Why do the syntax diagrams help us compute the value of the tree? If you look at the syntax trees, you will see that they accurately represent which operations should be carried out first. In the first tree, 4 and 5 should be multiplied, and then the result should be added to 3. In the second tree, 3 and 4 should be added, and the result should be multiplied with 5.

At the end of this section, you will find the implementation of the `Evaluator` class, which evaluates these expressions. The `Evaluator` makes use of an `ExpressionTokenizer` class, which breaks up an input string into tokens—numbers, operators, and parentheses. When you call `nextToken`, the next input token is returned as a string. However, unlike the `StringTokenizer`, we supply another method, `peekToken`, which lets you see the next token without consuming it. To see why this method is necessary, consider the syntax diagram of the factor type. If the next token is a "*" or "/", you want to continue adding and subtracting terms. But if the next token is another character, such as a "+" or "-", you want to stop without actually consuming it, so that the token can be considered later.

To compute the value of an expression, we implement three methods: `getExpression-Value`, `getTermValue`, and `getFactorValue`. The `getExpressionValue` method first

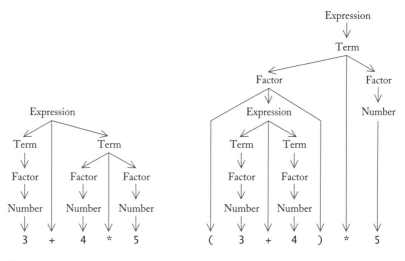

Figure 4

Syntax Trees for Two Expressions

calls `getTermValue` to get the value of the first term of the expression. Then it checks whether the next input token is one of + or -. If so, it calls `getTermValue` again and adds or subtracts it.

```
public int getExpressionValue()
{
    int value = getTermValue();
    boolean done = false;
    while (!done)
    {
        String next = tokenizer.peekToken();
        if ("+".equals(next) || "-".equals(next))
        {
            tokenizer.nextToken();
            int value2 = getTermValue();
            if ("+".equals(next)) value = value + value2;
            else value = value - value2;
        }
        else done = true;
    }
    return value;
}
```

The `getTermValue` method calls `getFactorValue` in the same way, multiplying or dividing the factor values.

Finally, the `getFactorValue` method checks whether the next input is a number, or whether it begins with a (token. In the first case, the value is simply the value of the number. However, in the second case, the `getFactorValue` method makes a recursive call to `getExpressionValue`. Thus, the three methods are mutually recursive.

```
public int getFactorValue()
{
   int value;
   String next = tokenizer.peekToken();
   if ("(".equals(next))
   {
      tokenizer.nextToken();
      value = getExpressionValue();
      next = tokenizer.nextToken(); // read ")"
   }
   else
      value = Integer.parseInt(tokenizer.nextToken());
   return value;
}
```

As always with a recursive solution, you need to ensure that the recursion terminates. In this situation, that is easy to see. If getExpressionValue calls itself, the second call works on a shorter subexpression than the original expression. At each recursive call, at least some of the tokens of the input string are consumed, so eventually the recursion must come to an end.

File Evaluator.java

```
 1  /**
 2      A class that can compute the value of an arithmetic expression.
 3  */
 4  public class Evaluator
 5  {
 6     /**
 7         Constructs an evaluator.
 8         @param anExpression a string containing the expression
 9         to be evaluated
10     */
11     public Evaluator(String anExpression)
12     {
13        tokenizer = new ExpressionTokenizer(anExpression);
14     }
15
16     /**
17         Evaluates the expression.
18         @return the value of the expression
19     */
20     public int getExpressionValue()
21     {
22        int value = getTermValue();
23        boolean done = false;
24        while (!done)
25        {
26           String next = tokenizer.peekToken();
27           if ("+".equals(next) || "-".equals(next))
28           {
29              tokenizer.nextToken();
30              int value2 = getTermValue();
```

```
31              if ("+".equals(next)) value = value + value2;
32              else value = value - value2;
33          }
34          else done = true;
35       }
36       return value;
37    }
38
39    /**
40       Evaluates the next term found in the expression.
41       @return the value of the term
42    */
43    public int getTermValue()
44    {
45       int value = getFactorValue();
46       boolean done = false;
47       while (!done)
48       {
49          String next = tokenizer.peekToken();
50          if ("*".equals(next) || "/".equals(next))
51          {
52             tokenizer.nextToken();
53             int value2 = getFactorValue();
54             if ("*".equals(next)) value = value * value2;
55             else value = value / value2;
56          }
57          else done = true;
58       }
59       return value;
60    }
61
62    /**
63       Evaluates the next factor found in the expression.
64       @return the value of the factor
65    */
66    public int getFactorValue()
67    {
68       int value;
69       String next = tokenizer.peekToken();
70       if ("(".equals(next))
71       {
72          tokenizer.nextToken();
73          value = getExpressionValue();
74          next = tokenizer.nextToken(); // read ")"
75       }
76       else
77          value = Integer.parseInt(tokenizer.nextToken());
78       return value;
79    }
80
81    private ExpressionTokenizer tokenizer;
82 }
```

File ExpressionTokenizer.java

```
1  /**
2     This class breaks up a string describing an expression
3     into tokens: numbers, parentheses, and operators.
4  */
5  public class ExpressionTokenizer
6  {
7     /**
8        Constructs a tokenizer.
9        @param anInput the string to tokenize
10    */
11    public ExpressionTokenizer(String anInput)
12    {
13       input = anInput;
14       start = 0;
15       end = 0;
16       nextToken();
17    }
18
19    /**
20       Peeks at the next token without consuming it.
21       @return the next token or null if there are no more tokens
22    */
23    public String peekToken()
24    {
25       if (start >= input.length()) return null;
26       else return input.substring(start, end);
27    }
28
29    /**
30       Gets the next token and moves the tokenizer to the
31       following token.
32       @return the next token or null if there are no more tokens
33    */
34    public String nextToken()
35    {
36       String r = peekToken();
37       start = end;
38       if (start >= input.length()) return r;
39       if (Character.isDigit(input.charAt(start)))
40       {
41          end = start + 1;
42          while (end < input.length()
43             && Character.isDigit(input.charAt(end)))
44             end++;
45       }
46       else
47          end = start + 1;
48       return r;
49    }
50
51    private String input;
```

```
52      private int start;
53      private int end;
54 }
```

File EvaluatorTest.java

```
1  import javax.swing.JOptionPane;
2
3  /**
4      This program tests the expression evaluator.
5  */
6  public class EvaluatorTest
7  {
8      public static void main(String[] args)
9      {
10         String input = JOptionPane.showInputDialog(
11            "Enter an expression:");
12         Evaluator e = new Evaluator(input);
13         int value = e.getExpressionValue();
14         System.out.println(input + "=" + value);
15         System.exit(0);
16     }
17 }
```

17.5 The Efficiency of Recursion

As you have seen in this chapter, recursion can be a powerful tool to implement complex algorithms. On the other hand, recursion can lead to algorithms that perform poorly. In this section, we will analyze the question of when recursion is beneficial and when it is inefficient.

Consider the Fibonacci sequence introduced in Chapter 5: a sequence of numbers defined by the equation

$$f_1 = 1$$
$$f_2 = 1$$
$$f_n = f_{n-1} + f_{n-2}$$

That is, each value of the sequence is the sum of the two preceding values. The first ten terms of the sequence are

1, 1, 2, 3, 5, 8, 13, 21, 34, 55

It is easy to extend this sequence indefinitely. Just keep appending the sum of the last two values of the sequence. For example, the next entry is $34 + 55 = 89$.

We would like to write a function that computes f_n for any value of n. Suppose we translate the definition directly into a recursive method:

File FibTest.java

```
1  import javax.swing.JOptionPane;
2
3  /**
```

```
 4      This program computes Fibonacci numbers using a recursive
 5      method.
 6  */
 7  public class FibTest
 8  {
 9     public static void main(String[] args)
10     {
11        String input = JOptionPane.showInputDialog(
12           "Enter n: ");
13        int n = Integer.parseInt(input);
14
15        for (int i = 1; i <= n; i++)
16        {
17           int f = fib(i);
18           System.out.println("fib(" + i + ") = " + f);
19        }
20        System.exit(0);
21     }
22
23     /**
24        Computes a Fibonacci number.
25        @param n an integer
26        @return the nth Fibonacci number
27     */
28     public static int fib(int n)
29     {
30        if (n <= 2) return 1;
31        else return fib(n - 1) + fib(n - 2);
32     }
33  }
```

That is certainly simple, and the method will work correctly. But watch the output closely as you run the test program. The first few calls to the fib method are quite fast. For larger values, though, the program pauses an amazingly long time between outputs.

That makes no sense. Armed with pencil, paper, and a pocket calculator you could calculate these numbers pretty quickly, so it shouldn't take the computer anywhere near that long.

To find out the problem, let us insert trace messages into the method:

File FibTrace.java

```
 1  import javax.swing.JOptionPane;
 2
 3  /**
 4      This program prints trace messages that show how often the
 5      recursive method for computing Fibonacci numbers calls itself.
 6  */
 7  public class FibTrace
 8  {
 9     public static void main(String[] args)
10     {
11        String input = JOptionPane.showInputDialog(
12           "Enter n: ");
13        int n = Integer.parseInt(input);
```

```
14
15        int f = fib(n);
16
17        System.out.println("fib(" + n + ") = " + f);
18        System.exit(0);
19     }
20
21     /**
22        Computes a Fibonacci number.
23        @param n  an integer
24        @return  the nth Fibonacci number
25     */
26     public static int fib(int n)
27     {
28        System.out.println("Entering fib: n = " + n);
29        int f;
30        if (n <= 2) f = 1;
31        else f = fib(n - 1) + fib(n - 2);
32        System.out.println("Exiting fib: n = " + n
33           + " return value = " + f);
34        return f;
35     }
36 }
```

Following is the trace for computing fib(5). Figure 5 shows the call tree

```
Entering fib: n = 6
Entering fib: n = 5
Entering fib: n = 4
Entering fib: n = 3
Entering fib: n = 2
Exiting fib: n = 2 return value = 1
```

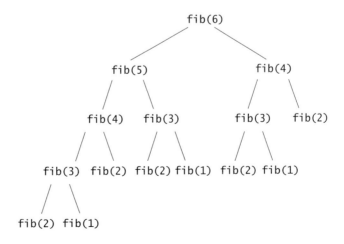

Figure 5

Call Pattern of the Recursive fib Method

```
Entering fib: n = 1
Exiting fib: n = 1 return value = 1
Exiting fib: n = 3 return value = 2
Entering fib: n = 2
Exiting fib: n = 2 return value = 1
Exiting fib: n = 4 return value = 3
Entering fib: n = 3
Entering fib: n = 2
Exiting fib: n = 2 return value = 1
Entering fib: n = 1
Exiting fib: n = 1 return value = 1
Exiting fib: n = 3 return value = 2
Exiting fib: n = 5 return value = 5
Entering fib: n = 4
Entering fib: n = 3
Entering fib: n = 2
Exiting fib: n = 2 return value = 1
Entering fib: n = 1
Exiting fib: n = 1 return value = 1
Exiting fib: n = 3 return value = 2
Entering fib: n = 2
Exiting fib: n = 2 return value = 1
Exiting fib: n = 4 return value = 3
Exiting fib: n = 6 return value = 8
```

Now it is becoming apparent why the method takes so long. It is computing the same values over and over. For example, the computation of fib(6) calls fib(4) twice and fib(3) three times. That is very different from the computation we would do with pencil and paper. There we would just write down the values as they were computed and add up the last two to get the next one until we reached the desired entry; no sequence value would ever be computed twice.

If we imitate the pencil-and-paper process, then we get the following program.

File FibLoop.java

```
1  import javax.swing.JOptionPane;
2
3  /**
4      This program computes Fibonacci numbers using an iterative method.
5  */
6  public class FibLoop
7  {
8      public static void main(String[] args)
9      {
10         String input = JOptionPane.showInputDialog(
11            "Enter n: ");
12         int n = Integer.parseInt(input);
13
14         for (int i = 1; i <= n; i++)
15         {
16            double f = fib(i);
17            System.out.println("fib(" + i + ") = " + f);
```

```
18          }
19          System.exit(0);
20      }
21
22      /**
23          Computes a Fibonacci number.
24          @param n  an integer
25          @return  the nth Fibonacci number
26      */
27      public static double fib(int n)
28      {
29          if (n <= 2) return 1;
30          double fold = 1;
31          double fold2 = 1;
32          double fnew = 1;
33          for (int i = 3; i <= n; i++)
34          {
35              fnew = fold + fold2;
36              fold2 = fold;
37              fold = fnew;
38          }
39          return fnew;
40      }
41  }
```

This method runs *much* faster than the recursive version.

In this example of the fib method, the recursive solution was easy to program because it exactly followed the mathematical definition, but it ran far more slowly than the iterative solution, because it computed many intermediate results multiple times.

Can you always speed up a recursive solution by changing it into a loop? Frequently, the iterative and recursive solution have essentially the same performance. For example, here is an iterative solution for the palindrome test.

```
public boolean isPalindrome()
{
    int start = 0;
    int end = text.length() - 1;
    while (start < end)
    {
        char first = Character.toLowerCase(
            text.charAt(start));
        char last = Character.toLowerCase(text.charAt(end));

        if (Character.isLetter(first)
            && Character.isLetter(last))
        {
            // both are letters
            if (first == last)
            {
                start++;
                end--;
            }
```

```
        else
            return false;
        if (!Character.isLetter(last))
            end--;
        if (!Character.isLetter(first))
            start++;
    }
    return true;
}
```

This solution keeps two index variables: `start` and `end`. The first index starts at the beginning of the string and is advanced whenever a letter has been matched or a nonletter has been ignored. The second index starts at the end of the string and moves towards the beginning. When the two index variables meet, then the iteration stops.

> Occasionally, a recursive solution runs much slower than its iterative counterpart. However, in most cases, the recursive solution is only slightly slower.

Both the iteration and the recursion run at about the same speed. If a palindrome has n characters, the iteration executes the loop between $n/2$ and n times, depending on how many of the characters are letters, since one or both index variables are moved in each step. Similarly, the recursive solution calls itself between $n/2$ and n times, because one or two characters are removed in each step.

In such a situation, the iterative solution tends to be a bit faster, because each recursive method call takes a certain amount of processor time. In principle, it is possible for a smart compiler to avoid recursive method calls if they follow simple patterns, but most compilers don't do that. From that point of view, an iterative solution is preferable.

> In many cases a recursive solution is easier to understand and implement correctly than an iterative solution.

There are quite a few problems that are dramatically easier to solve recursively than iteratively. For example, it is not at all obvious how you can come up with a nonrecursive solution for the permutation generator. As Exercise P17.11 shows, it is possible to avoid the recursion, but the resulting solution is quite complex (and no faster).

Often, recursive solutions are easier to understand and implement correctly than their iterative counterparts. There is a certain elegance and economy of thought to recursive solutions that makes them more appealing. As the computer scientist (and creator of the GhostScript interpreter for the PostScript graphics description language) L. Peter Deutsch put it: "To iterate is human, to recurse divine."

Random Fact 17.1

The Limits of Computation

Have you ever wondered how your instructor or grader makes sure your programming homework is correct? In all likelihood, they look at your solution and perhaps run it with some test inputs. But usually they have a correct solution available. That suggests that there might be an easier way. Perhaps they could feed your program and their correct program into a program comparator, a computer program that analyzes both programs

▼ and determines whether they both compute the same results. Of course, your solution and the program that is known to be correct need not be identical—what matters is that they produce the same output when given the same input.

▼ How could such a program comparator work? Well, the Java compiler knows how to read a program and make sense of the classes, methods, and statements. So it seems plausible that someone could, with some effort, write a program that reads two Java pro-

▼ grams, analyzes what they do, and determines whether they solve the same task. Of course, such a program would be very attractive to instructors, because it could automate the grading process. Thus, even though no such program exists today, it might be tempt-

▼ ing to try to develop one and sell it to universities around the world.

However, before you start raising venture capital for such an effort, you should know that theoretical computer scientists have proven that it is impossible to develop such a

▼ program, *no matter how hard you try.*

There are quite a few of these unsolvable problems. The first one, called the *halting problem,* was discovered by the British researcher Alan Turing in 1936 (see Figure 6).

▼ Because his research occurred before the first actual computer was constructed, Turing had to devise a theoretical device, the *Turing machine,* to explain how computers could work. The Turing machine consists of a long magnetic tape, a read/write head, and a

▼ program that has numbered instructions of the form: "If the current symbol under the head is x, then replace it with y, move the head one unit left or right, and continue with instruction n" (see Figure 7). Interestingly enough, with just these instructions, you can

▼ program just as much as with Java, even though it is incredibly tedious to do so. Theoretical computer scientists like Turing machines because they can be described using nothing more than the laws of mathematics.

▼

▼

▼

▼

▼

▼

Figure 6

Alan Turing

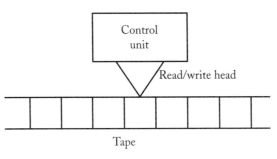

Instruction number	If tape symbol is	Replace with	Then move head	Then go to instruction
1	0	2	right	2
1	1	1	left	4
2	0	0	right	2
2	1	1	right	2
2	B	0	left	3
3	0	0	left	3
3	1	1	left	3
3	2	2	right	1
4	1	1	right	5
4	2	0	left	4

Program

Control unit

Read/write head

Tape

Figure 7

A Turing Machine

Expressed in terms of Java, the halting problem states: "It is impossible to write a program with two inputs, namely the source code of an arbitrary Java program P and a string I, and that decides whether the program P, when executed with the input I, will halt without getting into an infinite loop". Of course, for some kinds of programs and inputs, it is possible to decide whether the programs halt with the given input. The halting problem asserts that it is impossible to come up with a single decision-making algorithm that works with all programs and inputs. Note that you can't simply run the program P on the input I to settle this question. If the program runs for 1,000 days, you don't know that the program is in an infinite loop. Maybe you just have to wait another day for it to stop.

Such a "halt checker", if it could be written, might also be useful for grading homework. An instructor could use it to screen student submissions to see if they get into an infinite loop with a particular input, and then not check them any further. However, as Turing demonstrated, such a program cannot be written. His argument is ingenious and quite simple.

Suppose a "halt checker" program existed. Let's call it H. From H, we will develop another program, the "killer" program K. K does the following computation. Its input is a string containing the source code for a program R. It then applies the halting checker on the input program R and the input string R. That is, it checks whether the program R halts if its input is its own source code. It sounds bizarre to feed a program to itself, but it isn't impossible. For example, the Java compiler is written in Java, and you can use it to

▼ compile itself. Or, as a simpler example, you can use the word count program from Chapter 6 to count the words in its own source code.

▼ When *K* gets the answer from *H* that *R* halts when applied to itself, it is programmed to enter an infinite loop. Otherwise *K* exits. In Java, the program might look like this:

```
public class Killer
{
    public static void main(String[] args)
    {
        String r = read program input;
        HaltChecker checker = new HaltChecker();
        if (checker.check(r, r))
            while (true) { } // infinite loop
        else
            return;
    }
}
```

Now ask yourself: What does the halt checker answer when asked whether *K* halts when given *K* as the input? Maybe it finds out that *K* gets into an infinite loop with such an input. But wait, that can't be right. That would mean that `checker.check(r, r)` returns `false` when r is the program code of *K*. As you can plainly see, in that case, the `killer` method returns, so *K* didn't get into an infinite loop. That shows that *K* must halt when analyzing itself, so `checker.check(r, r)` should return `true`. But then the `killer` method doesn't terminate—it goes into an infinite loop. That shows that it is logically impossible to implement a program that can check whether *every* program halts on a particular input.

It is sobering to know that there are *limits* to computing. There are problems that no computer program, no matter how ingenious, can answer.

Theoretical computer scientists are working on other research involving the nature of computation. One important question that remains unsettled to this day deals with problems that in practice are very time-consuming to solve. It may be that these problems are intrinsically hard, in which case it would be pointless to try to look for better algorithms. Such theoretical research can have important practical applications. For example, right now, nobody knows whether the most common encryptions schemes used today could be broken by discovering a new algorithm (see Random Fact 15.1 for more information on encryption algorithms). Knowing that no fast algorithms exist for breaking a particular code could make us feel more comfortable about the security of encryption.

CHAPTER SUMMARY

1. A recursive computation solves a problem by using the solution of the same problem with simpler inputs.

2. For a recursion to terminate, there must be special cases for the simplest inputs.

3. Sometimes it is easier to find a recursive solution if you make a slight change to the original problem.

4. In a mutual recursion, a set of cooperating methods calls each other repeatedly.

5. Occasionally, a recursive solution runs much slower than its iterative counterpart. However, in most cases, the recursive solution is only slightly slower.

6. In many cases, a recursive solution is easier to understand and implement correctly than an iterative solution.

REVIEW EXERCISES

Exercise R17.1. Define the terms

- Recursion
- Iteration
- Infinite recursion
- Indirect recursion

Exercise R17.2. Outline, but do not implement, a recursive solution for finding the smallest value in an array.

Exercise R17.3. Outline, but do not implement, a recursive solution for sorting an array of numbers. *Hint:* First find the smallest value in the array.

Exercise R17.4. Outline, but do not implement, a recursive solution for generating all subsets of the set $\{1, 2, \ldots, n\}$.

Exercise R17.5. Exercise P17.11 shows an iterative way of generating all permutations of the sequence $(0, 1, \ldots, n - 1)$. Explain why the algorithm produces the right result.

Exercise R17.6. Write a recursive definition of x^n, where $n \geq 0$, similar to the recursive definition of the Fibonacci numbers. *Hint:* How do you compute x^n from x^{n-1}? How does the recursion terminate?

Exercise R17.7. Write a recursive definition of $n! = 1 \times 2 \times \cdots \times n$, similar to the recursive definition of the Fibonacci numbers.

Exercise R17.8. Find out how often the recursive version of `fib` calls itself. Keep a static variable `fibCount` and increment it once in every call of `fib`. What is the relationship between `fib(n)` and `fibCount`?

Exercise R17.9. How many moves are required in the "Towers of Hanoi" problem of Exercise P17.12 to move n disks? *Hint:* As explained in the exercises,

moves(1) = 1

moves(n) = 2 · moves($n - 1$) + 1

PROGRAMMING EXERCISES

Exercise P17.1. Write a recursive method `void reverse()` that reverses a sentence. For example:

```
Sentence greeting = new Sentence("Hello!");
greeting.reverse();
System.out.println(greeting.getText());
```

prints the string "!olleH". Implement a recursive solution by removing the first character, reversing a sentence consisting of the remaining text, and combining the two.

Exercise P17.2. Redo Exercise P17.1 with a recursive helper method that reverses a substring of the message text.

Exercise P17.3. Implement the reverse method of Exercise P17.1 as an iteration.

Exercise P17.4. Use recursion to implement a method boolean find(String t) that
tests whether a string is contained in a sentence:

```
Sentence s = new Sentence("Mississippi!");
boolean b = s.find("sip"); // returns true
```

Hint: If the text starts with the string you want to match, then you are done. If not, consider the sentence that you obtain by removing the first character.

Exercise P17.5. Use recursion to implement a method int indexOf(String t) that
returns the starting position of the first substring of the text that matches t. Return −1 if
t is not a substring of s. For example,

```
Sentence s = new Sentence("Mississippi!");
int n = s.find("sip"); // returns 6
```

Hint: This is a bit trickier than the preceding problem, because you need to keep track of
how far the match is from the beginning of the sentence. Make that value a parameter of
a helper method.

Exercise P17.6. Using recursion, find the largest element in an array.

```
public class DataSet
{
   public DataSet(int[] anArray) { . . . }
   public int getMaximum() { . . . }
   . . .
}
```

Hint: Find the largest element in the subset containing all but the last element. Then
compare that maximum to the value of the last element.

Exercise P17.7. Using recursion, compute the sum of all values in an array.

```
public class DataSet
{
   public DataSet(int[] anArray) { . . . }
   public int getSum() { . . . }
   . . .
}
```

Exercise P17.8. Using recursion, compute the area of a polygon. Cut off a triangle and
use the fact that a triangle with corners (x_1, y_1), (x_2, y_2), (x_3, y_3) has area

$$\left|x_1 y_2 + x_2 y_3 + x_3 y_1 - y_1 x_2 - y_2 x_3 - y_3 x_1\right| / 2$$

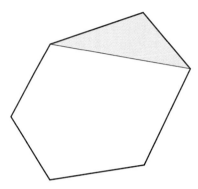

Exercise P17.9. Implement a `SubStringGenerator` that generates all substrings of a string. For example, the substrings of the string `"rum"` are the seven strings

   `"r"`, `"ru"`, `"rum"`, `"u"`, `"um"`, `"m"`, `""`

Hint: First enumerate all substrings that start with the first character. There are *n* of them if the string has length *n*. Then enumerate the substrings of the string that you obtain by removing the first character.

Exercise P17.10. Implement a `SubSetGenerator` that generates all subsets of characters of a string. For example, the subsets of characters of the string `"rum"` are the eight strings

   `"rum"`, `"ru"`, `"rm"`, `"r"`, `"um"`, `"u"`, `"m"`, `""`

Note that the subsets don't have to be substrings—for example, `"rm"` isn't a substring of `"rum"`.

Exercise P17.11. The following class generates all permutations of the numbers 0, 1, 2, ..., *n* − 1, without using recursion.

```
public class NumberPermutationGenerator
{
   public NumberPermutationGenerator(int n)
   {
      a = new int[n];
      done = false;
      for (int i = 0; i < n; i++) a[i] = i;
   }

   public int[] nextPermutation()
   {
      if (a.length <= 1) return a;

      for (int i = a.length - 1; i > 0; i--)
      {
         if (a[i - 1] < a[i])
         {
            int j = a.length - 1;
            while (a[i - 1] > a[j]) j--;
            swap(i - 1, j);
            reverse(i, a.length - 1);
```

```
            return a;
         }
      }
      return a;
   }

   public boolean hasMorePermutations()
   {
      if (a.length <= 1) return false;
      for (int i = a.length - 1; i > 0; i--)
      {
         if (a[i - 1] < a[i]) return true;
      }
      return false;
   }

   public void swap(int i, int j)
   {
      int temp = a[i];
      a[i] = a[j];
      a[j] = temp;
   }

   public void reverse(int i, int j)
   {
      while (i < j) { swap(i, j); i++, j  ; }
   }
   private int[] a;
}
```

The algorithm uses the fact that the set to be permuted consists of distinct numbers. Thus, you cannot use the same algorithm to compute the permutations of the characters in a string. You can, however, use this class to get all permutations of the character positions and then compute a string whose ith character is word.charAt(a[i]). Use this approach to reimplement the PermutationGenerator without recursion.

Exercise P17.12. *Towers of Hanoi.* This is a well-known puzzle. A stack of disks of decreasing size is to be transported from the leftmost peg to the rightmost peg. The middle peg can be used as a temporary storage. (See Figure 8.) One disk can be moved at one time, from any peg to any other peg. You can place smaller disks only on top of larger ones, not the other way around.

Write a program that prints the moves necessary to solve the puzzle for *n* disks. (Ask the user for *n* at the beginning of the program.) Print moves in the form

```
Move disk from peg 1 to peg 3
```

Hint: Implement a class DiskMover. The constructor takes

- The source peg from which to move the disks (1, 2, or 3)
- The target peg to which to move the disks (1, 2, or 3)
- The number of disks to move

Figure 8

Towers of Hanoi

A disk mover that moves a single disk from one peg to another simply has a `nextMove` method that returns a string

```
Move disk from peg source to peg target
```

A disk mover with more than disk to move must work harder. It needs another `Disk-Mover` to help it. In the constructor, construct a `DiskMover(source, other, disks - 1)` where `other` is the peg other than `from` and `target`.

The `nextMove` asks that disk mover for its next move until it is done. The effect is to move the first `disks - 1` disks to the other peg. Then the `nextMove` method issues a command to move a disk from the `from` peg to the `to` peg. Finally, it constructs another disk mover `DiskMover(other, target, disks - 1)` that generates the moves that move the disks from the other peg to the target peg.

Hint: It helps to keep track of the state of the disk mover:

- `BEFORE_LARGEST`: The helper mover moves the smaller pile to the other peg.
- `LARGEST`: Move the largest disk from the source to the destination.
- `AFTER_LARGEST`: The helper mover moves the smaller pile from the other peg to the target.
- `DONE`: All moves are done.

Test your program as follows:

```
DiskMover mover = new DiskMover(1, 3, n);
while (mover.hasMoreMoves())
    System.out.println(mover.nextMove());
```

Exercise P17.13. Implement a graphical version of the Towers of Hanoi program. Every time the user clicks on a button labeled "Next", draw the next move.

Sorting and Searching

CHAPTER GOALS

To study the several sorting and searching algorithms

▶ To appreciate that algorithms for the same task can differ widely in performance

▶ To understand the big-Oh notation

▶ To learn how to estimate and compare the performance of algorithms

▶ To learn how to measure the running time of a program

One of the most common tasks in data processing is sorting. For example, a collection of employees needs to be printed out in alphabetical order or sorted by salary. We will study several sorting methods in this chapter and compare their performance. This is by no means an exhaustive treatment on the subject of sorting. You will likely revisit this topic at a later time in your computer science studies. Reference [1] gives a good overview of the many sorting methods available.

Once a sequence of objects is sorted, one can locate individual objects rapidly. We will study the *binary search* algorithm, which carries out this fast lookup.

18.1 Selection Sort

To keep the examples simple, we will discuss how to sort an array of integers before going on to sorting strings or employee data. Consider the following array a:

| 11 | 9 | 17 | 5 | 12 |

> The selection sort algorithm sorts an array by repeatedly finding the smallest element of the unsorted tail region and moving it to the front.

An obvious first step is to find the smallest element. In this case the smallest element is 5, stored in `a[3]`. We should move the 5 to the beginning of the array. Of course, there is already an element stored in `a[0]`, namely 11. Therefore we cannot simply move `a[3]` into `a[0]` without moving the 11 somewhere else. We don't yet know where the 11 should end up, but we know for certain that it should not be in `a[0]`. We simply get it out of the way by *swapping* it with `a[3]`.

Now the first element is in the correct place. In the foregoing figure, the color indicates the portion of the array that is already sorted from the unsorted remainder.

Next we take the minimum of the remaining entries `a[1]` . . . `a[4]`. That minimum value, 9, is already in the correct place. We don't need to do anything in this case and can simply extend the sorted area by one to the right:

| 5 | 9 | 17 | 11 | 12 |

We repeat the process. The minimum value of the unsorted region is 11, which needs to be swapped with the first value of the unsorted region, 17:

Now the unsorted region is only two elements long, but we keep to the same successful strategy. The minimum value is 12, and we swap it with the first value, 17.

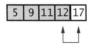

That leaves us with an unprocessed region of length 1, but of course a region of length 1 is always sorted. We are done.

Let us program this algorithm. For this program as well as the other programs in this chapter, we will use two utility methods—one to generate an array with random entries, and the other to print the values of an array—which we pack up in a class `ArrayUtil` so that we don't have to repeat them for every code example.

This algorithm will sort any array of integers. If speed were not an issue for us, or if there simply were no better sorting method available, we could stop the discussion of sorting right here. As the next section shows, however, this algorithm, while entirely correct, shows disappointing performance when run on a large data set.

Exercise R18.13 discusses insertion sort, another simple (and equally inefficient) sorting algorithm.

File SelectionSorter.java

```java
1  /**
2      This class sorts an array, using the selection sort
3      algorithm.
4  */
5  public class SelectionSorter
6  {
7      /**
8          Constructs a selection sorter.
9          @param anArray the array to sort
10     */
11     public SelectionSorter(int[] anArray)
12     {
13         a = anArray;
14     }
15
16     /**
17         Sorts the array managed by this selection sorter.
18     */
19     public void sort()
20     {
21         for (int i = 0; i < a.length - 1; i++)
22         {
23             int minPos = minimumPosition(i);
24             swap(minPos, i);
25         }
26     }
27
28     /**
29         Finds the smallest element in a tail range of the array.
30         @param from the first position in a to compare
31         @return the position of the smallest element in the
32             range a[from]...a[a.length - 1]
33     */
34     private int minimumPosition(int from)
35     {
36         int minPos = from;
37         for (int i = from + 1; i < a.length; i++)
```

```
38              if (a[i] < a[minPos]) minPos = i;
39          return minPos;
40      }
41
42      /**
43          Swaps two entries of the array.
44          @param i the first position to swap
45          @param j the second position to swap
46      */
47      private void swap(int i, int j)
48      {
49          int temp = a[i];
50          a[i] = a[j];
51          a[j] = temp;
52      }
53
54      private int[] a;
55 }
56 File SelectionSortTest.java
57 /**
58      This program tests the selection sort algorithm by
59      sorting an array that is filled with random numbers.
60 */
61 public class SelectionSortTest
62 {
63      public static void main(String[] args)
64      {
65          int[] a = ArrayUtil.randomIntArray(20, 100);
66          ArrayUtil.print(a);
67
68          SelectionSorter sorter = new SelectionSorter(a);
69          sorter.sort();
70
71          ArrayUtil.print(a);
72      }
73 }
```

File ArrayUtil.java

```
1 import java.util.Random;
2
3 /**
4      This class contains utility methods for array
5      manipulation.
6 */
7 public class ArrayUtil
8 {
9      /**
10          Creates an array filled with random values.
11          @param length the length of the array
12          @param n the number of possible random values
```

```
13          @return an array filled with length numbers between
14              0 and n-1
15      */
16      public static int[] randomIntArray(int length, int n)
17      {   int[] a = new int[length];
18          Random generator = new Random();
19
20          for (int i = 0; i < a.length; i++)
21              a[i] = generator.nextInt(n);
22
23          return a;
24      }
25
26      /**
27          Prints all elements in an array.
28          @param a the array to print
29      */
30      public static void print(int[] a)
31      {
32          for (int i = 0; i < a.length; i++)
33              System.out.print(a[i] + " ");
34          System.out.println();
35      }
36  }
```

18.2 Profiling the Selection Sort Algorithm

To measure the performance of a program, you could simply run it and measure how long it takes by using a stopwatch. However, most of our programs run very quickly, and it is not easy to time them accurately in this way. Furthermore, when a program does take a noticeable time to run, a certain amount of that time may simply be used for loading the program from disk into memory (for which we should not penalize it) or for screen output (whose speed depends on the computer model, even for computers with identical CPUs). We will instead create a StopWatch class. This class works just like a real stopwatch. You can start it, stop it, and read out the elapsed time. The class uses the System.current-TimeMillis method, which returns the milliseconds that have elapsed since midnight at the start of January 1, 1970. Of course, you don't care about the absolute number of seconds since this historical moment, but the *difference* of two such counts gives us the number of milliseconds of a time interval. Here is the code for the StopWatch class:

File StopWatch.java

```
1  /**
2      A stopwatch accumulates time when it is running. You can
3      repeatedly start and stop the stopwatch. You can use a
4      stopwatch to measure the running time of a program.
5  */
6  public class StopWatch
7  {
```

```
 8    /**
 9        Constructs a stopwatch that is in the stopped state
10        and has no time accumulated.
11    */
12    public StopWatch()
13    {
14       reset();
15    }
16
17    /**
18        Starts the stopwatch. Time starts accumulating now.
19    */
20    public void start()
21    {
22       if (isRunning) return;
23       isRunning = true;
24       startTime = System.currentTimeMillis();
25    }
26
27    /**
28        Stops the stopwatch. Time stops accumulating and is
29        is added to the elapsed time.
30    */
31    public void stop()
32    {
33       if (!isRunning) return;
34       isRunning = false;
35       long endTime = System.currentTimeMillis();
36       elapsedTime = elapsedTime + endTime - startTime;
37    }
38
39    /**
40        Returns the total elapsed time.
41        @return  the total elapsed time
42    */
43    public long getElapsedTime()
44    {
45       if (isRunning)
46       {
47          long endTime = System.currentTimeMillis();
48          elapsedTime = elapsedTime + endTime - startTime;
49          startTime = endTime;
50       }
51       return elapsedTime;
52    }
53
54    /**
55        Stops the watch and resets the elapsed time to 0.
56    */
57    public void reset()
```

```
58       {
59          elapsedTime = 0;
60          isRunning = false;
61       }
62
63       private long elapsedTime;
64       private long startTime;
65       private boolean isRunning;
66    }
```

Here is how we will use the stopwatch to measure the performance of the sorting algorithm:

File SelectionSortTimer.java

```java
1  import javax.swing.JOptionPane;
2
3  /**
4      This program measures how long it takes to sort an
5      array of a user-specified size with the selection
6      sort algorithm.
7  */
8  public class SelectionSortTimer
9  {
10     public static void main(String[] args)
11     {
12        String input = JOptionPane.showInputDialog(
13           "Enter array size:");
14        int n = Integer.parseInt(input);
15
16        // construct random array
17
18        int[] a = ArrayUtil.randomIntArray(n, 100);
19        SelectionSorter sorter = new SelectionSorter(a);
20
21        // use stopwatch to time selection sort
22
23        StopWatch timer = new StopWatch();
24
25        timer.start();
26        sorter.sort();
27        timer.stop();
28
29        System.out.println("Elapsed time: "
30           + timer.getElapsedTime() + " milliseconds");
31        System.exit(0);
32     }
33  }
```

By starting to measure the time just before sorting, and stopping the stopwatch just afterwards, you don't count the time it takes to initialize the array or the time during which the program waits for the user to type in n.

Figure 1

Time Taken by Selection Sort

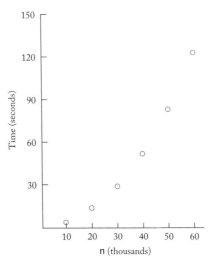

Here are the results of some sample runs:

n	Milliseconds
10,000	3,460
20,000	13,240
30,000	28,290
40,000	51,520
50,000	82,670
60,000	121,820

These measurements were obtained with a Pentium processor with a clock speed of 166 MHz, with 96MB of memory, and running Windows 98. On another computer the actual numbers will look different, but the relationship between the numbers will be the same. Figure 1 shows a plot of the measurements. As you can see, doubling the size of the data set more than doubles the time needed to sort it.

18.3 Analyzing the Performance of the Selection Sort Algorithm

Let us count the number of operations that the program must carry out to sort an array by the selection sort algorithm. We don't actually know how many machine operations are generated for each Java instruction or which of those instructions are more time-consuming than others, but we can make a simplification. We will simply count how often an array element is *visited*. Each visit requires about the same amount of work by other operations, such as incrementing subscripts and comparing values.

Let n be size of the array. First, we must find the smallest of n numbers. To achieve that, we must visit n array elements. Then we swap the elements, which takes 2 visits. (You may argue that there is a certain probability that we don't need to swap the values. That is true, and one can refine the computation to reflect that observation. As we will soon see, doing so would not affect the overall conclusion.) In the next step, we need to visit only $n - 1$ elements to find the minimum. In the following step, $n - 2$ elements are visited to find the minimum. The last step visits two elements to find the minimum. Each step requires 2 visits to swap the elements. Therefore, the total number of visits is

$$n + 2 + (n - 1) + 2 + \cdots + 2 + 2$$
$$= n + (n - 1) + \cdots + 2 + (n - 1) \cdot 2$$
$$= 2 + \cdots + (n - 1) + n + (n - 1) \cdot 2$$
$$= \frac{n \cdot (n + 1)}{2} - 1 + (n - 1) \cdot 2$$

because

$$1 + 2 + \cdots + (n - 1) + n = \frac{n \cdot (n + 1)}{2}$$

After multiplying out and collecting terms of n, we find that the number of visits is

$$\tfrac{1}{2} \cdot n^2 + \tfrac{5}{2} \cdot n - 3$$

We obtain a quadratic equation in n. That explains why the graph of Figure 1 looks approximately like a parabola.

Now let us simplify the analysis further. When you plug in a large value for n (for example, 1000 or 2000), then $\tfrac{1}{2} \cdot n^2$ is 500,000 or 2,000,000. The lower term, $\tfrac{5}{2} \cdot n - 3$, doesn't contribute much at all; it is just 2,497 or 4,997, a drop in the bucket compared to the hundreds of thousands or even millions of comparisons specified by the $\tfrac{1}{2} \cdot n^2$ term. We will just ignore these lower-level terms. Next, we will ignore the constant factor $\tfrac{1}{2}$. We are not interested in the actual count of visits for a single n. We want to compare the ratios of counts for different values of n. For example, we can say that sorting an array of 2000 numbers requires 4 times as many visits as sorting an array of 1000 numbers:

$$\frac{\tfrac{1}{2} \cdot 2000^2}{\tfrac{1}{2} \cdot 1000^2} = 4$$

> Computer scientists use the big-Oh notation $f(n) = O(g(n))$ to express that the function f grows no faster than the function g.

The factor cancels out in comparisons of this kind. We will simply say, "The number of visits is of order n^2". That way, we can easily see that the number of comparisons increases fourfold when the size of the array doubles: $(2n)^2 = 4n^2$.

To indicate that the number of visits is of order n^2, computer scientists often use *big-Oh notation:* The number of visits is $O(n^2)$. This is a convenient shorthand.

In general, the expression $f(n) = O(g(n))$ means that f grows no faster than g, or, more formally, that for all n larger than some threshold, the ratio $f(n)/g(n) \leq C$ for some constant value C. The function g is usually chosen to be very simple, such as n^2 in our example.

To turn an exact expression like

$$\tfrac{1}{2} \cdot n^2 + \tfrac{5}{2} \cdot n - 3$$

into big-Oh notation, simply locate the fastest-growing term, n^2, and ignore its constant coefficient, no matter how large or small it may be.

We observed before that the actual number of machine operations, and the actual number of microseconds that the computer spends on them, is approximately proportional to the number of element visits. Maybe there are about 10 machine operations (increments, comparisons, memory loads and stores) for every element visit. The number of machine operations is then approximately $10 \cdot \frac{1}{2} \cdot n^2$. Again, we aren't interested in the coefficient, so we can say that the number of machine operations, and hence the time spent on the sorting, is of the order of n^2 or $O(n^2)$.

> Selection sort is an $O(n^2)$ algorithm. Doubling the data set means a fourfold increase in processing time.

The sad fact remains that doubling the size of the array causes a fourfold increase in the time required for sorting it with selection sort. When the size of the array increases by a factor of 100, the sorting time increases by a factor of 10,000. To sort an array of a million entries (for example, to create a telephone directory) takes 10,000 times as long as sorting 10,000 entries. If 10,000 entries can be sorted in 3.5 seconds (as in our example), then a million entries require over 9 hours. That is a problem. We will see in the next section how one can dramatically improve the performance of the sorting process by choosing a more sophisticated algorithm.

18.4 Merge Sort

Suppose we have an array of 10 integers. Let us engage in a bit of wishful thinking and hope that the first half of the array is already perfectly sorted, and the second half is too, like this:

| 5 | 9 | 10 | 12 | 17 | 1 | 8 | 11 | 20 | 32 |

Now it is an easy matter to *merge* the two sorted arrays into a sorted array, simply by taking a new element from either the first or the second subarray, choosing the smaller of the elements each time:

```
5  9  10 12 17 | 1̶ 8  11 20 32 | 1
5̶ 9  10 12 17 | 1̶ 8  11 20 32 | 1  5
5̶ 9  10 12 17 | 1̶ 8̶ 11 20 32 | 1  5  8
5̶ 9̶ 10 12 17 | 1̶ 8̶ 11 20 32 | 1  5  8  9
5̶ 9̶ 10̶ 12 17 | 1̶ 8̶ 11 20 32 | 1  5  8  9  10
5̶ 9̶ 10̶ 12 17 | 1̶ 8̶ 11̶ 20 32 | 1  5  8  9  10 11
5̶ 9̶ 10̶ 12̶ 17 | 1̶ 8̶ 11̶ 20 32 | 1  5  8  9  10 11 12
5̶ 9̶ 10̶ 12̶ 17̶ | 1̶ 8̶ 11̶ 20 32 | 1  5  8  9  10 11 12 17
5̶ 9̶ 10̶ 12̶ 17̶ | 1̶ 8̶ 11̶ 20̶ 32 | 1  5  8  9  10 11 12 17 20
5̶ 9̶ 10̶ 12̶ 17̶ | 1̶ 8̶ 11̶ 20̶ 32̶ | 1  5  8  9  10 11 12 17 20 32
```

In fact, you probably performed this merging before when you and a friend had to sort a pile of papers. You and the friend split up the pile in the middle, each of you sorted your half, and then you merged the results together.

That is all good and well, but it doesn't seem to solve the problem for the computer. It still has to sort the first and the second half of the array, because it can't very well ask a few buddies to pitch in. As it turns out, though, if the computer keeps dividing the array into smaller and smaller subarrays, sorting each half and merging them back together, it carries out dramatically fewer steps than the selection sort requires.

> The merge sort algorithm sorts an array by cutting the array in half, recursively sorting each half, and then merging the sorted halves.

Let us write a `MergeSorter` class that implements this idea. When the `MergeSorter` sorts an array, it makes two arrays, each half the size of the original, and sorts them recursively. Then it merges the two sorted arrays together:

```
public void sort()
{
   if (a.length <= 1) return;
   int[] first = new int[a.length / 2];
   int[] second = new int[a.length - first.length];
   System.arraycopy(a, 0, first, 0, first.length);
   System.arraycopy(a,
      first.length, second, 0, second.length);
   MergeSorter firstSorter = new MergeSorter(first);
   MergeSorter secondSorter = new MergeSorter(second);
   firstSorter.sort();
   secondSorter.sort();
   merge(first, second);
}
```

The `merge` method is tedious but quite straightforward. You will find it in the code at the end of this section.

File MergeSorter.java

```
1  /**
2     This class sorts an array, using the merge sort algorithm.
3  */
4  public class MergeSorter
5  {
6     /**
7        Constructs a merge sorter.
8        @param anArray the array to sort
9     */
10    public MergeSorter(int[] anArray)
11    {
12       a = anArray;
13    }
14
15    /**
16       Sorts the array managed by this merge sorter.
17    */
18    public void sort()
19    {
20       if (a.length <= 1) return;
21       int[] first = new int[a.length / 2];
22       int[] second = new int[a.length - first.length];
```

```
23          System.arraycopy(a, 0, first, 0, first.length);
24          System.arraycopy(a,
25             first.length, second, 0, second.length);
26          MergeSorter firstSorter = new MergeSorter(first);
27          MergeSorter secondSorter = new MergeSorter(second);
28          firstSorter.sort();
29          secondSorter.sort();
30          merge(first, second);
31       }
32
33       /**
34          Merges two sorted arrays into the array to be sorted by this
35          merge sorter.
36          @param first the first sorted array
37          @param second the second sorted array
38       */
39       private void merge(int[] first, int[] second)
40       {
41          // merge both halves into the temporary array
42
43          int iFirst = 0;
44             // next element to consider in the first array
45          int iSecond = 0;
46             // next element to consider in the second array
47          int j = 0;
48             // next open position in a
49
50          // as long as neither i1 nor i2 past the end, move
51          // the smaller element into a
52          while (iFirst < first.length
53             && iSecond < second.length)
54          {
55             if (first[iFirst] < second[iSecond])
56             {
57                a[j] = first[iFirst];
58                iFirst++;
59             }
60             else
61             {
62                a[j] = second[iSecond];
63                iSecond++;
64             }
65             j++;
66          }
67
68          // Note that only one of the two calls to arraycopy
69          // below is executed.
70
71          // Copy any remaining entries of the first array.
72          System.arraycopy(first,
73             iFirst, a, j, first.length - iFirst);
74
```

```
75              // Copy any remaining entries of the second half.
76              System.arraycopy(second,
77                  iSecond, a, j, second.length - iSecond);
78          }
79
80      private int[] a;
81  }
```

File MergeSortTest.java

```
1  /**
2      This program tests the merge sort algorithm by
3      sorting an array that is filled with random numbers.
4  */
5  public class MergeSortTest
6  {
7      public static void main(String[] args)
8      {
9          int[] a = ArrayUtil.randomIntArray(20, 100);
10         ArrayUtil.print(a);
11         MergeSorter sorter = new MergeSorter(a);
12         sorter.sort();
13         ArrayUtil.print(a);
14     }
15 }
```

18.5   Analyzing the Merge Sort Algorithm

The merge sort algorithm looks a lot more complicated than the selection sort algorithm, and it appears that it may well take much longer to carry out these repeated subdivisions. However, the timing results for merge sort look much better than those for selection sort:

n	Merge sort (milliseconds)	Selection sort (milliseconds)
10,000	110	3,460
20,000	160	13,240
30,000	220	28,290
40,000	280	51,520
50,000	360	82,670
60,000	450	121,820

Figure 2 shows a graph comparing both sets of performance data. That is a tremendous improvement. To understand why, let us estimate the number of array element visits that are required to sort an array with the merge sort algorithm. First, let us tackle the merge process that happens after the first and second half have been sorted.

Figure 2

Merge Sort Timing (Rectangles) versus
Selection Sort (Circles)

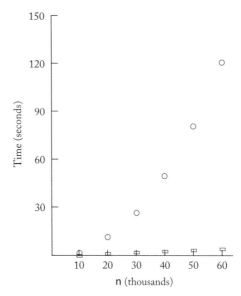

Each step in the merge process adds one more element to a. That element may come from first or second, and in most cases the elements from the two halves must be compared to see which one to take. Let us count that as 3 visits (one for a and one each for first and second) per element, or $3n$ visits total, where n denotes the length of a. Moreover, at the beginning, we had to copy from a to first and second, yielding another $2n$ visits, for a total of $5n$.

If we let $T(n)$ denote the number of visits required to sort a range of n elements through the merge sort process, then we obtain

$$T(n) = T\left(\frac{n}{2}\right) + T\left(\frac{n}{2}\right) + 5n$$

because sorting each half takes $T(n/2)$ visits. Actually, if n is not even, then we have one subarray of size $(n-1)/2$ and one of size $(n+1)/2$. Although it turns out that this detail does not affect the outcome of the computation, we will nevertheless assume for now that n is a power of 2, say $n = 2^m$. That way, all subarrays can be evenly divided into two parts.

Unfortunately, the formula

$$T(n) = 2T\left(\frac{n}{2}\right) + 5n$$

does not clearly tell us the relationship between n and $T(n)$. To understand the relationship, let us evaluate $T(n/2)$, using the same formula:

$$T\left(\frac{n}{2}\right) = 2T\left(\frac{n}{4}\right) + 5\frac{n}{2}$$

Therefore

$$T(n) = 2 \times 2T\left(\frac{n}{4}\right) + 5n + 5n$$

Let us do that again:

$$T\left(\frac{n}{4}\right) = 2T\left(\frac{n}{8}\right) + 5\frac{n}{4}$$

hence

$$T(n) \;=\; 2 \times 2 \times 2\,T\!\left(\frac{n}{8}\right) + 5n + 5n + 5n$$

This generalizes from 2, 4, 8, to arbitrary powers of 2:

$$T(n) \;=\; 2^{k} T\!\left(\frac{n}{2^{k}}\right) + 5nk$$

Recall that we assume that $n \;=\; 2^{m}$; hence, for $k \;=\; m$,

$$T(n) \;=\; 2^{m} T\!\left(\frac{n}{2^{m}}\right) + 5nk$$

$$= \; nT(1) + 5nm$$

$$= \; n + 5n\log_{2}(n)$$

Because $n \;=\; 2^{m}$, we have $m \;=\; \log_2(n)$.

To establish the growth order, we drop the lower-order term n and are left with $5n\log_2(n)$. We drop the constant factor 5. It is also customary to drop the base of the logarithm, because all logarithms are related by a constant factor. For example,

$$\log_2(x) \;=\; \log_{10}(x) \,/\, \log_{10}(2) \approx \log_{10}(x) \times 3.32193$$

> Merge sort is an $O(n \log (n))$ algorithm. The $n \log (n)$ function grows much more slowly than n^2.

Hence we say that merge sort is an $O(n \log(n))$ algorithm.

Is the $O(n \log(n))$ merge sort algorithm better than an $O(n^2)$ selection sort algorithm? You bet it is. Recall that it took $100^2 \;=\; 10{,}000$ times as long to sort a million records as it took to sort 10,000 records with the $O(n^2)$ algorithm. With the $O(n \log(n))$ algorithm, the ratio is

$$\frac{1{,}000{,}000 \,\log(1{,}000{,}000)}{10{,}000 \,\log(10{,}000)} \;=\; 100 \cdot \left(\frac{6}{4}\right) \;=\; 150$$

Suppose for the moment that merge sort takes the same time as selection sort to sort an array of 10,000 integers, that is, 3.5 seconds on the test machine. (Actually, it is much faster than that.) Then it would take about 3.5×150 seconds, or about 9 minutes, to sort a million integers. Contrast that with selection sort, which would take over 9 hours for the same task. As you can see, even if it takes you nine hours to learn about a better algorithm, that can be time well spent.

In this chapter we have barely begun to scratch the surface of this interesting topic. There are many sorting algorithms, some with even better performance than the merge sort algorithm, and the analysis of these algorithms can be quite challenging. If you are a computer science major, you will revisit these important issues in a later computer science class.

> The Arrays class implements a sorting method that you should use for your Java programs.

However, when you write Java programs, you don't have to implement your own sorting algorithm. The Arrays class contains static sort methods to sort arrays of integers and floating-point numbers. For example, you can sort an array of integers simply as

```
int[] a = . . .;
Arrays.sort(a);
```

That sort method uses the Quicksort algorithm—see Advanced Topic 18.1 for more information about that algorithm.

Random Fact   18.1

The First Programmer

Before pocket calculators and personal computers existed, navigators and engineers used mechanical adding machines, slide rules, and tables of logarithms and trigonometric functions to speed up computations. Unfortunately, the tables—whose values had to be computed by hand—were notoriously inaccurate. The mathematician Charles Babbage (1791–1871) had the insight that if a machine could be constructed that produced printed tables automatically, both calculation and typesetting errors could be avoided. Babbage set out to develop a machine for this purpose, which he called a *Difference Engine* because it used successive differences to compute polynomials. For example, consider the function $f(x) = x^3$. Write down the values for $f(1)$, $f(2)$, $f(3)$, and so on. Then take the *differences* between successive values:

```
1
        7
8
        19
27
        37
64
        61
125
        91
216
```

Repeat the process, taking the difference of successive values in the second column, and then repeat once again:

```
1
        7
8            12
        19        6
27           18
        37        6
64           24
        61        6
125          30
        91
216
```

Now the differences are constant. You can retrieve the function values by a pattern of additions—you need to know the values at the fringe of the pattern and the constant difference. This method was very attractive, because mechanical addition machines had been known for some time. They consisted of cog wheels, with ten cogs per wheel, to represent digits, and mechanisms to handle the carry from one digit to the next. Mechanical multiplication machines, on the other hand, were fragile and unreliable. Babbage built a successful prototype of the Difference Engine (see Figure 3) and, with his own money and government grants, proceeded to build the table-printing machine. However, because of funding problems and the difficulty of building the machine to the required precision, it was never completed.

While working on the Difference Engine, Babbage conceived of a much grander vision that he called the *Analytical Engine*. The Difference Engine was designed to carry out a limited set of computations—it was no smarter than a pocket calculator is today. But Babbage realized that such a machine could be made *programmable* by storing programs as well as data. The internal storage of the Analytical Engine was to consist of

Figure 3

Babbage's Difference Engine

▼ 1,000 registers of 50 decimal digits each. Programs and constants were to be stored on punched cards—a technique that was at that time commonly used on looms for weaving patterned fabrics.

▼ Ada Augusta, Countess of Lovelace (1815–1852), the only child of Lord Byron, was a friend and sponsor of Charles Babbage. Ada Lovelace was one of the first people to realize the potential of such a machine, not just for computing mathematical tables but

▼ for processing data that were not numbers. She is considered by many the world's first programmer. The Ada programming language, a language developed for use in U.S. Department of Defense projects (see Random Fact 10.1), was named in her honor.

▼ ## Advanced Topic   18.1

The Quicksort Algorithm

▼ Quicksort is a commonly used algorithm that has the advantage over merge sort that no temporary arrays are required to sort and merge the partial results.

▼ The quicksort algorithm, like merge sort, is based on the strategy of divide and conquer. To sort a range a[from] . . . a[to] of the array a, first rearrange the elements in the range so that no element in the range a[from] . . . a[p] is larger than any ele-

▼ ment in the range a[p + 1] . . . a[to]. This step is called *partitioning* the range.

For example, suppose we start with a range

| 5 | 3 | 2 | 6 | 4 | 1 | 3 | 7 |

▼ Here is a partitioning of the range. Note that the partitions aren't yet sorted.

| 3 | 3 | 2 | 1 | 4 | | 6 | 5 | 7 |

▼ You'll see later how to obtain such a partition. In the next step, sort each partition, by recursively applying the same algorithm on the two partitions. That sorts the entire range, because the largest element in the first partition is at most as large as the smallest

▼ element in the second partition.

| 1 | 2 | 3 | 3 | 4 | | 5 | 6 | 7 |

Quicksort is implemented recursively as follows:

```
public void sort(int from, int to)
{
   if (from >= to) return;
   int p = partition(from, to);
   sort(from, p);
   sort(p + 1, to);
}
```

▼ Let us return to the problem of partitioning a range. Pick an element from the range and call it the *pivot*. There are several variations of the quicksort algorithm. In the simplest one, we'll pick the first element of the range, a[from], as the pivot.

Figure 4

Partitioning a Range

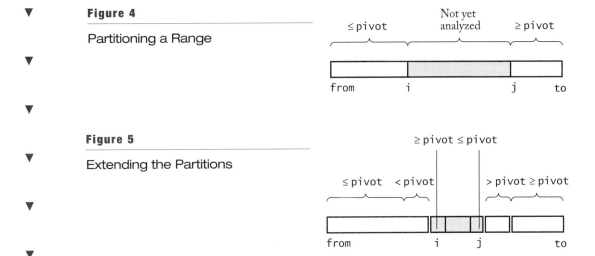

Figure 5

Extending the Partitions

Now form two regions a[from] . . . a[i], consisting of values at most as large as the pivot and a[j] . . . a[to], consisting of values at least as large as the pivot. The region a[i + 1] . . . a[j - 1] consists of values that haven't been analyzed yet. (See Figure 4.) At the beginning, both the left and right areas are empty; that is, i = from - 1 and j = to + 1.

Then keep incrementing i while a[i] < pivot and keep decrementing j while a[j] > pivot. Figure 5 shows i and j when that process stops.

Now swap the values in positions i and j, increasing both areas once more. Keep going while i < j. Here is the code for the partition method:

```
private int partition(int from, int to)
{
   int pivot = a[from];
   int i = from - 1;
   int j = to + 1;
   while (i < j)
   {
      i++; while (a[i] < pivot) i++;
      j--; while (a[j] > pivot) j--;
      if (i < j) swap(i, j);
   }
   return j;
}
```

On average, the quicksort algorithm is an $O(n \log(n))$ algorithm. Because it is simpler, it runs faster than merge sort in most cases. There is just one unfortunate aspect to the quicksort algorithm. Its *worst-case* runtime behavior is $O(n^2)$. Moreover, if the pivot element is chosen as the first element of the region, that worst-case behavior occurs when the input set is already sorted—a common situation in practice. By selecting the pivot element more cleverly, we can make it extremely unlikely for the worst-case behavior to occur. Such "tuned" quicksort algorithms are commonly used, because their performance

▼ is generally excellent. For example, as was mentioned, the sort method in the Arrays class uses a quicksort algorithm.

18.6 Searching

Suppose you need to find the telephone number of your friend. You look up his name in the telephone book, and naturally you can find it quickly, because the telephone book is sorted alphabetically. Quite possibly, you may never have thought how important it is that the telephone book is sorted. To see that, think of the following problem: Suppose you have a telephone number and you must know to what party it belongs. You could of course call that number, but suppose nobody picks up on the other end. You could look through the telephone book, a number at a time, until you find the number. That would obviously be a tremendous amount of work, and you would have to be desperate to attempt that.

> A linear search examines all values in an array until it finds a match or reaches the end.

This thought experiment shows the difference between a search through an unsorted data set and a search through a sorted data set. The following two sections will analyze the difference formally.

If you want to find a number in a sequence of values that occur in arbitrary order, there is nothing you can do to speed up the search. You must simply look through all elements until you have found a match or until you reach the end. This is called a *linear* or *sequential search*.

> A linear search locates a value in an array in $O(n)$ steps.

How long does a linear search take? If we assume that the element v is present in the array a, then the average search visits $n/2$ elements, where n is the length of the array. If it is not present, then all n elements must be inspected to verify the absence. Either way, a linear search is an $O(n)$ algorithm.

Here is a class that performs linear searches through an array a of integers. When searching for the value v, the search method returns the first index of the match, or −1 if v does not occur in a.

File LinearSearcher.java

```
1  /**
2      A class for executing linear searches through an array.
3  */
4  public class LinearSearcher
5  {
6      /**
7          Constructs the LinearSearcher.
8          @param anArray an array of integers
9      */
10     public LinearSearcher(int[] anArray)
11     {
12         a = anArray;
13     }
```

```
14
15     /**
16         Finds a value in an array, using the linear search algorithm.
17         @param v the value to search
18         @return the index at which the value occurs, or -1
19             if it does not occur in the array
20     */
21     public int search(int v)
22     {
23         for (int i = 0; i < a.length; i++)
24         {
25             if (a[i] == v)
26                 return i;
27         }
28         return -1;
29     }
30
31     private int[] a;
32 }
```

File LinearSearchTest.java

```
1  import javax.swing.JOptionPane;
2
3  /**
4      This program tests the linear search algorithm.
5  */
6  public class LinearSearchTest
7  {
8      public static void main(String[] args)
9      {
10         // construct random array
11
12         int[] a = ArrayUtil.randomIntArray(20, 100);
13         ArrayUtil.print(a);
14         LinearSearcher searcher = new LinearSearcher(a);
15
16         boolean done = false;
17         while (!done)
18         {
19             String input = JOptionPane.showInputDialog(
20                 "Enter number to search for, "
21                 + "Cancel to quit:");
22             if (input == null)
23                 done = true;
24             else
25             {
26                 int n = Integer.parseInt(input);
27                 int pos = searcher.search(n);
28                 System.out.println(
```

```
29                      "Found in position " + pos);
30            }
31         }
32         System.exit(0);
33      }
34 }
```

18.7   Binary Search

Now let us search an item in a data sequence that had been previously sorted. Of course, we could still do a linear search, but it turns out we can do much better than that.

Consider the following example: The data set is

a[0]	a[1]	a[2]	a[3]	a[4]	a[5]	a[6]	a[7]
14	43	76	100	115	290	400	511

We would like to see whether the value 123 is in the data set. Let's narrow our search by finding whether the value is in the first or second half of the array. The last point in the first half of the data set, a[3], is 100, which is smaller than the value we are looking for. Hence, we should look in the second half of the array for a match, that is, in the sequence

a[4]	a[5]	a[6]	a[7]
115	290	400	411

Now the last value of the first half of this sequence is 290; hence, the value must be located in the sequence

a[4]	a[5]
115	290

The last value of the first half of this very short sequence is 115, which is smaller than the value that we are searching, so we must look in the second half:

a[5]
290

> A binary search locates a value in a sorted array by determining whether the value occurs in the first or second half, then repeating the search in one of the halves.

It is trivial to see that we don't have a match, because 123 ≠ 290. If we wanted to insert 123 into the sequence, we would need to insert it just before a[5].

This search process is called a *binary search*, because we cut the size of the search in half in each step. That cutting in half works only because we know that the sequence of values is sorted.

The following class implements binary searches in a sorted array of integers. The search method returns the position of the match if the search succeeds, or −1 if v is not found in a:

File BinarySearcher.java

```
1  /**
2      A class for executing binary searches through an array.
3  */
```

```
 4  public class BinarySearcher
 5  {
 6      /**
 7          Constructs a BinarySearcher.
 8          @param anArray a sorted array of integers
 9      */
10      public BinarySearcher(int[] anArray)
11      {
12          a = anArray;
13      }
14
15      /**
16          Finds a value in a sorted array, using the binary
17          search algorithm.
18          @param v the value to search
19          @return the index at which the value occurs, or -1
20          if it does not occur in the array
21      */
22      public int search(int v)
23      {
24          int low = 0;
25          int high = a.length - 1;
26          while (low <= high)
27          {
28              int mid = (low + high) / 2;
29              int diff = a[mid] - v;
30
31              if (diff == 0) // a[mid] == v
32                  return mid;
33              else if (diff < 0) // a[mid] < v
34                  low = mid + 1;
35              else
36                  high = mid - 1;
37          }
38          return -1;
39      }
40
41      private int[] a;
42  }
```

Let us determine the number of visits of array elements required to carry out a search. We can use the same technique as in the analysis of merge sort. Since we look at the middle element, which counts as one comparison, and then search either the left or the right subarray, we have

$$T(n) \;=\; T\!\left(\frac{n}{2}\right) + 1$$

Using the same equation,

$$T\!\left(\frac{n}{2}\right) \;=\; T\!\left(\frac{n}{4}\right) + 1$$

By plugging this result into the original equation, we get

$$T(n) \;=\; T\!\left(\frac{n}{4}\right) + 2$$

That generalizes to

$$T(n) \;=\; T\!\left(\frac{n}{2^k}\right) + k$$

As in the analysis of merge sort, we make the simplifying assumption that n is a power of 2, $n \;=\; 2^m$, where $m \;=\; \log_2(n)$. Then we obtain

$$T(n) \;=\; 1 + \log_2(n)$$

Therefore, binary search is an $O(\log(n))$ algorithm.

> A binary search locates a value in an array in $O(\log(n))$ steps.

That result makes intuitive sense. Suppose that n is 100. Then after each search, the size of the search range is cut in half, to 50, 25, 12, 6, 3, and 1. After seven comparisons we are done. This agrees with our formula, since $\log_2(100) \approx 6.64386$, and indeed the next larger power of 2 is $2^7 \;=\; 128$.

Since a binary search is so much faster than a linear search, is it worthwhile to sort an array first and then use a binary search? It depends. If you search the array only once, then it is more efficient to pay for an $O(n)$ linear search than for an $O(n \log(n))$ sort and an $O(\log(n))$ binary search. But if you will be making many searches in the same array, then sorting it is definitely worthwhile.

The `Arrays` class contains a static `binarySearch` method that implements the binary search algorithm, but with a useful enhancement. If a value is not found in the array, then the returned value is not -1, but $-k - 1$, where k is the position before which the element should be inserted. For example,

```
int[] a = { 1, 4, 9 };
int v = 7;
int pos = Arrays.binarySearch(a, v);
    // returns -3; v should be inserted before position 2
```

18.8   Searching and Sorting Real Data

In this chapter we have studied how to search and sort arrays of integers. Of course, in real programming there is rarely a need to search through a collection of integers. However, it is easy to modify these techniques to search through real data.

The `Arrays` class contains methods for sorting and searching collections of objects. You can sort objects of any class that implements the `Comparable` interface. That interface has a single method:

```
public interface Comparable
{
    int compareTo(Object otherObject);
}
```

The call

```
a.compareTo(b)
```

must return a negative number if a should come before b, 0 if a and b are the same, and a positive number otherwise.

Several classes in the standard Java library, such as the `String` and `Date` classes, implement the `Comparable` interface.

You can implement the `Comparable` interface for your own classes as well. For example, to sort a collection of bank accounts, the `BankAccount` class would need to implement this interface and define a `compareTo` method:

```
public class BankAccount
{
   . . .
   public int compareTo(Object otherObject)
   {
      BankAccount other = (BankAccount)otherObject;
      if (balance < other.balance) return -1;
      if (balance == other.balance) return 0;
      return 1;
   }
   . . .
}
```

When you implement the `compareTo` method of the `Comparable` interface, you must make sure that the method defines a *total ordering relationship*, with the following three properties:

- *Antisymmetric:* $\text{sign}(x.\text{compareTo}(y)) = -\text{sign}(y.\text{compareTo}(x))$
- *Reflexive:* $x.\text{compareTo}(x) = 0$
- *Transitive:* If $x.\text{compareTo}(y) \leq 0$ and $y.\text{compareTo}(z) \leq 0$, then $x.\text{compareTo}(z) \leq 0$

> The `Arrays` class contains a `sort` method that can sort arrays of objects that implement the `Comparable` interface.

The `Arrays` class implements both sorting and binary search for arrays of objects that implement the `Comparable` interface. Thus, you can easily sort and search arrays of strings. If you are willing to implement the `Comparable` interface in your own classes, then you can also sort and search arrays of objects.

```
BankAccount[] accounts = . . .;
Arrays.sort(accounts);
```

> The `Arrays` class contains another `sort` method that requires a `Comparator` object. That method can sort arrays of arbitrary objects.

However, sometimes it is impossible for you to modify a class so that it implements the `Comparable` interface. If you don't own the class, or if you already implemented the `Comparable` interface but you want to sort the objects in a different way, then you need to use an alternate approach. Define a class that realizes the *strategy interface* `Comparator`.

```
public interface Comparator
{
   public int compare(
      Object firstObject, Object secondObject);
}
```

If comp is a comparator object, then the call

```
comp.compare(a, b)
```

must return a negative number if a should come before b, 0 if a and b are the same, and a positive number otherwise.

For example, here is a Comparator class for coins:

```
public class CoinComparator implements Comparator
{
   public int compare(
      Object firstObject, Object secondObject)
   {
      Coin first = (Coin)firstObject;
      Coin second = (Coin)secondObject;
      if (first.getValue() < second.getValue())
         return -1;
      if (first.getValue() == second.getValue())
         return 0;
      return 1;
   }
}
```

Then you can sort an array of coins like this:

```
Coin[] a = . . .;
Comparator comp = new CoinComparator();
Arrays.sort(a, comp);
```

> The Collections class contains sort methods that can sort array lists.

The Coin class does not have to implement the Comparable interface.

Finally, the Collections class contains static sort and binarySearch methods that work with ArrayList collections.

```
ArrayList coins = new ArrayList();
// add coins
. . .
Comparator comp = new CoinComparator();
Collections.sort(coins, comp);
```

This sort method uses the merge sort algorithm. The example at the end of this section shows a Purse class whose toString method sorts the coins in the purse by increasing value.

As a practical matter, you should use the sorting and searching methods in the Arrays and Collections classes and not those that you write yourself. The library algorithms have been fully debugged and optimized. Thus, the primary purpose of this chapter was not to teach you how to implement practical sorting and searching algorithms.

Instead, you have learned something more important, namely that different algorithms can vary widely in performance, and that it is worthwhile to learn more about the design and analysis of algorithms.

File PurseTest.java

```
1 import javax.swing.JOptionPane;
2
3 /**
4     This class tests the Purse class by prompting the
5     user to add coins into a purse and printing the
6     purse contents, sorted by coin value.
7 */
8 public class PurseTest
9 {
10     public static void main(String[] args)
11     {
12         double NICKEL_VALUE = 0.05;
13         double DIME_VALUE = 0.1;
14         double QUARTER_VALUE = 0.25;
15
16         Purse myPurse = new Purse();
17
18         boolean done = false;
19         while (!done)
20         {
21             String input = JOptionPane.showInputDialog(
22                     "Enter coin name or Cancel");
23             if (input == null)
24                 done = true;
25             else
26             {
27                 double value = 0;
28                 if (input.equals("nickel"))
29                     value = NICKEL_VALUE;
30                 else if (input.equals("dime"))
31                     value = DIME_VALUE;
32                 else if (input.equals("quarter"))
33                     value = QUARTER_VALUE;
34                 if (value != 0)
35                 {
36                     Coin c = new Coin(value, input);
37                     myPurse.add(c);
38                     System.out.println(
39                         "The contents of the purse is "
40                         + myPurse);
41                 }
42             }
43         }
```

```
44        System.exit(0);
45    }
46 }
```

CHAPTER SUMMARY

1. The selection sort algorithm sorts an array by repeatedly finding the smallest element of the unsorted tail region and moving it to the front.

2. Computer scientists use the big-Oh notation $f(n) = O(g(n))$ to express that the function f grows no faster than the function g.

3. Selection sort is an $O(n^2)$ algorithm. Doubling the data set means a fourfold increase in processing time.

4. The merge sort algorithm sorts an array by cutting the array in half, recursively sorting each half, and then merging the sorted halves.

5. Merge sort is an $O(n \log(n))$ algorithm. The $n \log(n)$ function grows much more slowly than n^2.

6. The `Arrays` class implements a sorting method that you should use for your Java programs.

7. A linear search examines all values in an array until it finds a match or reaches the end.

8. A linear search locates a value in an array in $O(n)$ steps.

9. A binary search locates a value in a sorted array by determining whether the value occurs in the first or second half, then repeating the search in one of the halves.

10. A binary search locates a value in an array in $O(\log(n))$ steps.

11. The `Arrays` class contains a `sort` method that can sort arrays of objects that implement the `Comparable` interface.

12. The `Arrays` class contains another `sort` method that requires a `Comparator` object. That method can sort arrays of arbitrary objects.

13. The `Collections` class contains `sort` methods that can sort array lists.

Further Reading

[1] Michael T. Goodrich and Roberto Tamassia: *Data Structures and Algorithms in Java*, John Wiley & Sons, 1998.

CLASSES, OBJECTS, AND METHODS INTRODUCED IN THIS CHAPTER

```
java.lang.Comparable
   compareTo
java.lang.System
```

```
    currentTimeMillis
java.util.Arrays
    binarySearch
    sort
java.util.Collections
    binarySearch
    sort
java.util.Comparator
    compare
```

REVIEW EXERCISES

Exercise R18.1. *Checking against off-by-1 errors.* When writing the selection sort algorithm of Section 18.1, a programmer must make the usual choices of < against <=, a.length against a.length - 1, and from against from + 1. This is a fertile ground for off-by-1 errors. Conduct code walkthroughs of the algorithm with arrays of length 0, 1, 2, and 3 and check carefully that all index values are correct.

Exercise R18.2. What is the difference between searching and sorting?

Exercise R18.3. For the following expressions, what is the order of the growth of each?

$$n^2 + 2n + 1$$
$$n^{10} + 9n^9 + 20n^8 + 145n^7$$
$$(n + 1)^4$$
$$(n^2 + n)^2$$
$$n + 0.001n^3$$
$$n^3 - 1000n^2 + 10^9$$
$$n + \log(n)$$
$$n^2 + n\log(n)$$
$$2^n + n^2$$
$$\frac{n^3 + 2n}{n^2 + 0.75}$$

Exercise R18.4. We determined that the actual number of visits in the selection sort algorithm is

$$T(n) = \tfrac{1}{2}n^2 + \tfrac{5}{2}n - 3$$

We then characterized this method as having $O(n^2)$ growth. Compute the actual ratios

$$T(2000)/T(1000)$$
$$T(4000)/T(1000)$$
$$T(10000)/T(1000)$$

and compare them with

$$f(2000)/f(1000)$$
$$f(4000)/f(1000)$$
$$f(10000)/f(1000)$$

where $f(n) = n^2$.

Exercise R18.5. Suppose algorithm A takes 5 seconds to handle a data set of 1000 records. If the algorithm A is an $O(n)$ algorithm, how long will it take to handle a data set of 2000 records? Of 10,000 records?

Exercise R18.6. Suppose an algorithm takes 5 seconds to handle a data set of 1,000 records. Fill in the following table, which shows the approximate growth of the execution times depending on the complexity of the algorithm.

	$O(n)$	$O(n^2)$	$O(n^3)$	$O(n \log n)$	$O(2^n)$
1000	5	5	5	5	5
2000					
3000		45			
10000					

For example, since $3000^2/1000^2 = 9$, the algorithm would take 9 times as long, or 45 seconds, to handle a data set of 3000 records.

Exercise R18.7. Sort the following growth rates from slowest growth to fastest growth.

$$O(n)$$
$$O(n^3)$$
$$O(n^n)$$
$$O(\log(n))$$
$$O(n^2 \log(n))$$
$$O(1)$$
$$O(n \log(n))$$
$$O(2^n)$$
$$O(\sqrt{n})$$
$$O(n\sqrt{n})$$
$$O(n^{\log(n)})$$

Exercise R18.8. What is the growth rate of the standard algorithm to find the minimum value of an array? Of finding both the minimum and the maximum?

Exercise R18.9. What is the growth rate of the following method?

```
public static int count(int[] a, int c)
{
```

```
        int i;
        int count = 0;

        for (i = 0; i < a.length; i++)
        {
            if (a[i] == c) count++;
        }
        return count;
    }
```

Exercise R18.10. Your task is to remove all duplicates from an array. For example, if the array has the values

4 7 11 4 9 5 11 7 3 5

then the array should be changed to

4 7 11 9 5 3

Here is a simple algorithm. Look at a[i]. Count how many times it occurs in a. If the count is larger than 1, remove it. What is the growth rate of the time required for this algorithm?

Exercise R18.11. Consider the following algorithm to remove all duplicates from an array. Sort the array. For each element in the array, look at its next neighbor to decide whether it is present more than once. If so, remove it. Is this a faster algorithm than the one in the preceding exercise?

Exercise R18.12. Develop a fast algorithm for removing duplicates from an array if the resulting array must have the same ordering as the original array.

Exercise R18.13. *Insertion sort.* Consider the following sorting algorithm. To sort a, make a second array b of the same size. Then insert elements from a into b, keeping b in sorted order. Whenever you insert an element a[i] into the sorted range b[0] . . . b[i - 1], compare all elements until you find an element b[j] > a[i]. Then move the subrange b[j] . . . b[i - 1] by one position and insert a[i] into position j.

Is this an efficient algorithm? Estimate the number of array element visits in the sorting process. Assume that on average half of the elements of b need to be moved to insert a new element.

Exercise R18.14. Consider the following speedup of the insertion sort algorithm of the preceding exercise. For each element, call the binary search method of Exercise P18.8 to determine where it needs to be inserted. Does this speedup have a significant impact on the efficiency of the algorithm?

PROGRAMMING EXERCISES

Exercise P18.1. Modify the selection sort algorithm to sort an array of integers in descending order.

Exercise P18.2. Modify the selection sort algorithm to sort an array of coins by their value.

Exercise P18.3. Write a program that generates the table of sample runs of the selection sort times automatically. The program should ask for the smallest and largest value of n and the number of measurements and then make all sample runs.

Exercise P18.4. Modify the merge sort algorithm to sort an array of strings in lexicographic order.

Exercise P18.5. Write a telephone lookup program. Read a data set of 1000 names and telephone numbers from a file that contains the numbers in random order. Handle lookups by name and also reverse lookups by phone number. Use a binary search for both lookups.

Exercise P18.6. Implement the insertion sort algorithm described in Exercise R18.13.

Exercise P18.7. Modify the `Purse` class at the end of Section 18.8 so that the `toString` method lists the coins with the most valuable ones first.

Exercise P18.8. Consider the binary search algorithm in Section 18.7. If no match is found, the `search` method returns −1. Modify the method so that if `a` is not found, the method returns $-k - 1$, where k is the position before which the element should be inserted.

Exercise P18.9. Use the modification of the binary search method of the preceding exercise to sort an array as described in Exercise R18.14. Implement this algorithm and measure its performance.

Exercise P18.10. Implement the `sort` method of the merge sort algorithm without recursion, where the length of the array is a power of 2. First merge adjacent regions of size 1, then adjacent regions of size 2, then adjacent regions of size 4, and so on.

Exercise P18.11. Implement the `sort` method of the merge sort algorithm without recursion, where the length of the array is an arbitrary number. Keep merging adjacent regions whose size is a power of 2, and pay special attention to the last area whose size is less.

Exercise P18.12. Give a *graphical animation* of selection sort as follows: Fill an array with a set of random numbers between 1 and 100. Draw each array element as a stick, as in Figure 6. Whenever the algorithm changes the array, display an option pane and wait for the user to click OK, then call the `repaint` method.

Exercise P18.13. Write a graphical animation of merge sort.

Exercise P18.14. Write a graphical animation of binary search. Highlight the currently inspected element and the current values of `from` and `to`.

Exercise P18.15. Supply a class `Person` that implements the `Comparable` interface. Compare persons by their names. Ask the user to input ten names and generate ten `Person` objects. Using the `compareTo` method, determine the first and last person among them and print them.

Exercise P18.16. Sort an array list of strings by increasing *length*. *Hint:* Supply a `Comparator`.

Figure 6

Graphical Animation

Exercise P18.17. Sort an array list of strings by increasing length, so that strings of the same length are sorted lexicographically. *Hint:* Supply a `Comparator`.

Exercise P18.18. Write a program that keeps an appointment book. Make a class `Appointment` that stores a description of the appointment, the appointment day, the starting time, and the ending time. Your program should keep the appointments in a sorted array list. Users can add appointments and print out all appointments for a given day. When a new appointment is added, use binary search to find where it should be inserted in the array list. Do not add it if it conflicts with another appointment.

An Introduction to Data Structures

Chapter 19

CHAPTER GOALS

To learn how to use linked lists provided in the standard library

▶ To be able to use iterators to traverse linked lists

▶ To understand the implementation of linked lists

▶ To distinguish between abstract and concrete data types

▶ To know the efficiency of fundamental operations of lists and arrays

▶ To become familiar with the stack and queue types

Up to this point, we used `ArrayList` objects as a "one size fits all" mechanism for collecting objects. However, computer scientists have developed many different data structures that have varying performance tradeoffs. In this chapter, you will learn about the linked list, a data structure lets you add and remove elements efficiently, without moving any existing elements. You will also learn about the distinction between concrete and abstract data types. An abstract type spells out what fundamental operations should be supported efficiently, but it leaves the implementation unspecified. The stack and queue types, introduced at the end of this chapter, are examples of abstract types.

19.1 Using Linked Lists

Imagine a program that maintains an array of employee objects, sorted by the last names of the employees. When a new employee is hired, an object needs to be inserted into the array. Unless the company happened to hire employees in dictionary order, the new object probably needs to be inserted somewhere near the middle of the array. Then all objects following the new hire must be moved toward the end.

Conversely, if an employee leaves the company, the object must be removed, and the hole in the sequence needs to be closed up by moving all employee objects that come after it. Moving a large number of values can involve a substantial amount of computer time. We would like to discover a method that minimizes this cost.

> A linked list consists of a number of links, each of which has a reference to the next link.

To minimize movement of values, let us change the structure of the storage. Rather than storing the object references in an array, let us break up the array into a sequence of *links*. Each link stores an element and a reference to the next link in the sequence (see Figure 1). Such a data structure is called a *linked list*.

> Adding and removing elements in the middle of a linked list is efficient.

When you insert a new element into a linked list, only the neighboring link references need to be updated. The same is true when you remove an element.

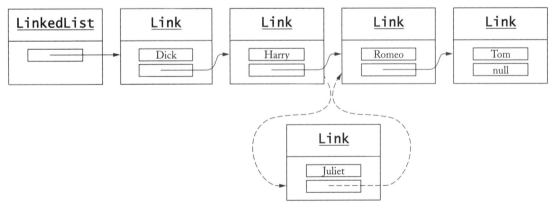

Figure 1

Inserting an Element Into a Linked List

> Visiting the elements of a linked list in sequential order is efficient, but random access is not.

What's the catch? Linked lists allow speedy insertion and removal, but *element access* is slow. To locate the fifth element, you have to traverse the first four. This is a problem if you need to access the elements in random order. But if you mostly visit all elements in sequence (for example, to display or print the elements), the lack of random access is not a problem. You use linked lists when you are concerned about the efficiency of inserting or removing elements and you don't need element access in random order.

The Java library provides a linked-list class. In this section you will learn how to use this class. In the next section you will peek under the hood and see how some of its key methods are implemented.

The `LinkedList` class in the `java.util` package implements linked lists. This linked list remembers both the first and the last link in the list. You have easy access to both ends of the list with the methods

```
void addFirst(Object obj)
void addLast(Object obj)
Object getFirst()
Object getLast()
Object removeFirst()
Object removeLast()
```

How do you add and remove elements in the middle of the list? The list will not give you references to the links. If you had direct access to them and somehow messed them up, you would break the linked list. As you will see in the next section, where you implement some of the linked list operations yourself, keeping all links intact is not trivial.

> You use a list iterator to access elements inside a linked list.

For your protection, the Java library supplies a `ListIterator` type. A list iterator encapsulates a position anywhere inside the linked list (see Figure 2).

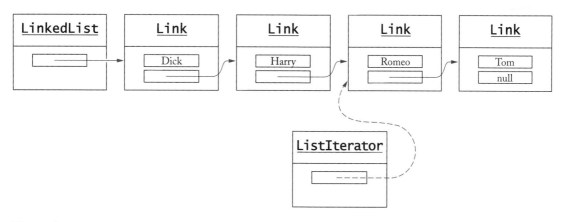

Figure 2

A List Iterator

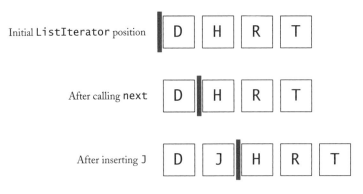

Initial ListIterator position

After calling next

After inserting J

Figure 3

A Conceptual View of the List Iterator

Conceptually, you should think of the iterator as pointing between two links, just as the cursor in a word processor points between two characters (see Figure 3). In the conceptual view, think of each link element as being like a letter in a word processor, and think of the iterator as being like the blinking cursor between letters.

You obtain a list iterator with the listIterator method of the LinkedList class:

```
LinkedList list = . . .;
ListIterator iterator = list.listIterator();
```

Initially, the iterator points before the first element. You can move the iterator position with the next method:

```
iterator.next();
```

The next method throws a NoSuchElementException if you are already past the end of the list. You should always call the method hasNext before calling next—it returns true if there is a next element.

```
if (iterator.hasNext())
    iterator.next();
```

The next method returns the object of the link that it is passing. Therefore, you can traverse all elements in a linked list with the following loop:

```
while (iterator.hasNext())
{
    Object obj = iterator.next();
    do something with obj
}
```

Actually, the links of the LinkedList class store two links: one to the next element and one to the previous one. Such a list is called a *doubly linked list*. You can use the previous and hasPrevious methods of the iterator class to move the list position backwards.

The add method adds an object after the iterator, and then moves the iterator position past the new element.

```
iterator.add("Juliet");
```

You can visualize insertion to be like typing text in a word processor. Each character is inserted after the cursor, and then the cursor moves past the inserted character (see Figure 3). Most people never pay much attention to this—you may want to try it out and watch carefully how your word processor inserts characters.

The remove method removes and returns the object that was returned by the last call to next or previous. For example, the following loop removes all objects that fulfill a certain condition:

```
while (iterator.hasNext())
{
    Object obj = iterator.next();
    if (obj fulfills condition)
        iterator.remove();
}
```

You have to be careful when calling remove. It can be called only once after calling next or previous, and you cannot call it immediately after a call to add. If you call the method improperly, it throws an IllegalStateException.

Here is a sample program that inserts elements into a list and then iterates through the list, adding and removing elements. Finally, the entire list is printed. The comments indicate the iterator position.

File ListTest.java

```
 1  import java.util.LinkedList;
 2  import java.util.ListIterator;
 3
 4  /**
 5      A program that demonstrates the LinkedList class.
 6  */
 7  public class ListTest
 8  {
 9      public static void main(String[] args)
10      {
11          LinkedList staff = new LinkedList();
12          staff.addLast("Dick");
13          staff.addLast("Harry");
14          staff.addLast("Romeo");
15          staff.addLast("Tom");
16
17          // | in the comments indicates the iterator position
18
19          ListIterator iterator =
20              staff.listIterator(); // |DHRT
21          iterator.next(); // D|HRT
22          iterator.next(); // DH|RT
```

```
23
24          //  add more elements after second element
25
26          iterator.add("Juliet"); // DHJ|RT
27          iterator.add("Nina"); // DHJN|RT
28
29          iterator.next(); // DHJNR|T
30
31          //  remove last traversed element
32
33          iterator.remove(); // DHJN|T
34
35          //  print all elements
36
37          iterator = staff.listIterator();
38          while (iterator.hasNext())
39              System.out.println(iterator.next());
40      }
41  }
```

19.2 Implementing Linked Lists

In the last section you saw how to use the linked list class that is supplied by the Java library. In this section, we will look at the implementation of a simplified version of this class. This shows you how the list operations manipulate the links as the list is modified.

To keep this sample code simple, we will not implement all methods of the linked-list class. We will implement only a singly linked list, and the list class will supply direct access only to the first list element, not the last one. The result will be a fully functional list class that shows how the links are updated in the add and remove operations and how the iterator traverses the list.

A Link object stores an object and a reference to the next link. Because the methods of both the linked list class and the iterator class have frequent access to the Link instance variables, we do not make the instance variables private. Instead, we make Link a private inner class of the LinkedList class. Since none of the list methods returns a Link object, it is safe to leave the instance variables public.

```
class LinkedList
{   . . .
    private class Link
    {
        public Object data;
        public Link next;
    }
}
```

The LinkedList class holds a reference first to the first link (or null, if the list is completely empty).

```
class LinkedList
{
   public LinkedList()
   {
      first = null;
   }

   public Object getFirst()
   {
      if (first == null)
         throw new NoSuchElementException();
      return first.data;
   }


   . . .
   private Link first;
}
```

Now let us turn to the `addFirst` method (see Figure 4). When a new link is added to the list, it becomes the head of the list, and the link that was the old list head becomes its next link:

```
class LinkedList
{  . . .
   public void addFirst(Object obj)
   {
      Link newLink = new Link();
      newLink.data = obj;
      newLink.next = first;
      first = newLink;
   }
   . . .
}
```

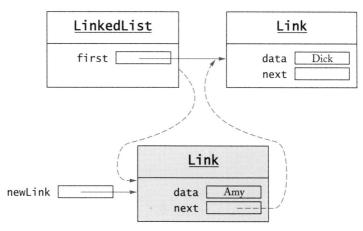

Figure 4

Adding a Link to the Head of a Linked List

Figure 5

Removing the First Link from a Linked List

Removing the first element of the list works as follows. The data of the first link are saved and later returned as the method result. The successor of the first link becomes the first link of the shorter list (see Figure 5). Then there are no further references to the old link, and the garbage collector will eventually recycle it.

```
class LinkedList
{  . . .
   public Object removeFirst()
   {
      if (first == null)
         throw new NoSuchElementException();
      Object obj = first.data;
      first = first.next;
      return obj;
   }
   . . .
}
```

Next, let us turn to the iterator class. The ListIterator interface in the standard library defines nine methods. We omit four of them (the methods that move the iterator backwards and the methods that report an integer index of the iterator).

The LinkedList class defines a private inner class LinkedListIterator, which implements the simplified ListIterator interface. Because LinkedListIterator is an inner class, it has access to the private features of the LinkedList class—in particular, the first field and the private Link class.

Note that clients of the LinkedList class don't actually know the name of the iterator class. They only know it is a class that implements the ListIterator interface.

```
class LinkedList
{
   . . .
   public ListIterator listIterator()
   {
      return new LinkedListIterator();
```

```
      }

      private class LinkedListIterator
      {
         public LinkedListIterator()
         {
            position = null;
            previous = null;
         }


         . . .
         private Link position;
         private Link previous;
      }
      . . .
   }
```

Each iterator object has a reference `position` to the last visited link. We also store a reference to the last link before that. We will need that reference to adjust the links properly in the `remove` operation.

The `next` method is simple. The `position` reference is advanced to `position.next`, and the old position is remembered in `previous`. There is a special case, however—if the iterator points before the first element of the list, then the old `position` is `null`, and `position` must be set to `first`.

```
   private class LinkedListIterator
      implements ListIterator
   {
      . . .
      public Object next()
      {
         if (!hasNext())
            throw new NoSuchElementException();
         previous = position; // remember for remove

         if (position == null)
            position = first;
         else
            position = position.next;

         return position.data;
      }
      . . .
   }
```

The `next` method is supposed to be called only when the iterator is not yet at the end of the list. The iterator is at the end if the list is empty (that is, `first == null`) or if there is no element after the current position (`position.next == null`).

```
   private class LinkedListIterator
      implements ListIterator
```

```
     {
        . . .
        public boolean hasNext()
        {
           if (position == null)
              return first != null;
           else
              return position.next != null;
        }
        . . .
     }
```

> Implementing operations that modify a linked list is challenging—you need to make sure that you update all link references correctly.

Removing the last visited link is more involved. If the element to be removed is the first element, we just call removeFirst. Otherwise, an element in the middle of the list must be removed, and the link preceding it needs to have its next reference updated to skip the removed element (see Figure 6). If the previous reference is null, then this call to remove does not immediately follow a call to next, and we throw an IllegalStateException.

According to the definition of the remove method, it is illegal to call remove twice in a row. Therefore, the remove method sets the previous reference to null.

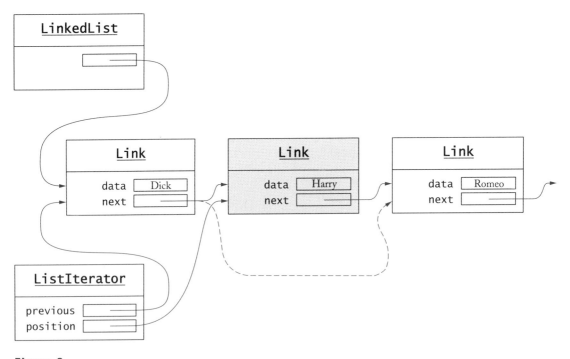

Figure 6

Removing a Link from the Middle of a Linked List

```
private class LinkedListIterator
   implements ListIterator
{  . . .
   public void remove()
   {
      if (position == first)
      {
         removeFirst();
         position = first;
      }
      else
      {
         if (previous == null)
            throw new IllegalStateException();
         previous.next = position.next;
         position = previous;
      }
      previous = null;
   }
   . . .
}
```

The set method changes the data stored in the previously visited element. Its implementation is straightforward because our linked lists can be traversed in only one direction. The linked-list implementation of the standard library must keep track of whether the last iterator movement was forward or backward. For that reason, the standard library forbids a call to the set method following an add or remove method. We do not enforce that restriction.

```
public void set(Object obj)
{
   if (position == null)
      throw new NoSuchElementException();
   position.data = obj;
}
```

Finally, the most complex operation is the addition of a link. You insert the new link after the current position, and set the successor of the new link to the successor of the current position (see Figure 7).

```
private class LinkedListIterator
   implements ListIterator
{  . . .
   public void add(Object obj)
   {
      if (position == null)
      {
         addFirst(obj);
         position = first;
      }
      else
```

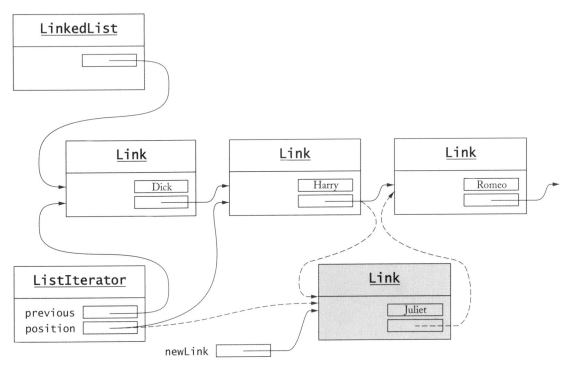

Figure 7

Adding a Link to the Middle of a Linked List

```
      {
         Link newLink = new Link();
         newLink.data = obj;
         newLink.next = position.next;
         position.next = newLink;
         position = newLink;
      }
      previous = null;
   }
   . . .
}
```

At the end of this section is the complete implementation of our LinkedList class. You can test it with the test program of the preceding section.

You now know how to use the LinkedList class in the Java library, and you have had a peek "under the hood" to see how linked lists are implemented.

File LinkedList.java

```
1  import java.util.NoSuchElementException;
2
3  /**
```

```
 4       A linked list is a sequence of links with efficient
 5       element insertion and removal. This class
 6       contains a subset of the methods of the standard
 7       java.util.LinkedList class.
 8  */
 9  public class LinkedList
10  {
11      /**
12          Constructs an empty linked list.
13      */
14      public LinkedList()
15      {
16          first = null;
17      }
18
19      /**
20          Returns the first element in the linked list.
21          @return  the first element in the linked list
22      */
23      public Object getFirst()
24      {
25          if (first == null)
26              throw new NoSuchElementException();
27          return first.data;
28      }
29
30      /**
31          Removes the first element in the linked list.
32          @return  the removed element
33      */
34      public Object removeFirst()
35      {
36          if (first == null)
37              throw new NoSuchElementException();
38          Object obj = first.data;
39          first = first.next;
40          return obj;
41      }
42
43      /**
44          Adds an element to the front of the linked list.
45          @param obj  the object to add
46      */
47      public void addFirst(Object obj)
48      {
49          Link newLink = new Link();
50          newLink.data = obj;
51          newLink.next = first;
52          first = newLink;
53      }
```

```
54
55      /**
56          Returns an iterator for iterating through this list.
57          @return  an iterator for iterating through this list
58      */
59      public ListIterator listIterator()
60      {
61          return new LinkedListIterator();
62      }
63
64      private Link first;
65
66      private class Link
67      {
68          public Object data;
69          public Link next;
70      }
71
72      private class LinkedListIterator
73          implements ListIterator
74      {
75          /**
76              Constructs an iterator that points to the front
77              of the linked list.
78          */
79          public LinkedListIterator()
80          {
81              position = null;
82              previous = null;
83          }
84
85          /**
86              Moves the iterator past the next element.
87              @return the traversed element
88          */
89          public Object next()
90          {
91              if (!hasNext())
92                  throw new NoSuchElementException();
93              previous = position; // remember for remove
94
95              if (position == null)
96                  position = first;
97              else
98                  position = position.next;
99
100             return position.data;
101         }
102
103         /**
```

```
104              Tests whether there is an element after the iterator
105              position.
106              @return true if there is an element after the iterator
107              position
108        */
109        public boolean hasNext()
110        {
111            if (position == null)
112                return first != null;
113            else
114                return position.next != null;
115        }
116
117        /**
118            Adds an element before the iterator position
119            and moves the iterator past the inserted element.
120            @param obj the object to add
121        */
122        public void add(Object obj)
123        {
124            if (position == null)
125            {
126                addFirst(obj);
127                position = first;
128            }
129            else
130            {
131                Link newLink = new Link();
132                newLink.data = obj;
133                newLink.next = position.next;
134                position.next = newLink;
135                position = newLink;
136            }
137            previous = null;
138        }
139
140        /**
141            Removes the last traversed element. This method may
142            be called only after a call to the next() method.
143        */
144        public void remove()
145        {
146            if (position == first)
147            {
148                removeFirst();
149                position = first;
150            }
151            else
152            {
153                if (previous == null)
```

```
154                   throw new IllegalStateException();
155               previous.next = position.next;
156               position = previous;
157           }
158           previous = null;
159       }
160
161       /**
162           Sets the last traversed element to a different
163           value.
164           @param obj  the object to set
165       */
166       public void set(Object obj)
167       {
168           if (position == null)
169               throw new NoSuchElementException();
170           position.data = obj;
171       }
172
173       private Link position;
174       private Link previous;
175   }
176 }
```

File ListIterator.java

```
1  import java.util.NoSuchElementException;
2
3  /**
4      A list iterator allows access to a position in a linked list.
5      This interface contains a subset of the methods of the
6      standard java.util.ListIterator interface. The methods for
7      backward traversal are not included.
8  */
9  public interface ListIterator
10 {
11     /**
12         Moves the iterator past the next element.
13         @return  the traversed element
14     */
15     Object next();
16
17     /**
18         Tests whether there is an element after the iterator position.
19         @return  true  if there is an element after the iterator
20         position
21     */
22     boolean hasNext();
23
24     /**
```

```
25              Adds an element before the iterator position
26              and moves the iterator past the inserted element.
27              @param obj  the object to add
28         */
29         void add(Object obj);
30
31         /**
32              Removes the last traversed element. This method may
33              be called only after a call to the next() method.
34         */
35         void remove();
36
37         /**
38              Sets the last traversed element to a different value.
39              @param obj  the object to set
40         */
41         void set(Object obj);
42  }
```

▼ AT **Advanced Topic** 19.1

Static Inner Classes

▼

You first saw the use of inner classes for event handlers. Inner classes are useful in that
context, because their methods have the privilege of accessing private data members of
▼ outer-class objects. The same is true for the LinkedListIterator inner class in the
sample code for this section. The iterator needs to access the first instance variable of
its linked list.
▼   However, the Link inner class has no need to access the outer class. In fact, it has no
methods. Thus, there is no need to store a reference to the outer list class with each Link
object. To suppress the outer-class reference, you can declare the inner class as static:

▼
```
class LinkedList
{
   . . .
▼   private static class Link
   {
      . . .
   }
▼ }
```

The purpose of the keyword static in this context is to indicate that the inner-class
▼ objects do not depend on the outer-class objects that generate them. In particular, the methods of a static inner class cannot access the outer-class instance variables. Declaring the
inner class static is efficient, because its objects do not store an outer-class reference.

▼

19.3 Abstract and Concrete Data Types

> An abstract data type defines the fundamental operations on the data but does not specify an implementation.

> An abstract list is an ordered sequence of items that can be traversed sequentially and that allows for insertion and removal of elements at any position.

> An abstract array is an ordered sequence of items with random access by specifying an integer index.

There are two ways of looking at a linked list. One way is to think of the concrete implementation of such a list, with its link nodes that have references to data items and to their successor nodes (see Figure 8).

On the other hand, you can think of the *abstract* concept of the linked list. In the abstract, a linked list is an ordered sequence of data items that can be traversed with an iterator (see Figure 9).

Similarly, there are two ways of looking at an array list. Of course, an array list has a concrete implementation: a partially filled array of object references (see Figure 10). But you don't usually think about the concrete implementation when using an array list. You take the abstract point of view. An array list is an ordered sequence of data items, each of which can be accessed by an integer index (see Figure 11).

The concrete implementations of a linked list and an array list are quite different. The abstractions, on the other hand, seem to be similar at first glance. To see the difference, consider the public interfaces, stripped down to their minimal essentials.

An array list allows *random access* to all elements. You specify an integer index, and you can get or set the corresponding element.

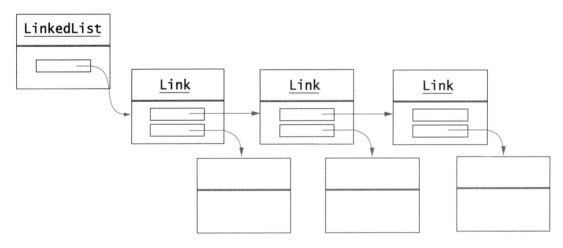

Figure 8

A Concrete View of a Linked List

Figure 9

An Abstract View of a Linked List

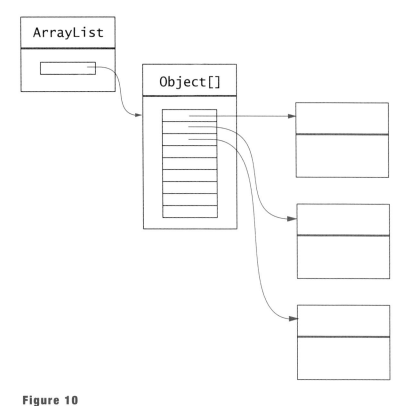

Figure 10

A Concrete View of an Array List

Figure 11

An Abstract View of an Array List

```
public class ArrayList
{
    public Object get(int index) { . . . }
    public void set(int index, Object value) { . . . }
    . . .
}
```

With a linked list, on the other hand, element access is a bit more complex. A linked list allows sequential access. You need to ask the linked list for an iterator. Using that iterator, you can easily traverse the list elements one at a time. But if you want to go to a particular element, say the 100th one, you first have to skip all elements before it.

```
public class LinkedList
{
    public ListIterator listIterator() { . . . }
    . . .
}

public interface ListIterator
{
    Object next();
    boolean hasNext();
    void add(Object value);
    void remove();
    void set(Object value);
    . . .
}
```

Here we show only the *fundamental* operations on array lists and linked lists. Other operations can be composed from these fundamental operations. For example, you can add or remove an element in an array list by moving all elements beyond the insertion or removal index, calling get and set multiple times.

Of course, the ArrayList class has methods to add and remove elements in the middle, even if they are slow. Conversely, the LinkedList class has get and set methods that let you access any element in the linked list, albeit very inefficiently, by performing repeated sequential accesses.

In fact, the term ArrayList signifies that its implementors wanted to combine the interfaces of an array and a list. Somewhat confusingly, both the ArrayList and the LinkedList class implement an interface called List that defines operations both for random access and for sequential access.

That terminology is not in common use outside the Java library. Instead, let us adopt a more traditional terminology. We will call the abstract types *array* and *list*. The Java library provides concrete implementations ArrayList and LinkedList for these abstract types. Other concrete implementations are possible in other libraries. In fact, Java arrays (Object[]) are another implementation of the abstract array type.

To understand an abstract data type completely, you need to know not just its fundamental operations but also their relative efficiency.

In a linked list, an element can be added or removed in constant time (assuming that the iterator is already in the right position). A fixed number of link references need to be modified to add or remove a link, regardless of the size of the list. Using the big-Oh notation, an operation that requires a bounded amount of time, regardless of the total number of elements in the structure, is denoted as $O(1)$. Random access in an array list also takes $O(1)$ time.

Adding or removing an arbitrary element in an array takes $O(n)$ time, where n is the size of the array list, because on average $n/2$ elements need to be moved. Random access in a linked list takes $O(n)$ time because on average $n/2$ elements need to be skipped.

Table 1 shows this information for arrays and lists.

Table 1

Efficiency of Operations for Arrays and Lists

Operation	Array	List
Random access	$O(1)$	$O(n)$
Linear traversal step	$O(1)$	$O(1)$
Add/remove an element	$O(n)$	$O(1)$

Why consider abstract types at all? If you implement a particular algorithm, you can tell what operations you need to carry out on the data structures that your algorithm manipulates. You can then determine the abstract type that supports those operations efficiently.

For example, suppose you have a sorted collection of items and you want to locate items using the binary search algorithm (see Section 18.7). That algorithm makes a random access to the middle of the collection, followed by other random accesses. Thus, fast random access is essential for the algorithm to work correctly. Once you know that an array supports fast random access and a linked list does not, you then look for concrete implementations of the abstract array type. You won't be fooled into using a `LinkedList`, even though the `LinkedList` class actually provides `get` and `set` methods.

In the next section and in Chapter 20, you will see additional examples of abstract data types.

19.4   Stacks and Queues

> A stack is a collection of items with "last in first out" retrieval.

In this section we will consider two common abstract data types that allow insertion and removal of items at the ends only, not in the middle. A *stack* lets you insert and remove elements at only one end, traditionally called the *top* of the stack. To visualize a stack, think of a stack of books (see Figure 12).

New items can be added to the top of the stack. Items are removed at the top of the stack as well. Therefore, they are removed in the order that is opposite from the order in

Figure 12

A Stack of Books

which they have been added, called *last in, first out* or *LIFO* order. For example, if you add items A, B, and C and then remove them, you obtain C, B, and A. Traditionally, the addition and removal operations are called push and pop.

There is a Stack class in the Java library that implements the abstract stack type and the push and pop operations. The following sample code shows how to use that class.

```
Stack s = new Stack();
s.push("A");
s.push("B");
s.push("C");
// the following loop prints C, B, and A
while (s.size() > 0)
   System.out.println(s.pop());
```

The Stack class in the Java library uses an Object[] array to implement a stack. Exercise P19.8 shows how to use a linked list instead.

A *queue* is similar to a stack, except that you add items to one end of the queue (the *tail*) and remove them from the other end of the queue (the *head*). To visualize a queue, simply think of people lining up (see Figure 13). People join the tail of the queue and wait until they have reached the head of the queue. Queues store items in a *first in, first out* or *FIFO* fashion. Items are removed in the same order in which they have been added.

> A queue is a collection of items with "first in first out" retrieval.

There are many uses of queues in computer science. For example, the Java graphical user interface system keeps an event queue of all events, such as mouse and keyboard events. The events are inserted into the queue whenever the operating system notifies the application of the event. Another thread of control removes them from the queue and passes them to the appropriate

Figure 13

A Queue

event listeners. Another example is a print queue. A printer may be accessed by several applications, perhaps running on different computers. If each of the applications tried to access the printer at the same time, the printout would be garbled. Instead, each application places all bytes that need to be sent to the printer into a file and inserts that file into the print queue. When the printer is done printing one file, it retrieves the next one from the queue. Therefore, print jobs are printed using the "first in, first out" rule, which is a fair arrangement for users of the shared printer.

There is no implementation of a queue in the standard Java library; however, it is a simple matter to create your own.

```java
public class Queue
{
    /**
        Constructs an empty queue.
    */
    public Queue()
    {
        list = new LinkedList();
    }

    /**
        Adds an item to the tail of the queue.
        @param x  the item to add
    */
    public void add(Object x)
    {
        list.addLast(x);
    }

    /**
        Removes an item from the head of the queue.
        @return  the removed item
    */
    public Object remove()
    {
        return list.removeFirst();
    }

    /**
        Gets the number of items in the queue.
        @return  the size
    */
    int size()
    {
        return list.size();
    }

    private LinkedList list;
}
```

You would definitely not want to use the **add** and `remove` methods of an array to implement a queue. Removing the first element of an array is inefficient—all other elements must be moved towards the beginning. However, Exercise P19.9 shows you how to implement a queue efficiently as a "circular" array, in which all elements stay at the position at which they were inserted, but the index values that denote the head and tail of the queue change when elements are added and removed.

In this chapter, you have seen the two most fundamental abstract data types, arrays and lists, and their concrete implementations. You also learned about the stack and queue types. In the next chapter, you will see additional data types that require more sophisticated implementation techniques.

 Random Fact   19.1

Standardization

You encounter the benefits of standardization every day. When you buy a light bulb, you can be assured that it fits the socket without having to measure the socket at home and the light bulb in the store. In fact, you may have experienced how painful the lack of standards can be if you have ever purchased a flashlight with nonstandard bulbs. Replacement bulbs for such a flashlight can be difficult and expensive to obtain.

Programmers have a similar desire for standardization. Consider the important goal of platform independence for Java programs. After you compile a Java program into class files, you can execute the class files on any computer that has a Java virtual machine. For this to work, the behavior of the virtual machine has to be strictly defined. If virtual machines don't all behave exactly the same way, then the slogan of "write once, run anywhere" turns into "write once, debug everywhere". In order for multiple implementors to create compatible virtual machines, the virtual machine needed to be *standardized*. That is, someone needed to create a definition of the virtual machine and its expected behavior.

Who creates standards? Some of the most successful standards have been created by volunteer groups such as the Internet Engineering Task Force (IETF) and the World Wide Web Consortium (W3C). You can find the Requests for Comment (RFC) that standardize many of the Internet protocols at the IETF site, http://www.ietf.org/rfc.html. For example, RFC 822 standardizes the format of email, and RFC 2616 defines the Hypertext Transmission Protocol (HTTP) that is used to serve web pages to browsers. The W3C standardizes the Hypertext Markup Language (HTML), the format for web pages—see http://www.w3c.org. These standards have been instrumental in the creation of the World Wide Web as an open platform that is not controlled by any one company.

Many programming languages, such as C++ and Scheme, have been standardized by independent standards organizations such as the American National Standards Institute (ANSI) and the International Organization for Standardization, called ISO for short (not an acronym; see http://www.iso.ch/iso/en/aboutiso/introduction/whatisISO.html). ANSI and ISO are associations of industry professionals who develop standards for everything from car tires and credit card shapes to programming languages.

▼ The process of standardizing the C++ language turned out to be very painstaking and time-consuming, and the standards organization followed a rigorous process to ensure fairness and to avoid being influenced by companies with vested interests.

▼ When a company invents a new technology, it has an interest in its invention becoming a standard, so that other vendors produce tools that work with the invention and thus increase its likelihood of success. On the other hand, by handing over the invention to a standards committee, especially one that insists on a fair process, the company may lose control over the standard. For that reason, Sun Microsystems, the inventor of Java, never agreed to have a third-party organization standardize the Java language. They run their own standardization process, involving other companies but refusing to relinquish control. Another unfortunate but common tactic is to create a weak standard. For example, Netscape and Microsoft chose the European Computer Manufacturers Association (ECMA) to standardize the JavaScript language (see Random Fact 11.1). ECMA was willing to settle for something less than truly useful, standardizing the behavior of the core language and just a few of its libraries. Since most useful JavaScript programs need to use more libraries than those defined in the standard, programmers still go through a lot of tedious trial and error to write JavaScript code that runs identically on Netscape's and Microsoft's browsers.

▼ Often, competing standards are developed by different coalitions of vendors. For example, at the time of this writing, hardware vendors are in disagreement whether to use the IEEE 1394 (also called "FireWire" or iLink) or High-Speed USB for connecting external devices to computers. As Grace Hopper, the famous computer science pioneer, observed: "The great thing about standards is that there are so many to choose from".

▼ Of course, many important pieces of technology aren't standardized at all. Consider the Windows operating system. Although Windows is often called a de-facto standard, it really is no standard at all. Nobody has ever attempted to define formally what the Windows operating system should do. The behavior changes at the whim of its vendor. That suits Microsoft just fine, because it makes it impossible for a third party to create its own version of Windows.

▼ As a computer professional, there will be many times in your career when you need to make a decision whether to support a particular standard. Consider a simple example. In this chapter, we use the LinkedList class from the standard Java library. However, many computer scientists dislike this class because the interface muddies the distinction between abstract lists and arrays, and the iterators are clumsy to use. Should you use the LinkedList class in your own code, or should you implement a better list? If you do the former, you have to deal with an implementation that is less than optimal. If you do the latter, other programmers may have a hard time understanding your code because they aren't familiar with your list class.

CHAPTER SUMMARY

1. A linked list consists of a number of links, each of which has a reference to the next link.

2. Adding and removing elements in the middle of a linked list is efficient.

3. Visiting the elements of a linked list in sequential order is efficient, but random access is not.

4. You use a list iterator to access elements inside a linked list.

5. Implementing operations that modify a linked list is challenging—you need to make sure that you update all link references correctly.

6. An abstract data type defines the fundamental operations on the data but does not specify an implementation.

7. An abstract list is an ordered sequence of items that can be traversed sequentially and that allows for insertion and removal of elements at any position.

8. An abstract array is an ordered sequence of items with random access by specifying an integer index.

9. A stack is a collection of items with "last in first out" retrieval.

10. A queue is a collection of items with "first in first out" retrieval.

CLASSES, OBJECTS, AND METHODS INTRODUCED IN THIS CHAPTER

```
java.util.AbstractList
    listIterator
java.util.LinkedList
    addFirst
    addLast
    getFirst
    getLast
    removeFirst
    removeLast
java.util.ListIterator
    add
    hasNext
    hasPrevious
    next
    previous
    remove
    set
```

REVIEW EXERCISES

Exercise R19.1. Explain what the following code prints. Draw pictures of the linked list after each step. Just draw the forward links, as in Figure 1.

```
LinkedList staff = new LinkedList();
staff.addFirst("Harry");
staff.addFirst("Dick");
staff.addFirst("Tom");
System.out.println(staff.removeFirst());
System.out.println(staff.removeFirst());
System.out.println(staff.removeFirst());
```

Exercise R19.2. Explain what the following code prints. Draw pictures of the linked list after each step. Just draw the forward links, as in Figure 1.

```
LinkedList staff = new LinkedList();
staff.addFirst("Harry");
staff.addFirst("Dick");
staff.addFirst("Tom");
System.out.println(staff.removeLast());
System.out.println(staff.removeFirst());
System.out.println(staff.removeLast());
```

Exercise P19.3. Explain what the following code prints. Draw pictures of the linked list after each step. Just draw the forward links, as in Figure 1.

```
LinkedList staff = new LinkedList();
staff.addFirst("Harry");
staff.addLast("Dick");
staff.addFirst("Tom");
System.out.println(staff.removeLast());
System.out.println(staff.removeFirst());
System.out.println(staff.removeLast());
```

Exercise R19.4. Explain what the following code prints. Draw pictures of the linked list and the iterator position after each step.

```
LinkedList staff = new LinkedList();
ListIterator iterator = staff.listIterator();
iterator.add("Tom");
iterator.add("Dick");
iterator.add("Harry");
iterator = staff.listIterator();
if (iterator.next().equals("Tom"))
    iterator.remove();
while (iterator.hasNext())
    System.out.println(iterator.next());
```

Exercise R19.5. Explain what the following code prints. Draw pictures of the linked list and the iterator position after each step.

```
LinkedList staff = new LinkedList();
ListIterator iterator = staff.listIterator();
iterator.add("Tom");
iterator.add("Dick");
iterator.add("Harry");
iterator = staff.listIterator();
iterator.next();
iterator.next();
iterator.add("Romeo");
iterator.next();
iterator.add("Juliet");
iterator = staff.listIterator();
iterator.next();
```

```
    iterator.remove();
    while (iterator.hasNext())
        System.out.println(iterator.next());
```

Exercise R19.6. The linked-list class in the Java library supports operations `addLast` and `removeLast`. To carry out these operations efficiently, the `LinkedList` class has an added reference `last` to the last node in the linked list. Draw a "before/after" diagram of the changes of the links in a linked list under the `addLast` and `removeLast` methods.

Exercise R19.7. The linked-list class in the Java library supports bidirectional iterators. To go backward efficiently, each `Link` has an added reference, `previous`, to the predecessor node in the linked list. Draw a "before/after" diagram of the changes of the links in a linked list under the `addFirst` and `removeFirst` methods that shows how the `previous` links need to be updated.

Exercise R19.8. What advantages do lists have over arrays? What disadvantages do they have?

Exercise R19.9. Suppose you needed to organize a collection of telephone numbers for a company division. There are currently about 6,000 employees, and you know that the phone switch can handle at most 10,000 phone numbers. You expect several hundred lookups against the collection every day. Would you use an array or a list to store the information?

Exercise R19.10. Suppose you needed to keep a collection of appointments. Would you use a list or an array of `Appointment` objects?

Exercise R19.11. Suppose you write a program that models a card deck. Cards are taken from the top of the deck and given out to players. As cards are returned to the deck, they are placed on the bottom of the deck. Would you store the cards in a stack or a queue?

Exercise R19.12. Suppose the strings "A" . . . "Z" are pushed onto a stack. Then they are popped off the stack and pushed onto a second stack. Finally, they are all popped off the second stack and printed. In which order are the strings printed?

PROGRAMMING EXERCISES

Exercise P19.1. Using just the public interface of the linked-list class, write a method

```
    public static void downsize(LinkedList staff)
```

that removes every other employee from a linked list.

Exercise P19.2. Using just the public interface of the linked-list class, write a method

```
    public static void reverse(LinkedList staff)
```

that reverses the entries in a linked list.

Exercise P19.3. Add a method `reverse()` to our implementation of the `LinkedList` class that reverses the links in a list. Implement this method by directly rerouting the links, not by using an iterator.

Exercise P19.4. Write a method `draw` to display a linked list graphically. Draw each element of the list as a box, and indicate the links with arrows.

Exercise P19.5. Add a method `size()` to our implementation of the `LinkedList` class that computes the number of elements in the list, by following links and counting the elements until the end of the list is reached.

Exercise P19.6. Add a `currentSize` field to our implementation of the `LinkedList` class. Modify the add and remove methods of both the linked list and the list iterator to update the `currentSize` field so that it always contains the correct size. Change the `size()` method of the preceding exercise so that it simply returns the value of this instance variable.

Exercise P19.7. Write a class `Polynomial` that stores a polynomial such as

$$p(x) = 5x^{10} + 9x^7 - x - 10$$

Store it as a linked list of terms. A term contains the coefficient and the power of x. For example, you would store $p(x)$ as

$(5, 10), (9, 7), (-1, 1), (-10, 0)$

Supply methods to add, multiply, and print polynomials. For example, the polynomial p can be constructed as

```
Polynomial p = new Polynomial();
p.addTerm(-10, 0);
p.addTerm(-1, 1);
p.addTerm(9, 7);
p.addTerm(5, 10);
```

Then compute $p(x) \times p(x)$.

```
Polynomial q = p.multiply(p);
q.print();
```

Exercise P19.8. Implement a `Stack` class by using a linked list to store the elements.

Exercise P19.9. Implement a queue as a *circular array* as follows: Use two index variables `head` and `tail` that contain the index of the next element to be removed and the next element to be added. After an element is removed or added, the index is incremented (see Figure 14).

Figure 14

Adding and Removing Queue Elements

Figure 15

A Queue Element Set That Wraps
Around the End of the Array

After a while, the `tail` element will reach the top of the array. Then it "wraps around" and starts again at 0—see Figure 15. For that reason, the array is called "circular".

```
public class CircularArrayQueue
{
    public CircularArrayQueue(int capacity) { . . . }
    public void add(Object x) { . . . }
    public Object remove() { . . . }
    public int getLength() { . . . }
    private int head;
    private int tail;
    private int length;
    private Object[] elements;
}
```

This implementation supplies a *bounded* queue—it can eventually fill up. See the next exercise on how to remove that limitation.

Exercise P19.10. The queue in the preceding exercise can fill up if more elements are added than the array can hold. Improve the implementation as follows. When the array fills up, allocate a larger array, copy the values to the larger array and assign it to the `elements` instance variable. *Hint:* You can't just copy the elements into the same position of the new array. Move the head element to position 0 instead.

Advanced Data Structures

To learn about the set and map data types

▶ To understand the implementation of hash tables

▶ To be able to program hash functions

▶ To learn about binary trees

▶ To be able to use tree sets and tree maps

In this chapter we study data structures that are more complex than arrays or lists. These data structures take control of organizing their elements, rather than keeping them in a fixed position. In return, they can offer better performance for adding, removing, and finding elements.

You will learn about the abstract set and map data types and the implementations that the standard library offers for these abstract types. You will see how two completely different implementations—hash tables and trees—can be used to implement these abstract types efficiently.

20.1 Sets

In the preceding chapter you encountered two important data structures: arrays and lists. Both have one characteristic in common: These data structures keep the elements in the same order in which you inserted them. However, in many applications, you don't really care about the order of the elements in a collection. For example, a server may keep a collection of objects representing available printers (see Figure 1). The order of the objects doesn't really matter.

> A set is an unordered collection of distinct elements. Elements can be added, located, and removed.

In mathematics, such an unordered collection is called a *set*. You have probably learned some set theory in a course in mathematics, and you may know that sets are a fundamental mathematical notion.

But what does that mean for data structures? If the data structure is no longer responsible for remembering the order of element insertion, can it give us better performance for some of its operations? It turns out that it can indeed, as you will see later in this chapter.

Figure 1

A Set of Printers

Let's list the fundamental operations on a set:

- Adding an element

- Removing an element

- Containment testing (does the set contain a given object?)

- Listing all elements (in arbitrary order)

> Sets don't have duplicates. Adding a duplicate of an element that is already present is silently ignored.

In mathematics, a set rejects duplicates. If an object is already in the set, an attempt to add it again is ignored. That's useful in many programming situations as well. For example, if we keep a set of available printers, each printer should occur at most once in the set. Thus, we will interpret the add and remove operations of sets just as we do in mathematics: Adding an element has no effect if the element is already in the set, and attempting to remove an element that isn't in the set is silently ignored.

Of course, we could use a linked list to implement a set. But adding, removing, and containment testing would be relatively slow, because they all have to do a linear search through the list. (Adding requires a search through the list to make sure that we don't add a duplicate.) As you will see later in this chapter, there are data structures that can handle these operations much more quickly.

> Both the HashSet and TreeSet classes realize the Set interface.

In fact, there are two different data structures for that purpose, called *hash tables* and *trees*. The standard Java library provides set implementations based on both data structures, called HashSet and TreeSet. Both of these data structures realize the Set interface (see Figure 2).

You will see later in this chapter when it is better to choose a hash set or a tree set. For now, let's look at an example where we choose a hash set. To keep the example simple, we'll just store strings, not Printer objects.

```
Set names = new HashSet();
```

Note that we store the reference to the HashSet object in a Set variable. After you construct the collection object, it no longer matters what kind of set implementation it is; only the interface is important.

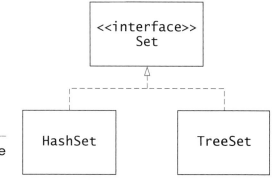

Figure 2

Set Classes and Interfaces in the Standard Library

Adding and removing set elements is straightforward:

```
names.add("Romeo");
names.remove("Juliet");
```

The `contains` method tests whether an element is contained in the set:

```
if (names.contains("Juliet")) . . .
```

> Use an iterator to list all elements in a set.

Finally, to list all elements in the set, you get an iterator. As with list iterators, you use the `next` and `hasNext` methods to step through the set.

```
Iterator iter = names.iterator();
while (iter.hasNext())
{
    String name = (String)iter.next();
    do something with name
}
```

> A set iterator does not visit the elements in the order in which you inserted them. The set implementation rearranges the elements so that it can locate them quickly.

> You cannot add an element to a set at an iterator position.

Note that the elements are *not* visited in the order in which you inserted them. Instead, they are visited in the order in which the `HashSet` keeps them for rapid execution of its methods.

There is an important difference between the `Iterator` that you obtain from a set and the `ListIterator` that a list yields. The `ListIterator` has an `add` method to add an element at the list iterator position. The `Iterator` interface has no such method. It makes no sense to add an element at a particular position in a set, because the set can order the elements any way it likes. Thus, you always add elements directly to a set, never to an iterator of the set.

However, you can remove a set element at an iterator position, just as you do with list iterators.

Also, the `Iterator` interface has no `previous` method to go backwards through the elements. Since the elements are not ordered, it is not meaningful to distinguish between "going forward" and "going backward".

The following test program lets you add and remove elements from a set. After each command, it prints out the current contents of the set. When you run this program, try adding strings that are already contained in the set and removing strings that aren't present in the set.

File SetTest.java

```
1  import java.util.HashSet;
2  import java.util.Iterator;
3  import java.util.Set;
4  import javax.swing.JOptionPane;
5
6  /**
7      This program demonstrates a set of strings. The user
8      can add and remove strings.
```

```
 9  */
10  public class SetTest
11  {
12     public static void main(String[] args)
13     {
14        Set names = new HashSet();
15
16        boolean done = false;
17        while (!done)
18        {
19           String input = JOptionPane.showInputDialog(
20              "Add name, Cancel when done");
21           if (input == null)
22              done = true;
23           else
24           {
25              names.add(input);
26              print(names);
27           }
28        }
29
30        done = false;
31        while (!done)
32        {
33           String input = JOptionPane.showInputDialog(
34              "Remove name, Cancel when done");
35           if (input == null)
36              done = true;
37           else
38           {
39              names.remove(input);
40              print(names);
41           }
42        }
43        System.exit(0);
44     }
45
46     /**
47        Prints the contents of a set.
48        @param s a set
49     */
50     private static void print(Set s)
51     {
52        Iterator iter = s.iterator();
53        System.out.print("{ ");
54        while (iter.hasNext())
55        {
56           System.out.print(iter.next());
57           System.out.print(" ");
58        }
```

```
59          System.out.println("}");
60      }
61  }
```

▼

⚜ Quality Tip 20.1

Use Interface References to Manipulate Data Structures

It is considered good style to store a reference to a `HashSet` or `TreeSet` in a variable of type `Set`.

```
Set names = new HashSet();
```

That way, you have to change only one line if you decide to use a `TreeSet` instead.

Also, methods that operate on sets should specify parameters of type `Set`:

```
public static void print(Set s)
```

Then the method can be used for all set implementations.

In theory, we should make the same recommendation for linked lists, namely to save `LinkedList` references in variables of type `List`. However, in the Java library, the `List` interface is common to both the `ArrayList` and the `LinkedList` class. In particular, it has `get` and `set` methods for random access, even though these methods are very inefficient for linked lists. You can't write efficient code if you don't know whether random access is efficient or not. This is plainly a serious design error in the standard library, and I cannot recommend using the `List` interface for that reason. (To see just how embarrassing that error is, have a look at the source code for the `binarySearch` method of the `Collections` class. That method takes a `List` parameter, but binary search makes no sense for a linked list. The code then clumsily tries to discover whether the list is a linked list, and then switches to a linear search!)

The `Set` interface and the `Map` interface, which you will see in the next section, are well-designed, and you should use them.

20.2 Maps

> A map keeps associations between key and value objects.

A map is a data type that keeps associations between *keys and values*. Figure 3 gives a typical example: a map that associates names with colors. This map might describe the favorite colors of various people.

Mathematically speaking, a map is a function from one set, the *key set*, to another set, the *value set*. Every key in the map has a unique value, but a value may be associated with several keys.

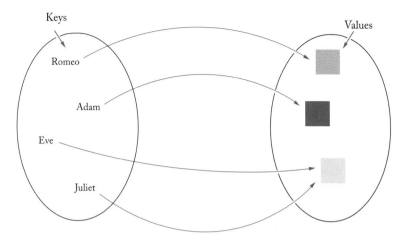

Figure 3

A Map

Both the HashMap and TreeMap classes realize the Map interface.

Just as there are two kinds of set implementations, the Java library has two implementations for maps: HashMap and TreeMap. Both of them realize the Map interface (see Figure 4).

After constructing a HashMap or TreeMap, you should store the reference to the map object in a Map reference:

```
Map favoriteColors = new HashMap();
```

Use the put method to add an association:

```
favoriteColors.put("Juliet", Color.pink);
```

You can change the value of an existing association, simply by calling put again:

```
favoriteColors.put("Juliet", Color.red);
```

The get method returns the value associated with a key.

```
Color julietsFavoriteColor =
    favoriteColors.get("Juliet");
```

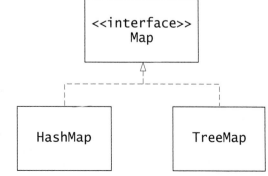

Figure 4

Map Classes and Interfaces in the Standard Library

If you ask for a key that isn't associated with any values, then the get method returns null. To remove a key and its associated value, use the remove method:

```
favoriteColors.remove("Juliet");
```

> To find all keys and values in a map, iterate through the key set and find the values that correspond to the keys.

Sometimes you want to enumerate all keys in a map. The keySet method yields the set of keys. You can then ask the key set for an iterator and get all keys. From each key, you can find the associated value with the get method. Thus, the following instructions print all key/value pairs in a map m:

```
Set keySet = m.keySet();
Iterator iter = keySet.iterator();
while (iter.hasNext())
{
   Object key = iter.next();
   Object value = m.get(key);
   System.out.println(key + "->" + value);
}
```

The sample program at the end of this section shows a map in action.

File MapTest.java

```
1  import java.awt.Color;
2  import java.util.HashMap;
3  import java.util.Iterator;
4  import java.util.Map;
5  import java.util.Set;
6
7  /**
8      This program tests a map that maps names to colors.
9  */
10 public class MapTest
11 {
12    public static void main(String[] args)
13    {
14
15       Map favoriteColors = new HashMap();
16       favoriteColors.put("Juliet", Color.pink);
17       favoriteColors.put("Romeo", Color.green);
18       favoriteColors.put("Adam", Color.blue);
19       favoriteColors.put("Eve", Color.pink);
20       print(favoriteColors);
21    }
22
23    /**
24        Prints the contents of a map.
25        @param m a map
26    */
27    private static void print(Map m)
28    {
29       Set keySet = m.keySet();
```

```
30          Iterator iter = keySet.iterator();
31          while (iter.hasNext())
32          {
33             Object key = iter.next();
34             Object value = m.get(key);
35             System.out.println(key + "->" + value);
36          }
37       }
38 }
```

20.3   Hash Tables

In this section, you will see how the technique of *hashing* can be used to find elements in a data structure quickly, without making a linear search through all elements. Hashing gives rise to the *hash table*, which can be used to implement sets and maps.

> A hash function computes an integer value from an object.

A *hash function* is a function that computes an integer value, the *hash code*, from an object, in such a way that different objects are likely to yield different hash codes. The `Object` class has a `hashCode` method that other classes need to redefine. The call

```
int h = x.hashCode();
```

computes the hash code of the object x.

> A good hash function minimizes *collisions*, identical hash codes for different objects.

It is possible that two or more distinct objects have the same hash code. That is called a *collision*. A good hash function minimizes collisions. For example, the String class defines a hash function for strings that does a good job of producing different integer values for different strings. Table 1 shows some examples of strings and their hash codes. You will see in Section 20.4 how these values are obtained.

String	Hash Code
"Adam"	2035631
"Eve"	70068
"Harry"	69496448
"Jim"	74478
"Joe"	74656
"Juliet"	−2065036585
"Katherine"	2079199209
"Sue"	83491

Table 1

Sample Strings and Their Hash Codes

Figure 5

Figure 5

A Simplistic Implementation of a
Hash Table

Section 20.4 explains how you should redefine the hashCode method for other classes.

A hash code is used as an array index into a hash table. In the simplest implementation of a hash table, you could make an array and insert each object at the location of its hash code (see Figure 5).

Then it is a very simple matter to find out whether an object is already present in the set or not. Compute its hash code and check whether the array position with that hash code is already occupied. This doesn't require a search through the entire array!

However, there are two problems with this simplistic approach. First, it is not possible to allocate an array that is large enough to hold all possible integer index positions. Therefore, we must pick an array of some reasonable size and then reduce the hash code to fall inside the array:

```
int h = x.hashCode();
if (h < 0) h = -h;
h = h % size;
```

> A hash table can be implemented as an array of *buckets,* sequences of links that hold elements with the same hash code.

Furthermore, it is possible that two different objects have the same hash code. After reducing the hash code modulo a smaller array size, it becomes even more likely that several objects collide and need to share a position in the array.

To store multiple objects in the same array position, we use (short, we hope) link sequences for the elements with the same hash code (see Figure 6). These link sequences are called *buckets.*

Now the algorithm for finding an object x in a hash table is quite simple.

1. Compute the hash code and reduce it modulo the table size. This gives an index h into the hash table.

2. Iterate through the elements of the bucket at position h. For each element of the bucket, check whether it is equal to x.

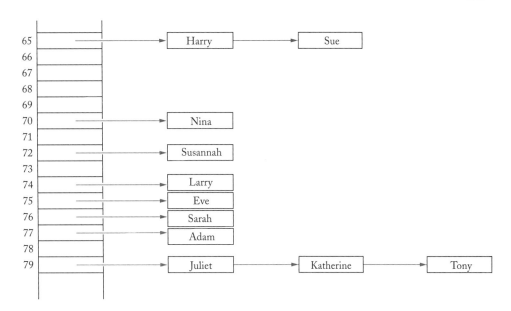

Figure 6

A Hash Table with Linked Lists to Store Elements with the Same Hash Code

3. If a match is found among the elements of that bucket, then x is in the set. Otherwise, it is not.

> If there are no or only a few collisions, then adding, locating, and removing hash table elements takes constant or $O(1)$ time.

In the best case, in which there are no collisions, all buckets either are empty or have a single element. Then checking for containment takes constant or $O(1)$ time.

More generally, for this algorithm to be effective, the bucket sizes must be small. If the table only has a few entries, then collisions are unavoidable, and each bucket will get quite full. Then the linear search through a bucket is time-consuming. In the worst case, where all elements end up in the same bucket, a hash table degenerates into a linked list!

> The table size should be a prime number, larger than the expected number of elements.

Therefore, it is recommended to make the table somewhat larger than the number of elements that you expect to insert. Then there is a good chance for avoiding collisions altogether. An excess capacity of about 30 percent is typical. According to some researchers, the hash table size should be chosen to be a prime number to minimize the number of collisions.

Adding an element is a simple extension of the algorithm for finding an object. First compute the hash code to locate the bucket in which the element should be inserted. Try finding the object in that bucket. If it is already present, do nothing. Otherwise, insert it.

Removing an element is equally simple. First compute the hash code to locate the bucket in which the element should be inserted. Try finding the object in that bucket. If it is present, remove it. Otherwise, do nothing.

As long as there are few collisions, an element can also be added or removed in constant or $O(1)$ time.

At the end of this section you will find the code for a simple implementation of a hash set. That implementation takes advantage of the `AbstractSet` class, which already implements most of the methods of the `Set` interface.

In this implementation you must specify the size of the hash table. In the standard library, you don't need to supply a table size. If the hash table gets too full, a new table of twice the size is created, and all elements are inserted into the new table.

File HashSet.java

```
1  import java.util.Iterator;
2  import java.util.AbstractSet;
3
4  /**
5     A hash set stores an unordered collection of objects, using
6     a hash table.
7  */
8  public class HashSet extends AbstractSet
9  {
10    /**
11       Constructs a hash table.
12       @param bucketsLength the length of the buckets array
13    */
14    public HashSet(int bucketsLength)
15    {
16       buckets = new Link[bucketsLength];
17       size = 0;
18    }
19
20    /**
21       Tests for set membership.
22       @param x an object
23       @return true if x is an element of this set
24    */
25    public boolean contains(Object x)
26    {
27       int h = x.hashCode();
28       if (h < 0) h = -h;
29       h = h % buckets.length;
30
31       Link current = buckets[h];
32       while (current != null)
33       {
34          if (current.data.equals(x)) return true;
35          current = current.next;
36       }
37       return false;
38    }
39
40    /**
41       Adds an element to this set.
```

```
42          @param x an object
43          @return true if x is a new object, false if x was
44             already in the set
45      */
46      public boolean add(Object x)
47      {
48          int h = x.hashCode();
49          if (h < 0) h = -h;
50          h = h % buckets.length;
51
52          Link current = buckets[h];
53          while (current != null)
54          {
55             if (current.data.equals(x))
56                return false; // already in the set
57             current = current.next;
58          }
59          Link newLink = new Link();
60          newLink.data = x;
61          newLink.next = buckets[h];
62          buckets[h] = newLink;
63          size++;
64          return true;
65      }
66
67      /**
68          Removes an object from this set.
69          @param x an object
70          @return true if x was removed from this set, false
71             if x was not an element of this set
72      */
73      public boolean remove(Object x)
74      {
75          int h = x.hashCode();
76          if (h < 0) h = -h;
77          h = h % buckets.length;
78
79          Link current = buckets[h];
80          Link previous = null;
81          while (current != null)
82          {
83             if (current.data.equals(x))
84             {
85                if (previous == null)
86                   buckets[h] = current.next;
87                else previous.next = current.next;
88                size--;
89                return true;
90             }
91             previous = current;
```

```
 92            current = current.next;
 93        }
 94        return false;
 95    }
 96
 97    /**
 98        Returns an iterator that traverses the elements of this set.
 99        @param a  hash set iterator
100    */
101    public Iterator iterator()
102    {
103        return new HashSetIterator();
104    }
105
106    /**
107        Gets the number of elements in this set.
108        @return  the number of elements
109    */
110    public int size()
111    {
112        return size;
113    }
114
115    private Link[] buckets;
116    private int size;
117
118    private class Link
119    {
120        public Object data;
121        public Link next;
122    }
123
124    private class HashSetIterator implements Iterator
125    {
126
127        /**
128            Constructs a hash set iterator that points to the
129            first element of the hash set.
130        */
131        public HashSetIterator()
132        {
133            bucket = 0;
134            previous = null;
135            previousBucket = buckets.length;
136
137            // set bucket to the index of the first nonempty bucket
138            while (bucket < buckets.length
139                    && buckets[bucket] == null)
140                bucket++;
141            if (bucket < buckets.length)
```

```
142            current = buckets[bucket];
143         else current = null;
144      }
145
146      public boolean hasNext()
147      {
148         return current != null;
149      }
150
151      public Object next()
152      {
153         Object r = current.data;
154
155         if (current.next == null) // move to next bucket
156         {
157            previousBucket = bucket;
158            bucket++;
159
160            while (bucket < buckets.length
161                  && buckets[bucket] == null)
162               bucket++;
163            if (bucket < buckets.length)
164               current = buckets[bucket];
165            else
166               current = null;
167         }
168         else // move to next element in bucket
169         {
170            previous = current;
171            current = current.next;
172         }
173
174         return r;
175      }
176
177      public void remove()
178      {
179         if (previous != null)
180            previous.next = previous.next.next;
181         else if (previousBucket < buckets.length)
182            buckets[previousBucket] = null;
183         else
184            throw new IllegalStateException();
185         previous = null;
186         previousBucket = buckets.length;
187      }
188
189      private int bucket;
190      private Link current;
191      private int previousBucket;
```

```
192          private Link previous;
193      }
194 }
```

File SetTest.java

```
 1 import java.util.Iterator;
 2 import java.util.Set;
 3
 4 /**
 5     This program tests the hash set class.
 6 */
 7 public class SetTest
 8 {
 9     public static void main(String[] args)
10     {
11         Set names = new HashSet(101); // 101 is a prime
12
13         names.add("Sue");
14         names.add("Harry");
15         names.add("Nina");
16         names.add("Susannah");
17         names.add("Larry");
18         names.add("Eve");
19         names.add("Sarah");
20         names.add("Adam");
21         names.add("Tony");
22         names.add("Katherine");
23         names.add("Juliet");
24         names.add("Romeo");
25         names.remove("Romeo");
26         names.remove("George");
27
28         Iterator iter = names.iterator();
29         while (iter.hasNext())
30             System.out.println(iter.next());
31     }
32 }
```

20.4   Computing Hash Codes

A hash function computes an integer hash code from an object, so that different objects are likely to have different hash codes. Let us first look at how you can compute a hash code from a string. Clearly, you need to combine the character values of the string to yield some integer. You could, for example, add up the character values:

```
int h = 0;
for (int i = 0; i < s.length(); i++)
    h = h + s.charAt(i);
```

However, that would not be a good idea. It doesn't scramble the character values enough. Strings that are permutations of another (such as "eat" and "tea") all have the same hash code.

Here is the method that the standard library uses to compute the hash code for a string.

```
final int HASH_MULTIPLIER = 31;
int h = 0;
for (int i = 0; i < s.length(); i++)
   h = HASH_MULTIPLIER * h + s.charAt(i);
```

For example, the hash code of "eat" is

```
31 * (31 * 'e' + 'a') + 't' = 100184
```

The hash code of "tea" is quite different, namely

```
31 * (31 * 't' + 'e') + 'a' = 114704
```

> Define hashCode methods for your own classes by combining the hash codes for the instance variables.

(Use the Unicode table from Appendix A6 to look up the character values: 'a' is 97, 'e' is 101, and 't' is 116.)

For your own classes, you should make up a hash code that combines the hash codes of the instance fields in a similar way. For example, let us define a hashCode method for the Coin class. There are two instance fields: the coin name and the coin value. First, compute their hash code. You know how to compute the hash code of a string. To compute the hash code of a floating-point number, first wrap the floating-point number into a Double object, and then compute its hash code.

```
class Coin
{
   public int hashCode()
   {
      int h1 = name.hashCode();
      int h2 = new Double(value).hashCode();
      . . .
   }
}
```

Then combine the two hash codes.

```
final int HASH_MULTIPLIER = 29;
int h = HASH_MULTIPLIER * h1 + h2;
return h;
```

Use a prime number as the hash multiplier—it scrambles the values better.

If you have more than two instance fields, then combine their hash codes as follows:

```
int h = HASH_MULTIPLIER * h1 + h2;
h = HASH_MULTIPLIER * h + h3;
h = HASH_MULTIPLIER * h + h4;
. . .
return h;
```

Your hashCode method must be compatible with the equals method.

If one of the instance fields is an integer, just use the field value as its hash code.

When you add objects of your class into a hash table, you need to double-check that it is *compatible* with the equals method of your class. Two objects that are equal must yield the same hash code:

```
If x.equals(y), then x.hashCode() == y.hashCode()
```

After all, if x and y are equal to another, then you don't want to insert both of them into a set—sets don't store duplicates. But if their hash codes are different, x and y may end up in different buckets, and the add method would never notice that they are actually duplicates.

Of course, the converse of the compatibility condition is generally not true. It is possible for two objects to have the same hash code without being equal.

For the Coin class, the compatibility condition holds. We define two coins to be equal to another if their names and values are equal. In that case, their hash codes will also be equal, because the hash code is computed from the hash codes of the name and value fields.

You get into trouble if your class defines an equals method but not a hashCode method. Suppose we forget to define a hashCode method for the Coin class. Then it inherits the hash code method from the Object superclass. That method computes a hash code from the *memory location* of the object. The effect is that any two objects are very likely to have a different hash code.

```
Coin coin1 = new Coin(0.25, "quarter");
Coin coin2 = new Coin(0.25, "quarter");
```

Now coin1.hashCode() is derived from the memory location of coin1, and coin2.hashCode() is derived from the memory location of coin2. Even though coin1.equals(coin2) is true, their hash codes differ.

However, if you define *neither* equals or hashCode, then there is no problem. The equals method of the Object class considers two objects equal only if their memory location is the same. That is, the Object class has compatible equals and hashCode methods. Of course, then the notion of equality is very restricted: Only identical objects are considered equal. That is not necessarily a bad notion of equality: If you want to collect a set of coins in a purse, you may not want to lump coins of equal value together.

Whenever you use a hash set, you need to make sure that an appropriate hash function exists for the type of the objects that you add to the set. Check the equals method of your class. It tells you when two objects are considered equal. There are two possibilities. Either equals hasn't been defined or it has been. If equals has not been defined, only identical objects are considered equal. In that case, don't define hash-Code either. However, if the equals method has been defined, look at its implementation. Typically, two objects are considered equal if some or all of the instance fields are equal. Sometimes, not all instance fields are used in the comparison. Two Student objects may be considered equal if their studentID fields are equal. Define the hash-Code method to combine the hash codes of the fields that are compared in the equals method.

When you use a HashMap, only the keys are hashed. They need compatible hashCode and equals methods. The values are never hashed or compared. The reason is simple—the map only needs to find, add, and remove keys quickly.

What can you do if the objects of your class have equals and hashCode methods defined that don't work for your situation, or if you don't want to bother defining an appropriate hashCode method? Maybe you can use a TreeSet or TreeMap instead. Trees are the subject of the next section.

File Coin.java

```
 1  /**
 2      A coin with a monetary value.
 3  */
 4  public class Coin
 5  {
 6      /**
 7          Constructs a coin.
 8          @param aValue the monetary value of the coin
 9          @param aName the name of the coin
10      */
11      public Coin(double aValue, String aName)
12      {
13          value = aValue;
14          name = aName;
15      }
16
17      /**
18          Gets the coin value.
19          @return the value
20      */
21      public double getValue()
22      {
23          return value;
24      }
25
26      /**
27          Gets the coin name.
28          @return the name
29      */
30      public String getName()
31      {
32          return name;
33      }
34
35      public boolean equals(Object otherObject)
36      {
37          if (otherObject == null) return false;
38          if (getClass() != otherObject.getClass())
39              return false;
```

```
40        Coin other = (Coin)otherObject;
41        return (
42           value == other.value
43           && name.equals(other.name));
44     }
45
46     public int hashCode()
47     {
48        int h1 = name.hashCode();
49        int h2 = new Double(value).hashCode();
50        final int HASH_MULTIPLIER = 29;
51        int h = HASH_MULTIPLIER * h1 + h2;
52        return h;
53     }
54
55     public String toString()
56     {
57        return
58           "Coin[value=" + value + ",name=" + name + "]";
59     }
60
61     private double value;
62     private String name;
63 }
```

File HashCodeTest.java

```
1  import java.util.HashSet;
2  import java.util.Iterator;
3  import java.util.Set;
4
5  /**
6     A program to test hash codes of coins.
7  */
8  public class HashCodeTest
9  {
10     public static void main(String[] args)
11     {
12        Coin coin1 = new Coin(0.25, "quarter");
13        Coin coin2 = new Coin(0.25, "quarter");
14        Coin coin3 = new Coin(0.05, "nickel");
15
16        System.out.println("hash code of coin1="
17           + coin1.hashCode());
18        System.out.println("hash code of coin2="
19           + coin2.hashCode());
20        System.out.println("hash code of coin3="
21           + coin3.hashCode());
22
23        Set coins = new HashSet();
```

```
24          coins.add(coin1);
25          coins.add(coin2);
26          coins.add(coin3);
27
28          Iterator iter = coins.iterator();
29          while (iter.hasNext())
30              System.out.println(iter.next());
31      }
32 }
```

⊗ Common Error   20.1

Forgetting to Define hashCode

When putting elements into a hash table, make sure that the hashCode method is defined. (The only exception is that you don't need to define hashCode if equals isn't defined either, and you consider any two objects of your class different, even if they have matching contents.)

If you forget to implement the hashCode method, then you inherit the hashCode method of the Object class. That method computes a hash code of the memory location of the object. For example, suppose that you do *not* define the hashCode method of the Coin class. Then the following code is likely to fail:

```
Coin coin1 = new Coin(0.25, "quarter");
Set coins = new HashSet();
coins.add(new Coin(0.25, "quarter"));
// the following comparison will probably fail if hashCode not defined
if (coins.contains(new Coin(0.25, "quarter"))
    System.out.println("The set contains a quarter.");
```

The two Coin objects are constructed at different memory locations, so the hashCode method of the Object class will probably compute different hash codes for them. (As always with hash codes, there is a small chance that the hash codes happen to collide.) Then the contains method will inspect the wrong bucket and never find the matching coin.

The remedy is to define a hashCode method in the Coin class.

20.5   Binary Search Trees

A set implementation is allowed to rearrange its elements in any way it chooses so that it can find elements quickly. Suppose a set implementation *sorts* its entries. Then it can use *binary search* to locate elements quickly. Binary search takes $O(\log(n))$ steps, where n is the size of the set. For example, binary search in an array of 1000 elements is able to locate an element in about 10 steps by cutting the size of the search interval in half in each step.

There is just one wrinkle with this idea. We can't use an array to store the elements of a set, because insertion and removal in an array is slow; an $O(n)$ operation.

> A binary tree consists of nodes, each of which has two child nodes.

In this section we will introduce the simplest of many *treelike* data structures that computer scientists have invented to overcome that problem. Binary search trees allow fast insertion and removal of elements, *and* they are specially designed for fast searching.

> All nodes in a binary search tree fulfill the property that the descendants to the left have smaller data values than the node data value, and the descendants to the right have larger data values.

A linked list is a one-dimensional data structure. Every link has a reference to the next link. You can imagine that all links are arranged in line. In contrast, a *binary tree* is made of nodes with *two* references, called the *left* and *right children*. You should visualize it as a tree, except that it is traditional to draw the tree upside down, like a family tree or hierarchy chart (see Figure 7). In a binary tree, every node has at most two children; hence the name *binary*.

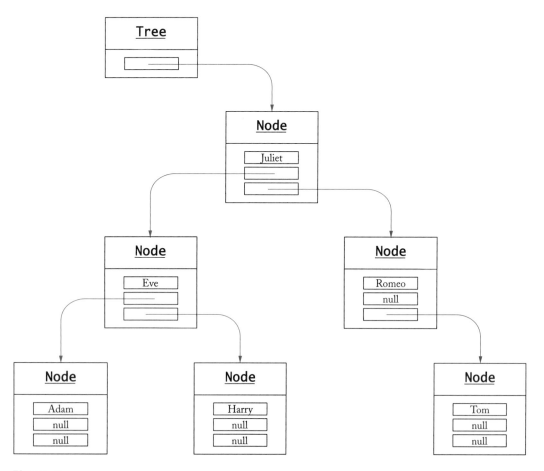

Figure 7

A Binary Search Tree

Finally, a *binary search tree* is carefully constructed to have the following important property:

- The data values of *all* descendants to the left of *any* node are less than the data value stored in that node, and *all* descendants to the right have greater data values.

The tree in Figure 7 has this property. To verify the binary search property, you must check each node. Consider the node "Juliet". All descendants to the left have data before "Juliet". All descendants on the right have data after "Juliet". Move on to "Eve". There is a single descendant to the left, with data "Adam" before "Eve", and a single descendant to the right, with data "Harry" after "Eve". Check the remaining nodes in the same way.

Figure 8 shows a binary tree that is not a binary search tree. Look carefully—the root node passes the test, but its two children do not.

Let us implement these tree classes. Just as you needed classes for lists and their links, you need one class for the tree, containing a reference to the *root node*, and a separate

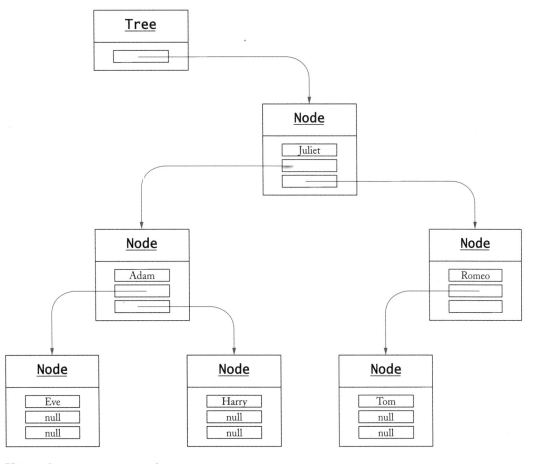

Figure 8

A Binary Tree That Is Not a Binary Search Tree

class for the nodes. Each node contains two references (to the left and right child nodes) and a data field. At the fringes of the tree, one or two of the child references are null. The data field has type Comparable, not Object, because you must be able to compare the values in a binary search tree in order to place them into the correct position.

```
class Tree
{
   public Tree() { . . . }
   public void insert(Comparable obj) { . . . }
   public void print() { . . . }

   private Node root;

   private class Node
   {
      public void insertNode(Node newNode) { . . . }
      public void printNodes() { . . . }

      public Comparable data;
      public Node left;
      public Node right;
   }
}
```

To insert data into the tree, use the following algorithm:

- If you encounter a non-null node pointer, look at its data value. If the data value of that node is larger than the one you want to insert, continue the process with the left subtree. If the existing data value is smaller, continue the process with the right subtree.

- If you encounter a null node pointer, replace it with the new node.

For example, consider the tree in Figure 9. We want to insert a new element Romeo into it.

Start with the root, Juliet. Romeo comes after Juliet, so you move to the right subtree. You encounter the node Tom. Romeo comes before Tom, so you move to the left subtree. But there is no left subtree. Hence, you insert a new Romeo node as the left child of Tom (see Figure 10).

You should convince yourself that the resulting tree is still a binary search tree. When Romeo is inserted, it must end up as a right descendant of Juliet—that is what the binary search tree condition means for the root node Juliet. The root node doesn't care where in the right subtree the new node ends up. Moving along to Tom, the right child of Juliet, all it cares about is that the new node Romeo ends up somewhere on its left. There is nothing to its left, so Romeo becomes the new left child, and the resulting tree is again a binary search tree.

Here is the code for the insert method of the Tree class:

```
class Tree
{
```

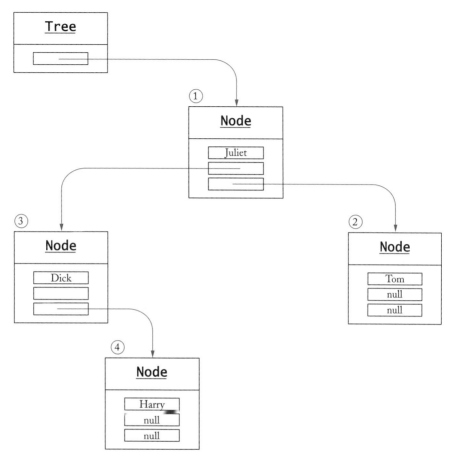

Figure 9

Binary Search Tree after Four Insertions

```
   . . .
   public void insert(Comparable obj)
   {
      Node newNode = new Node();
      newNode.data = obj;
      newNode.left = null;
      newNode.right = null;
      if (root == null) root = newNode;
      else root.insertNode(newNode);
   }
   . . .
}
```

If the tree is empty, simply set its root to the new node. Otherwise, you know that the new node must be inserted somewhere within the nodes, and you can ask the root node

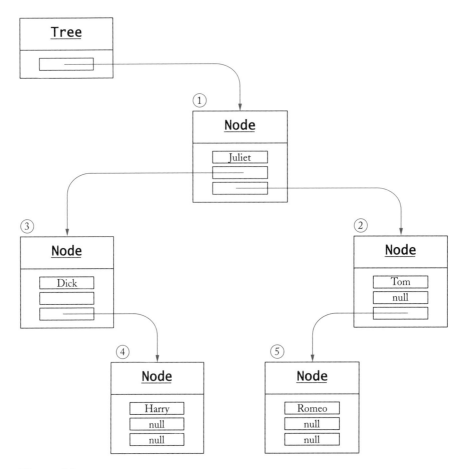

Figure 10

Binary Search Tree after Five Insertions

to perform the insertion. That node object calls the `insertNode` method of the `Node` class, which checks whether the new object is less than the object stored in the node. If so, the element is inserted in the left subtree; if not, it is inserted in the right subtree:

```
private class Node
{
    . . .
    public void insertNode(Node newNode)
    {
        if (newNode.data.compareTo(data) < 0)
        {
            if (left == null) left = newNode;
            else left.insertNode(newNode);
        }
        else
```

```
          {
             if (right == null) right = newNode;
             else right.insertNode(newNode);
          }
      }
      . . .
   }
```

Let us trace the calls to insertNode when inserting Romeo into the tree in Figure 9. The first call to insertNode is

```
root.insertNode(newNode)
```

Because root points to Juliet, you compare Juliet with Romeo and find that you must call

```
root.right.insertNode(newNode)
```

The node root.right is Tom. Compare the data values again (Tom vs. Romeo) and find that you must now move to the left. Since root.right.left is null, set root.right.left to newNode, and the insertion is complete (see Figure 10).

Now that the data are inserted in the tree, what can you do with them? It turns out to be surprisingly simple to print all elements in sorted order. You *know* that all data in the left subtree of any node must come before the node and before all data in the right subtree. That is, the following algorithm will print the elements in sorted order:

1. Print the left subtree.
2. Print the data.
3. Print the right subtree.

Let's try this out with the tree in Figure 10. The algorithm tells us to

1. Print the left subtree of Juliet; that is, Dick and children.
2. Print Juliet.
3. Print the right subtree of Juliet; that is, Tom and children.

How do you print the subtree starting at Dick?

1. Print the left subtree of Dick. There is nothing to print.
2. Print Dick.
3. Print the right subtree of Dick, that is, Harry.

That is, the left subtree of Juliet is printed as

```
Dick
Harry
```

The right subtree of Juliet is the subtree starting at Tom. How is it printed? Again, using the same algorithm:

1. Print the left subtree of Tom, that is, Romeo.
2. Print Tom.
3. Print the right subtree of Tom. There is nothing to print.

Thus, the right subtree of Juliet is printed as

```
Romeo
Tom
```

Now put it all together: the left subtree, Juliet, and the right subtree:

```
Dick
Harry
Juliet
Romeo
Tom
```

The tree is printed in sorted order.

Let us implement the print method. You need a worker method printNodes of the Node class:

```
private class Node
{
    . . .
    public void printNodes()
    {
        if (left != null)
            left.printNodes();
        System.out.println(data);

        if (right != null)
            right.printNodes();
    }
    . . .
}
```

To print the entire tree, start this recursive printing process at the root, with the following method of the Tree class.

```
class Tree
{
    . . .
    public void print()
    {
        if (root != null)
            root.printNodes();
    }
    . . .
}
```

At the end of this section you will find a complete program to insert data into a tree and to print them out in sorted order.

Unlike a linked list or an array, and like a hash table, a binary tree has no *insert positions.* You cannot select the position where you would like to insert an element into a binary search tree. The data structure is *self-organizing;* that is, each element finds its own place.

Deleting an element from a binary search tree is a little more complicated, because the children of the deleted node must be rearranged. We will leave that topic to a course on data structures. You can find the details in reference [1].

> If a binary search tree is approximately balanced, then adding an element takes $O(\log(n))$ time.

Now that you have implemented this complex data structure, you may well wonder whether it is any good. Like links in a list, nodes are allocated one at a time. No existing elements need to be moved when a new element is inserted in the tree; that is an advantage. How fast insertion is, however, depends on the shape of the tree. If the tree is *balanced*—that is, if each node has approximately as many children on the left as on the right—then insertion is very fast, because about half of the nodes are eliminated in each step. On the other hand, if the tree happens to be *unbalanced*, then insertion can be slow—perhaps as slow as insertion into a linked list. (See Figure 11.)

If new elements are fairly random, the resulting tree is likely to be well balanced. However, if the incoming elements happen to be already in sorted order, then the resulting tree is completely unbalanced. Each new element is inserted at the end, and the entire tree must be traversed every time to find that end!

Binary search trees work well for random data, but if you suspect that the data in your application might be sorted or have long runs of sorted data, you should not use a binary search tree. There are more sophisticated tree structures whose methods keep trees balanced at all times. In these tree structures, one can guarantee that finding, adding, and removing elements takes $O(\log(n))$ time. To learn more about those advanced data structures, you may want to enroll in a course about data structures.

The standard Java library uses *red-black trees*, a special form of balanced binary trees, to implement sets and maps. You will see in the next section what you need to do to use the `TreeSet` and `TreeMap` classes. For information on how to implement a red-black tree yourself, see reference [1].

File TreeTest.java

```
1  /**
2      This program tests the binary search tree class.
3  */
4  public class TreeTest
5  {
6     public static void main(String[] args)
7     {
8        Tree names = new Tree();
9        names.insert("Romeo");
10       names.insert("Juliet");
11       names.insert("Tom");
12       names.insert("Dick");
13       names.insert("Harry");
14
15       names.print();
16    }
17 }
```

File Tree.java

```
1  /**
2      This class implements a binary search tree whose
3      nodes hold objects that implement the Comparable
```

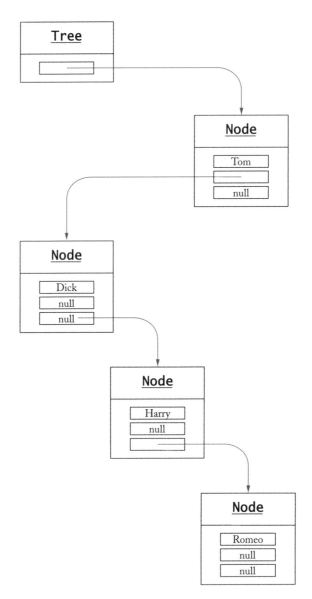

Figure 11

An Unbalanced Binary Search Tree

```
4      interface.
5  */
6  public class Tree
7  {
8      /**
```

```
 9          Constructs an empty tree.
10      */
11      public Tree()
12      {
13          root = null;
14      }
15
16      /**
17          Inserts a new node into the tree.
18          @param obj the object to insert
19      */
20      public void insert(Comparable obj)
21      {
22          Node newNode = new Node();
23          newNode.data = obj;
24          newNode.left = null;
25          newNode.right = null;
26          if (root == null) root = newNode;
27          else root.insertNode(newNode);
28      }
29
30      /**
31          Prints the contents of the tree in sorted order.
32      */
33      public void print()
34      {
35          if (root != null)
36              root.printNodes();
37      }
38
39      private Node root;
40
41      /**
42          A node of a tree stores a data item and references
43          to the child nodes on the left and on the right.
44      */
45      private class Node
46      {
47          /**
48              Inserts a new node as a descendant of this node.
49              @param newNode the node to insert
50          */
51          public void insertNode(Node newNode)
52          {
53              if (newNode.data.compareTo(data) < 0)
54              {
55                  if (left == null) left = newNode;
56                  else left.insertNode(newNode);
57              }
58              else
```

```
59              {
60                  if (right == null) right = newNode;
61                  else right.insertNode(newNode);
62              }
63          }
64
65          /**
66              Prints this node and all of its descendants
67              in sorted order.
68          */
69          public void printNodes()
70          {
71              if (left != null)
72                  left.printNodes();
73              System.out.println(data);
74              if (right != null)
75                  right.printNodes();
76          }
77
78          public Comparable data;
79          public Node left;
80          public Node right;
81      }
82  }
```

20.6 Using Tree Sets and Tree Maps

> The TreeSet class uses a form of balanced binary trees that guarantees that adding and removing an element takes $O(\log(n))$ time.

Both the HashSet and the TreeSet classes implement the Set interface. Thus, if you need a set of objects, you have a choice which one to use.

If you have a good hash function for your objects, then hashing is usually faster than tree-based algorithms. But the balanced trees used in the TreeSet class can *guarantee* reasonable performance, whereas the HashSet is entirely at the mercy of the hash function.

If you don't want to define a hash function, then a tree set is an attractive option. Tree sets have another advantage: The iterators visit elements in *sorted order* rather than the completely random order given by the hash codes.

> To use a tree set, the elements must be comparable.

To use a TreeSet, either your objects must belong to a class that realizes the Comparable interface, or you must supply a Comparator object. That is exactly the same requirement that you saw in Section 18.8 for using the sort and binarySearch methods in the standard library.

To use a TreeMap, the same requirement holds for the *keys*. There is no requirement for the values.

For example, the String class realizes the Comparable interface. The compareTo method compares strings in dictionary order. Thus, you can form tree sets of strings, and use strings as keys for tree maps.

If the class of the tree set elements doesn't implement the Comparable interface, you must supply a comparator.

If your class doesn't realize the `Comparable` interface, or the sort order of the `compareTo` method isn't the one you want, then you can define your own comparison by supplying a `Comparator` object to the `TreeSet` or `TreeMap` constructor. For example,

```
Comparator comp = new CoinComparator();
Set s = new TreeSet(comp);
```

Recall from Section 18.8 that a `Comparator` object compares two elements and returns a negative integer if the first is less than the second, zero if they are identical, and a positive value otherwise. The example program at the end of this section constructs a `TreeSet` of `Coin` objects, using the coin comparator of Section 18.8.

File TreeSetTest.java

```
1  import java.util.Comparator;
2  import java.util.Iterator;
3  import java.util.Set;
4  import java.util.TreeSet;
5
6  /**
7      A program to test hash codes of coins.
8  */
9  public class TreeSetTest
10 {
11     public static void main(String[] args)
12     {
13        Coin coin1 = new Coin(0.25, "quarter");
14        Coin coin2 = new Coin(0.25, "quarter");
15        Coin coin3 = new Coin(0.01, "penny");
16        Coin coin4 = new Coin(0.05, "nickel");
17
18        class CoinComparator implements Comparator
19        {
20           public int compare(
21              Object firstObject, Object secondObject)
22           {
23              Coin first = (Coin)firstObject;
24              Coin second = (Coin)secondObject;
25              if (first.getValue() < second.getValue())
26                 return -1;
27              if (first.getValue() == second.getValue())
28                 return 0;
29              return 1;
30           }
31        }
32
33        Comparator comp = new CoinComparator();
34        Set coins = new TreeSet(comp);
35        coins.add(coin1);
```

```
36          coins.add(coin2);
37          coins.add(coin3);
38          coins.add(coin4);
39
40          Iterator iter = coins.iterator();
41          while (iter.hasNext())
42              System.out.println(iter.next());
43      }
44  }
```

▼ Advanced Topic   20.1

Priority Queues

A priority queue is an abstract data type that has many practical applications. It has two fundamental operations:

- Add an element.

- Remove the element with the highest priority.

One example of a priority queue is an event queue. User interface events are inserted in random order. Whenever there is time to process an event, the one with the smallest time stamp is removed. Generally, the "highest" priority is often the one with the minimum value. We will follow that convention in this section.

To implement a priority queue, it is not necessary to sort the entire set of elements. In fact, the fastest implementations of priority queues do not keep the elements sorted but instead use a tree structure that is optimized for quickly finding the minimum and for efficiently reorganizing the elements when the minimum is removed. We refer you to reference [1] for more information on the implementation of priority queues.

The standard Java library does not supply any priority queue interfaces or implementations. But you can easily turn a `TreeSet` into a priority queue as follows:

```
public class TreePriorityQueue
{
    public TreePriorityQueue(Comparator comp)
    {
        tree = new TreeSet(comp);
    }

    public void add(Object x)
    {
        tree.add(x);
    }

    public int size()
    {
        return tree.size();
```

```
      }

      public Object removeFirst()
      {
         Iterator iter = tree.iterator();
         Object r = iter.next();
         iter.remove();
         return r;
      }

      private TreeSet tree;
}
```

Random Fact   20.1

Software Piracy

As you read this, you have written a few computer programs, and you have experienced firsthand how much effort it takes to write even the humblest of programs. Writing a real software product, such as a financial application or a computer game, takes a lot of time and money. Few people, and fewer companies, are going to spend that kind of time and money if they don't have a reasonable chance to make more money from their effort. (Actually, some companies give away their software in the hope that users will upgrade to more elaborate paid versions. Other companies give away the software that enables users to read and use files but sell the software needed to create those files. Finally, there are individuals who donate their time, out of enthusiasm, and produce programs that you can copy freely.)

When selling software, a company must rely on the honesty of its customers. It is an easy matter for an unscrupulous person to make copies of computer programs without paying for them. In most countries that is illegal. Most governments provide legal protection, such as copyright laws and patents, to encourage the development of new products. Countries that tolerate widespread piracy have found that they have an ample cheap supply of foreign software, but that no local manufacturer is stupid enough to design good software for their own citizens, such as word processors in the local script or financial programs adapted to the local tax laws.

When a mass market for software first appeared, vendors were enraged by the money they lost through piracy. They tried to fight back by various schemes to ensure that only the legitimate owner could use the software. Some manufacturers used *key disks:* floppy disks with a special pattern of holes burned in by a laser, which couldn't be copied. Others used *dongles:* devices that are attached between the computer and a printer port. Legitimate users hated these measures. They paid for the software, but they had to suffer through the inconvenience of inserting a key disk every time they started the software or having multiple dongles stick out from the back of their computer. In the United States, market pressures forced most vendors to give up on these copy protection schemes, but they are still commonplace in other parts of the world.

Because it is so easy and inexpensive to pirate software, and the chance of being found out is minimal, you have to make a moral choice for yourself. If a package that you would really like to have is too expensive for your budget, do you steal it, or do you stay honest and get by with a more affordable product?

Of course, piracy is not limited to software. The same issues arise for other digital products as well. You may have had the opportunity to obtain copies of songs or movies without payment. Or you may have been frustrated by a copy protection device on your music player that made it difficult for you to listen to songs that you paid for. Admittedly, it can be difficult to have a lot of sympathy for a musical ensemble whose publisher charges a lot of money for what seems to have been very little effort on their part, at least when compared to the effort that goes into designing and implementing a software package. Nevertheless, it seems only fair that artists and authors receive some compensation for their effort. How to pay artists, authors, and programmers fairly, without burdening honest customers, is an unsolved problem at the time of this writing, and many computer scientists are engaged in research in this area.

HOWTO 20.1

Choosing a Container

Suppose you need to store objects in a container. You have now seen a number of different data structures. This HOWTO reviews how to pick an appropriate container for your application.

Step 1 Determine how you access the elements

You store elements in a container so that you can later retrieve them. How do you want to access individual elements? You have several choices.

- It doesn't matter. Elements are always accessed "in bulk", by visiting all elements and doing something with them.

- Access by key. Elements are accessed by a special key. Example: Retrieve a bank account by the account number.

- Access by integer index. Elements have a position that is naturally an integer or a pair of integers. Example: A piece on a chess board is accessed by a row and column index.

If you need keyed access, use a map. If you need access by integer index, use an array list or array. For an index pair, use a two-dimensional array.

Step 2 Determine whether element order matters

When you retrieve elements from a container, do you care about the order in which they are retrieved? You have several choices.

▼

- It doesn't matter. As long as you get to visit all elements, you don't care in which order.

▼

- Elements must be sorted.

- Elements must be in the same order in which they were inserted.

▼

To keep elements sorted, use a `TreeSet`.
To keep elements in the order in which you inserted them, use a `LinkedList`, `ArrayList`, or array.

▼

Step 3   Determine which operations need to be fast

You have several choices.

▼

- It doesn't matter. You collect so few elements that you aren't concerned about speed.

▼

- Adding and removing elements must be fast.

- Finding elements must be fast.

▼

Linked lists let you add and remove elements efficiently, provided you are already near the location of the change. Changing either end of the linked list is always fast.
If you need to find an element quickly, use a set.

▼

At this point, you should have narrowed down your selection to a particular container. If you answered "It doesn't matter" for each of the choices, then just use an `ArrayList`. It's a simple container that you already know well.

▼

Step 4   For sets and maps, choose between hash tables and trees

If you decided that you need a set or map, you need to pick a particular implementation, either a hash table or a tree.
If your elements (or keys, in case of a map) are strings, use a hash table. It's more efficient.

▼

If your elements or keys belong to a type that someone else defined, check whether the class implements its own `hashCode` and `equals` methods. The inherited `hashCode` method of the `Object` class takes only the object's memory address into account, not its

▼

contents. If there is no satisfactory `hashCode` method, then you must use a tree.
If your elements or keys belong to your own class, you usually want to use hashing. Define a `hashCode` and compatible `equals` method.

▼

Step 5   If you use a tree, decide whether to supply a comparator

Look at the class of the elements or keys that the tree manages. Does that class implement the `Comparable` interface? If so, is the sort order given by the `compareTo` method the one you want. Then you don't need to do anything further.

▼

Otherwise, you need to define a class that implements the `Comparator` interface and define the `compare` method. Supply an object of the comparator class to the `TreeSet` or `TreeMap` constructor.

CHAPTER SUMMARY

1. A set is an unordered collection of distinct elements. Elements can be added, located, and removed.

2. Sets don't have duplicates. Adding a duplicate of an element that is already present is silently ignored.

3. Both the `HashSet` and `TreeSet` classes realize the `Set` interface.

4. Use an iterator to list all elements in a set.

5. A set iterator does not visit the elements in the order in which you inserted them. The set implementation rearranges the elements so that it can locate them quickly.

6. You cannot add an element to a set at an iterator position.

7. A map keeps associations between key and value objects.

8. Both the `HashMap` and `TreeMap` classes realize the `Map` interface.

9. To find all keys and values in a map, iterate through the key set and find the values that correspond to the keys.

10. A hash function computes an integer value from an object.

11. A good hash function minimizes *collisions*, identical hash codes for different objects.

12. A hash table can be implemented as an array of *buckets*, sequences of links that hold elements with the same hash code.

13. If there are no or only a few collisions, then adding, locating, and removing hash table elements takes constant or $O(1)$ time.

14. The table size should be a prime number, larger than the expected number of elements.

15. Define `hashCode` methods for your own classes by combining the hash codes for the instance variables.

16. Your `hashCode` method must be compatible with the `equals` method.

17. In a hash map, only the keys are hashed.

18. A binary tree consists of nodes, each of which has two child nodes.

19. All nodes in a binary search tree fulfill the property that the descendants to the left have smaller data values than the node data value, and the descendants to the right have larger data values.

20. If a binary search tree is approximately balanced, then adding an element takes $O(\log(n))$ time.

21. The `TreeSet` class uses a form of balanced binary trees that guarantees that adding and removing an element takes $O(\log(n))$ time.

22. To use a tree set, the elements must be comparable.

23. If the class of the tree set elements doesn't implement the `Comparable` interface, you must supply a comparator.

CLASSES, OBJECTS, AND METHODS INTRODUCED IN THIS CHAPTER

```
java.util.HashMap
java.util.HashSet
java.util.Iterator
    hasNext
    next
    remove
java.util.Map
    get
    put
    keySet
    remove
java.util.Set
    add
    contains
    iterator
    remove
    size
java.util.TreeMap
java.util.TreeSet
```

Further Reading

[1] Thomas H. Cormen, Charles E. Leiserson, Ronald L. Rivest, *Introduction to Algorithms*, MIT Press, 1990

REVIEW EXERCISES

Exercise R20.1. What is the difference between a set and a map?

Exercise R20.2. What implementations does the Java library provide for the abstract set type?

Exercise R20.3. What are the fundamental operations on the abstract set type? What additional methods does the `Set` interface provide? (Look up the interface in the API documentation.)

Exercise R20.4. The union of two sets *A* and *B* is the set of all elements that are contained in *A*, *B*, or both. The intersection is the set of all elements that are contained in *A* and *B*. How can you compute the union and intersection of two sets, using the fundamental set operations?

Exercise R20.5. How can you compute the union and intersection of two sets, using some of the methods that the `Set` interface provides? (Look up the interface in the API documentation.)

Exercise R20.6. Can a map have two keys with the same value? Two values with the same key?

Exercise R20.7. A map can be implemented as a set of (*key, value*) pairs. Explain.

Exercise R20.8. When implementing a hash map as a set of (*key, value*) pairs, what hash function should be used?

Exercise R20.9. Verify the hash codes of the strings "Jim" and "Joe" in Table 1.

Exercise R20.10. From the hash codes in Table 1, show that Figure 6 accurately shows the locations of the strings if the hash table size is 101.

Exercise R20.11. What is the difference between a binary tree and a binary search tree? Give examples of each.

Exercise R20.12. What is the difference between a balanced tree and an unbalanced tree? Give examples of each.

Exercise R20.13. The following elements are inserted into a binary search tree. Make a drawing that shows the resulting tree after each insertion.

Adam

Eve

Romeo

Juliet

Tom

Dick

Harry

Exercise R20.14. Insert the elements of the preceding exercise in opposite order. Then determine how the `Tree.print` method prints out both the tree from the preceding exercise and this tree. Explain how the printouts are related.

Exercise R20.15. Consider the following tree. In which order are the nodes printed by the `Tree.print` method?

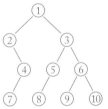

PROGRAMMING EXERCISES

Exercise P20.1. Write a program that reads text from `System.in` and breaks it up into individual words, just like the `Split` program in Chapter 6. Insert the words into a tree set. At the end of the input file, print all words, followed by the size of the resulting set. This program determines how many unique words a text file has.

Exercise P20.2. Insert the 13 standard colors that the `Color` class predefines (that is, `Color.pink`, `Color.green`, and so on) into a set. Prompt the user to enter a color by specifying red, green, and blue values between 0 and 1. Then tell the user whether the resulting color is in the set.

Exercise P20.3. Add a `debug` method to the `HashSet` implementation in Section 20.3 that prints the nonempty buckets of the hash table. Run the test program at the end of Section 20.3. Call the `debug` method after all additions and removals and verify that Figure 6 accurately represents the state of the hash table.

Exercise P20.4. Write a program that keeps a map in which both keys and values are strings—the names of students and their course grades. Prompt the user of the program to add or remove students, to modify grades, or to print all grades. The printout should be sorted by name and formatted like this:

```
Carl: B+
Joe: C
Sarah: A
```

Exercise P20.5. Reimplement the preceding exercise so that the keys of the map are objects of class `Student`. A student should have a first name, a last name, and an integer ID. The printout should be sorted by last name. If two students have the same last name, then use the first name as tie breaker. If the first names are also identical, then use the integer ID.

Exercise P20.6. Supply compatible `hashCode` and `equals` methods to the `Student` class described in the preceding exercise. Test the hash code by adding `Student` objects to a hash set.

Exercise P20.7. Supply compatible `hashCode` and `equals` methods to the `BankAccount` class. Test the `hashCode` method by printing out hash codes and by adding `BankAccount` objects to a hash set.

Exercise P20.8. Design a data structure `IntSet` that can hold a set of integers. Hide the private implementation: a tree set of `Integer` objects. Provide the following methods:

- A constructor to make an empty set
- `add(int x)` to add x if it is not present
- `remove(int x)` to remove x if it is present
- `print()` to print all elements currently in the set

Exercise P20.9. Enhance the set class from the previous example by supplying an iterator object that supports *only* the `hasNext/next` methods.

```
IntSetIterator iterator = mySet.iterator();
while (iterator.hasNext())
    System.out.println(iterator.next());
```

Note that the `next` method returns an `int`, not an object. For that reason, you cannot simply return the iterator of the tree set.

Exercise P20.10. Enhance the set class from the previous examples by supplying methods

```
IntSet union(IntSet other)
IntSet intersection(IntSet other)
```

that compute the union and intersection of two sets.

Exercise P20.11. Implement the *sieve of Eratosthenes:* a method for computing prime numbers, known to the ancient Greeks. Choose an n. This method will compute all prime numbers up to n. First insert all numbers from 2 to n into a set. Then erase all multiples of 2 (except 2); that is, 4, 6, 8, 10, 12, ... Erase all multiples of 3; that is, 6, 9, 12, 15, ... Go up to $\sqrt{n}$. The remaining numbers are all primes. Of course, you should use only the public interface of the `IntSet` data structure.

Exercise P20.12. Design an `IntTree` class that stores just integers, not objects. Support the same methods as the `Tree` class in the book.

Exercise P20.13. Write a method of the `Tree` class

```
    Comparable smallest()
```

that returns the smallest element of a tree. You will also need to add a method to the `Node` class.

Exercise P20.14. Change the `print` method to print the tree as a tree shape. You can print the tree sideways. Extra credit if you instead display the tree graphically, with the root node centered on the top.

Exercise P20.15. The `print` method of the tree class prints a tree according to the following algorithm:

1. Print the left subtree.
2. Print the current node.
3. Print the right subtree.

This is called *inorder traversal.* There are two other traversal schemes, namely *preorder traversal,*

1. Print the current node.
2. Print the left subtree.
3. Print the right subtree.

and *postorder traversal,*

1. Print the left subtree.
2. Print the right subtree.
3. Print the current node.

Write a program that builds a tree of strings from user input and then prints the user's choice of preorder, inorder, or postorder traversal.

Multithreading

To understand how multiple thread can execute in parallel

▶ To learn how to implement threads

▶ To understand race conditions and deadlocks

▶ To be able to avoid corruption of shared objects by using synchronized methods

▶ To be able to use threads for programming animations

I t is often useful for a program to carry out two or more tasks at the same time. For example, a web browser can load multiple images of a web page at the same time. Or an animation program can show moving figures, with separate tasks computing the positions of each separate figure. Of course, you can program effects such as these by implementing a loop that first does a little bit of the first task, then a little bit of the second, and so on. But such programs get complex quickly, because you have to mix the code for doing the work with code to control the timing.

In this chapter, you will see how you can instead implement each task as a *thread*. A thread is a program unit that is executed independently of other parts of the program. The Java virtual machine, not the programmer, executes each thread for a short amount of time and then switches to another thread. This gives the illusion of executing the threads in parallel to each other. Actually, if a computer has multiple central processing units (CPUs), then some of the threads can really run in parallel, one on each processor.

A thread is a program unit that is executed independently of other parts of the program.

Threads are convenient for programmers. They let you concentrate on the task that you want to carry out, without having to worry how that task is alternated with other tasks. If you need to carry out two tasks in parallel, you simply implement a thread for each of them and start each thread. There are, of course, a couple of complexities. You sometimes need some way of synchronizing the threads. One thread may need a result that is being computed by another thread. Another common problem occurs when multiple threads simultaneously try to modify a shared object. You will see in this chapter how to deal with these issues.

CHAPTER CONTENTS

21.1 Thread Basics

21.1.1 — Running Threads

Running a thread is simple—just follow these steps:

1. Implement a class that extends the Thread class.
2. Place the code for your task into the run method of your subclass.
3. Create an object of your subclass.
4. Call the start method to start the thread.

When a Thread object is started, the code in its run method is executed in a new thread.

Let us look at a concrete example. We just want to print ten greetings "Hello, World!", one greeting every second. We add a time stamp to each greeting to see when it is printed.

```
Thu Dec 28 23:12:03 PST 2000 Hello, World!
Thu Dec 28 23:12:04 PST 2000 Hello, World!
Thu Dec 28 23:12:05 PST 2000 Hello, World!
Thu Dec 28 23:12:06 PST 2000 Hello, World!
```

```
Thu Dec 28 23:12:07 PST 2000 Hello, World!
Thu Dec 28 23:12:08 PST 2000 Hello, World!
Thu Dec 28 23:12:09 PST 2000 Hello, World!
Thu Dec 28 23:12:10 PST 2000 Hello, World!
Thu Dec 28 23:12:11 PST 2000 Hello, World!
Thu Dec 28 23:12:12 PST 2000 Hello, World!
```

Following the instructions for creating a thread, we define a class that extends the Thread class:

```
public class GreetingThread extends Thread
{
   public void run()
   {
      // thread action
      . . .
   }
   // variables used by the thread action
   . . .
}
```

Here are the thread actions for our thread:

- Print a time stamp.

- Print the greeting.

- Wait a second.

The thread should loop through them 10 times.

We get the time stamp by constructing a Date object. Its default constructor produces a date that is set to the current date and time.

```
Date now = new Date();
System.out.println(now + " " + greeting);
```

> The sleep method puts the current thread to sleep for a given number of milliseconds.

To wait a second, we use the sleep method of the Thread class. The call

```
sleep(milliseconds)
```

puts the current thread to sleep for a given number of milliseconds. In our case, we sleep for 1,000 milliseconds, or one second.

There is, however, one technical problem. Putting a thread to sleep is potentially risky—a thread might sleep for so long that it is no longer useful and should be terminated. As you will see in Section 21.1.2, to terminate a thread, you interrupt it. When a sleeping thread is interrupted, an InterruptedException is generated. You need to catch that exception in your run method and terminate the thread. The simplest way to handle thread interruptions is to give your run method the following form:

```
public void run()
{
```

```
        try
        {
            thread action
        }
        catch (InterruptedException exception)
        {
            cleanup, if necessary
        }
    }
```

> When a thread is interrupted, the most common response is to terminate the run method.

We follow that structure in our example. Here is the complete code for the thread class:

Code GreetingThread.java

```java
 1  import java.util.Date;
 2
 3  /**
 4      A thread that repeatedly prints a greeting.
 5  */
 6  public class GreetingThread extends Thread
 7  {
 8      /**
 9          Constructs the thread object.
10          @param aGreeting the greeting to display
11      */
12      public GreetingThread(String aGreeting)
13      {
14          greeting = aGreeting;
15      }
16
17      public void run()
18      {
19          try
20          {
21              for (int i = 1; i <= REPETITIONS; i++)
22              {
23                  Date now = new Date();
24                  System.out.println(now + " " + greeting);
25                  sleep(DELAY);
26              }
27          }
28          catch (InterruptedException exception)
29          {
30          }
31      }
32
33      private String greeting;
```

```
34
35     private static final int REPETITIONS = 10;
36     private static final int DELAY = 1000;
37 }
```

To start a thread, you first construct an object of the thread class.

```
GreetingThread t = new GreetingThread("Hello, World!");
```

Then you call the start method.

```
t.start();
```

Now a new thread is started, executing the code in the run method of your thread in parallel with any other threads in your program.

In our sample program, we start two threads: one that prints "Hello, World!" and one that prints "Goodbye, World!"

Code GreetingThreadTest.java

```
1  import java.util.Date;
2
3  /**
4      This program tests the greeting thread by running two
5      threads in parallel.
6  */
7  public class GreetingThreadTest
8  {
9      public static void main(String[] args)
10     {
11        GreetingThread t1 =
12           new GreetingThread("Hello, World!");
13        GreetingThread t2 =
14           new GreetingThread("Goodbye, World!");
15
16        t1.start();
17        t2.start();
18     }
19 }
```

Here is a sample output. Because both threads are running in parallel, the two messages appear interleaved.

```
Thu Dec 28 23:12:03 PST 2000 Hello, World!
Thu Dec 28 23:12:03 PST 2000 Goodbye, World!
Thu Dec 28 23:12:04 PST 2000 Hello, World!
Thu Dec 28 23:12:05 PST 2000 Hello, World!
Thu Dec 28 23:12:04 PST 2000 Goodbye, World!
Thu Dec 28 23:12:05 PST 2000 Goodbye, World!
Thu Dec 28 23:12:06 PST 2000 Hello, World!
Thu Dec 28 23:12:06 PST 2000 Goodbye, World!
Thu Dec 28 23:12:07 PST 2000 Hello, World!
Thu Dec 28 23:12:07 PST 2000 Goodbye, World!
```

```
Thu Dec 28 23:12:08 PST 2000 Hello, World!
Thu Dec 28 23:12:08 PST 2000 Goodbye, World!
Thu Dec 28 23:12:09 PST 2000 Hello, World!
Thu Dec 28 23:12:09 PST 2000 Goodbye, World!
Thu Dec 28 23:12:10 PST 2000 Hello, World!
Thu Dec 28 23:12:10 PST 2000 Goodbye, World!
Thu Dec 28 23:12:11 PST 2000 Goodbye, World!
Thu Dec 28 23:12:11 PST 2000 Hello, World!
Thu Dec 28 23:12:12 PST 2000 Goodbye, World!
Thu Dec 28 23:12:12 PST 2000 Hello, World!
```

> The thread scheduler runs each thread for a short amount of time, called a *time slice*.

If you look closely, you will find that the two threads aren't *exactly* interleaved. Sometimes, the second thread seems to jump ahead of the first thread. This shows an important characteristic of threads. The thread scheduler gives no guarantee about the order in which threads are executed. Each thread runs for a short amount of time, called a *time slice*. Then the scheduler activates another thread, choosing from the *runnable* threads at its disposal. A thread is runnable if it isn't currently sleeping or blocked in some other way. However, there will always be slight variations in running times, especially when calling operating system services (such as input and output). Thus, you should expect that the order in which each thread gains control is somewhat random.

Common Error 21.1

Calling the run Method of a Thread

When you implement a thread class, you labor hard to produce a run method that contains the thread action. It seems only natural to call that method:

```
MyThread thread = new MyThread();
thread.run(); // Does NOT start new thread!
```

But then the run method is executed in the *current* thread, not a new thread!

To start a new thread, you must call thread.start(). The start method starts a new thread, and then invokes the run method.

Advanced Topic 21.1

The Runnable Interface

Instead of supplying the thread action in the run method of a subclass of Thread, you can use the Runnable interface:

```
public interface Runnable
{
    void run();
}
```

▼   Define a class that realizes the `Runnable` interface:

```
public class MyRunnable implements Runnable
{
    public void run()
    {
        // thread action
        . . .
    }
    // other methods and fields
    . . .
}
```

You then construct a `Thread` object from an instance of the class, and start the thread in the normal way.

```
MyRunnable runnable = new MyRunnable();
Thread myThread = new Thread(runnable);
myThread.start();
```

Before inner classes were added to the Java language, this was a useful construct. By adding the `run` method to another class, you can access the private instance fields. However, nowadays it is just as easy to make the thread class an inner class.

Advanced Topic   21.2

Thread Priorities

You can assign different *priorities* to threads, by calling the `setPriority` method with a priority parameter between 1 (or `Thread.MIN_PRIORITY`) and 10 (or `Thread.MAX_PRIORITY`). The value `Thread.NORM_PRIORITY` is defined as 5. For example,

```
myThread.setPriority(Thread.NORM_PRIORITY + 2);
myThread.start();
```

Whenever the thread scheduler needs to make a decision which thread to run, it picks the thread with the highest priority. If there are multiple threads with the same high priority, the scheduler picks one of them. For example, if a higher-priority thread wakes up from its call to `sleep` while a lower-priority thread is running, the scheduler will run it and suspend the current thread.

However, priorities are pretty unreliable in practice. For example, the thread system of Windows NT has only seven priority levels, so some priority differences do not actually have an impact on the scheduler.

Priorities aren't all that useful for most thread programming. If you find yourself tinkering with priority levels to get your multithreaded program to work, you are probably doing something else wrong. In Section 21.2, you will learn about thread synchronization, a more reliable scheme for controlling the behavior of your threads.

21.1.2 — Terminating Threads

A thread terminates when its run method returns. This is the normal way of terminating a thread—implement the run method so that it returns when it determines that no more work needs to be done.

> A thread terminates when its run method terminates.

However, sometimes you need to terminate a running thread. For example, you may have several threads try to find a solution to a problem. As soon as the first one has succeeded, you may want to terminate the other ones. In the initial release of the Java library, the Thread class had a stop method to terminate a thread. However, that method is now *deprecated*—computer scientists have found that stopping a thread can lead to dangerous situations when multiple threads share objects. (We will discuss access to shared objects in Section 21.2.) Instead of simply stopping a thread, you should notify the thread that it should be terminated. The thread needs to cooperate, by releasing any resources that it is currently using and doing any other required cleanup.

To notify a thread that it should clean up and terminate, you use the interrupt method.

```
t.interrupt();
```

> A thread should occasionally check whether it has been interrupted, by calling the isInterrupted method.

The thread's run method should occasionally check whether it has been interrupted, by calling the isInterrupted method. In that case, it should do any necessary cleanup and exit. For example, the run method of the GreetingThread could check at the begining of each loop iteration:

```
public void run()
{
    for (int i = 1;
            i <= REPETITIONS && !isInterrupted();
            i++)
    {
        do work
    }
    clean up
}
```

However, if a thread is sleeping, it can't execute code that checks for interruptions. Therefore, the sleep method throws an InterruptedException whenever a sleeping thread is interrupted. You need to catch that exception and also terminate the thread if it occurs. The easiest way to do that is to surround the entire work portion of the run method with a try block, like this:

```
public void run
{
    try
    {
```

```
        for (int i = 1;
             i <= REPETITIONS && !isInterrupted();
             i++)
        {
            do work
        }
    }
    catch (InterruptedException exception)
    {
    }
    clean up
}
```

Strictly speaking, there is nothing in the Java language specification that says that a thread must terminate when it is interrupted. It is entirely up to the thread what it does when it is interrupted. Interrupting is a general mechanism for getting the thread's attention, even when it is sleeping. However, in this chapter, we will always terminate a thread that is being interrupted.

▼ Quality Tip   21.1

Check for Thread Interruptions in the run Method of a Thread

By convention, a thread should terminate itself (or at least act in some other well-defined way) when it is interrupted. You should implement your threads to follow this convention.

Simply do the following:

- In an appropriate loop of your thread, call the `isInterrupted` method. If it returns `true`, do any cleanup and exit the `run` method.

- Put the thread action inside a `try` block that catches the `InterruptedException`. That exception occurs when your thread is interrupted while it is not running, for example inside a call to `sleep`. When you catch the exception, do any required cleanup and exit the `run` method.

Many programmers don't understand the purpose of the `InterruptedException` and, out of ignorance and desperation, muzzle it by surrounding just the call to `sleep` inside a `try` block.

```
public void run()
{
    while (. . .)
    {
        . . .
        try
```

```
            {
                sleep(delay);
            }
            catch (InterruptedException e) {} // DON'T
            . . .
        }
    }
```

Don't do that. If you do, users of your thread class can't get your thread's attention by interrupting it. It is just as easy to place the entire thread action inside a single `try` block. Then interrupting the thread terminates the thread action.

```
    public void run()
    {
        try
        {
            while (. . .)
            {
                . . .
                sleep(delay);
                . . .
            }
        }
        catch (InterruptedException e) {} // OK
    }
```

⚛ Advanced Topic   21.3

Thread Groups

A program that has many threads can place them into thread groups. You start a new thread group with the constructor

```
    String name = ". . .";
    ThreadGroup group = new ThreadGroup(name);
```

Then you add threads to the group by supplying the group in the constructor, for example:

```
    Thread myThread = new Thread(group, myRunnable);
```

Any threads that `myThread` starts are automatically in the new thread group as well.

The principal advantage of thread groups is that you can manage all the threads in the group at once. For example, to interrupt all threads in the group, call

```
    group.interrupt();
```

As a practical application, you can place all threads that load the various parts of a web page into a group. If the user doesn't want the page loaded after all, you can simply interrupt all threads at once.

21.2 Synchronization

21.2.1 — Observing Corruption Caused by Unsynchronized Threads

When threads share access to a common object, they can conflict with each other. To demonstrate the problems that can arise, we will investigate a sample program in which multiple threads manipulate a bank account. Each thread repeatedly deposits or withdraws an amount of money, and then sleeps for a short amount of time. Here is the `run` method of the `DepositThread` class:

```java
public void run()
{
   try
   {
      for (int i = 1;
            i <= REPETITIONS && !isInterrupted();
            i++)
      {
         account.deposit(amount);
         sleep(DELAY);
      }
   }
   catch (InterruptedException exception)
   {
   }
}
```

The `WithdrawThread` class is similar—it withdraws money instead.

In our sample program, we construct a bank account that starts out with a zero balance. We create two threads:

- `t0` deposits $100 into the bank account for 10 iterations.

- `t1` withdraws $100 from the bank account for 10 iterations.

The `deposit` and `withdraw` methods of the `BankAccount` class have been modified to print messages that show what is happening. For example, here is the code for the `deposit` method:

```java
public void deposit(double amount)
{
   System.out.print("Depositing " + amount);
   double newBalance = balance + amount;
   System.out.println(", new balance is "
      + newBalance);
   balance = newBalance;
}
```

You can find the complete source code at the end of this section.

Normally, the program output looks somewhat like this:

```
Depositing 100.0, new balance is 100.0
Withdrawing 100.0, new balance is 0.0
Depositing 100.0, new balance is 100.0
Depositing 100.0, new balance is 200.0
Withdrawing 100.0, new balance is 100.0
. . .
Withdrawing 100.0, new balance is 0.0
```

In the end, the balance should be zero. However, when you run this program repeatedly, you may sometimes notice messed-up output, like this:

```
Depositing 100.0Withdrawing 100.0, new balance is 100.0
, new balance is -100.0
```

And if you look at the last line of the output, you will notice that the final balance is not always zero. Clearly, something problematic is happening.

You may have to try the program several times to see this effect.

Here is a scenario that explains how a problem can occur.

1. The first thread executes the lines

   ```
   System.out.print("Depositing " + amount);
   double newBalance = balance + amount;
   ```

   in the deposit method of the BankAccount class. The value of the balance field is still 0, and the value of the newBalance local variable is 100.

2. Immediately afterwards, the first thread reaches the end of its time slice, and the second thread gains control.

3. The second thread calls the withdraw method, which prints a message and withdraws $100 from the balance variable. It is now −100.

4. The second thread goes to sleep.

5. The original thread regains control and picks up where it was interrupted. It now executes the lines

   ```
   System.out.println(", new balance is " + newBalance);
   balance = newBalance;
   ```

   The value of balance is now 100 (see Figure 1).

Thus, not only are the messages interleaved, but the balance is wrong. The balance after a withdrawal and deposit should again be 0, not 100. Because the deposit method was interrupted, it used the *old* balance (before the withdrawal) to compute the value of its local newBalance variable. Later, when it was activated again, it used that newBalance value to overwrite the changed balance field.

> A race condition occurs if the effect of multiple threads on shared data depends on the order in which the threads are scheduled.

As you can see, each thread has its own local variables, but both threads share access to the balance instance field. That shared access creates a problem. This problem is often called a *race condition*. Both threads, in their race to complete their respective tasks, manipulate a shared field, and the end result depends on which of them happens to win the race.

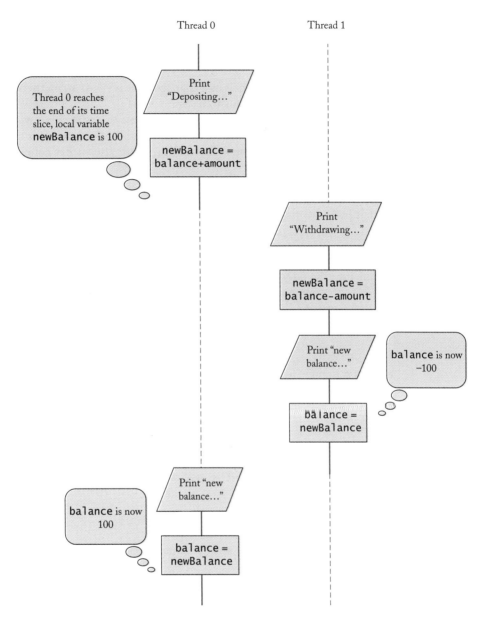

Figure 1

Corrupting the Contents of the `balance` Field

You might argue that the reason for this problem is that we made it too easy to interrupt the balance computation. Suppose the code for the `deposit` method is reorganized like this:

```
public void deposit(double amount)
{
```

```
        balance = balance + amount;
        System.out.print("Depositing " + amount
            + ", new balance is " + newBalance);
    }
```

Suppose further that you make the same change in the `withdraw` method. If you run the resulting program, everything seems to be fine.

However, that is a *dangerous illusion*. The problem hasn't gone away; it just has become much less frequent, and therefore more difficult to observe. It is still possible for the `deposit` method to reach the end of its time slice after it has computed the right-hand-side value

```
    balance + amount
```

but before it performs the assignment

```
    balance = the right-hand-side value
```

When the method regains control, it finally carries out the assignment, putting the wrong value into the `balance` field.

File BankAccountThreadTest.java

```
1  import java.util.Random;
2
3  /**
4      This program runs two threads that deposit and withdraw
5      money from the same bank account.
6  */
7  public class BankAccountThreadTest
8  {
9      public static void main(String[] args)
10     {
11         BankAccount account = new BankAccount();
12
13         DepositThread t0 =
14             new DepositThread(account, 100);
15         WithdrawThread t1 =
16             new WithdrawThread(account, 100);
17
18         t0.start();
19         t1.start();
20     }
21 }
```

File DepositThread.java

```
1  /**
2      A deposit thread makes periodic deposits to a bank account.
3  */
4  class DepositThread extends Thread
5  {
```

```
6     /**
7         Constructs a deposit thread.
8         @param anAccount the account into which to deposit money
9         @anAmount the amount to deposit in each repetition
10    */
11    public DepositThread(BankAccount anAccount,
12       double anAmount)
13    {
14       account = anAccount;
15       amount = anAmount;
16    }
17
18    public void run()
19    {
20       try
21       {
22          for (int i = 1;
23             i <= REPETITIONS && !isInterrupted();
24             i++)
25          {
26             account.deposit(amount);
27             sleep(DELAY);
28          }
29       }
30       catch (InterruptedException exception)
31       {
32       }
33    }
34
35    private BankAccount account;
36    private double amount;
37
38    private static final int REPETITIONS = 10;
39    private static final int DELAY = 10;
40 }
```

File WithdrawalThread.java

```
1  /**
2     A withdraw thread makes periodic withdrawals from a bank account.
3  */
4  class WithdrawThread extends Thread
5  {
6     /**
7         Constructs a withdraw thread.
8         @param anAccount the account from which to withdraw money
9         @anAmount the amount to withdraw in each repetition
10    */
11    public WithdrawThread(BankAccount anAccount,
12       double anAmount)
```

```
13     {
14        account = anAccount;
15        amount = anAmount;
16     }
17
18     public void run()
19     {
20        try
21        {
22           for (int i = 1;
23                i <= REPETITIONS && !isInterrupted();
24                i++)
25           {
26              account.withdraw(amount);
27              sleep(DELAY);
28           }
29        }
30        catch (InterruptedException exception)
31        {
32        }
33     }
34
35     private BankAccount account;
36     private double amount;
37
38     private static final int REPETITIONS = 10;
39     private static final int DELAY = 10;
40  }
```

File BankAccount.java

```
1  /**
2     A bank account has a balance that can be changed by
3     deposits and withdrawals.
4  */
5  public class BankAccount
6  {
7     /**
8        Constructs a bank account with a zero balance.
9     */
10    public BankAccount()
11    {
12       balance = 0;
13    }
14
15    /**
16       Deposits money into the bank account.
17       @param amount the amount to deposit
18    */
19    public void deposit(double amount)
```

```
20      {
21         System.out.print("Depositing " + amount);
22         double newBalance = balance + amount;
23         System.out.println(", new balance is "
24            + newBalance);
25         balance = newBalance;
26      }
27
28      /**
29         Withdraws money from the bank account.
30         @param amount the amount to withdraw
31      */
32      public void withdraw(double amount)
33      {
34         System.out.print("Withdrawing " + amount);
35         double newBalance = balance - amount;
36         System.out.println(", new balance is "
37            + newBalance);
38         balance = newBalance;
39      }
40
41      /**
42         Gets the current balance of the bank account.
43         @return the current balance
44      */
45      public double getBalance()
46      {
47         return balance;
48      }
49
50      private double balance;
51   }
```

21.2.2— Synchronizing Object Access

To solve problems such as the one that you observed in the preceding section, a thread must be able to *lock* an object temporarily. While the thread has the object locked, no other thread should be able to modify the state of the object.

In the Java programming language, you use *synchronized* methods for object locking. You must tag all methods that contain thread-sensitive code (such as the deposit and withdraw methods of the BankAccount class) with the synchronized keyword.

```
public class BankAccount
{
   public synchronized void deposit(double amount)
   {
      . . .
```

```
      }

      public synchronized void withdraw(double amount)
      {
            . . .
      }

            . . .
   }
```

> By executing a synchronized method, a thread acquires the object lock. Then no other thread can acquire the lock.

Each object has a lock. By default, an object is unlocked. A thread can lock it by executing a synchronized method. Then that thread *owns the lock* until it returns from the method and thereby unlocks the object. When an object is locked by one thread, no other thread can enter a synchronized method for that object. When another thread makes a call to a synchronized method for that object, the other thread is automatically deactivated, and it needs to wait until the first thread has unlocked the object again.

One way to visualize this behavior is to imagine that the object is a rest room and the threads are people. (See Figure 2.) The rest room has facilities for only one person to be using it at one time. If the rest room is empty, then the first person wanting to use it just goes inside and locks the door. If another person wants to use the rest room and finds it locked, then the second person needs to wait until the first person leaves the room. If multiple people want to gain access to the rest room, they all wait outside. They don't necessarily form an orderly queue; a randomly chosen person may gain access when the rest room becomes available again.

By declaring both the deposit and withdraw methods to be synchronized, we ensure that our program will always run correctly. Only one thread at a time can execute either method on a given object. Whenever a thread starts, it is guaranteed to execute the method to completion before the other thread gets a chance to execute a synchronized method on the same object.

21.3   Avoiding Deadlocks

> A deadlock occurs if no thread can proceed because each thread is waiting for another to do some work first.

You can use object locks and synchronized methods to ensure that your objects are in a consistent state when several threads access them. However, they can also lead to another problem. It can happen that one thread locks an object but then waits for another thread to do some essential work. If that other thread is currently waiting to lock the same object, then neither of the two threads can proceed, and the program is locked up. Such a situation is called a *deadlock* or *deadly embrace*. Let's look at an example.

Suppose we want to disallow negative bank balances in our program. Here's a naive way of doing that. In the run method of the WithdrawThread, we can check the balance before withdrawing money:

```
if (account.getBalance() >= amount)
   account.withdraw(amount);
```

That works if there is only a single thread running that withdraws money. But suppose we have multiple threads that withdraw money. Then the time slice of the current thread may expire after the check account.getBalance() >= amount passes, but before the withdraw method is called. If in the interim another thread withdraws more money, then the test was useless, and we still have a negative balance.

Clearly, the test should be moved inside the synchronized withdraw method. That ensures that the test for sufficient funds and the actual withdrawal cannot be separated. Thus, the withdraw method should look like this:

```
public synchronized void withdraw(double amount)
{
   while (balance < amount)
      wait for the balance to grow
   . . .
}
```

But how can we wait for the balance to grow? You can't simply call sleep inside the withdraw method. If a thread sleeps inside a synchronized method, it still locks the object. No other thread can execute the synchronized deposit method. Other threads will call deposit, but they will simply be blocked until the withdraw method exits. But the withdraw method doesn't exit until it has funds available. This is the deadlock situation that we mentioned earlier.

> Calling wait inside a synchronized method makes the current thread wait and allows another thread to acquire the object lock.

This situation is common, and there is a special set of methods that were designed to help. The wait method temporarily releases an object lock and deactivates the current thread.

In the rest room analogy, you don't want the person in the rest room to go to sleep if there is no toilet paper. Instead, think of the person in the rest room giving up and leaving the stall. That gives another person a chance to enter the rest room and refill the toilet paper.

Here is the correct `withdraw` method.

```
public synchronized void withdraw(double amount)
    throws InterruptedException
{
    while (balance < amount)
        wait();
    . . .
}
```

The `wait` method can throw an `InterruptedException`. The `withdraw` method propagates that exception, because it has no way of knowing what the thread that calls the `withdraw` method wants to do if it is interrupted.

When a thread calls `wait`, it is not simply deactivated in the same way as a thread that reaches the end of its time slice. Instead, it is in a blocked state, and it will not be activated by the thread scheduler until it is unblocked. To unblock, another thread must execute the `notifyAll` method. The `notifyAll` method unblocks all threads waiting on the object. They can then compete with all other threads that are waiting for the object lock. Eventually, one of them will gain access to the object.

> A waiting thread is blocked until another thread calls `notifyAll` or `notify` on the object for which the thread is waiting.

In the rest room analogy, the thread calling `wait` corresponds to the person who enters the rest room and finds that there is no toilet paper. That person then leaves the rest room and waits outside, depressed, doing absolutely nothing, even as other people enter and leave the rest room. The person knows it is pointless to try again. At some point, an attendant enters the rest room, refills the toilet paper, and shouts a notification. Now all the people waiting for toilet paper stop being depressed and again compete for the rest room.

You call the `notifyAll` method whenever the state of an object has changed in a way that might benefit waiting threads. In our bank account example, this is the case after a deposit has been made. At that time, the threads that are waiting for a larger balance should be unblocked so that they can reinspect the balances. Here is how you should modify the `deposit` method:

```
public synchronized void deposit(double amount)
{
    . . .
    notifyAll(); // unblock all waiting threads
}
```

You can call the `notifyAll` method only from a thread that has locked the object. In other words, the call to `notifyAll` must be in a synchronized method or in a method that is called directly or indirectly from a synchronized method.

There is also a `notify` method, which randomly picks just *one* thread that is waiting on the object and unblocks it. The `notify` method can be more efficient, but it is useful only if you know that *every* waiting thread can actually proceed. In general, you don't know that, and `notify` can lead to deadlocks. For that reason, we recommend that you always call `notifyAll`.

Note that the wait, notifyAll, and notify methods belong to the Object class. Every object has a queue of waiting threads. If you call x.wait(), the current thread is added to the queue of the object x. Most commonly, you will call wait(), which adds the current thread to the queue of this. Similarly, the call notifyAll() unblocks all threads that are waiting for this.

With the calls to wait and notifyAll in the withdraw and deposit methods, we can launch any number of withdrawal and deposit threads without a deadlock. If you run the sample program, you will note that all transactions are carried out without ever reaching a negative balance. Here is a sample program with four threads: two for withdrawals and two for deposits.

File BankAccountThreadTest.java

```
1  import java.util.Random;
2
3  /**
4     This program runs four threads that deposit and withdraw
5     money from the same bank account.
6  */
7  public class BankAccountThreadTest
8  {
9     public static void main(String[] args)
10    {
11       BankAccount account = new BankAccount();
12
13       DepositThread t0 =
14          new DepositThread(account, 100);
15       WithdrawThread t1 =
16          new WithdrawThread(account, 100);
17       DepositThread t2 =
18          new DepositThread(account, 100);
19       WithdrawThread t3 =
20          new WithdrawThread(account, 100);
21
22       t0.start();
23       t1.start();
24       t2.start();
25       t3.start();
26    }
27 }
```

File BankAccount.java

```
1  /**
2     A bank account has a balance that can be changed by
3     deposits and withdrawals.
4  */
5  public class BankAccount
6  {
```

```
 7     /**
 8         Constructs a bank account with a zero balance.
 9     */
10     public BankAccount()
11     {
12         balance = 0;
13     }
14
15     /**
16         Deposits money into the bank account.
17         @param amount  the amount to deposit
18     */
19     public synchronized void deposit(double amount)
20     {
21         System.out.print("Depositing " + amount);
22         double newBalance = balance + amount;
23         System.out.println(", new balance is "
24             + newBalance);
25         balance = newBalance;
26         notifyAll();
27     }
28
29     /**
30         Withdraws money from the bank account.
31         @param amount  the amount to withdraw
32     */
33     public synchronized void withdraw(double amount)
34         throws InterruptedException
35     {
36         while (balance < amount)
37             wait();
38         System.out.print("Withdrawing " + amount);
39         double newBalance = balance - amount;
40         System.out.println(", new balance is "
41             + newBalance);
42         balance = newBalance;
43     }
44
45     /**
46         Gets the current balance of the bank account.
47         @return  the current balance
48     */
49     public double getBalance()
50     {
51         return balance;
52     }
53
54     private double balance;
55 }
```

▼ ⊗ **Common Error** `21.2`

Calling wait **without Calling** notifyAll

It is intuitively clear when to call `wait`. If a thread finds out that it can't do its job, it has to wait. But once a thread has called `wait`, it temporarily gives up all hope and doesn't try again until some other thread calls `notifyAll` on the object for which the thread is waiting. In the rest room analogy, if the attendant who brings in new toilet paper doesn't notify the waiting people, they'll wait forever.

A common error is to have threads call `wait` without matching calls to `notifyAll` by other threads. Whenever you call `wait`, ask yourself which call to `notifyAll` will notify your thread.

▼ ⊗ **Common Error** `21.3`

Calling notifyAll **without Locking the Object**

The thread that calls `notifyAll` must own the lock on the object on which `notifyAll` is called. Otherwise, an `IllegalMonitorState` exception is thrown.

In the rest room analogy, the attendant must shout the notification while *inside* the rest room after refilling the toilet paper.

In practice, this should not be a problem. Remember that `notifyAll` is called when some thread has just changed the state of some object in a way that may benefit waiting threads. That change should be inside a synchronized method in any case. As long as you tag all methods that change a shared object as `synchronized`, and you are in the habit of calling `notifyAll` after every beneficial change, you won't run into problems. But if you use `notifyAll` in a haphazard way, you may encounter the `IllegalMonitor-StateException`.

▼ 🄰🄣 **Advanced Topic** `21.4`

Complex Deadlocks

Using the `wait` and `notify` methods doesn't solve all deadlocks. Here is an example. We have three accounts: `account0`, `account1`, and `account2`. We have three *transfer threads*. A transfer thread transfers money from two accounts into a third.

- t0 repeatedly transfers $500 each from `account1` and `account2` to `account0`.

- t1 repeatedly transfers $500 each from `account2` and `account0` to `account1`.

- t2 repeatedly transfers $500 each from `account1` and `account0` to `account2`.

▼   If the three threads take turns and each thread executes one iteration before losing control, then the program runs indefinitely:

	account0	account1	account2
Initial balance	$1000	$1000	$1000
After t0 iteration	$2000	$500	$500
After t1 iteration	$1500	$1500	0
After t2 iteration	$1000	$1000	$1000

But if it happens that t0 executes two iterations before t1 and t2 get a chance, then the program deadlocks:

	account0	account1	account2
Initial balance	$1000	$1000	$1000
After t0 iteration	$2000	$500	$500
After t0 iteration	$3000	$0	$0

Now none of the three threads can progress, and the program deadlocks. You can try out the program. Most of the time, it will carry out the transfers successfully, but once in a while you may be able to observe a deadlock.

       It is possible to avoid *this* deadlock by reordering the withdrawals. But there is no known general method for mechanically avoiding *all* deadlocks. Also, as you already saw, running a few experiments can be very misleading. Programmers who create multi-threaded programs must make an effort to prove rigorously why their threads can't deadlock, no matter in which order they are executed.

File BankAccountThreadTest.java

```
1  import java.util.Random;
2
3  /**
4     This program uses three threads that transfer money between
5     three accounts. It can occasionally deadlock.
6  */
7  public class BankAccountThreadTest
8  {
9     public static void main(String[] args)
10    {
11       BankAccount account0 = new BankAccount(1000);
12       BankAccount account1 = new BankAccount(1000);
13       BankAccount account2 = new BankAccount(1000);
14
15       TransferThread t0 = new TransferThread(
16          account1, account2, account0, 500);
17       TransferThread t1 = new TransferThread(
18          account2, account0, account1, 500);
19       TransferThread t2 = new TransferThread(
```

```
▼   20              account1, account0, account2, 500);
    21
    22         t0.start();
▼   23         t1.start();
    24         t2.start();
    25      }
▼   26 }
```

TransferThread.java

```
▼    1 /**
     2      A transfer thread repeatedly transfers money between three
     3      bank accounts.
▼    4 */
     5 class TransferThread extends Thread
     6 {
     7      /**
▼    8          Constructs a transfer thread.
     9          @param account1 the first account from which to withdraw
    10          @param account2 the second account from which to withdraw
▼   11          @param account3 the account to which to deposit
    12          @param anAmount the amount to withdraw from each of the
    13              first two accounts
    14      */
▼   15      public TransferThread(BankAccount account1,
    16         BankAccount account2, BankAccount account3,
    17         double anAmount)
▼   18      {
    19         from1 = account1;
    20         from2 = account2;
▼   21         to = account3;
    22         amount = anAmount;
    23      }
    24
▼   25      public void run()
    26      {
    27         try
▼   28         {
    29            for (int i = 1;
    30                 i <= REPETITIONS && !isInterrupted();
▼   31                 i++)
    32            {
    33               from1.withdraw(amount);
▼   34               from2.withdraw(amount);
    35               to.deposit(2 * amount);
    36               sleep(DELAY);
    37            }
▼   38         }
    39         catch (InterruptedException exception)
    40         {
```

```
41          }
42      }
43
44      private BankAccount from1;
45      private BankAccount from2;
46      private BankAccount to;
47      private double amount;
48
49      private static final int REPETITIONS = 10;
50      private static final int DELAY = 10;
51  }
```

BankAccount.java

```
1   /**
2       A bank account has a balance that can be changed by
3       deposits and withdrawals.
4   */
5   public class BankAccount
6   {
7       /**
8           Constructs a bank account with a given balance.
9           @param initialBalance the initial balance
10      */
11      public BankAccount(double initialBalance)
12      {
13          balance = initialBalance;
14      }
15
16      /**
17          Deposits money into the bank account.
18          @param amount the amount to deposit
19      */
20      public synchronized void deposit(double amount)
21      {
22          balance = balance + amount;
23          System.out.println(Thread.currentThread().getName()
24              + " Depositing " + amount
25              + ", new balance is " + balance);
26          notifyAll();
27      }
28
29      /**
30          Withdraws money from the bank account.
31          @param amount the amount to withdraw
32      */
33      public synchronized void withdraw(double amount)
34          throws InterruptedException
35      {
36          while (balance < amount)
```

```
▼    37        {
     38            System.out.println(
     39                Thread.currentThread().getName()
▼    40                + " Waiting...");
     41            wait();
     42        }
     43        balance = balance - amount;
▼    44        System.out.println(
     45            Thread.currentThread().getName()
     46            + " Withdrawing " + amount
▼    47            + ", new balance is " + balance);
     48    }
     49
▼    50    /**
     51        Gets the current balance of the bank account.
     52        @return the current balance
     53    */
▼    54    public double getBalance()
     55    {
     56        return balance;
▼    57    }
     58
     59    private double balance;
▼    60 }
```

21.4 An Application of Threads: Algorithm Animation

One popular use for thread programming is animation. A program that displays an animation shows different objects moving or changing in some way as time progresses. This is often achieved by launching one or more threads that compute how parts of the animation change.

You can use the Swing Timer class for simple animations without having to do any thread programming—see Exercise 21.8 for an example. However, more advanced animations are best implemented with threads.

In this section, you will see a particular kind of animation, namely the visualization of the steps of an algorithm. Algorithm animation is an excellent technique for gaining a better understanding of how an algorithm works. Following tradition, we will implement the animation as an applet—posting animations on a web page seems to be a favorite activity of programmers. (As with all the applets of this book, a Java 2-enabled browser such as Netscape 6 or Opera is required to view them.) Many algorithms can be animated—type "Java algorithm animation" into your favorite web search engine, and you'll find lots of links to web pages with animations of various algorithms.

All algorithm animations have a similar structure. The algorithm runs in a separate thread that periodically updates an image of the current state of the algorithm and then pauses so that the user can view the image. After a short amount of time, the algorithm thread wakes up again and runs to the next point of interest in the algorithm. It then updates the image and pauses again. This sequence is repeated until the algorithm has finished.

Let's take the selection sort algorithm of Chapter 18 as an example. That algorithm sorts an array of values. It first finds the smallest element, by inspecting all elements in the array, and bringing the smallest element to the leftmost position. It then finds the smallest element among the remaining elements and brings it into the second position. It keeps going in that way. As the algorithm progresses, the sorted part of the array grows.

How can you visualize this algorithm? It is useful to show the part of the array that is already sorted in a different color. Also, we want to show how each step of the algorithm inspects another element in the unsorted part. That demonstrates why the selection sort algorithm is so slow—it first inspects all elements of the array, then all but one, and so on. If the array has n elements, the algorithm inspects $n + (n - 1) + (n - 2) + \cdots = n(n - 1)/2 = O(n^2)$ elements. To demonstrate that, we mark the currently visited element in red.

Thus, the algorithm state is described by three items:

- The array of values

- The size of the already sorted area

- The currently marked element

First, you need to add an `applet` instance variable to the algorithm class and augment the constructor to set it. That instance variable is needed for repainting the applet and to find out the dimensions of the applet when drawing the algorithm state.

```
public class SelectionSorter
{
    public SelectionSorter(int[] anArray, Applet anApplet)
    {
        a = anArray;
        applet = anApplet;
    }
    . . .
    private Applet applet;
}
```

At each point of interest, the algorithm needs to pause so that the user can admire the graphical output. Supply the `pause` method shown here, and call the applet's `pause` method at various places in the algorithm. The `pause` method repaints the applet and sleeps for a small delay that is proportional to the number of steps involved. However, if the thread was interrupted, then this method throws an `InterruptedException`, which will terminate the `run` method. (By turning the "interrupted" flag into an exception, you don't need to add a check for interruption to the algorithm code.)

```
public void pause(int steps)
    throws InterruptedException
{
    if (Thread.currentThread().isInterrupted())
```

```
      throw new InterruptedException();
   repaint();
   Thread.sleep(steps * DELAY);
}
```

You need to add a `draw` method to the algorithm class that can draw the current state of the data structure, with the items of special interest highlighted. The `draw` method is specific to the particular algorithm. This `draw` method draws the array elements as a sequence of sticks in different colors. The already sorted portion is blue, the marked position is red, and the remainder is black.

```
public void draw(Graphics2D g2)
{
   int deltaX = applet.getWidth() / a.length;
   for (int i = 0; i < a.length; i++)
   {
      if (i == markedPosition)
         g2.setColor(Color.red);
      else if (i <= alreadySorted)
         g2.setColor(Color.blue);
      else
         g2.setColor(Color.black);
      g2.draw(new Line2D.Double(i * deltaX, 0,
         i * deltaX, a[i]));
   }
}
```

You need to update the special positions as the algorithm progresses and pause the animation whenever something interesting happens. The pause should be proportional to the number of steps that are being executed. For a sorting algorithm, pause one unit for each visited array element.

Here is the `minimumPosition` method from Chapter 18, before the animation code is inserted.

```
public int minimumPosition(int from)
{
   int minPos = from;
   for (int i = from + 1; i < a.length; i++)
      if (a[i] < a[minPos]) minPos = i;
   return minPos;
}
```

After each iteration of the `for` loop, we want to update the marked position of the algorithm state; then we want to pause the applet. To measure the cost of each step fairly, we pause two units of time, because two array elements were inspected. The `pause` method might throw an `InterruptedException`, which we must declare.

```
public int minimumPosition(int from)
throws InterruptedException
{
   int minPos = from;
```

```
        for (int i = from + 1; i < a.length; i++)
        {
            if (a[i] < a[minPos]) minPos = i;
            markedPosition = i;
            applet.pause(2);
        }
        return minPos;
    }
```

The sort method is augmented in the same way. You will find the code at the end of this section. This concludes the modification of the algorithm class. Let us now turn to the applet class.

First, we need a user interface to start a new animation. In this example, we keep it simple. When the user clicks within the area of the applet, the animation starts. If an animation is already running, we interrupt that thread to terminate it. This is achieved in the usual way, by attaching a mouse listener to the applet.

```
public class SelectionSortApplet extends Applet
{
    public SelectionSortApplet()
    {
        class MousePressListener extends MouseAdapter
        {
            public void mousePressed(MouseEvent event)
            {
                if (animation != null && animation.isAlive())
                    animation.interrupt();
                startAnimation();
            }
        }

        MouseListener listener = new MousePressListener();
        addMouseListener(listener);
        . . .
        animation = null;
    }


    . . .
    private Thread animation;
}
```

The applet's paint method calls the draw method of the algorithm object.

```
    public void paint(Graphics g)
    {
        if (sorter == null) return;
        Graphics2D g2 = (Graphics2D)g;
        sorter.draw(g2);
    }
```

The startAnimation method constructs a SelectionSorter object, which supplies a new array and the this reference to the applet. Then the method constructs a thread whose run method calls the sorter's sort method.

```
public void startAnimation()
{
    class AnimationThread extends Thread
    {
        public void run()
        {
            try
            {
                sorter.sort();
            }
            catch (InterruptedException exception)
            {
            }
        }
    }

    int[] values = ArrayUtil.randomIntArray(30, 300);
    sorter = new SelectionSorter(values, this);
    animation = new AnimationThread();
    animation.start();
}
```

The classes for the animation applet and the HTML file to start the applet are at the end of this section. Run the applet and click within the applet's area. The animation starts. You can run the animation until the array is completely sorted, or you can interrupt it at any time. Each time you click on the applet, a new animation with a different randomly filled array is started (see Figure 3).

Exercise 21.9 asks you to animate the merge sort algorithm of Chapter 18. If you do that exercise, then start both applets and run them in parallel to see which algorithm is

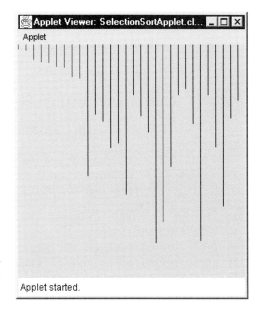

Figure 3

A Step in the Animation of the Selection
Sort Algorithm

faster. Actually, you may find the result surprising. If you build fair delays into the merge sort animation to account for the copying from and to the temporary array, you will find that it doesn't perform all that well for small arrays. But if you increase the array size, then the advantage of the merge sort algorithm becomes clear.

File SelectionSortApplet.html

```
1  <html>
2     <body>
3        <p>Click on the applet to start the animation.</p>
4        <applet code="SelectionSortApplet.class"
5           width="300" height="300">
6        </applet>
7     </body>
8  </html>
```

File SelectionSortApplet.java

```
1  import java.applet.Applet;
2  import java.awt.Color;
3  import java.awt.Graphics;
4  import java.awt.Graphics2D;
5  import java.awt.event.MouseEvent;
6  import java.awt.event.MouseAdapter;
7  import java.awt.event.MouseListener;
8
9  /**
10     This applet animates the selection sort algorithm.
11  */
12  public class SelectionSortApplet extends Applet
13  {
14     /**
15        Constructs the applet and sets up the mouse handler.
16        Click on the surface of the applet to start the animation.
17     */
18     public SelectionSortApplet()
19     {
20        class MousePressListener extends MouseAdapter
21        {
22           public void mousePressed(MouseEvent event)
23           {
24              if (animation != null && animation.isAlive())
25                 animation.interrupt();
26              startAnimation();
27           }
28        }
29
30        MouseListener listener = new MousePressListener();
31        addMouseListener(listener);
32        setBackground(Color.lightGray);
33
```

```
34        sorter = null;
35        animation = null;
36     }
37
38     public void paint(Graphics g)
39     {
40        if (sorter == null) return;
41        Graphics2D g2 = (Graphics2D)g;
42        sorter.draw(g2);
43     }
44
45     /**
46        Starts a new animation thread.
47     */
48     public void startAnimation()
49     {
50        class AnimationThread extends Thread
51        {
52           public void run()
53           {
54              try
55              {
56                 sorter.sort();
57              }
58              catch (InterruptedException exception)
59              {
60              }
61           }
62        }
63
64        int[] values = ArrayUtil.randomIntArray(30, 300);
65        sorter = new SelectionSorter(values, this);
66        animation = new AnimationThread();
67        animation.start();
68     }
69
70     private SelectionSorter sorter;
71     private Thread animation;
72 }
```

File SelectionSorter.java

```
1 import java.applet.Applet;
2 import java.awt.Color;
3 import java.awt.Graphics2D;
4 import java.awt.geom.Line2D;
5
6 /**
7    This class sorts an array, using the selection sort algorithm.
8 */
```

```
 9  public class SelectionSorter
10  {
11     /**
12        Constructs a selection sorter.
13        @param anArray  the array to sort
14     */
15     public SelectionSorter(int[] anArray, Applet anApplet)
16     {
17        a = anArray;
18        applet = anApplet;
19     }
20
21     /**
22        Sorts the array managed by this selection sorter.
23     */
24     public void sort()
25        throws InterruptedException
26     {
27        for (int i = 0; i < a.length - 1; i++)
28        {
29           int minPos = minimumPosition(i);
30           swap(minPos, i);
31           // for animation
32           alreadySorted = i;
33           pause(2);
34        }
35     }
36
37     /**
38        Finds the smallest element in a tail range of the array.
39        @param from  the first position in a to compare
40        @return  the position of the smallest element in the
41           range a[from]...a[a.length - 1]
42     */
43     private int minimumPosition(int from)
44        throws InterruptedException
45     {
46        int minPos = from;
47        for (int i = from + 1; i < a.length; i++)
48        {
49           if (a[i] < a[minPos]) minPos = i;
50           // for animation
51           markedPosition = i;
52           pause(2);
53        }
54        return minPos;
55     }
56
57     /**
58        Swaps two entries of the array.
```

```
59          @param i the first position to swap
60          @param j the second position to swap
61       */
62       private void swap(int i, int j)
63       {
64          int temp = a[i];
65          a[i] = a[j];
66          a[j] = temp;
67       }
68
69       /**
70          Draws the current state of the sorting algorithm.
71          @param g2 the graphics context
72       */
73       public void draw(Graphics2D g2)
74       {
75          int deltaX = applet.getWidth() / a.length;
76          for (int i = 0; i < a.length; i++)
77          {
78             if (i == markedPosition)
79                g2.setColor(Color.red);
80             else if (i <= alreadySorted)
81                g2.setColor(Color.blue);
82             else
83                g2.setColor(Color.black);
84             g2.draw(new Line2D.Double(i * deltaX, 0,
85                i * deltaX, a[i]));
86          }
87       }
88
89       /**
90          Pauses the animation.
91          @param steps the number of steps to pause
92       */
93       public void pause(int steps)
94          throws InterruptedException
95       {
96          if (Thread.currentThread().isInterrupted())
97             throw new InterruptedException();
98          applet.repaint();
99          Thread.sleep(steps * DELAY);
100      }
101
102      private int[] a;
103
104      // the applet is needed for pausing the animation
105      private Applet applet;
106
107      // these fields are needed for drawing
108      private int markedPosition = -1;
```

```
109     private int alreadySorted = -1;
110
111     private static final int DELAY = 100;
112 }
```

▼ Random Fact 21.1

Embedded Systems

▼ An embedded system is a computer system that controls a device. The device contains a processor and other hardware and is controlled by a computer program. Unlike a personal computer, which has been designed to be flexible and run many different computer programs, the hardware and software of an embedded system are tailored to a specific device. Computer-controlled devices are becoming increasingly common, ranging from washing machines to medical equipment, automobile engines, and spacecraft.

▼ Several challenges are specific to programming embedded systems. Most importantly, a much higher standard of quality control applies. Vendors are often unconcerned about bugs in personal computer software, because they can always make you install a patch or upgrade to the next version. But in an embedded system, that is not an option. Few consumers would feel comfortable upgrading the software in their washing machines or automobile engines. If you ever handed in a programming assignment that you believed to be correct, only to have the instructor or grader find bugs in it, then you know how hard it is to write software that can reliably do its task for many years without a chance of changing it.

▼ Quality standards are especially important in devices whose failure would destroy property or human life—see Random Facts 8.2 and 14.1.

▼ Many personal computer purchasers buy computers that are fast and have a lot of storage, because the investment is paid back over time when many programs are run on the same equipment. But the hardware for an embedded device is not shared—it is dedicated to one device. A separate processor, memory, and so on, are built for every copy of the device (see Figure 4). If it is possible to shave off a few pennies off the manufacturing cost of every unit, the savings can add up quickly for devices that are produced in large volumes. Thus, the embedded-system programmer has a much larger economic incentive to conserve resources than the programmer of desktop software. Unfortunately, trying to conserve resources usually makes it harder to write programs that work correctly.

▼ Generally, embedded systems are written in lower-level programming languages to avoid the overhead of a complex runtime system. The Java runtime system, with its safety mechanisms, garbage collector, support for multithreading, and so on, would be too costly to add to every washing machine. However, some devices are now being built with a scaled-down version of Java: the Java 2 Micro Edition. Examples are smart cell phones and onboard computers for automobiles. The Java 2 Micro Edition is a good candidate for devices that are connected to a network and that need to be able to run new applications safely. For example, you can download a program into a Java-enabled cell phone and be assured that it cannot corrupt other parts of the cell phone software.

Figure 4

The Controller of an Embedded System

CHAPTER SUMMARY

1. A thread is a program unit that is executed independently of other parts of the program.

2. When a Thread object is started, the code in its run method is executed in a new thread.

3. The sleep method puts the current thread to sleep for a given number of milliseconds.

4. When a thread is interrupted, the most common response is to terminate the run method.

5. The thread scheduler runs each thread for a short amount of time, called a *time slice*.

6. A thread terminates when its run method terminates.

7. A thread should occasionally check whether it has been interrupted, by calling the isInterrupted method.

8. A race condition occurs if the effect of multiple threads on shared data depends on the order in which the threads are scheduled.

9. By executing a synchronized method, a thread acquires the object lock. Then no other thread can acquire the lock.

10. A deadlock occurs if no thread can proceed because each thread is waiting for another to do some work first.

11. Calling wait inside a synchronized method makes the current thread wait and allows another thread to acquire the object lock.

12. A waiting thread is blocked until another thread calls notifyAll or notify on the object for which the thread is waiting.

CLASSES, OBJECTS, AND METHODS INTRODUCED IN THIS CHAPTER

```
java.lang.InterruptedException
java.lang.Object
    notify
    notifyAll
    wait
java.lang.Thread
    currentThread
    isInterrupted
    run
    sleep
    start
```

REVIEW EXERCISES

Exercise R21.1. Run a program with the following instructions:

```
GreetingThread t1 = new GreetingThread("Hello, World!");
GreetingThread t2 =
    new GreetingThread("Goodbye, World!");
t1.run();
t2.run();
```

Note that the threads don't run in parallel. Explain.

Exercise R21.2. In the program of Section 21.1, is it possible that both threads are sleeping at the same time? That neither of the two threads is sleeping at a particular time? Explain.

Exercise R21.3. In Java, a graphical user interface program has more than one thread. Explain how you can prove that.

Exercise R21.4. Why is the `stop` method for stopping a thread deprecated? How do you terminate a thread?

Exercise R21.5. Give an example why you would want to terminate a thread.

Exercise R21.6. Suppose you surround each call to the `sleep` method with a `try/catch` block to catch an `InterruptedException` and ignore it. What problem do you create?

Exercise R21.7. Suppose the following threads are alive.

Thread	State	Priority
Thread-0	Runnable	5
Thread-1	Sleeping	5
Thread-2	Runnable	5
Thread-3	Waiting	5

The scheduler is about to give a time slice to a new thread. Among which of these threads does it choose?

Exercise R21.8. Suppose the following threads are alive.

Thread	State	Priority
Thread-0	Runnable	5
Thread-1	Sleeping	6
Thread-2	Runnable	5
Thread-3	Waiting	6
Thread-4	Runnable	4

The scheduler is about to give a time slice to a new thread. Among which of these threads does it choose?

Exercise R21.9. What is a race condition? How can you avoid it?

Exercise R21.10. What is a deadlock? How can you avoid it?

Exercise R21.11. What is the difference between a thread that sleeps by calling `sleep` and a thread that waits by calling `wait`?

Exercise R21.12. What happens when a thread calls `wait` and no other thread calls `notifyAll` or `notify`?

Exercise R21.13. How can you change the threads in Advanced Topic 21.4 to avoid the deadlock?

Exercise R21.14. In the algorithm animation program of Section 21.4, we do not use `wait` and `notify`. Why not?

Exercise R21.15. Consider the algorithm animation program of Section 21.4. Suppose you click with the mouse after the animation has started but before it has finished. Then the animation thread is interrupted. Suppose the thread is currently sleeping. Explain how its `run` method is terminated. On the other hand, if it is not sleeping when it is interrupted, how is the `run` method terminated?

PROGRAMMING EXERCISES

Exercise P21.1. Implement a `Queue` class whose `add` and `remove` methods are synchronized. Supply one thread, called the producer, which keeps inserting strings into the queue as long as there are fewer than 10 elements in it. When the queue gets too full, the thread waits. As sample strings, simply use time stamps `new Date().toString()`. Supply a second thread, called the consumer, that keeps removing and printing strings from the queue as long as the queue is not empty. When the queue is empty, the thread waits. Both the consumer and producer threads should run for 1,000 iterations.

Exercise P21.2. Enhance the preceding exercise by supplying a variable number of producer and consumer threads. Prompt the program user for the numbers.

Exercise P21.3. Implement the `Purse` class of Chapter 13 so that the `addCoin` method is synchronized. Also implement a synchronized `removeCoin` method. Implement one thread that adds pennies, another thread that adds quarters, and one thread that removes and prints coins.

Exercise P21.4. Modify the car applet of Chapter 4 so that the cars are moving. Use a separate thread for each car.

Exercise P21.5. Modify the preceding exercise so that the cars change direction when they hit an edge of the window.

Exercise P21.6. Write a program `WordCount` that counts the words in one or more files. Start a new thread for each file. For example, if you call

```
java WordCount report.txt address.txt Homework.java
```

then the program might print

```
address.txt: 1052
Homework.java: 445
report.txt: 2099
```

Exercise P21.7. Write a program `Find` that searches all files specified on the command line and prints out all lines containing a keyword. Start a new thread for each file. For example, if you call

```
java Find Buff report.txt address.txt Homework.java
```

then the program might print

```
report.txt: Buffet style lunch will be available at the
address.txt: Buffet, Warren|11801 Trenton Court|Dallas|TX
```

```
Homework.java: BufferedReader in;
address.txt: Walters, Winnie|59 Timothy Circle|Buffalo|MI
```

Exercise P21.8. Instead of using a thread and a `pause` method, use the `Timer` class of Chapter 9 to animate an algorithm. Whenever the timer sends out an action event, run the algorithm to the next step and display the state. That requires a more extensive recoding of the algorithm. You need to implement a `runToNextStep` method that is capable of running the algorithm one step at a time. Add sufficient instance fields to the algorithm to remember where the last step left off. For example, in the case of the selection sort algorithm, if you know the values of `alreadySorted` and `markedPosition`, you can determine the next step.

Exercise P21.9. Implement an animation of the merge sort algorithm of Chapter 18. Reimplement the algorithm so that the recursive calls sort the elements inside a subrange of the the original array, rather than in their own arrays:

```
public void mergeSort(int from, int to)
{
   if (from == to) return;
   int mid = (from + to) / 2;
   mergeSort(from, mid);
   mergeSort(mid + 1, to);
   merge(from, mid, to);
}
```

The `merge` method merges the sorted ranges `a[from]` . . . `a[mid]` and `a[mid + 1]` . . . `a[to]`.

Pause in the `merge` method whenever you inspect an array element. Color the range `a[from]` . . . `a[to]` in blue, and the currently inspected element in red.

Exercise P21.10. Implement the merge sort algorithm of Chapter 18 by spawning a new thread for each smaller `MergeSorter`.

Internet Networking

▶ To learn how to send and receive data through sockets

▶ To implement network clients and servers

▶ To communicate with web servers and server-side applications through the Hypertext Transfer Protocol (HTTP)

Y

The *Internet* is a worldwide collection of networks, routing equipment, and computers using a common set of protocols to define how each party will interact with each other.

ou probably have quite a bit of experience with the *Internet:* the global network that links together millions of computers. In particular, you use the Internet whenever you browse the World Wide Web. Note that the Internet is not the same as the "web". The World Wide Web is only one of many services that are offered over the Internet. Email, another popular service, also uses the Internet, but its implementation differs from that of the Web. In this chapter, you will see what goes on "under the hood" when you send an email message or when you retrieve a web page from a remote server. You will also learn how to write your own programs that fetch data from sites across the Internet and how to write server programs that can serve information to other programs.

22.1   The Internet Protocol

Computers can be connected with each other through a variety of physical media. In a computer lab, for example, computers are connected by network cabling. Electrical impulses representing information flow across the cables. If you use a modem to connect your own computer to the Internet, the signals travel across a regular telephone wire, encoded as tones. On a wireless network, signals are sent by transmitting a modulated radio frequency. The physical characteristics of these transmissions differ widely, but they ultimately consist of sending and receiving streams of zeroes and ones along the network connection.

These zeroes and ones represent two kinds of information: *application data*, the data that one computer actually wants to send to another, and *network protocol data*, the data that describe how to reach the intended recipient and how to check for errors and data loss in the transmission. The protocol data follow certain rules set forth by a particular *network protocol*. Various network protocols are in common use, such as Microsoft Networking, Novell NetWare, or AppleTalk; these are protocols for local area networks (see Random Fact 4.1). The *Internet Protocol* (IP), on the other hand, was developed to enable different local area networks to communicate with each other and has become the basis for connecting computers around the world together over the Internet. We will discuss IP in this chapter.

Suppose that a computer A wants to send data to a computer B, both on the Internet. The computers aren't connected directly with a cable, as they could be if both were on the same local area network. Instead, A may be someone's home computer and connect by phone to an *Internet service provider* (ISP), which is in turn connected to an *Internet access point*; B might be a computer on a local area network belonging to a large firm that has an Internet access point of its own, which may be half a world away from A. The Internet itself, finally, is a complex collection of pathways on which a message can travel from one Internet access point to, eventually, any other Internet access point (see Figure 1). Those connections carry millions of messages, not just the data that A is sending to B.

For the data to arrive at their destination, they must be marked with a *destination address*. In IP, addresses are denoted by sequences of four numbers, each one byte (that is, between 0 and 255); for example, 130.65.86.66. (Because there aren't enough 4-byte addresses for all devices that would like to connect to the Internet, these addresses will be extended to six numbers in the near future.) In order to send data, A needs to know the Internet address of B and include it in the protocol portion when sending the data across the Internet. The routing software that is distributed across the Internet can then deliver the data to B.

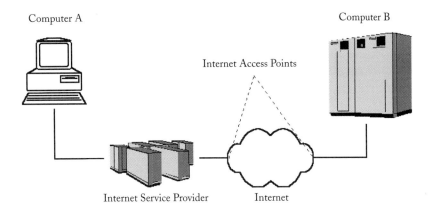

Computer A

Computer B

Internet Access Points

Internet Service Provider

Internet

Figure 1

Two Computers Communicating across the Internet

Of course, addresses such as 130.65.86.66 are not easy to remember. You would not be happy if you had to use number sequences every time you sent email or requested information from a web server. On the Internet, computers can have so-called *domain names* that are easier to remember, such as `cs.sjsu.edu` or `java.sun.com`. A special service called the *Domain Naming Service* (DNS) translates between domain names and Internet addresses. Thus, if computer A wants to have information from `java.sun.com`, it first asks the DNS to translate this domain name into a numeric Internet address; then it includes the numeric address with the request.

One interesting aspect of IP is that it breaks large chunks of data up into more manageable *packets*. Each packet is delivered separately, and different packets that are part of the same transmission can take different routes through the Internet. Packets are numbered, and the recipient reassembles them in the correct order.

The Internet Protocol has just one function—to attempt to deliver data from one computer to another across the Internet. If some data get lost or garbled in the process, IP has safeguards built in to make sure that the recipient is aware of that unfortunate fact and doesn't rely on incomplete data. However, IP has no provisions for notifying the sender to retry the transmission. That is the job of a higher-level protocol, the *Transmission Control Protocol* (TCP). This protocol attempts reliable delivery of data, with retries if there are failures, and it notifies the sender whether or not the attempt succeeded. Most, but not all, Internet programs use TCP for reliable delivery. (Exceptions are "streaming media" services, which bypass the slower TCP for the fastest possible throughput and tolerate occasional information loss. However, the most popular Internet services—the World Wide Web and email—use TCP.) TCP is independent of the Internet Protocol; it could in principle be used with another lower-level network protocol. However, in practice, TCP over IP (often called TCP/IP) is the most commonly used combination. We will focus on TCP/IP networking in this chapter.

> TCP/IP is the abbreviation for *Transmission Control Protocol over Internet Protocol*, the pair of communication protocols that is used to establish reliable transmission of data between two computers on the Internet.

A computer that is connected to the Internet may have programs for many different purposes. For example, a computer may run both a web server program and a mail server program. When data are sent to that computer, they need to be marked so that they can be forwarded to the appropriate program. The Internet Protocol uses *port numbers* for this purpose. A port number is an integer between 0 and 65,535. The sending computer must know the port number of the receiving program and include it with the transmitted data. Some application use "well-known" port numbers. For example, by convention, web servers use port 80, whereas mail servers running the Post Office Protocol (POP) use port 110. TCP packets, therefore, must contain

- The Internet address of the recipient
- The port number of the recipient
- The Internet address of the sender
- The port number of the sender

> A TCP connection requires the Internet addresses and port numbers of both endpoints.

You can think of a TCP connection as a "pipe" between two computers that links the two ports together. Data flow in either direction through the pipe. In practical programming situations, you simply establish a connection and send data across it without worrying about the details of the TCP/IP mechanism. You will see how to establish such a connection in Section 22.3.

Random Fact 22.1

The OSI Model

In 1984, the International Organization for Standardization (ISO) released a theoretical description of network protocols called the Open Systems Interconnection (OSI) reference model. The OSI model describes the various layers of abstraction for network software and hardware, and it sets rules for how the layers can communicate with each other. As Figure 2 shows, the layers form a stack. Each layer calls on services only from the layer immediately below it. This design shields the upper layers from implementation details of the lower layers.

Here is a detailed description of the layers.

- The *physical layer* is concerned with transmitting bits over a physical medium such as a copper cable, optical fiber, or wireless link.

- The *data link layer* groups bits of data into larger packages that are transmitted as a unit, and ensures that packages are delivered without transmission errors.

▼ **Figure 2**

▼ The OSI Reference Model

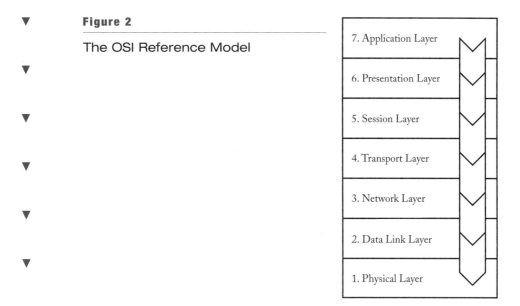

- The *network layer* manages connections across the network, such as routing packages and avoiding congestion.

- The *transport layer* ensures that packages are delivered from one computer to the other, requests retransmission of lost packages, and rearranges packages that arrived out of order.

- The *session layer* establishes connection sessions between two computers and regulates which side transmits data, and for how long.

- The *presentation layer* implements standardized data presentation services such as data encryption, compression, and format conversion.

- The *application layer* is concerned with network applications such as web browsing and electronic mail.

The OSI model is a theoretical model to which actual network implementations conform to various degrees. In the case of the Internet, IP lies at level 3, and TCP lies at level 4. That is, IP is responsible for delivering packets across the network. The job of IP is to make sure that packets are either delivered in their entirety to their intended recipient, or not delivered at all. TCP is responsible for guaranteed delivery of a stream of packets. If the TCP layer finds that a packet is missing, it uses the IP layer (but not a lower layer) to ask the sender to retransmit the missing packet.

22.2 Application Level Protocols

> HTTP, which stands for Hypertext Transfer Protocol, is the protocol that defines communication between web browsers and web servers.

> An URL or *Uniform Resource Locator*, is a pointer to an information resource (such as a web page or an image) on the World Wide Web.

In the preceding section you saw how the TCP/IP mechanism can establish an Internet connection between two ports on two computers so that the two computers can exchange data. Each Internet application has a different *application protocol*, which describes how the data for that particular application are transmitted.

Consider, for example, HTTP: the *Hypertext Transfer Protocol*, which is used for the World Wide Web. Suppose you type a web address, called a Uniform Resource Locator (URL, often pronounced like "Earl"), such as `http://java.sun.com/index.html`, into the Address window of your browser and ask the browser to load the page. The browser now takes the following steps:

1. It examines the part of the URL between the double slash and the first single slash ("`java.sun.com`"), which identifies the computer to which you want to connect. Because this part of this URL contains letters, it must be a domain name rather than an Internet address, so the browser sends a request to a DNS server to obtain the Internet address of the computer with domain name `java.sun.com`.

2. From the `http:` prefix of the URL, the browser deduces that the protocol you want to use is HTTP, which by default uses port 80.

3. It establishes a TCP/IP connection to port 80 at the Internet address it obtained in step 1.

4. It deduces from the `/index.html` suffix that you want to see the file `/index.html`, so it sends a request, formatted as an HTTP command, through the connection that was established in step 3. The request looks like this:

   ```
   GET /index.html HTTP/1.0
   blank line
   ```

5. The web server running on the computer whose Internet address is the one the browser obtained in step 1 receives the request and decodes it. It then fetches the file `/index.html` and sends it back to the browser on your computer.

6. The browser displays the contents of the file for you to see. Since it happens to be an HTML file, the browser translates the HTML codes into fonts, bullets, separator lines, and so on (see Chapter 4). If the HTML file contains images, then the browser makes more `GET` requests, one for each image, through the same connection, to fetch the image data.

You can try the following experiment to see this process in action. The *telnet* program enables a user to type characters for sending to a remote computer and view characters that the remote computer sends back. On Windows, the Telnet program is usually already installed, but you probably won't see it on your desktop; try clicking on the Start button, selecting "Run...", and type `telnet` at the "Open" window. On the Macintosh, you should download and install NCSA Telnet from http://www.ncsa.uiuc.edu/SDG/Software/MacTelnet/.

Figure 3

Using *telnet* to Connect to a Web
Server

UNIX (and Linux) systems normally have *telnet* preinstalled. For this experiment, you want to start *telnet* with a host of `java.sun.com` and port 80. The details depend on your *telnet* program. If you start the program from the command line, simply type

```
telnet java.sun.com 80
```

With some versions of *telnet*, you need to enter the host and port into a dialog box. Figure 3 shows the dialog of the Windows version.

Once the program starts, type very carefully, without making any typing errors and without hitting the backspace key,

```
GET /index.html HTTP/1.0
```

Then hit the Enter key twice.

> The *telnet* program is a useful tool to establish test connections with servers.

You will not see what you type, because the *telnet* program sends your keystrokes directly to the server. (Some versions of *telnet* have a "local echo" option that show you what you typed. If yours does, it is a good idea to turn it on for this experiment.)

The server now sends a response to the request—see Figure 4. The response, of course, consists of the index.html file. The *telnet* program is not a

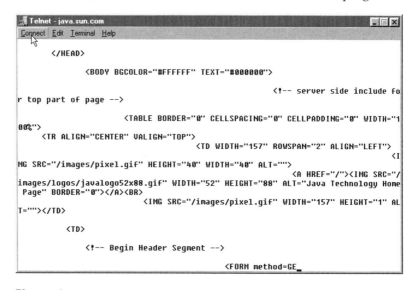

Figure 4

The Web Server Sends the Response

Command	Meaning
GET	Return the requested item
HEAD	Request only the header information of an item
OPTIONS	Request communications options of an item
POST	Supply input to a server-side command and return the result
PUT	Store an item on the server
DELETE	Delete an item on the server
TRACE	Trace server communication

Table 1

HTTP Commands

browser and does not understand HTML tags, so it simply displays the HTML file, text, tags, and all.

The GET command is one of the commands of HTTP. Table 1 shows the other commands of the protocol. As you can see, the protocol is pretty simple.

> The HTTP GET command requests information from a web server. The web server returns the requested item, which may be a web page, an image, or other data.

By the way, be sure not to confuse HTML with HTTP. HTML is a *document format* (with commands such as <h1> or <ul>) that describes the structure of a document, including headings, bulleted lists, images, hyperlinks, and so on. HTTP is a *protocol* (with commands such as GET and POST) that describes the command set for web server requests. Web *browsers* know how to display HTML documents and how to issue HTTP commands. Web *servers* know nothing about HTML. They merely understand HTTP and know how to fetch the requested items. Those items may be HTML documents, GIF or JPEG images, or any other data that a web browser can display.

HTTP is just one of many application protocols in use on the Internet. Another commonly used protocol is the Post Office Protocol (POP), which is used to download received messages from email servers. To *send* messages, you use yet another protocol called the Simple Mail Transfer Protocol (SMTP). We don't want to go into the details of these protocols, but Figure 5 gives you a flavor of the commands used by the Post Office Protocol.

Both HTTP and POP use plain text. That makes it particularly easy to test and debug client and server programs (see HOWTO 22.1).

Figure 5

A Sample POP Session

```
+OK San Quentin State POP server
USER harryh
+OK Password required for harryh
PASS secret
+OK harryh has 2 messages (320 octets)
STAT
+OK 2 320
RETR 1
+OK 120 octets
the message is included here
DELE 1
+OK message 1 deleted
QUIT
+OK POP server signing off
```

Black = mail client requests
Color = mail server responses

22.3   A Client Program

In this section you will see how to write a Java program that establishes a TCP/IP connection to a server, sends a request to the server, and prints the response.

In the terminology of TCP/IP, there is a *socket* on each side of the connection (see Figure 6). In Java, a client establishes a socket with a call

```
Socket s = new Socket(hostname, portnumber);
```

For example, to connect to the HTTP port of the server java.sun.com, you use

```
final int HTTP_PORT = 80;
Socket s = new Socket("java.sun.com", HTTP_PORT);
```

The socket constructor throws an UnknownHostException if it can't find the host.

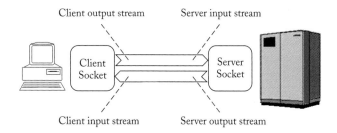

Figure 6

Client and Server Sockets

Once you have a socket, you obtain its input and output streams:

```
InputStream in = s.getInputStream();
OutputStream out = s.getOutputStream();
```

When you send data to output stream out, the socket automatically forwards them to the server. The socket catches the server's response, and you can read the response through the input stream in (see Figure 6).

When you are done communicating with the server, you should close the socket:

```
s.close();
```

In Chapter 15, you saw that the InputStream and OutputStream classes are used for reading and writing bytes. If you want to communicate with the server by sending and receiving text, you should turn the streams into readers and writers, as follows:

```
BufferedReader reader = new BufferedReader(
    new InputStreamReader(in));
PrintWriter writer = new PrintWriter(out);
```

A print writer *buffers* the characters that you send to it. That is, characters are not immediately sent to their destination. Instead, they are placed into an array. When the array is full, then the print writer sends all characters in the array to its destination. The advantage of buffering is increased performance—it takes some amount of time to contact the destination and send it data, and it is expensive to pay for that contact time for every character. However, when communicating with a server that responds to requests, you want to make sure that the server gets a complete request at a time. Therefore, you need to *flush* the buffer manually whenever you send a command:

```
writer.print(command);
writer.flush();
```

The flush method empties the buffer and forwards all waiting characters to the destination.

The WebGet program at the end of this section lets you retrieve any item from a web server. You need to specify the host and the item from the command line. For example,

```
java WebGet java.sun.com index.html
```

The program simply establishes a connection to the host, sends a GET command to the host, and then receives input from the server until the server closes its connection.

Program WebGet.java

```
1 import java.io.BufferedReader;
2 import java.io.InputStream;
```

```
 3  import java.io.InputStreamReader;
 4  import java.io.IOException;
 5  import java.io.OutputStream;
 6  import java.io.PrintWriter;
 7  import java.net.Socket;
 8
 9  /**
10     This program demonstrates how to use a socket to communicate
11     with a web server. Supply the name of the host and the
12     resource on the command line, for example
13        java WebGet java.sun.com index.html
14  */
15  public class WebGet
16  {
17     public static void main(String[] args)
18        throws IOException
19     {
20        // get command line arguments
21
22        if (args.length != 2)
23        {
24           System.out.println(
25              "usage: java WebGet host resource");
26           System.exit(0);
27        }
28        String host = args[0];
29        String resource = args[1];
30
31        // open socket
32
33        final int HTTP_PORT = 80;
34        Socket s = new Socket(host, HTTP_PORT);
35
36        // get streams
37
38        InputStream in = s.getInputStream();
39        OutputStream out = s.getOutputStream();
40
41        // turn streams into readers and writers
42
43        BufferedReader reader = new BufferedReader(
44           new InputStreamReader(in));
45        PrintWriter writer = new PrintWriter(out);
46
47        // send command
48
49        String command = "GET /" + resource
50           + " HTTP/1.0\n\n";
51        writer.print(command);
52        writer.flush();
```

```
53
54        // read server response
55
56        boolean done = false;
57        while (!done)
58        {
59            String input = reader.readLine();
60            if (input == null) done = true;
61            else System.out.println(input);
62        }
63
64        // always close the socket at the end
65
66        s.close();
67    }
68 }
```

22.4 A Server Program

Now that you have seen how to write a network client, we will turn to the server side. In this section we will develop a server program that enables clients to manage a set of bank accounts in a bank.

Whenever you develop a server application, you need to specify some application-level protocol that clients can use to interact with the server. For the purpose of this example, we will create a "Simple Bank Access Protocol". Table 2 shows the protocol format. Of course, this is just a toy protocol to show you how to implement a server.

The server program waits for clients to connect to a particular port. We choose port 8888 for this service. To listen to incoming connections, you use a *server socket*. To construct a server socket, you need to supply the port number.

```
ServerSocket server = new ServerSocket(8888);
```

Client Request	Server Response	Meaning
BALANCE *n*	*n* and the balance	Get balance of account *n*
DEPOSIT *n a*	*n* and the new balance	Deposit amount *a* into account *n*
WITHDRAW *n a*	*n* and the new balance	Withdraw amount *a* from account *n*
QUIT	None	Quit the connection

Table 2

A Simple Bank Access Protocol

The `accept` method of the `ServerSocket` class waits for client connection. When a client connects, then the server program obtains a socket through which it communicates with the client.

```
Socket s = server.accept();
```

> The ServerSocket class is used by server applications to listen for client connections.

You now obtain the input and output streams from s in the same way as we discussed in the preceding section:

```
BufferedReader in = new BufferedReader(
    new InputStreamReader(s.getInputStream()));

PrintWriter out = new PrintWriter(
    s.getOutputStream());
```

Next, the server reads a command from the client:

```
String line = in.readLine();
```

If the line is null (which means the client has disconnected) or equals the `"QUIT"` command, then the server closes the socket `s`. The *server* socket is never closed—the server keeps waiting for incoming connections.

To analyze the client command further, we use a string tokenizer. The first token is the command, and the second is the account number:

```
StringTokenizer tokenizer = new StringTokenizer(line);
String command = tokenizer.nextToken();
int account = Integer.parseInt(tokenizer.nextToken());
```

If the command is DEPOSIT, then we carry out the deposit.

```
double amount = Double.parseDouble(
    tokenizer.nextToken());
bank.deposit(account, amount);
```

We handle the `WITHDRAW` command in the same way.

Finally, we send the account number and new balance to the client.

```
out.println(n + " " + bank.getBalance(account));
```

Note that the server program never stops. When you are done running the server, you need to kill it. For example, if you started the server in a shell window, hit Ctrl+C.

To try out the program, run the server. Then use the telnet program to connect to `localhost`, port number 8888. Start typing commands. Here is a typical dialog:

```
BALANCE 5
5 0
DEPOSIT 5 2000
5 2000
WITHDRAW 5 1000
5 1000
QUIT
```

See Figure 7.

Figure 7

Using the telnet program to Connect to the Bank Server

Alternatively, you can use a client program that connects to the server. You will find a sample client program at the end of this section.

This server program has one major limitation: Only one client can connect to it at any point in time. This limitation would be serious in practice—typically many clients connect to a server at any time. To implement that behavior, server programs spawn a new *thread* whenever a client connects. Multiple threads can run in parallel. Each thread is responsible for serving one client. See Exercise P22.5 for the implementation of a multithreaded server.

File BankServer.java

```
1  import java.io.IOException;
2  import java.net.ServerSocket;
3  import java.net.Socket;
4
5  /**
6      A server that executes the Simple Bank Access Protocol.
7  */
8  public class BankServer
9  {
10     public static void main(String[] args )
11        throws IOException
12     {
13        final int ACCOUNTS_LENGTH = 10;
14        Bank bank = new Bank(ACCOUNTS_LENGTH);
```

```
15        final int SBAP_PORT = 8888;
16        ServerSocket server = new ServerSocket(SBAP_PORT);
17        System.out.println(
18           "Waiting for clients to connect...");
19
20        while (true)
21        {
22           Socket s = server.accept();
23
24           BankService service = new BankService(s, bank);
25           service.doService();
26           s.close();
27        }
28     }
29  }
```

File BankService.java

```
 1  import java.io.BufferedReader;
 2  import java.io.InputStream;
 3  import java.io.InputStreamReader;
 4  import java.io.IOException;
 5  import java.io.OutputStream;
 6  import java.io.PrintWriter;
 7  import java.net.Socket;
 8  import java.util.StringTokenizer;
 9
10  /**
11      Executes Simple Bank Access Protocol commands
12      from a socket.
13  */
14  public class BankService
15  {
16     /**
17         Constructs a service object that processes commands
18         from a socket for a bank.
19         @param aSocket the socket
20         @param aBank the bank
21     */
22     public BankService(Socket aSocket, Bank aBank)
23     {
24        s = aSocket;
25        bank = aBank;
26     }
27
28     /**
29         Executes all commands until the QUIT command or the
30         end of input.
31     */
32     public void doService() throws IOException
```

```
33     {
34        BufferedReader in = new BufferedReader(
35           new InputStreamReader(s.getInputStream()));
36        PrintWriter out = new PrintWriter(
37           s.getOutputStream());
38
39        while (true)
40        {
41           String line = in.readLine();
42           System.out.println("Received: " + line);
43           if (line == null || line.equals("QUIT"))
44              return;
45
46           String response = executeCommand(line);
47
48           System.out.println("Sending: " + response);
49           out.println(response);
50           out.flush();
51        }
52     }
53
54     /**
55        Executes a single command.
56        @param line the command
57        @return the reply to send to the client
58     */
59     public String executeCommand(String line)
60     {
61        StringTokenizer tokenizer
62           = new StringTokenizer(line);
63        String command = tokenizer.nextToken();
64        int account = Integer.parseInt(
65           tokenizer.nextToken());
66        if (command.equals("DEPOSIT"))
67        {
68           double amount = Double.parseDouble(
69              tokenizer.nextToken());
70           bank.deposit(account, amount);
71        }
72        else if (command.equals("WITHDRAW"))
73        {
74           double amount = Double.parseDouble(
75              tokenizer.nextToken());
76           bank.withdraw(account, amount);
77        }
78        else if (!command.equals("BALANCE"))
79           return "Invalid command";
80
81        return account + " " + bank.getBalance(account);
82     }
```

```
83
84    private Socket s;
85    private Bank bank;
86 }
```

File BankClient.java

```
1 import java.io.BufferedReader;
2 import java.io.InputStream;
3 import java.io.InputStreamReader;
4 import java.io.IOException;
5 import java.io.OutputStream;
6 import java.io.PrintWriter;
7 import java.net.Socket;
8
9 /**
10    This program tests the bank server.
11 */
12 public class BankClient
13 {
14    public static void main(String[] args)
15       throws IOException
16    {
17       final int SBAP_PORT = 8888;
18       Socket s = new Socket("localhost", SBAP_PORT);
19       InputStream in = s.getInputStream();
20       OutputStream out = s.getOutputStream();
21       BufferedReader reader = new BufferedReader(
22          new InputStreamReader(in));
23       PrintWriter writer = new PrintWriter(out);
24
25       String command = "DEPOSIT 3 1000\n";
26       System.out.print("Sending: " + command);
27       writer.print(command);
28       writer.flush();
29       String response = reader.readLine();
30       System.out.println("Receiving: " + response);
31
32       command = "WITHDRAW 3 500\n";
33       System.out.print("Sending: " + command);
34       writer.print(command);
35       writer.flush();
36       response = reader.readLine();
37       System.out.println("Receiving: " + response);
38
39       command = "QUIT\n";
40       System.out.print("Sending: " + command);
41       writer.print(command);
42       writer.flush();
43
```

```
44        s.close();
45     }
46 }
```

File Bank.java

```
1  /**
2      A bank consisting of multiple bank accounts.
3  */
4  public class Bank
5  {
6      /**
7          Constructs a bank account with a given number of accounts.
8          @param size the number of accounts
9      */
10     public Bank(int size)
11     {
12        accounts = new BankAccount[size];
13        for (int i = 0; i < accounts.length; i++)
14           accounts[i] = new BankAccount();
15     }
16
17     /**
18         Deposits money into a bank account.
19         @param accountNumber the account number
20         @param amount the amount to deposit
21     */
22     public void deposit(int accountNumber, double amount)
23     {
24        BankAccount account = accounts[accountNumber];
25        account.deposit(amount);
26     }
27
28     /**
29         Withdraws money from a bank account.
30         @param accountNumber the account number
31         @param amount the amount to withdraw
32     */
33     public void withdraw(int accountNumber, double amount)
34     {
35        BankAccount account = accounts[accountNumber];
36        account.withdraw(amount);
37     }
38
39     /**
40         Gets the balance of a bank account.
41         @param accountNumber the account number
42         @return the account balance
43     */
44     public double getBalance(int accountNumber)
```

```
45    {
46        BankAccount account = accounts[accountNumber];
47        return account.getBalance();
48    }
49
50    private BankAccount[] accounts;
51 }
```

? HOWTO   22.1

Designing Client/Server Programs

The bank server of this section is a typical example of a client/server program. A web browser and web server are another example. Follow these steps when designing a client/server application.

Step 1 Determine whether it really makes sense to implement a stand-alone server and a matching client

Many times it makes more sense to build a web application instead. Chapter 25 discusses the construction of web applications in detail. For example, the bank application of this section could easily be turned into a web application, using an HTML form with Withdraw and Deposit buttons. However, programs for chat or peer-to-peer file sharing cannot easily be implemented as web applications.

Step 2 Design a communications protocol

Figure out exactly what messages the client and server send to each other and what the success and error responses are.

With each request and response, ask yourself how the *end of data* is indicated.

- Do the data fit on a single line? Then the end of the line serves as the data terminator.

- Can the data be terminated by a special line (such as a blank line after the HTTP header or a line containing a period in SMTP)?

- Does the sender of the data close the socket? That's what a web server does at the end of a GET request.

- Can the sender indicate how many bytes are contained in the request? Web browsers do that in POST requests.

Use text, not binary data, for the communication between client and server. A text-based protocol is easier to debug.

▼ Step 3 Implement the server program

▼ The server listens for socket connections and accepts them. It then receives commands, interprets them, and sends a response back to the client.

Step 4 Test the server with the telnet program

▼ Try out all commands in the communications protocol.

▼ Step 5 Once the server works, write a client program

The client program interacts with the program user, turns user requests into protocol commands, sends the commands to the server, receives the response, and displays the response for the program user.

22.5 URL Connections

In Section 22.3, you saw how to use sockets to connect to a web server and how to retrieve information from the server by sending HTTP commands. However, because HTTP is such an important protocol, the Java library contains an URLConnection class, which provides convenient support for the HTTP. The URLConnection class takes care of the socket connection, so you don't have to fuss with sockets when you want to retrieve from a web server. As an additional benefit, the URLConnection class can also handle FTP, the *file transfer protocol*.

> The URLConnection class makes it easy to communicate with a web server without having to issue HTTP commands.

The URLConnection class makes it very easy to fetch a file from a web server given the file's URL as a string. First, you construct an URL object from the URL in the familiar format, starting with http or ftp prefix. Then you use the URL object's openConnection() method to get the URLConnection object itself.

```
URL u = new URL("http://java.sun.com/index.html");
URLConnection connection = u.openConnection();
```

Then you call the getInputStream method to obtain an input stream:

```
InputStream in = connection.getInputStream();
```

Sometimes you can just give that input stream to another method. But if you want to read the contents yourself, you need to turn the stream into a reader.

```
BufferedReader reader = new BufferedReader(
    new InputStreamReader(in));
```

Now you can read the contents of the resource a line at a time:

```
boolean done = false;

while (!done)
```

```
{
   String input = reader.readLine();
   if (input == null)
      done = true;
   else do something with input
}
```

> The URLConnection and HttpURLConnection classes can give you additional information about HTTP requests and responses.

The `URLConnection` class can give you additional useful information. To understand those capabilities, we need to have a closer look at HTTP requests and responses. You saw in Section 22.1 that the command for getting an item from the server is

```
GET item HTTP/1.0
blank line
```

You may have wondered why you need to provide a blank line. This blank line is a part of the general request format. The first line of the request is a command such as `GET` or `POST`. The command may be followed by *request properties*, and some commands—in particular, the `POST` command—send input data to the server. (We will look at the `POST` command in the next section.) The reason for the blank line is to denote the boundary between the command, with its request property section, and the input data section.

A typical request property is `If-Modified-Since`. If you request an item with

```
GET item HTTP/1.0
If-Modified-Since: date
blank line
```

the server sends the item only if it is newer than the date. Browsers use this feature to speed up redisplay of previously loaded web pages. When a web page is loaded, the browser stores it in a *cache* directory. When the user wants to see the same web page again, the browser asks the server to get a new page only if it has been modified since the date of the cached copy. If it isn't, the browser simply redisplays the cached copy without spending time on downloading another identical copy.

The `URLConnection` class has methods to set request properties. For example, you can set the `If-Modified-Since` property with the `setIfModifiedSince` method:

```
connection.setIfModifiedSince(date);
```

You need to set request properties before calling the `getInputStream` method. The `URLConnection` class then sends to the web server all the request properties that you set.

Similarly, the response from the server starts with a status line followed by a set of response parameters. The response parameters are terminated by a blank line and followed by the requested data (for example, an HTML page). Here is a typical response:

```
HTTP/1.1 200 OK
Date: Sun, 29 Aug 1999 00:15:48 GMT
Server: Apache/1.3.3 (Unix)
Last-Modified: Thu, 24 Jun 1999 20:53:38 GMT
Content-Length: 4813
```

```
Content-Type: text/html
```
blank line
requested data

Normally, you don't see the response code. However, you may have run across bad links and seen a page that contained a response code `404 Not Found`. (A successful response has status `200 OK`.)

To retrieve the response code, you need to cast the `URLConnection` object to the `HttpURLConnection` subclass. You can retrieve the response code (such as the number 200 in this example, or the code 404 if a page was not found) and response message with the `getResponseCode` and `getResponseMessage` methods:

```
HttpURLConnection httpConnection =
    (HttpURLConnection)connection;
int code = httpConnection.getResponseCode(); // e.g., 404
String message =
    httpConnection.getResponseMessage(); // e.g., "Not found"
```

As you can see from the response example, the server sends some information *about* the requested data, such as the content length and the content type. You can request this information with methods from the `URLConnection` class:

```
int length = connection.getContentLength();
String type = connection.getContentType();
```

You need to call these methods after calling the `getInputStream` method.

To summarize: You don't need to use sockets to communicate with a web server, and you need not master the details of the HTTP protocol. Simply use the `URLConnection` and `HttpURLConnection` classes to obtain data from a web server, to set request parameters, or to obtain response information.

The program at the end of this section puts the `URLConnection` class to work. The program fulfills the same purpose as that of Section 22.1—to retrieve a web page from a server—but it works at a higher level of abstraction. There is no longer a need to issue an explicit GET command. The `URLConnection` class takes care of that. Similarly, the parsing of the HTTP request and response headers is handled transparently to the programmer. Our sample program takes advantage of that fact. It checks whether the server response is `200 OK`. If not, it prints the server response and exits. You can try that out by testing the program with a bad URL, like `http://java.sun.com/wombat.html`. Then the program prints the server response `404 Not Found`.

In the next section you will see another use for the `HttpURLConnection` class: to send input to server-side programs.

File URLGet.java

```
1 import java.io.BufferedReader;
2 import java.io.InputStream;
3 import java.io.InputStreamReader;
4 import java.io.IOException;
5 import java.io.OutputStream;
6 import java.io.PrintWriter;
```

```
 7  import java.net.HttpURLConnection;
 8  import java.net.URL;
 9  import java.net.URLConnection;
10
11  /**
12     This program demonstrates how to use an URL connection
13     to communicate with a web server. Supply the URL on the
14     command line, for example
15        java URLGet http://java.sun.com/index.html
16  */
17  public class URLGet
18  {
19     public static void main(String[] args)
20        throws IOException
21     {
22        // get command line arguments
23
24        if (args.length != 1)
25        {
26           System.out.println("usage: java UrlGet URL");
27           System.exit(0);
28        }
29
30        // open connection
31
32        URL u = new URL(args[0]);
33        URLConnection connection = u.openConnection();
34
35        // check whether response code is HTTP OK (200)
36
37        HttpURLConnection httpConnection =
38           (HttpURLConnection)connection;
39        int code = httpConnection.getResponseCode();
40        if (code != HttpURLConnection.HTTP_OK)
41        {
42           String message =
43              httpConnection.getResponseMessage();
44           System.out.println(code + " " + message);
45           return;
46        }
47
48        // read server response
49
50        InputStream in = connection.getInputStream();
51        BufferedReader reader = new BufferedReader(
52           new InputStreamReader(in));
53
54        boolean done = false;
55        while (!done)
56        {
57           String input = reader.readLine();
58           if (input == null) done = true;
```

```
59          else System.out.println(input);
60       }
61    }
62 }
```

22.6 Posting Form Data

> Dynamic web content is generated by programs that the web server invokes when the data are requested.

When you request a web page such as `index.html` from a web server, the web server simply fetches the file and sends its contents back to you. Of course, if you request the same page multiple times, you will get the same contents every time, until someone replaces the file on the web server. However, many web pages have *dynamic content*—information that changes by the minute, such as weather information or stock prices. These web pages are not stored in files; instead, they are generated by programs that run on the web server. Whenever you request such a page, the web server starts the appropriate program, supplies it with input from the request, and sends its output back (see Figure 8). Usually, these programs generate output that is a mixture of data (such as the requested weather information or stock prices) and HTML code for formatting the data. The result can be displayed in any browser.

A web server needs to know when a URL denotes a file and when it denotes a program. Typically, web servers look at the directory of the URL—for example, all URLs whose suffixes start with `/servlet/` or `/cgi-bin/` are commonly considered programs. The details depend on the web server configuration. There are different methods for starting up server-side programs. We will look at one of the mechanisms—JavaServer Pages—in Chapter 25. For now, we assume that the web server knows how to locate and start up the appropriate application when it receives a request with an URL that denotes a program.

Figure 8

Dynamic Weather Data

> There are two HTTP commands for supplying input to server-side programs: GET and POST. The GET syntax is simpler, but it can be used only for short inputs.

When the web server starts the program, it feeds the program the input that the client provided in the HTTP request. There are two methods for supplying input, called the GET method and the POST method. In the GET method, the input is appended after the program URL, following a ? character. For example, consider the URL

```
http://mach.usno.navy.mil/cgi-bin/aa_moonphases?year=2000
```

This URL tells the web server at `mach.usno.navy.mil` to start up the program associated with `/cgi-bin/aa_moonphases` and to provide it the input

```
year=2000
```

This input method is called the GET method because it uses the HTTP GET command to transmit the request to the web server. The request looks like

```
GET /cgi-bin/aa_moonphases?year=2000 HTTP/1.0
```
blank line

Typically, server-side programs receive inputs that are name/value pairs. In this example, the program received a single input with name `year` and value `2000`. Multiple name/value pairs are separated by an ampersand (&) character, like this:

```
city=Chicago&zip=60614
```

> Data in GET and POST requests must be encoded. Use the URLEncoder class for that purpose.

If the names or values contain characters that are not ASCII letters or numbers, then they are encoded according a scheme called *URL encoding*. Spaces are encoded as + characters, for example

```
city=San+Francisco
```

Other bytes are encoded as %*xy*, where *xy* is the hexadecimal value of the byte. For example, to encode a / character (which has an encoding of 47 decimal or 2F hexadecimal), you use %2F:

```
city=Raleigh%2FDurham
```

You can use the static methods `URLEncoder.encode` and `URLDecoder.decode` to encode and decode strings. For example,

```
String encoding = URLEncoder.encode(name)
    + "=" + URLEncoder.encode(value);
```

The GET method has a major disadvantage: Many browsers put a limit on the number of bytes permitted in an URL (sometimes just 255 characters). Thus, you can supply only a small amount of information to a server-side program through a GET request. If you want to supply more information, you need to use a POST request. The format of a POST request is

```
POST url
Content-Type: type
```

Content-Length: *length*
other request headers
blank line
input data

The input data can be in any format. However, a common source for POST requests is the submission of HTML form data. (See Figure 9 for an HTML form.) Browsers use URL encoding when transmitting form data. Thus, a typical POST might look like this:

```
POST /cgi-bin/zip4/zip4inq2
Content-Type: application/x-www-form-urlencoded
Content-Length: 91
```
blank line
```
Firm=&Urbanization=&Delivery+Address=100+Main+Street&City=Ann+
Arbor&State=MI&Zip+Code=48104
```

> Use the URLConnection class to send POST requests to a web server.

Fortunately, when you use the URLConnection class, you don't have to worry about formatting the POST request. You simply call the set-DoOutput method to tell the URLConnection that you want to send output to it. Then you call getOutputStream to obtain an output stream and send data to that stream. If you are posting to a server-side program that processes form data, you send URL-encoded name/value pairs to the output stream. When you are done, close the output stream. Your output then becomes the input data of the POST request. Here is a typical code segment:

```
connection.setDoOutput(true);
OutputStream out = connection.getOutputStream();
```

Figure 9

An HTML Form

```
PrintWriter writer = new PrintWriter(out);
writer.print(URLEncoder.encode(name_1)
   + "=" + URLEncoder.encode(value_1) + "&");
 . . .
writer.print(URLEncoder.encode(name_n)
   + "=" + URLEncoder.encode(value_n) + "\n");
writer.close();
```

The following sample program makes a ZIP code lookup by calling a server-side program hosted by the United States Postal Service. The server-side program has the URL `http://www.usps.gov/cgi-bin/zip4/ctystzip`. It expects a POST input with a single name `ctystzip` and a value that is either a ZIP code or a city and state (such as `"Beverly Hills, CA"`).

To run the sample program, provide an input on the command line such as

```
java PostZipQuery 12345
```

or

```
java PostZipQuery Beverly Hills, CA
```

The program first concatenates all command-line arguments into a variable `input` or sets `input` to a default value of `"90210"`—the zip code of Beverly Hills, California—if you don't give any command-line arguments. Then the program passes the query input data to the `URLConnection` object, connects to the post office server, and prints out the reply that it receives from the server-side program. The reply is formatted in HTML, but if you look closely, you can read the answer. Exercise P22.6 asks you to clean up the output.

This program completes our introduction into Internet programming with Java. You have seen how to use sockets to connect client and server programs. You also saw how to use the higher-level `URLConnection` class to obtain information from web servers. The `URLConnection` class is more convenient to use, because it takes care of the details of the socket connection and it implements HTTP.

Program PostZipQuery.java

```
 1  import java.io.BufferedReader;
 2  import java.io.InputStream;
 3  import java.io.InputStreamReader;
 4  import java.io.IOException;
 5  import java.io.OutputStream;
 6  import java.io.PrintWriter;
 7  import java.net.URL;
 8  import java.net.URLConnection;
 9  import java.net.URLEncoder;
10
11  /**
12      This program posts a query to a United States Postal Service
13      server that can look up the ZIP code for a city name. Supply
14      the city name and an optional state on the command line,
15      such as
16      java PostZipQuery Los Angeles, CA
17  */
```

```
18  public class PostZipQuery
19  {
20     public static void main(String[] args)
21        throws IOException
22     {
23        // concatenate all command line arguments
24
25        String input;
26        if (args.length > 0)
27        {
28           input = args[0];
29           for (int i = 1; i < args.length; i++)
30              input += " " + args[i];
31        }
32        else
33           input = "90210";
34
35        // establish URL connection
36
37        URL u = new URL(
38           "http://www.usps.gov/cgi-bin/zip4/ctystzip");
39        URLConnection connection = u.openConnection();
40
41        // send POST data
42
43        connection.setDoOutput(true);
44        OutputStream out = connection.getOutputStream();
45        PrintWriter writer = new PrintWriter(out);
46        writer.print("ctystzip="
47           + URLEncoder.encode(input) + "\n");
48        writer.close();
49
50        // print server response
51
52        InputStream in = connection.getInputStream();
53        BufferedReader reader = new BufferedReader(
54           new InputStreamReader(in));
55
56        boolean done = false;
57        while (!done)
58        {
59           String inputLine = reader.readLine();
60           if (inputLine == null)
61              done = true;
62           else
63              System.out.println(inputLine);
64        }
65        reader.close();
66     }
67  }
```

▼ ⟳ **Productivity Hint** ◤ **22.1** ▶

Use High-Level Libraries

▼ When you communicate with a web server to obtain data, you have two choices. You can make a socket connection and send GET and POST commands to the server over the socket. Or you can use the URLConnection class and have it issue the commands on
▼ your behalf.

Similarly, to communicate with a mail server, you can write programs that send SMTP and POP commands, or you can learn how to use the Java mail extensions. (See
▼ http://java.sun.com/products/javamail/index.html for more information on the Java Mail API.)

In such a situation, you may be tempted to use the low-level approach and send com-
▼ mands over a socket connection. It seems simpler than learning a complex set of classes. However, that simplicity is often deceptive. Once you go beyond the simplest cases, the low-level approach usually requires hard work. For example, to send binary mail attach-
▼ ments, you may need to master complex data encodings. The high-level libraries have all that knowledge built in, and you don't have to reinvent the wheel.

For that reason, you should not actually use sockets to connect to web servers. Always
▼ use the URLConnection class instead. Why did this book teach you about sockets if you aren't expected to use them? There are two reasons. Some client programs don't commu-nicate with web or mail servers, and you may need to use sockets when a high-level
▼ library is not available. And, just as importantly, knowing what the high-level library does under the hood helps you understand it better. For the same reason, you saw in Chapter 19 how to implement linked lists, even though you probably will never program
▼ your own lists and will just use the LinkedList class.

CHAPTER SUMMARY

1. The *Internet* is a worldwide collection of networks, routing equipment, and computers using a common set of protocols to define how each party will interact with each other.

2. TCP/IP is the abbreviation for *Transmission Control Protocol over Internet Protocol,* the pair of communication protocols that is used to establish reliable transmission of data between two computers on the Internet.

3. A TCP connection requires the Internet addresses and port numbers of both end-points.

4. HTTP, which stands for *Hypertext Transfer Protocol,* is the protocol that defines communication between web browsers and web servers.

5. An URL, or *Uniform Resource Locator,* is a pointer to an information resource (such as a web page or an image) on the World Wide Web.

6. The *telnet* program is a useful tool to establish test connections with servers.

7. The HTTP GET command requests information from a web server. The web server returns the requested item, which may be a web page, an image, or other data.

8. A *socket* is an object that encapsulates a TCP/IP connection. To communicate with the other endpoint of the connection, you use the input and output streams attached to the socket.

9. When transmission over a socket is complete, remember to close the socket.

10. For text protocols, turn the socket streams into readers and writers.

11. Flush the writer attached to a socket at the end of every command. Then the command is sent to the server, even if the writer's buffer isn't completely filled.

12. The ServerSocket class is used by server applications to listen for client connections.

13. The URLConnection class makes it easy to communicate with a web server without having to issue HTTP commands.

14. The URLConnection and HttpURLConnection classes can give you additional information about HTTP requests and responses.

15. Dynamic web content is generated by programs that the web server invokes when the data are requested.

16. There are two HTTP commands for supplying input to server-side programs: GET and POST. The GET syntax is simpler, but it can be used only for short inputs.

17. Data in GET and POST requests must be encoded. Use the URLEncoder class for that purpose.

18. Use the URLConnection class to send POST requests to a web server.

Classes, Objects, and Methods Introduced in This Chapter

```
java.net.ServerSocket
   accept
   close
java.net.Socket
   getInputStream
   getOutputStream
java.net.URL
   openConnection
java.net.URLConnection
   getInputStream
   setIfModifiedSince
   getContentLength
   getContentType
   getOutputStream
```

```
      setDoOutput
java.net.HttpURLConnection
   getResponseCode
   getResponseMessage
java.util.StringTokenizer
   nextToken
java.net.URLDecoder
   decode
java.net.URLEncoder
   encode
```

REVIEW EXERCISES

Exercise R22.1. What is a server? What is a client? How many clients can connect to a server at one time?

Exercise R22.2. What is a socket? What is the difference between a Socket object and a ServerSocket object?

Exercise R22.3. Under what circumstances would an UnknownHostException be thrown?

Exercise R22.4. What happens if the Socket constructor's second parameter is not the same as the port number at which the server waits for connections?

Exercise R22.5. When a socket is created, which Internet address is used?
- The address of the computer to which you want to connect
- The address of your computer
- The address of your ISP

Exercise R22.6. What is the purpose of the accept method of the ServerSocket class?

Exercise R22.7. After a socket establishes a connection, what mechanism will your client program use to read data from the server computer?
- The Socket will fill a buffer with bytes.
- You will use an Reader obtained from the Socket.
- You will use an InputStream obtained from the Socket.

Exercise R22.8. Why is it not common to work directly with the InputStream and OutputStream objects obtained from a Socket object?

Exercise R22.9. When a client program communicates with a server, it sometimes needs to flush the output stream. Explain why.

Exercise R22.10. In the BankService example, what is the significance of using StringTokenizer?

Exercise R22.11. How can you communicate with a web server without using sockets?

Exercise R22.12. What is the difference between HTTP and HTML?

Exercise R22.13. What is an URL? How do you create an URL? How do you connect to an URL?

Exercise R22.14. What is the difference between a URL instance and a URLConnection instance?

Exercise R22.15. What is the difference between the GET method and the POST method?

Exercise R22.16. True or false?
- The ServerSocket class is used only by the client program.
- The Socket class is used only by the server program.
- A web server knows when an URL denotes a file and when it denotes a program.
- You can supply as much information as you like to a server-side program through a GET request.
- When you use the URLConnection class, you don't have to worry about formatting the POST request.
- The URL constructor throws a MalformedURLException whenever an URL is not specified properly.

PROGRAMMING EXERCISES

Exercise P22.1. Modify the WebGet program to print only the HTTP header of the returned HTML page. The HTTP header is the beginning of the response data. It consists of several lines such as

```
HTTP/1.1 200 OK
Date: Sun, 10 Jun 2001 16:10:34 GMT
Server: Apache/1.3.19 (Unix)
Cache-Control: max-age=86400
Expires: Mon, 11 Jun 2001 16:10:34 GMT
Connection: close
Content-Type: text/html
```

followed by a blank line.

Exercise P22.2. Modify the WebGet program to print only the *title* of the returned HTML page. An HTML page has the structure

```
<html><head><title>. . .</title></head><body>. . .</body></html>
```

For example, if you run the program by typing at the command line `java WebGet java.sun.com index.html`, the output should be `java.sun.com - The Source for Java(TM) Technology`.

Exercise P22.3. Rewrite the PostZipQuery program so that you don't use an URLConnection. Instead, format the POST data manually and send them to the server.

Exercise P22.4. Modify the BankServer program to provide complete error checking. For example, one thing to check is to make sure that there is enough money in the account when withdrawing. Send appropriate error reports back to the client. Enhance the protocol to be similar to HTTP, in which each server response starts with a number indicating the success or failure condition, followed by a string with response data or an error description.

Exercise P22.5. Modify the `BankServer` program so that it can accept simultaneous connections from multiple clients. You need to make the following changes:

- The `BankService` class should extend `Thread`. Rename the `doService` method to `run`.
- When the server socket accepts a connection, it should construct a new `Bank-Service` thread and start it.
- The `BankAccount` methods should be synchronized.

Try out your program by establishing two simultaneous *telnet* sessions to the bank server.

Exercise P22.6. Modify the `PostZipQuery` program by cleaning up the output so that the answer to the query can be seen clearly. *Hint:* Implement a class that will convert HTML to text by removing unwanted tags and translating <br> or <p> tags to '\n' characters.

Exercise P22.7. Write a client application that executes an infinite loop that does the following: (*a*) prompts the user for a number, (*b*) sends that value to the server, (*c*) receives the number, and (*d*) displays the new number. Also write a server that executes an infinite loop to read a number from a client, compute the square root of the value, and write the result to the client.

Exercise P22.8. Implement a client-server program in which the client will print the date and time given by the server. Two classes should be implemented: `DateClient` and `DateServer`. The `DateServer` simply prints `new Date().toString()` whenever it accepts a connection and then closes the socket.

Exercise P22.9. Write a program to display the protocol, host, port, and file components of an URL. *Hint:* Look at the API documentation of the URL class.

Exercise P22.10. Write a simple web server that recognizes only the GET request. When a client connects to your server and sends a command such as GET *filename* `HTTP/1.0`, then return a header

```
HTTP/1.1 200 OK
```

followed by a blank line and all lines in the file. If the file doesn't exist, return `404 Not Found` instead.

Test your web server by starting up your web browser and loading a page such as `local-host/c:\cs1\myfile.html`.

Exercise P22.11. Write a chat server and client program. The chat server accepts connections from clients. Whenever one of the clients sends a chat message, it is displayed for all other clients to see. Use a protocol with three commands: `LOGIN` *name*, `CHAT` *message*, `LOGOUT`. You need separate threads for this program to work. Follow the approach of Exercise 22.5.

Exercise P22.12. A query such as

```
http://mach.usno.navy.mil/cgi-bin/aa_moonphases?year=2001
```

returns a page containing the moon phases in a given year. Write a program that asks the user for a year, month, and day and then prints the phase of the moon on that day.

23

Relational Databases

▶ To learn how to query a database with the Structured Query Language (SQL)

▶ To connect to databases with Java Database Connectivity (JDBC)

▶ To write database programs that insert, update, and query data in a relational database

In Chapter 15 you saw how to store data in a file. When you store data, you will want to be able to add more data items, remove data, change data items, and find items that match certain criteria. However, if you have a lot of data, it can be difficult to carry out these operations quickly and efficiently. Because data storage is such a common task, special *database management systems* (DBMS) have been invented that let the programmer think in terms of the data rather than file storage. Database management systems are commonly used to keep customer records, medical information, and many other kinds of data.

The most common type of databases is a *relational database*. In such a database, you can use a *structured query language* to formulate queries and update instructions in a natural way, without having to worry about where and how the information is stored. In this chapter you will learn how to query and update information in a relational database and how to access database information from Java. Of course, database management is a complex topic, and many issues are important for the implementation of professional database systems. This chapter ends with a brief discussion of some of the more advanced database topics.

CHAPTER CONTENTS

23.1   Organizing Database Information

23.1.1 — Database Tables

> A relational database stores information in tables. Each table column has a name and a data type.

A relational database stores information in *tables*. Figure 1 shows a typical table. As you can see, each *row* in this table corresponds to a product. The *column headers* correspond to attributes of the product: the product code, description, and unit price. Note that all items in a particular column have the same type: product codes and description are strings, unit prices are floating-point numbers. The allowable column types differ somewhat from one database to another. Table 1 shows types that are commonly available in relational databases that follow the SQL (for Structured Query Language; often pronounced "sequel") standard. (See [1] for more information on the SQL standard.)

> SQL (Structured Query Language) is a command language for interacting with a database.

Most relational databases follow the SQL standard. You will see in the next section how to use SQL commands to carry out queries, but there are other SQL commands besides queries. There is no relationship between SQL and Java—they are different languages. However, as you will see later in this chapter, you can use Java to send SQL commands to a database.

Product_Code	Description	Unit_Price
116-064	Toaster	24.95
257-535	Hair dryer	29.95
643-119	Car vacuum	19.99

Figure 1

A Product Table in a Relational Database

SQL Data Type	Java Data Type
INTEGER or INT	int
REAL	float
DOUBLE	double
DECIMAL *(m, n)*	Fixed-point decimal numbers with *m* total digits and *n* digits after the decimal point. Similar to BigDecimal
BOOLEAN	boolean
CHARACTER *(n) or* CHAR *(n)*	Fixed-length string of length *n*. Similar to String

Table 1

Some Standard SQL Types and Their Corresponding Java Types

For example, here is the SQL command to create a product table:

```
CREATE TABLE Products
(
    Product_Code CHAR(11),
    Description CHAR(10),
    Unit_Price DECIMAL(10, 2)
)
```

> Use the CREATE TABLE and INSERT SQL commands to add data to a database.

Unlike Java, SQL is not case-sensitive. For example, you could have spelled the command `create table` instead of CREATE TABLE. However, as a matter of convention, we will use uppercase letters for SQL keywords and mixed case for table and column names.

To insert rows into the table, you use the INSERT command. You issue one command for each row, such as

```
INSERT INTO Products
    VALUES ('3554-0632-1', 'Hair dryer', 29.95)
```

As you can see, SQL uses single quotes ('), not double quotes, to delimit strings. What if you have a string that contains a single quote? Rather than using an escape sequence (such as \') as in Java, you just write the single quote twice, such as

```
'Sam''s Small Appliances'
```

If you create a table and subsequently want to remove it, use the DROP TABLE command. For example,

```
DROP TABLE Test
```

Productivity Hint 23.1

Stick with the Standard

The Java language is highly standardized. You will rarely find compilers that allow you to specify Java code that differs from the standard, and if they do, it is always a compiler bug. However, SQL implementations are often much more forgiving. For example, many SQL vendors allow you to use a Java-style escape sequence such as

```
'Sam\'s Small Appliances'
```

in a SQL string. Probably the vendor thought that this would be "helpful" to programmers who are familiar with Java or C. (The C language uses the same escape mechanism for denoting special characters.)

However, this is an illusion. If you deviate from the standard, you limit portability. Suppose you later want to move your database code to another vendor, perhaps to improve performance or to lower the cost of the database software. If the other vendor hasn't implemented a particular deviation, then your code will no longer work and you need to spend time fixing it.

To avoid these problems, you should stick with the standard. With SQL, you cannot rely on your database to flag all errors—some of them may be considered "helpful" extensions. That means that you need to *know* the standard and have the discipline to follow it.

23.1.2 Linking Tables

If you have objects whose instance fields are strings, numbers, dates, or other types that are permissible as table column types, then you can easily store them as rows in a database table. For example, consider a `Customer` class similar to that used in Chapter 14:

```
class Customer
{
   . . .
   private String name;
   private String address;
   private String city;
   private String state;
   private String zip;
}
```

It is simple to come up with a table structure that lets you store customers—see Figure 2.

For other objects, it is not so easy. Consider an invoice. Each invoice object contains a reference to a customer object.

```
class Invoice
{
   . . .
   private int invoiceNumber;
```

Name	Address	City	State	Zip
CHAR (40)	CHAR (40)	CHAR (30)	CHAR (2)	CHAR (10)
Sam's Small Appliances	100 Main Street	Anytown	CA	98765

Figure 2

A Customer Table

```
        private Customer theCustomer;
          . . .
    }
```

You cannot simply come up with a single column holding a customer, because `Customer` isn't a SQL type. In this regard, table entries are very different from Java variables. The types of table entries are restricted to SQL types.

Of course, you might consider simply entering all the customer data into the invoice tables—see Figure 3. However, this is actually not a good idea. If you look at the sample data in Figure 3, you will notice that Sam's Small Appliances had two invoices, number 11731 and 11733. Yet all information for the customer was *replicated* in two rows.

This replication has two problems. First, it is wasteful to store the same information multiple times. If the same customer places many orders, then the replicated information can take up a lot of space. More importantly, the replication is *dangerous*. Suppose the customer moves to a new address. Then it would be an easy mistake to update the customer information in some of the invoice records and leave the old address in place in others.

Invoice_ Number	Customer_ Name	Customer_ Address	Customer_ City	Customer_ State	Customer_ Zip	...
INTEGER	CHAR (40)	CHAR (40)	CHAR (30)	CHAR (2)	CHAR (10)	...
11731	Sam's Small Appliances	100 Main Street	Anytown	CA	98765	...
11732	Electronics Unlimited	1175 Liberty Ave	Pleasantville	MI	45066	...
11733	Sam's Small Appliances	100 Main Street	Anytown	CA	98765	...

Figure 3

A Poor Design for an Invoice Table with Replicated Customer Data

> You should avoid rows with replicated data. Instead, distribute the data over multiple tables.

In a Java program, you don't have either of the two problems. Multiple `Invoice` objects can contain references to a single shared `Customer` object.

The first step in achieving the same effect in a database is to organize your data into multiple tables as in Figure 4. Dividing the columns into two tables solves the replication problem. The customer data are no longer replicated—the Invoice table contains no customer information, and the Customer table contains a single record for each customer. But how can we refer to the customer to which an invoice is issued? Notice in Figure 4 that there is now a Customer_Number column in *both* the Customer table and the Invoice table. Now all invoices for Sam's Small Appliances share only the customer number. The two tables are *linked* by the Customer_Number field. To find out more details about this customer, you need to use the customer number to look up the customer in the customer table.

Note that the customer number is a *unique identifier*. We introduced the customer number because the customer name by itself may not be unique. For example, there may well be multiple Electronics Unlimited stores in various locations. Thus, the customer

Invoice

Invoice__ Number	Customer_ Number	Payment
INTEGER	INTEGER	DECIMAL (10, 2)
11731	3175	0
11732	3176	249.95
11733	3175	0

Customer

Customer_ Number	Name	Address	City	State	Zip
INTEGER	CHAR (40)	CHAR (40)	CHAR (30)	CHAR (2)	CHAR (10)
3175	Sam's Small Appliances	100 Main Street	Anytown	CA	98765
3176	Electronics Unlimited	1175 Liberty Ave	Pleasantville	MI	45066

Figure 4

Two Tables for Invoice and Customer Data

> A primary key is a column (or combination of columns) whose value uniquely specifies a table record.

name alone does not uniquely identify a record, so we cannot to use the name as a link between the two tables.

In database terminology, a column (or combination of columns) that uniquely identifies a row in a table is called a *primary key*. In our Customer table, the Customer_Number column is a primary key. Not all database tables need a primary key. You need a primary key only if you want to establish a link from another table. For example, the Customer table needs a primary key so that you can link customers to invoices.

> A foreign key is a reference to a primary key in a linked table.

When a primary key is linked to another table, the matching column (or combination of columns) in that table is called a *foreign key*. For example, the Customer_Number in the Invoice table is a foreign key, linked to the primary key in the Customer table. Unlike primary keys, foreign keys need not be unique. For example, in our Invoice table we have several records that all have the same value for the Customer_Number foreign key.

Productivity Hint 23.2

Avoid Unnecessary Data Replication

It is very common for beginning database designers to replicate data in an Invoice table. Whenever you find yourself replicating data in a table, ask yourself if you can move the replicated data into a separate table and use a key such as a code or ID number to link the tables.

Consider this example:

...	Product_Code	Product_Description	Product_Price	...
...	CHAR (10)	CHAR (20)	DECIMAL (10, 2)	...
...	116-064	Toaster	24.95	...
...	116-064	Toaster	24.95	...
...	...	...	...	...

As you can see, some product information is replicated. Is this replication an error? It depends. The product description for the product with code 116-064 is always going to be "Toaster". Therefore, that correspondence should be stored in an external Product table.

The product price, however, can change over time. When it does, the old invoices don't automatically use the new price. Thus, it makes sense to store the price that the customer was actually charged in an Invoice table. The current list price, however, is best stored in an external Product table.

23.1.3— Implementing One-to-Many Relationships

Each invoice is linked to exactly one customer. That is called a *one-to-one* relationship. On the other hand, each invoice has many items. (As in Chapter 16, an *item* identifies the product, quantity, and unit price.) Thus, there is a *one-to-many* relationship between invoices and items. In the Java class, the Item objects are stored in an array list:

```
class Invoice
{
    . . .
    private int invoiceNumber;
    private Customer theCustomer;
    private ArrayList items; // contains Item objects
    private double payment;
}
```

However, in a relational database, you need to store the information in tables. Surprisingly many programmers, when faced with this situation, commit a major faux pas and replicate columns, one for each item, as in Figure 5.

Clearly, this design is not satisfactory. What should we do if there are more than three items on an invoice? Perhaps we should have ten columns instead? But that is wasteful if the majority of invoices have only a couple of items, and it still does not solve our problem for the occasional invoice with lots of items.

Instead, you should again distribute the information into two tables: one for invoices and another for items. Link each item back to its invoice with an Invoice_Number foreign key in the item table—see Figure 6.

Our database now consists of four tables:

- Invoice
- Customer
- Item
- Product

Figure 7 shows the links between these tables. In the next section you will see how to query this database for information about invoices, customers, and products. The queries will take advantage of the links between the tables.

Invoice_ Number	Customer_ Number	Product_ Code1	Quantity1	Product_ Code2	Quantity2	Product_ Code3	Quantity3	Payment
INTEGER	INTEGER	CHAR (10)	INTEGER	CHAR (10)	INTEGER	CHAR (10)	INTEGER	DECIMAL (10, 2)
11731	3175	116-064	3	257-535	1	643-119	2	0

Figure 5

A Poor Design for an Invoice Table with Replicated Columns

Invoice

Invoice_Number	Customer_Number	Payment
INTEGER	INTEGER	DECIMAL (10, 2)
11731	3175	0
11732	3176	249.50
11733	3175	0

Item

Invoice_Number	Product_Code	Quantity
INTEGER	CHAR (10)	INTEGER
11731	116-064	3
11731	257-535	1
11731	643-119	2
11732	116-064	10
11733	116-064	2
11733	643-119	1

Figure 6

Linked Invoice and Item Tables Implement a One-to-Many Relationship

▼ Productivity Hint **23.3**

Don't Replicate Columns in a Table

▼

If you find yourself numbering columns in a table with suffixes 1, 2, and so forth (such as Quantity1, Quantity2, Quantity3 in the preceding example), then you are probably on the wrong track. How do you know there are exactly three quantities? In that case, it's

▼ time for another table again.

Add a table to hold the information for which you replicated the columns. In that table, add a column that links back to a key in the first table, such as the invoice number in our

▼ example. By using an additional table, you can implement a one-to-many relationship.

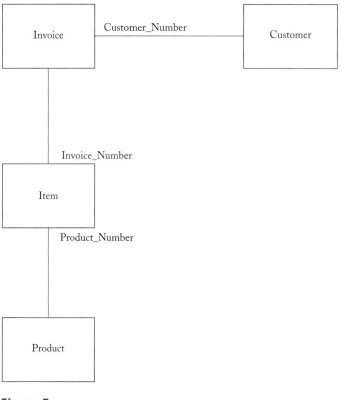

Figure 7

The Links between the Tables in the Sample Database

23.2 Queries

Let us assume that the tables in our database have been created and that records have been inserted. Once a database is filled with data, you will want to *query* the database for information, such as

- What are the names and addresses of all customers?

- What are the names and addresses of all customers in California?

- What are the names and addresses of all customers who buy toasters?

- What are the names and addresses of all customers with unpaid invoices?

- . . .

In this section you will learn how to formulate both simple and complex queries in SQL. We will use the data shown in Figure 8 for our examples.

Invoice

Invoice_Number	Customer_Number	Payment
INTEGER	INTEGER	DECIMAL (10, 2)
11731	3175	0
11732	3176	249.50
11733	3175	0

Item

Invoice_Number	Product_Code	Quantity
INTEGER	CHAR (10)	INTEGER
11731	116-064	3
11731	257-535	1
11731	643-119	2
11732	116-064	10
11733	116-064	2
11733	643-119	1

Customer

Customer_Number	Name	Address	City	State	Zip
INTEGER	CHAR (40)	CHAR (40)	CHAR (30)	CHAR (2)	CHAR (10)
3175	Sam's Small Appliances	100 Main Street	Anytown	CA	98765
3176	Electronics Unlimited	1175 Liberty Ave	Pleasantville	MI	45066

Product

Product_Code	Description	Unit_Price
CHAR (10)	CHAR (40)	DECIMAL (10, 2)
116-064	Toaster	24.95
257-535	Hair dryer	29.95
643-119	Car vacuum	19.99

Figure 8

A Sample Database

23.2.1 — Simple Queries

> Use the SQL SELECT statement to query a database.

In SQL, you use the SELECT command to issue queries. For example, the command to select all data from the Customer table is

```
SELECT * FROM Customer
```

The result is

Customer_Number	Name	Address	City	State	Zip
3175	Sam's Small Appliances	100 Main Street	Anytown	CA	98765
3176	Electronics Unlimited	1175 Liberty Ave	Pleasantville	MI	45066

The outcome of the query is a *view*—a set of rows and columns that provides a "window" through which you can see some of the database data. If you select all rows and columns from a single table, of course you get a view into just that table.

Many database systems have tools that let you issue interactive SQL commands—Figure 9 shows a typical example. When you issue a SELECT command, the tool displays

Figure 9

An Interactive SQL Tool

the resulting view. You may want to skip ahead to Section 23.5 and install a database. Or perhaps your computer lab has a database installed already. Then you can run the interactive SQL tool of your database and try out some queries yourself.

23.2.2 — Selecting Columns

Often, you don't care about all columns in a table. Suppose your traveling salesperson is planning a trip to all customers. To plan the route, the salesperson just wants to know the cities and states of all customers. Here is the query:

```
SELECT City, State FROM Customer
```

The result is

City	State
Anytown	CA
Pleasantville	MI

As you can see, the syntax for selecting columns is straightforward. You simply specify the names of the columns you want, separated by commas.

23.2.3 — Selecting Subsets

You just saw how you can restrict a view to show selected columns. Sometimes you want to select certain rows that fit a particular criterion. For example, you may want to find all customers in California. Whenever you want to select a subset, you use the WHERE clause, followed by the condition that describes the subset. Here is an example.

```
SELECT * FROM Customer WHERE State = 'CA'
```

The result is

Customer_Number	Name	Address	City	State	Zip
3175	Sam's Small Appliances	100 Main Street	Anytown	CA	98765

You have to be a bit careful with expressing the condition in the WHERE clause, because SQL syntax differs from the Java syntax. As you already know, in SQL you use single quotes to delimit strings, such as 'CA'. You also use a single =, not a double ==, to test for equality. To test for inequality, you use the <> operator. For example

```
SELECT * FROM Customer WHERE State <> 'CA'
```

selects all customers that are not in California.

You can match patterns with the LIKE operator. The right-hand side must be a string that can contain the special symbols _ (match exactly one character) and % (match any character sequence). For example, the expression

```
Name LIKE '_o%'
```

matches all strings whose second character is an "o". Thus, "Toaster" is a match but "Crowbar" is not.

You can combine expressions with the logical connectives AND, OR, and NOT. (Do not use the Java &&, ||, and ! operators.) For example,

```
SELECT *
   FROM Product
   WHERE Price < 100
      AND Description <> 'Toaster'
```

selects all products whose price is less than 100 that are not toasters.

Of course, you can select both row and column subsets, such as

```
SELECT Name, City FROM Customer WHERE State = 'CA'
```

23.2.4 — Calculations

Suppose you want to find out *how many* customers there are in California. Use the COUNT function:

```
SELECT COUNT(*) FROM Customer WHERE State = 'CA'
```

In addition to the COUNT function, there are four other functions: SUM, AVG (average), MAX, and MIN.

The * means that you want to calculate entire records. That is appropriate only for the COUNT function. For other functions, you have to access a specific column. Put the column name inside the parentheses:

```
SELECT AVG(Price) FROM Product
```

23.2.5 — Joins

The queries that you have seen so far all involve a single table. However, usually the information that you want is distributed over multiple tables. For example, suppose you are asked to find all invoices that include an item for a car vacuum. From the Product table, you can issue a query to find the product code:

```
SELECT Product_Code
   FROM Product
   WHERE Description = 'Car vacuum'
```

You will find out that the car vacuum has product code 643-119. Then you can issue a second query

```
SELECT Invoice_Number
   FROM Item
   WHERE Product_Code = '643-119'
```

But it makes sense to combine these two queries so that you don't have to keep track of the intermediate result. When combining queries, note that the two tables are linked by the Product_Code field. We want to look at matching rows in both tables. In other words, we want to restrict the search to rows where

```
Product.Product_Code = Item.Product_Code
```

Here, the syntax

TableName . ColumnName

denotes the column in a particular table. Whenever a query involves multiple tables, you should specify both the table name and the column name. Thus, the combined query is

```
SELECT Item.Invoice_Number
   FROM Product, Item
   WHERE Product.Description = 'Car vacuum'
      AND Product.Product_Code = Item.Product_Code
```

The result is

Invoice_Number
11731
11733

In this query, the FROM clause contains the names of multiple tables, separated by commas. (It doesn't matter in which order you list the tables.) Such a query is often called a *join* because it involves joining multiple tables.

> A join is a query that involves multiple tables.

You may want to know in what cities hair dryers are popular. Now you need to add the Customer table to the query—it contains the customer addresses. The customers are referenced by invoices, so you need that table as well. Here is the complete query:

```
SELECT Customer.City, Customer.State, Customer.Zip
   FROM Product, Item, Invoice, Customer
   WHERE Product.Description = 'Hair dryer'
      AND Product.Product_Code = Item.Product_Code
      AND Item.Invoice_Number = Invoice.Invoice_Number
      AND Invoice.Customer_Number
         = Customer.Customer_Number
```

The result is

City	State	Zip
Anytown	CA	98765

Whenever you formulate a query that involves multiple tables, remember to do all of the following:

- List all tables that are involved in the query in the FROM clause.
- Use the *TableName*.*ColumnName* syntax to refer to column names.
- List all join conditions (*TableName1*.*ColumnName1* = *TableName2*.*ColumnName2*) in the WHERE clause.

As you can see, these queries can get a bit complex. However, databases are very good at answering these queries (see Productivity Hint 23.4). One remarkable aspect of SQL is that you tell the database *what* you want, not *how* it should find the answer. It is entirely up to the database to come up with a plan for how to find the answer to your query in the shortest number of steps. Commercial database manufacturers take great pride in coming up with clever ways to speed up queries: query optimization strategies, caching of prior results, and so on. In this regard, SQL is a very different language from Java. SQL statements are descriptive and leave it to the database how to execute them. Java statements are prescriptive—you spell out exactly the steps you want your program to carry out.

Common Error 23.1

Joining Tables without Specifying a Link Condition

If you select data from multiple tables without a restriction, the result is somewhat surprising—you get a result set containing *all combinations* of the values, whether or not one of the combinations exists with actual data. For example, the query

```
SELECT Invoice.Invoice_Number, Customer.Name
    FROM Invoice, Customer
```

returns the result set

Invoice.Invoice_Number	Customer.Name
11731	Sam's Small Appliances
11732	Sam's Small Appliances
11733	Sam's Small Appliances
11731	Electronics Unlimited
11732	Electronics Unlimited
11733	Electronics Unlimited

As you can see, the result set contains all six combinations of invoice numbers (11731, 11732, 11733) and customer names (Sam's Small Appliances and Electronics

▼

▼

▼

▼

▼

▼

Unlimited), even though three of those combinations don't occur with real invoices. You need to supply a WHERE clause to restrict the set of combinations. For example,

```
SELECT Invoice.Invoice_Number, Customer.Name
    FROM Invoice, Customer
    WHERE Invoice.Customer_Number
        = Customer.Customer_Number
```

yields

Invoice.Invoice_Number	Customer.Name
11731	Sam's Small Appliances
11732	Electronics Unlimited
11733	Sam's Small Appliances

23.2.6 — Updating and Deleting Data

> The UPDATE and DELETE SQL commands modify the data in a database.

Up to now, you have been seeing how to formulate increasingly complex SELECT queries. The outcome of a SELECT query is a *result set* that you can view and analyze. Two related statement types, UPDATE and DELETE, don't produce a result set. Instead, they modify the database. The DELETE statement is the easier of the two. It simply deletes the rows that you specify. For example, to delete all customers in California, you issue the statement

```
DELETE FROM Customer WHERE State = 'CA'
```

The UPDATE query lets you update columns of all records that fulfill a certain condition. For example, here is how you can add another unit to the quantity of every item in invoice number 11731.

```
UPDATE Item
    SET Quantity = Quantity + 1
    WHERE Invoice_Number = '11731'
```

You can update multiple column values by specifying multiple update expressions in the SET clause, separated by commas.

Both the DELETE and the UPDATE statements return a value, namely the number of rows that are deleted or updated.

▼ **Random Fact** **23.1** ▶

Databases and Privacy

▼

▼

Most companies use computers to keep huge data files of customer records and other business information. Databases not only lower the cost of doing business; they improve the quality of service that companies can offer. Nowadays it is almost unimaginable how time-consuming it used to be to withdraw money from a bank branch or to make travel reservations.

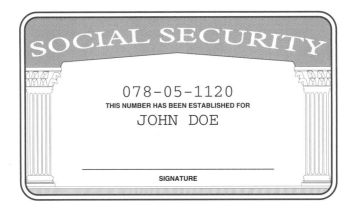

Figure 10

A Social Security Card

Many companies collect large amounts of data on their customers and often share the data with other companies. The data are used not just for good customer service but for other commercial purposes—for example, to select targets for advertising. A company may have a file of addresses of car owners and a file of people with good payment history. It can then send special offers to all of its customers who placed an order in the last month, drive an expensive car, and pay their bills on time.

This kind of query is, of course, much faster if all customer files use the *same* key, which is why so many organizations in the United States try to collect the Social Security numbers of their customers.

The Social Security Act of 1935 provided that each contributor be assigned a Social Security number to track contributions into the Social Security Fund. These numbers have a distinctive format, such as 078-05-1120. (This particular number is not actually a Social Security number belonging to any person. It was printed on sample cards that were inserted in wallets in the 1940s and 1950s.) Figure 10 shows a Social Security card.

Although they had not originally been intended for use as a universal identification number, Social Security numbers have become just that in the last 60 years. The tax authorities and many other government agencies are required to collect the numbers, as are banks (for the reporting of interest income) and, of course, employers. Many other organizations find it convenient to use the number as well.

From a technical standpoint, Social Security numbers are a lousy method for indexing a database. There is a risk of having two records with the same number, because many illegal immigrants use fake numbers. Not everyone has a number—in particular, foreign customers. Because there is no checksum, a clerical error (such as transposing two digits) cannot be detected. (Credit card numbers have a checksum.) For the same reason, it is easy for anyone to make up a number.

Some people are very concerned about the fact that just about every organization wants to store their Social Security number. Unless there is a legal requirement, such as for banks, one can usually fight it or take one's business elsewhere. Even when an organi-

▼

▼

zation is required to collect the number, such as an employer, one can insist that the number be used only on tax and Social Security paperwork, not on the face of an ID card. Unfortunately, it usually takes near-superhuman effort to climb the organizational

▼ ladder to find someone with the authority to process paperwork with no Social Security number or to assign another identification number.

As the Internet becomes a more pervasive part of our lives, you can witness firsthand the voracious appetite for personal information by marketers of products and services. There are many opportunities to obtain free services (such as free email), if you are will-

▼ ing to divulge some personal information, and if you agree to the monitoring of your browsing and purchasing habits.

The discomfort that many people have about the computerization of their personal information is understandable. There is the possibility that companies and the govern-

▼ ment can merge multiple databases and derive information about us that we may wish they did not have or that simply may be untrue. An insurance company may deny coverage, or charge a higher premium, if it finds that you have too many relatives with a cer-

▼ tain disease. You may be denied a job because of an inaccurate credit or medical report, and you may not even know the reason. These are very disturbing developments that have had a very negative impact for a small but growing number of people. See [3] and

▼ [4] for more information.

23.3 Installing a Database

A wide variety of database systems are available. Among them are

- High-performance commercial databases such as Oracle, DB2, Informix, Sybase, and Microsoft SQL Server

- Open-source databases such as PostgreSQL , MySQL, mSQL, and Interbase

- Lightweight Java databases such as Cloudscape and Pointbase

- Desktop databases such as Paradox and Access

Which one should you choose for learning database programming? That depends greatly on your available budget, computing resources, and experience with installing complex software. In a laboratory environment with a trained administrator, it makes a lot of sense to install a commercial database such as Oracle, but the products themselves, the hardware to run them, and the staff to administer them are expensive. Open-source alternatives are available free of charge, and their quality has greatly increased in recent years. Although they may not be suited for large-scale applications, they work fine for learning purposes. However, installation is generally not for the faint of heart. Lightweight Java databases are much easier to install and work on a variety of platforms. This makes them a good choice for the beginner. But there are drawbacks—these programs typically offer low performance and may not support complex SQL commands. Desktop databases such as Access are generally a poor choice and should be avoided if possible.

If you work in a computing laboratory, someone will have installed a database for you, and you should be able to find instructions on how to use it. If you install your own database, we recommend that you start out with a lightweight Java database.

Detailed instructions for installing a database vary widely. Here we give you a general sequence of steps on how to install a database and test your installation.

1. Obtain the database program, either on CD-ROM or by downloading it from the web.

2. Read the installation instructions.

3. Install the program. Details vary greatly. This may be as simple as running an installation program, or you may need to recompile the program from its source code.

4. Start the database. With most database systems (but not some of the lightweight Java database systems), you need to start the database server before you can carry out any database operations. Read the installation instructions for details.

5. Set up user accounts. This typically involves running an administration program, logging in as administrator with a default administration account, and adding user names and passwords. If you are the only user of the database, you may be able just to use a default account. Again, details vary greatly among databases, and you should consult the documentation.

6. Run a test. Most databases come with a program that lets you execute interactive SQL instructions. Locate that program and find out how to log on as a database user. Then run the following SQL instructions:

```
CREATE TABLE Test (Name CHAR(20))
INSERT INTO Test VALUES ('Romeo')
SELECT * FROM Test
DROP TABLE Test
```

At this point, you should get a display that shows a single row and column of the Test database, containing the string "Romeo". If not, carefully read the documentation of your SQL tool to see how you need to enter SQL statements. For example, with some SQL tools, you need a special terminator for each SQL statement.

> You need a JDBC (Java Database Connectivity) driver to access a database from a Java program.

Once your database is set up and functioning correctly, you need to install a *JDBC driver*. The acronym JDBC stands for Java Database Connectivity, the name of the technology that enables Java programs to interact with databases. Different databases require different drivers, which may be supplied by either the database manufacturer or by a third party. You need to locate and install the driver that matches your database. When your Java program issues SQL commands, the driver forwards them to the database and lets your program analyze the results (see Figure 11).

The Java Software Development Kit includes a "JDBC/ODBC" bridge driver, which can connect to any database that follows the ODBC (Open Database Connectivity) standard. When the JDBC technology was first released, that bridge driver made sense, because most databases at the time had ODBC drivers. However, nowadays most databases have JDBC drivers that are more powerful and easier to configure than the JDBC/ODBC

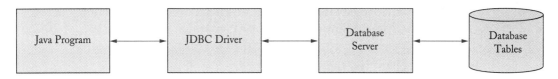

Figure 11

JDBC Architecture

bridge driver. For that reason, we recommend that you use a JDBC driver instead of an ODBC driver and the JDBC/ODBC bridge.

> Make sure the JDBC driver is on the class path when you launch the Java program.

After you install the JDBC driver, you should run a test program to verify that the installation was successful. For this test program, we assume that you already created a Test table in your database, as described in the database test instructions. Here are the steps for testing the JDBC driver.

1. Every JDBC driver contains some Java code that your Java programs require to connect to the database. From the JDBC driver documentation, find the *class path* for the driver. Here is a typical example—the class path for the Cloudscape JDBC driver, installed on the C drive of a computer running the Windows operating system.

   ```
   c:\cloudscape\lib\cloudscape.jar
   ```

   One version of the Oracle database uses a class path

   ```
   /usr/local/oracle/jdbc/classes111b.zip
   ```

   You will find this information in the documentation of the JDBC driver.

2. Find the name of the driver class that you need to load. Here is a typical driver class, also from the InstantDB database:

   ```
   COM.cloudscape.core.JDBCDriver
   ```

   The Oracle database uses a driver

   ```
   oracle.jdbc.driver.OracleDriver
   ```

   In general, you should expect the class name to be in a package that matches the vendor name (such as `COM.cloudscape` or `oracle`), followed by some vendor-specific class name. Your JDBC driver documentation will have this documentation.

3. Find the name of the *database URL* that your driver expects. All database URLs have the format

   jdbc:*subprotocol*:*driver-specific data*

   The subprotocol is a code that identifies the driver manufacturer, such as `cloudscape` or `oracle`. The driver-specific data encode the database name and the location of the database. Here are typical examples:

   ```
   jdbc:cloudscape:InvoiceDB;create=true
   jdbc:oracle:thin:@larry.mathcs.sjsu.edu:1521:InvoiceDB
   ```

Again, consult your JDBC driver information for details on the format of the database URL and how to specify the database that you use.

4. In the TestDB.java program at the end of this section, edit the file `data-base.properties` and supply

   - The driver class name
   - The database URL
   - Your database user name
   - Your database password

5. Compile the program as

   ```
   java TestDB.java
   ```

6. Run the program as

   ```
   java -classpath driver_class_path;. TestDB database.properties
   ```

   In UNIX/Linux, use a : separator in the class path:

   ```
   java -classpath driver_class_path:. TestDB database.properties
   ```

If everything works correctly, you will get an output that lists all data in the Test table. If you followed the test instructions precisely, you will see one line of output with the name "Romeo".

If your program doesn't work, there are several possible causes.

- If you get an error message about a missing driver, then the program cannot load the JDBC driver. Check the class path and the driver name.

- If you get an error message that the driver cannot connect to the database, then the database may not be started, or, if the database is located on another computer, then the database may not be reachable. Check that the database is working by connecting with a SQL tool.

- If you get an error message about failed login, check the database name in the database URL, the user name, and the password.

- If you get an error message about a missing Test table, make sure you create and populate the table as described in the database test.

Here is the test program. We will explain the Java instructions of this program in the following section.

File TestDB.java

```
1  import java.sql.Connection;
2  import java.sql.ResultSet;
3  import java.sql.Statement;
4
5  /**
6     Tests a database installation by creating and querying
7     a sample table. Call this program as
8     java -classpath driver_class_path;. TestDB database.properties
9  */
```

```
10  public class TestDB
11  {
12     public static void main(String[] args)
13        throws Exception
14     {
15        if (args.length == 0)
16        {
17           System.out.println(
18              "Usage: TestDB propertiesFile");
19           System.exit(0);
20        }
21        else
22           SimpleDataSource.init(args[0]);
23
24        Connection conn = SimpleDataSource.getConnection();
25
26        Statement stat = conn.createStatement();
27
28        stat.execute("CREATE TABLE Test (Name CHAR(20))");
29        stat.execute("INSERT INTO Test VALUES ('Romeo')");
30
31        ResultSet result = stat.executeQuery(
32           "SELECT * FROM Test");
33        result.next();
34        System.out.println(result.getString("Name"));
35        result.close();
36
37        stat.execute("DROP TABLE Test");
38
39        stat.close();
40        conn.close();
41     }
42  }
```

File SimpleDataSource.java

```
1   import java.sql.Connection;
2   import java.sql.DriverManager;
3   import java.sql.SQLException;
4   import java.io.FileInputStream;
5   import java.io.IOException;
6   import java.util.Properties;
7
8   /**
9      A simple data source for getting database connections.
10  */
11  public class SimpleDataSource
12  {
13     /**
14        Initializes the data source.
15        @param fileName the name of the property file that
16        contains the database driver, url, username, and password
```

```
17      */
18    public static void init(String fileName)
19        throws IOException, ClassNotFoundException
20    {
21        Properties props = new Properties();
22        FileInputStream in = new FileInputStream(fileName);
23        props.load(in);
24
25        driver = props.getProperty("jdbc.driver");
26        url = props.getProperty("jdbc.url");
27        username = props.getProperty(
28           "jdbc.username");
29        password = props.getProperty(
30           "jdbc.password");
31
32        Class.forName(driver);
33    }
34
35    /**
36        Gets a connection to the database.
37        @return the database connection
38    */
39    public static Connection getConnection()
40        throws SQLException
41    {
42        return DriverManager.getConnection(url,
43           username, password);
44    }
45
46    private static String url;
47    private static String username;
48    private static String password;
49 }
```

Sample File database.properties

```
1 jdbc.driver=COM.cloudscape.core.JDBCDriver
2 jdbc.url=jdbc:cloudscape:BankDB;create=true
3 jdbc.username=username
4 jdbc.password=password
```

23.4 Database Programming in Java

23.4.1 Connecting to the Database

| Use a Connection object to access a database from a Java program. |

To connect to a database, you need an object of the class Connection. The following code fragment shows you how to obtain such a connection. First you load the database driver; then you ask the DriverManager for a connection. You need to initialize the driver, url, username, and password strings with the values that apply to your database.

```
String driver = . . .;
String url = . . .;
String username = . . .;
String password = . . .;

Class.forName(driver); // load driver
Connection conn = DriverManager.getConnection(url,
    username, password);
```

When you are done issuing your database commands, you should close the database connection by calling the `close` method:

```
conn.close();
```

This is actually a somewhat simplistic view of connection management. Two problems occur in practice. Larger programs (such as the bank example in Section 23.5) need to connect to the database from many classes. You don't want to propagate the database login information to a large number of classes. Also, it is usually not feasible to use a single connection for all database requests. In particular, as you will see in Chapter 25, a container for Java server pages can run many simultaneous web page requests from different browsers. Each page request needs its own database connection. But because opening a database connection is quite slow and page requests come so frequently, database connections need to be pooled rather than closed and reopened. The details can be complex, and there is currently no standard implementation available.

It is always a good idea to decouple connection management from the other database code. We supply a `SimpleDataSource` class for this purpose. You can find the implementation at the end of the preceding section. This class is a very simple tool for connection management. At the beginning of your program, call the static `init` method with the name of the database configuration file, for example

```
SimpleDataSource.init("database.properties");
```

The configuration file is a text file containing four lines

```
jdbc.driver=. . .
jdbc.url=. . .
jdbc.username=. . .
jdbc.password=. . .
```

The `init` method uses the `Properties` class, which has been designed to make it easy to read such a file.

The `Properties` class has a `load` method to read a file of key/value pairs from a stream:

```
Properties props = new Properties();
FileInputStream in = new FileInputStream(fileName);
props.load(in);
```

The `getProperty` method returns the value of a given key:

```
String driver = props.getProperty("jdbc.driver");
```

You don't actually have to think about this—the `init` method takes care of the details.

Whenever you need a connection, call

```
Connection conn = SimpleDataSource.getConnection();
```

You need to close the connection by calling

```
conn.close();
```

when you are done using it.

Real-world connection managers have slightly different methods, but the basic principle is the same.

Quality Tip   23.1

Don't Hardwire Database Connection Parameters into Your Program

It is considered inelegant to hardwire the database parameters into a program.

```
public class MyProg
{
    public static void main(String[] args)
    {
        // don't do this:
        String driver = "COM.cloudscape.core.JDBCDriver";
        String url = "jdbc:cloudscape:InvoiceDB;create=true";
        String username = "username";
        String password = "password";
        . . .
    }
}
```

If you want to change to a different database, you must locate these strings, update them, and recompile.

Instead, place the strings into a separate configuration file. The `SimpleData-Source.java` file reads in a configuration file with the database connection parameters. To connect to a different database, you simply supply a different configuration file name on the command line.

23.4.2 — Executing SQL Statements

> A `Connection` object can create `Statement` objects. You use statements to execute SQL commands.

Once you have a connection, you can use it to create `Statement` objects. You need `Statement` objects to execute SQL statements.

```
Statement stat = conn.createStatement();
```

The `execute` method of the `Statement` class executes a SQL statement. For example,

```
stat.execute("CREATE TABLE Test (Name CHAR(20))");
stat.execute("INSERT INTO Test VALUES ('Romeo')");
```

> The result of a SQL query is returned in a `ResultSet` object.

To issue a query, use the `executeQuery` method of the `Statement` class. The query result is returned as a `ResultSet` object. For example,

```
String queryStatement = "SELECT * FROM Test";
ResultSet result = stat.executeQuery(queryStatement);
```

You will see in the next section how to use the `ResultSet` object to analyze the result of the query.

For UPDATE statements, you can use the `executeUpdate` method. It returns the number of rows affected by the statement:

```
String updateStatement = "UPDATE Item "
   + "SET Quantity = Quantity + 1 "
   + "WHERE Invoice_Number = '11731'";
int count = stat.executeUpdate(updateStatement);
```

Alternatively, you can use the generic `execute` statement to execute queries and results. It returns a `boolean` value to indicate whether the SQL command yields a result set. If so, you can obtain it with the `getResultSet` method. Otherwise, you can get the update count with the `getUpdateCount` method.

```
String command = . . .;
boolean hasResultSet = stat.execute(command);
if (hasResultSet)
{
   ResultSet result = stat.getResultSet();
   . . .
}
else
{
   int count = stat.getUpdateCount();
   . . .
}
```

You can reuse a `Statement` object to execute as many SQL commands as you like. However, for each `Statement` object, you should only have one active `ResultSet`. If your program needs to look at several result sets at the same time, then you need to create multiple `Statement` objects.

When you are done using a `ResultSet`, you should close it before issuing a new query on the same statement.

```
result.close();
```

When you are done with a `Statement` object, you should close it. That automatically closes the associated result set.

```
stat.close();
```

23.4.3 — Analyzing Query Results

A `ResultSet` lets you fetch the query result, a row at a time. You iterate through the rows, and for each row, you can inspect the column values. Like the collection iterators that you saw in Chapter 19, the `ResultSet` class has a `next` method to visit the next row. However, the behavior of the `next` method is somewhat different. The `next` method does not return any data but a `boolean` value that indicates whether more data are available. Moreover, when you first get a result set from the `executeQuery` method, no row data are available. You need to call `next` to move to the first row. This appears curious, but it makes the iteration loop simple:

```
while (result.next())
{
    inspect column data from the current row
}
```

If the result set is completely empty, then the first call to `result.next()` returns `false`, and the loop is never entered. Otherwise, the first call to `result.next()` fetches the data for the first row from the database. As you can see, the loop ends when the `next` method returns `false`, which indicates that all rows have been fetched.

Once the result set object has fetched a particular row, you can inspect its columns. Various `get` methods return the column value formatted as a number, string, date, and so on. In fact, for each data type, there are two `get` methods. One of them has an integer parameter that indicates the column position. The other has a string parameter for the column name. For example, you can fetch the product code as

```
String productCode = result.getString(1);
```

or

```
String productCode = result.getString("Product_Code");
```

Note that the integer index starts at one, not at zero; that is, `getString(1)` inspects the first column. Database column indexes are different from array subscripts.

Accessing a column by an integer index is marginally faster and perfectly acceptable if you explicitly named the desired columns in the SELECT statement, such as

```
SELECT Invoice_Number FROM Invoice WHERE Payment = 0
```

However, if you make a SELECT * query, it is a good idea to use a column name instead of a column index. It makes your code easier to read, and you don't have to update the code when the column layout changes.

In the preceding example, you saw the `getString` method in action. To fetch a number, use the `getInt` and `getDouble` instead, for example

```
int quantity = result.getInt("Quantity");
double unitPrice = result.getDouble("Price");
```

Productivity Hint 23.4

Let the Database Do the Work

You now know how to issue a SQL query from a Java program and iterate through the result set. A common error that students make is to iterate through one table at a time to find a result. For example, suppose you want to find all invoices that contain car vacuums. You could use the following plan:

1. Issue the query SELECT * FROM Product and iterate through the result set to find the product code for a car vacuum
2. Issue the query SELECT * FROM Item and iterate through the result set to find the items with that product code

However, that plan is *extremely inefficient*. Such a program does in very slow motion what a database has been designed to do quickly.

Instead, you should let the database do all the work. Give the complete query to the database:

```
SELECT Item.Invoice_Number
    FROM Product, Item
    WHERE Product.Description = 'Car vacuum'
        AND Product.Product_Code = Item.Product_Code
```

Then iterate through the result set to read off all invoice numbers.

Beginners are often afraid of issuing complex SQL queries. However, you are throwing away a major benefit of a relational database if you don't take advantage of SQL.

23.4.4 — Result Set Meta Data

> Meta data are data about an object. Result set meta data describe the properties of a result set.

When you have a result set from an unknown table, you may want to know the names of the columns. You can use the ResultSetMeta-Data class to find out about properties of a result set. Start by requesting the meta data object from the result set:

```
ResultSetMetaData metaData = result.getMetaData();
```

Then you can get the number of columns with the getColumnCount method. The get-ColumnLabel method gives you the column name for each column. Finally, the get-ColumnDisplaySize method returns the column width, which is useful if you want to print table rows and have the columns line up. Note that the indexes for these methods start with 1. For example,

```
for (int i = 1; i <= metaData.getColumnCount(); i++)
{
    String columnName = metaData.getColumnLabel(i);
```

```
        int columnSize = metaData.getColumnDisplaySize(i);
        . . .
    }
```

At the end of this section, you will find a useful program that puts these concepts to work. The program reads a file containing SQL statements and executes them all. When a statement has a result set, the result set is printed, using the result set meta data to determine the column count and column labels.

For example, suppose you have the following file:

File product.sql

```
1  CREATE TABLE Product (Product_Code CHAR(10),Description CHAR(40),
   Price DECIMAL(10, 2))
2  INSERT INTO Product VALUES ('116-064', 'Toaster', 24.95)
3  INSERT INTO Product VALUES ('257-535', 'Hair dryer', 29.95)
4  INSERT INTO Product VALUES ('643-119', 'Car vacuum', 19.95)
5  SELECT * FROM Product
```

Then run the program as

```
java ExecSQL database.properties product.sql
```

The program executes the statements in the file and prints out the result of the SELECT query.

You can also use the program as an interactive testing tool. Run

```
java ExecSQL database.properties
```

Type in SQL commands at the command line. Every time you hit the Enter key, the command is executed.

File ExecSQL.java

```
1  import java.sql.Connection;
2  import java.sql.ResultSet;
3  import java.sql.ResultSetMetaData;
4  import java.sql.Statement;
5  import java.sql.SQLException;
6  import java.io.BufferedReader;
7  import java.io.FileReader;
8  import java.io.InputStreamReader;
9  import java.io.IOException;
10 import java.io.Reader;
11
12 /**
13     Executes all SQL statements in a file.
```

```
14      Call this program as
15      java -classpath driver_class_path;. ExecSQL
16          database.properties commands.sql
17  */
18  class ExecSQL
19  {
20      public static void main (String args[])
21          throws Exception
22      {
23          if (args.length == 0)
24          {
25              System.out.println(
26                  "Usage: java ExecSQL propertiesFile"
27                  + " [statementFile]");
28              System.exit(0);
29          }
30
31          SimpleDataSource.init(args[0]);
32
33          Connection conn = SimpleDataSource.getConnection();
34          Statement stat = conn.createStatement();
35
36          Reader reader;
37          if (args.length > 1)
38              reader = new FileReader(args[1]);
39          else
40              reader = new InputStreamReader(System.in);
41          BufferedReader in = new BufferedReader(reader);
42
43          boolean done = false;
44          while (!done)
45          {
46              String line = in.readLine();
47              if (line == null)
48                  done = true;
49              else
50              {
51                  try
52                  {
53                      boolean hasResultSet = stat.execute(line);
54                      if (hasResultSet)
55                          showResultSet(stat);
56                  }
57                  catch (SQLException exception)
58                  {
59                      exception.printStackTrace();
60                  }
61              }
62          }
63
```

```
64          in.close();
65          stat.close();
66          conn.close();
67       }
68
69       /**
70          Prints a result set.
71          @param stat the statement whose result set should be
72          printed
73       */
74       public static void showResultSet(Statement stat)
75          throws SQLException
76       {
77          ResultSet result = stat.getResultSet();
78          ResultSetMetaData metaData = result.getMetaData();
79          int columnCount = metaData.getColumnCount();
80
81          for (int i = 1; i <= columnCount; i++)
82          {
83             if (i > 1) System.out.print(", ");
84             System.out.print(metaData.getColumnLabel(i));
85          }
86          System.out.println();
87
88          while (result.next())
89          {
90             for (int i = 1; i <= columnCount; i++)
91             {
92                if (i > 1) System.out.print(", ");
93                System.out.print(result.getString(i));
94             }
95             System.out.println();
96          }
97          result.close();
98       }
99    }
```

23.5   Case Study: A Bank Database

In this section, we will develop a complete database program. We will reimplement the
ATM simulation of Chapter 16, storing the customer and account data in a database.
Recall that in the simulation, every customer has a customer number, a PIN, and two
bank accounts: a checking account and a savings account. We'll store the information in
two tables:

Customer

Customer_ Number	PIN	Checking_ Account_ Number	Savings_ Account_ Number
INTEGER	INTEGER	INTEGER	INTEGER

Account

Account_Number	Balance
INTEGER	DECIMAL (10, 2)

The Bank class now needs to connect to the database whenever it is asked to find a customer. Here is the implementation of the method that finds a customer. The method makes a query

```
SELECT * FROM Customer WHERE Customer_Number = . . .
```

It then checks that the PIN matches, and it constructs a Customer object. This method turns the row-and-column information of the database into object-oriented data.

```java
public Customer find(int customerNumber, int pin)
    throws SQLException
{
    Customer c = null;
    Connection conn = SimpleDataSource.getConnection();
    Statement stat = conn.createStatement();
    ResultSet result = stat.executeQuery("SELECT *"
        + " FROM Customer WHERE Customer_Number = "
        + customerNumber);

    if (result.next() && pin == result.getInt("PIN"))
        c = new Customer(customerNumber,
            result.getInt("Checking_Account_Number"),
            result.getInt("Savings_Account_Number"));
    result.close();
    stat.close();
    conn.close();
    return c;
}
```

Note that the method throws a SQLException. Why don't we catch that exception and return null if an exception occurs? There are many potential reasons for a SQL exception, and the Bank class doesn't want to hide the exception details. But the Bank class also doesn't know anything about the user interface of the application, so it can't display information about the exception to the user. By throwing the exception to the caller, the information can reach the part of the program that interacts with the user.

The `BankAccount` class in this program is quite different from the implementation you have seen throughout the book. Now we do not store the balance of the bank account in the object; instead, we look it up from the database:

```
public double getBalance()
    throws SQLException
{
    double balance = 0;
    Connection conn = SimpleDataSource.getConnection();
    Statement stat = conn.createStatement();
    ResultSet result = stat.executeQuery(
        "SELECT Balance"
        + " FROM Account WHERE Account_Number = "
        + accountNumber);
    if (result.next())
        balance = result.getDouble(1);
    result.close();
    stat.close();
    conn.close();
    return balance;
}
```

The `deposit` and `withdraw` operations immediately update the database as well:

```
public void deposit(double amount)
    throws SQLException
{
    Connection conn = SimpleDataSource.getConnection();
    Statement stat = conn.createStatement();
    stat.execute("UPDATE Account"
        + " SET Balance = Balance + " + amount
        + " WHERE Account_Number = " + accountNumber);
    stat.close();
    conn.close();
}
```

It seems somewhat inefficient to connect to the database whenever the bank balance is accessed, but it is much safer than storing it in an object. Suppose you have two instances of the ATM program running at the same time. Then it is possible that both programs modify the same bank account. If each of them copied the bank balances from the database into objects, then the modifications made by one user would not be seen by the other.

You can try out this simultaneous access yourself, simply by running two instances of the ATM simulation. Alternatively, you can modify the `main` method of the `ATMSimulation` to pop up two ATM frames. But you will need to get an "industrial-strength" database—some databases won't allow simultaneous connections from multiple programs.

Clearly, access by multiple users is very important in practice. Most real database applications have many simultaneous users. Therefore, you must design the translation from the database data to program objects with some care. You can't just copy data into objects that other users might modify. On the other hand, database lookups are pretty slow compared to object lookups, so you want to hold immutable data in objects. Programming real-world database applications that run quickly and correctly can get quite complex. In recent years, *application servers* have become available that manage some of this burden for developers. An application server monitors the objects that mirror database information and makes sure that the object and database data are always synchronized. The Java 2 Enterprise Edition defines a technology standard for Java-based application servers.

File ATMSimulation.java

```java
1  import javax.swing.JFrame;
2
3  /**
4     A simulation of an automatic teller machine.
5  */
6  public class ATMSimulation
7  {
8     public static void main(String[] args)
9     {
10       if (args.length == 0)
11       {
12          System.out.println(
13             "Usage: ATMSimulation propertiesFile");
14          System.exit(0);
15       }
16       else
17       {
18          try
19          {
20             SimpleDataSource.init(args[0]);
21          }
22          catch (Exception ex)
23          {
24             ex.printStackTrace();
25             System.exit(0);
26          }
27       }
28
29       JFrame frame = new ATM();
30       frame.setTitle("First National Bank of Java");
31       frame.setDefaultCloseOperation(
32          JFrame.EXIT_ON_CLOSE);
33       frame.pack();
34       frame.show();
35    }
36 }
```

File ATM.java

```java
1  import java.awt.Container;
2  import java.awt.FlowLayout;
```

```
 3  import java.awt.GridLayout;
 4  import java.awt.event.ActionEvent;
 5  import java.awt.event.ActionListener;
 6  import java.io.FileInputStream;
 7  import java.io.IOException;
 8  import java.sql.SQLException;
 9  import java.util.Properties;
10  import javax.swing.JButton;
11  import javax.swing.JFrame;
12  import javax.swing.JOptionPane;
13  import javax.swing.JPanel;
14  import javax.swing.JTextArea;
15
16  /**
17     A frame displaying the components of an ATM.
18  */
19  class ATM extends JFrame
20  {
21     /**
22        Constructs the user interface of the ATM application.
23     */
24     public ATM()
25     {
26        theBank = new Bank();
27
28        // construct components
29
30        pad = new KeyPad();
31
32        display = new JTextArea(4, 20);
33
34        aButton = new JButton("  A  ");
35        aButton.addActionListener(new AButtonListener());
36
37        bButton = new JButton("  B  ");
38        bButton.addActionListener(new BButtonListener());
39
40        cButton = new JButton("  C  ");
41        cButton.addActionListener(new CButtonListener());
42
43        // add components to content pane
44
45        JPanel buttonPanel = new JPanel();
46        buttonPanel.setLayout(new GridLayout(3, 1));
47        buttonPanel.add(aButton);
48        buttonPanel.add(bButton);
49        buttonPanel.add(cButton);
50
51        Container contentPane = getContentPane();
52        contentPane.setLayout(new FlowLayout());
```

```
53           contentPane.add(pad);
54           contentPane.add(display);
55           contentPane.add(buttonPanel);
56           try
57           {
58              setNextState(START_STATE);
59           }
60           catch (SQLException exception)
61           {
62              JOptionPane.showMessageDialog(null,
63                 exception.getMessage());
64           }
65        }
66
67        /**
68           Sets the current customer number to the keypad value
69           and sets state to PIN.
70        */
71        public void setCustomerNumber() throws SQLException
72        {
73           customerNumber = (int)pad.getValue();
74           setNextState(PIN_STATE);
75        }
76
77        /**
78           Gets PIN from keypad, finds customer in bank.
79           If found, sets state to ACCOUNT, else to START.
80        */
81        public void selectCustomer() throws SQLException
82        {
83           int pin = (int)pad.getValue();
84           currentCustomer = theBank.find(
85              customerNumber, pin);
86           if (currentCustomer == null)
87              setNextState(START_STATE);
88           else
89              setNextState(ACCOUNT_STATE);
90        }
91
92        /**
93           Sets current account to checking or savings. Sets
94           state to TRANSACT.
95           @param account one of CHECKING_ACCOUNT
96              or SAVINGS_ACCOUNT
97        */
98        public void selectAccount(int account)
99           throws SQLException
100        {
101           if (account == CHECKING_ACCOUNT)
102              currentAccount
```

```
103                       = currentCustomer.getCheckingAccount();
104          else
105             currentAccount
106                = currentCustomer.getSavingsAccount();
107          setNextState(TRANSACT_STATE);
108       }
109
110       /**
111          Withdraws amount typed in keypad from current account.
112          Sets state to ACCOUNT.
113       */
114       public void withdraw() throws SQLException
115       {
116          currentAccount.withdraw(pad.getValue());
117          setNextState(ACCOUNT_STATE);
118       }
119
120       /**
121          Deposits amount typed in keypad to current account.
122          Sets state to ACCOUNT.
123       */
124       public void deposit() throws SQLException
125       {
126          currentAccount.deposit(pad.getValue());
127          setNextState(ACCOUNT_STATE);
128       }
129
130       /**
131          Sets state and updates display message.
132          @param state the next state
133       */
134       public void setNextState(int newState)
135          throws SQLException
136       {
137          state = newState;
138          pad.clear();
139          if (state == START_STATE)
140             display.setText("Enter customer number\n"
141                + "A = OK");
142          else if (state == PIN_STATE)
143             display.setText("Enter PIN\nA = OK");
144          else if (state == ACCOUNT_STATE)
145             display.setText("Select Account\n"
146                + "A = Checking\nB = Savings\nC = Exit");
147          else if (state == TRANSACT_STATE)
148             display.setText("Balance = "
149                + currentAccount.getBalance()
150                + "\nEnter amount and select transaction\n"
151                + "A = Withdraw\nB = Deposit\nC = Cancel");
152       }
```

```
153
154    private class AButtonListener
155       implements ActionListener
156    {
157       public void actionPerformed(ActionEvent event)
158       {
159          try
160          {
161             if (state == START_STATE)
162                setCustomerNumber();
163             else if (state == PIN_STATE)
164                selectCustomer();
165             else if (state == ACCOUNT_STATE)
166                selectAccount(CHECKING_ACCOUNT);
167             else if (state == TRANSACT_STATE)
168                withdraw();
169          }
170          catch (SQLException exception)
171          {
172             JOptionPane.showMessageDialog(null,
173                exception.getMessage());
174          }
175       }
176    }
177
178    private class BButtonListener
179       implements ActionListener
180    [
181       public void actionPerformed(ActionEvent event)
182       {
183          try
184          {
185             if (state == ACCOUNT_STATE)
186                selectAccount(SAVINGS_ACCOUNT);
187             else if (state == TRANSACT_STATE)
188                deposit();
189          }
190          catch (SQLException exception)
191          {
192             JOptionPane.showMessageDialog(null,
193                exception.getMessage());
194          }
195       }
196    }
197
198    private class CButtonListener
199       implements ActionListener
200    {
201       public void actionPerformed(ActionEvent event)
202       {
```

```
203              try
204              {
205                  if (state == ACCOUNT_STATE)
206                      setNextState(START_STATE);
207                  else if (state == TRANSACT_STATE)
208                      setNextState(ACCOUNT_STATE);
209              }
210              catch (SQLException exception)
211              {
212                  JOptionPane.showMessageDialog(null,
213                      exception.getMessage());
214              }
215          }
216      }
217
218      private int state;
219      private int customerNumber;
220      private Bank theBank;
221      private Customer currentCustomer;
222      private BankAccount currentAccount;
223
224      private JButton aButton;
225      private JButton bButton;
226      private JButton cButton;
227
228      private KeyPad pad;
229      private JTextArea display;
230
231      private static final int START_STATE = 1;
232      private static final int PIN_STATE = 2;
233      private static final int ACCOUNT_STATE = 3;
234      private static final int TRANSACT_STATE = 4;
235
236      private static final int CHECKING_ACCOUNT = 1;
237      private static final int SAVINGS_ACCOUNT = 2;
238  }
```

File Bank.java

```
1   import java.sql.Connection;
2   import java.sql.ResultSet;
3   import java.sql.Statement;
4   import java.sql.SQLException;
5
6   /**
7       A bank consisting of multiple bank accounts.
8   */
9   public class Bank
10  {
11      /**
```

```
12          Finds a customer with a given number and PIN.
13          @param conn  the database connection
14          @param customerNumber  the customer number
15          @param pin  the personal identification number
16          @return  the matching customer, or null if none found
17      */
18      public Customer find(int customerNumber, int pin)
19          throws SQLException
20      {
21          Customer c = null;
22          Connection conn = SimpleDataSource.getConnection();
23          Statement stat = conn.createStatement();
24          ResultSet result = stat.executeQuery("SELECT *"
25              + " FROM Customer WHERE Customer_Number = "
26              + customerNumber);
27
28          if (result.next() && pin == result.getInt("PIN"))
29              c = new Customer(customerNumber,
30                  result.getInt("Checking_Account_Number"),
31                  result.getInt("Savings_Account_Number"));
32          result.close();
33          stat.close();
34          conn.close();
35          return c;
36      }
37 }
```

File BankAccount.java

```
 1 import java.sql.Connection;
 2 import java.sql.ResultSet;
 3 import java.sql.Statement;
 4 import java.sql.SQLException;
 5
 6 /**
 7     A bank account has a balance that can be changed by
 8     deposits and withdrawals.
 9 */
10 public class BankAccount
11 {
12     /**
13         Constructs a bank account with a given balance.
14         @param anAccountNumber  the account number
15     */
16     public BankAccount(int anAccountNumber)
17     {
18         accountNumber = anAccountNumber;
19     }
20
21     /**
```

```
22          Deposits money into a bank account.
23          @param accountNumber the account number
24          @param amount the amount to deposit
25       */
26       public void deposit(double amount)
27          throws SQLException
28       {
29          Connection conn = SimpleDataSource.getConnection();
30          Statement stat = conn.createStatement();
31          stat.execute("UPDATE Account"
32             + " SET Balance = Balance + " + amount
33             + " WHERE Account_Number = " + accountNumber);
34          stat.close();
35          conn.close();
36       }
37
38       /**
39          Withdraws money from a bank account.
40          @param accountNumber the account number
41          @param amount the amount to withdraw
42       */
43       public void withdraw(double amount)
44          throws SQLException
45       {
46          Connection conn = SimpleDataSource.getConnection();
47          Statement stat = conn.createStatement();
48          stat.execute("UPDATE Account"
49             + " SET Balance = Balance - " + amount
50             + " WHERE Account_Number = " + accountNumber);
51          stat.close();
52          conn.close();
53       }
54
55       /**
56          Gets the balance of a bank account.
57          @param accountNumber the account number
58          @return the account balance
59       */
60       public double getBalance()
61          throws SQLException
62       {
63          double balance = 0;
64          Connection conn = SimpleDataSource.getConnection();
65          Statement stat = conn.createStatement();
66          ResultSet result = stat.executeQuery(
67             "SELECT Balance"
68             + " FROM Account WHERE Account_Number = "
69             + accountNumber);
70          if (result.next())
71             balance = result.getDouble(1);
```

```
72          result.close();
73          stat.close();
74          conn.close();
75          return balance;
76       }
77
78       private int accountNumber;
79  }
```

File Customer.java

```
1   /**
2       A bank customer with a checking and savings account.
3   */
4   public class Customer
5   {
6       /**
7           Constructs a customer with a given number and PIN.
8           @param aCustomerNumber  the customer number
9           @param checkingAccountNumber  the checking account number
10          @param savingsAccountNumber  the savings account number
11      */
12      public Customer(int aCustomerNumber,
13          int checkingAccountNumber,
14          int savingsAccountNumber)
15      {
16          customerNumber = aCustomerNumber;
17          checkingAccount = new BankAccount(
18              checkingAccountNumber);
19          savingsAccount = new BankAccount(
20              savingsAccountNumber);
21      }
22
23      /**
24          Gets the checking account of this customer.
25          @return  the checking account
26      */
27      public BankAccount getCheckingAccount()
28      {
29          return checkingAccount;
30      }
31
32      /**
33          Gets the savings account of this customer.
34          @return  the checking account
35      */
36      public BankAccount getSavingsAccount()
37      {
38          return savingsAccount;
39      }
```

```
40
41     private int customerNumber;
42     private BankAccount checkingAccount;
43     private BankAccount savingsAccount;
44 }
```

23.6   Advanced Database Concepts

In this section we will briefly touch on a few more advanced database concepts that are important in real-world applications. If you take a class in database programming, you will encounter these concepts again in much greater detail. At this point, you may just want to read through this section to gain an appreciation that real-world database programming is quite a bit more complex than issuing a few SQL queries.

23.6.1 — Transactions

> A transactions is a set of database updates that should either succeed in their entirety or not happen at all.

An important part of database processing is *transaction handling*. A transaction is a set of database updates that should either succeed in their entirety or not happen at all. For example, consider a banking application that transfers money from one account to another. This operation involves two steps: reducing the balance of one account and increasing the balance of another account. No software system is perfect, and there is always the possibility of an error. The banking application, the database program, or the network connection between them could exhibit an error right after the first part—then the money would be withdrawn from the first account but never deposited to the second account. Clearly, this would be very bad. There are many other similar situations. For example, if you change an airline reservation, you don't want to give up your old seat until the new one is confirmed.

What all these situations have in common is that there is a set of database operations that are grouped together to carry out the transaction. All operations in the group must be carried out together—a partial completion cannot be tolerated. In SQL, you use the COMMIT and ROLLBACK commands to manage transactions. For example, to transfer money from one account to another, you issue the commands

```
UPDATE Account SET Balance = Balance - 1000
   WHERE Account_Number = '95667-2574'
UPDATE Account SET Balance = Balance + 1000
   WHERE Account_Number = '82041-1196'
COMMIT
```

The COMMIT command makes the updates permanent. Conversely, the ROLLBACK command undoes all changes up to the last COMMIT.

When you program with JDBC, by default the JDBC library automatically commits all database updates. That is convenient for simple programs, but it is not what you want for transaction processing. Thus, you should first turn the autocommit mode off:

```
Connection conn = . . . ;
conn.setAutoCommit(false);
Statement stat = conn.createStatement();
```

Then issue your updates that form the transaction and call the `commit` method of the `Statement` class.

```
stat.executeUpdate(
    "UPDATE Accounts SET Balance = Balance - "
    + amount + " WHERE Account_Number = " + fromAccount);
stat.executeUpdate(
    "UPDATE Accounts SET Balance = Balance + "
    + amount + " WHERE Account_Number = " + toAccount);
stat.commit();
```

Conversely, if you encounter an error, then call the `rollback` method. This typically happens in an exception handler:

```
try
{
    . . .
}
catch(SQLException exception)
{
    stat.rollback();
}
```

You may wonder how a database can undo updates when a transaction is rolled back. The database actually stores your changes in a set of temporary tables. If you make queries within a transaction, the information in the temporary tables is merged with the permanent data for the purpose of computing the query result, giving you the illusion that the updates have already taken place. When you commit the transaction, the temporary data are made permanent. When you execute a rollback, the temporary tables are simply discarded.

23.6.2 — Scrollable and Updatable Result Sets

When you obtain a result set from a query, you can inspect the result one row at a time, moving forward with the `next` method. However, you may want to go back as well. This most commonly happens when the result is displayed in a user interface component such as a table with scroll bars (see Figure 12). The user may well want to scroll backward to look at some data again.

Of course, if the result set is small, it is a simple matter to copy the result into an array. But query results can be huge. For example, suppose that a query has 100,000 possible results. (You may know from personal experience that some queries that you make with a web search engine have huge numbers of results.) In this case, it is not practical to read in the entire result set and copy it into an array. Keep in mind that the database may well be located on another computer. Thus, it can be quite slow to transport large amounts of data from the database to your application. For that reason, the `ResultSet` object does *not* contain the entire result set. It is just a gateway to the result set that is

	CUSTOMER_NUMBER	PIN	CHECKING_ACCOUNT_NUMBER	
3	3	3692	301	▲
4	4	4826	401	
5	5	5050	501	
6	6	6284	601	
7	7	7418	701	
8	8	8642	801	▼

stored in the database. Each time you call the `next` method, a single row is transferred into the `ResultSet` object.

At any rate, a user probably doesn't want to see all results of a large query. Typically, users look at the first few rows of the result and then try to figure out how to narrow the query down. Still, in the process of inspecting the result, users may want to look backward. To make this easier to program, you can use a *scrollable* result set.

To obtain scrollable result sets, you need to create a `Statement` object with type and concurrency parameter constants from the `ResultSet` class. Here are your choices:

- Do you want a scrollable result set? If not, use TYPE_FORWARD_ONLY (the default).

- When scrolling through the result set, do you want the result set to be updated when other processes change the information in the database? If so, use TYPE_SCROLL_SENSITIVE. Otherwise, use TYPE_SCROLL_INSENSITIVE.

- Do you want to be able to update the database by editing the result set (instead of issuing an UPDATE statement)? If so, use CONCUR_UPDATABLE. If not, use CONCUR_READ_ONLY. We discuss updatable result sets later in this section.

For example, suppose you want scroll, but you don't care about sensing changes by other processes, and you don't need an updatable result set. Then construct the `Statement` object as follows:

```
Statement stat =
conn.createStatement(ResultSet.TYPE_SCROLL_SENSITIVE,
    ResultSet.CONCUR_READ_ONLY);
ResultSet result = stat.executeQuery(. . .);
```

When you get a scrollable result set from a query, you have several methods to navigate through the result:

- `previous()` moves to the previous row.

- `first()` and `last()` move to the first and last row, respectively.

- `relative(n)` and `absolute(n)` move by n rows, or to row number n.

> A scrollable result set gives random access to query results.

In effect, a scrollable result set gives you random access to the result set. If you obtain an updatable result set, then you can use a `set` method to update the corresponding value in the database. For example, suppose you obtain an account record.

```
Statement stat = con.createStatement(
```

```
    ResultSet.TYPE_FORWARD_ONLY,
    ResultSet.CONCUR_UPDATABLE);
String accountQuery =
    "SELECT * WHERE Account_Number = " + account;
ResultSet result = stat.executeQuery(accountQuery);
double balance = result.getDouble("Balance");
```

Then you can call

```
result.updateDouble("Balance", balance + deposit);
```

This call updates the current row but does not yet update the database. You can update other fields in the current row. Then call

```
result.updateRow()
```

to change the data in the database. You can also use updatable result sets to insert new rows. First, move the cursor to a special position called the *insert row*. Then update all column values and call the **updateRow** method:

```
result.moveToInsertRow();
result.updateString("Account_Number", "54382-5516");
result.updateString("Customer_Number", "992345");
result.updateDouble("Balance", 1000);
result.updateRow();
```

> An updatable result set makes it easy to modify the contents of a database without using SQL commands.

Many programmers find updatable result sets easier to use than UPDATE or INSERT SQL commands.

Not all JDBC drivers implement scrollable or updatable result sets. If you use a driver that lacks these capabilities, the result set that you obtain from a query does not have scrolling or update capabilities. When you invoke one of the unsupported methods (such as **previous** or an **update** method), the method throws an exception.

23.6.3 — Speeding Queries Up

There are a number of methods for speeding queries up. In this section, we discuss three of them:

- Indexing

- Prepared statements

- Stored procedures

> Table indexes can speed database queries up. To use indexes, you must specify primary keys when creating tables.

Recall that a *primary key* is a column (or combination of columns) that uniquely identifies a row in a table. When a table has a primary key, then the database can build an *index file:* a file that stores information on how to access a row quickly when the primary key is known. Indexing can greatly increase the speed of joins.

If the primary key is contained in a single column, then you can tag the column with the keyword PRIMARY KEY, like this:

```
CREATE TABLE Products
(
    Product_Code CHAR(10) PRIMARY KEY,
    Description CHAR(40),
    Price DECIMAL(10, 2)
)
```

If the primary key is contained in multiple columns, then you add a PRIMARY KEY clause to the end of the CREATE TABLE command, like this:

```
CREATE TABLE Items
(
    Invoice_Number INTEGER,
    Product_Code CHAR(10),
    Quantity INTEGER,
    PRIMARY KEY (Invoice_Number, Product_Code)
)
```

> Use prepared statements for frequently repeated database queries and updates, to avoid the repeated computation of query strategies.

Occasionally, it is possible to speed queries up by building *secondary indexes:* index files that index other column sets, which are not necessarily unique. That is an advanced technique that we will not discuss here.

When you issue a query to the database, the database program must figure out in which order it should search the tables that you want to query. Coming up with a strategy for answering your query takes time. If you issue the same query many times, it makes sense to use a *prepared statement*. When you send a prepared statement to the database, the database formulates a query strategy and saves it with the prepared statement. Every time you issue the prepared statement, the database uses that precomputed strategy. Thus, prepared statements make sense for statements that you issue frequently.

For example, here is how you prepare the query to get the bank account information for a given account number:

```
String query = "SELECT * WHERE Account_Number = ?";
PreparedStatement prepStat =
    conn.prepareStatement(query);
```

The ? symbols in the query string denote variables that you fill in when you make an actual query. You use a set command for that purpose, for example

```
prepStat.setString(1, accountNumber);
```

The first parameter of the set methods denotes the variable position: 1 is the first ?, 2 the second, and so on.

Finally, when you have set all variables, you call the **executeQuery** method, as you would with a regular statement.

```
ResultSet result = prepStat.executeQuery();
```

You can keep reusing the prepared query object—just keep setting the variables and calling executeQuery.

Stored procedures are another method of formulating repeated statements. Stored procedures are executed in the database kernel and are thus much faster than sequences of SQL commands, each of which is separately transmitted to the database. Not all databases have the ability to execute stored procedures, and the databases that do don't all use the same syntax for them. (In fact, some databases—namely those that support the SQLJ standard—even let you formulate stored procedures in Java! However, we will not discuss SQLJ in this book.) Thus, you should consult your database documentation before trying out the code that follows.

> Stored procedures are executed in the database kernel, which is much faster than issuing sequences of SQL commands.

Before you can call it, you first need to download a stored procedure into the database. A typical way of doing that is to issue the CREATE PROCEDURE command. Here is an example of a procedure that transfers money from one account to another:

```
CREATE PROCEDURE transfer(
    :from INTEGER, :to INTEGER, :amount DECIMAL(10, 2))
BEGIN
    UPDATE Accounts SET Balance = Balance - :amount
        WHERE Account_Number = :from;
    UPDATE Accounts SET Balance = Balance + :amount
        WHERE Account_Number = :to;
END
```

Note that the exact syntax for stored procedures differs among databases. Some databases don't support stored procedures at all.

In Java, you can download the stored procedure by executing the SQL statement that defines the procedure.

```
String definition =
    "CREATE PROCEDURE transfer("
    + . . .
    + ") BEGIN"
    + . . .
    + "END";
stat.execute(definition);
```

To call the procedure, you use the CallableStatement class. You get a CallableStatement object from the prepareCall method of the Connection class.

```
CallableStatement callStat = conn.prepareCall(
    "{call transfer(?, ?, ?)}");
```

The ? placeholders have the same function as in prepared statements—you need to set values before calling the procedure. The { } delimiters tell the JDBC driver that the enclosed call command is not standard SQL and needs to be translated into the call syntax of the particular database.

Next, you set the parameter values:

```
callStat.setInt(1, fromAccount);
callStat.setInt(2, toAccount);
callStat.setDouble(3, amount);
```

Finally, you make the call:

```
callStat.execute();
```

Using stored procedures for frequently occurring SQL statement sequences can dramatically improve the performance of a database application. However, since stored procedures differ from one database to the next, using stored procedures limits portability. It is always a good idea to get your application working correctly and then profile the performance before turning to stored procedures.

In this section you have seen a number of advanced techniques for database programming. Although you can express the logic of most database applications with just the basic commands introduced earlier in this chapter, professional database programmers use these and other advanced techniques to produce database applications with good performance.

This discussion of advanced techniques completes our chapter on Java database programming. You have seen how you can use SQL to query and update data in a database and how the JDBC library makes it easy for you to issue SQL commands in a Java program.

CHAPTER SUMMARY

1. A relational database stores information in tables. Each table column has a name and a data type.

2. SQL (Structured Query Language) is a command language for interacting with a database.

3. Use the CREATE TABLE and INSERT SQL commands to add data to a database.

4. You should avoid rows with replicated data. Instead, distribute the data over multiple tables.

5. A primary key is a column (or combination of columns) whose value uniquely specifies a table record.

6. A foreign key is a reference to a primary key in a linked table.

7. Use the SQL SELECT statement to query a database.

8. A join is a query that involves multiple tables.

9. The UPDATE and DELETE SQL commands modify the data in a database.

10. You need a JDBC (Java Database Connectivity) driver to access a database from a Java program.

11. Make sure the JDBC driver is on the class path when you launch the Java program.

12. Use a Connection object to access a database from a Java program.

13. A Connection object can create Statement objects. You use statements to execute SQL commands.

14. The result of a SQL query is returned in a ResultSet object.

15. Meta data are data about an object. Result set meta data describe the properties of a result set.

16. A transaction is a set of database updates that should either succeed in their entirety or not happen at all.

17. A scrollable result set gives random access to query results.

18. An updatable result set makes it easy to modify the contents of a database without using SQL commands.

19. Table indexes can speed database queries up. To use indexes, you must specify primary keys when creating tables.

20. Use prepared statements for frequently repeated database queries and updates, to avoid the repeated computation of query strategies.

21. Stored procedures are executed in the database kernel, which is much faster than issuing sequences of SQL commands.

Further Reading

[1] Chris J. Date and Hugh Darwen, *A Guide to the SQL Standard: A User's Guide to the Standard Database Language SQL*, Addison-Wesley, 1997.
[2] Seth White, Maydene Fisher, Rick Cattell, Graham Hamilton, and Mark Hapner, *JDBC API Tutorial and Reference, 2nd edition*, Addison-Wesley, 1999.
[3] http://www.cpsr.org/cpsr/privacy/ssn/ssn.faq.html A list of frequently asked questions about Social Security numbers, by Computer Professionals for Social Responsibility.
[4] http://www.ftc.gov/privacy/ A web site on information privacy by the Federal Trade Commission.

CLASSES, OBJECTS, AND METHODS INTRODUCED IN THIS CHAPTER

```
java.lang.Class
   forName
java.sql.Connection
   close
   commit
   createStatement
   prepareCall
   prepareStatement
   rollback
   setAutoCommit
java.sql.DriverManager
   getConnection
java.sql.PreparedStatement
```

```
      execute
      executeQuery
      executeUpdate
      setInt
      setDouble
      setString
  java.sql.ResultSet
      absolute
      close
      first
      getInt
      getDouble
      getMetaData
      getString
      last
      moveToInsertRow
      next
      previous
      relative
      updateInt
      updateDouble
      updateRow
      updateString
  java.sql.ResultSetMetaData
      getColumnCount
      getColumnDisplaySize
      getColumnLabel
  java.sql.SQLException
  java.sql.Statement
      close
      execute
      executeQuery
      executeUpdate
      getResultSet
      getUpdateCount
  java.util.Properties
      load
      getProperty
```

Review Exercises

Exercise R23.1. Design a set of database tables to store people and cars. A person has a name, a unique driver license number, and an address. Every car has a unique vehicle identification number, manufacturer, type, and year. Every car has one owner, but one person can own multiple cars.

Exercise R23.2. Design a set of database tables to store library books and patrons. A book has an ISBN (International Standard Book Number), an author, and a title. The library may have multiple copies of each book, each with a different book ID. A patron has a name, a unique ID, and an address. A book may be checked out by at most one patron, but one patron can check out multiple books.

Exercise R23.3. Design a set of database tables to store sets of coins in purses. Each purse has an owner name and a unique ID. Each coin type has a unique name and a value. Each purse contains some quantity of coins of a given type.

Exercise R23.4. Design a set of database tables to store students, classes, professors, and classrooms. Each student takes zero or more classes. Each class has one professor, but a professor can teach multiple classes. Each class has one classroom.

Exercise R23.5. Give SQL commands to create a Book table, with columns for the ISBN, author, and title, and to insert all textbooks that you are using this semester.

Exercise R23.6. Give SQL commands to create a Car table, with columns for the vehicle identification number, manufacturer, type, and year of cars, and to insert all cars that your family members own.

Exercise R23.7. Give a SQL query that lists all products in the invoice database.

Exercise R23.8. Give a SQL query that lists all customers in California.

Exercise R23.9. Give a SQL query that lists all customers in California or Nevada.

Exercise R23.10. Give a SQL query that lists all customers not in Hawaii.

Exercise R23.11. Give a SQL query that lists all customers who have an unpaid invoice.

Exercise R23.12. Give a SQL query that lists all products that have been purchased by a customer in California.

Exercise R23.13. Give a SQL query that lists all items that are part of invoice number 11731.

Exercise R23.14. Give a SQL query that computes the sum of all quantities that are part of invoice number 11731.

Exercise R23.15. Give a SQL query that computes the total cost. `SUM(Product.Price * Item.Quantity)` of all items in invoice number 11731.

Exercise R23.16. Give a SQL update statement that raises all prices by 10%.

Exercise R23.17. Give a SQL statement that deletes all customers in California.

Exercise R23.18. Pick a database system (such as DB2, Oracle, Postgres, SQL Server) and find out from the web documentation:
- What JDBC driver do you need?
- What is the database URL?

Exercise R23.19. What is the difference between a `Connection` and a `Statement`?

Exercise R23.20. Of the SQL commands introduced in this chapter, which yield result sets, which yield an update count, and which yield neither?

Exercise R23.21. How is a `ResultSet` different from an `Iterator`?

Exercise R23.22. How can you make the `deposit` method of the `BankAccount` class "bulletproof" so that the connection and statement objects get closed even when an exception occurs? This is not as simple as it sounds. For example, consider the case in which the `getStatement` method throws an exception. Then the connection needs to be closed, but the statement object is still `null`.

Exercise R23.23. How can one speed up the bank simulation in Section 23.5 to avoid the cost of frequent connections to the database?

PROGRAMMING EXERCISES

Exercise P23.1. Write a Java program that creates a Coin table with coin names and values; inserts coin types penny, nickel, dime, quarter, half dollar, and dollar; and prints out the sum of the coin values. Use CREATE TABLE, INSERT, and SELECT SUM SQL commands.

Exercise P23.2. Write a Java program that creates a Car table with car manufacturers, types, model years, and fuel efficiency ratings. Insert several cars. Print out the average fuel efficiency. Use CREATE TABLE, INSERT, and SELECT AVG SQL commands.

Exercise P23.3. Reimplement the bank data program from Section 15.7 using a database table for the bank accounts.

Exercise P23.4. Improve the ExecSQL program and make the columns of the output line up. *Hint:* Use the `getColumnDisplaySize` method of the `ResultSetMetaData` class.

Exercise P23.5. Write a Java program that uses the database tables from the invoice database. Prompt the user for an invoice number and print out the invoice, formatted as in Chapter 16.

Exercise P23.6. Write a Java program that uses the database tables from the invoice database. Produce a report that lists all customers, their invoices, the amounts paid, and the unpaid balances.

Exercise P23.7. Write a Java program that uses a library database of books and patron data, as described in Exercise R23.2. Patrons should be able to check out and return books. Supply commands to print the books that a patron has checked out and to find who has checked out a particular book. You may create and populate Patron and Book tables before running the program.

Exercise P23.8. Write a Java program that creates a grade book for a class. You may create and populate a Student table and other tables that you need before running the program. The program should be able to display all grades for a given student. It should allow the instructor to add a new grade (such as "Homework 4: 100") or modify an existing grade.

Exercise P23.9. Write a program that assigns seats on an airplane as described in Exercise P16.11. Keep the passenger and seating information in a database.

Exercise P23.10. Write a program that keeps an appointment calendar in a database. An appointment includes a date, the starting time, the ending time, and a description; for example,

```
Dentist 2001/10/1 17:30 18:30
CS1 class 2001/10/2 08:30 10:00
```

Supply a user interface to add appointments, remove canceled appointments, and print out a list of appointments for a particular day. Your user interface can be text-based or graphical.

Exercise P23.11. Modify the ATM simulation program of Section 23.5 so that the program pops up two ATM frames. Verify that the database can be accessed simultaneously by two users.

XML

Understanding XML elements and attributes

▶ Understanding the concept of an XML parser

▶ Being able to read and write XML documents

▶ Being able to design Document Type Definitions for XML documents

Y ou saw in Chapter 23 how to store data in a database. Databases are excellent for storing large quantities of data and for retrieving the data quickly. In this chapter we are concerned with a different data storage issue, namely, how to transmit data from one program to another in a structured form. Of course, you can turn any data into strings, by encoding them in some way. For example, if you want to exchange product information, you can encode each product as a string, such as

    Car vacuum 24.95

But there are problems with such an *ad hoc* encoding. For example, suppose the product name contains spaces. Then it becomes difficult to *parse* the string. That is, the recipient has a harder time telling which part of the string is the product name and which is the price. Alternatively, you can use *object serialization* (which we discussed in Chapter 15) to exchange binary data that describe the objects. There are problems with that approach as well—in particular, the recipient must be a Java program that uses the same versions of the classes as the sending program.

In this chapter, you will learn about the Extensible Markup Language (XML), a mechanism for encoding data that is independent of any programming language. XML lets you encode complex data in a form that the recipient can parse easily. XML is becoming very popular for data exchange. It is simple enough that a wide variety of programs can easily generate XML data. XML data has a nested structure, so you can use it to describe hierarchical data sets—for example, an invoice that contains many items, each of which

> XML lets you encode complex data, independent from any programming language, in a form that the recipient can parse easily.

consists of a product and a quantity. Because the XML format is standardized, libraries for parsing the data are widely available and—as you will see in this chapter—easy to use for a programmer.

It is particularly easy to read and write XML documents in Java. In fact, it is generally easier to use XML than it is to use an "*ad hoc*" file format. Thus, using XML makes your programs easier to write and more professional.

CHAPTER CONTENTS

24.1   XML Tags and Documents

24.1.1 — Advantages of XML

You use XML to encode data. Let's look at a typical example. We want to encode coin descriptions. In Chapter 14, we used a naïve encoding like this:

```
0.5
half dollar
```

The value and name were placed on separate lines so that we didn't have to work too hard if the name had spaces.

In contrast, here is an XML encoding of the same data:

```
<coin>
    <value>0.5</value>
    <name>half dollar</name>
</coin>
```

The advantage of the XML version is clear: You can look at the data and understand what they mean. Of course, this is a benefit for the programmer, not for a computer program. A computer program has no understanding what a "price" is. As a programmer, you still need to write code to extract the price as the contents of the `price` element. Nevertheless, the fact that an XML document is comprehensible by humans is a huge advantage for program development.

> XML files are readable by computer programs and by humans.

A second advantage of the XML version is that it is *resilient to change*. Suppose the coin data change, and an additional field is introduced, to denote the year in which the coin was issued. In the naïve format, the year field might be added below the name field:

```
0.5
half dollar
1982
```

Now, a program that can process the old format might choke when reading a sequence of coins in the new format. The program would think that the name is followed by the value of the next coin. Thus, the program needs to be updated to work with the new data format. Then the updated program cannot read the old data format any longer. (Of course, one can overcome these issues with some amount of ingenuity, but as data get more complex, programming for multiple versions of a data format can be difficult and time-consuming.)

> XML formatted data files are resilient to change.

When using XML, on the other hand, it is easy to add new elements:

```
<coin>
    <value>0.5</value>
    <name>half dollar</name>
    <year>1982</year>
</coin>
```

Now a program that processes the new data can still extract the old information in the same way—as the contents of the `value` and `name` elements. The program need not be updated, and it can tolerate different versions of the data format.

24.1.2 — Differences between XML and HTML

You may have noticed that the XML format of the product data looked somewhat like HTML code. In particular, the XML tag pairs such as `<value>` and `</value>` look just like HTML tag pairs such as `<h1>` and `</h1>`. Both in XML and in HTML, tags are enclosed in angle brackets `< >`, and an opening tag is paired with a closing tag that starts with a slash `/` character.

> Both HTML and XML are descendants of SGML, the Standard Generalized Markup Language.

This similarity is no accident. Both HTML and XML are descendants of SGML, the Standard Generalized Markup Language. SGML was developed in the 1970s to specify structure rule sets for different documents and to create documents that fit those rule sets. For example, an organization using SGML might define rule sets for brochures, instruction manuals, shareholder reports, and so on. Then each document would be prepared according to its rule set, using the syntax of SGML. In fact, HTML defines one such rule set—namely the structure rules for hypertext documents. When you prepare an HTML document, you use the tags such as <h1> or <li> to *mark up* your document. That is, the tags show the structure of your particular web page. The structure must confom to certain rules—for example, an li element must be contained inside an ul or ol list. We say that HTML is an *instance* of SGML—it is one particular rule set that uses the general SGML syntax.

However, in one perhaps unfortunate aspect, HTML, as it is used on the web today, is not quite an SGML instance. SGML is very strict. For example, if a document contains an li element that is not inside a ul or ol list, the document is invalid and should not be processed. But browsers will somehow display the element anyway. Of course, each browser manufacturer may show such an invalid element in a different fashion. Superficially, finding a way to display the element sounds "nicer" than refusing to display an invalid document, but in practice it is a major problem. A web designer who checks a particular page in one or two browsers may think that the page is correct because these browsers happened to display it correctly, but another browser may display the invalid portions quite differently. It would have been better if the page had been diagnosed as incorrect. Of course, HTML syntax-checking tools are available, and it is a good idea to use them for your own web pages. One example of such a tool is the HTML validator from the World Wide Web Consortium (W3C), a nonprofit organization that sets web standards. You can find the validator at http://validator.w3.org/.

SGML is quite complex, because the designers wanted to make it easy for typists to enter text. For example, when you type a paragraph that starts with a <p> tag, you don't have to enter a </p> if the end of the paragraph is clear from the context. If you start another paragraph, then you can just enter another <p> tag and the preceding paragraph is closed automatically. This is a convenience for the typist, but it complicates the logic of the rule sets and file processing. Because of these complications, it is not easy to implement SGML tools. SGML was used extensively in some industries (such as the aircraft industry) where the need to manage huge volumes of documents outweighed the complexity of SGML, but it never quite caught on as a universal document description language. In 1996, the World Wide Web Consortium started discussions about the use of SGML on the web. The outcome was XML, a greatly simplified version of SGML. The XML 1.0 specification was released in 1998. It was 26 pages long, as opposed to the more than 500 pages of the SGML specification. There is also an annotated version with good explanations of the specification ([1]).

One reason for the simplicity of the XML specification is its strictness.

- In XML, you *must* pay attention to the letter case of the tags; for example, <li> and <LI> are different tags that bear no relation to each other.

- Every start tag *must* have a matching end tag. You cannot omit tags such as `</p>`. However, if a tag has no end-tag, it must end in `/>`, for example

  ```
  <img src="hamster.jpeg"/>
  ```

  When the parser sees the `/>`, it knows not to look for a matching end tag.

- Finally, attribute values must be enclosed in quotes. For example,

  ```
  <img src="hamster.jpeg" width=400 height=300/>
  ```

  is not acceptable. You must use

  ```
  <img src="hamster.jpeg" width="400" height="300"/>
  ```

> XML describes the meaning of data, not how to display them.

Most people who first see XML wonder how an XML document looks inside a browser. However, that is *not* generally a useful question to ask. Some browsers make some effort to display XML documents, and there is a *transformation* mechanism that can transform XML into HTML that is suitable for display in a browser (see Advanced Topic 24.2). However, most data that are encoded in XML have nothing to do with browsers. For example, it would probably not be exciting to display an XML document with nothing but product records (such as the ones in the previous section) in a browser. Instead, you will learn in this chapter how to write programs that analyze XML data. The fundamental difference between XML and HTML is that XML tells you what the data *mean*, not how to display them.

▼ Random Fact 24.1

Word Processing and Typesetting Systems

You have almost certainly used a *word processor* for writing letters or reports. A word processor is a program to write and edit documents made up of text and images. The text can contain characters in various fonts. It can be arranged in paragraphs, tables, and footnotes. Paragraphs can be formatted in various ways, such as ragged right (that is, the left ends of the lines of text are aligned under each other, but the right ends aren't), centered, and fully justified (that is, both the left and right ends of the lines are aligned). What is characteristic of modern word processors is their "what you see is what you get" operation. You enter text and commands, using the keyboard and the mouse. The computer screen instantly shows what the printed document will look like (see Figure 1).

However, there are disadvantages to the "what you see is what you get" nature of a word processor. You may labor to arrange various related images and tables to be together on the same page. Later, you find that you need to add a couple of paragraphs on the preceding page. Now half of the material moves to the next page, and you have do the arranging all over again. It would have been more useful if you could have told the word processor your intention, namely: "Always keep these images and tables together on the same page". In general, "what you see is what you get" programs are very good in letting you arrange material, but they don't know *why* you arranged the material in a certain way.

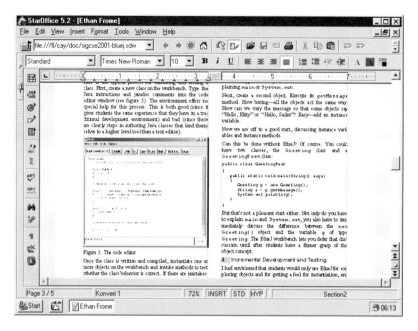

Figure 1

A "What You See Is What You Get" Word Processor

Thus, they can't keep the arrangement when your document changes. Some people call these programs "what you see is all you've got".

More fundamentally, "what you see is what you get" programs break down when you need to publish the same material in multiple ways. You may want to format product information as a product parts list and an advertising brochure. Or you may want to publish the information in printed form, on the web, and in spoken form for telephone retrieval. Now you no longer want to "get" a single result, so it isn't as helpful to see what you get. Instead, it becomes much more important to visualize the *structure* of the information.

A program for editing structured text needs to capture three pieces of information:

- The text itself

- The structural element (paragraph, bulleted list, heading, and so on) to which each part of the text belongs

- The rules for formatting the structural elements

To make it easy to interchange structured documents between computer systems, the structural information is often encoded in *markup tags*. For example, XML and HTML use tags that are enclosed in angle brackets such as the familiar <p>, <ul>, and <h1> tags.

In the 1970s, when publishers began to move away from traditional manual typesetting to computer-based typesetting, the result at first was much inferior quality, particu-

▼

Figure 2

A Formula Typeset in the $\mathrm{T_{\!E}X}$ Typesetting System

A sum inside text: $\sum_{i=1}^{n} i^2$.
The same sum as a displayed formula:

$$\sum_{i=1}^{n} i^2$$

▼

▼

▼

larly for mathematical formulas. Arranging the symbols in complex formulas in a way
that makes mathematical sense is an art that requires practice and good judgment, and
the first typesetting programs were definitely not up to the job. Frustrated by this situation, the famous computer scientist Donald Knuth of Stanford University decided to do
something about it and invented a typesetting program that he called $\mathrm{T_{\!E}X}$ (pronounced
"tek" because the "X" is a capital Greek chi). Input to that program consists of text with
markup tags that start with a backslash; curly braces {} for grouping; and other special
markup symbols, such as _ and ∧ to indicate subscript and superscript. For example, to
specify a summation, you type

```
\sum_{i=1}^n i^2
```

The $\mathrm{T_{\!E}X}$ program typesets the summation as shown in Figure 2. Note that the expression is formatted one way when it occurs inside text and another way when it appears as
part of a displayed formula.

A markup tag such as <h1> in HTML or \sum in $\mathrm{T_{\!E}X}$ is a benefit mainly for
exchanging documents among different computer systems. Only the most hardened
HTML or $\mathrm{T_{\!E}X}$ authors produce the markup by hand. For HTML in particular, many
programs are available that display the structure of an HTML document and allow
authors to edit both text and structure in a convenient way that combines the benefits of
visual feedback and structure editing.

24.1.3 — The Structure of an XML Document

> An XML data set is called a
> document. It starts out with
> a header and contains
> elements and text.

In this section, you will see the rules for properly formatted XML
data. For historical reasons—namely, SGML's roots in document
processing—an XML data set is called a *document*, even though most
XML data have little, if anything, to do with traditional documents.

The XML standard recommends that every XML document
starts out with a header

```
<?xml version="1.0"?>
```

Next, the XML document contains the actual data. The data are contained in a *root element*. For example,

```
<?xml version="1.0"?>
<purse>
    more data
</purse>
```

The root element is an example of an XML *element*. An element has one of two forms:

<elementTag optional attributes> content *</elementTag>*

or

`<elementTag` *optional attributes/>*

In the first case, the element has *content*—elements, text, or a mixture of both. A good example is a paragraph in an HTML document:

```
<p>Use XML for <strong>robust</strong> data formats.</p>
```

The **p** element contains

1. The text: "Use XML for"
2. A `strong` subelement
3. More text: " data formats."

> An element can contain text, subelements, or both ("mixed content"). For data descriptions, avoid mixed content.

For XML files that contain documents in the traditional sense of the term, the mixture of text and elements is useful. The XML specification calls this type of contents *mixed content*. But for files that describe data sets—such as our coin data—it is better to stick with elements that contain *either* other elements *or* text. The XML specification calls content that consists only of elements *element content*.

Each element can also contain *attributes*. For example, the **a** element of HTML has an `HREF` attribute that specifies the URL of a hyperlink:

```
<a href="http://java.sun.com"> . . . </a>
```

> Elements can have attributes. Use attributes to describe how to interpret the element content.

An attribute has a name (such as `href`) and a value. In XML, the value must be enclosed in single or double quotes.

Programmers often wonder whether it is better to use attributes or subelements. For example, should a coin be described as

```
<coin value="0.5" price="half dollar"/>
```

or

```
<coin>
    <value>0.5</value>
    <name>half dollar</name>
</coin>
```

The former is shorter. However, it violates the spirit of attributes. Attributes are intended to provide information *about* the element content. For example, the `value` element might have an attribute `currency` that helps interpret the element content. The content 0.5 has a different interpretation in the element

```
<value currency="USD">0.5</value>
```

than it does in the element

```
<value currency="EUR">0.5</value>
```

An element can have multiple attributes, for example

```
<img src="hamster.jpeg" width="400" height="300"/>
```

And, as you have already seen, an element can have both attributes and content.

```
<a href="http://java.sun.com">Sun's Java web site</a>
```

You have now seen the components of an XML document that are needed to use XML for encoding data. There are other XML constructs for more specialized situations—see [1] for more information. In the next section, you will see how to use Java to parse XML documents.

Quality Tip   24.1

Prefer XML Elements over Attributes

Attributes are shorter than elements. For example,

```
<coin value="0.5" price="half dollar"/>
```

seems simpler than

```
<coin>
    <value>0.5</value>
    <name>half dollar</name>
</coin>
```

There is the temptation to use attributes because they are "easier to type". But of course, you don't type XML documents, except for testing purposes. In real-world situations, XML documents are generated by programs.

Attributes are less flexible than elements. Suppose we want to add a currency indication to the value. With elements, that's easy to do:

```
<value currency="USD">0.5</value>
```

or even

```
<value>
    <currency>USD</currency>
    <amount>0.5</amount>
</value>
```

With attributes, you are stuck—you can't refine the structure. Of course, you could use

```
<coin value="USD 0.5" price="half dollar"/>
```

But then your program has to *parse* the string USD 0.5 and manually take it apart. That's just the kind of tedious and error-prone coding that XML is designed to avoid.

▼ In HTML, there is a simple rule when to use attributes. All strings that are not part of the displayed text are attributes. For example, consider a link.

```
<a href="http://java.sun.com">The Java web page</a>
```

The text inside the a element, The Java web page, is part of what the user sees on the web page, but the href attribute string http://java.sun.com is not displayed on the page.

▼ Of course, HTML is a little different from the XML documents that you construct to describe data such as product lists, but the same basic rule applies. Anything that's a part of your data should not be an attribute. An attribute is appropriate only if it tells something *about* the data but isn't a part of the data itself. If you find yourself engaged in metaphysical discussions to settle whether an item is part of the data or tells something about the data, make the item an element, not an attribute.

Quality Tip 24.2

Avoid Children with Mixed Elements and Text

The children of an element can be

1. Elements
2. Text
3. A mixture of both

In HTML, it is common to mix elements and text, for example

```
<p>Use XML for <strong>robust</strong> data formats.</p>
```

But when describing data sets, you should not mix elements and text. For example, you should not do the following:

```
<value>
    <currency>USD</currency>
    0.5
</value>
```

Instead, the children of an element should be either text

```
<value>0.5</value>
```

or elements

```
<value>
    <currency>USD</currency>
    <amount>0.5</amount>
</value>
```

There is an important reason for this design rule. As you will see later in this chapter, you can specify much stricter rules for elements that have only child elements than for elements whose children can contain text.

▼ ❓ **HOWTO** 24.1
▶

Designing an XML Document Format

▼
This HOWTO walks you through the process of designing an XML document format. You will see in Section 24.4 how to describe the format formally with a document type
▼
definition. Right now, we focus on an informal definition of the document content. The "output" of this activity is a sample document.

Step 1 Gather the data elements that you need to include in the XML document
▼
Write them on a sheet of paper. If at all possible, work from some real-life examples.
For example, suppose you need to design an XML document for an invoice. An
▼
invoice has

- An invoice number
▼
- A shipping address

- A billing address
▼
- A list of items ordered

If possible, gather some actual invoices. Decide which features of the actual invoices you
▼
need to include in your XML document.

Step 2 Analyze which data elements need to be refined
▼
Continue refinement until you reach data values that can be described by single strings or numbers. Make a note of all data items that you discovered during the refinement process. When done, you should have a list of data elements, some of which can be broken down
▼
further and some of which are simple enough to be described by a single string or number.
For example, the "shipping address" actually contains the customer name, street, city, state, and ZIP code.
▼
The "list of items ordered" contains items. Each item contains a product and the quantity ordered. Each product contains the product name and price.
Thus, our list now contains
▼
- Invoice number

- Address
▼
- Name

- Street
▼
- City

- State
▼
- ZIP code

▼

- List of items ordered

- Item

▼

- Product

- Description

▼

- Price

- Quantity

▼
Keep breaking the data items down until each of them can be described by a single *string* or *number*. For example, an address cannot be described by a single string, but a city can be described by a single string.

▼

Step 3 Come up with a suitable element name that describes the entire XML document

▼
This element becomes the root element. For example, the invoice data would be contained in an element named `invoice`.

▼
Step 4 Come up with suitable element names for the top-level decomposition that you found in Step 1

▼
These become the children of the root element. For example, the `invoice` element has children

- `number`

▼

- `address`

- `itemlist`

▼
Step 5 Repeat this process to give names to the other elements that you discovered in Step 2

▼
As you do this, make a comprehensive example that shows all elements at work. For the invoice problem, here is such an example.

▼
```
<invoice>
   <number>11365</number>
   <address>
      <name>John Meyers</name>
      <company>ACME Computer Supplies Inc.</company>
      <street>1195 W. Fairfield Rd.</street>
      <city>Sunnyvale</city>
      <state>CA</state>
      <zip>94085</zip>
   </address>
   <items>
      <item>
         <product>
```

```
                        <description>Ink Jet Refill Kit</description>
                        <price>29.95</price>
                    </product>
                    <quantity>8</quantity>
                </item>
                <item>
                    <product>
                        <description>4-port Mini Hub</description>
                        <price>19.95</price>
                    </product>
                    <quantity>4</quantity>
                </item>
            </items>
        </invoice>
```

Step 6 Check that the document doesn't have mixed content

That is, make sure each element has as its children either additional elements or text, but not both. If necessary, add more child elements to wrap any text.

For example, suppose the product had looked like this:

```
<product>
<description>Ink Jet Refill Kit</description>
29.95
</product>
```

Perhaps someone thought it was "obvious" that the last entry was the price. However, following Quality Tip 24.2, it is best to wrap the price inside a price element, like this:

```
<product>
<description>Ink Jet Refill Kit</description>
<price>29.95</price>
</product>
```

24.2   Parsing XML Documents

> A parser is a program that reads a document, checks whether it is syntactically correct, and takes some action as it processes the document.

To read and analyze the contents of an XML document, you need an XML *parser.* A parser is a program that reads a document, checks whether it is syntactically correct, and takes some action as it processes the document.

Two kinds of XML parsers are in common use. One of them follows the a specification called SAX (Simple Access to XML), and the other follows a specification called DOM (Document Object Model). A SAX parser is *event-driven.* Whenever the parser encounters a particular construct (for example, an opening tag such as <price>), then it calls a method that you must provide. In contrast, a DOM parser builds up a tree that represents the parsed document. Once the parser is done, you can analyze the tree. SAX parsers have one advantage—they are more efficient for handling large XML documents since they don't have to build up a tree. DOM parsers, however, are easier to use for most applications—the parse tree gives you a complete overview of the data, whereas a SAX parser gives you the information in bits and pieces. In this section, you will learn how to use a DOM parser.

> There are two kinds of XML parsers. SAX fires events as it analyzes a document. DOM builds a document tree.

The DOM standard defines an interface `Document` in the `org.w3c.dom` package. This interface provides methods to analyze and modify the tree structure that represents an XML document. However, the current version of the DOM standard is silent on how to turn an XML document into a `Document` object. Several DOM parsers are available that can read input with XML markup and turn it into a `Document`. In the past, each parser had a different interface, making it difficult for programmers to switch from one parser to another. To solve this problem, Sun Microsystems defined a specification called JAXP (Java API for XML Processing; recall that API stands for Application Programming Interface). The JAXP specification provides a standard mechanism for DOM parsers to read and create documents. JAXP is a part of Java 1.4 and above. If you use an earlier version of Java, you need to download additional libraries—see the book's companion web site for instructions.

> A `DocumentBuilder` can read an XML document from a file, URL, or input stream. The result is a `Document` object, which contains a tree.

As already mentioned, the `Document` interface describes the tree structure of an XML document. To generate an object of a class that implements the `Document` interface, you need a `DocumentBuilder`. You get a `DocumentBuilder` by calling the static `newInstance` method of the `DocumentBuilderFactory` class. Then call the `newDocumentBuilder` method on the factory object.

```
DocumentBuilderFactory factory =
    DocumentBuilderFactory.newInstance();
DocumentBuilder builder = factory.newDocumentBuilder();
```

Once you have a `DocumentBuilder`, you can read a document in. To read a document from a file, first construct a `File` object from the filename, then call the `parse` method of the `DocumentBuilder` class.

```
String fileName = . . .;
File f = new File(fileName);
Document doc = builder.parse(f);
```

If the document is located on the Internet, use an URL instead of a file:

```
String urlName = . . .;
URL u = new URL(urlName);
Document doc = builder.parse(u);
```

You can also read a document from an arbitrary input stream:

```
InputStream in = . . .;
Document doc = builder.parse(in);
```

Once you have created a new document or read a document from a file, you can inspect and modify it. You start with the root element. The `getDocumentElement` method of the `Document` interface returns the root element.

```
Element root = doc.getDocumentElement();
```

> The document tree consists of nodes. The most important node types are `Element` and `Text`.

Like `Document`, the `Element` type is an interface, not a class. It is up to the document builder to produce an object that implements the interface. The same is true for all types that the DOM standard defines—they are all interfaces.

The `Element` interface is a subinterface of the more general `Node` interface. Besides the `Element` interface, there are several other node types that are subinterfaces of the `Node` interface. In this chapter, the only other subinterface of interest to us is the `Text` interface (see Figure 3).

If an element has just one or two children, you can use the `getFirstChild` and `getLastChild` method to retrieve just one child. These methods return `null` if the requested node doesn't exist.

> Use a `NodeList` to visit the child nodes of an element.

However, most elements have more than one or two children. Then use the `getChildNodes` method of the `Element` interface to get the child elements of an element, stored in an object of a class that implements the `NodeList` interface. For example, consider the item list in Figure 4. You can consider the document as a tree whose root is the `items` element (see Figure 5). Calling the `getChildNodes` method on the root element yields a node list containing two `item` elements.

Sadly, a `NodeList` does not implement the standard `List` interface that we saw in Chapter 19. To use a `NodeList`, you have to learn yet another set of methods. Use the `getLength` method to obtain the number of nodes in the list. Then call the `item` method to get an item in the node list. Here is how you access the child element with index i of the root.

```
NodeList nodes = root.getChildNodes();
int i = . . .; // a value between 0 and nodes.getLength() - 1
Node childNode = nodes.item(i);
```

> If you don't use a DTD, the XML parser keeps all white spaces.

By default, the XML parser *keeps all white space* (that is, spaces, tabs, and newline characters) between elements, just in case you want to analyze it. As a result, an element's children include text (the white space) as well as elements. When your XML document describes data records, you never care about that white space. If you have made sure not to mix meaningful text with elements, as described in Quality Tip 24.2, ignoring the white space is easy: If you have an element whose children are also elements (such as the `item` element in our example), just skip all child nodes that aren't element nodes. Use the following loop:

```
for (int i = 0; i < nodes.getLength(); i++)
{
    Node childNode = nodes.item(j);
    if (childNode instanceof Element)
    {
        Element childElement = (Element)childNode;
        // do something with childElement
    }
}
```

In Section 24.5, you will see how to tell the parser not to report this white space. To do so, you will have to provide a Document Type Definition (DTD) that specifies the structure of your XML document. Right now, it is simpler to include a test to ignore white space.

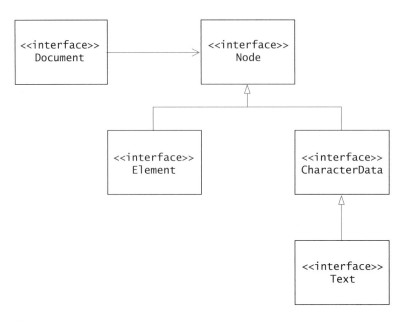

Figure 3

UML Diagram of DOM Interfaces Used in This Chapter

```
<?xml version="1.0"?>
<items>
   <item>
      <product>
         <description>Ink Jet Refill Kit</description>
         <price>29.95</price>
      </product>
      <quantity>8</quantity>
   </item>
   <item>
      <product>
         <description>4-port Mini Hub</description>
         <price>19.95</price>
      </product>
      <quantity>4</quantity>
   </item>
</items>
```

Figure 4

An XML Document

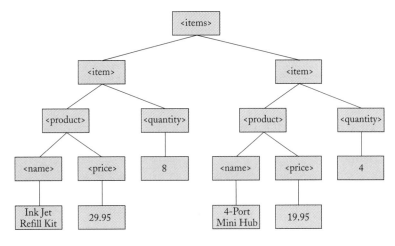

Figure 5

The Tree View of the Document

Once you have an element, you can get the element name (such as `price`) by calling the `getTagName` method.

```
Element priceElement = . . .;
String name = priceElement.getTagName();
    // returns a tag name such as price
```

You can also look up attributes by name. For example, here is how you look up the `currency` attribute:

```
String attributeValue = priceElement.getAttribute(
    "currency");
```

> Use a NamedNodeMap to visit the attributes of an element. Each attribute is stored in a Node.

If you don't know an attribute's name, you can iterate through all attributes. For that purpose you use a `NamedNodeMap`, which, like the `NodeList` interface, is an interface that is proprietary to the DOM library. The `NamedNodeMap` is conceptually similar to the standard Java `Map` interface that you saw in Chapter 19, but the usage details are different. The `getAttributes` method returns a map of all pairs of attribute names and values:

```
NamedNodeMap attributes = priceElement.getAttributes();
```

The `getLength` method tells you how many attributes this element has. To get a particular attribute, call the `item` method, just as you would for a `NodeList`. Then call `getNodeName` and `getNodeValue` on the returned `Node` object:

```
int i = . . .;
// a value between 0 and attributes.getLength() - 1
Node anAttributeNode = attributes.item(i);
String attributeName = anAttributeNode.getNodeName();
// e.g., "currency"
String attributeValue = anAttributeNode.getNodeValue();
// e.g., "USD"
```

Now you know how to analyze elements and their attributes, and how to find their children if they themselves are elements. However, some elements have children that contain text. In our example, those are the description, price, and quantity elements. The document builder creates nodes of type Text for these children. If you follow the recommendation of Quality Tip 24.2, then any elements containing text have a *single* Text child node, which you can retrieve with the get-FirstChild method. To read the text in such a node, you use the getData method. That method returns a string, which you may need to parse to convert it to a number. For example, here is how you determine the price that is stored in a price element:

```
Element priceNode = . . .;
Text priceData = (Text)priceNode.getFirstChild();
String priceString = priceData.getData(); // e.g., "24.95"
double price = Double.parseDouble(priceString);
```

Now you know how to read and analyze an XML document. The example program at the end of this section puts these techniques to work. The class ItemListParser can parse an XML document that contains a list of product descriptions. Its parse method takes the file name and returns an array list of Item objects:

```
ItemListParser parser = new ItemListParser();
ArrayList items = parser.parse("items.xml");
```

The ItemListParser class translates each item element into an object of the Java class Item and each product element into an object of the Java class Product. It turns the items element into an ArrayList of items. For this purpose, there are static helper methods

```
private Product getProduct(Element e)
private Item getItem(Element e)
private ArrayList getItems(Element e)
```

However, there are no helper methods for parsing the description, price, and quantity elements. Parsing these elements is so simple that it is done inside the getProduct and getItem methods. In general, it is a good idea to make one helper method for each XML element that contains subelements.

File ItemListParser.java

```
 1  import java.io.File;
 2  import java.io.IOException;
 3  import java.util.ArrayList;
 4  import javax.xml.parsers.DocumentBuilder;
 5  import javax.xml.parsers.DocumentBuilderFactory;
 6  import javax.xml.parsers.ParserConfigurationException;
 7  import org.w3c.dom.Attr;
 8  import org.w3c.dom.Document;
 9  import org.w3c.dom.Element;
10  import org.w3c.dom.NamedNodeMap;
```

```
11  import org.w3c.dom.Node;
12  import org.w3c.dom.NodeList;
13  import org.w3c.dom.Text;
14  import org.xml.sax.SAXException;
15
16  /**
17      An XML parser for item lists.
18  */
19  public class ItemListParser
20  {
21      /**
22          Constructs a parser that can parse item lists.
23      */
24      public ItemListParser()
25          throws ParserConfigurationException
26      {
27          DocumentBuilderFactory factory
28              = DocumentBuilderFactory.newInstance();
29          builder = factory.newDocumentBuilder();
30      }
31
32      /**
33          Parses an XML file containing an item list.
34          @param fileName  the name of the file
35          @return  an array list containing all items in the XML file
36      */
37      public ArrayList parse(String fileName)
38          throws SAXException, IOException
39      {
40          File f = new File(fileName);
41          Document doc = builder.parse(f);
42
43          // get the <items> root element
44
45          Element root = doc.getDocumentElement();
46          return getItems(root);
47      }
48
49      /**
50          Obtains an array list of items from a DOM element.
51          @param e  an <items> element
52          @return  an array list of all <item> children of e
53      */
54      private static ArrayList getItems(Element e)
55      {
56          ArrayList items = new ArrayList();
57
58          // get the <item> children
59
60          NodeList children = e.getChildNodes();
```

```
 61          for (int i = 0; i < children.getLength(); i++)
 62          {
 63             Node childNode = children.item(i);
 64             if (childNode instanceof Element)
 65             {
 66                Element childElement = (Element)childNode;
 67                if (childElement.getTagName().equals("item"))
 68                {
 69                   Item c = getItem(childElement);
 70                   items.add(c);
 71                }
 72             }
 73          }
 74          return items;
 75       }
 76
 77       /**
 78          Obtains an item from a DOM element.
 79          @param e an <item> element
 80          @return the item described by the given element
 81       */
 82       private static Item getItem(Element e)
 83       {
 84          NodeList children = e.getChildNodes();
 85          Product p = null;
 86          int quantity = 0;
 87          for (int j = 0; j < children.getLength(); j++)
 88          {
 89             Node childNode = children.item(j);
 90             if (childNode instanceof Element)
 91             {
 92                Element childElement = (Element)childNode;
 93                String tagName = childElement.getTagName();
 94                if (tagName.equals("product"))
 95                   p = getProduct(childElement);
 96                else if (tagName.equals("quantity"))
 97                {
 98                   Text textNode
 99                      = (Text)childElement.getFirstChild();
100                   String data = textNode.getData();
101                   quantity = Integer.parseInt(data);
102                }
103             }
104          }
105          return new Item(p, quantity);
106       }
107
108       /**
109          Obtains a product from a DOM element.
110          @param e a <product> element
```

```
111          @return  the product described by the given element
112      */
113      private static Product getProduct(Element e)
114      {
115         NodeList children = e.getChildNodes();
116         String name = "";
117         double price = 0;
118         for (int j = 0; j < children.getLength(); j++)
119         {
120            Node childNode = children.item(j);
121            if (childNode instanceof Element)
122            {
123               Element childElement = (Element)childNode;
124               String tagName = childElement.getTagName();
125               Text textNode
126                  = (Text)childElement.getFirstChild();
127
128               String data = textNode.getData();
129               if (tagName.equals("description"))
130                  name = data;
131               else if (tagName.equals("price"))
132                  price = Double.parseDouble(data);
133            }
134         }
135         return new Product(name, price);
136      }
137
138      private DocumentBuilder builder;
139 }
```

File ItemListParserTest.java

```
1  import java.util.ArrayList;
2
3  /**
4      This program parses an XML file containing an item list.
5      It prints out the items that are described in the XML file.
6  */
7  public class ItemListParserTest
8  {
9      public static void main(String[] args)
10        throws Exception
11     {
12        ItemListParser parser = new ItemListParser();
13        ArrayList items = parser.parse("items.xml");
14        for (int i = 0; i < items.size(); i++)
15        {
16           Item anItem = (Item)items.get(i);
17           System.out.println(anItem.format());
```

```
18        }
19     }
20 }
```

This program uses the `Item` and `Product` classes from Chapter 16.

HOWTO 24.2

Writing a Parser for an XML Document Type

If you are asked to write a parser, you need to write a class that can be used to read in an XML document and produce a Java object of some type:

```
public class MyParser
{
    public SomeClass parse(String fileName)
    . . .
}
```

Step 1 Look at the XML document format

Consider all elements with element content (that is, elements that contain subelements). For each such element, ask yourself what *class* it should belong to. That may be an existing Java class; a Java class that you need to write; or, if an element simply contains a sequence of child elements of the same type, the `ArrayList` class.

Consider the invoice example from HOWTO 24.1. The following elements have element content:

- `invoice`
- `address`
- `items`
- `item`
- `product`

The `invoice`, `address`, `item`, and `product` tags correspond to the Java types `Invoice`, `Address`, `Item`, and `Product`. The `items` tag contains a sequence of `item` objects, so we can simply use an `ArrayList`.

Step 2 For each class found in Step 1, add a static `get` method to your parser class

The `get` method should have a structure like this:

```
private static ClassForElement getElementName(Element e)
{
    NodeList children = e.getChildNodes();
```

```
        for (int i = 0; i < children.getLength(); i++)
        {
            Node childNode = children.item(i);
            if (childNode instanceof Element)
            {
                Element childElement = (Element)childNode;
                convert child element to Java object
            }
        }
        use the child element values to construct and
        return a ClassForElement object
    }
```

There are two cases in looking at the child elements. If the child element contains text, then you should convert the element data:

```
Text textNode = (Text)childElement.getFirstChild();
String data = textNode.getData();
```

If necessary, convert that string to a number, using `Integer.parseInt` or `Double.parseDouble`.

If the child element doesn't contain text, then call *its* get*ChildElementName* method:

```
ClassForChildElement childObject =
    getChildElementName(childElement);
```

For example, here is what the `getItem` method for the `item` element looks like:

```
private static Item getItem(Element e)
{
    Product p = null;
    int quantity = 0;
    NodeList children = e.getChildNodes();
    for (int i = 0; i < children.getLength(); i++)
    {
        Node childNode = children.item(i);
        if (childNode instanceof Element)
        {
            Element childElement = (Element)childNode;
            // convert child element to Java object
            if (childElement.getTagName().equals(
                "quantity"))
            {
                // get text data and convert to a number
                Text textNode
                    = (Text)childElement.getFirstChild();
                String data = textNode.getData();
                quantity = Integer.parseInt(data);
            }
            else if (childElement.getTagName().equals(
                "product"))
```

```
            {
                // get child element object
                p = getProduct(childElement);
            }
        }
    }
    // use the child element values to construct and
    // return a ClassForElement object
    Item r = new Item(quantity, p);
    return r;
}
```

Altogether, the `InvoiceParser` class has five helper methods:

```
public class InvoiceParser
{
    . . .
    private static Invoice getInvoice(Element e) {...}
    private static Address getAddress(Element e) {...}
    private static ArrayList getItems(Element e) {...}
    private static Item getItem(Element e) {...}
    private static Product getProduct(Element e) {...}
}
```

You may find it helpful to implement these "bottom up", starting with the simplest method (such as `getProduct`) and finishing with the method for the root element (`get-Invoice`).

Step 3 Finish off your parser by writing a constructor and the `parse` method

```
public class MyParser
{
    public MyParser()
        throws ParserConfigurationException
    {
        DocumentBuilderFactory factory
            = DocumentBuilderFactory.newInstance();
        builder = factory.newDocumentBuilder();
    }
    public parse(String fileName)
        throws SAXException, IOException
    {
        File f = new File(fileName);
        Document doc = builder.parse(f);
        Element root = doc.getDocumentElement();
        return getRootElementName(root);
    }
    // helper methods
    . . .
    private DocumentBuilder builder;
}
```

▼ For example, in an `InvoiceParser`, you call

```
return getInvoice(root)
```

▼ in the last line of the `parse` method.

▼ ⊗ **Common Error**   **24.1**

XML Elements Describe Instance Fields, Not Classes

▼ HOWTO 24.2 explains how to convert XML documents to Java classes. You need to
determine a class for each element type. This can be confusing. For example, consider a
▼ slightly different invoice description, with separate shipping and billing addresses:

```
<invoice>
   <number>11365</number>
   <shipto>
      <name>John Meyers</name>
      <company>ACME Computer Supplies Inc.</company>
      <street>1195 W. Fairfield Rd.</street>
      <city>Sunnyvale</city>
      <state>CA</state>
      <zip>94085</state>
   </shipto>
   <billto>
      <name>Accounts Payable</name>
      <company>ACME Computer Supplies Inc.</company>
      <street>P.O. Box 11098</street>
      <city>Sunnyvale</city>
      <state>CA</state>
      <zip>94080-1098</state>
   </billto>
   <items>
      . . .
   </items>
</invoice>
```

▼ Should you have a class `Shipto` to match the `shipto` element and another class `Billto`
to match the `billto` element? That makes no sense, because both of them have the
same contents: elements that describe an address.

▼ Instead, you should think of the XML element as the equivalent of an instance field
and then determine an appropriate class. For example, an invoice object has instance
fields

- `billto`, of type `Address`

- `shipto`, also of type `Address`

Note that you don't see the classes in the XML document. There is no notion of a class `Address` in the XML document describing an invoice. To make element classes explicit, you use an XML *schema*—see Advanced Topic 24.1 for more information.

Random Fact 24.2

Grammars, Parsers, and Compilers

Grammars are very important in many areas of computer science to describe the structure of computer programs or data formats. To introduce the concept of a grammar, consider this set of rules for a set of simple English language sentences:

1. A sentence has a noun phrase followed by a verb and another noun phrase.
2. A noun phrase consists of an article followed by an adjective list followed by a noun.
3. An adjective list consists of an adjective or an adjective followed by an adjective list.
4. Articles are "a" and "the".
5. Adjectives are "quick", "brown", "lazy", and "hungry".
6. Nouns are "fox", "dog", and "hamster".
7. Verbs are "jumps over" and "eats".

Here are two sentences that follow these rules:

• The quick brown fox jumps over the lazy dog.

• The hungry hamster eats a quick brown fox.

Symbolically, these rules can be expressed by a formal grammar:

```
<sentence> ::= <noun-phrase> <verb> <noun-phrase>
<noun-phrase> ::= <article> <adjective-list> <noun>
<adjective-list> ::=
    <adjective> | <adjective> <adjective-list>
<article> ::= a | the
<adjective> ::= quick | brown | lazy | hungry
<noun> ::= fox | dog | hamster
<verb> ::= jumps over | eats
```

Here the symbol `::=` means "can be replaced with". For example, `<article>` can be replaced with a or the.

The grammar symbols such as `<noun>` happen to be enclosed in angle brackets just like XML tags, but they are different from tags. One purpose of a grammar is to produce strings that are *legal* according to the grammar, by starting with the start symbol (`<sentence>` in this example) and applying replacement rules until the resulting string is free from symbols. For example,

String	Rule
<sentence>	Start
<noun-phrase> <verb> <noun-phrase>	1
<noun-phrase> eats <noun-phrase>	7
<article> <adjective-list> <noun> eats <noun-phrase>	2
the <adjective-list> <noun> eats <noun-phrase>	4
the <adjective> <noun> eats <noun-phrase>	3
the hungry <noun> eats <noun-phrase>	5
the hungry hamster eats <noun-phrase>	6
the hungry hamster eats <article> <adjective-list> <noun>	2
the hungry hamster eats a <adjective-list> <noun>	4
the hungry hamster eats a <adjective> <adjective-list> <noun>	3
the hungry hamster eats a quick <adjective-list> <noun>	5
the hungry hamster eats a quick <adjective> <noun>	3
the hungry hamster eats a quick brown <noun>	5
the hungry hamster eats a quick brown fox	6

If you have a grammar and a string, such as "the hungry hamster eats a quick brown fox" or "a brown jumps over hamster quick lazy", you can *parse* the sentence: that is, check whether the sentence is described by the grammar rules and, if it is, show how it can be derived from the start symbol. One way to show the derivation is to construct a *parse tree* (see Figure 6).

A *parser* is a program that reads strings and decides whether the input conforms to the rules of a certain grammar. Some parsers—such as the DOM XML parser—build a parse tree in the process or report an error message when a parse tree cannot be constructed. Other parsers—such as the SAX XML parser—call user-specified methods whenever a part of the input was successfully parsed.

The most important use for parsers is inside compilers for programming languages. Just as our grammar can describe (some) simple English language sentences, the legal "sentences" in a programming language can be described by a grammar. The actual grammar for the Java programming language occupies about 15 pages in the *Java Language Specification* [2]. To give a flavor of a small subset of such a grammar, here is a grammar that describes arithmetic expressions.

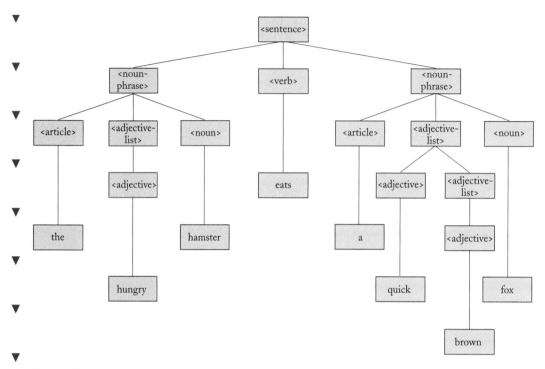

Figure 6

A Parse Tree for a Simple Sentence

```
<expression> ::=
    <term> | <term> <additive-operator> <expression>
<additive-operator> ::= + | -
<term> ::=
    <factor> | <factor> <multiplicative-operator> <term>
<multiplicative-operator> ::= * | /
<factor> ::= <integer> | ( <expression> )
<integer> ::= <digits> | - <digits>
<digits> ::= <digit> | <digit> <digits>
<digit> ::= 0 | 1 | 2 | 3 | 4 | 5 | 6 | 7 | 8 | 9
```

An example of a legal expression in this grammar is

```
-2 * (3 + 10)
```

Figure 7 shows the parse tree for this expression.

In a compiler, parsing the program source is the first step towards generating code that the target processor (the Java virtual machine in the case of Java) can execute. Writing a parser is a challenging and interesting task. You may at one point in your studies take a course in compiler construction, in which you learn how to write a parser and how to generate code from the parsed input. Fortunately, to use XML you don't have to know

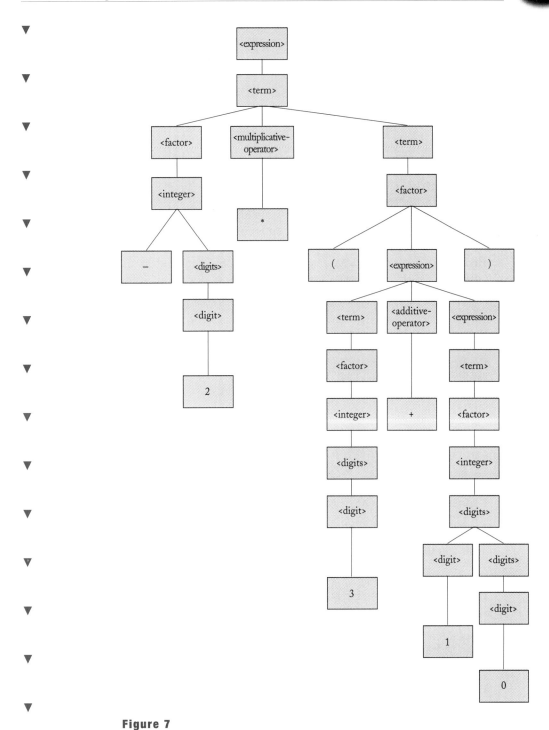

Figure 7

A Parse Tree for an Expression

▼

how the parser does its job. You simply ask the XML parser to read the XML input and then process the resulting Document tree.

24.3   Creating XML Documents

In the preceding section, you saw how to read an XML document into a Document object and how to analyze the contents of that object. In this section, you will see how to do the opposite—build up a Document object and then save it as an XML document. Of course, you can also generate an XML document simply as a sequence of print statements. However, that is not a good idea—it is easy to build an illegal XML document in this way, as when names contain special characters such as < or &.

Recall that you needed a DocumentBuilder object to read in an XML document. You also need such an object to create a new, empty document. Thus, to create a new document, first make a document builder factory, then a document builder, and finally the empty document:

```
DocumentBuilderFactory factory =
    DocumentBuilderFactory.newInstance();
DocumentBuilder builder = factory.newDocumentBuilder();
Document doc = builder.newDocument();
// an empty document
```

> The Document class has methods to create elements and text nodes.

Now you are ready to insert nodes into the document. The document object is a factory for nodes. You use the createElement and createTextNode methods of the Document interface to create the element and text nodes that you need. Pass a tag name to the createElement method.

```
Element itemElement = doc.createElement("item");
```

Pass a text string to the createTextNode method.

```
Text quantityText = doc.createTextNode("8");
```

You set element attributes with the setAttribute method. For example,

```
priceElement.setAttribute("currency", "USD");
```

To construct the tree structure of a document, start with the root, then add children with the appendChild method. For example, here we build an XML tree that describes an item (see Figure 8).

```
// create elements
Element itemElement = doc.createElement("item");
Element productElement = doc.createElement("product");
Element descriptionElement
    = result.createElement("description");
Element priceElement = result.createElement("price");
```

Figure 8

An XML Tree That Describes a Product

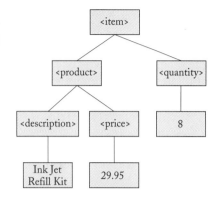

```
Element quantityElement
   = result.createElement("quantity");
Text descriptionText
   = result.createTextNode("Ink Jet Refill Kit");
Text priceText = result.createTextNode("29.95");
Text quantityText = result.createTextNode("8");

// add elements to the document
doc.appendChild(itemElement);
itemElement.appendChild(productElement);
itemElement.appendChild(quantityElement);
productElement.appendChild(descriptionElement);
productElement.appendChild(priceElement);
descriptionElement.appendChild(descriptionText);
priceElement.appendChild(priceText);
quantityElement.appendChild(quantityText);
```

At the time that this book was written, the DOM standard has no "official" method to write a Document object to a stream. That omission is surprising, because generating XML documents is such a common task. (Version 3 of that standard— which was under development as this book was written—promises a method for saving a Document object.)

> Use a Transformer to write an XML document to stream.

In the meantime, the easiest way to write an XML document is to use a couple of classes from the XML transformation library. (See Advanced Topic 24.2 for more information on transformations.) Fortunately, you don't need to know anything about XML transformations for this purpose. Simply create a transformer like this:

```
Transformer t = TransformerFactory
   .newInstance().newTransformer();
```

Then turn your Document into a DOMSource and your output stream into a Stream-Result, and call the transform method:

```
t.transform(new DOMSource(doc),
   new StreamResult(System.out));
```

The `Transformer` writes the XML document without spaces or line breaks. As a result, the output looks less pretty, but it is actually more suitable for parsing by another program because it is free from unnecessary white space.

The example program at the end of this section shows how to build an XML document and print it out. The program uses an `ItemListBuilder` class that turns an array list of items into an XML document.

The `ItemListBuilder` has several helper methods:

```
private Element createItemList(ArrayList items)
private Element createItem(Item anItem)
private Element createProduct(Product p)
```

Note that these methods are the reverse of the helper methods of the `ItemListParser` class of the preceding sections. The parser class helper methods turned elements into Java objects. The builder helper methods turn Java objects into elements. As with the `ItemListParser`, we use one helper method for each XML element that has child elements.

File ItemListBuilder.java

```java
 1 import java.util.ArrayList;
 2 import javax.xml.parsers.DocumentBuilder;
 3 import javax.xml.parsers.DocumentBuilderFactory;
 4 import javax.xml.parsers.ParserConfigurationException;
 5 import org.w3c.dom.Document;
 6 import org.w3c.dom.Element;
 7 import org.w3c.dom.Text;
 8
 9 /**
10     Builds a DOM document for an array list of items.
11 */
12 public class ItemListBuilder
13 {
14     /**
15         Constructs an item list builder.
16     */
17     public ItemListBuilder()
18         throws ParserConfigurationException
19     {
20         DocumentBuilderFactory factory
21             = DocumentBuilderFactory.newInstance();
22         builder = factory.newDocumentBuilder();
23     }
24
25     /**
26         Builds a DOM document for an array list of items.
27         @param items the items
28         @return a DOM document describing the items
29     */
30     public Document build(ArrayList items)
```

```
31     {
32        doc = builder.newDocument();
33        Element root = createItemList(items);
34        doc.appendChild(root);
35        return doc;
36     }
37
38     /**
39        Builds a DOM element for an array list of items.
40        @param items the items
41        @return a DOM element describing the items
42     */
43     private Element createItemList(ArrayList items)
44     {
45        Element itemsElement = doc.createElement("items");
46        for (int i = 0; i < items.size(); i++)
47        {
48           Item anItem = (Item)items.get(i);
49           Element itemElement = createItem(anItem);
50           itemsElement.appendChild(itemElement);
51        }
52        return itemsElement;
53     }
54
55     /**
56        Builds a DOM element for an item.
57        @param anItem the item
58        @return a DOM element describing the item
59     */
60     private Element createItem(Item anItem)
61     {
62        Element itemElement = doc.createElement("item");
63        Element productElement
64           = createProduct(anItem.getProduct());
65        Text quantityText = doc.createTextNode(
66           "" + anItem.getQuantity());
67        Element quantityElement
68           = doc.createElement("quantity");
69        quantityElement.appendChild(quantityText);
70
71        itemElement.appendChild(productElement);
72        itemElement.appendChild(quantityElement);
73        return itemElement;
74     }
75
76     /**
77        Builds a DOM element for a product.
78        @param p the product
79        @return a DOM element describing the product
80     */
```

```
81      private Element createProduct(Product p)
82      {
83         Text descriptionText
84            = doc.createTextNode(p.getDescription());
85         Text priceText
86            = doc.createTextNode("" + p.getPrice());
87
88         Element descriptionElement
89            = doc.createElement("description");
90         Element priceElement = doc.createElement("price");
91
92         descriptionElement.appendChild(descriptionText);
93         priceElement.appendChild(priceText);
94
95         Element productElement
96            = doc.createElement("product");
97
98         productElement.appendChild(descriptionElement);
99         productElement.appendChild(priceElement);
100
101        return productElement;
102     }
103
104     private DocumentBuilder builder;
105     private Document doc;
106  }
```

File ItemListBuilderTest.java

```
1  import java.util.ArrayList;
2  import org.w3c.dom.Document;
3  import javax.xml.transform.Transformer;
4  import javax.xml.transform.TransformerFactory;
5  import javax.xml.transform.dom.DOMSource;
6  import javax.xml.transform.stream.StreamResult;
7
8  /**
9     This program tests the item list builder. It prints the
10    XML file corresponding to a DOM document containing a list
11    of items.
12  */
13  public class ItemListBuilderTest
14  {
15     public static void main(String[] args)
16        throws Exception
17     {
18        ArrayList items = new ArrayList();
19        items.add(
20           new Item(new Product("Toaster", 29.95), 3));
21        items.add(
```

```
·("Hair dryer", 24.95), 1));

      new ItemListBuilder();
       '(items);
         ˉtory
            r();
```

ın Chapter 16. The `Item` class has
antity methods.

24.3

↳ Document

...ourse write an XML document as a series of `println` calls. But that's
...d you also have to search manually for characters such as < in any output
and replace them with their encodings. Instead, you should build a `Document`
...ect and write it to a stream, using a class such as the `Transformer`.

To construct the `Document` object from an object of some class, you should implement a class such as this one:

```
public class MyBuilder
{
    public Document parse(SomeClass x)
    . . .
}
```

The steps are the reverse of the steps in HOWTO 24.?.

Step 1 Look at the format of the XML document that you want to create

As in step 1 of HOWTO 24.?, consider all elements with element content and find their
matching Java classes.

Step 2 For each class in Step 1, add a helper method to your parser class

The helper method should be structured like this:

```
private Element createElementName(ClassForElement x)
{
    Element e = doc.createElement("element name");
    Element child1 = . . .;
```

```
      e.appendChild(child1);
      Element child2 = . . . .;
      e.appendChild(child2);

      . . .
      return e;
   }
```

There are two cases for creating a child element. If the child
then you should create a text node and a child node:

```
   Text childText = doc.createNode(text value);
   Element child = doc.createElement("child element name");
   child.appendChild(childText);
```

If the child element doesn't contain text, then query the object x for the
become part of the child element and call *its* create*ChildElementName* me

```
   ClassForChildElement y = x.getChildData();
   Element child = createChildElementName(y);
```

For example, here is what the createItem method for the item element looks li

```
   private Element createItem(Item x)
   {
      Element e = doc.createElement("element name");
      Element quantityChild = doc.createElement("quantity");
      Text quantityText =
         doc.createTextNode("" + x.getQuantity());
      quantityChild.appendChild(quantityText);
      e.appendChild(quantityChild);
      Product y = x.getProduct();
      Element productChild = createProduct(y);
      e.appendChild(productChild);
      return e;
   }
```

Altogether, an InvoiceBuilder class needs five helper methods:

```
public class InvoiceBuilder
{
   . . .
   private Element createInvoice(Invoice x) {...}
   private Element createAddress(Address x) {...}
   private Element createItems(ArrayList x) {...}
   private Element createItem(Item x) {...}
   private Element createProduct(Product x) {...}
}
```

You may find it helpful to implement these "bottom up", starting with the simplest method (such as createProduct) and finishing with the method for the root element (createInvoice).

▼   Step 3 Finish off your builder by writing a constructor and the `build` method

▼
```
public class MyBuilder
{
    public MyBuilder()
        throws ParserConfigurationException
    {
        DocumentBuilderFactory factory
            = DocumentBuilderFactory.newInstance();
        builder = factory.newDocumentBuilder();
    }
    public Document build(ClassForRootElement x)
    {
        doc = builder.newDocument();
        Element root = createRootElementName(x);
        doc.appendChild(root);
        return doc;
    }
    // helper methods
    . . .
    private DocumentBuilder builder;
    private Document doc;
}
```

▼   For example, in an `InvoiceBuilder`, you call

```
Element root = createInvoice(x)
```

▼   in the second line of the `build` method.

▼   Step 4 Use a class such as the `Transformer` to write the `Document` to an output stream

▼   For example,

```
Invoice x = . . .;
InvoiceBuilder builder = new InvoiceBuilder();
Document doc = builder.build(x);
Transformer t = TransformerFactory
    .newInstance().newTransformer();
t.transform(new DOMSource(doc),
    new StreamResult(System.out));
```

▼

24.4   Document Type Definitions

In the preceding two sections, you saw how to read and write XML documents. In this section you will learn how to produce Document Type Definitions (DTDs), which are sets of rules for correctly formed documents of a particular type.

For example, consider a document of type `items`. Intuitively, `items` denotes a sequence of `item` elements. Each `item` element contains a `product` and a `quantity`. A

> A DTD is a sequence of rules that describe the legal child elements and attributes for each element type.

product contains a description and a price. Each of these element contains text describing the product's description, price, and quantity. The purpose of a DTD is to formalize this description.

A DTD is a sequence of rules that describe

- The legal attributes for each element type

- The legal child elements for each element type

Let us first turn to child elements. The legal child elements of an element are described by an ELEMENT rule:

```
<!ELEMENT items (item*)>
```

This means that an item list must contain a sequence of 0 or more item elements.

As you can see, the rule is delimited by <! ...>, and it contains the name of the element whose children are to be constrained (items), followed by a description of what children are allowed.

Next, let us turn to the definition of an item node:

```
<!ELEMENT item (product, quantity)>
```

This means that the children of a item node must be a product node, followed by a quantity node.

The definition for a product is similar:

```
<!ELEMENT product (description, price)>
```

Finally, here are the definitions of the three remaining node types:

```
<!ELEMENT quantity (#PCDATA)>
<!ELEMENT description (#PCDATA)>
<!ELEMENT price (#PCDATA)>
```

The symbol #PCDATA refers to text, called "parsable character data" in XML terminology. The character data can contain any characters. However, certain characters, such as < and &, have special meaning in XML and need to be encoded if they occur in character data. Table 1 shows the encodings for special characters.

Character	Encoding	Name
<	<	Less than (left angle bracket)
>	>	Greater than (left angle bracket)
&	&	Ampersand
'	&apos	Apostrophe
"	"	Quotation mark

Table 1

Encodings for Special Characters

```
22              new Item(new Product("Hair dryer", 24.95), 1));
23
24          ItemListBuilder builder = new ItemListBuilder();
25          Document doc = builder.build(items);
26          Transformer t = TransformerFactory
27              .newInstance().newTransformer();
28          t.transform(new DOMSource(doc),
29              new StreamResult(System.out));
30      }
31 }
```

This program uses the **Product** and **Item** classes from Chapter 16. The **Item** class has been modified by adding **getProduct** and **getQuantity** methods.

 HOWTO   **24.3**

Writing an XML Document

You could of course write an XML document as a series of **println** calls. But that's tedious, and you also have to search manually for characters such as < in any output strings and replace them with their encodings. Instead, you should build a **Document** object and write it to a stream, using a class such as the **Transformer**.

To construct the **Document** object from an object of some class, you should implement a class such as this one:

```
public class MyBuilder
{
    public Document parse(SomeClass x)
        . . .
}
```

The steps are the reverse of the steps in HOWTO 24.2.

Step 1 Look at the format of the XML document that you want to create

As in step 1 of HOWTO 24.2, consider all elements with element content and find their matching Java classes.

Step 2 For each class in Step 1, add a helper method to your parser class

The helper method should be structured like this:

```
private Element createElementName(ClassForElement x)
{
    Element e = doc.createElement("element name");
    Element child1 = . . .;
```

```
      e.appendChild(child1);
      Element child2 = . . .;
      e.appendChild(child2);
      . . .
      return e;
   }
```

There are two cases for creating a child element. If the child element contains text, then you should create a text node and a child node:

```
Text childText = doc.createNode(text value);
Element child = doc.createElement("child element name");
child.appendChild(childText);
```

If the child element doesn't contain text, then query the object x for the data that is to become part of the child element and call *its* create*ChildElementName* method:

```
ClassForChildElement y = x.getChildData();
Element child = createChildElementName(y);
```

For example, here is what the createItem method for the item element looks like:

```
private Element createItem(Item x)
{
   Element e = doc.createElement("element name");
   Element quantityChild = doc.createElement("quantity");
   Text quantityText =
      doc.createTextNode("" + x.getQuantity());
   quantityChild.appendChild(quantityText);
   e.appendChild(quantityChild);
   Product y = x.getProduct();
   Element productChild = createProduct(y);
   e.appendChild(productChild);
   return e;
}
```

Altogether, an InvoiceBuilder class needs five helper methods:

```
public class InvoiceBuilder
{
   . . .
   private Element createInvoice(Invoice x) {...}
   private Element createAddress(Address x) {...}
   private Element createItems(ArrayList x) {...}
   private Element createItem(Item x) {...}
   private Element createProduct(Product x) {...}
}
```

You may find it helpful to implement these "bottom up", starting with the simplest method (such as createProduct) and finishing with the method for the root element (createInvoice).

▼ Step 3 Finish off your builder by writing a constructor and the `build` method

```
public class MyBuilder
{
    public MyBuilder()
        throws ParserConfigurationException
    {
        DocumentBuilderFactory factory
            = DocumentBuilderFactory.newInstance();
        builder = factory.newDocumentBuilder();
    }
    public Document build(ClassForRootElement x)
    {
        doc = builder.newDocument();
        Element root = createRootElementName(x);
        doc.appendChild(root);
        return doc;
    }
    // helper methods
    . . .
    private DocumentBuilder builder;
    private Document doc;
}
```

For example, in an `InvoiceBuilder`, you call

```
Element root = createInvoice(x)
```

in the second line of the `build` method.

▼ Step 4 Use a class such as the Transformer to write the Document to an output stream

For example,

```
Invoice x = . . .;
InvoiceBuilder builder = new InvoiceBuilder();
Document doc = builder.build(x);
Transformer t = TransformerFactory
    .newInstance().newTransformer();
t.transform(new DOMSource(doc),
    new StreamResult(System.out));
```

24.4 Document Type Definitions

In the preceding two sections, you saw how to read and write XML documents. In this section you will learn how to produce Document Type Definitions (DTDs), which are sets of rules for correctly formed documents of a particular type.

For example, consider a document of type `items`. Intuitively, `items` denotes a sequence of `item` elements. Each `item` element contains a `product` and a `quantity`. A

> A DTD is a sequence of rules that describe the legal child elements and attributes for each element type.

product contains a description and a price. Each of these element contains text describing the product's description, price, and quantity. The purpose of a DTD is to formalize this description.

A DTD is a sequence of rules that describe

- The legal attributes for each element type
- The legal child elements for each element type

Let us first turn to child elements. The legal child elements of an element are described by an ELEMENT rule:

```
<!ELEMENT items (item*)>
```

This means that an item list must contain a sequence of 0 or more item elements.

As you can see, the rule is delimited by `<! ... >`, and it contains the name of the element whose children are to be constrained (items), followed by a description of what children are allowed.

Next, let us turn to the definition of an item node:

```
<!ELEMENT item (product, quantity)>
```

This means that the children of a item node must be a product node, followed by a quantity node.

The definition for a product is similar:

```
<!ELEMENT product (description, price)>
```

Finally, here are the definitions of the three remaining node types:

```
<!ELEMENT quantity (#PCDATA)>
<!ELEMENT description (#PCDATA)>
<!ELEMENT price (#PCDATA)>
```

The symbol #PCDATA refers to text, called "parsable character data" in XML terminology. The character data can contain any characters. However, certain characters, such as < and &, have special meaning in XML and need to be encoded if they occur in character data. Table 1 shows the encodings for special characters.

Character	Encoding	Name
<	&lt;	Less than (left angle bracket)
>	&gt;	Greater than (left angle bracket)
&	&amp;	Ampersand
'	&apos	Apostrophe
"	&quot;	Quotation mark

Table 1

Encodings for Special Characters

The complete DTD for an item list has six rules, one for each element type:

```
<!ELEMENT items (item)*>
<!ELEMENT item (product, quantity)>
<!ELEMENT product (description, price)>
<!ELEMENT quantity (#PCDATA)>
<!ELEMENT description (#PCDATA)>
<!ELEMENT price (#PCDATA)>
```

Let us have a closer look at the descriptions of the allowed children. Table 2 shows the expressions that you can use to describe the children of an element. The EMPTY keyword is self-explanatory: an element that is declared as EMPTY may not have any children. For example, the HTML DTD defines the img element to be EMPTY–an image has only attributes, specifying the image source, size, and placement, and no children.

More interesting child rules can be formed with the *regular expression* operations (* + ? , |). (See Table 1 and Figure 9. Also see Productivity Hint 7.2 for more information on regular expressions.) You have already seen the * ("0 or more") and , (sequence) operations. The children of an items element are 0 or more item elements, and the children of an item are a sequence of product and description elements.

You can also combine these operations to form more complex expressions. For example,

```
<!ELEMENT section (title, (paragraph | (image, title?))+)
```

defines an element section whose children are:

1. A title element
2. A sequence of one or more of the following:
   - paragraph elements
   - image elements followed by optional title elements

Rule Description	Element Content
EMPTY	No children allowed
$(E*)$	Any sequence of 0 or more elements E
$(E+)$	Any sequence of 1 or more elements E
$(E?)$	Optional element E (0 or 1 occurrences allowed)
$(E1, E2, \ldots)$	Element $E1$, followed by $E2$ or ...
$(E1 | E2 | \ldots)$	Element $E1$ or $E2$ or ...
(#PCDATA)	Text only
$(\#PCDATA | E1 | E2 | \ldots)*$	Any sequence of text and elements $E1, E2,\ldots$, in any order.
ANY	Any children allowed

Table 2

Regular Expressions for Element Content

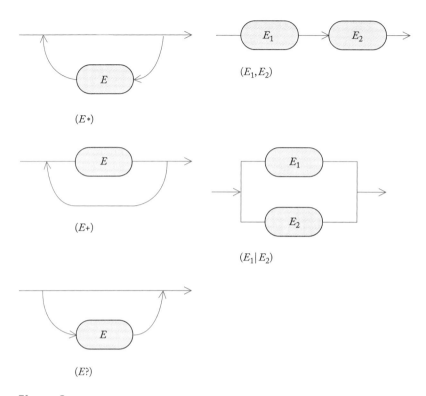

Figure 9

DTD Regular Expression Operations

Thus,

```
<section>
    <title/>
    <paragraph/>
    <image/>
    <title/>
    <paragraph/>
</section>
```

is legal, but

```
<section>
    <paragraph/>
    <paragraph/>
    <title/>
</section>
```

is not—there is no starting title, and the title at the end doesn't follow an image. Fortunately, such complex rules are not very common in practice.

You already saw the (#PCDATA) rule. It means that the children can consist of any character data. For example, in our product list DTD, the `product` element can have any character data inside.

You can also allow *mixed content*—any sequence of character data and specified elements. However, in mixed content, you *lose control* over the order in which the elements appear. As explained in Quality Tip 24.2, you should avoid mixed content for DTDs that describe data sets. This feature is intended for documents that contain both text and markup instructions such as HTML pages.

Finally, you can allow a node to have children of any type—you should avoid that for DTDs that describe data sets.

You now know how to specify what children a node can have. A DTD also gives you control over the allowed attributes of an element. An attribute description looks like this:

```
<!ATTLIST Element Attribute Type Default>
```

The most useful attribute type descriptions are listed in Table 3. The `CDATA` type describes any sequence of character data. As with #PCDATA, certain characters such as < and & need to be encoded (as <, & and so on). There is no practical difference between the `CDATA` and `#PCDATA` types. Simply use `CDATA` in attribute declarations and `#PCDATA` in element declarations.

Rather than allowing arbitrary attribute values, you can specify a finite number of choices. For example, you may want to restrict a `currency` attribute to U.S. dollar, euro, and Japanese yen. Then use the following declaration:

```
<!ATTLIST price currency (USD | EUR | JPY) #REQUIRED>
```

Each of the choices must consist of letters, numbers, or the special characters

```
-  _  .
```

There are other type descriptions that are less common in practice. You can find them in the XML reference [1].

The attribute type description is followed by a "default" declaration. The keywords that can appear in a "default" declaration are listed in Table 4.

For example, this attribute declaration describes that each `price` element must have a `currency` attribute whose value is any character data:

```
<!ATTLIST price currency CDATA #REQUIRED>
```

To fulfill this declaration, each `price` element must have a `currency` attribute, such as `<price currency="USD">`. It would be illegal to specify a price without a currency.

Type description	Attribute type
CDATA	Any character data
$(N_1 \mid N_2 \mid \ldots)$	One of $N_1, N_2, \ldots$

Table 3

Common Attribute Types

Default declaration	Explanation
#REQUIRED	Attribute is required
#IMPLIED	Attribute is optional
N	Default attribute, to be used if attribute is not specified
#FIXED N	Attribute must either be unspecified or contain this value

Table 4

Attribute Defaults

For an optional attribute, you use the #IMPLIED keyword instead.

```
<!ATTLIST price currency CDATA #IMPLIED>
```

That means that you can supply a currency attribute in a price element, or you can omit it. If you omit it, then the application that processes the XML data implicitly assumes some default currency.

A better choice would be to supply the default value explicitly:

```
<!ATTLIST price currency CDATA "USD">
```

That means that the currency attribute is understood to mean USD if the attribute is not specified. An XML parser will then report the value of currency as USD if the attribute was not specified.

Finally, you can state that an attribute can only be identical to a particular value. For example, the rule

```
<!ATTLIST price currency CDATA #FIXED "USD">
```

means that a price element must either not have a currency attribute at all (in which case the XML parser will report its value as USD), or specify the currency attribute as USD. Naturally, this kind of rule is not very common.

You have now seen the most common constructs for DTDs. Using these constructs, you can define your own DTDs for XML documents that describe data sets. In the next section, you will see how to specify which DTD an XML document should use, and how to have the XML parser check that a document conforms to its DTD.

Of course, you can't place text and elements anywhere you like. The rules in the DTD tell you which elements can go where. For example, the DTD for product lists, which we will develop later in this chapter, will tell you that the price element can be inside a product element but not inside an item element.

? HOWTO 24.4

Writing a DTD

You write a DTD to describe a set of XML documents of the same type. The DTD specifies which elements contain child elements (and the order in which they may appear) and which elements contain text. It also specifies which elements may have attributes, which attributes are required, and which defaults are used for missing attributes.

These rules are for DTDs that describe program data. DTDs that describe documents generally have a much more complex structure.

Step 1 Get or write a couple of sample XML documents

Step 2 Make a list of all elements that can occur in the XML document

Step 3 For each of the elements, decide whether its children are elements or text

Following Quality Tip 24.2, it is best to avoid elements whose children are a mixture of both.

Step 4 For elements that contain text, the DTD rule is

```
<!ELEMENT element name (#PCDATA)>
```

Step 5 For each element that contains other elements, make a list of the possible child elements

Step 6 For each of those elements, decide in which order the child elements should occur, and how often each element should occur

Then form the rule

```
<!ELEMENT element name    child1 count1, child2 count2, . . .>
```

where each *count* is one of the following:

Quantity	Count
0 or 1	?
1	omit
0 or more	*
1 or more	+

▼ Step 7 Decide whether any elements should have attributes

▼ Following Quality Tip 24.1, it is best to avoid attributes altogether or to minimize the use of attributes.

Let us carry out these steps to make a DTD for XML documents that describe an invoice.

▼ Step 1 calls for a sample XML document. You can find one in HOWTO 24.1.

Step 2 asks us to list all elements. They are

▼ - invoice

- number

- address

▼ - name

- company

▼ - street

- city

▼ - state

- zip

▼ - items

- item

▼ - product

- description

▼ - quantity

▼ Step 3 asks us to separate the elements that contain other elements from those that contain text. The following have element content:

- invoice

▼ - description

- items

▼ - item

- product

▼ The remainder contain text.

Step 4 says that the elements that contain text can be disposed of simply:

▼ ```
<!ELEMENT number (#PCDATA)>
<!ELEMENT name (#PCDATA)>
<!ELEMENT company (#PCDATA)>
```
```

```
<!ELEMENT street (#PCDATA)>
<!ELEMENT city (#PCDATA)>
<!ELEMENT state (#PCDATA)>
<!ELEMENT zip (#PCDATA)>
<!ELEMENT quantity (#PCDATA)>
<!ELEMENT description (#PCDATA)>
```

Step 5 asks us to list the child elements for each of the remaining elements:

* `invoice`
* `quantity`
* `address`
* `items`
* `address`
* `name`
* `company`
* `street`
* `city`
* `state`
* `zip`
* `items`
* `item`
* `item`
* `product`
* `quantity`
* `product`
* `description`
* `price`

In step 6, you now need to decide what regular expressions you should use to combine these child elements. The `items` element can contain any number of items, so the rule is

```
<!ELEMENT items (item*)>
```

In the remaining cases, each child element occurs exactly once. That leads to the rules

```
<!ELEMENT invoice (number,address,items)>
<!ELEMENT address (name,company,street,city,state,zip)>
```

```
<!ELEMENT item (product,quantity)>
<!ELEMENT product (descripton,price)>
```

Step 7 suggests not to add any attribute unless there is a good reason. There isn't, so the DTD is complete.

Advanced Topic   24.1

The XML Schema Specification

A limitation of DTDs is that you can't really specify what you want each XML element to contain. For example, you can't force an element to contain just a number or a date—any text string is allowed for a (#PCDATA) element. The XML Schema specification overcomes these limitations. An XML schema is like a DTD in that it is a set of rules that documents of a particular type need to follow, but a schema can contain far more precise rule descriptions.

At the time of this writing, the XML Schema Specification was a recommendation, and only experimental implementations were available. However, by the time that you read this, XML schema support may be much more widespread.

Here is just a flavor of how an XML schema is specified. For each element, you specify the element name and the type. The element names are the same as in a DTD, but the types are new. There are many basic types; Table 5 lists several.

Here is a typical definition:

```
<xsd:element name="quantity" type="xsd:integer"/>
```

This defines the quantity element as an element that contains text, where the text can't be arbitrary but must be an integer. The xsd: prefix is a *name space* prefix to denote that

XML Schema Type	Meaning
string	Any string
integer	An integer
double	A floating-point number
boolean	false or true
date	A date such as 2001-01-23
time	A time of day such as 20:15

Table 5

A Subset of the XML Schema Basic Types

▼   `xsd:element` and `xsd:integer` are part of the XML Schema Definition name space. See Advanced Topic 24.2 for more information about name spaces.

▼   Furthermore, you can define complex types, much as you define classes in Java. Here is the definition of an `Address` type:

```
<xsd:complexType name="Address">
   <xsd:sequence>
      <xsd:element name="name" type="xsd:string"/>
      <xsd:element name="company" type="xsd:string"/>
      <xsd:element name="street" type="xsd:string"/>
      <xsd:element name="city" type="xsd:string"/>
      <xsd:element name="state" type="xsd:string"/>
      <xsd:element name="zip" type="xsd:string"/>
   </xsd:sequence>
</xsd:complexType>
```

▼   To indicate that an element can be repeated, you use `minOccurs` and `maxOccurs`:

```
<xsd:complexType name="ItemList">
   <xsd:element name="item" type="Item"
       minOccurs="0" maxOccurs="unbounded"/>
</xsd:complexType>
```

▼   Then you can specify that an invoice should have `shipto` and `billto` fields that are both of type `Address`:

```
<xsd:element name="shipto" type="Address"/>
<xsd:element name="billto" type="Address"/>
```

▼   These examples show that an XML schema can be both simpler and more precise than a DTD. For that reason, it is likely that DTDs will be of lesser importance over the long run and that XML schema definitions will become the method of choice for describing XML document types.

▼   The XML Schema specification has many advanced features—see the W3C web site [3] for details.

24.5   Parsing with Document Type Definitions

So far, you have seen how to parse an XML document without a DTD. However, it is always a good idea to reference a DTD with every XML document and to instruct the parser to check that the document follows the rules of the DTD. That way, the parser can check errors in the document. Furthermore, it can be more intelligent about parsing. For example, if the parser knows that the children of an element are again elements, then it can suppress white space, and you can save yourself the trouble of checking for white space.

> An XML document can contain its DTD or refer to a DTD that is stored elsewhere.

In the preceding section you saw how to develop a DTD for a class of XML documents. The DTD specifies the permitted elements and attributes in the document. An XML document has two ways of referencing a DTD:

1. The document may contain the DTD.
2. The document may refer to a DTD that is stored elsewhere.

A DTD is introduced with the DOCTYPE declaration. If the document contains its DTD, then the declaration looks like this:

```
<!DOCTYPE rootElement [ rules ]>
```

For example, an item list can include its DTD like this:

```
<?xml version="1.0"?>
<!DOCTYPE items [

<!ELEMENT items (item*)>
<!ELEMENT item (product, quantity)>
<!ELEMENT product (description, price)>
<!ELEMENT quantity (#PCDATA)>
<!ELEMENT description (#PCDATA)>
<!ELEMENT price (#PCDATA)>

]>
<items>
   <item>
      <product>
         <description>Ink Jet Refill Kit</description>
         <price>29.95</price>
      </product>
      <quantity>8</quantity>
   </item>
   <item>
      <product>
         <description>4-port Mini Hub</description>
         <price>19.95</price>
      </product>
      <quantity>4</quantity>
   </item>
</items>
```

When referencing an external DTD, you must supply a file name or URL.

However, if the DTD is more complex, then it is better to store it outside the XML document. In that case, you use the SYSTEM keyword inside the DOCTYPE declaration to indicate that the system that hosts the XML processor must locate the DTD. The SYSTEM keyword is followed by the location of the DTD. For example, a DOCTYPE declaration might point to a local file

```
<!DOCTYPE items SYSTEM "items.dtd">
```

Alternatively, the resource might be an URL anywhere on the web:

```
<!DOCTYPE items
    SYSTEM "http://www.mycompany.com/dtds/items.dtd">
```

For commonly used DTDs, the DOCTYPE declaration can contain a PUBLIC keyword. For example,

```
<!DOCTYPE web-app
    PUBLIC
    "-//Sun Microsystems, Inc.//DTD Web Application 2.3//EN"
    "http://java.sun.com/j2ee/dtds/web-app_2_3.dtd">
```

> When your XML document has a DTD, use validation when parsing.

A program parsing the DTD can look at the public identifier. If it is a familiar identifier, then it need not retrieve the DTD from the URL.

When you include a DTD with an XML document, then you should tell the parser to *validate* the document. That means that the parser will check that all child elements and attributes of an element conform to the ELEMENT and ATTLIST rules in the DTD. If a document is invalid, then the parser throws an exception. To turn on validation, you use the setValidating method of the DocumentBuilderFactory class before calling the newDocumentBuilder method:

```
DocumentBuilderFactory factory =
    DocumentBuilderFactory.newInstance();
factory.setValidating(true);
DocumentBuilder builder = factory.newDocumentBuilder();
Document doc = builder.parse(. . .);
```

A great advantage of validation is that you know that the document is correct if it has been read in and validated. For example, if the DTD specifies that the child elements of each item element are product and quantity elements in that order, then you can rely on that fact and don't need to put tedious checks in your code. Compare the ItemList-Parser at the end of this section with the one from Section 24.3, and see how much simpler the code is.

> When you parse an XML file with a DTD, tell the parser to ignore white space.

If the parser has access to the DTD, it can make another useful improvement. Recall that in the preceding example program we had to skip the spaces that the parser reported. In that program, the parser didn't have access to the DTD, so it had no way of knowing whether spaces are significant or not. But if the parser knows the DTD, it can strip out white space in elements that don't have #PCDATA text as children (that is, elements that have element content). For example, in the product list DTD, the children of a product element are all elements, not text. Thus, any spaces between the elements can be ignored. To generate parsers with that behavior, you need to call the setIgnoringElement-ContentWhiteSpace method of the DocumentBuilderFactory class.

```
factory.setValidating(true);
factory.setIgnoringElementContentWhitespace(true);
```

Finally, if the parser has access to the DTD, it can fill in default values for attributes. For example, suppose a DTD defines a currency attribute for a price element:

```
<!ATTLIST price currency CDATA "USD">
```

If a document contains a price element without a currency attribute, then the parser can supply the default:

```
String attributeValue
    = priceElement.getAttribute("currency");
// gets "USD" if no currency specified
```

As these arguments show, it is always a good idea to construct DTDs and to supply them with all XML documents.

This concludes our discussion of XML. You now know enough XML to put it to work for describing data formats. Whenever you are tempted to use a "quick and dirty" file format, you should consider using XML instead. By using XML for data interchange, your programs become more professional, robust, and flexible. This chapter covers the most important aspects of XML for everyday programming. For more advanced features that can be useful in specialized situations, please see [1]. Furthermore, XML technology is still undergoing rapid change at the time of this writing. Therefore, it is a good idea to check out the latest developments. Good web sites are [3] and [4].

File ItemListParser.java

```
 1  import java.io.File;
 2  import java.io.IOException;
 3  import java.util.ArrayList;
 4  import javax.xml.parsers.DocumentBuilder;
 5  import javax.xml.parsers.DocumentBuilderFactory;
 6  import javax.xml.parsers.ParserConfigurationException;
 7  import org.w3c.dom.Attr;
 8  import org.w3c.dom.Document;
 9  import org.w3c.dom.Element;
10  import org.w3c.dom.NamedNodeMap;
11  import org.w3c.dom.Node;
12  import org.w3c.dom.NodeList;
13  import org.w3c.dom.Text;
14  import org.xml.sax.SAXException;
15
16  /**
17      An XML parser for item lists.
18  */
19  public class ItemListParser
20  {
21      /**
22          Constructs a parser that can parse item lists.
23      */
24      public ItemListParser()
25          throws ParserConfigurationException
26      {
27          DocumentBuilderFactory factory
28              = DocumentBuilderFactory.newInstance();
29          factory.setValidating(true);
30          factory.setIgnoringElementContentWhitespace(true);
```

```java
31          builder = factory.newDocumentBuilder();
32       }
33
34       /**
35          Parses an XML file containing an item list.
36          @param fileName the name of the file
37          @return an array list containing all items in the XML file
38       */
39       public ArrayList parse(String fileName)
40          throws SAXException, IOException
41       {
42          File f = new File(fileName);
43          Document doc = builder.parse(f);
44
45          // get the <items> root element
46
47          Element root = doc.getDocumentElement();
48          return getItems(root);
49       }
50
51       /**
52          Obtains an array list of items from a DOM element.
53          @param e an <items> element
54          @return an array list of all <item> children of e
55       */
56       private static ArrayList getItems(Element e)
57       {
58          ArrayList items = new ArrayList();
59
60          // get the <item> children
61
62          NodeList children = e.getChildNodes();
63          for (int i = 0; i < children.getLength(); i++)
64          {
65             Element childElement
66                = (Element)children.item(i);
67             Item c = getItem(childElement);
68             items.add(c);
69          }
70          return items;
71       }
72
73       /**
74          Obtains an item from a DOM element.
75          @param e an <item> element
76          @return the item described by the given element
77       */
78       private static Item getItem(Element e)
79       {
80          NodeList children = e.getChildNodes();
```

```
81
82          Product p = getProduct((Element)children.item(0));
83
84          Element quantityElement
85              = (Element)children.item(1);
86          Text quantityText
87              = (Text)quantityElement.getFirstChild();
88          int quantity
89              = Integer.parseInt(quantityText.getData());
90
91          return new Item(p, quantity);
92       }
93
94       /**
95          Obtains a product from a DOM element.
96          @param e a <product> element
97          @return the product described by the given element
98       */
99       private static Product getProduct(Element e)
100      {
101         NodeList children = e.getChildNodes();
102
103         Element descriptionElement
104             = (Element)children.item(1);
105         Text descriptionText
106             = (Text)descriptionElement.getFirstChild();
107         String description = descriptionText.getData();
108
109         Element priceElement = (Element)children.item(1);
110         Text priceText
111             = (Text)priceElement.getFirstChild();
112         double price
113             = Double.parseDouble(priceText.getData());
114
115         return new Product(description, price);
116      }
117
118      private DocumentBuilder builder;
119 }
```

File ItemListParserTest.java

```
1 import java.util.ArrayList;
2
3 /**
4    This program parses an XML file containing an item list.
5    The XML file should reference the file items.dtd.
6 */
7 public class ItemListParserTest
8 {
```

```
 9   public static void main(String[] args)
10      throws Exception
11   {
12      ItemListParser parser = new ItemListParser();
13      ArrayList items = parser.parse("items.xml");
14      for (int i = 0; i < items.size(); i++)
15      {
16         Item anItem = (Item)items.get(i);
17         System.out.println(anItem.format());
18      }
19   }
20 }
```

▼ Productivity Hint   24.1

Use DTDs with Your XML Files

It is an additional effort to develop a DTD for a set of XML files. However, that effort is repaid almost immediately, because the code that translates a document to a Java object becomes much simpler. For example, contrast the getItem methods of the parser in Section 24.2 (which doesn't use a DTD) and that in Section 24.5 (which validates a DTD and skips white space). The first version doesn't know in which order the elements come, and it must manually skip white-space nodes. That makes the method somewhat tedious to implement:

```
private static Item getItem(Element e)
{
   NodeList children = e.getChildNodes();
   Product p = null;
   int quantity = 0;
   for (int j = 0; j < children.getLength(); j++)
   {
      Node childNode = children.item(j);
      if (childNode instanceof Element)
      {
         Element childElement = (Element)childNode;
         String tagName = childElement.getTagName();
         if (tagName.equals("product"))
            p = getProduct(childElement);
         else if (tagName.equals("quantity"))
         {
            Text textNode
               = (Text)childElement.getFirstChild();
            String data = textNode.getData();
            quantity = Integer.parseInt(data);
         }
      }
```

```
        }
        return new Item(p, quantity);
    }
```

The second version is much shorter. It simply follows the DTD rule

```
    <!ELEMENT item (product, quantity)>
```

It knows that an item has two children: product and quantity.

```
    private static Item getItem(Element e)
    {
        NodeList children = e.getChildNodes();
        Product p = getProduct((Element)children.item(0));
        Element quantityElement
            = (Element)children.item(1);
        Text quantityText
            = (Text)quantityElement.getFirstChild();
        int quantity
            = Integer.parseInt(quantityText.getData());
        return new Item(p, quantity);
    }
```

If there is an error in the XML file, then the parser will refuse to parse the file. Your code doesn't have to worry about bad inputs, which is a real time saver.

⊗ Common Error 24.2

You Cannot Read an XML Document with an External DTD from a Stream

If your document references an external DTD, for example

```
    <!DOCTYPE productlist SYSTEM "dtds/productlist.dtd">
```

then you cannot use an InputStream to read the document.

```
    InputStream in = . . .;
    // an input stream containing the XML document
    Document doc = builder.parse(in);
    // won't work for an external DTD
```

Instead, you must read the document from a file or URL. For example,

```
    File f = . . .;
    Document doc = builder.parse(f);
```

will work. The DTD is then loaded relative to the directory containing the file. But if you read from a stream, the parser has no idea how to locate the DTD. After all, a stream is just a sequence of bytes that could come from anywhere.

▼ ⬛ **Advanced Topic** ▶ **24.2**

▼

Other XML Technologies

▼

This chapter covers the subset of the XML 1.0 specification that is most useful for common programming situations. Since version 1.0 of the XML specification was released,
▼
there has been a huge amount of interest in advanced XML technologies. A number of useful developments are currently emerging. Among them are:

▼
- Schema Definitions

- Name Spaces

▼
- XHTML

- XSL and Transformations

▼
Advanced Topic 24.1 contains more information about schema definitions.

Name spaces were invented to ensure that many different people and organizations can develop XML documents without running into conflicts with element names. For
▼
example, if you look inside Advanced Topic 24.1, you will see that XML schema definitions have element names that are prefixed with a tag `xsd:`, such as

▼
```
<xsd:element name="city" type="xsd:string"/>
```

That way, the tag and attribute names such as `element` and `string` don't conflict with other names. In that regard, name spaces are similar to Java packages. However, a name
▼
space prefix such as `xsd:` is just a shortcut for the actual name space identifier, which is a much longer, unique string. The full name space for XML Schema definitions is `http:/
/www.w3.org/2000/08/XMLSchema`. Each schema definition starts out with the statement

▼
```
<xsd:schema
    xmlns:xsd="http://www.w3.org/2000/08/XMLSchema">
```

which binds the `xsd` prefix to the full name space.
▼
XHTML is the most recent recommendation of the W3C for formatting web pages. Unlike HTML, XHTML is fully XML-compliant. Once web editing tools switch to XHTML, it will become much easier to write programs that parse web pages. The
▼
XHTML standard has been carefully designed to be backwards compatible with existing browsers.

While XHTML documents are intended to be viewed by browsers, general XML
▼
documents are not designed to be viewed at all. Nevertheless, it is often desirable to *transform* an XML document into a viewable form. XSL (Extensible Style Language) was created for this purpose. A style sheet indicates how to change an XML document
▼
into an HTML document, or even a completely different format such as PDF.

For more information on these and other emerging technologies, see the W3C web
▼
site [3].

CHAPTER SUMMARY

1. XML lets you encode complex data, independent from any programming language, in a form that the recipient can parse easily.

2. XML files are readable by computer programs and by humans.

3. XML-formatted data files are resilient to change.

4. Both HTML and XML are descendants of SGML, the Standard Generalized Markup Language.

5. XML describes the meaning of data, not how to display them.

6. An XML data set is called a document. It starts out with a header and contains elements and text.

7. An element can contain text, subelements, or both ("mixed content"). For data descriptions, avoid mixed content.

8. Elements can have attributes. Use attributes to describe how to interpret the element content.

9. A parser is a program that reads a document, checks whether it is syntactically correct, and takes some action as it processes the document.

10. There are two kinds of XML parsers. SAX fires events as it analyzes a document. DOM builds a document tree.

11. A `DocumentBuilder` can read an XML document from a file, URL, or input stream. The result is a `Document` object, which contains a tree.

12. The document tree consists of nodes. The most important node types are `Element` and `Text`.

13. Use a `NodeList` to visit the child nodes of an element.

14. If you don't use a DTD, the XML parser keeps all white space.

15. Use a `NamedNodeMap` to visit the attributes of an element. Each attribute is stored in a `Node`.

16. The `Document` class has methods to create elements and text nodes.

17. Use a `Transformer` to write an XML document to a stream.

18. A DTD is a sequence of rules that describe the legal child elements and attributes for each element type.

19. An XML document can contain its DTD or refer to a DTD that is stored elsewhere.

20. When referencing an external DTD, you must supply a file name or URL.

21. When your XML document has a DTD, use validation when parsing.

22. When you parse an XML file with a DTD, tell the parser to ignore white space.

Further Reading

[1] http://www.xml.com/axml/axml.html Annotated XML specification.
[2] James Gosling et al., *The Java Language Specification*, 2nd ed., Addison-Wesley, 2000.
[3] http://www.w3c.org/xml The W3C XML web site.
[4] http://java.sun.com/xml The Sun Microsystems XML web site.

CLASSES, OBJECTS, AND METHODS INTRODUCED IN THIS CHAPTER

```
javax.xml.parsers.DocumentBuilder
   newDocument
   parse
javax.xml.parsers.DocumentBuilderFactory
   newInstance
   newDocumentBuilder
   setIgnoreElementContentWhitespace
   setValidating
javax.xml.transform.Transformer
   transform
javax.xml.transform.TransformerFactory
   newInstance
   newTransformer
javax.xml.transform.dom.DOMSource
javax.xml.transform.stream.StreamResult
org.w3c.dom.Document
   createElement
   createTextNode
   getDocumentElement
org.w3c.dom.Element
   getAttribute
   getAttributes
   getTagName
   setAttribute
org.w3c.dom.NamedNodeMap
   getLength
   item
org.w3c.dom.Node
   getChildNodes
   getFirstChild
   getLastChild
org.w3c.dom.NodeList
   getLength
   item
org.w3c.dom.Text
   getData
```

REVIEW EXERCISES

Exercise R24.1. Give some examples to show the differences between XML and HTML.

Exercise R24.2. Design an XML document that describes a bank account.

Exercise R24.3. Draw a tree view for the XML document you created in the preceding exercise.

Exercise R24.4. Write the XML document that corresponds to the parse tree in Figure 6.

Exercise R24.5. Write the XML document that corresponds to the parse tree in Figure 7.

Exercise R24.6. Make an XML document describing a book, with child elements for the author name, the title, and the publication year.

Exercise R24.7. Add a description of the book's language to the document of the preceding exercise. Should you use an element or an attribute?

Exercise R24.8. What is mixed content? What problems does it cause?

Exercise R24.9. Design an XML document that describes a purse containing three quarters, a dime, and two nickels.

Exercise R24.10. Explain why a paint program such as Microsoft Paint is a WYSIWYG program that is also "what you see is all you've got".

Exercise R24.11. How can you visit the children of a node without using a `NodeList`? (*Hint:* `getNextSibling`)

Exercise R24.12. What are the differences between a `NodeList` and an `ArrayList`?

Exercise R24.13. What are the differences between a `NodeList` and a `LinkedList`?

Exercise R24.14. What are the differences between a `NodeList` and a `NamedNodeMap`?

Exercise R24.15. Design a DTD that describes a bank with bank accounts.

Exercise R24.16. Design a DTD that describes a library patron who has checked out a set of books. Each book has an ID number, an author, and a title. The patron has a name and telephone number.

Exercise R24.17. Write the DTD file for the following XML document

```
<?xml version="1.0"?>
<productlist>
  <product>
    <name>Comtrade Tornado</name>
    <price currency = "USD">2495</price>
    <score>60</score>
  </product>
  <product>
```

```
            <name>AMAX Powerstation 75</name>
            <price>2999</price>
            <score>62</score>
        </product>
    </productlist>
```

Exercise R24.18. Design a DTD for invoices, as described in HOWTO 24.2.

Exercise R24.19. Design a DTD for simple English sentences, as described in Random Fact 24.2.

Exercise R24.20. Design a DTD for arithmetic expressions, as described in Random Fact 24.2.

Programming Exercises

Exercise P24.1. Write a program that can read XML files such as

```
<purse>
    <coin>
        <value>0.5</value>
        <name>half dollar</name>
    </coin>
    . . .
</purse>
```

Your program should construct a `Purse` object and print the total value of the coins in the purse.

Exercise P24.2. Building on Exercise P24.1, make the program read an XML file as described in that exercise. Then print out an XML file of the form

```
<purse>
    <coins>
        <coin>
            <value>0.5</value>
            <name>half dollar</name>
        </coin>
        <quantity>3</quantity>
    </coins>
    <coins>
        <coin>
            <value>0.25</value>
            <name>quarter</name>
        </coin>
        <quantity>2</quantity>
    </coins>
</purse>
```

Exercise P24.3. Repeat Exercise P24.1, using a DTD for validation.

Exercise P24.4. Write a program that can read XML files such as

```
<bank>
    <account>
        <number>3</number>
        <balance>1295.32</balance>
    </account>
    . . .
</bank>
```

Your program should construct a `Bank` object and print the total value of the balances in the accounts.

Exercise P24.5. Repeat the preceding exercise, using a DTD for validation.

Exercise P24.6. Enhance Exercise P24.4 as follows: First read the XML file in, then add 10% interest to all accounts, and write an XML file that contains the increased account balances.

Exercise P24.7. Write a program that can read an XML document of the form

```
<rectangle>
    <x>5</x>
    <y>10</y>
    <width>20</width>
    <height>30</height>
</rectangle>
```

Draw the shape in a window.

Exercise P24.8. Write a program that can read an XML document of the form

```
<ellipse>
    <x>5</x>
    <y>10</y>
    <width>20</width>
    <height>30</height>
</ellipse>
```

Draw the shape in a window.

Exercise P24.9. Write a program that can read an XML document of the form

```
<rectangularshape shape="ellipse">
    <x>5</x>
    <y>10</y>
    <width>20</width>
    <height>30</height>
</rectangularshape>
```

Support shape attributes `"rectangle"`, `"diamond"`, and `"ellipse"`.

Draw the shape in a window.

Exercise P24.10. Write a program that can read an XML document of the form

```
<drawing>
    <rectangle>
```

```
        <x>5</x>
        <y>10</y>
        <width>20</width>
        <height>30</height>
     </rectangle>
     <line>
        <x1>5</x1>
        <y1>10</y1>
        <x2>25</x2>
        <y2>40</y2>
     </line>
     <message>
        <text>Hello, World!</text>
        <x>20</x>
        <y>30</y>
     </message>
  </drawing>
```

Show the drawing in a window.

Exercise P24.11. Repeat the preceding exercise, using a DTD for validation.

Exercise P24.12. Write a program that can read an XML document of the form

```
<polygon>
   <point>
      <x>5</x>
      <y>10</y>
   <point>
   . . .
</polygon>
```

Draw the shape in a window.

Exercise P24.13. Write a DTD file which describes documents that contain information about countries: name of the country, its population and its area. Create an XML file that has five different countries. The DTD and XML should be in different files. Write a program which uses the XML file you wrote and prints:

- The country with the largest area
- The country with the largest population
- The country with the largest population density (people per square kilometer)

Exercise P24.14. Write a parser to parse invoices, as described in HOWTO 24.1. The parser should create a tree structure of the invoice first, then print it out in the format used in chapter 16.

Exercise P24.15. Modify the preceding exercise to support separate shipping and billing addresses.

Exercise P24.16. Write a document builder that turns an invoice object, as defined in chapter 16, into an XML file of the format described in HOWTO 24.1.

Exercise P24.17. Modify the preceding exercise to support separate shipping and billing addresses.

Exercise P24.18. Following exercise P16.10, design an XML format for the appointments in an appointment calendar. Write a parser for the appointment file format that generates an `AppointmentCalendar` object containing `Appointment` objects.

Exercise P24.19. Enhance the preceding exercise so that the program first reads in a file with appointment, then another file of the format

```
<commands>
   <add>
      <appointment>
         . . .
      </appointment>
   </add>
   . . .
   <remove>
      <appointment>
         . . .
      </appointment>
   </remove>
</commands>
```

Your program should process the commands and then produce an XML file that consists of the updated appointments.

Exercise P24.20. Write a program to simulate an airline seat reservation system, using XML documents. Reference Exercise P16.11 for the airplane seats information. The program reads a seating chart, in an XML format of your choice, and a command file, in an XML format of your choice, similar to the command file of the preceding exercise. Then the program processes the commands and produces an updated seating chart.

25

JavaServer Pages and Servlets

W hen a web browser requests an HTML page from a web server, the server locates the file and sends its content back to the client. The content is static—the same content is displayed every time the page is requested, until the HTML file is replaced with another. However, most interesting web sites serve dynamic content. Whenever you revisit a news or shopping web site, you receive changing information, often tailored to your personal preferences. In this chapter, you will see how to implement dynamic web content using JavaServer Pages and servlets.

CHAPTER CONTENTS

25.1   Dynamic Web Content

To use JavaServer Pages™ (JSP) technology to produce dynamic web content, you need a web server that is integrated with a *JSP container*. Several JSP containers are available. One excellent and freely available product is the Apache Tomcat server ([1]); please turn to the companion web site to the book for installation instructions. We will assume that you have installed a web server and JSP container to try out the programs in this chapter.

Let's start with a very simple JSP page.

File date.jsp

```
1  <html>
2     <head>
3        <title>Date JSP</title>
4     </head>
5     <body>
6        <h1>Date JSP</h1>
7        <p>The current time is:
8           <%= new java.util.Date() %>
9        </p>
10    </body>
11 </html>
```

> A JavaServer Pages (JSP) page contains HTML tags and Java instructions.

As you can see, the JSP page looks almost like a regular HTML page. However, inside the HTML code, you find the instruction

```
<%= new java.util.Date() %>
```

This instruction is executed whenever the web page is served to a browser. The value of the expression is inserted into the page. Each time you request this page, a different date and time are displayed. Figure 1 shows the result.

Executing the Date Page

To deploy this page, follow these steps:

1. Use a text editor to type the JSP file.
2. Place the file into a *web application* directory of your JSP engine. For example, if you use Tomcat, you should create a subdirectory such as

   ```
   c:\jakarta-tomcat\webapps\bigjava
   ```

3. Place the `date.jsp` file into that directory.
4. Start the web server.
5. Point your browser to `localhost:8080/bigjava/date.jsp`.

> The JSP container removes all JSP tags and inserts the strings that result from evaluating Java expressions.

This example shows one important construct of JavaServer Pages. The JSP container reads the requested JSP page and transforms it into an HTML page. Regular HTML tags are left unchanged. However, any expression enclosed in JSP tags of the form

```
<%= . . . %>
```

is evaluated and converted to a string (through the `toString` method). The resulting string is inserted into the HTML page. You will see other JSP tags later in this chapter; the JSP container removes and processes them all. The resulting document contains only HTML. The web server sends that document to the browser (see Figure 2).

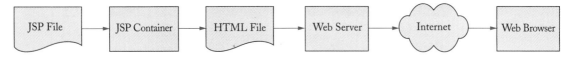

Figure 2

The JSP Container Rewrites the Requested Page

Encapsulating Computations in JavaBeans

In the preceding example, the dynamic portion of the JSP page was very simple—a single Java expression. In most cases, a JSP page has to do many more computations to generate interesting output. Although it is theoretically possible to add more Java code directly into a JSP page, it is rarely a good idea to do so. The reason is simple. Most professional web pages need design input from two different experts—a programmer who understands how to compute the results that the page should display, and a graphic designer who determines how to display those results. The programmer is concerned with the computational logic—that is, the Java code. The graphic designer is concerned with the presentation—that is, the HTML tags. If the two are intermingled, the programmer and graphic designer need to be careful not to interfere with each other's work; even worse, they might inadvertently cause errors by messing up code or tags.

> A JavaBean is a class with a default constructor that exposes properties through its get and set methods.

Therefore, the inventors of JavaServer Pages recommend that any nontrivial computation should be carried out in a separate Java class. There is a JSP mechanism that makes this easy. You can connect one or more *JavaBeans* to a JSP page. Just about any Java class can be a JavaBean—there is only one technical requirement: A JavaBean must have a public constructor with no parameters.

More importantly, a JavaBean is, conceptually, a class that exposes *properties*. Properties are accessed and modified by methods that follow a particular naming convention. If the name of the property is *propertyName*, and its type is *Type*, then the accessor and mutator methods must be of the form

```
Type getPropertyName()
void setPropertyName(Type newValue)
```

For example, if a property of a JavaBean is called lastName and has the type String, then the property accessor and mutator method names are

```
String getLastName()
void setLastName(String newValue)
```

This is, of course, a convention that we have used for most accessor and mutator methods.

There is one exception to the naming convention. A Boolean property must have accessors and mutators of the form

```
boolean isPropertyName()
void setPropertyName(boolean newValue)
```

For example, a Boolean property `married` has methods

```
boolean isMarried()
void setMarried(boolean newValue)
```

Finally, most programmers follow the additional convention that the name of a bean class should end in `Bean`, but that is not a requirement.

Here is a simple example of a bean class:

```
public class PersonBean
{
    // required default constructor
    public PersonBean() { . . . }

    // name property
    public String getLastName() { . . . }
    public void setLastName(String newValue) { . . . }

    // married property
    public boolean isMarried() { . . . }
    public void setMarried(boolean newValue) { . . . }

    // instance variables
    . . .
}
```

This class has two properties: `lastName` and `married`. Note that the name of a property starts with a lowercase letter (such as `lastName`), but the corresponding methods have an uppercase letter (`getLastName`). The only exception is that property names can be all capitals, such as `ID` or `URL`, with corresponding methods `getID` or `setURL`.

In this example, the two properties are read-write properties. You can also have read-only properties (with just a `get` or `is` method) or write-only properties (with just a `set` method).

You should *not* make any assumptions about the internal representation of properties in the bean class. The bean class *may* simply have an instance field for every property:

```
private String name;
private boolean married;
```

On the other hand, perhaps the bean class stores the object state in a database, so that the `get` and `set` methods actually contain database operations.

What's so special about beans? Some programming environments—in particular, JSP—give you convenient access to bean properties without having to call any Java methods.

> A JSP page gives you access to the properties of a bean without having to write Java code.

To use a bean in a JSP page, you use the `jsp:useBean` directive. Give a name to the bean object and the class name of the bean. For example,

```
<jsp:useBean id="user" class="PersonBean"/>
```

This directive invokes the default constructor of the `PersonBean` class to make an object with name `user`. Recall that every bean must have a default constructor.

To set a property, use the `setProperty` directive:

```
<jsp:setProperty name="user" property="married" value="true"/>
```

The `jsp:setProperty` directive figures out the name of the mutator method (`setMarried`), converts the string `"true"` to the Boolean value `true`, and invokes the method on the `user` object.

Conversely, the `jsp:getProperty` directive invokes the correct method to read a property and converts the result to a string. That string becomes part of the HTML page that the JSP page produces.

```
<jsp:getProperty name="user" property="married"/>
```

Note that the name of the bean object is specified with an `id` attribute only in the `jsp:useBean` directive:

```
<jsp:useBean id="user" . . ./>
```

The `jsp:setProperty` and `jsp:getProperty` directives use the `name` attribute:

```
<jsp:setProperty name="user" . . ./>
```

When you use beans, the JSP page contains only the bean directives, no Java code. Of course, the implementation of the bean class contains Java code. Thus, by using beans in JSP pages, you separate the code from the presentation.

Now let's put these concepts to work in an actual JSP page. Suppose we want to display the current time, not the whole date. There is no `Time` class that gets just the time. Instead, you need to format the date with a formatter that ignores the day, month, and year and just formats the time. You get such a formatter by calling the static `getTime-Instance` method of the `DateFormat` class. (That class is related to the `NumberFormat` class, which you saw in Chapter 3.)

```
DateFormat timeFormatter = DateFormat.getTimeInstance();
```

The resulting formatter object converts a `Date` object to a string containing the current time:

```
Date now = new Date(); // sets now to current date and time
String timeString = timeFormatter.format(now);
// e.g.,"7:35:21 AM"
```

Let's put this code into a bean class:

File TimeFormatterBean.java

```
 1  import java.text.DateFormat;
 2  import java.util.Date;
 3
 4  /**
 5     This bean formats the time of day from a given date.
 6  */
 7  public class TimeFormatterBean
 8  {
 9     /**
```

```
10          Initializes the formatter.
11      */
12      public TimeFormatterBean()
13      {
14          timeFormatter = DateFormat.getTimeInstance();
15      }
16
17      /**
18          Write-only date property.
19          @param aDate the date to be formatted.
20      */
21      public void setDate(Date aDate)
22      {
23          theDate = aDate;
24      }
25
26      /**
27          Read-only time property.
28          @return the formatted time
29      */
30      public String getTime()
31      {
32          String timeString = timeFormatter.format(theDate);
33          return timeString;
34      }
35
36      private DateFormat timeFormatter;
37      private Date theDate;
38 }
```

To use this bean, you *first* set the date property to the Date object that you want to have formatted. Then you get the time property to retrieve the formatted time string.

Here is the JSP page that invokes the time formatter bean.

File time.jsp

```
1 <jsp:useBean id="formatter" class="TimeFormatterBean"/>
2 <jsp:setProperty name="formatter" property="date"
3     value="<%= new java.util.Date() %>"/>
4
5 <html>
6     <head>
7         <title>Date JSP</title>
8     </head>
9     <body>
10        <h1>Date JSP</h1>
11        <p>The current time is:
12            <jsp:getProperty name="formatter"
13                property="time"/>
14        </p>
```

```
15    </body>
16  </html>
```

The first two lines construct the formatter bean and set the date property to the current date. In general, it is a good idea to put the directives for constructing beans and setting properties at the beginning of the JSP file, before the HTML contents.

Inside the body of the HTML document, the `jsp:getProperty` directive inserts the formatted time.

To try out this JSP, you need to deploy both the `time.jsp` file and the `TimeFormatter-Bean.class` file. Place them in the following directories:

- `time.jsp` into `c:\jakarta-tomcat\webapps\bigjava`

- `TimeFormatterBean.class` into
  `c:\jakarta-tomcat\webapps\bigjava\WEB-INF\classes`

> Use beans to separate HTML presentation from Java computation.

This example demonstrates the separation of the presentation from the Java code. A graphic designer can improve the look of the page by editing the HTML document only, to change the layout, add images, and so on, without having to do any programming. Conversely, a programmer can modify the code of the bean class without doing any web design.

Admittedly, the bean class in our example is very simple. However, we will enhance it in the following sections by adding significant functionality. This is of course typical. Many web applications start out simple, and more features are added over time. Some programmers yield to temptation and start putting Java code inside their JSP files, because for simple code it seems not to be worth the trouble to implement a separate bean class. However, as the application gets more complex, that code ends up more and more tangled. If you use JavaBeans from the outset, even for simple cases, then you can easily manage an increase in complexity.

▼ ⊗ Common Error

Fussy JSP Syntax

It is very easy to make errors in the JSP syntax, because it is a mixture of HTML, JSP-specific tags, and Java code. Also, because the JSP compilation step is hidden from the programmer, you don't get good error messages. Here are some of the most common errors:

- Forgetting the / before a closing angle bracket such as `<jsp:useBean ... />`. The JSP tags use the XML syntax, and a closing / is required (unless you supply a separate `</jsp:useBean>` tag).

- Letter case errors, such as `jsp:usebean` instead of `jsp:useBean`. HTML is not case-sensitive, but the JSP tags are.

- Forgetting the = after an <%. There is a separate <% ... %> tag that does not include the result in the output.

- Confusing id and name. You use the id attribute in the useBean tag and the name attribute in the getProperty and setProperty tags.

- Forgetting quotation marks for attribute values. In HTML it is OK to omit these quotation marks, but the JSP tags follow the stricter XML syntax. For example, <jsp:useBean id=formatter . . ./> is an error. Use id="formatter" instead.

- Quotes in quoted strings. When you include a Java expression as the value attribute of a JSP bean tag, then you need to quote it, such as

  ```
  <jsp:setProperty name="formatter" property="date"
      value="<%= new java.util.Date() %>"
  ```

  If the expression itself has quotation marks, you must escape them with backslashes:

  ```
  <jsp:setProperty name="formatter" property="zone"
      value="<%= java.util.TimeZone(\"Asia/Tokyo\")) %>" />
  ```

  Alternatively, you can use single quotes for the attribute values:

  ```
  <jsp:setProperty name='formatter' property='zone'
      value='<%= java.util.TimeZone("Asia/Tokyo")) %>' />
  ```

 Quality Tip 25.1

Minimize the Java Code in JSP

It is always a good idea to separate presentation from computation. Then user interface experts can perfect the presentation, and programmers can optimize the computation.

You can defeat that principle by putting lots of Java code inside the JSP tags. For example, suppose you want to generate a web page that generates a set of lottery numbers. Here is an example that doesn't use beans:

```
<html>
   <head>
      <title>Lottery JSP</title>
   </head>
   <body>
      <h1>Lottery JSP</h1>
      <p>Bet these numbers. They'll make you rich!
      </p>
      <ul>
      <%
          java.util.Random generator
```

```
            = new java.util.Random();
         int[] values = new int[49];
         for (int i = 0; i < 49; i++)
            values[i] = i + 1;
         for (int i = 0; i < 6; i++)
         {
            int r = generator.nextInt(49 - i);
            int c = values[r];
            values[r] = values[48 - i];
            out.print("<li>");
            out.print(c);
            out.print("</li>");
         }
      %>
      </ul>
   </body>
</html>
```

Can you see what modifications to make to the HTML page to add some graphics and other beautifications? Can you see what modifications you would need to make if you wanted the numbers to be sorted? Because the page mixes presentation and computation, it becomes very hard to make any changes. It makes a lot more sense to use a **Lottery-Bean** instead:

```
<jsp:useBean id="lottery" class="LotteryBean"/>
<jsp:setProperty name="lottery" property="numbers"
   value="49"/>
<jsp:setProperty name="lottery" property="choices"
   value="6"/>
<html>
   <head>
      <title>Lottery JSP</title>
   </head>
   <body>
      <h1>Lottery JSP</h1>
      <p>Bet these numbers. They'll make you rich!
      </p>
      <jsp:getProperty name="lottery"
         property="combination"/>
   </body>
</html>
```

A well-designed JSP page uses beans for all significant Java code, gluing the beans together with small code snippets as required. If you find yourself putting variable declarations, branches, and loops into a JSP page, then you should implement a new bean instead.

There is just one exception to this rule. In Section 25.6, you will see JSP pages that do only computation, followed by a request to forward to another page. Since those pages do not contain any HTML tags at all, it is acceptable for them to contain lots of Java code.

HOWTO **25.1**

Designing a Bean

A bean is just a regular Java class, with two special characteristics.

- The bean must have a default constructor.
- Methods of the form

```
Type getPropertyName()
void setPropertyName(Type x)
```

can be called from JSP tags.

In the context of JSP, the most common use for a bean is to implement the equivalent of a method call. However, since you can't supply parameters to a `get` method, you need to use `set` methods to set the inputs of the computation, then use a `get` method to retrieve the result. That is, a method call

```
result = method(param1, param2, . . .)
```

turns into

```
<%jsp:useBean id="aBean" class="MethodBean" />
<%jsp:setProperty name="aBean" property="param1Name"
   value="<%= param1 %>" />
<%jsp:setProperty name="aBean" property="param2Name"
   value="<%= param2 %>" />
. . .
<%jsp:getProperty name="aBean" property="resultName"/>
```

Here are step-by-step instructions for designing the bean class.

Step 1 Decide what computation the bean is supposed to carry out

What are the inputs? What is the desired output?

Step 2 Give property names for each of the inputs and the output

Step 3 Settle on the *format* of the desired output

Should it be a string? An object whose `toString` method yields the appropriate string? HTML code to generate a bulleted list or a table?

Step 4 Implement the default constructor

It initializes any fields that are reused whenever the bean's computation is executed. Examples are formatters, random number generators, and so on.

▼   **Step 5** Implement the `set` methods for all the inputs of the computation

These methods simply store the values in instance variables.

▼   **Step 6** Supply a `get` method that retrieves the parameters, computes the result, and returns it

▼   Since the result will be included in the surrounding HTML page, it should be a string or an object whose `toString` method yields the desired string. The result string often includes HTML tags.

▼   Here is an example. Suppose we want to generate a web page that contains a set of randomly generated lottery numbers, as in Quality Tip 25.1. We want to simulate a call

▼   ```
result = combinations(49, 6)
```

In the lottery bean, we need two `set` methods to set the numbers to choose from and the number of choices we get. Let's call the properties `numbers` and `choices`. Then the

▼   methods are

```
void setNumbers(int n)
void setChoices(int n)
```

▼   The computation is triggered by a `get` method. Let's call the property `combination`. Then the method becomes

```
String getCombination()
```

▼   It returns a string such as

```
<ul><li>22</li><li>17</li><li>18</li><li>16</li>
<li>27</li><li>36</li></ul>
```

▼   Here is the code for the entire bean:

```
public class LotteryBean
{
   public LotteryBean()
   {
      generator = new Random();
   }

   public void setNumbers(int n)
   {
      numbers = n;
   }

   public void setChoices(int n)
   {
      choices = n;
   }

   public String getCombination()
```
```

```
      {
          StringBuffer buffer = new StringBuffer();
          buffer.append("<ul>");
          int[] values = new int[numbers];
          for (int i = 0; i < numbers; i++)
             values[i] = i + 1;
          for (int i = 0; i < choices; i++)
          {
             int r = generator.nextInt(numbers - i);
             int c = values[r];
             values[r] = values[numbers - 1 - i];
             buffer.append("<li>");
             buffer.append("" + c);
             buffer.append("</li>");
          }
          buffer.append("</ul>");
          return buffer.toString();
      }

      private Random generator;
      private int numbers;
      private int choices;
   }
```

Now the JSP page looks nice and code-free, but you can argue that the bean itself isn't quite clean—it generates some HTML. What if we want to have the lottery combination in a table instead of a bulleted list? That is a valid complaint. Exercise P25.5 shows how you can use two beans—a computational bean that computes an array list of numbers, and a formatter bean that formats any array list as a bulleted list.

25.3   Handling Request Parameters

The program of the preceding section was not very typical, because it did not receive user input. Also, because it gave the user the time *at the server location,* it is not very useful if the user is in another time zone. In this section, we will improve this JSP page to take as user input the city in which the user is located, and to return the time in the user's time zone.

The Java library contains a convenient `TimeZone` class that knows about time zones across the world. A time zone is identified by a string such as `"America/Los_Angeles"` or `"Asia/Tokyo"`. The static method `getAvailableIDs` returns a string array containing all IDs:

```
String[] zoneIDs = TimeZone.getAvailableIDs();
```

There are several hundred time zone IDs. (We are using time zones in this example because the `TimeZone` class gives us an interesting data source with lots of data. Later in this chapter, you will see how to access data from a database, but of course that's more complex.)

The static `getTimeZone` method returns a `TimeZone` class for a given ID string:

```
String zoneID = "America/Los_Angeles";
TimeZone zone = TimeZone.getTimeZone(zoneID);
```

Once you have a `TimeZone` object, you can use it in conjunction with a `DateFormat` to get a time string in that time zone.

```
DateFormat formatter = DateFormat.getTimeInstance();
formatter.setTimeZone(zone);
Date now = new Date();
// suppose the server is in New York, and it's noon there
System.out.println(formatter.format(now));
// prints 9:00:00 AM
```

Of course, we don't expect the user to know about time zone ID strings such as `"America/Los_Angeles"`. Instead, we assume that the user will simply enter the city name such as `Los Angeles`. We will write a time zone bean that checks whether that string, with spaces replaced by underscores, appears at the end of one of the valid time zone IDs. If so, the JSP page formats the current time in that time zone. If not, it prints a message that the city name is not found.

We now need to tackle the issue of how the user supplies the input to the JSP page. You need to design an HTML form—see Figure 3. The form contains a text field with the city name and a button to submit the form data to the JSP page.

Here is the HTML code for that form:

File timezone.html

```
 1  <html>
 2     <head>
 3        <title>Time Zone Form</title>
 4     </head>
 5     <body>
 6        <form action="timezone.jsp" method="POST">
 7           <p>City:
 8              <input type="text" name="city"/>
 9              <input type="submit" value="Get Time"/>
10           </p>
11        </form>
12     </body>
13  </html>
```

> When a browser submits a form, it sends the names and values of all form elements to the web server.

Figure 3 shows the form, after a user has filled in a city.

In Section 25.4 you'll see in detail how to make an HTML form. Right now, we'll just have a closer look at this simple form. First note the `value` attribute of the submit button. As you can see in Figure 3, that attribute specifies the button label, "Get Time". The text field has a `name` attribute. That attribute is not displayed on the form. Instead, when the form is submitted to the server, the server receives a pair of strings, namely the name of the text field (that is, `city`) and its contents (the city that the user entered).

Figure 3

The HTML Form for Entering the City Name

> In a JSP page, you can access the form data through the predefined request object.

The `action` attribute of the `form` element specifies the URL of the server-side program that processes the form data. In our case, we want the `timezone.jsp` page to read the user input.

A JSP page can find out what the user typed into the input fields of a form by asking the special `request` object. This is an object that is defined for every JSP document. It is an instance of the `Servlet-Request` class. (As you will see later in this chapter, servlets and server pages are closely related.) The `getParameter` method returns the value of the form element with a given name. For example,

```
<%= request.getParameter("city") %>
```

yields the city that the user typed.

To obtain the time in a particular time zone, we will define a `TimeZoneBean` with a `city` property. There are two ways for setting that property to the city that the user provided. Of course, you can simply place the call to the `getParameter` method inside the `jsp:setProperty` directive:

```
<jsp:setProperty name="zone" property="city"
    value="<%= request.getParameter(\"city\") %>" />
```

> There is a convenient shorthand for supplying a request parameter to a bean.

(Note that the quotes of the string `"city"` must be escaped by backslashes, because they are contained inside the quotes of the `value` attribute.)

Figure 4

The Output of the Time Zone JSP Page

But there is a convenient shorthand:

```
<jsp:setProperty name="zone" property="city"
   param="city"/>
```

When you use the `param` attribute inside a `jsp:setProperty` directive, the value of the property is set to the value of the request parameter with the given name. This shorthand notation makes it very easy to initialize beans with request parameters.

Here are the JSP file and the time zone bean. Figure 4 shows the output of the JSP.

File timezone.jsp

```
1  <jsp:useBean id="zone" class="TimeZoneBean"/>
2  <jsp:setProperty name="zone" property="date"
3     value="<%= new java.util.Date() %>"/>
4  <jsp:setProperty name="zone" property="city"
5     param="city"/>
6
7  <html>
8     <head>
9        <title>Time Zone JSP</title>
10    </head>
11    <body>
12       <h1>Time Zone JSP</h1>
13       <p>The current time in
```

```
14          <%= request.getParameter("city") %> is:
15          <jsp:getProperty name="zone" property="time"/>
16       </p>
17    </body>
18 </html>
```

File TimeZoneBean.java

```
1  import java.text.DateFormat;
2  import java.util.Date;
3  import java.util.TimeZone;
4
5  /**
6      This bean formats the local time of day for a given date
7      and city.
8  */
9  public class TimeZoneBean
10 {
11     /**
12         Initializes the formatter.
13     */
14     public TimeZoneBean()
15     {
16         timeFormatter = DateFormat.getTimeInstance();
17     }
18
19     /**
20         Write-only date property.
21         @param aDate the date to be formatted
22     */
23     public void setDate(Date aDate)
24     {
25         theDate = aDate;
26     }
27
28     /**
29         Write-only city property.
30         @param aCity the city for which to report the local time
31     */
32     public void setCity(String aCity)
33     {
34         city = aCity;
35     }
36
37     /**
38         Read-only available property.
39         @return true if time zone information is available for
40         this city
41     */
42     public boolean isAvailable()
```

```
43      {
44          return getTimeZone(city) != null;
45      }
46
47      /**
48          Read-only time property.
49          @return the formatted time
50      */
51      public String getTime()
52      {
53          TimeZone zone = getTimeZone(city);
54          if (zone == null) return "not available";
55          timeFormatter.setTimeZone(zone);
56          String timeString = timeFormatter.format(theDate);
57          return timeString;
58      }
59
60      /**
61          Looks up the time zone for a city.
62          @param aCity the city for which to find the time zone
63          @return the time zone or null if no match is found
64      */
65      private static TimeZone getTimeZone(String city)
66      {
67          String[] ids = TimeZone.getAvailableIDs();
68          for (int i = 0; i < ids.length; i++)
69              if (timeZoneIDmatch(ids[i], city))
70                  return TimeZone.getTimeZone(ids[i]);
71          return null;
72      }
73
74      /**
75          Checks whether a time zone ID matches a city.
76          @param id the time zone ID (e.g., "America/Los_Angeles")
77          @param aCity the city to match (e.g., "Los Angeles")
78          @return true if the ID and city match
79      */
80      private static boolean timeZoneIDmatch(String id,
81          String city)
82      {
83          String idCity = id.substring(id.indexOf('/') + 1);
84          return idCity.replace('_', ' ').equals(city);
85      }
86
87      private DateFormat timeFormatter;
88      private Date theDate;
89      private String city;
90  }
```

▼ ⊗ **Common Error**   **25.2**
▶

▼

Mismatch between Form and Parameter Names

It is important that the name of the form field or button equals the request parameter
name. If the names don't match, then the call to `getParameter` returns `null` or, worse,
▼   the contents of a different form element.

   If you change the form names, you also need to change the JSP code. For example, if
you update the form to

▼   `<input type="text" name="cityname"/>`

you also need to change the code in the JSP page to

▼   `<jsp:setProperty name="zone" property="city"`
        `param="cityname"/>`

▼ 🎗 **Quality Tip**   **25.2**
▶

▼

Use Relative URLs

Look at the `action` attribute of the form tags in the `timezone.html` and `time-
zone.jsp` files.

▼   `<form action="timezone.jsp" method="POST">`

Always use a *relative* URL, not an absolute URL such as

▼   `<form action="http://localhost:8080/bigjava/timezone.jsp"`
        `method="POST">`

▼   When you use all relative URLs, it is easy to move the web application to another location.

25.4 **HTML Forms**

An HTML form contains
user interface elements
such as text fields and
buttons.

In the preceding section you saw how a JSP page reads information
from an HTML form. Specifically, the user fills out the form, and
the browser sends a set of pairs, consisting of field names and values,
to the web server.

   In this section, you will see the field types that you can place on an
HTML form. We will cover the following types (see also Figure 5).

- Text fields
- Password fields
- Text areas

Figure 5

The HTML Form Elements

- Radio buttons
- Check boxes
- Selection lists
- Submit buttons
- Hidden fields

Most form elements have the syntax

```
<input type=type name  additional attributes/>
```

You will always want to include a `name` attribute with every element. (There is one exception—a single submit button on a form doesn't require a name.) You can also include a `value` attribute with a default value. For example,

```
<input type="text" name="country" value="USA"/>
```

You have already seen text fields in the time zone example. In addition to the name and a possible default value, there are two useful attribute. The `size` attribute indicates the number of characters to that are displayed in the field. The `maxlength` attribute limits the number of characters that the user can enter.

The `password` type is similar to the text type, except that all characters that the user enters are displayed as a special character, often an * or bullet. You use password fields for sensitive information that onlookers shouldn't be able to spot, such as passwords and account numbers. For example,

```
<input type="password" name="accountnumber" size="16"
   maxlength="16"/>
```

Attribute	Used in Elements
name	All
value	All input elements
size	text, password
maxlength	text, password
rows	textarea
cols	textarea
checked	radio, checkbox

To collect input that extends over multiple lines, you use a text area. Text areas do not use an `input` element. Instead, use the `textarea` element and enclose the default value, like this:

```
<textarea name="..." rows="..." cols="...">
default text
</textarea>
```

The `rows` and `cols` specify the number of rows and columns that are displayed. Users can type in more text—the contents of the text area scroll to accommodate text of any size.

Radio buttons have the form

```
<input type="radio"
   name=name of button group
   value=value of selection
   additional attributes/>
```

Radio buttons come in groups. If the user clicks on a button in the group, then the browser automatically unchecks the previously selected button. The HTML form should specify which element is checked when the form is first displayed, by supplying a `checked="checked"` attribute. Here is an example:

```
<input type="radio" name="shirtsize"
   value="S"/>Small
<input type="radio" name="shirtsize"
   value="M"/>Medium
```

```
<input type="radio" name="shirtsize"
   value="L" checked="checked"/>Large
<input type="radio" name="shirtsize"
   value="XL"/>Extra large
```

See Figure 5 for the layout that results from this button group. Note that the button *label* is not part of the `input` element. You specify it with a regular HTML text string or perhaps an image. The `value` attribute specifies the value that the browser sends to the server when the form is submitted. For example, if the user selected the button next to the "Large" label, the browser sends the name/value pair `shirtsize=L` (and not `shirtsize=Large`) to the server.

Check box elements are coded similarly to radio buttons. For example,

```
<input type="checkbox" name="topping"
   value="mushrooms" checked="checked"/>Mushrooms
<input type="checkbox" name="topping"
   value="anchovies"/>Anchovies
```

More than one check box in a group can have the `checked` attribute set to `"checked"`. If both the boxes are checked, the browser sends the string

```
topping=mushrooms+topping=anchovies
```

to the server.

If you want to supply a large number of options in compact form, use a selection list. This is the second form element that doesn't use an `input` element. Instead, you enclose `option` elements inside a `select` element. Here is an example:

```
<select name="month">
<option value="1" selected="selected">January</option>
<option value="2">February</option>
<option value="3">March</option>
<option value="4">April</option>
<option value="5">May</option>
<option value="6">June</option>
<option value="7">July</option>
<option value="8">August</option>
<option value="9">September</option>
<option value="10">October</option>
<option value="11">November</option>
<option value="12">December</option>
</select>
```

Each option has a value that is sent to the server, and it contains the associated text that is displayed in the pull-down menu.

In its most basic form, a submit button is simply

```
<input type="submit"/>
```

This displays a standard submit button (see Figure 5). You can also change the button label by specifying the `value` attribute:

```
<input type="submit" value="Get time"/>
```

You can have multiple submit buttons on the same page. Then you should use the `name` and `value` attributes so that the JSP page can tell which button was pressed. For example,

```
<input type="submit" name="show" value="Next"/>
<input type="submit" name="show" value="Previous"/>
```

Finally, you can place *hidden fields* into a form. The browser does not display a hidden field, but it sends the name/value pairs in the field to the server when the user submits the form. Some web applications use hidden fields to pass information from a previous interaction, for example the user's account number, to the program that processes this form. The syntax is straightforward:

```
<input type="hidden" name="accountnumber"
   value="YVV-11534-449-6"/>
```

> An HTML form must specify the URL of the server program that processes the form data.

However, this technique is not common with JSP pages. As you will see in the next section, JSP pages can use session tracking to store information conveniently across multiple forms.

Finally, you place all fields that belong to a form into a `form` element.

```
<form action="timezone.jsp" method="POST">
   . . .
</form>
```

The `action` attribute of the `form` tag contains the URL of the JSP page that processes the form data. The `method` attribute should be set to POST. (Recall from Chapter 22 that there are two methods of sending data to a web server: the GET method and the POST method. The POST method is more appropriate for form data because there is no length limit.)

25.5   Session Tracking

> A session is a sequence of page requests from the same browser to the same web server.

Consider a typical web shopping application. When you add items to your shopping cart, the shopping cart remembers what you added. To implement such a behavior in a web application, you need to track user *sessions*. A session is a sequence of page requests from the same browser to the same web server.

> To track a session in a sequence of JSP pages, use a bean with session scope.

In JSP, session tracking is very easy. If you tag a bean with the attribute `scope="session"`, then the *same object* is used for all sessions. For example, the following directive declares a shopping cart object that is available throughout a user session.

```
<jsp:useBean id="cart" class="ShoppingCartBean"
   scope="session"/>
```

When the user requests the JSP page containing this directive for the first time, a new `cart` object is constructed. When the user returns to the same web page or visits another web page in the same web application, the `cart` object is still alive. Thus, when items are added to the cart, the items stay in it when the user returns to a web page that belongs to this web application. However, a separate cart is created for each user.

In contrast, if a bean directive has no `scope` attribute, the bean object has *page scope*. In that case, a new object is created every time when the page is visited.

Use session scope for all information that should persist when the user returns to your web application. Typical information with session scope are the user name, items ordered, personalization options, and so on.

Let us write a simple program that shows session scope at work. Rather than showing the time at a single location, we'll allow users to keep adding cities. In the initial HTML form, this web application asks for the name of the first city (see Figure 6).

The JSP page displays the first city, together with a form to enter the next city (see Figure 7).

You can add as many cities as you like, and the JSP page displays a list of all cities and their current times (see Figure 8). All cities are stored in an object of time `MultiZone-Bean`. The `setCity` method adds a city to the bean object. Since the object has session scope, the same object holds an ever-growing list of cities.

As in the preceding section, we use an HTML form for the first user input. That form posts the city name to a JSP file, which displays a list of cities and their local times. The JSP file itself contains a form. The form in the JSP file posts input to itself. Each time the user submits the form, another city is added to the list (see Figure 9).

Figure 6

Asking for the First of Several Cities

Figure 7

Asking for the Next City

Figure 8

Displaying the Times in Multiple Locations

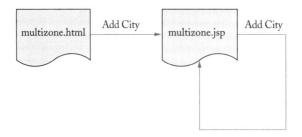

Figure 9

The Structure of the Multiple Time Zone Web Application

We keep cities in a `MultiZoneBean`. An instance of the bean is created for each session:

```
<jsp:useBean id="zones" class="MultiZoneBean"
   scope="session"/>
```

Its `setCity` method *adds* a city to the list of cities. It gets invoked whenever the page is requested. The new city is the value of the text field whose name is `city`:

```
<jsp:setProperty name="zones" property="city"
   param="city"/>
```

The `times` property of the `MultiZoneBean` yields the HTML code for a bulleted list that contains the city names and local times.

You can check that the `MultiZoneBean` has session scope, by starting two separate browsers (such as Netscape Navigator and Internet Explorer). Point both browsers to the `multizone.html` file. You can then build two lists of cities. Each list remembers your prior entries, because the web server establishes a session for each browser connection. But the city lists are are independent of each other, because they are contained in two different objects, one for each session.

File multizone.html

```
1  <html>
2     <head>
3        <title>Multiple Time Zone Form</title>
4     </head>
5     <body>
6        <form action="multizone.jsp" method="POST">
7           <p>First City:
8              <input type="text" name="city"/>
9              <input type="submit" value="Add City"/>
10          </p>
11       </form>
12    </body>
13 </html>
```

File multizone.jsp

```
1  <jsp:useBean id="zones" class="MultiZoneBean"
2     scope="session"/>
3  <jsp:setProperty name="zones" property="date"
4     value="<%= new java.util.Date() %>"/>
5  <jsp:setProperty name="zones" property="city"
6     param="city"/>
7
8  <html>
9     <head>
10        <title>Multiple Time Zone JSP</title>
11     </head>
12     <body>
13        <h1>Current time lookup</h1>
14        <ul>
15           <jsp:getProperty name="zones" property="times"/>
16        </ul>
17        <form action="multizone.jsp"
18           method="POST">
19           <p>Next City:
20              <input type="text" name="city"/>
21              <input type="submit" value="Add City"/>
22           </p>
23        </form>
24     </body>
25  </html>
```

File MultiZoneBean.java

```
1  import java.text.DateFormat;
2  import java.util.ArrayList;
3  import java.util.Date;
4  import java.util.TimeZone;
5
6  /**
7     This bean formats the local times of day for a given date
8     and list of cities.
9  */
10 public class MultiZoneBean
11 {
12    /**
13       Initializes the formatter and city list.
14    */
15    public MultiZoneBean()
16    {
17       timeFormatter = DateFormat.getTimeInstance();
18       cities = new ArrayList();
19    }
20
21    /**
```

```
22          Write-only date property.
23          @param aDate  the date to be formatted
24      */
25      public void setDate(Date aDate)
26      {
27          theDate = aDate;
28      }
29
30      /**
31          Write-only city property.
32          @param aCity  the city to add to the city list
33      */
34      public void setCity(String aCity)
35      {
36          cities.add(aCity);
37      }
38
39      /**
40          Read-only times property.
41          @return  a string containing the HTML code for an unnumbered
42          list of cities and local times
43      */
44      public String getTimes()
45      {
46          StringBuffer buffer = new StringBuffer();
47          for (int i = 0; i < cities.size(); i++)
48          {
49              String city = (String)cities.get(i);
50
51              buffer.append("<li>");
52              buffer.append(city);
53              buffer.append(": ");
54
55              TimeZone zone = getTimeZone(city);
56              if (zone == null)
57                  buffer.append("not available");
58              else
59              {
60                  timeFormatter.setTimeZone(zone);
61                  String timeString
62                      = timeFormatter.format(theDate);
63                  buffer.append(timeString);
64              }
65              buffer.append("</li>");
66          }
67          return buffer.toString();
68      }
69
70      /**
71          Looks up the time zone for a city.
```

```
72            @param aCity the city for which to find the time zone
73            @return the time zone or null if no match is found
74       */
75       private static TimeZone getTimeZone(String city)
76       {
77           String[] ids = TimeZone.getAvailableIDs();
78           for (int i = 0; i < ids.length; i++)
79               if (timeZoneIDmatch(ids[i], city))
80                   return TimeZone.getTimeZone(ids[i]);
81           return null;
82       }
83
84       /**
85           Checks whether a time zone ID matches a city.
86           @param id the time zone ID (e.g., "America/Los_Angeles")
87           @param aCity the city to match (e.g., "Los Angeles")
88           @return true if the ID and city match
89       */
90       private static boolean timeZoneIDmatch(String id,
91           String city)
92       {
93           String idCity = id.substring(id.indexOf('/') + 1);
94           return idCity.replace('_', ' ').equals(city);
95       }
96
97       private DateFormat timeFormatter;
98       private Date theDate;
99       private ArrayList cities;
100 }
```

▼ 𝐀𝐓 Advanced Topic   25.1

Session State

You may recall from Chapter 22 that HTTP is a *stateless* protocol. A browser sends a request to a web server. The web server sends the reply and then disconnects. This is different from other protocols such as POP, where the mail client first logs in to the mail server and then issues commands to retrieve and delete mail messages. The mail client stays connected until it explicitly closes the connection. In contrast, a browser makes a new connection to the web server for each web page, and the web server has no way of knowing that those connections originate from the same browser.

Cookies were invented to overcome this restriction. A cookie consists of a small string that the web server sends to a browser, and that the browser sends back to the same server with all further requests. That way, the server can tie the stream of requests together. You may have heard some privacy advocates complaining about cookies, but they aren't inherently evil. When used to establish a session or to remember login information, they

▼

can make web applications more user-friendly. But when cookies are used to track your identity while you surf the web, there can be privacy concerns.

▼

Some people turn off cookies, and then web applications need to use another scheme to establish a session, typically by embedding a session identifier in the request URL or a hidden field of a form. Fortunately, the JSP session mechanism is smart enough to use URLs with session identifiers if the client browser doesn't support cookies.

▼

25.6 Branching and Forwarding Pages

When building a web application with Java server pages, you use HTML tags to build a user interface. If parts of the user interface are dynamic—dependent on the data that is being shown to the user—you use JavaBeans to produce the dynamic portions. However, sometimes the *entire page* depends on the data to be shown. For example, consider the common situation of error handling. If the user makes an input error, you want to show a web page that tells the user about the input error and provides a chance to correct the error. On the other hand, if the user input was correct, you want to show a web page with the information that the user requested.

> A JSP page can forward a request to another page. Forwarding is useful for implementing branches.

In such a situation, you can use the "branch and forward" technique that we will introduce in this section. For this technique, you post the user query to a JSP page that checks the user data but *has no HTML output.* Instead, the page evaluates a condition and uses the `jsp:forward` directive to select another JSP page. The directive

```
<jsp:forward page="url">
```

causes the JSP engine to load another page instead of the current one. The request data of the current page, and all beans with `scope="request"`, are forwarded to the new page. The "branch and forward page" feeds request data to a bean and then ends with a test like this:

```
<%
    if (some condition)
    {
%>
        <jsp:forward page="url1"/>
<%
    }
    else
    {
%>
        <jsp:forward page="url2"/>
<%
    }
%>
```

Note that the Java statements are enclosed in <% . . . %> delimiters. These delimiters are different from the <%= . . . %> delimiters that you saw for simple expressions. As we

Figure 10

Starting the Time Lookup

already mentioned, it is legal to add Java statements to any JSP page, although it violates the separation of presentation and business logic. However, Java code is acceptable in pages that don't contain any presentation. The presentation is contained in the JSP pages that are loaded through the `jsp:forward` directives.

In the following example, we use this technique to handle the names of cities for which no time zone is known. We start with the same HTML form as usual (see Figure 10 and the `zonebranch.html` file). However, we post the form data to the nonvisual `zonebranch.jsp` page.

File zonebranch.html

```
1  <html>
2     <head>
3        <title>Time Zone Branch Form</title>
4     </head>
5     <body>
6        <form action="zonebranch.jsp">
7           <p>City:
8              <input type="text" name="city"/>
9              <input type="submit" value="Get Time"/>
10          </p>
11       </form>
12    </body>
13 </html>
```

File zonebranch.jsp

```
1   <jsp:useBean id="zone" class="TimeZoneBean"
2      scope="request"/>
3   <jsp:setProperty name="zone" property="date"
4      value="<%= new java.util.Date() %>"/>
5   <jsp:setProperty name="zone" property="city"
6      param="city"/> <html>
7   <%
8      if (zone.isAvailable())
9      {
10  %>
11         <jsp:forward page="zoneresult.jsp"/>
12  <%
13     }
14     else
15     {
16  %>
17         <jsp:forward page="zoneerror.jsp"/>
18  <%
19     }
20  %>
```

> A bean with request scope persists when a request is forwarded to another page.

The `zonebranch.jsp` page constructs a `TimeZoneBean` and sets its `date` and `city` properties. Then the branch logic calls the `isAvailable` method of the `TimeZoneBean` class to find out whether a time zone is available for this city. If that method returns `true`, the request is forwarded to the `zoneresult.jsp` page. That page shows the result of the successful lookup (see Figure 11).

Note the `scope` attribute of the `TimeZoneBean` in the `zonebranch.jsp` page:

```
<jsp:useBean id="zone" class="TimeZoneBean"
   scope="request"/>
```

Request scope indicates that the bean is available to the current page and to any other pages to which this request is forwarded. Therefore, the `zoneresult.jsp` page can continue to access the `zone` bean. Furthermore, the original `request` object is also passed to the forwarded page. Note how the `zoneresult.jsp` page obtains the value of the `city` parameter that was posted to the `zonebranch.jsp` page.

File zoneresult.jsp

```
1   <html>
2      <head>
3         <title>Time Zone Branch Result JSP</title>
4      </head>
5      <body>
6         <h1>Time Zone Branch Result JSP</h1>
7         <p>The current time in
8            <%= request.getParameter("city") %>
9            is:
```

Figure 11

A Successful Time Lookup

```
10              <jsp:getProperty name="zone" property="time"/>
11          </p>
12      </body>
13  </html>
```

Finally, let us see what happens if the lookup is not successful. In that case, the request is forwarded to the zoneerror.jsp page (see Figure 12). In that page, the user is given the chance to enter another city name. When the form is submitted, it is again sent to zonebranch.jsp. Figure 13 shows the structure of this web application.

File zoneerror.jsp

```
1  <html>
2     <head>
3        <title>Time Zone Error JSP</title>
4     </head>
5     <body>
6        <p>Unfortunately, no information is available for
7           <%= request.getParameter("city") %>.
8           Please enter another city.
9        </p>
10       <form action="zonebranch.jsp">
11          <p>City:
12             <input type="text" name="city"/>
```

Figure 12

An Unsuccessful Time Lookup

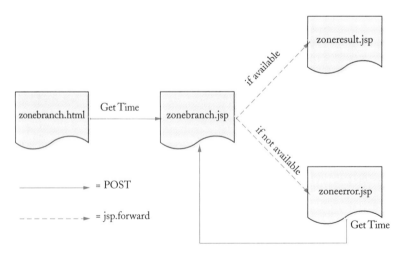

Figure 13

The Structure of the Time Lookup Web Application

```
13                  <input type="submit" value="Get Time"/>
14          </p>
15       </form>
16    </body>
17 </html>
```

? HOWTO   25.2

Building a Web Application

Step 1 On separate sheets of paper, sketch a screen for each web page of the application

Start out with the initial screen, often a login screen. On each screen will be one or more buttons that post data to the server and switch to another page (or maybe the same page with more information added). Be sure to include error screens for invalid inputs.

Step 2 Draw a transition diagram similar to the one in Figure 13

For each page, draw an arrow to its successor page and label it with the button name. If a decision needs to be made (for example, for error checking), introduce a nonvisual JSP page.

Step 3 On each web page, mark the static and the dynamic parts

The static parts always stay the same (such as titles, logos, instructions, and so on). The dynamic parts change according to user input.

Step 4 The dynamic parts need to be generated by beans

Design a set of beans that can yield the dynamic parts. Settle on the `get` and `set` methods. Often you can find the same information on different pages; then you can share the beans.

Step 5 Look at the decisions that the decision-making nonvisual JSP pages need to make (such as error-checking)

Do the nonvisual JSP pages need help from the beans you already developed? Do you need to add methods or new beans?

Step 6 Using an HTML editor, design the basic web pages

If your HTML editor lets you add the JSP tags, then use that feature. Otherwise add the JSP tags with a text editor. You need `jsp:getProperty` tags to generate the dynamic portions of the page. On the first JSP page of the application, you need to instantiate all beans with session scope, with the `jsp:useBean` tag. (That is usually the most sensible

▼ default for a bean in a web application.) On the top of each page, place `jsp:setProp-erty` tags to set the request parameters and other settings.

▼ **Step 7** Implement the Java code for the beans and compile it

Step 8 Deploy your application

▼ Place the JSP files into the web application directory and the class files into the `WEB-INF/classes` subdirectory.

25.7   A Three-Tier Application

> A three-tier application has separate tiers for presentation, business logic, and data storage.

In the final JSP example, you will see a web application with a very common structure. In this example, we will use a database for information storage. We will enhance the time zone example by storing additional cities that are not known to the `TimeZone` class in a database. Such an application is called a *three-tier* application because it consists of three separate layers or tiers:

- The presentation tier: the web browser
- The "business logic" tier: the JSP engine, the JSP pages, and the JavaBeans
- The storage tier: the database

The middle tier is often called the "business logic" because, in commercial applications, it contains the rules that are used for business decisions: what products to offer, how much to charge, to whom to extend credit, and so on. In our simple examples, the time zone logic is the equivalent of the business logic. Thus, the brains of the application are in the business logic. The presentation and storage tiers use off-the-shelf browsers and database systems, with application-specific forms and tables. See Figure 14 for a schematic diagram of the tiers. It is also common to subdivide the middle tier into additional layers, leading to an *n*-tier application.

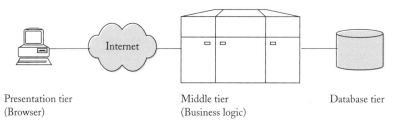

Presentation tier   Middle tier   Database tier
(Browser)   (Business logic)

Figure 14

Three-Tier Architecture

Figure 15

Two-Tier Client-Server Architecture

Client
(Presentation and
Business Logic)

Server (Database)

Contrast the three-tier architecture with a more traditional *client-server* or *two-tier* architecture that you saw in the database programs of Chapter 23. In that architecture, one of the tiers is the database server, which is accessed by multiple client programs on desktops. Each client module has a presentation layer—usually with a specially programmed graphical user interface—and business logic code. (See Figure 15.) Note that the client module is specific to the application. When the business logic changes, a new client module must be distributed over all desktops. In contrast, in a three-tier application, the business logic resides on a server. When the logic changes, the server code is updated, while the presentation tier—the browser—remains unchanged. That is much simpler to manage than updating multiple desktops.

In our example, we will have a single database table, `CityZone`, with city and time zone names (see Table 1). When the user supplies a city name, the `ZoneDBBean` first consults the database to find the matching zone name. If there is no match, then the bean looks through the available zone IDs, as in the preceding examples.

File cityzone.sql

```
1 CREATE TABLE CityZone (City CHAR(30), Zone CHAR(45))
2 INSERT INTO CityZone
     VALUES ('San Francisco', 'America/Los_Angeles')
3 INSERT INTO CityZone
     VALUES ('Kaoshiung', 'Asia/Taipei')
4 . . .
```

To query the database, the bean needs a `Connection` object. You saw in Chapter 23 that the static `getConnection` method of the `DriverManager` class yields such an object:

```
Connection conn = DriverManager.getConnection(
    url, username, password);
```

Where should we place this code? We don't want to store the database username and password inside the `ZoneDBBean` class (and all other classes that make database calls).

City	Zone
San Francisco	America/Los_Angeles
Kaohsiung	Asia/Taipei
...	...

Table 1

The `CityZone` Table

Instead, we supply a second class, `DataSourceBean`, whose sole purpose is to manage database connections. The implementation of that class is very simple—there are four methods to set the driver, database URL, username, and password and one `getConnection` method to get a connection. The `DataSource-Bean` is a bean version of the `Simple-DataSource` in Chapter 23.

> A bean with application scope is initialized once and exists throughout the life of the web application.

We need only a single instance of the `DataSourceBean` to serve all JSP pages that make up the web application. To achieve that, we set the scope of the bean to `"application"`:

```
<jsp:useBean id="db" class="DataSourceBean"
    scope="application"/>
```

Where should we place the database access parameters? It would be a mistake to hard-code them into the `DataSourceBean` class (see Quality Tip 23.1). In Chapter 23, we used a property file for the database properties, but it is awkward to deploy a property file in a JSP application, because a bean does not know how to locate relative file names, and we don't want to hardwire an absolute file name either. Fortunately, the designers of JSP have anticipated issues such as this one and provide a better way to supply information to a web application.

When it is started, the JSP engine reads a setup file with the name `web.xml` from the `WEB-INF` subdirectory of the web application directory. This file is a central location for storing configuration parameters such as database properties. This file is in XML format. (See Chapter 24 for more information on XML.) The file has the following structure:

```
<?xml version="1.0"?>

<!DOCTYPE web-app
PUBLIC
"-//Sun Microsystems, Inc.//DTD Web Application 2.3//EN"
"http://java.sun.com/j2ee/dtds/web-app_2_3.dtd">

<web-app>
    configuration parameters
    other options
</web-app>
```

Note that the `DOCTYPE` may be different for your JSP engine.

Configuration parameters that are of interest to all JSP files in the web application are contained in `<context-param>` elements. Each parameter has a name and a value. For example, here is how you can supply database properties:

```
<context-param>
    <param-name>jdbc.drivers</param-name>
    <param-value>
        COM.cloudscape.core.JDBCDriver</param-value>
</context-param>
<context-param>
    <param-name>jdbc.url</param-name>
    <param-value>
        jdbc:cloudscape:InvoiceDB;create=true
```

```
        </param-value>
    </context-param>
    <context-param>
        <param-name>jdbc.username</param-name>
        <param-value>username</param-value>
    </context-param>
    <context-param>
        <param-name>jdbc.password</param-name>
        <param-value>password</param-value>
    </context-param>
```

> You can place initialization parameters into the `web.xml` file and access them through the predefined `application` object.

To access the parameter values in a JSP page, you use the `getInitParameter` method of the predefined `application` object. That object is defined in every JSP page, similar to the `request` object that you already used. It is an object of the `ServletContext` class. For example, you obtain the database username as

```
<%= application.getInitParameter("jdbc.username"); %>
```

You need to retrieve these values to initialize the database connection bean. Now there is a slight complication. We want the initialization to happen only *once*, when the bean is first constructed, and not every time the page is accessed. This is a common situation, and the `jsp:useBean` directive has a mechanism to deal with it. Any directives that you place as child elements of the `jsp:useBean` directives are executed only once, when the bean is first constructed. Here are the directives for constructing the database connection bean:

```
<jsp:useBean id="db" class="DataSourceBean" scope="application">
    <jsp:setProperty name="db" property="driver"
        value=
        "<%= application.getInitParameter(\"jdbc.drivers\") %>"/>
    <jsp:setProperty name="db" property="url"
        value=
        "<%= application.getInitParameter(\"jdbc.url\") %>"/>
    <jsp:setProperty name="db" property="username"
        value=
        "<%= application.getInitParameter(\"jdbc.username\") %>"/>
    <jsp:setProperty name="db" property="password"
        value=
        "<%= application.getInitParameter(\"jdbc.password\") %>"/>
</jsp:useBean>
```

As already mentioned in Chapter 23, professional programs use a more sophisticated method for managing database connections, using *pooled connections*. When a pooled connection is closed, it is not physically terminated but instead returned to a queue and given out again to another caller of the `getConnection` method. However, at the time of this writing, there is no standard mechanism for connection pooling in either the Java SDK or the JSP standard. Therefore, you will need to look for a data source with connection pooling. Both database and JSP container vendors often supply them. You can also find many implementations—of varying quality—on the Internet.

The ZoneDBBean class is a slight modification of the TimeZoneBean class. Before looking up the among the standard time zone IDs, it makes a database query:

```
SELECT Zone FROM CityZone WHERE City = the requested city
```

If there is a matching entry in the database, that time zone is returned.

Here is the complete code for this web application:

File zonedb.html

```
1   <html>
2      <head>
3         <title>Time Zone Database Form</title>
4      </head>
5      <body>
6         <form action="zonedb.jsp" method="POST">
7            <p>City:
8               <input type="text" name="city"/>
9               <input type="submit" value="Get Time"/>
10           </p>
11        </form>
12     </body>
13  </html>
```

File zonedb.jsp

```
1   <jsp:useBean id="db" class="DBConnBean" scope="application">
2      <jsp:setProperty name="db" property="driver"
3         value=
4         "<%= application.getInitParameter(\"jdbc.drivers\") %>"/>
5      <jsp:setProperty name="db" property="url"
6         value=
7         "<%= application.getInitParameter(\"jdbc.url\") %>"/>
8      <jsp:setProperty name="db" property="username"
9         value=
10        "<%= application.getInitParameter(\"jdbc.username\") %>"/>
11     <jsp:setProperty name="db" property="password"
12        value=
13        "<%= application.getInitParameter(\"jdbc.password\") %>"/>
14  </jsp:useBean>
15
16  <jsp:useBean id="zone" class="ZoneDBBean"/>
17  <jsp:setProperty name="zone" property="city"
18     param="city"/>
19  <jsp:setProperty name="zone" property="connection"
20     value="<%= db.getConnection() %>"/>
21  <jsp:setProperty name="zone" property="date"
22     value="<%= new java.util.Date() %>"/>
23
24  <html>
25     <head>
```

```
26          <title>Zone Database JSP</title>
27      </head>
28      <body>
29          <h1>Zone Database JSP</h1>
30          <p>The current time in
31              <%= request.getParameter("city") %> is:
32              <jsp:getProperty name="zone" property="time"/>
33          </p>
34      </body>
35  </html>
```

File DataSourceBean.java

```
1  import java.sql.DriverManager;
2  import java.sql.Connection;
3  import java.sql.SQLException;
4
5  /**
6      A simple data source bean for getting database connections.
7  */
8  public class DataSourceBean
9  {
10     /**
11         Write-only driver property.
12         @param driver the database driver name
13     */
14     public void setDriver(String driver)
15         throws ClassNotFoundException
16     {
17         Class.forName(driver);
18     }
19
20     /**
21         Write-only url property.
22         @param aUrl the JDBC URL
23     */
24     public void setUrl(String aUrl)
25     {
26         url = aUrl;
27     }
28
29     /**
30         Write-only username property.
31         @param aUsername the database user name
32     */
33     public void setUsername(String aUsername)
34     {
35         username = aUsername;
36     }
37
```

```
38     /**
39         Write-only password property.
40         @param aUsername the database user's password
41     */
42     public void setPassword(String aPassword)
43     {
44         password = aPassword;
45     }
46
47     /**
48         Gets a connection to the database.
49         @return the database connection
50     */
51     public static Connection getConnection()
52         throws SQLException
53     {
54         return DriverManager.getConnection(
55             url, username, password);
56     }
57
58     private static String url;
59     private static String username;
60     private static String password;
61 }
```

File ZoneDBBean.java

```
1 import java.text.DateFormat;
2 import java.util.Date;
3 import java.util.TimeZone;
4 import java.sql.Connection;
5 import java.sql.Statement;
6 import java.sql.ResultSet;
7 import java.sql.SQLException;
8
9 /**
10     This bean formats the local time of day for a given date
11     and city, consulting a database in addition to the standard
12     time zone ID list.
13 */
14 public class ZoneDBBean
15 {
16     /**
17         Initializes the formatter.
18     */
19     public ZoneDBBean()
20     {
21         timeFormatter = DateFormat.getTimeInstance();
22     }
23
```

```
24      /**
25          The city property.
26          @return the city for which to report the local time
27      */
28      public String getCity()
29      {
30          return city;
31      }
32
33      /**
34          The city property.
35          @param aCity the city for which to report the local time
36      */
37      public void setCity(String aCity)
38      {
39          city = aCity;
40      }
41
42      /**
43          Write-only date property.
44          @param aDate the date to be formatted.
45      */
46      public void setDate(Date aDate)
47      {
48          theDate = aDate;
49      }
50
51      /**
52          Read-only time property.
53          @return the formatted time
54      */
55      public String getTime() throws SQLException
56      {
57          TimeZone zone = null;
58          zone = getTimeZoneDB();
59          if (zone == null) // not found in database
60              zone = getTimeZone(city);
61          if (zone == null) return "not available";
62          timeFormatter.setTimeZone(zone);
63          return timeFormatter.format(theDate);
64      }
65
66      /**
67          Looks up the time zone for a city in the database and
68          the list of time zone IDs.
69          @param aCity the city for which to find the time zone
70          @return the time zone or null if no match is found
71      */
72      private TimeZone getTimeZoneDB() throws SQLException
73      {
```

```
74          Connection conn = null;
75          try
76          {
77             conn = DataSourceBean.getConnection();
78             Statement stat = conn.createStatement();
79             String query = "SELECT Zone FROM CityZone"
80                + " WHERE City = '" + city + "'";
81             ResultSet result = stat.executeQuery(query);
82             if (result.next())
83                return TimeZone.getTimeZone(
84                   result.getString(1));
85             else
86                return null;
87          }
88          finally
89          {
90             if (conn != null) conn.close();
91          }
92       }
93
94       /**
95          Looks up the time zone for a city in the list of time
96          zone IDs.
97          @param aCity the city for which to find the time zone
98          @return the time zone or null if no match is found
99       */
100      private static TimeZone getTimeZone(String city)
101      {
102         String[] ids = TimeZone.getAvailableIDs();
103         for (int i = 0; i < ids.length; i++)
104            if (timeZoneIDmatch(ids[i], city))
105               return TimeZone.getTimeZone(ids[i]);
106         return null;
107      }
108
109      /**
110         Checks whether a time zone ID matches a city.
111         @param id the time zone ID (e.g., "America/Los_Angeles")
112         @param aCity the city to match (e.g., "Los Angeles")
113         @return true if the ID and city match
114      */
115      private static boolean timeZoneIDmatch(String id,
116         String city)
117      {
118         String idCity = id.substring(id.indexOf('/') + 1);
119         return idCity.replace('_', ' ').equals(city);
120      }
121
122      private Date theDate;
123      private DateFormat timeFormatter;
```

```
124     private String city;
125  }
```

25.8 Servlets

In the preceding sections you saw how to use JSP to build web applications. A JSP page specifies the static HTML code and the dynamic information that the user of the web application sees in a browser. It also provides a connection to JavaBeans that carry out computations.

> A servlet is a Java program that carries out computations and emits data that are returned to the browser.

Java *servlets* are an alternate mechanism for building web applications. A servlet is a Java program that carries out computations, some of which emit HTML code. As you will see in the next section, servlets and JavaServer Pages are closely related—each JSP page is automatically translated into a servlet.

When you write a servlet, you provide a class that extends the `HttpServlet` class and implement one or both of the following methods:

```
void doGet(
   HttpServletRequest request,
   HttpServletResponse response)
void doPost(
   HttpServletRequest request,
   HttpServletResponse response)
```

depending on whether you want your servlet to handle GET requests, POST requests, or both.

For our first servlet, we will process only GET requests. In fact, we won't send any request information. The servlet will simply obtain the current time, create an HTML document containing that information, and send it back to the browser.

The `request` parameter contains details about the request—we will take up that class in the next example. In this sample servlet, the returned information does not depend on any user input, so we don't care about the request.

The `response` parameter lets you specify what to send back to the browser. If you want to send an HTML document back (the most common case), then you need to do the following:

1. Set the content type to HTML:

   ```
   response.setContentType("text/html");
   ```
2. Get a print writer to collect the document that is to be returned to the browser:

   ```
   PrintWriter out = response.getWriter();
   ```
3. Print the HTML document to the print writer.

4. Close the print writer.

Here is the complete servlet. Note the code that produces the HTML document by printing the tags (such as <html>, <head>, and so on) together with the information for the user. In our case, the information is simply the current date and time.

File DateServlet.java

```java
1  import java.io.PrintWriter;
2  import java.io.IOException;
3  import java.util.Date;
4  import javax.servlet.ServletException;
5  import javax.servlet.http.HttpServlet;
6  import javax.servlet.http.HttpServletRequest;
7  import javax.servlet.http.HttpServletResponse;
8
9  /**
10     This servlet prints out the current date and time.
11 */
12 public class DateServlet extends HttpServlet
13 {
14    public void doGet(HttpServletRequest request,
15       HttpServletResponse response)
16       throws ServletException, IOException
17    {
18       // get information
19       String now = new Date().toString();
20
21       // set content type to HTML
22       response.setContentType("text/html");
23
24       // print formatted information
25       PrintWriter out = response.getWriter();
26
27       String title = "Date Servlet";
28       out.println("<html><head><title>");
29       out.println(title);
30       out.println("</title></head><body><h1>");
31       out.print(title);
32       out.println("</h1><p>The current time is: ");
33       out.println(now);
34       out.println("</p></body></html>");
35
36       out.close();
37    }
38 }
```

> You must provide a deployment descriptor in order to deploy servlets.

Figure 16 shows the output of the servlet.

As you can see, the basic structure of a servlet is simple. You need to obtain the information that the user requested and return the HTML code to display the response in a pleasing and informative way.

Deploying a servlet is a bit more involved than deploying a JSP page. You need to write a *deployment descriptor*. In the deployment descriptor, you give a name to your servlet, which can be different from the class name. You then specify two pieces of information:

Figure 16

The Output of the Date Servlet

- How to locate the servlet class

- Which URLs map to the servlet

Here is an example deployment descriptor for our date servlet. We give the servlet the name Date. The deployment descriptor tells the servlet engine that it is implemented by the DateServlet class, and that a URL with suffix /date should activate the servlet.

The deployment descriptor must be in a file called web.xml (see below). Note that the DOCTYPE can be different on your system.

File web.xml

```
1  <?xml version="1.0"?>
2  <!DOCTYPE web-app
3  PUBLIC
4  "-//Sun Microsystems, Inc.//DTD Web Application 2.3//EN"
5  "http://java.sun.com/j2ee/dtds/web-app_2_3.dtd">
6  <web-app>
7     <servlet>
8        <servlet-name>Date</servlet-name>
9        <servlet-class>DateServlet</servlet-class>
10    </servlet>
11    <servlet-mapping>
12       <servlet-name>Date</servlet-name>
13       <url-pattern>/date</url-pattern>
14    </servlet-mapping>
15  </web-app>
```

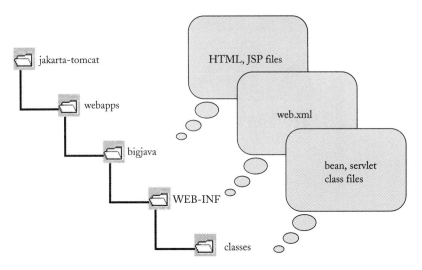

Figure 17

Placement of Web Application Files

You need to place the web.xml file into the WEB-INF subdirectory of your web application directory, such as

```
c:\jakarta-tomcat\webapps\bigjava\WEB-INF
```

Finally, you need to place the class files into the classes subdirectory of the WEB-INF directory, just as you would for bean classes (see Figure 17)

In the web.xml file, you are free to choose any names for the URL suffix and servlet that you like. That flexibility isn't usually necessary, so you may want to give both the same name as the class file. You can also choose different names, as in the preceding example.

The complete URL to launch the servlet is the web application name followed by the URL suffix, such as

```
http://localhost:8080/bigjava/date
```

We now look at a second servlet that lets the user specify a city name. In this servlet we use the request parameter of the doPost method to obtain the value that the user supplied. This parameter is identical to the request variable in a JSP page. You use the getParameter method to get a request parameter:

```
String cityName = request.getParameter("city");
```

File zoneservlet.html

```
1  <html>
2     <head>
3        <title>Time Zone Servlet Form</title>
4     </head>
5     <body>
```

```
6              <form action="timezone">
7                 <p>City:
8                    <input type="text" name="city"/>
9                    <input type="submit" value="Get Time"/>
10                </p>
11             </form>
12          </body>
13       </html>
```

File TimeZoneServlet.java

```
1  import java.io.PrintWriter;
2  import java.io.IOException;
3  import java.text.DateFormat;
4  import java.util.Date;
5  import java.util.TimeZone;
6  import javax.servlet.ServletException;
7  import javax.servlet.http.HttpServlet;
8  import javax.servlet.http.HttpServletRequest;
9  import javax.servlet.http.HttpServletResponse;
10
11 /**
12     This servlet prints out the current local time.
13     The city name must be posted as value of the
14     city parameter.
15 */
16 public class TimeZoneServlet extends HttpServlet
17 {
18    public void doPost(HttpServletRequest request,
19       HttpServletResponse response)
20       throws ServletException, IOException
21    {
22       // get information
23
24       String cityName = request.getParameter("city");
25       TimeZone zone = getTimeZone(cityName);
26
27       // set content type to HTML
28       response.setContentType("text/html");
29
30       // print formatted information
31       PrintWriter out = response.getWriter();
32
33       String title = "Time Zone Servlet";
34       out.println("<html><head><title>");
35       out.println(title);
36       out.println("</title></head><body><h1>");
37       out.print(title);
38       out.println("</h1><p>");
39
```

```
40        if (zone == null)
41           out.println("Sorry--unknown city");
42        else
43        {
44           out.print("The current time in <b>");
45           out.print(cityName);
46           out.print("</b> is: ");
47           DateFormat formatter
48              = DateFormat.getTimeInstance();
49           formatter.setTimeZone(zone);
50           Date now = new Date();
51           out.print(formatter.format(now));
52        }
53        out.println("</p></body></html>");
54
55        out.close();
56     }
57
58     /**
59        Looks up the time zone for a city.
60        @param aCity the city for which to find the time zone
61        @return the time zone or null if no match is found
62     */
63     private static TimeZone getTimeZone(String city)
64     {
65        String[] ids = TimeZone.getAvailableIDs();
66        for (int i = 0; i < ids.length; i++)
67           if (timeZoneIDmatch(ids[i], city))
68              return TimeZone.getTimeZone(ids[i]);
69        return null;
70     }
71
72     /**
73        Checks whether a time zone ID matches a city.
74        @param id the time zone ID (e.g., "America/Los_Angeles")
75        @param aCity the city to match (e.g., "Los Angeles")
76        @return true if the ID and city match
77     */
78     private static boolean timeZoneIDmatch(String id,
79        String city)
80     {
81        String idCity = id.substring(id.indexOf('/') + 1);
82        return idCity.replace('_', ' ').equals(city);
83     }
84 }
```

Apart from the parameter processing, this servlet is similar to the first servlet example. However, if you look at the program code, you will notice that it is not easy to tell what the output of this servlet looks like. You have to look carefully at what gets printed to the out stream. In contrast, a JSP page makes it very easy to see what the output looks like.

JavaServer Pages technology also encourages the separation of presentation and computation much more than servlets do.

For this reason, the Java 2 enterprise deployment guidelines recommend use of JavaServer Pages as the primary technology for producing web interfaces. Why bother with servlets at all? Servlets have their place—for example, when the result of a web query is not HTML but binary data, such as an image or a program file to be downloaded. Also, as you will see in the next section, JSP pages are compiled into servlets. Knowing the basic facts about servlets can help you understand how to write JSP pages.

▼ ⊗ **Common Error**   **25.3**

Instance Variables in Servlets

▼

If you look carefully at the program listing of the `TimeZoneServlet` class, you will note that the `doPost` method passes the data to be formatted to various static methods. Could you have used an instance variable for the `city` field instead of passing it around? This seemingly logical idea does *not* work for servlets. The servlet container constructs a *single* servlet object. That single object serves all requests. If multiple requests arrive simultaneously, they are executed in parallel in separate threads. (See Chapter 21 for more information about threads.) All requests share the same object and therefore the same instance variables. Therefore, you can use instance variables only for information that you want to share between servlet requests. Since the city names are *different* for each request, you cannot store them in instance variables.

Local variables are safe—each thread uses a separate copy of local variables.

25.9   Compilation of JSP Pages

> The JSP container translates JSP pages into servlets.

When you write a JSP page, the JSP engine translates the page into a servlet when it is requested for the first time or when the page changed since the last request. You may have noticed that it sometimes takes a long time for a JSP page to send a response to the browser—the delay is caused by this translation process. In a production environment, this is not a problem because a JSP page, once tested, will stay unchanged for a long time.

Consider our first example for JSP, the date page:

```
<html>
   <head>
      <title>Date JSP</title>
   </head>
   <body>
```

```
        <h1>Date JSP</h1>
        <p>The current time is:
            <%= new java.util.Date() %>
        </p>
    </body>
</html>
```

This page is translated into a servlet with the following doPost method:

```
public void doPost(HttpServletRequest request,
    HttpServletResponse response)
    throws ServletException, IOException
{
    response.setContentType("text/html");
    PrintWriter out = response.getWriter();
    out.println(
        "<html><head><title>Date JSP</title></head>"
        + "<body><h1>Date JSP</h1>"
        + "<p>The current time is:");
    out.println(new java.util.Date());
    out.println("</p></body></html>");
    out.close();
}
```

Bean directives are translated into Java code. For example,

```
<jsp:setProperty name="zone" property="city"
    param="city"/>
```

becomes

```
zone.setCity(reqest.getParameter("city"));
```

Here is how the branch and forward code of Section 25.6 gets translated.

```
<%
    if (zone.isAvailable())
    {
%>
        <jsp:forward page="zoneresult.jsp"/>
<%
    }
    else
    {
%>
        <jsp:forward page="zoneerror.jsp"/>
<%
    }
%>
```

becomes

```
if (zone.isAvailable())
{
```

```
         out.clear();
         pageContext.forward("zoneresult.jsp");
         return;
      }
      else
      {
         out.clear();
         pageContext.forward("zoneerror.jsp");
         return;
      }
```

Now you can see why the braces are needed around the jsp:forward directives: Each directive is translated into multiple Java statements.

This overview of the JSP compilation process concludes the chapter on JavaServer Pages. You have now seen how to develop server-side applications in Java and how to achieve separation of presentation (that is, the HTML code in the JSP page) from business logic (that is, the Java code in the beans).

▼ **Productivity Hint**   **25.1**

Inspecting the Servlet Code

You can actually have a look at the source code of the servlets into which the JSP files are translated—they are stored in the work subdirectory of the JSP engine directory, such as c:\jakarta-tomcat\work. This can be quite helpful to spot errors in your JSP page.

Here is a typical servlet—the compiled multizone.jsp page. Some of the code has been removed for the sake of simplicity. Also, to fit the code on the page, line breaks have been introduced and output strings have been broken up.

```
import statements removed

public class _0002fmultizone_0002ejspmultizone_jsp_1
   extends HttpJspBase
{
   routine code removed
   public void _jspService(
      HttpServletRequest request,
      HttpServletResponse  response)
      throws IOException, ServletException
   {
      routine code removed
      MultiZoneBean zones = (MultiZoneBean)
         pageContext.getAttribute("zones",
            PageContext.SESSION_SCOPE);
      pageContext.setAttribute("zones", zones,
         PageContext.SESSION_SCOPE);
```

```
            JspRuntimeLibrary.handleSetProperty(
                pageContext.findAttribute("zones"),
                 "date", new java.util.Date() );
            JspRuntimeLibrary.introspecthelper(
                pageContext.findAttribute("zones"), "city",
                request.getParameter("city"), request,
                "city", false);
            JspRuntimeLibrary.introspecthelper(
                pageContext.findAttribute("zones"), "city",
                "<jsp:getProperty name=\"zones\""
            + " property=\"times\"/>",
            null, null, false);
        out.write(
            "\n\n<html>\n<head>\n"
            + "<title>Multiple Time Zone JSP</title>\n"
            + "</head>\n<body>\n"
            + "<h1>Current time lookup</h1>\n<ul>\n");
        out.print(JspRuntimeLibrary.toString(
            (((MultiZoneBean)
                pageContext.findAttribute("zones"))
                    .getTimes())));
        out.write("\n</ul>\n"
            + "<form action=\"multizone.jsp\""
            + " method=\"POST\">\n<p>Next City:\n"
            + "<input type=\"text\" name=\"city\"/>\n"
            + "<input type=\"submit\" value=\"Add City\"/>"
            + "\n</p>\n</form>\n</body>\n</html>\n");
        routine code removed
    }
  }
```

Of course, much of the code will be mysterious, but it is sometimes possible to see why a particular JSP construct doesn't seem to be compiling properly.

Random Fact   25.1

Cataloging Your Necktie Collection

People and companies use computers to organize just about every aspect of our lives. On the whole, computers are tremendously good for collecting and analyzing data. In fact, the power offered by computers and their software makes them seductive solutions for just about any organizational problem. It is easy to lose sight of the fact that using a computer is not always the best solution to a problem.

In 1983, the author John Bear wrote about a person who had come up with a novel use for the personal computers that had recently become available. That person cataloged his necktie collection, putting descriptions of the ties into a database and generating reports that listed them by color, price, or style. We can hope he had another use to justify the purchase of a piece of equipment worth several thousand dollars, but that particular application was so dear to his heart that he wanted the world to know about it. Perhaps not surprisingly, few other computer users share that excitement, and you don't find the store shelves of your local software store lined with necktie-cataloging software.

The phenomenon of using technology for its own sake is quite widespread. In the mid-1990s, several large corporations showed great enthusiasm for using computer networks to deliver movies to home viewers on demand. With the available technology, that was an expensive way of getting a movie to a person's home. Fast network connections and new receiving equipment were required. However, initial field experiments were sobering. In these experiments, the network lines and computers were simulated by employees putting tapes into remote video tape players. Few customers were willing to pay a sufficient premium for this service to warrant the huge investments needed. At some point in the future it may be economical to send movies over computer networks, but today the inexpensive video players and rental movies do a better job more cheaply.

In the "Internet bubble" of 2000, hundreds of companies were founded on the premise that the Internet made it technologically possible to order items such as groceries and pet food from a home computer, and therefore the traditional stores would be replaced by web stores. Again, technological feasibility did not ensure economic success. Trucking groceries and pet food to households wasn't economical enough, and few customers were willing to pay a premium for the added convenience.

At the time of this writing, many elementary schools are spending tremendous resources to bring computers and the Internet into the classroom. Indeed, it is easy to understand why teachers, school administrators, parents, and politicians are in favor of computers in classrooms. Isn't computer literacy absolutely essential for youngsters in the new millennium? Isn't it particularly important to give low-income kids, whose parents may not be able to afford a home computer, the opportunity to master computer skills? However, schools have found that computers are enormously expensive. The initial cost of purchasing the equipment, while substantial when compared to the cost of books and other teaching materials, is not beyond the budget of most schools. However, the *total cost of ownership*—that is, the initial cost plus the cost of keeping the computers in working order and of replacing them when they become outdated, all too quickly—is staggering. As schools purchased more equipment than could be maintained by occasional volunteers, they had to make hard choices—should they lay off librarians and art instructors to hire more computer technicians, or should they let the expensive equipment become useless? What were the educational benefits anyway? Interestingly, many schools were so caught up in the hype that they never asked themselves that question until after the computers arrived.

As computer programmers, we like to program everything. As computer professionals, though, we owe it to our employers and clients to understand what problems they want to solve and to deploy computers and software only where they add more value than cost.

CHAPTER SUMMARY

1. A JavaServer Pages (JSP) page contains HTML tags and Java instructions.

2. The JSP container removes all JSP tags and inserts the strings that result from evaluating Java expressions.

3. A JavaBean is a class with a default constructor that exposes properties through its `get` and `set` methods.

4. A JSP page gives you access to the properties of a bean without having to write Java code.

5. Use beans to separate HTML presentation from Java computation.

6. When a browser submits a form, it sends the names and values of all form elements to the web server.

7. In a JSP page, you can access the form data through the predefined `request` object.

8. There is a convenient shorthand for supplying a request parameter to a bean.

9. An HTML form contains user interface elements such as text fields and buttons.

10. An HTML form must specify the URL of the server program that processes the form data.

11. A session is a sequence of page requests from the same browser to the same web server.

12. To track a session in a sequence of JSP pages, use a bean with session scope.

13. A JSP page can forward a request to another page. Forwarding is useful for implementing branches.

14. A bean with request scope persists when a request is forwarded to another page.

15. A three-tier application has separate tiers for presentation, business logic, and data storage.

16. A bean with application scope is initialized once and exists throughout the life of the web application.

17. You can place initialization parameters into the `web.xml` file and access them through the predefined `application` object.

18. A servlet is a Java program that carries out computations and emits data that are returned to the browser.

19. You must provide a deployment descriptor in order to deploy servlets.

20. The JSP container translates JSP pages into servlets.

Further Reading

[1] http://jakarta.apache.org/tomcat/index.html The web page for the Apache Tomcat server.
[2] Marty Hall, *Core Servlets and JavaServer Pages*, Sun Microsystems Press/Prentice Hall, 2000.
[3] Damon Hougland and Aaron Tavistock, *Core JSP*, Prentice Hall, 2001.

Classes, Objects, and Methods Introduced in This Chapter

```
java.util.DateFormat
   format
   getTimeInstance
   setTimeZone
java.util.TimeZone
   getTimeZone
   getAvailableIDs
javax.servlet.ServletContext
   getInitParameter
javax.servlet.http.HttpServlet
   doGet
   doPost
javax.servlet.http.HttpServletRequest
   getParameter
javax.servlet.http.HttpServletResponse
   setContentType
   getWriter
```

Review Exercises

Exercise R25.1. What is the difference between a JSP page and a JSP container?

Exercise R25.2. What is a bean?

Exercise R25.3. What is a bean property?

Exercise R25.4. Is a JButton a bean? Why or why not?

Exercise R25.5. What is the software engineering purpose of using beans in conjunction with JSP pages?

Exercise R25.6. JSP offers two unique services to beans that make them more flexible than Java variables: scope and request parameter initialization. Explain.

Exercise R25.7. What are the choices for the scope of a bean. What is the default? When should you choose which scope?

Exercise R25.8. How can you implement error checking in a form using JSP pages? Explain, using a login dialog as an example.

Exercise R25.9. What information does a browser send to a web application when a form is being posted? How can the web application analyze the information?

Exercise R25.10. What input elements can you place on an HTML form? What are their Swing equivalents?

Exercise R25.11. What is a session? Why is a session mechanism needed for web applications? Why isn't it provided by the HTTP protocol?

Exercise R25.12. What is the difference between a client-server application and a three-tier application?

Exercise R25.13. How can you store and retrieve initialization parameters in a web application without hardwiring them into JSP or bean code?

Exercise R25.14. What is the connection between JSP pages and servlets?

Exercise R25.15. On your JSP engine, find the servlet code that the `multizone.jsp` page generates. Where did you find it? What is the Java code to construct a bean with session scope?

Programming Exercises

Exercise P25.1. Write a JSP page that reports the values of the following system properties of the web server:
- The Java version (`java.version`)
- The operating system name (`os.name`)
- The operating system version (`os.version`)

Use the `getProperties` method of the `System` class.

Exercise P25.2. Write a JSP page that simulates two rolls of a die, producing an output such as "Rolled a 4 and a 6". When the user reloads the page, a new pair of values should be displayed. Use the `Math.random` method to avoid having to instantiate a `Random` object.

Exercise P25.3. Enhance the preceding exercise by producing a web page that shows *images* of the rolled dice. Find GIF images of dice with numbers 1 through 6 on the front, and generate an HTML page that references the appropriate images.

Exercise P25.4. Add a property `format` to the `LotteryBean` from HOWTO 25.1. If `format` is `"ul"`, the output is an unnumbered list. If it is `"table"`, the output is an HTML table.

Exercise P25.5. Split the `LotteryBean` from HOWTO 25.1 into two beans. The first bean should return an array list of `Integer` objects, wrapping the chosen numbers. The second bean should format an arbitrary array list into the HTML code for an unnumbered list.

Exercise P25.6. Write a web application that lets a user specify six lottery numbers. Generate your own combination on the server, and then print out both combinations together with a count of matches.

Exercise P25.7. Add error checking to the preceding exercise. If the lottery numbers are not within the correct range, or if there are duplicates, show an appropriate message and allow the user to fix the error.

Exercise P25.8. Write a shopping cart application. Show the user a list of items that can be purchased. The user can select one item to purchase. (Use radio buttons.) Then ask for the quantity. Then show the current shopping cart. Then ask if the user wants to purchase more or check out. If the user wants to purchase more, go back to the initial screen. If the user wants to check out, ask for the name and address, then display an invoice.

Exercise P25.9. Change the multicity application of Section 25.5 so that each entry of the city list is prefixed by a checkbox. Add a "Delete checked" button that deletes all cities that the user checked.

Exercise P25.10. Personalize the time zone application of Section 25.3. Have a user log in and then specify a city in their profile. The next time the user logs in, the time of their favorite city is displayed automatically. Store users, passwords, and favorite cities in a database. You need a logout button to switch users.

Exercise P25.11. Extend the preceding exercise so that a user can choose multiple cities and all cities chosen by the user are remembered on the next login.

Exercise P25.12. Write a web version of the ExecSQL utility of Chapter 23. Allow users to type arbitrary SQL queries into a text area. Then submit the query to the database and display the result.

Exercise P25.13. Produce a web front end for the ATM program in Chapter 16.

Exercise P25.14. Combine the web front end of the preceding exercise with the bank database of Chapter 23.

Exercise P25.15. Produce a web front end for the appointment book application of Exercise P16.10.

Exercise P25.16. Produce a web front end for the airline reservation program of Exercise P16.11.

Exercise P25.17. Write a LotteryServlet that produces a random set of lottery numbers, like the LotteryBean of HOWTO 25.1.

Java Language Coding Guidelines

Introduction

This coding style guide is a simplified version of one that has been used with good success both in industrial practice and for college courses.

A style guide is a set of mandatory requirements for layout and formatting. Uniform style makes it easier for you to read code from your instructor and classmates. You will really appreciate that advantage if you do a team project. It is also easier for your instructor and your grader to grasp the essence of your programs quickly.

A style guide makes you a more productive programmer because it *reduces gratuitous choice*. If you don't have to make choices about trivial matters, you can spend your energy on the solution of real problems.

In these guidelines, several constructs are plainly outlawed. That doesn't mean that programmers using them are evil or incompetent. It does mean that the constructs are not essential and can be expressed just as well or even better with other language constructs.

If you already have programming experience, in Java or another language, you may be initially uncomfortable at giving up some fond habits. However, it is a sign of professionalism to set aside personal preferences in minor matters and to compromise for the benefit of your group.

These guidelines are necessarily somewhat dull. They also mention features that you may not yet have seen in class. Here are the most important highlights:

- Tabs are set every three spaces.

- Variable and method names are lowercase, with occasional upperCase characters in the middle.

- Class names start with an Uppercase letter.

- Constant names are UPPERCASE, with an occasional UNDER_SCORE.

- There are spaces after keywords and surrounding binary operators.

- Braces must line up horizontally or vertically.

- No magic numbers may be used.

- Every method, except for `main` and overridden library methods, must have a comment.

- At most 30 lines of code may be used per method.

- No `continue` or `break` is allowed.

- All non-`final` variables must be private.

Note to the instructor: Of course, many programmers and organizations have strong feelings about coding style. If this style guide is incompatible with your own preferences or with local custom, please feel free to modify it. For that purpose, this coding style guide is available in electronic form from the author.

Source Files

Each Java program is a collection of one or more source files. The executable program is obtained by compiling these files. Organize the material in each file as follows:

- `package` statement, if appropriate

- `import` statements

- A comment explaining the purpose of this file

- A `public` class

- Other classes, if appropriate

The comment explaining the purpose of this file should be in the format recognized by the `javadoc` utility. Start with a `/**`, and use the `@author` and `@version` tags:

```
/**
    COPYRIGHT (C) 1997 Harry Hacker. All Rights Reserved.
    Classes to manipulate widgets.
    Solves CS101 homework assignment #3
    @author  Harry Hacker
```

```
    @version  1.01 1997-02-15
*/
```

Classes

Each class should be preceded by a class comment explaining the purpose of the class.

First list all public features, then all private features.

Within the public and private sections, use the following order:

1. Constructors
2. Instance methods
3. Static methods
4. Instance fields
5. Static fields
6. Inner classes

Leave a blank line after every method.

All non-`final` variables must be private. (However, instance variables of a `private` inner class may be public.) Methods and final variables can be either public or private, as appropriate.

All features must be tagged `public` or `private`. Do not use the default visibility (that is, package visibility) or the `protected` attribute.

Avoid static variables (except `final` ones) whenever possible. In the rare instance that you need static variables, you are permitted one static variable per class.

Methods

Every method (except for `main`) starts with a comment in `javadoc` format.

```
/**
    Convert calendar date into Julian day.
    Note: This algorithm is from Press et al., Numerical Recipes
    in C, 2nd ed., Cambridge University Press, 1992.
    @param day  day of the date to be converted
    @param month  month of the date to be converted
    @param year  year of the date to be converted
    @return  the Julian day number that begins at noon of the
    given calendar date.
*/
public static int dat2jul(int day, int month, int year)
{
    . . .
}
```

Methods must have at most 30 lines of code. The method signature, comments, blank lines, and lines containing only braces are not included in this count. This rule forces you to break up complex computations into separate methods.

Variables and Constants

Do not define all variables at the beginning of a block:

```
{
    double xold;
    double xnew; // Don't
    boolean more;
    . . .
}
```

Define each variable just before it is used for the first time:

```
{
    . . .
    double xold = Integer.parseInt(input);
    boolean more = false;
    while (more)
    {
        double xnew = (xold + a / xold) / 2; // OK
        . . .
    }
    . . .
}
```

Do not define two variables on the same line:

```
int dimes = 0, nickels = 0; // Don't
```

Instead, use two separate definitions:

```
int dimes = 0; // OK
int nickels = 0;
```

In Java, constants must be defined with the keyword `final`. If the constant is used by multiple methods, declare it as `static final`. It is a good idea to define static final variables as `private` if no other class has an interest in them.

Do not use *magic numbers!* A magic number is a numeric constant embedded in code, without a constant definition. Any number except $-1, 0, 1$, and 2 is considered magic:

```
if (p.getX() < 300) // Don't
```

Use `final` variables instead:

```
final double WINDOW_WIDTH = 300;
. . .
if (p.getX() < WINDOW_WIDTH) // OK
```

Even the most reasonable cosmic constant is going to change one day. You think there are 365 days per year? Your customers on Mars are going to be pretty unhappy about your silly prejudice. Make a constant

```
public static final int DAYS_PER_YEAR = 365;
```

so that you can easily produce a Martian version without trying to find all the 365s, 364s, 366s, 367s, and so on, in your code.

When declaring array variables, group the [] with the type, not the variable.

```
int[] values; // OK
int values[]; // Ugh—this is an ugly holdover from C
```

Control Flow

The if Statement

Avoid the "if ... if ... else" trap. The code

```
if ( ... )
   if ( ... ) ...;
else ...;
```

will not do what the indentation level suggests, and it can take hours to find such a bug. Always use an extra pair of { ... } when dealing with "if ... if ... else":

```
if ( ... )
{
   if ( ... ) ...;
} // {...} are necessary
else ...;

if ( ... )
{
   if ( ... ) ...;
   else ...;
} // {...} not necessary, but they keep you out of trouble
```

The for Statement

Use for loops only when a variable runs from somewhere to somewhere with some constant increment/decrement:

```
for (int i = 0; i < a.length; i++)
   System.out.println(a[i]);
```

Do not use the for loop for weird constructs such as

```
for (a = a / 2; count < ITERATIONS;
   System.out.println(xnew))
   // Don't
```

Make such a loop into a while loop. That way, the sequence of instructions is much clearer.

```
a = a / 2;
while (count < ITERATIONS) // OK
{  . . .
   System.out.println(xnew);
}
```

Nonlinear Control Flow

Avoid the `switch` statement, because it is easy to fall through accidentally to an unwanted case. Use `if/else` instead.

Avoid the `break` or `continue` statements. Use another `boolean` variable to control the execution flow.

Exceptions

Do not tag a method with an overly general exception specification:

```
Widget readWidget(Reader in)
    throws Exception // Bad
```

Instead, specifically declare any checked exceptions that your method may throw:

```
Widget readWidget(Reader in)
    throws IOException, MalformedWidgetException // Good
```

Do not "squelch" exceptions:

```
try
{
    double price = in.readDouble();
}
catch (Exception e)
{} // Bad
```

Beginners often make this mistake "to keep the compiler happy". If the current method is not appropriate for handling the exception, simply use a `throws` specification and let one of its callers handle it.

Lexical Issues

Naming Convention

The following rules specify when to use upper- and lowercase letters in identifier names.

- All variable and method names and all data fields of classes are in lowercase (maybe with an occasional upperCase in the middle); for example, `firstPlayer`.

- All constants are in uppercase (maybe with an occasional UNDER_SCORE); for example, `CLOCK_RADIUS`.

- All class and interface names start with uppercase and are followed by lowercase letters (maybe with an occasional UpperCase letter); for example, `BankTeller`.

Names must be reasonably long and descriptive. Use `firstPlayer` instead of `fp`. No drppng f vwls. Local variables that are fairly routine can be short (`ch`, `i`) as long as they are really just boring holders for an input character, a loop counter, and so on. Also, do not use `ctr`, `c`, `cntr`, `cnt`, `c2` for variables in your method. Surely these variables all have specific purposes and can be named to remind the reader of them (for example, `current`, `next`, `previous`, `result`, ...).

Indentation and White Space

Use tab stops every three columns. That means you will need to change the tab stop setting in your editor!

Use blank lines freely to separate parts of a method that are logically distinct.

Use a blank space around every binary operator:

```
x1 = (-b - Math.sqrt(b * b - 4 * a * c)) / (2 * a);
// Good

x1=(-b-Math.sqrt(b*b-4*a*c))/(2*a);
// Bad
```

Leave a blank space after (and not before) each comma or semicolon. Do not leave a space before or after a parenthesis or bracket in an expression. Leave spaces around the (. . .) part of an `if`, `while`, `for`, or `catch` statement.

```
if (x == 0) y = 0;

f(a, b[i]);
```

Every line must fit on 80 columns. If you must break a statement, add an indentation level for the continuation:

```
a[n] = ...........................................
     + ................;
```

Start the indented line with an operator (if possible).

If the condition in an `if` or `while` statement must be broken, be sure to brace the body in, *even if it consists of only one statement:*

```
if ( ......................................................
     && ..................
     || .......... )
{
   . . .
}
```

If it weren't for the braces, it would be hard to separate the continuation of the condition visually from the statement to be executed.

Braces

Opening and closing braces must line up, either horizontally or vertically:

```
while (i < n) { System.out.println(a[i]); i++; }

while (i < n)
{
```

```
        System.out.println(a[i]);
        i++;
    }
```

Some programmers don't line up vertical braces but place the { behind the keyword:

```
    while (i < n) { // DON'T
        System.out.println(a[i]);
        i++;
    }
```

Doing so makes it hard to check that the braces match.

Unstable Layout

Some programmers take great pride in lining up certain columns in their code:

```
    firstRecord = other.firstRecord;
    lastRecord  = other.lastRecord;
    cutoff      = other.cutoff;
```

This is undeniably neat, but the layout is not *stable* under change. A new variable name that is longer than the preallotted number of columns requires that you move *all* entries around:

```
    firstRecord = other.firstRecord;
    lastRecord  = other.lastRecord;
    cutoff      = other.cutoff;
    marginalFudgeFactor = other.marginalFudgeFactor;
```

This is just the kind of trap that makes you decide to use a short variable name like mff instead.

Do not use // comments for comments that extend for more than two lines. You don't want to have to move the // around when you edit the comment.

```
    // comment—don't do this
    // more comment
    // more comment
```

Use /* . . . */ comments instead. When using /* . . . */ comments, don't "beautify" them with additional asterisks:

```
    /* comment—don't do this
     * more comment
     * more comment
     */
```

It looks neat, but it is a major disincentive to update the comment. Some people have text editors that lay out comments. But even if you do, you don't know whether the next person who maintains your code has such an editor.

Instead, format long comments like this:

```
    /*
    comment
    more comment
```

```
      more comment
  */
```

or this:

```
  /*
  comment
  more comment
  more comment
  */
```

These comments are easier to maintain as your program changes. If you have to choose between pretty but unmaintained comments and ugly comments that are up to date, truth wins over beauty.

A2

Java Syntax Summary

In this syntax summary, we use a monospaced font for actual Java keywords and tokens such as `while`. An italic font denotes language constructs such as *condition* or *variable*. Items enclosed in brackets [...] are optional. Items separated by vertical bars | are alternatives. Do not include the brackets or vertical bars in your code!

The summary reflects the parts of the Java language that were covered in this book. For a full overview of the Java syntax, see [1].

Types

A type is a primitive type or a reference type.
The primitive types are

- The numeric types `int`, `long`, `short`, `char`, `byte`, `float`, `double`
- The `boolean` type

The reference types are

- Classes such as `String` or `Employee` (see "Classes")
- Interfaces such as `Comparable`
- Array types such as `Employee[]` or `int[][]`

Variables

Local variable declarations have the form

```
[final] Type variableName [= initializer];
Examples:
int n;
double x = 0;
String harry = "Harry Handsome";
Rectangle box = new Rectangle(5, 10, 20, 30);
int[] a = { 1, 4, 9, 16, 25 };
```

The variable name consists only of letters, numbers, and underscores. It must begin with a letter or underscore. Names are case-sensitive: `totalscore`, `TOTALSCORE`, and `total-Score` are three different variables.

The scope of a local variable extends from the point of its definition to the end of the enclosing block.

A variable that is declared as `final` can have its value set only once.

Instance variables will be discussed under "Classes".

Expressions

An expression is a variable, a method call, or a combination of subexpressions joined by operators. Examples are:

```
x
Math.sin(x)
x + Math.sin(x)
x * (1 + Math.sin(x))
x++
x == y
x == y && (z > 0 || w > 0)
p.x
e.getSalary()
v[i]
```

Operators can be *unary*, *binary*, or *ternary*. A unary operator acts on a single expression, such as `x++`. A binary operator combines two expressions, such as `x + y`. A ternary operator combines three expressions. Java has one ternary operator, `? :` (see Advanced Topic 5.1).

Unary operators can be *prefix* or *postfix*. A prefix operator is written before the expression on which it operates, as in `-x`. A postfix operator is written after the expression on which it operates, such as `x++`.

Operators are ranked by *precedence* levels. Operators with a higher precedence bind more strongly than operators with a lower precedence. For example, `*` has a higher precedence than `+`, so `x + y * z` is the same as `x + (y * z)`, even though the `+` comes first.

Most operators are *left-associative*. That is, operators of the same precedence are evaluated from the left to the right. For example, `x - y + z` is interpreted as `(x - y) + z`, not x - (y + z). The exceptions are the unary prefix operators and the assignment operator which are right-associative. For example, z = y = Math.sin(x) means the same as z = (y = Math.sin(x)).

Appendix A3 has a list of all Java operators.

Classes

The syntax for a *class* is

```
[public] [abstract|final] class ClassName
    [extends SuperClassName]
    [implements InterfaceName₁, InterfaceName₂, . . .]
{
    feature₁
    feature₂
    . . .
}
```

Each *feature* is either a declaration of the form

modifiers constructor|method|field|class

or an initialization block

```
[static] { body }
```

See the section "Constructors" for more information about initialization blocks.

Potential *modifiers* include public, private, protected, static, and final. A *constructor* has the form

```
ClassName(parameter₁, parameter₂, . . .)
    [throws ExceptionType₁, ExceptionType₂, . . .]
{
    body
}
```

A *method* has the form

```
Type methodName(parameter₁, parameter₂, . . .)
    [throws ExceptionType₁, ExceptionType₂, . . .]
{
    body
}
```

An abstract method has the form

```
abstract Type methodName(parameter₁, parameter₂, . . .);
```

A *field* declaration has the form

```
Type variableName [= initializer];
```

Here is an example:

```
public class Point
{
   public Point() { x = 0; y = 0; }
   public Point(double xx, double yy) { x = xx; y = yy; }
   public double getX() { return x; }
   public double getY() { return y; }
   private double x;
   private double y;
}
```

A class can have both instance fields and `static` fields. Each object of the class has a separate copy of the instance fields. There is only one per-class copy of the `static` fields.

A class that is declared as `abstract` cannot be instantiated. That is, you can't construct objects of that class.

A class that is declared as `final` cannot be extended.

Interfaces

The syntax for an interface is

```
[public] interface InterfaceName
    [extends InterfaceName₁, InterfaceName₂, . . .]
{
    feature₁
    feature₂
    . . .
}
```

Each feature has the form

modifiers   method | field

Potential *modifiers* are `public`, `static`, `final`. However, modifiers are never necessary because methods are automatically `public` and fields are automatically `public static final`.

A *method* declaration has the form

Type methodName(parameter₁, parameter₂, . . .);

A *field* declaration has the form

Type variableName = initializer;

Here is an example:

```
public interface Measurable
{
   int getMeasure();
   int CM_PER_INCH = 2.54;
}
```

Methods

A method definition has the form

> *modifiers Type methodName(parameter$_1$, parameter$_2$, . . .)*
>   [`throws` *ExceptionType$_1$, ExceptionType$_2$, . . .*]
> {
>   *body*
> }

The return type *Type* is any Java type, or the special type `void` to indicate that the method returns no value.

Each *parameter* has the form

> [`final`] *Type parameterName*

In Java, all parameters are passed by *value*. Each parameter is a local variable whose scope extends to the end of the method body. It is initialized with a copy of the value supplied in the call. That value may be a primitive type or a reference type. If it is a reference type, invoking a mutator on the reference will modify the object whose reference has been passed to the method.

Changing the value of the parameter variable has no effect outside the method. Tagging the parameter as `final` disallows such a change altogether. This is commonly done to allow access of the parameter from an inner class defined in the method.

We distinguish between *instance* methods and *static* methods. Instance methods have a special parameter, the *implicit* parameter, supplied in the method call with the syntax

> *implicitParameterValue . methodName(*
>   *parameterValue$_1$, parameterValue$_2$, . . .)*

Example:

```
harry.setSalary(30000)
```

The type of the implicit parameter must be the same as the type of the class containing the method definition. A static method does not have an implicit parameter.

In the method body, the `this` variable is initialized with a copy of the implicit parameter value. Using a field name without qualification means to access the field of the implicit parameter. For example,

```
public void setSalary(double s)
{
    salary = s; // i.e., this.salary = s
}
```

By default, methods are *dynamically bound*. The virtual machine determines the class to which the implicit parameter object belongs and invokes the method defined in that class. However, if a method is invoked on the special variable `super`, then the method defined in the superclass is invoked on `this`. For example,

```
public class MyPanel extends JPanel
{
```

```
public void paintComponent(Graphics g)
{
   super.paintComponent(g);
   // calls JPanel.paintComponent
   . . .
}
. . .
}
```

The `return` statement causes a method to exit immediately. If the method type is not `void`, you must return a value. The syntax is

```
return [value];
```

For example,

```
public double getSalary()
{
   return salary;
}
```

A method can call itself. Such a method is called *recursive*:

```
public static int factorial(int n)
{
   if (n <= 1) return 1;
      return n * factorial(n - 1);
}
```

Constructors

A constructor definition has the form

modifiers ClassName(*parameter*$_1$, *parameter*$_2$, . . .)
   [`throws` *ExceptionType*$_1$, *ExceptionType*$_2$, . . .]
{
   body
}

You invoke a constructor to allocate and construct a new object with a `new` expression

`new` *ClassName*(*parameterValue*$_1$, *parameterValue*$_2$, . . .)

A constructor can call the body of another constructor of the same class with the syntax

`this`(*parameterValue*$_1$, *parameterValue*$_2$, . . .)

For example,

```
public Employee()
{
   this("", 0);
}
```

It can call a constructor of its superclass with the syntax

    super($parameterValue_1$, $parameterValue_2$, . . .)

The call to `this` or `super` must be the first statement in the constructor.
    Arrays are constructed with the syntax

    new $ArrayType$ [= {$initializer_1$, $initializer_2$, . . .}]

For example,

    `new int[] { 1, 4, 9, 16, 25 }`

When an object is constructed, the following actions take place:

- All fields are initialized with 0, `false`, or `null`.

- The initializers and initialization blocks are executed in the order in which they are declared.

- The body of the constructor is invoked.

When a class is loaded, the following actions take place:

- All static fields are initialized with 0, `false`, or `null`.

- The initializers of static fields and static initialization blocks are executed in the order in which they are declared.

Statements

A statement is one of the following:

- An expression followed by a semicolon

- A branch or loop statement

- A `return` statement

- A `throw` statement

- A *block*, that is, a group of variable declarations and statements enclosed in braces {. . .}

- A `try` block

Java has two branch statements (`if` and `switch`), three loop statements (`while`, `for`, and `do`), and two mechanisms for nonlinear control flow (`break` and `continue`).
    The `if` statement has the form

    `if` (*condition*) *statement*$_1$ [`else` *statement*$_2$]

If the *condition* is true, then the first *statement* is executed. Otherwise, the second *statement* is executed.

The `switch` statement has the form

```
switch (expression)
{
   case constant₁₁:
   case constant₁₂:
   . . .
      statement₁₁
      statement₁₂
      . . .
   case constant₂₁:
   case constant₂₂:
   . . .
      statement₂₁
      statement₂₂
      . . .

   . . .
   [default:
      statement₁
      statement₂
      . . .]
}
```

The *expression* must have an integer value. Depending on its value, control is transferred to the first statement following the matching `case` label, or to the first statement following the `default` label if none of the `case` labels match. Execution continues with the next statement until a `break` or `return` statement is encountered, an exception is thrown, or the end of the `switch` is reached. Execution skips over any `case` labels.

The `while` loop has the form

```
while (condition) statement
```

The *statement* is executed while the *condition* is true.

The `for` loop has the form

```
for (initExpression|variableDeclaration;
        condition;
        updateExpression₁, updateExpression₂, . . .)
     statement
```

The initialization expression or the variable declaration are executed once. While the *condition* remains true, the loop *statement* and the update expressions are executed. Examples:

```
for (i = 0; i < 10; i++) sum = sum + i;
for (int i = 0, j = 9; i < 10; i++, j--) a[j] = b[i];
```

The do loop has the form

```
do statement while (condition);
```

The *statement* is repeatedly executed until the *condition* is no longer true. In contrast to a `while` loop, the statement of a **do** loop is executed at least once.

The `break` statement exits the innermost enclosing `while`, **do**, `for`, or `switch` statement (not counting `if` or block statements).

Any statement (including if and block statements) can be tagged with a label:

label: *statement*

The labeled break statement

break *label*;

exits the labeled statement.

The continue statement skips past the end of the *statement* part of a while, do, or for statement. In the case of the while or do statement, the loop condition is executed next. In the case of the for statement, the update expressions are executed next.

The labeled continue statement

continue *label*;

skips past the end of the *statement* part of a while, do, or for statement with the matching label.

Exceptions

The throw statement

throw *expression*;

abruptly terminates the current method and resumes control inside the innermost matching catch clause of a surrounding try block. The *expression* must evaluate to a reference to an object of a subclass of Throwable.

The try statement has the form

```
try tryBlock
[catch (ExceptionType₁ exceptionVariable₁) catchBlock₁
catch (ExceptionType₂ exceptionVariable₂) catchBlock₂
. . .]
[finally finallyBlock]
```

- The try statement must have at least one catch or finally clause.

- All blocks are block statements in the usual sense, that is, { . . . }-delimited statement sequences.

The statements in the *tryBlock* are executed. If one of them throws an exception object whose type is a subtype of one of the types in the catch clauses, then its *catchBlock* is executed. As soon as the catch block is entered, that exception is handled.

If the *tryBlock* exits for any reason at all (because all of its statements executed completely; because one of its statements was a break, continue, or return statement; or because an exception was thrown), then the *finallyBlock* is executed.

If the *finallyBlock* was entered because an exception was thrown and it itself throws another exception, then that exception masks the prior exception.

Packages

A class can be placed in a package, by putting the package declaration

```
package packageName;
```

as the first non-`import` declaration of the source file.

A package name has the form

identifier$_1$.identifier$_2$. . . .

For example,

```
java.util
com.horstmann.bigjava
```

A fully qualified name of a class is

packageName.ClassName

Classes can always be referenced by their fully qualified class names. However, this can be inconvenient. For that reason, you can reference *imported* classes by just their *ClassName*. All classes in the package `java.lang` and in the package of the current source file are always imported. To import additional classes, use an import directive

```
import packageName.ClassName;
```

or

```
import packageName.*;
```

The second version imports all classes in the package.

Comments

There are three kinds of comments:

```
/* comment */
// one-line-comment
/** documentationComment */
```

The one-line comment extends to the end of the line. The other comments can span multiple lines and extend to the */ delimiter.

Documentation comments are further explained in Appendix A10.

Further Reading

[1] James Gosling et al., *The Java Language Specification,* 2nd ed., Addison-Wesley, 2000.

Java Operator Summary

Operator	Description	Associativity
.	Access class feature	Left to right
[ ]	Array subscript	
( )	Function call	
++	Increment	Right to left
--	Decrement	
!	Boolean not	
~	Bitwise not	
+ (unary)	(Has no effect)	
- (unary)	Negative	
(*TypeName*)	Cast	
new	Object allocation	
*	Multiplication	Left to right
/	Division or integer division	
%	Integer remainder	
+	Addition, string concatenation	Left to right
-	Subtraction	
<<	Shift left	Left to right
>>	Arithmetic shift right	
>>>	Bitwise shift right	

Operator	Description	Associativity
<	Less than	Left to right
<=	Less than or equal	
>	Greater than	
>=	Greater than or equal	
==	Equal	
!=	Not equal	
instanceof	Tests whether an object's type is a given type or a subtype thereof	
&	Bitwise and	Left to right
^	Bitwise exclusive or	Left to right
|	Bitwise or	Left to right
&&	Bitwise "short circuit" and	Left to right
||	Boolean "short circuit" or	Left to right
=	Assignment	Right to left
op=	Assignment with binary operator (*op* is one of +, -, *, /, &, |, ^, <<, >>, >>>)	

Java Keyword Summary

Keyword	Description
abstract	An abstract class or method
boolean	The Boolean type
break	Breaks out of the current loop or labeled statement
byte	The 8-bit signed integer type
case	A label in a switch statement
catch	The handler for an exception in a try block
char	The 16-bit Unicode character type
class	Defines a class
const	Not used
continue	Skip the remainder of a loop body
default	The default label in a switch statement
do	A loop whose body is executed at least once
double	The 64-bit double-precision floating-point type
else	The alternative clause in an if statement
extends	Indicates that a class is a subclass of another class
final	A value that cannot be changed after it has been initialized, a method that can't be overridden, or a class that can't be executed
finally	A clause of a try block that is always executed
float	The 32-bit single-precision floating-point type
for	A loop with initialization, condition, and update expressions
goto	Not used
if	A conditional branch statement
implements	Indicates that a class realizes an interface
import	Allows the use of class names without the package name

Keyword	Description
`instanceof`	Tests whether an object's type is a given type or a subtype thereof
`int`	The 32-bit integer type
`interface`	An abstract type with only abstract methods and constants
`long`	The 64-bit integer type
`native`	A method implemented in non-Java code
`new`	Allocates an object
`package`	A collection of related classes
`private`	A feature that is accessible only by methods of the same class
`protected`	A feature that is accessible only by methods of the the same class, a subclass, or another class in the same package
`public`	A feature that is accessible by all methods
`return`	Returns from a method
`short`	The 16-bit integer type
`static`	A feature that is defined for a class, not for individual instances
`strictfp`	Use strict rules for floating-point computations
`super`	Invoke the superclass constructor or a superclass method
`switch`	A selection statement
`synchronized`	A block of code that is accessible to only one thread at a time
`this`	The implicit parameter of a method; or invocation of another constructor of the same class
`throw`	Throws an exception
`throws`	The exceptions that a method may throw
`transient`	Fields that should not be serialized
`try`	A block of code with exception handlers or a `finally` handler
`void`	Tags a method that doesn't return a value
`volatile`	A field that may be updated by multiple threads without synchronization
`while`	A loop statement

The Java Library

This appendix lists all classes and methods from the standard Java library that are used in this book.

In the following inheritance diagram, superclasses that are not used in this book are shown in parentheses. Some classes implement interfaces not covered in this book; they are omitted. Classes are sorted first by package, then alphabetically within a package.

```
java.awt.Shape
java.awt.Stroke
java.lang.Cloneable
java.lang.Object
    java.awt.BasicStroke implements Stroke
    java.awt.Color implements Serializable
    java.awt.Component implements Serializable
        java.awt.Container
            javax.swing.JComponent
                javax.swing.AbstractButton
                    javax.swing.JButton
                    javax.swing.JMenuItem
                        javax.swing.JMenu
                    (javax.swing.JToggleButton)
                        javax.swing.JCheckBox
                        javax.swing.JRadioButton
                javax.swing.JComboBox
                javax.swing.JFileChooser
                javax.swing.JMenuBar
                javax.swing.JPanel
                javax.swing.JOptionPane
                javax.swing.JSlider
                javax.swing.text.JTextComponent
                    javax.swing.JTextArea
                    javax.swing.JTextField
            (java.awt.Panel)
```

```
              java.applet.Applet
              javax.swing.JApplet
         java.awt.Window
            java.awt.Frame
               javax.swing.JFrame
java.awt.FlowLayout implements Serializable
java.awt.Font implements Serializable
java.awt.Graphics
   java.awt.Graphics2D;
java.awt.GridLayout implements Serializable
java.awt.event.MouseAdapter implements MouseListener
java.awt.event.WindowAdapter
   implements WindowListener
java.awt.font.FontRenderContext
java.awt.font.TextLayout implements Cloneable
java.awt.geom.Line2D
   implements Cloneable, Shape
   java.awt.geom.Line2D.Double
java.awt.geom.Point2D implements Cloneable
   java.awt.geom.Point2D.Double
java.awt.geom.RectangularShape
   implements Cloneable, Shape
  (java.awt.geom.Rectangle2D)
      java.awt.Rectangle implements Serializable
      java.awt.Rectangle2D.Double
   java.awt.geom.Ellipse2D
      java.awt.geom.Ellipse2D.Double
java.io.File implements Comparable, Serializable
java.io.InputStream
   java.io.FileInputStream
   java.io.ObjectInputStream
java.io.OutputStream
   java.io.FileOutputStream
   java.io.ObjectOutputStream
java.io.RandomAccessFile
java.io.Reader
   java.io.BufferedReader
   java.io.InputStreamReader
      java.io.FileReader
java.io.Writer
   java.io.PrintWriter
  (java.io.OutputStreamWriter)
      java.io.FileWriter
java.lang.Boolean implements Serializable
java.lang.Class implements Serializable
java.lang.Math
(java.lang.Number implements Serializable)
   java.math.BigDecimal implements Comparable
   java.math.BigInteger implements Comparable
   java.lang.Double implements Comparable
```

```
      java.lang.Float implements Comparable
      java.lang.Integer implements Comparable
  java.lang.String implements Comparable, Serializable
  java.lang.System
  java.lang.Thread implements Runnable
  java.lang.Throwable
    java.lang.Error
    java.lang.Exception
      java.lang.CloneNotSupportedException
      java.lang.InterruptedException
      java.io.IOException
        java.io.EOFException
        java.io.FileNotFoundException
      java.lang.RuntimeException
        java.lang.IllegalArgumentException
           java.lang.NumberFormatException
        java.lang.NullPointerException
      java.sql.SQLException
(java.text.Format implements Cloneable, Serializable)
    java.text.DateFormat
    java.text.NumberFormat
(java.util.AbstractCollection)
    java.util.AbstractList
      (java.util.AbstractSequentialList)
          java.util.LinkedList
      (java.util.AbstractSet)
          java.util.HashSet
            implements Cloneable, Serializable, Set
          java.util.TreeSet
            implements Cloneable, Serializable,
              SortedSet
       java.util.ArrayList
          implements Cloneable, List, Serializable
(java.util.AbstractMap)
    java.util.HashMap
        implements Cloneable, Map, Serializable
    java.util.TreeMap
        implements Cloneable, Serializable, SortedMap
  java.util.logging.Level implements Serializable
  java.util.logging.Logger
  java.net.ServerSocket
  java.net.Socket
  java.net.URL implements Serializable
  java.net.URLConnection
     java.net.HttpURLConnection
  java.net.URLDecoder
  java.net.URLEncoder
  java.sql.DriverManager
  java.util.Arrays
  java.util.EventObject implements Serializable
```

```
            (java.awt.AWTEvent)
                java.awt.event.ActionEvent
                (java.awt.event.ComponentEvent)
                    java.awt.event.InputEvent
                        java.awt.event.MouseEvent
                    java.awt.event.WindowEvent
                javax.swing.event.ChangeEvent
        java.util.Random implements Serializable
        java.util.StringTokenizer
        java.util.TimeZone implements Cloneable, Serializable
        (javax.servlet.GenericServlet)
            javax.servlet.http.HttpServlet
        javax.swing.ButtonGroup implements Serializable
        javax.swing.ImageIcon implements Serializable
        javax.swing.Timer implements Serializable
        (javax.swing.border.AbstractBorder
            implements Serializable)
            javax.swing.border.EtchedBorder
            javax.swing.border.TitledBorder
        javax.xml.parsers.DocumentBuilder
        javax.xml.parsers.DocumentBuilderFactory
        javax.xml.transform.Transformer
        javax.xml.transform.TransformerFactory
        javax.xml.transform.dom.DOMSource implements Source
        javax.xml.transform.stream.StreamResult
            implements Result
java.lang.Serializable
java.sql.Connection
java.sql.ResultSet
java.sql.ResultSetMetaData
java.sql.Statement
    java.sql.PreparedStatement
        java.sql.CallableStatement
java.util.Collection
    java.util.List
    java.util.Set
        java.util.SortedSet
java.util.EventListener
    java.awt.event.ActionListener
    java.awt.event.MouseListener
    java.awt.event.WindowListener
    javax.swing.event.ChangeListener
java.util.Iterator
    java.util.ListIterator
java.util.Map
    java.util.SortedMap
javax.servlet.ServletContext
javax.servlet.ServletRequest
    javax.servlet.http.HttpServletRequest
javax.servlet.ServletResponse
```

```
    javax.servlet.http.HttpServletResponse
javax.xml.transform.Result
javax.xml.transform.Source
org.w3c.dom.NamedNodeMap
org.w3c.dom.Node
    org.w3c.dom.Attr
    org.w3c.dom.CharacterData
        org.w3c.dom.Text
    org.w3c.dom.Document
    org.w3c.dom.Element
org.w3c.dom.NodeList
```

In the following descriptions, the phrase "this object" ("this component", "this container", and so forth) means the object (component, container, and so forth) on which the method is invoked (the implicit parameter, `this`).

Package `java.applet`

Class `java.applet.Applet`

- `void destroy()`

  This method is called when the applet is about to be terminated, after the last call to `stop`.

- `void init()`

  This method is called when the applet has been loaded, before the first call to `start`. Applets override this method to carry out applet-specific initialization and to read applet parameters.

- `void start()`

  This method is called after the `init` method and each time the applet is revisited.

- `void stop()`

  This method is called whenever the user has stopped watching this applet.

Package `java.awt`

Class `java.awt.BasicStroke`

- `BasicStroke(float width)`

  This constructs a stroke object that draws lines of a given width.

  Parameters:

  `width`—The stroke width

Class `java.awt.BorderLayout`

- `BorderLayout()`

This constructs a border layout. A border layout has five regions for adding components, called "North", "East", "South", "West" and "Center".

- `static final int CENTER`

This value identifies the center position of a border layout.

- `static final int EAST`

This value identifies the east position of a border layout.

- `static final int NORTH`

This value identifies the north position of a border layout.

- `static final int SOUTH`

This value identifies the south position of a border layout.

- `static final int WEST`

This value identifies the west position of a border layout.

Class `java.awt.Color`

- `Color(float red, float green, float blue)`

This creates a color with the specified red, green, and blue values between `0.0F` and `1.0F`.

Parameters:

 `red`—The red component
 `green`—The green component
 `blue`—The blue component

Class `java.awt.Component`

- `int getHeight()`

This method gets the height of this component.

Returns: The height in pixels.

- `int getWidth()`

This method gets the width of this component.

Returns: The width in pixels.

- `void repaint()`

This method repaints this component by scheduling a call to the `paint` method.

- `void setPreferredSize(int width, int height)`

This method sets the preferred size for this component.

Parameters:

> width—The preferred width
>
> height—The preferred height

Class java.awt.Container

- void add(Component c)
- void add(Component c, Object position)

These methods add a component to the end of this container. If a position is given, the layout manager is called to position the component.

Parameters:

> c—The component to be added
>
> position—An object expressing position information for the layout manager

- void paint(Graphics g)

This method is called when the surface of the container needs to be repainted.

Parameters:

> g—The graphics context

- void setLayout(LayoutManager manager)

This method sets the layout manager for this container.

Parameters:

> manager—A layout manager

- void setSize(int width, int height)

This method changes the size of this container.

Parameters:

> width—The new width
>
> height—The new height

Class java.awt.FlowLayout

- FlowLayout()

This constructs a new flow layout. A flow layout places as many components as possible in a row, without changing their size, and starts new rows when necessary.

Class java.awt.Font

- Font(String name, int style, int size)

This constructs a font object from the specified name, style, and point size.

Parameters:

> name—The font name, either a font face name or a logical font name, which must be one of "Dialog", "DialogInput", "Monospaced", "Serif", or "SansSerif"

> style—One of Font.PLAIN, Font.ITALIC, Font.BOLD, or Font.ITALIC +Font.BOLD

> size—The point size of the font

- Rectangle2D getStringBounds(String s, FontRenderContext context)

This method measures the size of a string.

Parameters:

> s—The string to measure

> context—The font render context to use for measuring

Returns: A rectangle enclosing the string, whose basepoint is positioned at (0, 0).

Class java.awt.Frame

- void setTitle(String title)

This method sets the frame title.

Parameters:

> title—The title to be displayed in the border of the frame

Class java.awt.Graphics

- void setColor(Color c)

This method sets the current color. From now on, all graphics operations use this color.

Parameters:

> c—The new drawing color

- void setFont(Font font)

This method sets the current font. From now on, all text operations use this font.

Parameters:

> font–The font

Class java.awt.Graphics2D

- void draw(Shape s)

> This method draws the outline of the given shape. Many classes—among them Rectangle and Line2D.Double—implement the Shape interface.

Parameters:

> s—The shape to be drawn

- void drawString(String s, int x, int y)
- void drawString(String s, float x, float y)

These methods draw a string in the current font.

Parameters:

> s—The string to draw
>
> x,y—The basepoint of the first character in the string

- void fill(Shape s)

This method draws the given shape and fills it with the current color.

Parameters:

> s—The shape to be filled

- FontRenderContext getFontRenderContext()

This method gets the font render context, an object that is used for measuring and drawing fonts.

Returns: The font render context.

- void setStroke(Stroke s)

This method sets the current stroke for drawing lines and curves.

Parameters:

> s—The stroke to use

Class java.awt.GridLayout

- GridLayout(int rows, int cols)

This constructor creates a grid layout with the specified number of rows and columns. The components in a grid layout are arranged in a grid with equal widths and heights. One, but not both, of rows and cols can be zero, in which case any number of objects can be placed in a row or in a column, respectively.

Parameters:

> rows—The number of rows in the grid
>
> cols—The number of columns in the grid

Class java.awt.Rectangle

- Rectangle()

This constructs a rectangle whose top left corner is at (0, 0) and whose width and height are both zero.

- `Rectangle(int x,int y,int width,int height)`

This constructs a rectangle with given top left corner and size.

Parameters:

> `x,y`—The upper left corner
> `width`—The width
> `height`—The height

- `Rectangle intersection(Rectangle other)`

This method computes the intersection of this rectangle with the specified rectangle.

Parameters:

> `other`—A rectangle

Returns: The largest rectangle contained in both `this` and `other`.

- `void setLocation(int x, int y)`

This method moves this rectangle to a new location.

Parameters:

> `x,y`—The new top left corner

- `void setSize(int width, int height)`

This method changes the size of this rectangle.

Parameters:

> `width`—The new width
> `height`—The new height

- `void translate(int dx, int dy)`

This method moves this rectangle.

Parameters:

> `dx`—The distance to move along the *x*-axis
> `dy`—The distance to move along the *y*-axis

- `Rectangle union(Rectangle other)`

This method computes the union of this rectangle with the specified rectangle. This is not the set-theoretic union but the smallest rectangle that contains both `this` and `other`.

Parameters:

> `other`—A rectangle

Returns: The smallest rectangle containing both `this` and `other`.

Interface `java.awt.Shape`

The `Shape` interface describes shapes that can be drawn and filled by a `Graphics2D` object.

Class `java.awt.Window`

- `void addWindowListener(WindowListener listener)`

This method adds a window listener. The window listener is notified whenever a window event originates from this window.

Parameters:

    `listener`—The window listener to be added

- `void pack()`

This method lays out the components in the window to occupy as little space as possible, and sizes the window to enclose the components.

- `void show()`

This method makes the window visible and brings it to the front.

Package `java.awt.event`

Class `java.awt.event.ActionEvent`

- `String getActionCommand()`

This method returns a string describing this action event, such as the label of the button or menu that caused it. These strings are subject to change, so you should generally not use them to identify the event source.

Returns: The action command string.

Interface `java.awt.event.ActionListener`

- `void actionPerformed(ActionEvent e)`

The event source calls this method when an action occurs.

Class `java.awt.event.MouseAdapter`

- `void mouseClicked(MouseEvent e)`

This method is called when the mouse has been clicked (that is, pressed and released in quick succession).

- `void mousePressed(MouseEvent e)`

This method is called when a mouse button has been pressed.

- `void mouseReleased(MouseEvent e)`

This method is called when a mouse button has been released.

Class `java.awt.event.MouseEvent`

- `int getX()`

  This method returns the horizontal position of the mouse as of the time the event occurred.

  Returns: The *x*-position of the mouse.

- `int getY()`

  This method returns the vertical position of the mouse as of the time the event occurred.

  Returns: The *y*-position of the mouse.

Interface `java.awt.event.MouseListener`

- `void mouseClicked(MouseEvent e)`

  This method is called when the mouse has been clicked (that is, pressed and released in quick succession).

- `void mousePressed(MouseEvent e)`

  This method is called when a mouse button has been pressed.

- `void mouseReleased(MouseEvent e)`

  This method is called when a mouse button has been released.

Class `java.awt.event.WindowAdapter`

- `void windowClosing(WindowEvent e)`

  This method is called when a window is in the process of being closed. Override this method if you want to exit the program when the window is closed.

Interface `java.awt.event.WindowListener`

- `void windowClosing(WindowEvent e)`

  This method is called when a window is in the process of being closed. Override this method if you want to exit the program when the window is closed.

Package `java.awt.font`

Class `java.awt.font.FontRenderContext`

A font render context is an object that is used for measuring and drawing fonts. It is obtained by the `getFontRenderContext()` method of the `java.awt.Graphics2D` class and used by the `java.awt.font.TextLayout` constructor.

Class `java.awt.font.TextLayout`

- `TextLayout(String s, Font f, FontRenderContext context)`

  This constructs a text layout to measure and draw a string in a particular font.

Parameters:

> s—The string to lay out
>
> f—The font to use
>
> context—The font render context of the output device

- float getAdvance()

This method gets the total width of the string laid out by this TextLayout object.

Returns: The advance (width in pixels) of the string.

- float getAscent()

This method gets the height above the base line of the string laid out by this Text-Layout object.

Returns: The ascent of the string in pixels.

- float getDescent()

This method gets the depth below the base line of the string laid out by this Text-Layout object.

Returns: The descent of the string in pixels.

- float getLeading()

This method gets the distance between two lines in the font used by this Text-Layout object.

Returns: The leading of the font in pixels.

Package java.awt.geom

Class java.awt.geom.Ellipse2D.Double

- Ellipse2D.Double(double x, double y, double w, double h)

This constructs an ellipse from the specified coordinates.

Parameters:

> x,y—The top left corner of the bounding rectangle
>
> w—The width of the bounding rectangle
>
> h—The height of the bounding rectangle

Class java.awt.geom.Line2D

- double getX1()
- double getX2()
- double getY1()
- double getY2()

These methods get the requested coordinate of an endpoint of this line.

Returns: The *x*- or *y*-coordinate of the first or second endpoint.

● `void setLine(double x1, double y1, double x2, double y2)`

This methods sets the endpoints of this line.

Parameters:

> `x1,y1`—A new endpoint of this line
>
> `x2,y2`—The other new endpoint

Class `java.awt.geom.Line2D.Double`

● `Line2D.Double(double x1, double y1, double x2, double y2)`

This constructs a line from the specified coordinates.

Parameters:

> `x1, y1`—One endpoint of the line
>
> `x2, y2`—The other endpoint

● `Line2D.Double(Point2D p1, Point2D p2)`

This constructs a line from the two endpoints.

Parameters:

> `p1, p2`—The endpoints of the line

Class `java.awt.geom.Point2D`

● `double getX()`

● `double getY()`

These methods get the requested coordinates of this point.

Returns: The *x*- or *y*-coordinate of this point.

● `void setLocation(double x, double y)`

This method sets the *x*- and *y*-coordinates of this point.

Parameters:

> `x,y`—The new location of this point

Class `java.awt.geom.Point2D.Double`

● `Point2D.Double(double x, double y)`

This constructs a point with the specified coordinates.

Parameters:

> `x,y`—The coordinates of the point

Class `java.awt.geom.Rectangle2D.Double`

- `Rectangle2D.Double(double x, double y, double w, double h)`

  This constructs a rectangle.

  Parameters:

  > `x, y`—The upper left corner
  >
  > `w`—The width
  >
  > `h`—The height

Class `java.awt.geom.RectangularShape`

- `int getHeight()`
- `int getWidth()`

  These methods get the height or width of the bounding rectangle of this rectangular shape.

  Returns: The height or width, respectively.

- `double getCenterX()`
- `double getCenterY()`
- `double getMaxX()`
- `double getMaxY()`
- `double getMinX()`
- `double getMinY()`

  These methods get the requested coordinate value of the corners or center of the bounding rectangle of this shape.

  Returns: The minimum, center, or maximum *x*- and *y*-coordinates.

- `void setFrame(double x, double y, double w, double h)`

  This method sets the bounding rectangle of this rectangular shape.

  Parameters:

  > `x, y`—The upper left corner
  >
  > `w`—The width
  >
  > `h`—The height

- `void setFrameFromDiagonal(double x1, double y1, double x2, double y2)`

  This method sets the bounding rectangle of this rectangular shape.

  Parameters:

  > `x1, y1`—A corner point
  >
  > `x2, y2`—The diametrically opposite corner point

Package `java.io`

Class `java.io.BufferedReader`

- `BufferedReader(Reader in)`

  This constructs a buffered reader, an object that stores characters in a buffer for more efficient reading.

  Parameters:

  > `in`—A reader

- `String readLine()`

  This method reads a line of input from this buffered reader.

  Returns: The input line, or `null` if the end of input has been reached.

Class `java.io.EOFException`

- `EOFException(String message)`

  This constructs an "end of file" exception object.

  Parameters:

  > `message`—The detail message

Class `java.io.File`

This class describes a disk file or directory. Objects of this class are returned by the `getSelectedFile()` method of the `javax.swing.JFileChooser` class.

Class `java.io.FileInputStream`

- `FileInputStream(File f)`

  This constructs a file input stream and opens the chosen file. If the file cannot be opened for reading, a `FileNotFoundException` is thrown.

  Parameters:

  > `f`—The file to be opened for reading

- `FileInputStream(String name)`

  This constructs a file input stream and opens the named file. If the file cannot be opened for reading, a `FileNotFoundException` is thrown.

  Parameters:

  > `name`—The name of the file to be opened for reading

Class `java.io.FileNotFoundException`

This exception is thrown when a file could not be opened.

Class java.io.FileOutputStream

- FileOutputStream(File f)

  This constructs a file output stream and opens the chosen file. If the file cannot be opened for writing, a FileNotFoundException is thrown.

  Parameters:

  > f—The file to be opened for writing

- FileOutputStream(String name)

  This constructs a file output stream and opens the named file. If the file cannot be opened for writing, a FileNotFoundException is thrown.

  Parameters:

  > name—The name of the file to be opened for writing

Class java.io.FileReader

- FileReader(File f)

  This constructs a file reader and opens the chosen file. If the file cannot be opened for reading, a FileNotFoundException is thrown.

  Parameters:

  > f—The file to be opened for reading

- FileReader(String name)

  This constructs a file reader and opens the named file. If the file cannot be opened for reading, a FileNotFoundException is thrown.

  Parameters:

  > name—The name of the file to be opened for reading

Class java.io.FileWriter

- FileWriter(File f)

  This constructs a file writer and opens the chosen file. If the file cannot be opened for writing, a FileNotFoundException is thrown.

  Parameters:

  > f—The file to be opened for writing

- FileWriter(String name)

  This constructs a file writer and opens the named file. If the file cannot be opened for writing, a FileNotFoundException is thrown.

  Parameters:

  > name—The name of the file to be opened for writing

Class `java.io.InputStream`

- `void close()`

  This method closes this input stream (such as a `FileInputStream`) and releases any system resources associated with the stream.

- `int read()`

  This method reads the next byte of data from this input stream.

  Returns: The next byte of data, or −1 if the end of the stream is reached.

Class `java.io.InputStreamReader`

- `InputStreamReader(InputStream in)`

  This constructs a reader from a specified input stream.

  Parameters:

    `in`—The stream to read from

Class `java.io.IOException`

This type of exception is thrown when an input/output error is encountered.

Class **java.io.ObjectInputStream**

- `ObjectInputStream(InputStream in)`

  This constructs an object input stream.

  Parameters:

    `in`—The stream to read from

- `Object readObject()`

  This method reads the next object from this object input stream.

  Returns: The next object.

Class **java.io.ObjectOutputStream**

- `ObjectOutputStream(OutputStream out)`

  This constructs an object output stream.

  Parameters:

    `out`—The stream to write to

- `Object writeObject(Object obj)`

  This method writes the next object to this object output stream.

  Parameters:

    `obj`—The object to write

Class `java.io.OutputStream`

- `void close()`

  This method closes this output stream (such as a `FileOutputStream`) and releases any system resources associated with this stream. A closed stream cannot perform output operations and cannot be reopened.

- `void write(int b)`

  This method writes the lowest byte of b to this output stream.

  Parameters:

  > b—The integer whose lowest byte is written

Class `java.io.PrintStream`

- `void print(int x)`
- `void print(double x)`
- `void print(Object x)`
- `void print(String x)`
- `void println()`
- `void println(int x)`
- `void println(double x)`
- `void println(Object x)`
- `void println(String x)`

  These methods print a value to this print stream. The `println` methods print a newline after the value. Objects are printed by converting them to strings with their `toString` methods.

  Parameters:

  > x—The value to be printed

Class `java.io.PrintWriter`

- `PrintWriter(Writer out)`

  This constructs a print writer from a specified writer (such as a `FileWriter`).

  Parameters:

  > out—The writer to write output to

- `void print(int x)`
- `void print(double x)`
- `void print(Object x)`
- `void print(String x)`
- `void println()`

- void println(int x)
- void println(double x)
- void println(Object x)
- void println(String x)

These methods print a value to this print writer. The println methods print a newline after the value. Objects are printed by converting them to strings with their toString methods.

Parameters:

x—The value to be printed

Class java.io.RandomAccessFile

- RandomAccessFile(String name, String mode)

This method opens a named random access file for reading or read/write access.

Parameters:

name—The file name

mode—"r" for reading or "rw" for read/write access

- long getFilePointer()

This method gets the current position in this file.

Returns: The current position for reading and writing.

- long length()

This method gets the length of this file.

Returns: The file length.

- char readChar()
- double readDouble()
- int readInt()

These methods read a value from the current position in this file.

Returns: The value that was read from the file.

- void seek(long position)

This method sets the position for reading and writing in this file.

Parameters:

position—The new position

- void writeChar(int x)
- void writeChars(String x)

- void writeDouble(double x)
- void writeInt(int x)

These methods write a value to the current position in this file.

Parameters:

x—The value to be written

Class java.io.Reader

- int read()

This method reads the next character from this reader (such as a FileReader).

Returns: The next character, or −1 if the end of the input is reached.

Interface java.io.Serializable

A class must implement this interface to enable its objects to be written to object streams.

Class java.io.Writer

- void write(int b)

This method writes the lowest two bytes of b to this writer (such as a File-Writer).

Parameters:

b—The integer whose lowest two bytes are written

Package java.lang

Class java.lang.Boolean

- Boolean(boolean value)

This constructs a wrapper object for a boolean value.

Parameters:

value—The value to store in this object

- boolean booleanValue()

This method returns the boolean value stored in this Boolean object.

Returns: The Boolean value of this object.

Class java.lang.Class

- static Class forName(String className)

This method loads a class with a given name. Loading a class initializes its static fields.

Parameters:

> className—The name of the class to load

Returns: The type descriptor of the class.

Interface java.lang.Cloneable

A class implements this interface to indicate that the Object.clone method is allowed to make a shallow copy of its instance variables.

Class java.lang.CloneNotSupportedException

This exception is thrown when a program tries to use Object.clone to make a shallow copy of an object of a class that does not implement the Cloneable interface.

Interface java.lang.Comparable

- int compareTo(Object other)

This method compares this object with the other object.

Parameters:

> other—The object to be compared

Returns: A negative integer if this object is less than the other, zero if they are equal, or a positive integer otherwise.

Class java.lang.Double

- Double(double value)

This constructs a wrapper object for a double-precision floating-point number.

Parameters:

> value—The value to store in this object

- double doubleValue()

This method returns the floating-point value stored in this Double wrapper object.

Returns: The value stored in the object.

- static double parseDouble(String s)

This method returns the floating-point number that the string represents. If the string cannot be interpreted as a number, a NumberFormatException is thrown.

Parameters:

> s—The string to be parsed

Returns: The value represented by the string parameter.

- `static String toString(double x)`

This method converts a number to a string representation.

Parameters:

x—The number to be converted

Returns: The string representing the number parameter.

Class `java.lang.Error`

This is the superclass for all unchecked system errors.

Class `java.lang.Float`

- `static float parseFloat(String s)`

This method returns the single-precision floating-point number that the string represents. If the string cannot be interpreted as such a number, a `NumberFormat-Exception` is thrown.

Parameters:

s—The string to be parsed

Returns: The value represented by the string parameter.

Class `java.lang.IllegalArgumentException`

- `IllegalArgumentException()`

This constructs an `IllegalArgumentException` with no detail message.

Class `java.lang.Integer`

- `Integer(int value)`

This constructs a wrapper object for an integer.

Parameters:

value—The value to store in this object.

- `int intValue()`

This method returns the integer value stored in this wrapper object.

Returns: The value stored in the object.

- `static int parseInt(String s)`

This method returns the integer that the string represents. If the string cannot be interpreted as an integer, a `NumberFormatException` is thrown.

Parameters:

s—The string to be parsed

Returns: The value represented by the string parameter.

- `static Integer parseInt(String s,int base)`

This method returns the integer value that the string represents in a given number system. If the string cannot be interpreted as an integer, a `NumberFormat-Exception` is thrown.

Parameters:

> s—The string to be parsed
>
> base—The base of the number system (such as 2 or 16)

Returns: The value represented by the string parameter.

- `static String toString(int i)`
- `static String toString(int i, int base)`

This method creates a string representation of an integer in a given number system. If no base is given, a decimal representation is created.

Parameters:

> i—An integer number
>
> base—The base of the number system (such as 2 or 16)

Returns: A string representation of the number parameter in the specified number system.

- `static final int MAX_VALUE`

This constant is the largest value of type `int`.

- `static final int MIN_VALUE`

This constant is the smallest (negative) value of type `int`.

Class `java.lang.InterruptedException`

This exception is thrown to interrupt a thread, usually with the intent of terminating it.

Class `java.lang.Math`

- `static double abs(double x)`

This method returns the absolute value $|x|$.

Parameters:

> x—A floating-point value

Returns: The absolute value of the parameter.

- `static double acos(double x)`

This method returns the angle with the given cosine, $\cos^{-1} x \in [0, \pi]$.

Parameters:

> x—A floating-point value between −1 and 1

Returns: The arc cosine of the parameter, in radians.

- `static double asin(double x)`

  This method returns the angle with the given sine, $\sin^{-1} x \in [-\pi/2, \pi/2]$.

  Parameters:

  x—A floating-point value between −1 and 1

  Returns: The arc sine of the parameter, in radians.

- `static double atan(double x)`

  This method returns the angle with the given tangent, $\tan^{-1} x$ $(-\pi/2, \pi/2)$.

  Parameters:

  x—A floating-point value

  Returns: The arc tangent of the parameter, in radians.

- `static double atan2(double y, double x)`

  This method returns the arc tangent, $\tan^{-1} (y/x) \in (-\pi, \pi)$. If x can equal zero, or if it is necessary to distinguish "northwest" from "southeast" and "northeast" from "southwest", use this method instead of `atan(y/x)`.

  Parameters:

  y,x—Two floating-point values

  Returns: The angle, in radians, between the points (0,0) and (x,y).

- `static double ceil(double x)`

  This method returns the smallest integer $\leq x$ (as a `double`).

  Parameters:

  x—A floating-point value

  Returns: The "ceiling integer" of the parameter.

- `static double cos(double radians)`

  This method returns the cosine of an angle given in radians.

  Parameters:

  radians—An angle, in radians

  Returns: The cosine of the parameter.

- `static double exp(double x)`

  This method returns the value e^x, where e is the base of the natural logarithms.

  Parameters:

  x—A floating-point value

  Returns: e^x.

- `static double floor(double x)`

  This method returns the largest integer $\geq x$ (as a `double`).

  Parameters:

  x—A floating-point value

  Returns: The "floor integer" of the parameter.

- `static double log(double x)`

  This method returns the natural (base *e*) logarithm of *x*, ln *x*.

  Parameters:

    x—A number greater than 0.0

  Returns: The natural logarithm of the parameter.

- `static int max(int x, int y)`
- `static double max(double x, double y)`

  This method returns the larger of the given parameter values.

  Parameters:

    x, y—Two integers or floating-point values

  Returns: The maximum of the parameter values.

- `static int min(int x, int y)`
- `static double min(double x, double y)`

  This method returns the smaller of the given parameter values.

  Parameters:

    x, y—Two integers or floating-point values

  Returns: The minimum of the parameter values.

- `static double pow(double x, double y)`

  This method returns the value x^y ($x > 0$, or $x = 0$ and $y > 0$, or $x < 0$ and y is an integer).

  Parameters:

    x,y   Two floating point values

  Returns: The value of the first parameter raised to the power of the second parameter.

- `static long round(double x)`

  This method returns the closest `long` integer to the parameter.

  Parameters:

    x—A floating-point value

  Returns: The value of the parameter rounded to the nearest `long` value.

- `static double sin(double radians)`

  This method returns the sine of an angle given in radians.

  Parameters:

    radians—An angle, in radians

  Returns: The sine of the parameter.

- `static double sqrt(double x)`

  This method returns the square root of *x*, $\sqrt{x}$.

  Parameters:

    x—A nonnegative floating-point value

  Returns: The square root of the parameter.

- `static double tan(double radians)`

  This method returns the tangent of an angle given in radians.

  Parameters:

    `radians`—An angle, in radians

  Returns: The tangent of the parameter.

- `static double toDegrees(double radian)`

  This method converts radians to degrees.

  Parameters:

    `radians`—An angle, in radians

  Returns: The angle in degrees.

- `static double toRadians(double degrees)`

  This methods converts degrees to radians.

  Parameters:

    `degrees`—An angle, in degrees

  Returns: The angle in radians.

- `static final double E`

  This constant is the value of *e*, the base of the natural logarithms.

- `static final double PI`

  This constant is the value of π.

Class `java.lang.NullPointerException`

This exception is thrown when a program tries to use an object through a `null` reference.

Class `java.lang.NumberFormatException`

This exception is thrown when a program tries to parse the numerical value of a string that is not a number.

Class `java.lang.Object`

- `protected Object clone()`

  This method constructs and returns a shallow copy of this object whose instance variables are copies of the instance variables of this object. If an instance variable of the object is an object reference itself, only the reference is copied, not the object itself. However, if the class does not implement the `Cloneable` interface, a `CloneNotSupportedException` is thrown. Subclasses should redefine this method to make a deep copy.

  Returns: A copy of this object.

- `boolean equals(Object other)`

  This method tests whether `this` and the other object are equal. This method tests only whether the object references are to the same object. Subclasses should redefine this method to compare the instance variables.

  Parameters:

  > `other`—The object with which to compare

  Returns: `true` if the objects are equal, `false` otherwise.

- `void notify()`

  This method notifies one of the threads that is currently on the wait list for the lock of this object.

- `void notifyAll()`

  This method notifies all of the threads that are currently on the wait list for the lock of this object.

- `String toString()`

  This method returns a string representation of this object. This method produces only the class name and locations of the objects. Subclasses should redefine this method to print the instance variables.

  Returns: A string describing this object.

- `void wait()`

  This method blocks the currently executing thread and puts it on the wait list for the lock of this object.

Class `java.lang.RuntimeException`

This is the superclass for all unchecked exceptions.

Class `java.lang.String`

- `int compareTo(String other)`

  This method compares this string and the other string lexicographically.

  Parameters:

  > `other`—The other string to be compared

  Returns: A value less than 0 if this string is lexicographically less than the other, 0 if the strings are equal, and a value greater than 0 otherwise.

- `boolean equals(String other)`
- `boolean equalsIgnoreCase(String other)`

  These methods test whether two strings are equal, or whether they are equal when letter case is ignored.

Parameters:

> other—The other string to be compared

Returns: `true` if the strings are equal.

- `int length()`

This method returns the length of this string.

Returns: The count of characters in this string.

- `String substring(int begin)`
- `String substring(int begin, int pastEnd)`

These methods return a new string that is a substring of this string, made up of all characters starting at position `begin` and up to either position `pastEnd - 1` is given, or the end of the string.

Parameters:

> begin—The beginning index, inclusive
>
> pastEnd—The ending index, exclusive

Returns: The specified substring.

- `String toLowerCase()`

This method returns a new string that consists of all characters in this string converted to lowercase.

Returns: A string with all characters of this string converted to lowercase.

- `String toUpperCase()`

This method returns a new string that consists of all characters in this string converted to uppercase.

Returns: A string with all characters of this string converted to uppercase.

Class `java.lang.System`

- `static void arraycopy(Object from, int fromStart, Object to, int toStart, int count)`

This method copies values from one array to the other. (The array parameters are of type `Object` because you can convert an array of numbers to an `Object` but not to an `Object[]`.)

Parameters:

> from—The source array
>
> fromStart—Start position in the source array
>
> to—The destination array
>
> toStart—Start position in the destination data
>
> count—The number of array elements to be copied

- `static long currentTimeMillis()`

This method returns the difference, measured in milliseconds, between the current time and midnight, Universal Time, January 1, 1970.

Returns: The current time in milliseconds.

- `static void exit(int status)`

This method terminates the program.

Parameters:

> `status`—exit status. A nonzero status code indicates abnormal termination.

- `static final InputStream in`

This object is the "standard input" stream. Reading from this stream typically reads keyboard input.

- `static final PrintStream out`

This object is the "standard output" stream. Printing to this stream typically sends output to the console window.

Class `java.lang.Thread`

- `static Thread currentThread()`

This method gets the thread object that represents the thread that executes this method call.

Returns: The current thread.

- `boolean isInterrupted()`

This method tests whether another thread has called the `interrupt` method on this thread.

Returns: `true` if the thread has been interrupted.

- `void run()`

This method should be overridden by subclasses of the `Thread` class. When the thread is started, this method is executed.

- `static void sleep(int millis)`

This method puts the calling thread to sleep.

Parameters:

> `millis`—the number of millseconds to sleep

- `void start()`

This method starts the thread and executes its `run` method.

Class `java.lang.Throwable`

This is the superclass of exceptions and errors.

- `Throwable()`

  This constructs a `Throwable` with no detail message.

- `void printStackTrace()`

  This method prints a stack trace to the "standard error" stream. The stack trace contains a printout of this object and of all calls that were pending at the time it was created.

Package `java.math`

Class `java.math.BigDecimal`

- `BigDecimal(String value)`

  This constructs an arbitrary-precision floating-point number from the digits in the given string.

  Parameters:

  > `value`—A string representing the floating-point number

- `BigDecimal add(BigDecimal other)`
- `BigDecimal subtract(BigDecimal other)`
- `BigDecimal multiply(BigDecimal other)`
- `BigDecimal divide(BigDecimal other, int roundingMode)`

  These methods return a `BigDecimal` whose value is the sum, difference, product, or quotient of this number and the other.

  Parameters:

  > `other`—The other number
  >
  > `roundingMode`—The rounding mode to apply to division (use `BigDecimal-.ROUND_HALF_EVEN` for general-purpose calculations)

  Returns: The result of the arithmetic operation.

Class `java.math.BigInteger`

- `BigInteger(String value)`

  This method constructs an arbitrary-precision integer from the digits in the given string.

  Parameters:

  > `value`—A string representing an arbitrary-precision integer

- `BigInteger add(BigInteger other)`
- `BigInteger subtract(BigInteger other)`

- `BigInteger multiply(BigInteger other)`
- `BigInteger divide(BigInteger other)`
- `BigInteger mod(BigInteger other)`

These methods return a `BigInteger` whose value is the sum, difference, product, quotient, or remainder of this number and the other.

Parameters:

    `other`—The other number

Returns: The result of the arithmetic operation.

Package `java.net`

Class `java.net.HttpURLConnection`

- `int getResponseCode()`

This method gets the response status code from this connection. A value of `HTTP_OK` indicates success.

Returns: The HTTP response code.

- `String getResponseMessage()`

This method gets the response message of this connection's HTTP request.

Returns: The message, such as `"OK"` or `"File not found"`

- `static int HTTP_OK`

This response code indicates a successful fulfillment of the request.

Class `java.net.ServerSocket`

- `ServerSocket(int port)`

This constructs a server socket that listens to the given port.

Parameters:

    `port`—The port number to listen to

- `Socket accept()`

This method waits for a client to connect to the port to which this server socket listens. When a connection occurs, the method returns a socket through which the server can communicate with the client.

Returns: The socket through which the server can communicate with the client.

- `void close()`

This method closes the server socket. Clients can no longer connect.

Class `java.net.Socket`

- `Socket(String host, int port)`

  This constructs a socket that connects to a server.

  Parameters:

  > `host`—The host name
  >
  > `port`—The port number to connect to

- `void close()`

  This method closes the connection with the server.

- `InputStream getInputStream()`

  This method gets the input stream through which the client can read the information that the server sends.

  Returns: The input stream associated with this socket.

- `OutputStream getOutputStream()`

  This method gets the output stream through which the client can send information to the server.

  Returns: The output stream associated with this socket.

Class `java.net.URL`

- `URL(String s)`

  This constructs an URL object from a string containing the URL.

  Parameters:

  > `s`—The URL string, such as `"http://java.sun.com/index.html"`

- `InputStream openConnection()`

  This method gets the input stream through which the client can read the information that the server sends.

  Returns: The input stream associated with this URL.

Class `java.net.URLConnection`

- `URLConnection(URL u)`

  This constructs an `URLConnection` object from an URL object.

  Parameters:

  > `u`—The resource to which you intend to connect

- `int getContentLength()`

This method gets the value of the `content-length` header of this URL connection.

Returns: The number of bytes in the content that the server is sending.

- `String getContentType()`

This method gets the value of the `content-type` header of this URL connection.

Returns: The MIME type of the content that the server is sending, such as `"text/plain"` or `"image/gif"`.

- `InputStream getInputStream()`

This method gets the input stream through which the client can read the information that the server sends.

Returns: The input stream associated with this URL.

- `OutputStream getOutputStream()`

This method gets the output stream through which the client can send information to the server.

Returns: The output stream associated with this socket.

- `void setDoOutput(boolean b)`

This method sets the output mode of this connection. By default, connections are not enabled for output.

Parameters:

> b—`true` to enable the sending of data to the server

- `void setIfModifiedSince(Date d)`

This method instructs the connection to request that the server send data only if the content has been modified since a given date.

Parameters:

> d—The modification date

Class `java.net.URLDecoder`

- `static String decode(String s)`

This method decodes an URL-encoded string.

Parameters:

> s—The string to decode

Returns: The decoded string.

Class `java.net.URLEncoder`

- `static String encode(String s)`

  This method URL-encodes a string.

  Parameters:

  > s—The string to encode

  Returns: The encoded string.

Package `java.sql`

Interface `java.sql.Connection`

- `void close()`

  This method closes the connection with the database.

- `void close()`

  This method commits all database changes since the last call to `commit` or `rollback`.

- `Statement createStatement()`

  This method creates a statement object, which can be used to issue database commands.

  Returns: A statement object.

- `CallableStatement prepareCall(String command)`

  This method creates a callable SQL statement for a stored procedure call.

  Parameters:

  > command—The command to call the procedure

  Returns: The SQL statement object for setting parameters and executing the call.

- `PreparedStatement prepareStatement(String command)`

  This method creates a prepared statement for a SQL command that is issued repeatedly.

  Parameters:

  > command—The SQL command

  Returns: The statement object for setting parameters and executing the call.

- `void close()`

  This method abandons all database changes since the last call to `commit` or `rollback`.

- void setAutoCommit(boolean b)

This method sets the auto commit mode. By default, it is true. If it is set to false, then transactions are indicated with calls to commit or rollback. Creates a prepared statement for a SQL command that is issued repeatedly.

Parameters:

> command—The SQL command
>
> b—The desired auto commit mode

Class java.sql.DriverManager

- static Connection getConnection(String url, String username, String password)

This method obtains a connection to the database specified in the database URL.

Parameters:

> url—The database URL
>
> username—The database user name
>
> password—The password for the database user

Returns: A connection to the database.

Interface java.sql.PreparedStatement

- boolean execute()

This method executes this prepared statement.

Returns: true if the execution yielded a result set.

- ResultSet executeQuery()

This method executes this prepared query.

Returns: The query result.

- int executeUpdate()

This method executes this prepared update command.

Returns: The number of records affected by the update.

- void setDouble(int index, double value)

This method sets a floating-point parameter for a call of this prepared statement.

Parameters:

> index—The parameter index (starting with 1)
>
> value—The parameter value

- void setInt(int index, int value)

This method sets an integer parameter for a call of this prepared statement.

Parameters:

> index—The parameter index (starting with 1)
>
> value—The parameter value

- void setString(int index, String value)

This method sets a parameter for a call of this prepared statement.

Parameters:

> index—The parameter index (starting with 1)
>
> value—The parameter value

Interface java.sql.ResultSet

- boolean absolute(int row)

This method positions the cursor to a row with a given row index. This method works only for scrollable result sets.

Parameters:

> row—The row index (starting with index 1), or, if negative, the row index from the last row (starting with −1)

Returns: true if the cursor has been positioned on a row.

- boolean relative(int rows)

This method positions the cursor to a row that is a given distance away from the current row. This method works only for scrollable result sets.

Parameters:

> rows—The number of rows to move the cursor

Returns: true if the cursor has been positioned on a row.

- void close()

This method closes the result set.

- boolean first()

This method positions the cursor to the first row. This method works only for scrollable result sets.

Returns: true if the cursor has been positioned on a row.

- int getDouble(int column)

This method returns the floating-point value at the cursor row and the given column.

Parameters:

   column—The column index (starting with 1)

Returns: The data value.

- `int getDouble(String columnName)`

This method returns the floating-point value at the cursor row and the given column.

Parameters:

   columnName—The column name

Returns: The data value.

- `int getInt(int column)`

This method returns the integer value at the cursor row and the given column.

Parameters:

   column—The column index (starting with 1)

Returns: The data value.

- `int getInt(String columnName)`

This method returns the integer value at the cursor row and the given column.

Parameters:

   columnName—The column name

Returns: The data value

- `ResultSetMetaData getMetaData()`

This method returns the meta data associated with this result set.

Returns: The meta data.

- `String getString(int column)`

This method returns the value at the cursor row and the given column.

Parameters:

   column—The column index (starting with 1)

Returns: The data value, as a string.

- `int getString(String columnName)`

This method returns the value at the cursor row and the given column.

Parameters:

   columnName—The column name

Returns: The data value, as a string.

- boolean last()

This method positions the cursor to the last row. This method works only for scrollable result sets.

Returns: true if the cursor has been positioned on a row.

- void moveToInsertRow()

This method positions the cursor to the insert row. This method works only for updatable result sets.

- boolean next()

This method positions the cursor to the next row. You must call next once before calling any of the get methods to move the cursor to the first row.

Returns: true if the cursor has been positioned on a row, false at the end of the result set.

- boolean previous()

This method positions the cursor to the previous row. This method works only for scrollable result sets.

Returns: true if the cursor has been positioned on a row.

- void updateDouble(int column, double value)

This method updates the floating-point value at the cursor row and the given column. This method works only for updatable result sets.

Parameters:

   column—The column index (starting with 1)

   value—The new value

- void updateDouble(String columnName, double value)

This method updates the floating-point value at the cursor row and the given column. This method works only for updatable result sets.

Parameters:

   columnName—The column name

   value—The new value

- void updateInt(int column, int value)

This method updates the integer value at the cursor row and the given column. This method works only for updatable result sets.

Parameters:

   column—The column index (starting with 1)

   value—The new value

- `void updateInt(String columnName, int value)`

This method updates the integer value at the cursor row and the given column. This method works only for updatable result sets.

Parameters:

> `columnName`—The column name
>
> `value`—The new value

- `void updateRow()`

This method saves the changes in the current row to the database. This method works only for updatable result sets.

- `void updateString(int column, String value)`

This method updates the value at the cursor row and the given column. This method works only for updatable result sets.

Parameters:

> `column`—The column index (starting with 1)
>
> `value`—The new value

- `void updateString(String columnName, String value)`

This method updates the value at the cursor row and the given column. This method works only for updatable result sets.

Parameters:

> `columnName`—The column name
>
> `value`—The new value

Interface `java.sql.ResultSetMetaData`

- `void getColumnCount()`

This method returns the number of columns of this result set.

Returns: the number of columns.

- `int getColumnDisplaySize(int column)`

This method returns the number of characters that should be used to display the specified column in this result set.

Parameters:

> `column`—The column index (starting with 1)

Returns: The number of characters that should be used to display this column.

- `String getColumnLabel(int column)`

This method returns the label for a column in this result set.

Parameters:

       `column`—The column index (starting with 1)

Returns: The column label.

Class `java.sql.SQLException`

This exception is thrown when a database error occurs.

Interface `java.sql.Statement`

- `void close()`

  This method closes this statement.

- `boolean execute(String command)`

  This method executes a SQL command.

  Parameters:

         `command`—The command to execute

  Returns: `true` if the execution yielded a result set.

- `ResultSet executeQuery(String command)`

  This method executes a SQL query.

  Parameters:

         `command`—The query command to execute

  Returns: The query result.

- `int executeUpdate(String command)`

  This method executes a SQL update command.

  Parameters:

         `command`—The update command to execute

  Returns: The number of records affected by the update.

- `ResultSet getResultSet()`

  This method gets the result of the last command.

  Returns: The query result from the last command.

- `int getUpdateCount()`

  This method gets the update count of the last command.

  Returns: The number of records affected by the last command.

Package `java.text`

Class `java.text.DateFormat`

- `String format(Date aDate)`

  This method formats a date.

  Parameters:

  > aDate—The date to format

  Returns: A string containing the formatted date.

- `static DateFormat getTimeInstance()`

  This method returns a formatter that formats only the time portion of a date.

  Returns: The formatter object.

- `void setTimeZone(TimeZone zone)`

  This method sets the time zone to be used when formatting dates.

  Parameters:

  > zone—The time zone to use

Class `java.text.NumberFormat`

- `String format(double x)`

  This method formats a number according to the formatting rules of this object

  Parameters:

  > x—The number to format

  Returns: A string representing x.

- `static NumberFormat getCurrencyInstance()`

  This method returns a currency formatter, which formats numbers with a currency symbol and a fixed number of fractional digits.

- `static NumberFormat getNumberInstance()`

  This method returns a number formatter, which formats numbers with decimal separators and a user-selectable number of fractional digits.

- `void setMaximumFractionDigits(int digits)`

  This method sets the maximum number of fraction digits used when formatting numbers. Numbers will be rounded if they have more digits.

  Parameters:

  > digits—The maximum number of to digits to use

- void setMinimumFractionDigits(int digits)

This method sets the minimum number of fraction digits used when formatting numbers. Formatted numbers are padded with trailing zeroes if they have fewer digits.

Parameters:

digits—The minimum number of digits to use

Package java.util

Class java.util.ArrayList

- ArrayList()

This constructs an empty array list.

- boolean add(Object element)

This method appends an element to the end of this array list.

Parameters:

element—The element to add

Returns: true. (This method returns a value because it overrides a method in the List interface.)

- void add(int index, Object element)

This method inserts an element into this array list.

Parameters:

index—Insert position

element—The element to insert

- void copyInto(Object[] array)

This method copies the components of this array list into an array. The array must be big enough to hold all the objects in this array list.

Parameters:

array—The array into which the components get copied

- Object get(int index)

This method gets the element at the specified position in this array list.

Parameters:

index—Position of the element to return

Returns: The requested element.

- `Object remove(int index)`

  This method removes the element at the specified position in this array list and returns it.

  Parameters:

  > `index`—Position of the element to remove

  Returns: The removed element.

- `Object set(int index, Object element)`

  This method replaces the element at a specified position in this array list.

  Parameters:

  > `index`—Position of element to replace

  > `element`—Element to be stored at the specified position

  Returns: The element previously at the specified position.

- `int size()`

  This method returns the number of elements in this array list.

  Returns: The number of elements in this array list.

Class `java.util.Arrays`

- `static int binarySearch(Object[] a, Object key)`

  This method searches the specified array for the specified object using the binary search algorithm. The array elements must implement the `Comparable` interface. The array must be sorted in ascending order.

  Parameters:

  > `a`—The array to be searched
  > `key`—The value to be searched for

  Returns: The position of the search key, if it is contained in the list; otherwise, −*index* − 1, where *index* is the position where the element may be inserted.

- `static void sort(Object[] a)`

  This method sorts the specified array of objects into ascending order. Its elements must implement the `Comparable` interface.

  Parameters:

  > `a`—The array to be sorted

Interface `java.util.Collection`

- `boolean add(Object element)`

  This method adds an element to this collection.

Parameters:

element—The element to add

Returns: true if adding the element changes the collection.

- boolean contains(Object element)

This method tests whether an element is present in this collection.

Parameters:

element—The element to find

Returns: true if the element is contained in the collection.

- Iterator iterator()

This method returns an iterator that can be used to traverse the elements of this collection.

Returns: An object of a class implementing the Iterator interface.

- boolean remove(Object element)

This method removes an element from this collection.

Parameters:

element—The element to remove

Returns: true if removing the element changes the collection.

- int size()

This method returns the number of elements in this collection.

Returns: The number of elements in this collection.

Class java.util.EventObject

- Object getSource()

This method returns a reference to the object on which this event initially occurred.

Returns: The source of this event.

Class java.util.HashMap

- HashMap()

This constructs an empty hash map.

Class java.util.HashSet

- HashSet()

This constructs an empty hash set.

Interface java.util.Iterator

- boolean hasNext()

  This method checks whether the iterator is past the end of the list.

  Returns: true if the iterator is not yet past the end of the list.

- Object next()

  This method moves the iterator over the next element in the linked list. This method throws an exception if the iterator is past the end of the list.

  Returns: The object that was just skipped over.

- void remove()

  This method removes the element that was returned by the last call to next or previous. This method throws an exception if there was an add or remove operation after the last call to next or previous.

Interface java.util.List

- ListIterator listIterator()

  This method gets an iterator to visit the elements in this list.

  Returns: An iterator that points before the first element in this list.

Interface java.util.ListIterator

Objects implementing this interface are created by the listIterator methods of list classes.

- void add(Object element)

  This method adds an element after the iterator position and moves the iterator after the new element.

  Parameters:

  element—The element to be added

- boolean hasPrevious()

  This method checks whether the iterator is before the first element of the list.

  Returns: true if the iterator is not before the first element of the list.

- Object previous()

  This method moves the iterator over the previous element in the linked list. This method throws an exception if the iterator is before the first element of the list.

  Returns: The object that was just skipped over.

Class java.util.LinkedList

- void addFirst(Object element)
- void addLast(Object element)

These methods add an element before the first or after the last element in this list.

Parameters:

> `element`—The element to be added

- `Object getFirst()`
- `Object getLast()`

These methods return a reference to the specified element from this list.

Returns: The first or last element.

- `Object removeFirst()`
- `Object removeLast()`

These methods remove the specified element from this list.

Returns: A reference to the removed element.

Interface `java.util.Map`

- `Object get(Object key)`

Gets the value associated with a key in this map.

Parameters:

> `key`—The key for which to find the associated value

Returns: The value associated with the key, or `null` if the key is not present in the table.

- `Set keySet()`

This method returns all keys in the table of this map.

Returns: A set of all keys in the table of this map.

- `Object put(Object key, Object value)`

This method associates a value with a key in this map.

Parameters:

> `key`—The lookup key
> `value`—The value to associate with the key

Returns: The value previously associated with the key, or `null` if the key was not present in the table.

- `Object remove(Object key)`

This method removes a key and its associated value from this map.

Parameters:

> `key`—The lookup key

Returns: The value previously associated with the key, or `null` if the key was not present in the table.

Class `java.util.Properties`

- `String getProperty(Object key)`

  This method gets the value associated with a key in this properties map.

  Parameters:

    key—The key for which to find the associated value

  Returns: The value, or `null` if the key is not present in the table.

- `void load(InputStream in)`

  This method loads a set of key/value pairs into this properties map from a stream.

  Parameters:

    in—The stream from which to read the key/value pairs (it must be a sequence of lines of the form `key=value`)

Class `java.util.Random`

- `Random()`

  This constructs a new random number generator.

- `double nextDouble()`

  This method returns the next pseudorandom, uniformly distributed floating-point number between 0.0 (inclusive) and 1.0 (exclusive) from this random number generator's sequence.

  Returns: The next pseudorandom floating-point number.

- `int nextInt(int n)`

  This method returns the next pseudorandom, uniformly distributed integer between 0 (inclusive) and the specified value (exclusive) drawn from this random number generator's sequence.

  Parameters:

    n—Number of values to draw from

  Returns: The next pseudorandom integer.

Class `java.util.StringTokenizer`

- `StringTokenizer(String s)`

  This constructs a string tokenizer that breaks the specified string into tokens. Tokens are delimited by white space.

  Parameters:

    s—The string to break up into tokens

- `int countTokens()`

This method counts the number of tokens in the string being processed by this tokenizer.

Returns: The token count.

`boolean hasMoreTokens()`

This method checks whether all tokens in the string being processed by this tokenizer have been skipped over by `nextToken()`.

Returns: `true` if more tokens are available.

- `String nextToken()`

This method skips over and returns the next token in the string being processed by this tokenizer.

Returns: A string containing the token that was just skipped over.

Class `java.util.TimeZone`

- `static String[] getAvailableIDs()`

This method gets the supported time zone IDs.

Returns: An array of ID strings.

- `static TimeZone getTimeZone(String id)`

This method gets the time zone for a time zone ID.

Parameters:

> id—The time zone ID, such as `"America/Los_Angeles"`

Returns: The time zone object associated with the ID, or `null` if the ID is not supported.

Class `java.util.TreeMap`

- `TreeMap()`

This constructs an empty tree map.

Class `java.util.TreeSet`

- `TreeSet()`

This constructs an empty tree set.

Package `java.util.logging`

Class `java.util.logging.Level`

- `static final int ALL`

This value indicates logging of all messages.

- static final int INFO

  This value indicates informational logging.

- static final int NONE

  This value indicates logging of no messages.

Class java.util.logging.Logger

- static Logger getLogger(String id)

  This method gets the logger for a given ID. Use the ID "global" to get the default global logger.

  Parameters:

  > id—the logger ID such as "global" or "com.mycompany.mymodule"

  Returns: The logger with the given ID.

- void info(String message)

  This method logs an informational message.

  Parameters:

  > message—The message to log

- void setLevel(Level aLevel)

  This method sets the logging level. Logging messages with a lesser severity than the current level are ignored.

  Parameters:

  > aLevel—The minimum level for logging messages

Package javax.servlet

Interface javax.servlet.ServletContext

- String getInitParameter(String key)

  This method retrieves an initialization parameter. Details depend on the configuration mechanism of the servlet container.

  Parameters:

  > key—The key for looking up the parameter

  Returns: The parameter value, or null if no such parameter exists.

Interface javax.servlet.ServletRequest

- String getParameter(String name)

  This method retrieves a request parameter.

Parameters:

name—The parameter name

Returns: The parameter value, or **null** if no such parameter exists.

Interface `javax.servlet.ServletResponse`

- `PrintWriter getWriter()`

This method retrieves the writer to which this servlet sends its output.

Returns: The writer.

- `void setContentType(String type)`

This method sets the content type of this servlet's output.

Parameters:

type—The MIME type, such as `"text/plain"` or `"image/gif"`

Package `javax.servlet.http`

Class `javax.servlet.http.HttpServlet`

- `void doGet(HttpServletRequest request, HttpServletResponse response)`

You should override this method in servlet subclasses. It is called whenever a client issues an HTTP GET request.

Parameters:

request—The request data

response—The response data

- `void doPost(HttpServletRequest request, HttpServletResponse response)`

You should override this method in servlet subclasses. It is called whenever a client issues an HTTP POST request.

Parameters:

request—The request data

response—The response data

Package `javax.swing`

Class `javax.swing.AbstractButton`

- `void addActionListener(ActionListener listener)`

This method adds an action listener to the button.

Parameters:

> listener—The action listener to be added

- boolean isSelected()

This method returns the selection state of the button.

Returns: true if the button is selected.

- void setSelected(boolean state)

This method sets the selection state of the button. This method updates the button but does not trigger an action event.

Parameters:

> state—true to select, false to deselect

Class javax.swing.ButtonGroup

- void add(AbstractButton button)

This method adds the button to the group.

Parameters:

> button—The button to add

Class javax.swing.ImageIcon

- ImageIcon(String filename)

This constructs an image icon from the specified graphics file.

Parameters:

> filename—A string specifying a file name

Class javax.swing.JApplet

- Container getContentPane()

This method returns the content pane of this applet.

Returns: The content pane.

Class javax.swing.JCheckBox

- JCheckBox(String text)

This constructs a check box, having the given text, initially deselected. (Use the set-Selected() method to make the box selected; see the javax.swing.Abstract-Button class.)

Parameters:

> text—The text displayed next to the check box

Class `javax.swing.JComboBox`

- `JComboBox()`

  This constructs a combo box with no items.

- `void addItem(Object item)`

  This method adds an item to the item list of this combo box.

  Parameters:

     `item`–The item to add

- `Object getSelectedItem()`

  This method gets the currently selected item of this combo box.

  Returns: The currently selected item.

- `boolean isEditable()`

  This method checks whether the combo box is editable. An editable combo box allows the user to type into the text field of the combo box.

  Returns: `true` if the combo box is editable.

- `void setEditable(boolean state)`

  This method is used to make the combo box editable or not.

  Parameters:

     `state`—`true` to make editable, `false` to disable editing

Class `javax.swing.JComponent`

- `protected void paintComponent(Graphics g)`

  Override this method to paint the surface of a component. Your method needs to call `super.paintComponent(g)`.

  Parameters:

     `g`—The graphics context used for drawing

- `void setBorder(Border b)`

  This method sets the border of this component.

  Parameters:

     `b`—The border to surround this component

- `void setFont(Font f)`

  Sets the font used for the text in this component.

  Parameters:

     `f`—A font

Class javax.swing.JFileChooser

- JFileChooser()

  This constructs a file chooser.

- File getSelectedFile()

  This method gets the selected file from this file chooser.

  Returns: The selected file.

- int showOpenDialog(Component parent)

  This method displays an "Open File" file chooser dialog.

  Parameters:

  parent—The parent component or null

  Returns: The return state of this file chooser after it has been closed by the user: either APPROVE_OPTION or CANCEL_OPTION. If APPROVE_OPTION is returned, call getSelectedFile()on this file chooser to get the file.

- int showSaveDialog(Component parent)

  This method displays a "Save File" file chooser dialog.

  Parameters:

  parent—The parent component or null

  Returns: The return state of the file chooser after it has been closed by the user: either APPROVE_OPTION or CANCEL_OPTION.

Class javax.swing.JFrame

- static final int EXIT_ON_CLOSE

  This value indicates that when the user closes this frame, the application is to exit.

- Container getContentPane()

  This method returns the content pane of this frame.

  Returns: The content pane.

- void setContentPane(Container pane)

  This method sets the content pane of this frame to a new container.

  Parameters:

  pane—The new content pane

- void setDefaultCloseOperation(int operation)

  This method sets the default action for closing the frame.

Parameters:

> operation–The desired close operation. Choose among
> DO_NOTHING_ON_CLOSE, HIDE_ON_CLOSE (the default),
> DISPOSE_ON_CLOSE, or EXIT_ON_CLOSE

- void setJMenuBar(JMenuBar mb)

This method sets the menu bar for this frame.

Parameters:

> mb—The menu bar. If mb is null, then the current menu bar is removed.

Class javax.swing.JLabel

- JLabel(String text,int alignment)

This container creates a JLabel instance with the specified text and horizontal alignment.

Parameters:

> text—The label text to be displayed by the label
>
> alignment—One of SwingConstants.LEFT, SwingConstants.CENTER, or SwingConstants.RIGHT

Class javax.swing.JMenu

- JMenu()

This constructs a menu with no items.

- JMenuItem add(JMenuItem menuItem)

This method appends a menu item to the end of this menu.

Parameters:

> menuItem—The menu item to be added

Returns: The menu item that was added.

Class javax.swing.JMenuBar

- JMenuBar()

This constructs a menu bar with no menus.

- JMenu add(JMenu menu)

This method appends a menu to the end of this menu bar.

Parameters:

> menu—The menu to be added

Returns: The menu that was added.

Class `javax.swing.JMenuItem`

- `JMenuItem(String text)`

This constructs a menu item.

Parameters:

> `text`—The text to appear in the menu item

Class `javax.swing.JOptionPane`

- `static String showInputDialog(Object prompt)`

This method brings up a modal input dialog, which displays a prompt and waits for the user to enter an input in a text field, preventing the user from doing anything else in this program.

Parameters:

> `prompt`—The prompt to display

Returns: The string that the user typed.

- `static void showMessageDialog(Component parent,Object message)`

This method brings up a confirmation dialog that displays a message and waits for the user to confirm it.

Parameters:

> `parent`—The parent component or `null`
>
> `message`—The message to display

Class `javax.swing.JPanel`

This class is a component without decorations. It can be used as an invisible container for other components. A subclass can implement its own `paintComponent` method.

Class `javax.swing.JRadioButton`

- `JRadioButton(String text)`

This constructs a radio button having the given text that is initially deselected. (Use the `setSelected()` method to select it; see the `javax.swing.Abstract-Button` class.)

Parameters:

> `text`—The string displayed next to the radio button

Class `javax.swing.JSlider`

- `JSlider(int min,int max,int value)`

This constructor creates a horizontal slider using the specified minimum, maximum, and value.

Parameters:

> min—The smallest possible slider value
>
> max—The largest possible slider value
>
> value—The initial value of the slider

- void addChangeListener(ChangeListener listener)

This method adds a change listener to the slider.

Parameters:

> listener—The change listener to add

- int getValue()

This method returns the slider's value.

Returns: The current value of the slider.

Class javax.swing.JTextArea

- JTextArea()

This constructs an empty text area.

- JTextArea(int columns)

This constructs an empty text area with the specified number of rows and columns.

Parameters:

> rows—The number of rows
>
> columns—The number of columns

Class javax.swing.JTextField

- JTextField()

This constructs an empty text field.

- JTextField(int columns)

This constructs an empty text field with the specified number of columns.

Parameters:

> columns—The number of columns

- void addActionListener(ActionListener listener)

This method adds an action listener to be notified when the user hits the Enter key in this text field.

Parameters:

> listener—The action listener

Class javax.swing.Timer

- Timer(int millis, ActionListener listener)

This constructor constructs a timer that notifies an action listener whenever a time interval has elapsed.

Parameters:

> millis—The number of milliseconds between timer notifications
>
> listener—The object to be notified when the time inverval has elapsed

- void start()

This method starts the timer. Once the timer has started, it begins notifiying its listener.

- void stop()

This method stops the timer. Once the timer has stopped, it no longer notifies its listener.

Package javax.swing.border

Class javax.swing.border.EtchedBorder

- EtchedBorder()

This constructor creates a lowered etched border.

Class javax.swing.border.TitledBorder

- TitledBorder(Border b,String title)

This constructor creates a titled border that adds a title to a given border.

Parameters:

> b—The border to which the title is added
>
> title—The title the border should display

Package javax.swing.event

Class javax.swing.event.ChangeEvent

A slider emits change events when it is adjusted.

Class javax.swing.event.ChangeListener

- void stateChanged(ChangeEvent e)

This event is called when the event source has changed its state.

Parameters:

> e—A change event

Package `javax.swing.text`

Class `javax.swing.text.JTextComponent`

- `String getText()`

  This method returns the text contained in this text component.

  Returns: The text.

- `boolean isEditable()`

  This method checks whether this text component is editable.

  Returns: `true` if the component is editable.

- `void setEditable(boolean state)`

  This method is used to make this text component editable or not.

  Parameters:

  > `state`—`true` to make editable, `false` to disable editing

- `void setText(String text)`

  This method sets the text of this text component to the specified text. If the text is empty, the old text is deleted.

  Parameters:

  > `text`—The new text to be set

Package `javax.xml.parsers`

Class `javax.xml.parsers.DocumentBuilder`

- `Document newDocument()`

  This method constructs a new document object.

  Returns: An empty document.

- `Document parse(File in)`

  This method parses an XML document in a file.

  Parameters:

  > `in`—The file containing the document

  Returns: The parsed document.

- `Document parse(InputStream in)`

  This method parses an XML document in a stream.

Parameters:

in—The stream containing the document

Returns: The parsed document.

Class `javax.xml.parsers.DocumentBuilderFactory`

- `DocumentBuilder newDocumentBuilder()`

This method creates a new document builder object.

Returns: The document builder.

- `static DocumentBuilderFactory newInstance()`

This method creates a new document builder factory object.

Returns: The document builder factory.

- `void setIgnoreElementContentWhiteSpace(boolean b)`

This method sets the parsing mode for ignoring white space in element content for all document builders that are generated from this factory.

Parameters:

b—`true` if white space should be ignored

- `void setValidating(boolean b)`

This method sets the validation mode for all document builders that are generated from this factory.

Parameters:

b—`true` if documents should be validated during parsing

Package `javax.xml.transform`

Class `javax.xml.transform.Transformer`

- `void transform(Source doc, Result out)`

This method transforms an XML document into a result format.

Parameters:

doc—The XML source to be transformed

out—The result that holds the transformed output

Class `javax.xml.transform.TransformerFactory`

- `static TransformerFactory newInstance()`

This method creates a new transformer factory object.

Returns: The transformer factory.

- `Transformer newTransformer()`

This method creates a transformer for the "identity" transformation. It can be used to send an XML document to a stream.

Returns: An identity transformer.

Package `javax.xml.transform.dom`

Class `javax.xml.transform.dom.DOMSource`

- `DOMSource(Node in)`

This constructs a source object from a document node.

Parameters:

> in—The top-level node of the source document

Package `javax.xml.transform.stream`

Class `javax.xml.transform.stream.StreamResult`

- `StreamResult(File out)`

This constructs a result object from a file.

Parameters:

> out—The output destination

- `StreamResult(OutputStream out)`

This constructs a result object from a stream.

Parameters:

> out—The output destination

Package `org.w3c.dom`

Interface `org.w3c.dom.CharacterData`

- `String getText()`

This method returns the text of this character data element.

Returns: The text string.

Interface `org.w3c.dom.Document`

- `Attr createAttribute(String attributeName)`

This method creates a new attribute node with a given attribute name.

Parameters:

> attributeName—The name of the XML attribute

Returns: The created node.

- Element createElement(String tagName)

This method creates a new document element with a given tag.

Parameters:

> tagName—The name of the XML tag

Returns: The created element.

- Element getDocumentElement()

This method returns the root element of the document.

Returns: The document root.

Interface org.w3c.dom.Element

- String getAttribute(String attributeName)

This method returns the value of a given attribute.

Parameters:

> attributeName—The name of the XML attribute

Returns: The attribute value, or the empty string "" if that attribute does not exist for this element.

- String getTagName()

This method returns the tag name of this element.

Returns: The tag name.

- void setAttribute(string name, String value)

This method sets the value of a given attribute.

Parameters:

> name—The name of the XML attribute
> value—The desired value of the XML attribute

Interface org.w3c.dom.NamedNodeMap

- int getLength()

This method returns the length of this map.

Returns: The number of name/value pairs in this map.

- `Node item(int index)`

  This method returns a name/value pair at a given index position.

  Parameters:

  > `index`—The (zero-based) index

  Returns: The node containing the attribute name/value.

Interface `org.w3c.dom.Node`

- `NamedNodeMap getAttributes()`

  This method returns a node map with all attributes of this node.

  Returns: The node map.

- `NodeList getChildNodes()`

  This method returns a node list with all children of this node.

  Returns: The node list.

- `Node getFirstChild()`

  This method returns the first child node of this node.

  Returns: The child node.

- `Node getLastChild()`

  This method returns the last child node of this node.

  Returns: The child node.

Interface `org.w3c.dom.NodeList`

- `int getLength()`

  This method returns the length of this list.

  Returns: The number of nodes in this map.

- `Node item(int index)`

  This method returns a node at a given index position.

  Parameters:

  > `index`—The zero-based index

  Returns: The node at the specified position.

Appendix A6

The Basic Latin and Latin-1 Subsets of Unicode

Char.	Code	Dec.	Char.	Code	Dec.	Char.	Code	Dec.
			0	'\u0030'	48	@	'\u0040'	64
!	'\u0021'	33	1	'\u0031'	49	A	'\u0041'	65
"	'\u0022'	34	2	'\u0032'	50	B	'\u0042'	66
#	'\u0023'	35	3	'\u0033'	51	C	'\u0043'	67
$	'\u0024'	36	4	'\u0034'	52	D	'\u0044'	68
%	'\u0025'	37	5	'\u0035'	53	E	'\u0045'	69
&	'\u0026'	38	6	'\u0036'	54	F	'\u0046'	70
'	'\u0027'	39	7	'\u0037'	55	G	'\u0047'	71
(	'\u0028'	40	8	'\u0038'	56	H	'\u0048'	72
)	'\u0029'	41	9	'\u0039'	57	I	'\u0049'	73
*	'\u002A'	42	:	'\u003A'	58	J	'\u004A'	74
+	'\u002B'	43	;	'\u003B'	59	K	'\u004B'	75
,	'\u002C'	44	<	'\u003C'	60	L	'\u004C'	76
–	'\u002D'	45	=	'\u003D'	61	M	'\u004D'	77
.	'\u002E'	46	>	'\u003E'	62	N	'\u004E'	78
/	'\u002F'	47	?	'\u003F'	63	O	'\u004F'	79

Table 1

The Basic Latin (ASCII) Subset of Unicode (*continues*)

Char.	Code	Dec.	Char.	Code	Dec.	Char.	Code	Dec.
P	'\u0050'	80	`	'\u0060'	96	p	'\u0070'	112
Q	'\u0051'	81	a	'\u0061'	97	q	'\u0071'	113
R	'\u0052'	82	b	'\u0062'	98	r	'\u0072'	114
S	'\u0053'	83	c	'\u0063'	99	s	'\u0073'	115
T	'\u0054'	84	d	'\u0064'	100	t	'\u0074'	116
U	'\u0055'	85	e	'\u0065'	101	u	'\u0075'	117
V	'\u0056'	86	f	'\u0066'	102	v	'\u0076'	118
W	'\u0057'	87	g	'\u0067'	103	w	'\u0077'	119
X	'\u0058'	88	h	'\u0068'	104	x	'\u0078'	120
Y	'\u0059'	89	i	'\u0069'	105	y	'\u0079'	121
Z	'\u005A'	90	j	'\u006A'	106	z	'\u007A'	122
[	'\u005B'	91	k	'\u006B'	107	{	'\u007B'	123
\	'\u005C'	92	l	'\u006C'	108	|	'\u007C'	124
]	'\u005D'	93	m	'\u006D'	109	}	'\u007D'	125
^	'\u005E'	94	n	'\u006E'	110	~	'\u007E'	126
_	'\u005F'	95	o	'\u006F'	111			

Table 1 (*continued*)

The Basic Latin (ASCII) Subset of Unicode

Table 2

Selected Control Characters

Char.	Code	Dec.
Space	' '	32
Newline	'\n'	10
Return	'\r'	13
Tab	'\t'	9

Char.	Code	Dec.	Char.	Code	Dec.	Char.	Code	Dec.
			À	`'\u00C0'`	192	à	`'\u00E0'`	224
¡	`'\u00A1'`	161	Á	`'\u00C1'`	193	á	`'\u00E1'`	225
¢	`'\u00A2'`	162	Â	`'\u00C2'`	194	â	`'\u00E2'`	226
£	`'\u00A3'`	163	Ã	`'\u00C3'`	195	ã	`'\u00E3'`	227
¤	`'\u00A4'`	164	Ä	`'\u00C4'`	196	ä	`'\u00E4'`	228
¥	`'\u00A5'`	165	Å	`'\u00C5'`	197	å	`'\u00E5'`	229
¦	`'\u00A6'`	166	Æ	`'\u00C6'`	198	æ	`'\u00E6'`	230
§	`'\u00A7'`	167	Ç	`'\u00C7'`	199	ç	`'\u00E7'`	231
¨	`'\u00A8'`	168	È	`'\u00C8'`	200	è	`'\u00E8'`	232
©	`'\u00A9'`	169	É	`'\u00C9'`	201	é	`'\u00E9'`	233
ª	`'\u00AA'`	170	Ê	`'\u00CA'`	202	ê	`'\u00EA'`	234
«	`'\u00AB'`	171	Ë	`'\u00CB'`	203	ë	`'\u00EB'`	235
¬	`'\u00AC'`	172	Ì	`'\u00CC'`	204	ì	`'\u00EC'`	236
	`'\u00AD'`	173	Í	`'\u00CD'`	205	í	`'\u00ED'`	237
®	`'\u00AE'`	174	Î	`'\u00CE'`	206	î	`'\u00EE'`	238
¯	`'\u00AF'`	175	Ï	`'\u00CF'`	207	ï	`'\u00EF'`	239
°	`'\u00B0'`	176	Ð	`'\u00D0'`	208	ð	`'\u00F0'`	240
±	`'\u00B1'`	177	Ñ	`'\u00D1'`	209	ñ	`'\u00F1'`	241
²	`'\u00B2'`	178	Ò	`'\u00D2'`	210	ò	`'\u00F2'`	242
³	`'\u00B3'`	179	Ó	`'\u00D3'`	211	ó	`'\u00F3'`	243
´	`'\u00B4'`	180	Ô	`'\u00D4'`	212	ô	`'\u00F4'`	244
µ	`'\u00B5'`	181	Õ	`'\u00D5'`	213	õ	`'\u00F5'`	245
¶	`'\u00B6'`	182	Ö	`'\u00D6'`	214	ö	`'\u00F6'`	246
·	`'\u00B7'`	183	×	`'\u00D7'`	215	÷	`'\u00F7'`	247
¸	`'\u00B8'`	184	Ø	`'\u00D8'`	216	ø	`'\u00F8'`	248
¹	`'\u00B9'`	185	Ù	`'\u00D9'`	217	ù	`'\u00F9'`	249
º	`'\u00BA'`	186	Ú	`'\u00DA'`	218	ú	`'\u00FA'`	250
»	`'\u00BB'`	187	Û	`'\u00DB'`	219	û	`'\u00FB'`	251
¼	`'\u00BC'`	188	Ü	`'\u00DC'`	220	ü	`'\u00FC'`	252
½	`'\u00BD'`	189	Ý	`'\u00DD'`	221	ý	`'\u00FD'`	253
¾	`'\u00BE'`	190	Þ	`'\u00DE'`	222	þ	`'\u00FE'`	254
¿	`'\u00BF'`	191	ß	`'\u00DF'`	223	ÿ	`'\u00FF'`	255

Table 3

The Latin-1 Subset of Unicode

Metric Conversion Factors

Measure	Name	Type
m	meter	Distance
L	liter	Volume (= 1000 cm^3)
g	gram	Weight
°C	degree Celsius	Temperature

Table 1

Metric Measurement

Table 2

Metric Unit Factors

Unit	Name	Factor
μ	micro	10^{-6}
m	milli	10^{-3}
c	centi	10^{-2}
k	kilo	10^3

To convert from	To	Perform this operation
Fluid ounce (fl. oz.)	mL	Multiply by 29.586
Gallon	L	Multiply by 3.785
Ounce (oz)	g	Multipy by 28.3495
Pound (lb)	kg	Multiply by 0.4536
Inch (in)	cm	Multiply by 2.54
Foot (ft)	cm	Multiply by 30.5
Mile	km	Multiply by 1.609
Degrees Fahrenheit (°F)	°C	Subtract 32, then multiply by 5 and divide by 9

Table 3

Conversions from Nonmetric Units to Metric Units

HTML Summary

Tag	Meaning	Children	Commonly Used Attributes
html	HTML document	head, body	
head	Head of an HTML document	title	
title	Title of an HTML document		
body	Body of an HTML document		
h1 ... h6	Heading level 1 ... 6		
p	Paragraph		
ul	Unnumbered list	li	
ol	Ordered list	li	
dl	Definition list	dt, dd	
li	List item		
dt	Term to be defined		
dd	Definition data		
table	Table	tr	
tr	Table row	th, td	
th	Table header cell		
td	Table cell data		
a	Anchor		href, name
img	Image		src, width, height
applet	Applet		code, width, height
pre	Preformatted text		
hr	Horizontal rule		
br	Line break		
i or em	Italic		

Table 1

Selected HTML Tags (*continues*)

Tag	Meaning	Children	Commonly Used Attributes
b or strong	Bold		
tt or code	Typewriter or code font		
s or strike	Strike through		
u	Underline		
super	Superscript		
sub	Subscript		
form	Form		action, method
input	Input field		type, name, value, size, checked
select	Combo box style selector	option	name
option	Option for selection		
textarea	Multiline text area		name, rows, cols

Table 1 (*continued*)

Selected HTML Tags

Attribute	Description	Commonly Contained in Element
name	Name of form element or anchor	input, select, textarea, a
href	Hyperlink reference	a
src	Source (as of image)	img
code	Applet code	applet
width, height	Width, height of image or applet	img, applet
rows, cols	Rows, columns of text area	textarea
type	Type of input field, such as text, password, checkbox, radio, submit, hidden	input
value	Value of input field, or label of submit button	input
size	Size of text field	input
checked	Check radio button or checkbox	input
action	URL of form action	form
method	GET or POST	form

Table 2

Selected HTML Attributes

Entity	Description	Appearance
`&lt;`	Less than	<
`&gt;`	Greater than	>
`&amp;`	Ampersand	&
`&quot;`	Quotation mark	"
` `	Nonbreaking space	
`&copy;`	Copyright symbol	©

Table 3

Selected HTML Entities

A9

Tool Summary

In this syntax summary, we use a monospaced font for actual commands such as javac. An italic font denotes descriptions of tool command components such as *options*. Items enclosed in brackets [...] are optional. Items separated by vertical bars | are alternatives. Do not include the brackets or vertical bars when typing in the commands.

The Java Compiler

javac [*options*] *sourceFile1*|*@fileList1* *sourceFile2*|*@fileList2*. . .

A file list is a text file that contains one file name per line. For example,

File Greeting.list

```
1 Greeting.java
2 GreetingTest.java
```

Then you can compile all files with the command

javac @Greeting.list

The Java compiler options are summarized in Table 1.

Option	Description
-classpath *locations*	The compiler is to look for classes on this path, overriding the CLASSPATH environment variable. If neither is specified, the current directory is used. Each *location* is a directory, JAR file, or ZIP file. Locations are separated by a platform-dependent separator (: on Unix, ; on Windows).
-sourcepath *locations*	The compiler is to look for source files on this path. If not specified, source files are searched in the class path.
-g	Generate debugging information.
-verbose	Include information about all classes that are being compiled (useful for troubleshooting).
-deprecation	Give detailed information about the usage of deprecated messages.

Table 1

Common Compiler Options

The Java Interpreter

> java [*options*] *className* [*argument*$_1$ *argument*$_2$ . . .]

This command loads the given class and starts its `main` method, passing it an array containing the provided command line arguments.

> java [*options*] -jar *jarFileName* [*argument*$_1$ *argument*$_2$ . . .]

This command loads the main class of the given JAR file and starts its `main` method, passing it an array containing the provided command line arguments.

The Java interpreter options are summarized in Table 2.

The Applet Viewer

> appletviewer [*options*] *url*$_1$ *url*$_2$ . . .

The *url*s are searched for applets, and each applet is displayed in a separate window.

An applet should be specified as an HTML tag of the form

```
<applet
    code=appletClassFile
    width=pixels
    height=pixels
    [codebase=relativeURL]>
    <param name=parameterName1 value=parameterValue1>
    <param name=parameterName2 value=parameterValue2>

</applet>
```

or

```
<object
    code=appletClassFile
    width=pixels
    height=pixels>
```

Option	Description
`-classpath` *locations* or `-cp` *locations*	Look for classes on this path, overriding the CLASSPATH environment variable. If neither is specified, the current directory is used. Each *location* is a directory, JAR file, or ZIP file. Locations are separated by a platform-dependent separator (: on Unix, ; on Windows).
`-verbose`	Trace class loading
`-D`*property*=*value*	Set a system property that you can retrieve with the `System.getProperties` method.

Table 2

Common Interpreter Options

Option	Description
`-J`*option*	Pass the *option* to the Java interpreter, for example `-J-Djava.security.policy=mypolicy`

Table 3

Common Applet Viewer Options

```
<param name=type value=application/x-java-applet>
<param name=code value=appletClassFile>
[<param name=codebase value=relativeURL>]
<param name=parameterName₁ value=parameterValue₁>
<param name=parameterName₂ value=parameterValue₂>
   . . .
</object>
```

The `codebase` parameter is an URL that is relative to the URL of the HTML file containing the applet or object tag.

The applet viewer options are summarized in Table 3.

The JAR Tool

To combine one or more files into a JAR (Java Archive) file, use the command

    jar cvf *jarFile* *file*₁ *file*₂ . . .

The resulting JAR file can be included in a class path.

To build a program that can be launched with `java -jar`, you must create a *manifest file,* such as

File myprog.mf

1 `Main-Class: com/horstmann/MyProg`

The manifest must specify the path name of the class file that launches the application, but with the `.class` extension removed. Then build the JAR file as

    jar cvfm *jarFile* *manifestFile* *file*₁ *file*₂ . . .

You can also use JAR as a replacement for a ZIP utility, simply to compress and bundle a set of files for any purpose. Then you may want to suppress the generation of the JAR manifest, with the command

    jar cvfM *jarFile* *file*₁ *file*₂ . . .

To extract the contents of a JAR file into the current directory, use

    jar xvf *jarFile*

To see the files contained in a JAR file without extracting the files, use

    jar tvf *jarFile*

javadoc Summary

Setting Documentation Comments in Source

A documentation comment is delimited by /** and */. You can comment

- Classes

- Methods

- Fields

Each comment is placed *immediately above* the feature it documents.

Each /** . . . */ documentation comment contains introductory text followed by tagged documentation. A tag starts with an @ character, such as @author or @param. Tags are summarized in Table 1. The *first sentence* of the introductory text should be a summary statement. The javadoc utility automatically generates summary pages that extract these sentences.

You can use HTML tags such as em for emphasis, code for a monospaced font, img for images, ul for bulleted lists, and so on.

Here is a typical example. The summary sentence (in boldface) will be included with the method summary.

```
/**
    Withdraws money from the bank account. Increments the
    transaction count.
    @param amount the amount to withdraw
    @return the balance after the withdrawal
    @throws IllegalArgumentException if the balance is not sufficient
*/
public double withdraw(double amount)
{
    if (balance - amount < minimumBalance)
        throw new IllegalArgumentException();
```

Tag	Description
@param *parameter explanation*	A parameter of a method. Use a separate tag for each parameter.
@return *explanation*	The return value of a method.
@throws *exceptionType explanation*	An exception that a method may throw. Use a separate tag for each exception.
@deprecated	A feature that remains for compatibility but that should not be used for new code.
@see *packageName . ClassName* @see *packageName . ClassName#methodName*($Type_1$, $Type_2$, . . .) @see *packageName . ClassName#fieldName*	A reference to a related documentation entry.
@author	The author of a class or interface. Use a separate tag for each author.
@version	The version of a class or interface.

Table 1

Common javadoc Tags

```
        balance = balance - amount;
        transactions++;
        return balance;
    }
```

Generating Documentation from Commented Source

To extract the comments, run the javadoc program:

> javadoc *[options] sourceFile₁|packageName₁|@fileList₁*
>   *sourceFile₂|packageName₂|@fileList₂* . . .

See the documentation of the javac command in Appendix A9 for an explanation of file lists. Commonly used *options* are summarized in Table 2.

To document all files in the current directory, use (all on one line)

```
javadoc -link http://java.sun.com/products/jdk/1.4/docs/api
    -d docdir *.java
```

Option	Description
-link *URL*	Link to another set of Javadoc files. You should include a link to the standard library documentation, either locally or at the Sun web site, http://java.sun.com/products/jdk/1.4/docs/api.
-d *directory*	Store the output in *directory*. This is a useful option, because it keeps your current directory from being cluttered up with javadoc files.
-classpath *locations*	Look for classes on the specified paths, overriding the CLASSPATH environment variable. If neither is specified, the current directory is used. Each *location* is a directory, JAR file, or ZIP file. Locations are separated by a platform-dependent separator (: on Unix, ; on Windows)
-sourcepath *locations*	Look for source files on the specified paths. If not specified, source files are searched in the class path.
-author, -version	Include author, version information in the documentation. This information is omitted by default.

Table 2

Common javadoc Command Line Options

A11

Number Systems

Binary Numbers

Decimal notation represents numbers as powers of 10, for example

$$1728_{\text{decimal}} = 1 \times 10^3 + 7 \times 10^2 + 2 \times 10^1 + 8 \times 10^0$$

There is no particular reason for the choice of 10, except that several historical number systems were derived from people's counting with their fingers. Other number systems, using a base of 12, 20, or 60, have been used by various cultures throughout human history. However, computers use a number system with base 2 because it is far easier to build electronic components that work with two values, which can be represented by a current being either off or on, than it would be to represent 10 different values of electrical signals. A number written in base 2 is also called a *binary* number.

For example,

$$1101_{\text{binary}} = 1 \times 2^3 + 1 \times 2^2 + 0 \times 2^1 + 1 \times 2^0 = 8 + 4 + 1 = 13$$

For digits after the "decimal" point, use negative powers of 2.

$$1.101_{\text{binary}} = 1 \times 2^0 + 1 \times 2^{-1} + 0 \times 2^{-2} + 1 \times 2^{-3}$$

$$= 1 + \frac{1}{2} + \frac{1}{8}$$

$$= 1 + 0.5 + 0.125 = 1.625$$

In general, to convert a binary number into its decimal equivalent, simply evaluate the powers of 2 corresponding to digits with value 1, and add them up. Table 1 shows the first powers of 2.

Table 1

Powers of Two

Power	Decimal Value
2^0	1
2^1	2
2^2	4
2^3	8
2^4	16
2^5	32
2^6	64
2^7	128
2^8	256
2^9	512
2^{10}	1,024
2^{11}	2,048
2^{12}	4,096
2^{13}	8,192
2^{14}	16,384
2^{15}	32,768
2^{16}	65,536

To convert a decimal integer into its binary equivalent, keep dividing the integer by 2, keeping track of the remainders. Stop when the number is 0. Then write the remainders as a binary number, starting with the *last* one. For example,

$$100 \div 2 = 50 \text{ remainder } 0$$
$$50 \div 2 = 25 \text{ remainder } 0$$
$$25 \div 2 = 12 \text{ remainder } 1$$
$$12 \div 2 = 6 \text{ remainder } 0$$
$$6 \div 2 = 3 \text{ remainder } 0$$
$$3 \div 2 = 1 \text{ remainder } 1$$
$$1 \div 2 = 0 \text{ remainder } 1$$

Therefore, $100_{\text{decimal}} = 1100100_{\text{binary}}$.

Conversely, to convert a fractional number less than 1 to its binary format, keep multiplying by 2. If the result is greater than 1, subtract 1. Stop when the number is 0. Then use the digits before the decimal points as the binary digits of the fractional part, starting with the *first* one. For example,

$$0.35 \cdot 2 = 0.7$$
$$0.7 \cdot 2 = 1.4$$
$$0.4 \cdot 2 = 0.8$$
$$0.8 \cdot 2 = 1.6$$
$$0.6 \cdot 2 = 1.2$$
$$0.2 \cdot 2 = 0.4$$

Here the pattern repeats. That is, the binary representation of 0.35 is 0.01 0110 0110 0110 . . .

To convert any floating-point number into binary, convert the whole part and the fractional part separately.

Two's Complement Integers

To represent negative integers, there are two common representations, called "signed magnitude" and "two's complement". Signed magnitude notation is simple: use the leftmost bit for the sign (0 = positive, 1 = negative). For example, when using 8-bit numbers,

$$-13 = 10001101_{\text{signed magnitude}}$$

However, building circuitry for adding numbers gets a bit more complicated when one has to take a sign bit into account. The two's complement representation solves this problem. To form the two's complement of a number,

- Flip all bits.

- Then add 1.

For example, to compute −13 as an 8-bit value, first flip all bits of 00001101 to get 11110010. Then add 1:

$$-13 = 11110011_{\text{two's complement}}$$

Now no special circuitry is required for adding two numbers. Just follow the normal rule for addition, with a carry to the next position if the sum of the digits and the prior carry is 2 or 3. For example,

```
      1 1111 111
+13    |0000|1101
-13    |1111|0011
      ─────────────
      1|0000|0000
```

But only the last 8 bits count, so +13 and −13 add up to 0, as they should.

In particular, −1 has two's complement representation 1111 . . . 1111, with all bits set.

The top bit of a two's complement number is 0 if the number is positive or zero, 1 if it is negative.

Two's complement notation with a given number of bits can represent one more negative number than positive numbers. For example, the 8-bit two's complement numbers range from −128 to +127.

This phenomenon is an occasional cause for a programming error. For example, consider the following code:

```
byte b = . . .;
if (b < 0) b = -b;
```

This code does not guarantee that b is nonnegative afterwards. If b happens to be −128, then computing its negative again yields −128. (Try it out—take 10000000, flip all bits, and add 1.)

IEEE Floating-Point Numbers

The Institute for Electrical and Electronics Engineering (IEEE) defines standards for floating-point representations in the IEEE-754 standard. Figure 1 shows how single-precision (`float`) and double-precision (`double`) values are decomposed into

- A sign bit

- An exponent

- A mantissa

Floating-point numbers use scientific notation, in which a number is represented as

$$0.b_1b_2b_3\ldots \times 2^e$$

In this representation, e is the exponent, and the digits $b_1b_2b_3\ldots$ form the mantissa. The *normalized* representation is the one where $b_1 \neq 0$. For example,

$$100_{\text{decimal}} = 1100100_{\text{binary}} = 0.1100100_{\text{binary}} \times 2^7$$

Because in the binary number system the first bit of a normalized representation must be 1, it is not actually stored in the mantissa. Therefore, you always need to add it on to represent the actual value. For example, the mantissa 0.1100100 is stored as 100100.

The exponent part of the IEEE representation uses neither signed magnitude nor two's complement representation. Instead, a *bias* is added to the actual exponent. The bias is 127 for single-precision numbers, 1023 for double-precision numbers. For example, the exponent $e = 7$ would be stored as 134 in a single-precision number. Thus,

$$100_{\text{decimal}} = 0\,|\,10000110\,|\,10010000000000000000000_{\text{single-precision IEEE}}$$

In addition, there are several special values. Among them are:

- *Zero:* biased exponent $= 0$, mantissa $= 0$.

- *Infinity:* biased exponent $= 11\ldots1$, mantissa $= 0$.

- *NaN* (not a number): biased exponent $= 11\ldots1$, mantissa $\neq 10\ldots0$.

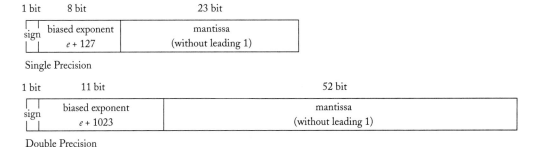

1 bit	8 bit	23 bit
sign	biased exponent $e + 127$	mantissa (without leading 1)

Single Precision

1 bit	11 bit	52 bit
sign	biased exponent $e + 1023$	mantissa (without leading 1)

Double Precision

Figure 1

IEEE Floating-Point Representation

Table 2

Hexadecimal Digits

Hexadecimal	Decimal	Binary
0	0	0000
1	1	0001
2	2	0010
3	3	0011
4	4	0100
5	5	0101
6	6	0110
7	7	0111
8	8	1000
9	9	1001
A	10	1010
B	11	1011
C	12	1100
D	13	1101
E	14	1110
F	15	1111

Hexadecimal Numbers

Because binary numbers can be hard to read for humans, programmers often use the hexadecimal number system, with base 16. The digits are denoted as 0, 1, . . . , 9, A, B, C, D, E, F. (see Table 2).

Four binary digits correspond to one hexadecimal digit. That makes it easy to convert between binary and hexadecimal values. For example,

$$11\,|1011\,|0001_{\text{binary}} \;=\; 3B1_{\text{hexadecimal}}$$

In Java, hexadecimal numbers are used for Unicode character values, such as \u03B1 (the Greek lowercase letter alpha). Hexadecimal integers are denoted with a 0x prefix, such as 0x3B1.

Bit and Shift Operations

There are four bit operations in Java: the unary negation ($\sim$) and the binary and ($\&$), or ($|$), and exclusive or ($\wedge$), often called xor.

Tables 1 and 2 show the truth tables for the bit operations in Java. When a bit operation is applied to integer values, the operation is carried out on corresponding bits.

For example, suppose we want to compute 46 & 13. First convert both values to binary. $46_{decimal} = 101110_{binary}$ (actually 00000000000000000000000000101110 as a 32-bit integer), and $5_{decimal} = 101_{binary}$. Now combine corresponding bits:

```
  0.....0101110
& 0.....0001101
---------------
  0.....0001100
```

The answer is $1100_{binary} = 12_{decimal}$.

Table 1

The Unary Negation Operation

a	~a
0	1
1	0

Table 2

The Binary And, Or, and Xor Operations

a	b	a&b	a|b	a∧b
0	0	0	0	0
0	1	0	1	1
1	0	0	1	1
1	1	1	1	0

You sometimes see the | operator being used to combine two bit patterns. For example, Font.BOLD is the value 1, Font.ITALIC is 2. The combination Font.BOLD | Font.ITALIC has both the bold and the italic bit set:

```
  0.....0000001
| 0.....0000010
  ─────────────
  0.....0000011
```

Don't confuse the & and | bit operators with the && and || operators. The latter work only on **boolean** values, not on bits of numbers.

Besides the operations that work on individual bits, there are three *shift* operations that take the bit pattern of a number and shift it to the left or right by a given number of positions. There are three shift operations: shift left (<<), arithmetic shift right (>>), and bitwise shift right (>>>).

The left shift moves all bits to the left, filling in zeroes in the least significant bits. Shifting to the left by *n* bits yields the same result as multiplication by 2^n. The arithmetic right shift moves all bits to the right, *propagating* the sign bit. Therefore, the result is the same as integer division by 2^n, both for positive and negative values. Finally, the bitwise right shift moves all bits to the right, filling in zeroes in the most significant bits. (See Figure 1.)

Left shift (<<)

Arithmetic right shift (>>)

Bitwise right shift (>>>)

Figure 1

The Shift Operations

Note that the right-hand-side value of the shift operators is reduced modulo 32 (for `int` values) or 64 (for `long` values) to determine the actual number of bits to shift. For example, `1 << 35` is the same as `1 << 3`. Actually shifting 1 by 35 bits to the left would make no sense—the result would be 0.

The expression

```
1 << n
```

yields a bit pattern in which the nth bit is set (where the 0 bit is the least significant bit).

To set the nth bit of a number, carry out the operation

```
x = x | 1 << n
```

To check whether the nth bit is set, execute the test

```
if ((x & 1 << n) != 0) . . .
```

Note that the parentheses around the & are required—the & operator has a lower precedence than the relational operators.

UML Summary

In this book, we use a very restricted subset of the UML notation. This appendix lists the components of the subset. For a complete discussion of the UML notation, see reference [1].

Figure 1 shows the notation for classes and interfaces. Table 1 shows the arrows that indicate relationships between them.

Further Reading

[1] Grady Booch, James Rumbaugh, and Ivar Jacobson, *The Unified Modeling Language User Guide,* Addison-Wesley, 1999.

Figure 1

UML Symbols for Classes and Interfaces

Relationship	Symbol	Line style	Arrow tip
Inheritance	——————▷	Solid	Closed
Realization	- - - - - -▷	Dotted	Closed
Association	——————→	Solid	Open
Dependency	- - - - - ->	Dotted	Open

Table 1

UML Symbols for Relationships between Classes

Glossary

Abstract array An ordered sequence of items that can be efficiently accessed at random through an integer index.

Abstract class A class that cannot be instantiated.

Abstraction The process of finding the essential feature set for a building block of a program such as a class.

Abstract list An ordered sequence of items that can be traversed sequentially and that allows for efficient insertion and removal of elements at any position.

Abstract method A method with a name, parameter types, and return type but without an implementation.

Accessor method A method that accesses an object but does not change it.

Actual parameter The expression supplied for a formal parameter of a method by the caller.

ADT (abstract data type) A specification of the fundamental operations that characterize a data type, without supplying an implementation.

Aggregation The "has-a" relationship between classes.

Algorithm An unambiguous, executable, and terminating specification of a way to solve a problem.

API (application programming interface) A code library for building programs.

Applet A graphical Java program that executes inside a web browser or applet viewer.

Argument An actual parameter in a method call, or one of the values combined by an operator.

Array A collection of values of the same type stored in contiguous memory locations, each of which can be accessed by an integer index.

Array list A Java class that implements a dynamically growing array of objects.

Assertion A claim that a certain condition holds in a particular program location.

Assignment Placing a new value into a variable.

Association A relationship between classes in which one can navigate from objects of one class to objects of the other class, usually by following object references.

Balanced tree A tree in which *each* subtree has the property that the number of descendants to the left is approximately the same as the number of descendants to the right.

Big-Oh notation The notation $g(n) = O(f(n))$, which denotes that the function g grows at a rate that is bounded by the growth rate of the function f with respect to n. For example, $10n^2 + 100n - 1000 = O(n^2)$.

Binary file A file in which values are stored in their binary representation and cannot be read as text.

Binary operator An operator that takes two arguments, for example $+$ in $x + y$.

Binary search A fast algorithm to find a value in a sorted array. It narrows the search down to half of the array in every step.

Binary search tree A binary tree in which *each* subtree has the property that all left descendants are smaller than the value stored in the root, and all right descendants are larger.

Binary tree A tree in which each node has at most two child nodes.

Bit Binary digit; the smallest unit of information, having two possible values: 0 and 1. A data element consisting of n bits has 2^n possible values.

Black-box testing Testing a method without knowing its implementation.

Block A group of statements bracketed by {}.

Blocked thread A thread that cannot proceed because it is waiting for some external event.

Boolean operator → **Logical operator**

Boolean type A type with two possible values: `true` and `false`.

Border layout A layout management scheme in which components are placed into the center or one of the four borders of their container.

Boundary test case A test case involving values that are at the outer boundary of the set of legal values. For example, if a function is expected to work for all nonnegative integers, then 0 is a boundary test case.

Bounds error Trying to access an array element that is outside the legal range.

Breakpoint A point in a program, specified in a debugger, at which it stops executing the program and lets the user inspect the program state.

break statement A statement that terminates a loop or `switch` statement.

Buffer A temporary storage location for holding values that have been produced (for example, characters typed by the user) and are waiting to be consumed (for example, read a line at a time).

Buffered input Input that is gathered in batches, for example, a line at a time.

Byte A number made up of eight bits. Essentially all currently manufactured computers use a byte as the smallest unit of storage in memory.

Bytecode Instructions for the Java virtual machine.

Call by reference A method call mechanism in which the method receives the location in memory of a variable supplied as an actual parameter. Call by reference enables a method to change the contents of the original variable so that the change remains in effect after the method returns.

Call by value A method call mechanism in which the method receives a copy of the contents of a variable supplied as an actual parameter. Java uses only call by value. If a parameter variable's type is a class, its value is an object reference, so the method can alter that object but cannot make the parameter variable refer to a different object.

Call stack The ordered set of all methods that currently have been called but not yet terminated, starting with the current method and ending with `main`.

Case-sensitive Distinguishing upper- and lowercase characters.

Cast Explicitly converting a value from one type to a different type. For example, the cast from a floating-point number x to an integer is expressed in Java by the cast notation `(int)x`.

catch clause A part of a `try` block that is executed when a matching exception is thrown by any statement in the `try` block.

Check box A user interface component that can be used for a binary selection.

Checked exception An exception that the compiler checks. All checked exceptions must be declared or caught.

Class A programmer-defined data type.

Client A computer program or system that issues requests to a server and processes the server responses.

Cloning Making a copy of an object whose state can be modified independently of the original object.

Cohesion A class is cohesive if its features support a single abstraction.

Combo box A user interface component that combines a text field with a drop-down list of selections.

Command line The line the user types to start a program in DOS or UNIX or a command window in Windows. It consists of the program name followed by any necessary arguments.

Comment An explanation to help the human reader understand a section of a program; ignored by the compiler.

Compiler A program that translates code in a high-level language (such as Java) to machine instructions (such as bytecode for the Java virtual machine).

Compile-time error An error that is detected when a program is compiled.

Component → User interface component

Compound statement A statement such as `if` or `while` that is made up of several parts such as a condition and a body.

Concatenation Placing one string after another to form a new string.

Console program A Java program that does not have a graphical window. A console program reads input from the keyboard and writes output to the terminal screen.

Constant A value that cannot be changed by a program. In Java, constants are defined with the keyword `final`.

Construction Setting a newly allocated object to an initial state.

Constructor A method that initializes a newly instantiated object.

Container A user interface component that can hold other components and present them together to the user. Also, a data structure, such as a list, that can hold a collection of objects and present them individually to a program.

Content pane The part of a Swing frame that holds the user interface components of the frame.

Coupling The degree to which classes are related to each other by dependency.

CPU (Central Processing Unit) The part of a computer that executes the machine instructions.

CRC card An index card representing a class, listing its responsibilities and its collaborating classes.

Deadlock A state in which no thread can proceed because each thread is waiting for another to do some work first.

Debugger A program that lets a user run another program one or a few steps at a time, stop execution, and inspect the variables in order to analyze it for bugs.

Default constructor A constructor that is invoked with no parameters.

Dependency The "uses" relationship between classes, in which one class needs services provided by another class.

Dictionary ordering → Lexicographic ordering

Directory A structure on a disk that can hold files or other directories; also called a folder.

Documentation comment A comment in a source file that can be automatically extracted into the program documentation by a program such as javadoc.

Dot notation The notation *object*.*method*(*parameters*) or *object*.*field* used to invoke a method or access a field.

Doubly linked list A linked list in which each link has a reference to both its predecessor and successor links.

DTD (Document Type Definition) A sequence of rules that describe the legal child elements and attributes for each element type in an SGML or XML document.

Early binding Choosing at compile time among several methods with the same name but different parameter types.

Encapsulation The hiding of implementation details.

End of file The condition that is true when all characters of a file have been read. Note that there is no special "end of file character". When composing a file on the keyboard, you may need to type a special character to tell the operating system to end the file, but that character is not part of the file.

Escape character A character in text that is not taken literally but has a special meaning when combined with the character or characters that follow it. The \ character is an escape character in Java strings.

Event class A class that contains information about an event, such as its source.

Event adapter A class that implements an event listener interface by defining all methods to do nothing.

Event listener An object that is notified by an event source when an event occurs.

Event source An object that can notify other classes of events.

Exception A class that signals a condition that prevents the program from continuing normally. When such a condition occurs, an object of the exception class is thrown.

Exception handler A sequence of statements that is given control when an exception of a particular type has been thrown and caught.

Explicit parameter A parameter of a method other than the object on which the method is invoked.

Expression A syntactical construct that is made up of constants, variables, method calls, and operators combining them.

Extension The last part of a file name, which specifies the file type. For example, the extension .java denotes a Java file.

Extreme Programming A development methodology that strives for simplicity, by removing formal structure and focusing on best practices.

Fibonacci numbers The sequence of numbers 1, 1, 2, 3, 5, 8, 13, ..., in which every term is the sum of its two predecessors.

File A sequence of bytes that is stored on disk.

File pointer The position within a random-access file of the next byte to be read or written. It can be moved so as to access any byte in the file.

finally clause A part of a `try` block that is executed no matter how the `try` block is exited.

Floating-point number A number that can have a fractional part.

Flow layout A layout management scheme in which components are laid out left to right.

Flushing a stream Sending all characters that are still held in a buffer to its destination.

Folder → **Directory**

Font A set of character shapes in a particular style and size.

Foreign key A reference to a primary key in a linked table.

Formal parameter A variable in a method definition; it is initialized with an actual parameter value when the method is called.

Frame A window with a border and a title bar.

Garbage collection Automatic reclamation of memory occupied by objects that are no longer referenced.

GET An HTTP command to request information from a web server when the server needs only a small amount of information to fulfill the request.

goto statement A statement that transfers control to some other statement, which is tagged with a label. Java does not have a goto statement.

Grammar A set of rules that specifies which sequences of tokens are legal for a particular document set.

Graphics context A class through which a programmer can cause shapes to appear on a window or off-screen bitmap.

grep The "generalized regular expression pattern" search program, useful for finding all strings matching a pattern in a set of files.

Grid layout A layout management scheme in which components are placed into a two-dimensional grid.

GUI (graphical user interface) A user interface in which the user supplies inputs through graphical components such as buttons, menus, and text fields.

Hash collision Two different objects for which a hash function computes identical values.

Hash function A function that computes an integer value from an object in such a way that different objects are likely to yield different values.

Hash table A data structure in which elements are mapped to array positions according to their hash function values.

HTML (Hypertext Markup Language) The language in which web pages are described.

HTTP (Hypertext Transfer Protocol) The protocol that defines communication between web browsers and web servers.

IDE (integrated development environment) A programming environment that includes an editor, compiler, and debugger.

Immutable class A class without a mutator method.

Implementing an interface → **Realizing an interface**

Implicit parameter The object on which a method is invoked. For example, in the call x.f(y), the object x is the implicit parameter of the method f.

Inheritance The "is-a" relationship between a more general superclass and a more specialized subclass.

Initialization Setting a variable to a well-defined value when it is created.

Inner class A class that is defined inside another class.

Instance method A method with an implicit parameter; that is, a method that is invoked on an instance of a class.

Instance of a class An object whose type is that class.

Instance field A variable defined in a class for which every object of the class has its own value.

Instantiation of a class Constructing an object of that class.

Integer A number that cannot have a fractional part.

Integer division Taking the quotient of two integers, discarding the remainder. In Java the / symbol denotes integer division if both arguments are integers. For example, 11/4 is 2, not 2.75.

Interface A type with no instance variables and only abstract methods and constants.

Internet A worldwide collection of networks, routing equipment, and computers using a common set of protocols that define how participants interact with each other.

Interpreter A program that reads a set of codes and carries out the commands specified by them. The Java virtual machine is an interpreter that reads and executes Java bytecode.

Iterator An object that can inspect all elements in a container such as a linked list.

JavaBean A class with a default constructor that exposes properties through its get and set methods.

javadoc The documentation generator in the Java SDK. It extracts documentation comments from Java source files and produces a set of linked HTML files.

JDBC (Java Database Connectivity) The technology that enables a Java program to interact with relational databases.

Join A database query that involves multiple tables.

JSP (JavaServer Pages) A technology that uses Java to produce dynamic web page content. A JSP page can contain HTML and Java, and it is compiled into a servlet.

JSP container A program that processes requests for a JSP page, by evaluating the Java code in the page and returning an HTML document that contains both the non-Java content and the result of the Java code.

Late binding Choosing at run time among several methods with the same name invoked on objects belonging to subclasses of the same superclass.

Layout manager A class that arranges user interface components inside a container.

Lexicographic ordering Ordering strings in the same order as in a dictionary, by skipping all matching characters and comparing the first nonmatching characters of both strings. For example, "orbit" comes before "orchid" in lexicographic ordering. Note that in Java, unlike a dictionary, the ordering is case-sensitive: Z comes before a.

Library A set of precompiled classes that can be included into programs.

Linear search Searching a container (such as an array or list) for an object by inspecting each element in turn.

Linked list A data structure that can hold an arbitrary number of objects, each of which is stored in a link object, which contains a pointer to the next link.

Local variable A variable whose scope is a block.

Lock A data structure to regulate the scheduling of multiple threads. Once a thread has acquired a lock, other threads that also wish to acquire it must wait until the first thread relinquishes it.

Logging Sending messages that trace the progress of a program to a file or window.

Logical operator An operator that can be applied to Boolean values. Java has three logical operators: &&, ||, and !.

Logic error An error in a syntactically correct program that causes it to act differently from its specification.

Loop A sequence of instructions that is executed repeatedly.

Loop and a half A loop whose termination decision is neither at the beginning nor at the end.

Loop invariant A statement about the program state that is preserved when the statements in the loop are executed once.

Machine code Instructions that can be executed directly by the CPU.

Magic number A number that appears in a program without explanation.

main method The method that is first called when a Java application executes.

Map A data structure that keeps associations between key and value objects.

Markup Information about data that is added as humanly readable instructions. An example is the tagging of HTML documents with elements such as <h1> or <b>.

Merge sort A sorting algorithm that first sorts two halves of a data structure and then merges the sorted subarrays together.

Meta data Data that describe properties of a data set.

Method A sequence of statements that has a name, may have formal parameters, and may return a value. A method can be invoked any number of times, with different values for its parameters.

Method signature The name of a method and the types of its parameters.

Mixed content In XML, a markup element that contains both text and other elements.

Mutator method A method that changes the state of an object.

Mutual recursion Cooperating methods that call each other.

Name clash Accidentally using the same name to denote two program features in a way that cannot be resolved by the compiler.

Negative test case A test case that is expected to fail. For example, when testing a root-finding program, an attempt to compute the square root of −1 is a negative test case.

Nested block A block that is contained inside another block.

Newline The '\n' character, which indicates the end of a line.

new operator An operator that allocates new objects.

Null reference A reference that does not refer to any object.

Object A value of a class type.

Object-oriented design Designing a program by discovering objects, their properties, and their relationships.

Object reference A value that denotes the location of an object in memory. In Java, a variable whose type is a class contains a reference to an object of that class.

Off-by-one error A common programming error in which a value is one larger or smaller than it should be.

Opening a file Preparing a file for reading or writing.

Operating system The software that launches application programs and provides services (such as a file system) for those programs.

Operator A symbol denoting a mathematical or logical operation, such as + or &&.

Operator associativity The rule that governs in which order operators of the same precedence are executed. For example, in Java the - operator is left-associative because a - b - c is interpreted as (a - b) - c, and = is right-associative because a = b = c is interpreted as a = (b = c).

Operator precedence The rule that governs which operator is evaluated first. For example, in Java the && operator has a higher precedence than the || operator. Hence a || b && c is interpreted as a || (b && c).

Oracle A program that predicts how another program should behave.

Overloading Giving more than one meaning to a method name.

Overriding Redefining a method in a subclass.

Package A collection of related classes. The import statement is used to access one or more classes in a package.

Panel A user interface component with no visual appearance. It can be used to group other components, or as the superclass of a component that defines a method for painting.

Parallel arrays Arrays of the same length, in which corresponding elements are logically related.

Parameter An item of information that is specified to a method when the method is called. For example, in the call `System.out.println("Hello,World!")`, the parameters are the implicit parameter `System.out` and the explicit parameter `"Hello,World!"`.

Parameter passing Specifying expressions to be actual parameter values for a method when it is called.

Parser A program that reads a document, checks whether it is syntactically correct, and takes some action as it processes the document.

Partially filled array An array that is not filled to capacity, together with a companion variable that indicates the number of elements actually stored.

Polymorphism Selecting a method among several methods that have the same name on the basis of the actual types of the implicit parameters.

Positive test case A test case that a method is expected to handle correctly.

POST An HTTP command to request information from a web server. Unlike the GET command, the POST command can send request information of arbitrary size to the server.

Postfix operator A unary operator that is written after its argument.

Precondition A condition that must be true when a method is called if the method is to work correctly.

Predicate method A method that returns a Boolean value.

Prefix operator A unary operator that is written before its argument.

Prepared statement A SQL statement with a precomputed query strategy.

Primary key A column (or combination of columns) whose value uniquely specifies a table record.

Primitive type In Java, a number type or `boolean`.

Priority queue An abstract data type that enables efficient insertion of elements and efficient removal of the smallest element.

Private feature A feature that is accessible only by methods of the same class or an inner class.

Project A collection of source files and their dependencies.

Prompt A string that tells the user to provide input.

Protected feature A feature that is accessible by a class, its inner classes, its subclasses, and the other classes in the same package.

Public feature A feature that is accessible by all classes.

Qualified name A name that is made unambiguous because it starts with the package name.

Queue A collection of items with "first in, first out" retrieval.

Quicksort A generally fast sorting algorithm that picks an element, called the pivot, partitions the sequence into the elements smaller than the pivot and those larger than the pivot, and then recursively sorts the subsequences.

Race condition A condition in which the effect of multiple threads on shared data depends on the order in which the threads are scheduled.

Radio button A user interface component that can be used for selecting one of several options.

RAM (random-access memory) Electronic circuits in a computer that can store code and data of running programs.

Random access The ability to access any value directly without having to read the values preceding it.

Reader In the Java input/output library, a class from which to read characters.

Realizing an interface Implementing a class that defines all methods specified in the interface.

Recursive method A method that can call itself with simpler values. It must handle the simplest values without calling itself.

Redirection Linking the input or output of a program to a file instead of the keyboard or display.

Reference → **Object reference**

Regression testing Keeping old test cases and testing every revision of a program against them.

Regular expression A string that defines a set of matching strings according to their content. Each part of a regular expression can be a specific required character; one of a set of permitted characters such as `[abc]`, which can be a range such as `[a-z]`; any character not in a set of forbidden characters, such as `[^0-9]`; a repetition of one or more matches, such as `[0-9]+`, or zero or more, such as `[ACGT]*`; one of a set of alternatives, such as `and|et|und`; or various other possibilities. For example, `"[A-Za-z]*[0-9]+"` matches `"Cloud9"` or `"007"` but not `"Jack"`.

Relational database A data repository that stores information in tables and retrieves data as the result of queries that are formulated in terms of table relationships.

Reserved word A word that has a special meaning in a programming language and therefore cannot be used as a name by the programmer.

Return value The value returned by a method through a `return` statement.

Roundoff error An error introduced by the fact that the computer can store only a finite number of digits of a floating-point number.

Runnable thread A thread that can proceed provided it is given a time slice to do work.

Run-time error → **Logic error**

Run-time stack The data structure that stores the local variables of all called methods as a program runs.

Scope The part of a program in which a variable is defined.

SDK (Software Development Kit) A collection of tools for developing software.

Selection sort A sorting algorithm in which the smallest element is repeatedly found and removed until no elements remain.

Sentinel A value in input that is not to be used as an actual input value but to signal the end of input.

Sequential access Accessing values one after another without skipping over any of them.

Serialization The process of saving an object, and all the objects that it references, to a stream.

Server A computer program or system that receives requests from a client, obtains or computes the requested information, and sends it to the client.

Servlet A Java program that carries out computations and emits data that are returned to the browser.

Session A sequence of page requests from the same browser to the same web server.

Set An unordered collection that allows efficient addition, locating, and removal of elements.

SGML (Standard Generalized Markup Language) A format for structured data in which the structure is indicated by markup instructions. Unlike XML, SGML has provisions to minimize markup effort by human typists.

Shadowing Hiding a variable by defining another one with the same name.

Shell A part of an operating system in which the user types command lines to execute programs and manipulate files.

Shell script A file that contains commands for running programs and manipulating files. Typing the name of the shell script file on the command line causes those commands to be executed.

Side effect An effect of a method other than returning a value.

Signature → **Method signature**

Simple statement A statement consisting only of an expression.

Single-stepping Executing a program in the debugger one statement at a time.

Socket An object that encapsulates a TCP/IP connection. To communicate with the other endpoint of the connection, you use the input and output streams attached to the socket.

Software life cycle All activites related to the creation and maintenance of the software from initial analysis until obselescence.

Source file A file containing instructions in a programming language such as Java.

Spiral model An iterative process model of software development in which design and implementation are repeated.

SQL (Structured Query Language) A command language for interacting with a database.

Stack A data structure with "last in, first out" retrieval. Elements can be added and removed only at one position, called the top of the stack.

Stack trace A printout of the call stack, listing all currently pending method calls.

Statement A syntactical unit in a program. In Java a statement is either a simple statement, a compound statement, or a block.

Static method A method with no implicit parameter.

Static field A variable defined in a class that has only one value for the whole class, which can be accessed and changed by any method of that class.

Stored procedures A database procedure that is executed in the database kernel.

Stream An abstraction for a sequence of bytes from which data can be read or to which data can be written.

String A sequence of characters.

Stub A method with no or minimal functionality.

Subclass A class that inherits variables and methods from a superclass but adds instance variables, adds methods, or redefines methods.

Superclass A general class from which a more specialized class (a subclass) inherits.

Swing A Java toolkit for implementing graphical user interfaces.

Synchronized block A block of code that is controlled by a lock. To start execution, a thread must acquire the lock. Upon completion, it relinquishes the lock.

Syntax Rules that define how to form instructions in a particular programming language.

Syntax error An instruction that does not follow the programming language rules and is rejected by the compiler.

Tab character The '\t' character, which advances the next character on the line to the next one of a set of fixed positions known as tab stops.

TCP/IP (Transmission Control Protocol/Internet Protocol) The pair of communication protocols that is used to establish reliable transmission of data between two computers on the Internet.

Ternary operator An operator with three arguments. Java has one ternary operator, a ? b : c.

Test coverage The instructions of a program that are executed in a set of test cases.

Test harness A program that calls a function that needs to be tested, supplying parameters and analyzing the function's return value.

Test suite A set of test cases for a program.

Text field A user interface component that allows a user to provide text input.

Text file A file in which values are stored in their text representation.

Thread A program unit that is executed independently of other parts of the program.

Three-tier application An application that is composed of separate tiers for presentation, business logic, and data storage.

Throwing an exception Indicating an abnormal condition by terminating the normal control flow of a program and transferring control to a matching `catch` clause.

throws specifier Indicates the types of the checked exceptions that a method may throw.

Time slicing Scheduling threads by giving each thread a small amount of time in which to do its work, then giving control to another thread.

Token A sequence of consecutive characters from an input source that belongs together for the purpose of analyzing the input. For example, a token can be a sequence of characters other than white space.

Trace message A message that is printed during a program run for debugging purposes.

Transaction A set of database operations that should either succeed in their entirety, or not happen at all.

try block A block of statements that contains exception processing clauses. A `try` block contains at least one `catch` or `finally` clause.

Turing machine A very simple model of computation that is used in theoretical computer science to explore computability of problems.

Two-dimensional array A tabular arrangement of elements in which an element is specified by a row and a column index.

Unary operator An operator with one argument.

Unchecked exception An exception that the compiler doesn't check.

Unicode A standard code that assigns code values consisting of two bytes to characters used in scripts around the world. Java stores all characters as their Unicode values.

Uninitialized variable A variable that has not been set to a particular value. In Java, using an uninitialized local variable is a syntax error.

Unit test A test of a method by itself, isolated from the remainder of the program.

URL (Uniform Resource Locator) A pointer to an information resource (such as a web page or an image) on the World Wide Web.

User interface component A building block for a graphical user interface, such as a button or a text field. User interface components are used to present information to the user and allow the user to enter information to the program.

Variable A symbol in a program that identifies a storage location that can hold different values.

Virtual machine A program that simulates a CPU that can be implemented efficiently on a variety of actual machines. A given program in Java bytecode can be executed by any Java virtual machine, regardless of which CPU is used to run the virtual machine itself.

Visual programming Programming by arranging graphical elements on a form, setting program behavior by selecting properties for these elements, and writing only a small amount of "glue" code linking them.

void keyword A keyword indicating no type or an unknown type.

Watch window A window in a debugger that shows the current values of selected variables.

Waterfall model A sequential process model of software development, consisting of analysis, design, implementation, testing, and deployment.

White-box testing Testing functions taking their implementations into account, in contrast to black-box testing; for example, by selecting boundary test cases and ensuring that all branches of the code are covered by some test case.

White-space Any sequence of only space, tab, and newline characters.

Writer In the Java input/output library, a class to which characters are to be sent.

XML (Extensible Markup Language) A simple format for structured data in which the structure is indicated by markup instructions.

Index*

*Page numbers in color refer to terms found in the boxes set in margins throughout the text, which contain the key concepts of each chapter.

Photo Credits

Chapter 1
Page 4: Courtesy of Intel Corporation.
Page 5: Courtesy of Seagate Technology, Inc.
Page 6: Courtesy of Intel Corporation.
Page 7: Courtesy of Sperry Univac, Division of Sperry Corporation.

Chapter 2
Page 70: Courtesy of International Business Machines Corporation.

Chapter 4
Page 162: Courtesy of SAS Institute, Inc.
Page 163 (top): Courtesy of AutoDesk, Inc.
Page 163 (bottom): M. Tcherevkoff/The Image Bank.

Chapter 5
Page 202: Courtesy of Digital Equipment Corporation, Corporate Photo Library.
Page 203: ©Sun Microsystems.
Page 210: ©1997 by Sidney Harris.

Chapter 8
Page 354: Naval Surface Weapons Center, Dhalgren, VA.

Chapter 14
Page 577 (center, right, left): AP/Wide World Photos.

Chapter 17
Page 695: Science Photo Library/Photo Researchers.

Chapter 18
Page 719: Photo by Robert Godfrey. Courtesy International Business Machines Corporation. Unauthorized use not permitted.

Chapter 19
Page 758: AP/Wide World Photos.

Chapter 21
Page 845: Courtesy of Professor Naehyuck Chang, Computer Systems Lab, Dept. of Computer Engineering, Seoul National University.